LIST OF ORGANIZATIONS
FILING AS PRIVATE FOUNDATIONS

Compiled by THE FOUNDATION CENTER

Distributed by

COLUMBIA UNIVERSITY PRESS

New York   1973

Library of Congress Catalog Card Number: 73-78321
ISBN: 087954-002-8
Printed in the United States of America

The Foundation Center

888 Seventh Avenue, New York, N.Y. 10019; Tel. (212) 489-8610
1001 Connecticut Avenue, N.W., Washington, D.C. 20036; Tel. (202) 347-1400

The Foundation Center was incorporated in 1956 as an educational institution by the Board of Regents of the University of the State of New York. It is an independent agency, dedicated to the public interest and governed by its own board of trustees, usually half of whom are foundation officials and half public members from outside the foundation field.

The Center gathers and disseminates factual information on the philanthropic foundations through programs of library service, publication, and research. The Center's libraries in New York and Washington, D.C., contain extensive collections of books, documents, and reports on the foundation field and current files on the activities and program interests of more than 26,000 foundations in the United States.

The Center prepares and publishes *The Foundation Directory,* a standard reference work; the latest, *Edition 4,* published in 1971, contains basic data on 5,454 foundations. *The Foundation Center Information Quarterly,* the first issue of which was published in October 1972, includes updated information on the larger foundations listed in the *Directory* as well as listings of foundation annual reports on film, bibliographies, information on the foundation grants data bank, and announcements of new Center publications and services. The Center also compiles and publishes *The Foundation Grants Index,* a cumulative record of foundation grants, which appears in *Foundation News.*

Contents

Introduction

This preliminary list is a transcription of approximately 30,000 organization names as they appear on the microfilm of the 1970 returns (Forms 990 and 990-AR) supplied by the Internal Revenue Service. It will serve as a finding aid for locating particular foundation reports on the microfilm as well as for requesting film records (aperture cards) for subsequent years. The list is arranged in the same order as the records on film, geographically by state and alphabetically by foundation name within each state. For each state there are two alphabetical sequences, representing the two filmings by IRS. Each listing includes foundation name and city location followed by two numbers separated by a diagonal mark. The number preceding the diagonal indicates the microfilm reel number, while the number following the diagonal is an odometer reading which locates the foundation record on the film.

Due to inconsistencies in the filing order of some returns, there may be irregularities in the alphabetical sequence. If a foundation is not listed under the surname of an individual, for example, it may be located under the first or middle name. On the other hand, some hyphenated corporate names are alphabetized under the last rather than the first element in the name. Some organizations filing as trusts are listed under "T" for trust, followed by the name of the creator in approximate alphabetical order. In the second filming for California, records for foundations whose names begin with H, I, J, and the early K's were inadvertently omitted and consequently do not appear in this list. Instead, foundation names beginning with E and F were refilmed following the names beginning with G. It is expected that a complete list for California will be available in future refinements of this list.

The records for foundations located in Washington, D.C. were interfiled alphabetically with those in Maryland and appear on the Maryland film. A few foundations located in Hawaii were recorded on the second reel of microfilm for the Office of International Operations (O.I.O.), which covers certain foundations located outside the United States.

Returns for some foundations which received extensions for filing or whose status as a private foundation had not been determined at that time may not appear. Finally, because of certain provisions of the Tax Reform Act of 1969, there are a number of organizations included in this list which do not meet The Foundation Center's definition of a private foundation: ". . .a foundation may be defined as a nongovernmental, nonprofit organization, with funds and program managed by its own trustees or directors, and established to maintain or aid social, educational, charitable, religious, or other activities serving the common welfare."

Internal Revenue Service information returns 990 and 990-AR for 1971 will be available on aperture cards in the spring of 1973. Each card contains up to 15 images, and the majority of foundation records can be accommodated on two cards.

To order aperture cards for individual foundations from the Center, submit a list by state with foundation names, together with city location, in alphabetical sequence. This method will greatly facilitate the filling of orders. In ordering paper copies, please also indicate what portion of the return is required such as "list of grants paid" or "officers and trustees." Institutions will be billed on the following basis.

Prices: Aperture cards — $.15 per card (15 microimages, one image for each page of the original return)

Paper copies — $.25 per page

Postage and handling charge of $1.00 will be added for orders of six or more aperture cards or paper copies.

Order from: The Foundation Center, 888 Seventh Avenue, New York, New York 10019

Large blocks by state should be ordered directly from the Internal Revenue Service as follows:

Internal Revenue Service Price List

Aperture cards of public information data filed by foundations, on Return of Organization Exempt From Income Tax, (IRS Form 990), can be obtained from the Director, Internal Revenue Service Center, Post Office Box 187, Cornwells Heights, Pennsylvania 19020. Prices for complete sets of aperture cards for 1971 returns (by state) processed during 1972 follow.

State	Price	State	Price	State	Price
Alabama	$ 24.00	Louisiana	$ 26.00	Oklahoma	$ 28.00
Alaska	2.00	Maine	31.00	Oregon	37.00
Arizona	19.00	Maryland	57.00	Pennsylvania	238.00
Arkansas	17.00	Massachusetts	229.00	Rhode Island	23.00
California	306.00	Michigan	118.00	South Carolina	22.00
Colorado	43.00	Minnesota	81.00	South Dakota	5.00
Connecticut	97.00	Mississippi	9.00	Tennessee	41.00
Delaware	28.00	Missouri	94.00	Texas	160.00
District of Columbia	56.00	Montana	7.00	Utah	12.00
Florida	79.00	Nebraska	19.00	Vermont	7.00
Georgia	61.00	Nevada	4.00	Virginia	50.00
Hawaii	14.00	New Hampshire	25.00	Washington	41.00
Idaho	6.00	New Jersey	86.00	West Virginia	10.00
Illinois	256.00	New Mexico	4.00	Wisconsin	105.00
Indiana	78.00	New York	787.00	Wyoming	3.00
Iowa	40.00	North Carolina	61.00	OIO (Office	
Kansas	24.00	North Dakota	6.00	of International	
Kentucky	29.00	Ohio	257.00	Operations)	2.00

Complete set: $3,864.00

ALABAMA

First Filming

Adler (Emanuel A.) Testamentary Charitable Trust, Birmingham, 1/001
Advance Foundation, Birmingham, 1/002
Alabama Christian College, Montgomery, 1/003
Alabama Journalism Scholarship Trust, Birmingham, 1/003
Alabama Safety Council, Inc., Montgomery, 1/004
Aland (Leon & Leanore) Fdn., Birmingham, 1/004
Albright (E. Roy) Fdn. Merchants, Mobile, 1/004
Annville Institute Endowment Fund, Gadsden, 1/005
Avondale Educational and Charitable Fdn., Sylacauga, 1/005
Avondale Presbyterian Church Trust, Birmingham, 1/007
Baker (Raymon J.) Foundation, Decatur, 1/008
Batre (Lloyd) Scholarship Trust Fund, Mobile, 1/009
Bear (T. L.) Fdn., Montgomery, 1/010
Bedsole (J.L.) Fdn., Mobile, 1/010
Bartlett (Bessie) Loan Fund, Montgomery, 1/011
Blount Fdn., Montgomery, 1/012
Blount (Roberts & Mildred) Educational Charitable Fdn., Montgomery, 1/012
Brackin (Nelson) Fdn., Mobile, 1/013
Brightwell (A.T.) School Trust, Montgomery, 1/013
Britton (Margaret and William R.) Charitable Trust, Montgomery, 1/014
Cabaniss Fdn., Birmingham, 1/015
Caldwell Foundry Employee Credit Union, Birmingham, 1/016
Cemetery Care Fund, Montgomery, 1/016
Charico Non Profit Corp., Birmingham, 1/016
Charity Fund of White Employees of American Cast Iron Pipe Company, Birmingham, 1/017
Charity Fund of Colored Employees of American Cast Iron Pipe Company, Birmingham, 1/017
Children's Fresh Air Farm Trust, Birmingham, 1/018
Clark (Allen) Fdn., Birmingham, 1/019
Cohen (Mortimer & Josephine) Fund, Montgomery, 1/020
Comer (E. T. & B. B.) Irrevocable Trust, Birmingham, 1/020
Cowikee Educational & Charitable Fdn., Birmingham, 1/020
Cross (Emma T. Martin) Fdn. for the Aged, Birmingham, 1/022
Dean (Maude B.) Test Tr for Children's Hospital, Birmingham, 1/023
Dix (Britt) Memorial Scholarship Fund, Birmingham, 1/024
Dorsey (Claude E.), Jr. Memorial Scholarship Fund, Birmingham, 1/025
Dunlap (David R.) Memorial Trust, Mobile, 1/026
Dunlap (George H.) IV Memorial Trust, Mobile, 1/027
Elmore, (Stanhope E.) Charitable Trust, Montgomery, 1/027
First Presbyterian Church, Montgomery, 1/028
Flack (J. Hunter) Fdn., Montgomery, 1/028
Gallalee Fdn., Mobile, 1/029
Gartrell Fdn., Oneonta, 1/029
Gaston (A.G.) Fdn., Birmingham, 1/030
Gaston Youth Fdn., Birmingham, 1/031
Goltsman (Sidney S.) Fdn., Montgomery, 1/031
Grayson Family Fdn., Birmingham, 1/032
Greil (Gaston J. and Faye S.) Fund, Montgomery, 1/032
Gulf Foundation, Mobile, 1/033

Hanson Fdn., Sipsey, 1/033
Health Workers Association of Jefferson County, Birmingham, 1/034
Held Foundation, Birmingham, 1/034
Hendon (John F.) Fdn., Birmingham, 1/034
Hess Fdn., Birmingham, 1/035
Hodgson (James & Elizabeth) Memorial Fdn., Montgomery, 1/037
Holberg (Abe and Dora) Memorial Trust, Birmingham, 1/037
Hutson (Melvin & Virginia) Fdn., Decatur, 1/037
Hyde (Oscar) Christian Fdn., Birmingham, 1/038
Ingalls Fdn., Birmingham, 1/039
Ingalls (Elesabeth & Barbara) Fdn., Birmingham, 1/040
Ireland Fdn., Birmingham, 1/041
Jackson (Mozelle Harris) Scholarship, Albertville, 1/042
Jackson (Sara Ann) Fdn., Albertville, 1/042
Jemison (John) Fdn., Birmingham, 1/043
Johnston Fdn., Huntsville, 1/044
Johnson (Caroline) Trust for Community Chest, Birmingham, 1/044
Johnson (Crawford T.) Trust for Children's Hospital, Birmingham, 1/045
Johnson (Crawford T.) Trust for Community Chest, Birmingham, 1/045
Jordan Family Fdn., Centre, 1/045
Kincey (Robert W.) Scholarship Trust, Tuscaloosa, 1/046
King (O. Harvey) Charitable Trust, Birmingham, 1/046
Linly-Heflin Scholarship Trust Fund, Birmingham, 1/047
Linn-Henley Charitable Trust, Birmingham, 1/047
Loeb (James L. and Joan B.) Fund, Montgomery, 1/048
Loeb (Lucien S. & Helen W.) Fund, Montgomery, 1/048
Loh Charitable and Educational Fdn., Mobile, 1/049
Lowry Foundation, Montgomery, 1/049
Manes (Agnes MacIntyre) Fdn., Mobile, 1/050
Magnes (Sidney) Fdn., Mobile, 1/050
Malbis Memorial Fdn., Daphne, 1/051
Marshall County Fdn. for Fine Arts, Guntersville, 1/052
Martin Fdn., Birmingham, 1/052
Mayer (Sol) Fdn., Mobile, 1/053
McGowin (Lillian C.) Fdn., Mobile, 1/054
McMillan (D. W.) Fdn., Brewton, 1/054
McWane Fdn., Birmingham, 1/055
Meyer (Robert R.) Fdn., Birmingham, 1/057
Meyer (Robert R.), Jr. Memorial Scholarship Trust, Birmingham, 1/057
Miller (H.S.) Trust for Jewish Community Center, Birmingham, 1/058
Mitchell Fdn., Mobile, 1/058
Moody (Lula J.) Item Nine Trust, Birmingham, 1/059
Morgan (L. D.) Trust, Montgomery, 1/059
Murray (Harriet) Memorial Trust, Birmingham, 1/059
Nash (James G.) Fdn., Birmingham, 1/060
New Williams Fdn., Birmingham, 1/061
Newhouse (Stanley & Eda) Fund, Montgomery, 1/062
Norton (Edward L.) Trust for Birmingham So. College, Birmingham, 1/064
Patterson (Christina) Trust for Children's Hospital, Birmingham, 1/065
Patterson (Christina) Trust for Hillman Hospital, Birmingham, 1/066
Patterson (Christina) Trust for the Neighborhood House, Birmingham, 1/066
Patterson (Christina) Trust for Presbyterian Home, Birmingham, 1/066
Patterson (Christina) Trust for So. Highland Church, Birmingham, 1/066
Pelzer (Eva L.) Fund, Montgomery, 1/067
Pelzer (Arthur) Presbyterian Home for Children, Montgomery, 1/067

Pelzer (Arthur & Eva L.) Trust for the Children's Protective Association, Montgomery, 1/068
Pelzer (Eva L.) Presbyterian Home for Children Fund, Montgomery, 1/068
Perdue (Graham) Fdn., Birmingham, 1/069
Phifer (Reese), Jr. Memorial Trust, Tuscaloosa, 1/070
Randa Inc., Montgomery, 1/070
Reese Fdn., Birmingham, 1/071
Robertson (Maude Davis) Test Trust, Birmingham, 1/071
Rose (Wm. Alfred) Fdn., Birmingham, 1/072
Rothschild (Carol W. & Myron J.) Fund, Montgomery, 1/072
Rucker Agee Fund, Birmingham, 1/073
Rushton Lectures Voluntary Trust, Birmingham, 1/074
Ryding (Herbert C.) Physics Fellowship Fund, Birmingham, 1/075
Russell (Benjamin & Roberta) Educational & Charitable, Alexander City, 1/075
St. John's Episcopal Church Seele Fund, Montgomery, 1/076
Salit Foundation, Birmingham, 1/076
Samford Fdn., Birmingham, 1/077
Sealy-Wilbanks Charitable Fdn. of Alexander City, Inc., Alexander City, 1/078
Seaman's Club of Mobile, Inc., Mobile, 1/078
Shores (Fred H.) Educational Scholarships Trust, Decatur, 1/079
Smith (Don McQueen) 1963 Charitable Trust, Montgomery, 1/080
Smith (Gordon) Fdn., Inc., Mobile, 1/080
Smith (Louise Maytag) Charitable Trust, Montgomery, 1/081
Smith (Louis Maytag) Memorial Trust, Montgomery, 1/082
Smith (M. W.) Jr., Fdn., Mobile, 1/082
Stockham (William H. and Kate F.) Fdn., Inc., Birmingham, 1/084
Styles (Mattie A.) Charitable Trust, Birmingham, 1/085
G. M. & O. - Tigrett Fdn., Mobile, 1/086
Tisdale (Mary W.) Fund for the Protestant Episcopal Church in The Diocese of Alabama, Montgomery, 1/087
Turner (Tommy C.) Memorial Fdn., Werumpka, 1/087
Tutwiler (Margaret C.) Etal Trust, Birmingham, 1/087
United States Pipe and Foundry Contributions Trust, Birmingham, 1/088
University of Alabama Huntsville Fdn., Huntsville, 1/088
Upchurch Charitable Trust, Birmingham, 1/089
Vick (Marjorie Dixon) Memorial Scholarship Trust, Andalusia, 1/090
Weil (Adolph Jr. and Robert S.) Fund, Montgomery, 1/091
Weil (Cecile & Leonel) Fund, Inc., Montgomery, 1/091
Wendland (Diane) 1962 Charitable Trust, Montgomery, 1/092
Wendland (Don Smith-Diane) Trust, Montgomery, 1/093
Wiener (Kathryn & Julian) Fund, Montgomery, 1/093
Williams (Thomas W.) Test Trust, Birmingham, 1/093
Vestavia Hills Baptist Church, Birmingham, 1/094
Ward (Lyman) Military Academy, Montgomery, 1/094

Second Filming

Alabama Friends of the Institutes, Montgomery, 2/001
All Charities Trust Inc., Birmingham, 2/001
Americas Junior Miss Scholarship Fdn., Mobile, 2/002
Associated Charities Fdn., Inc., Bessemer, 2/003
Bradford Fdn., Inc., Birmingham, 2/004
Chandler Fdn., Mobile, 2/004

Chappell Fdn., Birmingham, 2/005

Dothan Chamber of Commerce, Dothan, 2/006

Civitan International Hamilton, Hamilton, 2/006

Crampton Scholarship Endowment Trust, Mobile, 2/007

Dearmon (James S. & Bessie F.) Fdn., Bladon Springs, 2/007

Elmore County Farm Bureau, Inc., Wetumpka, 2/008

Faith (Edward W.) Life Insurance Trust, Mobile, 2/008

Friedman (V. Hugo) Trust for Tuscaloosa City Schools, Tuscaloosa, 2/009

Goldsmith (Mamie E.) Trust, Mobile, 2/010

Gordy-Mead-Britton Fdn., Montgomery, 2/010

Hadassah & National Council of Jewish Women Tr. U/W of Milton Fichold, Mobile, 2/011

Mobile Female Benevolent Society Inc. Trust, Mobile, 2/011

Hargis (Estes) Charitable Fdn., Birmingham, 2/012

Hargis Christian Retreat Charitable Trust, Birmingham, 2/013

Held Fdn., Inc., Birmingham, 2/013

Hicks (James L.) Charitable Trust, Talladega, 2/013

Hillman (Emily S.) Testamentary Trust, Birmingham, 2/014

Huntsville Association of Folk Musicians, Huntsville, 2/014

Ingalls Fdn., Inc. Trust for University of Ala., Birmingham, 2/014

Jackson (Sallie E.) Testamentary Trust, Birmingham, 2/014

Johnson Fdn., Inc., Geneva, 2/015

Johnson (Crawford) Jr., Charitable Trust, Birmingham, 2/015

Killgore (J. A. & Ophelia) Scholarship Trust Fund, 2/017

Le Moyne Trust Fund, Fairhope, 2/017

Linn-Henley Charitable Trust, Birmingham, 2/018

Magnes (Sidney) Fdn., Inc., Mobile, 2/019

Matthews Fdn., Inc., Phenix City, 2/020

Memorial Institute of Pathology, Inc., Birmingham, 2/020

Middleton (Robert) Theological Endowment, Mobile, 2/021

M. & M. Charitable Fdn., Montgomery, 2/022

Nitsos Frangista Fdn., Mobile, 2/022

O'Neal (Kirkman & Elizabeth) Fdn., Inc., Birmingham, 2/022

Peterson (John A.) Charitable Trust, Montgomery, 2/024

Phantom Host, Montgomery, 2/024

Presbyterian Home for Children Perpetual Trust, Montgomery, 2/025

Ramsey Fdn., Dothan, 2/026

Ruby Fund of Alpha Omicron Pi, Montgomery, 2/028

Samford Fdn., Birmingham, 2/028

Scholarship Fdn. of the Alabama Pharmeceutical, Birmingham, 2/029

Shades Valley Presbyterian Church Irrevocable Trust, Birmingham, 2/029

S. O. S. Fdn. of Jefferson County, Birmingham, 2/031

South Central Alabama Girl Scout Council, Inc., Montgomery, 2/031

Steiner Fdn., Birmingham, 2/032

Hicks (Elizabeth) Charitable Trust, Birmingham, 2/032

Trust Under Article Fifteen of the Will of Kate K. Middleton for Christ Church, Mobile, 2/033

Vann (J. A.) Charitable Trust, Birmingham, 2/034

Warner (David) Fdn. Trust, Tuscaloosa, 2/034

ALASKA

First Filming

International Brotherhood of Painters and Allied Trades, Fairbanks, 1/002

Carlquist-Howell Fdn., Inc., Anchorage, 1/003

Goldstein Scottish Rite Trust, Juneau, 1/004

Loussac Fdn., Anchorage, 1/004

Loussac Trust, Anchorage, 1/004

Rasmuson Fdn., Anchorage, 1/005

Second Filming

Atwood Fdn., Inc., Anchorage, 2/003

Clement Fdn., Inc., Anchorage, 2/004

Sitka Longshoremen's Benevolent Association, Sitka, 2/004

ARIZONA

First Filming

B G Y Fdn., Tucson, 1/001

du Bois (E. Blois) Fdn., Pheonix, 1/001

Bross Fdn., Prescott, 1/002

Capin Charitable Fdn., Nogales, 1/002

Carver (Harry E.) Trust Fund, Sun City, 1/002

Casa de Usted Fdn., Scottsdale, 1/003

Chambers (Gordon R.) Fdn., Phoenix, 1/003

Choate Fdn., Phoenix, 1/003

Cohen (Maurice & Fannie) Fdn. for Social Welfare, Tucson, 1/003

Cochise College Fdn., Douglas, 1/004

Davis (Selma & Lew) Fdn., Tucson, 1/004

Demund Fdn., Phoenix, 1/005

Earl (Eddie & Madelon) Charitable Fdn., Tucson, 1/005

Eaton (Ralph H. & Frances M.) Fdn., Phoenix, 1/006

Ellsworth (Leo) Fdn., Queen Creek, 1/006

Engineering College Endowment Fund, Phoenix, 1/007

Flinn Fdn., Phoenix, 1/007

Forsman (Anne N.) Fdn., Phoenix, 1/008

Freeman Fdn., Tucson, 1/008

French Fdn., Scottsdale, 1/009

Freudenthal (James H. & Margaret E.) Fdn., Tucson, 1/010

General Time Fdn., Phoenix, 1/010

Goor Fdn., Phoenix, 1/011

Grimshaw Fdn., Phoenix, 1/012

Grossman (Esther & Morris) Fdn., Tucson, 1/012

Grunon (Lois) Memorial Clinic, Phoenix, 1/013

Halstead Fdn., Phoenix, 1/014

Harber Fdn., Phoenix, 1/014

Herberger Fdn., Scottsdale, 1/015

Horrigan (Mabel) Fdn., Phoenix, 1/015

Horwitch (Albert A.) Fdn., Phoenix, 1/016

Jackson Charitable Fund, Scottsdale, 1/017

Jacobson (L.C.) Fdn., Phoenix, 1/017

Kieckhefer (J. W.) Fdn., Prescott, 1/017

Kieckhefer (Thelma H.) Charitable Fdn., Phoenix, 1/019

Kingston Philanthropic Trust Formerly New York, Tucson, 1/019

Kopmeier (Loretta Miller) Charitable Fdn., Paradise Valley, 1/020

Levy (Leon) Charitable Fdn., Tucson, 1/021

Lime (Paul) Plant Employees Insurance Fund, Douglas, 1/021

Lincoln (David C.) Fdn., Phoenix, 1/022

Long (John F.) Fdn., Phoenix, 1/022

Louis (Paul) Fdn., Phoenix, 1/023

Lutfy (William P.) Fdn., Phoenix, 1/023

Mamer (Kehoe) Fdn. Formerly Michigan, Tucson, 1/024

Marshall Fdn., Tucson, 1/024

Mathews Fdn., Tucson, 1/025

McDonald (J.M.) Fdn., Scottsdale, 1/026

Morris (Margaret T.) Fdn., Prescott, 1/028

Mullan (Read & Frances B.) Fdn., Phoenix, 1/029

Murphey (John & Helen) Fdn., Tucson, 1/029

O'Connell (Daniel & Marjorie) Fdn., Tucson, 1/030

Pantano Fdn., Tucson, 1/031

Parkman (Elizabeth Ann) Fdn., Tucson, 1/031

Phoenix Welfare Fdn., Phoenix, 1/032

Phoenix Welfare Fdn., Phoenix, 1/033

Rich Fdn., Phoenix, 1/033

Rosenbaum (Morris & Marye) Philanthropies, Tucson, 1/034

Seventh Day Adventist Missionary Fdn., Phoenix, 1/035

Silver-Brier Fdn., Scottsdale, 1/035

Simon (A.C.) Fdn., Tucson, 1/036

Spalding (Eliot) Fdn., Tucson, 1/037

Stewart (Spencer D.) Charitable Trust, Phoenix, 1/037

Vance Fdn., Tucson, 1/037

Volk (Celia & Marvin H.) Fdn., Tucson, 1/038

Webb (Del E.) Fdn., Phoenix, 1/038

Webb-Jacobson Fdn., Phoenix, 1/038

Wright (David & Gladys) Fdn., Phoenix, 1/039

Wright (Frank Lloyd) Memorial Fdn., Scottsdale, 1/039

Second Filming

Adamson (Dr. E.W.) Scholarship Fund, Pheonix, 2/001

Advance Allied Fdn., Phoenix, 2/002

Allergy and Asthma Fdn. of Arizona, Phoenix, 2/003

Amerind Fdn., Inc., The, Dragoon, 2/004

Anchor Fdn. for Alcoholics, Inc., Phoenix, 2/005

Arnold (Arthur A.) Fdn., Inc., Kingman, 2/005

Babbitt (Madeline and George), Jr. Fdn., Phoenix, 2/005

Bennett (Josephine F.) Fdn., Phoenix, 2/006

Bergh (Henry) Fdn., 2/006

Catalina Flying Eagle, Inc., Tucson, 2/006

Corday (Ruth) Fdn., The, Scottsdale, 2/007

duBois (E. Blois) Fdn., Inc., Phoenix, 2/007

Echols - Reynolds Memorial Fund, Fort Smith, 2/008

Elm Street Fdn. Questionnaire, Tucson, 2/008

Flagg (A. L.) Fdn. for the Advancement of Earth Science, Phoenix, 2/008

Fdn. for the Science of Spiritual Law, Tonopah, 2/009

Genematas (Nicholas W.) Fdn., Tucson, 2/009

Grand (Richard) Fdn. for Legal Research and Education, Tucson, 2/010

Grimshaw Fdn., Inc., Phoenix, 2/010

Heller (Max T.) Fdn., Tucson, 2/011

Indoor and Good Sports Building Corporation, Tucson, 2/012

Jordan (B. F.) Fdn., Inc., Scottsdale, 2/012

Kai Fdn. for Agricultural Research, Marana, 2/013

Knoell Bros. Construction, Inc., Fdn., Tempe, 2/014

Sheldon Kotz Memorial Fdn., Tucson, 2/015

K 2 Fdn., Tucson, 2/015

Langerman Fdn., Phoenix, 2/016

Long (John F.) Fdn., Inc., Phoenix, 2/017

Mason (Lloyd W.) Charitable Fdn., Scottsdale, 2/017

Millar (Gregory) Music Fdn., Tucson, 2/018

Jacoby (Milton and Dorothy) Fdn., Tucson, 2/020

Mulcahy Fdn., Tucson, 2/021

Murrell (M.C.) Fdn., Inc., Scottsdale, 2/022

National Railroad Historical Society, Tucson, 2/022

O'Rielly (Frank C.) Fdn., Inc., Tucson, 2/023

Paulin Fdn., The, Tucson, 2/024

Payne (Ann) Fdn., Phoenix, 2/024

Pima County Republican Women Educational Trust Fund, The, Tucson, 2/025

Prevo Fdn., The, Tucson, 2/025

Producers Cotton Oil Agricultural Fdn., Phoenix, 2/025
Raymond Educational Fdn., Flagstaff, 2/026
Sahara - Nevada Fdn., Phoenix, 2/027
Simpson (Robert E.) Memorial Trust Fund, The, Phoenix, 2/027
Simroe Fdn., Tucson, 2/028
Snyder (Lois M.) Memorial Trust Fund, Phoenix, 2/028
Southwest Fdn. for Medical Research and Education, The, Phoenix, 2/029
Stanley (Dean) Fdn., The, Phoenix, 2/029
Stonewall Fdn., The, Tucson, 2/030
Sun City Community Fund, Inc., Sun City, 2/031
Sunshine Kiwanis Community Service Fdn. of Tucson, Tucson, 2/031
Tell Fdn., The, Phoenix, 2/031
Van Ness Fdn., Phoenix, 2/033
Waddell (Donald Ware) Fdn., Waddell, 2/033
Whiteman (Edna Rider) Fdn., Phoenix, 2/034
Witten Fdn., The, Phoenix, 2/035

ARKANSAS

First Filming

Arkansas Association for Retarded Children, Little Rock, 1/001
Arkansas Gazette Fdn., Little Rock, 1/001
Arkansas Opportunity Fund, Little Rock, 1/002
Arkansas Society of Certified Public Accountants Student Loan Fund, Texarkana, 1/002
Ayers Fdn., Fort Smith, 1/003
Ayers (Walter W.) Trust, Fort Smith, 1/003
Barton Fdn., El Dorado, 1/004
Blass (Gus) Company Fdn., Little Rock, 1/005
Black (L.A.) & J.H. Boone Fdn., DeWitt, 1/006
Boston Store Fdn., Fort Smith, 1/006
Brown Fdn., Little Rock, 1/007
Bryant Fdn., Clarksville, 1/008
Caldwell (Walter O.) Fdn., Fort Smith, 1/009
Camden Furniture Fdn., Camden, 1/009
Cargile (Stark & Mary Frances) Fund, Little Rock, 1/010
Coca-Cola Bottling Company of Arkansas Charitable Trust, Little Rock, 1/011
Cohn (M.M.) Company Fdn., Little Rock, 1/011
Cook Fdn., Pine Bluff, 1/012
Crowe Fdn., Stuttgart, 1/012
Crowley Benevolent Association, Little Rock, 1/013
Darragh Fdn., Little Rock, 1/013
Dunklin (George H.) Association, Pine Bluff, 1/014
Dunklin (M.E. Black) Trust, Pine Bluff, 1/015
Fausett Fdn., Little Rock, 1/015
Forsgren (Gilbert) Charitable Trust, Fort Smith, 1/016
Easy K Fdn., Zion, 1/016
Forsgren (Raymond) Charitable Trust, Fort Smith, 1/016
Fulbright Fdn., Fayetteville, 1/017
Gandhi Fdn. of America, Pine Bluff, 1/017
Garnett (Dr. Algernon Sidney) Memorial Fund, Little Rock, 1/018
Godfrey (Bitha) & Maude J. Thomas Charitable Fdn., Fort Smith, 1/018
Grundfest Fdn. of Arkansas, Little Rock, 1/020
Hennessy (William Thomas & May Pitman) Fdn., Fort Smith, 1/021
Home - Church - School Fdn., Little Rock, 1/022
Inglewood Fdn., Little Rock, 1/022
Ingram Fdn., Pine Bluff, 1/023
Jones (Harvey & Bernice) Fdn., Springdale, 1/023

Jones (Kenneth G.) Charitable Trust, Little Rock, 1/024
Hough (Edward C.) & Mary Hough Kimble Fdn., Rogers, 1/024
Lyon Fdn., Little Rock, 1/025
Magale (John F. & Joanna G.) Trust for Southern State College, Magnolia, 1/026
Magale (John F. & Joanna G.) Trust for Columbia County Library, Magnolia, 1/026
Magale (John F. & Joanna G.) Endowment Trust for United Methodist Children's Home & United Methodist Church in Arkansas, Magnolia, 1/026
Markham (Joy Pratt) Charitable Fdn., Fayetteville, 1/027
Ney Fdn., Fort Smith, 1/027
O'Daniel (F.A.) Fdn., DeWitt, 1/028
Odom (Jess) Fdn., Little Rock, 1/028
P & J Fdn., Pine Bluff, 1/029
Peterson Fdn., Decatur, 1/029
Pine Bluff Fdn., Pine Bluff, 1/030
Pine Bluff Boys Club Fdn., Pine Bluff, 1/031
Pine Bluff Junior College Fdn., Pine Bluff, 1/031
Matthews (John Pope) Fdn., North Little Rock, 1/031
Rich Family Charitable Fdn., West Memphis, 1/032
Riggs Benevolent Fund, Little Rock, 1/032
Riggs Family Charitable Trust, Little Rock, 1/033
Rockwin Fund, Morrilton, 1/033
Ross Fdn., Arkadelphia, 1/034
Rust (John) Fdn., Pine Bluff, 1/035
Seabrook - Bellingrath Fdn., Pine Bluff, 1/036
Siebert Fdn., Little Rock, 1/036
Smith (Pete & Betty) Fdn., Hot Springs, 1/036
Stevenson (Lillian Magale) Endowment Trust for Mount St. Mary Academy, Little Rock, 1/037
Stevenson (Lillian Magale) Endowment Trust, Magnolia, 1/038
Strauss McCaskill Fdn., Little Rock, 1/038
Sugarman (Barney) Memorial Trust, Fort Smith, 1/038
Sutton (Doss T.) Charitable Fdn., Fort Smith, 1/039
Taylor Fdn., Fort Smith, 1/039
Tenenbaum Fdn., Little Rock, 1/040
Thomas (Godfrey) Fdn., DeWitt, 1/040
Tilles Fdn., Fort Smith, 1/041
Trotter Fdn., Pine Bluff, 1/042
Turpin Memorial Association, Stuttgart, 1/042
Tyson Fdn., Little Rock, 1/043
Union National Fdn., Little Rock, 1/043
Rockefeller (Winthrop) Fund, Little Rock, 1/044
Wrape Family Charitable Trust, Little Rock, 1/044

Second Filming

Adkins - Phelps Fdn., North Little Rock, 2/001
Arkansas Congress of Parents & Teachers, Little Rock, 2/002
Arkansas Pharmaceutical Fdn., Little Rock, 2/002
Arnold (Hale) Fdn., Jonesboro, 2/003
Bailey Fdn., Little Rock, 2/003
Hamilton (Barrett) Fdn., Little Rock, 2/004
Brown (Russell) & Company Fdn., Little Rock, 2/005
Clark (L.W.) Fdn., Fordyce, 2/005
Coleman Dairy Fdn., Little Rock, 2/005
Dantes Scholarship Fdn., Dumas, 2/006
Darby Fdn., Little Rock, 2/007
Cullum (E.L.) Fdn., Little Rock, 2/007
Stonecypher (Evelyn L.) Fund, Fort Smith, 2/008
Franklin (Harold & Marjorie) Fdn., Pine Bluff, 2/008
Freudenberg Fdn., Stuttgart, 2/008
Gibson - Duncan Educational Trust, Little Rock, 2/008
Thomas (Godfrey) Fdn., DeWitt, 2/009
Young (Gordon E.) Fdn., Pine Bluff, 2/009

Grand Prairie Art Council, Stuttgart, 2/010
Grapette Fdn., Camden, 2/010
Gray (John T.) Fdn., Jonesboro, 2/011
Hogan Fdn., Little Rock, 2/011
Dunklin (James P.) Trust, Pine Bluff, 2/012
Wadley (J.K.) Fdn., Texarkana, 2/012
Wallace (Johnnie Donaghey) Fdn., Little Rock, 2/013
Johnson - Knoop Fdn., Clarksville, 2/015
Speer (Melanie Holt) Fdn., Fort Smith, 2/016
McCord (M.S. & Myrtle) Fdn., Little Rock, 2/017
Christian Camp Fdn., Little Rock, 2/018
Morevski Fdn., Little Rock, 2/018
Murphy Fdn., El Dorado, 2/018
Nolan (William C. & Theodosia Murphy) Fdn., El Dorado, 2/019
Navy League of Hot Springs, Hot Springs, 2/020
Ottenheimer Brothers Fdn., Little Rock, 2/021
Palmer Fdn., Texarkana, 2/021
Peace (M.E.) Charitable Trust, Magnolia, 2/022
Reynolds (Donald W.) Fdn., Fort Smith, 2/022
Terry (Seymour) Memorial Scholarship Trust Fund, Little Rock, 2/023
Smith - Holloway Fdn., Little Rock, 2/024
Smith - Williams, Friday, & Bowen Fdn., Little Rock, 2/024
Tennyson (L.E.), Jr. Fdn., Smackover, 2/025
Union Carbide Employees Acitivty Club, Hot Springs, 2/026
Walker (Billy) Evangelistic Association, College City, 2/026
Worthen Charitable Trust, Little Rock, 2/026
Sturgis (W.P.) Fdn., Arkadelphia, 2/026

CALIFORNIA

First Filming

Abramson (Jacob) Fdn., Salinas, 1/001
Adams Fund, Los Angeles, 1/001
Adams (Berle H.) Fdn., North Hollywood, 1/002
Adler (Ben & Pauline) Fdn., Los Angeles, 1/003
Adler (Cyrus Max) Fund, Pacific Palisades, 1/004
Adler (John Robert) Family Fund, Los Angeles, 1/004
Adolph's Fdn., Burbank, 1/005
Aeronca Fdn., Torrance, 1/007
Aftergood (George), Sr. Fdn., Van Nuys, 1/008
Agape Fdn., Los Angeles, 1/008
Aid-Mates, Beverly Hills, 1/008
A.J.S. Fdn., Los Angeles, 1/009
Alabaster Fdn., Riverside, 1/010
Alanson (Mabel B.) Memorial Fund, San Francisco, 1/010
Albertson Fdn., Los Angeles, 1/011
Alexander (De Witt & Edith) Fund, Berkeley, 1/011
Alhambra First Methodist Fdn., Alhambra, 1/011
Alhambra Foundry Co. Ltd. Scholarship Fdn., Alhambra, 1/012
Allen-Ewing Fdn., La Jolla, 1/013
Allen (Winifred & Harry B.) Fdn., San Francisco, 1/013
Allen (H. Clifford) Scholarship Fund, Los Angeles, 1/014
Allequash Fdn., Pasadena, 1/014
Allgemeiner Deutscher Frauen Verein, San Francisco, 1/015
Allied Post N. 302 Youth Fdn., Los Angeles, 1/016
Almanor Scholarship Fund, Chester, 1/017
Alpert Family Fdn., Hollywood, 1/018
Alpert (J. Norman) Fdn., Beverly Hills, 1/019

Alpha Omega Fdn., Orinda, 1/020
Alschuler (Leon S. Evelyn G.) Fdn., Beverly Hills, 1/020
Alta Vista Fdn., Santa Barbara, 1/021
Ambrose Fdn., Santa Monica, 1/022
American BroTherhood for the Blind, Los Angeles, 1/023
American Building Maintenance Charitable Fdn., Los Angeles, 1/023
American Cement Fdn., Los Angeles, 1/024
American Fdn. for Oceanography, Los Angeles, 1/025
American Institute of Family Relations, Los Angeles, 1/026
Amzalak (James) Fdn., La Jolla, 1/026
Anderson (Harry W.) Charitable Fdn., Menlo Park, 1/027
Anderson Fdn., San Diego, 1/028
Anderson (Frederick & Elizabeth) Fdn., Menlo Park, 1/030
Andreas (Frank A.) Scholarship Fdn., Delano, 1/030
Angel on My Shoulder Fdn., Newport Beach, 1/031
Anthroposophical Fdn. of California, Los Angeles, 1/031
Appel Fdn., Los Angeles, 1/032
Apple Valley Fdn., Apple Valley, 1/032
Arakelian (K.) Fdn., Fresno, 1/033
Argo Fdn., Berkeley, 1/035
Argonaut Charitable Fdn., Los Angeles, 1/035
Arkelian (Ben H. & Gladys) Fdn., Bakersfield, 1/036
Rutter Armey Fdn., Fresno, 1/038
Arnell Family Fdn., Los Angeles, 1/038
Arnovitz (J.B.), Inc., San Francisco, 1/039
Artevel Fdn., Los Angeles, 1/040
Arthur Fdn., Woodland Hills, 1/041
Ashford (Lucille) Fdn., Los Angeles, 1/042
Ashrule Fdn., Beverly Hills, 1/042
Assurance Sciences Fdn., Mount View, 1/043
Atkinson Fdn., South San Francisco, 1/043
Atkinson (Myrtle L.) Fdn., Los Angeles, 1/046
Avery Fdn., San Marino, 1/048
Avery (Alice O'Neill) Fdn., Santa Monica, 1/049
Babcock (Katharine) Trust, San Francisco, 1/050
Bach (Karl) Fdn., San Francisco, 1/050
Bacon (Francis) Fdn., Claremont, 1/051
Baez (Joan C.) Charitable Trust, San Jose, 1/053
Baker Family Fdn., Newport Beach, 1/054
Baker (R.C.) Fdn., Los Angeles, 1/054
Ball (Lucille) Fdn., Century City, 1/056
Ballard (Virginia) Memorial Scholarship Fund, Long Beach, 1/057
Ballman Charitable Fdn., Los Angeles, 1/057
Bamberger-Allen Health & Education Fdn., Salt Lake City (Utah), 1/058
Bank of America Fdn., San Francisco, 1/059
Bank of America-Giannini Fdn., San Francisco, 1/061
Bannan (Arline & Thomas J.) Fdn., Lynwood, 1/065
Banta (Merle H.) Fdn., San Marino, 1/067
Barness, Candiotty, Finkle Fdn., Beverly Hills, 1/068
Barnum (Helen W.) Fdn., Eureka, 1/069
Barshop (Nathan & Coe) Fdn., Los Angeles, 1/070
Bart Family Fdn., San Francisco, 1/071
Bartman Fdn., Beverly Hills, 1/071
Baskin Fdn., Vallejo, 1/072
Bates (John) Fdn., San Francisco, 1/073
Battistone Fdn., Santa Barbara, 1/074
Baughn (Rod) & Joel Copeland Memorial Scholarship Fdn., Orange, 1/075
Baum (Dwight C.) Fdn., San Marino, 1/075
Baxter (Donald E.) Fdn., Los Angeles, 1/075
B & D Fdn., Los Angeles, 1/076
Beals (Gale & Marie) Fdn., Palm Springs, 1/077
Beaver Fdn., Oakland, 1/077
Bechtel (Elizabeth Hay) Fund, San Francisco, 1/078

Bechtel (S.D.), Jr. Fdn., San Francisco, 1/078
Behrstock Fdn., Los Angeles, 1/079
Beidner (George & Lillian) Fdn., Los Angeles, 1/079
Bekins (Milo W.) Fdn., Los Angeles, 1/081
Bell (Lionel & Theresa) Fdn., Beverly Hills, 1/082
Belvedere Scientific Fund, San Francisco, 1/083
Benbough (Legler) Fdn., San Diego, 1/084
Bendix (Herman M.) & Betty L. Bendix Fdn., Studio City, 1/084
Benjamin (Morley & Janet) Fdn., Los Angeles, 1/085
Berg (Mischa F.) Fdn., Beverly Hills, 1/085
Bergen Fdn., Los Angeles, 1/086
Bergen (William B.) Fdn., El Segundo, 1/086
Berger (H.N. & Frances C.) Fdn., Arcadia, 1/087
Berliner (Robert A.) Family Fdn., Los Angeles, 1/087
Beta Theta Pi Scholastic Fdn., Newport Beach, 1/089
Beverly Hills Clinic Non-Profit Fdn., Beverly Hills, 1/090
Biblical Colloquium, San Anselmo, 1/091
Bidart Family Fdn., Bakersfield, 1/091
Bing Fund, Los Angeles, 1/091
Bing Fund, Inc., Los Angeles, 1/093
Biological Research Fdn., San Francisco, 1/094
Bird-Pohndorf Fdn., Palm Springs, 1/095
Bireley Fdn., Los Angeles, 1/096
Birnbaum (David Saul) Fdn., Los Angeles, 1/098
Birnkrant (Michael C.) Fdn., Los Angeles, 1/099
Birnkrout (Michael C. & Cecele) Fdn., Los Angeles, 1/099
Bisagno (Pete) Scholarship Fund, Placerville, 1/099
Bissinger (Paul A.) Fdn., San Francisco, 1/100
B & J Scholarship, San Marino, 1/101
Blabon (Anna C.) Trust, Corning, 1/101
Blackburn Fdn., Los Angeles, 1/102
Blazina Fdn. of Sports Medicine, Los Angeles, 1/103
Bleitz Wildlife Fdn., Hollywood, 1/103
B.L.E.-692 (Brotherhood of Locomotive Engineers), Tracy, 1/104
Bloomfield Fdn., Los Angeles, 1/105
Bloomfield (Sam & Rie) Fdn., Los Angeles, 1/106
Blum (Richard C.) Fdn., San Rafael, 1/106
Blume (John A. & Ruth C.) Fdn., Hillsborough, 1/106
Blumenfield (Joseph) Fdn., San Francisco, 1/107
Blumenthal (Julius) Fdn., San Francisco, 1/107
Blumenthal (Mr. & Mrs. Harold) Fund, Rancho Santa Fe, 1/108
Blywise (Richard A.) Fdn., Beverly Hills, 1/108
Bock Fdn., Los Angeles, 1/109
Boehn-Buzzell Fdn., Pasadena, 1/110
Bolotin (Hyman) Fdn., Santa Monica, 1/111
Bon Air Fdn., Los Angeles, 1/111
Bontems Fdn., Montebello, 1/112
Booth Fdn., Atherton, 1/113
Booth-Holt-Carlson Fdn., Laguna Beach, 1/113
Borkey Fdn., Paso Robles, 1/114
Boswell (James G.) Fdn., Los Angeles, 1/114
Bothin Helping Fund, San Francisco, 1/115
Bowes-English Education Fund, Los Angeles, 1/118
Bowles Family Fdn., San Francisco, 1/118
Boyd (Katherine & William) Fund, San Francisco, 1/119
Boye (Mary August) Fdn., Los Angeles, 1/119
Bradshaw Fdn., La Jolla, 1/121
Brant (David O.) Fdn., Los Angeles, 1/122
Brantman (Joyce & William) Fdn., Tiburon, 1/122
Breslow Fdn., Beverly Hills, 1/122
Bridge Mountain Fdn., Ben Lommond, 1/123
Bridges (Robert & Alice) Fdn., San Francisco, 1/123

Broad (Eli & Edythe L.) Fdn., Los Angeles, 1/125
Broadcast Fdn. of California, Los Angeles, 1/125
Brody (Frances & Sidney) Charitable Fund, Beverly Hills, 1/126
Brooks (Alton M.) Fdn., Santa Ana, 1/127
Brooks-Mathews Fdn., San Leandro, 1/128
Brotman Fdn. of California, Los Angeles, 1/129
Brotman (Alix) Fdn., Los Angeles, 1/130
Brown (E.C.) Fdn., San Francisco, 1/130
Brown (Emil) Fund, Los Angeles, 1/131
Bryan Fdn., San Francisco, 1/132
Brydegaard Fdn., San Diego, 1/133
Buchalter, Nemer, Fields & Savitch Charitable Fdn., Los Angeles, 1/134
Buffum (Betty Upham) Charitable Fdn., Long Beach, 1/135
Bull (Henry W.) Fdn., Beverly Hills, 1/135
Bullocks Fdn., Los Angeles, 1/137
Bunnell (Sterling) Memorial Fdn., San Francisco, 1/137
Bureau of Home Applicances of San Diego County, San Diego, 1/138
Burnand (Alphonse A.) Medical & Educational Fdn., Borrego Springs, 1/138
Burnand (A.A.) Memorial Fund, Santa Barbara, 1/139
Burns-Dumphy Fdn., San Francisco, 1/139
Burns Family Fdn., Garden Grove, 1/140
Burke (Edmund A. & Marguerite L.A.) Fdn., Los Angeles, 1/141
Butts (John H.) Fdn., Santa Barbara, 1/141
Caddock Fdn., Riverside, 1/141
California Alpha Delta Phi Memorial Fdn., Berkley, 1/142
California Center on Environment, San Francisco, 1/143
California County Government Education Fdn., Sacramento, 1/143
California Jockey Club Fdn., San Francisco, 1/144
California Real Estate Association Scholarship Fdn., Los Angeles, 1/145
Cannon (Frank H. & Laura I.) Charitable Fdn., Fallbrook, 1/145
Cannon (James H.) Fdn., Los Angeles, 1/145
Cantor (Eddie) Charitable Fdn., Sunland, 1/146
Carnation Company Fdn., Los Angeles, 1/147
Carnation Company Scholarship Fdn., Los Angeles, 1/148
Carr (Fred & Dianne) Fdn., Beverly Hills, 1/149
Carr (George Russell) Fdn., Los Angeles, 1/150
Carrell (Tommy) Fdn., San Fernando, 1/151
Caughey (John & LaRee) Fdn., Los Angeles, 1/152
Cave Research Associates, Castro Valley, 1/153
Central California National Hemophilia Fdn., West Sacramento, 1/153
Chalek (Marvin M. & Carmen) Fdn., Los Angeles, 1/153
Chapman (Charles C.) Memorial Fdn., Fullerton, 1/155
Chapman Research Fund, Carmel, 1/156
Chapple-Macaulay Fdn., Los Angeles, 1/156
Charis Fund, Berkeley, 1/158
Cheesewright (Gwendolyn Milner) Fdn., Los Angeles, 1/159
Chelew (William E.) Fdn., Los Angeles, 1/160
Chen (Rose T.Y.) Charitable Fdn., San Francisco, 1/161
Child View Fdn., Beaumont, 1/161
Christadelphian Joy Fund, San Mateo, 1/162
Christensen Fund, Palo Alto, 1/163
Christian Day School Fdn., Supulveda, 1/164
Christian Freedom Fdn., Buena Park, 1/164
City Terrace Cultural Center, Los Angeles, 1/165
Claremont Fdn., Claremont, 1/166
Claremore Fund, Los Angeles, 1/166
Clark (Erna P.) Fdn., San Diego, 1/167

Clark (Frank W.), Jr. Charities, Los Angeles, 1/168

Clumeck Fdn., Rose, 1/169

Coberly (Victoria N.) Fdn., Los Angeles, 1/170

Cochran (Annette Gillette) Fund - Franklin Hospital, Santa Barbara, 1/170

Codding Fdn., Santa Rosa, 1/171

Cohan Family Fdn., Los Angeles, 1/173

Cohn (Daniel E.) Fdn., Beverly Hills, 1/174

Cohn (Edgar M.) Fdn., Los Angeles, 2/001

Colburn (Richard D.) Fdn., Los Angeles, 2/001

Combined British Charitable Fund, Los Angeles, 2/002

Commons Family Fdn., Hollywood, 2/003

Condie (John D. & Alvina M.) Fdn., Saratoga, 2/004

Consolidated Frieghtways Fdn., San Francisco, 2/005

Conyes Fdn., Oakland, 2/006

Cooper Ornithological Society, Berkeley, 2/008

Cooper (Daniel William) Scholastic Fdn., Los Angeles, 2/009

Cooperman (Ben) Memorial Fdn., Malibu, 2/009

Copeland (Jack) Fdn., Los Angeles, 2/010

Copley Charities, La Jolla, 2/010

Corwin (Louis W. & Ethabelle) Fdn., Beverly Hills, 2/012

Corwin (Sherrill C.) Fdn., Los Angeles, 2/012

Cowell (Ernest V.) Scholarship Fund, Santa Cruz, 2/014

Crane (W.E. & Mary C.) Fdn., Santa Ana, 2/015

Crary Fdn., Los Angeles, 2/015

Cravens (Malcolm) Fdn., San Francisco, 2/017

Crenshaw Medical Fdn., Los Angeles, 2/018

Crick Fdn., Altadena, 2/019

Crocker (Roy P.) & Josephine S. Crocker Fdn., Los Angeles, 2/020

Crocker (Mary A.) Trust, San Francisco, 2/020

Crosley (Willard) Fdn., Glendale, 2/021

Crown City Rebekah Lodge #325, Pasadena, 2/022

Crown Zellerbach Fdn., San Francisco, 2/022

Cruse (Albert F.) Fdn., Palm Springs, 2/026

CTU44ME in U.S.A. Scholarship Fdn., Pasadena, 2/027

Cummings Research Fdn., Beverly Hills, 2/027

Curtis Fdn., Los Angeles, 2/028

Cutter (Albert B.) Memorial Fund, Riverside, 2/028

Dailey (Frank) Cancer Fund, Oakland, 2/030

Dakin (Roger & Joan) Family Memorial Fund, Brisbane, 2/031

Daly (Edward J.) Fdn., Oakland, 2/032

Damask (Irving & Fae) Fdn., Los Angeles, 2/032

Danish Cheer Committee, Newport Beach, 2/033

Darrow Fdn., San Rafael, 2/033

Dart (Jane & Justin) Fdn., Los Angeles, 2/034

Dart Industries Fdn., Los Angeles, 2/035

Darwin Fdn., Sherman Oaks, 2/036

Dawson Fdn., Los Altos Hills, 2/037

Day (Willametta K.) Fdn., Los Angeles, 2/037

Deane (B.C.) Fdn., Newport Beach, 2/038

Deblar Fdn., Oakland, 2/038

Deeter Fdn., Bakersfield, 2/039

De Guigne (Christian) Memorial Fdn., San Francisco, 2/039

De Karman (Josephine) Trust, Pasadena, 2/040

Dekela Education Fdn., Los Angeles, 2/041

Del Amo Fdn. Educational Trust, Los Angeles, 2/042

Del Amo Fdn. Trust #1, Los Angeles, 2/045

Delaney (Edwin D. & Rose) Fdn., Los Alamitos, 2/046

Del Mar Science Fdn., Los Angeles, 2/047

De Marin (Dora Stillman) Fdn., Beverly Hills, 2/048

De Mille (Cecil B.) Trust, Hollywood, 2/048

DeMolay Fdn. of California, Richmond, 2/049

Demos Fdn., San Francisco, 2/050

den Dulk Christian Fdn., Ripon, 2/050

Deer Fdn., San Francisco, 2/051

Desert Radiological Fdn., Palm Springs, 2/052

De Tessan Fdn., San Francisco, 2/053

Di Giorgio Fdn., San Francisco, 2/053

Dinner (Richard S. & Betty S.) Charitable Fdn., San Francisco, 2/054

Dipacific Fdn., Riverside, 2/055

Djerassi Fdn., Portola Valley, 2/055

Doe (Marguerite) Fdn., Santa Barbara, 2/056

Doehring Fdn., Glendale, 2/057

Doheny (Carrie Estelle) Fdn., Los Angeles, 2/058

Doolan (Jerome & Elvira) Fdn., Santa Barbara, 2/062

Dorandu Scholarship Fund, Los Angeles, 2/062

Douglas Charitable Fdn., Beverly Hills, 2/063

Douglas (Kirk) Fdn., Beverly Hills, 2/064

Drake Steel Charitable & Educational Fdn., Beverly Hills, 2/064

Dreisen Fdn., Los Angeles, 2/065

Dr. Seuss Fdn., La Jolla, 2/066

Drudis (Jose) Fdn., Los Angeles, 2/066

Drum (Frank G.) Fdn., San Francisco, 2/068

Ducommun (Charles E. & Palmer G.) Fdn., Beverly Hills, 2/068

Ducommun (Edmond F.) Fdn., Los Angeles, 2/069

Ducommun (Emil C. & Bessie S.) Fdn., Los Angeles, 2/070

Duggan (Daniel L. & Jean D.) Fdn., Los Angeles, 2/071

Dumm (Wesley I.) Fdn., La Jolla, 2/071

Dumont Fdn., Beverly Hills, 2/073

Dunitz (Gerald & Maxine) Family Fdn., Beverly Hills, 2/073

Early (Fred J.), Jr. Fdn., San Francisco, 2/073

Ebsen-Wolcott Family Fdn., Los Angeles, 2/074

Edwards Fdn., East Highlands, 2/075

Edwards Fdn., Inc., Atherton, 2/076

Feig (J.A.M.S.) Fdn., Beverly Hills, 2/077

Edwards (Ralph & Barbara) Fdn., Hollywood, 2/077

Ehrenfreund (Kurt & Irma) Charitable Fdn., Los Angeles, 2/079

Ehrlich (Annie) Fdn., Beverly Hills, 2/079

Ehrlich (J.W.) Fdn., San Francisco, 2/079

Ehrlich (Philip S. & Frances) Fund, San Francisco, 2/080

Ehrlich Fund, San Francisco, 2/081

Eichenbaum (J.K.) Fdn., Beverly Hills, 2/083

Eisendrath (Phil & Vinnie) Fdn., Beverly Hills, 2/083

Eldorado Fdn., San Francisco, 2/083

Eldridge Fdn., Atherton, 2/084

Elfstrom Family Fdn., Fullerton, 2/085

Elmore (John J.) Fdn., San Clemente, 2/086

El Solyo Fdn., Patterson, 2/087

Epstein (Warren G.) Charitable Fdn., San Francisco, 2/088

Essick Fdn., Los Angeles, 2/088

Euphrat Fdn., San Francisco, 2/090

Factor (Ted H.) Fdn., Los Angeles, 2/091

Fairchild-Martindale Fdn., Newport Beach, 2/092

Fairfield (Freeman E.) Fdn., Long Beach, 2/093

Familian (Gary & Elisabeth) Family Fdn., Los Angeles, 2/095

Family Fund, San Francisco, 2/096

Family Unity Fdn., San Juan Capistrano, 2/096

Farman Charitable Fdn., San Diego, 2/097

Faude (C. Fredrick) Fdn., Sausalito, 2/098

Fellowship Center Fdn., Palm Desert, 2/098

Femino Fdn., Rosemead, 2/099

Fibreboard Fdn., San Francisco, 2/099

Field (Irwin & Joanna) Fdn., Norwalk, 2/100

Filippi (Elio & Reno) Fdn., San Francisco, 2/101

Fingerhut (William & Freda) Fdn., Woodland Hills, 2/102

Fireman's Fund American Fdn., San Francisco, 2/103

First Methodist of San Jose Fdn., San Jose, 2/104

First Myrtle Fund, San Francisco, 2/104

Fisher (Montgomery R.) Fdn., Los Angeles, 2/105

Flagg Family Fdn., Monterey, 2/106

Fleet Fdn., San Diego, 2/106

Floret Fund, Berkeley, 2/108

Fluor (Dea & Fred) Fdn., Santa Ana, 2/108

Flynn Fdn., Vernon, 2/109

FMC Fdn., San Jose, 2/110

Fogg Fdn., Pasadena, 2/111

Foleys (Edward T.) Fdn., Pasadena, 2/111

Follis (R. Gwin) Fdn., San Francisco, 2/114

Food Technology Fdn., San Francisco, 2/115

Ford (Robert F.) Charitable Fdn., Pasadena, 2/115

Ford, Markson, Swig & Weiler Fdn., San Francisco, 2/116

Foremost-McKesson Fdn., San Francisco, 2/117

Forest Lawn Fdn., Glendale, 2/118

Forty First Medical Trust, Los Angeles, 2/118

Foster Fdn, A National Educational Fdn. for Study of The Democratic Process, Oakland, 2/119

Foundation for Brotherhood, Oakland, 2/119

Foundation for Educational & Behavioral Therapy, Long Beach, 2/120

Foundation for Independence, La Crescenta, 2/120

Foundation for Social Research, San Jacinto, 2/120

Foundation for The Establishment of an International Criminal Court, Beverly Hills, 2/121

Foundation Funds of Norton Simon, Los Angeles, 2/121

Foundation Honoring California Women, Los Angeles, 2/122

Four R's Fdn., San Diego, 2/122

Fowler (Francis E.), Jr. Fdn., Los Angeles, 2/123

Fox Fdn., Richmond, 2/125

Fox (Rose & Howard) Fdn., Beverly Hills, 2/125

Frank (Lawrence L.) Fdn., Los Angeles, 2/126

Frank (Harry J.L.), Jr. Fdn., Beverly Hills, 2/126

Freedle Fdn., Sacramento, 2/127

Freitas Fdn., San Rafael, 2/127

Fremont Physicians Fdn. for Special Education, Fremont, 2/128

Andrews-French Fdn., Redding, 2/128

Fresno-Madera Dental Fdn., Fresno, 2/129

Fresno Relief Society, Fresno, 2/130

Friars Club Charity Fdn., Beverly Hills, 2/130

Friedman (Charlotte) Fdn., Los Angeles, 2/131

Friedman (Mendel) Fdn., Downey, 2/132

Friendly Fellowship Fdn., Los Angeles, 2/133

Fromm (Alfred) Fund, San Francisco, 2/133

Fuller (Arthur Dodd) Fdn., Los Angeles, 2/135

Fuller (Delmarie) Fund, San Francisco, 2/135

Fund for Job Corps Graduates, Beverly Hills, 2/136

Fusenot (Georges & Germaine) Charity Fdn., Los Angeles, 2/137

G.A.G. Charitable Corporation, Beverly Hills, 2/138

Gallo (Ernest) Fdn., Modesto, 2/138

Gallo (Julio R.) Fdn., Modesto, 2/139

Gamble Fdn., San Francisco, 2/140

Gang Tyre & Brown Charitable Fdn., Los Angeles, 2/141

Gardiner (Thomas & Margaret) Fdn., Oakland, 2/141

Garfield (Harriet) Charitable Fdn., Beverly Hills, 2/142

Garrett (Paul) Fdn., Los Angeles, 2/143

Gates (Mary Irwin) Fdn., Palos Verdes Estates, 2/143

Gates (Randall Mason) Fdn., Foster City, 2/144

Gauer (Edward & Marion) Fdn., San Francisco, 2/145

Gealer (Saul B.) & Nathan Gealer Fdn., Los Angeles, 2/146

Gelber (Felix & Ruth) Fdn., Century City, 2/146

Gellert (Carl) Fdn., San Francisco, 2/147

Gellert (Fred) Fdn., San Francisco, 2/148

Gelson Fdn., Encino, 2/148

Gelu Fdn., La Habra, 2/148

Gemco Charitable & Scholarship Fund, Buena Park, 2/149

George (Lieutenant General Harold L. & Violette H.) Fdn., Beverly Hills, 2/150

George (Julia) Library Trust Fund, San Francisco, 2/150

Gerbode (Wallace Alexander) Fdn., San Francisco, 2/151

Getty (Timothy Christopher Ware) Fdn., Los Angeles, 2/152

Getty Oil Company Fdn., Los Angeles, 2/153

Chidotti Fdn., Nevada City, 2/154

Giannini (A.P.) Scholarship Fdn., San Francisco, 2/155

Gillin Fdn., Los Angeles, 2/156

Gilmore (Earl B.) Fdn., Los Angeles, 2/156

Gilmore (Howard N.) Fdn., San Francisco, 2/158

Gindi (E.J.) Fdn., Los Angeles, 2/161

Ginsburg (H.M. & Clara) Fdn., Fresno, 2/161

Given (Samuel & Rena) Fdn., Los Angeles, 2/162

Gladman (Everett A.) Memorial Fdn., Oakland, 2/163

Glaser (Walter A.) Fdn., San Francisco, 2/163

Glassick (W.B.) Fdn., Los Angeles, 2/164

Gleason (Katherine) Fdn., San Francisco, 2/164

Glenn (Anna J. & Harold T.) Fdn., Long Beach, 2/165

Glennon Club, Lynwood, 2/166

Glickman (Mannes N.) Fdn., Beverly Hills, 2/166

Golan (Louis E.) Fdn., Santa Monica, 2/167

Golden (Robert M.) Fdn., San Diego, 2/167

Goldenberg (Carl & Ann) Fdn., Palm Springs, 2/168

Goldenberg (Harry K. & Tess) Charitable Fdn., Beverly Hills, 2/168

Goldman (Bruce) Fdn., Oakland, 2/169

Goldman (Harry & Barbara) Fdn., Beverly Hills, 2/170

Goldman (Robert & Judith) Fdn., Beverly Hills, 2/171

Goldsmith-Konheim Fdn., Beverly Hills, 2/172

Goldstone (Phil) Fdn., Los Angeles, 2/172

Goldwyn (Samuel) Fdn., Los Angeles, 2/173

Goodman (David M.) & Florence S. Goodman Fdn., Palos Verdes Estates, 2/175

Goodrich-Schaller Memorial Trust, Ojai, 2/176

Goodwin Fdn., San Diego, 2/177

Gorman (Stephanie) Memorial Scholarship Fund, Los Angeles, 2/178

Gould (Robert T.) Family Fdn., Beverly Hills, 2/178

Gould Medical Fdn., Modesto, 2/179

Gourrich Fdn., Los Angeles, 2/180

Graduate Physiology Fund, Hillsborough, 2/180

Graff Fdn., Los Angeles, 2/181

Grandview Fdn., Pasadena, 2/182

Grant Fdn., Newport Beach, 2/182

Grass Valley Ladies Relief Society, Grass Valley, 2/183

Green (Robert) & Co. Fdn., Los Angeles, 2/184

Green (Burton E.) Fdn., Beverly Hills, 2/184

Green (Irving H.) & Faye B. Green Fdn., Los Angeles, 2/185

Greenberg (Mayer) Fdn., Los Angeles, 2/185

Greenberg (Audrey & Arthur N.) Fund, Los Angeles, 2/186

Greenvile Fdn., Pacific Palisades, 2/187

Griffin (Frances D. & Irene D.) Fdn., Los Angeles, 2/188

Gross (Gary Stephen) Fdn., Beverly Hills, 2/189

Grubb (James B.) Oakland Scottish Rite Scholarship Fdn., Oakland, 2/189

Gruenhagen (Kenny) Fdn., San Francisco, 2/190

Guenther (Henry L.) Fdn., Los Angeles, 2/190

Guggenheim (Carrie) Shelter, Beverly Hills, 2/191

Gunther (Richard S.) Fdn., Beverly Hills, 2/192

Guymon Fdn., San Diego, 2/192

Haas (Walter & Elise) Fund, San Francisco, 2/193

Hachmeister (Harry C. & Myrtle W.) Charitable Fdn., Los Angeles, 2/194

Haddad Brothers, Encino, 2/195

Hagadorn Family Trust Charitable Trust, Costa Mesa, 2/195

Hale (Crescent Porter) Fdn., San Francisco, 2/196

Halladay (Elsie Smith) Hospital Fund, Pasadena, 2/197

Halper (Louis M. & Birdie) Fdn., Beverly Hills, 2/197

Halpern (Jackie) Fdn., Los Angeles, 2/198

Hamilton (Pierpont) Fdn., Santa Barbara, 2/199

Hampton (Jack) Fdn. (Troupe 10 Alumni Assoc.), Altadena, 2/200

Hancock (John W.) Fdn., Long Beach, 2/200

Handler (Elliot & Ruth) Fdn., Century City, 2/202

Hanley Fdn., Los Angeles, 2/202

Hare Fdn., Grass Valley, 2/203

Harkson (U.S.) Fdn., Burlingame, 2/204

Harrington (Mark H. & Blanche M.) Fdn., Pasadena, 2/205

Harriwil Fund, San Francisco, 2/206

Hart (Eva P.) Fdn., Atherton, 2/207

Hart (George D.) Fdn., San Francisco, 2/207

Hayden (Samuel) Fdn., Beverly Hills, 2/209

Hayden (William R.) Fdn., San Marino, 2/211

Haytin (Harold A. & Lois) Fdn., Los Angeles, 2/211

Hayward (N. Cary) Fdn., Walnut Creek, 2/212

Hazan (Morris A.) Fdn., Los Angeles, 2/213

Hazen (Lita Annenberg) Fdn., Los Angeles, 2/213

Heart & Lung Surgery Fdn., Los Angeles, 2/214

Heffernan Fdn., San Francisco, 2/215

Heims Trust for Talented Children, Oakland, 2/216

Heller Charitable & Educational Fund, San Francisco, 2/217

Heller (Douglas M. & Mary E.) Fdn., San Francisco, 2/218

Heller (William S. & Sylvia) Fdn., Encino, 2/220

Hellman (I.W.) Fund, San Francisco, 2/220

Helmaur Fdn., San Francisco, 2/220

Heltzer (George J.) & Lillian Heltzer Fdn., Los Angeles, 2/221

Helwig (A.A.) Fdn., Los Angeles, 2/221

Henry B. Fdn., Beverly Hills, 2/221

Hewlett Fdn., Palo Alto, 2/222

Heymann (Martha, Rex & Juliane) Charitable Fdn., Beverly Hills, 2/223

Hi-Crest Fdn., Inglewood, 2/223

Hillman (Francis & Myrtle) Fdn., Los Angeles, 2/224

Hills (Herbert Gray) Fund, San Francisco, 2/224

Hilp (Harry H.) Fdn., San Francisco, 2/225

Hinchcliffe (Stephen F.), Jr. Fdn., Palos Verdes Estates, 2/225

Hinckley (William & Alice) Fund, San Francisco, 2/226

Hindes (Barrett & Margaret) Fdn., San Francisco, 2/228

Hoag Fdn., Pasadena, 3/001

Hobart Fdn., San Diego, 3/002

Hoefer Family Fdn., Menlo Park, 3/002

Hoffman (H. Leslie) & Elaine S. Hoffman Fdn., San Marino, 3/003

Hollander Fdn., Scotts Valley, 3/004

Honig (Louis & Miriam) Fdn., San Francisco, 3/004

Hoover (Margaret W & Herbert), Jr., Fdn., Los Angeles, 3/005

Hopkins Charitable Fund, Santa Barbara, 3/005

Hotchkis Fdn., Los Angeles, 3/006

Hotchkiss (lester C. & Alpha L.) Fdn., Fresno, 3/007

Houchin (C.E. & Kathryn) Fdn., Los Angeles, 3/008

How Family Fdn., Burlingame, 3/009

Howard Fdn., Los Angeles, 3/010

Hubbs (Ken) Fdn., Colton, 3/011

Hughes (Bertha M.) Memorial Scholarship, Placerville, 3/011

Hawaii (Hui O.) of San Diego, San Diego, 3/012

Humboldt State College Alumni Fdn., Arcata, 3/012

Hunt (Reed & Sarah) Fund, San Francisco, 3/012

Hunte Fdn., Rancho Sante Fe, 3/013

Hunting Bowmen, Inc., San Francisco, 3/014

Huntsinger Fdn., Ventura, 3/014

Hyland Research Fdn., Los Angeles, 3/015

Hyman Family Fdn., Culver City, 3/015

Ice Capades Ten Year Club, Hollywood, 3/016

Inasmuch Fund, Glendale, 3/016

Independent Order of Odd Fellows, Hanford, 3/016

Industrial Indemnity Fdn., San Francisco, 3/017

Ingraham Memorial Fund, Pasadena, 3/018

Institute for the Study of Economic Systems, San Francisco, 3/019

International Friendship Charitable Fdn., Gardena, 3/021

Irell Family Fdn., Los Angeles, 3/021

Irvine (William M.) Jr., Scholarship Fund, Salinas, 3/022

Irwin (William G.) Charity Fdn., San Francisco, 3/023

Isaacs Brothers Fdn., Beverly Hills, 3/025

Iseli Fdn., Los Angeles, 3/026

Ishiyama Fdn., San Francisco, 3/026

Isotope Fdn., Los Angeles, 3/027

Israel (Hyman & Bessie) - Irell (Lawrence E.) Fdn., Los Angeles, 3/028

Italian Welfare Agency, San Francisco, 3/028

Jacuzzi (Kenneth A.) Fdn., Walnut Creek, 3/028

Jaeger Family Fdn., Oakland, 3/028

Janus Fdn., San Francisco, 3/029

Jeffer (Harris C.) Fdn., Sierta Madre, 3/030

Jefferson (John Percival) Trust Fund, Santa Barbara, 3/030

Jenkins (Gordon W.) Charitable Fdn., San Marino, 3/031

Jenkins Fdn. for Research, Salinas, 3/031

Jensen (Jon Philip) Memorial Fdn., San Francisco, 3/032

Jerome Fdn., Los Angeles, 3/032

JMS Fdn., Beverly Hills, 3/033

Johnson Fdn., Riverside, 3/033

John 23rd Memorial Trust, Stockton, 3/035

Jones (Merle & Frances) Fdn., Los Angeles, 3/035

Jones (John Clifton) Trust, Los Angeles, 3/036

Jopat Fdn., San Francisco, 3/036

Jordan (Dennis) Fdn., Hayward, 3/037

Jorgensen (Earle M.) Fdn., Los Angeles, 3/037

Joseph (Irving & Zaz) Fdn., Los Angeles, 3/038

Josepho (Anatol & Ganna) Fdn., Los Angeles, 3/039

Juda (Felix & Helen) Fdn., Los Angeles, 3/040

Juda (Tom & Nancy) Fdn., Los Angeles, 3/041

Judean Youth Fdn., Los Angeles, 3/042

Kaiser (Henry J.) Family Fdn., Oakland, 3/042

Kallis (Albert J.) Fdn., Beverly Hills, 3/043

Kagothos (Kalos) Fdn., Los Angeles, 3/044

Kane (Irwin E.) Fdn., Los Angeles, 3/044

Kaplan (Charles H.) & Lillian S. Kaplan Fdn., Beverly Hills, 3/046

Kaufman (Loretta & Seymour) Fdn., Beverly Hills, 3/046

Keane (Walter & Margaret) Fdn., Redwood City, 3/047

Keck (Howard B. & Elizabeth A.) Fdn., Los Angeles, 3/047

Keck (W.M.) Fdn., Los Angeles, 3/048

K E Fdn., San Francisco, 3/048

Kellogg (Evelyn & Irving) Fdn., Beverly Hills, 3/049

Kelly (Eugene C.) Fdn., Beverly Hills, 3/050

Kelly (Paul B.) Fdn., Santa Rosa, 3/050

Kelton Fund, Beverly Hills, 3/052

Keren-Or, Los Angeles, 3/052

Kesten (Louis) Charitable Fdn., Los Angeles, 3/053

Kettenhofen Family Fdn., Sausalito, 3/054

Kettlewell Fund, Piedmont, 3/054

Kevin Fdn., San Francisco, 3/054

Kiely (John & Margaret Lee) Fdn., San Francisco, 3/055

Kilner Fdn., Palm Springs, 3/056

Kinsey (G.E. & Mattie B.) Fdn., Los Angeles, 3/057

Kingston (Virginia W.) Fdn., Los Angeles, 3/057

Kirchheimer (Barbara & Joseph) Fund, Palm Springs, 3/058

Kirkcudbright Fdn., Los Angeles, 3/059

Kirshbaum (Joanne & Ira) Family Fdn., Los Angeles, 3/060

Kirshbaum (Joseph B.) Family Fdn., Los Angeles, 3/061

Kiwanis Fdn. of Eagel Rock, Los Angeles, 3/062

Kiwanis Fdn. of Greater Canoga Park, Canogo Park, 3/062

Klein (Eugene V.) Fdn., Beverly Hills, 3/063

Klein (H.H. & Gertrude) Fdn., Beverly Hills, 3/063

Kleiner, Bell Fdn., Beverly Hills, 3/064

Kleiner Fdn., Beverly Hills, 3/064

Kleiman (Joseph & Shirley) Fdn., Los Angeles, 3/065

Klicka (Jessie) Fdn., San Diego, 3/065

Knapp (George Owen) Memorial Fund, Eureka, 3/067

Kneller (George F.) Fdn., Los Angeles, 3/068

Knudsen (R.) & Valley M. Knudsen Fdn., Los Angeles, 3/068

Kohn (Eva Heller) Helping Fund, San Francisco, 3/070

Komaroff (Lillian & Revan) Fdn., Long Beach, 3/072

Komes Fdn., San Francisco, 3/072

Kopelove (Ralph & Marian) Fdn., Beverly Hills, 3/073

Koret Fdn., San Francisco, 3/074

Krausz Fdn., Los Angeles, 3/075

Kunze Fdn., Yucaipa, 3/075

Ladd (George S.) Memorial Fund, San Francisco, 3/076

Laing Fdn., Los Angeles, 3/076

La Jolla Visiting Nurse Association, La Jolla, 3/077

Lakeside Fdn., San Francisco, 3/078

Lampert Fdn., Los Angeles, 3/079

Lancaster Family Fdn., Century City, 3/079

Land Fdn., San Francisco, 3/080

Landes Fdn., San Carlos, 3/081

Landis Fdn., San Francisco, 3/082

Lappen (Chet & Jon) Fdn., Los Angeles, 3/084

Lasky (Ruth & Moses) Fund, San Francisco, 3/085

Latham (Olive & Dana) Fdn., Los Angeles, 3/086

Latz (Ida S.) Fdn., Los Angeles, 3/087

Laucks Fdn., Santa Barbara, 3/088

Laurel & Hardy Fund, San Diego, 3/088

Layton (Alfred B.) Fund, Diablo, 3/089

Lazarus (J.M.) Fdn., Beverly Hills, 3/089

Lear (William P. & Moya Olsen) Fdn. Los Angeles, Century City, 3/091

Lear (Milton J.) Fund, Los Angeles, 3/091

Leavey (Thomas & Dorothy) Fdn., Los Angeles, 3/092

Lebus (Bertha) Trust, Los Angeles, 3/092

Ledler Fdn., Burbank, 3/093

Lee (Russell V. & Dorothy W.) Charitable Fdn., Palo Alto, 3/094

Lee (Raymond) Fdn., Beverly Hills, 3/095

Lee (Ruth L.) Fund, Los Angeles, 3/096

Leibovitz (Maury P. & Ginger) Fdn., Los Angeles, 3/098

Lejoy Fdn., San Francisco, 3/099

Leonard Fdn., San Francisco, 3/099

Leonardt Fdn., Los Angeles, 3/099

Leppo Fdn., San Francisco, 3/100

Le Roy (Mervyn) Fdn., Beverly Hills, 3/101

Lesley Fdn., Burlingame, 3/102

Lesser (Fadiman, Stephen & John) Fund, Los Angeles, 3/103

Levenson (Sydney T.) MD, Fdn., Los Angeles, 3/104

Levi (Ursula & Myron) Fdn. Los Angeles, Century City, 3/105

Levine (Hyman) Family Fdn., Beverly Hills, 3/105

Levinson (Marshall) Fdn., Los Angeles, 3/106

Levitas (Robert B. & Leah A.) Charitable Fdn., Brisbane, 3/107

Lidow Fdn., Los Angeles, 3/107

Lipsey (Abe & Muriel) Charitable Fdn., Beverly Hills, 3/108

Lipsky (Gerald & Nancy) Fdn., Beverly Hills, 3/109

Little (Winifred) Fdn., San Francisco, 3/110

Littlefield (Edmund Wattis) Fdn., San Francisco, 3/111

Littman Family Fdn., Palm Springs, 3/111

Litz Fdn., Beverly Hills, 3/112

Lloyd (Ralph B.) Fdn., Beverly Hills, 3/113

Lockheed Leadership Fund, Burbank, 3/115

Lockman Fdn., La Habra, 3/116

Logan (Hugh H.) Fdn., Glendale, 3/118

Long Beach Landscape Gardeners Association, Long Beach, 3/119

Long Fdn., Walnut Creek, 3/119

Los Angeles Black Service Center, Los Angeles, 3/120

Los Angeles Post Office Employees' Cafeteria Association, Los Angeles, 3/120

Los Angeles Programs for Education, Santa Monica, 3/121

Los Angeles Retail Plant Owners Association of Dry Cleaners, Los Angeles, 3/122

Los Angeles Rod & Reel Club Fdn., Los Angeles, 3/123

Los Angeles Society for the Hard of Hearing, Los Angeles, 3/123

Los Angeles West Berlin Sister City Affiliation, Los Angeles, 3/123

Loube Fdn., Oakland, 3/124

Lowden (George M. Pullman) Fdn., Santa Ana, 3/124

Lowy (Marcus) Charitable Fdn., Los Angeles, 3/124

Loyola Fdn. of California, Lynwood, 3/125

L S Fdn., Santa Clara, 3/125

Lucidi - Von Ah Memorial Fdn., La Habra, 3/126

Ludekens Fdn., Belvedere, 3/127

Luper (Archie) Fdn., Ventura, 3/127

Lurie (Louis R.) Fdn., San Francisco, 3/130

Lyman (Arthur S.) Memorial Fund, Ukiah, 3/132

Mackenzie Fdn., Los Angeles, 3/133

Mackintosh Fund, Los Angeles, 3/134

Pierce (MacNeel) Fdn., Ontario, 3/134

Madison Fund, San Francisco, 3/134

Magnin (Donald) Family Fdn., San Francisco, 3/137

Magnin (Joseph) Fdn., San Francisco, 3/138

Mailliard Fdn., San Francisco, 3/139

Malouf (Anees B.) Fdn., Los Angeles, 3/140

Malough (Bert B.) Fdn., Los Angeles, 3/141

Mandel Family Fdn., Beverly Hills, 3/142

Manella (Arthur & Nancy) Fdn., Los Angeles, 3/143

Marci Fdn., Ojai, 3/144

Margaret Fdn., Glendale, 3/144

Markson California Fdn., Los Angeles, 3/145

Markus (Eli) Fdn. & Charitable Trust, Beverly Hills, 3/146

Marmelzat (Willard L.) Fdn., Beverly Hills, 3/147

Marschak (Deborah) Memorial Fund, Berkeley, 3/148

Marti (Jose) Fdn., Los Angeles, 3/148

Martin (Marcus) Memorial Scholarship Trust, Santa Cruz, 3/149

Marx (Melville & Louise) Fund, San Francisco, 3/150

Maschal Fdn., San Francisco, 3/150

Masonic Hall Association, Chico, 3/151

Mate Fdn., San Francisco, 3/151

Factor (Max) Memorial Fund, Los Angeles, 3/152

Maxwell (Windslow) Fdn., Los Angeles, 3/153

Mayer (Louis B.) Fdn., Beverly Hills, 3/154

Mazer (Eleanor Ellis) Fund, San Francisco, 3/155

McCammon (Charles & Ruth) Fdn., Palm Springs, 3/156

McClatchy Fdn., Sacramento, 3/156

McCone Fdn., Los Angeles, 3/157

McConnell (Carl R. & Leah F.) Fdn., San Francisco, 3/158

McElhinny (Robert & Mary) Memorial, Los Angeles, 3/159

McGuinness Fdn., Beverly Hills, 3/160

McGuire (Thomas G.) Fund, San Francisco, 3/161

McInnes (Alice) Scholarship Fund, Stockton, 3/162

McKenna (William E. & Mary N.) Fdn., Beverly Hills, 3/162

McKeon Fdn., Sacramento, 3/163

McKuen (Rod) Fdn., Los Angeles, 3/164

McLain Fdn., Palm Desert, 3/164

McMahan Charitable & Educational Fdn., Fresno, 3/165

McMahan Fdn., El Cajon, 3/166

McMillan (John Christian & Margaret Edna) Fdn., Los Angeles, 3/166

Mead Fdn., Los Angeles, 3/167

Mead Housing Trust, Los Angeles, 3/168

Mead Redevelopment Corporation, Los Angeles, 3/170

Mead Residuary Trust, Los Angeles, 3/171

Medical Students Fdn., Los Angeles, 3/173

Mehren (Paul & Madeleine) Fdn., Pasadena, 3/173

Mel (Charles) Search & Rescue Fdn., Oakland, 3/174

Memorex Fdn., Santa Clara, 3/174

Meningitis Research Fdn., San Francisco, 3/175

Menkin Fdn., Los Angeles, 3/175

Meselson Fdn., Beverly Hills, 3/176

Metro, Goldwyn-Mayer Employees' Welfare Fund, Culver City, 3/176

Metzner (Robert & Esther) Fdn., Beverly Hills, 3/176

Meyer (Bertha G. & Louis), Jr., Fdn., Los Angeles, 3/177

Meyer (A.H.) Fdn., St. Helena, 3/178

Meyer (Howard P.) Fdn., El Centro, 3/179

Michillinda Community Woman's Club, West Arcadia, 3/179

Mier (Harry & Joan) Fdn., Beverly Hills, 3/180

Milens Fdn., Oakland, 3/180

Miles (Ida S.) Fdn., Pacific Palisades, 3/181

Millard (Marie D.) Trust, Palo Alto, 3/182

Miller (Earl Burns) Trust, Long Beach, 3/183

Miller-Howard Fund, Santa Barbara, 3/183

Minifree Fdn., Piedmont, 3/184

Mintz Fdn., Palo Alto, 3/185

Mission Linen Fdn., Santa Barbara, 3/185

Mitchell (Edward D. & Anna) Family Fdn., Los Angeles, 3/186

Mitchell Fdn., Pacific Palisades, 3/189

Mitchell (Clinton) Fdn., Palm Springs, 3/190

Mitchell (Ruth Wattis) Fdn., Beverly Hills, 3/191

Mizzy Family Fdn., Los Angeles, 3/191

M O D Fdn., San Francisco, 3/192

Monterey International Pop Festival, Los Angeles, 3/192
Monte Sano Memorial Fdn., Los Angeles, 3/193
Moore (Richard Harrison) Student Memorial Fund, Porterville, 3/193
Moore-White Medical Fdn., Los Angeles, 3/194
Morrison (Alice G.) Memorial Fdn., Oakland, 3/194
Morshead (John Stuart) Fdn., San Francisco, 3/195
Moseley Fdn., Glendale, 3/195
Moseley (Thomas Jefferson) Fdn., San Carlos, 3/197
Moskowitz (Irving I.) Fdn., Long Beach, 3/198
Moss Fdn., Hollywood, 3/198
Mountain View Fdn., Pasadena, 3/199
Mudd (Seeley W.) Fdn., Los Angeles, 3/200
Mudd (Seeley G.) Fund, Los Angeles, 3/201
Muhs (Fred R.) Family Fdn., Pebble Beach, 3/202
Mulago Fdn., San Francisco, 3/203
Muller Fdn., Tarzana, 3/204
Murdy Fdn., Newport Beach, 3/204
Murphy (Dan) Fdn., Los Angeles, 3/204
Murphy (Lluella Morey) Fdn., Los Angeles, 3/207
Myers-Kelly Memorial Fund Charitable Trust, San Francisco, 3/207
Nathan (Elinor & Frank) Fdn., Beverly Hills, 3/207
National Turf Fdn., La Jolla, 3/208
Neil (William P.) Fdn., Azusa, 3/209
Nesbitt Fdn., Los Angeles, 3/209
New Horizons Fdn., Azusa, 3/210
Newell Fdn., San Jose, 3/210
Newhall (Henry Mayo) Fdn., San Francisco, 3/211
Newhouse Fdn., San Francisco, 3/212
Newman (Ellen Magnin) Family Fdn., San Francisco, 3/213
Newton Fdn., Los Angeles, 3/214
Nigg (Cyril C.) Fdn., Los Angeles, 3/214
Nihewan Fdn., Sherman Oaks, 3/216
Nixon Birthplace Fdn., Yorba Linda, 3/216
N.J.J. Fdn., Beverly Hills, 3/216
Noble Fund, San Francisco, 3/217
Norman (Andrew) Fdn., Los Angeles, 3/218
Northern Lights Guild Memorial Hospital of Long Beach, Long Beach, 3/220
Nott (Grace O.) Fdn., San Francisco, 3/221
Nu Sigma Nu Alumni Fdn., San Francisco, 3/221
Nutrilite Fdn., Buena Park, 3/222
Oak Tree Fdn., Arcadia, 3/222
Obernauer (Marne & Joan) Fdn., Los Angeles, 3/223
O'Brien (Rena Mannex) Fdn., Los Angeles, 3/224
O'Brian (Hugh) Youth Fdn., Beverly Hills, 3/225
Occidental Petroleum Charitable Fdn., Los Angeles, 3/225
Ocean View Fdn., Halfmoon, 3/226
Odell (Robert Stewart & Helen Pfeiffer) Fund, San Francisco, 3/227
Offer Family Fdn., Los Angeles, 3/228
Old Bofie Fdn., San Francisco, 3/228
Olender Fdn., Los Angeles, 4/001
O'Malley (Walter F.) Fdn., Los Angeles, 4/002
One Eleven Fdn., Los Angeles, 4/004
O'Neill (Richard J.) Fdn., Santa Monica, 4/005
Ormsby Hill Trust, La Crescenta, 4/005
Oro Grande Fdn., Oro Grande, 4/006
Osherenko (Margo & Joe) Fdn., Beverly Hills, 4/007
Ostrow (Jack M. & Bel) Fdn., Los Angeles, 4/008
Our Youth Fdn., San Francisco, 4/009
Overholser Fdn., Beverly Hills, 4/009
Owen Charitable Fund, Palm Springs, 4/011
Owings (Nathaniel & Margaret Wentworth) Fdn., San Francisco, 4/012

Packard (David & Lucile) Fdn., Palo Alto, 4/013
Paddock (Charles W.) Memorial Fdn., Los Angeles, 4/014
Page (Charles & Mary Catherine), San Francisco, 4/014
Palmer (Nina) Memorial Scholarship Trust, Santa Cruz, 4/015
Pardee (George C. & H.N.) Fdn., Oakland, 4/016
Park (Arthur & Merril) Fdn., Beverly Hills, 4/016
Parker (Patrick S.) Fdn., Culver City, 4/017
Parmelee (Helen Wegman) Educational Fdn., Oakland, 4/018
Parr (Fred D.) Fdn., San Francisco, 4/018
Parsons (Ralph M.) Fdn., Los Angeles, 4/018
Parvin (Albert) Fdn., Los Angeles, 4/019
Pasadena Child Health Fdn., Pasadena, 4/021
Pategian (Charles K.) Fdn., San Francisco, 4/023
Pattiz Family Fdn., Beverly Hills, 4/024
Paul (Susan W.) Fdn., Los Angeles, 4/027
Pauley (Edwin W.) Fdn., Los Angeles, 4/027
Peck (C.L.) Fdn., Los Angeles, 4/028
Pelavin Fund, San Francisco, 4/028
Pennebaker Fdn., Beverly Hills, 4/029
Pep Boys of California Educational Fdn., Los Angeles, 4/029
Peppers (Ann) Fdn., Los Angeles, 4/031
Peralta Medical Fdn., Oakland, 4/031
Jefferson (John Percival & Mary C.) Endowment Fund, Santa Barbara, 4/031
Permanente Fdn. (f/k/a Kaiser Fdn.), Oakland, 4/032
Little Perry Fdn., Berkeley, 4/033
Person (Zoe H.) Life Interest Trust, Long Beach, 4/034
Pest Control Operators of California, Los Angeles, 4/034
Peterson (Patricia Price) Fdn., San Francisco, 4/035
Petri (Louis & Fiori) Fdn., San Francisco, 4/036
Pfaffinger Fdn., Los Angeles, 4/037
Pfleger (George T.) Fdn., Newport Beach, 4/038
Phelps (Winifred Y.) Trust, Santa Cruz, 4/042
Philandria Fdn., Los Angeles, 4/043
Phillips Fdn., Los Angeles, 4/043
Plesset (Ernst & Pauline) Fdn., Santa Monica, 4/045
Plumbing Heating Cooling Contractors of Tahoe Employers Trust Fund, South Lake Tahoe, 4/045
Polinsky (A.B. & Jessie W.) Family Fdn., San Diego, 4/046
Polland Family Fdn., Los Angeles, 4/047
Queen of the Valley Hospital Fdn., Napa, 4/047
Quay Charitable Fdn., Sacramento, 4/048
Pythian Youth Fdn. of California, Hayward, 4/048
Quay Charitable Fdn., Sacramento, 4/048
Ponitoff (Alexander M.) Fdn., Atherton, 4/048
Portola Fdn., San Francisco, 4/048
Prescott (Nellie S.) Trust, San Francisco, 4/049
Press (Morris & Mary) Fdn., Beverly Hills, 4/050
Price Fdn., Upland, 4/050
Pryne Fdn., Claremont, 4/051
Psoriasis, Skin & Cancer Fdn., San Francisco, 4/051
Puente (Ruth Buhles) Fdn., Lafayette, 4/052
Purcell Fdn., Pasadena, 4/052
Putnam Charitable Trust, Santa Barbara, 4/052
Poniatoff (Alexander M.) Fdn., Atherton, 4/053
Rabin (Bruce & Joy) Fdn., Beverly Hills, 4/053
Rabin (Joseph) Fdn., Los Angeles, 4/054
Raney (Jack) Memorial Trust Fund, Chula Vista, 4/054
Rankin (Walker) Family Fdn., Bakersfield, 4/055

Rawlinson (J.E. & E.A.) Fdn., Los Angeles, 4/055
Raybrook Fdn., Pacific Palisades, 4/056
Rayner Fdn., Mill Valley, 4/056
Reade (George) Fdn., Riverside, 4/057
Refrigeration & Air Conditioning Training Trust, San Francisco, 4/058
Regensburg (Jerome & Flora) Fdn., Los Angeles, 4/059
Reilly Fdn., Whittier, 4/060
Reinert (Howard & Marilyn) Fdn., N.Y.C., N.Y., 4/061
Religious Research Fdn., San Francisco, 4/061
Religious Youth Fdn., San Diego, 4/062
Resetar (Mitchell L.) Jr., Family Fdn., Watsonville, 4/062
Reyman (Allison H. & Irma H.) Fund, San Francisco, 4/062
Reynolds Family Fdn., Pacoima, 4/063
Rhoades (Donald A.) Family Fdn., Oakland, 4/065
Richards (Edgar G. & Florence) Charitable Fdn., Los Angeles, 4/065
Richman (Irving M.) Memorial Fdn., Los Angeles, 4/065
Rivers (Johnny) Fdn., Los Angeles, 4/066
RML - GML, San Francisco, 4/067
Robbins (Irvine & Irma) Fdn., Encino, 4/068
Robertson (J.D.) Fdn., San Francisco, 4/069
Rochlin (Abraham & Sonia) Fdn., Arcata, 4/069
Rock Fdn., San Francisco, 4/071
Roe (Milius) Fdn., Los Angeles, 4/072
Roeber Fdn., Oakland, 4/072
Roland Fdn., Atherton, 4/073
Rolph-Nicol Fund, San Francisco, 4/074
Romberger Fund, Newport Beach, 4/074
Rose (David) Fdn., Los Angeles, 4/075
Rose (Don H. & Edessa H.) Fdn., San Marino, 4/076
Rosenberg (Theodore) Charitable Fdn., San Francisco, 4/076
Rosenberg Family Fdn., Century, 4/078
Rosenberg Fdn., San Francisco, 4/078
Rosenberg (Albert H. & Beatrice G.) Fdn., Beverly Hills, 4/085
Rosenkranz (J.A.) Fdn., Los Angeles, 4/086
Rosenberg (S.J.) Fdn., Los Angeles, 4/087
Rosenberg (Adolph) Trust Fund, San Francisco, 4/088
Rosenus Fdn. Trust, Beverly Hills, 4/088
Ross (Robert C.) Fdn., Woodside, 4/090
Ross (Gordon) Medical Fdn., Pasadena, 4/090
Roth (Lurline B.) Charity Fdn., San Francisco, 4/091
Rothschild (Edward & Ann) Fdn., Beverly Hills, 4/091
Rosseau (Oliver M.) Fdn., Hayward, 4/092
Rowles Fdn., Sacramento, 4/093
Royce (Donald) Fdn., Los Angeles, 4/093
Royce (Ken) Fdn., South San Francisco, 4/095
Rubenstein (David) Memorial Scholarship Fdn., San Francisco, 4/095
Rubottom (Corinne Precourt) Fdn., Carpenteria, 4/096
Rudel (Julius) Award Trust Fund, Burbank, 4/097
Rupley (Joseph Robert) Charitable Trust, Walnut Creek, 4/098
Rural Gospel & Medical Missions of India, Pasadena, 4/098
Rusalem (Frank & Edna) Fdn., San Francisco, 4/099
Ruser Fdn., Beverly Hills, 4/100
Russell Fdn., Los Angeles, 4/101
Russell (S. & C.G.) Fdn., Arcadia, 4/101
Ryan Aeronautical Library, San Diego, 4/101
Ryan (David Claude) Fdn., San Diego, 4/102
Sacramento Fdn., Sacramento, 4/103
Sacramento Board of Realtors Scholarship Fdn., Sacramento, 4/103
S.A.E. Leadership Fdn., San Francisco, 4/104
Salinas Y's Man Club, Salinas, 4/105
Salud Fdn., Earlimart, 4/106
Salvatori (Henry & Grace) Fdn., Los Angeles, 4/106

Samoville (Edward & Geraldine) Fdn., Sacramento, 4/108

Sanders (Edward & Rose E.) Fdn., Los Angeles, 4/109

Sandlin (Dorothy) Fdn., Los Angeles, 4/109

San Fernando Valley Sportsmans Club, Van Nuys, 4/110

Sanford (D.E.) Fdn., Beverly Hills, 4/110

San Francisco Aquarium Society, San Francisco, 4/111

San Joaquin Pioneer & Historical Society, Stockton, 4/112

San Jose Quota Club Scholarship Fund, San Jose, 4/113

San Mateo County Building Trades Fdn., San Mateo, 4/113

Santa Barbara Educational Load Fund, Los Angeles, 4/114

Santa Barbara Medical Clinic Fdn. for Medical Research & Education, Santa Barbara, 4/115

Santa Ynez Fdn., Santa Barbara, 4/116

Sarian Fdn., Los Angeles, 4/117

Sawyer Fdn., Los Angeles, 4/118

Scan Charities, La Jolla, 4/119

Schaefer Fdn., Calistoga, 4/120

Schafer Fdn., San Francisco, 4/121

Schapiro-Tyre Fdn., Los Angeles, 4/121

Schlesinger (Albert E. & Irma C.) Fdn., San Francisco, 4/121

Schmidt (Marjorie Mosher) Fdn., Los Angeles, 4/122

Schmier (Walter D.) Fdn., San Diego, 4/123

Schoepe (Martha) Memorial Fdn., Araheim, 4/124

Schillo Family Fdn., Los Angeles, 4/125

Schultz Fdn., Greenbrae, 4/126

Schuman Fdn., Beverly Hills, 4/126

Schwartz (Alice & Sidney L.) Fdn., San Francisco, 4/127

Schwartz (Daniel) Fdn., Cathedral City, 4/130

Schweiger, Segel & Rubinstein Fdn., Los Angeles, 4/130

Science of the Golden Dawn Fdn., Long Beach, 4/131

Scott (James J.) Fdn., Los Angeles, 4/131

Scripps (Josephine Stedem) Fdn., San Diego, 4/131

Seaton (George & Phyllis) Fdn., Los Angeles, 4/132

See (Charles) Fdn., Los Angeles, 4/132

Sefton (J.W.) Fdn., San Diego, 4/136

Sence Fdn., Burbank, 4/138

Shafton (Robert & Sally) Fdn., Los Angeles, 4/139

Shanedling (Donald H.) Fdn., Culver City, 4/140

Shapiro (Joseph M. & Ednah Root) Fdn., Palm Springs, 4/141

Shapiro (Ralph & Martin) Fdn., Beverly Hills, 4/141

Shawnigan Fdn., San Francisco, 4/142

Shea (J.F.) Company Fdn., Walnut, 4/142

Shea Fdn., Walnut, 4/143

Shearer (Lloyd & Marva) Scholarship Fdn., Beverly Hills, 4/144

Sheinbaum Fdn., Los Angeles, 4/145

Sheldon (Sidney) Fdn., Beverly Hills, 4/145

Shenandoah Fdn., San Francisco, 4/146

Sherman (Marshall & Sara) Fdn., Beverly Hills, 4/147

Shlens Fdn., Los Angeles, 4/147

Shragge (Mollie E. & A.J.) Fdn., San Francisco, 4/148

Sibert (Pearson) Fdn., Beverly Hills, 4/149

Sifford (Pearl) Fund, Stockton, 4/149

Sigall (Marie Stauffer) Fdn., San Francisco, 4/150

Sigmann (Jacob & Fanny) Fdn., Beverly Hills, 4/151

Signal Companies Fdn., Los Angeles, 4/152

Sigoloff Fdn., Los Angeles, 4/152

Sikh Fdn., Woodside, 4/152

Silberberg (Mendel B.) Fdn., Beverly Hills, 4/153

Silbert (Harvey & Lillian) Fdn., Beverly Hills, 4/154

Silliman (Will C.) Memorial, San Bernardino, 4/154

Silverstein Family Fdn., Beverly Hills, 4/156

Simon (Albert & Mariam) Fdn., Oakland, 4/158

Simon (Al & Judith) Fdn., Hollywood, 4/159

Simon (Lucille Ellis) Fdn., Los Angeles, 4/161

Simon (Norton) Fdn., Los Angeles, 4/162

Simon (Robert Ellis) Fdn., Los Angeles, 4/163

Simon (Gerald H.) Fund, San Francisco, 4/164

Simon Foundation Funds of Norton, Los Angeles, 4/164

Simpson Fund, San Francisco, 4/165

Sinatra (Frank) Charitable Fdn., Beverly Hills, 4/166

Sinay (Joseph) Fdn., Los Angeles, 4/166

Sinsheimer (A.Z.) Family Memory Fund, San Luis Obispo, 4/167

Siskiyou County Historical Society, Yreka, 4/168

Skaggs Fdn., Oakland, 4/169

Skaggs (L.J.) & Mary Skaggs Fdn., Oakland, 4/170

Skouras (Charles P.) Fdn., Encino, 4/171

Slenczynski (Ruth) Scholarship Fund, San Francisco, 4/172

SLG Fdn., Los Angeles, 4/172

Sloan (Dr. Howard) Memorial Fdn., Pacific Palisades, 4/172

Sloss (Margaret K.) Fdn., San Francisco, 4/173

Slotkin (Stanley S.) Fdn., Los Angeles, 4/174

Smith Fdn., Oakland, 4/175

Smith (Earl W.) Fdn., El Cerrito, 4/176

Smith (Grace Pepper) Fdn., Balboa Island, 4/177

Smith (Lon V.) Fdn., Beverly Hills, 4/178

Smith-Hobson Fdn., Ventura, 4/178

Smith Memorial Cultural Fdn., San Jose, 4/179

Smits Fdn., San Marino, 4/179

Society for the Study of Intelligent Telecommunication Signals Emanating from Quasi-Stellar Radiation Sources, Carson, 4/180

Sommer (Allan & Jeanne) Fdn., San Francisco, 4/180

Song Line Fdn., Palm Springs, 4/180

Sons in Retirement, Sacramento, 4/181

Soule (Edward L. & Addie M.) Fdn., San Francisco, 4/181

Southern California Improvement Fdn., Los Angeles, 4/182

Spain (J.E.) Memorial Fdn., San Bernardino, 4/182

Sparling (Ray C.) Fdn., El Monte, 4/183

Sperling Fdn., Los Angeles, 4/184

Sperry (Leonard M.) Jr. Charitable Fund, Belvedere, 4/184

Sperry (Leonard & Rose A.) Fund, Los Angeles, 4/185

Sperry (Leonard M.) Research Center Fund, Los Angeles, 4/186

Spiegel (Adele Lehrer) Fdn., Los Angeles, 4/186

Spitzer (Jack J. & Charlotte B.) Fdn., Riverside, 4/187

Spivak (Morris & Rae) Fdn., Beverly Hills, 4/188

Sprague (Caryle M. & Norman F.) Fdn., Los Angeles, 4/189

Springer (Charles) Fdn., Burbank, 4/190

Stahl (John M. & Rosalie K.) Fdn., Los Angeles, 4/190

Stamps (James L.) Fdn., Downey, 4/191

Stang (Patricia Ann) Fdn., Orange, 4/192

Stanlee (Gene) Fdn., Redondo Beach, 4/193

Stauffer (John & Beverly) Fdn., Los Angeles, 4/193

Steel (Marshall) Sr. Fdn., Oakland, 4/195

Steelworkers Old Timers Fdn., Fontara, 4/196

Stein (Bley) Fdn., Studio City, 4/197

Stein (Jules & Doris) Fdn., Universal City, 4/197

Stein (Bennie) Memoral Fdn., Montebello, 4/199

Steinberg (Morris) Family Fdn., Van Nuys, 4/199

Steiner (Rudolf) Libraries, Los Angeles, 4/200

Steinhart (John H. & Helene T.) Charitable Fdn., San Francisco, 4/201

Steinhart (Genevieve & Jesse) Trust, San Francisco, 4/201

Stephens (John Lloyd) Fdn., San Marino, 4/202

Sterling (Mitzi) Memorial Fdn., Los Angeles, 4/202

Stern (Lucie) Fdn., San Francisco, 4/203

Stewart (James) Fdn., Beverly Hills, 4/204

Stilson (Elizabeth M.) Fdn., Coma Linda, 4/205

Stoller (Morris & Gertrude) Fdn., Beverly Hills, 4/206

Stone (Irving & Jean) Fdn., Beverly Hills, 4/206

Stone (Norman & Karen) Fdn., Woodside, 4/207

Stoner Fdn., Aurora, Illinois, 4/208

Stover Fdn., San Francisco, 4/208

Straub Family Fdn., Los Angeles, 4/209

Strauss (Levi) Fdn., San Francisco, 4/210

Strough (J. Val), Piedmont, 4/211

Strouse (Norman H. & Charlotte A) Trustees u/i, St. Helena, 4/212

Stuart (Elbridge & Mary) Fdn., Los Angeles, 4/212

Stulsaft (Morris) Fdn., San Francisco, 4/214

Sue (Julius F. & Eleanor Y.) Fdn., Los Angeles, 4/215

Suite 900 Fdn., Los Angeles, 4/215

Sullivan (Dorothy Grannis) Fdn., Los Angeles, 4/216

Sullivan (Louise A. & Walter H.) Fdn., San Francisco, 4/217

Sunflower Fdn., Santa Barbara, 4/219

Sun Valley Private School, Fort Bragg, 4/221

Swanson (W. Clarke) Family Fdn., Los Angeles, 4/221

Swedlow Fdn., Beverly Hills, 4/223

Swerdlow Family Fdn., Beverly Hills, 4/224

Swig (Benjamin H.) Charitable Fdn., San Francisco, 4/225

Swig (Mae & Benjamin) Charity Fdn., San Francisco, 4/225

Symons (Stanley E.) Fund, San Francisco, 4/226

Talent Bank Fdn., San Francisco, 4/227

Tamkin Fdn., Beverly Hills, 4/227

Tancer-Von Feldringen (Renee Bullard) Fdn., San Francisco, 4/228

Taubman (Morris B. & Janice L.) Fdn., Los Angeles, 4/230

Taubman (Ruthe & Louis) Fdn., Beverly Hills, 4/230

Teale Memorial Scholarship Fdn., Mokelumne Hill, 4/230

Techalloy Fdn. of California, Pomona, 4/231

Teledyne Charitable Trust, Los Angeles, 4/231

Thayer (Byron J.) Fdn., Stockton, 5/001

Theka Educational & Religious Fdn., Los Angeles, 5/001

Thille (Albert) Fdn., Santa Paula, 5/002

Thompson Fdn., Balboa Island, 5/003

Thompson (Fannie) Memorial Fund, Los Angeles, 5/004

Thomson Family Fdn., Los Angeles, 5/004

Thornburg (Jack) Medical Research Fdn., Santa Ysabel, 5/005

Thornton Fdn., Beverly Hills, 5/005

TI Corporation (of California) Fdn., Los Angeles, 5/006

Time Fdn., San Francisco, 5/010

Time's Tiny Tots Fdn., Los Angeles, 5/011

Tissue Fdn., Los Angeles, 5/013

Tomato Genetics Cooperative University of California, Davis, 5/013

Tomlinson-Howekamp Fdn., San Francisco, 5/014

Torrey Family Fdn., Menlo Park, 5/014

Towne Fdn., Los Angeles, 5/014

Townhouse Fdn., San Diego, 5/015

Townsend (Calvin K. & Doreen) Fdn., San Jose, 5/016

Transamerica Fdn., San Francisco, 5/016

Transition Fdn., Los Angeles, 5/017

Traynor (Stephen Pierre) Fdn., Berkeley, 5/017

Teadwell (Nora Eccks) Fdn., Oakland, 5/018

Trevarno Fdn., Pleasanton, 5/018

Trione Fdn., Santa Rosa, 5/019

True Fellowship Lodge #52, I.O.O.P., Santa Clara, 5/019

Trust Funds, San Francisco, 5/019

Brown (Samuel R.) Trust u/w, Los Angeles, 5/021

Disney (Walter E.) Charitable Trust u/w, Burbank, 5/023

Moore (J.M.) Residuary Trust u/w, San Francisco, 5/024

Seaver (Frank R.) Trust u/w, Los Angeles, 5/024

Walker (Kate Ellen) Trust u/w, Los Angeles, 5/025

Twelveacres, Trustees of, San Jose, 5/026

Try Fdn., Los Angeles, 5/027

Tuerk (Fred Reynolds) Fund, Los Angeles, 5/029

Turk (Gladys) Fdn., Beverly Hills, 5/030

Turman (Laurence) Fdn., Beverly Hills, 5/032

Tyler Clinic Research Fdn., Los Angeles, 5/033

Tyler (John & Alice) Fdn., Los Angeles, 5/033

Union Oil Company of California Fdn., Los Angeles, 5/034

Union-Tribune Charities, La Jolla, 5/037

U.S. Charitable Fdn., San Francisco, 5/038

Valentine Fdn., Santa Barbara, 5/039

Van Camp Fdn., Long Beach, 5/039

Vanderwilt (John W.) Fdn., Sun City, 5/040

Van Gogh Street School, Granada Hills, 5/040

Van Nuys (J.B. & Emily) Charities, Los Angeles, 5/041

Van Oppen (James F.) Memorial Fund, Torrance, 5/041

Van Winkle (Emma C.) Educational Fdn., Concord, 5/041

Varian Fdn., San Francisco, 5/042

Vaughn Water Co., Bakersfield, 5/043

Verfred Fdn., San Marcos, 5/044

Veterans of World War I of the United States of America, Mojave, 5/044

Victor (Alexander F.) Fdn., Carmel, 5/044

Vidor (Charles) Fdn., Los Angeles, 5/045

Vignolo Fdn., Shafter, 5/046

Vinnell Fdn., Los Angeles, 5/046

Vista Hill Psychiatric Fdn., San Diego, 5/047

Vitale Fdn., Los Angeles, 5/048

Voegelin (Harold S.) Fdn., Los Angeles, 5/049

Von's Grocery Fdn., Los Angeles, 5/049

Vukasovich Fdn., Watsonville, 5/050

Wade (Elizabeth Firth) Endowment Fund, Santa Barbara, 5/051

Wain Fdn., Los Angeles, 5/054

Waldier Fdn., Woodside, 5/054

Walker and Lee Fdn., Anaheim, 5/054

Walker (Clinton) Fdn., San Francisco, 5/055

Walker (Morley) Fdn., Berkeley, 5/056

Wallis Fdn., Universal City, 5/056

Waltmar Fdn., Garden Grove, 5/058

Ward Fdn., Hollywood, 5/058

Warde (Charles R.) Fdn., Beverly Hills, 5/058

Warner (Ann B. & Jack L.) Fdn., Inc., Century City, 5/060

Kendrick (Warren Charles) Trust, San Francisco, 5/061

Waste Family Fund, San Francisco, 5/062

Wattis (Paul L. & Phyllis) Fdn., San Francisco, 5/063

Weber (Daniel A. & Doris L.) Fdn., Los Angeles, 5/064

Webster (C.A.) Fdn., Linden, 5/065

Weed Fdn., Inc., Los Angeles, 5/066

Weeks (Lucina) Trust for Handicapped Children, San Francisco, 5/067

Weinberg (Bernard) Fdn., Los Angeles, 5/069

Weinberg (Chas M.) Fund, Newport Beach, 5/070

Weiss (Benjamin & Betty) Fdn., Los Angeles, 5/070

Weiss (Julian D. & Shirley W.) Fdn., Los Angeles, 5/071

Welfund Inc., Los Angeles, 5/071

Wells Fdn., Pasadena, 5/073

Werner-Phillips Fdn., Los Angeles, 5/074

Wesix Fdn., Tiburon, 5/075

West Coast Baptist Children's Home, Lodi, 5/075

Western Cardiac Fdn., Beverly Hills, 5/075

Western Fdn. of Vertebrate Zoology, Los Angeles, 5/076

Western Medical Research Fdn. of America, San Francisco, 5/077

Western Physics Fdn., Santa Monica, 5/077

Western State University Fdn., Anahgim, 5/077

Weston (Alan E.) Fdn., Los Angeles, 5/078

Whitfield Fund, San Diego, 5/078

Whitman Fdn., San Francisco, 5/079

Whitney Fdn., San Diego, 5/079

Whitsett (W.P.) Fdn., Van Nuys, 5/081

Wilbur (Brayton) Fdn., San Francisco, 5/081

Willens Family Fdn., Los Angeles, 5/082

Burgess (William H.) Fdn., Pasadena, 5/082

Williams (Harold M. & Estelle F.) Fdn., Beverly Hills, 5/082

Williams (Frank) Fund, Inc., San Diego, 5/083

Wilson (J.E.) Fdn., Beverly Hills, 5/083

Wilson (Lorin H.) Fdn., Los Angeles, 5/084

Winnett Fdn., Los Angeles, 5/084

Winston Family Fdn, Inc., Cathedral City, 5/085

Winters Family Fdn., Los Angeles, 5/086

Witherbee-Gilpin Fdn., Beverly Hills, 5/088

Witherspoon (Gertrude Ralphs) Fdn., Los Angeles, 5/089

Witter (Dean) Fdn., San Francisco, 5/090

Witter (Jean C.) Fdn., San Francisco, 5/090

Wolf (Bennett L.) Fdn., Los Angeles, 5/091

Wolf (Donald S.) Fdn., Los Angeles, 5/092

Wolf (Julius R.) Fdn., Los Angeles, 5/092

Wolfen Family Fdn., Century City, 5/093

Wolfskill (John & Lucretta) Fdn., El Monte, 5/094

Wollenberg Fdn., San Francisco, 5/094

Wolper Fdn., Beverly Hills, 5/095

Woodard Fdn., La Jolla, 5/096

Wooldridge (Dean E. & Helene) Fdn., Santa Barbara, 5/096

Worden (James S.) Memorial Fund, San Carlos, 5/097

Worldwide Visual Alliance, La Crescenta, 5/098

Wrather (J.D. & Mazie) Fdn., Beverly Hills, 5/098

Wrigley (William) Jr., Memorial Fdn., Avalon, 5/099

Wunderlich (Martin) Fdn., Palo Alto, 5/099

Wyatt Fdn., Oakland, 5/099

Wyle Fdn., El Segundo, 5/100

Wynn Fdn., Azusa, 5/100

Yager (Judge Thomas C. & Eileen K.J.) Fdn., Los Angeles, 5/101

Yates (Sybil & Perry) Fund, San Francisco, 5/103

Yellin (Edward) Fdn., Encino, 5/104

Yolo County Medical Society, Woodland, 5/105

Young Saints Scholarship Fdn., Los Angeles, 5/107

Zaffaroni Fdn., Atherton, 5/107

Zarem Fdn., Beverly Hills, 5/107

Zelinsky (D.) & Sons Fdn., San Francisco, 5/108

Zellerbach (Harold L.) Art Fdn., San Francisco, 5/109

Zellerbach Family Fdn., San Francisco, 5/110

Zellerbach (William & Margery) Fdn., San Francisco, 5/112

Zellerbach (Hana) Fund, San Francisco, 5/113

Zellerbach (Harold & Doris) Fund, San Francisco, 5/113

Zellerbach-Loew Fdn., Beverly Hills, 5/114

Zerner Fdn., Los Angeles, 5/115

Ziegler Family Fdn., Los Angeles, 5/117

Zuckerman (E.K.) Fdn., Santa Monica, 5/117

Zuckerman (Kenneth A.) Fdn., Santa Monica, 5/118

102 Fdn., Los Angeles, 5/119

Second Filming

Aaron (Mary M.) Memorial Trust Scholarship Fund, Yuba City, 6/001

Aaron (Mary M.) Memorial Trust Museum Fund, Yuba City, 6/001

A.B.O.Y., Inc., San Jose, 6/002

Adams (Berle H.) Fdn., North Hollywood, 6/003

Aetna Fdn., Los Angeles, 6/003

Agricultural Education Fdn., San Mateo, 6/004

Alameda Boys Club Fdn., Alameda, 6/004

Albert (Agnes) Trust, San Francisco, 6/005

Alexander Educational Fund, Santa Barbara, 6/005

Alexian Brothers Hospital Fdn., San Jose, 6/007

Alta California Eye Research Fdn., San Francisco, 6/007

Amaranth Homes of California, Needles, 6/007

American Association for Inhalation Therapy Fdn., Riverside, 6/008

American Brotherhood for the Blind, Los Angeles, 6/008

American Christian History Institute, San Francisco, 6/009

American Legion Post 0724, Weott, 6/009

American Redirection Medicine Association, Orinda, 6/010

American Right of Way Association, San Diego, 6/010

Ampex Fdn., Redwood City, 6/010

Anderson (Arthur C. & Gertrude H.) Trust, San Diego, 6/014

Griffith (Andy) Fdn., Beverly Hills, 6/015

Anderton (Nina) Fdn., Los Angeles, 6/015

Armitage (Herbert Dewey) Memorial Fdn., Hayward, 6/016

Armstrong (Robert A.) Research Fdn., Santa Monica, 6/017

Assurance Sciences Fdn., Mt. View, 6/018

Avery - Fuller Children's Center, San Francisco, 6/018

Babcock (William) Memorial Endowment, San Francisco, 6/020

Bailey (Fred) Charitable Fdn., Malibu, 6/022

Baker Family Fdn., Newport Beach, 5/023

Baker (Solomon R.) Fdn., Beverly Hills, 6/023

Balfour Medical Fdn., Pasadena, 6/024

Bannan (Bernard J.) Fdn., Lynwood, 6/025

Bannerman (William C.) Fdn., Los Angeles, 6/025

Banner (James) Charitable Fdn., Beverly Hills, 6/026

Barlow (William P.) Fdn., San Francisco, 6/027

Barnett (Lawrence R. & Isabel B.) Fdn., Los Angeles, 6/027

Barrett (Barbara L. & Richard C.) Fdn., Los Angeles, 6/028

Beaver Medical Clinic Fdn., Redlands, 6/029

Beachy (Walter F. & Kathleen S.) Charitable Fdn., Woodland Hills, 6/030

Bay (Sam S. & Phyllis) Fdn., Los Angeles, 6/030

Bay Area Fdn. for Human Resources, Berkeley, 6/031

Bartlett Trust Fund, Porterville, 6/032

Bee (Anna H. & Albert W.) Scholarship Fund, Santa Barbara, 6/032

Free (William C. & Mazy Bell) Scholarship Fund, Pasadena, 6/034

Beneficial Standard Fdn., Los Angeles, 6/035

Bennett (A.E.) Neuropsychiatric Research Fdn., Berkeley, 6/036

Berkman (Irving & Sam) Fdn., Van Nuys, 6/038

Berlin (Lela M.) Trust, Oxnard, 6/038

Berman Family Fdn., Los Angeles, 6/039

Beverly Hills Cancer Research Fdn., Beverly Hills, 6/039

Binder (Miriam Muller) Scholarship Trust, Los Angeles, 6/040
Birks Family Fdn., Montreal, Canada, 6/040
Pike (Bishop) Fdn., Santa Barbara, 6/041
Bissinger Fdn., San Francisco, 6/042
B & J Association of California, Studio City, 6/043
Blatteis (S & C) Fdn., San Francisco, 6/045
Bluebird Fdn., Los Angeles, 6/045
Blywise Fdn. Formerly Ohio, Palm Springs, 6/046
Rancho Santa Ana Botanic Garden Trust, Claremont, 6/047
Hope (Bob & Dolores) Charitable Fdn., North Hollywood, 6/048
Bodman (Julia B. & Edward W.) Fdn., Los Angeles, 6/049
Bolker (Joseph) Fdn. Formerly Bolker (Jan & Joe) Fdn., Los Angeles, 6/050
Bohnett (Vi) Memorial Fdn., Santa Barbara, 6/051
Borrego Springs Educational Scholarship Committee, Borrego Springs, 6/051
Bothin Convelescent Home, San Raphael, 6/052
Bowers (Charles W.) Memorial Museum Fdn., Santa Ana, 6/053
B.P.O. Elks Lodge No. 2045, Corona, 6/053
B.P.O.E. Lodge 1382, Calexico, 6/053
Bradley (Frederick Worthen) Fdn., San Francisco, 6/054
Bramila Charitable Fdn., Beverly Hills, 6/055
Bramwell (L.W. & B.S.) Fdn., La Jolla, 6/056
Brandeis (Louis D.) House, San Francisco, 6/056
Brandler (Henry & Mona) Fdn., Los Angeles, 6/057
Braun Fdn., Los Angeles, 6/058
Brodovsky (Hyman) Memorial Fund, Sacramento, 6/059
Brodovsky (Louis & Dorothy) Fdn., Sacramento, 6/060
Brooks (Harold & Evelyn) Fdn., Los Angeles, 6/060
Brown (Charles I.) Fdn., Los Angeles, 6/061
Bruck (Ellen Hindes) Fdn., San Francisco, 6/061
Bryant Oil Company Fdn., Huntington Park, 6/062
Buckley Education Fdn., Los Angeles, 6/062
Bushnell (Nina C.) Fdn., Altadena, 6/063
Butler (Marjorie E.) Trust, Eureka, 6/063
B.W. Fdn., Los Angeles, 6/064
Cachelin Fdn., Santa Barbara, 6/065
California Fdn. for Biochemical Research, Los Angeles, 6/065
California Masonic Fdn., San Francisco, 6/066
California Pharmacy Fdn. Trust Fund, Sacramento, 6/067
California Pioneer Fdn., San Francisco, 6/067
California School Counselor Association, Fullerton, 6/067
California Surgical Research Fdn., Los Angeles, 6/068
Callendar (Robert S. & Wynnefred W.) Charitable Fdn., Palm Desert, 6/068
Callison Memorial Hospital, San Francisco, 6/068
Calmerton Educational Fdn., Los Angeles, 6/069
Cambium Corporation Formerly District of Columbia, San Francisco, 6/069
Campini (Frank A.) Fdn., Berkeley, 6/070
Canfield Fdn., Beverly Hills, 6/071
Cardea Fdn., Los Angeles, 6/072
Careers for Retired Military, San Francisco, 6/073
Carlton Fdn., Santa Barbara, 6/074
Carpenters Local Union No. 1976 Mortuary Trust Fund, Los Angeles, 6/075
Carter (Victor M. & Adrea) Fdn., Los Angeles, 6/075
Catalyst Fund, Menlo Park, 6/083
Catholic Professional Women's Club, San Francisco, 6/087
Cecil (Earl J.) Educational Fdn., Fresno, 6/088

Cedu Fdn., San Bernardino, 6/088
Century City Cardiovascular Research Fdn., Los Angeles, 6/090
Chai Fdn., Los Angeles, 6/091
Chalek (Marvin M. & Carmen) Fdn., Los Angeles, 6/092
Chapman Research Fund, Carmel, 6/092
Chase (Del & Gail) Fdn., Walnut Creek, 6/094
Children's Kaleidoscope of San Diego, San Diego, 6/095
Children's Welfare Fdn., Corona del Mar, 6/095
Christadelphian Joy Fund, San Mateo, 6/095
Christian Counseling Service, Garden Grove, 6/097
Christian Witness Fdn., Sacramento, 6/097
Civitan Fdn. of Pasadena, Pasadena, 6/098
Clark (Willis W. & Ethel M.) Fdn., Pebble Beach, 6/098
Clarke (Amy Bassett) Trust, San Francisco, 6/099
Claremont Fdn., Claremont, 6/099
Clarke (Chauncey) Fellowship Testamentary Trust, Claremont, 6/101
Colburn (Richard D.) Fdn., Los Angeles, 6/102
Collins Fdn., North Hollywood, 6/103
Columbia Fdn., San Francisco, 6/103
Community Projects Fdn., San Francisco, 6/105
Community Scholarship Fdn., La Canada, 6/106
Conn (Harry) Fdn., Encino, 6/107
Connell (Michael J.) Fdn., Los Angeles, 6/107
Connor (Edward H.) Fdn., Lafayette, 6/108
Consolidated Fdn., Los Angeles, 6/109
Consumer Research Fdn., San Rafael, 6/109
Contra Costa Labor, Health & Welfare Council, Martinez, 6/110
Cotton Fdn., Pasadena, 6/110
Cox (Joseph B.) Fdn., Santa Barbara, 6/110
Crummey (John D.) Benevolent Trust, San Jose, 6/110
Crummey (Vivan G.) Benevolent Trust, San Jose, 6/111
Cunningham (Briggs) Automotive Museum, Pasadena, 6/112
Danish Relief Society of East Bay Cities, Oakland, 6/113
Darin (Robert) Fdn., Beverly Hills, 6/113
Davis (Allen V.C.) Fdn., Beverly Hills, 6/114
Davis (Stanley M.) Fdn., Davis, 6/114
Dawn (Alma) Fdn., Los Angeles, 6/115
DeFord (William A.) Trust, San Diego, 6/115
Del Monte Fdn., Pebble Beach, 6/117
Dental Fdn. of California, Los Angeles, 6/117
Dermal Pathology Institute, Los Angeles, 6/119
Des Baillets (Emilie) Trust, Los Angeles, 6/120
Deutsch Fund, Los Angeles, 6/121
Devine (Agnes) Trust, San Diego, 6/121
De Wolfe (Elsie) Fdn., Los Angeles, 6/122
Diabetes & Nutrition Fdn., Redwood City, 6/123
Diablo Symphony Association, Walnut Creek, 6/125
Diamond (Leo L.) Fdn., Los Angeles, 6/125
Dickranian Fdn., Beverly Hills, 6/125
Diener (Frank C.) Fdn., Five Points, 6/126
Diller (Richard S. & Eudice Linsey) Fdn., Beverly Hills, 6/127
Disney (Roy) Fdn., Burbank, 6/128
Dollard (Laura) Scholarship Fund, San Francisco, 6/129
Donner Summit Fdn., San Francisco, 6/130
Downer (Edward M. & Gertrude T.) Fund, Richmond, 6/131
Drews Fdn., San Francisco, 6/132
Drown (Francis) Fdn., Los Angeles, 6/133
Drum Fdn., San Francisco, 6/134
Drug Abuse Information Service, San Jose, 6/135
Moore Dry Dock Fdn., San Francisco, 6/136
Dumbarton Research Council, Menlo Park, 6/136

Ebell Rest Cottage Association, Los Angeles, 6/137
Ebell of Los Angeles Scholarship Endowment Fund, Los Angeles, 6/138
Eckstrom Memorial Cancer Detection Fdn., Los Angeles, 6/139
Edgewood Botanic Garden, Mill Valley, 6/140
Edwards (Frank) Fdn., Burlingame, 6/141
Elan Fdn., San Francisco, 6/142
Elek Research Fund, Beverly Hills, 6/143
Enterprises Fdn., Los Angeles, 6/144
Ericsson (Annie L.P.) Trust, Santa Barbara, 6/145
Erickson (Lennart) Fdn., San Meteo, 6/145
Esperance Fdn., Balboa Island, 6/146
Evangelical Press Association, La Canada, 6/146
Factor (John & Rella) Fdn., Los Angeles, 6/147
Familian (Isadore & Sunny) Family Fdn., Pacoima, 6/148
Feigon (Gershon J. & Beylah) Fdn. Formerly New York, El Cajon, 6/149
Fels (Helen & Herman) Fdn., Beverly Hills, 6/150
Fenmore (Terry) Memorial Fund, Marina del Rey, 6/151
Field (William) Charitable Fund, Point Reyes, 6/151
Field (Martin) Fdn., San Francisco, 6/152
Finkelstein (Lester M. & Irene C.) Fdn., Los Angeles, 6/152
Finley (Ernest L. & Ruth) Fdn., Santa Rosa, 6/153
Fletcher Fdn., Arcadia, 6/153
Fleishhacker (Mortimer) Fdn., San Francisco, 6/154
Fletcher (Willis & Jane) Fdn., San Diego, 6/156
Flesch Family Fdn., Beverly Hills, 6/156
Fletcher (Willis & Jane) Fdn., San Diego, 6/156
Fligelman (Julius & Molly) Fdn., Los Angeles, 6/156
Flint (Mr. & Mrs. Charles N.) Scholarship Fdn. Fund, Los Angeles, 6/157
Fluor (Marjorie L. & J. Simon) Fdn., Santa Ana, 6/157
Park Flyers, Fullterton, 6/158
Foss (Robert B.) Fdn., San Diego, 6/159
Foundation for American Christian Education, San Francisco, 6/159
Foundation for Hearing Research, Redwood City, 6/161
Foundation for Human Potentials, Beverly Hills, 6/161
Foundation of the Litton Industries, Beverly Hills, 6/162
Foundation for Nutrition & Stress Research, Redwood City, 6/163
Foundation for Radio Theosophy, Ojai, 6/164
Foundation for Reconstructive Facial Surgery, Studio City, 6/164
Foundation for Research & Community Development, San Jose, 6/164
Foundation for the Study of the Behavioral Sciences, Downey, 6/165
Foundation for the Study of Voluntary Control of Psychophysiological States, Van Nuys, 6/165
Fourtees Fdn., Beverly Hills, 6/166
Fowle Fdn., Los Altos Hills, 6/167
Freedman (Charles & Ruth) Fdn., Los Angeles, 6/167
Freeman Family Fdn., Los Angeles, 6/167
French Hospital Fdn. for Research & Education, San Francisco, 6/168
Fresno State College Alumni Association, Fresno, 6/168
Fresno State College Alumni Trust Council, Fresno, 6/169
Friedberger Educational Fund, Stockton, 6/170
Friedman Brothers Fdn., Los Angeles, 6/171
Friedman (Howard A. & Phyllis K.) Fdn., San Francisco, 6/172

Friedman (Harry & Olga) Fdn., Los Angeles, 6/173

Friedman (Samuel) Fdn., Los Angeles, 6/173

Friend Family Fdn., San Francisco, 6/175

Fullen - Smith Fdn., Los Angeles, 6/177

Fundtastics Toastmistress Club, San Francisco, 6/178

Furniture Manufacturers Association of California, Los Angeles, 6/178

Gage (Sanford & Marion) Charitable Fdn., Beverly Hills, 6/179

Gallo Fdn., Modesto, 6/180

Galster Fdn., West Covina, 6/180

Garfield (David H. & Dorothea) Charitable Fdn., La Jolla, 6/181

Garland (John Jewett & Helen Chandler) Fdn. Trust, Los Angeles, 6/182

Gassin (Robert & Carol) Fdn., Walnut Creek, 6/183

Ceazan - Geist Charitable Fdn., Los Angeles, 6/184

Geller (A.J. & Thelma) Fdn. Formerly Minnesota, Los Angeles, 6/184

Giannini (Clorinda) Memorial Benefit Fund, San Francisco, 6/185

Giannini (George J.) Fdn., San Francisco, 6/186

Gilbert Fdn., Beverly Hills, 6/187

Gildred Fdn., San Diego, 7/001

Ginsberg (Herbert A.) Fdn., San Francisco, 7/001

Given (Sherman & Doris) Fdn., Los Angeles, 7/002

Gjoa Fdn., San Francisco, 7/002

Glaser Fdn., San Francisco, 7/002

Gleich Fdn., San Diego, 7/003

Gold Star Memorial Scholarship Fund, Palo Alto, 7/004

Goldman (Harry A. & Hilda) Fdn., Beverly Hills, 7/004

Gonzalez (Faye Dobbs) Fdn., San Diego, 7/005

Goodman Jewelers Fdn., San Bernardino, 7/005

Gordon Fdn., San Diego, 7/006

Gospel Meeting Rooms, Los Angeles, 7/006

Gotham Fund, Los Angeles, 7/006

Gottlieb (Milton & Pat) Fdn., Beverly Hills, 7/007

Graham (Marie Luise) Charitable Fdn., San Francisco, 7/007

Grancell (I.H. & Anna) Fdn., Los Angeles, 7/008

Grand Counselors, Century City, 7/009

Grass Valley Ladies Relief Society, Grass Valley, 7/009

Griffin (Alice M.) Fund, San Francisco, 7/010

Gross (Stella B.) Charitable Trust, San Jose, 7/011

Gruen (Victor) Fdn. for Environmental Planning, Los Angeles, 7/013

Guedel's Dinky Fdn., Los Angeles, 7/014

Ebell Rest Cottage Association, Los Angeles, 7/015

Ebell of Los Angeles Scholarship Endowment Fund, Los Angeles, 7/017

Eckstrom Memorial Cancer Detection Fdn., Los Angeles, 7/018

Edgewood Botanic Garden, Mill Valley, 7/019

Edwards (Frank) Fdn., Burlingame, 7/019

Elan Fdn., San Francisco, 7/021

Elek Research Fund, Beverly Hills, 7/022

Enterprises Fdn., Los Angeles, 7/022

Ericsson (Annie L.P.) Trust, Santa Barbara, 7/023

Erikson (Lennart) Fdn., San Mateo, 7/023

Esperance Fdn., Balboa Island, 7/024

Evangelical Press Association, La Canada, 7/025

Factor (John & Rella) Fdn., Los Angeles, 7/025

Familian (Isadore & Sunny) Family Fdn., Pacoima, 7/026

Feigon (Gershon J. & Beylah) Fdn. Formerly New York, El Cajon, 7/027

Fels (Helen & Herman) Fdn., Beverly Hills, 7/028

Fenmore (Terry) Memorial Fund, Marina del Rey, 7/029

Field (William) Charitable Fund, Point Reyes, 7/029

Field (Martin) Fdn., San Francisco, 7/029

Finkelstein (Lester M. & Irene C.) Fdn., Los Angeles, 7/030

Finley (Ernest L. & Ruth) Fdn., Santa Rosa, 7/031

Fletcher Fdn., Arcadia, 7/031

Fleishhacker (Mortimer) Fdn., San Francisco, 7/032

Fletcher (Willis & Jane) Fdn., San Diego, 7/033

Flesch Family Fdn., Beverly Hills, 7/034

Fletcher (Willis & Jane) Fdn., San Diego, 7/034

Fligelman (Julius & Molly) Fdn., Los Angeles, 7/034

Flint (Mr. & Mrs. Charles N.) Scholarship Fdn. Fund, Los Angeles, 7/035

Flour (Marjorie L. & J. Simon) Fdn., Santa Ana, 7/035

Park Fliers, Fullerton, 7/036

Foss (Robert B.) Fdn., San Diego, 7/037

Foundation for American Christian Education, San Francisco, 7/037

Foundation for Hearing Research, Redwood City, 7/038

Foundation for Human Potentials, Beverly Hills, 7/038

Foundation of the Litton Industries, Beverly Hills, 7/039

Foundation for Nutrition & Stress Research, Redwood City, 7/041

Foundation for Radio Theosophy, Ojai, 7/041

Foundation for Reconstructive Facial Surgery, Studio City, 7/041

Foundation for Research & Community Development, San Jose, 7/042

Foundation for the Study of the Behavioral Sciences, Downey, 7/042

Foundation for the Study of the Voluntary Control of Psychophysiological States, Van Nuys, 7/043

Fourtees Fdn., Beverly Hills, 7/043

Fowle Fdn., A Charitable Trust, Los Altos Hills, 7/044

Freedman (Charles & Ruth) Fdn., Los Angeles, 7/044

Freeman Family Fdn., Los Angeles, 7/044

French Hospital Fdn. for Research & Education, San Francisco, 7/046

Kinnoull Fdn., Monterey, 7/046

Kiwanis International, Chula Vista Kiwanis Club, Chula Vista, 7/047

Kiwanis International Club of Chula Vista, Chula Vista, 7/047

Kodimer (Paul) Fdn., Beverly Hills, 7/048

Kofman (Abraham) Fdn., Alameda, 7/049

Kornwasser Charitable Fdn., Los Angeles, 7/049

Kotzin Fund, Los Angeles, 7/050

K & R Fdn., Ojai, 7/051

Kratz Fdn., Van Nuys, 7/051

Kudler (Moe & Berdie) Fdn., Los Angeles, 7/052

L & M Fdn., Thousand Oaks, 7/053

Lacma Fdn. for Medical Education, Los Angeles, 7/053

Laing Fdn., Los Angeles, 7/054

Lamp Research Fdn., Los Angeles, 7/054

Land (Charles H.) Family Fdn., San Francisco, 7/055

Langendorf (Stanley S.) Charitable Trust, San Francisco, 7/055

Lantin Fdn., Beverly Hills, 7/056

Lapierre (Albert L.) Fdn., Indio, 7/057

Lasher (Edward A. & Alma) Fdn., Beverly Hills, 7/057

Lasker (Edward & Cynthia) Fdn., Los Angeles, 7/058

Lastfogel (Abe & Frances) Fdn., Beverly Hills, 7/058

Lear - Siegler Fdn., Santa Monica, 7/059

Lee (Norma & Sidney) Fdn., Pebble Beach, 7/060

Lee (S. Charles) Fdn., Beverly Hills, 7/060

Cocuzza - Lenchner Fdn., San Francisco, 7/061

Levi (John & Judy) Charitable Fdn., Beverly Hills, 7/062

Lewis (Jarma) Fdn., Beverly Hills, 7/062

Lewis (Ed & Mary) Fdn., Pacific Palisades, 7/063

Lewis (Mabelle McLeod) Memorial Fund, San Francisco, 7/064

Liberal Arts 677 Benevolent Fdn., Los Angeles, 7/066

Library Association of La Jolla, La Jolla, 7/066

Lifton (Sam & Beatrice) Fdn., Los Angeles, 7/068

Link - Care Fdn., Fresno, 7/068

Linke (Richard O.) Fdn., Beverly Hills, 7/069

Linkletter Fdn., Irvine, 7/069

Lions International - Lake Arrowhead Lions Club, Blue Jay, 7/070

Lipschutz (Dora) Memorial Fdn., North Hollywood, 7/070

Li - Ro Lodge, Glendale, 7/070

Live Oak P.T.A., Santa Cruz, 7/070

Living Memorials Fdn., Los Angeles, 7/071

Livingston (Rebecca Payne) Fdn., Pasadena, 7/073

Lomas (Stella & Max) Fdn., Los Angeles, 7/073

Long (Walter H.) Charitable Fdn., Burbank, 7/074

Los Angeles County Painting Industry Administrative Trust Fund, Los Angeles, 7/075

Los Angeles Junior Chamber of Commerce Golf Fdn., Los Angeles, 7/075

Los Angeles Medical Research Fdn., West Los Angeles, 7/076

Los Angeles Transplant Fdn., Los Angeles, 7/077

Loveman (Harold & Saralyn) Fdn., Rolling Hills Estates, 7/077

Los Angeles Center for Group Psychotherapy, Los Angeles, 7/078

Loveman (Harold & Saralyn) Fdn., Rolling Hills Estates, 7/078

Lowitz Fdn., Beverly Hills, 7/079

Loyal Order of Moose, Palmdale, 7/080

Lustgarfen (Edward) Fdn., Encino, 7/080

Lux (Miranda) Fdn., San Francisco, 7/080

Lyman (Maude E.) Memorial Fund, Ukiah, 7/081

Magnin (Cyril) Fdn., San Francisco, 7/082

Mahl Memorial Fund, San Francisco, 7/083

Maier (Henry) Education & Research Fdn., San Leandro, 7/083

Malton (Marvin & Sonia) Charitable Fdn., Beverly Hills, 7/083

Mancini (Ione) Estate of, Modesto, 7/084

Mandel (Robert & Stella) Fdn., Beverly Hills, 7/085

Marian Charitable Trust, Los Angeles, 7/085

Marks (Walter N.) Fdn., Beverly Hills, 7/086

Marquis Fdn. Formerly New York, Los Angeles, 7/087

Marriage Guidance Institute, Beverly Hills, 7/087

Marshall Family Charitable Trust, Palo Alto, 7/087

Schoepe (Martha) Memorial Fdn., Anaheim, 7/088

Martin Family Fdn., Beverly Hills, 7/088

Marvine (Helen) Trust, San Francisco, 7/088

Mared Fdn., San Francisco, 7/089

Marci Fdn., Ojai, 7/090

Marks (Walter N.) Fdn., Beverly Hills, 7/090

Martin (Blanche E.), Los Angeles, 7/091

Padway (Martin) Fdn., Sun Valley, 7/091

Masonic Board of Relief of Los Angeles, Los Angeles, 7/092

Mave Diagnostic Training & Education Ct., Sunnyvale, 7/092

May (David), II Fdn., Los Angeles, 7/092

May Educational Fdn., Los Angeles, 7/094

May (Wilbur) Fdn., Los Angeles, 7/095

Mayhew Trust for Brigham Young University, Davis, 7/096

McAlister (Harold) Charitable Fdn., Los Angeles, 7/097

McAteer (J. Eugene) Memorial Fdn., San Francisco, 7/099

McBean (Atholl) Fdn., San Francisco, 7/100

McCheyney (Josephine) Fdn., San Diego, 7/101

McCulloch (Robert P.) Charitable Trust, Los Angeles, 7/102

McMillan (John Christian & Margaret Edna) Fdn., Los Angeles, 7/103

McGah Fdn., Orinda, 7/104

McCarthy (John A.) Fdn., Los Angeles, 7/104

McDonald (Louis) Pollution Abatement Fdn., Los Angeles, 7/106

Mead Improvement Corporation, Los Angeles, 7/106

Meltzer (Edward) Fdn., Beverly Hills, 7/107

Men's & Boy's Apparel Club of Southern California, Westmac, Los Angeles, 7/108

Metaphysical Research Fdn., Los Angeles, 7/108

Millbrae Community Players, Millbrae, 7/108

Miller (Avy L. & Roberta L.) Fdn., Encino, 7/109

Miller (Earl Burns) Trust, Long Beach, 7/109

Miller (Earl B. & Loraine H.) Fdn., Long Beach, 7/110

Millfield School Fdn., Beverly Hills, 7/110

Miracle Fdn., Turlock, 7/111

Mirisch Family Fdn., Los Angeles, 7/112

Missionary Enterprises, La Habra, 7/112

Mogilner (Samuel) Family Fdn., San Diego, 7/113

P.T.A. - Del Rey, Victorville, 7/113

Moore (Cornelia M.) Memorial Free Dental Fdn., Santa Barbara, 7/114

Moore (Ethel) Memorial, San Leandro, 7/115

Moore (E. Ray & Dora May) Fdn., Santa Ana, 7/116

Morrison (Alice G.) Memorial Fdn., Oakland, 7/117

Mudd (Henry T.) Fdn., Los Angeles, 7/118

Mudd (Mildred E. & Harvey S.) Fdn., Los Angeles, 7/119

Murrell (Robert B.) Trust, Los Angeles, 7/120

Mzuri Safari Club Fdn., Santa Rosa, 7/121

Nagel (Jack & Gitta) Fdn., Los Angeles, 7/121

Nahas (Robert T.) Company Fdn., Castro Valley, 7/122

Nasser Fund, Beverly Hills, 7/122

National Association of Legal Secretaries, Los Angeles, 7/123

National Fdn. for Treatment of Emotionally Handicapped, Sepulveda, 7/123

National Handicappers' Fellowship, Victorville, 7/124

National Sight Fdn., La Crescenta, 7/124

Native Sons of the Golden West Charitable Fdn., San Francisco, 7/124

Navsky (Albert W. & Seena) Fdn., Los Angeles, 7/124

Neil (William P.) Fdn., Azusa, 7/125

New Arts & Science Fdn., Palmdale, 7/125

New Horizons Fdn., Azusa, 7/126

Nevonen Family Fdn., Los Angeles, 7/126

Newfield (Arthur A. & Katheryn N.) Fdn., Los Angeles, 7/127

Nigh (Sam H.) Family Trust, San Francisco, 7/127

Niven Charitable Fund, Los Angeles, 7/128

Nixon Birthplace Fdn., Yorba Linda, 7/128

Noble (Bert) Fdn., Orange, 7/129

Northern California Pharmaceutical Association, San Francisco, 7/129

Nosutch Fdn., Los Angeles, 7/130

Nye (Jessica) Fdn., Mill Valley, 7/131

Oakes (Roscoe & Margaret) Fdn., San Francisco, 7/132

Oakland Junior Chamber of Commerce Charitable Trust, Oakland, 7/134

Oakland Scottish Rite Scaife Scholarship Fdn., Oakland, 7/134

Oakmont League of Glendale, California, Glendale, 7/135

Odlum - Cochran Fdn., Indio, 7/135

Ojai Civic Association, Ojai, 7/136

Oppenheimer (Harry L.) Fdn., Los Angeles, 7/137

Oppenheimer (Harry L. & Adele A.) Fdn., Los Angeles, 7/137

Orange Coast College Fdn., Costa Mesa, 7/138

Ornstein (Jack A.) Fdn., San Francisco, 7/141

Orthopedic Research & Educational Fdn., Beverly Hills, 7/142

Pacific Smelting Fdn., Torrance, 7/142

Pacific Center for Emotionally Disturbed Children, Beverly Hills, 7/143

Pacific Egg & Poultry Association, Los Angeles, 7/143

Palevsky (Mary J.) Fdn., Los Angeles, 7/144

Palo Alto Congregational Fdn., Palo Alto, 7/145

Park (C.C.) Trust, Santa Barbara, 7/145

Parsons (Richard C.) Trust, Santa Barbara, 7/146

Boone (Pat) Fdn., Los Angeles, 7/147

Pauley (Edwin W.) Fdn., Los Angeles, 7/147

Peat, Marwick, Mitchell - L.A. Fdn., Los Angeles, 7/147

Perry (David S.) Fdn., Beverly Hills, 7/148

Pelletier (Donalda Precourt) Fdn., Pasadena, 7/150

Peninsula Endowment, Palo Alto, 7/150

Pennish (John S.) Fdn., Los Angeles, 7/150

Performing Arts Social Society, San Francisco, 7/151

Phi Delta Phi Fdn., Los Angeles, 7/152

Philanthropy Fund of the Oakmont League of Glendale, California, Glendale, 7/153

Piatigorsky Chess Fdn., Los Angeles, 7/154

Pilgrim Place Trust, Pomona, 7/154

Pillsbury (Mary K. & Edith) Fdn., Santa Barbara, 7/155

Pitzer Endowment Trust, Los Angeles, 7/155

Piedmont Fdn., Beverly Hills, 7/157

Plantation Trust, Long Beach, 7/157

Platt (George E.) Fdn., Los Angeles, 7/158

Podell (Michael H.) Fdn., Burlingame, 7/159

Pollack (Saul & Sarah) Fdn., Beverly Hills, 7/159

Polverini (Celso) Fdn., Los Angeles, 7/160

Polland Family Fdn. Formerly Wisconsin, Los Angeles, 7/160

Ponty (George & Margaret) Fdn., Marina del Rey, 7/160

Procurement Service, Inc., Los Angeles, 7/160

Professional Action for Community Education & Research Fdn., San Diego, 7/161

Prytanean Alumnae, Inc., Berkeley, 7/161

Psychology Fdn. of San Diego, San Diego, 7/162

P T A - California Congress, San Gabriel, 7/162

P T A - San Lorenzo High, San Lorenzo, 7/162

Putnam (Tracy J.) Fdn., Los Angeles, 7/162

Mighty Quinn Fdn., San Francisco, 7/163

Rabinovitch (Benjamin & Anita) Fdn., Beverly Hills, 7/164

Rabinovitch (George & Dora) Fdn., Los Angeles, 7/165

Rahn (Paul) Fdn., North Palm Springs, 7/165

Rainbow Fdn., Los Angeles, 7/165

Ramo (Simon & Virginia) Fdn., Beverly Hills, 7/166

Reid (Will J.) Fdn., Long Beach, 7/167

R - K Family Corporation, Los Angeles, 7/167

Research Fdn. for Circulatory Diseases, Los Angeles, 7/167

Research Society for Parkinson's Disease & Movement Disorders, San Gabriel, 7/168

Rhodes (Theodore & Marjorie) Fdn., Beverly Hills, 7/168

Rich Fdn., Los Angeles, 7/170

Rifkind - Grant Fdn., Beverly Hills, 7/170

Risley (Thomas E. & Gladys K.) Trust, Fresno, 7/171

Roberts Fdn., Pasadena, 7/171

Rockwell Family Fdn., Sun City, 7/171

Lahai Roi Fdn., Aptos, 7/172

Roselynn Company, Los Angeles, 7/172

Rosenberg (Joyce) Fdn., Los Angeles, 7/172

Rosenthal (Sol Roy) Fdn. Formerly Illinois, Rancho Sante Fe, 7/174

Rosensweig (Saul & Carol) Fdn., Palm Springs, 7/175

Rosencrans Fdn., Los Angeles, 7/176

Roth Family Fdn., Los Angeles, 7/181

Roush (Caroll J. & Emma P.) Fdn., San Francisco, 7/181

Sales & Marketing Council, Home Builders Association of Los Angeles, Los Angeles, 7/183

Salisbury (Arthur G.) Trust, Santa Barbara, 7/184

Sandy (George H.) Fdn., San Francisco, 7/185

San Chez (Belmont J.) Fdn., Garden Grove, 7/186

Sanders (Edward & Rose E.) Fdn. Formerly Sanders Family Fdn., Los Angeles, 7/187

San Diego Education Fund, San Diego, 7/187

San Diego Interfaith Housing Fdn., San Diego, 7/187

San Francisco Mime Troup, San Francisco, 7/188

San Joaquin College of Law, Fresno, 7/189

San Jose Medical Research Fdn., San Jose, 7/189

Santa Barbara Rescue Mission, Santa Barbara, 7/189

Santa Rosa Boys' Club Fdn., Santa Rosa, 7/190

Santa Rosa Fdn., Santa Rosa, 7/191

Sattler (Daniel A. & Edna J.) Beneficial Trust, Santa Barbara, 7/191

Sargent - Dyak Fund, Garden Grove, 7/191

Satya Sai Society of America, Pacific Palisades, 7/192

Saunders (Eunice Knight) Fdn., Rosemead, 7/192

Scharf Fdn., Los Angeles, 7/192

Schenck (Joseph M.) Fdn., Beverly Hills, 7/193

Schmer (Leah) Fdn., Los Angeles, 7/194

Schmidt (Marjorie Mosher) Fdn., Los Angeles, 7/195

Schneider (Otto H.) Memorial Prize Fund, San Diego, 7/196

Scott Fdn., San Diego, 7/196

Scripps (Ellen Browning) Fdn., San Diego, 7/197

Scudder Memorial Student Aid Fund, Sacramento, 7/198

Seabury (David) School of Psychology, Los Angeles, 7/198

Seaver Institute, Los Angeles, 7/199

Seljan (John W.) Fdn., Costa Mesa, 7/200

Setzer Fdn., Sacramento, 7/201

Shapell Fdn., Los Angeles, 7/203

Shapiro (Marvin & Natalie) Fdn., Los Angeles, 7/203

Shapiro (L.K.) Family Fdn., Los Angeles, 7/204

Shawl - Anderson Modern Dance Center, Berkeley, 7/205

Sheet Metal Journeyman & Apprentice Training Fund, Stockton, 7/205

Shenson (Walter) Fdn., Beverly Hills, 7/205

Thomas (Sherman) Fdn., Madera, 7/206

Sidell - Kagan Scientific & Medical Research Fdn., Beverly Hills, 7/207

Silverstein Family Fdn., Beverly Hills, 7/207

Shoong (Joe) Fdn., San Francisco, 7/207

Sicular (Henry & Geraldyn) Fdn., San Francisco, 7/209

Siemon Fdn., Redondo Beach, 7/210

Silbert (Harvey & Lillian) Fdn., Beverly Hills, 7/210

Simon (Donald E.) Fdn., Los Angeles, 7/211

Lyman (Mike) & William H. Simon Fdn., Los Angeles, 7/213

Simon (William H. & Fanchon) Fdn., Los Angeles, 7/213

Sinaiko (Isaac D. & Ruth G.) Fdn., Norwalk, 7/214

Sinay (Samuel B. & Charlotte) Fdn., Los Angeles, 7/214
Slavik Family Fdn., Pasadena, 7/215
Slavonic Mutual Benevolent Society of San Francisco, San Francisco, 7/216
Sleeper - Thayer Fdn., Los Angeles, 7/217
Smalley (Marvin & Sondra) Family Fdn., Pacoima, 7/217
Smith (Corinna & Chadwick) Fdn., Los Angeles, 7/218
Smith - Farris Fdn. for Surgical Research, Los Angeles, 7/219
Sheet Metal Workers Local Union 495, Modesto, 7/219
Sobel (Maxwell & Selma Davis) Fdn., Beverly Hills, 8/001
Soiland (Albert) Cancer Fdn., Los Angeles, 8/001
Soroptimist Club of Perris - Sun City, Sun City, 8/002
Soroptimist International Club of Whittier, Whittier, 8/002
Southern California Protective Society, Los Angeles, 8/003
Southern California Surveyors Joint Apprenticeship Trust, Los Angeles, 8/005
Southern Monterey County Memorial Hospital Fdn., King City, 8/005
Southern Pacific Fdn., San Francisco, 8/006
Southwest Arts Fdn., San Marcos, 8/007
Sperling Family Fdn., Los Angeles, 8/007
Spiegel (Abraham & Edita) Fdn., Beverly Hills, 8/008
Spiegel (Bernard) Fdn., Los Angeles, 8/009
Sta - Hi Fdn., Newport Beach, 8/010
Smith (Stanley) Horticultural Trust, San Francisco, 8/011
Statham (Louis Dee) Fdn., Anaheim, 8/012
Steinman (Robert) Family Charitable Fdn., Los Angeles, 8/014
Stern (Robert & Adele) Fdn., Palm Springs, 8/015
Stockwitz (Anna & Charles) Fund Formerly Stockwitz (Anna) Trust, San Francisco, 8/015
Stone (Albert H.) Educational Fund, Los Angeles, 8/016
Storke (Thomas More) Fdn., Santa Barbara, 8/017
Stratford Fdn., Los Angeles, 8/017
Strimling (Theodore & Esther) Fdn., Los Angeles, 8/017
Stuart (Dwight L.) Fdn., Los Angeles, 8/018
Stuart (Elbridge) Fdn., Los Angeles, 8/019
Social Service Auxiliary, La Mesa, 8/020
Stewart (W.L.), Jr. Memorial Fdn., Los Angeles, 8/021
Stuart (Elbridge & Evelyn) Fdn., Los Angeles, 8/022
Sully - Miller Fdn., Long Beach, 8/023
Swig Fdn., San Francisco, 8/023
Taper (Barry) Fdn., Los Angeles, 8/025
Taper (Mark) Fdn., Beverly Hills, 8/026
Taubman (Ruthe & Louis) Fdn., Beverly Hills, 8/027
Techalloy Fdn. of California, Claremont, 8/027
Thomas (Judith S.) Fdn., Los Angeles, 8/028
Thompson (Sara & Harold Lincoln) Fdn. for Medical Education & Research, Los Angeles, 8/029
Thora Fdn., Lakewood, 8/029
Thagard Fdn., South Gate, 8/030
Tibbians, Los Angeles, 8/031
Times Mirror Fdn., Los Angeles, 8/032
Tracy (Perry S. & Stella H.) Scholarship Fund, Sacramento, 8/033
Trader Vic's Fdn., San Francisco, 8/034
Trousdale Fdn., Los Angeles, 8/035
Trust U/A Everett F. Armington, Los Angeles, 8/035
Braun (Carl F.) Trust, Los Angeles, 8/036
Briggs (Ella P.) Charitable Trust, Sacramento, 8/037
Doheny (Carrie Estelle) Trust for Edward L. Doheny Memorial Vincential Fathers, Los Angeles, 8/039

Doheny (Carrie Estelle) Trust for Edward Laurence Doheny Memorial Library, Los Angeles, 8/040
Doheny (Carrie Estelle) Trust for St. Vincent de Paul Church, Los Angeles, 8/040
Koulaieff (Ivan V.) Educational Fund, The Trustees of, San Francisco, 8/041
Marian Charitable Trust, Los Angeles, 8/041
Tulare - King's Employers Council, Visalia, 8/041
Tuohy (Alice Lyon Tweed) Charitable Fdn., Santa Barbara, 8/041
Turlock of Industrial Park, Turlock, 8/042
Turlock Chamber of Commerce, Turlock, 8/043
Blochman (L.E. & Ida M.) Scholarship Fund, Santa Maria, 8/043
Twychin (Kybald) Fdn., Los Angeles, 8/044
Uncle Claude, Inc., Beverly Hills, 8/045
Unifran Fdn., San Francisco, 8/046
Union Bank Welfare Fund, Los Angeles, 8/047
University Hill Fdn., Los Angeles, 8/048
Univista Development Company, San Francisco, 8/049
Vacaville Community Fdn., Vacaville, 8/049
Val Verde Trust, Santa Barbara, 8/049
Vanderwilt (John) Fdn., Sun City, 8/050
Vandruff Fdn. Trust, Yorba Linda, 8/050
Van Horne (Betty Offield) Fdn., Alhambra, 8/051
Van Loben Sels (Ernst D. & Eleanor Slate) Charitable Fdn., Manteca, 8/052
Van Mouwerik Fdn., Redlands, 8/054
Van Nuys (I.N. & Susanna H.) Fdn., Los Angeles, 8/055
Vasa Park Association, Los Angeles, 8/058
Verdant Vales Fdn., Middletown, 8/058
Verdi Fdn., San Francisco, 8/059
Vo - Co Fdn., Burlingame, 8/059
Volk Fdn., Los Angeles, 8/060
Vose (Clara Edith) Fdn., Santa Ana, 8/061
Wallach (Nathan F.) Fdn., Los Angeles, 8/063
Walter (Judith Scott) Trust, Los Angeles, 8/064
Warner (Mr. & Mrs. Harry M.) Fdn., Los Angeles, 8/064
Warschaw (Carmen & Louis) Fdn., Los Angeles, 8/065
Waxler (Amelia) Fdn., Los Angeles, 8/066
Watchorn - Lincoln Memorial Association, Redlands, 8/066
Weber (Capt. Charles M.) Memorial Fdn., Stockton, 8/067
Wednesday Morning Club, Los Angeles, 8/068
Weeden Fdn., Alameda, 8/068
Weill (Blanche & Irma) Fdn., Bakersfield, 8/069
Weiler (Ralph J.) Fdn., Los Angeles, 8/070
Weingart (Stella) Trust No. 2., Los Angeles, 8/070
Weisman (Frederick & Marcia) Fdn., Los Angeles, 8/072
West Torrance Lions Club, Torrance, 8/073
Western Center Consultants, Culver City, 8/073
Western Indian Fdn., Norwalk, 8/074
Weston (Alan E.) Fdn., Los Angeles, 8/074
White Memorial Medical Fdn., Glendale, 8/075
Whittier Fdn., Los Angeles, 8/075
Whittaker Fdn., Los Angeles, 8/075
Whittier Academy of Medicine, Los Angeles, 8/075
Widows', Orphans' & Disabled Firemen's Fund, Los Angeles, 8/077
Wikel (Peter James & Florence Ruth) Fdn., Larkspur, 8/077
Wilcox (Ray C.), Sr. Fdn., Los Angeles, 8/077
Wilsey Fdn., San Francisco, 8/078
Richards (Mabel Wilson) Scholarship Fund, San Francisco, 8/078
Winans (L.) Fdn., Idyllwild, 8/083
Varian (Sigurd F. & Winifred H.) Charitable Fdn., Portola Valley, 8/085
Witter (Lucy) Memorial Trust, Los Altos, 8/085
Witzman (M.A.) Charities, Los Angeles, 8/086

Women's University Club of Los Angeles, Los Angeles, 8/086
Wong (Bing) Scholarship Fdn., San Bernardino, 8/086
Wood (Frank C.) Memorial Fund #2053, San Diego, 8/087
Worden (James S.) Memorial Fund, Menlo Park, 8/088
Wyman, Finell & Rothman Fdn., Beverly Hills, 8/088
Youth Benefit Trust, Santa Ana, 8/088
Young Home Builders Council, Los Angeles, 8/089
Zabala Family Fdn., San Francisco, 8/089
Familian (Zalec) Fdn., South Gate, 8/089
Zalk (Louis & Erma) Fdn., Beverly Hills, 8/090
Ziffren Family Fdn., Los Angeles, 8/091
Zimmer (Max & Pauline) Fdn., Los Angeles, 8/092
Zuckerman (Theodore E.) Fdn., South Gate, 8/093

COLORADO

First Filming

A B C Fdn., Denver, 1/002
Ackerman (Anna Kessling) Trust, Colorado Springs, 1/002
Adelstein Fdn., Denver, 1/003
Adler (Jacques H. & May Evans) Fdn., Denver, 1/004
Alpert (Joe & Betty) Fdn., Denver, 1/005
Amter (Helen Kohn) Fdn., Denver, 1/005
Amter (Joseph A.) Fdn., Denver, 1/006
Anderson (T.W.) Fdn., Denver, 1/007
Arapahoe County 4-H Fdn., Englewood, 1/007
Balke (Rudy) Trust, Colorado Springs, 1/009
Ballantine Family Charitable Fund, Durango, 1/010
Bancroft (Hugh, Jr.) Fdn., Denver, 1/011
Weld County Bank Fdn., Greeley, 1/011
Barth Fdn., Indian Hills, 1/012
Baum (Dr. Harry L.) Memorial Fdn., Denver, 1/013
Baum (Sam & Patty) Fdn., Denver, 1/013
Bemis-Taylor Fdn., Colorado Springs, 1/014
Bernstein Brothers Parapsychology Fdn., Pueblo, 1/015
Bitzl (Therese) Trust, Denver, 1/016
Bixler (Dr. C.W.) Family Fdn., Longmont, 1/016
Bloedorn Fdn., Fort Morgan, 1/017
Boettcher Fdn., Denver, 1/018
Bonell Trust, Denver, 1/021
Bonell (B.W.) Trust, Denver, 1/022
Bonfils (Frederick G.) Fdn., Denver, 1/022
Bonfils (Helen G.) Fdn., Denver, 1/024
Bonforte Fdn., Pueblo, 1/025
Bosworth Fdn., Denver, 1/025
Brockhurst Fdn., Green Mountain Falls, 1/026
Brown (Ruth H.) Fdn., Denver, 1/026
Buell (Temple Hoyne) Fdn., Denver, 1/027
Burghardt Trust (Denver Fdn.), Denver, 1/027
Burham (Elizabeth M.) Trust (Denver Fdn.), Denver, 1/028
Burns (Franklin L.) Fdn., Denver, 1/029
Cassidy (Elizabeth) Trust, Denver, 1/030
Central Bank Fdn., Denver, 1/031
Charitable Trust of the American National Bank of Denver, Denver, 1/032
Charsky Fdn., Denver, 1/033
Coleman (Alice) Trust, Denver, 1/034
Colorado College Faculty Salary Fund Trust, Colorado Springs, 1/035
Colorado Bar Fdn., Denver, 1/035
Colorado Medical Fdn. General Fund, Denver, 1/037
Colorado Pipe Trades Industry Program, Denver, 1/038

Colorado Springs Kiwanis Fdn., Colorado
Springs, 1/038
Continental Airlines Fdn., Denver, 1/039
Cooper (Walter B.) Fdn., Fort Collins, 1/040
Coulter (Viola Vestal) Fdn., Denver, 1/040
Cox (Charles C. & Agnes Freiberg) Fdn.,
Colorado Springs, 1/041
Cragmor Fdn., Colorado Springs, 1/042
Crippled Children's Aid Fund, Denver, 1/042
Cultural Advancement Fund of Golden, Golden,
1/043
Curtis (Effie H. & Edward H.) Trust Fund, Fort
Collins, 1/043
Davis (Sam & Freda) Fdn., Denver, 1/044
Davison Family Fdn., Denver, 1/044
Degen Fund, Denver, 1/045
Delatour (Ben C.) Fdn., Fort Collins, 1/045
Denver Medical Society Stop Polio Sundays
(Denver Fdn.), Denver, 1/046
Denver Opera Fdn., Denver, 1/047
Denver United States National Bank Fdn.,
Denver, 1/047
Dobbins Fdn., Denver, 1/048
Douglas Trust, Denver, 1/049
Dower (Mary M.) Benevolent Corporation,
Denver, 1/049
Duncan (John G.) Trust, Denver, 1/050
East High School Alumni Trust, Denver, 1/052
Edelweiss Fdn., Colorado Springs, 1/053
Educators Life Fdn., Denver, 1/054
Ellis Fdn., Denver, 1/054
Empson Trust, Denver, 1/054
Emrich Fdn., Denver, 1/055
Evangelical Christian Union, Denver, 1/056
Farkas Family Fdn., Denver, 1/057
Farley (John B.) Fdn., Pueblo, 1/057
First National Bank of Greeley, Greeley, 1/057
Fisher (Frank E. & Florence A.) Fdn., Fort
Collins, 1/058
Flatirons Fdn., Aspen, 1/058
Foss Fdn., Denver, 1/058
Fountain Valley School Endowment Trust,
Colorado Springs, 1/059
Fox (Michael) Trust B/O Fuks Memorial,
Denver, 1/059
Frankel (Lulu) Fdn., Denver, 1/060
Freudenthal (Alfred) Memorial Fdn., Trinidad,
1/060
Friedman (Sam & Anna) Fdn., Denver, 1/061
Gates Fdn., Denver, 1/062
Gilliam (Judge) Trust Fund, Denver, 1/065
Glassman (M.B. & Shana) Fdn., Denver,
1/065
God's Truth Fdn., Alamosa, 1/066
Greeley National Bank Fdn., Greeley, 1/066
Greenberg (Arnold L.) Fdn., Denver, 1/067
Hagestead (Vern) Fdn., Denver, 1/068
Hall (J.N.) Trust, Denver, 1/068
Halstead (Gene) Fdn., Sterling, 1/069
Hamilton Fdn., Denver, 1/069
Harris Trust (Denver Fdn), Denver, 1/070
Havasu Fdn., Aspen, 1/071
Hayes (John Nelson) Fdn., Boulder, 1/071
Heginbotham (Will E.) Trust, Holyoke, 1/072
Heiserman Trust, Denver, 1/072
Henry (Mabel) Fund, Pueblo, 1/073
Herbert (John W.) Fdn., Aspen, 1/074
Hockmuth (Ronald B.) Memorial Scholarship
Trust, Denver, 1/074
Hoddy (J. Stanley) Fdn., Colorado Springs,
1/075
Hogge (Grant) Memorial Fdn., Denver, 1/076
Hospital Visitation Group, Denver, 1/076
Hover (Charles) Family Fdn., Longmont,
1/076
Hughes (Mabel Y.) - Denver Childrens Home,
Denver, 1/077
Humphreys Fdn., Denver, 1/077
Hunter (A.V.) Trust, Denver, 1/078
Hunter (Estelle) Trust, Denver, 1/080
Hutchinson (T.A.) Fdn., Denver, 1/081
Jean Charitable Trust, Denver, 1/081
Johnson (Arthur E.) Fdn., Denver, 1/083
Kejr Fdn. - Christian Service Fellowship, Fort
Morgan, 1/084
Kenney Trust, Denver, 1/085

Aurora Kiwanis Fdn., Aurora, 1/085
Kortz (Jess & Rose) Fdn., Denver, 1/086
Laff Fdn., Denver, 1/086
Lanyon (Ray) Educational Loan Fund,
Longmont, 1/087
Lawrence (David) Fdn., Denver, 1/087
Levoy Trust, Denver, 1/088
Levy (Raphael) Memorial Fdn., Denver, 1/089
Liebhardt Trust, Denver, 1/089
Liszt (Franz) Fdn. of America, Denver, 1/090
Livingston Family Fdn., Denver, 1/090
Loveland (Sarah E.) Hospital Fund, Fort
Collins, 1/092
Lovell (J.B.) Trust, Denver, 1/092
Manitou Springs Kiwanis Fdn., Manitou
Springs, 1/093
Markley Trust [Denver Foundation], Denver,
1/094
Marshall Trust, Denver, 1/095
Martin Trust, Denver, 1/095
Maurer Fdn., Denver, 1/096
McCombe Trust [Denver Foundation], Denver,
1/097
McDonald (Della B.) Scholarship Trust,
Greeley, 1/098
McNaught (Grace Isabelle) Trust, Denver,
1/098
Midwest Oil Fdn., Denver, 1/100
Midwest Steel & Iron Works Co. Fdn., Denver,
1/101
Miller Fdn., Denver, 1/102
Miller (Dora J.) Fdn., Denver, 1/103
Miller (George K.) Trust [Denver Fdn.],
Denver, 1/103
Miller (Max) Fdn., Denver, 1/104
Miller (Morris) Fdn., Denver, 1/105
Miller (Philip & Ruchiel) Fdn., Denver, 1/105
Mitchell (Miriam) Trust, Denver, 1/107
Morris Trust [Denver Fdn.], Denver, 1/107
Morris (Fay S.) Fdn. Formerly Morris (Bertram
& Fay) Fdn., Denver, 1/108
Murphey Trust, Denver, 1/109
Music Fdn. of Denver, Englewood, 1/111
Needham (Joslin) Family Fdn., Brush, 1/111
Neufeld (Jean Kohn) Fdn., Denver, 1/112
Norgren (Carl A.) Fdn., Littleton, 1/113
Norgren (Leigh H.) Fdn., Denver, 1/115
North Star Fdn., Aspen, 1/116
Oberfelder (Robert S.) Trust, Denver, 1/117
O'Connor (John M.) Benevolent Corporation,
Denver, 1/118
Opera Fdn. of Denver, Denver, 1/119
Ormiston (Clara M.) Trust, Denver, 1/119
Page (John, Jr.) Fdn., Boulder, 1/120
Peace Research Organization Fund, Denver,
1/121
Perry Fdn., Denver, 1/121
Peterson (Elmer H.) Fdn., Denver, 1/121
Petteys (Jack) Memorial Fdn., Brush, 1/122
Phipps (Lawrence) Fdn., Denver, 1/122
Pilot Trust, Denver, 1/125
Proctor Fdn., Denver, 1/125
Radinsky (A.D.) Fdn., Denver, 1/126
Randles (B.W.) Family Fdn., Englewood,
1/126
Reclamation Employees Hope Fund, Denver,
1/126
Remington Fdn., Boulder, 1/126
Reuler-Lewin Fdn., Denver, 1/126
Rittenberg Fdn., Englewood, 1/127
Rocky Mountain Fdn., Denver, 1/128
Roof (Freda T.) Memorial Scholarship Fund,
Denver, 1/128
Rosenbaum (Lt. Alvin) Fdn., Denver, 1/130
Sachs Fdn., Colorado Springs, 1/131
St. Johns Church in The Wilderness Trust,
Denver, 1/133
Houghton (John Henry) Endowment Fund, St.
Marks Parish and the Diocese of Colorado,
Denver, 1/134
Samelson Family Fdn., Denver, 1/135
Schlessman Fdn., Denver, 1/135
Schriber-Freedman Fdn., Denver, 1/137
Seldin Fdn., Denver, 1/137
Sell (Louisa) Trust, Denver, 1/137
Sharoff Family Fdn., Denver, 1/138

Shwayder, Inc., Denver, 1/139
Shwayder (King & Rose) Fdn., Denver, 1/139
Silver Fdn., Denver, 1/140
Stanton (May Bonfils) Trust, Denver, 1/142
Stein (Morris) Fdn., Denver, 1/148
Stratton (Myron) Home, Colorado Springs,
1/149
Taylor (Frederick M.P.) Memorial Organ Fund,
Colorado Springs, 1/151
Teachers Award Fdn., Denver, 1/151
Thatcher Fdn., Pueblo, 1/152
Thompson Trust, Denver, 1/154
Tipton & Kalmbach, Inc. - Graduate Fellowship
Fund, Denver, 1/155
Tipton (Natalie Knight) Scholarship Trust,
Denver, 1/155
Toltz Fdn., Denver, 1/156
Truss (Catherine) Trust, Denver, 1/156
Bonell Trust, Denver, 1/158
Cochems (Jane Nugent) Trust for Prize Fund,
Denver, 1/158
Cochems (Jane Nugent) Trust to Provide for
Old Indigent Doctors, Denver, 1/159
Crater Trust B/O First Unitarian Society,
Denver, 1/160
DeRicqles Trust for Colorado School of Mines
Students, Denver, 1/161
DeRicqles Trust for Denver University Students,
Denver, 1/162
Enosh Trust B/O Emily Griffith Boys Home,
Denver, 1/163
Hodges Trust B/O Needlework Guild, Denver,
1/164
Holland (M.B.) Trust B/O Charities, Denver,
1/164
Lovell Trust B/O First Baptist Church, Denver,
1/165
Lovell Trust B/O Temple Buell College, Denver,
1/166
McMurray Trust B/O Needlework Guild,
Denver, 1/167
Muller Trust B/O Masons Charity Committee,
Denver, 1/167
Phipps Fdn. B/O Colorado Academy, Denver,
1/168
Stickley Trust B/O Leadville Public Library,
Denver, 1/169
Van Hummell-Howard Fdn., Denver, 1/170
Van Vleet Fdn., Denver, 1/171
Wann (Ralph J.) Fdn., Denver, 1/172
Weckbaugh (Ella M.) Benevolent Corporation,
Denver, 1/173
Wiesbart (Sam) Fdn. Trust No. 2, Denver,
1/174
Weisbart (Sam) Fdn., Denver, 1/174
Weiss Fund, Denver, 1/175
Weld County General Hospital Educational
Trust Fund, Greeley, 1/175
Weller Investment Company, Denver, 1/176
Wheeler Trust, Denver, 1/177
Willens (Minnie K.) Trust, Denver, 1/179
Williams Family Fdn., Fort Morgan, 1/180
Wilson Fdn., Denver, 1/181
Woodward Governor Company Charitable
Trust, Fort Collins, 1/182
Yellow Cab Fdn., Denver, 1/183
Zeppelin Fdn., Denver, 1/184
Zerobnick Fdn., Aurora, 1/184

Second Filming

Aardvark Ltd., Denver, 2/002
American Natl. Center for Educational
Research, Boulder, 2/003
Baldridge - Iliff Scholarship Trust, Grand
Junction, 2/004
Barnes Corporation, Denver, 2/004
Bates (Dr. Mary E.) Trust Fund, Denver,
2/005
Beet Sugar Development Fdn., Fort Collins,
2/007
Bein (Eleanor M.) Historical Endowmt., Denver,
2/008
Bell (Ezra M.) Estate of,, 2/010
Borwick (Charles and Maurine) Fdn., Denver,
2/010

Breeden (Charline H.) Fdn., The, Denver, 2/011

Brown (Lucille R.) Fdn., Inc., Denver, 2/012

Temple Hoyne Buell Fdn., The, Denver, 2/013

Cenikor Fdn., Inc., Lakewood, 2/014

Centennial Turf Club Fdn., Inc., Littleton, 2/015

Cerasa (Arthur) Fdn., The, Denver, 2/016

Cook (Ben) Fdn., Denver, 2/016

Cowperthwaite Fdn., Inc., The, Denver, 2/017

Daly Fund, The, Denver, 2/017

Davis (Sam & Freda) Fdn., Denver, 2/018

Denver Altrusa Club Fdn., Denver, 2/018

Dericoles Trust for Colorado State University Stud., Denver, 2/020

El Pomar Fdn., Colorado Springs, 2/021

Dierks (Eugene Herbert and Irene C.) Charitable Trust, Canon City, 2/023

Martin (Euphrasia) Fdn., Denver, 2/024

Farr Farms Fdn., Greeley, 2/024

Flanders Fdn., Inc., Longmont, 2/025

Fdn. for Research in Ocular Diseases, Colorado Springs, 2/026

Fdn. for Senior Citizens, Inc., Grand Junction, 2/027

Gaiser Fdn., The, Denver, 2/027

Glorious Gospel Association, Denver, 2/028

Goldberg Brothers Fdn., Denver, 2/028

Golden Family Fdn., Longmont, 2/030

Greeley Concerts Assoc., Greeley, 2/030

Hart (Robert Ira) Fdn., The, Boulder, 2/031

Herbert (John W.) Fdn., Inc., Aspen, 2/032

Holland Trust 1 7923 00, Denver, 2/032

Holt (R.B.) Corporate Fdn., The, Springfield, 2/033

Homemakers Guild Fdn. Ltd., Denver, 2/033

Houck (Frank M.) Charitable Trust, Denver, 2/033

Hughes (Mabel Y.) Denver Children's Home, Denver, 2/034

Hughes-Dumb (Mabel Y.) Friends League, Denver, 2/035

Hynd Blind Fund of the James Hynd Trust, Boulder, 2/035

Jackson (Robert Allan) Fdn., Peublo, 2/037

Jean Stan Inc., Denver, 2/037

Keith (A.A.) Fdn., Denver, 2/038

Kidney Fdn. of the Rocky Mountain Region, Inc., Denver, 2/038

Marlar (William F.) Memorial Fdn., Inc., The, Denver, 2/039

McArthur Fdn., The, Greeley, 2/040

Miller (Myron and Louann) Fdn., Denver, 2/041

Monfort Charitable Fdn., Denver, 2/041

Mullen (John K. and Catherine S.) Benevolent Corp., The, Denver, 2/041

Neusteter Colorado Company, The, Denver, 2/043

Occhiato (Mike) Fdn., The, Pueblo, 2/044

Page (John) Jr. Fdn., Boulder, 2/046

Palmer Lake Little Art Group, Palmer Lake, 2/046

Phipps (Lawrence C.) Jr., Starzl (Thomas E.) Fund, Denver, 2/047

Raycon Fdn., Boulder, 2/047

Ripley Et AL B/O Steinberg Memorial, Denver, 2/048

Rocky Mountain Ballet Fdn., Colorado Springs, 2/048

Rocky Mountain Camps Inc., Golden, 2/048

Rominger Fdn., Sterling, 2/049

Rowe Fdn., Steamboat Spring, 2/050

Shwayder (Elizabeth B.) Ltd., Denver, 2/051

Schramm Fdn., The, Denver, 2/052

Star Bread Fdn., The, Denver, 2/052

Swingle (John W.) Fdn., The, Denver, 2/053

Tipton (Royce J.) & Associates Scholarship Fund, Denver, 2/055

Trianon Fdn., Denver, 2/056

Trueblood (Harry) Fdn., Denver, 2/057

United States Ski Association, Denver, 2/057

United States Ski Educational Fdn., Inc., Denver, 2/058

Van Derbur Fdn., Denver, 2/059

Vestal (Don & Maxine) Fdn., Denver, 2/059

Von Trotha Educational Trust, Greeley, 2/060

Walker Fdn. Inc., Grand Junction, 2/061

Waterbury National Bank Trustee for Charitable Donations u/t/a The Conrex Corp., Waterbury, Conn., 2/061

Weld County General Hospital Medical Staff, Greeley, 2/062

Winograd Fdn., Greeley, 2/062

Yetter (Edward Joseph & Helen Dean) Fdn., Denver, 2/063

CONNECTICUT

First Filming

A B C Fund, Woodbridge, 1/001

Abrahamson (D.L.) Fdn., West Hartford, 1/001

Acme Shear Fdn., Bridgeport, 1/002

Adams (Mary Lane) Cemetery Fund, Waterbury, 1/002

Ariadne Fdn., New Haven, 1/003

Clark (May Austin) Trust, Hartford, 1/004

Aibel (Howard & Katherine) Fdn., Westport, 1/005

Albert (Lawrence & Marilyn) Fdn., Bloomfield, 1/005

Alexander (Jack & Charlotte) Fdn., Stamford, 1/006

American Institute for Foreign Study Scholarship Fdn., Greenwich, 1/007

Anderson (Harlan E.) Fdn., New Canaan, 1/007

Anderson (Robert M.) Memorial Scholarship Fund, Norwich, 1/008

Ariadne Fdn., New Haven, 1/009

Armar Fdn., Darien, 1/009

Arons (Hubert M.) Fdn., West Hartford, 1/010

Armstrong (Benjamin A.) Trust, Hartford, 1/010

Atwood Educational Fdn., Bristol, 1/010

Auerbach (Beatrice Fox) Fdn., West Hartford, 1/011

Atkins (Thomas J.) Memorial Fund Trust, Hartford, 1/012

Ball (Frank R.) Fdn., Meriden, 1/013

Ball (Thomas) Fdn., Hartford, 1/013

Ballet Etudes, Incorporated, Norwalk, 1/014

Banks Fdn., Hartford, 1/014

Barnes Fdn., Bristol, 1/015

Batt (Herbert L.) Memorial Fdn., New Haven, 1/016

Bauer Fdn., Lakeville, 1/016

Bauer (Frederick R.) Fund, Lakeville, 1/017

Beckerman Fdn., Hartford, 1/017

Scoville (William Beecher) Fdn., Hartford, 1/018

Beinecke Fdn., Greenwich, 1/018

Belding (Alvah N.) Fund, Greenwich, 1/020

Benham (Robert J.) Trust for Scholarships, Waterbury, 1/021

Bernhard (Arnold) Fdn., Westport, 1/022

Bialek (Norman) Fdn., Westport, 1/022

Bierman (Samuel D. & Rosalie K.) Fdn., Norwalk, 1/023

Birnbaum (Samuel Sigh) Fdn., New Britain, 2/001

Bissell (J. Walton) Fdn., Hartford, 2/002

Blakeslee (Henry L. & Nellie E.) Scholarship Fund, Waterbury, 2/004

Blue Horizon Health & Welfare Trust, Lakeville, 2/005

Bluenose Fdn., Greenwich, 2/005

Blumenthal (Samuel) Family Fdn., West Hartford, 2/006

Bodine Fdn., Bridgeport, 2/007

Boller - Thomas Fdn., Greenwich, 2/008

Borck (Jay) Fdn., Bridgeport, 2/008

Botwinik Fdn., New Haven, 2/008

Brainerd (Lyman B.) Charitable Trust, Hartford, 2/009

Branigan (Mary E.) Trust, New London, 2/009

Breslav Fdn. Trust, New Haven, 2/010

Bristol Brass Fdn., Bristol, 2/011

Brooks (Frederic & Jane) Fdn., Greenwich, 2/012

Brown (Elsie A.) Fund, Norwich, 2/013

Brown (Philip) Memorial Fdn., Stamford, 2/013

Brumberger Fdn., New Haven, 2/013

Bucalate Fdn., Stamford, 2/014

Bullard Company Charity Fdn., Bridgeport, 2/014

Burdick Memorial Fund, Wilton, 2/015

Burger (Zoltan) Fdn., Bridgeport, 2/016

Burke (Priscilla Alden) Memorial Professorship in American History, Waterbury, 2/016

Burndy Library, Inc., Norwalk, 2/017

Burns (Beryl S. & John L.) Fdn., Darien, 2/020

Buxton (Robert W.) Student Aid Fund, Waterbury, 2/020

Bye & Bye Fdn., Stamford, 2/021

Byram Rotary Fdn., Byram, 2/022

Calhoun (Flora J.) Trust, Hartford, 2/022

Case (Edward H.) Trust, Hartford, 2/023

Case (Jane E.) Fund, Hartford, 2/023

Christian Businessmen's Fdn., Fairfield, 2/025

Clapp Fdn., Milford, 2/026

Clark (Timothy D. & Elizabeth Ann F.) Charitable Trust, Darien, 2/026

Clifton Fdn., Byram, 2/026

Coe (Jennie F.) Trust, Hartford, 2/027

Coe (Marion Isabele) Fund, Waterbury, 2/028

Coffin (Elizabeth Dorr) Memorial Fdn., Windsor Locks, 2/032

Coggins Fdn., Meriden, 2/033

Cohn (Maury) Fdn., Coventry, 2/034

Cohen (Benjamin & Freda) Fdn., New Haven, 2/035

Cohn Fdn., New Haven, 2/036

Cole (Marguerite N.) Fdn., Greenwich, 2/036

Colin (Justin & Cynthia) Fdn., Ridgefield, 2/037

Colt Industries Fdn., Hartford, 2/038

Cowles (C.) & Company Community Trust, Hartford, 2/039

Community Workshop, Inc., Waterbury, 2/040

Concordia Fdn. Trust, Hartford, 2/040

ConMunited Fund, Hartford, 2/042

Connecticut National Bank Employees Scholarship Fund, Bridgeport, 2/042

Connell (Joan) Fdn., Middletown, 2/042

Conroy (Katherine L.) Trust, Hartford, 2/043

Cooke (Dick) Memorial Fund Trust, Hartford, 2/044

Corning (John J.) Trust, Hartford, 2/044

Cottonwood Fdn., Hartford, 2/046

Covey (Lois Lenski) Trust, Hartford, 2/047

Cone (Joseph H.) Fdn., Bridgeport, 2/048

Crocker (James) Testamentary Trust, Winsted, 2/049

Crosby (Isabel S.) Trust, Hartford, 2/049

Culbertson (William H.) Fdn., Kent, 2/050

Cuno Fdn., Meriden, 2/052

Curtis (Lemuel) Charitable Trust, Hartford, 2/053

Cushman Industries Charitable Fdn., Hartford, 2/053

Daggett (Frederick Kimball) Fdn., Guilford, 2/054

Dameshek (William) Research Fdn., Newington, 2/054

Dana (Charles A.) Fdn., Greenwich, 2/055

Davis (Eddie S.) Fund Trust, Hartford, 2/057

Deeds (Charles W.) Trust, Hartford, 2/057

Dibble (Lewis A.), Sr. Fund, Naugatuck, 2/059

Dibner Fund, Norwald, 2/059

Dinkeloo Family Fdn., Hamden, 2/059

Donenfeld (Harry) Fdn., Westport, 2/060

Doubl - Glo Fdn., Stamford, 2/060

Duffek (John) Memorial Trust, Hartford, 2/061

Duke - Lab Fdn., South Norwalk, 2/062

East Haddam Community Service Trust, Hartford, 2/063

East Hartford Rotary Club Scholarship Trust, Hartford, 2/064

17

Echlin Fdn., Branford, 2/064
Echo Fdn., Orange, 2/065
Eder (Sidney & Arthur) Fdn., Stamford, 2/066
Edgerton Fdn., New Haven, 2/067
Electrical Historical Fdn., Norwalk, 2/068
Elinco Fdn., Wilton, 2/069
Emery Educational Fdn., Wilton, 2/069
Engineering Education Fdn., Stamford, 2/070
Eno Fdn. for Transportation, Saugatuck, 2/070
Ensign - Bickford Fdn., Simsbury, 2/072
Ensworth Charitable Fdn., Hartford, 2/073
Emhart Fdn. Trust, Hartford, 2/073
Rathbun (Norris W. Estate & F.L.) Special Book Fund, Hartford, 2/074
Thayer (George B. Estate) Trust, Hartford, 2/076
Fafnir Bearing Fund, New Britain, 2/076
Favre Fdn., Stamford, 2/077
Feldmann (C. Russell) Fdn., Greenwich, 2/077
Feltman (Philip D.) Family Charitable Fdn., Hartford, 2/078
Fink (Doris) Fund, Greenwich, 2/078
Fisher Fdn., Farmington, 2/079
Flaxman Fdn., West Hartford, 2/080
Foundation for Mankind, Greenwich, 2/081
Fox Fdn., Orange, 2/082
Fox (Jacob L.) Fdn., Hartford, 2/082
Fry (Lily Palmer) Memorial Trust, Greenwich, 2/083
Fuller (Alfred C.) Trust, Hartford, 2/085
Fuller (Alfred C.) Fdn., Hartford, 2/085
Funston (Elizabeth K. & G. Keith) Trust, Greenwich, 2/086
Gant Fdn., New Haven, 2/087
Garvan (John S.) Fdn., Hartford, 2/087
Geisinger (Frederick J.) Fdn., New Haven, 2/088
G.F. & G. Fdn., New Haven, 2/089
Gillespie (Doris & Kingsley) Charitable Fdn., Stamford, 2/091
Gilman (Herbert) Family Charitable Fdn., Hartford, 2/092
Gilman (Milton A.) Family Charitable Fdn., Hartford, 2/092
Gilman (Irving) Family Charitable Fdn., Hartford, 2/093
Gimbel (Richard) Fdn. for Literary Research Formerly Pennsylvania, New Haven, 2/094
Smith (Mabel Glidden) Trust, Hartford, 2/094
Goodman (Clara M.) Trust, Hartford, 2/095
Goodman (Maurice) Fdn., Norwalk, 2/096
Goodwin Charitable Fdn., New Haven, 2/096
Gosman (Abraham O. & Betty C.) Fdn., Hartford, 2/097
Graceman Fdn., Hartford, 2/097
Graham Fdn. Trust, Hartford, 2/097
Greene (T.D.) Charitable Trust, Hartford, 2/098
Greenberg (Maurice) Family Fdn., Hartford, 2/098
Greenfield Fdn., Bridgeport, 2/100
Grinold (Raymond W. & Cleo C.) Fdn., West Hartford, 2/101
Grody (Israel) Family Fdn., Hartford, 2/101
Gross (Benjamin, Ethel, & Paul) Fdn., Hartford, 2/103
Gross (William A.O.) Fdn., Greenwich, 2/103
Grossman Fdn., Westport, 2/103
Haas Fdn., Hartford, 2/104
Hadley Fdn., Greenwich, 2/104
Hager Family Fdn., Southbury, 2/105
Harden (Frank A.) Trust, New Milford, 2/105
Harrington Fdn., Greenwich, 2/106
Hartford Insurance Group Fdn., Hartford, 2/106
Hart (Adelle Wise) Fdn., Hartford, 2/109
Harrison (Nathan & Minnie) Fdn., New Haven, 2/110
Harrison Fdn., Bridgeport, 2/111
Hartford Special Machinery Fdn., Simsbury, 2/112
Hatfield Fund, Bridgeport, 2/112
Havemeyer (Loomis) Trust, Hartford, 2/113
Hazen (Edward W.) Fdn., New Haven, 2/114
Heald (William Howard) Trust, Hartford, 2/116

Heise (Otto W.) Fdn., Bridgeport, 2/116
Heritage Fdn., Trumbull, 2/117
Hershey (Paul H.) Fdn., Orange, 2/118
Hershman (Samuel I. & Esther G.) Fdn., Hamden, 2/119
Hess Fdn., Waterbury, 2/119
Hills (Irene H.) Trust, Hartford, 2/120
Hilltop Fdn., Bridgeport, 2/121
Hixon Fdn., Essex, 2/122
Hodson (James W.) Charitable Fdn., New Haven, 2/122
Hollander (Aaron) Fund Trust, Hartford, 2/123
Hollander Family Fdn., Bridgeport, 2/124
Hope Fdn., Stamford, 2/125
Horowitz (William) Fdn., Rockville, 2/126
Horowitz (William) Trust, Rockville, 2/126
Hotchkiss (Gertrude F.) Trust, Hartford, 2/127
Howard & Bush Fdn., Hartford, 2/128
Howland Fdn., Wilton, 2/130
Hubbell (Harvey) Fdn., Bridgeport, 2/130
Humphrey (Lucius E.) Trust, Hartford, 2/130
Huisking (Frank R.) Fdn., Greenwich, 2/131
Hurlbutt (Horace) Memorial Fund Trust, Westport, 2/132
Local #350 International Alliance of Theatrical Stage Employees & Moving Picture Machine Operators of U.S.A. & Canada, Meriden, 2/133
Insilco Fdn., Meriden, 2/134
International Art Fdn., Meriden, 2/134
International Center of Medieval Art, New Haven, 2/135
Ives (H.B.) Company Charitable Fdn., Hartford, 2/136
Jacobs (Herb W.) Fdn., Greenwich, 2/137
Jewish Home for Children Trust, New Haven, 2/138
J.J.C. Fdn., West Hartford, 2/139
Johansen (John C. & Jean MacLane) Fdn., Norwalk, 2/140
Johnson (Wilbur J.) Fund, Cornwall, 2/140
Joseloff (Anna & Robert) Trust, Norwalk, 2/140
Joseloff (Hugh M.) Fdn., West Hartford, 2/141
Joseloff (Morris) Fdn., West Hartford, 2/141
Jost (Charles & Mabel P.) Fdn., Easton, 2/143
Kaplan Fdn., Bridgeport, 2/144
Kauffman (James D. & Marion) Fdn., New Haven, 2/145
Kavanewsky (John F. & Caroline Y.) Fund, East Norwalk, 2/145
Kazanjian (Calvin K.) Economics Fdn., Waterbury, 2/146
Knights of Columbus Supreme Council Educational Trust Fund, New Haven, 2/147
Knights of Columbus Supreme Council Italian Welfare Fund, New Haven, 2/149
Kearns (William H.) Fdn., Riverside, 2/150
Keeney Fdn., Somersville, 2/151
Keeney (Robert A.) Charitable Fdn., Wethersfield, 2/151
Kent (Sidney A.) Trust, Hartford, 2/152
Kerite Community Trust Fund, Seymour, 2/153
King (Dr. Alexander) House Trust, Hartford, 2/154
Kitchings (Chester W.) Fdn., Waterford, 2/154
Klaff (William R.) Charitable Trust, South Norwalk, 2/155
Knapp Fdn., Greenwich, 2/155
Knight (Agnes L. & Harry W.) Fdn., Darien, 2/157
Knobloch (William R.) Charitable Trust, Stamford, 2/157
Kollmorgen Fdn. Formerly Massachusetts, Hartford, 2/158
Knox Fdn., Hartford, 2/158
Koopman Fund, West Hartford, 2/163
H P K Fdn., Hartford, 2/164
Kopplemann (Rae & Abraham) Fdn., Hartford, 2/165
Kossack (John & Evelyn) Fdn., Fairfield, 2/166
Krall (Irving H. & Alice F.) Fdn., Hartford, 2/167
Kramer (Esther S.) Fdn., Greenwich, 2/167
Kuriansky (Louis J.) Fdn., Stamford, 2/168

Lamport (Saide & Arthur) Fdn. Formerly New York, Stamford, 2/168
Larrabee Fund Trust, Hartford, 2/169
Lavieri (Madeline M.) Scholarship Fund, Winsted, 2/170
Lavitt (Sol) Fdn., Hartford, 2/170
Leahy (John W.) Fdn., Danbury, 2/171
Leavenworth (Elisha) Fdn., Waterbury, 2/171
Lee (Marvin & Annette) Fdn., Wilton, 2/172
Lee (Thomas) House Fdn. East Lyme Historical Society Trust, Hartford, 2/173
Lefer Fdn., Bridgeport, 2/173
Leon (Marion A. & A. Percy) Fdn., Bridgeport, 2/174
Levine (Martin) Family Fdn., New Haven, 2/175
Levine (Morris M.) Fdn., New Haven, 2/175
Levine Fdn., Hartford, 2/176
Libbin (Ephram) Family Charitable Fdn., Hartford, 2/177
Liebeskind Fdn., Middlebury, 2/177
Lindquist Fdn., Bridgeport, 2/177
Linton (James M.) Trust, Hartford, 2/178
Lipman (Morris) Fdn., West Hartford, 2/178
Long (George A. & Grace L.) Fdn., Hartford, 2/180
Look-Out Fund, Hartford, 2/182
Lorber Fdn., Westport, 2/182
Lotstein Family Fdn., Stamford, 2/183
Luce (Theodore) Fdn., New Canaan, 2/183
Lunin (Arthur A.) Fdn., Bridgeport, 2/183
Lunin (Gladys Jacoby) Fdn., Bridgeport, 2/184
Lyon Charitable Trust, Hartford, 2/184
Maguire Fdn., Stamford, 2/184
Main Street Fdn., Fairfield, 2/186
Mandeville (Ann Adams) Fdn., Bridgeport, 2/187
Mandeville Fdn., Fairfield, 2/187
Mannweiler (Emil) Scholarship Fund, Waterbury, 2/189
Mannweiler (Mary B.) Trust f/b/o Grove Cemetery Association, Waterbury, 2/190
Hubbard (Marsden) Student Aid Fund Trust, Hartford, 2/191
Marinescu (Mihail) Fdn., Stamford, 2/192
Marks Family Fdn., Hartford, 2/193
Marsilius (Newman M.) Charitable Trust, Bridgeport, 2/193
Marsilius (Philip R.) Charitable Trust, Bridgeport, 2/194
Martin (Jane & John) Fdn., Hartford, 2/195
Masonic Charitable Society of Collinsville, Collinsville, 2/195
Mead (Richard Harlow) Fdn., Greenwich, 2/196
McLean Fund, Hartford, 2/197
McLean Association, Incorporated, Hartford, 2/199
McLean (George P.) Fund, Hartford, 2/200
McLean (George P.) Trust, Hartford, 2/201
McManus (Ella Burr) Trust, Hartford, 2/202
McManus (James) Fund of Hartford Dental Society, Hartford, 2/203
Meadow Falls Fdn., Greenwich, 2/204
Meek Fdn., Greenwich, 2/205
Meredith Fdn., Greenwich, 2/208
Meyers (George L.) Fdn., Norwalk, 2/208
Michaeljon Fdn., Westport, 2/209
Michaels Fdn., New Haven, 2/209
Mitchell (Charles) Memorial Fund, Waterbury, 2/209
Michelson (Elizabeth & Martin) Charitable Trust, West Hartford, 2/210
Milford Automatics Fdn., Milford, 2/211
Milikowsky (Matthew & Esther) Fdn., New Haven, 2/211
Morgan (Ebenezer) Trusts, Hartford, 2/212
Moses (Rachel R.) Fdn., Ellington, 2/213
National Shooting Sports Educational Fund, Riverside, 2/214
National Union Electric Charitable & Educational Fund, Greenwich, 2/215
New Britain Machine Charitable Trust, New Britain, 2/215
Newman (Robert W.) Fdn., West Hartford, 2/215

Ney (J.M.) Fund Trust, Hartford, 2/216
Noble (Edward John) Fdn., Washington Depot, 2/216
Noyes (Eliot) Fdn., New Canaan, 2/218
Nutmeg Fdn., Hartford, 2/219
Nyselius Fdn., Stamford, 2/220
OJO-DOR, Incorporated, Greenwich, 2/221
Olsen Fdn., New Haven, 2/222
O'Neil (Tom & Claire) Fdn., Greenwich, 2/223
Paine (Richard P.) Trust, Hartford, 2/223
Palen-klar (Countess Frances Thorley) Scholarship Fund, Greenwich, 2/223
Palmer (Grace Humphreys) Fund, Branford, 2/224
Panneton (Eunice A.) Fund, Waterbury, 2/225
Paolella (Ciro) Fdn., Hamden, 2/225
Pardee (Sarah N.) Estate Trust, Hartford, 2/226
Parker Fdn., Stamford, 3/001
Knox Parks Fdn., Hartford, 3/001
Peter Paul Fdn., Naugatuck, 3/002
Peterson (Victor N.) Memorial Scholarship Fund, Waterbury, 3/002
Peaslee (Arthur F.) Fdn., South Windsor, 3/002
Peltz (Harvey A.) Fdn., Stamford, 3/003
Peltz (Joseph J.) Fdn., Stamford, 3/004
Peninsula Charities Fdn., Darien, 3/004
Pennybacker Fdn., Westport, 3/006
Perakos (Peter) Scholarship Fund, New Britain, 3/007
Phi Kappa Educational Fdn., Glastonbury, 3/007
Pierce (John B.) Fdn. of Connecticut, New Haven, 3/007
Pine Level Fdn., Fairfield, 3/009
Plainville General Electric Assistance Fund, Plainville, 3/011
Porter (James J.) Memorial Trust, Litchfield, 3/011
Porter (Sarah) Fund, Hartford, 3/012
Powers (Ralph Averill) Fdn., Montville, 3/012
Pratt (Eliot) Fdn., New Milford, 3/014
Price (Lucien E. & Katherine E.) Fdn., Greenwich, 3/014
Proctor Fdn., New Haven, 3/016
Progress Fund of Norwalk, Norwalk, 3/016
Putnam (Colonel Daniel) Association, Hartford, 3/017
Putnam - Prospect Fdn., Hartford, 3/017
Rachlin Fdn. Charitable Trust, New Britain, 3/018
Rathbun (F.L.) Trust for Alms House, Hartford, 3/018
Rebay (Hilla) Fdn., Stamford, 3/018
Rentschler (Faye Belden) Memorial Fdn., Hartford, 3/019
Reynolds (Kate E.) Trust, Hartford, 3/019
Laural Ridge Fdn., Hartford, 3/020
Roberts (Alan Kirk) Scholarship Fund Trust, Hartford, 3/020
Roberts (Edward C. & Ann T.) Fdn., Hartford, 3/021
Robinson (Barclay & Mary) Trust, Hartford, 3/023
Robinson (Charles N.) Estate Trust, Hartford, 3/023
Roerich (Helena) Fdn., Stamford, 3/025
Rogers (Philip A.) Fdn., Hartford, 3/026
Rosen (James M.) Family Fdn., New Haven, 3/026
Rosenstein (Max) Fdn., Unionville, 3/027
Middletown Rotary Club Trust, Hartford, 3/028
Rubinow (Mary B. & William) Scholarship Fund, Manchester, 3/028
Russell (Edward S.) Memorial Scholarship Fund, Hamden, 3/029
Sachem Fund, New Haven, 3/029
Salem Fdn., Naugatuck, 3/031
Salerno Scholarship Fund, Greenwich, 3/031
Salisbury Recreation, Inc., Lakeville, 3/032
Salmon (Grace K.) Trust, Westport, 3/032
Savitt Fdn., Hartford, 3/033
Saxe Fdn., New Canaan, 3/034

Scherer Fdn., East Hartford, 3/035
Schilthuis Fdn., Westport, 3/036
Schiro Fund, West Hartford, 3/036
Schwartz (Morris & Fannie) Fdn., Bloomfield, 3/038
Schneller (Nancy & Richard) Fdn., Hartford, 3/039
Schwedel Fdn., Manchester, 3/040
Second National Bank Charitable Trust, New Haven, 3/040
Seery (William N. & Virginia C.) Fdn., West Hartford, 3/041
Shepherd (Herman R. & Carol Ruth) Fdn., Rowayton, 3/041
Sherman Higher Education Fund, Sherman, 3/042
Shulansky Fdn., Hartford, 3/043
Shoor (Julian C.) Fdn., West Hartford, 3/043
Shulman (Joseph L.) Fdn., Hartford, 3/044
Sigel Family Fdn., West Hartford, 3/044
Sitrin (Florence R.) Fdn., Hartford, 3/044
Sluyter (Elizabeth Lee) Memorial Fund Trust, Hartford, 3/045
Smith (Olcott & Lucy) Fdn., Hartford, 3/046
Smith (Ray C.) Memorial Burial Fund, Hartford, 3/047
Smyth Manufacturing Company Fdn., Bloomfield, 3/048
Snyder (Anna K. & Harry L.) Charitable Trust, Westport, 3/049
Solomkin (Mark & Ruth) Fdn., Hartford, 3/049
Soltz (Dr. Thomas) Education Trust, Hartford, 3/050
Sondik Fdn., Hartford, 3/050
Sorenson Family Fdn., West Hartford, 3/051
Southwell (Kate) Fund, Simsbury, 3/051
Spear (L.Y.) Fdn., Hartford, 3/052
Spencer Turbine Fdn. Trust, Hartford, 3/052
Spring Brook Fund, Hartford, 3/053
Stamford Kiwanis Trust Fund, Stamford, 3/054
Stamford Fdn., Stamford, 3/055
Standish (Miles) Fdn., Litchfield, 3/055
Stanley Works Fdn., New Britain, 3/056
Stanley (Alix W.) Charitable Fdn., New Britain, 3/056
Stanley (Charles B.) Testamentary Trust, Hartford, 3/057
Stark Fdn., East Norwalk, 3/058
Starlite Farm Fdn., North Stonington, 3/059
Steinkraus (Herman W. & Gladys C.) Fdn., Westport, 3/059
Sterling Fund & Fellowship Fdn., Bridgeport, 3/060
Stern & Company Charitable Fdn., Hartford, 3/061
Stern (George W. & Wilma P.) Charitable Trust, Hartford, 3/061
Stich Fdn., Hartford, 3/062
Stillman (Harriet) Trust, Hartford, 3/063
Stoeckel (Ellen B.) Residue Trust, Hartford, 3/063
Stone (Georgia Safford) Trust, Hartford, 3/064
Rocking Stone Lodge Charitable Trust, Hartford, 3/065
Stoner Charitable Fdn., West Hartford, 3/066
Stowe, Beecher, Hooker, Seymour, Day Memorial Library & Historical Fdn., Hartford, 3/066
Sunset Fdn., Hartford, 3/067
Taylor & Fenn Fdn., Windsor, 3/069
Thalberg (Reuben E.) Fdn., Southington, 3/069
Thomas (William S.) Trust, Hartford, 3/070
Thompson (Franklin R.) Fdn., Darien, 3/070
Todd (Vera H. & William R.) Fdn., Bridgeport, 3/071
Tomberg (Charles) Memorial Fdn., Cos Cob, 3/072
Torin Trust, Torrington, 3/072
Traurig Fdn., Waterbury, 3/073
Beach (Charles L.) Trust, Hartford, 3/074
Alfred (Henry A.) Trust, Waterbury, 3/075
Andrews (Randall T.) Trust, Waterbury, 3/075
Atta (William S.) Trust, Waterbury, 3/076

Atwood (Joseph W.) Trust, Waterbury, 3/076
Averill (Horace P.) Trust, Waterbury, 3/077
Baker (Alden A.) Trust, Hartford, 3/077
Bancroft (Horace) Trust, Waterbury, 3/078
Barber (Elizabeth) Trust, Waterbury, 3/078
Basham (Martha J.) Trust, Waterbury, 3/079
Lumberger (Julia O.) Trust, Waterbury, 3/079
Blakeslee (Russell C.) Trust, Waterbury, 3/080
Bradley (Howard H.) Trust, Waterbury, 3/081
Bronson (Eleanor L.) Trust, Waterbury, 3/081
Buck (Roswell C.) Trust, Waterbury, 3/081
Capen (Charles A.) Trust, Hartford, 3/082
Buckley Family Charitable Trust, Hartford, 3/083
Carlisle (Alice L.) Trust, Waterbury, 3/084
Chappell (Walter F.) Trust, Waterbury, 3/087
Chipman (Sarah V.) Trust, Waterbury, 3/088
Chase (Isadore) Trust, Waterbury, 3/089
Coe (Marion Isabell) Trusts, Waterbury, 3/089
Curtis (Laura W.) Trust, Waterbury, 3/091
Davey (John S.) Trusts, Waterbury, 3/091
Corning (Bertie) Memorial Trust, Waterbury, 3/092
Dibble (Lewis A.) Trust, Waterbury, 3/093
Donovan (M.C.) Latin Prize Fund of Crosby High School, Waterbury, 3/093
Doughty (James A.) Trust, Waterbury, 3/093
Elton (John P.) Trusts, Waterbury, 3/094
Epstein (Benjamin) Trust, Waterbury, 3/095
Fehrer (Emma B.) Trust, Hartford, 3/096
Fetzenko (Joseph) Trust, Waterbury, 3/097
Forbes (William Trust, Waterbury, 3/098
Fulton (Lewis) Trust, Waterbury, 3/098
Gannon (Anna M.) Trust, Waterbury, 3/099
Gardner (I.I.) Trust, Waterbury, 3/099
Gordon (Gurdon W.) Trust, Hartford, 3/099
Goss (Emily Marlin) Charitable Trust, New Haven, 3/100
Hablitzel (Eugenie C.) Trust, Waterbury, 3/101
Hall (Orinda E.) Trust, Waterbury, 3/101
Hampson (R. William) Trust, Waterbury, 3/102
Harrington (James L.) Trust, Hartford, 3/102
Harrub (Charles H.) Trusts, Waterbury, 3/103
Hart (Charles E. & Katherine) Trust, Waterbury, 3/104
Henry (Ida M.) Trust, Waterbury, 3/104
Hopkins (Samuel E.) Trust, Waterbury, 3/105
Hewitt (Lyman) Trust, Hartford, 3/105
Hopkins (Abbie C.) Trust, Waterbury, 3/106
Hopkins (Samuel E.) Trust f/b/o Lake Helen Congregational Church, Waterbury, 3/107
Hudner (Julia A.) Trust, Waterbury, 3/107
Kaiser (Babette) Trust, Waterbury, 3/107
Keeling (Frank) Trust, Waterbury, 3/108
Keeling (Jacob) Trust, Waterbury, 3/108
Kirk (Elizabeth) Trust, Waterbury, 3/109
Kellogg (Frank W.) Trust, Waterbury, 3/110
Kenea (Edith Lee) Trusts, Waterbury, 3/110
Langdon (Virginia C.) Trusts, Waterbury, 3/117
Leavenworth (Elisha) Trust, Waterbury, 3/118
Lewis (Truman S.) Trusts, Waterbury, 3/118
Fulton (Lewis) Memorial Fund Trust, Lewis (Truman S.) Trusts, 3/120
Lott (Rose A.) Trusts, Waterbury, 3/121
Mannweiler (Mary B.) Trust, Waterbury, 3/122
Marley (Anna A.) Trust, Waterbury, 3/122
Nuckols (Florence B.) Trust, Greenwich, 3/123
Meigs (Mary L.) Trust f/b/o Brookside Cemetery, Waterbury, 3/123
Meigs (Mary L.) Trust f/b/o Christ Church Parish, Oxford, Waterbury, 3/124
Meigs (Mary L.) Trust f/b/o Episcopal & Congregational Cemetery of Oxford, Waterbury, 3/124
Munson (Marion A.) Trust, Waterbury, 3/125
Mygatt (Henry D.) Trust, Waterbury, 3/125
Noble (Bertha P.) Trust, Waterbury, 3/125
Nolan (Joseph J.) Trust, Waterbury, 3/126
Nuckols (Florence B.) Trust, Greenwich, 3/127
Osborne (Hartwell C.) Trust, Waterbury, 3/127
Peck (Henry H.) Trusts, Waterbury, 3/127
Peck (Katherine L.) Trusts, Waterbury, 3/128
Hart (Bertha Platt) Trust, Waterbury, 3/133

Pomeroy (Katherine H.) Trust, Waterbury, 3/134

Pomeroy (Nelson A.) Trust, Waterbury, 3/134

Pond (E. Leroy) Trust, Hartford, 3/135

Rathbun (Norris W.) Trust, Hartford, 3/136

Russell (Edward) Trust, Waterbury, 3/137

Sackett (Frank) Trust f/b/o Methodist Episcopal Church, Winsted, Waterbury, 3/138

Sackett (Frank) Trust f/b/o Y.M.C.A., Winsted, Waterbury, 3/138

Scovill (Ellen Hyde) Trusts, Waterbury, 3/139

Skilton (Alice K.) Trust, Waterbury, 3/139

Smith (Charles F.) Trust, Waterbury, 3/140

Smith (Easton) Trusts, Waterbury, 3/141

Smith (Henry A.) Trust, Waterbury, 3/143

Swayze (Clara M.) Trust, Waterbury, 3/143

Tiffany (L.W.) Trust, Hartford, 3/144

Travis (Frank M.) Trust, Waterbury, 3/144

Tuttle (Jeannette S.) Trust, Waterbury, 3/145

Wadhams (Sanford H.) Trust, Waterbury, 3/145

Wakelee (William Howard) Trust, Waterbury, 3/146

Walker (Gertrude B.) Trusts, Waterbury, 3/146

Warner (Oscar L.) Trusts, Waterbury, 3/147

Wilson (William H.) Trust, Hartford, 3/149

Whittemore (Gertrude B.) Trust, Waterbury, 3/150

Tunxis Fdn., Bristol, 3/150

American Republican, Inc. Trust, Waterbury, 3/151

Bronson (Homer D.) Company Trust, Waterbury, 3/152

Camp (Hilda M. M.) Trust, Waterbury, 3/152

Griffin (Robert W.) Trust, Waterbury, 3/153

Griswold (Harlan) Trust, Waterbury, 3/154

Hall (Edward F. & Mary P.K.) Trust, Waterbury, 3/154

Hutchinson (Henry G.) Trust, Waterbury, 3/154

Jones (Edward R.) Trust, Waterbury, 3/155

Jones (Eleanor W.) Trust, Waterbury, 3/155

MacDermid, Inc. Trust, Waterbury, 3/156

Ottley (Marian W.) Trust, Waterbury, 3/156

Goss (Pamela Pond & Donald W.) Trust, Waterbury, 3/157

Platt Brothers & Company Trust, Waterbury, 3/157

Reinbrecht (Downing A.) Trust, Waterbury, 3/158

Smith (Edmund S. & Eleanor M.) Trust, Waterbury, 3/158

Smith (J.E.) & Company Trust, Waterbury, 3/159

Stanton (Josephine K.) Trust, Waterbury, 3/159

Waterbury Ready Mixed Concrete Co. Trust, Waterbury, 3/160

Watkinson Prisoners' Aid Society Trust, Hartford, 3/161

Wise (Selma S.) Trusts, Hartford, 3/162

Weiss (Henrietta) Trust, Waterbury, 3/165

Wien (Minnie) Trust, Waterbury, 3/165

Welton (Nelson J.) Trust, Waterbury, 3/166

Whitemore (Gertrude B.) Memorial Fund, Waterbury, 3/166

Whittemore (Gertrude B.) Trust, Waterbury, 3/167

Whittemore (J.H.) Trust, Waterbury, 3/167

Woodruff (George M.) Trust, Waterbury, 3/167

Woodruff (James P.) Trust, Waterbury, 3/168

Workman (Andrew) Trust, Waterbury, 3/169

Workman (Anna F.) Trust, Waterbury, 3/169

Underhill Burying Ground, Greenwich, 3/170

Underhill Society of America, Inc., Greenwich, 3/170

United Aircraft Fdn., East Hartford, 3/171

United Philanthropy Fdn., Greenwich, 3/172

Vance (Robert C.) Charitable Fdn., New Britain, 3/173

Veeder Industries Trust, Hartford, 3/173

Vitamaur Fdn., Hartford, 3/174

Vitramon Fdn., Bridgeport, 3/175

Wahlstrom Fdn., Easton, 3/176

Walker (Louis) Charitable Fdn., Hartford, 3/177

Walker (William S.) Trust, Hartford, 3/178

War Memorial Scholarship of National League of Women's Service, Danbury, 3/179

Warner Fdn., Greenwich, 3/180

Warren Fdn., Greenwich, 3/180

Waterbury Companies Fdn., Waterbury, 3/181

Weinerman Fdn., Hartford, 3/182

Weissman Charitable & Eudcational Fund, New Haven, 3/183

Westport Weston Fdn. Trust, Westport, 3/183

Wetstone Fdn., Manchester, 3/184

White (Benjamin V.) Fdn., West Hartford, 3/184

White (Linford C. & Mildred I.) Fdn., Waterbury, 3/185

Wickersham Fund Trust, Hartford, 3/185

Wickham City Hall Clock Fund Trust, Hartford, 3/185

Wickham Park Trust, Hartford, 3/186

Wilcox (C.H. & G.G.) Fdn., New Britain, 3/187

Wilkins (Edward C. & Mary W.) Fdn., Wethersfield, 3/188

D.A.R. Willard Chapter - Pinches Fund Trust, Hartford, 3/188

Williams (Vianda Playter) Fdn., Greenwich, 3/188

Wimpfheimer Fdn., Stonington, 3/190

Wiremold Fdn., West Hartford, 3/191

Wise (Isidore & Selma) Travel Fdn. Trust, Hartford, 3/192

Woman's Seamen's Friend Society of Connecticut, New Haven, 3/193

Yale Club of Hartford Fdn., Hartford, 3/194

Youmans Fdn., West Hartford, 3/195

Young (Robert R.) Fdn., Greenwich, 3/196

Zell (David H. & Sophie B.) Memorial Fdn., Norwalk, 3/196

Zell (Esther & Charles M.) Fdn. Formerly New York, Stamford, 3/197

Second Filming

Adelphic Educational Fund, Hartford, 4/001

Alling (George E.) Trust, New Haven, 4/002

Allison Fund, Fairfield, 4/002

Ambrook Fdn., Norwich, 4/002

American Can Fdn., Greenwich, 4/003

Ames Fdn., Hartford, 4/005

Amity Educational Fund, New Haven, 4/006

Aned Fdn., Lakeville, 4/007

Anthony (Graham H.), Jr. Scholarship Fund, Hartford, 4/007

Ardolino (Edward J.) Fdn., Branford, 4/008

Armstrong Rubber Company Fdn., New Haven, 4/008

Aspell (William P.) Trust, Hartford, 4/009

Associated Construction Company Fdn. for Charitable Purposes, Hartford, 4/010

Auerbach (Beatrice Fox) Fdn., West Hartford, 4/011

Babbitt (Elizabeth E.) Trust, New Haven, 4/011

Bannow Fdn., Easton, 4/011

Banquer (I.S. & A.J.) Family Fdn., New Haven, 4/012

Barber (William J. & Julie A.) Memorial Fund Trust, Hartford, 4/013

Barkhamsted Center Cemetery Trusts, Hartford, 4/013

Batcheller (William H.) Trust, Hartford, 4/014

Associated Contrution Company Fdn. for Charitable Purposes, Hartford, 4/015

Bates (Vernal W. & Florence H.) Fdn., Branford, 4/015

Bayview Rest, Bridgeport, 4/016

Beecher (L. Wheeler) Trust, New Haven, 4/017

Behrend (Mary B.) Fdn., Greenwich, 4/017

Bethany Memorial Scholarship Fund, New Haven, 4/020

Bradley (Andrew R.) Residuary Trust, New Haven, 4/021

Bradley (Howard H.) Trusts, New Haven, 4/021

Bingham (Edwin H.) Trust, Hartford, 4/022

Bingham (Mary G.) Trust, Hartford, 4/022

Bissell (Lebbeus F.) Supplementary Scholarship Fund, Hartford, 4/023

Bissell (Dr. William) Fund for Hospital Aid, Lakeville, 4/024

Bland Fdn., West Hartford, 4/025

Blechner (Adolf C. & Marie J.) Fdn., Woodbury, 4/026

B.P.O. Elks of U.S.A. Lodge # 36, Bridgeport, 4/027

Bridge Fdn., Hazardville, 4/027

Bridgeport Machines Fdn., Bridgeport, 4/027

Bristol Yale Scholarship Fund, Bristol, 4/028

Killingly-Brooklyn Scholarship Fund, Hartford, 4/029

Brown (Kate W.) Trust, New Haven, 4/029

Brown (Martha W.) Trust, Hartford, 4/030

Brynwood Fdn., Greenwich, 4/030

Bufferd (Chester Edward) Prize Fund, Waterbury, 4/031

Bull (Dorothy) Memorial Fund, Waterbury, 4/031

Burnham (Harriet T.) Trusts, Hartford, 4/032

Cagenello - Martocchi Fdn., New Haven, 4/034

Cairns (Margaret R.) Trust, Hartford, 4/035

Johnny Cake Child Study Center Fdn., Hartford, 4/036

Carbonari (Edith F. & Albert F.) Fdn., Woodbridge, 4/037

Cartin (Morris B. & Edith S.) Family Fdn., Hartford, 4/037

Case (A. Willard) Trust, Hartford, 4/038

Central Burial Association of Haddam, Connecticut, Hartford, 4/039

Chaffee (Charles E.) Trust, Hartford, 4/041

Chaffee (Etta C.) Trust, Hartford, 4/041

Anaconda American Brass Company Charitable Donations Trust, Waterbury, 4/042

Connrex Corporation Charitable Donations Trust, Waterbury, 4/043

Lunan (I. Douglas) Charitable Donations Trust, Waterbury, 4/043

Sealy, New York Charitable Donations Trust (Greater), Waterbury, 4/045

Waterbury Mattress Company Charitable Donations Trust, Waterbury, 4/045

Walzer (William H.) Charitable Donations Trust, Waterbury, 4/046

Colony Fdn., New Haven, 4/046

Cone (Helen) Trust, Hartford, 4/047

Conklin (William D.) Charity Trust, New Canaan, 4/048

Connecticut Society for Medical Research, Farmington, 4/048

Connecticut State Dental Association - Relief Fund, Hartford, 4/049

Connecticut Troopers Memorial Scholarship Fund, Hartford, 4/049

Copelon (Herman H. & Kathryn S.) Fdn., New Haven, 4/049

Corning (John J.) Trust, Hartford, 4/050

Citizen's Scholarship Fdn. of Bloomfield, Hartford, 4/051

Clinton Museum Trust, Hartford, 4/051

Crippled Children's Aid Society, Branford, 4/052

Crosby (Sarah) & Henry J. Dunleavy Scholarship Trust Fund, Hartford, 4/054

Dann (Paul N.) Trust, New Haven, 4/054

David (Joseph P.) Trust, New Haven, 4/055

Foster - Davis Fdn., Westport, 4/056

David (Joseph P.) Trust, New Haven, 4/057

Day (Patrick F.), Sr. Trust, Hartford, 4/057

Phelps (James De Forest) Trust, Hartford, 4/058

Dickinson (Helen F.) Trust, Hartford, 4/058

Dickerman (Wilton E.) Trust, New Haven, 4/059

Dodge (Linsley V.) Charitable Trust, Greenwich, 4/059

Eberle (William D. & Jean Q.) Charitable Trust, Riverside, 4/059

Educational Fdn. of America, Westport, 4/060
Ellis (Jonathan George) Leukemia Fdn., Manchester, 4/061
Madison Historical Society Endowment Fund, Madison, 4/062
Ensworth Charitable Fdn., Hartford, 4/062
Walker (Ethel) Charitable & Educational Fdn., Simsbury, 4/064
Ensworth Charitable Fdn., Hartford, 4/064
Fafnir Bearing Company Rehabilitation, New Britain, 4/064
Farmington Fdn., Farmington, 4/065
Foote (Grace Salisbury) Fund, New Haven, 4/065
Farrel (Franklin) Memorial Fund, New Haven, 4/066
Framarb Fdn., Greenwich, 4/066
Friedberg (Milton H.) Fund, Bridgeport, 4/067
Fitch (Charles P.) Trust, Hartford, 4/068
Gilbert (Agnes H.) Trust, New Haven, 4/069
Goddard (Flora H.) Trust, New Haven, 4/069
Goodwin (Anna M.) Trust, Hartford, 4/069
Goodwin (Charles L.) Trust, Hartford, 4/071
Goodwin (George R.) Trust, Hartford, 4/072
Graff Fdn., Hartford, 4/073
Greer (Josephine L.) & Philip Lauter Fdn., Willimantic, 4/074
Griffing (Bruce N.) Trust, New Haven, 4/077
Hagaman (Isaac) Trust, New Haven, 4/079
Hale Fdn., New Haven, 4/080
Hall Fdn., Hartford, 4/081
Hall (Fred) Trust, New Haven, 4/081
Hall Fdn. Trusts, Hartford, 4/083
Hall (Rosa O.) Trust, Hartford, 4/086
Keogh (Sarah F.) & Florence K. Hall Fdn., Stamford, 4/087
Hamden Library Gift Fund Trust, New Haven, 4/087
Harcourt (Alfred) Fdn. Formerly New York, New Milford, 4/087
Hartford County Medical Fdn., Hartford, 4/088
Hartford Public High School Alumni Association, Hartford, 4/089
Hatch (George) Trust, Hartford, 4/091
Hendrick (Hobart & Mary) Charitable Trust, New Haven, 4/091
Heris (Alcibiades G.) Trust, New Haven, 4/092
Hersey Fdn., New Haven, 4/092
Heublein Fdn., Hartford, 4/093
Hicks (Mary C.) Trust, Hartford, 4/094
Higley Educational & Historical Fdn., New Canaan, 4/095
Hills (Eliza W.) Trust, Hartford, 4/096
Hills (Henry W.) Trust, Hartford, 4/096
Hills (Stephen) Trust, Hartford, 4/097
Hixon Fdn., Essex, 4/098
Holley (Myron) Trust, Hartford, 4/098
Humiston (Julia A.) Trust, New Haven, 4/099
Hunter (William & Alice) Fund, Hartford, 4/101
Hyde (Elizabeth A.) Memorial Fund, Waterbury, 4/101
Hyde (Elizabeth Alvina) Fund, Waterbury, 4/102
Institute for the Future, Middletown, 4/102
International Doll Library Fdn., Greenwich, 4/103
Isis, Inc., New Haven, 4/105
Ives (Frederick A.) Trust, New Haven, 4/105
Jacoby (Frank) Fdn., Bridgeport, 4/106
Jackson (John Day) Trust, New Haven, 4/106
Jackson Fdn., New Haven, 4/107
Jost (Charles & Mabel P.) Fdn., Easton, 4/107
Kane (Mary M.) Fdn., Westport, 4/108
Kingsley Trust Association, New Haven, 4/109
Kohn Fdn., Bloomfield, 4/110
Korn (Ruth B. & Samuel H.) Fdn. Formerly New York, Greenwich, 4/110
Krechevsky Fdn., West Hartford, 4/111
Ledbetter Fdn., Greenwich, 4/112
Licht Fdn., New Haven, 4/112
Liftig Fdn., Beacon Falls, 4/113
List (Albert A.) Fdn., Byram, 4/113

Litchfield County University Club, Woodbury, 4/114
Litchfield Nature Center & Museum, Litchfield, 4/117
Hiram Lodge Trust, New Haven, 4/117
Lowman (Lawrence W.) Fdn., Stamford, 4/117
MacJannet Fdn., Bridgeport, 4/118
Madison Historical Society, Madison, 4/119
Marrod Fdn., West Hartford, 4/120
McDonough Fdn., Bloomfield, 4/121
McGraft Park Trust, Hartford, 4/122
McLaughlin - Whipple Trust, Stamford, 4/123
McLean Fund, Hartford, 4/123
McLean (John) Fund Trust, Hartford, 4/124
McManus (Ella Burr) Trust, Hartford, 4/125
Michaeljon Fdn., Westport, 4/125
Miller (Edward) Trusts, Hartford, 4/126
Catlin (Frederick A. & Justine Millspaugh) Fdn., New Haven, 4/131
Mittelman (Reuben) Family Charitable Fdn., West Hartford, 4/132
Montague (John) Charitable Fdn., Stamford, 4/133
Moeller (August) Memorial Fdn., Wethersfield, 4/133
Moore (Richard & Mary) Fdn., Bridgeport, 4/133
Moore (Marjorie) Charitable Fdn., New Britain, 4/134
Morse (William Inglis) Trust, New Haven, 4/134
Morton (Willie T.) Trusts, Hartford, 4/135
Morton (W.T.) East Windsor Cemetery Trust, Hartford, 4/136
Morton (Willie T.) Trust, Hartford, 4/137
Manger (William Muir) Research Fdn., Stamford, 4/138
O'Connor (Maurice) Charitable Fdn., New Haven, 4/138
Naugatuck Rotary Fdn., Naugatuck, 4/139
New Britain Day Nursery, New Britain, 4/139
New Britain Fdn. for Public Giving, New Britain, 4/140
New Canaan Woman's Club, New Canaan, 4/141
New Haven Paint & Clay Club Trust, New Haven, 4/141
Noank Arts Fdn., Noank, 4/142
O'Meara Fdn., West Hartford, 4/142
Padden (Katherine McManns) Fund, New Haven, 4/143
Page (May Rockwell) Trust, Bristol, 4/143
Palmer (Frank Loomis) Fund Trust, Hartford, 4/144
Pardee (Wilbur W.) Trust, New Haven, 4/145
Porter (Sarah) Centenary Memorial Fund Trust, Hartford, 4/146
Portland Fdn., Portland, 4/146
Price (Miriam Sutro) Scholarship Fund, Waterbury, 4/147
Putnam - Prospect Fdn., Hartford, 4/148
Queenan Fdn., Greenwich, 4/148
Rathbun (Norris W.) Trust, Hartford, 4/149
Record - Journal Fdn., Meriden, 4/150
Regional District Eleven Scholarship Loan Fund, Chaplin, 4/150
Rho Psi Brothers Fdn., Fairfield, 4/150
Laurel Ridge Fdn., Hartford, 4/151
Ridgefield Library & Historical Assoc., Ridgefield, 4/151
Riggs (T. Lawrason) Trust, New Haven, 4/152
Robinson (Henry N.) Trust, Hartford, 4/152
Rock Ledge Institute, Darien, 4/153
Rosenberg (J. & B.) Fdn., Stratford, 4/154
Rosenthal (Herbert I. & Shirley C.) Fdn., Westport, 4/155
Rubin (Albert & Augusta) Fdn., West Hartford, 4/155
Ruddell (H. Louise) Charitable Fdn., Manchester, 4/156
Rudkin Fdn., Southport, 4/157
Safety Industries Community Trust Fund, New Haven, 4/157
St. Andrews Cemetery Fund Trust, Hartford, 4/158

St. Lukes Home, Hartford, 4/159
Saginor (David & Shirley) Fdn., Woodbridge, 4/160
Sargent (Daniel I.) Charitable Trust, New Canaan, 4/161
Schatz Fdn., Hartford, 4/162
Scholarship Fund of the Polish Business & Professional Men's Assoc. of New Haven, Orange, 4/163
Scovill Fdn., Waterbury, 4/164
Scranton (E.C.) Memorial Library Trusts, New Haven, 4/164
Service Bureau for Connecticut Organizations, Formerly Service Bureau for Women's Organizations, West Hartford, 4/167
Shaffer (Elizabeth B.) Fdn., New Haven, 4/167
Sherman (Irving J.) Fdn., Bridgeport, 4/168
Skinner Precision Industries, Inc. Charitable Trust, New Britain, 4/168
Ely (John Slade) Fund, New Haven, 4/169
Danbury Slovak Gym Union Sokol, Danbury, 4/169
Smith (Lester W.) Fund, Stamford, 4/169
Smith (Wilbur) Fdn., New Haven, 4/170
Sorensen Fdn., Bridgeport, 4/172
Spalding (Helen E.) Fdn., New Haven, 4/172
Stambol Family Fdn., South Windsor, 4/173
Stanley (William) Trust, Hartford, 4/173
Starr (William F.) Fellowship Fund, Hartford, 4/174
Stern (Moses) Memorial Fund Trust, Hartford, 4/175
Stratfield Fund, Bridgeport, 4/176
Strong (Emerette L.) Trust, Hartford, 4/176
Strong (Susan E.) Trust, New Haven, 4/177
Suisman Fdn., Hartford, 4/177
Sweet Life Fdn., Suffield, 4/180
Swindells Charitable Fdn. Trust, Hartford, 4/180
Talcott Art Fund, New Britain, 4/181
Toffolon Charitable Fdn., Plainville, 4/182
Torrington Company Charitable Trust, Hartford, 4/183
Tourtellotte (Jacob F.) Trusts, Hartford, 4/184
Alling (George F.) Trust, New Haven, 4/186
Alford (F.) Trust, New Britain, 4/187
Alling (George F.) Trust, New Haven, 4/187
Ardenghi (Anna F.) Trust, New Haven, 4/188
Arnold (Marie) Trust, New Haven, 4/188
Ardenghi (Anna F.) Trust, New Haven, 4/189
Barclay (William C.) Trust, New Haven, 4/190
Beers (Seth P.) Trust, Waterbury, 4/192
Blakeslee (Dennis A.) Trust, New Haven, 4/192
Goffe Street Special School Trust, New Haven, 4/194
Pomeroy (Nelson A.) Trust, Waterbury, 4/194
Barclay (William C.) Trust, New Haven, 4/195
Bolles (Arthur H.) Trust, Waterbury, 4/196
Bissell (Henry) Trust, Waterbury, 4/197
New Britain Machine Company Charitable Trust, New Britain, 4/197
Bufferd (Celia) Trust, Waterbury, 4/198
Catlin (Anson & Caroline) Trust, Waterbury, 4/198
Carlisle (Alice L.) Trust, Waterbury, 4/199
Godfrey (Adelaide Coe) Trust, Waterbury, 4/200
Coe (Francis M.) Trusts, Waterbury, 4/201
Cornwall Bridge Methodist Church Trust, Waterbury, 4/204
Dunbar (Adeline) Trust, Waterbury, 4/204
Eames (William Scott) Trusts, New Haven, 4/205
Gillmore (Gertrude A.) Trust, New Haven, 4/207
Hall (Fred) Trust, New Haven, 4/208
Hanchett (Harry B.) Trust, Waterbury, 4/209
Harris (Etta M.) Trust, New Haven, 4/210
Hawley (B.) Trust, New Britain, 4/211
Heris (Alcibiades G.) Trust, New Haven, 4/211
Holcomb (Walter) Trust, Waterbury, 4/212
Hull (Arabelle A. Meigs) Trust, New Haven, 4/213
Hunn (Flora L.) Trust, New Haven, 4/214

Hungerford (Newman) Trusts, Waterbury, 4/215
Johnson (B.) Trusts, New Haven, 4/216
Kingsbury (Edith) Trust, Waterbury, 4/219
Marlin (Mary M.) Trust, New Haven, 4/219
Marlin (Mahlon H.) Trust, New Haven, 4/221
Martin (Alice) Trust, New Britain, 4/223
Meeker (Dora P.) Trust, New Haven, 4/224
Mulford (William M.) Trust, Hartford, 4/225
Mulford (William M.) Trust, Hartford, 5/001
Osborn (John S.) Trust, New Haven, 5/002
Patrick (Elise K.) Trust, New Haven, 5/003
Perakos (Peter) Scholarship Fund, New Britain, 5/004
Prudden (Martha E.) Trust, New Haven, 5/005
Ransom (William L.) Trust, Waterbury, 5/006
Rockhill (Edith P.) Trust, Waterbury, 5/007
Ryan (Frank L.) Trust, Waterbury, 5/007
Scanlon (Eliza L.) Trust, New Haven, 5/008
Coe (Ella Seymour) Trusts, Waterbury, 5/009
Skinner Precision Industries, Inc. Charitable Fund, New Britain, 5/011
Smith (Mary L.) Trust, Waterbury, 5/012
Squires (Charles L.) Trust, New Haven, 5/012
Thorpe (George W.) Trust, New Haven, 5/013
Dann (Paul N.) Trust, New Haven, 5/015
Thorpe (George W.) Trust, New Haven, 5/015
Tomkins (Bennett H. & Elizabeth H.) Fund, Waterbury, 5/016
Poole (Edith F.) Trust, Waterbury, 5/016
Tsunami Fdn., Greenwich, 5/017
Tunxis Fdn., Bristol, 5/017
Vilonat (William) Memorial Scholarship Fund, Norwalk, 5/018
Vogt Research Fdn., Weston, 5/019
Vose (Alden H.) Fdn., Westport, 5/020
Bozzuto's, Inc. Charitable Donations Trust, Waterbury, 5/021
Camp (Orton P.), Jr. Charitable Donations Trust, Waterbury, 5/021
Leever (Harold & Ruth Ann) Charitable Donations Trust, Waterbury, 5/022
Williams (Selden T. & Ella V.) Charitable Donations Trust, Waterbury, 5/024
Whitehead (J. Paul & Corinne) Charitable Donations Trust, Waterbury, 5/024
Ward (Henry) Trust, New Haven, 5/025
Waterman Fdn., Greenwich, 5/026
Waugh (Samuel G.) Fdn., Southport, 5/026
Wells (Horace) Trust Fund, Hartford, 5/027
Wells (Jean & Wayne) Fdn., Greenwich, 5/028
Winter Trust, West Hartford, 5/028
Wheeler (Wilmot) Fdn., Bridgeport, 5/028
Woodward (Charles G.) Trust, Hartford, 5/030
Wohl (Solomon & Katie) Fdn., Hartford, 5/031
Wrexham Fdn., New Haven, 5/031
Yale Club of Hartford Fdn., Hartford, 5/033
Yolen (William & Esther) Fdn., Hartford, 5/033
Young (Robert R.) Fdn., Greenwich, 5/034

DELAWARE

First Filming

Action Task Force Fund, Wilmington, 1/002
Aeolian Fdn., Wilmington, 1/002
Angustura, Wilmington, 1/003
Atlanta Fdn., Wilmington, 1/003
Arguild Fdn., Wilmington, 1/004
Averell - Ross Fdn., Wilmington, 1/004
Ball (Russell C.) Fdn., Wilmington, 1/005
Beekhuis (Albert) Fdn., Wilmington, 1/005
Beneficial Fdn., Wilmington, 1/006
Bernstein Development Fdn., Wilmington, 1/009
Birch (Stephen & Mary) Fdn. Formerly New Jersey, Dover, 1/009

Bishop (Edward E. & Lillian H.) Fdn. (1953), Wilmington, 1/010
Bishop (Edward E. & Lillian H.) Fdn. (1964), Wilmington, 1/011
Borkee - Hagley Fdn., Wilmington, 1/011
Brittingham Charitable Fdn., Wilmington, 1/012
Bradford Fdn., Wilmington, 1/012
Bredin Fdn., Wilmington, 1/013
Brownington Fdn., Dover, 1/014
Brown (Florence H.) Trusts, Wilmington, 1/014
Carlson Fdn., Wilmington, 1/017
Carpenter Fdn., Wilmington, 1/017
Caspersen (O. W.) Fdn. for Aid to Health and Education, Wilmington, 1/018
Catalyst Fund, Wilmington, 1/019
Champlin Fdn., Wilmington, 1/020
Charitable Research Fdn., Wilmington, 1/021
Charron Fdn., Wilmington, 1/022
Chichester Dupont Fdn., Wilmington, 1/022
Choptank Fdn., Middletown, 1/023
Christiana Fdn., Wilmington, 1/024
Clifton Center, Inc., Wilmington, 1/024
Copeland Andelot Fdn., Wilmington, 1/025
Coverdale Fdn., Wilmington, 1/026
Crawford (Harry S.) f/b/o Mt. Horeb Presbyterian Church, Wilmington, 1/026
Crestlea Fdn., Wilmington, 1/027
Crystal Trust, Wilmington, 1/027
Curran Fdn., Wilmington, 1/030
Dean Fdn., Wilmington, 1/031
Delaware Mental Health Fdn., Wilmington, 1/031
Devonwood Fdn., Wilmington, 1/032
Dietrich Brothers Americana Corporation, Wilmington, 1/032
Dillon (Herbert L.) Fdn., Wilmington, 1/032
Eberman Family Fdn., Dover, 1/033
Ederic Fdn., Wilmington, 1/034
Eleutherian Mills - Hagley Fdn., Wilmington, 1/035
Evergreen Plan, Inc., Greenville, 1/038
Field - Wiltsie Fdn., Wilmington, 1/039
Fleitas Fdn., Wilmington, 1/039
Forney Family Fdn., Wilmington, 1/041
Good Samaritan, Inc., Wilmington, 1/041
Grasselli (Mary A. & Thomas F.) Endowment Fdn., Wilmington, 1/042
Handy (Margaret I.) Fdn. for Children, Wilmington, 1/042
Hartefeld Fund, Wilmington, 1/043
Hanby (Albert T.) Trust, Wilmington, 1/043
Hebb Memorial Fund, Misses, Wilmington, 1/044
Holpont Fdn., Wilmington, 1/045
Inniskilling Fdn., Wilmington, 1/046
Irwin Fdn., Wilmington, 1/047
Iselin (O'Donnell) Fdn., Wilmington, 1/047
J. B. L. Scholarship Trust, Wilmington, 1/048
Kent (Atwater) Fdn., Wilmington, 1/049
Kingsley Fdn. Formerly Connecticut, Wilmington, 1/055
Kirby (F. M.) Fdn., Wilmington, 1/056
Laffey - McHugh Fdn., Wilmington, 1/058
Lesesne Fdn., Wilmington, 1/060
Lynch (John B.) Scholarship Fdn., Wilmington, 1/061
Madison Trust, Wilmington, 1/063
Mancill Fdn., Wilmington, 1/064
Mariner Fdn., Wilmington, 1/065
Marmot Fdn., Wilmington, 1/065
Martin (Aaron J.) Fdn., Wilmington, 1/066
Martinez Fdn., Greenville, 1/067
Martineau (Maud Morris) Fdn., Wilmington, 1/068
Milliken (Gerrish H.) Fdn., Wilmington, 1/068
Milliken (Agnes G.) Fdn., Wilmington, 1/069
Minquadale Home, Wilmington, 1/071
National Vulcanized Fibre Company Community Service Trust Fund, Wilmington, 1/071
Newton Fdn., Bridgeville, 1/072
Oberod Fdn., Wilmington, 1/062
Old Kennett Fdn., Greenville, 1/072
Palmer Home, Inc., Dover, 1/073

Kennett Pike Association, Greenville, 1/075
Pollack Fdn., Wilmington, 1/075
Rabinowitz Fdn., Harbeson, 1/076
R A Fdn., Dover, 1/076
Raskob (Bill) Fdn., Wilmington, 1/077
Raskob Fdn. for Catholic Activities, Wilmington, 1/078
Red Clay Reservation, Inc., Wilmington, 1/079
Rencourt Fdn., Wilmington, 1/080
Rock Spring Fdn., Montchanin, 1/080
Rorer Fdn., Wilmington, 1/081
Schlumberger Horizons, Inc., Wilmington, 1/082
Second Champlin Fdn., Wilmington, 1/082
Sharp Fdn., Wilmington, 1/084
Spanel Fdn., Dover, 1/084
Silva (Cristovam) Fdn., Wilmington, 1/085
Stubbins (John Russell) Fdn., Dover, 1/085
Student Exchange Fdn., Wilmington, 1/086
Theano Fdn., Wilmington, 1/087
Hughes (Wilhelmina D.) Trust, Wilmington, 1/088
Kollock (Henry G. M.) Trust b/o Newark Public Library, Wilmington, 1/088
Lister (Sarah H.) Trust b/o Kent General Hospital, Wilmington, 1/089
Rhodes (George) Trust b/o St. John the Baptist Church, Wilmington, 1/089
Simpson (Sallie E.) Trust b/o Kent General Hospital, Wilmington, 1/089
Simpson (William J.) Trust b/o Kent General Hospital, Wilmington, 1/089
Skelly (Mary A.) Trust b/o St. Peter's Church, Wilmington, 1/090
University of Wisconsin Trust, Wilmington, 1/090
Van Leer (Charles) Trust, Wilmington, 1/092
Van Leer (Bernard) Fdn., Wilmington, 1/093
Ware Fdn., Wilmington, 1/093
Welfare Fdn., Wilmington, 1/095
Weymouth Fdn., Wilmington, 1/096
Wilmington Trust Company Fdn., Wilmington, 1/097
Du Pont (Henry Francis) Winterthur Museum, Inc., Winterthur, 1/097
Woodstock Fdn., Wilmington, 1/099
Wunsch Americana Fdn., Dover, 1/100
Young Fdn., Wilmington, 1/100
Zacharia (Isaac Herman) Fdn., Wilmington, 1/101

Second Filming

Andante Corp., Wilmington, 2/002
Asbury Methodist Trust 3577, Wilmington, 2/003
Baymere Fdn., Wilmington, 2/003
Bennett (C. E.) Fdn., Wilmington, 2/003
Brittingham Arts Fdn., Inc., Wilmington, 2/004
Brinser (Donald C.) Mem. Fdn., Wilmington, 2/005
Burton (David G.) Successor Trustee U/A T R DTD 5/6/69, Wilmington, 2/005
Carlisle (Tryphena V.) T/W, Wilmington, 2/006
Charis Fdn., Inc., Wilmington, 2/006
Chippey (Annie P.) TR U/W, Wilmington, 2/007
Clark (Emma) T/W, Wilmington, 2/007
Cohen (Harry) Fdn., Inc., Wilmington, 2/008
Crawford (Anna Louise) T/W 3439, Wilmington, 2/009
Crawford (Anna Louise) T/W 3459, Wilmington, 2/010
Israel (A. Cremieux) Fdn., Inc., Dover, 2/011
Cummins (Albert W.) T/W, Wilmington, 2/012
Delaware Fdn. Golding T/A, Wilmington, 2/013
Delaware King Memorial Fdn., Wilmington, 2/014
Delaware Park Inc., Wilmington, 2/015
Delaware Fdn. Quigley, Wilmington, 2/016
Doherty (Hannah A.) T/A, Wilmington, 2/016
Dupont (Jean K. F.) T/A, Wilmington, 2/017
Edgell Fdn., Inc., Dover, 2/017

English (Henry C.) T/W, Wilmington, 2/018
Etchells-McCann Immanuel P. E. Church, Wilmington, 2/019
Etlon Fdn., Inc., Wilmington, 2/020
Evans (Mary R.) T/W 6785, Wilmington, 2/020
Evans (Mary R.) T/A 4950, Wilmington, 2/021
Eykamp Fdn., Wilmington, 2/021
Foundation Internationale de Delaware, Greenville, 2/022
Gerard (Sumner) Fdn., Wilmington, 2/022
Gillett (Lucy B.) T/A, Wilmington, 2/023
Greenwood Fdn., Wilmington, 2/024
Grier (Charles) T/W, Wilmington, 2/025
Hartefeld Endeavor Inc., Wilmington, 2/025
Hanover St. Presbyterian Church Sabbath School, Wilmington, 2/026
Historical Society of Delaware T/W, Wilmington, 2/027
Justis (Mary E.) T/A, Wilmington, 2/027
Kent-Lucas Fdn., Inc., Wilmington, 2/028
Kollock (Henry G. M.) T/W, Wilmington, 2/029
Kruse (Edwina B.) T/W, Wilmington, 2/030
Layton (Annie E.) Cem. T/W, Wilmington, 2/030
Lewes Historical Society, Lewes, 2/031
Lower Brandywine Presbyterian Chruch U/W WMB 1980, Wilmington, 2/032
Masonic Club of Delaware Educational Fdn., Inc., Wilmington, 2/032
McLaughlin (Ellen) T/W 5068, Wilmington, 2/032
McLaughlin (Ellen) T/W 5085, Wilmington, 2/034
Miller (Sarah A.) T/W, Wilmington, 2/034
Miller (Clara) T/W, Wilmington, 2/035
Morris (Elizabeth) T/W, Wilmington, 2/036
Murphy (Elizabeth W.) School, Inc., Dover, 2/036
Milliken (Gerrish H.) Fdn., Wilmington, 2/037
National Society of The Colonial Dames of America in the State of Delaware, Wilmington, 2/039
Nautilus Fdn., Wilmington, 2/039
Orr (Martha G.) T/W, Wilmington, 2/040
Plunkett (Anna) Police Pension Fund, Wilmington, 2/041
Quigley (Elizabeth) V/A, Wilmington, 2/041
Rencourt Fdn., Inc., Wilmington, 2/042
Reynolds (Sarah B.) T/W, Wilmington, 2/043
Rollins (John W.) Fdn. Inc., Wilmington, 2/043
Romill Fdn., Wilmington, 2/044
Ross Fdn., Inc., Wilmington, 2/045
Heald (William H.) Scholarship Fund #4256, Wilmington, 2/045
Silva (Christovam) Fdn., Wilmington, 2/046
Sudler (Emory) T/W, Wilmington, 2/047
Society of Economic Geologists Fdn., Inc., Wilmington, 2/047
Stone Masons No. 3 Welfare Fund, Wilmington, 2/048
Stubbins (John Russell) Fdn., Dover, 2/048
Trust U/W of Frederick E. Bennett for Slaughter, Wilmington, 2/049
Trust U/W of Henrietta Bennett, Wilmington, 2/049
Trust U/A with Board of Education of the Alexis, Wilmington, 2/050
Trust U/W of Ella M. Brown for Old Pencader Presbyterian, Wilmington, 2/050
Trust U/W of George S. Capelle Jr., Wilmington, 2/051
Trust U/W of George S. Capelle Jr. for University of Pennsylvania, Wilmington, 2/051
Trust U/W with Walter Carpenter Jr. for Delaware Academy of Medicine, Inc., Wilmington, 2/052
Trust U/W of Annie R. Carmean, Wilmington, 2/053
Trust U/W of Della M. Coverdale for Ellendale Cemet., Wilmington, 2/053

Trust U/A with Crystal Fount Lodge, Wilmington, 2/054
Trust U/W of Emma R. Davis for Slaughter Neck Church, Wilmington, 2/055
Trust U/W of Henry F. du Pont for Christ Church, Wilmington, 2/055
Trust U/A with Pierre S. du Pont for Alexis 1 du Pont, Wilmington, 2/056
Trust U/A with David Flett du Pont, Wilmington, 2/056
Trust U/D with Philip F. du Pont for University of Virginia, Wilmington, 2/057
Trust U/A with 1st Central Presbyterian Church of Wilmington, Delaware, Wilmington, 2/058
Trust U/A M/B with First & Central Presbyterian Church of Wilmington, Delaware, Wilmington, 2/058
Trust U/W of Victorine E. Foster for Christ Church, Wilmington, 2/059
Trust U/W of A.L. Foster for Christ Church, Wilmington, 2/059
Trust U/A with Anna V. Graham Charitable Trust, Wilmington, 2/060
Trust U/W of George H. Hall for Avenue Methodist Episcopal Church, Wilmington, 2/060
Trust of U/W George H. Hall for Milford Memorial Hosp., Wilmington, 2/061
Trust U/W of Sallie M. Hobson, Wilmington, 2/062
Trust U/W with Eugene Kelley for Initial Teaching Alphabet Fdn., Inc., Wilmington, 2/062
Trust U/A Sarah H. Lister B/O Kent General Hospital, Wilmington, 2/063
Trust U/I Eight U/W of Ida J. Miller for Designated Charitable Organization, Wilmington, 2/064
Trust U/W with Montefiore Mutual Benefit Society, Wilmington, 2/065
Trust U/A with Mount Salem M.E. Church, 2/065
Trust U/A with Nileb Fdn., Inc. for Boys Club of Wilmington, Delaware, Inc., Wilmington, 2/066
Trust U/A with Nileb Fdn., Inc. for Waverly Community House, Wilmington, 2/066
Trust U/A H. Rodney Sharp for Paoli Mem. Hosp., Wilmington, 2/067
Trust U/A with H. Rodney Sharp for Chester County Hosp. of West Chester, Wilmington, 2/068
Trust U/W of Jennie Shepherd for Walter Chapel Cem., Wilmington, 2/068
Trust U/W of Katherine C. Smalley for Christina Presbyterian Church, Wilmington, 2/069
Trust U/W of John B. Smith for Old Presbyterian Church, Wilmington, 2/070
Trust U/W of J. Gerard Wayne Stegner for Catholic Diocese of Wilmington, Wilmington, 2/070
Trust U/I Third of Will of Robert J. Clendaniel for Red Mens Cemetery, Wilmington, 2/071
Trust U/A with Wilmington High School Alumni Association, Wilmington, 2/071
Trust U/A with Trustees of West Presbyterian Church, Wilmington, 2/072
Trust U/W of Annie B. Wilson for Cedar Neck Church, Wilmington, 2/073
Trust U/W of Annie B. Wilson for Slaughter Neck Church, Wilmington, 2/073
Trust U/W of Elizabeth Virginia White for University of Delaware, Wilmington, 2/074
Vale (Ruby R.) Fdn., Philadelphia, Pa., 2/074
Warner (Daniel C.) End Fd., Wilmington, 2/075
Wemyss Fdn., Wilmington, 2/076
Winer Fdn., Inc., Dover, 2/076
Wright (Margaret S.), Wilmington, 2/076
Young (George F.), Wilmington, 2/077
Zallea Fdn., Wilmington, 2/077

FLORIDA

First Filming

Adair Charities, Maitland, 1/002
Alpha Fdn. Formerly Kentucky, Vero Beach, 1/003
Ansin Fdn., Miami Beach, 1/003
Adams (Arthur F.) Fdn., Miami, 1/004
Adams (Joe A.) Fdn., Jacksonville, 1/004
Albrecht (Henry) Fdn., Naples, 1/005
Alexander (Sidney & Inez) Family Fdn., Hollywood, 1/005
Allen (Don) Fdn., Miami, 1/006
Allen (Evans C.) Fdn., Tallahassee, 1/007
Allyn Musuem of Entomology, Inc. Formerly Allyn Fdn. of Illinois, Sarasota, 1/007
American Fdn., Jacksonville, 1/008
Argo Fdn., Orlando, 1/008
Arnold Fdn., Palm Beach, 1/009
Atkins Fdn., Ft. Lauderdale, 1/010
Bach Festival Society of Winter Park, Winter Park, 1/010
Bailey (James Maxwell) Fdn., Ft. Myers, 1/011
Baking Arts Guild, Miami, 1/011
Ball (Edward) Wildlife Fdn., Jacksonville, 1/012
Meyer (Baron de Hirsch) Fdn., Miami Beach, 1/012
Bassett Fdn., Miami, 1/013
Barry (Benjamin & Frances) Family Fdn., Miami Beach, 1/014
Basic Fdn., Sarasota, 1/015
Bay Branch Fdn., Ft. Lauderdale, 1/015
Beacham (Charles R.) Fdn., Ponte Vedra Beach, 1/016
Benson (George B. & Irene) Charitable Fund, Lighthouse Point, 1/016
Berger (Joseph) Fdn., Hollywood, 1/017
Bessey (Hubert Wilbur) Scholarship Fund, West Palm Beach, 1/017
Black (F.) Fdn., Tampa, 1/018
Blank (Samuel) & Family Fdn., Miami, 1/018
Blank (Solo & Dorothy G.) Fdn., Bay Harbor Island, 1/019
Blun Fdn., Sarasota, 1/019
Bofa Fdn., Sarasota, 1/020
Bohmfalk (John Frederick) Fdn., Palm Beach, 1/020
Boka Fdn., Miami, 1/020
Bolles School Endowment Fdn. Trust, Jacksonville, 1/021
Boyce Fdn. Formerly Ohio, New Port Richey, 1/021
Bresler (Louis & Helene) Family Fdn., Miami Beach, 1/022
Briggs Family Fdn., Naples, 1/023
Briggs (John & Jane) Fdn. Formerly California, Naples, 1/023
Buckley (A. C.) Fdn., Winter Park, 1/024
Buckner (Thad & Loca Lee) Fdn., Jacksonville, 1/025
Buchwald Charitable Fdn., Miami Beach, 1/026
Cafiero (Michael J.), Sr. Fdn., Ft. Lauderdale, 1/026
Calkins (William B.) Fdn., Orlando, 1/027
Carlton Fdn., Tampa, 1/029
Carpenter (W. J.) Memorial Fdn., Sarasota, 1/029
Cary (Frances W. & Elton M.) Charitable Trust, Miami, 1/030
Charity Inc., Jacksonville, 1/031
Chastain (Robert Lee & Thomas M.) Charitable Fdn., West Palm Beach, 1/032
Childress (Francis B. & Miranda Y.) Fdn., Jacksonville, 1/032
Chiropractic Research Fdn., Clearwater, 1/033
Chope (W. E.) Fdn., Coral Gables, 1/033
Clinton Family Fdn., Miami Springs, 1/033
Coddington Fdn., Winter Park, 1/034
Coffin (Lloyd & Ruth) Charitable Fdn., Naples, 1/034
Cohen (Ruth & James) Fdn., Miami Beach, 1/035

Community Service Fdn., Largo, 1/036

Cornelius (Joseph F.) Family Fdn., Clearwater, 1/036

Coughlin (Paul H.) Fdn., West Palm Beach, 1/037

Courshon (Arthur H.) Fdn., Miami Beach, 1/038

Courshon (Jack R.) Fdn., Miami Beach, 1/038

Craig Fdn., Winter Park, 1/039

Crandall Memorial Scholarship Trust Fund, Miami, 1/039

Crane (Raymond E. & Ellen F.) Fdn., Miami, 1/040

Cruickshank Fdn., Boca Raton, 1/041

Davis (A. Darius) Family Fdn., Jacksonville, 1/041

Daugherty Fdn., Eustis, 1/042

Davis (Arthur Vining) Fdn., Miami, 1/042

Davis (Elsworth) Family Fdn., Jacksonville, 1/044

Davis (Milton Austin) Fdn., Jacksonville, 1/045

Davis (Polly) Fdn., Miami Beach, 1/046

Davis (Tine Wayne) Fdn., Jacksonville, 1/046

Davidson (Louis & Tillie) Fdn., Miami Beach, 1/047

Dearholt Fdn., Naples, 1/048

Dee (Virginia P.) Charitable Fund, Palm Beach, 1/049

Deering Fdn. for Jackson Memorial Hospital, Miami, 1/049

Delta Sigma Theta Sorority Ft. Pierce Alumni Chapter, Ft. Pierce, 1/050

Denius Fdn., Ft. Lauderdale, 1/051

Dixie Home Stores Fdn., Jacksonville, 1/051

Drusin Fdn., Miami Beach, 1/052

Dube (Harry S.) Fdn., Miami Beach, 1/052

DuBois (T. V.) Fdn. Formerly Ohio, Palm Beach, 1/053

Duda Fdn., Oviedo, 1/053

Duke Charitable Fdn., Jacksonville, 1/054

Dunspaugh - Dalton Fdn., Miami, 1/054

DuPont (Alfred I.) Fdn., Jacksonville, 1/055

Dyer (Gene T. & Evelyn M.) Fdn., Palm Beach, 1/056

Eakin (Perry V.) Trust, Riviera Beach, 1/057

Education & Research Fdn. of Florida, Jacksonville, 1/057

Elizabeth Fdn. Formerly Ohio, Ft. Lauderdale, 1/057

Evans Fdn. Formerly Ohio, Ft. Lauderdale, 1/058

Evans (J. E.) Fdn., Dade City, 1/059

Exley (Edward Wilkes) Fdn., Jacksonville, 1/059

Falk Mandel Charity Fdn., Tampa, 1/060

Feuerstein (Harold) Fdn., Miami Beach, 1/061

First National Bank of Miami Fdn., Miami, 1/061

Fitzgerald Brothers Fdn., Miami Shores, 1/062

Fitzpatrick (Roney) Fdn., Miami, 1/062

Flagler (Henry Morrison) Museum, Palm Beach, 1/062

Flanigan (Aimee M. & Horace C.) Fdn. Formerly New York, Palm Beach, 1/064

Fleigh (Bob) Fdn., Ft. Lauderdale, 1/065

Fleming Fdn., Boca Raton, 1/065

Florence & Bama Fdn., Jacksonville, 1/066

Florida Association of Architects Fdn., Coral Gables, 1/066

Florida D. H. I. A. Board, Inc., Gainesville, 1/067

Florida Plumbing & Mechanical Contractor Self Insurers Fund, Lakeland, 1/067

Forman (Hamilton M. & Blanche C.) Christian Fdn., Ft. Lauderdale, 1/067

Foulkrod Fdn., Ft. Lauderdale, 1/068

Friedman Fdn. Formerly Ohio, Ft. Lauderdale, 1/069

Friedman (Robert Taft) Fdn., Ft. Lauderdale, 1/069

Friedman (Rosalie) Fdn., Ft. Lauderdale, 1/070

Friedwald (Lynne) Fdn., Miami Beach, 1/071

Gabel Family Fund, Hollywood, 1/072

Gadsden Educational Fdn., Quincy, 1/072

Gahagan Fdn., Tampa, 1/073

Gallagher (Lorraine) Fdn., Palm Beach, 1/074

Galloway Fdn., Winter Park, 1/074

Genius (Elizabeth Morse) Fdn., Winter Park, 1/075

Gibson Fdn., Winter Park, 1/075

Goldstein (Arnold & Vivien) Fdn., Hollywood, 1/076

Goldstein (Charles) Family Fdn., Mimi, 1/076

Gordon-Goldstein Fdn., Hollywood, 1/077

Goldstein (Nat & Besse) Fdn., Hollywood, 1/078

Goldstein (Sam A. & B. B.) Family Fdn., Miami Beach, 1/078

Golub (Rachel & David) Fdn., Hallandale, 1/078

Graham (David) Fdn., Delray Beach, 1/079

Graves (Harold N. & Ferne L.) Fdn., Boca Raton, 1/079

Green (Tom) Fdn., Ft. Lauderdale, 1/080

Greenberg (Archie) Fdn., Miami Beach, 1/080

Greene Fdn., Bradenton, 1/080

Griffin (C. V.), Sr. Fdn., Howey-in-the-Hills, 1/081

Griffis Fdn., Palm Beach, 1/082

Grotto (Selama) Cerebral Palsy Endowment, Inc., St. Petersburg, 1/083

Gusman (Maurice) Fdn., Maimi, 1/084

Haven (Nina) Charitable Fdn., Stuart, 1/086

Hecht (I.) Fdn., Miami, 1/087

Hector (Louis J.) Fdn., Miami, 1/087

Heede (B. M. & Ruth C.) Fdn., Palm Beach, 1/088

Henderson (A. D.) Fdn., Pompano Beach, 1/089

Henry Fdn., Bartow, 1/089

Hirschberg (Morton R.) Fdn., Jacksonville, 1/090

Hollingsworth (J. E. & Mildred) Fdn., Palm Beach, 1/090

Hopkins (Lenora B.) Fdn., Miami, 1/091

Hopkins Research Fdn., Miami, 1/092

Houck (May K.) Fdn., Sarasota, 1/093

Howard (J. Alex) Fdn., Jacksonville, 1/094

Howard (J. Blaine) Fund for Charitable Giving, Vero Beach, 1/094

Hubbard Fdn., Orlando, 1/094

Hulitar (Mary & Philip) Fdn., West Palm Beach, 1/097

Human Research Fdn., Ft. Lauderdale, 1/097

Humphrey (David E. & Lois S.) Fdn., Jacksonville, 1/098

Hunt (James S.) Charitable and Educational Fdn., Coral Springs, 1/098

Grubb (Hunter) Fdn., Ft. Lauderdale, 1/099

Hutzler (Ida) Fund, Miami, 1/100

I. B. E. W. Electricians Local 323 Health & Welfare Fund, West Palm Beach, 1/101

International Association of Heat & Frost Insulators & Asbestos Workers Local Union #50 Vacation Fund, Coral Gables, 1/101

Jacobson (Bob) Memorial Fdn., Tampa, 1/102

Jane Fdn. Formerly Ohio, Ft. Lauderdale, 1/102

Janirve Fdn., Palm Beach, 1/102

Jasspon (William Henry) Fdn., Winter Park, 1/103

Jenkins (George W.) Fdn., Lakeland, 1/103

Jennifer Fdn. Formerly Ohio, Ft. Lauderdale, 1/104

Jennings (Alma) Fdn., Coral Gables, 1/105

Jewett Fdn., Maitland, 1/105

Johnson (Thomas E. & Agnes M.) Charitable Trust, Pompano Beach, 1/106

Johnson (Charles F.) Fdn., Palm Beach, 1/107

Johnson (D. Mead) Fdn., Palm Beach, 1/107

Johnson (Edward H.) Fdn., Ft. Lauderdale, 1/108

Johnson (Harold F.) Fund, Delray Beach, 1/108

Jones (Waldon) Fdn., Ft. Lauderdale, 1/109

Katz Fdn., Coral Gables, 1/110

Keene Family Fdn., Winter Garden, 1/110

Kelly Fdn., Clewiston, 1/110

Kennedy (Ethel M.) Charitable Fdn., Miami, 1/111

Kern (Herbert) Charitable Fdn., Miami, 1/112

Kerver (William R. & Laurie L.) Fdn., Ft. Lauderdale, 1/112

Keyes Fdn., Miami, 1/112

K-F Fdn., Bradenton, 1/114

Kipnis (Jerome & Norma) Fdn., Jacksonville, 1/115

Kipnis (Samuel) Family Fdn., Jacksonville, 1/116

Lane (James T.) Trust, Jacksonville, 1/116

Laney Charitable Fdn., Jacksonville, 1/117

Leban Fdn., Hollywood, 1/117

Lee Fdn., Orlando, 1/118

Lehigh Acres Welfare Fund, Lehigh Acres, 1/119

Leipold Fdn., Delray Beach, 1/119

L'Engle (Mary E.) Trust u/w - Orchestral Fund, Jacksonville, 1/119

Leo Fdn., Boca Raton, 1/120

Leonard Brothers Trucking Fdn., Orlando, 1/121

Levine (Jay & Mabel) Fdn., Miami Beach, 1/121

Lewis (Ghislaine & J. Norman) Fdn., Miami Beach, 1/122

Lichtenstein (Samuel & Lillian) Charitable & Educational Fdn., Miami Beach, 1/122

Liggett (R. A. & Dorothy) Fdn., Tampa, 1/122

Leonard & Lipton Charity Fdn., Miami, 1/123

Lowry (Sumter L.) Fdn., Tampa, 1/123

MacDonald (John D. & Dorothy P.) Fdn., Sarasota, 1/124

Manly (J. D.) Fdn., Leesburg, 1/125

Mann (Lola) Memorial Fund, Winter Haven, 1/125

Merrick Manor Fdn., Coral Gables, 1/126

Marcus (Joseph P. & Rosanna B.) Fdn. Formerly New York, Palm Beach, 1/126

Markowitz (Ben) Family Fdn., Miami, 1/126

Marks (Herbert), Ltd., Hollywood, 1/127

Maroon (Hoke) Fdn., West Miami, 1/127

Mary Fdn. Formerly Ohio, Ft. Lauderdale, 1/128

Massey (W. W.) Fdn., Jacksonville, 1/128

Maxcy Fdn., Frostproof, 1/129

McArthur (J. N.) Fdn., Miami, 1/130

McConnell (Robert Earll) Fdn., Palm Beach, 1/131

McDonald Benevolent Fdn., Coral Gables, 1/132

McKillips (Sara H.) Fdn., Miami, 1/133

McKim (Robert J.) Fdn. Formerly New York, Lake Wales, 1/134

McMullin (C. M.) Fdn., New Port Richey, 1/135

Mead (Edwin Budge) Scholarship Trust, Eustis, 1/135

Meatcutters & Butcher Workmen Local 282 Welfare Fund, Tampa, 1/136

Medical Research Fdn. of Dade County, Miami Beach, 1/136

Mendez (C. E.) Fdn., Tampa, 1/136

Meyer (John J.) Fdn. Formerly Massachusetts, Hollywood, 1/137

Meyer (Sidney & Zenia) Fdn., Miami, 1/137

Miller (George T.) Fdn., Jacksonville, 1/138

Miller (Jack) & Family Fdn., Miami Beach, 1/138

Moore (Coyle E.), Jr. Memoral Fdn., Tallahassee, 1/139

Morgan (Louie R. & Gertrude) Fdn., Arcadia, 1/139

Morse (Joseph Laffan) Fdn., Palm Beach, 1/140

Moseley Title Fdn., Fort Meyers, 1/140

Mote Scientific Fdn., Sarasota, 1/141

Nelson Fdn., Naples, 1/141

Newcombe Fdn., Naples, 1/142

Newtown (Helen R. Payne) Day Nursery Fdn., Sarasota, 1/142

Nichols (Perry) Fdn., Miami, 1/143

Nichelsburg (David) Fdn., Miami Beach, 1/143

Nien Tsi Fdn., Miami, 1/143

Noonan (W. J.) Fdn., Pensacola, 1/144
Open House Fdn., Miami, 1/144
Orlich (William A.) Charity Fund, Winter Haven, 1/144
O'Shea (Charles M.) Fdn., Sarasota, 1/144
Other's, Inc., Boca Raton, 1/145
Our Lords Fund Charitable Trust, Sarasota, 1/146
Overstreet Fdn., Orlando, 1/147
American Legion Memorial Scholarship Funds, West Palm Beach, 1/147
Padolf (Lou & Lillian) Fdn., Clearwater, 1/148
Parker Theatre, Inc., Ft. Lauderdale, 1/150
Parsons (Vera Davis) Fdn., Jacksonville, 1/152
Peacock Fdn., Miami, 1/153
Peebles Fdn., Palm Beach, 1/154
Phipps Florida Fdn., Tallahassee, 1/154
Phipps (Michael G.) Fdn., Palm Beach, 1/155
Pinellas Fdn., Tallahassee, 1/156
Plumer (Richard) Fdn., Miami, 1/157
Polasek (Albin) Fdn., Winter Park, 1/158
Pollak (Albert) Fdn., Miami Beach, 1/158
Poynter Fund, St. Petersburg, 1/159
Price Fdn., Ormond Beach, 1/160
Price Fdn., Sarasota, 1/161
Price Fdn., Ormond Beach, 1/161
Prior (Frank O.) Fdn., Palm Beach, 1/162
Purple Heart Fdn., Jacksonville, 1/162
Radebaugh, Orlando, 1/162
Rahall (Ferris E. & Victoria B.) Fdn., St. Petersburg, 1/163
R-C Motor Lines Fdn., Jacksonville, 1/164
Redfield (Charles E.) Fdn., Coral Gables, 1/165
Redstone (Michael) Charitable Trust, Bal Harbour, 1/166
Reinhold (Paul E. & Ida Klare) Fdn., Jacksonville, 1/166
Reuter Fdn., Palm Beach, 1/167
Rex Fdn., Orlando, 1/167
Reynolds Fdn., Pompano Beach, 1/168
Reynolds (Janet R. & Wiley R.), Jr. Fdn., Palm Beach, 1/168
Merited Riegel Charitable Trust, Delray Beach, 1/169
River Branch Fdn., Jacksonville, 1/169
Roberts (George Scarboro) Fdn., Miami, 1/170
Robinson (Donald H. & Margaret R.) Fdn., Naples, 1/171
Rosenfelt Fdn., Tallahassee, 1/171
Rothman (Maurice A.) Fdn., St. Petersburg, 1/172
Rountree Fdn., Sarasota, 1/173
Russell Fdn. of Jacksonville, Jacksonville, 1/174
Ryder Fdn., Miami, 1/175
Salhaven Fdn., Jupiter, 1/175
Sanson Fdn., Miami, 1/175
Sarasota Garden Club, Inc. Endowment Fund, Sarasota, 1/177
Saunders Fdn., Tampa, 1/177
Schechter (Barbara M.) Family Fdn., Miami, 1/178
Schizophrenia Biological Research Fdn., Miami, 1/178
Schramm (Edward R.) Fdn., Clearwater, 1/179
Schultz Fdn., Jacksonville, 1/179
Selig Fdn., Miami, 1/180
Broad (Shepard) Fdn., Miami Beach, 1/181
Shuler (John & Catherine) Charitable Trust, Longboat Key, 1/182
Simone (Harry) Fdn., Miami Beach, 1/183
Singer Family Fdn., Miami, 1/183
Sisler (Mary) Fdn., Palm Beach, 1/184
Smith (A. J. & M. R.) Fdn., Naples, 1/184
Soref (Samuel M.) Chartiable Trust, Ft. Lauderdale, 1/185
Smith (McGregor) Fdn., Miami, 1/186
Soref (Samuel M.) Charitable Trust, Ft. Lauderdale, 1/187
Sorey (Vincent) Music Fdn., Miami Beach, 1/189
Southern Fruit Distributors Fund, Orlando, 1/189
St. Denis Fdn., Jacksonville, 1/189
Starck Fdn., Seminole, 1/190

Stein Family Fdn., Jacksonville, 1/191
Steinberg Fdn., Miami, 1/191
Storer (George B.) Fdn., Miami Beach, 1/193
Sugarman (Joseph & Charlotte) Charitable Fdn., Miami, 1/194
Sutherland Fdn., Naples, 1/194
Suwannee River Area Council, Boy Scouts of America Trust, Tallahassee, 1/195
Sweeney (Catherine Hauberg) Charitable Trust, Miami, 1/195
Sweet Fdn., Winter Haven, 1/195
Swenson Fdn., Miami, 1/195
Swisher (Carl S.) Fdn., Jacksonville, 1/196
Tamp Court 89 Royal Order of Jesters, Tampaa, 1/198
Taylor (Harry Benjamin) Trust, Miami, 1/198
Taylor (Jack) Fdn., Miami, 1/198
Telford Fdn., Naples, 1/199
Thomas (Bert L.) Fdn., Jacksonville, 1/200
Thompson Fdn., Clearwater, 1/200
Titusville Chapter No. 6 O. E. S., Titusville, 1/201
Toor (H. O.) Fdn., Palm Beach, 1/201
Towey (James P.) Fdn., St. Petersburg, 1/202
Travers Fdn., Naples, 1/203
Traylor (W. LeRoy and Elizabeth) Fdn., Orlando, 1/203
Triangle Fdn., Clearwater, 1/203
Truesdell (Leonard C. & Maudine) Fdn., Reddick, 1/205
Tucker Fdn., Winter Park, 1/205
United Fdns., Jacksonville, 1/206
United Fund of Greater Tampa, Tampa, 1/207
Van Hoy (James H. & Hilda A.) Education Fdn., Jacksonville, 1/207
Vero Beach Fdn. for The Elderly, Palm Beach, 1/208
Veterans of World War I-Miami Barracks 732, Miami, 1/208
Wagner Fund Trust, Miami, 1/209
Ward (William F.) Fdn., Avon Park, 1/210
Wasmuth (Thomas C.) Fdn., Miami Beach, 1/210
Weinkle (Carl) and Family Fdn., Miami Beach, 1/210
Wellhouse (Rhoda & Louis), Jr. Fdn., Jacksonville, 1/212
Wentworth Fdn., Clearwater, 1/212
Whatley Fdn., Jacksonville, 1/212
Whitfield Fdn., Orlando, 1/213
Wicklanding Fdn., Punta Gorda, 1/214
Wien (Leonard A.) Charity Fdn., Miami Springs, 1/214
Wilderman Memorial Fdn., Tampa, 1/214
Williams (Charles J.) Fdn., Jacksonville, 1/215
Winer (Samuel & Evelyn) Charitable Trust, Miami Beach, 1/216
Winn Fdn. Trust, Vero Beach, 1/217
Winn-Dixie Stores Fdn., Jacksonville, 1/217
Winston (James H.) Fdn., Jacksonville, 1/222
Wiseheart Fdn., Miami, 1/223
Wolfson Family Fdn., Jacksonville, 1/223
Wolfson (Mitchell) Family Fdn., Miami, 1/225
Wolfson (Richard F.) Family Fdn., Coral Gables, 1/225
Wolfson (Loulyfran) Fdn., Miami, 1/225
Women's Club of Winter Haven Scholarship Fund, Winter Haven, 1/226
Wood (Gar) Fdn., Miami, 1/226
Wright (Rev. Robert H.), III Trust, Jacksonville, 1/227
Yardley Memorial Trust, Winter Haven, 1/228
Zivian (Max J. & Rose) Fdn., Palm Beach, 1/228

Second Filming

Alpha Xi Delta Building Corporation, Tallahassee, 2/001
Ambassadors of Friendship, Miami, 2/001
Andersen (Martin & Gracia) Fdn., Orlando, 2/002
Avalone (Ronnie) Evangelistic Association, Delray Beach, 2/003
Bacon (Edward A.) Fdn., Coral Gables, 2/004
Bahia Temple Widows Fund, Orlando, 2/005

Barnett (Gordon J.) Fdn. Trust, Orlando, 2/005
Bateman (Will Paul) Scholarship Fund, Miami, 2/006
Beaux Arts of the Joe & Emily Lowe Gallery of the University of Miami, Coral Gables, 2/007
Berachah Colony, Ocala, 2/008
Bethelstone Fdn., Delray Beach, 2/008
Big Brothers of Greater Jacksonville, Jacksonville, 2/008
Biscayne Fdn., Miami, 2/010
Bloom (Sol W. & Josepha K.) Fdn., Hollywood, 2/011
Boalt Fdn., Palm Beach, 2/011
Boca Raton Rotary Fund, Boca Raton, 2/013
Boley (Bessie) Fdn. Trust, St. Petersburg, 2/013
Borns (Harry) Trust, Bradenton, 2/014
Bradshaw (Charles H. & Ruth D.) Fdn., Boca Raton, 2/015
Brown Charity Fdn., Miami Beach, 2/017
Brown (Victor & Lillian) Fdn., Miami, 2/018
Bultman (Fred M.) Memorial Fund, Jacksonville, 2/018
Carlson Fdn., Pompano Beach, 2/019
Cathedral Fdn., Orlando, 2/019
Chapin Fdn., Palm Beach, 2/019
Chapman (Alvah H. & Wyline P.) Fdn., Miami, 2/020
Children's Fdn. of Lake Wales, Lake Wales, 2/020
Coleman (Ray K. & P.N.) Fdn., Jacksonville, 2/021
Conn Memorial Fdn., Tampa, 2/022
Conquistadore Historical Fdn., Bradenton, 2/023
Dade County Bar Association Educational Fdn., Miami, 2/024
De Peyster Fdn., Palm Beach, 2/024
Dermer Fdn., Miami, 2/025
Diehl Fdn. for Shriners' Hospitals, Miami, 2/025
Donnell - Kay Fdn., Palm Beach, 2/026
duPont (Alfred I.) Awards Fdn., Jacksonville, 2/027
Eidlitz (Dorothy Meigs) Fdn., Winter Park, 2/028
Einstein (Albert & Birdie) Fund, Hollywood, 2/029
Eisenberg Fdn., Miami, 2/029
Elliott (Frances Porter) Fdn., Miami, 2/030
Emphysema Fdn. of the U.S.A., Hollywood, 2/030
Ensworth Charitable Fdn., Hartford, Conn., 2/031
Epstein (Samuel P.) Fdn. Formerly New York, Palm Beach, 2/031
Falk (George & Mildred) Charitable Trust, Palm Beach, 2/031
Farris (Victor W.) Fdn., Palm Beach, 2/032
Feamster (Maude Inez) Fdn. Trust, St. Petersburg, 2/032
Fellows (J. Hugh & Earle W.) Memorial Fund, Pensacola, 2/033
Florida Charities Fdn., Orlando, 2/035
Florida Citrus Research Fdn., Lakeland, 2/037
Frantz Fdn. for Lighthouse for the Blind, Miami, 2/037
Geiger (Ruth & August) Charity Fdn., Bal Harbour, 2/038
Golden Gate Community Theatre, Naples, 2/039
Goldstein (Arnold & Vivien) Fdn., Hollywood, 2/040
Good Will Trust, Nokomis, 2/040
Graham Fdn., Miami Lakes, 2/041
Graham (Letitia V.) Testamentary Trust, Tampa, 2/041
Greater Miami Progress Fdn., Miami, 2/043
Grundwerg Fdn., Miami, 2/043
Harders Fdn., Panama City, 2/044
Hear Fdn. of Florida, North Miami Beach, 2/044
Herbert (Jerome & Grace) Fdn., Hollywood, 2/045

Herskowitz (Bernard J.) Fdn., Miami Beach, 2/045
Hoffman (Carl T.) Fdn., Miami, 2/046
Holiday Isles Elks #1912, Madeira Beach, 2/047
Holloway (Jack) Fdn., Orlando, 2/047
Hotchkiss Fdn., Hallandale, 2/047
Houck (May K.) Fdn., Sarasota, 2/048
Hubbell Scholarship Fdn., Miami, 2/048
Hughey Fdn., Tampa, 2/049
Grubb (Hunter) Fdn., Ft. Lauderdale, 2/050
International Fdn. for Gifted Children, Delray Beach, 2/050
International Medical Fdn., Jacksonville, 2/050
Johnson (Julian E. & Jean W.) Family Charitable Fdn., Jacksonville, 2/052
Kanter (Morris & Beatrice) Family Fdn., Miami Beach, 2/053
Kearns (William P. & Rosemarie) Fdn., North Palm Beach, 2/054
Keller Fdn., Miami Beach, 2/054
Keys Community Hospital Fdn., Islamorada, 2/055
Kramer (Harry & Fannie) Fdn., Fort Lauderdale, 2/055
Kugelman (Sylvia K. & Edgar M.) Fdn., Jacksonville, 2/057
Lafferty Family Fdn., Miami Shores, 2/057
Land (Harry L.) Trust, Bradenton, 2/058
Las Olas Fdn., Fort Lauderdale, 2/059
Lauffer (Charles A.) Trust, St. Petersburg, 2/060
Lee (John M.) Fdn., Pensacola, 2/061
Lee (Louis F. & Selma) Fdn., Sarasota, 2/061
Levinson (Jo Ellen) Fdn., Miami, 2/062
Levowich Fdn., Miami, 2/063
Longacre Fdn., Coral Gables, 2/064
Longden (Ralph L.) Scholarship Fund Fdn., South Miami, 2/064
Lord (F. & W.) Fdn., Lakeland, 2/065
Luby Fdn., Miami, 2/066
Lyons (Lena) Baptist Mission Fdn., Pompano Beach, 2/066
Manasota Medical Fdn., Sarasota, 2/066
Marbito Fdn., Jacksonville, 2/066
McArthur (Charles) Fdn., Okeechobee, 2/067
McCann (Henry C.) Trust, St. Petersburg, 2/068
McCrea Fdn., Miami, 2/068
McGeary Fdn., Miami, 2/069
McKaig Educational Fdn., Sarasota, 2/070
Meeks (James Edward), Jr. Memorial Scholarship Fund, La Belle, 2/070
Meltzer (Herman & David) Fdn., Palm Beach, 2/071
Metal Industries Fdn., Clearwater, 2/071
Miami Lions Club Fdn., Miami, 2/071
Midnight Cry Publishing Corporation, Tequesta, 2/072
Migrant Services Fdn., Miami, 2/072
Mills, Charles Memorial Fdn., Miami, 2/073
Moore (Gene & Margaret) Research Fdn., Titusville, 2/074
Morris (Allen) Fdn., Miami, 2/074
National Dividend Fdn., Palm Beach, 2/076
National Fdn. for Highway Safety, Clearwater, 2/076
Norman (Harold & Mirian) Fdn., Lake Wales, 2/076
Novack (Ben) Fdn., Miami Beach, 2/077
Organized Migrants in Community Action, Homestead, 2/078
Ormond War Memorial Art Gallery, Ormond Beach, 2/079
Pace Fdn., Orange Park, 2/079
Paddock (Jerome & Mildred) Fdn., Sarasota, 2/080
Palm Beach County Scholarship Fdn., West Palm Beach, 2/080
Phillips (A.P.), Jr. Fdn., Orlando, 2/082
Phipps Florida Fdn., Tallahassee, 2/083
Popick (Ruth & Jack) Fdn., Miami Beach, 2/084
Porter Fdn., Miami, 2/084
Porter (Nathan) Trust, Kissimmee, 2/084
Posner (Victor) Fdn., Miami Beach, 2/085

Princeton University Educational Fdn., Clearwater, 2/086
Prosser Fdn., Pompano Beach, 2/087
Rahall (Sam G.) Fdn., St. Petersburg, 2/088
Rainforth Fdn., Coral Gables, 2/088
Rinker Companies Fdn., West Palm Beach, 2/091
Rodeheaver - Westbury Trust for Boys, Jacksonville, 2/092
Rosenberg (William J. & Tina) Fdn., Miami, 2/092
Rosenthal (Edwin M. & Ester L.) Fdn., North Miami Beach, 2/093
Rost (Libby) Charitable Trust, Miami, 2/094
Rotary Club of St. Petersburg Trust Fund, St. Petersburg, 2/095
Rothkopf Fdn., Hollywood, 2/096
Rowntree (Leonard) Fund, Coral Gables, 2/097
Russack Family Fdn., Miami Beach, 2/098
Ruwitch (Lee) Fdn., Miami, 2/098
Sabel Fdn., Jacksonville, 2/099
Sadler (Luke) Fdn., Jacksonville, 2/099
Saferian (Paul) Trust, St. Petersburg, 2/100
St. Augustine Restoration, St. Augustine, 2/100
Sarasota County Educational Fdn., Sarasota, 2/101
Sapiro (Samuel T.) Fdn., Coral Gables, 2/101
Sargent (Harry J.) Trust, St. Petersburg, 2/101
Scadron (Irene Haas) Memorial Educational Fund, Quincy, 2/102
Schippmann (J.W.) Fdn., Jacksonville, 2/103
Schuster Fdn., Surfside, 2/104
Scottish Rite Fdn. of Tampa, Tampa, 2/104
Seacamp Association, Miami, 2/105
Selby (William G. & Marie) Fdn., Sarasota, 2/106
Shaw (Sarah & Herman L.) Fdn., Miami, 2/107
Slater Fdn., Naples, 2/108
Smith (Buckingham) Benevolent Association, St. Augustine, 2/108
Smith (F. Burton) Fdn., Orlando, 2/109
Smith (Paul) Fdn., Tampa, 2/109
Soule (Charles) Fdn., Pensacola, 2/110
South Florida Air Academy, Plantation, 2/111
Stuart (Edward C.) Fdn., Bartow, 2/111
Students Aid Fdn., Miami, 2/112
Thomas (Dorothy) Fd., Tampa, 2/114
Timoner Family Fdn., Miami, 2/115
Titusville Chapter No. 6 O.E.S., Titusville, 2/116
Tisch Family Fdn., Bal Harbour, 2/116
Tobin (Ben) Fdn., Hollywood, 2/118
Trismen Fdn., Winter Park, 2/118
Berkowitz (H.C.) Trust, North Miami, 2/118
Doyle (John) Trust, St. Petersburg, 2/119
Ungar - Abess Fdn., Miami, 2/119
Vance (L. Alexander & Jane K.) Library Acquisition Fdn., Sarasota, 2/120
Versaggi Brothers Fdn., St. Augustine, 2/121
Ward (Harry E.) Fdn., Palm Beach, 2/121
W C K T Fdn., Miami, 2/122
Weber (Kate C.) Memorial Trust, Jacksonville, 2/123
Weymer Fdn., Fort Lauderdale, 2/124
White Belt Fdn., Miami, 2/124
Willey (Tom) Fdn., Winter Park, 2/124
Winter Haven Hospital Charity Fund, Winter Haven, 2/125
Woman's Club Charitable & Educational Fdn., Jacksonville, 2/126
Yacht Club, Fort Lauderdale, 2/126
Zwerner (Carl R. & Sally T.) Fdn., Miami, 2/126
Young Men's Christian Association of Sarasota, Sarasota, 2/126

GEORGIA

First Filming

Abrams (A.R.) Family Fdn., Atlanta, 1/001
Achenbach Fdn., Vidalia, 1/002
Adelphean Fdn., Atlanta, 1/004
Alpha Alpha Delta Educational Fdn., Athens, 1/005
American Institute of Architects (North Georgia Chapter), Atlanta, 1/005
Anderson (Peyton) Fdn., Macon, 1/005
Ani Employees One-Pledge-Plan Fund, Atlanta, 1/006
Anncox Fdn., Atlanta, 1/006
Anthony (William A. & Jospeh T.) Memorial Fund, Columbus, 1/007
Arnold Fund, Atlanta, 1/007
A.T.H., Thomaston, 1/008
Atlanta Claims Association, Atlanta, 1/009
Atlanta Steel Fdn., Atlanta, 1/009
Augusta National Fdn., Augusta, 1/010
Balfour Fdn., Thomasville, 1/011
Banks (W.N.) Fdn., Newnan, 1/011
Barge Fdn., Atlanta, 1/012
Bell (C.V.) Fdn., Augusta, 1/013
Bellman (Katherine & Russell) Fdn., Atlanta, 1/014
Benefit Association, Columbus, 1/015
Bentley (Kate F.) Trust Fund, Valdosta, 1/015
Bernard (Guy T.) Tumor Clinic, Augusta, 1/016
Berry Fdn., Atlanta, 1/016
Bibb Benevolent Fund, Macon, 1/017
Bono-Yellin Fdn., Savanah, 1/018
Bowe (William F. & Dorothea A.) Trust, Augusta, 1/019
Bowen (R.A.) Trust, Macon, 1/020
Bradley (W.C. & Sarah H.) Fdn., Columbus, 1/020
Bradshaw (Frank B.), Jr. Fdn., Atlanta, 1/023
Brown (George M.) & Corrie Hoyt Brown Fund of Second Ponce de Leon Baptist Chruch, Atlanta, 1/023
Brown (Mary) Fund, Atlanta, 1/024
Brown (Salley Eugenia) Fund of Second Ponce de Leon Baptist Church, Atlanta, 1/025
Callaway (Fuller E.) Fdn., La Grange, 1/026
Cannon (Richard & Edna) Fdn., Atlanta, 1/028
Carmichael (James V.) Fdn., Marietta, 1/029
Castleway Fdn., Atlanta, 1/030
Cates (Alvin B.) Fdn., Atlanta, 1/030
Center (Dave) Fdn., Atlanta, 1/031
Chanin (Henry & Herma) Fdn., Atlanta, 1/032
Cherokee Fdn., Thomasville, 1/032
Christian Arms, Atlanta, 1/033
Christian Projects Fdn., Atlanta, 1/034
Christian Service, Augusta, 1/034
Citizens and Southern Fund, Atlanta, 1/034
Clifton (Walter) Fdn., Atlanta, 1/036
Cobb (Cully A. & Lois D.) Trust Fund, Atlanta, 1/037
Cobb (George S. & Edna L.) Fdn., La Grange, 1/037
Coggins Granite Welfare Fdn., Elberton, 1/039
Colonial Stores Fdn., Atlanta, 1/040
Columbus Bank & Trust Company Charitable Trust, Columbus, 1/041
Commins (Randolph W.) & Dorothy S. Commins Fdn., Atlanta, 1/041
Connally (Mary V.) Fund of the Second Baptist Church, Atlanta, 1/042
Community Welfare Association, Moultrie, 1/042
Cooper Fdn., Atlanta, 1/043
Courts Fdn., Atlanta, 1/043
Cox (James M.) Fdn. of Georgia, Atlanta, 1/044
Crusaders Fund, Decatur, 1/046
Cuba Fdn., Atlanta, 1/046
Davenport (William L.), Jr. Fdn., Atlanta, 1/047
Davis (Lucy Whatley) Trust Fund, Columbus, 1/047

Davidson (Florre Jo & Charles L.) Fdn., Lithonia, 1/048

Delta Air Lines Fdn., Atlanta, 1/048

Derst (John & Emma) Fdn., Savannah, 1/049

Diamond (Bernard F.) Fdn., Savannah, 1/049

Dobbs (Helen & Howard) Fdn., Atlanta, 1/050

Dodson (James Glenwell & Clara May) Fdn., Atlanta, 1/050

Dorminy (John Henry) Fdn., Fitzgerald, 1/051

Drawdy (Sherman & Fairy H.) Family Charitable Trust, Augusta, 1/052

Dubrof (Jerry) Fdn., Atlanta, 1/053

DuVall Fdn., Atlanta, 1/053

Dwoskin (Harry & Mary) Fdn., Atlanta, 1/054

Dyess (Maurice E.) Trust, Augusta, 1/054

Ellis (Harriet W. & Edward P.) Trust, Atlanta, 1/055

Estroff (Naomi P. & Maxwell J.) Fdn., Augusta, 1/056

Evans (Lettie Pate) Fdn., Atlanta, 1/056

Felchlin (Frank Lyons) Fdn., Athens, 1/059

Ferst (M. & H.) Fdn., Atlanta, 1/059

Ferst (R. & J.) Fdn., Atlanta, 1/060

Ferst (Sylvia M. & Frank W.) Fdn., Atlanta, 1/060

Fink (Libby P.) Fdn., Augusta, 1/061

Foundation of the Civitan Club of Atlanta, Atlanta, 1/061

Fox (Alfred) Fdn., Atlanta, 1/061

Fox (Lawrence) Fdn., Atlanta, 1/062

Cocke (Emory, Frances & Jane) Fdn., Atlanta, 1/063

Frank (Lawrence M.) Fdn., Atlanta, 1/064

Frank (Moses) Testamentary Trust, Atlanta, 1/065

Frank (Sarah M.) Trust for the Blind, Atlanta, 1/065

Fraser (Carlyle) Employees Benefit Fund, Atlanta, 1/066

Fraser (Carlyle) Fdn., Atlanta, 1/068

Fraser (Isobel A.) Fdn., Atlanta, 1/068

Freeman Fdn., Newnan, 1/069

Freeman (Sam P.) Fdn., Atlanta, 1/069

Friedman Charitable Trust, Brunswick, 1/070

Friedman (B.I.) Fdn., Savannah, 1/070

Hitch (Harry Fulenwider) Trust, Savannah, 1/071

Fulton County Medical Society Fdn., Atlanta, 1/071

Fulton Charitable Trust, Atlanta, 1/072

Garson Fund, Atlanta, 1/073

Georgia Youth Fdn., Albany, 1/073

Ginsberg (Paul) Fdn., Atlanta, 1/074

Green (Hix) Fdn., Atlanta, 1/074

Griggs (A.C.) Scholarship Fdn., Augusta, 1/074

Haas (Elliot I.) Fdn., Atlanta, 1/075

Habersham Mills Fdn., Habersham, 1/075

Hardaway Fdn., Columbus, 1/077

Harland (John H.) Company Fdn., Atlanta, 1/077

Harris (Arthur) Fdn., Atlanta, 1/080

Harrison (Dr. J. Harold) Fdn., Atlanta, 1/081

Haverty (Mary E.) Fdn., Atlanta, 1/081

Hay (P.L.) Fdn., Macon, 1/083

Herndon (Alonzo F. & Norris B.) Fdn., Atlanta, 1/083

Hightower (Julian T.), Thomaston, 1/084

Hofmayer (Fannie & Louis) Trust, Atlanta, 1/085

Hollis Fdn., Columbus, 1/087

Honey (William E.) Fdn., Atlanta, 1/087

Jamison Fdn., Doraville, 1/088

Johnson (Eleanor Dallis Dunson) Fdn., La Grange, 1/088

Johnson (George S.) Fdn., La Grange, 1/088

Kaufmann Fdn., Atlanta, 1/089

Kercher Fdn., Atlanta, 1/089

Kessler Fdn., Atlanta, 1/090

Kinnett Fdn., Columbus, 1/091

Kinnett (F.M.) Fdn., Atlanta, 1/091

Laird Fdn., Atlanta, 1/092

Lane (Mills B.) Research Fdn. in Banking at the University of Georgia, Atlanta, 1/093

Lane (Mills B.) Lecturship in Finance and Banking Management at Georgia Institute of Technology, Atlanta, 1/094

Lane (Mills B.) Professional Chair in Finance & Banking at Atlanta University, Atlanta, 1/094

Lane (Mills Bee) Chair of Banking & Finance at Georgia State University, Atlanta, 1/095

Lane (Mills Bee) Memorial Fdn., Savannah, 1/097

Lane (Mills B.) Lecturship in Finance & Banking at Emory University, Atlanta, 1/097

Lanier (Helen S.) Fdn., Atlanta, 1/098

Lewis (J.C.) Fdn., Savannah, 1/099

Libowsky (Esther & Irving) Fdn., Atlanta, 1/100

Lipscomb (Blanche) Fdn., Atlanta, 1/101

Love (Albert) Fdn., Atlanta, 1/102

Lane (Malvern) Fdn., Augusta, 1/102

Markham (William) Fund, Atlanta, 1/102

Marks (Belle S.) Fdn., Augusta, 1/103

Markwalter (Agnes & Victor) Fdn., Augusta, 1/103

Massell (Ben J.) Fdn., Atlanta, 1/104

Maxwell (Bertram) Charitable Trust, Augusta, 1/105

Maxwell (Gilbert M.) Trust, Augusta, 1/105

Maxwell (Robert J. & Annie V.) Family Charitable Trust, Augusta, 1/106

McCamish Fdn., Atlanta, 1/106

McCurdy Fdn., Decatur, 1/106

McCutchen (Joe & Christine) Fdn., Dalton, 1/107

McKellar (Ella Hand) Trust Fund, Tifton, 1/107

McNeely Fdn., Toccoa, 1/107

Meyer Family Fdn., Atlanta, 1/108

Mingledorff (Walter L.) Fdn., Savannah, 1/109

Mix (Charles L.) Memorial Fund, Americus, 1/109

Monroe-Bashlor Education Fdn., Savannah, 1/110

Montgomery (Jeannette & Lafayette) Fdn., Atlanta, 1/110

Moore (James Starr) Memorial Fdn., Atlanta, 1/111

Morgan (Fred) Scholarship Fund, Atlanta, 1/112

Mothner Fdn., Augusta, 1/112

Muscogee Mills Fdn., Columbus, 1/112

Neighbors Fund, West Point, 1/113

Newnan Cotton Mills Fdn., Newnan, 1/114

Tuttle-Newton Home, Augusta, 1/115

Nixon (Lucy Lanier) Fdn., La Grange, 1/116

Nochumson (Ira N.) Fdn., Atlanta, 1/116

Nunn (R.J.) Trust Fund, Savannah, 1/117

Orkin (Sanford H.) Fdn., Atlanta, 1/117

Owens (Anne Grant) Fdn., Atlanta, 1/118

Owens (Frank C.) Fdn., Atlanta, 1/118

Oxford Fdn., Atlanta, 1/119

Parker Fdn., Claxton, 1/120

Patterson-Barclay Memorial Fdn., Atlanta, 1/120

Pattillo Fdn., Decatur, 1/121

Penningroth Fdn., Atlanta, 1/122

Phillips-Shoop-Kirtley Fdn., Albany, 1/123

Pirrung Fdn., Bainbridge, 1/124

Plantation Pipe Line Fdn., Atlanta, 1/124

Poer-Underwood-Hinton Fdn., Atlanta, 1/128

Poole (James P. & Dorothy G.) Fdn., Atlanta, 1/128

Porter (James Hyde) Testamentary Trust, Macon, 1/129

Porter (Louisa) Fdn., Savannah, 1/129

Porter (Oliver S.) Fund, Macon, 1/130

Ray (H.G.), Sr. Fdn., Atlanta, 1/131

Regenstein Fdn., Atlanta, 1/131

Reinsch Fdn., Atlanta, 1/132

Relief Fdn., Pine Mountain, 1/133

Rich Fdn., Atlanta, 1/134

Robert Fdn., Atlanta, 1/135

Robinson (Josephine C.) Fdn., Atlanta, 1/136

Rochfort Fdn., Madison, 1/138

Roddenbery Fdn., Cairo, 1/138

Roddenbery Memorial Library Building Maintenance Trust Fund, Cairo, 1/138

Rollins (O. Wayne) Fdn., Atlanta, 1/139

Rosenzweig Fdn., Savannah, 1/139

Rothman (Max) Fdn., Dalton, 1/139

Rothschild (Dora G. & Jac H.) Fdn., Columbus, 1/140

Sandler (Nat) Fdn., Atlanta, 1/141

Savannah Benevolent Association, Savannah, 1/142

Schwob (Ruth Schutzbank) Music Fund, Columbus, 1/143

Schwarz (Herman & Greta) Fdn., Atlanta, 1/143

Scott (William Fred), Sr. Memorial Trust, Thomasville, 1/143

Sears (Claud A.) Fdn., Cols, 1/144

Selig Fdn., Atlanta, 1/144

Shapiro Family Fdn., Atlanta, 1/145

Sheehan Fdn., Augusta, 1/145

Sherman (Louis & Mary L.) Trust, Atlanta, 1/146

Ships of the Sea, Savannah, 1/146

Short Cardiovascular Research Fdn., Augusta, 1/147

Silver Fdn., Augusta, 1/147

Simowitz (Hannah E.) Fdn., Augusta, 1/148

Smith (Aquilla) Fdn., Augusta, 1/148

Smith (C.C.), Jr. Fdn., Moultrie, 1/149

Smith (Hal L. & Julia T.) Fdn., Atlanta, 1/149

Smith (Jack C.) Fdn., Moultrie, 1/150

Smith (Jeannette Early) Fdn., Moultrie, 1/151

Smith (Rhett J.) Fdn., Moultrie, 1/151

Southern G.F. Fdn., Atlanta, 1/152

Southern Orthopedic Research Fdn., Douglasville, 1/153

Southern Regional Council, Atlanta, 1/153

Southern Tennis Patrons Fdn., Atlanta, 1/154

Sparks (George McIntosh) Scholarship Fund, Atlanta, 1/154

Stanton Fdn., Augusta, 1/155

Star Fdn., Tallapoosa, 1/155

Steiner (Albert), Estate of, Atlanta, 1/156

Swift Spinning Mills Fdn., Columbus, 1/158

Tabaka Fdn., Atlanta, 1/158

Taiwan-American Educational Trust, Macon, 1/159

Taylor (Esther K.) Fdn., Atlanta, 1/159

Terhune (Cornelius) Memorial Fund, Rome, 1/161

Timmers Fdn., Atlanta, 1/161

Tippie (Henry B.) Fdn., Atlanta, 1/161

Tomlinson (Kate & Elwyn) Fdn., Atlanta, 1/162

Trebor Fdn., Atlanta, 1/163

Trend Fdn., Rome, 1/164

Trotter Fdn., La Grange, 1/165

United Daughters of the Confederacy u/a with Mrs. C.E. Bulloch, Atlanta, 1/165

Campbell (John Bulow) Fdn., u/w, Atlanta, 1/166

Camp Younts Fdn. u/a Mrs. Willia Camp Younts & Charles R. Younts, Atlanta, 1/169

Cobb (Ty) Educational Fund, u/a, Atlanta, 1/170

Conklin (Anne Mays) & Charles Ashmore Conklin Trust u/a Daniel E. Conklin, Atlanta, 1/171

English (Florence C. & Harry L.) Memorial Fund u/w Mrs. Florence Cruft English, Atlanta, 1/171

Fine Arts Fdn. of Atlanta, Atlanta, 1/173

Georgia Baptist Hospital & Georgia Baptist Children's Home u/w Hugh R. Todd, Atlanta, 1/173

Glenn (Wilbur Fisk) Memorial Fdn., Atlanta, 1/174

Greene-Sawtell Fdn. u/a with Forest Greene & Mrs. Alice Greene Sawtell, Atlanta, 1/174

Hall (John T.) Student Loan Fund, u/w, Atlanta, 1/175

Hillyer Memorial Fund u/a with Second Ponce de Leon Baptist Church and Mrs. Edith Carter Hillyer, Atlanta, 1/178

Hohenberg (Gertrude & Irving) Fdn. u/a Miss Bertie Hohenberg, Atlanta, 1/178
Howell Fund, u/a, Atlanta, 1/179
Hunt (Robert G.) u/w, Atlanta, 1/180
Hunt (Agnes B.) Trust u/w Robert G. Hunt, Atlanta, 1/180
Jones (Sallie Maude) u/w Asbury Seminary et al, Atlanta, 1/181
King (Clyde L.) Sr., Atlanta, 1/182
Kuhrt (Mary Ryan & Henry G.) Fdn. u/a Henry G. Kuhrt, Atlanta, 1/182
Lampkin (Lois & Lucy) Fdn. u/a Lucy Phelps Lampkin, Atlanta, 1/182
Lanier Brothers Fdn. u/a with Sartain Lanier, J. Hicks Lanier & John Reese Lanier, Atlanta, 1/183
Marshall (Mattie H.) Fdn. u/a with Mrs. Mattie H. Marshall, Atlanta, 1/184
McRae (Floyd W.) u/a with Eleven-Eleven Fund, Atlanta, 1/185
McBurney (Helen Sterrett) Fdn. u/w Helen Sterrett McBurney, Atlanta, 1/186
Moss (Sarah H.) Fellowship Fund u/w Sarah H. Moss, Atlanta, 1/187
Murphy (Katherine John) Fdn., u/a, Atlanta, 1/187
Pitts (W.I.H. & Lula E.) Fdn. u/w W.I.H. Pitts, Atlanta, 1/188
Porter (James Hyde), u/w, Macon, 1/189
Rhodes (J.D.) u/w Trust for Charitable Bequests, Atlanta, 1/189
Rountree (Minnie Lewis) Charitable Trust u/a with Samuel S. Rountree, Atlanta, 1/190
Godfrey (J.E.), Estate of, Atlanta, 1/190
Trust Company of Georgia Fdn. u/a with Trust Company of Georgia, Atlanta, 1/190
Wardlaw (Gertrude & William C.) Fund u/a, Atlanta, 1/191
Warren (Virgil P.) Fdn. u/a with Virgil P. Warren, Atlanta, 1/192
Woolford (Thomas Guy) Charitable Trust of Will of U/I, Atlanta, 1/194
Woolford (Mrs. Frances Tremere), One of Will of U/I, Atlanta, 1/194
Tull (J.M.) Fdn., Atlanta, 1/195
Turner (D.A. & Elizabeth B.) Fdn., Columbus, 1/197
Turner (W.B. & Sue T.) Fdn., Columbus, 1/197
Union Manufacturing Co. Fdn., Union Point, 1/199
Walker (Charles M.) Fdn., Monroe, 1/200
Warren (William C.), Jr. Fdn., Atlanta, 1/200
Wasden Fdn., Millen, 1/201
Watts (Purvie B. & Margaret Y.) Fdn., Augusta, 1/201
West Fdn., Atlanta, 1/201
Whitehead (Joseph B.) Fdn., Atlanta, 1/202
Whitehead (Lettie Pate) Fdn., Atlanta, 1/2-5
Williamson (Charles H.) Memorial Scholarship, Macon, 1/207
Woodruff (Emily & Ernest) Fdn., Atlanta, 1/207
Yonan Codex Fdn., Decatur, 1/209
Zimmerman (Jeannette & Ben H.) Fdn., Atlanta, 1/209
Wormsloe Fdn., Savannah, 1/210
Zimmerman (Lila & Jerome) Fdn., Atlanta, 1/210

Second Filming

Abrams Fdn., Atlanta, 2/001
Adler (Elinor & Sam G.) Fund, Savannah, 2/002
Allen Fdn., Atlanta, 2/002
Allen (John C.) - Bible Fund, Atlanta, 2/003
Alterman Foods Fdn., Atlanta, 2/003
Amilsco Charitable & Educational Fdn., Atlanta, 2/004
Atlanta Claims Association, Atlanta, 2/004
Atlanta Medical Research Fdn., Atlanta, 2/005
Baird Fdn., Atlanta, 2/006
Balfour Fdn., Thomasville, 2/006
Barringer (Flora M.) Fdn., Augusta, 2/007
Barwick (E.T.) Fdn., Atlanta, 2/007

Beck (Lewis H.) Fdn., Atlanta, 2/008
Beck (Lewis H.) Scholarship Fund, Atlanta, 2/010
Beloco Fdn., Columbus, 2/011
Benedictine Memorial Fdn., Savannah, 2/012
Birnie (Wilton Earle) Memorial Trust, Atlanta, 2/012
Boatwright (James) Fdn., LaGrange, 2/012
Branan (C.I.) Trust, Atlanta, 2/012
Breman Fdn., Atlanta, 2/013
Brown (Sally E.) Fund, Atlanta, 2/013
Bulloch County Hospital Fdn., Statesboro, 2/014
C & H Fund, Atlanta, 2/014
Castleberry (Clement L.) Fdn., Augusta, 2/015
Chatham Valley Fdn., Atlanta, 2/015
Christian Vision, Augusta, 2/016
Clarke (Harrison) Fdn., Atlanta, 2/017
Cloudman (Josephine) Trust, Atlanta, 2/018
Cousins Fdn., Atlanta, 2/018
Critz (H. Dale) Fdn., Savannah, 2/019
Cullum's Fdn., Augusta, 2/020
Custer Park, Marietta, 2/021
DeKalb Medical Education Trust, Atlanta, 2/021
Dellinger (Ray) Scholarship Fund, Cartersville, 2/022
Duncan (Sue B. & Clarke W.) Fdn., Buena Vista, 2/024
Ecological Fdn., Macon, 2/024
Etheridge (J. Lee) Trust Fund, Augusta, 2/025
Atlanta Falcons Fdn., Atlanta, 2/025
Fernbank, Inc., Atlanta, 2/025
Fox - Heyman Fdn., Rome, 2/026
Franklin (John & Mary) Fdn., Atlanta, 2/027
Franklin Fund, Atlanta, 2/029
Friedlander Fdn., Moultrie, 2/031
Friedman (Harold L.) Fdn., Brunswick, 2/032
Galloway (Sam Harris) Memorial Scholarship Fund, Vidalia, 2/032
Gary (Irene Von Camp) Fdn., Augusta, 2/032
Georgia Distilled Spirits Fdn., Atlanta, 2/033
Georgia Southern College Fdn., Statesboro, 2/033
Gerson (Morris & Rosa) Trust Fund Fdn., Columbus, 2/034
Glancy (Lenora & Alfred) Fdn., Atlanta, 2/034
Glenn Fdn., Formerly Hatcher Memorial Fund, Columbus, 2/035
Gordon (Edward McGuire) Educational Trust Fund, Savannah, 2/036
Gottlieb (Martin) Charitable Trust, Atlanta, 2/036
Graham Fdn., Atlanta, 2/037
Grantville Mills Fdn., Grantville, 2/038
Graves (Mary A.) Trust, Atlanta, 2/039
Great Dane Fdn., Savannah, 2/040
Gym - Medic - Medical Physical Fitness Fdn., Atlanta, 2/041
Haas (Betty G. & Joseph F.) Fdn., Atlanta, 2/041
Haley (W.B.) Fdn., Albany, 2/042
Harley (Howard) Charity Trust, Waycross, 2/042
Harrison (Julian) Fdn., Rome, 2/042
Harvard (L.B. & Grace C.) Fdn., Thomasville, 2/043
Pickett & Hatcher Educational Fund, Columbus, 2/044
Hinton (Claude) Trust, Atlanta, 2/045
Hirsch (Harold) Scholarship Fund, Atlanta, 2/045
Hughes (Herbert H.) Scholarship Award, Columbus, 2/047
Hughes (William Sylvester & Ruth J.) Fdn., College Park, 2/048
Johnson Fdn., Atlanta, 2/048
Jones (R.T.) Memorial Community Fdn., Canton, 2/049
Kennedy (William & Nancy) Fdn., Atlanta, 2/049
Kennesaw Junior College Fdn., Marietta, 2/049
Dobbs (S.C.) Trust, Atlanta, 2/050
Kinser Fdn., Atlanta, 2/051

Kirk (Anna M. & James L.) Fdn., Atlanta, 2/052
Kiwanis Fdn. of Peachtree - Atlanta, Atlanta, 2/053
Kiwanis Fdn. of Atlanta, Atlanta, 2/053
Lacy Fdn., Atlanta, 2/054
Largo, Inc., Sandersville, 2/054
Lilburn Middle School P.T.A., Lilburn, 2/054
Livingston (Robele) Fdn., Atlanta, 2/055
Loridans (Charles) Fdn., Atlanta, 2/055
Lubo Fund, Atlanta, 2/056
Marks (Yetta & Matthew) Fdn., Augusta, 2/059
Maynard (Albert D. & Mary Smith) Educational Trust, Atlanta, 2/059
McAliley Endowment Trust, Atlanta, 2/060
McCay (Walter W.) - Daisey Hayes Fund, Toccoa, 2/061
Medical Association of Georgia Fdn., Atlanta, 2/061
Medical College of Georgia Fdn., Augusta, 2/061
Miller (Martha) Memorial Fund, West Point, 2/063
Monroe Welfare Fdn., Waycross, 2/064
Mouhot (Donna Jean) Fdn., Chamblee, 2/065
National Service Fdn., Atlanta, 2/065
Newsom (James) Scholarship Award, Columbus, 2/066
Nodvin (Morris M.) Memorial Fdn., Atlanta, 2/066
Oconee Hill Cemetery Trustees, Athens, 2/067
Ottley (Dr. Charles W.) Fdn., Atlanta, 2/067
Ousley (Odille) Fdn., Decatur, 2/067
Painting Industry Apprenticeship Program, Atlanta, 2/068
Pennington Fdn., Madison, 2/068
Perkins - Ponder Fdn., Macon, 2/068
Peroda Fdn., Atlanta, 2/069
Pine Mountain Benevolent Fdn., Columbus, 2/070
P M P W 802, Waynesboro, 2/071
Poer - Underwood - Hinton Fdn., Atlanta, 2/071
Porter (Louisa) Fdn., Savannah, 2/071
Rainbow Fund, Fort Valley, 2/072
Raines Fdn., Atlanta, 2/073
Rice (Jack M.) Fund, Atlanta, 2/074
Rich's Employees Once-for-All Fund, Atlanta, 2/074
Rich (Mr. & Mrs. M.) Scholarship Fund, Atlanta, 2/075
Rossville Memorial Center, Rossville, 2/075
Rutland (Guy W.) Fdn., Decatur, 2/077
Samaritan Fund of Gainesville, Georgia, Gainesville, 2/077
Westcott (Sanford) Memorial Youth Fdn., Rossville, 2/077
Sapelo Island Research Fdn., Sapelo Island, 2/077
Wardlaw (William C.) Trust, Atlanta, 2/080
Schwob (Simon) Fdn., Columbus, 2/080
Scripto Employees Scholarship Fund, Atlanta, 2/081
Seretean (M.B.) Fdn., Formerly Tennessee, Dalton, 2/081
Sewell (Warren P. & Ava F.) Fdn., Breman, 2/083
S & F Fdn., Atlanta, 2/084
Shapiro Family Fdn., Atlanta, 2/085
Shepherd Fdn., Atlanta, 2/085
Sherrill (George) Memorial Junior Golf Fund, Atlanta, 2/085
Sibley (Alan B.) Fdn., Milledgeville, 2/086
Silverstein (Samuel) Family Fdn., Augusta, 2/086
Society of American Archivists - Special Project Fund, Atlanta, 2/087
South Dougherty Community Center, Albany, 2/087
Southern Cross Industries Fdn., Atlanta, 2/088
Southern Sates Educational Fdn., Savannah, 2/089
Spiegelberg Memorial Fund, Rome, 2/089
Stein Fdn., Atlanta, 2/090

Stevens (Ed) Memorial Education Fund,
Dawson, 2/091
Student Aid Fdn., Atlanta, 2/091
Swint Fdn., Augusta, 2/094
Edmondson - Telford Fdn., Gainesville, 2/095
Textile Education Fdn., Atlanta, 2/095
Tillman (Thomas McKey) Fdn., Athens, 2/096
Trustees of the Augusta Free School, Augusta,
2/097
Alexander (F.P.) Trust, Augusta, 2/098
Bray (Vivian L.) Trust, Atlanta, 2/098
Lyon (Kate P.) Trust, Augusta, 2/098
McBurney (E.P.) Trust, Atlanta, 2/099
Sears Memorial Fund, Columbus, 2/099
Setze (J. Adolphus) Trust, Augusta, 2/099
Van Deventer Memorial Scout Fdn., Jackson,
2/100
Vaughan Family Fdn., Atlanta, 2/101
West Point - Pepperell Fdn., West Point, 2/101
Davis (Lucy Whatley) Trust Fund, Columbus,
2/102
White (J.B.) Fdn., Augusta, 2/103
Whitehead (Richard K.) Fdn., Atlanta, 2/103
Wilder (Fannie) Educational Fund, Atlanta,
2/104
Wilkins Fdn., Athens, 2/104
Wilson (Frances Wood) Fdn., Decatur, 2/104
Woodruff (J.W. & Ethel I.) Fdn., Columbus,
2/106
Woolley (Vasser) Fdn., Atlanta, 2/106
Zaban Fdn., Atlanta, 2/107

HAWAII

First Filming

Advertiser Contemporary Arts Center of
Hawaii, Honolulu, 1/001
Agena (Paul R.) Fdn., Honolulu, 1/002
Akeroyed (Brilly & Richard) Fdn. for Mental
Health, Honolulu, 1/003
American Fdn. for the Study of Man, Honolulu,
1/004
Anthony (Barbara Cox) Fdn., Honolulu, 1/004
Atherton (F.C.) Trust, Honolulu, 1/004
Atherton (Juliette M.) Trust, Honolulu, 1/006
Baldwin (Fred) Memorial Fdn., Kahului,
1/008
Barstow (Frederic Duclos) Fdn., Honolulu,
1/009
Brown (Francis H.I.) Fdn., Honolulu, 1/010
Capital Investment Fdn., Honolulu, 1/011
Castle (Harold K.L.) Fdn., Kaneohe, 1/012
Castle (Samuel N. & Mary) Fdn., Honolulu,
1/013
Chaminade College Educational Fdn., Honolulu,
1/015
Ching (Clarence T.C.) Fdn., Honolulu, 1/015
Chow (Harry) & Nee Chang Chock Wong
Fdn., Honolulu, 1/016
Chung Kun A. Fdn., Honolulu, 1/016
DeNossa (Irmande)/Senhora Do Monte Fdn.,
Honolulu, 1/017
Finance Factors Fdn., Honolulu, 1/018
Frear (Mary D. & Walter F.) Eleomosynary
Trust, Honolulu, 1/019
Mosher Galt Fdn., Honolulu, 1/021
Gillette (David O.) Fdn., Honolulu, 1/022
Greenwill (Frank R.) Memorial Trust,
Honolulu, 1/023
Hawaii 4-H Fdn., Honolulu, 1/024
Hawaii Veterans Memorial Fund, Honolulu,
1/024
Hawaii Veterinary Research Fdn., Honolulu,
1/026
Hawaii Botanical Gardens Fdn., Honolulu,
1/026
Hawaii Civic Club of Honolulu Scholarship
Fund, Honolulu, 1/027
Hemenway (Charles R.) Scholarship Trust,
Honolulu, 1/029

Kings Daughters Circle of Honolulu, Honolulu,
1/030
Mackenzie Fdn., Honolulu, 1/032
McNaughton (Boyd and Roberta P.) Fdn.,
Honolulu, 1/033
Pang (Dr. and Mrs. L. Q.) Fdn., Honolulu,
1/034
Stranger's Friend Society, Honolulu, 1/034
Sultan Fdn., Honolulu, 1/035
Public Health Fund of the Chamber of
Commerce, Honolulu, 1/035
Tax Fdn. of Hawaii, Honolulu, 1/037
VFW Post Hana, Maui, Hana, 1/037
Teruya (Albert T. and Wallace T.) Fdn.,
Honolulu, 1/037
Wilcox (Elsie H.) Fdn., Honolulu, 1/038
Wilcox (G. N.) General Trust, Honolulu, 1/039
Wilcox (Mabel I.) Fdn., Honolulu, 1/041
Wilcox (S. W.) Trust, Honolulu, 1/042
Wood (Hart) Fdn., Honolulu, 1/043
Yee (Clifford K. F.) Fdn., Honolulu, 1/043
Zimmerman (Hans and Clara Davis) Fdn.,
Honolulu, 1/044
Zukerkorn (James and Sally) Fdn., Honolulu,
1/045

Second Filming

Atherton (Kate M.) Trust Estate F. B. O.
Salvation Army Boys & Girls Home,
Honolulu, 2/002
Booth (Lani) Trust Estate, Honolulu, 2/003
Brown (Julia Temple Davis) Fdn., Honolulu,
2/004
Campbell (James) School Library Fdn.,
Honolulu, 2/004
Cooke (Charles M. and Anna C.) Trust
Limited, Honolulu, 2/006
Damon (Richard C.) Fdn., Honolulu, 2/007
Dillingham (Lowell S.) Fdn., The, Honolulu,
2/007
Dillingham (Walter & Louise) Fdn., The,
Honolulu, 2/008
Earle (J. C.) Family Fdn., Honolulu, 2/009
Fukunaga Scholarship Fdn., Honolulu, 2/010
Hawaii Laborers Training Trust Fund,
Honolulu, 2/011
Hawaii Nurses Association, Honolulu, 2/011
Hawaii Preparatory Academy Huntington
Taylor Fund, Honolulu, 2/012
Honolulu Commandery No. 1 Knights Templar,
Honolulu, 2/013
Honolulu County Medical Library Endowment
Fund, Honolulu, 2/013
Horita (Herbert K.) Fdn., Honolulu, 2/013
Jones (Margaret) Memorial Fund, Honolulu,
2/014
Kahanamoku (Duke) Fdn., Honolulu, 2/014
Kahelekukona (George K.) Trust, Honolulu,
2/014
Keller (Arthur S.) Trust Estates, Honolulu,
2/015
Kun (Mrs. Lau) Memorial Fdn., Honolulu,
2/015
Leahi Fdn., Honolulu, 2/016
Liliuokalani Trust, Honolulu, 2/016
Makaha Historical Society Incorp., Honolulu,
2/018
Manaolana (Hui) Fdn., Inc., Honolulu, 2/019
Maui Quarantine Fund, Honolulu, 2/020
McInerny Fdn., Honolulu, 2/020
McWayne (Robinson A.) Memorial Fund,
Honolulu, 2/022
Moanalua Gardens Fdn., Inc., Honolulu, 2/022
Pope (Ida M.) Memorial Scholarship Fund,
Honolulu, 2/023
Prisanlee Trust Yates (Andrew L.) Ward Ttee,
Honolulu, 2/024
Daughters of Cincinnati, New York, N.Y.,
2/025
Ross (John M.) Fdn., Hilo, 2/025
Straub (George F.) Trust Estate Art 6,
Honolulu, 2/026
Sultan Foundation, Honolulu, 2/026
Trust (Huntington Taylor T.) Hawaii
Preparatory Academy, Honolulu, 2/026

Tulloch (Alexander R.) Trust, Honolulu, 2/027
Watumull Fdn., Honolulu, 2/028
Wichman (Juliet Rice) Fdn., The, Honolulu,
2/029
Woodford (Frank F. & Katharine L.) Memorial
Trust, Honolulu, 2/031

IDAHO

First Filming

Arens (A.E.) f/b/o American Cancer Society,
Boise, 1/002
Arens (A.E.) f/b/o Idaho Heart Association,
Boise, 1/002
Arens (A.E.) f/b/o Salvation Army, Boise,
1/003
Beckman (Leland D.) Fdn., Idaho Falls, 1/004
Boise Cascade Corporation Fdn, Inc., Boise,
1/004
Daugherty Fdn., Idaho Falls, 1/006
Day (Henry L.) Fdn., Wallace, 1/006
Dufresne (Walter) and Leona Dufresne Fdn.,
Inc., Boise, 1/007
Fowler Memorial Trust, Cedar Falls, 1/008
Hancock County Historical Society, Britt, 1/008
Galli-Curci (Ameltia) Fdn., Ketchum, 1/008
Horsley (M.L. & Emma) Scholarship Trust,
Boise, 1/009
Kingsbury (Mr. and Mrs. Henry B.) Scholarship
Fund, Wallace, 1/010
Magnuson (Harry F.) Charitable Trust,
Wallace, 1/010
Malakoff Fdn., Des Moines, 1/011
Morrison (Harry W.) Family Fdn., Inc., Boise,
1/011
Morrison-Knudsen Employees Fdn., Inc., Boise,
1/012
Paddock (E.A.) Scholarship Trust, Boise, 1/012
Potlatch Forests Fdn., Inc., Lewiston, 1/012
Swendsen (Warren & Mabel) Scholarship Fund,
Boise, 1/014
Swim (Arthur L.) Fdn., Twin Falls, 1/014
Title Insurance Company Fdn., Boise, 1/015
Tri Bli Fdn., Tama, 1/016

Second Filming

Amalgamated Meat Cutters and Butcher
Workmen, Local 368 Welfare Trust Fund -
Packinghouse Division, Nampa, 2/004
Anderson (C.C. and Henrietta W.) Fdn., Inc.,
Boise, 2/004
Boise Cascade Corporation Fdn., Boise, 2/005
Caldwell Memorial Hospital Fdn., Caldwell,
2/008
Gray (William J.) Scholarship Trust, Genesee,
2/010
Inspiration, Incorporated, Boise, 2/010
King (M. H.) Fdn., Burley, 2/011
Rouch (A. P. and Louise) Boys Fdn., Twin
Falls, 2/011
Shattuck (W. L.) Fdn., Boise, 2/011
Shirrod (Fred and Emma) Scholarship Trust,
Genessee, 2/012
Sun Valley Forum on National Health, Sun
Valley, 2/013

ILLINOIS

First Filming

Abbott Fdn., North Chicago, 1/001
Abbott Laboratories Fund, North Chicago,
1/003
Abeles (B & J) Fdn., Winnetka, 1/005
Abelson (Lester S.) Fdn., Chicago, 1/006
Abelson (Morton S.) Fdn., Chicago, 1/007
Abler Fund, Libertyville, 1/008

Ackermann (M.G.A.) Memorial Fund, Chicago, 1/008

Ackley (William & Margaret) Fdn., Chicago, 1/009

Adler (Arthur M.) Jr. Charitable Trust, Chicago, 1/009

Adler (Max & Sophie R.) Fund, Chicago, 1/010

Adler (Robert S.) Family Fund, Chicago, 1/011

Adler (Susan) Fdn., Chicago, 1/013

Admiral Corporation Fdn., Chicago, 1/013

Adventurers Club Fdn., Chicago, 1/014

A E S Fdn., Chicago, 1/014

A. F. Fund, Chicago, 1/014

Aignel (G. J.) Fdn., Chicago, 1/015

Akiba Fdn., Chicago, 1/015

Albin Fdn., Chicago, 1/016

Aldeen (Norris A.) Charitable Fdn., Rockford, 1/017

Aldeen (Reuben A.) Charitable Fdn., Rockford, 1/018

Aldworth (Richard James) Fdn., Oak Park, 1/019

Alexander Fdn., Decatur, 1/019

Alfaye Fdn., Chicago, 1/020

Allbright Fdn., Chicago, 1/020

Allen Fdn. (f/k/a Taylor Fdn.), Chicago, 1/021

Allen-Heath Memorial Fdn., Chicago, 1/022

Allen (James L.) Fdn., Chicago, 1/022

Allied Products Corporation Charitable Fund, Chicago, 1/023

Allison Fund, Bloomington, 1/025

Allocation Fund, Chicago, 1/025

Allport Charitable Trust, Chicago, 1/026

Allstate Fdn., Northbrook, 1/027

Allyn Fdn., Chicago, 1/029

Alsdorf Fdn., Chicago, 1/031

Altman (David) Fdn., Chicago, 1/032

Alton Woman's Home Association, Alton, 1/033

Altruistic Club, Chicago, 1/034

Altschuler (Melvoin & Glasser) Fund, Chicago, 1/034

Alumnae Club of Springfield, Illinois, Springfield, 1/035

American Dietetic Association Fdn., Chicago, 1/035

American National Bank & Trust Company of Chicago Association, Chicago, 1/036

American Institute for the Medical Research of Trauma, Chicago, 1/037

American Institute of Real Estate Appraisers -- Illinois Chapter 6, Chicago, 1/038

Amerock Charities Trust, Rockford, 1/038

Anderson Electric Fdn., Leeds, Ala., 1/039

Andrews (E. F.) Fdn., Chicago, 1/040

Anton (Nickolas T.) Fdn., Chicago, 1/041

A. P. Fdn., Chicago, 1/041

Appleton (Arthur I.) Fdn., Chicago, 1/042

Apollo Musical Club, Chicago, 1/042

ARGUS - WHBF Fdn., Rock Island, 1/043

Aries (Leon) Fdn., Chicago, 1/044

Arkin (Maurice E.) Fdn., Chicago, 1/044

Arkin (Norman) Fdn., Chicago, 1/045

Armour (Laurance H., Jr. & Margot B.) Family Fdn., Chicago, 1/045

Armour (Lester) Fdn., Chicago, 1/045

Armour (Philip D.) Fdn., Lake Forest, 1/046

Armour (Sarah & Watson) III Charity Fdn., Chicago, 1/047

Arnstein Fdn., Chicago, 1/048

Aronson (Harry) Family Fdn., Chicago, 1/048

Arrington Fdn., Chicago, 1/049

ARS Charitable Gift Fund, Chicago, 1/050

Arvey Fdn., Chicago, 1/051

Asher (Frederick & Frances) Fund, Highland Park, 1/051

Aspegren Charitable Fdn., Chicago, 1/052

Atwood Fdn., Rockford, 1/053

Augusta Fund, Peoria, 1/054

Averill (Anna B.) Memorial Fund, Chicago, 1/055

Avery Fund, Chicago, 1/055

Avery-Follansbee Fund, Chicago, 1/056

A. Y. & H. W. B. Family Fund, Chicago, 1/057

Gibbons (Elizabeth Ayres) Charitable Fdn., Chicago, 1/057

Azzarelli Fdn. Trust No. 1659, Kankakee, 1/057

Baker (Edward J.) Fdn., Chicago, 1/058

Baker (John L.) Family Fdn., Chicago, 1/059

Balaban & Katz Employees' Trust, Chicago, 1/059

Ballis Fdn., Chicago, 1/060

Barber - Colman Fdn., Rockford, 1/060

Barker (Robert A.) Fdn., Springfield, 1/061

Barker Welfare Fdn., Chicago, 1/062

Barnard (Eleanor & Morton John) Fdn., Chicago, 1/064

Barnard (George Hugh) Fdn., Chicago, 1/065

Barnow (David & Ruth) Fdn., Highland Park, 1/065

Barr (George) Fdn., Niles, 1/066

Barrett Fdn., Joliet, 1/067

Barrick (William H.) Family Charitable Fdn., Rockford, 1/068

Barry (Sarah G.) Charitable Trust, Chicago, 1/068

Barscott Fdn., Chicago, 1/069

Barth Fdn., St. Charles, 1/070

Bates (Alben F.) & Clara G. Bates Fdn., Elmhurst, 1/070

Batouri Mission Fdn., Wheaton, 1/071

Baudhuin (Ralph J.) Fdn., Rockford, 1/072

Bauer (M. R.) Fdn., Chicago, 1/073

Baum (Alvin H.) Family Fund, Chicago, 1/074

Baumgarten (Joseph & Gertrude) Fdn., Chicago, 1/075

B & B Fdn., Chicago, 1/076

Beber (Helen & Sam) Fdn., Park Forest, 1/076

Bech (Joseph) American Scholarship Fund, Chicago, 1/077

Beck (Adolph)-Jewish Federation, Chicago, 1/077

Beck (Adolph)-Home for Destitute Crippled Children, Chicago, 1/078

Beck (Adolph)-National Jewish Hospital for Consumptives, Chicago, 1/079

Beck (Adolph)-German Old Peoples Home of Forest Park, Chicago, 1/080

Beck (Lillian & Sylvan) Charitable Fdn., Chicago, 1/081

Becker (A. G.) Fdn., Chicago, 1/081

Becker (Jean M. & Benjamin M.) Fdn., Chicago, 1/082

Becker (Marion G. & S. Max), Jr. Fdn., Chicago, 1/083

Bederman Fdn., Highland Park, 1/085

Bederman (Ernest A.) Fund, Evanston, 1/086

Behavior Research & Action in the Social Sciences Fdn., Chicago, 1/087

Behr Charitable Trust, Rockford, 1/088

Beidler (Francis) Charitable Trust, Chicago, 1/088

Belden (Joseph C.) Fdn., Chicago, 1/090

Bell Fdn., Chicago, 1/091

Bell & Howell Fdn., Chicago, 1/092

Bell Tower Trust, Chicago, 1/093

Bellebyron Fdn., Chicago, 1/093

Bennett Family Fdn., Chicago, 1/095

Bennett (James O'Donnell) Trust, Chicago, 1/095

Bensinger (B. E.) Fdn., Chicago, 1/095

Bensinger (Peter B.) Fdn., Chicago, 1/096

Bensinger (Robert F.) Fdn., Chicago, 1/097

Bensinger (Roger G.) Fdn., Chicago, 1/097

Bentley (Julian T. & Milly M.) Fdn., Chicago, 1/098

Benton (Daniel L. & Rosalind) Fdn., Chicago, 1/098

Berg Fdn., Chicago, 1/099

Berger (Albert E.) Fdn., Chicago, 1/100

Berger (David & Sophia) Fdn., Chicago, 1/101

Berkey (Peter) Fdn., Santa Monica, Calif., 1/101

Berland (Abel) Fund, Chicago, 1/102

Berlin (M. H.) Fdn., Evanston, 1/103

Bernard Charitable Trust, Granite City, 1/103

Bernard (Frank C.) Fund, Chicago, 1/104

Bernhardt Charitable Trust, Rockford, 1/104

Bernstein (A. L.) Charitable Fdn., Chicago, 1/105

Bernstein (George & Ceil) Fdn., Chicago, 1/105

Bernstein (Samuel & Belle) Fdn., Chicago, 1/106

Bernstein (Samuel & Louis) Fund, Chicago, 1/106

B. F. Fdn., Medinah, 1/107

Biegler Fdn., Chicago, 1/107

Biel Fdn., Chicago, 1/108

Birginal Fdn., Bensenville, 1/110

B & J Association, Chicago, 1/111

B. K. N. Fund, Highland Park, 1/111

Bliss & Laughlin Fdn., Oak Brook, 1/112

Blitstein (Morton A.) Family Fdn., Lincolnwood, 1/113

Block (Louis) Scholarship Fund, Chicago, 1/113

Block (Mary & Leigh) Charitable Fund, Chicago, 1/113

Block (Philip D.) Jr. Family Fdn., Chicago, 1/115

Block (Roger & Ruth) Fund, Chicago, 1/117

Blommer (Bernard J. & Charlotte E.) Fdn., Chicago, 1/118

Blum (Harry & Maribel G.) Fdn., Chicago, 1/118

Bogardus (Katherine) Trust, Clinton, 1/120

Bogle (Walter S.) Trust A, Chicago, 1/120

Bohnen Family Fdn., Hinsdale, 1/121

Bonem (Leo & Erna) Charitable Fdn., Chicago, 1/122

Borg Fdn., La Grange Park, 1/122

Borg-Warner Fdn., Chicago, 1/123

Bosch (Katherine M.) Fdn., Chicago, 1/124

Bowes Fdn., Chicago, 1/125

Bowyer (Ambrose & Gladys) Fdn., Chicago, 1/126

Boynton-Gillespie Memorial Fund, Sparta, 1/127

Bradley (Arthur P. Mehlenbeck) Scholarship Fund, Peoria, 1/128

Brady (Harriet B. & Harold S.) Fdn., Chicago, 1/129

Brain Research Fdn., Chicago, 1/129

Bramsen (Svend & Elizabeth) Fdn., Chicago, 1/133

Brandt Fdn., Chicago, 1/134

Braun (Milton L.) Fdn., Flossmoor, 1/134

Braun (Theodore W.), Chicago, 1/136

Bremner (Aloysius J. & Loretta Hogan) Charities, Wilmette, 1/136

Breskin (Louis A. & Hazel) Fdn., Chicago, 1/137

Bressler Fdn., Chicago, 1/138

Bretzfelder Cancer Research Fdn., Chicago, 1/138

Bridgen (Clarence J.) Fdn., Chicago, 1/139

Bries Fdn., Chicago, 1/140

Bries (Katherine & Louis) Medical Fdn., Chicago, 1/141

Bright (David E.) Fdn., Chicago, 1/141

Brody-Davis Fdn., Chicago, 1/142

Brody (Helen A.) Fdn., Chicago, 1/142

Brown (Baird) Fdn., Chicago, 1/143

Brown (Cameron) Fdn., Chicago, 1/144

Brown, Connolly & Paddock Fdn., Rockford, 1/145

Brown (Daniel G.), Chicago, 1/146

Brown (George F.) & Sons, Inc. Fdn., Chicago, 1/147

Browne (Burton) Fdn., Chicago, 1/148

Brownstein (Bertha & Henry) Fdn., Chicago, 1/148

Brundage (Avery) Fdn., Chicago, 1/149

Bruning Fdn., Mount Prospect, 1/149

Brunner (Fred J.) Fdn., Franklin Park, 1/150

Brunswick Fdn., Chicago, 1/152

B & T Association, N.Y., N.Y., 1/154

Buchanan Family Fdn., Chicago, 1/155

Buik Fdn., Chicago, 1/156

Bundy Fdn., Streator, 1/156

Bunker-Ramo Fdn., Oak Brook, 1/157

Bunn (Jessie A.) Memorial Fdn., Alsip, 1/158

Bureau/Beaver Fdn., Chicago, 1/158
Burg (Harry) Family Fdn., Chicago, 1/158
Burgess Cellulose Fdn., Freeport, 1/159
Burgess (Frank A.) Fdn., Geneva, 1/159
Burgess (William H.) Fdn., Pasadena, Calif., 1/159
Burke (C. T.)-E. Burke Educational Fdn. Trust, Chicago, 1/160
Burnett (Leo) Fdn., Chicago, 1/160
Burns (William G. & M.) Fdn., Chicago, 1/161
Burnstein (Harold R. & Harriet) Charitable Fund, Highland Park, 1/161
Burroughs Fdn., Detroit, Michigan, 1/162
Butler (George W.) Fdn., River Forest, 1/163
Butler (Paul) Fdn., Oak Brook, 1/164
Butterworth (William) Memorial Trust, Moline, 1/165
Butz Fdn., Prescott, Ariz., 1/166
Byerly E. S.) Fdn., Peoria, 1/168
Byje Fdn., Chicago, 1/168
Caestecker (Charles & Marie) Fdn., Kenilworth, 1/169
Cahen (Ella Shure) Family Fdn., Chicago, 1/170
Callahan (Frank C.) & Marion C. Callahan Fdn., Chicago, 1/171
Callen Fdn., River Forest, 1/172
Callner (Milton H.) Fdn., Chicago, 1/172
Camp Fdn., Wheaton, 1/173
Campbell (Ruth Haney) Charitable Fdn., Chicago, 1/173
Canmann Family Fdn., Highland Park, 1/174
Cantigny First Division Fdn., Chicago, 1/175
Cantigny Trust u/w/o Robert R. McCormick, Chicago, 1/176
Capitol Dairy Fdn., Chicago, 1/177
Carlile (Florence Jeffrey) Fund, Chicago, 1/179
Carlin Fund, Chicago, 1/179
Carlin (Esther & Thomas) Fund, Chicago, 1/181
Carona Fdn., DeKalb, 1/181
Carson Charitable Trust, Hinsdale, 1/181
Cartier (E. Mae) Trust, Belleville, 1/182
Cartwright Fdn., Chicago, 1/182
Cash-Acme Fdn., Decatur, 1/183
Caslow (Paul & Pearl) Fdn., Chicago, 1/183
Caspers (Raymond I.) Trust, Chicago, 1/184
Cassady (Thomas G.) Fdn., Elmhurst, 1/185
Cassandra Fdn., Chicago, 1/185
Casteel (Russell R.) Trust, Belleville, 1/186
Castle Fdn., Franklin Park, 1/187
C E F Fdn., Chicago, 1/189
Centraila Fdn., Centralia, 1/190
Century Weavers Fdn., Chicago, 1/191
C F D A Fdn., Park Ridge, 1/191
Chaimovitz Charity Fdn., Chicago, 1/192
Chappell (Caroline S. & George S.), Jr. Charitable Fund, Chicago, 1/192
Chapin (Emily C.), Chicago, 1/193
Chapin (May) Fdn. of Illinois, Chicago, 1/194
Charitable & Educational Fund, Skokie, 1/194
Chaveriat Fdn., Chicago, 1/195
Checkers (Joseph M.) Family Fdn., Chicago, 1/195
Chemetron Fdn., Chicago, 1/196
Chicago Bridge & Iron Fdn., Oak Brook, 1/197
Chicago Charitable Fdn., Chicago, 1/198
Chicago Chemical Library Fdn., Des Plaines, 1/198
Chicago Extruded Metals Fund, Cicero, 1/198
Chicago Latin School Fdn., Chicago, 1/199
Chicago Tribune Fdn., Chicago, 1/199
Christian Charities Fdn., Peoria, 1/200
Christian Counselling Fdn., Warrenville, 1/200
Church of Christ, Iva M. Wood Testamentary Trust, Petersburg, 1/201
City National Bank & Trust Co. of Rockford Fdn., Rockford, 1/202
Clarendon Hills Lions Fdn., Clarendon Hills, 1/202
Clark (J. L.) Fdn., Rockford, 1/202
Clarke Fdn., Chicago, 1/203
Clarke (Philip R.) Fdn., Chicago, 1/204
Clayman Family Charitable Fdn., Wilmette, 1/205
Clevite Welfare Fund, Chicago, 1/206

Clow Fdn., Chicago, 1/207
CNA Fdn., Chicago, 1/208
Coblens Fdn., Chicago, 1/211
Coburn (Annie Swan), Chicago, 1/211
Cohen (Charles L.) Family Fdn., Chicago, 1/212
Cohen (Phillip J.) & Bertha Cohen Fdn., Chicago, 1/212
Cohen (Sam & Libby) Fdn., Chicago, 1/213
Cohen (Seymour) & Ethel A. Cohen Fdn., Chicago Heights, 1/213
Cohen (Yonnie) Heart Fdn., Chicago, 1/214
Cohn Family Fdn., Chicago, 1/214
Cohn (Albert H.) Fdn., Chicago, 1/216
Cohn (Jacob) Fdn., Chicago, 1/218
Brand (Marcus)-Elmond Cohn Memorial Fdn., Chicago, 1/219
Cohn (Richard & Patricia) Family Fdn., Glencoe, 1/219
Cole (Asher J. & Marilyn) Fdn., Glencoe, 1/220
Coleman Fdn., Chicago, 1/221
Coleman (Clarence L.) Jr. & Lillian S. Coleman Fdn., Winnetka, 1/222
Coleman (Marvin & Charlotte) Fdn., Morton Grove, 1/224
Collectors Club of Chicago, Chicago, 1/224
Collins (Arthur J. & Glenna B.) Charitable Fdn., Chicago, 1/225
Collins (Edward J.) Fdn., Chicago, 1/226
Colson (U. O. & Ada G.) Fdn., Paris, 1/227
Comar (Jerome M.) Fdn., Chicago, 1/227
Combs (Earle M.) & Virginia M. Combs Fdn., Chicago, 1/228
Community Assistance Fund, Chicago, 1/229
Community Babe Ruth League, Marengo, 1/229
Bresky (Constance Getz) Fdn., Chicago, 1/230
Container Corporation of America Fdn., Chicago, 1/231
Continental Bank Charitabl Fdn., Chicago, 1/234
Continental Charitable Fdn., Skokie, 1/236
Cook (David C.) Fdn., Elgin, 1/237
Cook (Richter E. E.) Memorial Fund, Chicago, 1/239
Continental Bank Charitable Fdn., Chicago, 2/001
Continental Charitable Foundation, Skokie, 2/002
Cook (David C.) Fdn., Elgin, 2/003
Cook (Richter E. E.) Memorial Fund, Chicago, 2/006
Coolidge Fdn., Chicago, 2/007
Coon (Owen L.) Fdn., Glenview, 2/007
Cooper (Richard H.) Fdn., Oakbrook, 2/008
Cooper (Robert & Dorothy) Fund, Chicago, 2/009
Coral Fdn., Waukegan, 2/010
Corrington (John W.) Fdn., Chicago, 2/011
Cotta Fdn., Rockford, 2/012
Cox Fdn., Orland Park, 2/012
Cox (A.G.) Charity Trust, Chicago, 2/013
Grain (G. D.), Jr. Fdn., Chicago, 2/014
Crawford Fdn., Chicago, 2/014
Crise (Tom) Memorial Fund, Villa Park, 2/015
Crescent Fdn., East Dubuque, 2/015
Croft Fdn., Wilmette, 2/016
Crosby Fdn., Chicago, 2/017
Crouse (John N.) Dental Endowment Fund, Chicago, 2/018
Crowell (Henry P. & Susan C.) Trust, Chicago, 2/018
Cruttenden Fdn., Chicago, 2/020
Cudahy (Edward I.) Fdn., Chicago, 2/020
Cummings (Herbert K. & Irene H.) Fdn., Chicago, 2/021
Cuneo Fdn., Chicago, 2/022
Cunningham (Oliver B.) Memorial Fund, Chicago, 2/023
Cusack (Thomas) for Jewish Federation, Chicago, 2/024
Daily Pantograph Fdn., Bloomington, 2/024
Damar Fdn., Waukegan, 2/025
Daniel (William & Lottie) Fdn., Rockford, 2/025

Dann Brothers Charitable Fdn., Chicago, 2/026
Darling (John & Norma) Fdn., Chicago, 2/026
Daubert (Ray B.) Fdn., Oakbrook, 2/027
Daughters of the American Revolution, Chicago, 2/027
Davee Fdn., Chicago, 2/018
Davis (Ruth Diane) Fdn., Chicago, 2/028
Dawson (Horace) Fdn., Evanston, 2/029
Dean (John Richmond) Fdn., Chicago, 2/031
Decalogue Fdn., Chicago, 2/031
Decker (O. Paul) Memorial Fdn., Chicago, 2/032
Deemar (Isidor & Sarah) Fdn., Niles, 2/033
Deicke (Edwin F.) Fdn., Wheaton, 2/033
De Jan Institute, Evanston, 2/035
De Jan Charitable Trust, Evanston, 2/035
Delta Fdn., Rock Island, 2/035
Demos (N.) Fdn., Chicago, 2/036
Deneen (Florence), Chicago, 2/037
Deree (William S. & Marion Z.) Fdn., Chicago, 2/037
De Soto Fdn., Des Plaines, 2/038
Development Fdn., Chicago, 2/039
Devitt (Thomas H.) Trust, Chicago, 2/040
Dick (A. B.) Fdn., Chicago, 2/041
Dickinson (Theodore G.) Fdn., Oglesby, 2/042
Disbursing Fund, Chicago, 2/043
Division Fund, Chicago, 2/044
Dixon Old Peoples Home Fund, Dixon, 2/045
D & K Fdn., Chicago, 2/046
Doane (F. B.) Fdn., Chicago, 2/046
Dobson Research Fdn., Evanston, 2/047
Dohrn Fdn., Rock Island, 2/047
Domsky (Ronald Z. & Judith G.) Charitable Fdn., Chicago, 2/048
Donahue (Mary Hartline) Fdn., Chicago, 2/048
Donnelley (Elliott & Ann) Fdn., Chicago, 2/049
Donnelley (Gaylord) Fdn., Chicago, 2/049
Donnelley (James R.) Fdn., Chicago, 2/050
Donnelley (Thomas E.) II & Cynthia C. Donnelley Fdn., Chicago, 2/051
Dooley (James A.) Fdn., Chicago, 2/051
Doppelt (Charles) Fdn., Chicago, 2/052
Dougherty Family Fdn., Chicago, 2/052
Drachler (Bella & Sam) Fdn., Chicago, 2/053
Drell (Hannah & Joseph B.) Fdn., Chicago, 2/053
D.R. Fund for Childrens' Clinics, Chicago, 2/054
Dressler (Max & Bertha) Fdn., Chicago, 2/055
D & R Fund, Chicago, 2/055
Drynan (Arthur Charles), Chicago, 2/057
DuBow (Jack & Shirley) Charitable Fdn., Chicago, 2/058
DuKane Fdn., St. Charles, 2/058
Duman Fdn., Highland Park, 2/059
Du Page County Medical Society, Glen Ellyn, 2/060
Eckerling (Joseph & Max) Fdn., Chicago, 2/060
Edelman (Daniel J.) Fdn., Chicago, 2/060
Edelstein (Marian & Arthur) Fdn., Chicago, 2/061
Edelstone (Sigmund E.) Fdn., Chicago, 2/062
Educational Fdn. for Nuclear Science, Chicago, 2/063
Eff Fdn., Chicago, 2/063
Ehlco Fdn., Chicago, 2/064
Eisenberg (George M.) Fdn., Chicago, 2/064
Eisenschiml Fdn., Chicago, 2/065
Eisenschiml (Carol & Ralph) Trust, Chicago, 2/065
Eisenschiml (Harry & Gerald) Fund, Chicago, 2/066
Ekvall (Mae W.) Memorial Trust, Chicago, 2/066
Elco Charitable Fdn., Rockford, 2/067
Eldel Fdn., Arlington Heights, 2/067
Eliel (Willard & Eleanor) Fdn., Highland Park, 2/068
Elliott (William S.) Memorial Fund, Chicago, 2/068

Ellis (Fred D.) Charitable Fdn., Chicago,
2/070
Elson Fdn., Highland Park, 2/071
Emaye Charities, Chicago, 2/072
Enelow Fund, Chicago, 2/072
English (Harold) Fdn., Barrington Hills, 2/073
Enivar Charitable Fund, Chicago, 2/073
Enterprise Paint Fdn., Chicago, 2/074
Epstein Fdn., Chicago, 2/075
Epton Fdn., Chicago, 2/076
Erkert (Roger William) Fdn., Rockford, 2/076
Erkert (James Sommer) Fdn., Rockford, 2/077
Esopus Fdn., Evanston, 2/077
Eureka Williams Employees Charitable Fdn.,
Bloomington, 2/077
Evans Fd., Chicago, 2/078
Eye Rehabilitation & Research Fdn., Chicago,
2/078
Faber Fdn., Chicago, 2/079
Factor (Jerome & Alida) Fdn., Chicago, 2/079
Falk (Marian C.) Fdn., Morton Grove, 2/080
Falkoff (Frank) Memorial, Chicago, 2/081
Farnham Charitable Fund, Chicago, 2/082
Stein Roe & Farnham Fdn., Chicago, 2/083
Farwell (A.W.) for Old Peoples Home, Chicago,
2/084
F.A.S.S. Benevolent Fdn., Chicago, 2/084
Fathauer (George) Fdn., Decatur, 2/085
Fauntleroy (Robert R.) Jr. Memorial Trust,
Chicago, 2/086
Fauntleroy (Robert R.) Jr. Memorial Trust
Accumulated Income, Chicago, 2/086
Fay Fdn., Chicago, 2/087
Feldman Family Fdn., Chicago, 2/088
Feldman (Sam J.) Fund, Chicago, 2/089
Fell Family Fdn., Highland Park, 2/089
Fetzer-Alexander Fdn., Chicago, 2/090
Fiedler (Louis P. & Saerree K.) Fund, Highland
Park, 2/091
Fine Arts Center of Clinton, Clinton, 2/091
Fine (Berta & Irving A.) Fdn., Chicago, 2/092
Fink (Barbara & Eli E.) Fund, Chicago, 2/092
First National Bank of Chicago Fdn., Chicago,
2/093
First National Bank of Elgin, Elgin, 2/097
First National Bank of Lake Forest, Lake
Forest, 2/098
First National Bank & Trust Company of
Rockford Charitable Trust, Rockford, 2/098
Fish Fdn., Chicago, 2/099
Fisher Charitable Trust, Rockford, 2/099
Fisher (Leonard N. & Sylvia) Fdn., Chicago,
2/100
Fixman (T.M. & Fannabell S.) Fdn., Oak Park,
2/101
Flanzer Family Fdn., Chicago, 2/102
Fleer (Herman Henry) Fdn., Evanston, 2/102
Florsheim (Lillian H.) Charity Fdn., Chicago,
2/103
Florsheim (Lillian H.) Fdn. for Fine Arts,
Chicago, 2/104
Florsheim Shoe Fdn., Chicago, 2/104
Foote, Cone & Belding Fdn., Chicago, 2/106
Foote, Erastus Wise Charity, Chicago, 2/106
Footlik (Irving M. & Sylvia) Fdn., Skokie,
2/107
Foreman (Alfred K.), Jr. Charitable Trust,
Chicago, 2/107
Forest Hospital Fdn., Des Plaines, 2/108
Lincoln Forest Fdn., Evanston, 2/108
Foster Humane Fund, Chicago, 2/108
Foundation for Childrens Therapeutic
Education, Chicago, 2/109
Foundation for Foreign Affairs, Chicago, 2/109
Foundation to Franchise Freedom, Oak Brook,
2/110
Frank Fdn., Chicago, 2/110
Frank (Clinton E.) Fdn., Chicago, 2/111
Frank (Zollie & Elaine) Fund, Chicago, 2/112
Frankel Fdn., Chicago, 2/114
Frankel (Gustave) Fdn., Chicago, 2/115
Frankenthal-McMillan Family Fdn., Chicago,
2/115
Fran-Mark Trust, Oak Park, 2/116
Freehling (Willard & Elaine) Fdn., Chicago,
2/116

Freeman (Artgrace) Charitable Fdn., Chicago,
2/117
Freier (Arthur) Fdn., Barrington, 2/118
Fremont (Robert S.) Fdn., Rosemont, 2/118
Freund (Edwin O. & Rosalind H.) Fdn.,
Chicago, 2/118
Freund (Maurice & Henry L.) Charitable Fdn.,
Chicago, 2/119
Freudenthal Fdn., Chicago, 2/120
Friedman Charitable Fund, Glencoe, 2/120
Friedman (G.) Family Fdn., Chicago, 2/121
Friedman (Marvin D. & Sandra) Fdn., Chicago,
2/122
Friedman (Michael J. & Blance L.) Fdn.,
Chicago, 2/122
Friedman (Samuel R.) Fdn., Chicago, 2/123
Friedman (William J. & Irene J.) Fdn.,
Chicago, 2/123
Friend (Henry & Milton) Fdn., Chicago, 2/124
Fritsch Charitable Fdn., Libertyville, 2/125
Froehling (Samuel) Fund, Chicago, 2/126
Fromm Music Fdn., Chicago, 2/127
Fry (Lloyd A.) Fdn., Summit, 2/128
Frye Fdn., Chicago, 2/129
Fulk Family Charitable Trust, Sinnetka, 2/129
Fullerton Metals Fdn., Northbrook, 2/130
Fund for Enlightenment, Chicago, 2/131
Fund for International Conference of
Agricultural Economists, Chicago, 2/132
Fusco (Joseph C.) Fdn., Chicago, 2/134
Futorian Fdn., Chicago, 2/135
Gaines (S. J.-Roslyn) Fund, Highland Park,
2/137
Gaines (Harry B. & Rolinda J.) Fdn., Chicago,
2/138
Gallagher (Arthur J.) Fdn., Chicago, 2/139
Galter Fdn., Chicago, 2/140
Galvin (Robert W.) Fdn., Franklin Park,
2/140
Garard (James L., Jr. & Irene C.) Fdn.,
Northfield, 2/142
Garcy Fdn., Chicago, 2/143
Gardner-Denver Fdn., Quincy, 2/144
Gaylord Fdn., Chicago, 2/145
Gehlbach (Marian S.) Charitable Trust,
Evanston, 2/145
Gelles (Sam) Fdn., Chicago, 2/146
General American Transportation Fdn.,
Chicago, 2/146
Genius (Arthur E.), Chicago, 2/147
Gerstley (Adelaide D.) Charitable Fund,
Chicago, 2/147
Getz Fdn., Chicago, 2/148
Getz (Emma & Oscar) Fdn., Chicago, 2/149
Gianaras Fdn., Deerfield, 2/150
Gibbs Fdn., Broadway, 2/151
Gidwitz (Michael & Carrie) Charitable Fdn.,
Chicago, 2/152
Gieser Missionary Foundation, Wheaton, 2/152
Gilbert & Wolf Fdn., Crestwood, 2/153
Gilbert (Morris & Rose) Fdn., Chicago, 2/153
Gilford (Fred A.) Family Fund, Chicago,
2/153
Gimbel (J. William Jr. & Odell B.) Fdn.,
Chicago, 2/154
Gingiss Fdn., Chicago, 2/155
Glaser (Beatrice & Gustave) Fund, Chicago,
2/155
Glaser (Mr. & Mrs. Leon S.) Trust, Chicago,
2/156
Glasser Philanthropic Fund, Chicago, 2/156
Glasser (Beatrice & Morris) Fdn., Oak Park,
2/157
Gleason (Mary Jane & John S.), Jr. Fdn.,
Winnetka, 2/157
Glore Fund, Chicago, 2/158
Glory B. Fdn., Chicago, 2/158
Glos (Albert H.) & Iona D. Glos Fdn.,
Elmhurst, 2/159
Goldberg (Jacob) Memorial Fund, Chicago,
2/160
Goldblatt Brothers Employees-Nathan Goldblatt
Cancer Research Fund, Chicago, 2/161
Goldblatt Brothers Fdn., Chicago, 2/162
Goldman (George J.) Home for the Jewish
Aged, Chicago, 2/162

Goldman (Morris & Rose) Fdn., Chicago,
2/162
Goldstein (Albert B.) Fdn., Chicago, 2/163
Goldstein (George J.) Fdn., Chicago, 2/164
Good (Sheldon F.) Family Fdn., Chicago,
2/165
Goodman (Philip D.) Family Fdn., Chicago,
2/166
Gordon Fdn., Chicago, 2/167
Gordon (James) Grant for Government,
Chicago, 2/167
Goldblatt Brothers Fdn., Chicago, 2/167
Gordon (Jane & Norman) Family Fdn.,
Chicago, 2/168
Gosselin Fdn., Joliet, 2/169
Gottlieb Fdn., Northlake, 2/169
Gould Fdn., Chicago, 2/171
Gould (William & Harriet) Fdn., Chicago,
2/172
Gradison (Jules T.) Family Fdn., Chicago,
2/172
Gradman (David J.) Fund, Chicago, 2/173
Graft (Everett D.) Charitable Fund, Winnetka,
2/174
Graff-Pinkert Fdn., Chicago, 2/174
Graham Fdn. for Advanced Studies in the Fine
Arts, Chicago, 2/175
Graham (Gerald J. & Helen J.) Fdn., Chicago,
2/177
Grainger Fdn., Chicago, 2/178
Gramm Fdn., Chicago, 2/180
Grant A f/b/o Wiscasset Cemetery, Chicago,
2/180
Grawoig (Allen) Family Fdn., Chicago, 2/181
Grawoig (Garrison & Rita) Fdn., Chicago,
2/182
Gray (Joseph J.) Family Fund, Glencoe, 2/182
Gray (Leon H.) Fdn., Highland Park, 2/183
Greene-Michel Fdn., Chicago, 2/184
Green (Harry L.) Jr. Charitable Fdn., Rockford,
2/184
Greenberg (Alex Louis) Charitable Fdn.,
Chicago, 2/185
Greenberg Brothers Fdn., Joliet, 2/185
Greenberg (Harold & Esther) Family Fdn.,
Chicago, 2/185
Greenfield (Sam & Hermine) Charitable Fdn.,
Chicago, 2/186
Greenspan Charitable Fdn., Chicago, 2/187
Griffith (Carroll L.) & Sylvia M. Griffith Fdn.,
Chicago, 2/188
Griffith (Dean & Lois) Fdn., Chicago, 2/188
Grill Fdn., Evanston, 2/189
Groom (Pat) Fdn., Chicago, 2/190
Gross Fdn., Decatur, 2/190
Gross (Seymour R.) Fdn., Chicago, 2/190
Grumman (David L.) Fdn., Evanston, 2/191
Gunner Fdn., Dixon, 2/192
Gunness (R.C.) Fdn., Chicago, 2/192
Grunsfeld (Ernest A.) Memorial Fund, Chicago,
2/193
Haag Fdn., Chicago, 2/194
Haas Family Charitable Fund, Glencoe, 2/194
Hadsall (John M.) Charitable Fdn., Glencoe,
2/195
Haffner Fdn., Chicago, 2/195
Hales Charitable Fund, Chicago, 2/196
Hamill (Hunt & Jean) Fdn., Chicago, 2/199
Hamm Family Charitable Trust, Chicago,
2/201
Hammerman (Meyer & Raena) Fdn., Chicago,
2/202
Hammerman (Sol & Celia) Fdn., Highland
Park, 2/202
Hammes (Romy & Dorothy) Trust, Kankakee,
2/203
Hanover Fdn., Chicago, 2/203
Hard (Louise A.) Trust, Chicago, 2/203
Hardin Fdn., Wilmette, 2/204
Hardin (Shirley & Louis) Fund, Chicago,
2/204
Harding Fdn., Loves Park, 2/205
Harper (H. Mitchell & Margaret L.), Morton
Grove, 2/206
Harper (Philip S.) Fdn., Hinsdale, 2/206
Harris Fdn., Chicago, 2/208

Harris Bank Fdn., Chicago, 2/210
Harris (Carl) Family Fdn., Chicago, 2/212
Harris (E.F.) Family Fdn., Lincolnwood, 2/212
Harris (G.H.), Chicago, 2/213
Harris (Jerome & Arlene) Fdn., Chicago, 2/214
Harris (S.H.) Jr. Fdn., Chicago, 2/214
Hart (Harry J.) Fdn., Chicago, 2/215
Hart Schaffner & Marx Charitable Fdn., Chicago, 2/216
Hartzer (Aileen J.) Fdn., Chicago, 2/216
Hauser (Charles & Minnie) Fdn., Litchfield, 2/217
Hawley Fdn., Chicago, 2/217
Hay (John I.) Fdn., Chicago, 2/218
Haynie (William Duff), Chicago, 2/218
Haugh Family Fdn., Chicago, 2/219
Hearst (Marjorie S.) Charitable Fdn., Chicago, 2/220
Heed (Thomas D.), Chicago, 2/220
Heffer Fdn., Chicago, 2/221
Hefner (Hugh M.) Fdn., Chicago, 2/222
Hefter (Edward G.) Fdn., Chicago, 2/223
Hegeler (Edward C.) Trust Fund, LaSalle, 2/223
Heidrick & Struggles Fdn., Chicago, 2/224
Heller (Florence G.) Fdn., Chicago, 2/224
Heller (Walter F.) Fdn., Chicago, 2/225
Hemphill (James C.) Fdn., Chicago, 2/226
Henning (Malcolm E.) Fdn., Chicago, 2/228
Henninger Benevolent Trust, River Fores, 2/228
Henry (Frances) Charitable Fund, Chicago, 2/228
Herley Fdn., Chicago, 2/230
Hermann (Grover) Fdn., Chicago, 2/230
Heron (Presly M.), Chicago, 2/233
Hertz (Fannie & John) Fdn., Chicago, 2/233
Herz (J.H.) Family Fdn., Winnetka, 2/234
Hesser (Bess & Erwin) Fdn., Glencoe, 2/235
Heyman (Herbert & Goldyne) Fdn., Chicago, 2/235
Hibben Fdn., Chicago, 2/236
Hickey Fdn., Chicago, 2/237
Hicks (C., Roberts, 2/238
Higgins (Edgar & Ellen) Scholarship Fdn., Chicago, 2/238
Highlands Fdn., Chicago, 2/239
Hill (Herbert L. & Ruth A.) Charitable Fdn., Skokie, 2/239
Hillman Charitable Fdn., Rockford, 2/240
Hills (Eleanor), Chicago, 2/240
Hills (Eleanor), Chicago, 3/001
Himmel Fdn., Chicago, 3/002
Himmelblau Fund, Chicago, 3/003
Hirsh Fund, Chicago, 3/004
Hirsh (Herbert W.) Charitable Fdn., Chicago, 3/004
Hirsh-Lowenstein Fdn., Chicago, 3/004
H & M Service Corporation, Chicago, 3/005
William (Hobart W.), Chicago, 3/006
Hoffman (S & D) Fdn., Chicago, 3/007
Hogan (O. T.) Family Fdn., Chicago, 3/007
Hokin (Dave) Fdn., Chicago Heights, 3/008
Hokin (Helen G. & Oscar E.) Charitable Fdn., Peoria, 3/008
Hokin (Samuel E.) Fdn., Chicago, 3/009
Holland Fdn., Chicago, 3/010
Holland (M. Z.) Memorial Fdn., Chicago, 3/011
Holm (Gladys) Fdn., Evanston, 3/012
Holtslander (Eugene S.), Chicago, 3/012
Holy Family Fdn. of Joliet, Joliet, 3/012
Holzheimer Fund, Chicago, 3/013
Hoover Fdn., Glencoe, 3/014
Hope Point Unlimited, Chicago, 3/015
Hopkins (Florence O.) Charitable Fund, Chicago, 3/016
Hopkins (John P.) Cemetery Trust, Chicago, 3/017
Hopper (Bertrand) Memorial Fdn., Taylorville, 3/017
Horton (John Todd & Helene A.) Charitable Fund, Oak Brook, 3/018
Horwich (Arthur & Lee) Family Fdn., Chicago, 3/018
Horwich (Ben) Fdn., Chicago, 3/019

Horwich (Franklin & Frances) Family Fdn., Chicago, 3/020
Horwich (Leonard J.) Family Fdn., Chicago, 3/021
Horwich (M. T.) Memorial Family Fdn., Chicago, 3/021
Horwich (Philip & Beatrice) Family Fdn., Chicago, 3/022
Horwitz (Sam & Faye) Fdn., Chicago, 3/023
Horwich (Theodore & Gertrude) Family Fdn., Chicago, 3/024
Hosbein (Louis) Family Fdn., Chicago, 3/025
Howe (Stewart) Fdn., Evanston, 3/028
Howell Neighborhood House Fdn., Chicago, 3/029
Hudson (R. C.) Memorial Fdn., Chicago, 3/030
Hulbert (E.) Cemetery Trust, Chicago, 3/030
Hull Fdn., Decatur, 3/031
Hummon Fdn., Chicago, 3/031
Huntly Charitable Trust, Berwyn, 3/031
Hurwitz (Paul) Fdn., Skokie, 3/032
Huston Fdn., Evanston, 3/032
Hyman-Michaels Fund, Chicago, 3/033
Hymen (Charles) Fund, Chicago, 3/033
Ideal Industries Fdn., Sycamore, 3/034
I & G Charitable Fdn., Chicago, 3/035
Illinois Federation of Women's Clubs, Chicago, 3/037
Illinois Federation of Women's Clubs Trust A, Chicago, 3/038
Illinois Institute for Arthritis Investigation & Research, Rockford, 3/038
Illinois Tool Works Fdn., Chicago, 3/039
Immanuel Bible Fdn., Normal, 3/040
Ingersoll Fdn., Rockford, 3/041
Inland Steel-Ryerson Fdn., Chicago, 3/042
Interlake Steel Fdn., Chicago, 3/048
Interocean Charitable Fdn., Chicago, 3/049
Inter-Science Research Fdn., Chicago, 3/050
Ioka Fund, Chicago, 3/050
Isenbert (Hans D.) Fdn., Chicago, 3/052
Jablonski, Chicago, 3/053
Jackson (Mary G.), Chicago, 3/053
Jacobs (Alan & Phyllis) Family Fdn., Highland Park, 3/053
Jacobs (Irwin & Selma) Family Fdn., Skokie, 3/054
Jacoby Fdn., Alton, 3/055
James (Walter C.) Fdn., Chicago, 3/055
Jay (Ross) Fdn., Winnetka, 3/056
J B Charitable Trust, Chicago, 3/057
Jefferson (Joseph) Award Committee, Chicago, 3/058
Jewel Fdn., Melrose Park, 3/058
J & I Fdn., Northfield, 3/059
J & M H Trust, Chicago, 3/059
Jocarno Fund, Highland Park, 3/061
Johnson (A. D.) Fdn., Chicago, 3/062
Johnson (Carl H. & Evelyn P.) Fund, Wilmette, 3/063
Johnson (Elmer) Fdn., Chicago, 3/063
Johnson (Elmer C.), Chicago, 3/063
Jones & McKnight Fdn., Chicago, 3/065
Jones (Otis L.) Trust, Chicago, 3/065
Joseph Fdn., Chicago, 3/066
Joseph (Janet & Gabe) Fdn., Glencoe, 3/066
Joslyn Fdn., Chicago, 3/066
Jovan (James N.) Fdn., Chicago, 3/068
Joyce Fdn., Chicago, 3/068
Kahane (David M. & Florence H.) Fdn., Chicago, 3/069
Kahn (Henry S.) Charitable Fund, Chicago, 3/070
Kahn (Harry H.) Fdn., Chicago, 3/070
Kahnweiler Family Fdn., Chicago, 3/070
Kamin Fdn., Chicago, 3/070
Kane (William H.) & Isabella A. Kane Memorial Scholarship Trust, Chicago, 3/071
Kaplan & Malki Family Fdn., Evanston, 3/072
Kaplan (Mayer & Morris) Fdn., Rosemont, 3/072
Kaplan (Philip) Fdn., Chicago, 3/072
Kaplan (Sollie) Fdn., Chicago, 3/073
Kaplan (Samuel & June) Fdn., Chicago, 3/074
Kapp (H. J.) Fdn., Decatur, 3/075

Karandjeff (Ethel) Charitable Fdn., Granite City, 3/075
Karger Fund, Chicago, 3/075
Karmin (Kurt B.) Family Fdn., Glencoe, 3/076
Karoll Fdn., Chicago, 3/077
Katz (Arthur & Sylvia) Fdn., Chicago, 3/078
Katz (Meyer) Family Fdn., Chicago, 3/078
Katz (Sidney M.) Family Fdn., Glencoe, 3/079
Kaymorn Fdn., Chicago, 3/080
Kearney (A. T.) Fdn., Chicago, 3/081
Keating (Edward) Family Fdn., Winnetka, 3/082
Kecaps Fdn., Chicago, 3/083
Keebler Company Fdn., Elmhurst, 3/083
Keeley (Leslie E.), Chicago, 3/085
Kelly (T. Lloyd) Fdn., Chicago, 3/085
Kemp (Parker) Fdn., Lexington, 3/086
Kempler (Charles & Frances) Fdn., Chicago, 3/087
Kenilworth Dental Research Fdn., Kenilworth, 3/088
Kenis Fdn., Chicago, 3/088
Keeney (Hattie Hannan), Chicago, 3/089
Kenny Fdn., Skokie, 3/090
Kernott (Doris J.) Memorial Fdn.--Cameron Ross, Chicago, 3/091
Kernott (Doris J.) Memorial Fdn.--Chicago Center, Chicago, 3/092
Kernott (Doris J.) Memorial Fdn., Chicago, 3/092
Kernott (Doris J.) Memorial Fdn.--Shrine Hospital, Chicago, 3/093
Kersten Family Fdn., Chicago, 3/094
Kestnbaum Fdn., Chicago, 3/095
Kilburg (Harold J.) Sr. Fdn., Chicago, 3/095
Kimbark Fdn., Chicago, 3/096
Kimbow Fund, Chicago, 3/096
Kinley (David) Educational Fdn., Palatine, 3/097
Kinney (Eugene M.) Fdn., Chicago, 3/098
Kirchheimer (Emil) Residuary Trust, Chicago, 3/099
Kirkland School Association, Chicago, 3/100
Kirshbaum (Milton & Charlotte) Fund, Chicago, 3/100
Kirsten (Herman) Fdn., Chicago, 3/101
Klauber (Edmond R.) Family Fdn., Flossmer, 3/102
Klauer Fdn., Chicago, 3/102
Klegar Fdn., Highland Park, 3/103
Klein (James) Scholarship Fund, Highland Park, 3/103
Kleinschmidt (Edward Frederick) Scholarship Trust, Park Ridge, 3/103
Klier Family Fdn., Chicago, 3/104
Kline Fdn., Chicago Heights, 3/105
Klutznick Fdn., Chicago, 3/105
Knapp (George O.) Benevolent Fund, Chicago, 3/106
Kneip (Elmer W.) Fdn., Chicago, 3/107
Knight (R. G. & E. M.) Fund, Glen Ellyn, 3/107
Kochton Family Fdn., Glenview, 3/108
Koenigsberg Bros. Fdn., Chicago, 3/108
Koff (Arthur K.) Welfare Fund, Chicago, 3/109
Kohn (A. Robert) Fdn., Chicago, 3/109
Kole Fdn., Oak Lawn, 3/110
Kolflat (Alf), Chicago, 3/111
Koolish (A. L.) Fdn., Chicago, 3/111
Kopstein (Juda & Eva) Fdn., Chicago, 3/111
Koretz Fund, Highland Park, 3/112
Korn (Carl & Frances) Fdn., Lincolnwood, 3/113
Korshak (Marshall) Fdn., Chicago, 3/114
Kortemeier (Elwood F.) Jr. Fdn., Wheaton, 3/114
Dore (Virginia Krafft), Chicago, 3/114
Kramer (H.) Fdn., Chicago, 3/115
Krando Fdn., Chicago, 3/115
Krashen (Leo) Fdn., Wilmette, 3/116
Krause (Edward R.) Family Fdn., Wilmette, 3/116
Kraus (Jay & Edna) Fdn., Chicago, 3/117
Kreeger (Dr. & Mrs. Morris H.) Charitable Trust, Chicago, 3/118

Kritcheyer Fdn., Winnetka, 3/118
Kritz (Alfred A.) Family Fdn., Chicago, 3/118
Kroc Fdn., Chicago, 3/119
Kroehler (Rodney Stuart) Memorial Fdn., Naperville, 3/120
Kroehler Fdn., Naperville, 3/120
Krueger Fdn., Chicago, 3/121
Kunstadter (Albert) Family Fdn., Chicago, 3/122
Lanners (Dr. Thomas) General Trust Fund, Decatur, 3/123
Laidlaw Educational Fdn., Chicago, 3/123
Laidlaw Fdn., Peoria, 3/124
Lake County Humane Society, Waukegan, 3/124
Lakewood Fdn., Chicago, 3/125
Landau (Howard & Pauline) Fdn., Chicago, 3/126
Lane (Edna S.), Chicago, 3/127
Landfield (Michael S.) Fund, Chicago, 3/127
Larchmont Fdn., Lombard, 3/128
LaSalle Adams Fund, Chicago, 3/128
LaSalle Steel Fdn., Chicago, 3/130
Laser (Celia) Fdn., Chicago, 3/131
Lash Fdn., Chicago, 3/131
Lavezzorio Fdn., Chicago, 3/132
Lavin (Leonard H.) Fdn., Glencoe, 3/133
Lavin (R.) & Sons, Inc. Charity Fdn., Chicago, 3/134
Lawson (Victor) For Community, Chicago, 3/135
L - B Fdn., Chicago, 3/136
Leaf Fdn., Chicago, 3/137
Leaf (Marshall) Family Fdn., Chicago, 3/138
Leaf (Martin & Norma) Charitable Fdn., Glencoe, 3/139
Leaf (Norman & Sallie) Charitable Fdn., Highland Park, 3/139
Leaf (Sol & Bertha) Charitable Fdn., Chicago, 3/140
Leavitt (Gerald B. & Edith) Fdn., Glencoe, 3/141
Lebeson (H & R) Fund, Chicago, 3/142
Lebolt Fdn., Chicago, 3/142
Lederer Fdn., Chicago, 3/143
Lederer (Anne Pollock) Fdn., Chicago, 3/144
Lederer (Francis L.) Fdn., Chicago, 3/145
Leffmann Fdn., Chicago, 3/145
Lehr (Chester G.) Jr. Memorial Scholarship for Men, Canton, 3/145
Leibman (Morris I.) Fdn., Chicago, 3/146
Leiferman (Silvia W. & Irwin H.) Fdn., Chicago, 3/146
Leiter (Winifred De Puy), Chicago, 3/148
Leopold (Herbert R. & Bernice) Fund, Chicago, 3/148
Leopold (Howard F.) Family Fdn., Chicago, 3/149
Levi (Stanley & Elaine) Fdn., Chicago, 3/149
Levie (Marcus & Theresa) Educational Fund, Chicago, 3/149
Levin (Ezra) Charitable Trust, Monticello, 3/152
Levin (Margot B. & Paul A.) Fdn., Chicago, 3/153
Levy (Joseph) Jr. Fdn., Chicago, 3/153
Levy (R. S.) Family Fdn., Chicago, 3/154
Lewers Scholarship Trust Fund, Mendota, 3/155
Lewis (Frank J.) Catholic Charities of the Archdiocese of Chicago, Chicago, 3/156
Lewis (Frank J.) Fdn., Chicago, 3/157
Lewis (Frank J.) Residuary Trust, Chicago, 3/158
Lewis (Frank J.) Trust for Lewis College, Chicago, 3/160
Lewis (Robert A.) Fund, Chicago, 3/161
Liberty Fdn., Teutopolis, 3/162
Lichtenberg (Leo & Eva) Fdn., Chicago, 3/163
Lidseen Fdn., Chicago, 3/163
Liff (Sam & Rose) Fdn., Chicago, 3/164
Limbert Fdn., Chicago, 3/165
Lindsay (Oakley) Fdn. of Quincy Newspapers, Inc. & Quincy Broadcasting Co., Quincy, 3/165

Linick (Sidney C.) Family Fdn., Chicago, 3/166
Lippman (Leo A. & Bertha) Fdn., Chicago, 3/166
Lipschultz (M. A.) Fdn., Chicago, 3/167
Lipsey (Maurie B. & Lillian H.) Fdn., Chicago, 3/168
Liss (Ben & Clara) Fund, Chicago, 3/168
Listeman (Marguerite) Fdn., Chicago, 3/169
Living Faith Fdn., Deerfield, 3/170
Lockformer Fdn., Lisle, 3/171
Lockrem (Constance & Dudley) Fdn., Chicago, 3/171
Loeb (Mr. & Mrs. Hamilton M.) Jr. Fdn., Chicago, 3/172
Logan Fund, Highland Park, 3/172
Logan (Robert L.) Fdn., Decatur, 3/173
Lopin (Julius & Janet) Charitable Fdn., Chicago, 3/174
Louis (John J.) Fdn., Chicago, 3/174
Loveland (George C.) Testamentary Trust, Dixon, 3/176
Lowenstine Fdn., Chicago, 3/176
Lowrey (Forest R.) Charitable Fdn., Evanston, 3/177
L. R. N. Fund, Chicago, 3/177
Lubin (Charles W. & Tillie K.) Fdn., Chicago, 3/178
Lumpkin Fdn., Chicago, 3/179
Lunding Fdn., Melrose Park, 3/181
Lutheran Fdn., Niles, 3/181
Lutz (George) Family Fdn., Chicago, 3/181
Lydia Fund, La Grange Park, 3/182
Lydon (Annie) Cemetery Trust, Chicago, 3/182
Lynch (John P.) Family Fdn., Chicago, 3/183
Mabley Fdn., Chicago, 3/183
MacArthur (John D. & Catherine T.) Fdn., Chicago, 3/184
Macfund, Lake Forest, 3/184
Mackler (Suzan R.) Fund, Chicago, 3/184
Macon County Lincoln Memorial Association, Decatur, 3/185
Mae Fdn., Chicago, 3/185
Magerstadt (Madeline) Charitable Fund, Chicago, 3/186
Maland-Ilg Charitable Trust, Wilmette, 3/187
Maltz (B. N.) Fdn., Chicago, 3/187
Maltz (M. M. & Dana G.) Fdn., Chicago, 3/189
Manaster (Florence) Fdn., Chicago, 3/189
Manhoff (Harold & Edna) Fdn., Chicago, 3/191
Mann (Henry & Belle) Charitable Fdn., Chicago, 3/192
Manowitz (Sidney) Fdn., Chicago, 3/192
Mansfield (Albert & Anne) Fnd., Chicago, 3/192
Maranz Fdn., Chicago, 3/193
Marcus Fdn., Chicago, 3/193
Marcus (Richard E. & Francelle W.) Family Fdn., Chicago, 3/194
Marder (S. Edward) Family Fdn., Chicago, 3/195
Maremont Corporation Fdn., Chicago, 3/195
Marks Family Charitable Trust, Chicago, 3/195
Markle Fdn., Chicago, 3/196
Markus (Jeanette & Henry) Family Fund, Chicago, 3/196
Marmel Charitable Trust, Chicago, 3/197
Marmor Fdn., Chicago, 3/198
Marquette Charitable Organization, Chicago, 3/199
Mars (Gerhardt C.) Fdn., Chicago, 3/200
Marsh & McLennan Fdn., Chicago, 3/201
Field (Marshall) & Company Fdn., Chicago, 3/202
Marshall (Zimmerman M.) Scholarship Fund, Chicago, 3/204
Marsteller Fdn., Chicago, 3/204
Martin (Bert William) Fdn., Chicago, 3/204
Martin (C. V.) Fdn., Chicago, 3/205
Martin (Irl C.) & Dorothy C. Martin Charitable Trust, Rockford, 3/205
Mason (Marcus D. & Dorothy) Fdn., Chicago, 3/206
Mason Scholarship Fund, Mattoon, 3/207

Material Service Fdn., Chicago, 3/208
Mather (Alonzo Clark) Trust, Chicago, 3/208
Mather (Alonzo) Fdn. Fund, Chicago, 3/210
Mathews Fdn., Alton, 3/211
Mauldin (William H.) Fdn., Chicago, 3/212
Mauranne Fdn., Chicago, 3/212
Maurose Fund, Chicago, 3/213
Gary (Elbert N.) For G. Mausoleum Trust, Chicago, 3/214
Maverick Fdn., Glencoe, 3/215
Mayer (Florence B.) Charitable Fdn., Chicago, 3/215
Mayer (Joseph) Jr. & Estelle C. Mayer Charitable Fdn., Chicago, 3/216
Mayer (Oscar) Fdn., Chicago, 3/217
Mayer (Oscar O. & Elsa S.) Charitable Trust, Chicago, 3/221
Mayer (Robert & Beatrice) Fdn., Chicago, 3/221
McAllister Fdn., Chicago, 3/222
McAvoy (Father John) Memorial Fdn., Chicago, 3/223
McCahey (James B. & Claire M.) Fdn., Chicago, 3/223
McClelland (L. S.) Fdn., Glenview, 3/224
McCormick (Brooks & Hope B.) Fdn., Chicago, 3/224
McCormick (Robert R.) Fdn., Chicago, 3/225
McCormick (Roger) Fdn., Chicago, 3/226
McCortney Fdn., Park Ridge, 3/226
McDougal (Winnifred & Bouton), Chicago, 3/227
McElwee (Robert H.), for Bethesda, Chicago, 3/228
McElwee (Robert H.) Trust, Chicago, 3/228
McElwee (William M. & A. H.), Chicago, 3/229
McFetridge Fdn., Chicago, 3/229
McGaw (Foster G.) Charitable Fdn., Evanston, 3/230
McGraw Fdn., Elgin, 3/230
McGraw Fdn., Elgin, 4/001
Wilton (McKinley) Charitable Trust, Chicago, 4/007
McShumwill Fdn., Chicago, 4/008
Mecklenburger (Albert & Erna) Fdn., Skokie, 4/009
Meitus Fdn., Chicago, 4/010
Melahn (E. M.) Fdn., Algonquin, 4/011
Melidones Family Fdn., Chicago, 4/011
Mellinger (Edward Arthur) Educational Fdn., Monmouth, 4/012
Mellon (Doris L.) Memorial Fund, Champaign, 4/019
Melrene Fund, Aurora, 4/019
Melvoin Fdn., Chicago, 4/019
Mendes-Goldstein Fdn., Chicago, 4/020
Merit Publishing Company Scholarship Fdn., Northfield, 4/021
Merkle (Arthur J.) & Clara C. Merkle Fdn., Danforth, 4/021
Merrell (Margaret & Richard) Fdn., Chicago, 4/021
Merrion Fdn., Chicago, 4/021
Merwin (Lorine & Marjorie) Fdn., Bloomington, 4/022
Metz (Arthur R.) Fdn., Chicago, 4/022
Metz (Carl J.) For Anna C., Chicago, 4/024
Metzenberg (John & Francelle) Fdn., Chicago, 4/024
Metzenberg (Robert & Eleanor) Fdn., Chicago, 4/025
Meyer (Arnold) Fdn., Chicago, 4/026
Meyer-Ceco Fdn., Chicago, 4/026
Meyerhoff (I. & R.) Fund, Highland Park, 4/027
Meyers (S. E.) Fdn., Chicago, 4/028
M. G. S. Charitable Fund, Chicago, 4/029
Mheda Insurance Trust Fund, Chicago, 4/030
Michelmann Fdn., Quincy, 4/030
Michels (Robert D.), Jr. Fdn., Winnetka, 4/031
Midas-International Corporation Scholarship Trust, Chicago, 4/032
Midas-International Corporation Fdn., Chicago, 4/032

Midwestern Society of Orthodontists, Northbrook, 4/033

Milby (Tom) Memorial Fdn., Springfield, 4/033

Miller (Glenn R.) Fdn., Glenview, 4/033

Miller (Loren C.) Fdn., Chicago, 4/034

Miller (Nathan & Isabel) Family Fdn., Chicago, 4/034

Milnot (Hauser) Fdn., Litchfield, 4/035

Milwaukee Valve Fdn., Highland Park, 4/035

Miner-Weisz Charitable Fdn., Chicago, 4/036

Minor (Edward & Lucy R.) Fdn., Chicago, 4/036

Minow (Newton & Josephine) Charitable Fund, Chicago, 4/036

Mira (Joseph J. & Ernest G.) Fdn., Alton, 4/037

Misco Fdn., Chicago, 4/038

Mizener (F. D.) Fdn., Downers Grove, 4/038

M. L. Fdn., Chicago, 4/038

Mogilner (Charles A. & Shirley) Family Fdn., Chicago, 4/039

Molner (Lillian L.) Fdn., Chicago, 4/040

Monroe Scholarship Fdn., Quincy, 4/041

Ward (Montgomery) Fdn., Chicago, 4/041

Moore (O. L.) Fdn., Chicago, 4/043

Moorman Company Fund, Quincy, 4/044

Moorman (Jessie) Trust, Quincy, 4/046

Moos (Naomie & Clifford) Fdn., Highland Park, 4/046

Morris (Philip & Fannie) Fdn., Chicago, 4/047

Morrison (Edward W.) Trust, Chicago, 4/048

Morton Fund, Chicago, 4/050

Morton (Sterling) Charitable Trust, Chicago, 4/050

Mossner (Alfred) Fdn., Chicago, 4/053

M. R. Fdn., Chicago, 4/053

Mueller Fdn. for Religious Charities, Palatine, 4/054

MUFA (f/k/a James J. Mullen Fdn.), Kankakee, 4/054

Murphy Fdn., Dixon, 4/055

Musical Education Fund, Chicago, 4/055

Nalco Fdn., Chicago, 4/056

Nathan (Cecile & Jerome) Fdn., Glencoe, 4/057

Nathanson Family Fund, Chicago, 4/058

National Industrial Recreation Research & Education Fdn., Chicago, 4/059

Navillus Charitable Trust, Wilmette, 4/059

Natovich (Hy & Anna) Fdn., Chicago, 4/060

Nayman Fdn., Chicago, 4/060

Nef (John U. & Evelyn) Fdn., Chicago, 4/061

Neisser Fund, Highland Park, 4/061

Neiman (Harry & Freida) Charitable Fdn., Chicago, 4/062

Nelson (Herbert U.) Memorial Fund, Chicago, 4/062

Nelson (L. M.) Family Charitable Trust, Evanston, 4/062

Nelson (L. R.) Trust, Brimfield, 4/062

Nemeroff (Victor) Fdn., Chicago, 4/063

New Prospect Fdn., Skokie, 4/064

Newberger (Arnold & Doris) Fund, Chicago, 4/064

Newbury (Michael) Family Fdn., Chicago, 4/065

Newman Medical Fdn., Chicago, 4/066

Newsman (Verna) Testamentary Trust, DeKalb, 4/066

Newton (Mary M.), Chicago, 4/066

Nichols Fdn., Jacksonville, 4/067

Nielsen (Arthur) Fdn., Chicago, 4/067

Nielsen (Arthur C.), Jr. Charitable Trust, Chicago, 4/068

Nierman (Eli A.) Fdn., Chicago, 4/069

Nixon (Alvan B. & Edna B.) Fund, Chicago, 4/071

Noer (O. J.) Research Fdn., Oak Park, 4/072

Norell Family Fdn., River Forest, 4/072

Norman (Harold) Fund, Chicago, 4/073

North (Esther L.) Charitable Trust, Chicago, 4/074

North (Francis S.) Fdn., Chicago, 4/074

Northern Illinois Fdn., Chicago, 4/075

Northern Trust Company Charitable Trust, Chicago, 4/075

Northwest Industries Fdn., Chicago, 4/076

Norton (Geraldi) Memorial Corporation, Chicago, 4/077

Norton (R. H.) Fund, Chicago, 4/078

Norton (Ralph H. & Elizabeth C.) Philanthropic Trust, Chicago, 4/079

Norville (Leo T.) Fdn., Chicago, 4/081

Norwell Fund, Chicago, 4/082

Notaro (Michael R.) Fdn., Chicago, 4/083

Novak (Lee) Fdn., Highland Park, 4/083

Nozette (Morris) Family Fdn., Chicago, 4/084

Nuveen Benevolent Trust, Chicago, 4/084

Oak Park-River Forest Community Fdn., Oak Park, 4/086

Offner (Franklin F.) Fdn., Deerfield, 4/086

Oguss Charitable Fdn., Glencoe, 4/087

H.B.C.L. Okawville Laborers, Lenzburg, 4/088

Olin (John M.) Fdn., Alton, 4/088

Oliphant (Walten) Fdn., Winnetka, 4/089

Olmstead (L. B.) Trust, Sycamore, 4/090

Oppenheimer Family Fdn., Chicago, 4/091

Orendorff (U. G.) for Canton Methodist Church, Chicago, 4/092

Orendorff (U. G.) for Canton Park District, Chicago, 4/093

Orendorff (U. G.) Educational Fund, Chicago, 4/093

Orendorff (U. G.) For Y.M.C.A. of Canton, Chicago, 4/094

Ottawa Silica Company Fdn., Chicago, 4/094

Ovitz (Virginia N.) Memorial Fund, Sycamore, 4/095

Ozite Fdn., Libertyville, 4/095

Page (John W.) Fdn., Chicago, 4/096

Page (Ruth) Fdn., Chicago, 4/096

Paidar Fund, Chicago, 4/097

Pajeau Children's Fdn., Chicago, 4/098

Pakula Fdn., Chicago, 4/099

Park (Francis) Fdn., Kewanee, 4/100

Parker (Don H.) Fdn., Chicago, 4/100

Parmelee (John W.), Chicago, 4/101

Patten Fdn., Chicago, 4/101

Pauley (C. & M.) for Cornell College, Chicago, 4/102

Pearlman & Pearlman Family Fdn., Chicago, 4/103

Pearson (Patsy) Memorial Fund, Chicago, 4/104

Pekin (Harry Jay) Memorial Fdn., Arlington Heights, 4/105

Pekow (Phil) Family Fdn., Chicago, 4/105

Penikoff (Fannie) Charitable Fdn., Chicago, 4/105

Perkins Fdn., Edwin E. Perkins--Trust under will, Chicago, 4/106

Perkins (Kitty M.) Fdn., Chicago, 4/107

Perlman (Joseph) Fdn., Chicago, 4/107

Perlman (Morris) Fdn., Chicago, 4/108

Perlman (Henry & Selma) Fdn., Chicago, 4/109

Perlstein (M.) Fund, Chicago, 4/110

Person-to-Person Fdn., Chicago, 4/111

Pesmen (Allen S.) Family Fdn., Chicago, 4/112

Peterborough Fdn., Chicago, 4/112

Petersen Family Fdn., Chicago, 4/113

Petersen (Esper A.) Fdn., Skokie, 4/114

Peterson Charitable Trust, Rockford, 4/115

Peterson-Martin Engineering Fdn., Reponset, 4/115

Petrie Fdn., Chicago, 4/115

Pfaelzer (Ellard L. & Oliva B.) Charitable Fund, Chicago, 4/117

Pfaelzer (Leonard & Elizabeth) Fdn., Glencoe, 4/117

Phi Chapter Educational Fdn. of Phi Gamma Delta Fraternity, Chicago, 4/118

Philo Fdn., Chicago, 4/118

Pick (Albert) Jr. Fund, Chicago, 4/119

Pick (Grant D.) Fdn., Chicago, 4/120

Pierce (H. A.) Fdn., Chicago, 4/121

Pink (Ira M. & Libbie P.) Fdn., Chicago, 4/122

Pinsof Fdn.. Chicago, 4/122

Pioneer Fund, Chicago, 4/123

Pip Fdn., Park Ridge, 4/124

Pittway Corporation Charitable Fdn., Northbrook, 4/124

Player (Annie Louise) Memorial Fund, Evanston, 4/124

Podall (Leslie Beth) Memorial Fund, Chicago, 4/124

Podulka (Gene J.) Fdn., Glenview, 4/125

Poe (Frances M.) Wildlife Salvage Trust, Wilmette, 4/125

Pokvitis (Zenon W.) Fdn., Chicago, 4/125

Polk Bros. Fdn., Melrose Park, 4/126

Polish Medical History & Science Fdn., Chicago, 4/126

Polo Training Fdn., Oak Brook, 4/127

Poncher (Jerry E.) Family Fdn., Chicago, 4/127

Poncher Fdn., River Forest, 4/128

Pope Fdn., Chicago, 4/129

Portes Charitable Trust, Chicago, 4/130

Portes (Herbert) Family Fdn., Chicago, 4/130

Pos (Arthur S.) & Company Charitable Fdn., Chicago, 4/130

Pos (Arthur S. & Mae L.) Fdn., Chicago, 4/131

Powell (Raymond R.) Charitable Trust, Springfield, 4/132

Preston Charitable Fdn., Chicago, 4/133

Price (Mary H. & Shelby A.) Fdn., Paris, 4/133

Priebe (Arthur F.) Fdn., Rockford, 4/134

Prince (Frederick Henry) Testamentary Trust, Chicago, 4/135

Prince (Frederick Henry) Trust, Chicago, 4/136

Prince Fdn., Chicago, 4/138

Prince Family Fdn., Chicago, 4/139

Pristo (Robert E.) Fdn., Chicago, 4/139

Proesel (Henry A.) Fdn., Chicago, 4/140

Prospect Fdn., Chicago, 4/140

Pullman Banking Group Charitable Fdn., Chicago, 4/143

Pullman Fdn., Chicago, 4/144

Purdy Fdn., Chicago, 4/145

Purvin Fdn., Riverside, 4/146

Rappaport (Eugene & Gertrude) Fdn., Chicago, 4/146

Rasmussen (Robert V.) Fdn., Antioch, 4/147

Ratcliffe (Myron F.) Fdn., Chicago, 4/148

Ratner (David & Milton) Fdn., Chicago, 4/149

Reade Industrial Fund, Chicago, 4/149

Red & White Fdn., Chicago, 4/150

Redhill Charities, Peoria, 4/151

Regenstein (Joseph & Helen) Fdn., Chicago, 4/152

Reich Fdn., Chicago, 4/155

Reich (Robert & Sonya) Fdn., Chicago, 4/155

Reingold (Jules J.) Trust, T/w, Chicago, 4/156

Replogle (Luther I.) Fdn., Oak Park, 4/157

Resnick Family Fdn., Chicago, 4/157

Resnick (Howard & Helaine) Fdn., Highland Park, 4/158

R. F. Fdn., Sycamore, 4/159

Rice (Dorothy & Wilbur) Charitable Fdn., Chicago, 4/161

Rice Fdn., Chicago, 4/161

Richards Fdn., Chicago, 4/162

Richardson (Robert J.) Fdn., Peioria, 4/162

Richman (Adolph) Family Fdn. for Geriatric Research & Shelter, Chicago, 4/163

Richter (Paul K.) Memorial Fund, Chicago, 4/163

Ringer (Lotta & Philip) Charitable Fund, Chicago, 4/164

R. I. S. Fdn., Chicago, 4/164

Rivco Fdn., Bellwood, 4/165

Robbins Charitable Fund, Elk Grove Village, 4/165 ˙

Robert Fdn., Chicago, 4/166

Roberts Fdn., Franklin Park, 4/166

Robin (Mr. & Mrs. Sidney L.) Fund, Glencoe, 4/166

Robinson (Ellen) Fund, Chicago, 4/166

Robinson (Sanger P. & Martha F.) Fdn., Chicago, 4/167

Robinson (Sidney R. & Frances W.) Fdn., Chicago, 4/167
Robson (Edwin O. & Elizabeth S.) Fdn., Glencoe, 4/168
Rochdale Institute, Chicago, 4/168
Rockford Fdn. for Plastic & Reconstructive Surgery, Rockford, 4/169
Rockford Real Estate Board Fdn., Rockford, 4/170
Roe-Sonnenschein Fdn., Chicago, 4/170
Roesing Family Fdn., Chicago, 4/170
Rohlen Fdn., Morton Grove, 4/171
Rolfe (Jane E. & Iver A.) Fdn., Rochelle, 4/172
Roper Fdn., Kankakee, 4/173
Rosca Fdn., Rosemont, 4/174
Rose (Gene) Fdn., Highland Park, 4/174
Rosenberg (Aaron A.) Family Fdn., Chicago, 4/174
Rosenberg (Ben L.) Family Fdn., Chicago, 4/175
Rosenberg (Michael) Memorial Fdn., Chicago, 4/176
Rosenbloom (Abe H.) Charitable Fdn., Rockford, 4/176
Rosenfield (Maurice & Losi) Fund, Chicago, 4/177
Rosemutter Fdn., Chicago, 4/178
Rosenstein Fdn., Chicago, 4/179
Rosenstein (Louis & Madeline) Fdn., Chicago, 4/180
Rosenthal (Morris & Ethel) Family Fdn., Chicago, 4/180
Rossi (James), Chicago, 4/180
Roth Fund, Chicago, 4/181
Roth (Herbert L.) Fdn., Olympia Fields, 4/181
Roth (Jerome M.)-Harold Seigle Fdn., Elgin, 4/182
Roth-Blackhawk Fdn., Chicago, 4/183
Rothschild (Ann & Edwin) Fund, Chicago, 4/184
Rothschild (Mr. & Mrs. A. Frank) Fund, Chicago, 4/186
Rothschild (G.W.V.M.) Fund, Evanston, 4/187
Rothschild (Helen) Fdn., Lake Zurich, 4/187
Rothschild (Melville N. & Mary F.) Fund, Chicago, 4/188
Rowin Fdn., Evanston, 4/189
Roxbury Fund, Chicago, 4/189
Rubert (Samual R. & Gertrude S.) Charitable Fdn., Lincolnwood, 4/190
Rubloff (Arthur) Fund, Chicago, 4/191
Ruby (S.D.) Fdn., Chicago, 4/192
Ruderman (Fannye & Norton E.) Fdn., Chicago, 4/193
Ruwitch (Shirley & Robert) Fdn., Northbrook, 4/194
Rusnak (Raymond L.) Family Fdn., Chicago, 4/194
Russell (Anna M.) Missionary, Chicago, 4/195
Rust-Oleum Fdn. f/k/a Fergusson Fdn., Evanston, 4/195
Ryerson (Morton Butler) Memorial Fund, Chicago, 4/196
Ryerson (Joseph T.) Charitable Fund, Chicago, 4/196
Sachs (Morris B.) Fdn., Chicago, 4/197
Saffir Fdn., Chicago, 4/198
Saganaga Corporation, Chicago, 4/199
St. Casimir Student Aid Fund, Chicago, 4/199
St. Charles Charities, St. Charles, 4/200
St. Mark's Parish, Chicago, 4/201
White (Catherine M.)-St. Mark's Church, Chicago, 4/202
St. Mary Magdaline Educational Fdn., Chicago, 4/203
Saks (Julien M. & Adele F.) Fdn., Highland Park, 4/204
Salomon Fdn., Chicago, 4/205
Saltz Family Fdn., Chicago, 4/205
Sampson (Frances C.) Testamentary Trust, Petersburg, 4/206
Samuels Family Fdn., Chicago, 4/206
Samuels (Robert & Hope) Fdn., Glencoe, 4/206

Sandberg (Virginia Walkinshaw) Fdn., Chicago, 4/207
Sandman (Sheldon J.) Family Fdn., Chicago, 4/207
Santa Fe Railway Fdn., Chicago, 4/208
Santucci Family Fdn., Skokie, 4/209
Satinover (Charles) Fund, Chicago, 4/210
Saul (Wesley W.) Charitable Trust, Des Plaines, 4/211
Sax Fdn., Chicago, 4/211
Sayler (Hildegarde H. & Charles E.) Fdn., Chicago, 4/212
Schaffner Family Fdn., Oak Park, 4/212
Schamberg Fdn., Skokie, 4/213
Scheel (Fred H.) Scholarship Fund, Chicago, 4/214
Schild (Edwin F.) Charitable Fdn., Chicago, 4/215
Schmidt (Casper) Fdn., Elgin, 4/216
Schmidt (Charles E. & Dorothy F.) Family Fdn., Chicago, 4/216
Schnadig (Lawrence & Dorothy) Family Fdn., Chicago, 4/217
Schneider (Herschel Lawrence) Charitable Fdn., Chicago, 4/218
Schneider (Robert E.) Fdn., Chicago, 4/218
Schoen (Armund & Rita) Fdn., Chicago, 4/219
Schoenberg (Samuel & Irene) Fdn., Chicago, 4/220
Schoenstadt Family Fdn., Chicago, 4/220
Scholl (William M.) Fdn., Chicago, 4/221
Schram (Leonard & Elvis B.) Fdn., Glencoe, 4/222
Schram (William S. & Lena G.) Fdn., Highland Park, 4/223
Schreiber (Ludwig D. & Jeanette) Fund, Chicago, 4/223
Schuessler Knitting Fdn., Chicago, 4/224
Schulman Fdn., Chicago, 4/224
Schwarten Family Fdn., Wilmette, 4/225
Schwartz (Charles P. & Lavinia S.) Fdn., Chicago, 4/225
Schwartz (Ida & Ben) Fdn., Chicago, 4/226
Schwartz (Kevie & Alan) Fdn., Chicago, 4/227
Schwartz (Nathan & Harriet) Fdn., Chicago, 4/227
Schwarz-Hart Family Fdn., Chicago, 4/228
Schweppe Fdn., Chicago, 4/229
Scott Fdn., Streator, 4/231
Scott (Carson Pirie) Fdn., Chicago, 4/231
Bromwell (Mari S. & M. Scott) Charitable Fund, Chicago, 4/234
Scully Fdn., Chicago, 4/235
Seabury Fdn., Chicago, 4/235
Searle Fdn., Chicago, 4/237
Sears-Roebuck Foundation, Chicago, 5/001
Sears Bank Foundation, Chicago, 5/004
Sebastian Fdn., Riverside, 5/005
Seder (Seymour & Frances) Fund, Chicago, 5/006
Seefurth Fdn., Chicago, 5/006
Seeley (John Harper) Fdn., Chicago, 5/007
Seifert Fdn., Chicago, 5/008
Serta Mattress of Chicago Fdn., Chicago, 5/009
Server Family Fdn., Chicago, 5/009
Settling Fdn., Chicago, 5/010
Seville Fdn., Chicago, 5/010
Sexton (Ellen Webb) Fdn., Chicago, 5/011
Seymour (Dr. Stephen) Memorial Fund, Chicago, 5/011
S & LB Fund, Highland Park, 5/012
Shankman (Sam & Helen) Charitable Fund, Glencoe, 5/013
Shapiro (Eugene & Marlene) Fdn., Skokie, 5/013
Shapiro (Lester & Edna) Fdn., Glencoe, 5/014
Shapiro (Nathan & Randy) Fdn., Highland Park, 5/014
Shapiro (Coretta & Henry) Family Fdn., Chicago, 5/015
Shapre (Byron & Helen) Fdn., Glencoe, 5/015
Shaw (Arch W.) Fdn., Chicago, 5/015
Shaw (Bradford W.) Fdn., Chicago, 5/016
Shaw-North Fdn., Chicago, 5/016

Shedd (John G. & M.R.) Library Trust A, Chicago, 5/017
Shelper (Billy) Memorial Fund, Bloomington, 5/018
Sherman-Jacobs Fdn., Chicago, 5/019
Sherman (Nate H.) Fdn., Chicago, 5/019
Sherry-Lu Fund, Springfield, 5/019
Sherwood Medical Industries Fdn., Chicago, 5/020
Shiller (Edith B.), Chicago, 5/021
Shilling Fund, Chicago, 5/022
Shinner Fdn., Berwyn, 5/022
Shipman (O.B. & L.M.) Charity Fund, Chicago, 5/023
Shlensky (Harold & Mildred) Family Fdn., Chicago, 5/025
Shmikler (Samuel) Fdn., Skokie, 5/025
Shore (Harry & Helen) Fdn., Chicago, 5/026
Shulman Fdn., Chicago, 5/027
Shure (Alan H.) Fund, Schiller Park, 5/027
Shure (Joseph N.) Family Fdn., Chicago, 5/028
Shure (Myron B.) Fund, Chicago, 5/029
Shure (Richard M.) Fund, Chicago, 5/029
Shure (Sam) Family Fdn., Chicago, 5/030
Siegel (Henry J.) Family Fdn., Chicago, 5/030
Signode Fdn., Chicago, 5/031
Silberman (Cleo & David B.) Charitable Fdn., Chicago, 5/032
Silberman (Hubert & Wilma) Charitable Fdn., Chicago, 5/032
Silberman (Sigmund) Fdn., Chicago, 5/033
Silbert Fdn., Chicago, 5/033
Silver (Michael & Rose) Fdn., Chicago, 5/034
Silver Spring Fdn., Chicago, 5/035
Silverstein (Harry & Constance) Fdn., Chicago, 5/036
Silverstein (Samuel) Charitable Fdn., Chicago, 5/037
Simmonds (Fanny R. & George L.) Fdn., Chicago, 5/037
Simmons Fdn., Chicago, 5/038
Simon (Oscar & Edith) Fdn., Lincolnwood, 5/039
Simon (William & Celeste W.) Fdn., Glencoe, 5/039
Simpson (John M.) Fdn., Chicago, 5/039
Simpson (William & Hope) Fdn., Chicago, 5/040
Singer (Sydney) Fdn., Chicago, 5/041
Six Point Fdn., Chicago, 5/041
Skoglund (Alice & Leonard) Fdn., Chicago, 5/042
Skoner Fdn., Wilmette, 5/042
Slavin-Malkin Fdn., Chicago, 5/043
Sloan (Noah & Belle) Fund, Chicago, 5/044
Small (Irwin H.) Charitable Fdn., Chicago, 5/045
Smart Family Fdn., Chicago, 5/045
Smith Charitable Trust, Rockford, 5/046
Smith (Edward Byron) Charitable Fund, Chicago, 5/046
Smith (Essie B.) Fdn., Sycamore, 5/047
Smith (George D.) Memorial Fund, Chicago, 5/048
Smith (Helen Lewis) Fdn., Fairbury, 5/048
Smith (Herman & Mary C.) Fdn., Chicago, 5/048
Smith (John V.) Fdn., Oak Park, 5/049
Smith (Solomon Byron) Charitable Fund, Chicago, 5/049
Smoler (Jerry) Family Fdn., Chicago, 5/050
Snow (Daisy J.), Chicago, 5/052
Solinsky (Robert S. & Marie V.) Fdn., Chicago, 5/052
Solomon (Jerome D.) Memorial Trust, Chicago, 5/052
Solomon (Julian M.) Fdn., Chicago, 5/053
Solomon (Lou-Eona) Fdn., Chicago, 5/053
Sommer (John R.) Fdn., Rockford, 5/054
Sommerfield (Nathaniel & Lillian G.) Fund, Chicago, 5/055
Sonnenschein Fund, Chicago, 5/056
Sonnenschein (Hugo & Virginia B.) Charitable Fund, Chicago, 5/056

Souder (William F.) Jr. Charitable Trust, Chicago, 5/056
Spertus Fdn., Chicago, 5/057
Spiegel (John & Babette) Fund, Chicago, 5/058
Speigel (M.J.) Family Fdn., Chicago, 5/058
Speigel (Ruth & Frederick) Fdn., Chicago, 5/059
Spiro (Harold M.) Fdn., Franklin Park, 5/060
Spitz (Joel & Maxine) Fdn., Glencoe, 5/060
Sports Shop Fdn., Lake Forest, 5/061
Sprad Fdn., Chicago, 5/061
Sprague (Otho S.A.) Memorial Institute, Chicago, 5/061
Square D Fdn., Park Ridge, 5/065
SRA Fdn., Chicago, 5/066
Staley (A.E.) Jr. Fdn., Decatur, 5/066
Staley (Emma L.) Fdn., Decatur, 5/067
Staley (Henry M.) Declaration of Charitable Tr., Decatur, 5/068
Stanadyne Fdn., Oak Park, 5/068
Standard Oil (Indiana) Fdn., Chicago, 5/069
Stanmart Fund, Chicago, 5/075
Stanray Fdn., Chicago, 5/076
Stans Fdn., Chicago, 5/077
Stans Student Loan Fdn., Chicago, 5/078
Star (Max & Yetta) Fdn., Chicago, 5/078
Starrett (Julius), Chicago, 5/079
Steber Gdn., Elmhurst, 5/080
Stefan Charitable Fdn., Winnetka, 5/082
Stein (Robert N.) Family Fdn., Skokie, 5/083
Steinberg (Jack & Gertrude) Fund, Chicago, 5/083
Steinberg (Jennie & Louis) Memorial Cancer Fdn., Chicago, 5/084
Stephens-Adamson Fdn., Aurora, 5/085
Sterling (John G.) Fdn., Richmond, 5/085
Stern (John N.) Charitable Fdn., Chicago, 5/087
Stetler (Pearl M.) Research Fund, Chicago, 5/087
Stevens Fund, Chicago, 5/088
Stewart Charitable Fund, Evanston, 5/088
Stewart-Warner Fdn., Chicago, 5/088
Stiffel (Lisbeth & Jules) Fdn., Chicago, 5/089
Stillwell Fdn., Quincy, 5/089
Stone Fdn., Chicago, 5/090
Stone (Avery & Patricia) Family Fdn., Chicago, 5/092
Stone (Clement) Fdn., Chicago, 5/093
Stone (Donna) Fdn., Chicago, 5/093
Stone (Ernted) Fund, Chicago, 5/094
Stone (Freda Komaiko) Heart Fund, Chicago, 5/095
Stone (Jerome & Evelyn) Family Fdn., Chicago, 5/095
Stone (Leo & Gladys) Fund, Chicago, 5/096
Stone (Lewis) Estate-W Art, III, Chicago, 5/096
Stone (Marvin & Anita) Family Fdn., Chicago, 5/096
Stone (Norman H.) Family Fdn., Chicago, 5/097
Stone (Roger & Susan) Family Fdn., Chicago, 5/098
Stone (W. Clement & Jessie V.) Fdn., Chicago, 5/099
Stonebridge Fdn., Chicago, 5/100
Stoskopf (Alice L.), Chicago, 5/101
Stoskopf (William B.), Chicago, 5/102
Stotler Charitable Trust, Champaign, 5/103
Straus (Madeline B. & Henry H.) Endowment Fund, Chicago, 5/103
Straus (Marjorie & Robert) Endowment Fund, Chicago, 5/104
Strauss (Beatrice H. & Leon) Fdn., Chicago, 5/105
Strauss (Harold E. & Lucille G.) Fdn., Chicago, 5/105
Strauss (Henry A.) & William Strauss Endowment, Chicago, 5/105
Strauss Surgical Group Fdn., Chicago, 5/106
Straut (Elizabeth A.) Estate, Chicago, 5/107
Streich (Edwin August) Trust, Chicago, 5/108
Struve (Fred C.) Charitable Trust, Chicago, 5/109

Stuart (Harold L.) Estate, Chicago, 5/110
Sturgis Family Fdn., Winnetka, 5/111
Sullivan (Joseph W.) Fund, Chicago, 5/112
Sunrise Fund, Chicago, 5/113
Sun-Times/Daily News Charity Trust, Chicago, 5/113
Superior Tanning Company Fdn., Chicago, 5/113
Susman & Asher Fdn., Chicago, 5/114
Svenson (Ernest J.) Fdn., Rockford, 5/115
Swanberg Collegiate Education Fdn., Quincy, 5/116
Swartz (William & Mary) Fdn., Chicago, 5/116
Swartzberg (Irvin) Family Fdn., Chicago, 5/117
Swearingen Fdn., Chicago, 5/118
Swett Family Fund, Chicago, 5/118
Swift & Company Fdn., Chicago, 5/120
Tallman (Sefton L.) Family Fdn., Chicago, 5/120
Tarahumara Fdn., Palatine, 5/121
Tark (L. Shirley) Charitable Fdn., Chicago, 5/121
Tarrson (Gilbert J.) Family Fdn., Chicago, 5/122
Tasner (Fred & Barbara) Fdn., Highland Park, 5/123
Tau Epsilon Rho Scholarship Fdn., Chicago, 5/123
Taub (Ethel & Ronald) Family Fdn., Highland Park, 5/123
Taussig (Stuart K. & Gloria) Charitable Fdn., Chicago, 5/124
Taylor (Allen S.) Fdn., Chicago, 5/124
Taylor (George W.) Charitable Trust, Rockford, 5/124
Taylor (J. Hall) Fdn., Chicago, 5/125
TCC Fdn., Chicago, 5/125
Tee-Pak Fdn., Chicago, 5/126
Teets Memorial Fund, Rosemont, 5/127
Teitelbaum (Fred) Charitable Fdn., Chicago, 5/127
Teller (Rabbi Morris) Memorial Fdn., Chicago, 5/128
Terry (Louis & Kate) Fdn., Chicago, 5/128
Thompson Fdn., Barrington, 5/129
Thompson (W.E. & E.P.) Educational Fund, Chicago, 5/129
Thompson Research Fdn., Monee, 5/130
Thompson (Earl L.) Fdn., Chicago, 5/131
Thorndale Fdn., Chicago, 5/131
Thorson Fdn., Chicago, 5/133
Thumb (Eugene W.), Chicago, 5/134
Tick (Jean Q. & Shirley J.) Family Fdn., Springfield, 5/134
Tompkins (Roscoe J.), Chicago, 5/135
Tourtelot Fdn., Chicago, 5/135
Town & Country Nursing Education Fdn., Petersburg, 5/136
Trend Charitable Fdn., Chicago, 5/136
Trienens (Howard J.) Fdn., Chicago, 5/137
Trieschmann Fdn., Chicago, 5/137
Tripp (Chester D.) Charitable Trust of 1967, Chicago, 5/138
Trojan Fdn., Park Ridge, 5/139
Chicago Title & Trust Company Fdn., Chicago, 5/140
Tryall Fund, Chicago, 5/141
Tuohy (Walter & Mary) Fdn., Chicago, 5/142
Turban (Gene & Shirley) Fdn., Chicago, 5/142
Turnbull (Dr. George C.) Fdn., Evanston, 5/143
Turoff (Lee & Inez) Fdn., Chicago, 5/143
Tyndale House Fdn., Wheaton, 5/143
Tyrrell Fdn., Elgin, 5/144
Uhlmann-Benjamin Fdn., Chicago, 5/144
Ukrainian Arts Club of Chicago, Chicago, 5/145
Underwood Fdn., Chicago, 5/145
Union Tank Car Fdn., Chicago, 5/146
Unit Machinery Charitable Trust, Rockford, 5/147
United Air Lines Fdn., Chicago, 5/147
United Conveyor Fdn., Chicago, 5/149
United Educators Fdn., Lake Bluff, 5/150

United-Greenfield Charitable & Educational Fdn., Northbrook, 5/151
United States Polo Association, Oak Brook, 5/153
U O P Fdn., Des Plaines, 5/153
Upton (Frederick S.) Fdn., Chicago, 5/156
Vawter (Elizabeth Epton) Fdn., Chicago, 5/157
Ursich (Joseph E.), Chicago, 5/158
DeMoulin (U.S.) Fund, Greenville, 5/158
Usiskin (Esther & Nathan) Fdn., Chicago, 5/159
Vale (Murray & Virginia) Fdn., Chicago, 5/160
Vanderveld (Christian) Fdn., Wheaton, 5/161
Vangelder (Henry) Residuary Trust, Chicago, 5/161
van Straaten (Virginia & Herbert) Fund, Chicago, 5/161
Vaughan (Harry A.) Family Fdn., Chicago, 5/162
Veritas Fund, Quincy, 5/162
Vermilion Fdn., Danville, 5/163
Victor Fdn., Chicago, 5/164
Vieleker (Ann M.), Chicago, 5/166
Vilas & Reid Fdn., Chicago, 5/166
Villa Park Bank Fdn., Chicago, 5/167
Vogl Family Fdn., Evanston, 5/168
Wadsworth (George S.) Charitable Trust, Chicago, 5/169
Wagenlis Fdn., Chicago, 5/170
Wagner Fdn., Chicago, 5/170
Wagner Products Fdn., Decatur, 5/171
Wahlin (Lois & Fred) Fdn., Chicago, 5/171
Walgreen (Mary Ann & Charles R.) Jr. Fund, Chicago, 5/172
Wallach (Leo & Howard) Family Fdn., Chicago, 5/173
Wallen Fdn., Chicago, 5/174
Waller (P.A.) Kewanee Hospital Association, Chicago, 5/174
Wallerstein Fdn., Chicago, 5/175
Walton (Arthur K. & Hazel C.) Fdn., Elmhurst, 5/175
Wanger (Ralph & Elaine) Fdn., Chicago, 5/176
War Memorial Fund of the Drama Club of Evanston, Chicago, 5/177
Ward Fund, Chicago, 5/177
Warner Electric Fdn., South Beloit, 5/178
Warren (Benedict O.) Fdn., Palos Park, 5/179
Watkins (Vine A.), Chicago, 5/179
Gailey (Watson) Eye Fdn., Bloomington, 5/180
Webb (Maria J. Wesley) Memorial Hospital, Chicago, 5/180
Webster (F.F.) Fdn., Chicago, 5/180
Webster (George H.), Chicago, 5/181
Wehr (C. Frederic) Charitable Trust, Chicago, 5/182
Weidner (Emma S.), Chicago, 5/183
Weil (David Maxwell) Fdn., Chicago, 5/183
Weil (Genevieve R.) Fdn., Chicago, 5/183
Weil (Victor), Chicago, 5/183
Weinberg (Jane G.) Fdn., Chicago, 5/184
Weinberg (Louis A.) Family Fdn., Glencoe, 5/184
Weinberg (Lewis C. & Sylvia M.) Fdn., Winnetka, 5/185
Weinberg (Louis A.) Family Fdn., Glencoe, 5/186
Weinberg (Max & Louise) Fdn., Glencoe, 5/186
Weiner (George H.) Fdn., Chicago, 5/186
Weiner (Sol S.) Family Fdn., Evanston, 5/187
Weinstein (Bert B.) Fdn., Chicago, 5/188
Weinstein (Edward B.) Fdn., Chicago, 5/188
Weinstein (Jack) & Richard Hirsch Charitable, Winnetka, 5/189
Weis (LeRoy & Sylvia) Fund, Chicago, 5/189
Weisman Family Fdn., Chicago, 5/190
Weiss (Howard A.) Fdn., Chicago, 5/191
Weiss (Jerome S.) Fund, Chicago, 5/192
Weiss (L.A.), Chicago, 5/193
Weiss (Robert G.) Family Fdn., Chicago, 5/194

Weitzman (Elsie) Memorial Fdn., Chicago,
5/195
Wells (K.A.) -- First Presbyterian, Chicago,
5/195
Wells (K.) for Chicago Hearing Society,
Chicago, 5/196
Wenske (Herbert C.) Fdn., Des Plaines, 5/196
Wertheimer (Ernest) Fdn., Chicago, 5/197
Westol (Theresa & Premo) Fdn., Chicago,
5/197
Wexler (Jerrold) Fdn., Chicago, 5/198
Kirkland (Weymouth) Fdn., Chicago, 5/198
Wharton Fdn., Hinsdale, 5/199
Wheeler (Robert C.) Fdn., Chicago, 5/200
Wheeler (Robert C.) Scholarship Fund,
Chicago, 5/201
White (Eugene E. & Jane B.) Fdn., Northfield,
5/202
White (George P.) Fdn., Chicago, 5/203
White (Robert P.) Fdn., Chicago, 5/203
White (W.P. & H.B.) Fdn., Chicago, 5/203
Whitting Home, Trustees of the, Kewanee,
5/204
Whitman (Albert) Trust, Chicago, 5/205
Wieboldt Fdn., Chicago, 5/205
Wilderness Research Fdn., Chicago, 5/208
Wilemal Fund, Chicago, 5/209
Wilkie Brothers Fdn., Des Plaines, 5/210
Wilkins (Edythe L.) Charities, Peoria, 5/212
Wilkow (Joseph & Mirjama) Fdn., Chicago,
5/213
Wilkow (William W. & Tamara) Fdn., Chicago,
5/213
Wilman Fund, Chicago, 5/214
Wilson Medical Research Fdn., Rockford,
5/214
Wiman (Charles Deere) Memorial Trust,
Moline, 5/215
Winkelman (Leon G. & Josephine) Fdn.,
Chicago, 5/215
Wineman Family Fdn., Chicago, 5/216
Winer (Louis & Esther) Fdn., Chicago, 5/218
Winneshiek Players Trust Fund, Freeport,
5/218
Witz Fdn., Chicago, 5/219
Wolfe Fdn., Decatur, 5/219
Wolfson (Howard & Harriet) Fdn., Chicago,
5/220
Wonderlic Fdn., Northfield, 5/221
Wood Family Fdn., Chicago, 5/222
Wood (Henry Clay) Fdn., Northfield, 5/223
Wood (L.S.) Charitable Trust, Chicago, 6/001
Wood (Iva M.) Testamentary Trust for
Oakland Cemetery, Petersburg, 6/001
Wood (Robert E.) Fdn., Chicago, 6/002
Wood (Steven) Fdn., Chicago, 6/003
Woodruff & Edwards Fdn., Elgin, 6/003
Woolford (Radcliffe O. & Hiawatha J.)
Memorial Scholarship Fdn., Chicago, 6/003
World War II Marshall High School
Scholarship, Chicago, 6/004
World War SVC Marshall Scholarship, Chicago,
6/004
De Woskin (Nathan) Family Fdn., Chicago,
6/004
Wright (Harold D. & Hazel C.) Fdn., Chicago,
6/004
Wright (Joseph S.) Fdn., Chicago, 6/005
Wrigley Fund, Chicago, 6/006
Wurlitzer Fdn., Chicago, 6/007
Wurlitzer (Farny & Grace K.) Fdn., Chicago,
6/008
Wyler (Silvain & Arma) Fdn., Chicago, 6/009
Wyne Fdn., Sterling, 6/010
Yoxall (Bertha A.), Chicago, 6/011
Yoxall (William), Chicago, 6/011
Zacharias (Beverly & Richard) Fdn., Chicago,
6/012
Zacharias (Bobette & James) Fdn., Chicago,
6/012
Zadek (Milton & Rose) Fund, Melrose Park,
6/013
Zahn (Louis) Fdn., Melrose Park, 6/013
Zalkind (Jerry) Fdn., Chicago, 6/014
Zavis Charitable Fdn., Chicago, 6/014
Zeisler (Claire P.) Fdn., Chicago, 6/014

Zell (Bernard & Rochelle) Fdn., Highland Park,
6/015
Ziegler Charitable Fdn., Chicago, 6/015

Second Filming

Aares Institute, Chicago, 7/001
Adler (Eugene M.) Family Fund, Glencoe,
7/003
Adventurers Club Fdn., Chicago, 7/004
Affiliated Industries Fdn., Chicago, 7/004
Ahern (Mary Eileen) Trust, Chicago, 7/005
Aigner (G.J.) Fdn., Chicago, 7/006
Aldeen (G.W.) Charitable Trust, Rockford,
7/006
Allerton (Robert) Endowment Fund, Chicago,
7/008
Altschuler - Seder Fund, Chicago, 7/011
Alumni Fdn. Fund of the Illinois Chapter of
Alpha Delta Phi Trust, Lake Forest, 7/012
Amalgamated Meat Cutters & Butcher
Workmen Scholarships, Chicago, 7/012
Amber Fdn., Chicago, 7/013
American Committee for South Asian Art,
Chicago, 7/013
American Gage & Machine Company Fdn.,
Chicago, 7/014
AMFUND a/k/a Mather (Alonzo) Fdn.,
Chicago, 7/015
Ward (A. Montgomery) Fdn., Chicago, 7/020
Anderson Brothers Manufacturing Company
Charitable Fdn., Rockford, 7/021
Annes Fdn., Chicago, 7/021
Arenberg (Frances & Milton) Fund, Chicago,
7/021
Arnold (William A.) Trust, Decatur, 7/023
Aronberg (Lester) Fdn., Chicago, 7/023
Aronberg (Lester & Bert) Fdn., Chicago, 7/024
Ausman (Donald C.) Family Fdn., Northbrook,
7/024
Bagus Charitable Trust, Rockford, 7/025
Barlu Fdn., Springfield, 7/025
Barrington Area Development Council,
Barrington, 7/025
Baird Fdn., Chicago, 7/026
Barron (S. Steven & Lynn K.) Fund, Glencoe,
7/026
Baskin (Samuel J.) Charitable Trust, Chicago,
7/027
Bates and Rogers Fdn., Chicago, 7/027
Baumgarth (John) Fdn., Chicago, 7/028
Baxter Fdn., Kenilworth, 7/029
Bayer (Kenneth M.) Fdn., Mt. Vernon, 7/029
Beacom (Thomas H.) Trust, Chicago, 7/029
Beck (Clare B.) Trust, Chicago, 7/030
Beeler Gdn., Sterling, 7/030
Beltone Institute for Hearing Research, Chicago,
7/031
Manaster (Benjamin & Liebe) Fdn., Chicago,
7/031
Berg (Joe) Fdn., Des Plaines, 7/033
Berlin (I.S.) Fdn., Chicago, 7/033
Bernstin (Russell & Barbara) Fdn., Evanston,
7/034
Best (Jacob) Fdn., Chicago, 7/035
B.F. Fdn., Medinah, 7/036
Blazek (Joseph) Residuary Trust, Chicago,
7/038
Blazek (Joseph) Fdn., Chicago, 7/039
Blinder Fdn., Chicago, 7/040
Blumberg Fdn., Chicago, 7/041
Blum - Kovler Fdn., Chicago, 7/041
Bobb (Allie) Trust, Decatur, 7/045
Boothroyd (Charles H. & Bertha L.) Fdn.,
Chicago, 7/046
Bowman (Lula E.) Trust, Chicago, 7/046
Brain Research Fdn., Chicago, 7/047
Brehm (C.E.) Fdn., Mt. Vernon, 7/048
Brennan (Bernard G.) Fdn., Chicago, 7/049
Bock (Anna M.) Memorial for the Blind,
Mattoon, 7/050
Breskin (Louis A. & Hazel) Fdn., Chicago,
7/051
Brown (David J.) Family Fdn., Chicago, 7/051
Burgess (William, Agnes & Elizabeth) Memorial
Scholarship Fund, Mattoon, 7/052

Burke (James O.) Fdn., Chicago, 7/053
Lord (Ruth Burns) Fdn., Palos Park, 7/054
Burpee (Harry & Della) Art Gallery
Association, Rockford, 7/054
Burton (Oliver M.) Charitable Trust, Chicago,
7/055
Businessmen for the Public Interest, Chicago,
7/056
Braverman Family Fdn., Chicago, 7/057
Brody Fdn., Chicago, 7/058
Cagney Fdn., Evanston, 7/059
Camp Fdn., Wheaton, 7/061
Carle Fdn., Urbana, 7/061
Carnes (Charles F.) Trust Fund A, Aurora,
7/062
Carylon Fdn., Chicago, 7/063
Cas Research, Sparta, 7/063
Caterpillar Fdn., East Peoria, 7/064
Cavanaugh (John W.) Family Fdn., Chicago,
7/064
Center for Curriculum Design, Evanston, 7/065
Chaffetz Family Fdn., Chicago, 7/066
Chapman (Morey & Anne) Family Fdn.,
Chicago, 7/067
Charles Fdn., Rockford, 7/068
Chemer (Sara & Benjamin) Family Memorial,
Chicago, 7/068
Chevra Shomer Hadas, Forest Park, 7/069
Bachroft (Lou) Chevrolet Charitable Fdn.,
Rockford, 7/070
Chicago Chapter Fdn., American Institute of
Architects, Chicago, 7/070
Chicago Molded Products Fdn., Chicago, 7/071
Buehler (Christian) Memorial Home, Peoria,
7/071
Christian Camps Fdn. of Michigan, Chicago,
7/073
Christian Laymen of Chicago, Chicago, 7/074
Christian Workers Fdn., Chicago, 7/075
Christiana Fdn., Chicago, 7/077
Chusid (Frederick) Fdn., Chicago, 7/078
Clark - Halladay Memorial Fdn., Chicago,
7/078
Cliff Dwellers Art Fdn., Chicago, 7/079
Coeli (Regina) Fdn., Mandelein, 7/080
Coen (J.W.) Fdn., Olney, 7/081
Cohen (J.W.) Fdn., Chicago, 7/081
Cohen (Howard H.) Family Fdn., Rock Island,
7/082
Cohen (Wolf P.) Fdn. for the General Bikur
Cholim Hospital of Jerusalem, Chicago,
7/082
Cohn (Lester & Florence) Fdn., Chicago,
7/083
Coleman Fdn., Chicago, 7/084
Collier - Swartchild Fdn., Glencoe, 7/084
Committee for One Society, Chicago, 7/085
Concerned Methodist Fdn., Oak Park, 7/086
Conpaco Fdn., Chicago, 7/086
Cowles Commission for Research in Economics,
Chicago, 7/087
Crane Pension Fund, Chicago, 7/088
Crane Fund for Widows & Children, Chicago,
7/094
Crosby Fdn., Chicago, 7/097
Crown (Arie & Ida) Memorial, Chicago, 7/097
Crossley Fdn., Chicago, 7/100
Crown (Robert) Navy Memorial, Chicago,
7/101
Cummings (Herbert K. & Irene H.) Fdn.,
Chicago, 7/101
Cummings (Nathan) Consolidated Foods
Scholarship Fund, Chicago, 7/103
Czechoslovak Foreign Institute in Exile Working
Gruop U S A, Chicago, 7/104
Archer - Daniels - Midland Fdn., Decatur,
7/104
Dalton (Edward J.) Fdn., Roscoe, 7/105
D.A.O. Fdn., Rockford, 7/105
Danielson (James Deering) Fdn., Chicago,
7/106
Davidow (Leonard S. & Claire S.) Fdn.,
Highland Park, 7/108
Dawson Fdn., Winnetka, 7/109
DeKalb Fdn., DeKalb, 7/109
Coleman (Delbert) Fdn., Chicago, 7/110

DeWitt (Lloyd R.) Journalism Scholarship
Trust, Mt. Vernon, 7/111
Smith (Dale DeWitt) Memorial Trust, Decatur,
7/111
Dessaver (Robert L.) Family Fdn., Chicago,
7/111
Donaldson (Eleanor Shay) Trust, Chicago,
7/113
Dorfman (Isaiah S.) Family Fund, Chicago,
7/113
Douglas Fdn., Mattoon, 7/114
Donaldson (Lewis A.) Trust, Chicago, 7/115
Dower (Thomas W.) Fdn., Chicago, 7/115
Doyle (Marguerite C.) Fdn., Chicago, 7/115
Duman Fdn., Highland Park, 7/116
Smith (Dunlap) Fund, Chicago, 7/117
Du Page Medical Society Fdn., Glen Ellyn,
7/119
Ecker (Morris) Memorial Fdn., Chicago, 7/120
Eclipse Fdn., Rockford, 7/120
Edelmann (Robert) Fdn., Chicago, 7/121
Effingham Dollars for Scholars, Effingham,
7/122
Eisenstein (Alexander) Residuary Trust,
Chicago, 7/122
Eisenstein (Alexander) Trust - Specific
Endowment Funds, Chicago, 7/123
Eliel (Willard & Eleanor S.) Fdn., Highland
Park, 7/123
Emmantee Fdn., Chicago, 7/124
Epaphroditus Fdn., Des Plaines, 7/125
Epstein (David Ellis) Memorial Fdn., Chicago,
7/126
Erickson (Eben W.) Fund, Evanston, 7/126
Eliel (Willard & Eleanor S.) Fdn., Highland
Park, 7/127
Epstein (Julius & Nancy) Fdn., Chicago, 7/128
Ettelson (Susan & Jerome) Fdn., Chicago,
7/129
Evangel Mission, Wheaton, 7/129
Everett (B.N. & M.C.) Fdn., Winnetka, 7/130
Everly Home for the Aged Trust, Macomb,
7/131
Levin (Ezra) Charitable Trust, Monticello,
7/131
Family Fund, Chicago, 7/132
Farm Fdn., Chicago, 7/132
Farrer (Margaret A.) Trust, Havanna, 7/135
Farwell Fdn., Chicago, 7/136
Farwell (A.W.) Trust for Christian Science
Benevolent Association, Chicago, 7/137
Farwell (A.W.) Trust for the Eleanor
Association of Chicago, Chicago, 7/138
Farwell (Ava W.) Trust for Fallen Women,
Chicago, 7/139
Farwell (Ava W.) Trust for Home for Destitute
Crippled Children of Chicago, Chicago,
7/139
Farwell (A.W.) Trust for Musical Educational
Fund, Chicago, 7/140
Farwell (Ava W.) Trust for Presbyterian
Hospital, Chicago, 7/141
Farwell (A.W.) Chicago Home for the
Friendless, Chicago, 7/142
Fauntleroy Fund, St. Charles, 7/142
F.D.M. Charitable Fund, Chicago, 7/143
Feinberg Fdn., Cicero, 7/143
Felmley Fdn. Trust, Springfield, 7/144
Field Fdn. of Illinois, Chicago, 7/144
Fink (Sidney C. & Edna F.) Fdn., Chicago,
7/146
First National Bank of Des Plaines Charitable
Fdn., Des Plaines, 7/147
Fishman (Rube S.) Trust, Chicago, 7/147
Fiterman (Reva & Morlan) Fdn., Chicago,
7/148
Fitzgerald (Matthew J.) Fdn., Chicago, 7/148
Fjord Fdn., Chicago, 7/149
Fleur de Lis Fdn., Chicago, 7/149
Flamm (Samuel H.) Fdn., Chicago, 7/149
Florsheim (Lillian H.) Fdn. for Fine Arts,
Chicago, 7/150
Follett Educational Fdn., Chicago, 7/150
Foot Health Educational Fdn., Chicago, 7/151
Forest Fund, Libertyville, 7/151
Forest Park Fund, Peoria Heights, 7/152

Forty Plus of Chicago, Chicago, 7/153
Foundation for Children's Therapeutic
Education, Chicago, 7/153
Foundation for Research on the Modification of
Behavior, Harvey, 7/154
Fralens Fdn., Chicago, 7/154
Frances Juvenile Home Association, Chicago,
7/155
Frankel (Harry & Ann) Fdn., Chicago, 7/156
Franson - Risberg Memorial Mission Home,
Chicago, 7/157
Fraternal Order of Eagles, Chicago, 7/157
Freeman (Jacqueline Ruth) Memorial Fdn.,
Glencoe, 7/157
Fried (Herbert & Marjorie) Fdn., Chicago,
7/158
Friedman (J.) Family Fdn., Highland Park,
7/161
Friedman (Samuel R.) Fdn., Chicago, 7/162
Fulton (Maurice & Muriel) Fdn., Chicago,
7/162
Funderburg Fdn., Belvidere, 7/162
Fox (Ellen B.) Fund, Chicago, 7/164
Funds for Latin American Poor, Chicago,
7/165
Funk (Paul A.) Charitable Trust, Bloomington,
7/165
Gallagher (Timothy) Fdn., Chicago, 7/166
Gantz Fdn., Northbrook, 7/166
Gary Fdn., Chicago, 7/167
Gatzert Family Fdn., Chicago, 7/168
Gatzert Fdn., Chicago, 7/169
Gaul Fdn., Chicago, 7/169
Geifman Family Fdn., Rock Island, 7/170
General Service Fdn., Chicago, 7/171
Geneva Scholarship Fund, Geneva, 7/173
Gerl (Joseph) Fdn., Chicago, 7/173
Germi (A.) Charitable Fdn., Chicago, 7/173
Goldberg (Bertrand & Nancy F.) Charitable
Fund, Chicago, 7/174
Goldberg (Fred & Harvey) Fdn., Chicago,
7/175
Goldberg (Irving H. & Jane W.) Charitable
Fdn., Chicago, 7/175
Goldberg (Joseph E.) Memorial Fdn., Mt.
Prospect, 7/175
Goldblatt Brothers Employees Fdn., Chicago,
7/176
Goldblatt (Maurice) Fdn., Chicago, 7/176
Goldenberg (Max) Fdn., Chicago, 7/177
Goldsmith (Kurt & Hanna) Charitable Fdn.,
Chicago, 7/179
Goodkoski (Erna Olga) Trust, Elgin, 7/180
Gosset (Earl J.) Fdn., Morton Grove, 7/180
Graham (William B.) Fdn., Morton Gtove,
7/181
Granite City Steel Company Thirty Minute
Club Charity Trust, Granite City, 7/182
Rockford Television Fdn. (Greater), Rockford,
7/182
Green (Harold J.) Fdn., Chicago, 7/182
Greenberg Fdn., Chicago, 7/184
Greenhill Research Fdn., Chicago, 7/185
Greenwald (Samuel & Pearl) Charitable Fdn.,
Chicago, 7/186
Griess-Pfleger Tanning Company Fdn.,
Waukegan, 7/187
Groom (Pat) Fdn., Chicago, 7/187
Groenings (John E.) Charitable Fdn., Chicago,
7/187
Grossinger (Sam & Sarah) Fdn., Chicago,
7/188
Grossman (Conrad & Rose) Fdn., Chicago,
7/189
Guthman (Leo S.) Fund, Chicago, 7/190
Haffner (Clarissa Donnelly) Charitable Trust,
Chicago, 7/192
Haines (June Ann) Memorial Fdn., Chicago,
7/193
Halligan (John R.) Charitable Fund, Chicago,
7/193
Hamilton (Frederick C.) Fdn. for Blind
Children, Kankakee, 7/194
Hammer (Armand) Fdn. Formerly California,
Chicago, 7/195
Hammond Fdn., Deerfield, 7/196

Handelman (Ira) Fdn., Chicago, 7/196
Hankeson (Florence P.) Scholarship Fund,
Chicago, 7/197
Chernin (Harris) Charitable Fdn., Chicago,
7/197
Harris (Dwight J.) Trust for Piney Woods
Country Life School, Chicago, 7/198
Harris (E.G.) - Bartlett Memorial Fund,
Chicago, 7/198
Harris (Emma Gale) - Gale Memorial Fund,
Chicago, 7/198
Harris (Emma Gale) - E.I. Gale Memorial
Mission Fund, Chicago, 7/199
Harris (Gerald H.) Charitable Fdn., Chicago,
7/199
Harris (Herman M.) Charitable Fdn., Glencoe,
7/199
Harris (Jerome & Arlene) Fdn., Chicago, 7/199
Harris (Squire R.) Trust for Verna R.H. Ewen,
Chicago, 7/200
Harrisburg Medical Fdn., Harrisburg, 7/201
Harrison (Fred G.) Fdn., Herrin, 7/202
Hartless Fdn., Chicago, 7/203
Harvey (Fred) Fine Arts Collection, Chicago,
7/204
Hayes (John T.) Fdn., Chicago, 7/205
H.B.B. Fdn., Oak Brook, 7/205
Health Services Fdn., Chicago, 7/206
Heidrick Fdn., Chicago, 7/206
Heled Charitable Fdn., Chicago, 7/207
Henderson (Fannie B.) Trust, Aurora, 7/208
Hesser (Bess & Erwin) Fdn., Glencoe, 7/209
Highland Community Fdn., Chicago, 8/001
Hill Fdn., Chicago, 8/001
H & M Service Corporation, Chicago, 8/002
Hoffer (Gertrude) Trust, Decatur, 8/003
Hoffman Family Fdn., Chicago, 8/003
Hokin (Samuel E.) Fdn., Chicago, 8/004
Holden (John L.) Trust Fund #2, Aurora,
8/005
Holtslander (Eugene S.) Trust, Chicago, 8/005
Horowitz (Ethel & Harold) Fdn., Springfield,
8/006
Horwich (Theodore & Gertrude) Family Fdn.,
Chicago, 8/006
Horwitz (Mark) Fdn., Northbrook, 8/007
Houston (Robert), Jr. Fdn., Oak Park, 8/008
Howell (Mae) Trust, Lewistown, 8/008
Huarisa Fdn., Chicago, 8/008
Human Development in Action, Flossmoor,
8/009
T/W Hunter (Helen Fay) - Crippled Children's
Fund, Chicago, 8/010
T/W Hunter (Helen Fay) - John E. Hunter
Memorial Heart Fund, Chicago, 8/011
Iglewski Family Fdn., Chicago, 8/012
Illinois Scottish Rite Fdn. Formerly Illinois
Scottish Rite Fund, Bloomington, 8/013
Illinois Hydraulic Fdn., Elgin, 8/013
Illinois St. Andrew Society, Chicago, 8/014
Independence Hall Association, Chicago, 8/016
Interlocking Trust Association, Morton, 8/016
Irwin (Richard D.) Fdn., Homewood, 8/017
Isgo Fdn., Chicago, 8/018
Jackson Park Hospital Fdn., Chicago, 8/020
Jacobs (Melvin H.) Fdn., Chicago, 8/023
Jacobs (Robert S. & Terri C.) Fdn., Chicago,
8/023
Janklow Fnd., East St. Louis, 8/024
J.I.H. Fdn., Chicago, 8/025
Bamberger (Arrie & Estelle Johnson)
Scholarship Fund, Chicago, 8/026
Jones (Paul) Fdn., Chicago, 8/026
Jospey (Shelden) Fdn., Broadview, 8/027
J.R.G. Charitable Fdn., Chicago, 8/028
Judy (Paul R.) Fdn., Chicago, 8/029
Just Fdn., Waukegan, 8/030
Kable Fdn., Mt. Morris, 8/030
Kaplan (Dr. Morris A. & Celia) Fdn., Chicago,
8/031
Kappa Sigma Centennial Fund, Chicago, 8/031
Karger (Robert S. & Jean F.) Fund, Chicago,
8/031
Katz (Helen & Isadore) Fdn., Chicago, 8/032
Keating Fdn., Bellwood, 8/033

Keeshin (John L. & Beatrice) Fdn., Chicago, 8/033
Kellogg Bird Sanctuary in Aid Trust, Chicago, 8/034
Kellogg (John L. & Helen) Fdn., Chicago, 8/034
Kellogg (W.K.) Farm Trust 11/28/27, Chicago, 8/035
Kelley (Nancy & Ann) Home, Canton, 8/036
Kemper Educational & Charitable Fund, Chicago, 8/036
Kempston (John & Nellie) Charitable Fdn., River Forest, 8/037
Kern Fdn., Chicago, 8/038
Kerwin (Edward M.) Fdn., Chicago, 8/039
Kewanee Machinery & Conveyor Company Fdn., Kewanee, 8/041
King (James C.), Chicago, 8/041
Kinneman Scholarship Fund in Sociology, Normal, 8/042
Kirchen Fdn., Lincolnwood, 8/042
Klein Fdn., Chicago, 8/043
Knights of Columbus Columbian Council # 2191, Batavia, 8/044
Kollsman Fdn., Melrose Park, 8/045
Korff Fdn., Chicago, 8/045
Korhumel Fdn., Chicago, 8/046
Koven (Howard R. & Eileen) Fdn., Chicago, 8/047
Kramer (H.) Fdn., Chicago, 8/047
Kroll (Larry & Betty) Fdn., Chicago, 8/048
Krom (Samuel H.) Charitable Fdn., Chicago, 8/049
Lake States Fdn., Wilmette, 8/049
Lakritz (Fannie F.) Memorial Fdn., Chicago, 8/049
Lannan Fdn., Chicago, 8/050
Lanza (Mario) Fdn. of Illinois, Berwyn, 8/051
Larson Fdn., Chicago, 8/051
LaSalle County Historical Society, Ottawa, 8/052
Laser (Celia) Fdn., Chicago, 8/053
Lasky (Harry & Sadie) Fdn., Chicago, 8/053
Lavin (Marshall & Charlene) Fdn., Chicago, 8/054
Lawndale Scholarship Fund, Chicago, 8/054
League of Women Voters of Illinois of Highland Park, Highland Park, 8/054
Leander (Russell J. & Kathryn S.) Fdn., Chicago, 8/055
Lederer (Anne Pollock) Fdn., Chicago, 8/056
Lederer (Francis L.) Fdn., Chicago, 8/057
Leff (Abe & Anna) Fdn., Chicago, 8/058
Leibnitz Fdn. for the Advancement of Science, Chicago, 8/059
Leiterman (Silvia W. & Irwin H.) Fdn., Chicago, 8/059
Leopold (Robert L.) Family Fdn., Chicago, 8/060
Leslie Fund, Chicago, 8/061
Levin (Albert J.) Memorial Fund, Northbrook, 8/061
Levinson (Marilyn & Harry) Fdn., Chicago, 8/061
Levy (Charles & Ruth) Fdn., Chicago, 8/062
Levy (Louis & Theresa) Fdn., Wheeling, 8/063
Lewis (Robert A.) Fund, Chicago, 8/065
Light (Rudolph A.) Charitable Trust, Chicago, 8/065
Lindsay - Schaub Fdn., Decatur, 8/066
Lipin Fdn., Chicago, 8/066
Lipschultz Brothers Family Fdn., Chicago, 8/067
Lipsky (Sydney E.) Fdn., Chicago, 8/068
Litchfield United Fund, Litchfield, 8/069
Little Friends of St. Martin, Chicago, 8/069
Livingston (Frederick & Benita) Fdn., Chicago, 8/070
Lizzadro (Joseph) Family Fdn., Chicago, 8/071
Local 142 Welfare Fund, Elgin, 8/072
Loeb (Allan & Elizabeth) Fund, Highland Park, 8/072
Logan (Reva & David) Fdn., Chicago, 8/073
Logan (Robert L.) Fdn., Decatur, 8/074
Long (Colette & Dale) Fdn., Chicago, 8/075
Lord (Ruth Burns) Fdn., Palos Park, 8/076

Lorig Fdn., Chicago, 8/076
Merwin (Loring & Marjorie) Fdn., Bloomington, 8/077
Huch (Louis J.) Fdn., Chicago, 8/078
Loundy Fdn., Chicago, 8/078
Luncheon Optimist Club of Springfield, Springfield, 8/080
Lusk (Alice E.) Trust Fund A, Chicago, 8/080
Madorin-Sirk Fdn., Chicago, 8/081
Jackson (Mahalia) Fdn., Chicago, 8/081
Mall Fdn., Chicago, 8/082
Manilow (Nathan) Fdn., Chicago, 8/083
March (Ruth K.) Fdn., Chicago, 8/084
Marcus Fdn., Chicago, 8/085
Markell Fdn., Chicago, 8/085
Mather (Alonzo C.) Trust, Chicago, 8/088
McKay (Helen & Wilbur) Fdn., Hampton, 8/088
McCormick (Robert R.) Charitable Trust, Chicago, 8/089
McCrink Fdn., Glen Ellyn, 8/090
McFarland Charitable Fdn., Havana, 8/091
McLucas (Annie May) Fdn., Chicago, 8/093
Meltzer Fdn., Chicago, 8/094
Memorial Loan & Scholarship Fund of the University of Illinois Women's Club at Chicago Circle, Chicago, 8/094
Carnes (Charles F.) Trust Fund B, Aurora, 8/095
Crawford (Adeline M.) Trust, Aurora, 8/095
Dewey (Howard) Educational Trust, Aurora, 8/096
Fox Valley Girl Scout Council of Illinois Trust, Aurora, 8/096
Holden (Alice M.) Trust, Aurora, 8/097
Schumacher (Rt. Rev. Msgr. M.A.) Trust, Aurora, 8/097
Yohng Women's Christian Association of Aurora Trust, Aurora, 8/098
Meyers Torah Fdn., Chicago, 8/098
M F A Fdn., Oak Park, 8/098
Michaels Fdn., Chicago, 8/099
Minann, Inc., Glenview, 8/099
Burt (Minnie Peterson) - Virginia W. Harker Memorial Scholarship Trust, Peoria, 8/100
Mira (Hoseph J. & Ernest G.) Fdn., Alton, 8/101
Mitchell Family Trust, Havana, 8/102
Mitchell (John R. & Eleanor R.) Fdn., Mt. Vernon, 8/102
Molner (Herbert R.) Fdn., Highland Park, 8/102
Ward (A. Montgomery) Fdn., Chicago, 8/103
Moore Family Fdn., Chicago, 8/104
Moorman Fdn., Quincy, 8/105
Morrison Family Fdn., Evanston, 8/107
Mortensen (Frederik) Memorial Library Fdn., Park Ridge, 8/107
Motorola Fdn., Franklin Park, 8/108
Murphy (Walter P.) Fdn., Chicago, 8/114
Musser (C.R. & Margaret K.) Trust, Chicago, 8/114
National Piano Fdn., Chicago, 8/115
National Restaurant Fdn., Chicago, 8/116
Harris (Neison) Fdn., Northbrook, 8/117
Nelson Charitable Trust, Chicago, 8/118
Nerad (John) Fdn., Riverside, 8/120
Nissman(Murray & Grace) Fdn., Chicago, 8/120
Norris (James) Fdn., Chicago, 8/121
O'Bryan Fdn., Chicago, 8/122
Odontographic Society of Chicago, Chicago, 8/122
Odontographic Society of Chicago Research & Education Fdn., Chicago, 8/122
Offield (Wrigley & Edna Jean) Fdn., Chicago, 8/123
Olson (Walter E.) Fdn., Chicago, 8/124
Ozmun Fdn., Wheeling, 8/124
Packard Research Fdn., Chicago, 8/125
Page (Roscoe A. & Helena B.) Charitable Fdn., Evanston, 8/125
Parents Association for Cerebral Palsy Children & Adults, Chicago, 8/126
Parker (Don H.) Fdn., Chicago, 8/126

Parker (Morris L.) Charitable Fund, Chicago, 8/128
Payne (Frank E. & Seba B.) Fdn., Chicago, 8/129
Pearce Hospital Fdn., Eldorado, 8/130
Perkins & Will Fdn., Chicago, 8/132
Perlman (Harold L.) Fdn., Chicago, 8/132
Perlstein Fdn., Chicago, 8/134
Peters (Donald & Evelyn) Fdn., Hinsdale, 8/135
Peterson (Robert E.) Fdn., Chicago, 8/136
Physical Distribution Research Center, Chicago, 8/137
Pick Benevolent Associaation, Chicago, 8/138
Pickus Fdn., Waukegan, 8/139
Pillsbury Hospital Residents Trust, Chicago, 8/139
Pilot Fdn., Chicago, 8/140
Plain (John) Fdn., Chicago, 8/141
Prehn (Harold) Fdn., Springfield, 8/141
Prince (Abbie Norman) Trust, Chicago, 8/142
Prime Mover Control Museum Association, Loves Park, 8/143
Prince (Abbie Norman) Trust, Chicago, 8/144
Pritzker Fdn., Chicago, 8/146
Prudential Plaza Fdn., Chicago, 8/147
Public Relations Board Fdn., Chicago, 8/147
Pullman (George M.) Trust, Chicago, 8/148
Quaker Oats Fdn., Chicago, 8/149
Raban Fdn., Chicago, 8/152
Ramis, Inc., Chicago, 8/153
Rapaport (Meyer B.) Fdn., Chicago, 8/154
Reed (William) Fdn., Chicago, 8/154
Research & Education Trust Fund of the American Institute of Real Estate Appraisers, Chicago, 8/155
Reserve Steel Fdn., Addison, 8/155
Reynolds (Harry Bertram) Trust, Mt. Vernon, 8/155
R.F. Fdn., Chicago, 8/156
RGDED Fdn., Chicago, 8/157
Ries Fdn., Chicago, 8/158
Robbins (Gen - Mort) Fdn., Chicago, 8/159
Robertson (Lois & Edward) Fdn., Chicago, 8/159
Robineau (Joseph F.) Family Fdn., Chicago, 8/160
Robinson (Jerome J.) Charitable Fdn., Chicago, 8/161
Robinson (Theodore W. & Annabel A.) Fdn., Chicago, 8/161
Rockford Morning Star & Register - Republic Fdn., Rockford, 8/161
Rockford Products Corporation Fdn., Rockford, 8/161
Rogers Charitable Trust A, Decatur, 8/162
Rooney (M.A.) Fdn., Lawrenceville, 8/163
Rosenberg (Jack) Memorial Fdn., Chicago, 8/164
Rosenberg (Michael) Memorial Fdn., Chicago, 8/164
Rosenberg (Miriam) Fund for the Promotion of Jewish Culture, Chicago, 8/165
Roseberry (Clarence Judson) Educational Fdn., Champaign, 8/165
Rosenthal (Benjamin J.) Fdn., Chicago, 8/166
Ross (Charles M.) Trust, Fairbury, 8/167
Rothschild (Hulda B.) Fdn., Chicago, 8/168
Roucher Fdn., Decatur, 8/168
Rubinstein (Albert & Joyce) Family Fdn., Chicago, 8/169
Rusnak (Raymond L.) Family Fdn., Chicago, 8/171
Russ (Kenneth & Elaine) Fdn., Wilmette, 8/172
Russell (Tom) Charitable Fdn., Chicago, 8/172
Sager (Ben W. & Florence H.) Fdn., Chicago, 8/172
St. Casimir Student Aid Fund, Chicago, 8/174
Sager (Ben W. & Florence H.) Fdn., Chicago, 8/174
Sandman (H.B.) Fdn., Lincolnwood, 8/175
Sandstone Fdn., Park Ridge, 8/176
Olin - Sang Fdn., Chicago, 8/176
Sarto Fdn., Winnetka, 8/177
Saxon Fdn., Aurora, 8/177

Scarborough (Henry) Fdn., Chicago, 8/177

Schecter (Abraham) Charitable Trust, Chicago, 8/178

Scheinfeld (Sylvia & Aaron) Fdn., Chicago, 8/178

Schlanger (Marvin) Fdn., Chicago, 8/180

Schoenbrod (Herbert & Alice) Fdn., Highland Park, 8/181

Schlossberg (Max) Fdn., Chicago, 8/181

Schmitt (Arthur J.) Fdn., Chicago, 8/183

Schultz (Arthur W. & Elizabeth M.) Fdn., Barrington, 8/185

Schwartz (Milton H. & Lillian Z.) Fdn., Chicago, 8/185

Schweppe Fdn., Chicago, 8/185

Scojew Charitable Trust, East Moline, 8/186

Scovill (Rose W.) Trust for Decatur Park District, Decatur, 8/186

Scovill (Guy N. & Rose W.) Trust for Decatur Memorial Hospital, Decatur, 8/187

Scovill (Guy N. & Rose W.) Trust for St. Paul's Lutheran & St. John's Episcopal Churches, Decatur, 8/187

Scovill (Guy N. & Rose W.) Trust for Parochial Schools, Decatur, 8/188

Scovill (Guy N. & Rose W.) Trust for St. Mary's Hospital, Decatur, 8/189

Scovill (Guy N. & Rose W.) Trust for Webster Hall, Decatur, 8/189

Simpson (Scott) Memorial Trust, Lincolnwood, 8/190

Scovill (Guy N. & Rose W.) Trust for Decatur & Macon County Opportunity Home for Boys, Decatur, 8/190

Seabury Fdn., Chicago, 8/191

Hess (Segel) Family Fund, Chicago, 8/194

Segil (L.J.) Fdn., Chicago, 8/194

S & C Fund Association, Chicago, 8/195

Seifer (Nathan) Fdn., Kankakee, 8/196

Semrow Fdn., Des Plaines, 8/196

Settle (Frank A.) Trust Student Loan Fund, Chicago, 8/197

Schmikler Charitable Trust, Champaign, 8/197

Scovill (Guy N.) Trust for St. John's Episcopal Church, Decatur, 8/197

Shapiro (Charles & M.R.) Fdn., Chicago, 8/198

Shapiro (Harry & Betty) Fdn., Skokie, 8/198

Shapiro (Philip A.) Fdn., Chicago, 8/199

Shaw (Walden W.) Fdn., Chicago, 8/200

Sheet Metal Industry Welfare Fund, Chicago, 8/201

Sheil (Bishop) Fdn., Chicago, 8/201

Shepard Fdn., Chicago, 8/201

Sherman (Leonard & Diane) Fdn., Chicago, 8/202

Shirk (Russell & Betty) Fdn., Bloomington, 8/203

Shure Fdn., Evanston, 8/203

Shure (Sidney N.) Fund, Evanston, 8/204

Simpson (Scott) Memorial Trust, Lincolnwood, 8/207

Singer (William & Etta) Fdn., Chicago, 8/207

Sinton (Lorraine L.) Charitable Trust, Chicago, 8/207

Siragusa Fdn., Chicago, 8/209

Smail Family Fdn., Chicago, 8/210

Smith - Dickerson Fdn., Decatur, 8/211

Smoler (Hymen & Harriet) Fdn., Chicago, 8/211

Smoller (Seymour & Clara) Fdn., Chicago, 8/212

Snite (Fred B.) Fdn., Chicago, 8/212

Society for Preservation of the American Musical Heritage, Wauconda, 8/213

Solo Cup Fdn., Chicago, 8/214

Sommer (Norman G.) Memorial Trust, Decatur, 8/217

Special Machine Fdn., Rockford, 8/218

Spencer Fdn., Chicago, 8/219

Spertus (Anita & Robert) Fdn., Glencoe, 8/221

Spertus (Herman & Sara) Fdn., Glencoe, 8/221

Spier (Jerome & Beatrice) Fdn., Wilmette, 8/222

Sprague (Edward S.) Fdn., Park Ridge, 8/223

Stanley (Mary E.) Trust, Chicago, 8/223

State Farm Companies Fdn., Bloomington, 8/224

Steel (Helen & Stephen) Charitable Fdn., Chicago, 8/225

Steinberg (Evelyn) Memorial Fdn., Chicago, 9/001

Steiner (Harry) Fdn., Chicago, 9/001

Steinfeld Fdn., Chicago, 9/002

Stein - Freiler Fdn., Skokie, 9/002

Sterling - Rock Falls Community Trust, Sterling, 9/004

Sternberg (Paul & Doris) Family Fdn., Glencoe, 9/005

Stevens (George R.) Fdn., Lake Forest, 9/005

Stillman Fund, Chicago, 9/006

Strieter (Martin E.) Family Fdn., Rock Island, 9/006

Stuart Fdn., Chicago, 9/007

Sullivan Charitable Trust, Northfield, 9/007

Sulzer Family Fdn., Chicago, 9/007

Swanson (Robert) Company Fdn., Chicago, 9/008

Elgin Sweeper Fdn., Elgin, 9/008

Swords (Miriam G. & Earl I.) Charitable Fdn., Peoria, 9/008

Targ (Fannie & Max) Fdn., Chicago, 9/008

Taylor (J. Hall) Fdn., Chicago, 9/009

Tepper (Norman & Paula) Fdn., Chicago, 9/009

Thorn River Fdn., Chicago, 9/010

Teschke (Almore H.) Family Fdn., Chicago, 9/011

Thornton (Edmund B.) Family Fdn., Chicago, 9/012

Thoresen Fdn., Chicago, 9/012

Toepfer (Francis H.) Family Fdn., Peoria, 9/013

Tomlinson (Clarence) Charitable Trust, Mt. Pulaski, 9/013

Todd (John O.) Fdn., Evanston, 9/013

Torosian (Peter G. & Elizabeth) Fdn., Chicago, 9/013

Tri-City Jewish Center Building Fund Fdn., Rock Island, 9/015

Tripp (Jane B.) Charitable Trust of 1969, Chicago, 9/016

Apperson (Ruth A.) Trust, Mattoon, 9/017

Axtell (Mary B.) Trust - Axtell Scholarship Fund, Chicago, 9/018

Bard (Mary Spear) Trust, Chicago, 9/019

Cohn (Tillie C.) Trust C - Fund B, Chicago, 9/019

Cohn (Tillie C.) Trust D, Chicago, 9/020

Barr (Cary C.) Trust, Chicago, 9/020

Fay (Jennie L.) Trust - Memorial Heart Fund, Chicago, 9/021

Fay (Jennie L.) Trust - Memorial Fund for Cancer Research, Chicago, 9/022

Galvin (Paul V.) Trust, Chicago, 9/023

T/W Hunter (Helen Fay) Memorial Fund for Cancer Research, Chicago, 9/025

Trust under the Article 3 of will McCormick (Marion Deering), Chicago, 9/026

Rankin (Lena M.) Trust - Willie H. Rankin Fund, Chicago, 9/028

Taylor (John R.) Trust, Chicago, 9/029

Christamore House Trust, Indianapolis, Ind., 9/030

Truckbreiter (George) Apprentice Training Fdn., Chicago, 9/030

Tunick Family Fdn., Rock Island, 9/031

Turner (William C.) Fdn., Casey, 9/031

Two Rivers Council, Boy Scouts of America Trust, Aurora, 9/032

United Fdn., Chicago, 9/032

Unterman (Melvin) Fdn., Chicago, 9/034

Urban Dynamics, Chicago, 9/034

Vainder Fdn., Glencoe, 9/035

Volid (Peter) Fdn., Chicago, 9/036

Voynow - Blumenthal Fdn., Chicago, 9/036

Walbridge Hospital Trust Fund, Decatur, 9/037

Walgreen Benefit Fund, Chicago, 9/037

Smith (Washington & Jane) Home, Chicago, 9/041

Webb (Herbert H.) - Reedsburg Trust 7/11/44, Chicago, 9/045

Wein (Hyman & Susan) Fdn., Chicago, 9/045

Weindruch Fdn., Rock Island, 9/046

Weinstein (Samuel) Family Fdn., Chicago, 9/046

Weinress (Morton) Family Fund, Chicago, 9/047

Weiss (Merle Diane) Fdn., Evanston, 9/048

Weissbourd Family Fdn., Chicago, 9/048

Weitzengeld (Burton Y. & Alice B.) Fdn., Chicago, 9/049

Welfare Fund for National Fire Employees, Chicago, 9/050

Wells Fdn., Chicago, 9/051

Miller (Olive S. & F. Wendell) Charitable Fund, Chicago, 9/051

Werner (Clara & Spencer) Fdn., Paris, 9/051

Wheeler (Robert C.) Fdn., Chicago, 9/052

Wiley (Morrison & Mary) Library, Elmwood, 9/052

Willett (Howard L.) Charitable Fdn., Chicago, 9/053

Williams (Edna B. & Ednyfed H.) Fdn., Chicago, 9/054

Williams (George J.) Charitable Trust, Chicago, 9/054

Williams - Steel Fdn., Robinson, 9/055

Williamson (Louise B.) Trust - Boy Scouts, Decatur, 9/056

Williamson (Louise B.) Trust - Y.M.C.A., Decatur, 9/056

Willner (Madeline B. & Benton J.) Fund, Chicago, 9/056

Friend (Peter Winston) Fdn., Chicago, 9/058

Witte (Lester) Fdn., Chicago, 9/060

Wood (Robert E.) Fdn., Chicago, 9/061

Woodruff & Edwards Fdn., Elgin, 9/062

World War II Marshall High School Scholarship Fund, Chicago, 9/062

Offield (Dorothy Wrigley) Charity Fund, Chicago, 9/063

Wyatt (Harry N. & Ruth F.) Fdn., Chicago, 9/065

Yellin Fdn., Chicago, 9/065

Zack Fdn., Chicago, 9/066

Zivin (Nathan & Jocelyn) Fdn., Highland Park, 9/067

Zukerman Fdn., Rock Island, 9/068

INDIANA

First Filming

Aid for the Blind Society of Plymouth, Plymouth, 1/002

Allen (Louise) Trust, Crawfordsville, 1/002

Amburn (Clifford L. & Daisie B.) Memorial Scholarship Fund, Muncie, 1/003

American Steel Dredge Company Fdn., Fort Wayne, 1/003

Amos Fdn., Edinburgh, 1/004

Anderson (John, Valparaiso, 1/005

Anderson (Viola) Trust, Muncie, 1/006

Angus (D.J.) - Scientech Educational Fdn., Indianapolis, 1/007

Anthony Fdn., Evansville, 1/008

Arvin Fdn., Columbus, 1/009

Associates Investment Company Fdn., South Bend, 1/009

Atkinson Fdn., Indianapolis, 1/011

Ayres Fdn., Indianapolis, 1/012

Ayres (Frederic & Janet) Fdn., Indianapolis, 1/013

Ball (George & Frances) Fdn., Muncie, 1/014

Bardsley Charities, Anderson, 1/014

Beech Grove Cemetery Trust, Mount Vernon, 1/015

Ben - Ephraim Fund, Indianapolis, 1/015

Bennett (John G.) Trust, Crawfordsville, 1/016

Bernell Fdn., South Bend, 1/017
Best Fdn., Indianapolis, 1/017
Bonsib (L.W.) Fdn., Fort Wayne, 1/018
Bowsher (Nelson P.) Fdn., South Bend, 1/019
Bronstein (Sol & Arlene) Charitable Trust, Evansville, 1/019
Bullen (Celia & Harry) Fdn. Trust, Evansville, 1/019
Byram (Stanley H.) Fdn., Indianapolis, 1/020
Burkhart Fdn., Indianapolis, 1/021
Byrket (W.F.) Education Fund, New Castle, 1/021
Cain Fdn., Indianapolis, 1/022
Carmack (Joan & Marvin) Fdn., Bloomington, 1/023
Carmichael Fdn., South Bend, 1/024
Carmichael (Ernestine Morris & Oliver C.), Jr. Fund, South Bend, 1/024
Centerboard Fdn., Indianapolis, 1/024
Central Broadcasting Corporation Charitable Trust, Richmond, 1/025
Jasper Chair Fdn., Jasper, 1/025
Chinese Club, Inc., Indianapolis, 1/026
Christian Fdn. of Indiana, Indianpolis, 1/026
Clegg (Jerry E.) Fdn., Lafayette, 1/026
Clements Fdn., Richmond, 1/027
Cloverdale Indiana Endowment Fund of the Rockwell & Cantwell Families, Cloverdale, 1/028
Clowes Fund, Indianapolis, 1/029
Cocos Fdn., Indianapolis, 1/030
Colby (Julian) Charitable Fdn., Hammond, 1/031
Cook (David M.) Fdn., Indianapolis, 1/032
Cook (Marvin H. & Gretchen V.) Educational Trust, Covington, 1/032
Cooling (Parke A.) Fdn., Indianapolis, 1/033
Cooper (George M.) Fdn., South Bend, 1/033
Cox Fdn., Alexandria, 1/034
Cragg Family Endowment Fund, Lafayette, 1/035
Crossman (Elizabeth Ann) Trust, Indianapolis, 1/035
Crowe (Charles W.) Fdn., Fort Wayne, 1/036
Crowe (Mary Jane M.) Fdn., Fort Wayne, 1/036
Krannert (Herman Charles & Ellnora Decker) Fdn., Indianapolis, 1/036
DeJong Fdn., Evansville, 1/037
Diggs (Elder) Memorial Fdn. of Kappa Alpha Psi Fraternity, Indianapolis, 1/038
Dinwiddie (Emma J.) Educational Fund Trust, Frankfort, 1/038
Doctors Hospital Fdn., Michigan City, 1/038
Domont Charitable Trust, Indianapolis, 1/039
Dunbar Fdn., Indianapolis, 1/039
Duncan Fdn., Lafayette, 1/040
Eagle Fdn., Indianapolis, 1/040
Eddy (Royal A. & Mildred D.) Student Loan Trust Fund, Gary, 1/041
Efroymson (Gustave Aaron) Fund Trust, Indianapolis, 1/042
Efroymson (Robert A.) Charitable Trust, Indianapolis, 1/042
E P H Fdn., Fort Wayne, 1/043
Fairbanks (Clara) Home for Aged Women, Terre Haute, 1/044
Fall Creek Fdn., Indianapolis, 1/045
Feinberg (Myron A.) Charitable Trust of 1962, Indianapolis, 1/046
Feinberg (Myron A.) Charitable Fdn., Indianapolis, 1/047
Findling (J.B.) Trust, Tipton, 1/047
First Bank & Trust Company Fdn., South Bend, 1/047
Fort Wayne Corrugated Paper Fdn., Fort Wayne, 1/049
Fort Wayne National Bank Fdn., Fort Wayne, 1/049
Freimann (Frank) Charitable Trust, Fort Wayne, 1/049
Frey (Henry) Fdn., Fort Wayne, 1/050
Freimann (Frank) Fdn., Fort Wayne, 1/050
Frey (Henry) Fdn., Fort Wayne, 1/051
Gary National Bank Charitable Trust, Gary, 1/051

Gemmer (H.C.) Family Christian Fdn., Indianapolis, 1/052
General Charities, Indianapolis, 1/052
General Fdn. for Ophthalmology, Indianapolis, 1/053
German American Fdn., Jasper, 1/053
Glasson (J.S. Sid) Trust, Shelbyville, 1/054
Glick (Eugene & Marilyn) Fdn., Indianapolis, 1/055
Golightly Fdn., Kokomo, 1/055
Graham Fdn., Washington, 1/056
Great Commission Fdn. Formerly Georgia, Warsaw, 1/056
Greenleaf Fdn., Elkhart, 1/056
Habig (Arnold F.) Fdn., Jasper, 1/057
Habig (Thomas L.) Fdn., Jasper, 1/057
Haindel (Roscoe E. & Rosa) Fdn., Richmond, 1/058
Hall (Charles E. & Sara A.) Memorial Fund, Tipton, 1/058
Hall (Donald A.) Memorial Trust, Portland, 1/059
Hamilton Fdn., Columbus, 1/059
Hammes (Romy) Charitable Trust, South Bend, 1/060
Haney (Francis J.) Scholarship Fund, Evansville, 1/061
Harrell Fdn., Indianapolis, 1/062
Harris (Benjamin) Home for Widows & Orphans, Rensselaer, 1/063
Harrison (President Benjamin) Fdn., Indianapolis, 1/063
Hayner Fdn., Fort Wayne, 1/064
Haynes (Elwood) Memorial Charitable Trust, Kokomo, 1/065
Hein (Silvio) Memorial Trust, Terre Haute, 1/065
Herman Charitable Trust, Indianapolis, 1/066
Hickey Fdn., South Bend, 1/066
Hillenbrand (George M.) Scholarship Gift Trust, Batesville, 1/067
Hillenbrand (George M.) Scholarship Loan Fund, Batesville, 1/067
Hodell (Lisle D. & Hazel M.) Fdn., Fort Wayne, 1/067
Honeywell Fdn., Wabash, 1/068
Hook Drug Fdn., Indianapolis, 1/071
Hoosier State Charitable Fdn., Hammond, 1/072
Huckleberry Fdn., Lafayette, 1/072
Hulman Public Building Trust, Terre Haute, 1/072
Hutner (David S. & Dorothy W.) Fdn., Fort Wayne, 1/072
Indiana Chemical Trust, Terre Haute, 1/073
Indiana Desk Fdn., Jasper, 1/074
Indiana Medical Fdn., Indianapolis, 1/075
Indiana Retired Teachers Community, Indianapolis, 1/076
Indianapolis Humane Society, Indianapolis, 1/076
Indianapolis Machinery Fdn., Indianapolis, 1/076
Indianapolis Motor Speedway Fdn., Speedway, 1/077
Inland Container Corporation Fdn., Indianapolis, 1/077
International Steel Company Fdn., Evansville, 1/079
Jasper Desk Fdn., Jasper, 1/079
Jasper Novelty Furniture Fdn., Jasper, 1/080
Jasper Office Furniture Fdn., Jasper, 1/081
Jasper Seating Fdn., Jasper, 1/082
Jasper Wood Products Fdn., Jasper, 1/083
Jenn Fdn., Indianapolis, 1/083
Johnson (Karl F. & Rosemary) Fdn., Indianapolis, 1/084
Kelling (Harry L.) Trust Fund, LaPorte, 1/084
Kemper Bothers Fdn., Richmond, 1/085
Kitselman (Alice Miriam) Scholarship Fund, Muncie, 1/085
Kiwanis Club of Elkhart, Elkhart, 1/086
Kiwanis Club of East Evansville Fdn., Evansville, 1/086
Twilight Optimist Club of Indianapolis, Indianapolis, 1/086

Kiwanis Club of North Side Evansville Fdn., Evansville, 1/086
Knoerzer (Leo P.) Fdn., Hammond, 1/087
Koch (Henry F.) Residual Charitable Trust, Evansville, 1/088
Koch (Henry F. & Minnie F.) Charitable Trust, Evansville, 1/088
Kokomo Labor Temple Association, Kokomo, 1/089
Krannert Charitable Trust, Indianapolis, 1/089
Krannert Graduate School of Industrial Administration Alumni Fdn., West Lafayette, 1/090
Kuehn Fdn., Evansville, 1/091
Kuhner Scholarship Fdn., Muncie, 1/092
Lakin (Sam) Fdn., Gary, 1/092
Lasky Fdn., Indianapolis, 1/093
Leeds (Rudolph Gaar) Fdn., Richmond, 1/093
Leve Fdn., Indianapolis, 1/094
Lilly (Eli) & Company Fdn., Indianapolis, 1/094
Lupke Fdn., Fort Wayne, 1/095
Lilly Endowment, Indianapolis, 1/096
Lilly (Lila A.) Fdn., Indianapolis, 1/100
Lincoln National Life Fdn., Fort Wayne, 1/100
Local 294 U.R.W.A. Building Corporation, Indianapolis, 1/101
Lupke Fdn., Fort Wayne, 1/101
Mallory (P.R.) Company Fdn., Indianapolis, 1/101
Marshall County Bank Fdn., South Bend, 1/103
McKee Fdn., Indianapolis, 1/103
McMillen Fdn., Fort Wayne, 1/104
McMillen (Dale, Jr. & Elizabeth) Fdn., Fort Wayne, 1/105
McMillen (Harold & Rachel) Fdn., Fort Wayne, 1/105
Mead Johnson & Company Fdn., Evansville, 1/106
Meridian Mutual Fdn., Indianapolis, 1/107
Merry Lea Nature & Religious Fdn., Wolf Lake, 1/107
Mesker (George L.) Music Trust, Evansville, 1/108
Michigan Public Broadcasting Corporation, South Bend, 1/109
Mid-West Ready-Mixed Concrete Association, Terre Haute, 1/109
Miholich Fdn., South Bend, 1/110
Miholich (Fred & Helen) Fdn., South Bend, 1/110
Mikesell Scholarship Fund, Warsaw, 1/112
Miles Laboratories Fdn., Formerly Miles - Ames Fdn., Elkhart, 1/113
Milner (Elva A.) Trust, Frankfort, 1/114
Moore (Walter H. & Vera I.) Educational Fund, Frankfort, 1/115
Morrill Fdn., Fort Wayne, 1/115
Morris (E.M.) Fdn., South Bend, 1/116
Morton Fdn., Evansville, 1/116
Morton (Robert Carter), Jr. French Award, Warsaw, 1/117
Levin (Mosette) Trust, Michigan City, 1/117
Muessel - Ellison Trust Fdn., South Bend, 1/118
Murphy College Fund Trust, Warsaw, 1/119
Muscatatuck Church Fdn., Butlerville, 1/119
Music Boosters, Richmond, 1/122
Naas (George H. & Erma N.) Memorial Trust, Portland, 1/122
Natco Fdn., Richmond, 1/122
Niccum Educational Trust Fdn., Goshen, 1/123
Nixon Newspapers Benevolent Association, Wabash, 1/123
Noll (John H.) Fdn., Fort Wayne, 1/123
Northwest Indiana Comprehensive Health Planning Council, Highland, 1/124
Norways Fdn., Indianapolis, 1/124
Notre Dame Club of St. Joseph Valley Scholarship Trust, South Bend, 1/125
Noyes (Nicholas H.), Jr. Memorial Fdn., Indianapolis, 1/127
Nugent (Elizabeth Ruddick) Fdn., Columbus, 1/129
Nugent (Walter C.) Fdn., Columbus, 1/130

Oakley (Hollie & Anna) Fdn., Terre Haute, 1/130
Oare (Robert L. & Mary Morris) Fdn., South Bend, 1/131
O'Brien Fdn., South Bend, 1/131
O'Brien (Cornelius) Fdn., Indianapolis, 1/132
Occidental Realty Company of Indiana Charitable Trust, Indianapolis, 1/132
Olivet Fdn., Indianapolis, 1/133
Oliver Memorial Trust Fdn., South Bend, 1/134
Outboard Boating Club of Evansville Fdn., Evansville, 1/134
Peninsula Fund, Indianapolis, 1/135
Plumsock Fund, Indianapolis, 1/135
Purdue Christian Fdn., West Lafayette, 1/137
Quigg Fund, Richmond, 1/137
Racoon Ridge Fdn., Fort Wayne, 1/138
R.B. Charitable & Educational Fdn., Rochester, 1/138
Redmon (Willard L.) & Family Fdn., Peru, 1/139
Regenstrief Fdn., Indianapolis, 1/139
Reilly Fdn., Indianapolis, 1/140
Repp Associates Fdn., Columbus, 1/140
Reuben Fdn., Indianapolis, 1/141
Reynolds (Janette) Aid Society for the Sick & Injured, South Bend, 1/141
Richardson Wildlife Sanctuary, Inc., Chesterton, 1/141
Ringle B. Franklin (Eleanore) Educational Trust, Warsaw, 1/142
Robertson (A.F.) Family Memorial Fund, Seymour, 1/142
Rodeheaver Fdn., Winona Lake, 1/142
Rothbaum Fdn., Indianapolis, 1/143
Rowe (Fred I. & Helen C.) Fdn., Fort Wayne, 1/143
Rubinson (Nathan) Fdn., South Bend, 1/144
Schemmel - Keck Fdn., Union City, 1/145
Schwanz (Phil J.) Fdn., Fort Wayne, 1/146
Scott (Donald W.) Fdn., Terre Haute, 1/146
Sengenberger (Ella C.) Scholarship Fdn., Indianapolis, 1/147
Severns (Edward P. & Barbara A.) Charitable Fdn. Trust, Indianapolis, 1/147
Sherman Educational Fund, Sullivan, 1/148
Shook (Luther V.) Trust, Tipton, 1/149
Shroyer (Benjamin F.) Scholarship Fund, Muncie, 1/150
Eta Chapter of Sigma Pi Scholarship Fdn., Lafayette, 1/151
Simon Educational Trust Fdn., South Bend, 1/151
Sims (Ernest M.) Fdn., Elkhart, 1/151
Sites (Venette & Mabel) Fdn., Fort Wayne, 1/152
Sleeth (Charlotte Frame) Trust, Rushville, 1/153
Smock (Frank & Laura) Fdn., Fort Wayne, 1/153
Sollitt Fdn., South Bend, 1/154
Sommers (Charles B.) Fdn., Indianapolis, 1/155
South Bend Tribune Fdn., South Bend, 1/155
Spencer (George A. & Marie G.) Education Fdn. Trust, Tipton, 1/156
Sperling Fdn., Indianapolis, 1/156
Spicer (Ted) Ministerial & Medical Scholarship Trust Fund, Salem, 1/157
Springer Fund, Indianapolis, 1/157
Stokely (William B.), Jr. Fdn., Indianapolis, 1/158
Sullivan Fdn., South Bend, 1/158
Sutphin (Samuel R.) Fdn., Indianapolis, 1/159
Sutton (Linda) Memorial Scholarship Fund, Muncie, 1/160
Swope (Sheldon) Trust, Terre Haute, 1/160
Teagarden (Stella I.) Trust for Liberty Cemetery Association of Orange County, Muncie, 1/161
Thomas (Adele M.) Trust, Indianapolis, 1/161
Treaty-Line Museum, Inc., Liberty, 1/162
Bartlett (Bessie) Trust, Indianapolis, 1/162
Bartlett (William) Trusts, Indianapolis, 1/163
Bassett (Ida M.) Trust, Indianapolis, 1/164

Brill (Esther & Henry) Scholarship Fund, Indianapolis, 1/164
Cheney (Alice) Trusts, Indianapolis, 1/165
Deitch (Guilford A.) Trust, Indianapolis, 1/165
Dinwiddie (Emma J.) Trusts, Frankfort, 1/166
Duncan (James R.) Trust, Evansville, 1/167
Ford (Charles) Trust, New Harmony, 1/168
Geuss (George B. & Sue M.) Religious, Charitable, & Educational Trust, Evansville, 1/170
Higgins (William L.) Trust, Indianapolis, 1/170
Children's Bureau of Indianapolis, Lt. James J. Mallon, Jr. Memorial Scholarship Trust, Indianapolis, 1/171
McDonald Memorial Fund Trust, Warsaw, 1/171
Tucker (Fred) Fdn., Indianapolis, 1/172
Union City Body Company Fdn., Union City, 1/173
United Fdn., Jasper, 1/174
Wabash Magnetics Scholarship Fdn., Wabash, 1/175
Weil - McLain Fdn., Michigan City, 1/176
West Fdn., Indianapolis, 1/176
Wheelabrator Fdn., Mishawaka, 1/177
Wheeler (Chuck) Christian Fdn., Chesterton, 1/177
Wheeler Second Fdn., Indianapolis, 1/178
White (Robert P.) Permanant Charitable Trust, Sullivan, 1/178
Wilkinson Fdn., Logansport, 1/179
Winchester Fdn., Winchester, 1/180
Winski Fdn., Michigan City, 1/182
Winski (Jack) Fdn., Michigan City, 1/183
Winski (Mortimer) Fdn., Michigan City, 1/184

Second Filming

Acme Fdn., Jasper, 2/001
Arbogast (Alfred C. & Ersa S.) Fdn., Elkhart, 2/001
American Legion, Mayberry Post 469, Frankton, 2/002
Appliance Fdn., Van Buren, 2/003
Armstrong Products Fdn., Warsaw, 2/003
Association of Foundations, Columbus, 2/003
Atlas Foundry Fdn., Marion, 2/004
Auburn Foundry Fdn., Auburn, 2/006
Baber (Weisell) Fdn., Peru, 2/007
Baker (Hugh J.) Memorial Fdn., Indianapolis, 2/008
Ball Brothers Fdn., Muncie, 2/008
Ball (George & Frances) Fdn., Muncie, 2/010
Baxter Fdn., Indianapolis, 2/010
Beardsley (Andrew Hubble) Fdn., Elkhart, 2/011
Beeth (Glendora) Trust, Muncie, 2/012
Berman (Herman & Pauline) Fdn., Evansville, 2/012
Besselman (John H. & Laura E.) Trust, Richmond, 2/013
Best (John G.) Fdn., Elkhart, 2/014
Bieberich Fdn., Fort Wayne, 2/015
Block (William H.) Fdn., Indianapolis, 2/015
Bostock (Albert O.) Fdn., Jeffersonville, 2/016
Bowker Fdn., Fort Wayne, 2/017
Brumfield (R.M.) Trust, Evansville, 2/017
Buehler Fdn., Indianapolis, 2/018
Jasper Cabinet Fdn., Jasper, 2/019
Caldwell (Jennie E.) Memorial Home, Earl Park, 2/019
Carson (W.A.) Student Loan Fund Trust, Evansville, 2/020
Carson (William A.) Fdn., Evansville, 2/021
Carson (William A.) Scholarship Fdn., Evansville, 2/022
Central Newspapers Fdn., Indianapolis, 2/023
Chicago Telephone Supply Fdn., Elkhart, 2/026
Christian Fdn., Columbus, 2/028
Clark (Stanley A. & Flora P.) Memorial Community Trust Fdn., South Bend, 2/029
Carmel Clay Educational Fdn., Carmel, 2/029
Colby (Julian) Charitable Fdn., Hammond, 2/029
Cole (Olive B.) Fdn., Fort Wayne, 2/030
Cooney (Thomas E.) Trust, Indianapolis, 2/032

Corley Family Fdn., Michigan City, 2/032
Crowe (Mary Jane M.) Fdn., Fort Wayne, 2/033
Crowley (Jerome J.) Fdn., South Bend, 2/033
Crume (Mary Powell) Trust, Indianapolis, 2/034
Cummins Engine Fdn., Columbus, 2/035
Da - Lite Screen Fdn., Warsaw, 2/038
Dalton (Donald J.) Fdn., Warsaw, 2/039
Delta Phi Delta Alumni Scholarship Fdn., Lafayette, 2/039
Dodge Fdn., Mishawaka, 2/041
Downtown Optimist Fdn., Indianapolis, 2/041
Duncan (James R. & Adelaide H.) Fdn., Evansville, 2/042
Eby (Henry W.) Trust, Indianapolis, 2/042
Edinburg Industries Youth Fdn., Edinburg, 2/043
Electrical Joint Apprenticeship & Training Committee of Northern Indiana, Evansville, 2/043
Elkhart Area Career Center Fdn., Elkhart, 2/044
Elkhart Bridge & Iron Fdn., Elkhart, 2/044
Elkhart General Hospital Fdn., Elkhart, 2/044
Ernie's Fdn., South Bend, 2/045
Evansville Philharmonic Orchestra Corp. Endowment Fund Trust, Evansville, 2/046
Evansville Serra Fdn., Evansville, 2/046
Evansville Typographical Union #35, Evansville, 2/047
Evansville Y M C A Endowment Fund Trust, Evansville, 2/047
Falender Charitable Trust, Indianapolis, 2/048
Farmer (Norman & Emma) Fdn., Gary, 2/048
Feinberg (Marcus A.) Charitable Trust, Indianapolis, 2/048
First Meridian Heights Presbyterian Church "Moreland Fund" Trust, Indianapolis, 2/049
First Meridian Heights Presbyterian Church "Wishard Fund" Trust, Indianapolis, 2/050
Lembke (Cora) Trust, Valparaiso, 2/050
Foellinger Fdn., Fort Wayne, 2/050
Fore (William E.) Trust, Indianapolis, 2/052
Freimann (Frank) Charitable Trust, Fort Wayne, 2/053
McKee Fdn., Indianapolis, 2/053
Frost (Robert J.) Family Fdn., Michigan City, 2/054
Gallahue (Edward) Fdn., Indianapolis, 2/054
Gates Fdn., South Bend, 2/054
Gemmer (H.C.) Family Christian Fdn., Indianapolis, 2/055
Gilbert (N.G.) Fdn., Muncie, 2/055
Goad Fdn., Gary, 2/055
Goodrich (John B.) Charitable Trust, Winchester, 2/056
Grantham Fdn., Gary, 2/059
Grossman Charitable Trust, Elkhart, 2/059
Gust (Edward G.) Family Fdn., Michigan City, 2/060
Hayes (Stanley W.) Research Fdn., Richmond, 2/061
Hill Fdn., Richmond, 2/062
Holliday (John H.) Trust #1, Indianapolis, 2/063
Holliday (John H.) Trust #2, Indianapolis, 2/063
Hoosier State Charitable Fdn., Hammond, 2/063
Howe Fund, Howe, 2/064
Hurley (Ruth M.) Trust, Indianapolis, 2/064
Hutner Guidance Center for Hearing & Speech, Fort Wayne, 2/065
Igleheart (Belle S.) Student Loan Fund, Evansville, 2/065
Indiana Cabinet Fdn., Dubois, 2/066
Indiana Delta Fdn., Franklin, 2/067
Indiana Educational, Cultural & Fine Arts Fdn., Fort Wayne, 2/067
Indiana 4-H Fdn., Lafayette, 2/068
Indiana Insurance Educational Fdn., Indianapolis, 2/068
Indianapolis Diabetes Association Fdn. Trust, Indianapolis, 2/069

Indianapolis - Michigan Fdn., Indianapolis, 2/069

Irwin - Sweeney - Miller Fdn., Columbus, 2/071

Irwin Union Fdn., Columbus, 2/074

Jackson (Dr. J.M.) Memorial Trust Fund, Lawrenceburg, 2/076

Jasper Fdn., Jasper, 2/077

Jewish Welfare Fund of Southeastern Indiana, Shelbyville, 2/078

Jewish Temple School Fund, Fort Wayne, 2/078

Johnson & Davisson Fdn., Elkhart, 2/078

Johnson Sheet Metal Works Fdn., Richmond, 2/079

Jordan (Arthur) Fdn., Indianapolis, 2/080

Kelling (Harry L.) Trust Fund, LaPorte, 2/081

Kilbourne (E.H. "Cap") Charitable, Educational & Religious Endowment Fund, Fort Wayne, 2/081

Kiwanis Club of Mishawaka Scholarship Loan Fdn., South Bend, 2/082

Kiwanis Indiana Fdn., Shelbyville, 2/082

Klein (Maude J.) Trust for Visiting Nurse Assoc. of Muncie, Muncie, 2/082

Kley (Charles F.) Trust, Evansville, 2/083

Laymen's Bible Study Fdn., Castleton, 2/084

Blazer (Lee) Studio Scholarship Fund, Greenfield, 2/085

Oakes (Frank Leonard) Trust, Indianapolis, 2/085

Leeds (Rudolph Gaar) Fdn., Richmond, 2/086

Letzter (Edwin E.) Charitable Trust, Indianapolis, 2/086

Lieber (Herman F.) Memorial Fund, Indianapolis, 2/087

Liberty Fund, Indianapolis, 2/087

Lilly (Evan F.) Memorial Fdn., Indianapolis, 2/091

Loeb Farm School for Jewish Children, Indianapolis, 2/091

Lowe Fdn., Pierceton, 2/093

Lupke Fdn., Fort Wayne, 2/093

Magnavox Fdn., Fort Wayne, 2/093

Malpas Trust, Lebanon, 2/094

Marsh Charitable Trust, Yorktown, 2/095

Martin Fdn., Elkhart, 2/096

Mavroulios (George Anastasios) Scholarship Fdn., Indianapolis, 2/097

Weil - McLain Fdn., Michigan City, 2/098

Meek (Frank) Memorial Trust, Indianapolis, 2/098

Mervis (David) Fdn., Kokomo, 2/099

Mitchell (John D.) Charitable Fdn., Goodland, 2/099

Morris (E.M.) Trust for YMCA for South Bend, South Bend, 2/100

Moore Fdn., Indianapolis, 2/100

Morgan Fdn., Indianapolis, 2/101

Muscatatuck Church Fdn., Indianapolis, 2/101

Mutual Service Fdn. Trust, Indianapolis, 2/105

Phillips (Dorothy Myers) Fund, Indianapolis, 2/105

Niccum Educational Trust Fdn., Goshen, 2/105

Nordmeyer Fdn., Batesville, 2/106

Notre Dame Club of St. Joseph Valley Scholarship Trust, South Bend, 2/106

Noyes (Nicholas H.), Jr. Memorial Fdn., Indianapolis, 2/107

Magee - O'Connor Fdn., Fort Wayne, 2/109

Old National Bank Charitable Trust, Evansville, 2/109

Petticrew Fdn., Indianapolis, 2/111

Petty (Margaret Ball) Fdn., Muncie, 2/111

Phi Chi Educational Fdn., Indianapolis, 2/112

Powell (William L.) Fdn., Lebanon, 2/112

Portland Fdn., Portland, 2/113

Prather (Calvin W.) Lodge #717 F. & A.M., Indianapolis, 2/113

Pulaski Memorial Hospital Fdn., Winamac, 2/114

Ramsey (Ada) Trust, Mt. Vernon, 2/114

Reynolds (Janette) Aid Society for the Sick & Injured, South Bend, 2/115

Rice Memorial Hospital & Welfare Fund, Evansville, 2/115

Roberts (James E.) Surgical Appliance Fund, Indianapolis, 2/116

Root Fdn., Terre Haute, 2/116

Rose (Chauncey) Home, Terre Haute, 2/117

St. Mary's Educational Trust, Anderson, 2/117

Santa Claus Samaritans, Evansville, 2/118

Schaefer (Edward J. & Hildegarde H.) Fdn., Fort Wayne, 2/119

Schwartz (Leo & Anna W.) Fdn., Muncie, 2/119

Schnuetgen (Henry) Trust, Evansville, 2/120

Scott (Ethel Voris) Trust, Indianapolis, 2/121

Shaw Fdn., Indianapolis, 2/121

Sims (Ernest M.) Fdn., Elkhart, 2/122

Sinning (Edward) Fdn., Elkhart, 2/122

Slaughter Scholarship Trust, South Bend, 2/122

Tefillia (Shara) Cemetery Trust, Indianapolis, 2/122

Shane (Norman A. & Margaret I.) Charitable Trust, Evansville, 2/123

Schultz (Kate W.) Trust, Mt. Vernon, 2/124

Sims (Ernest M.) Fdn., Elkhart, 2/124

Smelser (Elizabeth) Scholarship Fund, Richmond, 2/124

South Bend Scottish Rite Benevolent Trust, South Bend, 2/125

Storer (Oliver W.) Scholarship Fdn., Indianapolis, 2/125

Stout (C.B.) Fdn., Paoli, 2/127

Thirty Five Twenty, Inc., Indianapolis, 2/128

Thrush (H.A.) Fdn., Peru, 2/130

Binford (Mary H.) Memorial Fdn., Indianapolis, 2/130

Spencer Christian Church Trust, Indianapolis, 2/131

Boys Club Fdn. Trust, Indianapolis, 2/132

Askren (Caroline L.) Trust, Indianapolis, 2/132

Boy Scouts of America, Central Indiana Council Trust, Indianapolis, 2/133

Nafe Memorial School Fund, Indianapolis, 2/134

Lower (Dessie H.) Trust, Indianapolis, 2/134

East Tenth Street Methodist Church, Indianapolis, 2/135

English (Rosalind) Trust, Indianapolis, 2/135

East Tenth Street Methodist Church Trust, Indianapolis, 2/136

Higgins (William L.) Trust - Buren Fund, Indianapolis, 2/136

Hillenbrand (Sophia M.) Trust, Indianapolis, 2/137

Indianapolis Home for Aged - H.B. Higgins Fund, Indianapolis, 2/137

Indiana Science Education Fund Trust, Indianapolis, 2/137

Kresge (F.) Trust f/b/o Masonic Home Chapel, Indianapolis, 2/138

Kresge (Floyd L.) Trust, Indianapolis, 2/138

Kresge (Floyd L.) Trust a/c Falls Methodist Church, Indianapolis, 2/138

Landon (Jessie S.) Trust Item Y-#1, Indianapolis, 2/139

London (Jessie S.) Trust a/c Spalding Mem., Indianapolis, 2/139

Marble (Mitchell S.) Trust, Indianapolis, 2/140

McKinney (Leanna B.) Trust, Indianapolis, 2/141

Olson (Marks) Fdn. Trust, Indianapolis, 2/141

Proctor (Mary J.) Trust, Indianapolis, 2/142

Rhoades (William) Trust, Indianapolis, 2/142

English (Rosalind) Trust f/b/o Sick & Indigent Children, Indianapolis, 2/143

Tucker (Roscoe) Trust, Indianapolis, 2/143

Selmier (Frank) Trust f/b/o Girl Scouts, Indianapolis, 2/143

Teacher's College Trust, Eliza Blaker Fund, Indianapolis, 2/144

Teacher's College Trust, Louis Blaker Fund, Indianapolis, 2/144

Williams (Irving) Trust, Indianapolis, 2/144

Winningham (Mary E.D.) Trust, Indianapolis, 2/145

Woodsmall (Mary H.) Fdn. for Encouragement of Arts, Indianapolis, 2/145

Wright (John S.) Trust - J. Bass & Meridian St. Methodist Church, Indianapolis, 2/146

Wright (John S.) Trust u/w Lectania N. Wright, Indianapolis, 2/146

Zion United Church of Christ Trust, Indianapolis, 2/147

Tudor (Rev. Glenn L.) Fdn., Elkhart, 2/147

Turner (Basil S.) Fdn., Elkhart, 2/148

Tyson Fund, Indianapolis, 2/148

United Cabinet Fdn., Jasper, 2/149

Wallace (Walter E.) Fdn., Richmond, 2/150

Warner (Barbara K.) Charitable Trust, South Bend, 2/151

Welborn Fdn., Evansville, 2/152

Willkie (Wendell L.) Fund, Indianapolis, 2/152

Williams (Kenneth C.) Irrevocable Charitable Trust, Evansville, 2/154

Willkie (Wendell L.) Fund, Indianapolis, 2/154

Willkie Fdn., Rushville, 2/155

Willennar (William H.) Fdn., Auburn, 2/156

Wilson (John D.) Trust, Winchester, 2/157

Winchester Fdn., Winchester, 2/158

IOWA

First Filming

Aliber Fdn., Des Moines, 1/004

Amana Refrigeration Fdn., Cedar Rapids, 1/005

American Legion Post, Central City, 1/005

Anderson (A. O.) Fdn., Sac City, 1/006

Armstrong (Emma) Fund, Cedar Rapids, 1/006

Armstrong (Edith Curtis) and Florence E. Curtis Fdn., Clinton, 1/006

Armstrong (Samuel G. and Anna) Fund, Cedar Rapids, 1/007

Babcock (Quintus C.) Memorial Fund, Fayette, 1/007

Bechtel Fdn., Davenport, 1/008

Becker Fund, Cedar Rapids, 1/008

Benner Fdn., Burlington, 1/009

Bettendorf (W.E.) Fdn., Davenport, 1/010

Bezanson (P.F.) Charitable Trust, Cedar Rapids, 1/010

Bock (Lloyd R. and Ada) Fdn. Trust, Des Moines, 1/011

Bookey Trust Fdn., Des Moines, 1/011

Bookey (Morton-Lois) Fdn., Des Moines, 1/012

Bookey (Lester-Mary Jane) Fdn., Des Moines, 1/013

Booth Fdn., Davenport, 1/013

Boss Fdn., Des Moines, 1/014

Bossingham (Earl N. and Mabel Bragg) Fdn., Clarinda, 1/014

Brenton Fdn., Des Moines, 1/015

Brody (Julian and Irma) Fdn., Des Moines, 1/016

Brown-Iles-McKinney Charitable Trust, Des Moines, 1/016

Brown (Irene Larmon) Scholarship Fund, Stanton, 1/017

Brown (Rainsford A.) Fdn., Davenport, 1/017

Bucksbaum Fdn., Des Moines, 1/018

Campbell (John M.) Trust, Grinnell, 1/018

Chappell (E.E.) Fdn., Clear Lake, 1/021

Christopherson (Dr. J.E.) Memorial Scholarship Fund, Mason City, 1/021

Citizens First National Bank Fdn., Storm Lake, 1/022

Citizens First National Educational Trust, Storm Lake, 1/022

Cochrane (William) Memorial Trust, Red Oak, 1/022

Cohn (Esac and Eva) Fdn., Cedar Rapids, 1/023

Collins (Arthur) Charitable Trust, Cedar Rapids, 1/023

Collins (Merle) Fdn., Cedar Rapids, 1/024

Columbus Junction State Bank Fdn., Columbus Junction, 1/024

Cowles (Gardner) Fdn., Des Moines, 1/025

Crawford (William C. and Mildred) Charitable
Fdn., Cedar Rapids, 1/026
Crippen (Minnie M.) Fdn., Waterloo, 1/027
Crippen (Minnie M.) Trust, Waterloo, 1/028
Dahm (J.B.) Fdn., Des Moines, 1/030
Delzell (Earl B.) Fdn., Cedar Rapids, 1/031
Dial Fdn., Des Moines, 1/031
Doane (Grace O.) Charitable Fdn., Des
Moines, 1/033
Donnelly (M.J. and Alice G.) Charitable Trust,
Cedar Rapids, 1/033
Dubansky (Marvin H.) Fdn., Des Moines,
1/033
Dubuque Bank and Trust Company Fdn.,
Dubuque, 1/034
Duchen (Charles and Agnes Louise M.) Fdn.,
Des Moines, 1/034
Fahey (Bernard M.) Fund, Dubuque, 1/035
Fellman (Louis I. and Selma L.) Trust, Cedar
Rapids, 1/036
First National Bank of Dubuque Charitable
Trust, Dubuque, 1/036
Fisher Governor Fdn., Marshalltown, 1/037
Flynn (Elizabeth M.) Charitable Trust, Albia,
1/037
Galbraith (Melvin H.) Charitable Trust, Cedar
Rapids, 1/038
Gates Memorial Fund, Nevada, 1/039
Gazette Fdn., Cedar Rapids, 1/039
Glaser Fdn., Fort Dodge, 1/040
Glazer (Madelyn L.) Fdn., Des Moines, 1/041
Goldstein (Bernice and Harold) Fdn., Sioux
City, 1/041
Goodwin (Robert K.) Fdn., Des Moines,
1/042
Goodwin (W.J.) Fdn., Des Moines, 1/042
Goodwin (William) Fdn., Des Moines, 1/043
Gramma Fisher Fdn., Marshalltown, 1/043
Greenberg Fdn. of Sioux City, Sioux City,
1/044
Greenwood Fdn., Des Moines, 1/044
Grout (H.W.) Trust, Waterloo, 1/045
Guthrie Fdn., Iowa City, 1/046
Hall Fdn., Cedar Rapids, 1/046
Hawkeye Security Charitable Fdn., Des Moines,
1/048
Hawley Welfare Fdn., Des Moines, 1/048
Hockenberg (Harlan D.) Fdn., Des Moines,
1/048
Hoerner (Richard N.), Jr. Fdn., Keokuk, 1/048
Hubbell Brothers Trust, Des Moines, 1/049
Hubbell (Frederick Marion) Fdn., Des Moines,
1/049
Hubbell-Waterman Fdn., Davenport, 1/050
Hubinger Fdn., Keokuk, 1/051
Hyland Fdn., Des Moines, 1/051
Iowa Arboretum, Des Moines, 1/052
Iowa Manufacturing Fdn., Cedar Rapids,
1/052
Iowa Pharmacy Fdn., Des Moines, 1/053
Iowa Steel Fdn., Cedar Rapids, 1/053
Iowa Trust and Savings Bank Fdn., Estherville,
1/054
K A M Fdn., Davenport, 1/054
Kelloway (E.A.) Charitable Fdn., Atlantic,
1/055
Kelloway (Dorothy S.) Diagnostic and Research
Fdn., Atlantic, 1/055
Kem-Co Trust, Keokuk, 1/056
Kent-Stein Fdn., Muscatine, 1/056
King (Jane R.) Charity Fund, Jewell, 1/057
Kinney-Lindstrom Fdn., Mason City, 1/057
Kiowa Fdn., Marshalltown, 1/057
Klass-Belin Fdn., Sioux City, 1/058
Klinger (W.A.) Fdn., Sioux City, 1/058
Knalba Fdn., Des Moines, 1/058
Knapp (R.F.) Charitable Trust, Cedar Rapids,
1/061
Lake-Gidley Fdn., Shenandoah, 1/061
Lalor (Walter L.) Fdn., Des Moines, 1/062
Landis Charitable Trust, Cedar Rapids, 1/062
Levine (Arnold E. and Caroline W.) Fdn., Des
Moines, 1/063
Levitt (Richard S.) Fdn., Des Moines, 1/064
Levitt (Ellis I.) Welfare Fund, Des Moines,
1/064

Lindhart Educational Trust, Des Moines, 1/065
Lindholme (Doctor and Mrs. S.A.) Trust, Des
Moines, 1/066
Lindquist (M.W.) Fdn., Des Moines, 1/066
Lisle Fdn., Clarinda, 1/066
Lundy (Kathleen Walsh) Fdn., Davenport,
1/067
Lynch (C.J.) Charitable Trust, Cedar Rapids,
1/067
Mahoney Fund Trust, Sioux City, 1/068
Mandelbaum (Sidney) Fdn., Des Moines,
1/068
Mathis-Pfohl Fdn., Dubuque, 1/068
Maytag Company Fdn., Newton, 1/069
Maytag (Fred) Family Fdn., Newton, 1/072
Maytag (Fred) Park, Newton, 1/074
McDonald (A.Y.) Mfg. Co. Charitable Fdn.,
Dubuque, 1/075
McGowan (Mollie) Trust, Mason City, 1/077
Mid-America Fdn., Des Moines, 1/077
Moeller (Carl H.) Memorial Trust, Reinbeck,
1/078
Neiswanger Fdn., Davenport, 1/078
Nelson (Murray B.) Fdn., Newton, 1/079
Norris Fdn., Marshalltown, 1/080
Norris (Nick) Memorial Fdn., Marshalltown,
1/080
Noun (Louise) Charitable Trust, Des Moines,
1/081
Nussbaum (Louis I. and Rebecca) Fdn. Trust,
Des Moines, 1/082
O'Dea Fdn., Des Moines, 1/083
Peoples Charitable Trust Fund, Cedar Rapids,
1/084
Pidgeon (David D.) Charitable Fdn., Des
Moines, 1/085
Pierce (Frank) Trust, Marshalltown, 1/086
Plum Hill Trust, Newton, 1/087
Pomerantz Fdn., Des Moines, 1/088
Preacher (Ava M.) Memorial Trust, Davenport,
1/088
Preston (Elmer O. and Ida) Educational Trust,
Des Moines, 1/089
Pritchard Educational Fund, Cherokee, 1/090
Quail (John J.) Fdn., Davenport, 1/090
Quarton (Elnora H. and William B.) Fdn.,
Cedar Rapids, 1/090
Race (Frank and Margaret) Fdn., Cedar
Rapids, 1/091
Rath Charitable Fdn., Waterloo, 1/092
Reinbeck Educational Fund, Reinbeck, 1/093
Ringheim (William W.) Fdn., Des Moines,
1/093
Rolscreen (Pella) Fdn., Pella, 1/093
Rosenfield (Joseph F.) Charitable Trust, Des
Moines, 1/094
Salsbury (Dr. J.E.) Fdn., Charles City, 1/095
Sanborn (Clyde R. and Emily T.) Charitable
Trust, Cedar Rapids, 1/096
Saunders (Meredith R.) Fdn., Des Moines,
1/096
Schildberg (E.F. and S.K.) Charitable Trust,
Greenfield, 1/096
Schwartz Fdn., Marshalltown, 1/097
Self-Help Fdn., Waverly, 1/098
Shelton Fdn., Des Moines, 1/099
Sherman Fdn., Davenport, 1/099
Shloss (Sam M. and Gertrude B.) Fdn., Des
Moines, 1/099
Shulman Fdn., Iowa City, 1/100
Siefer Charitable Trust, Fort Dodge, 1/101
Sinaiko (Joseph M.) Fdn., Cedar Rapids,
1/101
Smith (Clemens J.) Charitable Fdn., New
Hampton, 1/102
Smith (Howard O.) Charitable Trust, Des
Moines, 1/102
Spaight Charitable Fdn., Cedar Rapids, 1/103
Spevak (Jack & Marjorie S.) Fdn., Des Moines,
1/103
Stamats Fund, Cedar Rapids, 1/103
Stanley Fdn., Muscatine, 1/104
Stoddard (John) Fdn., Des Moines, 1/105
Stoner System Charitable Fdn., Des Moines,
1/106

Struve (Hugo and Catherine) Charitable Trust,
Cedar Rapids, 1/106
Sumner (Mary) Fdn., Des Moines, 1/107
Sunshine Mission, Cedar Rapids, 1/107
Sweetheart Bread Charitable Trust, Burlington,
1/108
Telegraph-Herald Fdn., Dubuque, 1/108
Thomas Fdn., Coon Rapids, 1/110
Thompson Charitable Trust, Des Moines, 1/110
Treimer (Gustav) Memorial Trust, Reinbeck,
1/111
Turner-Evans Fdn., Cedar Rapids, 1/111
Tyler Fdn., Davenport, 1/112
Umbreit Trust, Newton, 1/112
University of Northern Iowa Fdn., Cedar Falls,
1/113
Valley Bank Fdn., Des Moines, 1/114
Vermeer Fdn., Pella, 1/114
Waldinger (Harry and Goldie) Fdn., Des
Moines, 1/115
Walsh Fund, Davenport, 1/115
Waterloo Savings Bank Charitable Fdn. Trust,
Waterloo, 1/115
Weitz Fdn., Des Moines, 1/116
White (George and Mildred) Fdn., Des Moines,
1/116
Wilson Fdn., Conrad, 1/116
Winegard Fdn., Burlington, 1/117
Wolco Charitable Fdn., Cedar Rapids, 1/118
Wolfe Cataract Fdn., Marshalltown, 1/118
Younkers Fdn., Des Moines, 1/118

Second Filming

Ames Area Committee for Human
Development, Ames, 2/004
Anderson (B.L.) Fdn., Cedar Rapids, 2/004
Berndes Family Trust, Monticello, 2/005
Beta Kappa Building Corporation, Ames, 2/005
Betts Fdn., Des Moines, 2/006
Bohen Fdn., Des Moines, 2/006
Brown (Miriam) Trust, Des Moines, 2/007
Brown (William C.) Company Charitable Fdn.,
Dubuque, 2/008
Bruns (Leonard) Fdn., Des Moines, 2/009
Bishop Cafeteria Charitable Trust, Cedar
Rapids, 2/009
Callahan (Nellie) Scholarship Fund, Des
Moines, 2/009
Colleges of Mid-America, Sioux City, 2/010
Camp (James M. and Betty J.) Fdn., Des
Moines, 2/010
Community Theater Building Corporation,
Cedar Rapids, 2/011
Congregation B North Jeshrun Cemetery Trust
Fund, Des Moines, 2/011
Des Moines Iron Workers Welfare Fund, Des
Moines, 2/011
Des Moines-Polk Co. Home Care-Homemaker
Service, Des Moines, 2/011
Dyer (William S.) Educational Trust, Ackley,
2/012
Engman Fdn., Des Moines, 2/012
Fowler Memorial Trust, Cedar Falls, 2/012
Gates Memorial Fund, Nevada, 2/013
Geisler-Penquite Corporation, Newton, 2/016
Goldberg (Louis and Dorothy) Charitable Fdn.,
Des Moines, 2/017
Goldman (Harry) Fdn., Des Moines, 2/017
Guaranty Bank and Trust Company Charitable
Trust, Cedar Rapids, 2/019
Gund (William L. and Ethel) Memorial Fund,
Cherokee, 2/019
Higley (Edward B.) Trust, Mason City, 2/020
Iowa Humane Society, Des Moines, 2/021
Iowa Medical Technologist Fdn., Des Moines,
2/021
Jay (George S. and Grace A.) Memorial Trust,
Shenandoah, 2/022
Iowa Realty Company Charitable Fdn., Des
Moines, 2/023
Jensen Fdn., Des Moines, 2/023
Kaplan (Israel E. and Sylvia C.) Fdn., Sioux
City, 2/024
Kenny (Pearl) Trust, Cherokee, 2/024

Kolls (Ernest W. and Vera Jane) Fdn., Des Moines, 2/025

Lake (Mr. and Mrs. Al) Trust, Mason City, 2/025

Levinger (Harold and Lerena) Fdn., Sioux City, 2/026

Kuyper (Peter H. and E. Lucille Gaass) Fdn., Pella, 2/027

Spahn and Rose Lumber Company Charitable Trust, Dubuque, 2/027

Mandelbaum (Robert J.) Fdn., Des Moines, 2/028

Martin (Dr.) Scholarship Fund for Fort Dodge Community College of Fort Dodge, Iowa, Fort Dodge, 2/029

McDonald (A.Y.) Mfg. Co. Charitable Trust, Dubuque, 2/030

McCutcheon (James and Ruth) Charitable Trust, Mt. Vernon, 2/030

Mentzer (John P.) Scholarship Trust, Cedar Rapids, 2/031

Martin (Dr.) Scholarship Fund for the Cornell College, Mount Vernon, 2/031

Meredith (Edwin T.) Fdn., Des Moines, 2/031

Mentzer (John P.) Scholarship Trust, Cedar Rapids, 2/032

Midwest Fdn., Cedar Rapids, 2/032

Moore (S.L.) Charity Fdn., Boone, 2/033

National Association of Letter Carriers, Des Moines, 2/032

Neurological Insitute Research Fdn. of Northeast Iowa, Cedar Falls, 2/033

Nelson (John W.) Trust, Sioux City, 2/033

Phelphs Fdn., Waterloo, 2/033

Pi Beta Phi Building Corporation, Ames, 2/034

Red Oak Scholarship Loan Fund, Red Oak, 2/034

Riverview Park Fdn., Des Moines, 2/034

Lund (Roger and Ruth) Charitable Trust, Ottumwa, 2/034

Rohle Memorial Clinic Fdn., Waverly, 2/035

Roosevelt Hotel Fdn., Cedar Rapids, 2/036

Rosenstock Fdn., Sioux City, 2/037

Ruan (John) Fdn. Trust, Des Moines, 2/037

Rural Neighbors Club, Des Moines, 2/038

Sanborn (Clyde R. and Emily T.) Charitable Trust, Cedar Rapids, 2/038

Stellart Sanford Fdn., Sioux City, 2/038

Sargent (Ernest) Family Fdn., Des Moines, 2/039

Saunders (Meredith R.) Fdn., Des Moines, 2/039

Schwartz (Don and Ruth) Fdn., Des Moines, 2/039

Sheaffer (W.A.) Memorial Fdn., Fort Madison, 2/039

Sheppley (William S.) Fdn., Dubuque, 2/041

Smith (Howard O.) Charitable Trust, Des Moines, 2/041

Stampfer Charitable Trust, Dubuque, 2/041

Sumner Community Charitable Trust, Sumner, 2/042

Sundholm Fdn., Albert City, 2/042

Swensrud (Sidney A.) Scholarship Fund, Northwood, 2/042

Trust under Paragraph 35, Will of James Callanan, Des Moines, 2/042

Trust under Paragraph 43, Will of James Callanan, Des Moines, 2/042

Trust under Paragraph 9, Will of James Leonard Callanan, Des Moines, 2/043

Trust u/w of Sam Raizes for Charities, Mason City, 2/043

University Towers Fdn., Tama, 2/044

Vail Medical Clinic, Denison, 2/044

Van Dyke (Carleton C.) Benevolence Fund, Sioux City, 2/045

Toy-Van Dyke Fdn., Sioux City, 2/045

Waldinger (Harry and Goldie) Fdn., Des Moines, 2/045

Wasta Charitable Trust, Cedar Rapids, 2/046

Woitishek Memorial Lecture Fund Trust, Cedar Rapids, 2/047

KANSAS

First Filming

Armstrong (A.W. and Nellie B.) Fdn., Inc., Phillipsburg, 1/002

Bar-Mar Charitable Fdn., Topeka, 1/003

Baughman Fdn., Liberal, 1/003

Beals (David T.) Fdn., Shawnee Mission, 1/003

Beren (Lois and Max) Fdn., Wichita, 1/004

Born (Harold J.) Charitable Fdn., Wichita, 1/005

Breidenthal (Willard J. and Mary G.) Fdn., Kansas City, 1/005

Bryant (B. K.) Fdn., Independence, 1/005

Brown Memorial Fdn., Abilene, 1/006

Butts (J. Arch) Fdn., Wichita, 1/007

Carey (Charles E.) Fdn., Hutchinson, 1/008

Calhoun Fdn., Emporia, 1/008

Carney (Danieal M.) Family Charitable Fdn., Wichita, 1/008

Carney (Frank L.) Family Charities Fdn., Wichita, 1/009

Carroll Fdn., St. Paul, 1/009

Casado (Luis and Vera) Fdn., Wichita, 1/010

Cessna Fdn., Wichita, 1/010

Charitable Fdn., Wichita, 1/011

Chisholm Family Charities Fdn., Wichita, 1/011

Coleman Charitable Trust, Wichita, 1/012

Coleman Employees Community Fund, Wichita, 1/012

Coleman Fdn., Wichita, 1/013

Coombs (Dorth L. and Virginia P.) Philanthropic Fund, Wichita, 1/013

Cray (Cloud L.) Fdn., Atchison, 1/014

Davis (James A. and Juliet L.) Fdn., Hutchinson, 1/014

Dean (W. Laird) Memorial Trust, Topeka, 1/014

Delta Tau Delta Education Fdn., Lawrence, 1/015

Dubbs (Rebecca) Memorial Fund Trust, Wichita, 1/015

Elliott (John and Ruth) Fdn., Wichita, 1/016

Emporia Teamwork, Emporia, 1/016

First National Bank Club, Wichita, 1/017

Garvey Fdn., Wichita, 1/017

Garvey Family Fdn., Wichita, 1/021

Garvey Kansas Fdn., Wichita, 1/021

Glendale Fund, Shawnee Mission, 1/022

Glickman Family Fdn., Wichita, 1/022

Glynn (Thomas C.) Charitable Trust, Wichita, 1/023

Great Plains Heritage Fdn., Wichita, 1/023

Hammond Fdn., Wichita, 1/024

Hedrick (Frank E.) Fdn., Wichita, 1/024

Heimple Charitable Fdn., Wichita, 1/025

Hess Fdn., McPherson, 1/025

Hesston Fdn., Hesston, 1/026

Hillcrest Fdn., Leawood, 1/027

Joscelyn (Verla Nesbitt) Fund, Salina, 1/027

Jellison Benevolent Society, Junction City, 1/029

Jordaan Fdn. Trust, Larned, 1/029

Joscelyn (Verla Nesbitt) Fdn., Salina, 1/030

Kansas Gas and Electric Charitable Fdn., Wichita, 1/031

Kansas State University Research Fdn., Manhattan, 1/032

Key Charitable Trust, Fort Scott, 1/032

Koch (Fred C.) Fdn., Wichita, 1/033

Kuhn (Walter) Fdn., Wichita, 1/034

Laybourn Fdn., Inc., Salina, 1/034

Levitt Charitable Fdn., Wichita, 1/035

Lew (James and Arlene) Fdn., Wichita, 1/037

Maloney (Carl V. and Honore G.) Fdn., Wichita, 1/037

Mammel (Clayton) Fdn., Wichita, 1/038

McFarland (Anna) Scholarship Fund, Kinsley, 1/038

McNally (Thomas and Mary) Fdn., Pittsburg, 1/039

McPherson County Fdn., McPherson, 1/039

Michaels Fdn., Inc., Wichita, 1/039

Midwest Orthopaedic Research Fdn., Topeka, 1/040

Mingenback (Julia J.) Fdn., McPherson, 1/041

Mission Fund, Shawnee Mission, 1/042

Morgan Fdn., Wichita, 1/043

Morning Star Trust Fund, Manhattan, 1/044

Muchnic Fdn., Atchison, 1/044

Naftzger Fund for Fine Arts, Wichita, 1/044

Neosho Memorial Hospital Fdn., Chanute, 1/045

Osteopathic Fdn. of Kansas, Topeka, 1/045

Ella Palmer Fdn., Wichita, 1/045

Parklane National Bank Fdn., Wichita, 1/046

Pi Beta Phi Educational Fdn., Kansas City, 1/046

Price Fdn., Wichita, 1/046

Ross (Paul) Charitable Fdn., Wichita, 1/047

Ross Fdn., Wichita, 1/048

Rouback Family Fdn., Russell, 1/048

Security Benefit Clinic & Hospital, Topeka, 1/050

Shanley (Laura & John) Charitable Trust, Wichita, 1/051

Short Family Fdn., Harper, 1/052

Smith (Kenneth L.) Fdn., Lenexa, 1/052

Smith-Putnam Trust, Junction City, 1/053

Snodgrass (Mabel Sites) Fdn., Wichita, 1/053

Spikes (Dr. Marion E.) Charitable Trust, Garden City, 1/053

Staley Fdn., Wichita, 1/054

Sutton (C. A.) Fdn., Wichita, 1/054

Towner Fdn., Pittsburgh, 1/054

Trembly (John E.) Fdn., Manhattan, 1/055

Trusler Fdn., Emporia, 1/056

Vesper (Dr. Vernon A. and Ada L.) Educational Trust, Hill City, 1/056

Wainscott (George E.) Fdn., Atchison, 1/057

Wallace (Dwane L.) Fdn., Wichita, 1/057

Wall-Diffenderfer Fdn., Topeka, 1/058

Watkins (E. A.) Fdn., Wichita, 1/058

Whetstone (Clayton & Beatrice) Memorial Scholarship Trust, Topeka, 1/059

Wichita Board of Realtors, Wichita, 1/060

Wichita Kiwanis Chorus Scholarship Fdn., Wichita, 1/061

Wiedemann (K. T.) Fdn., Wichita, 1/061

Second Filming

Anderson (E.T. & Cora F.) Fdn., Emporia, 2/003

Atchison Knights of Columbus Building Corp., Atchison, 2/003

Baehr (Louis W.) & Dolpha Baehr Fdn., Paola, 2/004

Baker (T.B.) Fdn. of Kansas, Fort Scott, 2/004

Beech Memorial Fdn., Wichita, 2/005

Bell (Uriah Porley) Memorial Scholarship Fund, Burlington, 2/005

Beren (Marian and S.O.) Fdn., Wichita, 2/006

Beren (Robert M.) and Joan S. Beren Fdn., Wichita, 2/006

Berry Fnd., Wichita, 2/007

Bowers Fdn., Prairie Village, 2/007

Boyer Educational Trust, Wellington, 2/007

Brinkman (Frank W.) Memorial Scholarship, Great Bend, 2/008

Carmean (Dale H.) Scholarships for Eagle Scouts, Topeka, 2/010

Congdon (Listle & Daisy) Trust, Wichita, 2/010

Cook Fdn., Concordia, 2/011

Davison (Faye Chambers) Testamentary Trust, Wichita, 2/012

Delt Alumni Fdn., Cleveland Park, 2/012

Dickinson (Glen W.) Fdn., Mission, 2/012

Dondlinger Fdn., Wichita, 2/013

First National Bank of Topeka Charitable Trust, Topeka, 2/015

First National Bank in Wichita Charitable Trust, Wichita, 2/016

Fourth National Bank in Wichita Charitable Trust, Wichita, 2/017

Truman Gates Trust, Ottawa, 2/017

Gaty (John P.) Charitable Trust, Wichita, 2/017
Gelvin-Haughey Clinic Research and Educational Fdn., Concordia, 2/018
Gosler Educational Fund, Matfield Green, 2/018
Graham Fdn., Wichita, 2/019
Hammond Fdn., Wichita, 2/019
Hawk (Eugene) Fdn., Wichita, 2/019
Hulme (Charles) Fdn., Great Bend, 2/020
Hutchinson National Bank and Trust Company Fdn., Hutchinson, 2/020
Jackman Charitable Trust, Wichita, 2/021
Jellison (Arthur D.) & Maude S. Jellison Charitable Trust, Topeka, 2/021
Joslyn (Richard O.) Fdn., Shawnee Mission, 2/024
Kansas Delta Upsilon Educational Fdn., Wichita, 2/025
Kansas Philanthropies Inc., Hutchinson, 2/025
Kansas State Alpha Tau Omega Students Aid Endowment Fund, Manhattan, 2/026
Kessler Fdn., Wichita, 2/026
Kopke (Fred F.) & Stella Kopke Fdn., Hutchinson, 2/027
Lusk Fdn., Wichita, 2/028
Marley Fund, Mission, 2/029
Martin (Cora E.) Testamentary Trust, Chanute, 2/031
Martin (Mary Elizabeth) Scholarship Trust, Prairie Village, 2/031
Mayer Fdn., Shawnee Mission, 2/033
McPherson Youth Fdn., McPherson, 2/033
Middlebrook (H.O.) Scholarship Fund, Hiawatha, 2/033
Misco Charitable Trust, Wichita, 2/035
Mount Carmel Alumnae Charitable Fdn., Wichita, 2/036
Murdock Charitable Fdn., Wichita, 2/036
Neosho Memorial Hospital Fdn., Chanute, 2/037
Nickerson Ch #33, Nickerson, 2/037
Page Fdn., Wichita, 2/037
Palace Fdn., Prairie Village, 2/037
Palmer (Ella) Fdn., Wichita, 2/039
Parr (Charles E.) Charitable Trust, Wichita, 2/039
Parrish (LW.) Fdn., Wichita, 2/039
Pfister Fdn., Wichita, 2/040
Porter (Laura E.) Trust, Pratt, 2/041
Sales & Marketing Executives of Wichita, Wichita, 2/041
St. James Episcopal Church Fdn., Wichita, 2/041
Sargent (J.C.) Fdn., Topeka, 2/042
Schowalter Fdn., Inc., Newton, 2/042
Sellens (W.H.) & Amelia Sellens Trust, Russell, 2/044
Short Family Fdn., Harper, 2/045
Staub (Mildred B. & Allen A.) Fdn., Wichita, 2/045
Steffen Fdn., Inc., Wichita, 2/046
Sullivan Charitable Fdn. Trust, Ulysses, 2/047
Thompson (Charles T. & Marion M.) Fdn., Kansas City, 2/048
Union National Bank Charitable Trust, Wichita, 2/049
Wallingford Fdn., Wichita, 2/049
Whelan Fdn., Topeka, 2/050
Wichita Tuberculosis Assoc., Wichita, 2/050

KENTUCKY

First Filming

Allen (Charles and Alberta) Fund, Louisville, 1/002
Alpha Gamma Rho Fraternity Alpha Omega Chapter, Murray, 1/003
American Air Filter Fdn., Louisville, 1/003
Anderson Fdn., Louisville, 1/003
Anderson (Sidney) Fdn., Louisville, 1/004

Appalachian Fund, Berea, 1/004
Ashland Oil Fdn., Ashland, 1/006
Atwood (Pierce Butler) Scholarship Fund, Louisville, 1/007
Barnett (Bernard H.) Fdn., Louisville, 1/007
Benovitz (William) Fdn., Louisville, 1/008
Blazer (Stuart) Fdn., Ashland, 1/008
Bleakley Fdn., Louisville, 1/009
Blue Fdn., Louisville, 1/010
Blue Grass Dental Student Loan Fund, Lexington, 1/010
Boys Club of Lexington, Kentucky, Lexington, 1/010
Brown (W.L. Lyons) Fdn., Louisville, 1/011
Brown (Eleanor and John Y.), Jr. Fdn., Louisville, 1/012
Byck Fdn., Lousiville, 1/013
Cherry (H. Wendell) Family Fdn., Lousiville, 1/013
Christian (Caroline) Fdn., Louisville, 1/014
Character-Building Fund, Louisville, 1/015
Clore (Carl) Fdn., Crestwood, 1/015
Cochran Fdn., Louisville, 1/015
College Scholarship Fdn., Bowling Green, 1/016
Walters Collegiate Institute, Richmond, 1/016
Congleton Childrens Home, Beattyville, 1/016
Cook (Henry J.) Memorial Fund, Newport, 1/017
Cooke (John) Fdn., Lexington, 1/018
Coolafinney Fdn., Louisville, 1/019
Courier-Journal and Louisville Times Fdn., Louisville, 1/019
Courtenay Fdn., Louisville, 1/020
Cronin (Ralph M. and Ruth Louis) Fdn., Louisville, 1/021
Crounse Fdn., Paducah, 1/022
Farmer (Glenn & Grace) Fdn., Grand Rivers, 1/022
Field Fdn., Owensboro, 1/022
Foundation for Clinical Pastoral Care, Lexington, 1/023
Gardner (Ed) Trust, Mayfield, 1/023
Giles Fdn., Louisville, 1/024
Miesthenia Gravis Fdn., Inc., Louisville, 1/025
Gray (James N.) Fdn., Glasgow, 1/025
Hadley (Mary Alice) Fdn., Louisville, 1/027
Hamilton Fdn., Louisville, 1/028
Haskin Fdn., Louisville, 1/028
Hensley (Robert B.) Family Fdn., Louisville, 1/028
Hertzman (Charles A.) Family Fdn., Louisville, 1/029
Highbaugh Fdn., Louisville, 1/030
Hoenig (Henry M.) Fund, Louisville, 1/031
Home of the Innocents, Louisville, 1/031
J.E.G. Fdn., Louisville, 1/032
Jones (Lillian Monroe) Memorial Fdn., Louisville, 1/032
Kane Fdn., Louisville, 1/032
Kanner Fdn., Lexington, 1/033
Kentucky Farm Bureau Scholarship Fdn., Louisville, 1/033
Klein (Bertram and Isadore) Family Fdn., Louisville, 1/033
Kosmos Portland Cement Company Fund, Anchorage, 1/034
Kunz Fdn., Louisville, 1/034
Kuns-Stuckey Charitable Fund, South Bend, Ind., 1/034
Linker (S. Harry) Fdn., Louisville, 1/035
Louisville Metabolic Research Fdn., Louisville, 1/035
Lykins (Dorsa B. & Edna R.) Fdn., Winchester, 1/036
Magee Christian Education Fdn., Ashland, 1/036
Mason County Recreation Fdn., Maysville, 1/037
McAvoy (H.J.) Trust, Henderson, 1/037
McBride (Pierre) Fund, Louisville, 1/038
Mills (Ralph E.) Fdn., Frankfort, 1/038
Mitchell Fdn., Inc., Glasgow, 1/040
Morrill (J.L.) Fund, Berea, 1/040
Morrill (Louisa S.) Fund, Berea, 1/041

National Labor Management Fdn., Louisville, 1/042
Odum Fdn., Louisville, 1/042
Paul's Workshop, Louisville, 1/043
Putnam Fdn., Ashland, 1/043
River Fields, Louisville, 1/044
Roseman (Ephraim) Fdn., Prospect, 1/044
Robertson Fdn., Louisville, 1/045
Rosenbaum (Irvin S.) Fdn., Louisville, 1/045
Rosenberg (Sam) Family Fdn., Louisville, 1/045
Society of Colonial Wars in The Commonwealth of Kentucky, Louisville, 1/046
Spragens Fund, Lebanon, 1/047
Sprayit Fdn., Louisville, 1/047
Starks (Franklin F.) Charitable Trust, Louisville, 1/048
Stodghill Fdn., Louisville, 1/048
Stoll-Dorsey Fdn., Louisville, 1/049
Story Real Estate Fdn., Lexington, 1/049
Sumner Fdn., Louisville, 1/049
Trover Clinic Fdn., Madisonville, 1/050
Virginia Educational Fund, Berea, 1/051
Watkins (J. Stephen) Fdn., Lexington, 1/051
Wave Fdn., Louisville, 1/052
Webber (William) Fdn., Cynthiana, 1/053
Weisberg (Charles and Marian) Family Fdn., Louisville, 1/053
Wimsatt (James I.) Fdn., Louisville, 1/054
Yale Scholarship Fund of Kentucky, Louisville, 1/054
Yarmuth (Stanley R.) Family Fdn., Louisville, 1/055

Second Filming

Abell (William H. and Abby S.) Fdn., Louisville, 2/002
Allen Fdn., Winchester, 2/003
Allen (Charles & Alberta) Fund, Louisville, 2/003
Alliance Francaise of Louisville, Kentucky, Louisville, 2/004
Baker-Hunt Fdn., Covington, 2/005
Bass (Lewis & Gladys) Family Fdn., Louisville, 2/005
Bayless Fdn., Anchorage, 2/006
Berg (Harold F.) Family Fdn., Louisville, 2/006
Blakely (Dorothy) Fdn., Louisville. 2/006
Breckenridge (Elizabeth) Scholarship Fund Trust, Louisville, 2/007
B & R Fdn., Louisville, 2/007
Brown (James Graham) Fdn., Louisville, 2/008
Brown-Pusey House, Elizabethtown, 2/009
Courier-Journal & Louisville Times Fdn., Louisville, 2/010
Dishman (J.A.) Fdn., Louisville, 2/011
Doll (A. Robert) Fdn., Louisville, 2/011
Dunbar Fdn., Louisville, 2/012
Duncan (William M.) Memorial Fdn., Louisville, 2/013
Duthie Family Fdn., Louisville, 2/013
Eastern High School Band Parents Association, Middletown, 2/014
Elk Creek Cemetery Company, Taylorsville, 2/015
Elkton Industrial Fdn., Elkton, 2/015
Fishman (Sam) Fdn., Louisville, 2/015
Gardner (Annie) Fdn., Mayfield, 2/016
Garth Educational Society, Lexington, 2/018
Goldstein (Isadore) Fdn., Louisville, 2/018
Heyburn (John Gilpin) Memorial Fund, Louisville, 2/018
Hildebrand Fdn., Louisville, 2/019
H.N.J.N. Fdn., Louisville, 2/020
Honey Locust Fdn., Louisville, 2/020
Houchens Fdn., Bowling Green, 2/021
Jays Fdn., Louisville, 2/023
Jones (David A.) Family Fdn., Louisville, 2/023
Jones (Martha R.) Fdn. for Health Education, Wilmore, 2/023
Kempac Education Fund, Louisville, 2/024

Kentucky Social Welfare Fdn., Louisville, 2/024

Kentucky State Humane Federation, Louisville, 2/025

KFEC Research & Development Fdn., Louisville, 2/025

King (Patrick M.) Family Fdn., Louisville, 2/025

Klein (Samuel H.) Family Fdn., Louisville, 2/026

Kopmeyer (M.R.) Fdn., Louisville, 2/026

Lebendiger Family Fdn., Louisville, 2/027

Levitch Fdn., Louisville, 2/027

L.K.J.B. Fdn., Louisville, 2/028

Louisville Medical Research Fdn., Louisville, 2/028

Maclean Fdn., Louisville, 2/028

Maysville & Mason County Library, Historical & Scientific Association, Maysville, 2/029

Medical Fdn. of the Jefferson County Medical Society, Louisville, 2/030

Ortner Fdn., Louisville, 2/030

Paul's Workshop, Louisville, 2/031

Perlstein (John I.) Memorial Fund, Louisville, 2/031

Presbyterian Institute for Human Development, Louisville, 2/032

Pressma Family Fdn., Louisville, 2/033

Pryor Fdn., Louisville, 2/033

Robinson (E.O.) Mountain Fund, Lexington, 2/034

Rosenberg (Max) Fdn., Louisville, 2/039

Roth (Louis T.) Fdn., Louisville, 2/039

Sanders (Colonel Harland) Fdn., Shelbyville, 2/040

Scottish Rite Fdn., Louisville, 2/040

Society of Colonial Wars in The Commonwealth of Kentucky, Louisville, 2/041

Thompson Fdn., Louisville, 2/042

McHenry Memorial Trust, Louisville, 2/042

Fdn. for United Methodists, Wilmore, 2/043

Vogt (Henry) Fdn., Louisville, 2/043

Welgo Fdn., Lexington, 2/045

Whayne Fdn., Louisville, 2/045

Willsales Fdn., Louisville, 2/045

Winn (Lizzie Mannen Turney) Testamentary Trust, Mt. Sterling, 2/045

Winn (Sarah E.) Home, Mt. Sterling, 2/046

WTY, Inc., Lexington, 2/047

Young (W. Hewitt) Merit Award Fund, Owensboro, 2/047

Young (John B. & Brownie) Memorial Fund, Owensboro, 2/048

LOUISIANA

First Filming

Achkinsky (Leon) Testamentary Trust, New Orleans, 1/001

Aldrich (W.R.) Fdn., Baton Rouge, 1/002

Aiken (Lieutenant John Gayle), III Memorial Fdn., New Orleans, 1/003

Alexander Fund, New Orleans, 1/003

Aloha Fdn., New Orleans, 1/003

Alpha XI Delta Building Corporation of Shreveport, Shreveport, 1/003

American Legion Hospital, Crowley, 1/004

Aron (J.) New Orleans Corporate Fund, New Orleans, 1/004

Atkins (J.B.) Foundation Trust, Shreveport, 1/005

Azby Fund, New Orleans, 1/007

Barmarob Fdn., New Orleans, 1/008

Beaird (Charles T.) Fdn., Shreveport, 1/009

Benjamin Fund, New Orleans, 1/010

Bernard (Victor) Fdn., New Orleans, 1/010

Biedenharn (Emy-Lou) Fdn. Trust "A", Monroe, 1/011

Brown (Joe W. & Dorothy Dorsett) Fdn., New Orleans, 1/011

Bradley Family Fdn., New Orleans, 1/012

Brownell Fdn., Morgan City, 1/012

BSA Trust Fund New Orleans Scout Fdn., Metairie, 1/014

Burkenroad Fdn., New Orleans, 1/014

Cahn Family, New Orleans, 1/015

Camp Street Fdn., Inc., New Orleans, 1/016

Central United Fdn., Monroe, 1/016

Clark (Russell) Fdn., New Orleans, 1/017

Cohn (Dr. Isidore), Jr. Surgical Research Fdn., New Orleans, 1/018

Common Street Fdn., New Orleans, 1/019

Cotton (Bill) Fdn., Alexandria, 1/020

Cotton (Hub) Fdn., Alexandria, 1/020

Crow Fdn., Shreveport, 1/021

Cunningham (Thomas F.) Research Library Fund, New Orleans, 1/021

Cunningham (Thomas F.) Award Fund, New Orleans, 1/022

Davis Family Fdn., New Orleans, 1/023

Dennery (Moise W.) Family Fund, New Orleans, 1/024

Dossett Fdn., Shreveport, 1/024

Dugas-Ford Fdn., New Orleans, 1/025

Eanda Fdn., New Orleans, 1/026

Eleven Hundred Fdn., Inc., New Orleans, 1/027

Freeman (Ella West) Fdn., New Orleans, 1/027

Employees Olinkraft United Fund, West Monroe, 1/029

FAF Fdn., Alexandria, 1/030

Favrot (Clifford F.) Family Fund, New Orleans, 1/031

Fidelis Fdn., New Orleans, 1/033

Foster Fdn., New Orleans, 1/033

Frey Fdn., New Orleans, 1/033

Friedler (Frances & Frank) Fdn., New Orleans, 1/035

Friedler (Frank & Patricia) Fdn., New Orleans, 1/035

Frost Fdn., Shreveport, 1/036

Garrett Fdn. for Christian Work, Shreveport, 1/037

Glazer (Jerome S.) Fdn., New Orleans, 1/038

Godchaux Brothers Fdn., Abbeville, 1/040

Godchaux Charitable Trust, New Orleans, 1/040

Godchaux (Frank & Mary) Fdn., New Orleans, 1/041

Gravier Street Fdn., New Orleans, 1/042

Greater New Orleans Housing Development Corporation, New Orleans, 1/042

Greater New Orleans Opera Fdn., New Orleans, 1/042

Guy (Charles) Fdn., Baton Rouge, 1/043

Hamilton Fdn., Shreveport, 1/043

Haring Fdn., Metairie, 1/044

Haspel Brothers Fdn., New Orleans, 1/044

Helis Fdn., New Orleans, 1/045

Heymann-Wolf Fdn., New Orleans, 1/046

Hutchinson (Henrietta Hardiner) Fdn., Alexandria, 1/046

Heymann (Mr. & Mrs. Jerry)-Special, New Orleans, 1/047

Hood (A.E.) Fdn., Amite, 1/048

Hunter (S.D.) Fdn., Shreveport, 1/048

Hurley (Ed E. & Gladys) Fdn., Shreveport, 1/049

Hyman Fund, New Orleans, 1/050

Ingram (F.B.) Fdn., New Orleans, 1/051

Jacobs Family Fdn., New Orleans, 1/051

Jung Fdn., New Orleans, 1/051

Katz (Harry & Ida) Fdn., New Orleans, 1/052

Keller Family Fdn., New Orleans, 1/053

Kirschman Fdn. for Health and Education, New Orleans, 1/053

Kirschman & Weil Fdn., New Orleans, 1/054

K & M Fdn., Shreveport, 1/056

Kolb (Allison R.) Fdn., Baton Rouge, 1/056

Kupperman Fdn., New Orleans, 1/056

Labouisse (John P. & Olive May) Fdn., New Orleans, 1/057

Lamar Fdn., New Orleans, 1/057

LaNasa-Greco Fdn., New Orleans, 1/058

Latter (Milton H.) Educational & Charitable Fdn., New Orleans, 1/059

Levy (Arnold J.) Fdn., Metairie, 1/060

Lewis (C. Huffman) Fdn., Shreveport, 1/061

McLean (Lilly Weaks) Trust, Metairie, 1/062

Lloyd (Hendrick) Fdn. of Highland Hospital, Shreveport, 1/062

Longue Vue Fdn., New Orleans, 1/063

Blanco (Alfred)-Albert Lawrence Loustalot Scholarship Fund, New Orleans, 1/063

Louisiana Research Fdn., Avery Island, 1/064

Lykes Fdn., New Orleans, 1/065

Megale (John F.) & Joanna G. Megale Trust for the Jesuit High School of Shreveport, Shreveport, 1/066

Megale (John F.) & Joanna G. Megale for the Library of Centenary College of Louisiana, Shreveport, 1/066

Administrators of the Rev. John W. Hynes, S.J. Manresa Memorial Endowment Fund, New Orleans, 1/067

Marcus Fdn., New Orleans, 1/067

Martin Cultural Fdn., Alexandria, 1/068

Masonic Educational Fdn., New Orleans, 1/069

McCain Charitable Trust, Shreveport, 1/069

McClure (Hattie) Testementary Trust, New Orleans, 1/070

McGee (Edith F. & Kenneth C.) Family Fund, New Orleans, 1/071

Mintz (A. & D.) Family Fdn., New Orleans, 1/071

Monroe (F. Lloyd) Family Fdn., New Orleans, 1/072

Monroe (J. Edgar) Fdn., New Orleans, 1/073

Moran Fdn., New Orleans, 1/073

Morgan City Fund, Morgan City, 1/074

Nelson Fdn., Shreveport, 1/075

New Orleans Literary Educational & Charitable Trust, New Orleans, 1/076

Newman (Ann & Isidore) Fund, New Orleans, 1/077

Norman (Hilda Loeb) Fdn., New Orleans, 1/077

Northeast State Fdn. Trust Fund (Ann Meyer Charities), Monroe, 1/078

Northeast State Fdn. Trust, Saul Adler Memorial Fund, Monroe, 1/078

Northeast State Fdn. Trust Fund "A", Monroe, 1/079

Norman (Sunny & Roussel) Fdn., New Orleans, 1/079

Norton (R.W.) Art Fdn., Shreveport, 1/079

O'Brien (Kathleen) Register Fdn., New Orleans, 1/081

Oreck (Paula & David) Family Fdn., New Orleans, 1/083

Palfrey (William T.) Testamentary Trust, New Orleans, 1/084

Parkside, New Orleans, 1/085

Pax Fdn. Fund, New Orleans, 1/086

Peters (Mary E.) & Robert W. Polchow Fdn., New Orleans, 1/086

Poindexter Fdn., Shreveport, 1/087

Poydras Home, New Orleans, 1/088

Pulitzer (Emanuel S.) Fdn., New Orleans, 1/089

Pulitzer (Samuel C.) Fdn., New Orleans, 1/089

Putnam (Oscar Lee) Cultural Endowment, New Orleans, 1/089

Querbes (Ann Olene & Justin P.), III Fdn., Shreveport, 1/091

Rasberry Foundation, Shreveport, 1/092

Reily Fdn., New Orleans, 1/092

Richards (E.V.), Jr. Fdn., New Orleans, 1/093

Rosamary Fdn., New Orleans, 1/094

Saal (Gertrude Goldsmith) Memorial Fdn., New Orleans, 1/097

St. Charles Fdn., New Orleans, 1/098

Salmen Family Fdn., New Orleans, 1/098

Schlieder (Edward G.) Educational Fdn., New Orleans, 1/099

Schreier (Leah Norman) Fdn., New Orleans, 1/100

Selber (Louis & Lillian) Fdn., Shreveport, 1/101

Six Fdn., New Orleans, 1/101

Six-Thirty-Five Fdn., New Orleans, 1/102
Six-Thirty-Four Fdn., New Orleans, 1/102
Standard Fruit Charities, New Orleans, 1/103
Stern (Percival) Fdn., New Orleans, 1/104
Stern Fund, New Orleans, 1/106
Strachan Trust, New Orleans, 1/108
Turman (Solon B. & Dolly H.) Fdn., New Orleans, 1/109
Uhl (Philip) Trust Fund, New Orleans, 1/110
Two-Twenty-Eight Fdn., Inc., New Orleans, 1/111
Walmsley (Virginia J. & Robert M.) Fdn., New Orleans, 1/111
WDSU Fdn., New Orleans, 1/112
Weil (Leo S.) Fdn., New Orleans, 1/113
Weiner Fdn., Gretna, 1/114
Wellan (Louis) Community Fund, Alexandria, 1/114
West Fdn., Minden, 1/115
West-Brandt Fdn., DeRider, 1/116
Wiener (S.G. & M.P.) Fund, Shreveport, 1/117
Wiener, Weiss & Wiener Fdn., Shreveport, 1/117
Wiener (William B.), Jr., Fdn., Shreveport, 1/118
Woldenberg Charitable and Educational Fdn., New Orleans, 1/119
Zemurray Fdn., New Orleans, 1/119
Zigler (Fred B. & Ruth B.) Fdn., Jennings, 1/120
Zigler Museum Fdn., Jennings, 1/122

Second Filming

Alma College Charitable Trust, New Orleans, 2/003
Barnard and Burk Fdn., Baton Rouge, 2/004
Berger (Alex) Fdn., New Orleans, 2/004
Brown-Roberts Fdn., Alexandria, 2/007
Brupbacher (Robert M. "Tiger") Educational Fdn., New Orleans, 2/008
Burden Fdn., Baton Rouge, 2/009
Burguieres (Louise M.) Fdn., The, New Orleans, 2/009
Burton (William T. & Ethel Lewis) Fdn., Sulphur, 2/010
Callicott Fdn., Baton Rouge, 2/010
Civic Fdn., New Orleans, 2/013
Eastland Fdn., Baton Rouge, 2/014
Erickson Educational Fdn., Baton Rouge, 2/014
Essex Club of New Orleans, New Orleans, 2/016
F. A. F. Fdn., Alexandria, 2/017
Farrnbacher Memorial Fdn., Baton Rouge, 2/017
First National Family Fdn., Shreveport, 2/018
First National Seventy-Fifth Anniversary Fund, Shreveport, 2/018
Foote (John M. and Vivian Cockerham) Fdn., Baton Rouge, 2/019
Forgotston (Mildred and Harold) Fdn., Metairie, 2/020
Frepala Fdn., New Orleans, 2/020
Friedler (Frances and Frank) Fdn., New Orleans, 2/021
George (William Holton) Testamentary Trust, New Orleans, 2/022
Gottesman (Charlotte and Frederick) Fdn., New Orleans, 2/022
Gulf States Eye Surgery Fdn., New Orleans, 2/023
Hicks Fund, Shreveport, 2/025
Jones (Eugenie & Joseph) Family Fdn., New Orleans, 2/026
LaFourche Medical Society Fdn., Thibodaux, 2/028
Board of Trustees of Libby-DuFour Fund, New Orleans, 2/028
Louisiana Fdn., Ruston, 2/030
Magale (John F.) Endowment Trust to St. Johns Education, Shreveport, 2/031
Marnie Fdn., New Orleans, 2/032
Mayer (Leonie & Gus) Fdn., New Orleans, 2/032
Moore (Edwin) Fdn., Shreveport, 2/034

Murphy Fdn. of Louisiana, Alexandria, 2/034
New Orleans Athletic Club, New Orleans, 2/035
New Orleans Educational Fdn., New Orleans, 2/036
Nicholson (Leonard Kimball) and Poitevent (Lolie) Fdn., New Orleans, 2/037
Norman (Bernice and William David) Fdn., New Orleans, 2/037
Phillips (Leonard W. & Betty) Fdn., Shreveport, 2/038
Plater Fdn., New Orleans, 2/038
Polson (M. E.) Fdn., New Orleans, 2/039
Raymond Fdn. of Louisiana, Shreveport, 2/040
Reynolds (Larry) Fdn., New Orleans, 2/041
Rubenstein (Morris & Helen) Fdn., New Orleans, 2/041
Rubenstein (Elkin & Fannie) Fdn., New Orleans, 2/042
Scott Fdn., Inc., Monroe, 2/043
Sklar (Albert & Miriam) Fdn., Shreveport, 2/044
Sklar (Sam & Ida) Fdn., Shreveport, 2/045
Southdown Fdn., New Orleans, 2/046
Strauss (Carolyn Rose) Fdn., Monroe, 2/046
Williams (Kemper and Leila) Fdn., New Orleans, 2/047
Williams (Margaret Ann) Fdn., New Orleans, 2/053
Woolf (William C.) Fdn., Shreveport, 2/053

MAINE

First Filming

Anthony (Kate J.) Memorial Book Fund f/b/o Auburn Public Library, Augusta, 1/003
Anthony (Kate J.) Memorial Book Fund f/b/o Lewiston Public Library, Augusta, 1/004
Anthony (Alfred Williams & Kate J.) Trusts, Augusta, 1/004
Anthony (Alfred W., Gertrude L. & Kate J.) Trust f/b/o United Baptist Parish, Augusta, 1/005
Bates Fdn., Lewiston, 1/005
Belknap (Robert W.), M.D. Free Bed Fund, Damariscotta, 1/006
B H S Alumni Association, Elizabeth Maud Nevins Trust Fund, Biddeford, 1/006
B H S Alumni Association, Harold W. Yeaton Fund, Biddeford, 1/007
B H S Alumni Association, Thursday Club Scholarship Fund, Biddeford, 1/007
B H S Alumni Association, Mary J. Crowley Fund, Biddeford, 1/007
B H S Alumni Association, Harry Haynes Burnham Fund, Biddeford, 1/008
B H S Alumni Association, Joseph E. Brooks Fund, Biddeford, 1/008
Boland (Rev. Maurice B.) Scholarship-Eastport, Biddeford, 1/008
Boland (Rev. Maurice B.) Scholarship-Augusta, Biddeford, 1/008
Boland (Maurice B.) Scholarship Fund f/b/o Male Seminary Students from St. Mary's Church, Orono, Maine, Portland, 1/009
Boland (Maurice B.) Scholarship Fund f/b/o Male Seminary Students from St. Thomas Church & Mission, Dover-Foxcroft, Maine, Portland, 1/009
Boland (Maurice B.) Scholarship Fund f/b/o Seminary Students from Trinity Church, Saco, Portland, 1/010
Boyd (Robert W.) Memorial Trust, Portland, 1/011
Bridge (Samuel J.) Trust, Portland, 1/011
Bridge Academy Trust, Portland, 1/012
Bridge Charitable Fund, Dresden, 1/012
Briggs (George M.) Fund Trust, Augusta, 1/013
Brown (Annette M.) Trust, Auburn, 1/014

Couri (Arthur R.) Award Trust, Portland, 1/014
Davenport Trust Fund, Bath, 1/015
Davis (Beatrice R.) Trust, Portland, 1/016
Robinson-Davis Trust Fund, Portland, 1/016
Depositors Trust Fdn., Augusta, 1/017
Drake Fdn., Portland, 1/017
Emple Fdn., Brewer, 1/018
Fairburn Marine Educational Fdn., Center Lovell, 1/019
Forest Fdn., Camden, 1/019
Forster Fdn., Wilton, 1/019
Friends of Nature, Inc., Brooksville, 1/020
Gannett (Guy P.) Fdn., Portland, 1/021
Greene Fdn., Bangor, 1/022
Hancock (Sumner O.) Scholarship Fund, Casco, 1/023
Jordan's Charitable Fdn., Portland, 1/024
Kenduskeag Fdn., Bangor, 1/025
La Verna Fdn., Round Pond, 1/025
Manson (John W.) Trust, Portland, 1/026
Mason (Hartley W.) Trust f/b/o York Hospital, Biddeford, 1/026
Mulford (Clarence E.) Trust, Fryeburg, 1/026
Murphy (Maxwell K.) Scholarship Fund, Bar Harbor, 1/027
Perreault (Ralph) Memorial Scholarship f/b/o Old Orchard Beach High School, Biddeford, 1/027
Perreault (Ralph) Memorial Scholarship f/b/o Biddeford High School, Biddeford, 1/028
Pertzoff Fdn., Boston, Mass., 1/028
Porteous, Mitchell & Braun Fdn., Portland, 1/029
Portland Academy, Trustees of, Portland, 1/030
Portland Camera Club Trust, Portland, 1/031
Proctor (J. Riker & Anne M. H.) Charitable Trust, Camden, 1/032
Rich (Chester A.) Trust f/b/o Bonney Eagle High School, Biddeford, 1/032
Robinson-Davis Fund Trust, Portland, 1/033
Rockland Fire Department Welfare Fund, Rockland, 1/034
Rohrbaugh Fdn., Rockport, 1/034
Sampson (Richard W.) Charitable Fdn., Auburn, 1/034
Searls (William) Scholarship Fdn., Southwest Harbor, 1/035
Skillings (Frederic) Trust, Portland, 1/035
Southwest Harbor Public Library, Southwest Harbor, 1/036
Striar (James) Family Fdn., Bangor, 1/037
Thaxter (Rosamond) Fdn., Portland, 1/037
Tibbetts Industries Fdn., Camden, 1/038
Turner (Solon E.) Trust, Portland, 1/039
Union Mutual Charitable Fdn., Portland, 1/040
Unmarried Parents Services & Adoption Program, Portland, 1/040
Vaill (Addie Kaler) Trust, Portland, 1/041
Vaughn (Elizabeth R.) Trust Fund, South Berwick, 1/042
Vincent (Adrien G.) Trust, Portland, 1/044
York County Children's Aid Society, Saco, 1/045

Second Filming

Abbe (Robert) Museum of Stone Age Antiquities, Bar Harbor, 2/001
Adams (Samuel) Fuel Fund Trust, Augusta, 2/001
Atkins (Will C.) Trust, Augusta, 2/002
Auburn Home for Aged Women, Auburn, 2/002
Averill (George & Frances) Trust, Waterville, 2/003
Averill (George G. & Frances M.) Endowment Trust, Augusta, 2/004
Ballard (Caroline M.) Trust, Augusta, 2/004
Bangor - Brewer Tuberculosis & Health Association, Bangor, 2/005
Bath Iron Works Charitable Trust, Portland, 2/005
Bean (William Furber) Trust, Augusta, 2/005
Blaisdell (J. Colby) Trust, Waterville, 2/006

Trustees of Bloomfield Academy, Skowhegan,
2/007
Bray (William H.) Trust, Augusta, 2/008
Bryant (George H.) Trust, Augusta, 2/008
Cape Elizabeth Home for Aged Women, South
Portland, 2/009
Castine Scientific Society, Perkins St. Wilson
Museum, Castine, 2/010
Centenary Methodist Church Trust, Waterville,
2/011
Coles Memorial Trust, Bar Harbor, 2/011
Crawford (William M.) Trusts, Waterville,
2/011
Cunningham (Charles H.) Trust, Augusta,
2/013
Daveis (Mabel S.) Trust, Portland, 2/013
Deering (Lucy B.) Trust, Portland, 2/014
Dick (Ralph T. & Betty) Trust, Augusta, 2/015
Dunn (William S.) Memorial Fdn., New
Gloucester, 2/015
Gingras (Adolph & Antoinette) Scholarship
Trust Fund, Augusta, 2/016
Greeley (Susanne) Trusts, Waterville, 2/016
Grumman Peace Fdn., Boston, Mass., 2/017
Gushee (R. Cynthia) Scholarship Trust,
Augusta, 2/018
Higgins (John W. & Florence S.) Educational
Fund Trust, Augusta, 2/018
Hilton (Peter Mark) Trust, Waterville, 2/018
Houghton (C. Gilbert) Trust, Augusta, 2/019
Huxford (May L.) Trust, Augusta, 2/019
Johnson (Henrietta Loring) Trust, Augusta,
2/019
Kagan (Max) Family Fdn., Bangor, 2/020
Kaler - Vaill Memorial Home, Scarborough,
2/020
Kenniston (George B.), Jr. Prize Speaking Trust
Fund, Augusta, 2/022
King Spruce Company, Bangor, 2/022
Kittredge (John Anson) Educational Fund,
Augusta, 2/023
Lawrence (Edna) Trusts, Waterville, 2/024
Lipman (Samuel & Esther) Fdn., Augusta,
2/025
Maine Charitable Mechanic Association,
Portland, 2/026
Maine Oil & Heating Equipment Dealers
Association Insurance Trust, Portland, 2/027
Marston (Ray G.) Trust, Augusta, 2/028
Maxim (Howard & Lauretta) Memorial Fund,
Norway, 2/028
Mearl Fdn., Eastport, 2/029
Merchant (L. D.) Fund Trust, Augusta, 2/029
Miller (Harold E.) Memorial Trust Fund,
Augusta, 2/029
Sanborn Weary Club Fund, Norway, 2/030
Nichols (James P.) Trust, Augusta, 2/030
Stephens Memorial Hospital Endowment Fund,
Norway, 2/031
Stiles (Moses P.) Trust, Norway, 2/031
Old Folks Home Association of Brunswick,
Maine, Brunswick, 2/031
Ovellette (Ludger D.) Trust, Augusta, 2/032
Peirce (Sarah Louise) Trust, Augusta, 2/032
Philbrick (William) Charitable Trust, Augusta,
2/032
Pillsbury (Ralph B.), III Trust, Augusta, 2/033
Pine Tree State 4-H Club Fdn., Bangor, 2/033
Plaisted (Richard C.) Trust, Augusta, 2/033
Portland Provident Association, Portland, 2/033
Reef (Samuel P. & Dora) Endowment Fund,
Portland, 2/035
Richardson (Betsy Barter) Scholarship Fund,
Stonington, 2/035
Roberts (Medora C.) Trusts, Augusta, 2/035
Seaward Fdn., Kittery, 2/037
Simmons Fdn., Portland, 2/038
Small (Amanda V.) Trust, Augusta, 2/039
Sowles Fdn., Falmouth, 2/039
Totman (Susan F.) Trust, Augusta, 2/040
Turner (Mark & Emily) Fdn., Presque Isle,
2/040
Anthony (Kate J.) Trust, Augusta, 2/040
Appleton (Alice) Trust, Bangor, 2/041
Appleton (Maria) Trust, Bangor, 2/041
Batchelder (William) Trusts, Sanford, 2/041

Bowden (William) Trust, Waterville, 2/042
Brackett (Wade) Trust, Bangor, 2/043
Cowan (Dorothy Bush) Trust, Bangor, 2/043
Crawford (William) Trust, Waterville, 2/044
Dearth (Freeman) Trust, Bangor, 2/044
Eaton (Emma Jane) Trust, Bangor, 2/045
Emery (George G.) Trust, Sanford, 2/045
Emery (Lucy E.) Trust, Sanford, 2/045
Emery (William O.) Trusts, Sanford, 2/046
Fenderson (George) Trust, Bangor, 2/047
Fish (Lucinda A.) Fund, Waterville, 2/047
Gardner (Harriet) Trust, Bangor, 2/048
Garvin (Edith W.) Trust, Sanford, 2/048
Gerald (Minnie) Trust, Waterville, 2/048
Gibson (Clara W.) Trust, Bangor, 2/049
Gould (Lillian W.) Trust, Sanford, 2/049
Hichborn (Della Whitney) Trust, Bangor,
2/050
Horne (Willena E.) Fund, Waterville, 2/050
Kennedy (Margaret) Trust, Bangor, 2/051
Littlefield (Carrie) Trust, Sanford, 2/051
Littlefield (Samuel) Trust, Sanford, 2/052
MacDonald (Annie Rummery) Trust, Bangor,
2/052
Magee (Marie F.) Trust, Bangor, 2/052
Maybury (Imogene M.) Trust, Bangor, 2/053
McKenney (Ella) Trust, Bangor, 2/054
Meder (George) Trusts, Bangor, 2/054
Moore (Josephine) Trusts, Bangor, 2/055
Nash (Ralph) Trust, Bangor, 2/057
Milliken (Mary W.) Trust, Bangor, 2/058
Oakes (Louis) Trust, Bangor, 2/058
Oakes (Myrtice) Trusts, Bangor, 2/059
Philbrook (Abby) Trust, Bangor, 2/060
Pitman (Woodman) Trust, Bangor, 2/060
Ross (H. Danforth) Trust, Sanford, 2/061
Sawyer (Edward M.) Trust, Bangor, 2/061
Sawyer (Josie) Trust, Bangor, 2/061
Sebec Community Church Trust, Bangor, 2/062
Sigma Kappa Fund, Waterville, 2/062
Smart (Winifred) Trust, Bangor, 2/063
Smith (Elvira) Trust, Bangor, 2/063
Whitter Memorial Fund, Bangor, 2/064
Woodman (Eleanor S.) Trust, Waterville,
2/064
Village Library & Reading Room Association,
New Field, 2/065
Viner Fdn., Bangor, 2/065
Whitehouse (Edward L.) Trust, Augusta, 2/066
Wilkins (Oscar) Scholarship Trust Fund,
Augusta, 2/066
Wilson (James W.) Trust, Augusta, 2/067
Wing - Benjamin Trust Fund, Augusta, 2/067
Woman's Literary Union, Portland, 2/068
Worthen (Harold) Trust, Bangor, 2/069
Women's Literary Union of Androscoggin
County, Auburn, 2/070
Young (Charles E.) Trust Fund, Augusta,
2/070

MARYLAND & D.C.

First Filming

A B C Crusade Fdn., D.C., 1/001
Abell (A.S.) Company Fdn., Baltimore, 1/001
Abeshouse (George & Sarah) Fdn., Pikesville,
1/002
Abrahams Family Fdn., Baltimore, 1/003
Abrams Fdn., Baltimore, 1/004
Abrams (David & Annie) Fdn., Baltimore,
1/005
Abrams (Esther R.) Family Fdn., Silver Spring,
1/005
Abramson-Libby-Reich Charitable Fdn., D.C.,
1/006
Abrams (Dr. & Mrs. Michael A.) Fdn. f/k/a
Marma Fdn., Baltimore, 1/006
A G C Education & Research Fdn., D.C.,
1/007
Alexander & Alexander Fdn., Baltimore, 1/007
A L H Fdn., Baltimore, 1/008

Allen Fund, Potomac, 1/009
Allen (George E.) Fdn., D.C., 1/010
Alperstein (Fred H. & Ruth) Fdn., Pikesville,
1/011
Altman Fund, D.C., 1/011
Alvord Fdn., D.C., 1/011
American Society of Appraisers Educational
Fdn., D.C., 1/013
April Fund, D.C., 1/013
Alumni Association of the Baltimore City
College Endowment Fund, Baltimore, 1/014
Appleby Fdn., D.C., 1/015
Appleby (Scott B. & Annie P.) Trust, D.C.,
1/016
Arundel Fdn., Baltimore, 1/017
Ayd Fdn., Baltimore, 1/018
Asian Cultural Exchange Fdn., D.C., 1/018
Atlas Fdn., D.C., 1/019
Baer (Lewis) Fdn., Baltimore, 1/019
Baetjer (Norman & Jeanne) Fdn., Garrison,
1/020
Baker, Watts & Co. Fdn., Baltimore, 1/021
Baker (Joseph D.) Fund, Frederick, 1/022
Balder Fdn., Baltimore, 1/023
Baldinger Family Fdn., D.C., 1/024
Baldinger Fdn., D.C., 1/024
Baldwin (Philip L.) Memorial Trust Fund, D.C.,
1/025
Baldwin (Summerfield, Jr.) Fdn., Baltimore,
1/025
Baltimore Colts Fdn., Baltimore, 1/027
Baltimore General Dispensary, Baltimore,
1/027
Barth Fdn., Baltimore, 1/029
Bank (Burton L.) Fdn., Baltimore, 1/029
Baylin (Joseph J.) Fdn., Baltimore, 1/029
Beachley Fdn., Hagerstown, 1/030
Behrend Fdn., Baltimore, 1/031
Behrend (Suevia & Rudolph) Fdn., D.C.,
1/031
Belmont Fdn., Baltimore, 1/032
Bender Fdn., D.C., 1/032
Benesch (Jerome W.) Charitable Fund,
Baltimore, 1/033
Berger Fdn., D.C., 1/033
Bernstein (Hyman & Freda) Family Fdn.,
Laurel, 1/033
Black & Decker Employees Combined Charities
Trust, Towson, 1/034
Blank (Isaac & Minnie) Fdn., Baltimore, 1/035
Blaustein (Louis & Henrietta) Fdn., Baltimore,
1/035
Blaustein (Jacob & Hilda) Fdn., Baltimore,
1/036
Bloedorn (Walter A.) Fdn., D.C., 1/037
Bloomberg (David & Estelle) Fdn., Owings
Mills, 1/038
Blozis (Al) Memorial Scholarship Fund, D.C.,
1/038
Blumenthal (Sydney C. & Ray Hess) Fund,
Owings Mills, 1/039
Bratman Charitable Fdn., Bethesda, 1/040
Braverman Fdn., D.C., 1/040
Brawner (Henry N., Jr.) Fdn., D.C., 1/041
Bright Star Fdn., Baltimore, 1/041
Brown (Bruce Ford) Charitable Trust,
Baltimore, 1/042
Brown (Vaughn W.) Charitable Trust,
Baltimore, 1/042
Brown (Keene C.) Charitable Trust, Baltimore,
1/043
Brown (Frank D., Jr.) Charitable Trust,
Baltimore, 1/044
Brown (H. Barksdale) Charitable Trust,
Baltimore, 1/045
Brown (Alex) And Sons Charitable Fdn.,
Baltimore, 1/046
Bruce (Mary Graham) - Howard Bruce Fund,
Baltimore, 1/046
Buchanan (Wiley & Ruth) Fdn., D.C., 1/048
Buckinham School of Frederick County,
Maryland, Monkton, 1/048
Buedel (Conrad G.) Scholarship Fund,
Baltimore, 1/049
Bugher (Henrietta B. & Frederick H.) Fdn.,
D.C., 1/050

Bunker Fdn., D.C., 1/050
Burka Family Fdn., Bethesda, 1/051
Burka (Harry & Fay) Fdn., D.C., 1/052
Burka (I.S.) Fdn., D.C., 1/052
Byram (Ira) Fdn., Cheverly, 1/053
Cafritz (Morris & Gwendolyn) Fdn., D.C., 1/053
Calvert Fdn., Baltimore, 1/055
Cambridge Rubber Fdn., Taneytown, 1/056
Campbell Fdn., Towson, 1/057
Caplin Fdn., D.C., 1/058
Cardin-Macks Fdn., Baltimore, 1/058
Carliner (Louis & Elsie) Fdn., Baltimore, 1/059
Carliner (Samuel & Reva) Family Fdn., Baltimore, 1/060
Carostead Fdn., D.C., 1/060
Carski Fdn., Baltimore, 1/061
Cemetery Association of Maryland & D.C., Baltimore, 1/062
Chambers (Emanuel) Fdn., Baltimore, 1/062
Chandler (Helen & George) Fdn., Salisbury, 1/062
Cheney Award Trust, D.C., 1/062
Chertkof (Ethel) Fdn., Baltimore, 1/063
Clapper (Raymond) Memorial Association, D.C., 1/063
Clark-Winchole Fdn., D.C., 1/064
Clarry Fdn., Baltimore, 1/065
Cleveland Fdn., Baltimore, 1/066
Coale (Edith Seville) MD Scholarships, D.C., 1/066
Cohen (Herman & Ben) Charitable Fdn., Baltimore, 1/066
Cohen-Solomon Family Fdn., D.C., 1/068
Cohen (Herman & Ben) Charitable Fdn., Baltimore, 1/068
Cohn (Marcus & Harryette) Fdn., Chevy Chase, 1/069
Combined Apartments Fdn., Baltimore, 1/069
Commodity Credit Company Fdn., Baltimore, 1/070
Community Fdn., D.C., 1/071
Cone (Maxwell) Fdn., Baltimore, 1/071
Cone (Sydney M.) Research Fdn., Baltimore, 1/071
Conference on Latin American History, D.C., 1/072
Consolidated Engineering Fdn., Baltimore, 1/072
Construction Industry Advancement Program of Baltimore, Lutherville, 1/073
Consumer Federation of America, D.C., 1/073
Conquest (Edwin P.) Memorial Trust, D.C., 1/074
Coventaros Fdn., Baltimore, 1/074
Crawford Fdn., Crofton, 1/075
C. & S. Fdn., Baltimore, 1/075
Daley (Arthur) Fdn., D.C., 1/076
Damil Fdn., Baltimore, 1/076
Daniels (C.R.) Fdn., Daniels, 1/076
Davies (Joe) Scholarship Fdn., D.C., 1/077
Davis (Norene S. & Floyd E.) Fdn., D.C., 1/077
Dechiaro (Ralph & Dorothy) Fdn., Towson, 1/077
Deiches Free Library Fund, Baltimore, 1/078
Delmar (Charles) Fdn., D.C., 1/078
Dickey (Allen) Fdn., Ellicott City, 1/079
Riggs Distler Fdn., Baltimore, 1/080
Dopkin (Lee L.) Fdn., Baltimore, 1/080
Dorsey Fdn., Easton, 1/081
DuFour (Raymond A.) Fdn., D.C., 1/081
Duncan (Kathleen) Fdn., D.C., 1/081
Dunning (H.A.B.) Fdn., Baltimore, 1/082
Dweck (Samuel R.) Fdn., D.C., 1/083
Eaton Fdn., D.C., 1/083
Eaton Fund, Baltimore, 1/084
Eckman Family Fdn., D.C., 1/085
Edmunds (Page) Fdn., Baltimore, 1/085
Eichler (John) Charitable Trust, Chevy Chase, 1/086
Eisenberg (Gerson Gutman) Fdn., Baltimore, 1/086
Elderkin (Clarence E.) Fdn., Baltimore, 1/086
Eliasberg Fund, Baltimore, 1/087
Flynn & Emerick Company, Baltimore, 1/089

Eppley (Constance R.) Fdn. Formerly D.C., Takoma Park, 1/089
Epstein (Jacob) Fdn., Baltimore, 1/089
Epstein Family Fdn., Baltimore, 1/090
Epstein (Samuel & Sidney) Charitable Trust, Baltimore, 1/090
Esperantic Studies Fdn., D.C., 1/091
Esskay Fund, Baltimore, 1/091
E T C Charitable Fdn., Baltimore, 1/091
Farber Fdn., Baltimore, 1/093
Feinberg (Harry & Jeanne) Fdn., D.C., 1/093
Feldman (Haskell & Ida) Fdn., Baltimore, 1/094
Fidelity & Deposit Company of Maryland Fdn., Baltimore, 1/094
Filbert Fdn., Baltimore, 1/095
Fine (M. Bruce) Fdn., Baltimore, 1/095
Firstman Family Fdn., Easton, 1/096
First Maryland Fdn., Baltimore, 1/096
Fitchett-Stick Fdn., Baltimore, 1/097
Fitzgerald Family Fund, D.C., 1/098
Forb Fdn., D.C., 1/098
Forconi Fdn., Baltimore, 1/098
Foundation to Enable Economic Development, D.C., 1/099
Fowler (John Edward) Memorial Fdn., D.C., 1/100
Fox (Marie & Ernest) Fdn., Baltimore, 1/101
Fox (Henry J.) Fund, D.C., 1/101
Fradkin Fdn., D.C., 1/102
Fradkin (I. Albert) Fdn., Baltimore, 1/102
Fradkin Brothers Charitable Trust, Baltimore, 1/103
Frank (Milton M.) Fdn., Baltimore, 1/103
Freedman (S.) & Sons Fdn., Landover, 1/104
Freeman (Carl M.) Fdn., Silver Spring, 1/105
Frenkil (Victor) Fdn., Baltimore, 1/105
Friedenwald Fdn., Baltimore, 1/107
Friedenwald (Mr. & Mrs. Leo W.) Memorial Fund, Baltimore, 1/107
Friedman & Lazinsky Fdn., Baltimore, 1/107
Friend (Philip R.) Fdn., D.C., 1/108
Fuld Fdn., Baltimore, 1/108
Fuld (Joseph, Bernice & Stuart) Fdn., Baltimore, 1/108
Fund for Public Policy Research, D.C., 1/109
Fund for The Future, Baltimore, 1/111
Furman Fdn., Baltimore, 1/111
Garfinkel (Gerry & Hy) Fdn., Bethesda, 1/112
Garrett (George A.) Fdn., D.C., 1/113
Gastrock Fdn., D.C., 1/113
Geist Church & Graveyard Fdn., Upperco, 1/114
Gelman (Melvin) Fdn., D.C., 1/114
Gerber (Thomas & Kay) Fdn., D.C., 1/116
German Society of Maryland, Baltimore, 1/116
Gerstell (Robert S.) Fdn., Baltimore, 1/117
Geschickter Fund for Medical Research, D.C., 1/117
Gettinger (Walter & Lillian) Fdn., Baltimore, 1/118
Gerwiz (Morris & Frances) Fdn., D.C., 1/119
Giant Food Fdn., D.C., 1/120
Gibson (Mary O'Brien & John T.) Fdn., D.C., 1/121
Gibson Island Country School Fdn., Gibson Island, 1/121
Gichner (Henry & Isabelle) Fdn., D.C., 1/121
Gilan Fdn., D.C., 1/122
Gildea Fdn., Baltimore, 1/123
Gilden Fdn., Annapolis, 1/123
Gilliam Fdn., D.C., 1/123
Gladding Fdn., Baltimore, 1/124
Glasmann Fdn., D.C., 1/124
Glen (Leonard & Adele) Family Fdn., Chevy Chase, 1/124
Goble (Ada M. & Gertrude) - Pearl Strickland Fdn., D.C., 1/125
Goetz (Albert F.) Fdn., Baltimore, 1/125
Goldstein (Albert E.) Memorial Fund, Baltimore, 1/125
Goodman (Morris M.) Fdn., D.C., 1/126
Gordon (Isaac & Annie) Fdn., Baltimore, 1/126
Gordon Fdn., D.C., 1/127
Gordon (Yale) Fdn., Baltimore, 1/127

Gorfine Fdn., Baltimore, 1/127
Gorn (Sarah) Fdn., Baltimore, 1/128
Grace Fdn. of Taylors Island, Pikesville, 1/128
Graham (Philip L.) Fund, D.C., 1/128
Green Spring Fdn., Baltimore, 1/129
Green (Benjamin) Fdn., Baltimore, 1/130
Greenfield Charitable Fund, Baltimore, 1/130
Greif (David & Irvin) Fdn., Lutherville, 1/131
Greif (Irvin) Fdn., Baltimore, 1/131
Gridiron Fdn., D.C., 1/132
Groh (Garland E.) Fdn., Hagerstown, 1/133
Gross (Murray Israel) Memorial Fdn., Baltimore, 1/133
Grossberg (Louis C.) Fdn., D.C., 1/133
Grotz (W. Arthur) Fdn., Baltimore, 1/134
Grumbacher (Marjorie & Richard) Fund, Hagerstown, 1/135
Gudelsky (Homer & Martha) Family Fdn., Baltimore, 1/135
Gumenick Fdn., D.C., 1/135
Gutman Trust, Baltimore, 1/136
G Charitable Fdn., Baltimore, 1/136
Hack Fdn., Baltimore, 1/137
Hampshire Fdn., Baltimore, 1/137
Hanauer (Jerome & Carrie) Fund, D.C., 1/137
Handleman (Myer C.) - Macke Educational Fdn., Cheverly, 1/138
Harms Fdn., Pasadena, 1/138
Head Fdn., Baltimore, 1/138
Hecht (Moses S. & Blanch H.) Fdn., Baltimore, 1/139
Hecht-Levi Fdn., Baltimore, 1/140
Helmos Fdn., Baltimore, 1/141
Hendler Fdn., Brooklandville, 1/142
Herman (Harry J.) Fdn., Baltimore, 1/143
Hertzberg (Dr. Herman & Katherine Wolf) Fdn., D.C., 1/144
Hessick Fdn., D.C., 1/144
Hettleman Fdn., Baltimore, 1/144
Higginson (Corina) Trust, D.C., 1/145
Fairchild Hiller Fdn., Germantown, 1/146
Himes (Joseph H.) Charitable Fdn., D.C., 1/147
Himmelfarb (Paul & Annetta) Fdn., D.C., 1/147
Himmelrich Fund, Baltimore, 1/148
Hoffberger Fdn., Baltimore, 1/148
Hoffman (Charles W.) Fdn., Hagerstown, 1/149
Hofmann (Julius) Memorial Fund, Baltimore, 1/149
Hoge Fdn., D.C., 1/150
Holtzman (Samuel J.) Family Fdn., Baltimore, 1/151
Home for the Aged of Frederick City, Frederick, 1/151
Hoover (J. Edgar) Fdn., D.C., 1/152
Hopkins (John Jay) Fdn. Formerly D.C., Takoma Park, 1/154
Hopkins (Ruth Smith) Fdn. Formerly D.C., Takoma Park, 1/154
Hosinger (Edward F., Jr.) Charitable Trust, Baltimore, 1/155
Howell (Harley W.) Charitable Fdn., Baltimore, 1/155
Hufty Fdn., D.C., 1/157
Human Needs Fdn., Bethesda, 1/158
Hurwitz (Philip & Shirley) Charity FUnd, Baltimore, 1/159
Hutzler Fund, Baltimore, 1/159
Hyman (George & Sadie) Fdn., D.C., 1/161
Hyman (Sigmund M.) Fdn., Baltimore, 1/162
International Group Plans Fdn., D.C., 1/162
Island Fdn., Baltimore, 1/164
Janal Fdn., Baltimore, 1/164
Jemicy Fund, Baltimore, 1/165
Jennings (Coleman) Fdn., D.C., 1/166
Johnston (James M.) Trust for Charitable & Educational Purposes, D.C., 1/166
Jones (Marguerite G. & Chester R.) Educational & Charitable Trust, D.C., 1/168
Kane (Francis J.) Charitable Trust, Tuxedo, 1/169
Kanfer Fdn., D.C., 1/169

Kann (S.) Sons Company Fdn., Baltimore, 1/170

Kaplan (Charles I. & Mary) Fdn., D.C., 1/171

Katz (Dorothy & Nathan) Fdn., Baltimore, 1/172

Kaufmann (Cora & Saul) Memorial Fdn., D.C., 1/173

Kay (A.S.) Fdn., D.C., 1/173

Keiser (George C.) Fdn., D.C., 1/175

Kelly-Springfield Employees Charity Fund, Cumberland, 1/176

Kelly (Ensign C. Markland, Jr.) Memorial Fdn., Baltimore, 1/177

Kennedy (Robert F.) Memorial Fdn., D.C., 1/178

Kerby (William J.) Fdn., D.C., 1/179

Kiplinger Fdn., D.C., 1/180

Kleff Fdn., Baltimore, 1/181

Klaven (Rabbi Joshua & Fannie D.) Memorial Fdn., D.C., 1/182

Klein (Hannah & Sidney) Family Fdn., D.C., 1/183

Kline (Ilene & Joel) Fdn., Silver Spring, 1/183

Klein (Lawrence R.) Fund, Silver Spring, 1/184

Klopman (Sidney) Memorial Fdn., Baltimore, 1/184

Knott Brothers Fdn., Baltimore, 1/184

Knox-Vincent Fdn., D.C., 1/185

Koenigsberger (Laurence & Irene) Fdn., D.C., 1/186

Kogod (Fred S.) Fdn., D.C., 1/187

Kohn (Irving) Fdn., Baltimore, 1/188

Kohn (Martin & Rosa) Fund, Baltimore, 1/189

Kolker (Benjamin & Miriam) Fdn., Baltimore, 1/189

Koteen Fdn., D.C., 1/190

Kramer (Victor H.) Fdn., D.C., 1/190

Kreeger (David Lloyd) Charitable Fdn., D.C., 1/192

Krieger Fund, Baltimore, 1/192

Kupersmidt Fdn., D.C., 1/193

Lablakehan Fdn., Baltimore, 1/194

Landa Educational Fdn., D.C., 1/195

Lansburgh (Sidney & Marion) Charitable Fdn., Baltimore, 1/195

Lanston (Tolbert) Trust, D.C., 1/196

Lapides Brothers Fdn., Baltimore, 1/196

Lapides Fdn., Baltimore, 1/197

Larson Fdn., Riverdale, 1/198

Lattman Fdn., D.C., 1/198

Lauer (Edith L.) Fund, Baltimore, 1/199

Lawson Charitable Fdn., Bethesda, 1/199

Layton (Greta Brown) Charitable Trust, Baltimore, 1/200

Leadership Grants, D.C., 1/201

League of Women Voters of Montgomery County, Maryland Memorial Library Fund, Kensington, 1/201

LeBaron Fdn., D.C., 1/201

Lebbin (Gary & Bernice) Fdn., D.C., 1/201

Legg & Co. Fdn., Baltimore, 1/202

Legum Distributing Charitable Fdn., Baltimore, 1/203

Legum Fdn., Baltimore, 1/204

Lehrman (Jacob & Charlotte) Fdn., D.C., 1/204

Leidy Chemicals Fdn., Baltimore, 1/205

Lesdor Fdn., D.C., 1/207

Levi (James H. & Adele S.) Fdn., Baltimore, 1/208

Lewis (John L.) Scholarship Fund, D.C., 1/208

Levenson & Klein Charitable Trust, Baltimore, 1/209

Levy (Philip) Fdn., D.C., 1/209

Lilliputian Fdn., Silver Spring, 1/209

Lime Kiln Valley Fdn., Baltimore, 1/210

Lifetime Sports Fdn., D.C., 1/210

Linsone, Inc., D.C., 1/211

Lion (Albert & Gloria) Fund, Owings Mills, 1/212

Lisanelly Fdn., Baltimore, 1/212

Lisner (Abraham & Laura) Home for Aged Women, D.C., 1/212

Londontown Fdn., Baltimore, 1/214

Long (W. Newton) Fdn., Baltimore, 1/214

Lovintellealth Fdn., Bethesda, 1/216

Lurie Fdn., Baltimore, 1/216

Macht (Ephraim & Annie) Fdn., Baltimore, 1/217

Magazine Family Fdn., D.C., 1/217

Mahr (Jacob & Ida) Fdn., Baltimore, 1/218

Manton Fdn., D.C., 1/219

McManus (George W.) Fdn., Baltimore, 1/219

Marcus (Louis) Fdn., Baltimore, 1/220

Marino (Dr. Frank C.) Fdn., Baltimore, 1/220

Marriott (J. Willard) Family Fdn., D.C., 1/221

Maryland National Bank, Baltimore, 1/222

Masur (Barbara F. & Jack) Fund, D.C., 1/224

Matthews (Ernestine) Trust, D.C., 1/224

Mazor (Meyer & Esther B.) Fdn., D.C., 1/225

McCarthy Historical Project, D.C., 1/226

McManus Fdn., Towson, 1/227

McNamara (Robert S. & Margaret C.) Fdn., D.C., 1/228

Mechanic (Morris A.) Fdn., Baltimore, 1/228

M E Fdn., Baltimore, 1/229

Mellett Fund for a Free & Responsible Press, D.C., 1/231

Merrick (Robert G. & Anne M.) Fdn., Baltimore, 1/231

Meserve-Basily Fund, Baltimore, 2/001

Meyer (Eugene & Agnes) Fdn., D.C., 2/001

Miller (Meyer M. & Lottie K.) Fdn., Baltimore, 2/006

Milnel Fdn., Baltimore, 2/006

Mitchell (James F.) Fdn. for Medical Education & Research, D.C., 2/007

Mitchell (Lloyd E.) Fdn., Baltimore, 2/007

Mitchell (E. Stewart) Fdn., Baltimore, 2/008

Chertkof (David W. & Annie) Mitzvah Fund, Baltimore, 2/009

Montgomery Fdn., D.C., 2/010

Morris (Arthur N.) Fdn., Baltimore, 2/011

Moss (Freda) Charity Trust Formerly Virginia, D.C., 2/012

Mulford (Vincent) Fdn., Baltimore, 2/013

Mullan (Thomas F. & Clementine L.) Fdn., Baltimore, 2/013

Mullendore-Freed Fdn., Hagerstown, 2/014

Munsell Color Fdn., Baltimore, 2/015

Murray (Oscar G.) Railroad Employees Benefit Fund, Baltimore, 2/016

Myers (D.) & Sons Fdn., Baltimore, 2/020

Nathan Fdn., Baltimore, 2/021

National Fdn. for Alcohol Education, Baltimore, 2/021

National Home Library Fdn., D.C., 2/022

National 4th (IVY) Division Association Scholarship Fund, D.C., 2/022

National Psychiatric Endowment Fund, Bethesda, 2/023

Nawapa Fdn., D.C., 2/024

Nelson (John M., Jr.) Fdn., Baltimore, 2/024

Foundation for Neuropsychiatric Research, Bethesda, 2/025

Norden (Carl & Ellen) Fdn., D.C., 2/026

Noxell Fdn., Formerly Noxzema Fdn., Baltimore, 2/027

O'Conor (James G.) Fdn., Baltimore, 2/029

Offen Fdn., Baltimore, 2/029

Oliphant (A.C. & R.L.) Charitable Fdn., D.C., 2/030

Orem Educational Trust, Hyattsville, 2/031

Ottenstein (Thomas R.) Charitable Fdn., Silver Spring, 2/031

Ourisman Fdn., Marlow Heights, 2/031

Oursler (George A. & Mary E.) Fdn., Baltimore, 2/032

Overlook Fdn., Pikesville, 2/033

Oxman (Maxwell & Beatrice) Fdn., D.C., 2/033

Pan American Health & Education Fdn., D.C., 2/033

Pariser (Inda & Henry) Fdn., Baltimore, 2/034

Passano Fdn., Baltimore, 2/034

Patterson (Jefferson) Fdn., D.C., 2/035

Peabody Library Association of Georgetown, D.C., D.C., 2/035

Perlman Fdn., Baltimore, 2/036

Phillips Collection, D.C., 2/037

Pike Fdn., Bethesda, 2/037

Pink Fdn., Cambridge, 2/038

Poland (Sidney & Iris) Fdn., Baltimore, 2/038

Poland (Morton & Suellen) Fdn., Baltimore, 2/039

Pollak (Ruth & Stephen) Fdn., D.C., 2/040

Pollin (Morris & Jennie) Fdn., D.C., 2/041

Pomerantz-Glazer Fdn., Owings Mills, 2/041

Porter (Katherine Anne) Fdn., College Park, 2/042

Posner (Lillian & Stanley) Fdn., D.C., 2/042

Post Fdn., Snow Hill, 2/043

Post (Marjorie Merriweather) Fdn., D.C., 2/043

Post (Marjorie Merriweather) Fdn. of D.C., D.C., 2/044

Potts (Isaac & Leah M.) Fdn., Baltimore, 2/045

Powder River Fdn., D.C., 2/046

Price Fdn., Baltimore, 2/046

Price (Rowe & Eleanor) Fdn., Baltimore, 2/047

Probert (Adelaide R.) Fund for the Washington Animal Rescue League, Sandy Spring, 2/047

Probert (Adelaide R.) Church Fund, Sandy Spring, 2/048

Probert (Adelaide R.) Humanity Fund, Sandy Spring, 2/048

Purnell (Tony) Fdn., Baltimore, 2/049

Radford (Arthur W.) Charitable Fdn., D.C., 2/050

Radner (William) Fund, Silver Spring, 2/050

Rall Fdn., Baltimore, 2/051

Rappaport Fdn., Baltimore, 2/052

Rau Fdn., D.C., 2/052

Rauh Family Fdn., D.C., 2/052

Read's Fdn., Baltimore, 2/053

R E C Fdn., Chevy Chase, 2/053

Rejon Fdn., Baltimore, 2/053

Religious Generations Fdn., Chillum, 2/054

Reynolds (Zachary Smith) Trust, Baltimore, 2/054

Rich (Edward N. Jr.) Charitable Trust, Baltimore, 2/055

Richardson (Lloyd A.) Fdn., Salisbury, 2/056

Richardson (Raymond I.) Fdn., Westminster, 2/056

Rietzke (Renah Blair) Family Fdn., D.C., 2/057

Ring Fdn., D.C., 2/058

Robinson (Herbert W.) Fdn., D.C., 2/059

Rockport Fund, D.C., 2/060

Roland Park Roads & Maintenance Corporation, Baltimore, 2/061

Rosenberg (Henry & Ruth Blaustein) Fdn., Baltimore, 2/061

Rosenberg (Solomon Morris) Fdn., Westminster, 2/062

Rosenzwog (Morris J.) Family Fdn., Baltimore, 2/064

Lazaron (Hilda Rothschild) Family Fdn., Baltimore, 2/064

Rouse Family Charitable Fdn., Columbia, 2/065

Rubin Fdn., Baltimore, 2/065

Rudick (Joseph R.) Fdn., Baltimore, 2/066

Rymland Fdn., Baltimore, 2/066

Sackett & Scherr Fdn., Landover, 2/067

St. James Educational Fund, Bethesda, 2/068

St. Joseph Fdn., Baltimore, 2/068

Salmon (Kurt) Fdn., Baltimore, 2/068

Salzberg Fdn., Chevy Chase, 2/069

Salzman (Herbert & Rita) Fdn., D.C., 2/070

Schapiro Fdn., Baltimore, 2/071

Schapiro (Morris) & Family Fdn., Baltimore, 2/071

Schattner (R.) Fdn., D.C., 2/072

Schloss (Rebecca) Memorial Fund, Baltimore, 2/073

Schluderberg Fdn., Baltimore, 2/073

Schnabel Fdn. Co. Charitable Trust, D.C., 2/073

Schoeneman-Weiler Fund, Baltimore, 2/074

Schuster (Frank & Marvin) Fdn., Baltimore, 2/074

Schwaber Fdn., Baltimore, 2/075

Schwartz (Theodore A. & Doris B.) Fdn.,
    Pikesville, 2/075
Sexton Fdn., D.C., 2/076
Sexton (Nathaniel G.) Fdn., Baltimore, 2/076
Shanks Fdn., D.C., 2/076
Shapiro (Jacob S.) Fdn., Baltimore, 2/076
Shear Family Fdn., Baltimore, 2/077
Shuger Fdn., Baltimore, 2/078
Siegel (Irvin L.) Fdn., D.C., 2/078
Silber Fdn., Baltimore, 2/079
Silberman (Ronnie & Dovera) Fdn., Baltimore,
    2/080
Silver0Burstein Fdn., D.C., 2/080
Silverstein Family Fdn., D.C., 2/081
Singer (Ben & Ide) Fdn., D.C., 2/081
Sisk Mailing Service of Washington, Inc.
    Charitable & Educational Fdn., D.C., 2/082
Sloan (Arthur W.) Fdn., D.C., 2/082
Smelkinson Fdn., Baltimore, 2/083
Smith (F. Bowie) Fdn., Baltimore, 2/083
Smith (Charles E.) Family Fdn., D.C., 2/084
Smith (John Thomas) Memorial Fdn., D.C.,
    2/085
Smith (Joseph & Anna) Fdn., D.C., 2/086
Smith (L.B.) Estates, D.C., 2/087
Smuck Fdn., Baltimore, 2/087
Society for the Preservation of Maryland
    Antiquities, Towson, 2/087
Society of the Cincinnati of Maryland,
    Baltimore, 2/088
Solomon (Jack & Irene Hayes) Fdn., D.C.,
    2/089
Speer (Talbot T.) Fdn., Baltimore, 2/089
Staiman (Aaron & Dora) Fdn., Silver Spring,
    2/090
Stein Brothers & Boyce Fdn., Baltimore, 2/091
Stern (Samuel & Elizabeth) Fund, D.C., 2/091
Steuart (James E.) Fdn., Baltimore, 2/093
Stouffer (Anne C.) Fdn., Baltimore, 2/093
Straus (Aaron & Lillie) Fdn., Baltimore, 2/094
Straus (Henry C.) Fdn., Baltimore, 2/097
Strauss (Lewis & Rosa) Memorial Fund, D.C.,
    2/098
Strauss Fdn., Baltimore, 2/099
Sugar (Isaac) Family Fdn., D.C., 2/099
Symington (J. Fife, III) Fdn., Baltimore, 2/100
Symington (Martha Frick) Fdn., Baltimore,
    2/100
Tager Family Fdn., Bethesda, 2/101
Thalheimer (Alvin & Fanny Blaustein) Fdn.,
    Baltimore, 2/101
Thistlewood, Ltd., Baltimore, 2/102
Thomas (G. Frank) Fdn., Frederick, 2/103
Thompson (Arthur Lee, III) Memorial Fdn.,
    D.C., 2/103
Thon (Robert & Evelyn) Fdn., Baltimore,
    2/104
Tompkins (Lida R. & Charles H.) Fdn., D.C.,
    2/104
True (Alice & Russell) Fdn., D.C., 2/105
Barker (Mary B.) Trust for Memorial Chapel,
    D.C., 2/105
Bright (Lynne A.) Trust, D.C., 2/105
Bryant (E.S.) Trust B/O Esther Memorial
    Church, D.C., 2/105
Bulloch (Liley W.R.) Trust, D.C., 2/106
Chase (Helen) Trust U/W Episcopal Home
    Memorial Fund, D.C., 2/106
Chase (Helen) Trust U/W Lincoln & Chase
    Fund, D.C., 2/107
Chase (Helen) Trust U/W B/O Washington
    Home for Incurables, D.C., 2/107
Clapp (Alice J.) Trust, D.C., 2/107
Conway (Albert P.) Trust, D.C., 2/108
Coope (Jessie) Trust, D.C., 2/108
Deiches Educational Fund, Baltimore, 2/109
Trigg (Ernest T.) Fdn., D.C., 2/109
Dickey (Robert J.) Trust, D.C., 2/110
First Cavalry Division Association Trust, D.C.,
    2/110
Snyder (Francoise R. & Sidney) Fdn.,
    Baltimore, 2/111
First Cavalry Division Association Trust, D.C.,
    2/111
Dickson (Henry) Trust, D.C., 2/111
Grandin (Emma P.) Trust, D.C., 2/111

Gray (Sarah) Trust, D.C., 2/111
Hartson (Nelson T.) Law Scholarship Trust,
    D.C., 2/112
Higgins (Mary Z.L.) Trust, D.C., 2/112
Hostetter (Horace J.) Trust, D.C., 2/112
Hoxie (Richard L.) Trust, D.C., 2/113
Hunter (Oscar B.) Memorial Fund Trust, D.C.,
    2/113
Johnson (Henry A.) Trust U/W B/O Herdon
    Lodge, D.C., 2/113
Johnson (Henry A.) Trust U/W Relief Fund,
    D.C., 2/114
Laughlin (William) Trust, D.C., 2/114
Lee (Jennie Browne) Trust, D.C., 2/114
Letts (Mary E.) Trust, D.C., 2/115
Marsden (Albert G.) Trust, D.C., 2/115
Marsh (Kate S.) Trust, D.C., 2/115
Phillips (Samuel) Trust Fund, D.C., 2/116
Prenner (Isadore S.) Trust, D.C., 2/116
Pumphrey (George C.) Trust U/W B/O
    Washington Lodge 15, D.C., 2/117
Ruffin (Sterlin) Trust, D.C., 2/117
Saltz (Lewis) Medical Fund Trust, D.C., 2/117
Smith (Lizzie C.) Trust, D.C., 2/117
Streater (William B.) Trust, D.C., 2/118
Stuart (Annie B.) Trust, D.C., 2/118
Collison (F.P.) Trust, D.C., 2/118
Walton (J. Roland) Trust, D.C., 2/118
Washington Fdn./Animal Relief Fund Trust,
    D.C., 2/119
Washington Fdn./Amelia Erback Fund Trust,
    D.C., 2/119
Washington Fdn./Emma Elizabeth Hawey
    Fund Trust, D.C., 2/119
Washington Fdn.-Unrestricted Trust, D.C.,
    2/120
Waterman (Anna R.) Trust, D.C., 2/120
Turk (Richard H.) Fdn., Baltimore, 2/120
Uhl Fdn., Hagerstown, 2/121
1922 Class of the United States Naval
    Academy/Memorial Scholarship Fund,
    Baltimore, 2/122
Urban Studies, D.C., 2/122
V F W Department of Maryland, Faulker,
    2/123
Viner Fdn., D.C., 2/123
Vinnick (Milton) Fdn. for College Education,
    D.C., 2/124
Virya Fdn., D.C., 2/125
Waller (Morris, Max & Minna) Fdn., Baltimore,
    2/125
Wareheim (E.C.) Fdn., Baltimore, 2/126
Warfield (Anna Emory) Memorial Fund,
    Baltimore, 2/127
Washington Children's Fund, D.C., 2/129
Wasserman (George) Fdn., D.C., 2/130
Webster (Marjorie) Junior College Educational
    Scholarship Fdn., D.C., 2/131
Weinberg (Edith Rothschild) Family Fdn.,
    Baltimore, 2/131
Weir Fdn. Trust, D.C., 2/132
Western Maryland Railway Fdn., Baltimore,
    2/133
White Coffee Pot Restaurants Fdn., Baltimore,
    2/133
White House-Security Fund, D.C., 2/134
Whitlock (Douglas) Student Grant Fund, D.C.,
    2/134
W.H.R. Memorial Fdn., Takoma Park, 2/134
Wilkoff (Arthur, Rachel & Susan) Fdn.,
    Baltimore, 2/135
Willard (Helen Parker) Fdn., D.C., 2/135
Willey (Gordon Fay) Trust, D.C., 2/136
Wilner Family Fdn., D.C., 2/137
Winchester Fdn., Baltimore, 2/137
Winer (Jacob) Trust, D.C., 2/138
Winer (Jacob & Eva) Fdn., Odenton, 2/138
Winslow (W.R.) Trust, D.C., 2/138
Wolf Pack Fdn., D.C., 2/139
Women's Board of the Hospital for
    Consumptives of Maryland, Baltimore,
    2/140
World Man Fund, Bethesda, 2/141
Wright (Bonnie & Jeannie) Fdn., Baltimore,
    2/141
Wright (John D.) Fdn., Baltimore, 2/142

Wyman Fund, Baltimore, 2/142
Yakov (Chunan Ben-Hillel) Fdn., Indianhead,
    2/143
Zerivitz (Joseph W. & Anna) Fdn., Baltimore,
    2/143
Zinder Family Fdn., D.C., 2/144
Zuckert (Eugene M. & Barbara J.) Charitable
    Trust, Chevy Chase, 2/144

Second Filming

Accokeek Fdn., D.C., 3/001
Aid Association for the Blind of D.C., D.C.,
    3/002
Altar Guild of Episcopal Churchwomen of the
    Diocese of Maryland Trust, Baltimore,
    3/003
American Fdn. for the Blind Trust, D.C., 3/003
American Israeli Fdn. for Insurance Education,
    D.C., 3/004
American Petroleum Institute, D.C., 3/004
D.C. Chapter of American Red Cross Trust,
    D.C., 3/005
American Youth Research Fdn., Baltimore,
    3/006
Americans for Indian Opportunity, D.C., 3/006
Amvets Memorial Scholarship Trust, D.C.,
    3/007
Andean Fdn., D.C., 3/007
Arent Charitable Fdn., D.C., 3/009
Arrow, Inc., D.C., 3/010
Asrael (Samuel & Rosa) Fdn., Pikesville, 3/011
Atlantica Fdn., D.C., 3/012
Ayd Fdn., Baltimore, 3/013
Azoans Charity Fund, Baltimore, 3/014
Baileys Neck Park Association, Easton, 3/014
Baker (Clayton) Trust, Baltimore, 3/015
Baker - King Fund, Baltimore, 3/015
Baldwin Fdn., Millersville, 3/016
Baltimore Council for Equal Business
    Opportunity, Baltimore, 3/016
Baltimore Eastern Dispensary Fund, Baltimore,
    3/017
Baltimore Opera Club, Baltimore, 3/017
Baltimore Rh Typing Laboratory, Inc.,
    Baltimore, 3/018
Baltimore Regional Joint Board of
    Amalgamated Clothing Workers of America
    Health & Welfare Fund, Baltimore, 3/018
Bank (Helen & Merrill) Fdn., Owings Mills,
    3/019
Barringer (Victor Clay) Memorial Fund Trust,
    D.C., 3/019
Andrews (Belle Fisk) Trust, D.C., 3/020
Bell (A.M.) Memorial Fund Trust, D.C., 3/020
Bell Volta Life Membership Fund Trust, D.C.,
    3/021
Bell Volta Fund Trust, D.C., 3/022
Bender Fdn., D.C., 3/022
Berea in Korea Fdn., D.C., 3/022
Berkow (Nathan & Jennie) Fdn., Linthicum
    Heights, 3/023
Bernard Memorial Fund Trust, D.C., 3/023
Bester (Henry A.), Jr. Fdn., Hagerstown, 3/024
Bethesda - Chevy Chase Rotary Club Fdn.,
    Bethesda, 3/024
Bethesda Methodist Church Cemetery Fund,
    Baltimore, 3/025
Blackburn Fdn., D.C., 3/025
Blades (A.T. & Mary H.) Fdn., Baltimore,
    3/025
Lee (Mrs. Blair) Memorial Fund Trust, D.C.,
    3/026
Blank (Raymond & Elaine) Fdn., Baltimore,
    3/026
Blum (Lois & Irving) Fdn., Baltimore, 3/027
Blum (Samuel) Fdn., Baltimore, 3/028
Bolljahn (John T.) Memorial Fdn., College
    Park, 3/030
Brady Scholarship Fund Trust, D.C., 3/041
Breezewood Fdn., Baltimore, 3/042
Breitenstein (Marie) Trust, Baltimore, 3/042
Brodie (Harry) Fdn., D.C., 3/043
Bowers Family Fdn., D.C., 3/043
Boston University School of Theology Trust,
    D.C., 3/043

Boyd (James S.) Trust, D.C., 3/043

Brenizer (Warren F.) Trust, D.C., 3/044

Brown (Alvin I. & Peggy S.) Charitable Fdn., D.C., 3/045

Budd (Michael W.) Trust Equity, D.C., 3/046

Burdett (Samuel S.) Trust, D.C., 3/046

Burlack (Eda) Trust, D.C., 3/047

Byrd (Robert C.) Scholastic Recognition Fund, D.C., 3/047

Carozza (Anthony & Anna L.) Fdn., D.C., 3/047

Casey - Clark Trust, D.C., 3/048

Casey (Annie L.) Trust, D.C., 3/049

Scagnelli (Caterina) Trust, D.C., 3/050

Catzen (Aaron) Fdn., Baltimore, 3/050

Center for Applied Linguistics, D.C., 3/051

Center for Community Change, D.C., 3/052

Central Union Mission Children's Emergency Home Trust, D.C., 3/053

Chandler (Helen & George) Fdn., Salisbury, 3/054

Charitable Fdn. of Prince Georges County Medical Society, Hyattsville, 3/054

Clagett Fdn., D.C., 3/055

Checket Family Fdn., Baltimore, 3/056

Clements (Cora T.) Trust, D.C., 3/057

Chesapeake Restaurant Fdn., Baltimore, 3/058

Children's Hospital Fund, Baltimore, 3/059

Cleaning Plant Employees Welfare Fund, St. Louis, Mo., 3/059

Cohen (Herman & Ben) Charitable Fdn., Baltimore, 3/061

Cole Fdn., D.C., 3/061

College Fdn., Silver Spring, 3/062

Commercial Credit Companies Fdn., Baltimore, 3/062

Community Consultants, Inc., D.C., 3/066

Coonley (Queene Ferry) Fdn., D.C., 3/067

Cooperative Assistance Fund, D.C., 3/067

Corcoran Charity Fund Trust Equity, D.C., 3/080

Cosmos Club Fdn., D.C., 3/080

Cotten (Bruce) Trust, Baltimore, 3/081

Council on Library Resources, D.C., 3/081

Dame (Harriet Patience) Trust, D.C., 3/085

Dashiell (Cassius M.) Trust, Baltimore, 3/085

Reasoner & Davis Charitable Trust, Bethesda, 3/085

Delano (Fred A. & Matilda) Trust, D.C., 3/086

Diffraction Fdn., Riderwood, 3/087

Dulany (John H.) Memorial, Fruitland, 3/087

Duncan (Alexander E.) Fdn., Baltimore, 3/087

Echo House Fdn., Baltimore, 3/088

Education & Scholarship Fdn. of Building Laborers' Local 74, D.C., 3/088

Educational Fund of Alumnae & Friends of Santiago College, Bethesda, 3/089

Electrical Local 26 Joint Apprenticeship & Training Trust Fund, D.C., 3/089

Emory (William Edwin) Trust, D.C., 3/090

Engel (Carrie & Jay) Fdn., Baltimore, 3/090

Environmental Law Institute, D.C., 3/091

Ferguson (Alice) Fdn., Accokeek, 3/091

Fink (Alice L.) Trust, Baltimore, 3/093

Fisher (Arthur) Trust, D.C., 3/093

Fitchett (T. Somerset) Fdn., Baltimore, 3/094

Fitzpatrick (F. Stuart) Award Fund, D.C., 3/094

Fleischmann (Marcelle & Edwin M.) Fdn., Baltimore, 3/105

Folger Fund, D.C., 3/106

Ford (Jefferson Lee), III Memorial Fdn., D.C., 3/107

Ford Union Military Academy Fund, Baltimore, 3/108

Foster Fdn., D.C., 3/108

Fox (Martin & Lillian) Fdn., Baltimore, 3/108

France (Jacob & Annita) Fdn., Baltimore, 3/109

Freed (Allie S. & Frances W.) Fdn., D.C., 3/110

Freudberg (Leopold & Rose) Fdn., D.C., 3/111

Friedman (Benjamin D. & Martha G.) Fdn., D.C., 3/111

Friedberg (Solomon & Jennie G.) Fdn., Baltimore, 3/112

Friends of German School Charitable Trust, D.C., 3/112

Fund for Public Policy Research, D.C., 3/113

Garwyn Fdn., Baltimore, 3/114

Gettinger (Walter & Lillian) Fdn., Baltimore, 3/114

Gibson (Roland) Art Fdn., Easton, 3/115

Glick (David & Rose S.) Fdn., Baltimore, 3/115

Goldseker (Morris) Fdn., Baltimore, 3/116

Golfer's Charitable Association, Baltimore, 3/117

Goodwin (Douglas & Anne) Fdn., Baltimore, 3/117

Grasmick (Madeline K. & Louis J.) Fdn., Baltimore, 3/118

Greggs (William R.) Agency Trust, D.C., 3/118

Grosvenor (A.G.B.) Memorial Fund, D.C., 3/118

Grosvenor (E.M.) Memroial Fund, D.C., 3/119

Group Health Fdn., D.C., 3/119

Gudelsky Fdn., Rockville, 3/120

Gutman Family Fdn., Baltimore, 3/121

Hack (Frank Newcomer) Memorial Hospital Trust, Baltimore, 3/122

Hoover (Halstead Pierce) Trust Equity, D.C., 3/122

Hammerman (S.L.) Fdn., Baltimore, 3/123

Health Services Research Fdn., Baltimore, 3/123

Hechinger (Sidney L.) Fdn., D.C., 3/124

Heckman (Jacob) Fdn., D.C., 3/125

Henley & Smith, Drs. Memorial Fund Trust, D.C., 3/126

Higginson (Corina) Trust, D.C., 3/127

Hilliard Custis Hospital Fund Trust, D.C., 3/129

Hirsch (Robert & Rosalyn) Fdn., D.C., 3/130

Hochschild, Kohn & Company Fdn., Baltimore, 3/131

Holt (Lawrence S.) Trust, D.C., 3/132

Holy Trinity Parish P.E. Church Trust, Baltimore, 3/133

Hunter (Anna Mae) Fdn., Baltimore, 3/133

Hurt (H.A.) Peoples Relief Fund, D.C., 3/134

Hutzler (Albert D. & Gretchen H.) Fdn., Baltimore, 3/135

Institute for International Social Research Formerly New Jersey, Chevy Chase, 3/135

Inter-American Institute of International Legal Studies, D.C., 3/136

Island Fdn., Baltimore, 3/137

Jacobson (Stanley Gene) Memorial Scholarship, Baltimore, 3/137

Jacobsson (Per) Fdn., D.C., 3/138

Jelleff (Frank R.) Charitable Trust, D.C., 3/139

Jett (Martha A.) Trust, D.C., 3/140

J. K. T. Fdn., D.C., 3/140

Kahn Fdn., Baltimore, 3/141

Kairys (Julia & Bernard) Fdn., Baltimore, 3/141

Kasson (John A.) Trust, D.C., 3/142

Kaufmann (Edmund I. & Lillian S.) Fdn., D.C., 3/143

Kay Associated Stores Fdn., D.C., 3/144

Keelty Fdn., Timonium, 3/144

Kiwanis Fdn. of D.C., D.C., 3/145

Kleinman Fdn., Baltimore, 3/145

Klopman (Sidney) Memorial Fdn., Baltimore, 3/146

Krooth Fund, D.C., 3/146

Lamoine Fdn., Santa Barbara, Cal., 3/147

Page (Florence Lathrop) Trust, D.C., 3/147

Lawrence (M.J.) Memorial Endowment Fund Trust, D.C., 3/148

Lawson Charitable Fdn., Bethesda, 3/148

Lawyer's Committee for Civil Rights Under Law, D.C., 3/149

Leaderman Fdn., Brooklandville, 3/151

Leakin (Susan D.) Trust, Baltimore, 3/151

Lee (Jabez) Scholarship Fund Trust, D.C., 3/152

Lending Hand, Inc., Baltimore, 3/152

Leonard Family Fdn., Chevy Chase, 3/153

Levy (M.S.) Trust, Baltimore, 3/153

Lewis (Lt. Earl) Memorial Fund for Advanced Police Training, Elkton, 3/153

Loats Female Orphan Asylum of Frederick City, Frederick, 3/153

Loudon County Hospital Trust, Baltimore, 3/154

Lucas (Anthony Francis) Fdn., D.C., 3/154

Macht (Morton & Sophia) Fdn., Baltimore, 3/155

Maloney (Charles P. & Eleanore) Fdn., Bethesda, 3/156

Mangan (Alma V.) Trust, Baltimore, 3/156

Markell (Ida M.) Trust, D.C., 3/157

Marks Fdn., Baltimore, 3/157

Marshall (James D.) Memorial Fund, D.C., 3/157

Maryland Pharmaceutical Fdn., Baltimore, 3/158

Maryland Shipbuilding & Drydock Fdn., Baltimore, 3/158

Mason Fdn., Newark, 3/158

McCarthy - Hicks Fdn., Timonium, 3/159

McGregor (Thomas & Frances) Fdn., D.C., 3/160

Medical Library Fdn., D.C., 3/160

Merkle (Edgar & Kathleen) Fdn., D.C., 3/160

Merowitz (Isaac & Lena) Fdn., Baltimore, 3/161

Metcalf (William P.) Trust, D.C., 3/162

Meyerhoff (Jack & Beatrice) Fund, Baltimore, 3/162

Meyerhoff (Joseph) Fund, Baltimore, 3/164

Michi Kawai Christian Fellowship, Inc., D.C., 3/167

Miller (Eli & Yetta) Fdn., Baltimore, 3/167

Anson Mills Fdn., D.C., 3/167

Moore (George W.) Trust, D.C., 3/168

Mortgage Opportunities, Inc., D.C., 3/169

Consaul (Fannie Moyers) Trust, D.C., 3/169

Mueller (Helen K. & Nicholas C.) Fdn., Baltimore, 3/170

Myerberg (N.J.) Fdn., Baltimore, 3/170

N A H B Scholarship Fdn., D.C., 3/171

National Committee on Household Employment, D.C., 3/172

National Conference of State Societies Charity Fund, D.C., 3/172

National Council on Hunger & Malnutrition in the U.S., D.C., 3/172

National Society for Prevention of Blindness, D.C., 3/173

National Symphony Orchestra Endowment Fund Trust, D.C., 3/173

National Tenants Information Service, D.C., 3/174

Oliver (Henry W.) Fdn., D.C., 3/175

Mitchell (Oscar L.) Trust, D.C., 3/176

Ottenstein (Joseph) Fdn., Cottage City, 3/176

Owens (William F. & Catherine) Fdn., Baltimore, 3/177

Palmer (Gordon) Christian Patriotism Broadcase, D.C., 3/177

Pangborn (Thomas W.) Residue Trust, Baltimore, 3/178

Patterson Memorial Association, Baltimore, 3/178

Perdue (Arthur W.) Fdn., Salisbury, 3/178

P H H Fdn., Baltimore, 3/179

Phi Delta Theta Fraternity, Westminster, 3/181

Pillsbury - McKee Fdn., Annapolis, 3/181

Poor of Manassas Trust, D.C., 3/181

Popick (Nat & Ethel) Fdn., D.C., 3/182

Potomac Fdn., D.C., 3/182

Potomac Institute, D.C., 3/183

Public Safety Research Institute, D.C., 3/184

Rainey (A. Sarah) Trust, D.C., 3/185

Raleigh Stores Fdn., D.C., 3/185

Religious Heritage Trust, D.C., 3/186

Rentaw Fdn., Baltimore, 3/187

Roffman Fdn., D.C., 3/187

Roberts (Bertha M.) Trust, D.C., 3/188

Rohrbeck Fund, D.C., 3/188

Rose (Charles) Fdn., D.C., 3/189

Rosen (Fannie) Fdn., Baltimore, 3/190

Rosen (I.S. & E.B.) Fdn., Baltimore, 3/191
Rosen (Julius J.) Fdn., Baltimore, 3/191
Ross (Walter G.) Fdn., D.C., 3/192
Rouse Company Fdn., Columbia, 3/193
Rubin Family Fdn., D.C., 3/194
Rubin (Nathan & Herman) Fdn., Baltimore, 3/194
Russell (Frank C.) Fdn., Chestertown, 3/194
Safety Systems Fdn., D.C., 3/195
Sahm (William) Fdn., D.C., 3/196
St. Alban's Parish Fund Trust, D.C., 3/196
Trust for St. Mary's Altar Guild of Grace & St. Peter's Church, Baltimore, 3/197
St. Mary Anne's Trust, Baltimore, 3/197
Trustees of the Salisbury Award, Salisbury, 3/197
Schenuit (Frank G.) Fdn., Baltimore, 3/197
Schoenfeld (John S.R. & Florence H.) Fdn., D.C., 3/198
Seiss (Margaret E.) Trust, D.C., 3/198
Shalom et Benedictus, Hancock, 3/198
Shapiro (Ida & Joseph) Fdn., Owings Mills, 3/199
Shavitz (Leon & Minna) Fdn., Baltimore, 3/200
Shine - Lazarus Fdn., Beltsville, 3/201
Shoemaker (Elizabeth R.) Home, D.C., 3/202
Sigma Delta Chi Fdn., D.C., 3/203
Sindler Family Fdn., Baltimore, 3/203
Slavin (Benjamin & Barbara) Fdn., D.C., 3/204
Slavin (Sanford & Doris) Fdn., D.C., 3/204
Society of the Cincinnati of Maryland, Baltimore, 3/205
Rosenbloom (Solomon & Anna) Fdn., Baltimore, 3/206
Sotterley Mansion Fdn., Hollywood, 3/207
Speert Fdn., Baltimore, 3/208
Stead (Mary Force) Playground Trust, D.C., 3/208
Steinberg (Bernard) Fdn., Bethesda, 3/209
Steinmann (Karl F. & Geraldine Y.) Fdn., Baltimore, 3/209
Stempler (Oscar & Lillian) Fdn., D.C., 3/210
Stern (Philip M.) Family Fund, D.C., 3/211
Stewart (Alexander & Margaret) Trust, D.C., 3/213
Storch Fdn., Baltimore, 3/215
Suffridge (James A.) - Retail Clerks International Association Scholarship Trust, D.C., 3/215
Sullivan (Patrick Henry) Trust, D.C., 3/216
Sweitzer (Charles McG.) School Trust, D.C., 3/217
Talbot Civic Trust, Easton, 3/217
Tauber Fdn., Bethesda, 3/217
Thompson (Arthur Lee), III Memorial Fdn., D.C., 3/218
Thompson (Robert M.) Prize Fund, D.C., 3/219
Thorpe (Merle), Jr. Fdn., D.C., 3/219
Transportation Research Fdn., D.C., 3/220
Trigg (Ernest T.) Fdn., D.C., 3/221
Anthony (Sarah Frances) Trust, Baltimore, 3/222
Ashland Presbyterian Church Trust, Baltimore, 3/222
Bethany Methodist Church Trust, Baltimore, 3/222
Bowie (Lucy Leigh) Trust, Baltimore, 3/222
Bowles (Louise O.) Trusts, Baltimore, 3/222
Brinsfield (Zoro) Trust, Baltimore, 3/223
Trust f/b/o Corpus Christi Church, Baltimore, 3/223
Dent (B. Gwynn & Opie T.) Memorial Fund Trust, D.C., 4/001
Fite (Kitty G.) Trust, Baltimore, 4/001
Linthicum (Edgar S.) Trusts, Baltimore, 4/001
Trust f/b/o Rector of Holy Trinity Church, Carroll County, Baltimore, 4/002
Trust f/b/o Roman Catholic Archbishop of Baltimore, Baltimore, 4/002
Slagle (Josephine) Trust f/b/o Grace & St. Peter's P.E. Church, Baltimore, 4/002
Smith (Helen T.) Trust, Baltimore, 4/002

Trust f/b/o Union Memorial Hospital, Baltimore, 4/002
Unger (Aber D.) Fdn., Baltimore, 4/003
Bowles (Louise C.) Trust f/b/o Union Memorial Hospital, Baltimore, 4/004
Trust for the Vestry of Emmanuel Church, Baltimore, Baltimore, 4/004
Vinnick (Milton) Fdn. for College Education, D.C., 4/004
Volta Bureau Fund Trust, D.C., 4/005
Walden (Augusta) Trust, Baltimore, 4/006
Walden (Erle D.) Trust, Baltimore, 4/006
Warren Memorial Fdn., D.C., 4/006
Washington Area Business Service, Inc., D.C., 4/006
Washington Home, Inc. Ice Cream Fdn. Trust, D.C., 4/007
Washington Home for Incurables Endowment Fund Trust, D.C., 4/007
Washington Home, Inc. Perry Fund Trust, D.C., 4/009
Washington Society for the Blind, D.C., 4/010
Weinberg (Harry & Jeannette) Fdn., Baltimore, 4/011
Weinberg (Louis) Fdn., Baltimore, 4/011
Eaton Fund Trust, Baltimore, 4/012
Whiteford (Robert L.) Memorial, Baltimore, 4/012
Widtsoe (John A.) Education Fdn., D.C., 4/012
Williams (Rufus M.G.) Fdn., Baltimore, 4/012
Winer (Sol & Sadie) Fdn., D.C., 4/013
Winslow Fdn., D.C., 4/014
Woodward Fdn., D.C., 4/015
Wright Brothers Memorial Trophy Fund Trust, D.C., 4/016
Wright (May B.) Trust, D.C., 4/017
Wye Institute, Queenstown, 4/017

MASSACHUSETTS

First Filming

Aaron Fdn., Longmeadow, 1/001
Abramowitz Family Fdn., Boston, 1/001
Acorn Charitable Trust, Brookline, 1/002
Adams Charitable Trust, West Newton, 1/002
Adams (C.F.), Jr. Fdn., Boston, 1/002
Agoos (Lassor and Fanny) Charity Fund, Boston, 1/003
Alecks Fdn., Dorchester, 1/004
Allen (Anne & Philip) Trust, Boston, 1/004
Almy (Helen Cabot) Fund, Cambridge, 1/005
Amdur Leather Associates Fdn., Woburn, 1/005
American Group Charitable Trust, Worcester, 1/006
American Bilrite Rubber Charitable Trust, Cambridge, 1/006
American Optical Fdn., Worcester, 1/007
American Pad & Paper Co. Charitable Trust, Holyoke, 1/008
Ames Fdn., Cambridge, 1/009
Ames Free Library Trust, Boston, 1/009
Ames (Chaterine Hobart) Scholarship, Boston, 1/010
Ames (Avis G.) Trust, Boston, 1/010
Anapol Fdn. Inc., Fall River, 1/011
Ansion Fdn., Lowell, 1/011
Anthony Advocate Fdn., Newton Centre, 1/012
Anthony-Arthur Fdn., Shrewsbury, 1/013
Antonelli (L.) Fdn., Quincy, 1/013
Apsley (Lewis Dewart) Fund for Aged, Boston, 1/013
Arakelian (Mary Alice) Fdn., Boston, 1/014
Armstrong Fdn., Boston, 1/015
Armstrong (John C.) Charitable Fdn., Milton, 1/015
Armstrong (Robert W.), Jr. Charitable Fdn., Worcester, 1/015
Arnold (Robert T.) Scholarship Fund, Pittsfield, 1/016

Arnold (Ethel Arow) Charitable Fund, Boston, 1/016
Ashworth (Arthur) Declaration Trust, Boston, 1/017
Asher Rdn., Fitchburg, 1/017
Association for the Relief of Aged, New Bedford, 1/018
Athassell Fdn., Watertown, 1/019
Atlantic Crossing Trust, Boston, 1/019
Auerbach Charitable Fdn., Boston, 1/020
August (Ann) Fdn., Northampton, 1/020
Aransky (David A.) Charitable Fdn., Boston, 1/021
Avon Home, Cambridge, 1/021
Babson (Paul & Edith) Fdn., Boston, 1/022
Babson (Grace Knight) Fund, Wellesley, 1/024
Babson (Isabel) Memorial, Gloucester, 1/025
Babson Webber-Mustard Fund, Wellesley, 1/025
Bach (Dudley) Charitable Trust, Boston, 1/026
Bacon (Ada B.W.) Trust u/w, Boston, 1/027
Baer (Claudia) Charitable Trust, Weston, 1/027
Bailey (Frederick A.) Charitable Trust, Boston, 1/028
Baker (Frances D.) Charitable Trust, Worcester, 1/029
Baker (M.E.) Charitable Fdn., Boston, 1/029
Baldwin Charitable Fdn., Boston, 1/029
Banks Charitable Fdn., Brookline, 1/030
Bannon (John F.) Fdn., Mansfield, 1/030
Bannon (William H.) Fdn., Mansfield, 1/031
Barnard (Frances Merry) Home, Hyde Park, 1/032
Baruch (Jordan J.) Fdn., Newton Centre, 1/032
Bass (Harry A.) Charity Fdn., Brookline, 1/033
Batcheller (Hugh W.) Family Fdn., Newton Highland, 1/033
Bauer Scientific Trust, Lynn, 1/034
Bay State Charitable Trust, Boston, 1/034
Bay State Rugby Football Fdn., Boston, 1/035
Bayrd (Adelaide Breed) Fdn., Boston, 1/035
Beaman Fdn., Boston, 1/036
Beard Family Charitable Trust, Boston, 1/037
Beebe (Frank Huntington) Fund for Musicians, Boston, 1/037
Benedict-Scholastica Society, West Springfield, 1/037
Benedict Scholarship, Boston, 1/038
Benedict Charitable Trust, Boston, 1/038
Berenson (Theodore W.) Charitable Fdn., Boston, 1/039
Berger Charitable Fdn., Brookline, 1/039
Berkowitz (Jean S. & Abram) Fdn., Boston, 1/040
Bernays (Edward L.) Fdn., Cambridge, 1/041
Berner (Robert & Hilda) Fdn., Brookline, 1/042
Best (Richard L.) Fdn., Wayland, 1/042
Berwick Boys Fdn. Development Trust Fund, West Bridgewater, 1/042
Beveridge (Frank Stanley) Fdn., Westfield, 1/043
Binney Fdn., Boston, 1/044
Binney (Elizabeth Peters) Charitable Fdn., Boston, 1/045
Bird (Adriel U.) Fdn., Boston, 1/046
Birmingham Fdn., Boston, 1/046
Bishins (Harold & Ericka) Family Fdn., Boston, 1/047
Blanchard (Henry Lawton) Fund, Brockton, 1/047
Blanchard Fdn., Boston, 1/047
Bloom (Inez & Joseph) Fdn., Newton, 1/049
Bloomberg Family Charitable Trust, Chelsea, 1/049
Blout (Elkan R.) Fdn., Boston, 1/050
Blundon Fdn., Boston, 1/051
Blythswood Charitable Trust, Winchester, 1/052
Bolt (Richard H.) Fdn., Cambridge, 1/053
Bolten (John) Charitable Fdn., Andover, 1/053
Booth Family Fdn., Beverly, 1/054
Boruchoff Mausoleum Trust, Boston, 1/054
Boston Druggists Association, Boston, 1/055

Boston Biophysics Research Fdn., Boston, 1/055

Boston City Hospital Social Service Fund, Boston, 1/055

Boutin (Rev.) Brothers Trust, Gardner, 1/056

Bowser (Richard L. & Lucille) Charitable Trust, Boston, 1/056

Boyer (Irving W. & Nellie R.) Fdn., Boston, 1/057

Boynton (John W.) Fund, Boston, 1/057

Boys Club Fdn. of Boston, Boston, 1/058

Bradlee 1959 Trust, Boston, 1/059

Braitmayer Fdn., Marion, 1/060

Brandegee Charitable Fdn., Boston, 1/061

Breck (Edward J.) Fdn., Springfield, 1/061

Breck (M. Constance) Fdn., Springfield, 1/062

Breed (M.E.L.) Fdn., Boston, 1/063

Bremner (Harriet & Herbert) Fdn., Brookline, 1/065

Brentano (Franz) Fdn., Boston, 1/065

Brezner (Nathan & Eva) Charitable Fdn., Brookline, 1/067

Bright (A.H.) Charitable Trust, Boston, 1/067

Bright (Horace O.) Charitable Fund, Boston, 1/068

Baiting Brook Charitable Trust, Framingham, 1/070

Brooks (J. Loring) Fdn., Springfield, 1/070

Brown Charitable Trust, Boston, 1/070

Brown (J. Frederick) Fdn., Boston, 1/071

Buckley (James B.) Family Charitable Trust, Fairhaven, 1/072

Buckner Family Fdn., Worcester, 1/073

Burke Fdn., Boston, 1/073

Burliss (Peter C.) Memorial Charitable Fdn., Chelmsford, 1/074

Buros Fdn., Boston, 1/074

Burroughs Family Fdn., Belmont, 1/075

Butchen (Charles) Fdn., Boston, 1/075

Buxton Fdn., Springfield, 1/075

B-W Charity Fund, Cambridge, 1/076

Byrd (The Admiral Richard E.) Fdn., Boston, 1/077

Cabot (Godfrey L.) Charitable, Boston, 1/077

Cabot-Saltonstall Charitable Trust, Boston, 1/078

Cabot (Ella Lyman) Trust Inc., Boston, 1/078

Calderwood Charitable Fdn., Boston, 1/079

Calvert Trust, Boston, 1/080

Cambridge Center for Social Sciences, Cambridge, 1/080

Cambridge Legal Services Inc., Cambridge, 1/081

Campanelli Family Fdn., South Braintree, 1/081

Capezio Fdn., Medford, 1/081

Candib (Murry A.) Family Fdn., Worcester, 1/082

Carder (Mort A.) Trust u/w, Boston, 1/082

Carlisle Conservation Fdn., Carlisle, 1/082

Carman Family Charitable Fdn., Springfield, 1/082

Carr (Hattie L.) Testamentary Trust, Brookline, 1/082

Carter (Eliot A.) Fdn., Boston, 1/083

Cary (Isaac Harris) Educational Fund, Lexington, 1/083

Casavant Family Charitable Trust, Worcester, 1/084

Casty (David & Libby) Charitable Trust, Brighton, 1/084

Casty & Associates Charitable Fdn., Brighton, 1/085

Cataldo (Wassimino) Fund, Jamaica Plain, 1/085

Cemetery Trust Fund, Boston, 1/085

Channing Home, Boston, 1/086

Chapelbrook Fdn., Boston, 1/087

Chapin (Homer N.) Fdn., Wilbraham, 1/087

Chapman (Leonard Boyd) Wildbird Sanctuary, Boston, 1/088

Charlotte Home, North Andover, 1/088

Chase (John P.) Fdn., Boston, 1/089

Chase (Alice P.) Charity Fdn., Boston, 1/089

Childs Park Fdn., Inc., Northampton, 1/091

Christian Charitable Trust, Watertown, 1/092

Claff Charitable Fdn., Brockton, 1/092

Clark (Forrester) Fdn., Boston, 1/093

Clyde Fdn., Boston, 1/093

Clyde Park Charitable Fdn., Brookline, 1/094

Coburn Charitable Society, Inc., Boston, 1/094

Cocaine (Christo & Mary) Charitable Fdn., Worcester, 1/095

Coffin (Bruce & Madeleine) Charitable Fdn., Marblehead, 1/095

Coffman (Max & Ann) Fdn., West Bridgewater, 1/096

Cohen (Abraham & Tillie) Family Fdn., Cambridge, 1/097

Cohen (Albert A. & Lillian) Family Fdn., Boston, 1/097

Cohen (Diana) Fdn., Chestnut Hill, 1/098

Cohen (Eli & Bessie) Fdn., Slonehun, 1/098

Cohn (Ollie A. & Eleanore) Family Fdn., Worcester, 1/099

Cohen (Herman B. & Jack O.) Fdn., Boston, 1/099

Colby Charitable Fdn., Wellesley Hills, 1/100

Colm (Blanche E.) Trust u/w, Boston, 1/101

Colgan (James W.) Trust, Palmer, 1/103

Colonial Charitable Fdn., Boston, 1/105

Colonial Provision Fdn., Boston, 1/105

Community Charitable Fdn., Boston, 1/106

Conat Charitable Trust, Boston, 1/107

Consiglio (Louis & Mary) Fdn., Springfield, 1/107

Consultek Charitable Fdn., Boston, 1/108

Cook Charitable Trust, Leominster, 1/108

Copper Range Fdn., Boston, 1/109

Corman (Louis) Charitable Fdn., Chelsea, 1/109

Cox Fdn., Inc., Boston, 1/109

Crane & Co. Fund, Dalton, 1/110

Crane (Zenas) Fund for Student Aid, Inc., Dalton, 1/110

Crapo (Henry H.) Charitable Fdn., New Bedford, 1/111

Creighton Family Fdn. Trust, Boston, 1/112

Crocker (Douglas & Isabelle) Fdn., Fitchburg, 1/113

Crompton & Knowles Fdn., Inc., Worcester, 1/113

Cross Student Fdn., Lunenburgh, 1/114

Cutler (Myer & Lucille) Fdn., Chestnut Hill, 1/114

Damon Charitable Fdn., Inc., Needham, 1/115

Dana Home of Lexington, Inc., Lexington, 1/116

Davenport (Horace E.) Fdn., Swampscott, 1/117

David (Nathan & Minnie J.) Memorial Fdn., Brookline, 1/119

Dean Fdn. for Little Children, Boston, 1/120

Dean Welfare Trust, Boston, 1/121

Deane (Wallace H.) Trust, Springfield, 1/123

Dedham Country Day School Teachers Trust, Boston, 1/123

Dedham Temporary Home for Women & Children, Boston, 1/123

Delphic Fdn., Boston, 1/124

Demoulas Fdn., Chelmsford, 1/124

Dennis Family Fdn., Boston, 1/125

Dennison Fdn., Framingham, 1/125

Devonshire Associates, Boston, 1/126

Dewey (Laura Stratton) Fdn., Lincoln, 1/126

Dewing (Frances R.) Fdn., Cambridge, 1/127

Dexter (Eugene A.) Charitable Fund, Springfield, 1/127

Dietrich Charitable Fdn., Boston, 1/128

Digregorid (Fileno) Fdn., Worcester, 1/129

Dirlam-Morris Charitable, Worcester, 1/129

Dockser (Charles E.) Charitable Fdn., Chestnut Hill, 1/129

Dolliver Fund for Poor & Deserving Persons at Gloucester, Mass., Gloucester, 1/130

Dover Historical & Natural History Society of Dover & Vicinity, Boston, 1/131

Dowd (Harry J.) Charitable Fdn., Cambridge, 1/132

Doyle Charitable Fdn., Boston, 1/132

Droper Charitable Fdn., Boston, 1/133

Drury Square Charitable Fdn., Auburn, 1/134

Dunbar Community Center in Springfield, Springfield, 1/134

Eagle-Tribune Santa Claus Trust, Lawrence, 1/135

Eastman Charitable Fdn., Boston, 1/137

Eaton Fdn., Inc., Boston, 1/137

Eaton Fdn., Boston, 1/139

E D S Fund, Weston, 1/139

Edelstein (Dr. Israel & Edith Putnam) Fdn., Quincy, 1/140

Edgerton (Harold E.) Fdn., Boston, 1/141

Edwards (Teresa Pastene) Fund, Boston, 1/141

Ehrlich (Harold L.) Charitable Fdn., Newton, 1/142

Eiseman (Marion & Philip) Fund, Boston, 1/142

Elion Fdn., Sherborn, 1/142

Elion (Maurice & Eunice) Fdn., Springfield, 1/142

Ellis (Mary G.) Fdn., Boston, 1/142

Ellsworth (Ruth H. & Warren A.) Fdn., Worcester, 1/143

Ember Fdn., Lexington, 1/143

Emerson (Ralph Waldo) Memorial Association, Boston, 1/144

Emerson (George) Trust, Boston, 1/144

Epstein (Rubin & Ethel) Fdn., Chestnut, 1/145

Esdaile (J. Newton) Charitable Trust, Boston, 1/146

Evans (Wilmot Roby) Corporation, Boston, 1/147

Evergreen Cemetery Association, Stoughton, 1/147

Falk (Myron P.) Charitable Trust, Leominster, 1/148

Faneuil (Ben & Charlotte) Charitable Fdn., Newton, 1/150

Farber Charitable Trust, Worcester, 1/150

Farnham Fdn., Carlisle, 1/150

Federal Street Fdn., Boston, 1/150

Feldberg Family Fdn., framingham, 1/151

Feldberg Family Charitable Trust, Worcester, 1/151

Feldman Family Charitable Trust, Worcester, 1/151

Fellows Fdn., Boston, 1/152

Fermon Charitable Fdn., Peabody, 1/152

Feyling Fdn., Belmont, 1/153

Fidgit Fdn., Boston, 1/153

Filene Charitable Fdn., Boston, 1/155

Filene (Edward A.) Goodwill Fund, Inc., Lynn, 1/156

Filene (Lincoln & Therese) Fdn., Inc., Boston, 1/156

Fine (Phil & Norma) Charitable Trust, Boston, 1/157

First Boston Fdn. Trust, Boston, 1/158

First Bank & Trust Company of Hampden County Charitable Donations Plan, Holyoke, 1/159

Fisher (Herman G. & Suzanne G.) Fdn., Boston, 1/160

Fitchburgh High School Class of 1879, Worcester, 1/160

Fitzgerald Chritable Fdn., Cohasset, 1/161

Forbes (Edith H.) Trust, Boston, 1/161

Forte (Orville W.) Charitable Fdn., Inc., Boston, 1/162

Foster Charitable Trust, Boston, 1/163

Foster Fdn. of Leominster, Leominster, 1/164

Foster (Joseph & Esther) Fdn., Leominster, 1/166

Foundation for Clinical Research, Boston, 1/166

Foundation for Education & Social Development, Boston, 1/167

Foundation for Housing Innovation, Inc., Boston, 1/168

Fox Club Endowment Fund, Boston, 1/168

Felix Fox Memorial Fund, Brookline, 1/169

Fox (J. John) Charitable Fdn., Allston, 1/170

Fox (Louis B.) Fdn., Swampscott, 1/171

Foxboro Company Fdn., Boston, 1/172

Freeman (Arthur M.) Charitable Trust, Norton, 1/172

French (Henry W.) Testamentary Trust, Boston, 1/195
District Nursing Association, Boston, 1/175
French Fdn., Boston, 1/176
French (Henry W.) Testamentary Trust, French (Susan E.) Scholarship, Boston, 1/177
French (Henry W.) Testamentary Trust, Parish Hall Association, Boston, 1/178
Friends of the French Protestant Library, Boston, 1/179
Fuller Fdn., Inc., Boston, 1/179
Fuller (George F. & Sybil H.) Fdn., Worcester, 1/180
Fuller Trust, Boston, 1/180
Fusaro Charitable Fdn., Worcester, 1/182
Gadsby (Dr. H.H.) Scholarship Fund of Drury High School, Pittsfield, 1/183
Gallagher (Paul) Trust, Peabody, 1/184
Gannon-Burke Charitable Trust, Boston, 1/185
Garelick (Daniel) Educational Trust, Boston, 1/186
Gardiner Shoe Co. Charity Trust, Boston, 1/186
Gasbarri (Fiorangelo) Trust u/w, Boston, 1/186
Gass (Samuel A.) & Carol Gass Fdn., Inc., Lowell, 1/187
Gates (Lester J.) Memorial Fund, No. Scitvate, Ma., 1/187
Geilich Charitable Fdn., Taunton, 1/188
Gens Charitable Trust, Newton, 1/188
Germeshausen (Kenneth J.) Fdn., Boston, 1/189
Gerondelis Fdn., Lynn, 1/189
Gerrity (Frank) Fdn. Trust, Boston, 1/190
Gerrity (Joe E.), Jr. Fdn., Boston, 1/191
Gifford (A. McK.) Student Loan & Scholarship Fund, Pittsfield, 1/192
Gifford (Albert J.) Charitable Trust, Worcester, 1/192
Gilbert (Horace D.) Fdn., Boston, 1/193
Gillett Charitable & Educational Fdn., Boston, 1/193
Ginn and Company Educational Fdn., Boston, 1/195
Gloucester Charitable Trust, Boston, 1/196
Glaziers Local #1044 Health & Welfare Fund, Boston, 1/196
Glick (Allen M.) Fdn., Framingham, 1/196
Glick Bros. Charitable Trust, Chelsea, 1/197
Gnotobiotic Research Fdn., Inc., N. Wilmington, 1/197
Goldberg (Merton & Edna J.) Charitable Fdn., Boston, 1/197
Goldenberg Fdn., Brighton, 1/197
Goldman (Robert H. & Janet) Charitable Trust, Worcester, 1/198
Goldrosen (David) Fdn., W. Boylston, 1/198
Goldrosen (Louis I.) Charitable Fdn., Worcester, 1/198
Goldston Family Fdn., Cleveland, Ohio, Boston, 1/199
Goode Family Charity Fund, Boston, 1/199
Goodman (Arnold G.) Family Fdn., Boston, 1/200
Goodman (Herbert M. & Phyllis R.) Charitable Trust, Worcester, 1/200
Goodman (Abraham & Etta) Fdn., Boston, 1/201
Goodrich Charitable Trust, Boston, 1/202
Goodwin (Mary B.) Trust, Springfield, 1/202
Gordon (Sarah A.) Charitable Trust, Boston, 1/203
Gordon (Albert I.) Family Charitable Trust, Boston, 1/203
Gordon (Selma & Louis M.) Charitable Trust, Boston, 1/203
Gordon (Barnett D.) Family Fdn., Chestnut Hill, 1/204
Gordon (Louis W.) Charitable Trust, Boston, 1/205
Gordon (Abraham L. & Mary S.) Family Charitable Fdn., Brookline, 1/205
Gordon (Sara R.) Heart Trust, Boston, 1/206
Gorin (Beryl David) Fdn., Boston, 1/206

Gornstein (Henry & Doris) Fdn., West Bridgewater, 1/206
Goulo (Morris & Lillian P.) Family Fdn., Northampton, 1/207
Gould (David F. & Sarah) Charitable Trust, Worcester, 1/208
Gowell (David & Harriet) Fdn., Marblehead, 1/208
Gross Charity Trust, Boston, 1/208
Grass Fdn., Boston, 1/208
Dewing Greek Numismatic Fdn., Cambridge, 1/210
Greenberg (Nathan & Mimi) Charitable Trust, Worcester, 1/211
Greenewalt (David) Charitable Trust, Boston, 1/212
Greenfield Library Association, Greenfield, 1/213
Greenfield Whitman Fdn., Whitman, 1/213
Greenough Fdn., Boston, 1/213
Green Shoe Stride Rite Charitable Fdn., Inc., Boston, 1/214
Greylock Fdn., Williamstown, 1/214
Griffith (Major Thomas B.) Fund, Middleboro, 1/216
Groman (Pesach & Trina) Family Fdn., East Boston, 1/216
Grosberg Family Charity Fund, Inc., Boston, 1/217
Grosberg Family Charity u/w/o Oscar Grosberg, Boston, 1/218
Gross (H.K.) Family Charitable Trust, Boston, 1/218
Groton Place, Boston, 1/219
Grunebaum Fdn., Peabody, 1/220
Gryzmish (Florence L. & Mortimer C.) Fdn., Boston, 1/220
Guaranty Fdn., Worcester, 1/221
Guillow (Gertrude H.) Fdn., Lynnfield, 1/221
Gummere (Francis B.) Charitable, Boston, 1/221
Gummo (Grace) Fund, Worcester, 1/221
Gurwitz Family Charitable Trust, Worcester, 1/222
Haffenreffer Benevolent Col, Boston, 1/223
Hale Memorial, Newburyport, 1/223
Hale (James W.) Trust u/w, f/b/o the deserving poor people of the city of Springfield, Springfield, 1/224
Hallowell (Richard P. 2nd) Fdn., Boston, 1/224
Hamilburg (Joseph H.) Fdn., Canton, 1/225
Hamilton (Sabra M.) Fdn., South Duxbury, 1/226
Hammon (Edmond E. & Bethea M.) Fdn., Boston, 1/227
Hammond (Thomas West) Fdn., Boston, 1/227
Hampden Glazed Paper & Card Co. Charitable Trust, Holyoke, 1/228
Hankins (Philip & Barbara) Charitable Trust, Boston, 1/228
Harley Street Fdn., Boston, 1/229
Harold (Raymond P.) Fdn., Worcester, 1/229
Harrington (Francis A.) Fdn., Worcester, 1/230
Harrington (Frank C.) Fdn., Worcester, 1/231
Harris (William H.) Fdn., Boston, 1/231
Harrower (Norman) Charitable Trust, Worcester, 1/232
Hartwell (Benjamin Hall) Testamentary Fund, Shirley, 1/233
Harvard Glee Club Fdn., Cambridge, 1/233
Haste (Peter J.) Fdn., New Bedford, 1/234
Haven Trust, Boston, 1/235
Haven (Charles B.) Home for Aged Men, Peabody, 1/235
Hayden (Josiah Willard) Recreation Center, Lexington, 1/236
Hayden (Josiah Willard) Recreation Center, Lexington, 2/001
Hayes (Eleanor) Fdn., Longmeadow, 2/001
Heald Machine Co. Fdn., Worcester, 2/003
Heald Fdn., Worcester, 2/004
Heald (Richard A.) Charitable Trust, Worcester, 2/004
Heald (Richard A.) Fund, Worcester, 2/005

Heald (Robert S.) Charitable Trust, Worcester, 2/005
Heart Research Fdn., Boston, 2/006
Heit (Jonas B.) Fdn., West Springfield, 2/006
Henderson Fdn., Wellesley Hills, 2/007
Hennessey (Walter R. & Helen P.) Charitable Fdn., Norwell, 2/008
Heritage Fdn., Old Deerfield, 2/009
Heritage Plantation of Sandwich, Sandwich, 2/012
Herman (Joseph H.) Trust Fund, West Newton, 2/012
Heydt (Nan & Matildo) Fund, Springfield, 2/012
Hiatt (Arnold & Anne) Fdn., Weston, 2/013
Higgins (Bradley C.) Fdn., Worcester, 2/014
Higgins (John Woodman) Armory, Worcester, 2/014
Higgins (John W. & Clara C.) Fdn., orcester, 2/015
Hinkle (James G.) Trust DTD 10/17/55, Boston, 2/016
Hoagland (Hudson & Anna P.) Charitable Trust, Worcester, 2/016
Hodgkinson (Harold D.) Charity Fdn., Boston, 2/017
Hoffman (Abraham J.) Fdn., Boston, 2/017
Hoffman (Max) Fdn., Boston, 2/018
Hofford (Ray) Memorial Library, Boston, 2/019
Holyoke Transcript Fdn., Holyoke, 2/020
Home for Aged People in Winchester, Winchester, 2/020
Hood (Charles H.) Dairy Fdn., Boston, 2/021
Hood (Charles H.) Educational & Charitable Trust, Boston, 2/023
Hood (Harvey P. & Charles H.) Educational Trust, Boston, 2/024
Hope Publications Fdn., Boston, 2/024
Hornblower (Henry) Fund, Boston, 2/024
Houghton (Henry D.) Charitable Trust, Cambridge, 2/025
Housen (Morris) Fdn., Erving, 2/026
Hoyt Fdn., Boston, 2/026
Hubbard (Ralph K.) Fdn., Worcester, 2/026
Huberman (Peter) Fdn., Wellesley Hill, 2/027
Hughes Family Fdn., Worcester, 2/028
Hunter Family Charitable Trust, Boston, 2/028
Hurdle Hill Fdn., Boston, 2/029
Hurley (Donald J.) Fdn., Boston, 2/030
Hurtig Charitable Trust, Boston, 2/031
Hyams (Godfrey M.) Trust, Boston, 2/032
Hyams (Isabel F.) Fund, Boston, 2/034
Hyams (Sarah A.) Fund, Boston, 2/035
Hyam (Mark) Fund, Boston, 2/036
Independence Fdn., Boston, 2/037
Information Sciences Fdn. of New England, Lexington, 2/038
Ipswich Historical Society, Ipswich, 2/039
Jacobs (William H. & Ruth) Family Fdn., Chestnut Hill, 2/039
Jaffe (Edwin & Lola) Fdn., Fall River, 2/040
Jaffe (Samuel & Frieda) Charity Fdn., Lynn, 2/041
Jampart Charitable Trust, Boston, 2/042
Jenks Charitable Fdn., Boston, 2/043
Jenks (James L.), Jr. Fdn., Winchester, 2/043
Jeppson Memorial Fund, Worcester, 2/044
Jewett (George frederick) Fdn., Boston, 2/045
Jewish Family Society of Chelsea, Chelsea, 2/047
Jingo Fdn., Boston, 2/048
Johann First Community Library of Boca Grande, Boston, 2/049
Johnson (Arthur W. & Marjorie W.) Charitable Trust, Shrewsbury, 2/049
Johnson (Carl E.) Fdn., Holyoke, 2/050
Johnson (Edward C.) Fund, Boston, 2/051
Johnson (Richard I.) Family Fdn., Chestnut Hill, 2/051
Johnson (Howard) Fdn., Dorchester, 2/052
Ellington & Jones Fdn., Boston, 2/053
Joslin Diabetes Fdn., Boston, 2/054
Juniper Fdn., Boston, 2/054
Kalman Fdn., Brookline, 2/054

Kamborian (J.S.) Charitable Fdn., Brighton, 2/055

Kane Charitable Trust, Chestnut Hill, 2/056

Kane-Smith Fdn., Boston, 2/057

Kaplan (Abraham) Charitable Fdn., Brookline, 2/057

Kaplan (Joseph L.) Family Fdn., Lowell, 2/058

Katz (Alan N.) Family Fdn., Longmeadow, 2/058

Katz (Benjamin H.) Family Fdn., Longmeadow, 2/059

Katz (Maurice N.) Family Fdn., Longmeadow, 2/060

Katz (S.J. & M.N.) Fdn., Springfield, 2/060

Katz (Simon J.) Family Fdn., Longmeadow, 2/060

Katz (Wolfie) Family Charitable Fdn., Chestnut Hill, 2/060

Kaufman (Mitchell B.) Charitable Fdn., Boston, 2/061

Kay Fdn., Boston, 2/062

Kaye (Sidney L.) Fdn., Somerville, 2/062

Keeler (Lawrence M. & Augusta L.) Scholarship Fund, Worcester, 2/062

Kendall Company Fdn., Boston, 2/062

Kendall (Henry P.) Fdn., Boston, 2/063

Kendall Square Fdn., Cambridge, 2/064

Kendall (Henry P.) Fdn. Trust, Boston, 2/065

Kendall Whaling Museum Trust, Sharon, 2/065

Kenilbrook Fdn., Boston, 2/066

Kenwood Fdn., Boston, 2/066

Kerubali Charitable Fdn., Watham, 2/067

Kimbell Fdn., Boston, 2/068

Kinsler (Herman & Raymond) Fund, Springfield, 2/069

Kirstein (Myer) Fdn., Boston, 2/069

Kirstein (Harold M.) Trust, Swampscott, 2/070

Klein (Thomas R.) Family Charitable Trust, Newton, 2/071

Kleven (Louis & Gertrude) Fdn., Haverhill, 2/071

Kleven (Paul I. & Ruth) Fdn., Andover, 2/072

Knight (Norman) Charitable Fdn., Boston, 2/072

Kohlrausch (Charles H.), Jr. Trust Fund, Billerica, 2/073

Kosow (Joseph) Charitable Fdn., Brighton, 2/073

Koussevitzky Memorial Trust, Pittsfield, 2/074

Krasner (Maurice) Fdn., Boston, 2/075

Krintzman Charitable Fdn., North Oxford, 2/075

Kruger (Leon & Anita) Charitable Trust, Longmeadow, 2/076

Kunian (David S. & Charlotte) Charitable Fund, Boston, 2/076

Labat (Samuel) Fdn., Lexington, 2/076

Laham (Mousour H.) Fdn., Brookline, 2/077

Lampert Fdn., Lowell, 2/077

Lancaster Fdn., Dedham, 2/077

Lane (Oliver J.) Memorial Fund, Bedford, 2/078

Lappin-Zaiger Charitable Fdn., Swampscott, 2/079

Lathrop Home for Aged Women in Northhampton, Northhampton, 2/079

Laven (Louis & Tess) Fdn., Springfield, 2/079

Leavitt (Max) Family Fdn., Brookline, 2/080

Lebo Charity Trust, Osterville, 2/080

Leclerc Charity Fund, Fitchburg, 2/081

Lee (Samuel Paul) Fdn., Brookline, 2/081

Lee Family Charitable Fdn., Boston, 2/081

Lee (Frances G.) Fdn., Boston, 2/082

Leghorn (Richard S.) Fdn., Boston, 2/083

Leibow (Saul) Fdn., Sharon, 2/083

Lenk Fdn., Boston, 2/084

Lerner (Louis C.) Charitable Trust, Boston, 2/084

Levin (Harry L.) Fdn., Boston, 2/084

Levy (June Rockwell) Fdn., Boston, 2/084

Lewis Family Fdn., Brookline, 2/086

Lincoln Old Town Hall Corporation, Lincoln, 2/086

Lindsay Charitable Trust, Boston, 2/086

Linenthal (Mark) Fdn., Boston, 2/087

Linsey (Joseph M.) Fdn., Boston, 2/088

Lipson Fdn., Newton, 2/088

List (William) Family Fdn., Fall River, 2/089

Little Harbor Fdn., Falmouth (Woods Hole), 2/089

Little (Arthur D.) Fdn., Cambridge, 2/090

Lockwood Family Charitable Trust, Worcester, 2/091

Loeser (Hans F. & Herta) Charitable Trust, Boston, 2/092

International Brotherhood of Electircal Workers, Lawrence, 2/093

Long (John A. & Ruth E.) Fdn., Boston, 2/093

Loomis (W. Farnsworth) Fdn., Boston, 2/093

Lothrop (Cyrus) Trust Fund, Boston, 2/094

Lowell Carpenters Apprenticeship Training Fund, Lowell, 2/094

Lown (Phil W.) Fdn., West Newton, 2/095

Lynn Historical Society, Lynn, 2/096

Lyons Fund, Brockton, 2/097

MacDougall Student Loan Fund, Middleboro, 2/098

MacPherson Fund, Cambridge, 2/098

Mades (Maurice & Mary) Charitable Fdn., Chestnut Hill, 2/098

MacNeil (Malcolm F.) Family Fdn., Watertown, 2/099

Malden Industrial Aid Society, Malden, 2/099

Maloney (William E.) Fdn., Lexington, 2/100

Manoog Fdn., Worcester, 2/100

Manchester Historical Society, Manchester, 2/101

Manos (Charles S.) Charitable Fdn., Boston, 2/102

Mantuck Fdn., Weston, 2/102

Mard Fund, Weston, 2/102

Charles & Marion Charitable Trust, Boston, 2/102

Marran (C. Charles) Charitable Fdn., Wabun, 2/103

Mascott (Frederick H.) Fdn., Lowell, 2/104

Mascott (Robert A.) Family Fdn., Lowell, 2/104

Mason (George H.) Fund, Holden, 2/104

Mason (Fanny Peabody) Music Fdn., Cambridge, 2/105

Massachusetts Alpha Association of Pi Beta Phi, Medford, 2/105

Mason (Edward & Ina) Charitable Trust, Worcester, 2/105

Massachusetts Indian Association, North Andover, 2/105

Massachusetts Library Aid Association, Ashburnham, 2/106

Massachusetts Pythian Sisters Home Association, West Springfield, 2/107

Massachusetts Charitable Mechanic Association, Boston, 2/108

Massachusetts Society for the University Education of Women, Boston, 2/108

Mattlin Fdn., Boston, 2/109

Mates Charitable Fdn., Boston, 2/109

Maudsley Fdn., Boston, 2/109

Mayer (Horace & Florence) Fdn., North Adams, 2/111

McCarthy Family Fdn., Beverly, 2/111

McCarthy (E.J.) Fdn., Boston, 2/111

McCarthy Family Fdn. Charity Fund, Boston, 2/112

McCarthy (Sarah G.) Memorial Fdn., Boston, 2/114

McCue (Gertrude L.) Trust u/i, Boston, 2/115

McCusker (Thomas B.) Charitable Fdn., Norwood, 2/116

McEvoy (Mildred H.) Fdn., Worcester, 2/117

McEachron (Karl Boyer) Fdn., Pittsfield, 2/118

McMillan (Edward N.) Fdn., S. Hamilton, 2/118

McNear (George P.), Jr. Fdn., Boston, 2/119

Mechanics National Bank Fdn., Worcester, 2/119

Medical Student & Resident Association Fdn., Boston, 2/120

Merrill (Everett F.) Fdn., Worcester, 2/121

Merrimac Charitable Trust, Boston, 2/122

Merrimack Valley Charitable Fdn., Lawrence, 2/123

Merrimack Valley Textile Museum, North Andover, 2/123

Merrimack Valley Charitable Fdn., Chelmsford, 2/124

Michelson Fdn., Chestnut Hill, 2/125

Middlecott Fdn., Boston, 2/125

Middlesex County Fdn., Concord, 2/126

Milender Charitable Trust, Boston, 2/126

Milhender (Joseph L.) Charitable Trust, Boston, 2/127

Miller Fdn., Pittsfield, 2/127

Minot (James Jackson & Miriam Sears) Family Fdn., Boston, 2/127

Mitton (George W.) Educational Fdn., Boston, 2/129

Mitton (George W.) Memorial Fdn., Boston, 2/129

Mock Fdn., Wellesley Hill, 2/129

Monks (Ann S.) Fdn., Boston, 2/130

Monks (G.G.) Fdn., Boston, 2/131

Moore (W. Gerald) Educational Fdn., Boston, 2/131

Moore (Robert L.) Fdn., Concord, 2/132

Morse (Alfred L. & Annette S.) Fdn., Canton, 2/134

Morin (Charles H.) Fdn., Boston, 2/135

Morse Shoe Fdn., Canton, 2/135

Mugar Fdn., Boston, 2/136

Mullare Family Fdn., Brockton, 2/138

Mullen (Miles J.) Trust, Boston, 2/138

Mydans (Max & Sophie) Fdn., Boston, 2/139

Nebhan Family Charitable Fdn., Worcester, 2/140

Nantucket Fdn., Nantucket, 2/141

Nantucket Ornithological Association, Boston, 2/141

National Shawmut Bank Trust, Boston, 2/142

Nehemias Gorin Fdn., Boston, 2/143

Neimon-Nymon Charitable Fdn., Braintree, 2/144

Nelson (Arthur T.), Jr. Memorial Fund, Boston, 2/145

Nelson (Harris J. & Geraldine S.) Fdn., Boston, 2/146

Nevins Memorial, Methuen, 2/146

Newburyport District Nursing Service, Newburyport, 2/146

New England High Carbon Wire, Millbury, 2/147

New England Theatres, Inc. Employees Trust, Newton, 2/147

Newman (Robert B.) Fdn., Lincoln, 2/148

New Ventures Association Charitable Fdn., Cambridge, 2/149

Northern Berkshire Santa Fund, North Adams, 2/149

Novakoff Charitable Fdn., Boston, 2/149

Noyes (John Calvin) Scholarship Fund, Newburyport, 2/150

Nulman Fdn., Belchertown, 2/151

Olivetti Fdn., Boston, 2/151

Olson (Gerturde Crane) Trust, Boston, 2/152

Orleans Recreation League, Orleans, 2/152

Fdn. for Research on Orthopedics & Related Medical Fields, Boston, 2/152

O'Toole (Francis A. & Dorothy D.) Charitable Trust, Worcester, 2/153

Ottmar (Jerome) Fdn. Trust, Attleboro, 2/153

Owens (Robert J.) Fdn., Boston, 2/154

Paine Charitable Trust, Boston, 2/154

Paine Charity Fund, Boston, 2/155

Paine (Stephen Davies & Susan Woods) Fund, Boston, 2/155

Paine (Charles J.) Scholarship Fund, Boston, 2/157

Pappas Charitable Trust, Boston, 2/158

Pappas Family Fdn., Boston, 2/158

Clyde Park Charitable Fdn., Brookline, 2/158

Parker Affiliated Companies Charitable Fdn., Worcester, 2/159

Parke Charitable Fdn., Boston, 2/159

Parker (Rev. Robert B.) Memorial Fund, Boston, 2/161

Parker (Theodore Edson) Fdn., Boston, 2/162

Parsons (Rose Peabody) Charitable Trust, Boston, 2/163

Patterson (Theodore O.) Charitable Fdn., Boston, 2/163

Peabody (Amelia) Fdn., Boston, 2/164

Gardner (G. Peabody & Rose) Charitable Trust, Boston, 2/165

Peabody (Margery) Charitable Trust, Boston, 2/167

Pearson (H.W.) Charitable Trust, Boston, 2/167

Pellegrino-Realmuto Charitable Fdn., Andover, 2/168

Pellegrino (Joseph) Family Fdn., Andover, 2/168

Percy (Charles) Fdn., Boston, 2/169

Perini (Joseph) Memorial Fdn., Framingham, 2/169

Peters (Frank R.) Trust, Boston, 2/170

Peters (Lovett & Ruth) Charitable Trust, Boston, 2/171

Phelon Fdn., East Longmeadow, 2/171

Phillips Lecture Fund, Springfield, 2/171

Phi Beta Phi-Massachusetts Alpha Assoc. Building Fund, Medford, 2/171

Pickering Fdn., Salem, 2/172

Pierce (S.S.) Co. Employees Aid Fund, Boston, 2/173

Pierni Family Fdn., Lynn, 2/174

Pietz Charitable Fdn., Watertown, 2/175

Pihl (Herman E.) Fdn., West Springfield, 2/175

Pilgrim Charitable Trust of Boston, Boston, 2/175

Pilgrim Fdn., Brockton, 2/176

Pioneer Fund, Boston, 2/177

Pittsfield Anti-Tuberculosis Association, Pittsfield, 2/178

Pokross (David R. & Muriel K.) Fdn., Boston, 2/179

Pomeroy (Gertrude A.) Charitable Trust, Boston, 2/180

Pomroy (Rebecca) Fdn., Newton, 2/181

Popkin Fdn., Longmeadow, 2/182

Porosky (Theodore R. & Marjorie) Charitable Fdn., Boston, 2/182

Post Charity Trust, Boston, 2/182

Pratt (Albert) Charitable Trust, Boston, 2/183

Praying Hands Charitable Trust, Winchester, 2/184

Prendergast (Rev. John E.) Scholarship Trust, Woburn, 2/185

Presteel Craftsmanship Educational Fund, Worcester, 2/186

Preston (Elwyn G.) Charitable Trust, Boston, 2/186

Preston (Jerome & Dorothy M.) Charitable Trust, Boston, 2/187

Pride (Harold L.) Fdn., Waltham, 2/187

Price (Daniel E. & Evelyn K.) Charitable Fdn., Boston, 2/187

Pringle (Charles G.) Fdn., Boston, 2/187

Staro Konstantinov Progressive Cemetery Association, Mattapan, 2/191

Putnam (William Lowell) Prize Fund for the Promotion of Scholarship, Boston, 2/191

Quinlan (Walter S.) Fdn., Boston, 2/192

Rabb (Irving & Charlotte) Charitable Fdn., Boston, 2/193

Rabb (Norman & Eleanor) Charitable Fdn., Boston, 2/194

Rabb (Sidney & Esther) Charitable Fdn., Boston, 2/195

Rabinovitz (Joseph) Family Fdn., Boston, 2/196

Radlo (Dora A.) Memorial Scholarship Fund, Pittsfield, 2/196

Rand (Eunice V. & Morris) Charitable Fdn., Boston, 2/196

Rantoul (Neal) Fdn., Boston, 2/197

Ratshesky (A.C.) Fdn., Boston, 2/198

Ravenswood Park Fund, Gloucester, 2/198

Recorder-Gazette Fdn., Greenfield, 2/199

Reed & Barton Fdn., Taunton, 2/200

Reisner (William H.) Fdn., Clinton, 2/200

Reopell (Albert V.) & Lena S. Reopell Charitable Fund, Springfield, 2/201

Revere Knitting Mills Charitable Fdn., Wakefield, 2/202

Riblet Fdn. Trust, Weston, 2/202

Rice (Albert W.) Charitable Fdn., Worcester, 2/203

Richardson (Mary T. & William A.) Fund Corp., Malden, 2/203

Richmond (Harold B.) Fdn., Boston, 2/204

Richter Family Charitable Trust, Lexington, 2/204

Riddell (George Robert) Charitable Trust, Marshfield, 2/204

Rigelhaupt Charitable Fdn., Wellfleet, 2/205

Riley (Charles Edward) Fdn., Boston, 2/205

Rimer Trust, Marblehead, 2/205

Rising Paper Company Charitable Fund, Housatonic, 2/206

Ritz (Henry M. & Roslyn S.) Charitable Trust, Worcester, 2/207

Charles River Fdn., Boston, 2/207

River Road Charitable Corporation, Boston, 2/207

Rizzi (Peter H.) Charitable Fdn., Dedham, 2/208

Rizika (Abraham W.) Fdn., Brookline, 2/208

Casey (Ruth Jones) Fdn., Osterville, 2/209

Robbins Charitable Fdn., Newton, 2/209

Robertson (Douglas) Fund, Taunton, 2/209

Robertson Trust, Taunton, 2/209

Robinson (Dwight) Charity Trust, Boston, 2/210

Robinson Family Charitable Trust, Hingham, 2/210

Robinson Family Fdn., Lowell, 2/211

Rocco (Salvatore & Grace) Charitable Trust, Everett, 2/212

Roche Bros. Charitable Fdn., Roslindale, 2/212

Rodman (Benjamin B. & Edith) Charitable Fdn., Brookline, 2/212

Roehl (Ora C.) Charitable Trust, Boston, 2/213

Rogers Family Fdn., Lawrence, 2/213

Rogerson House, Jamaica Plain, 2/214

Rose (Bertha C. & Edward) Trust, Boston, 2/215

Rose (Philip, Ralph & Sidney) Family Charitable Fdn., Worcester, 2/216

Rosenberg (William) Family Charitable Trust, Boston, 2/216

Ross (Paul P. & Sara W.) Charitable Trust, Boston, 2/217

Ross (Mrs. George L.) Nursing Scholarship Fund, Holyoke, 2/218

Rotch Travelling Scholarship Inc., Boston, 2/218

Roukas Scholarship Fund u/w-Frank A. Roukas, Middleboro, 2/219

Ruckert Family Fdn., Eastham, 2/219

Rudnick (Alford & Charlotte) Fdn., Brookline, 2/220

Ryan (Mary B. & William H.) Fdn., Lincoln, 2/220

Sacco Fdn., Brookline, 2/220

Sack (Abraham) Fdn., Worcester, 2/221

Sacred Heart School Guild, Holyoke, 2/221

Sagamore Fdn., Boston, 2/222

Sagansky (Harry & Lee) Fdn., Brookline, 2/223

St. Basil's Fund, Boston, 2/224

Salter (Leonard M. & Charlotte B.) Charitable Fdn., Boston, 2/224

Saltonstall (Richard) Charitable Fdn., Boston, 2/225

Salzer (Peter P.) Charitable Fdn., Worcester, 2/226

Samuel Archbishop Trust, Worcester, 2/226

Sanders (Theo M.) Fund, Boston, 2/226

Sanders Fund, Boston, 2/227

Charles Sanders, Trust u/w, Boston, 2/227

Sandman (Eli) Charitable Fdn., Worcester, 2/228

Sandler (Sylvia Hite) Charitable Trust, Chestnut Hill, 2/228

Sanford (Chaplain David) Fund, Boston, 2/228

Saquish Fdn., Boston, 2/229

Tay Fund, Boston, 2/229

Sawyer (Samuel E.) Chapel Fund, Gloucester, 2/230

Saxe Charitable Trust, Boston, 2/231

Schorr (Marvin G.) Charitable Fdn., Boston, 2/231

Schrafft (William E. & Bertha E.) Charitable Trust, Boston, 2/233

Schwartz (William & Lillian) Charitable Fdn., Boston, 2/234

Sciences & Art Fdn., Dedham, 2/235

Seamen's Widow & Orphan Association of Salem, Salem, 2/235

Seder Associates Fdn., Worcester, 2/236

Segal (Louise & Herbert) Charitable Fdn., Boston, 3/001

Segal (Maurice S. & Sylvia C.) Fdn., Cambridge, 3/002

Septimus Fdn., Boston, 3/002

Sexton Can Company Employee's Aid Fund, Everett, 3/003

Shamroth Family Charitable Fund, Boston, 3/004

Shankman (Joseph & Ruth B.) Fdn., Brookline, 3/004

Shapiro (Abraham) Charity Fdn., Boston, 3/005

Shapiro (Irving R.) Fdn., Brookline, 3/006

Shapiro (Maxwell & Evelyn) Charitable Fdn., Boston, 3/006

Sharf (Jean S. & Frederic A.) Fund, Newton, 3/007

Sharfman (Norman & Ethel) Charitable Trust, Worcester, 3/007

Sheldon (Samuel B. & Gloria R.) Charitable Fdn., Marblehead, 3/007

Sherr (Carl & Joyce) Charitable Trust, Worcester, 3/008

Shaw Fund for Mariners' Children, Boston, 3/008

Shea (James J.) Fdn., East Longmeadow, 3/009

Sher (Harry & Ida B.) Charitable Fdn., Boston, 3/009

Sherman (George) Charitable Fdn., Boston, 3/010

Shoolman Charitable Fdn., Newton, 3/011

Shore Fdn., Newton, 3/012

Shoul (Jacob W. & Ida B.) Fdn., Boston, 3/013

Shulman Fdn., Newton Centre, 3/013

Siegel (Isadore Arthur) Scholarship Fund, Boston, 3/013

Siff Charitable Fdn., Webster, 3/014

Silberg (Jacob, Sidney & Bernard) Charitable Trust, Lawrence, 3/014

Silbert Charitable Fdn., Swampscott, 3/014

Silbert (Newman) Fdn., Boston, 3/015

Silver Charitable Fdn., Springfield, 3/016

Silverman Family Charitable Fdn., Longmeadow, 3/016

Silverman (Joseph & Esther) Charitable Fdn., Boston, 3/016

Silverman (Milton J. & Elizabeth) Fdn., Boston, 3/017

Simon Family Fdn., Leominster, 3/018

Simons (Maurice C. & Adeline S.) Charitable Fdn., Swampscott, 3/018

Single Cell Research Fdn., Brockton, 3/019

Slate Family Charitable Trust, Quincy, 3/019

Slotnik Charitable Fund, Boston, 3/020

Smalley Fdn., Boston, 3/021

Smith (George O.) Trust, Lexington, 3/022

Smith (Dr. A. Vincent) & Harry E. Richmond Scholarship Fund Middleborough Trust Company, Middleboro, 3/023

Smith (Annie T.) Mercy Fund, Boston, 3/023

Smith-Petersen Fdn., Boston, 3/024

SML Fdn., Boston, 3/024

Sneath (Dorothy Melcher) Trust u/ind, Boston, 3/024

Snow & Jones Charitable Trust, Brockton, 3/025

Snyder (Joseph Emanuel) Memorial Fund, Springfield, 3/028

Solomon (Abraham) & Gertrude Solomon
  Charitable Trust, Worcester, 3/028
Solomon (Harry D.) & Anita Solomon
  Charitable Trust, Worcester, 3/028
Somerville Rotary Educational Fund, Somerville,
  3/028
Sonesta Charitable Fdn., Boston, 3/029
Sonnabend (Leopold M.) Fdn., Boston, 3/030
Southwell Fdn., Boston, 3/031
Sparks (Harold & Helen) Fdn., West Newton,
  3/031
Sparrell (Nellie L.) Trust, Norwell, 3/031
Spero Charitable Fdn., Brookline, 3/032
Spiegel (Felix) Fdn., Ashby, 3/032
Sprague Electric Company Fdn., North Adams,
  3/033
Sprague (Florence & Robert) Fdn.,
  Williamstown, 3/033
Sprague (Phileas W.) Memorial Fdn., Boston,
  3/033
Springfield Home for the Elderly, Springfield,
  3/035
S & R Trust, Brookline, 3/037
Star Fdn., Cambridge, 3/037
Stare Fund, Boston, 3/037
Starling Charitable Trust, Boston, 3/038
Starr (Max & Doris L.) Fdn., Boston, 3/039
Starr (Sherman H.) Fdn., Boston, 3/039
Stearns Charitable Trust, Boston, 3/040
Stearns (Ann B.) Charitable Fdn.,
  3/041
Stearns (George M.) Testamentary Trust,
  Springfield, 3/042
Steiger (Albert) Memorial Fund, Springfield,
  3/043
Stein (David & Grace) Charitable Trust,
  Boston, 3/043
Steir (Rose) Fdn., Boston, 3/044
Stevens (Abbot & Dorothy H.) Fdn., North
  Andover, 3/044
Stevens (Nathaniel & Elizabeth P.) Fdn., North
  Andover, 3/045
Stillman (R.D.) Memorial Fund, Inc.,
  Wareham, 3/046
Stockwell (Helen Wolcott) Trust u/w, Boston,
  3/046
Stoddard Charitable Trust, Worcester, 3/046
Stogel (Dorothy & Sidney S.) Fdn., Wahen,
  3/048
Stone (Samuel M.) Charitable Fund, Boston,
  3/049
Stone (Joseph) Fund, Brockton, 3/049
Stone (Albert H. & Reuben S.) Trust,
  Worcester, 3/050
Stop & Shop Fdn., Boston, 3/051
Storer Trust, Boston, 3/053
Stratford Trust, Boston, 3/053
Stull Family Fdn., Beverly, 3/053
Sudbury Fdn., Worcester, 3/054
Sundel (Jacob & Clarie) Fdn., Fall River,
  3/055
Sundell (Jeremiah) Family Fdn., Newton,
  3/055
Surgical Research Trust, Cambridge, 3/056
Surprenant (Albert H.) Charitable Trust,
  Boston, 3/056
Swampscott World War II Memorial Fund,
  Swampscott, 3/057
Swartz (Gertrude N. & Edward M.) Charitable
  Trust, Boston, 3/057
Swazey Fund, Newburyport, 3/057
Sweeney (Joseph L.) Charitable Fdn., Boston,
  3/058
Swift Charity, Boston, 3/058
Sylvester Fund, Boston, 3/059
Tamarack Fdn., Boston, 3/060
Taylor (Frank C. & Helen M.) Educational
  Fund, New Bedford, 3/061
Tedesco Country Club, Marblehead, 3/062
Terrazzo Workers Local 8 & 18 Health and
  Welfare Fund, Boston, 3/063
Thacher (Mary) Testamentary Trust f/b/o The
  Town of Yarmouth, Boston, 3/063
Thayer Museum, Lancaster, 3/063
Thompson (Richard H. & Barbara P.)
  Charitable Trust, Winchester, 3/064

Throne (Sidney) Family Fdn., Longmeadow,
  3/064
Tobie (Melinda W.) Trust, Boston, 3/066
Tobin (Alan D. and Judith) Charitable Fdn.,
  Brookline, 3/067
Tohoku Judo Club, Somerville, 3/068
Top Fund, Boston, 3/068
Touloukian Fdn., Brookline, 3/069
Towne (Richard R.) Charitable Trust, Holyoke,
  3/069
Trans-Sonics Fdn., Lexington, 3/070
Travelli (Emma R.) Jr., Boston, 3/070
Travelli (Charles irwin) Fund, Boston, 3/071
Tripp (C.K.) Memorial Scholarship Fdn., Lynn,
  3/071
Triton Fdn., Cambridge, 3/072
American Cancer Society, Boston, 3/072
American Class League of Miami University,
  Boston, 3/074
American Legion Auxiliary, Boston, 3/074
American Heart Association, Boston, 3/074
Ames Free Library, Boston, 3/074
Athol Memorial Hospital, Boston, 3/075
Bachelor (Charles O.) Trust, Worcester, 3/075
Baldwin (Mrs. Lena D.) Trust #1660, Boston,
  3/075
Baldwin (Mrs. Lena D.) Trust #1659, Boston,
  3/075
Baldwin (Mrs. Lena D.) Trust #1658, Boston,
  3/075
Baldwin (Mrs. Lena D.) Trust #1657, Boston,
  3/076
Baldwin (Mrs. Lena Dewey) Trust #2244,
  Boston, 3/076
Baptist Church of Westport, Boston, 3/076
Bayley (Harriet B.) Trust, Boston, 3/076
Belmont Public Library Trust #0580, Boston,
  3/077
Belmont Public Library Trust #0110, Boston,
  3/077
Bennett (Jane) Scholarship Fund, Middleboro,
  3/078
Beverly Hospital Trust #0005, Boston, 3/078
Beverly Hospital Trust #0006, Boston, 3/078
Bird (William W.) Trust, Worcester, 3/079
Bishop of Diocese of Mass., Boston, 3/079
Blind Service Association, Boston, 3/079
Board of Education School District #4746.03,
  Boston, 3/079
Board of Education, Boston, 3/080
Board of Ministerial Aid, Boston, 3/080
Boston Baptist Bethel, Boston, 3/080
Boston Council Inc., BSA, Boston, 3/080
Boston Dispensary, Boston, 3/081
Boston Floating Hospital, Boston, 3/081
Boston Marine Society, Boston, 3/081
Boy Scouts of America, Boston, 3/081
Boylston Medical Society Trust #0164, Boston,
  3/082
Boylston Medical Society Trust #0564, Boston,
  3/082
Boysville of Michigan, Boston, 3/082
Brattleboro Union H.S., Boston, 3/082
Bridgewater Public Library, Boston, 3/082
Brighton Evangelical Congregational Church,
  Boston, 3/083
Brighton Evangelical Congregational Sunday
  School, Boston, 3/083
Bullard Memorial Farm Assoc., Boston, 3/083
Bureau of Catholic Charities, Boston, 3/083
California School for the Deaf, Boston, 3/083
Canedy (Zebulon L.) Trust, Middleboro, 3/084
Carlisle Congregational Church, Boston, 3/084
Catholic Home for Children, Boston, 3/084
Chamber of Commerce, Boston, 3/085
Charitable Assn. of the Boston Fire Department
  Trust #0157, Boston, 3/085
Charitable Assn. of the Boston Fire Department
  Trust #0158, Boston, 3/085
Chelsea Public Library, Boston, 3/085
Chico State College Fdn., Boston, 3/086
Child Evangelism, Boston, 3/086
Children's Communities, Boston, 3/086
Children's Hospital Trust #1472.02, Boston,
  3/087

Children's Hospital Trust #2013.01, Boston,
  3/087
Children's Orthopedic Hospital, Boston, 3/087
Christ Church, Boston, 3/088
Choate (Charles F.) Jr., Trust, Boston, 3/088
City of Rockland, Boston, 3/089
Concord Home for the Aged, Boston, 3/089
Concord Home for the Aged Trust #0607,
  Boston, 3/089
Concordia Lutheran Church, Boston, 3/090
Congregational Church, Boston, 3/090
Congregational Church of Amherst, New
  Hampshire, Boston, 3/090
Congregational Church Trust, Boston, 3/090
Congregational Church in Cumberland, Boston,
  3/091
Congregational House, Boston, 3/091
Congregational Church in Cumberland, Boston,
  3/091
Cook (Richard) Trust, Boston, 3/091
Council of Churches, Boston, 3/091
Cox (Charles M.) Trust, Boston, 3/091
Crawford Memorial Trust, Boston, 3/092
Crittenton (Florence) League, Boston, 3/092
Crotched Mountain Foundation, Boston, 3/093
Curtis (John) Free Library, Boston, 3/093
Dana (Herman) Trust, Boston, 3/093
Daughters of Our King, Boston, 3/094
Dodge (Thomas H.) Trust, Worcester, 3/095
Donations for Education in the Near East,
  Boston, 3/095
Donations of Town of Concord Trust #0603,
  Boston, 3/095
Donations of Town of Concord Trust #0604,
  Boston, 3/095
Egan (Monsignor Francis C.) Trust, Boston,
  3/096
Endowment Association, Boston, 3/097
Evergreen Cemetery Assoc., Boston, 3/097
Fay (M. Irene) Trust, Boston, 3/097
First Church of Christian Scientist, Boston,
  3/097
First Church of Christ, Boston, 3/097
First Church in Roxbury, Boston, 3/098
First Church of Templeton, Boston, 3/098
First Church Unitarian, Boston, 3/098
First Church in Wenham, Boston, 3/098
First Congregational Church Trust #2584.01,
  Boston, 3/099
First Congregational Church Trust #2584.02,
  Boston, 3/099
First Evangelical United Trust, Boston, 3/099
First Parish Church, Boston, 3/100
First Presbyterian Church Trust #5873, Boston,
  3/100
First Presbyterian Church Trust #12388,
  Boston, 3/100
First Presbyterian Church of Glendale, Boston,
  3/100
Fisher Charitable Society, Boston, 3/100
Fitchburg H.S. Class of 1893 Trust, Worcester,
  3/101
Florida Beacon College Trust, Boston, 3/101
Foster Parents Plan, Boston, 3/101
Franklin Foundation, Boston, 3/101
General Charitable Society, Boston, 3/102
Gray Scholarship Fund, Boston, 3/102
Groveland Cemetery Corporation, Boston,
  3/102
Goodwill Industries of Oregon, Boston, 3/102
Monsignor John R. Hackett H.S., Boston,
  3/103
Haglund (Mrs. R.C.) Trust, Boston, 3/103
Hanson Public Library, Boston, 3/103
Hardens Creek Cemetery Assoc., Boston, 3/103
Harrington (George) Trust, Boston, 3/104
Holy Cross Cemetery, Boston, 3/104
Immaculate Conception Church, Boston, 3/105
Ind. School of Crippled and Deaf Children,
  Boston, 3/105
Jackson (Wilhelmina W.) Trust, Boston, 3/105
Joslin Diabetes Foundation, Boston, 3/106
Jamaica Plain Neighborhood House Association,
  Boston, 3/106
Lee (Anna) Trust, Boston, 3/107
Keene YMCA, Boston, 3/107

Kelly (Luke F. & Josephine M.) Charitable Trust, Middleboro, 3/107
King (Charles A.) Trust, Boston, 3/108
Lawrence Academy, Boston, 3/108
Lawrence Light Guard, Boston, 3/109
Leighton (Margaret W.) Trust, Boston, 3/109
Les Soeurs de L'Assumption, Boston, 3/110
Lorcott & Company, Boston, 3/110
Loring (Richard W.) Trust #103, Boston, 3/111
Loring (Richard W.) Trust #1217, Boston, 3/111
Lowell (Amy)-Tenth Clause Trust, Boston, 3/111
Lutheran Hospital School of Nursing, Boston, 3/112
Mariam Polan Aid Society, Boston, 3/112
Marshfield Historical Society, Boston, 3/112
Massachusetts Congregational Soc. Charitable Trust #153, Boston, 3/113
Massachusetts Congregational Soc. Charitable Trust #0569, Boston, 3/113
Massachusetts Medical Society, Boston, 3/113
Massachusetts Society of Mayflower Descendents, Boston, 3/114
Massachusetts Society for Prevention of Cruelty Trust #79.02, Boston, 3/114
Massachusetts Society for Prevention of Cruelty Trust #79.01, Boston, 3/114
Maxim (Charles W.) Trust f/b/o Selectmen of Roch., Middleboro, 3/114
Maxim (C.W.) Trust f/b/o St. Luke's Hospital, Middleboro, 3/115
Maxim (Clarence .) Trust f/b/o Salvation Army in New Bedford, Middleboro, 3/115
Medford Home for Aged, Boston, 3/115
Memorial Endowment for Educ. Pur. Trs., Boston, 3/116
Messinger (Charles A.) Trust, Worcester, 3/116
Methodist Church, Boston, 3/116
Helmes (Ruth H.) Trust, Middleboro, 3/116
Miles (Alice W.) Trust-William & Mary Miles Graduates of Rochester H.S. Scholarship Fund, Worcester, 3/117
Miles (Alice W.) Trust-W.P.I. Scholarship Fund, Worcester, 3/117
Missionaries of the Company of Mary, Boston, 3/117
Missionaries of the Company of Mary Prov. House, Boston, 3/118
Mount Vernon Church of Boston, Boston, 3/118
National Foundation, Boston, 3/118
N.D. Society for Crippled Children and Adults, Boston, 3/119
N.E. Anti-Vivisection Society, Boston, 3/119
N.H. Centennial Home for Aged, Boston, 3/119
No. Bennet S. Induatrial School, Boston, 3/119
Northfield and Mr. Herman School, Boston, 3/120
Notre Dame Training School, Boston, 3/120
Oakland Cemetery, Boston, 3/120
Old Fellow-Ribekah, Boston, 3/121
Old Bridgewater Historical Society, Boston, 3/121
Panaghuirishie City Hospital, Boston, 3/121
Park School Corporation, Boston, 3/121
Peirce (Maria L.H.) Trust f/b/o Church of Our Saviour, Choir Fund, Middleboro, 3/122
Peirce (Maria L.H.) Trust f/b/o Drinking Fountain Fund, Middleboro, 3/122
Peirce (Maria L.H.) Trust f/b/o Church of Our Saviour, Rectory Fund, Middleboro, 3/123
Pembroke Free Library, Boston, 3/123
Phi Beta Kappa, Boston, 3/123
Phillips (Edwin) Trust, Boston, 3/123
Phillips (Louise B.) Trust, Boston, 3/124
Pilgrim Society, Boston, 3/125
Pine Grove Cemetery, Boston, 3/125
Piney Woods County, Boston, 3/126
Pinkerton (Alfred S.) Trust, Worcester, 3/126
Plymouth Public Library, Boston, 3/126
Pres. & Fellow Harvard College Trust #073, Boston, 3/126

Pres. & Fellow Harvard College Trust #2075, Boston, 3/126
Principal Henry T. Wing School, Boston, 3/127
Protestant Episcopal Society of Christ Church, Boston, 3/127
Public Library of Chelsea, Mass., Boston, 3/128
Public School Department, Boston, 3/128
Radio Bible Class, Boston, 3/128
Reform Dutch Church of Mellenville, Boston, 3/129
Regs of Univ-Cal Off of Treasurer, Boston, 3/129
The Retreat Inc. Trust 5585, Boston, 3/129
The Retreat Inc. Trust 5584, Boston, 3/129
Richards (Adelia C.) Trust f/b/o Town of Middleboro, Playground Fund, Middleboro, 3/129
Richards (Adelia C.) Trust f/b/o Adelia C. Richards Scholarship Fund, Middleboro, 3/130
Richards (Ann Rebecca) Trust, Boston, 3/130
Ripley (Ellen C.) Trust, Boston, 3/131
Rivers Country Day School, Boston, 3/131
Runyon (Damon) Memorial Fund, Boston, 3/131
Romero (Sophie F.) Trust, Fall River, 3/132
St. Cecilia's Church, Boston, 3/133
St. Francis Roman Catholic Church, Boston, 3/133
St. John's Reformed Church, Boston, 3/133
St. Joseph's Hill Informary, Boston, 3/134
St. Joseph's Home for the Blind, Boston, 3/134
St. Mary's Catholic Church, Boston, 3/134
St. Mary's Infirmary Asylum Ly-In Hospital, Boston, 3/134
St. Michael's Parish, Boston, 3/134
St. Patrick's Church, Boston, 3/134
St. Patrick's School, Boston, 3/135
St. Patrick's Church, Boston, 3/135
St. Paul's Church, Boston, 3/135
St. Paul's Church in Brookline, Boston, 3/136
St. Paul's Episcopal Church, Boston, 3/136
St. Peter's Episcopal Church, Boston, 3/136
St. Peter's Lutheran Church, Boston, 3/137
Salamanca Hospital, Boston, 3/137
Salamanca Carnegie Library, Boston, 3/137
Salvation Army Trust #4284.07, Boston, 3/137
Salvation Army Trust #1575.02, Boston, 3/138
Schweinfurth (Julius A.) Trust, Boston, 3/138
Scoule Elementari del Comune, Boston, 3/139
Sears (Clara Endicott) Trust, Boston, 3/139
Sec of Caledonia Chapt. 97, Boston, 3/140
Select Men of the Town of Barnstable, Boston, 3/140
Select Men of the Town of Plymouth, Boston, 3/140
Select Men of the Town of Waynouth, Boston, 3/141
Self Help Home for the Aged, Boston, 3/141
Shaffer Memorial, Boston, 3/141
Shaw (Hannah B.G.) Trust, Middleboro, 3/141
Shriners Hospital for Crippled Children, Boston, 3/142
Sisterhood of Holy Nativity, Boston, 3/142
Sisters of St. Ann, Boston, 3/142
Sisters at St. Patrick's, Boston, 3/143
S M Chapter of Daughters of American Revolution, Boston, 3/143
Sparrow (Anna Taft) Trust f/b/o Sparrow Brothers Scholarship, Middleboro, 3/143
Tallot (Edna Beth) Trust, Boston, 3/144
Tappan (Eva March) Trust, Worcester, 3/144
Tauton Public Library, Boston, 3/144
Tenney (Clara L.) Trust, Worcester, 3/144
Thompson Academy, Boston, 3/144
Tidd Home, Boston, 3/145
Tillson (Clifford W.) Trust f/b/o Leonard O. Tillson Scholarship Fund, Middleboro, 3/145
Donations for Education in Liberia, Boston, 3/145
Town Treasurer, Boston, 3/146
Town Treasurer of Town of Duxbury, Boston, 3/146

Town Treasurer of Town of Milton, Boston, 3/146
Traip Trust, Boston, 3/147
Treasurer of W.A. Christ Episcopal Church, Boston, 3/147
Treasurer of Town of Highlands, Calif., Boston, 3/147
Treasurer of Town of Little Compton, R.I., Boston, 3/147
Treasurer of City of Newburyport, Mass., Boston, 3/148
Treasurer of Town of South Borough, Boston, 3/148
Trinitarian Congregational Church, Boston, 3/148
Town of New Ipswich, Boston, 3/148
Trustees of Trusts Funds, Boston, 3/148
Trustees of Trust #561, Boston, 3/148
Trustees of Trust #557, Boston, 3/149
Tuberculosis & Respiratory, Boston, 3/149
Tsai (Gerald) Charitable Trust, Boston, 3/149
Tucker (Lena) Testamentary Trust, Springfield, 3/150
Two Rivers Council, Boston, 3/150
Union Cemetery, Boston, 3/150
Unitarian Universalist Church Trust #0114, Boston, 3/150
Unitarian Universalist Church Trust #576, Boston, 3/151
Unitarian Universalist Church Trust #579, Boston, 3/151
United Church of Christ, Boston, 3/151
United Liberal Church, Boston, 3/152
United South End Settlements, Boston, 3/152
Unity of Lake Worth, Boston, 3/152
Ventress Library, Boston, 3/152
Villa Maria, Boston, 3/152
Jos Warren, Boston, 3/153
Weld (Helen) Fund, Boston, 3/153
Wells College, Boston, 3/153
Wenham College Imp. Soc., Boston, 3/153
Wilbraham Academy Student, Boston, 3/153
Woodland Cemetery Association, Boston, 3/154
YMCA, Boston, 3/154
Winchester Public Library, Boston, 3/154
Twelve Lawrence Trust, Winchester, 3/154
Vingo Trust II, Boston, 3/155
United-Carr Fdn., Boston, 3/155
United Fruit Company Fdn., Inc., Boston, 3/156
United States Envelope Fdn., Springfield, 3/157
Unity Fund, Boston, 3/158
Urann Fdn., Brockton, 3/158
Usen (Irving) Charitable Trust, Boston, 3/159
Valley Charitable Trust Fund, Springfield, 3/159
Vanderbilt (William H.) Fund, Boston, 3/160
Vatra's Educational Fdn., Boston, 3/161
Vaughan Fdn., Attleboro, 3/161
Veen (Jan) Educational Trust, Boston, 3/161
Veiner Charitable Fdn., Milford, 3/162
Venti Fdn., Longmeadow, 3/163
Viles (Marian Nichols) Memorial Fund, Boston, 3/163
Volpe (John A.) Fund, Malden, 3/164
Wald (Ellen & Harold) Charitable Trust, Boston, 3/165
Wald (Freda & Lewis) Trust, Worcester, 3/165
Walker (George H.) Milk Research Fund, Boston, 3/165
Walker (M.S.) & Family Trust Fund, Boston, 3/167
Wallace (George R.) Fdn., Gardner, 3/167
Wallace (George R.) Charitable Trust, Gardner, 3/167
Waltham Graduate Nurses Association, Waltham, 3/168
Warren Charitable Trust, Boston, 3/169
Warren (S.D.) Company Fdn., Boston, 3/170
Washburn (Ann White) Scholarship Fund, Middleboro, 3/171
Washington Mountain Arts Center, Inc., Washington, 3/171
Wasserman Family Fdn., Cambridge, 3/171
Wasserman (Leo) Fdn., Boston, 3/171

Watchmaker (David M.) Charitable Trust, Brookline, 3/172

Watkins (Curtis G.) Sales & Service Employees Scholarship Fund, Gardner, 3/173

Waters Fdn., Gramingham, 3/173

Watuppa Fdn., Fall River, 3/174

Ross-Webb Fund, New Bedford, 3/175

Webster Charitable Fdn., Lawrence, 3/175

Webster (Edwin S.) Fdn., Boston, 3/176

Weinberg (Benjamin) Charitable Trust, Boston, 3/177

Weiner (Alan D. & Phyllis F.) Charitable Fdn., Brockton, 3/178

Weinstein (Lewis H. & Selma) Charitable Trust, Boston, 3/178

Weiss (Mortimer & Ann) Family Fdn., Chestnut Hill, 3/179

Welch (James & Vedna) Fdn., Boston, 3/179

Wellesley Kiwanis Memorial Fund, Wellesley, 3/179

Wellman Fdn., Boston, 3/180

Wemyss (James C.) Fdn., Boston, 3/181

Wenham Village Improvement Society, Wenham, 3/182

Westfield Fdn., Boston, 3/183

Wexler (Robert H.) Fdn., Worcester, 3/183

Wexler (Jerold A.) Charitable Trust, Worcester, 3/184

Wexler (Samuel & Etta) Fdn., Worcester, 3/184

Weyman (Wesley) Testamentary Trust, Boston, 3/185

White (Annie Evans) Memorial, Winchendom, 3/185

White (Thomas J.) Fdn., Newton, 3/186

White (John A.) Trust, Boston, 3/186

Wiegand Memorial Fdn., Bernardston, 3/197

Wildlife Rehabilitation Center, Upton, 3/188

Wilder (Amos & Catherine) Fund, Cambridge, 3/188

Wilensky Fdn., Worcester, 3/188

Winer (Hy) Charitable Trust, Newton, 3/189

Winer (Irving) Charitable Trust, Boston, 3/189

Winter Street Charitable Fdn., Worcester, 3/190

Wise (Shirley & David M.) Fdn., Waban, 3/190

Wolfson (Louis E.) Fdn., Boston, 3/191

Wood (Cornelius A. & Muriel P.) Charity Fund, Boston, 3/192

Wyman-Gordon Fdn., Worcester, 3/193

Yerontitis (Kostas C.) Trust, Boston, 3/194

Yesley (Herschel I. & Ruth B.) Charitable Trust, Newton, 3/194

Zakon (William) & Sons Charity Fund, Brookline, 3/194

Zamcheck Research Fdn., Newton Centre, 3/195

Zayre Fdn., Framingham, 3/195

Zimble (Julius) Fdn., Norwood, 3/196

Zimman (Pvt. Robert) Memorial Fund, Lynn, 3/197

Ziskind (Jacob) Trust for Charitable Purposes, Boston, 3/197

Second Filming

Abrams (Dr. and Mrs. Jacob J.) Family Fdn., Brookline, 4/002

Abramson (Fisher) Charitable Trust, New Bedford, 4/003

Acorn Charitable Trust, Brookline, 4/003

Acushnet Fdn., New Bedford, 4/004

Adams Charitable Trust, West Newton, 4/005

Adams Memorial Society, Inc., Boston, 4/006

Adelman (Elliott & Barbara) Charitable Fdn., Boston, 4/007

Agoos (Lassor and Fanny) Charity Fund, Boston, 4/007

Allen (Quintus) Testamentary Trust, Bernardston, 4/008

Alperin (Jordan L.) Charitable Trust, Boston, 4/009

Alperin (Maurice G.) Charitable Trust, Boston, 4/010

Alumni Assoc. Framingham State College, Worcester, 4/011

American Employees Trust, Boston, 4/012

American London Symphony Orchestra Fdn., Boston, 4/012

American Mutual Charitable Fdn., Boston, 4/012

American Red Cross, Boston, 4/013

Amherst Home for Aged Women, Amherst, 4/013

Anderson (Hugh J.) Fdn., Bayport, Minn., 4/014

Trust U/A Andrews (Arthur I.), Boston, 4/015

Angino Charitable Fdn., Boston, 4/015

Apteker (Louis and Isabelle) Charitable Trust, Boston, 4/016

Archibald (Frederick W.) Fdn., Worcester, 4/017

Arlington Catholic High School Scholarship Fund, Boston, 4/017

Armstrong (John C.) Charitable Fdn., Milton, 4/019

Armstrong (Robert W.) Jr., Charitable Fdn., Winchester, 4/019

Aronson Fdn., Brookline, 4/019

Ashton (William J.), Springfield, 4/020

Ashworth (Earl) and Gladys Ashworth Fdn., Haverhill, 4/021

Association for the Works of Mercy in the Diocese of Massachusetts, Boston, 4/021

Associated Fdn. of Greater Boston, Boston, 4/022

Atoms for Peace Awards, Cambridge, 4/023

Babson Historical Assoc., Rockport, 4/024

Bailey Fdn., Boston, 4/025

Bailey (Lucretia Prentiss) Fdn., Kingston, 4/026

Bailey (Lucretia Prentiss) Trust of Massachusetts, Kingston, 4/026

Baker Brothers Fdn., Canton, 4/026

Baker (Sherman N.) Charitable Trust, Worcester, 4/027

Barger (Joseph V. and Anna) Charitable Fdn., Chestnut Hill, 4/028

Barnett Palley Fund, Worcester, 4/028

Barron Family Fdn., Boston, 4/029

Bator (Francis M. & Micheline) Fdn., Cambridge, 4/029

Batson (Ruth M.) Educational Fdn., Boston, 4/029

Bay State Abrasive Products Charitable Trust, Boston, 4/030

Bay State Charitable Trust, Boston, 4/030

Bay State Medical Rehabilitation Clinic, Boston, 4/031

Beckwith (Louis I.) Charity Fund, Inc., Boston, 4/031

Beneficient Soc. of the New England Conservatory of Music, Boston, 4/032

Bennett (Moses J. & Molly) Charitable Fdn., Swampscott, 4/033

Beranek (Leo L.) Fdn., Winchester, 4/033

Berean Presbyterian Church Trust, Boston, 4/034

Berkowitz (E. Sidney) Charitable Trust, Boston, 4/034

Berkshire County Home for Aged Women, Pittsfield, 4/035

Berman (Wendall & Bessie) Charitable Trust, Boston, 4/035

Berns Charitable Fdn., Inc., Chestnut Hill, 4/036

Bernstein (Eliot L. and Ruth E.) Charitable Trust, Boston, 4/037

Berwick Boys Fdn. Trust, Boston, 4/038

Besse (Lyman W.) Trust #29, 4/039

Besse (Lyman W.) Trust #30, Springfield, 4/039

Besse (Lyman W.) Trust #31, Springfield, 4/039

Besse (Lyman W.) Trust #32, Springfield, 4/039

Binney (Elizabeth Peters) Charitable Fdn., Boston, 4/039

Bird (Charles Sumner) Fdn., Boston, 4/039

Bird Companies Charitable Fdn., East Walpole, 4/041

Binney (Elizabeth Peters) Char. Fdn., Boston, 4/042

Blanchard (Henry Lawton) Fund Inc., Brockton, 4/042

Fuller (Harriet A. Bliss) Trust, Springfield, 4/044

Bloom (Inez and Joseph) Fdn., Newton, 4/044

Bombay Methodist Church Trust, Boston, 4/044

Bond (Rev. B. F.) Fdn. of N. E. Brown, Boston, 4/044

Boorky (Joseph) Charitable Trust, Worcester, 4/044

Borkum Fdn., Newton, 4/044

Bornstein (Samuel) And Lena Bornstein Fdn., Boston, 4/045

Boston Camera Club Fidelity Fund, Inc., Boston, 4/045

Boston Druggists Assoc. Trust, Boston, 4/047

Boston Stereotypers' Union #2 Old Age Assistance Plan, Boston, 4/047

Botolph Group, Boston, 4/048

Botsford (Eli Herbert) Testamentary Trust, Williamstown, 4/049

Bradley (Claruth W.) Trust, Springfield, 4/050

Breed M.-E.-L. Fdn., Boston, 4/050

Breitman (David and Joan) Charitable Fdn., Boston, 4/050

Bristol (Rexford A. & Margaret E.) Fdn., Boston, 4/051

British Charitable Society, Boston, 4/051

Trustees of the Bromfield School, Boston, 4/051

Brookledge Housing Corp., Boston, 4/052

Foundation for Brookline Housing, Boston, 4/053

Brown (Charles W.) Jr., Memorial Fdn., Boston, 4/053

Brown (Lucy Max), Springfield, 4/054

Brown (Matthew) Charitable Fdn., Boston, 4/054

Brown's (Obadiah) Benevolent Fund, Boston, 4/055

Brown (Ronald Goodrich) Music Fdn., Boston, 4/055

Burn (Brae) Charitable Fdn., Waltham, 4/055

Burbank (Mary C.) Trust, Springfield, 4/056

Burg (A. S.) Charitable Fdn., Boston, 4/056

Burstein Family Charitable Fund, Chelsea, 4/057

Cabot (Henry B.) Jr., Fdn., Boston, 4/057

Cahners Charitable Fund, Boston, 4/058

Calvin Institute Fdn., Boston, 4/058

Cambridge Historical Society, Cambridge, 4/060

Cameron (Randall P.) Charitable Fdn., Waltham, 4/061

Camp Menotomy Trust, Arlington, 4/061

Campbell (Bushrod H.) and Adah F. Hall Charity Fund, Boston, 4/061

Cannon (William L.) Memorial Fund, West Roxbury, 4/062

Cantor Family Fdn., Lowell, 4/062

Carleton (Elizabeth) House, Boston, 4/063

Carman (Walter T.) Trust, Springfield, 4/064

Carr (Hattie L.) Testamentary Trust, Brookline, 4/064

Carrick Fdn., Worcester, 4/064

Carroll Fdn., Springfield, 4/064

Cary (Isaac Harris) Educational Fund, Lexington, 4/065

Center House Fdn., Boston, 4/066

C - D Charitable Trust, Worcester, 4/068

Chafetz (Samuel and Zelda) Family Fdn., Worcester, 4/069

Fdn. for Character Education, Boston, 4/069

Charitable Trust U/I/D 4/28/59, Chestnut Hill, 4/069

Charles Bank Homes, Bouane, 4/071

Church (Frederic C.) Fdn., Boston, 4/072

Citizens Scholarship Fdn., Middleboro, 4/073

City Bank and Trust Company Scholarship Fdn., Boston, 4/073

V-8248 Trust U/Ind. Clark (F. Lyman), Boston, 4/074
Clark (Sterlin and Francine) Art Institute, Boston, 4/075
Clark Charitable Trust, Boston, 4/077
C. L. F. Fdn., Boston, 4/077
Close (Abraham) Charitable Trust, Needham, 4/079
Cohen (Hyman) Charitable Fdn., Brookline, 4/079
Collier-Keyworth Fdn., Gardner, 4/080
Committee of the Brockton Charitable Fund Incorporated, Brockton, 4/081
Congregational Church 50 Hadley Falls, Holyoke, 4/081
Connecticut River Watershed Council, Greenfield, 4/081
Consiglio (Louis and Mary) Fdn., Springfield, 4/081
Cooke (Lawrence E.) Memorial Fdn., Boston, 4/082
Cottle (Eleanor Cray) Charitable Trust, Boston, 4/082
Council of Central Bible, Boston, 4/083
Cove Charitable Trust, Boston, 4/083
Cox (Charles M.) 1940 Trust, Boston, 4/084
Crane (Clara K.) Trust, Springfield, 4/084
Cranston Fdn., Webster, 4/084
Cronin (Grover) Memorial Fdn., Waltham, 4/088
Cross (E. J.) Fdn., Worcester, 4/089
Fdn. for Cultural and Educational Affairs, Boston, 4/089
Mary Cousin Fund, Boston, 4/090
Curtis (Mary W. B.) Trust Under Will, Boston, 4/091
Cyker Charitable Fdn., Boston, 4/092
Dajer Charitable Fdn., Boston, 4/092
Dante Society of America, Cambridge, 4/093
Davies Fund, Boston, 4/093
Davis (Amelia) Fund for Incapacitated Teachers, Worcester, 4/094
Davis (Minerva J.), Springfield, 4/095
Dirlam (Arland A.) Charitable Fdn., Malden, 4/095
Dix (George A.) Trust U/A, Worcester, 4/095
Dreben (Robert) Charity Fdn., Marblehead, 4/096
Duxbury Yacht Club Charitable Fdn., Boston, 4/097
Dwight (Theodore F.) Trust, Springfield, 4/097
Dykema (Annette S. and Jere H.) Contributing Fund, Boston, 4/098
Eastern Charitable Fdn., Westwood, 4/098
Eaton (Georgiana Goddard) Memorial Fund, Boston, 4/099
Edelstein (Dr. Israel & Edith Putnam) Fdn., Quincy, 4/100
Edinburg (Joseph M. & Dorothy B.) Charitable Trust, Chestnut Hill, 4/100
Edwards Scholarship Fund, Boston, 4/101
Ehrlich (Harold L.) Charitable Fdn., Newton, 4/101
Ellison Fdn., Boston, 4/102
Elm St. Congregational Church, Boston, 4/103
Endicott (Samuel C.) Fund, Boston, 4/103
Trust u/agt Ericsson Post #109 Benefit Association, Worcester, 4/104
Farleys (Carl) Boys Ranch, Boston, 4/104
Farragaut (D. G.) Building Assoc., Worcester, 4/104
Fay (Aubert J.) Charitable Fund, Lowell, 4/104
Feinberg (Max L.) Charitable Fdn., Chelsea, 4/105
Feinsilver (Oscar and Goldie) Charitable Trust, Worcester, 4/106
Feuerstein (S. C.) Family Fdn., Malden, 4/106
Fidelity Fdn., Boston, 4/107
Firnabank Club Christmas Giving Fund, Boston, 4/108
First Baptist Society Fund, Holyoke, 4/109
First Boston Fdn. Trust, Boston, 4/109
Fisk (Lorin W.) Trust, Springfield, 4/111
Flagg (Lucretia F.) Trust, Holyoke, 4/111
Flynn Fdn., Salem, 4/111

F. N. B. Amherst Centennial Educational Trust Fund, Amherst, 4/112
Ford (Joseph F. and Clara) Fdn., Dorchester, 4/113
Foster (George E.) Trust, Springfield, 4/114
Fdn. for Medical Research, Boston, 4/114
Fdn. for Research In Bronchial Asthma and Related Diseases, Boston, 4/115
Foxboro Co. Ten Years Club, Foxboro, 4/116
Frame (Elizabeth F.) Trust, Springfield, 4/117
Fredkin (Edward) Charitable Fdn., Boston, 4/117
Freed (Manual) and Frances Freed Fdn., Brookline, 4/118
Freeman (Rev. Joseph B.) Memorial Fund, Springfield, 4/118
Freeman (Gilbert) Charitable Fdn., Weston, 4/118
Freilich (Joseph and Edith) Charitable Trust, Worcester, 4/119
French Fdn., Boston, 4/119
Freud (Martin) Trust, Boston, 4/121
Friedman (Sadie S. and Nathan H.) Fund, Chestnut Hill, 4/122
Friends of Albert Schweitzer in Boston, Brookline, 4/123
Friends of Paraguay Trust, Boston, 4/123
Friends of the University of New Brunswick, Boston, 4/124
Frost (Robert) Teaching Chairs Trust, Amherst, 4/124
Fruitlands Museums, Harvard, 4/125
Fuller (George E.) Trust, Springfield, 4/126
First Evangelical Reformed Church Memorial Fund, Boston, 4/126
Fuller (Louis M.) Fdn., Westfield, 4/126
Gardner (Isabella Stewart) Museum in the Fenway, Boston, 4/127
Gardner (Isabella Stewart) Museum, Boston, 4/128
Gass Family Charitable Trust, Boston, 4/129
Gebelein Fdn., Taunton, 4/131
General Charitable Fund, Leominster, 4/131
General Charitable Fund, Boston, 4/132
Genradco Trust, West Concord, 4/134
Gens (Charles Robert) Fdn., Boston, 4/135
German Aid Society of Boston Inc., Jamaica Plain, 4/136
Gifford (Albert J.) Charitable Trust, Worcester, 4/136
Gill (Emily F. A.) Voluntary Trust, Springfield, 4/137
Gill (Emily), Springfield, 4/137
Gillett (Frederick H.) Trust, Springfield, 4/137
Ginsburg (Carleton and Evelyn B.) Charitable Fdn., Boston, 4/137
Glasser (Hyman and Sarah) Charitable Trust, Brookline, 4/138
Glick Charitable Fdn., Worcester, 4/139
Gloucester Fishermens Institute, Gloucester, 4/140
Goldberg (Avram and Carol) Charitable Fdn., Boston, 4/141
Goldberg (Israel and Matilda) Family Fdn., Boston, 4/142
Goldman (Israel & Annie) Charitable Trust, Boston, 4/143
Goldstein Charitable Fdn., Longmeadow, 4/143
Gooding (George L.), Boston, 4/144
Goodstein (Eli D.) Fdn., Swampscott, 4/145
Gillett (Lucy D.) Trust, Springfield, 4/146
Gopen (David) Fdn., Boston, 4/146
Gordon (Frank B.) Fdn., Chelsea, 4/146
Gordon (Jack and Helena) Charitable Fdn., Newton, 4/147
Gordon (Sara R.) Heart Trust, Boston, 4/147
Gravity Research Fdn., Wellesley Hills, 4/147
Gray (Emma J.) Trust, Springfield, 4/148
Gray (James P.) Trust, Springfield, 4/148
Greenbaum (Joseph) Fdn., Boston, 4/148
Greene (Lucy W.) Trust, Springfield, 4/149
Greenspan Charitable Trust, Boston, 4/149
Greylock Fdn., Williamstown, 4/149
Grimm (Roland) Charitable Fdn., Boston, 4/152

Groper Charitable Trust, Westwood, 4/152
Grossman Family Trust, Braintree, 4/153
Grossman (David & Jill) Charitable Fdn., Newton, 4/154
Grossman (Everett and Naomi) Fdn., Braintree, 4/155
Grossman (Jacob) Charitable Fdn., Braintree, 4/155
Grossman (Nissie and Ethel) Fdn., Newton Center, 4/155
Grossman (Reuben A. and Lizzie) Fdn., Quincy, 4/156
Groton School Camp Association, Groton, 4/159
Gryzmish (Ethel & Reuben) Charitable Fdn., Boston, 4/159
Guebert (Mrs. Margaretha) Trust, Boston, 4/160
Hager (Albert) Trust, Holyoke, 4/160
Halladay (Fred P.) Trust, Springfield, 4/160
Halpern (Herbert M.) Charitable Fdn., Holyoke, 4/161
Hamilburg (Daniel M.) Fdn., Canton, 4/161
Hampden County Council of Congregational Women, Springfield, 4/163
Hanrahan (Paul B.) Fdn., Worcester, 4/163
Harrington Memorial Hospital Trust, Boston, 4/164
Harris (Marian U.) Charitable Fdn., Boston, 4/164
U/Ind. Hartman (Abraham, Louis, Samuel and Joseph) Charitable Trust, Boston, 4/165
Harvard Apparatus Fdn., Inc., Millis, 4/165
V-8304 U/Agmt. Harvard Class of 1902, Boston, 4/166
Harvard Musical Association, Boston, 4/167
Harvard Yearbook Publications, Inc., Cambridge, 4/168
Hathaway (George W.) Trust U/D, Fall River, 4/168
Hawes (Harry L.) Trust, Springfield, 4/169
Hawks (Helen B.), Springfield, 4/169
Hawks (Helen B.), Springfield, 4/169
Hayes (Maria) Home for The Aged Persons, Natick, 4/169
Hazard (Augusta G.) Beneficient Fund, Boston, 4/171
Helzel Fdn. Trust, Oakland, Calif., 4/171
Henderson (George B.) Fdn., Boston, 4/171
Hewitt (Charles Colby) Fdn., Boston, 4/174
Hiatt (Alexander) Charitable Trust, Worcester, 4/175
Hiatt (Jacob and Frances) Charitable Fdn., Inc., Worcester, 4/176
Hibbard (Nelson J.) Trust 792, Springfield, 4/177
Hibbard (Nelson J.) Trust 796, Springfield, 4/177
Hill (Wm. C.), Springfield, 4/178
Hill (Wm. C.) & Gertrude Hill, Springfield, 4/178
Hintlian Fdn., Cambridge, 4/178
Historical Society of Old Newbury, Newburyport, 4/179
Hitchcock (Dexter B.), Holyoke, 4/179
Hoffman (Abraham J.) Fdn., Boston, 4/179
Holstein Fdn., Springfield, 4/181
Holyoke Boys Club Assn., Holyoke, 4/181
Home for Aged Men in the City of Brockton, Brockton, 4/181
The Home for Aged People in Stoneham, Stoneham, 4/183
Trustees of the Home for Aged Women, Worcester, 4/184
Hood (Gilbert H.) Memorial Fund, Boston, 4/185
Hooper Fdn., Boston, 4/186
Hopedale Community House Inc., Hopedale, 4/187
Trustees of Hopkins Academy, Hadley, 4/188
Trustees of the Charity of Edward Hopkins, Boston, 4/188
Trustees of the Howard Funds in West Bridgewater, Boston, 4/190
Howland Fund for Aged Women, New Bedford, 4/190

Hudson (Clara E.) Trust, Springfield, 4/191
Huff (Richard S.) Scholarship Association, Waltham, 4/192
Hughes Family Fdn., Worcester, 4/192
Humane Society of The Commonwealth of Massachusetts, Boston, 4/192
Hyde (Ellen) Scholarship Alumni Assoc., Worcester, 4/193
Institute for Advanced Research, Cambridge, 4/194
Ipswich Heritage Trust, Ipswich, 4/195
Ives (Dwight H.), Holyoke, 4/195
Jackson Charitable Fdn., Needham, 4/195
Jacobson Fdn., Worcester, 4/196
Jacobson (Clarence N.) & Dorothy C. Jacobson Charitable Trust, Chestnut Hill, 4/197
Jaffe Fdn., Fall River, 4/197
Jaffe (Edwin and Lola) Fdn., Fall River, 4/199
James (Helen E.), Springfield, 4/199
Jo-Gal Charitable Fdn., Lawrence, 4/200
Johnson Charitable Fund, West Springfield, 4/200
Josephs (Russell and Roma) Charitable Trust, Worcester, 4/201
Josephs (Israel) and Lester Sadowsky Family Fdn., Worcester, 4/202
Kalker (Leona and Harry) Fdn., Williamstown, 4/202
Kaplan (Dorothy E. & Thomas) Charitable Fdn., Boston, 4/203
Kaplan (Ethyle and Archie) Charitable Fdn., Chestnut Hill, 4/204
Kaplan (Leonard & Glenyce) Charitable Fdn., Swampscott, 4/205
Kargman Charitable & Educational Fdn., Boston, 4/205
Katten (Adolph) Family Fdn., Longmeadow, 4/206
Katz (Louis and Ida) Fdn., Longmeadow, 4/207
Kauders Charitable Trust, Boston, 4/208
Kavanagh Fdn., Leominster, 4/208
Keller (Philip) Fdn., North Andover, 4/209
Kelley (Edward Bangs) and Elza Kelley Fdn., Hyannis, 4/210
Kelly (Dr. Clarence F.) Trust, Boston, 4/211
Kelly (Mary A.) Trust, Newburyport, 4/211
Kennedy (Frederick J.) Memorial Fdn., Boston, 4/211
Trustees of Kent State University, Boston, 4/212
Kenney (William F. & Dorothea C.) Charitable Trust, Worcester, 4/213
Ketover (Louis A. and Rose) Family Fdn., New Haven, 4/213
Keystone Charitable Fdn., Inc., Boston, 4/214
Kimball (Helen F.) Fund, Shirley, 4/214
King Family Fund Trust, Quincy, 4/215
Klein (Thomas R.) Family Charitable Trust, Newton, 4/216
Knapp (Mary B.), Springfield, 4/216
Krintzman (Iris L.) and Edward Krintzman Family Charitable Fdn., Longmeadow, 4/216
Krock (Aaron) Fdn., Worcester, 4/216
Krull (Leonard M. and Pauline F.) Fdn., Westboro, 4/217
Lahey Clinic Fdn., Boston, 4/217
L'Alliance Francaise Groupe de Boston-Cambridge, Boston, 4/218
Lamson Charitable Trust, Boston, 4/219
Lane Charitable Fund, Wellesley Hills, 4/220
Lane (William H.) Fdn., Leominster, 4/221
Larned (Elizabeth R.) Fund, Oxford, 4/221
Laven-Schaffer Fdn., Easthampton, 4/221
Lawrence Fdn., Brookline, 4/221
Lawrence Model Lodging House Trust, Boston, 4/222
Lawton (Stanley H.) Fund, Boston, 4/222
Leahy (Jennie B.) Trust, Holyoke, 4/222
Ledkote Charity Fdn., Boston, 4/223
LeGrow (Arthur R.), Jr. Memorial Scholarship Fund, W. Peabody, 4/223
Leland (Ella M. Ladd) Trust, Springfield, 4/224
Leland Home, Waltham, 4/224

Lend A Hand Society, Boston, 4/226
Levin (Benjamin & Charlotte D.) Charitable Trust, Boston, 4/229
Levine (Harry and Leona) Fdn., Worcester, 4/230
Levine (Harry & Louis) Fdn., Leominster, 5/001
Levine (Louis and Rae B.) Charitable Trust, Leominster, 5/001
Little (Arthur D.) Inc., Combined Service Fund-ADC, Combined Fund, Cambridge, 5/004
Looban (William) Fdn., Baltimore, 5/004
Lord Family Scholarship Fund, Malden, 5/004
Los Angeles Society for The Massachusetts Co., Boston, 5/005
Ludlow Fdn., Needham Heights, 5/005
Malden Home for Aged Persons, Malden, 5/005
Malden Trust Company, Malden, 5/007
Malik (Charles Habib) Educational Fund, Fall River, 5/008
Maliotis (Costas and Mary) Fdn., Belmont, 5/008
Malloch (Gertrude & Calra) Trust U/Ind., Boston, 5/009
Mansir (Newell C.) #472, Holyoke, 5/009
Mansir (Newill C.) #473, Holyoke, 5/010
Marblehead Female Humane Society, Marblehead, 5/010
Marcus (Richard J.) Family Charitable Trust, Chestnut Hill, 5/011
Marcus (Saul and Gertrude) Fdn., Worcester, 5/011
Marino (Maria) Scholarship Fund, Avon, 5/013
Marks (Maxine and Harry L.) Charitable Fdn., Boston, 5/013
Markus (Paula Anna) Fdn., Belmont, 5/014
Martin (Henry B.) Fund, Inc., Boston, 5/014
Martin (Joseph C.), Springfield, 5/016
Martin (Sarah E.), Springfield, 5/016
Mason (George H.) Fund, Holden, 5/016
Massachusetts Charitable Fire Society, Boston, 5/016
Massachusetts Co. Inc. Trustee, Boston, 5/017
Massachusetts Congregational Charitable Society, Salem, 5/017
Massachusetts Half-Way House, Boston, 5/018
Massachusetts Housing Association, Boston, 5/018
Massik (Paul) Fdn., Quincy, 5/019
Mass Maritime Academy Trust, Boston, 5/019
May (Geoffrey and Elizabeth S.) Fdn., Boston, 5/019
Mayburg Charitable Fund, Boston, 5/020
McCammon (Walter L.) Educational Trust, Boston, 5/021
McGovern-Hurley Scholarship Fund, Cambridge, 5/022
Medford Home for Aged Men and Women, Inc., Lexington, 5/022
Medical Research Institute of Worcester, Worcester, 5/024
Meditation and Philosophy Center, Milton, 5/025
Memorial Fund of Phi Beta Epsilon, Cambridge, 5/025
Merrimack Humane Society, Byfield, 5/026
Miami Jai Alai Charities, Boston, 5/026
Middleborough Trust Company, Trustee George A. Richards Playground Fund, Middleboro, 5/027
Middleborough Trust Company, Trustee Sparrow Brothers Scholarship, Middleboro, 5/027
Jackson (James) and Miriam Sears Minot Family Fdn., Boston, 5/027
Mintz (David J. and Edith) Fdn., Newton, 5/027
Mock Fdn., Boston, 5/027
Moeser (David E.) Ind/Trust, Boston, 5/028
Monadnock Fdn., Holden, 5/028
Mordecai (S. and L.) Charitable Fdn., Boston, 5/029
Morningstar Fdn., Cambridge, 5/030
Morris (Robert O.) #242, Springfield, 5/030

Morris (Roberto O.) #241, Springfield, 5/031
Morris (Robert O.) #240, Springfield, 5/031
Morrison (Archie T.) Fdn., Weymouth, 5/031
Morse (Lester S.) & Ruth Morse Fdn., Brookline, 5/032
Moseley (William O.) Fdn. Trust For, Boston, 5/033
Moses (Horace A.) Fdn., Boston, 5/034
Moses (Horace A.) Trust for Overseas Blind, Springfield, 5/035
Moses (Horace A.) Trust for The Industrial Home for the Blind, Springfield, 5/035
Moses (Horace A.) Trust for Guiding Eyes for The Blind, Springfield, 5/035
Moses (Horace A.) Trust for Connecticut Valley Historical Museum of the Springfield Lib. & Museum Assoc., Springfield, 5/036
Moses (Horace A.) Trust for Chestnut Knoll, Springfield, 5/036
Moses (Horace) Trust b/o Conn. Valley Historical Museum, Springfield, 5/036
Moses (Horace) Fdn. b/o Overseas Blind, Springfield, 5/036
Moses (Horace) Trust b/o Smith Art Museum, Springfield, 5/036
Moses (Horace A.) Trust for George Walter Vincent Smith Art Museum of the Springfield Lib. & Museum Association, Springfield, 5/036
Moses (Horace A.) Trust for Springfield City Library of the Springfield Library & Museum Assoc., Springfield, 5/036
Moses (Horace) Trust b/o Springfield Museum, Springfield, 5/037
Moses (Horace A.) Trust for Springfield Museum of Sci. of the Springfield Lib. & Museum Assoc., Springfield, 5/037
Moss (Edward S.) Memorial Fund, Boston, 5/037
Moye (Harold J.) Charitable Fdn., Chatham, 5/037
Munro (Martell) Trust, Boston, 5/037
Murdock Fund Trustees, Winchendon, 5/038
Murtha (Matthew J.) Charitable Trust, Waltham, 5/039
Nantuck Historical Trust, Nantuck, 5/039
Nathan (David G. and Jean F.) Charitable Trust, Cambridge, 5/041
Natl. Assoc. of St. Avia Offices Trust #3684, Boston, 5/041
Natl. Assoc. of St. Avia Offices Trust #3683, Boston, 5/041
Neurosciences Research Fdn., Brookline, 5/042
New England Education Society, Boston, 5/043
New England Heritage Trail Fdn., Boston, 5/043
New England Home for Deaf Mutes, Boston, 5/044
Newton-Waltham Bank and Trust Company Trustee Under Perpetual Benevolent Fund, Waltham, 5/048
New University Fdn., Boston, 5/050
Nexon (Philip J. and Elinor W.) Charitable Fdn., Boston, 5/051
Nichols Trust, Boston, 5/051
Nichols (John H.), Jr. Charitable Trust, Dedham, 5/052
Nieman (Philip & Adele) Charitable Fdn., Boston, 5/052
Noble Hospital, Springfield, 5/053
Nordisk Insulinfond Fdn., Boston, 5/053
Nordling Fdn., Boston, 5/055
Northern Baptist Education Society, Boston, 5/055
V-8364 U/Ind. Oaks Fdn., Boston, 5/056
Old Ladies Home Society, Beverly, 5/057
Omaha Home for Boys Trust, Boston, 5/058
Open Church Fdn., Gloucester, 5/058
Orchard Fdn., Inc., Boston, 5/060
Oregon State College Trust, Boston, 5/060
Orr Fdn. Newton-Waltham Bank & Trust, Waltham, 5/060
Osborne Charitable Fund, Boston, 5/061
Ostrow (John) Charitable Trust, Worcester, 5/061
Paine (Robert Treat) Assoc., Boston, 5/062

Parish (Jeffrey A.) Fdn., Springfield, 5/062
Park (Francis William) Trust, Boston, 5/063
Parker Affiliated Companies Charitable Fdn.,
    Worcester, 5/065
Parlin (Albert N.) House, Boston, 5/065
Parsons (Anne) Educational Trust, Cambridge,
    5/065
Patterson (Jessie T.), Springfield, 5/066
Peabody (Henry O.) School for Girls, Boston,
    5/066
Pease (James L.), Springfield, 5/067
Pechet (Maurice) Fdn., Boston, 5/067
Penn (Anne & Henry) Charitable Fdn.,
    Brookline, 5/068
Perini Memorial Fdn., Framingham, 5/069
Permanent Fund Trust for Harvard Travelers
    Club, Boston, 5/070
Perry (Thomas Andrew) Charitable Trust,
    Springfield, 5/070
Persky (A. S.) Fund, Worcester, 5/070
Persky (Joseph) Fdn., Worcester, 5/071
Peters (Gorham) Testamentary Trust, Boston,
    5/072
Pike School, Andover, 5/073
Pinanski (Abraham E.) Memorial Fund, Boston,
    5/073
Piper (Harold Scott) Fdn., Waban, 5/074
Platt Fdn., Cambridge, 5/075
Poland (Ted & Mildred S.) Charitable Fund,
    Boston, 5/075
Preston (Ina and Jerome) 1932 Charitable
    Trust, Boston, 5/075
Price (Dr. Joseph R. and Florence A.)
    Scholarship Fund, Boston, 5/076
Pringle (Charles G.) Fdn., Boston, 5/078
Prouty (Olive Higgins) Fdn., Boston, 5/081
Public Safety Committee Trust of Fitchburg,
    Worcester, 5/082
Quick (Joseph and Winifred) Fdn., Westboro,
    5/083
Quincy Oil Fund, Quincy, 5/083
Quogue Community Fdn., Harvard, 5/083
Rabb Fdn., Boston, 5/083
Rabinowitz (Sidney H.) Family Fdn., Boston,
    5/084
Ramlose (George A.) Fdn., Boston, 5/085
Raytheon Charitable Fdn., Lexington, 5/086
Reed (Lansing P.), Holyoke, 5/087
Reed (Mary T.), Boston, 5/087
Reigluth (Charles M.) Fdn., Boston, 5/087
Research FUnd of American Diabetes
    Association, Boston, 5/088
Revere Jewish Community Center Trust,
    Chestnut Hill, 5/088
Ribakoff (Eugene J. & Corinne A.) Charitable
    Fdn., Worcester, 5/090
Ricci-Goldberg Fdn., Fall River, 5/091
Rice (Albert W.) Charitable Fdn., Worcester,
    5/092
Richardson School Fund Trust, Attleboro,
    5/092
Richmond (Harold B.) Fdn., Boston, 5/092
Rickless (Herman A.) Family Fdn., Springfield,
    5/093
Riesman (Joseph and Sadie) Fdn., Boston,
    5/093
Rifchin Family Fdn., Watertown, 5/094
Robbie (J. Everett) Fdn., Quincy, 5/095
Robie (Samuel H. & Lizzie M.) Trust, Chelsea,
    5/096
Roby (Sara) Fdn., Nantucket, 5/097
Rogal (Helen and Sidney) Charitable Fdn.,
    Boston, 5/097
Romarlo Fdn., Vineyard Haven, 5/098
Ronthelym Charitable Trust, Boston, 5/098
Rosenbaum (Solomon and Rose) Fdn.,
    Fitchburg, 5/099
Rosenblum (Isidore and Bessie) Fdn., Natick,
    5/100
Rosenblum and Jaffe Charitable Trust,
    Worcester, 5/101
Rotenberg (Sol) Fdn., Brighton, 5/102
Roth (Hugo) Family Fdn., East Longmeadow,
    5/103
Roxbury Home for Aged Women, Boston,
    5/104

Roxco Fdn., Framingham, 5/105
Rubenstein (Harold) Family Charitable Fdn.,
    Brockton, 5/107
Rubenstein (Lawrence J. and Anne) Charitable
    Fdn., Boston, 5/108
Rudnick Charitable Fdn., Brookline, 5/108
Rudnick (Harold) Charitable Fdn., Cambridge,
    5/109
Sachs (Maxwell) Fdn., Chestnut Hill, 5/110
Sadowsky (William) Family Fdn., Worcester,
    5/111
Sailor's Snug Harbor of Boston, Boston, 5/112
St. Anthony's Welfare Center, Boston, 5/113
St. James Episcopal Church Trust, Boston,
    5/114
St. Johns Lutheran Church Trust, Boston,
    5/114
St. Pauls Church Mackintosh Fund, Holyoke,
    5/114
St. Pauls Church Metcalf, Holyoke, 5/114
St. Pauls Church Trust, Boston, 5/115
Salem Female Charitable Soc., Salem, 5/115
Salloway (Dr. Elliot W. and Regina) Charitable
    Trust, Worcester, 5/116
Salvation Army Trust, Boston, 5/116
Guido Salvucci Fdn., Newton, 5/116
Sanburn (Marion H.), Springfield, 5/117
Sanders (Sabra H.) Fund, Boston, 5/117
Sanford (Thomas A.), Boston, 5/118
Sapers (William R.) Fdn., Boston, 5/119
Sawyer Charitable Fdn., Boston, 5/119
Schwartz (Louis) Family Fdn., Boston, 5/120
Schwartz (Nathan and Ida) Charitable Trust,
    Boston, 5/121
Sciences and Arts Fdn., Dedham, 5/122
Trustees of the Sears and Other Funds Boston
    Safe, Boston, 5/122
Segregansett Country Club, Taunton, 5/124
Septimus Fdn., Boston, 5/125
Service League Fdn., Springfield, 5/126
Seveney (P. F. C. William F.) Scholarship
    Fund, Ware, 5/126
Shammash (Jacob B.) Family Charitable Fdn.,
    Longmeadow, 5/126
Shamroth Family Charitable Trust, Boston,
    5/128
Shaw (Gardiner Howland) Fdn., Boston, 5/128
Sheperd (Thomas M.) #T295, Springfield,
    5/129
Shepherd (Thomas M.) #300, Springfield,
    5/129
Sheraton Fdn., Boston, 5/129
Sherman (George and Beatrice) Family
    Charitable Trust, Boston, 5/131
Shipley Fdn., Newton, 5/131
U/W Shuman (Abraham) f/b/o Boston
    Floating Hospital, Boston, 5/132
Skinner (Joseph A.) #VT156, Holyoke, 5/133
Skinner (Joseph A.) Ins. Trust, Holyoke, 5/133
Skinner (Joseph A.) #VT313A, Holyoke,
    5/133
Smith (Belle T.), Springfield, 5/133
Smith Charities, Northampton, 5/134
Smith Family Charitable Fdn., Boston, 5/134
Smith (George W.), Springfield, 5/135
Smith (Henry B. and Edwin) Trust, Westfield,
    5/135
Smith (Horace) Fund, Springfield, 5/135
Smith (Lois G. and Charles L.), Jr. Charitable
    Fdn., 5/136
Smith (Rose M.) #T841, Springfield, 5/136
Smith (Rose M.) #T842, Springfield, 5/136
Smithies (Harry C.) Tr. U/5th C1 O/W,
    Springfield, 5/137
Snidier (Elliot L. and Ruth) Charitable Trust,
    Chestnut Hill, 5/137
Snider (Stanley and Mary Ann) Fdn., Chestnut
    Hill, 5/137
Snyder Family Charitable Fdn., Boston, 5/138
Society to Aid The Missions Trust, Boston,
    5/138
Society of the Cincinnati In The State of New
    Hamp., Boston, 5/138
Sohn (Donald R.) Fdn., Boston, 5/139
Solomont Charity Fdn., Lowell, 5/140
Solar Family Fdn., Boston, 5/140

Spaid (Charles J.), Springfield, 5/141
Sparrow (Marvin and Dorothy J.) Charitable
    Fdn., Boston, 5/141
Spaulding (Justin) Memorial Fund, Springfield,
    5/142
Spaulding (Woodward) Memorial Fund,
    Springfield, 5/142
Sprague (Florence & Robert) Fdn.,
    Williamstown, 5/143
Spruce Mountain Fdn., Wellesley, 5/143
S. S. & W. Charitable Fdn., Cambridge, 5/143
Stahl (Jacob I.) Fdn., Peabody, 5/144
Standard International Fdn., Andover, 5/144
Stanley Park of Westfield, Westfield, 5/145
Stearns (George M.), Springfield, 5/146
Stearns Fund, Boston, 5/146
Stein (Isadore and Goldie) Charitable Trust,
    Boston, 5/146
Stein (Renee & Herbert M.) Charitable Fdn.,
    Waban, 5/146
Stickney (Elsa P.), Springfield, 5/149
Stillwell (James M.) Trust, Springfield, 5/149
Strick (Helen & I L) Fdn., Springfield, 5/149
Stone (Faye G. and David G.) Charitable Fdn.,
    Brookline, 5/150
Stone Institute and Newton Home for Aged
    People, Newton Upper Falmass, 5/150
Stone Family Fdn., Chelmsford, 5/152
Stoneham Visiting Nurse Assoc., Stoneham,
    5/152
Stous (Richard Salter) Library of Longmeadow,
    Longmeadow, 5/153
Stromeyer (Charles F.) Fdn., Marblehead,
    5/154
Sullivan (John F. & Marian B.) Fdn.,
    Springfield, 5/154
Superv Prin Montrose Col Sch Trust, Boston,
    5/155
Sutton Home for Aged Women in Peabody,
    Peabody, 5/155
Tackeff (Bertram and Sterra) Charitable Fdn.,
    Brookline, 5/157
Tarbell (Dorothy J.) #T1022, Springfield,
    5/158
Tarbell (Dorothy J.) #T1023, Springfield,
    5/158
Tarlin (Lloyd D.) Fdn., Boston, 5/158
Taunton Female Charitable Assoc., Taunton,
    5/159
Taunton Greyhound Association Charitable
    Fdn., Boston, 5/160
Teamsters Union - 68 Welfare Fund, Boston,
    5/161
Tedeschi (Ralph D.) Charitable Trust,
    Rockland, 5/161
Tempo Theatre Co. Charitable Trust, Boston,
    5/161
Tenney Educational Fund, Andover, 5/161
Thayer (Julia B.) Testamentary Trust, Boston,
    5/162
Thayer (Pauline Revere) Memorial Pension
    Fdn., Boston, 5/162
Third Congregational Society of Springfield,
    Springfield, 5/163
Thresher (Herbert H.) #T902, Springfield,
    5/164
Thresher (Herbert H.) #T901, Springfield,
    5/164
Thompson (Thomas) Trust, Boston, 5/164
Tidd Home Trust, Boston, 5/166
Tobin (Alan D. and Judith) Charitable Fdn.,
    Brookline, 5/167
Trinity Lutheran Church, Boston, 5/167
Trust U/W Emma L. Borden, Fall River,
    5/167
Trust U/W Etta A. Allen, Springfield, 5/167
Trust U/Will Fred D. Allen, Boston, 5/168
T-7 U/Will Abbey B. Andrews, Boston, 5/168
Trust U/Agmt. Arthur I. Andrews, Boston,
    5/169
Trust u/w/o Allen J. Ash f/b/o Rebecca Ash
    Kenazy, Boston, 5/169
Tr. U/W Elizabeth F. Atwood Trust,
    Springfield, 5/170
Burbank (Mary C.) Testamentary Trust,
    Springfield, 5/170

Trust U/Will Mary E. Batchelder, Boston, 5/171

Trust U/W of Robert M. Birmingham, Lawrence, 5/172

Trust U/W Charles N. Blake, Boston, 5/173

Tr. U/W Edith L. Blanchard, Boston, 5/173

Trust Under Will of Milford Bliss, Attleboro, 5/175

Trust U/W of Helen C. S. Botsford #04-6130605, Williamstown, 5/175

Trust U/W of Helen C. S. Botsford, Williamstown, 5/175

Trust U/W John D. Bryant, Boston, 5/176

Tr. U/W Claruth W. Bradlwy, Springfield, 5/176

Tr. U/W Sarah S. Brayton, Fall River, 5/176

Trust U/W Herbert A. Chase, Boston, 5/177

T-73 U/Will Ira Cleveland, Boston, 5/178

Trust U/Will F. Lyman Clark, Boston, 5/178

Trustees U/W Lotta M. Crabtree, Boston, 5/179

Trust U/Will Matilda H. Crocker, Boston, 5/182

Dexter (Ernest J.) Trust, Springfield, 5/183

Trust U/W Charles J. Douglas, Boston, 5/184

Trust U/W Grace M. Edwards, Boston, 5/186

Trust U/W Hannah M. Edwards, Boston, 5/187

Trust U/W Robert J. Edwards, Boston, 5/187

Trust U/Art. 6 o/w/o Mary Alice Falvey, Boston, 5/187

T-8891 Tr. U/Will Laura S. Fiske, Boston, 5/190

Trust U/W Mary Alice Fitch, Boston, 5/193

Trust U/Will Richard & Mary Phipps Healy Charity, Worcester, 5/199

Hibbard (Gertrude) Trust, Springfield, 5/199

Hickey (Dorothy B.) Trust, Boston, 5/200

Hill (Gertrude L. G.) Trust, Springfield, 5/200

Hurley (John J.) Fund "A", Boston, 5/201

Hurley (John J.) Fund "B", Boston, 5/202

Hurley (John J.) Fund "C", Boston, 5/203

Kidder (Frederic) Trust, Boston, 5/204

Trust U/Will Nathaniel T. Kidder, Boston, 5/205

Kimball (Helen F.) Fund for the Promotion of Good Citizenship, Boston, 5/206

Lee (Margaret C.) Art. 15, Boston, 5/206

Life (Robert H.) Testamentary Trust, Springfield, 5/207

Longley (Harriet Dwight) T. Trust, Springfield, 5/208

Lutolf (Frances F.), Springfield, 5/209

Martin (Joseph C.) Trust, Springfield, 5/209

Will of Fanny P. Mason, Boston, 5/209

Will of Louise C. May, Boston, 5/210

Will of Daniel H. Maynard, Boston, 5/211

McCoy (Sarah H.) Testamentary Trust, Springfield, 5/211

Trust U/W of John McElandy, Boston, 5/212

Merritt (Louise C.) Testamentary Trust, Springfield, 5/213

Mulligan (Charles H.) Testamentary Trust, Springfield, 5/214

Trust U/Will Lena A. Thompson, Boston, 6/001

Lena A. Tucker Trust, Springfield, 6/002

T3246 U/W Elizabeth Vaughan, Boston, 6/002

Tr. U/W William B. Walker, Springfield. 6/003

Trust U/W Warner (Charles F.) Aid Worthy Students, Springfield, 6/003

Watson (Roy Garrett), Orr (Stewart G.) and Appleton (B. Earle), Boston, 6/003

Trust U/W White (Daniel) c/o Meller (James J.), Tr., Boston, 6/004

White (Harold) Testamentary Trust, Springfield, 6/004

Twenty-Fifth Inf. Div. Asso. Tr., Boston, 6/004

United Front Fdn., Roxbury, 6/004

United Fund of Southbridge Trust, Boston, 6/005

Univ. of Cincinnati Med. Sch. Tr., Boston, 6/005

University of Maine Trust, Boston, 6/005

Vance (Henry T.) Charitable Fdn., Boston, 6/005

Vash (Arthur M. and Lillian B.) Charitable Fdn., Newton Center, 6/006

Vatco Industries Charitable Fdn., Boston, 6/007

Veteran Association of the First Corps of Cadets, Boston, 6/007

Wallace (George R.) 3rd Charitable Trust, Fitchburg, 6/008

Walnut Medical Charitable Trust, Boston, 6/008

Walter (Henry & Ruth S.) Charitable Fdn., Wellesley, 6/09

Ward (Wilbur H. H.) Educational Trust, Amherst, 6/009

Warner (Charles F.), Springfield, 6/010

Warner (Herbert D.) Fund Boys and Girls Home, Sioux City, Iowa, 6/011

Warren Benevolent Fund, Ashland, 6/011

Wasmequia Charitable Trust, Boston, 6/012

Weaver (Howard) #T958, Springfield, 6/013

Weaver (Howard A.) #T961, Springfield, 6/013

Weber (Frederick E.) Charities Corporation, Boston, 6/013

Trust U/Ind. Rudolph L. Weber, Boston, 6/014

Webster (Edwin S.) Fdn., Boston, 6/015

Weinberg Family Fund, Auburndale, 6/016

Weinberg (Benjamin) Charitable Trust, Boston, 6/017

Weinstein (Aaron & Patricia) Charitable Fdn., Boston, 6/017

Weintraub (Gerald D. and Deborah S.) Fdn., Boston, 6/017

Weld Fdn., Boston, 6/018

Weltman (Esther Z.) Charitable Fdn., Boston, 6/018

Werkes (Leitung Des Dominicus), Boston, 6/019

Wesson Memorial Hospital Alumnae Assoc., Springfield, 6/019

Wesson (Daniel B.) #T365, Springfield, 6/020

Wesson (Daniel B.) #T364, Springfield, 6/020

West Scientific & Educational Fund for The Present Private Interest, Boston, 6/020

Wexler (Leo A.) Fdn., Newton, 6/021

White Fund, Lawrence, 6/022

White (Harvey and Dorothy) Charitable Trust, Boston, 6/022

Williams (Arthur Ashley) Fdn., Framingham, 6/023

Williams (Moses Pierce) House Assoc., Boston, 6/025

Wilson (Albert O.) Fdn., Cambridge, 6/025

Winokur (Harry & Etta) Charitable Fdn., Chestnut Hill, 6/026

Winthrop Ames Scholarship, Boston, 6/027

Witty (Carl) Charitable Trust, West Newton, 6/027

Wivern Trust, Cambridge, 6/028

Wolf (Natalie W. and Leo E.) Fdn., West Newton, 6/028

Wolfson (Jack and Marcia) Charitable Trust, Worcester, 6/028

Wollaston Mothers Club, North Qunicy, 6/029

Womens Fellowship of the Mass. Co., Boston, 6/029

Cornelius A. and Muriel P. Wood Charity Fund, Boston, 6/029

Wood (Frank) Testamentary Tr., Boston, 6/030

Wood (Mary E.) Fdn., Boston, 6/031

World Peace Fdn., Boston, 6/032

Worthen (F. P.) Fdn., Lowell, 6/034

Wright (Stevens T. M.) Fdn., Boston, 6/035

Wueth Endowment Fdn. for American Art, Boston, 6/036

Yamins Family Charitable Fdn., Brighton, 6/037

Yeomans (Peter Jeffe) Fdn., Needham, 6/037

Young (Mary Ida) Fdn., Springfield, 6/038

Zarling Charitable Fdn., Worcester, 6/038

Zartarian Fdn., Dorchester, 6/039

Zelkind Charitable Fdn., Worcester, 6/040

MICHIGAN

First Filming

Abernethy (Roy & Florence) Fdn., Detroit, 1/001

A.B.J. Fdn., Grand Rapids, 1/002

Abrams (Talbert & Leota) Fdn., Lansing, 1/003

Adler (Rabbi Morris) Memorial Fdn., Southfield, 1/003

Adrian Rotary Fdn., Adrian, 1/003

Aeroquip Fdn., Jackson, 1/003

Akers (Forest H.) Trust, East Lansing, 1/004

Albert (Harold) Fdn., Grand Rapids, 1/007

Albert (Silas F. & Estelle J.) Fdn., Grand Rapids, 1/007

Algar Fdn., Lincoln Park, 1/008

Alger (George F.) Company Fdn., Detroit, 1/008

Allan (George) Charitable Fdn., Battle Creek, 1/009

Alpena Museum Association, Alpena, 1/009

Alpern (E. Bryce & Harriet) Fdn., Detroit, 1/010

Alpert (Ida & Benjamin) Fdn., Detroit, 1/010

Americana Fdn., Farmington, 1/011

Ames [George M.] Trust (Grand Rapids Fdn.), Grand Rapids, 1/012

Anderson Family Fund, Detroit, 1/014

Anderson (Frank N.) Fdn., Saginaw, 1/015

Andrews (Claude D. & Etta H.) Charitable Trust, Detroit, 1/016

Angell (William R.) Fdn., Southfield, 1/017

Appco Fdn., Monroe, 1/017

Applegate Fdn., Grand Rapids, 1/018

Armstrong (Adam Elliott) Fdn., Three Rivers, 1/019

Armstrong (Jane E.) Trusts, Detroit, 1/019

Armstrong (John W. & Virginia C.) Fdn., Detroit, 1/020

Associated Truck Lines Fdn., Grand Rapids, 1/021

Atkinson (Annie Marie Nixon) Trust, Detroit, 1/022

Attwood Fdn., Wayne, 1/023

August (Harry E. & Helen S.) Fdn., Huntington Woods, 1/023

Ausco Employees Contribution Fund, St. Joseph, 1/024

Baldwin Fdn., Grand Rapids, 1/024

Bank of Alma Charitable Trust, Alma, 1/026

Bargman (Theodore & Mina) Fdn., Detroit, 1/027

Barnett (Harry & Edythe) Fdn., Oak Park, 1/028

Barstow Fdn., Midland, 1/029

Bartush (Stephen J.) Fdn., Detroit, 1/030

Bassett (Mary A.) Trust, Detroit, 1/031

Battjes (Dewey D. & Hattie) Fdn., Grand Rapids, 1/031

Bauer (Russell E.) Fdn., Warren, 1/031

Bay County Civic League, Bay City, 1/033

Becker (Harry) Fdn., Detroit, 1/033

Bennett (Earl W. & Eva V.) Fdn., Midland, 1/034

Beresford Fund, Birmingham, 1/034

Berger (Samuel & Clara) Fdn., Detroit, 1/035

Bernstein (Frank A.) Fdn., Detroit, 1/036

Berrien Community Fdn., Benton Harbor, 1/036

Berry Fdn., Detroit, 1/037

Besser Fdn., Alpena, 1/038

Besser (Jesse) Fund, Alpena, 1/039

Bishop (A.G.) Charitable Trust, Flint, 1/041

Bixby Fdn., Detroit, 1/042

Blesch Fund, Menominee, 1/043

Blesch (Bertha W.) Testamentary Trust, Menominee, 1/043

Bloom (Herbert & Betty) Fdn., Orchard Lake, 1/044

Blow (Arthur & Mary) Scholarship Fund, Royal Oak, 1/044

Bonner Fdn., Detroit, 1/045

Borin (Jacob) Fdn., Detroit, 1/045

Borman (Abraham & Molly) Fdn., Detroit, 1/046

Borman (Paul D.) Fdn., Detroit, 1/047

Borman (Tom & Sarah) Fdn., Detroit, 1/047

Boschan Family Fdn., Detroit, 1/047

Joy (Henry Bourne) Trust, Detroit, 1/047

Boutell (Marvin E.) Educational & Charitable Trust, Flint, 1/048

Bower Fdn., Grosse Pointe, 1/048

Bowie (Chester E. & Harriet F.) Fdn., Farmington, 1/050

Boyd (J. Fred & Helen Barnard) Fdn., Muskegon, 1/050

Bradley (Carl D.) Ship Disaster Children's Fund, Rogers City, 1/051

Breech Fdn., Detroit, 1/051

Brewer Fdn. of Grand Rapids, Grand Rapids, 1/053

Smith - Bridgman Charitable Trust, Flint, 1/053

Bright (Rinehart S. & Anne M.) Fdn., Southfield, 1/054

Bronner (Wallace) Family Trust, Frankenmuth, 1/054

Brown (Charles & Betty) Fdn., Birmingham, 1/054

Brown (Olive Marie McIntosh) Trust, Detroit, 1/056

Buek (Max W.) & Sloan (Elizabeth Jane) Trust Fund, Detroit, 1/057

Bugas Fund, Southfield, 1/057

Buhr Fdn., Ann Arbor, 1/058

Bundy Fdn., Detroit, 1/058

Bunting (Russell W.) Memorial Fdn., Oak Park, 1/060

Burns Fdn., Petoskey, 1/060

Byrne (Dan & Helen N.) Fdn., Detroit, 1/061

Cain Fund, Ann Arbor, 1/062

Campbell - Ewald Fdn., Detroit, 1/062

Campbell (Kenneth H.) Fdn. for Neurological Research, Grand Rapids, 1/063

Carey (Elaine & Walter) Fdn., Flint, 1/064

Caridad Fund, Grand Rapids, 1/064

Carls (William & Marie) Fdn., Detroit, 1/065

Carlson Fdn., Detroit, 1/065

Casey (E. Paul & Patricia P.) Fdn., Grosse Pointe, 1/066

C.C.I. Fdn., Detroit, 1/067

Challenge Stamping & Porcelain Co. Fdn., Grand Haven, 1/067

Chamberlin (Clarence & Grace) Fdn., Detroit, 1/067

Chapin (Roy D.) Fdn., Detroit, 1/070

Chapman Scholarship Trust, Niles, 1/071

Child Health Fdn. International, Detroit, 1/072

Christian Evangelical Fund, Bloomfield Hills, 1/073

Christopher Founders, Grand Rapids, 1/073

Chrysler Corporation Fund, Detroit, 1/074

Cisler (Walker & Gertrude) Library Fdn., Detroit, 1/076

Citrin (Jacob A.) & Sons Fdn., Romulus, 1/076

Clapp (Charles I. & Emma J.) Scholarship Fund, Kalamazoo, 1/077

Clarage Fdn., Kalamazoo, 1/078

Clark Fdn., Jackson, 1/079

Oleson Fdn., Traverse City, 1/079

Clifton (R.F.) Charitable Fdn., Three Rivers, 1/080

Clupper (John H.) Scholarship Trust, Niles, 1/080

Cogan (Harold L. & Jill A.) Fdn., Grand Rapids, 1/081

Cohen (Henry & Mary) Family Fdn., Southfield, 1/082

Community Health Center of Mesick, Mesick, 1/083

Cook (Peter C. & Emajean) Charitable Trust, Grand Rapids, 1/083

Cornwell (Edgar L.) Educational Trust, Flint, 1/084

Cramblet Fdn., St. Joseph, 1/086

Crawford (Anne I.) Fdn., Grand Rapids, 1/086

Cummings Fund, Fremont, 1/087

Dabco - Frank Fdn., Detroit, 1/088

Dailey Charitable Fund, Saginaw, 1/088

Dake Corporation Fdn., Grand Haven, 1/089

Darin & Armstrong Fdn., Detroit, 1/089

Darling Family Charitable Fdn., Grand Rapids, 1/090

Daverman Associates Fdn., Grand Rapids, 1/091

Daverman (Edward H.) Fdn., Grand Rapids, 1/092

Daverman (Herbert G.) Fdn., Grand Rapids, 1/092

Daverman (Joseph T.) Fdn., Grand Rapids, 1/093

Daverman (Robert J.) Fdn., Grand Rapids, 1/094

Davidson (W.M.) Fdn., Novi, 1/094

Davis (John R. & Ruth R.) Fdn., Bloomfield Hills, 1/095

De Bruyn Fdn., Zeeland, 1/095

Defoe Fdn., Bay City, 1/096

Denise Fdn., Dearborn, 1/097

Deroy (Helen L.) Fdn., Detroit, 1/097

Detroit Friends of Music, Southfield, 1/099

Detroit Steel Corporation Charitable Trust, Detroit, 1/100

Detroiter Fdn., St. Louis, 1/100

Deur Fdn., Giant, 1/101

Deutsch Family Fdn., Southfield, 1/101

Deutsch (William L. & Vivian) Charitale Fdn., Royal Oak, 1/102

DeVlieg (Charles B.) Fdn., Royal Oak, 1/102

Devos (Richard & Helen) Fdn., Grand Rapids, 1/103

DeWaters (Enos A.) Residue Trust, Flint, 1/105

Dexter Charitable Trust Fund, Grand Rapids, 1/106

Dexter Industries Charitable Fund, Grand Rapids, 1/108

D.H.C. Fdn., Grand Rapids, 1/110

Memorial Hospital Women's League, Iron Mountain, 1/111

Diehl (Edward & Ruth) Fdn., Pleasant Ridge, 1/111

Diehl (Lloyd & Irene) Fdn., Detroit, 1/112

Doan Fdn., Midland, 1/113

Doan (Herbert D. & Donalda L.) Fdn., Midland, 1/114

Doerfner (William H.) Fdn., Saginaw, 1/115

Doeren (Karl M.) Fdn., Ferndale, 1/115

Doty Educational Fund, Southfield, 1/116

Dow (Alden & Vada) Fund, Midland, 1/117

Dow (Herbert H. & Barbara C.) Fdn., Midland, 1/117

Dow (Herbert H. & Grace A.) Fdn., Midland, 1/118

Draper Family Fdn., Saginaw, 1/118

D.U. Memorial Fdn., Detroit, 1/119

Duffy (James E.) Fdn., Port Huron, 1/120

Dunn (Jack & Rose E.) & Son Fdn., Detroit, 1/120

Dyer - Ives Fdn., Grand Rapids, 1/121

Dykstra Fdn., Birmingham, 1/122

Earhart Fdn., Ann Arbor, 1/123

Earl - Beth Fdn., Grosse Pointe Famrs, 1/129

Edgar (Mary G.) Trust, Detroit, 1/130

E F O Fdn., Detroit, 1/131

Edison (L.W.) Charitable Fdn. of Grand Rapids, Grand Rapids, 1/131

Elder (William F. & Idella) Fdn., East Tawas, 1/132

Emerman (David & Edith) Fdn., Southfield, 1/132

Emmett Fdn., Detroit, 1/133

Endicott - Bohn Fdn., St. Clair Shores, 1/133

Enuresis Fdn., Galesburg, 1/134

Epsilon Educational Endowment, Ann Arbor, 1/135

Erb Fdn., Birmingham, 1/135

Erickson Fdn., Grand Haven, 1/136

Ervin (J.F.) Fdn., Ann Arbor, 1/136

Etruscan Fdn., Grosse Pointe Farms, 1/138

Ewald (H.T.) Fdn., Grosse Pointe, 1/138

Fachting (J.E.) Fdn., West Branch, 1/140

Feinberg Fdn., Detroit, 1/140

Feldman (Milton & Sally) Fdn., Detroit, 1/141

Fellrath Fdn., Dearborn, 1/141

Ferris (Effah Elizabeth) Revolving Fund, Muskegon, 1/142

Ferry (D.M.), Jr. Trustee Corporation, Detroit, 1/142

Field (Walter L.) Family Fdn., Detroit, 1/144

Fine Charitable Fdn., Lansing, 1/146

Fink (George R. & Elise M.) Fdn., Harper Woods, 1/147

Fischer (Wilhelmina S. & Frederick C.) Charitable Trust, Kalamazoo, 1/147

Fisher - Insley Fdn., St. Clair, 1/148

Fleet Fdn., Grosse Pointe, 1/149

Fleming Fdn., Alma, 1/150

F.M. & K. Fdn., Detroit, 1/151

Ford Motor Company Fund, Dearborn, 1/152

Ford (Benson & Edith) Fund, Detroit, 1/169

Ford (Eleanor Clay) Fund, Detroit, 1/171

Ford (Henry), II Fund, Detroit, 1/173

Ford (John B. & Mary H.) Fund, Detroit, 1/175

Ford (Walter & Josephine) Fund, Detroit, 1/175

Ford (William & Martha) Fund, Detroit, 1/177

Forest Haven Bible Camp Association, Harbor Springs, 1/179

Foundation for the Future, Bay City, 1/179

Frank (William Henry & Ruth Lambert) Charitable Fdn., Huntington Woods, 1/179

Frank (Harrison Jules Louis & Leon Harrison) Memorial Corporation, Huntington Woods, 1/180

Frankel (Samuel & Jean) Fdn., Birmingham, 1/181

Frankel (Stanley D.) Fdn., Birmingham, 1/182

Fredericks (Marshall) Fdn., Royal Oak, 1/184

Freedland (Nathan & Ruth) Fdn., Southfield, 1/184

Fremont Fdn., Fremont, 1/185

French (John S. & Elizabeth) Fdn., Bloomfield Hills, 1/186

Frenkel (Joseph) Family Fdn., Detroit, 1/186

Friedt Family Fdn., Detroit, 1/187

Fruehauf Corporation Charitable Fund, Detroit, 1/187

Fryfogle (W.D.) Medical Research Laboratory, Southfield, 1/188

Fusor Fdn., Benton Harbor, 1/189

Gage (Raymond D.) Fdn., Ferndale, 1/189

Gast Fdn., Benton Harbor, 1/189

Gehrke (Walter & Ruth) Fdn., Birmingham, 1/190

Gerstacker (Rollin M.) Fdn., Midland, 1/192

Gertz (Herman & Irene) Fdn., Monroe, 1/193

G F R Fdn., Flint, 1/194

Giles (William R. & Margaret) Fdn., Detroit, 1/194

Gilmore Fdn., Kalamazoo, 1/195

Gilmore (Genevieve & Donald) Fdn., Kalamazoo, 1/196

Gittlen (Alex & Ruth) Fdn., Grand Rapids, 1/197

Goad Fdn., Bloomfield Hills, 1/198

Goldberg (Adolph Irving & Adele) Fdn., Detroit, 1/198

Goldin (Nathan & Betty) Family Fdn., Southfield, 1/199

Goodman (Adolph & Herman) Family Trust, Detroit, 1/200

Goodman (Martha) Trust, Detroit, 1/200

Gordon (Frank & Doris) Fdn., Grand Rapids, 1/200

Gordon (Josephine E.) Fdn., Detroit, 1/202

Goudsmit Charitable Trust, Dearborn, 1/204

Grand Haven Stamped Products Company Fdn., Grand Haven, 1/204

Grand Rapids Fdn., Grand Rapids, 1/204

Grand Rapids Scholarship Association, Grand Rapids, 1/205

Grand Rapids Boiler Works Fdn., Grand Rapids, 1/207

Grand Rapids Steel & Supply Company Charitable Trust, Grand Rapids, 1/207

Gray (Roland) Youth Fund, Detroit, 1/208

Green Family Fdn., Detroit, 1/209
Green Hills Fdn., Ann Arbor, 1/210
Green (Irwin & Bethea) Fdn., Madison Heights, 1/211
Griffin (Jeanne) Fdn., Niles, 1/212
Grosse Pointe Rotary Fdn., Grosse Pointe Shores, 1/214
Gutmueller (Gus & Dorothy) Fdn., Grand Rapids, 1/214
Haass (Erwin & Virginia) Fdn., Detroit, 1/215
Haight (Floyd L. & Mary Dietrich) Charitable Trust, Detroit, 1/216
Hammers (Grace Paton) Charitable Trust, Detroit, 1/216
Hammond Fdn., Kalamazoo, 1/217
Hampson Fdn., Birmingham, 1/217
Hancock Fdn., Jackson, 1/218
Harder Fdn., Detroit, 1/218
Harding (Charles Stewart) Fdn., Flint, 1/219
Harlan Fdn., Detroit, 1/221
Harlow Fdn., Midland, 1/223
Harris Fdn., Detroit, 1/223
Hartman (Earl G. & Caroline M.) Fdn., Farmington, 1/224
Hartman (George H.) Scholarship Fund, Muskegon, 1/224
Harvey Memorial Fdn., Saginaw, 1/225
Hass Fdn., Detroit, 1/226
Haven Hill Fdn., Southfield, 1/226
Hayden (Donald C. & Agnes R.) Fdn., Dearborn, 1/226
Hauser Fdn., Detroit, 1/227
Hayes (Sheldon G.) Fdn., Southfield, 1/227
Header Fdn., Wayne, 1/228
Hekman (Edsko & Claire K.) Charitable Trust, Grand Rapids, 1/228
Herman (John R.) Fdn., Detroit, 1/229
Hill (Robert D.) Fdn., Birmingham, 1/229
Hinman (William & Sarah E.) Endowment Fund Corporation, Lansing, 1/230
Hofma (Drs. Edward & Elizabeth) Trust, Grand Haven, 1/230
Holden (James & Lynelle) Fund, Detroit, 1/232
Holley Fdn., Grosse Pointe Farms, 2/001
Hoobler (Madge & Raymond) Memorial, Ann Arbor, 2/002
Hopper (Florence V. H.) Trust, Detroit, 2/002
Horsley Fdn., Midland, 2/003
Hudson (Roberts P. & Ella B.) Fdn., Sault Ste. Marie, 2/004
Hungarian Sacred Heart Aid Society, Muskegon Heights, 2/005
Hurst Fdn., Jackson, 2/005
Iacocca Fdn., Birmingham, 2/006
Idema (Walter D.) Charitable Trust, Grand Rapids, 2/007
Iktinos Alumni Scholarship Fund, Detroit, 2/008
Imerman (John & Ella) Fdn., Detroit, 2/009
Imerman (Stanley) Charitable Trust, Detroit, 2/009
Ingham County Medical & Scientific Trust, Lansing, 2/010
Inman (May Lueder) Fdn., Niles, 2/010
Itzchok & Hendele Fdn., Ferndale, 2/011
Jackson (Corwill & Margie) Fdn., Detroit, 2/011
Jacobs (Roy W.) Fdn., Detroit, 2/013
Janssen Fdn., Rockford, 2/014
Jarecki Fdn., Grand Rapids, 2/014
Jarecki (Clare & Grace) Fdn., Grand Rapids, 2/014
Jeffers (Michael) Memorial Fdn., Saginaw, 2/015
Jensen Fdn., Jackson, 2/016
Jerome (Thomas S.) Lecture Fund, Detroit, 2/017
Jervis Corporation Fdn., Grandville, 2/018
Johns (Dr. Donald) Fdn., Grand Rapids, 2/018
Johnson (F. Martin & Dorothy A.) Fdn., Grand Haven, 2/019
Kabcenell Fdn., Pontiac, 2/020
Kahn (Albert) Associated Architects & Engineers Fdn., Detroit, 2/020

Kanat Fdn., Southfield, 2/021
Kanzler Fund, Detroit, 2/021
Kasle Fdn., Dearborn, 2/022
Katzman (Barney) Fdn., Huntington Woods, 2/023
Katzman (Sidney) Fdn., Huntington Woods, 2/024
Kaufman (Louis G.) Endowment Fund, Marquette, 2/024
Keith Fdn., Lansing, 2/025
Kellogg Company Twenty-five Year Employees Fund, Battle Creek, 2/026
Kelter Fdn., Southfield, 2/027
Kennedy (Elizabeth E.) Fund, Ann Arbor, 2/028
Kent (Floyd) Fdn., Pontiac, 2/029
Kent Medical Fdn., Grand Rapids, 2/029
Kent - Moore Fdn., Warren, 2/030
Kindel Fdn., Grand Rapids, 2/031
King (Cyrus H.) Charitable Trust, Detroit, 2/032
Kiwanis Club No. 2 Fdn. of Detroit, Detroit, 2/033
Komisaruk (Leon Kay) Fdn., Detroit, 2/034
Korman (Harry B. & Anna) Fdn., Detroit, 2/034
Kowalski Sausage Charitable Trust Fund, Detroit, 2/036
Kraft (Fannie) Fdn., Detroit, 2/036
Kraft (Jule & Shirley) Fdn., Southfield, 2/037
Kramer (Hyman A. & Bernice) Fdn., Detroit, 2/038
Kretschmer (Helen E. & Charles H.), Jr. Charitable Trust, Saginaw, 2/039
Kresge Fdn., Birmingham, 2/039
Krohn (Harry M. & Freda L.) Fdn., Southfield, 2/044
Kron (Joseph & Ida) Fdn., Detroit, 2/045
Kuhn (T.W.) Fdn., Southfield, 2/046
Kyes (Helen & Roger) Charity Fund, Detroit, 2/047
Laflin (William T.) Scholarship Fund, Barryton, 2/048
Major (LaMarre) Scholarship Fdn., Benton Harbor, 2/048
Laughlin (W.P.) Charitable Fdn., Kalamazoo, 2/049
Lee Fdn., Grand Haven, 2/051
Leflo Fdn., Muskegon Heights, 2/051
LeVine (David M. & Frieda G.) Fdn., Detroit, 2/052
Ligon (Robert G.) Fund, Ferndale, 2/053
Limbert Fdn., Grand Rapids, 2/054
Littler (Mark & Edith) Fdn., Grosse Pointe Shores, 2/055
Lord (John & Rhoda) Family Fund, Detroit, 2/055
Loutit Fdn., Grand Rapids, 2/056
Law (John L. & Rosa Lowry) Fdn., Ann Arbor, 2/058
L.T.R. Fdn., Detroit, 2/059
Lyon Fdn., Birmingham, 2/059
Maas (Benard L.) Fdn., Detroit, 2/061
Mackey (Helen H.) Memorial Educational Award Fund, Bay City, 2/062
MacCrone (Edward E.) Trust, Detroit, 2/062
Mahler (Sara & Irving) Fdn., Detroit, 2/063
Mahon (R.C.) Fdn., Detroit, 2/063
Manoogian (Marie & Alex) Fund, Detroit, 2/064
Maranatha Fdn., Franklin, 2/065
Marantette Fdn., Detroit, 2/066
Mardigian Fdn., Birmingham, 2/067
Marshall Civic Fdn., Marshall, 2/067
Marstan Fdn., Detroit, 2/067
Marstrand Fdn., Bloomfield Hills, 2/068
Marx (Helen Knowles & Harry Z.) Fdn., Bloomfield Hills, 2/069
Marx (Robert S.) Charitable Fdn. & Trust, Detroit, 2/069
Masco Screw Products Company Charitable Trust, Detroit, 2/070
Matthaei Fdn., Birmingham, 2/071
Matthaei (Litta) Trust, Detroit, 2/072
Matthes (Katherine M.) Trust, Detroit, 2/073

Matthias (Hans A. & Gertrude E.) Fdn., Birmingham, 2/073
McCabe (Evelyne) Fdn., Southfield, 2/074
McCarthy (Jerry) Fdn., Birmingham, 2/075
McCurdy Memorial Scholarship Fdn., Battle Creek, 2/076
McIntyre (B.D. & Jane E.) Fdn., Detroit, 2/077
McIntyre (C.S. & Marion F.) Fdn., Detroit, 2/077
McIntyre (W.D. & Prudence A.) Fdn., Detroit, 2/078
McLucas Family Charitable Trust, Detroit, 2/078
McMorran (Henry) Memorial Fdn., Port Huron, 2/079
Meckler (Irvin & Lillian) Fdn., Detroit, 2/080
Megdell (Joseph & Eleanor) Fdn., Flint, 2/080
Meyers (Allen H.) Fdn., Tecumseh, 2/080
Meynet (Maryanne Mott) Charitable Trust, Flint, 2/081
Michigan Dental Association Fund, Lansing, 2/082
Michigan Farm & Garden Fdn., Dearborn, 2/082
Michigan Fdn. for Advanced Research, Midland, 2/083
Michigan Press Association Fdn., East Lansing, 2/083
Miller (Abe & Rebecca) Fdn., Ferndale, 2/084
Miller (Arjay R. & Frances F.) Fdn., Detroit, 2/084
Miller (L.P.) Charitable Fdn., Southfield, 2/086
Miller (Milton J. & Jeanette X.) Fdn., Detroit, 2/086
Miro Fdn., Detroit, 2/087
Misco Scholarship Fund, Muskegon, 2/088
Mitchell Fdn., Owosso, 2/089
Modell Fdn., Birmingham, 2/089
Modell (Trudy & Harry) Fdn., Detroit, 2/090
Modell Fdn., Birmingham, 2/090
Molloy Fdn., Grosse Pointe Park, 2/091
Moore (Mary) Fdn., St. Clair, 2/093
Morley Brothers Fdn., Saginaw, 2/094
Morrison Fdn., Detroit, 2/095
Morrow (Thomas F. & Thirza S.) Fdn., Detroit, 2/096
Mott (Charles Stewart) Fdn., Flint, 2/096
Moulton Memorial Scholarship Fund, Grand Rapids, 2/101
Mueller Brass Fdn., Port Huron, 2/102
Mueller (Ebert B.) Trust, Detroit, 2/102
Muskegon Medical Fdn., Muskegon, 2/103
Muskegon Progress & Development Fund, Muskegon, 2/103
Muskegon Rotary Fdn., Muskegon, 2/104
National Bank of Detroit Charitable Trust Fund, Detroit, 2/105
National Fdn. of Rochester, Michigan, Rochester, 2/105
National - Standard Fdn., Niles, 2/106
Neithercut (Charles S.) Charitable Trust, Flint, 2/106
Neuman Charitable Trust, Grand Rapids, 2/107
Neumann (Frederick S.) Fdn., Detroit, 2/107
Newton (Charles R.) Memorial Scholarship Fdn., Detroit, 2/109
Nicolay (Ernest L.) Fdn., Detroit, 2/110
Nusbaum (Sol) Family Fdn., Southfield, 2/110
Oetjen (Johanna & Margaret) Fdn., Niles, 2/111
Orrell (Florence Whaley) Trust, Detroit, 2/112
Osuch (F.J.) Fdn., Detroit, 2/113
Owen Scholarship Trust, Niles, 2/113
Pardee (Elsa U.) Fdn., Midland, 2/114
Parkhurst (Cora B.) Scholarship Trust, Niles, 2/115
Parke - Davis Charitable Trust, Detroit, 2/116
Parsons Fdn., Traverse City, 2/117
Patterson (Charles H. & Elizabeth C.) Fdn., Birmingham, 2/118
Perkins (Elaine W. & Edward H.) Fdn., Birmingham, 2/118
Peterson (William W.) Charitable Trust Fund, Grand Rapids, 2/119

Wolverine Brass Works Fdn., Grand Rapids, 3/039

Wolverine Fdn., Kalamazoo, 3/040

Yeo (W.L. & Alma I.) Charitable Trust, Saginaw, 3/040

Yondotega Club, Detroit, 3/041

Youth Activities Fund Trust, Detroit, 3/041

Youth Fdn. of America, Petoskey, 3/041

Zahnow (Melvin J. & Lillian R.) Fdn., Saginaw, 3/042

Zeltzer (George M. & Pearl A.) Family Fdn., Southfield, 3/043

Zimmerman (Mary & George Herbert) Fdn., Detroit, 3/044

Zuckerman (Paul) Fdn., Livonia, 3/044

ZurSchmiede (W. Tom), Sr. Fdn., Detroit, 3/045

Zwerdling Fdn., Detroit, 3/046

Second Filming

Afro-American Cultural Development Fdn., Detroit, 4/001

Albion Civic Fdn., Albion, 4/002

Allan (George) Charitable Trust, Grand Rapids, 4/003

Allan (George) Charitable Fdn., Battle Creek, 4/003

Allen (A.D.) Fdn., Bay City, 4/004

Allen (George) Charitable Trust, Grand Rapids, 4/004

Alpena Exchange Charitable Trust, Alpena, 4/005

Ames (George M.) for Grand Rapids Fdn., Grand Rapids, 4/006

Anderson (Walter A. and Kathryn A.) Fdn., Detroit, 4/006

Ann Arbor Lodge #325 B. P. O. Elko, Ann Arbor, 4/007

Arcy (Edward T.) Fdn., Dearborn, 4/007

Area Resources Improvement Council, Benton Harbor, 4/008

Argus Cameras Charitable Trust Fund, Detroit, 4/010

Ash (Stanley & Blanche) Fdn., Greenville, 4/011

Bagley (Harry E.) Fdn., Dearborn, 4/012

Barnes (James T.) Fdn., Detroit, 4/012

Barnwell (E.W.) Fdn., Birmingham, 4/013

Barr (Edith and Andrew) Fund, Grosse Pointe, 4/014

Barris Sott Denn & Driker Fdn., Detroit, 4/014

Barton-Malow Company Fdn., Detroit, 4/015

Battle Creek Fdn., Battle Creek, 4/015

Beeghly (Lucile) Patrick Charitable Fdn., Battle Creek, 4/016

Bentley (Alvin M.) Fdn., Detroit, 4/017

Berkowitz (Hy and Greta) Fdn., Grands Rap, 4/018

Bernstein (Edward and June) Fdn., Ferndale, 4/019

Bernstein (Gerson & Lee) Fdn., Southfield, 4/019

Binder (Fred & Betty) Fdn., Detroit, 4/020

Birnbaum (Morris and Anna) Fdn., Wyandotte, 4/020

Bissell (Anna) aka Anna Bissell Charity Fund, Grand Rapids, 4/021

Blackmer Fdn., Grand Rapids, 4/021

Blackport Fdn., Grand Rapids, 4/021

Blumberg (Louis C.) Fdn., Detroit, 4/021

Braun Fdn., Detroit, 4/022

Brown (Ella E.M.) Charitable Circle Charitable Trust, Grand Rapids, 4/023

Boutell (Arnold and Gertrude) Memorial Fund, Saginaw, 4/023

Bower (Ferdinand A.) Trust; F.A. Bower Charitable Trust, Flint, 4/025

Brewer (Augusta H.) for Marian Louise Witney School of Nursing, Grand Rapids, 4/026

Cady (Mary Ida) Trust, Jackson, 4/026

Calvin Fdn., Grand Rapids, 4/027

Carleton (George N.) Fdn., Detroit, 4/027

Casgrain (Josephine P. & Wilfred V.) Charitable Trust, Detroit, 4/027

Catsman Fdn., Inc., Flint, 4/028

Center For Health Education, Detroit, 4/029

Chamberlin (Gerald W.) Fdn., Detroit, 4/030

Chapman (Bernard A.) Fdn., Bloomfield Hills, 4/032

Christian Advancement, Detroit, 4/032

Crysler (Sarah J.) Trust, Lansing, 4/033

Daily Tribune Trust, Royal Oak, 4/034

Dart (Harry A.) & Gladys M. Dart Fdn., Detroit, 4/034

Dearborn Rotary Fdn., Dearborn, 4/035

Demattia (W.H.) Fdn., Detroit, 4/035

Deneufville (J. & S.) Fdn., Birmingham, 4/036

DeNooyer Brothers Fdn., Kalamazoo, 4/036

DePree (D.J.) Charitable Trust, Zeeland, 4/037

Deseranno Educational Fdn., Detroit, 4/038

Detroit Ball Bearing Fdn., Detroit, 4/039

Detroit Community Trusts, Detroit, 4/041

DeVos (Jennie and Adrian A.) Fdn., Grand Haven, 4/046

DeWitt Fdn., Zeeland, 4/046

Diamond Crystal Fdn., St. Clair, 4/047

District Nursing Society, Detroit, 4/048

Dorsey (John M.) Trust, Highland Park, 4/049

Dow (Herbert H. and Grace A.) Fdn., Midland, 4/050

Dura Corporation, Southfield, 4/051

Elder (William and Idella) Fdn., East Tawas, 4/051

Elizabeth (Clara) Maternal Health Fund, Flint, 4/051

E. T. A. of Phi Sigma Delta Holding Co., Southfield, 4/052

Ettenheimer Fdn., Detroit, 4/052

Evenson (Charles Robert) Fdn., Grand Rapids, 4/052

Fabri-Kal Fdn., Kalamazoo, 4/052

Federal Screw Works Fdn., Detroit, 4/054

Feldmesser (Walter D.) Fdn., Detroit, 4/054

Fibre Converters Fdn., Three Rivers, 4/054

Fill (Dr. Leon) Fdn., Detroit, 4/055

Fink (Karl V.) Fdn., Ypsilanti, 4/055

First Methodist Church Charitable Trust #ID 38-604081, Flint, 4/055

First Methodist Church #ID 38-6097904, Flint, 4/056

First Presbyterian Church of Flint Trust, Flint, 4/057

Fisher (Max M. and Marjorie S.) Fdn., Detroit, 4/058

Fisher Trust for Shrine of Our Mother of Sorrows, Detroit, 4/057

Fishman (Nathan and Meyer M.) Family Fdn., Detroit, 4/058

Fleischman (Arthur) Family Fdn., Detroit, 4/059

Fleischman (Edward I.) Fdn., Detroit, 4/060

Flint Institute of Arts R. Spencer Bishop Trust, Flint, 4/060

Flodin Fdn., Iron Mountain, 4/061

Gordon Christian Fdn., Grand Rapids, 4/061

Citizens Com'l and Savings Bank Trustee U/A with Albert Sobey First Presbyterian Church, Flint, 4/062

Civic Affairs Research, Muskegon, 4/062

Civic Fund of Kalamazoo, Kalamazoo, 4/063

Clark Fund, Dryden, 4/064

Clement (Forney W.) Memorial Fdn., Detroit, 4/065

Cline Fdn., Huntington Woods, 4/065

Coleman Fdn., Hudson, 4/066

Collins (Lawrence and Violet) Music Fdn., Muskegon, 4/067

Comins (Franklin C.) & Francis M. Comins Charitable Trust, Flint, 4/069

Committee on Charities of The Miners First National Bank, Ishpeming, 4/070

T/U/A Cornelius (Louis A.), Grand Rapids, 4/070

Cotter (Florence V.) Fdn., Detroit, 4/071

Crane (Sallie A.) Scholars Aid Fund, Port Huron, 4/071

Cross, Wrock, Miller and Vieson Detroit Bar Assoc. Trust, Detroit, 4/071

Ford Fdn., Detroit, 4/071

Foster Welfare Fdn., Grand Rapids, 4/131

Fdn. for The Future, Bay City, 4/132

Frankel Fdn., Detroit, 4/132

Freedland Fdn., Warren, 4/133

Frey Fdn., Grand Rapids, 4/133

Freuhauf Fdn., Detroit, 4/134

Fruehauf (Angela and Harvey C.) Fdn., Detroit, 4/135

Fulks (James K.) Fdn., Birmingham, 4/137

Furniture Club of Detroit Fdn., Detroit, 4/138

Gage (Raymond D.) Fdn., Ferndale, 4/138

George Fund, Dryden, 4/138

Gerber Baby Foods Fund, Fremont, 4/139

Gerber (Louisa and Charles) Fdn., Fremont, 4/144

Gezon Fdn., Grand Rapids, 4/145

Glass (Sheldon C.) Memorial Fdn., Detroit, 4/146

Glick (Louis) Memorial Trust, Jackson, 4/146

Goodman (Adolph and Herman) Family Trust, Detroit, 4/147

Gooel Fdn., Detroit, 4/147

Gornick Fund, Bloomfield Hills, 4/148

Grand Rapids Fdn., Grand Rapids, 4/149

Grand Valley Cap 'N' Ballers Muzzle Loading Gun Club, Wayland, 4/149

Grander View Fdn., Milford, 4/149

Gray Fdn., Benton Harbor, 4/150

Greater International Metropolitan Area Council of The National Secretaries Assoc., Highland Park, 4/151

Green (R. Ellen) Trust, Lansing, 4/151

Greenberg (Hugh W. & Carolyn K.) Fdn., Detroit, 4/151

Greenhouse (N.Z.) Fdn., Detroit, 4/152

Griffin (Jeanne) Fdn., Niles, 4/153

Grinnell Fdn. of Music, Detroit, 4/153

Grosberg (Charles) Fdn., Oak Park, 4/154

H. A. J. Fdn., Pontiac, 4/154

Hall (Harry D. and Winifred K.) Fdn., Birmingham, 4/154

Hamburger (Louis and Ethel) Fdn., Detroit, 4/155

Hancock (James Edwin) Fdn., Detroit, 4/155

Hansen (Hans F.) Estate, Muskegon, 4/156

Hardy (O.D.) Trust, Lansing, 4/156

Harvard Fdn., Detroit, 4/157

Hayes (Bridget R.) Trust, Lansing, 4/157

Header Fdn., Wayne, 4/158

Heaney Charitable Fdn., Grand Rapids, 4/158

Heartland Fdn. Auxiliary Trust Fund, Grand Rapids, 4/159

Heavenrich (Osmond D. and Carrie V.) Scholarship Fund, Jackson, 4/162

Higby (Samuel) Camp Fdn., Jackson, 4/162

Higgins (George N.) Charitable Fdn. & Trust, Ferndale, 4/163

Hills Masonic Temple Assoc., Muskegon, 4/164

Hirchfield Family Fdn., Bay City, 4/165

Holden (James C. & Richard A.) Family Fdn., Bloomfield Hills, 4/165

Holka (Ralph G.) Fdn., Detroit, 4/165

Holmes (Charles H.) Trust, Lansing, 4/166

Hoover Fdn., Ann Arbor, 4/166

Hudson-Webber Fdn., Detroit, 4/168

Ingham County Fdn., Holt, 4/175

Irmax Fdn., Detroit, 4/176

Itin (Thomas W.) Charitable Trust, Detroit, 4/176

Jackson Memorial Camp for Children, Jackson, 4/177

Jacobson (Charles L.) Fdn., Detroit, 4/177

Johnson Corp. Scholarship Fdn., Three Rivers, 4/178

Johnson (George A.) Trust, Battle Creek, 4/178

Johnson (Mary Louise) Fdn., Detroit, 4/179

Jury (George H. and Jo Ann) Fdn., Grosse Pointe Park, 4/182

Kalamazoo Child Guidance Clinic, Kalamazoo, 4/182

Kales Fdn., Detroit, 4/183

Kaplan (Mabel) Fdn., Detroit, 4/185

Keith Fdn., Lansing, 4/185

Kellogg (W.K.) Bird Sanctuary, Battle Creek, 4/186

Kewaunee Fund, Andrian, 4/187

Keywell (Barney L. and Beatrice) Fdn., Detroit, 4/187

Kittler (Jack) Fdn., Bloomfield Hills, 4/188

Knape & Vogt Fdn., Grand Rapids, 4/188

Kogan Fdn., Detroit, 4/189

Kolla-Landwehr Fdn., Holland, 4/189

Kravitz (Sam and Jane) Fdn., Grand Rapids, 4/190

Kron (Joseph and Ida) Fdn., Detroit, 4/191

Lackey (L.S.) Fdn., River Rouge, 4/191

Lacks Fdn., Grand Rapids, 4/192

Ladies Library Assoc., Dawagiac, 4/192

LaMed (Louis & Esther) Fund, Southfield, 4/192

Lang Charitable Fund, Detroit, 4/193

Lapeer County Medical Fdn., Lapeer, 4/193

Latzer Keydel Fdn., Crosse Pointe Fami, 4/193

La-Z-Boy Fdn., Monroe, 4/194

Lemmen (Bernie J.) Fdn., Coopersville, 4/195

Leppien (Fred & Gertrude) Charitable Trust, Alma, 4/196

Leslie High School Scholarship Fund Assoc., Leslie, 4/196

Letts Fdn., Grand Blanc, 4/196

Levin (Saul R.) Memorial Fdn., Detroit, 4/196

Levison (Sydney & Robert) Fdn., Detroit, 4/196

Loud (Percy K. & Elizabeth P.) Fdn., Bloomfield Hills, 4/197

Loutit (William) Memorial Trust, Grand Rapids, 4/197

Lundy (J. Edward) Fdn., Dearborn, 5/001

Lurie-Polasky Fdn., Saginaw, 5/002

Magline Inc. Charitable Trust, Bay City, 5/002

Mailbach Fdn., Detroit, 5/002

T/U/A Mallery (Harvey J.), Grand Rapids, 5/003

Mann (Jessie E.) Trust, Jackson, 5/004

Manthel Charitable Trust, Petoskey, 5/004

Marcks (Oliver Dewey) Fdn., Detroit, 5/005

Marydale Center - A Michigan Non-Profit Corporation, Port Huron, 5/006

Mathews (Af & Clara G.) Fdn., Saginaw, 5/006

Mayerson (Allen & Dorli) Fdn., Detroit, 5/006

McCord Corp. Fdn., Detroit, 5/007

McDonnell Charitable Corp., Detroit, 5/007

McElmurry (Leland R. & Evelyn F.) Charitable Trust, Grand Rapids, 5/008

McGregor Fund, Detroit, 5/008

McInerney Fdn., Grand Rapids, 5/010

McKay (Ella Dole) Memorial Fund, Battle Creek, 5/011

McKinnon (Leonard A. & Zelpha E.) Educational & Charitable Trust, Flint, 5/011

Michell (Roy G.) Charitable Fdn. & Trust, Ferndale, 5/011

Michigan Academy of Science Arts and Letters, Ann Arbor, 5/012

Michigan Christian Youth Camp Inc., Attica, 5/012

Michigan Dairy Memorial and Scholarship Fdn., East Lansing, 5/013

Michigan Standard Alloys-Arthur S. Mendel Fdn., Benton Harbor, 5/013

Michi-Indi Pioneer Girls Camp Cherinth, Grand Rapids, 5/013

Michigan Knights Templar Charitable Trust, Detroit, 5/015

Michigan Seamless Tube Co. Fdn., South Lyon, 5/015

Mid-America Fdn., Coldwater, 5/016

Miller (Albert L. and Louise B.) Fdn., Battle Creek, 5/016

Miller (Joseph & Benjamin) Fdn., Detroit, 5/017

Miller (Arch) Flora M. Miller and Mary M. Miller Loan Fund, Grosse Pointe Farms, 5/018

Miller (Louise Tuller) Trust, Detroit, 5/018

Miner (Jack) Migratory Bird Fdn., Detroit, 5/020

Mitchell (Anthony Charles) Fdn., Detroit, 5/021

Modern American Living Inc., Detroit, 5/022

Monroe Catholic Central High School Scholarship Fund, Monroe, 5/022

Montview Fdn., Grand Rapids, 5/023

Moore (C.F.) Fdn., St. Clair, 5/023

M. & S. Fdn., Hudson, 5/024

Muir (John O.) Fdn., Grand Rapids, 5/024

Murray (Norbert T. and Marjorie I.) Fdn., Clare, 5/025

Moceri Family Fdn., Southfield, 5/025

Muskegon High School Scholarship Fdn., Muskegon, 5/026

McReynolds (Elsie L.) Trust, Detroit, 5/026

N. and B. Foundation, Montrose, 5/026

Nichamin Medical Research Fdn., Detroit, 5/027

Nickless (Allen E. and Marie A.) Memorial Fdn., Frankenmuth, 5/027

Nocolay (Ernest L.) Family Fdn., Detroit, 5/027

Northern National Fdn., Escanaba, 5/028

Oakland University Fdn., Bloomfield Hills, 5/028

Olson (Robert G. and Celia S.) Fdn., Highland Park, 5/028

Owens (Ralph L.) Trust #1647, Jackson, 5/029

Phillips (Myrtle Irene) Scholarship Fund Tr. #1477, Jackson, 5/029

Phinny (R.H. & Sally G.) Fdn., Fremont, 5/029

P.M. Fdn., Detroit, 5/031

Pool Fdn., Birmingham, 5/031

Portage Lake United Fund, Houghton, 5/031

Present (William A.) Trust, Lansing, 5/032

Packer (William M. & Suzanne V.) Charitable Trust, Detroit, 5/033

Parkhurst (Cora B.) Scholarship Trust, Niles, 5/034

Padnos (Louis and Helen) Fdn., Holland, 5/034

Palmer Fdn., Detroit, 5/035

Parkhurst (Cara B.) Scholarship Trust, Niles, 5/035

Pearlman (Joseph H.) Family Fdn., Warren, 5/036

Pheiffer (Eugene & Jayne) Fdn., Saginaw, 5/037

Petoskey Kiwanis Fdn., Petoskey, 5/037

Ranney Fdn., Greenville, 5/038

Rapaport Charities, Lansing, 5/038

Rapids-Standard Fdn., Grand Rapids, 5/038

Redfield (James M.) Fdn., Grand Rapids, 5/040

Reeder (Pansy Lee) Charitable Trust, Flint, 5/040

Riley (H.M.) Trust for Watch Tower Bible & Tract Soc., Battle Creek, 5/041

Robison (Harold & Carolyn) Fdn., Detroit, 5/042

Rohlik (Sigmund & Sophie) Fdn., Southfield, 5/042

Romney (George & Lenore) Fdn., Detroit, 5/043

Rosen (Harold) Fdn., Muskegon, 5/044

Rosenbaum (Meyer) Fdn., Detroit, 5/045

Roskam Fdn., Grand Rapids, 5/045

Rotary Forms Press Fdn., Pleasant Ridge, 5/047

Roth Fdn., Grand Rapids, 5/047

Safran Printing Company Fund, Detroit, 5/049

Safran (Hyman and Leah) Fdn., Detroit, 5/049

Savage Fdn., Detroit, 5/049

Schlafer (Nathan & Shirley K.) Fdn., Detroit, 5/050

Schneider Engstrom Fdn., Dearborn, 5/050

Scoutton (Margaret) Trust, Lansing, 5/051

Scudder (John) Fdn. for Old People, Detroit, 5/051

Seidman (William and Sarah) Fdn., Grand Rapids, 5/052

Semmes (Prewitt and Valerie D.) Fdn., Grosse Point Farm, 5/053

Service Employees International Union Local 582, Saginaw, 5/054

Shapero (Nate S. and Ruth B.) Fdn., Detroit, 5/054

Shaye (Rubin) Fdn., Detroit, 5/055

Shepard (Leon and Josephine Wade) Scholarship Fund Fdn., Kalamazoo, 5/056

Siegel Fdn., Detroit, 5/056

Silberstein (Ben L.) Fdn., Detroit, 5/057

Simmons Fdn., Ann Arbor, 5/057

Simons-Michelson Fdn., Detroit, 5/058

Simplicity Employees' Welfare and Recreation Fund, Niles, 5/059

Slemons Fdn., Grand Rapids, 5/059

Small Trinity Fdn., Jackson, 5/060

Smillie (Charles & Helen) Fdn., Bloomfield Hills, 5/061

Smith (Don & Dolly) Fdn., Lincoln Park, 5/062

Smith (H.A. and Carl H.) Charitable Fdn., Port Huron, 5/062

Smith (Lewis and Bernice) Fdn., Ann Arbor, 5/063

Smith (Tom-Anne) Smith Fdn., Southfield, 5/063

Snyder Fdn., Birmingham, 5/063

Sidney (Charles) & Martin Louis Srere Fdn., Detroit, 5/064

Stollman Fdn., Troy, 5/065

Stowe (Emma) Trust, Jackson, 5/066

Straus (Everet) Education Fund, Detroit, 5/066

Stroh Brewery Fdn., Detroit, 5/067

Strosacker (Charles J.) Fdn., Midland, 5/068

Student Aid Fdn. of Michigan, Detroit, 5/069

Student Benefit Club of Lansing Central High School Alumni Assn., Lansing, 5/071

Summerfield (Miriam W.) Fdn., Flint, 5/071

Sylvan Family Fdn., Southfield, 5/072

Tannahill (Robert H.) Fdn., Detroit, 5/073

Tecumseh Disaster Relief Fund, Tecumseh, 5/073

Thornapple Fdn., Hastings, 5/074

Timmer Fdn., Grand Rapids, 5/074

Tisdale (Wright and Miriam) Fdn., Bloomfield Hills, 5/075

Traub (Robert C.J.) Memorial Scholarship Travel Fund, Detroit, 5/075

T/U/A Barth (Charles F.) f/b/o St. Paul's Episcopal Church Mission Revolving Fund, Grand Rapids, 5/076

Citizens Com'l & Savings Bank Trustee U/W with J. Edington Burroughs & Louise H. Hubbard f/b/o Y.M.C.A., Flint, 5/076

Citizens Com'l & Savings Bank, Trustee u/w Wm. L. Plumer f/b/o First Presby. Church Holly Choir & Organ Fund, Flint, 5/076

T/U/W James M. Redfield Char. Trust, Grand Rapids, 5/076

Trust U/W of Alice Townsend Trust, Flint, 5/077

T/U/W William S. Dove for Grand Rapids, Fdn., Grand Rapids, 5/077

T/U/W Anna M. Douglas for Carmelite Sisters, Grand Rapids, 5/077

T/U/W Robert D. Graham, Grand Rapids, 5/078

Piper (Mark H.) Trust f/b/o First Methodist Church, Flint, 5/078

T/U/W Annette Richards, Grand Rapids, 5/078

Trust U/W of Harry S. Williams Deceased, Fremont, 5/078

Turkish Orphan Assn., Detroit, 5/079

Tyler (Dorothy) Fdn., Niles, 5/079

Tyner (Irving & Bess) Charitable Fdn., Detroit, 5/080

Ulrich (William J.) Fdn., Detroit, 5/080

Vandervoort (Frank S. & Mollie S.) Memorial Fdn., Grand Rapids, 5/081

Vlasic Fdn., Detroit, 5/082

Wajer Fdn., Detroit, 5/082

Gertrude (Jerry) Charitable Trust, Detroit, 5/083

Wayzata Memorial Educational Fdn., Wayzata, 5/084

Webber (Eloise and Richard) Fdn., Detroit, 5/084

Webber (Richard H. and Eloise Jenks) Charitable, Detroit, 5/086

Weiss (Lawrence and Mildred) Fund, Detroit, 5/087

Welch (James A.) Fdn., Flint, 5/087

Welded Products Fdn., Grand Haven, 5/088

Werner Endowment Fund, Marquette, 5/089

Werner (Charles R. & Marie) Fdn., Grand Rapids, 5/090

White Fdn., Bloomfield Hills, 5/091

Whiting Fdn., Flint, 5/092

Whitmer Chiropractic Fdn., Bloomfield Hills, 5/094

Whirlpool Opportunities Inc., Benton Harbor, 5/094

Wilder (H.W.) Fdn., Birmingham, 5/095

Weatherwax Fdn., Jackson, 5/095

Wilbur (Etta R.) Trust, Lansing, 5/096

Wilbur (Etta R.) Trust #38-6057655, Lansing, 5/096

Winston (Lydia K. & Harry L.) Art Collection, Detroit, 5/097

Woodall Fdn., Detroit, 5/097

Woodall Industries Fdn., Detroit, 5/098

Wright (Alice C. and James O.) Fdn., Birmingham, 5/099

Wyllys Fdn., Alma, 5/100

Y.M.C.A. Assn., Grand Haven, 5/100

Yonovitz (Sam) Memorial Fdn., Lathrup Village, 5/101

Young Womens Home Assn., Detroit, 5/101

Youth Guidance of Michigan, Oak Park, 5/103

Zurschmiede (W. Tom), Sr. Fdn., Detroit, 5/103

MINNESOTA

First Filming

Adams- Mastrovitch Family Fdn. Trust U/A 1569, Minneapolis, 1/004

Adler Fdn., St. Paul, 1/005

Advance Fdn., Spring Park, 1/005

Alexandra Fdn., St. Paul, 1/006

Alliss (Charles & Ellora) Educational Fdn., St. Paul, 1/007

Alworth (Marshall H. & Nellie) Memorial Fund, Duluth, 1/008

American Hoist & Derrick Fdn., St. Paul, 1/010

ply Fund, Minneapolis American Linen Sup, 1/010

Anderson Fdn., Bayport, 1/011

Anderson (Elmer I. & Eleanor J.) Fdn., St. Paul, 1/012

Anderson Trusts, Minneapolis, 1/013

Anderson (Z.A.F.) Fdn., Minneapolis, 1/014

Animal Human Society of Hennepin County Trust, Minneapolis, 1/014

Arend (Mark L.) Fdn., St. Paul, 1/015

Athwin Fdn., Minneapolis, 1/015

Atkinson (William M.) Memorial Fund, Minneapolis, 1/017

Badzin (Bernard & Fern) Fdn., Minneapolis, 1/018

Baker (Laura) Educational Fdn., Minneapolis, 1/019

Bakken Fdn., New Brighton, 1/019

Balfour (Carrie M. & Donald C.) Fund Trust 0723, Minneapolis, 1/019

Barry (Charles & Melanie) Family Fdn., Minneapolis, 1/020

Barry Fdn., Minneapolis, 1/021

Batzli Fdn., Minneapolis, 1/021

Bean (F.A.) Fdn., Minneapolis, 1/021

Beim Fdn. Midland Bank Building, Minneapolis, 1/023

Belford Fdn., Minneapolis, 1/023

Bell (David Winton) Fdn., Minneapolis, 1/024

Bell (James F.) Book Trust, Minneapolis, 1/024

Bell (James F.) Fdn., Minneapolis, 1/025

Bell (James F.) Testamentary Trust for the benefit of Univ. of Minn., Minneapolis, 1/026

Belzer Fdn., Minneapolis, 1/026

Bemis (Judson M.) Church & School Trust, Minneapolis, 1/026

Bemis Company Fdn., Minneapolis, 1/027

Beneficia Fdn., Bayport, 1/028

Benz (George & Louise) Fdn., St. Paul, 1/028

Berger Fdn., Minneapolis, 1/029

Berman Fdn., Minneapolis, 1/030

Beta Pi Memorial Trust, Minneapolis, 1/031

Bigelow (F.R.) Fdn. Trust 555, St. Paul, 1/031

Big Game club Special Projects Fdn., Minneapolis, 1/034

Bing Fdn., Wayzata, 1/034

Blandin (Charles K.) Cemetery T/W15963, Minneapolis, 1/035

Blandin (Charles K.) Fdn. 9890, Minneapolis, 1/036

Blue Ridge Fdn. Tr 18138, Minneapolis, 1/038

Bonhomie Fdn., Waverly, 1/039

Boys Club of MPLS T/A 20195, Minneapolis, 1/040

Brin Fdn., Minneapolis, 1/040

Bronstien Family Fdn., St. Paul, 1/041

Brown (Harry Rowatt) Tr U/A 18460, Minneapolis, 1/042

Budd Family Fdn., Minneapolis, 1/043

Buetow (Herbert P. & Lucille R.) Charitable Fdn., St. Paul, 1/044

Burlington Northern Fdn., St. Paul, 1/045

Busch (W.R.) Fdn., St. Paul, 1/047

Bush Fdn., St. Paul, 1/048

Business History Foundation, Northfield, 1/049

Butler (Patrick & Aimee) Family Fdn., St. Paul, 1/049

Buttrey Fdn., Minneapolis, 1/050

Callahan Fdn. Edward J. Callahan Sr. Et Al Truste, Minneapolis, 1/052

Campbell Charitable Trust, Duluth, 1/052

Capp (Martin and Esther) Fdn., Minneapolis, 1/053

Caridad Gift Trust, Duluth, 1/054

Carlen Fdn., Minneapolis, 1/054

Carlson Fdn., Minneapolis, 1/054

Carlson (Curtis L,) Fdn., Minneapolis, 1/055

Carolyn Fdn., Minneapolis, 1/056

Carr (Wilbur J.) Memorial Fund, Minneapolis, 1/057

Center Foundation Incorporated, Minneapolis, 1/058

Central Exchange Fdn., South St. Paul, 1/058

Central Livestock Fdn., South St. Paul, 1/059

Chadwick Fdn., Minneapolis, 1/059

Chamberlain (F.A.) Trust u/a #1798, Minneapolis, 1/061

C. Charitable Trust, Duluth, 1/061

C. Charitable Second Trust, Duluth, 1/062

Char-Lynn Fdn., Mound, 1/062

Chelgren-Haviland Fdn., Minneapolis, 1/063

Cherne Fdn., Minneapolis, 1/064

Chinese American Association of Minn., Minneapolis, 1/064

Clements (F.B.) Fdn., Mankato, 1/065

Comfort (Mary Ethel) Fdn., St. Paul, 1/066

Congdon (Edward C.) Memorial Trust, Duluth, 1/066

Conwed Fdn., St. Paul, 1/067

Cooke (Elbridge C.) Trust-4397, Minneapolis, 1/067

Cooke (Elbridge C.) Trust u/a No. 2, Minneapolis, 1/068

Cooke (Isabella T.) Trust, Minneapolis, 1/069

Cooperative Fdn., St. Paul, 1/071

Cornelius (Richard T.) Fdn., St. Paul, 1/072

Cretin High School Trust, St. Paul, 1/073

Dahlberg (Kenneth H.) Fdn., Goden Valley, 1/075

Dain Kalman & Quail Incorporated Fdn., Minneapolis, 1/075

Dansville Library Association Trust, Minneapolis, 1/076

Davis (Edwin W. and Catherine M.) Fdn., St. Paul, 1/077

Dean Trust, Minneapolis, 1/080

Deerwood Educational Fund, Duluth, 1/080

Deinard Fdn., Minneapolis, 1/081

Dellwood Fdn., St. Paul, 1/081

Deluxe Check Printers Fdn., St. Paul, 1/082

Denada Fdn., St. Paul, 1/083

Devereux Fdn. Trust, St. Paul, 1/084

Dietrich (Dolores G.) Memorial Fdn., Le Sueur, 1/086

Dodge (Thomas Irvine) Fdn., St. Paul, 1/086

Doerr Family Fund, Minneapolis, 1/087

Donaldson (Lawrence S.) II, Minneapolis, 1/088

Donnay Fdn., Minneapolis, 1/090

Donovan (George) Fdn., St. Paul, 1/091

Drew (Eliza A.) Memorial Fund, Minneapolis, 1/091

Dudley (W.H.) Fdn., Minneapolis, 1/092

Duke (Joseph C. and Lillian A.) Fdn., St. Paul, 1/093

Duluth Cathedral High School Educational Trust, Duluth, 1/094

Duluth Improvement Trust, Duluth, 1/095

Etoile Du Nord Fdn., St. Paul, 1/095

Dunwoody (Kate) Trust, Minneapolis, 1/095

Effress Family Fdn., St. Paul, 1/097

Eliel (Henry H.) Trust u/w The Sheltering Arms, Minneapolis, 1/097

Elliott Fdn., Rochester, 1/097

Elva Fund, Minneapolis, 1/098

Elwell Fdn., Minneapolis, 1/098

Enger (M.J.) Family Fdn., Minneapolis, 1/099

Erickson (Alfred W.) Fdn., Minneapolis, 1/100

Erickson (Arthur T.) Fdn., Minneapolis, 1/100

Estrem (Malcolm J.) Fdn., Minneapolis, 1/102

Faricy (Clare and Roland) Fdn., St. Paul, 1/102

Federal Cartridge Fdn., Minneapolis, 1/103

Feist Pet Memorial Cemetery, St. Paul, 1/104

Feller (George) Fdn., St. Paul, 1/104

Ferndale Fdn., St. Paul, 1/105

Ferguson (Charlotte Peet) Memorial Trust, St. Paul, 1/105

Fine (Adolph and Mildred) Fund, Minneapolis, 1/107

Finn (John F.) Fdn., Minneapolis, 1/107

First National Bank of Minneapolis Fdn. 1239, Minneapolis, 1/108

Fisher (S.S.) Fdn., St. Paul, 1/108

Fiterman (Edward) Fdn., Minneapolis, 1/108

Fitzgerald (Francis H.) Trust, Duluth, 1/110

Foundation for International Education In Neurological Surgery, Rochester, 1/110

Foundation for Minneapolis Area Boy Scouts Trust u/a, Minneapolis, 1/111

Frank (Dan & Ethel) Fdn., Minneapolis, 1/112

Freidson (Allen & Irene) Family Fdn., Minneapolis, 1/113

Freidson (Herman and Audrey) Family Fdn., Minneapolis, 1/113

Freidson Fdn., Minneapolis, 1/114

Freidson (Herman & Audrey) Family Fdn., Minneapolis, 1/114

Fuller Charitable Trust, Duluth, 1/114

Gainey Fdn., Owatonna, 1/115

Gamble (B.C.) Fdn., Minneapolis, 1/116

Gandrud Fdn., Owatonna, 1/117

Gasterland Charitable Trust-Richfield Bank and Trust Company, Minneapolis, 1/118

Gerot Fdn., Minneapolis, 1/119

Giertsen Fdn., Minneapolis, 1/119

Gilfillan (Fanny S.) Memorial, Redwood Falls, 1/120

Glaspel (George W. and Eva J.) Charitable Trust T/A, Minneapolis, 1/121

Goff (Sidney W.) Family Fdn., St. Paul, 1/121

Goldenberg (Jacob E.) Fdn., Minneapolis, 1/121

Goodin (Allan P.) Fdn., Minneapolis, 1/122

Goodman Brothers Fdn., St. Paul, 1/123

Goodman (Arthur & Constance) Family Fdn., St. Paul, 1/124

Gould (Ransford Rav) and Clara J. Gould Fdn., St. Paul, 1/125

Gould (Martha H.) Trust, Minneapolis, 1/126

Gowran (Edward A.) Trust, Minneapolis, 1/128

Graco Fdn., Minneapolis, 1/128
Granelda Fdn., Minneapolis, 1/129
Granite City Charitable Fdn., Minneapolis, 1/131
Graybrier Foundation, Excelsior, 1/131
Green (Myron B.) Fdn., Minneapolis, 1/131
Greenberg (S. David) Charitable Fdn., Newport, 1/132
Gregory (Lisa Brooks Gregory) Gdn., Minneapolis, 1/133
Gress (C.W.) Trust - Cong. Bd., Minneapolis, 1/133
Gress (Cliff W.) Trust u/a First Congregational Church, Minneapolis, 1/134
Grey (Ben & Abby) Fdn., St. Paul, 1/134
Greystone Fdn., Minneapolis, 1/135
Gross (William & Lisa) Charitable Fdn., Minneapolis, 1/136
Guardian Angels Foundation of Elk River, Elk River, 1/137
Halper (Harry) Family Fdn., St. Paul, 1/138
Halpin (George & Margaret) Fdn. Trust 9275, Minneapolis, 1/138
Hamer (Millard C.) Testamentary Trust, Minneapolis, 1/138
Hamlin (Oliver C.) Testamentary Trust, Minneapolis, 1/138
Hanson (Norris A.) Fdn., Mabel, 1/138
Harper (Josephine Louise) Memorial Fund Tr., Minneapolis, 1/139
Harrington (Helen) Charitable Trust u/w, Minneapolis, 1/140
Harris (B.W.) Fdn., West St. Paul, 1/141
Hartwell Fdn., Minneapolis, 1/142
Hartz Fdn., Thief River Falls, 1/143
Hawkins (Oscar and Madge) Fdn., Minneapolis, 1/143
Heimann (Jack) Family Fdn., St. Paul, 1/144
Hendel Fdn., Minneapolis, 1/144
Herz (Malvin E. & Josephine D.) Fdn., Excelsior, 1/146
Hibbs Family Fdn., Minneapolis, 1/146
Higgins (Bardon) Fdn., Duluth, 1/146
Hill (Mary B.) Charitable Trust-6419, Minneapolis, 1/147
Hill (Mary T.) Christian Brothers Trust, St. Paul, 1/148
Hill (Mary T.) Invalid Priests Trust, St. Paul, 1/148
Hill (Mary T.) Trust for The College of St. Thomas, St. Paul, 1/150
Hill (Mary T.) Trust for The House of The Good Shephe, St. Paul, 1/152
Hill (Mary T.) Trust for Little Sisters of The Poor, St. Paul, 1/153
Hill (Mary T.) Endowment Trust for St. Paul Seminary, St. Paul, 1/156
Hill (James Jerome) Reference Library, St. Paul, 1/158
Hill (N.B.) Fund Trust, Minneapolis, 1/163
Hormel Fdn., Austin, 1/163
Hormel (George A.) Testamentary Trust, Austin, 1/164
Hubbard Fdn., Minneapolis, 1/165
Hudson (Dayton) Fdn., Minneapolis, 1/166
Hudson (Laura & Walter) Hudson Fdn., Minneapolis, 1/169
Huested (Nevin N.) Fdn. for Handicapped Children, St. Paul, 1/171
Hull Educational Fdn., St. Paul, 1/171
Humphrey (Hubert H.) Fdn., Minneapolis, 1/175
Hunter Fdn., Minneapolis, 1/176
Hyslop (Ida Maud) Trust for The Benefit of Childrens, St. Paul, 1/176
Jaegerstaetter (Franz) Fdn., Stillwater, 1/179
Jaffray (Clive T.) Charitable Trust, Minneapolis, 1/179
Jaffray Employees Trust-6802 First National Bank, Minneapolis, 1/180
James (Sim) Fdn., Minneapolis, 1/180
Jimmerson (D.W.) Fdn., Wayzata, 1/180
J.N.M. 1966 Gift Trust, Duluth, 1/181
Johansen (Theodore H.) Family Fdn. Trust, Minneapolis, 1/182
Johnson (Al) Fdn., Minneapolis, 1/183

Johnson (Joseph E.) Trust, St. Paul, 1/184
Johnson (Lewis H.) Family Fdn., St. Paul, 1/185
Johnson (Edward M. and Effie R.) Fdn., Minneapolis, 1/187
Johnson (Marvin L. & Mildred L.) Fund - Trust 12999, Minneapolis, 1/188
Johnson (Everett R. & Ruth M.) Fund -12997, Minneapolis, 1/190
Johnston (Harry V.) Fdn., Edina, 1/191
Jones (Addie M.) Trust, Minneapolis, 1/192
Jones (Helen Winton) Fund, Minneapolis, 1/193
Jones (Herschel V.) Journalism Fund, Minneapolis, 1/194
Jones (Herschel V.) Fund, Minneapolis, 1/194
Joshua Fdn., Minneapolis, 1/195
JRD Fdn., Minneapolis, 1/197
Judd (Walter H.) Fdn., Minneapolis, 1/198
Judson Fund, Minneapolis, 1/198
Junell (John) Trust, Minneapolis, 1/199
Kaplan (George) Memorial Fdn., St. Paul, 1/200
Karleen-Valentine Fund, Minneapolis, 1/202
Kasper (Robert and Rita) Fdn., Minneapolis, 1/203
Kef Fdn., Duluth, 1/203
Kelm Fdn., Minneapolis, 1/204
Kitrick (Joseph) Charitable Trust, Minneapolis, 1/205
Kiwanis Fdn., West St. Paul, 1/205
Kingpin Fdn., St. Paul, 1/206
Klein (Harry J.) Family Fdn., Minneapolis, 1/207
Klein (Julius & Sophie) Family Fdn., St. Paul, 1/208
Kleven Fdn., Minneapolis, 1/208
Kline (Hess) Fdn., St. Paul, 1/209
Kline (Jaeson H.) Fdn., Minneapolis, 1/210
Kooiker Fdn., Minneapolis, 1/211
Lang (Harry) Fdn., Minneapolis, 1/212
Leach (Cora E. and Orrin A.) Charitable Trust, Minneapolis, 1/213
Lee (Mary G.) Trust, Minneapolis, 1/214
Leslie (Donald & Dorothy) Fdn.-Tr. 15213, Minneapolis, 1/214
Levine (George and Marion) Fdn., Minneapolis, 1/216
Coyle (Richard) Family Fdn., St. Paul, 1/217
Linsmayer (James B.) Fdn., Minneapolis, 1/218
Lipschultz (William) Fdn., St. Paul, 1/219
Longyear Tithe Trust R.D. Longyear Barbara L. Longyear, Minneapolis, 1/219
Loring Tree Trust, Minneapolis, 1/220
Lousetta-Cordelia Fdn. for Continuation of Congregational Principles, Minneapolis, 1/222
Lund (Russel T.) Charitable Trust - 7243, Minneapolis, 1/222
Lund Family Charitable Foundation, Minneapolis, 1/222
Luther (Rudy & Clair) Fdn. Trust, Minneapolis, 1/223
Lyman Memorial Fund, Minneapolis, 1/224
Lyndhurst Charitable Trust, St. Paul, 1/224
MacDonald Family Fdn., Duluth, 1/226
MacPherson (George A.) Fund, St. Paul, 1/227
Malakoff Fdn., Minneapolis, 1/229
Malmon (Joseph J. and Pauline K.) Fdn., St. Paul, 1/231
Manitou Fund, St. Paul, 1/231
Mar (Stan Don) Fdn., Minneapolis, 1/232
Marbrook Fdn., Minneapolis, 1/233
Mark (Lee) Fdn., St. Paul, 1/234
Marver (Gloria & Hillard) Fdn., St. Paul, 1/235
Mary & Robert Fdn., Minneapolis, 1/236
Marzahn Fdn., Waterville, 1/237
Maslon Fdn., Minneapolis, 1/237
Masterton (William J.) Memorial Trust, Minneapolis, 1/238
Mathison (Fred and Elvina) Fdn., Minneapolis, 1/239
McCannel Fund, Minneapolis, 1/239
McFarland Fdn., Minneapolis, 1/240

McKerrow (William) Scholarship Fund Trust u/a, Minneapolis, 1/241
McKinstry (William B. & Barbara D.) Fdn., Minneapolis, 1/242
McKnight Family Educational Fund, St. Paul, 1/243
McKnight Family Charitable Fdn., St. Paul, 1/244
McKnight Fdn., St. Paul, 2/017
McKnight Family Scientific Fund, St. Paul, 2/018
McKnight Family Endowment, St. Paul, 2/019
McKnight Family Literary Fund, St. Paul, 2/020
McKnight (Sumner T.) Fdn., Minneapolis, 2/022
McNally (Frank E.) Fdn., Minneapolis, 2/025
McNeely (Harry and Adelaide) Charitable Fdn., St. Paul, 2/025
Meadowood Fdn., Minneapolis, 2/027
Meeks Fdn., Minneapolis, 2/028
Melamed Fdn., Minneapolis, 2/028
Meyer (Roy E. and Merle) Fdn., Red Wing, 2/030
Meyer (Frank E.) Trust, St. Paul, 2/031
Patterson (M.F.) Fdn., Minneapolis, 2/032
Mickelson Fdn., Minneapolis, 2/034
Midwest Carriers Fund, Minneapolis, 2/034
Miller (Joseph) Fdn. of Winona, St. Paul, 2/034
Miller (Sam) Fdn., Minneapolis, 2/035
Minnesota Engineers Fdn., Inver Grove Hgtsmn, 2/035
Minnesota Historical Society Trust, Minneapolis, 2/036
Minn. Hospital Administration Alumni, Minneapolis, 2/037
Minnesota Mining and Manufacturing Fdn., St. Paul, 2/038
Minnesota Institute for Achievement of Human Potential, St. Paul, 2/039
Mooney Fdn., St. Paul, 2/039
Moore (Thomas & Kathleen) Fdn., Minneapolis, 2/039
Morton (John M.) Trust, Minneapolis, 2/041
Mott (Edward T.) Trust, St. Paul, 2/041
M.U. Chapter of PSI Upsilon Scholarship Trust, Minneapolis, 2/043
Murphy (Ina and Harry) Fdn., Minneapolis, 2/044
Murphy (Kingsley H.) Family Fdn., Minneapolis, 2/044
M. W. V. E. Fund, Duluth, 2/045
Myers Fdn., St. Paul, 2/045
Myers (Paul N.) Jr., Fdn., St. Paul, 2/046
Nash Fdn., Minneapolis, 2/046
Neilson (George W.) Fdn., Minneapolis, 2/048
Nelson (B.F.) Fdn., Minneapolis, 2/050
Nelson (R.C.) Family Fdn., Hallock, 2/051
Newell (Julia Augusta) Trust, Duluth, 2/051
Newman (Axel) Family Fdn., St. Paul, 2/051
Norling Brothers Fdn., St. Paul, 2/052
Norris (Jane & William) Fdn., St. Paul, 2/052
Northwest Paper Fdn., Cloquet, 2/055
Northwestern Fdn., Minneapolis, 2/056
Oakleaf Fdn., Minneapolis, 2/058
Ober Charitable Fdn., St. Paul, 2/059
O'Brien (Alice M.) Fdn., St. Paul, 2/041
O'Brien (Hannah F.) Trust, Minneapolis, 2/042
Onan Family Fdn., Minneapolis, 2/063
Ordean Fdn., Duluth, 2/063
Otteson (Paul M.) Fdn., Owatonna, 2/068
Pacific Fdn., Hibbing, 2/069
Page (Roger R.) Fdn., Minneapolis, 2/069
Palmer (George M.) Fdn., Mankato, 2/070
Palmgren (L.G.) Fdn., Long Prairie, 2/070
Paper (Lewis & Annie F.) Fdn., St. Paul, 2/071
Paper (Lewis & Janet S.) Fdn., St. Paul, 2/071
Paper (Joseph) Fdn., St. Paul, 2/073
Patton (George William & Mary Burnham) Scho. Fund, Minneapolis, 2/075
Paulucci Family Fdn., Duluth, 2/076
Perl (Norman) Fdn., St. Louis Park, 2/076
Perry Fdn., Minneapolis, 2/077

Second Filming

General Mills Fdn., Minneapolis, 3/054
Gilfillan (Charles D.) Memorial, St. Paul, 3/055
Glaspel (George and Eva) Charitable Trust, Minneapolis, 3/057
Gottstein Family Fdn., Minneapolis, 3/058
Gowran (Edward A.) Tr. U/A, Minneapolis, 3/059
Gowran (Edward A.) Tr. U/W Shrine Hospital, Minneapolis, 3/060
Grain Terminal Fdn., St. Paul, 3/061
Green Giant Fdn., Le Sueur, 3/062
Griggs (Mary Livingston) & Mary Griggs Burke Fdn., St. Paul, 3/063
Gross (Allen M.) Fdn., Minneapolis, 3/064
Grossman (Louis S.) Fdn., Minneapolis, 3/065
Grotto Fdn., St. Paul, 3/065
Hamm Fdn., St. Paul, 3/066
Harris (Edith) Fdn., St. Paul, 3/068
Henphil-Pillsbury Charitable Trust, Minneapolis, 3/068
Hermundslie Fdn., Minneapolis, 3/069
Hill Fdn. Company, St. Paul, 3/069
Hill (Louis W. and Maud) Family Fdn., St. Paul, 3/070
Hill (N.B.) Fund Trust, Minneapolis, 3/077
Honeywell Fund No. 1, Minneapolis, 3/078
Honeywell Fund No. 2, Minneapolis, 3/079
Hornby (Henry C.) Trust U/A Designated as Cloquet Cemt. Tr., St. Paul, 3/080
Hotchkiss (W.R.) Fdn., St. Paul, 3/082
Hulings (Mary Andersen) Fdn., Bayport, 3/082
Hunter Fdn., Minneapolis, 3/083
International Multifoods Charitable Fdn., Minneapolis, 3/085
Johnson (Al) Fdn., Minneapolis, 3/085
Johnson Fdn., Waseca, 3/086
Joseph Fdn., Minneapolis, 3/087
Kahler Corporation Fdn., Rochester, 3/088
Kegan (Lawrence P.) Fdn., St. Paul, 3/089
Kerkhof Fdn., Minneapolis, 3/090
Khurum (Carl Calvin-) Welfare Fund, Minneapolis, 3/090
Kierkegaard (David F. Swenson) Memorial Fund, Minneapolis, 3/090
Kugler (William & Ida) Fdn., St. Paul, 3/091
Ladd (J.B.) T W, Minneapolis, 3/092
Chancery Lane Fdn., St. Paul, 3/093
LaSalle Institute Trust, St. Paul, 3/094
Leavitt Fdn., St. Paul, 3/095
Leifman Memorial Fdn., St. Paul, 3/096
Little Sisters of the Poor Trust, Minneapolis, 3/096
Lyman Memorial Fund, Minneapolis, 3/096
Mankato Citizens Telephone Co. Fdn., Mankato, 3/097
Mann (Ted) Fdn., Minneapolis, 3/097
Masonic Fdn. of Minneapolis, Minneapolis, 3/097
Maternity Hospital Minneapolis Trust, Minneapolis, 3/098
McKinstry (William B. and Barbara D.) Fdn., Minneapolis, 3/098
Merci Inc., Minneapolis, 3/100
Merrill (Eugene A.) for Hillsdale College TRU, Minneapolis, 3/100
Meyers (J.E.) Memorial Park Association, Minneapolis, 3/100
Minneapolis Star and Tribune Fund, Minneapolis, 3/101
Minnesota Fdn., St. Paul, 3/102
Minnesota Landmarks, St. Paul, 3/104
Minnesota Natural Fdn., Minneapolis, 3/105
Morse Fdn., Minneapolis, 3/105
Moses (Leonard Wilk) Memorial Fund, Minneapolis, 3/106
Mullin (W.E. and M.H.) Fdn., Minneapolis, 3/107
Naftalin Fdn., Minneapolis, 3/108
National City Bank Fdn., Minneapolis, 3/108
National Fdn. for Public Safety, Minneapolis, 3/108
Needlework Guild Trust, Minneapolis, 3/109
Nelson (R.C.) Family Fdn., Hallock, 3/109
Newman (Malvin) Fdn., Minneapolis, 3/110
Nicollet Clinic Fdn., Minneapolis, 3/110

Norling Brothers Fund, Minneapolis, 3/111
North Star Research and Development Institute, Minneapolis, 3/112
Numero Fdn., Minneapolis, 3/114
Oberholtzer (Ernest C.) Fdn., St. Paul, 3/115
Olson (E.O.) Trust U/A Scholarship Fund, Minneapolis, 3/116
O'Neil (Albert T.) Fdn., St. Paul, 3/116
Ordway (Gladys and Richard) Charitable Fdn., Minneapolis, 3/117
Ouellette Fdn., St. Paul, 3/118
Owen Family Fund, Minneapolis, 3/120
Palmer (George M.) Fdn., Mankato, 3/120
Paulucci (Jeno F.) Fdn., Duluth, 3/121
P.C. Corp., Sleepy Eye, 3/122
Peerless Chain Fdn., Winona, 3/122
Perkins Family Fdn., Minneapolis, 3/123
Petombob Fdn., Minneapolis, 3/124
Phipps (William H.) Fdn., St. Paul, 3/125
Pierce (Elinore Mapes) Charitable Trust U/A 17198, Minneapolis, 3/126
Piper Jaffray & Hopwood Fdn., Minneapolis, 3/128
Plummer (Daisy) Rochester Art Center Trust U/A, Minneapolis, 3/129
Polyhymnia Society, St. Paul, 3/130
Radichel Family Fdn., Mankato, 3/130
Rau (Magdalena M.) Trust, St. Paul, 3/131
Raymond (E.F.) T/W, Minneapolis, 3/132
Religion and Society, Inc., Stillwater, 3/132
Research and Development Fdn. of Mankato State College, Mankato, 3/132
Anderson (Reuben L.) Fdn., Minneapolis, 3/133
Ringer Jr. Fdn., Crystal Bay, 3/134
Robins Davis & Lyons Fdn., Minneapolis, 3/134
Rockler (Vernon J.) Fdn., Minneapolis, 3/135
Ross (Gerald) Family Fdn., Golden Valley, 3/136
Ross Fdn., Minneapolis, 3/137
Rutman (George J.) Fdn., St. Paul, 3/138
Ryden (Arnold J.) Fdn., Minneapolis, 3/139
Salem Fdn., St. Paul, 3/139
Tanning (S.B. Foot) Co., Fdn., Red Wing, 3/140
Salet Fdn., Mankato, 3/141
Salkin Fdn., Minneapolis, 3/141
Sexton (Charles W.) Co., Fdn., Minneapolis, 3/142
Short (Robert E.) Fdn., St. Paul, 3/142
Smith Trust House of Hope Church, St. Paul, 3/143
Sparell (Delia S.) Memorial Fund T/A, Minneapolis, 3/145
Spencer (K.) Trust U/W Minneapolis Athenaeum, Minneapolis, 3/145
Steinberg (Charles L.) & Helen Steinberg Fdn., St. Paul, 3/146
Sveden House Fdn., Duluth, 3/146
Thomas Fdn., St. Paul, 3/147
Thompson (Charles) Memorial Hall, St. Paul, 3/148
Joseph Johnson Trust U/A, Minneapolis, 3/149
Mabee (Fred) Trust U/W Greene Public Library Board, Minneapolis, 3/150
Mabee (Fred L.) Trust U/W Mytle Mabee Public Library, Minneapolis, 3/151
Sister Joseph Trust U/A St. Mary's Hospital, Minneapolis, 3/151
Wells Memorial House (H.V. Jones) Trust U/W, Minneapolis, 3/152
Turnblad (Lillian Zenobia) Tru/W, Minneapolis, 3/152
Typographical Union Welfare Fund, St. Paul, 3/153
United Crippled Children's Fund, Coon Rapids, 3/153
United Fund of Mahnomen County, Mahnomen, 3/154
Vetter (Armin F.) Fdn., St. Paul, 3/154
Viking Land U.S.A., Battle Lake, 3/154
Watkins (J.R.) Fdn., Winona, 3/154
Watkins (Victor M.) Convalescent Home, St. Paul, 3/155

Watson (L.E.) Trust W/A J.S. Watson Scholarship, Minneapolis, 3/156
Webb Fdn., St. Paul, 3/157
Wedum Fdn., Alexandria, 3/158
Werner Fdn., Roseville, 3/159
Weyerhaeuser (Charles A.) Memorial Fdn., St. Paul, 3/160
Weyerhauser (Frederick and Margaret L.) Fdn., St. Paul, 3/161
Wilder (Amherst H.) Fdn., St. Paul, 3/162
Wilson (Alfred M.) Fund, Minneapolis, 3/165
Wurtele (V.) Fdn. Tr. U/A, Minneapolis, 3/165
Ziff Family Fdn., Minneapolis, 3/167
Zimmerman (Harry B.) Trust, St. Paul, 3/168

MISSISSIPPI

First Filming

Abroms & Seligman Charitable Trust, Shaw, 1/002
Allen (Barbara Ann) Memorial Fdn., Jackson, 1/002
Barrier Fdn., Yazoo City, 1/002
Bellamann (Henry H.) Fdn., Jackson, 1/003
Biglane (D.A.) Fdn., Natchez, 1/003
Bonelli Fdn., Vicksburg, 1/004
Brown (Harold Gibson) Memorial Library, Macon, 1/004
Bryan (J.H.) Fdn., West Point, 1/004
Chisolm Fdn., Laurel, 1/005
Christian Service Trust, Tupelo, 1/005
Crosby (Dorothy & Osmond) Fdn., Picayune, 1/006
Crosby (Ethel) Fdn. Fund, Picayune, 1/006
Crosby (Margaret Reed) Memorial Fdn., Picayune, 1/007
Delta Fdn., Greenville, 1/007
Deposit Guaranty Fdn., Jackson, 1/008
Fernwood Fdn., Fernwood, 1/009
Graeber Fdn., Marks, 1/010
Graeber (Lewis A.) Trust, Marks, 1/011
Greater Greenwood Fdn. of Arts, Greenwood, 1/011
Grundfest Fdn., Cary, 1/011
Self (Joan Hallett) Memorial Fund, Marks, 1/011
Hall Fdn., Bay Springs, 1/012
Hand (James) Fdn., Rolling Fork, 1/012
Hederman Fdn., Jackson, 1/012
Howell (Robert L.) Fdn., Greenwood, 1/013
Irby (Elizabeth M.) Fdn., Jackson, 1/013
Kent Fdn., Greenville, 1/014
Lewis (Celian H.) Family Fdn., Indianola, 1/014
Lewis (Morris) Family Fdn., Indianola, 1/015
Loewen Fund, Tougaloo, 1/016
Longenecker (I.R.) Fdn., Armory, 1/016
Magnolia State Fdn., Jackson, 1/016
Manker (David S. & Sara Jane) Charitable Trust, Clarksdale, 1/017
McClinton (S.W. & Ella C.) Memorial Fdn., Quitman, 1/018
McRae Fdn., Jackson, 1/018
Memorial Fdn., West Point, 1/018
Mississippi Farm Bureau Federation, Houston, 1/019
Mississippi Gulf Coast Fdn., Gulfport, 1/020
Mississippi Valley Gas Fdn., Jackson, 1/021
Nash Fdn., Greenville, 1/022
Paris Family Fdn., Lexington, 1/022
Phillips Fdn., Columbus, 1/022
Self Fdn., Marks, 1/023
Delta (Seymour) Trust Fund, Indianola, 1/023
Street Medical Fdn., Vicksburg, 1/024
Thompson (M. Ina) Fdn., Moss Point, 1/024
Urban Fdn., Brookhaven, 1/024
Hobgood (T.H. & Allie R.) Educational Trust, Meridian, 1/024

Second Filming

Chapman Trust Fund, Jackson, 2/001
Community Fdn., Jackson, 2/002
Davis Fdn., Okolona, 2/003
DeWeese (Mr. & Mrs. Ab) Youth Fdn.,
  Philadelphia, 2/004
Gardiner Fdn., Laurel, 2/004
Gilmore Sanitarium, Amory, 2/005
Gootman (Steven H.) Scholarship Fdn., Quincy,
  Mass., 2/006
Green (R.H.) Fdn., Jackson, 2/006
Hardin (Phil) Fdn., Meridian, 2/006
Lake (Robert E.) Fdn., Jackson, 2/007
Lewis (Celian H.) Family Fdn., Indianola,
  2/008
McRae Fdn., Jackson, 2/008
Mississippi Society of Certified Public
  Accountants Fdn., Jackson, 2/009
Mississippi State College Bass Memorial Loan
  Fund, Jackson, 2/010
Misticos (Alexander J.), Jackson, 2/010
Powers (R.V.) & Robert E. Lake Fdns.,
  Jackson, 2/010
Sanders (Robert D.) Fdn., Jackson, 2/011
Sixteenth Section Development Corp., Jackson,
  2/012
Stennis (Bessie C.) Memorial Fund, Jackson,
  2/013
Taylor (Marion E.) Christmas Fund, Natchez,
  2/013
Turner Fdn., Hattiesburg, 2/014
White (Dan M.) Family Fdn., Jackson, 2/015
Woods (Sam E.) Scholarship Fund, Jackson,
  2/015

MISSOURI

First Filming

Abbey (Adolph) Trust, St. Louis, 1/001
Adler (Jack) Fdn., St. Louis, 1/001
Allen (Terry W.) Scholarship Fund, St. Louis,
  1/002
Allendoerfer (Carl W.) Memorial Library Trust,
  Kansas City, 1/002
Aloe (A.S.) Company Charitable Trust, St.
  Louis, 1/003
Alton Box Board Charitable Trust, St. Louis,
  1/003
Altringer - Knight - Bunting Fdn., Kansas City,
  1/005
American Institute of Architects Scholarship
  Fund, St. Louis, 1/005
American Investment Company Fdn., St. Louis,
  1/006
American Legion Founders Trust, St. Louis,
  1/007
American Teke Fdn., Kansas City, 1/008
Anderson (Elizabeth Y.) Trust, St. Louis,
  1/008
Beatty (William J.) Scholarship Trust, St. Louis,
  1/009
Barnes (Robert A.) Trust, St. Louis, 1/009
Arndt (Joseph M.) Fdn., Clayton, 1/010
Atha (Russell E. & Helen) Gift Fund, Kansas
  City, 1/010
Baer (Arthur B.) Charitable Trust, St. Louis,
  1/011
Ashland Mausoleum Perpetual Care &
  Maintenance Fund, St. Joseph, 1/011
Baer (S. Charles) Charitable Trust, St. Louis,
  1/012
Baer (Sidney R.) Charitable Trust, St. Louis,
  1/013
Baer (Sigmond & Marie P.) Charitable Trust,
  St. Louis, 1/014
Barnes (Donald L.) Fdn., St. Louis, 1/015
Bartlett (John R.) Fdn., St. Louis, 1/016
Bascom (Elizabeth E. & Joseph H.) Charitable
  Fdn., St. Louis, 1/017
Battenfeld Fdn., Kansas City, 1/018

Beaumont (Louis D.) Employees Trust Fund,
  St. Louis, 1/018
Bentley (Frank C. & Georgia) Trust, St. Louis,
  1/019
Berkley (Richard L. & Janis D.) Fdn., Kansas
  City, 1/021
Berkowitz Fdn., Kansas City, 1/022
Berwitz - Gollin Hebrew University Fdn., St.
  Louis, 1/022
Better Business Bureau of Greater St. Louis
  Fdn., St. Louis, 1/023
Bitting Fdn., St. Louis, 1/024
Bixby (William K.) Trusts, St. Louis, 1/025
Smith (Cyril H. & Kathryn S.) Charitable
  Trust, St. Louis, 1/028
Black & Veatch Fdn., Kansas City, 1/028
Blake (C.D.) Trust, St. Louis, 1/029
Blanke (Albert G.), Jr. Charitable Trust, St.
  Louis, 1/029
Blewett (Ben) Memorial Fund Trust, St. Louis,
  1/029
Blind Girls Home, St. Louis, 1/029
Blossom (Marion C.) Fdn., St. Louis, 1/031
Blum (Ben & Martha) Fdn., Clayton, 1/032
Blumeyer Fdn., St. Louis, 1/033
Boatmen's National Bank of St. Louis
  Irrevocable Charitable Trust, St. Louis,
  1/034
Bradford (Frank E.) Trust, St. Louis, 1/034
Broderick & Bascom Rope Company Charitable
  Trust, St. Louis, 1/035
Brooks (Kenneth R.) Fund, St. Louis, 1/035
Brown (Barrett) Fdn., St. Louis, 1/036
Brown (George Warren) Fdn., St. Louis, 1/037
Brown (Melvin) Fdn., Kansas City, 1/038
Bruder (Leo R.) Fdn., St. Louis, 1/038
Butler Manufacturing Company Fdn., Kansas
  City, 1/039
Cannon Fdn., Elsberry, 1/039
Carp Charitable Fdn., St. Louis, 1/040
Carpenter (George O.), Sr. Trust, St. Louis,
  1/042
Cavin (Mary Ellen Kelley) Trust, St. Louis,
  1/042
Chance Fdn., Centralia, 1/042
Collins (Martin) Memorial Fund, St. Louis,
  1/043
Davis (G.H.) Trust f/b/o Nettleton Home,
  Kansas City, 1/044
Vita Cee Charitable Trust, St. Louis, 1/044
McFall Cemetery Association, McFall, 1/045
Chandeysson Fdn., St. Louis, 1/045
St. Louis Charitable Fdn., St. Louis, 1/046
Chase Hotel Charitable Trust, St. Louis, 1/046
Chetalie Fdn., Kansas City, 1/047
Christopher (Max A. & Sue Hargis) Trust,
  Kansas City, 1/047
CODASCO Class of 1950 Charitable Trust, St.
  Louis, 1/048
Collins (Horace C. & Mary A.) Memorial Fund
  Trust, St. Louis, 1/048
Columbia Charitable Fdn., St. Louis, 1/048
Columbia Terminals Company Charitable Trust,
  St. Louis, 1/049
Commerce Fdn., Kansas City, 1/050
Commerce Trust Company Fdn. for Education
  in the Fine Arts, Kansas City, 1/050
Connors Fdn., Richmond Heights, 1/051
Conzelman Benevolent Fund, St. Louis, 1/051
Coopersmith (Rudolph) Fdn., Clayton, 1/052
Cooter (E.L.) Trust f/b/o Holden Baptist
  Church, Kansas City, 1/052
Cooter (E.L.) Trust f/b/o First Presbyterian
  Church, Kansas City, 1/053
Cooter (E.L.) Trust f/b/o Holden Churches
  Trust, Kansas City, 1/053
Cornelius (Grover C.) Trust, St. Joseph, 1/054
Countryside Fund, Kansas City, 1/054
Cowden (Howard A.) Scholarship Fund,
  Kansas City, 1/055
Cowden (Louetta M.) Fdn., Kansas City,
  1/056
Creely (Walter J.) Fdn., St. Louis, 1/057
Cross Fdn., Kansas City, 1/058
Crunden Martin Manufacturing Company
  Charitable Trust, St. Louis, 1/059

Cumonow (Louis & Dorothy) Fdn., Kansas
  City, 1/060
Cupples Company Manufacturers Charitable
  Trust, St. Louis, 1/061
Curry Fdn., Kansas City, 1/062
Dalton (John M.) Educational Trust, Kennett,
  1/062
Dannen Fdn., St. Joseph, 1/063
D'Arcy (William C.) Trust, St. Louis, 1/064
Davis (Elizabeth O.) Trust, Kansas City, 1/065
Davis (G.H.) Trust f/b/o Nettleton Home,
  Kansas City, 1/066
Davis (G.H.) Trust f/b/o Central Christ
  Presbyterian Church, Kansas City, 1/067
Davis (G.H. & Elizabeth O.) Trust f/b/o Christ
  Presbyterian Church, Kansas City, 1/068
Davis (G.H. & Elizabeth O.) Trust f/b/o
  School of the Ozarks, Kansas City, 1/068
Davis (G.H. & Elizabeth O.) Trust f/b/o Park
  College, Kansas City, 1/069
Davis (Samuel C.) Charitable Trust, St. Louis,
  1/069
Dazor Manufacturing Corporation Charitable
  Trust, St. Louis, 1/071
Day (Dr. Carroll V. & Lew V.) Mission Trust
  Fund, Kansas City, 1/072
D.D.S. Fdn., Kansas City, 1/072
Deer Creek Fdn., St. Louis, 1/073
Deramus Fdn., Kansas City, 1/073
Diamant (Max) Fdn., St. Louis, 1/076
Diffenbaugh (H.J.) Trust f/b/o Baker
  University, Kansas City, 1/077
Diffenbaugh (H.J.) Trust f/b/o Illinois
  University, Kansas City, 1/078
Diffenbaugh (H.J.) Trust f/b/o Kansas
  University, Kansas City, 1/078
Diveley (George S.) Fund, Kansas City, 1/079
Doulos Fdn., Kansas City, 1/080
Dreyfoos (H.B.) Trust f/b/o Jewish Memorial
  Hospital, Kansas City, 1/080
Drury (George) Trust, Kansas City, 1/081
Dubinsky Fdn., St. Louis, 1/082
Dugdale (Harold P.) Charitable Trust, St.
  Joseph, 1/083
Dunn (J.E.) Fdn., Kansas City, 1/084
Dunn (Thomas) Memorials Trust, St. Louis,
  1/085
Dunn (Thomas) Trust, St. Louis, 1/087
Durwood Fdn., Kansas City, 1/089
Dwyer (John J.) Scholarship Fund, St. Louis,
  1/089
Eaton (Helen F.) Trust, St. Louis, 1/090
Edison Brothers Stores Fdn., St. Louis, 1/091
Edison (Harry) Fdn., St. Louis, 1/092
Edison (Simon) Fdn., St. Louis, 1/093
Educational Trust for Better Citizenship, Kansas
  City, 1/094
Edwards Charitable Trust, St. Louis, 1/095
Elgas (Rachel Baer) Trust, St. Louis, 1/095
Elko Charitable Trust & Foundation, Kansas
  City, 1/096
Elnel Fdn., Clayton, 1/096
Endowment Fund of the Memorial Home, St.
  Joseph, 1/097
Epple (John A. & Elizabeth K.) Fdn.,
  Columbia, 1/097
Erhardt (Louis) Trust, Kansas City, 1/098
Evans Family Fdn., St. Louis, 1/099
Ewald Charitable Trust, Kirkwood, 1/099
Fabick Charitable Trust, St. Louis, 1/100
Farm House Fdn., Columbia, 1/101
Fechner (Harold C. & Francine) Charitable
  Trust, St. Louis, 1/101
Feingold (Harry C. & Elaine E.) Fdn., Kansas
  City, 1/102
Feld (Milton W.) Fdn., Kansas City, 1/102
Fendell (M.M.) Charitable Fdn., Clayton,
  1/103
First Congregational Church of St. Louis
  Endowment Fund, St. Louis, 1/103
First National Bank in St. Louis Charitable
  Trust, St. Louis, 1/103
First National Fdn. of Kansas City, Kansas
  City, 1/105
Fischer Bauer Knirps Fdn., Clayton, 1/106
Fischer (Louis E.) Fdn., Clayton, 1/108

Fixman Fdn., Clayton, 1/109
Flower & Garden Fdn., Kansas City, 1/110
Foundation for Reformation Research, St. Louis, 1/110
Foundation for Junior Trapshooters of Missouri, St. Louis, 1/111
Four Six Six Fdn., St. Louis, 1/112
Francis (David R.) Trust, St. Louis, 1/112
Franklyn (Charles V.) Trust, St. Louis, 1/113
Freund (Eugene A. & Adlyne) Fdn., Richmond Heights, 1/113
Freund (Harry) Memorial Fdn., St. Louis, 1/115
Friedman (Joseph) Fdn., St. Louis, 1/116
Friend of the Boy Fdn., St. Louis, 1/117
Fruin - Colnon Fdn. Trust, St. Louis, 1/117
Fugate (Joseph F.) Trust, St. Louis, 1/118
Funk (Walter) Fdn., St. Louis, 1/119
Gaddis (Henry) Fdn., Kansas City, 1/119
Garland (Burton) Charitable Fdn., Clayton, 1/120
Garth (Helen K.) Trusts, St. Louis, 1/120
Gascosage Electric Cooperative, Dixon, 1/121
Gaylord (Clifford Willard) Fdn., St. Louis, 1/121
Geisse Fdn., St. Louis, 1/122
General Bancshares Charitable Corporation, St. Louis, 1/122
General Steel Industries Fdn., St. Louis, 1/122
Gerchen (Bernard) Fdn., St. Louis, 1/124
German School Association & Free Community of St. Louis, St. Louis, 1/124
Gerson Family Fdn., Kansas City, 1/124
Gillis (John Lamb & Carol Randolph) Charitable Trust, St. Louis, 1/126
Gladish (Sarah Cora) Endowment Fund, Higginsville, 1/127
Glaser (Joseph & Corinne Fuller) Charitable Trust, St. Louis, 1/127
Glen (Ida M. & Mabelle) Trust, Kansas City, 1/128
Goldstein (Ely & Mary) Charitable Fdn., St. Louis, 1/129
Goodall (John R.) Trust, St. Louis, 1/130
Goodman (Barney) Fdn., Kansas City, 1/131
Gordley (William T.) Trusts, St. Louis, 1/131
Green (A.P.) Refractories Company Scholarship Fund, Mexico, 1/131
Guy (William E.) Trust, St. Louis, 1/132
Grand (Joseph H. & Evalyne S.) Fdn., St. Louis, 1/132
Granite City Steel Company Charitable Trust, St. Louis, 1/133
Grant (William T. & Frances D.) Charitable Trust & Fdn., Kansas City, 1/134
Gray (M.H.) Charitable Trust, Kansas City, 1/134
Green (Allen P. & Josephine B.) Fdn., Mexico, 1/135
Greenberg (Julius & Faye) Fdn., Des Peres, 1/136
Gregg (Norris B.), Jr. Fdn., St. Louis, 1/137
Gudder Fdn., St. Louis, 1/137
Hagstrom Fdn., Kansas City, 1/138
Hall (J. Carl) Trust, St. Louis, 1/138
Hall (Herbert F.) Trust, Kansas City, 1/138
Halliday (William W. & Betty) Fdn., Normandy, 1/139
Hallmark Educational Fdn. of Kansas, Kansas City, 1/140
Hallmark Educational Fdn., Kansas City, 1/141
Hamra (Sam Farris) Fdn., St. Louis, 1/152
Happel (Roberta Parks) Memorial Trust, St. Louis, 1/153
Hardesty (Sallie M.) Trust, Kansas City, 1/154
Hardy (T. Walter), Jr. Charitable Trust, St. Louis, 1/155
Harris Fdn., St. Louis, 1/155
Harzfeld Fdn., Kansas City, 1/156
Hayes (W. Alfred) Fdn., St. Louis, 1/157
H.B.S. Fund, St. Louis, 1/158
Hedrick (Minnie B.) Trust, Kansas City, 1/158
Hein (J.B. & Anna) Trust, St. Joseph, 1/160
Helpers Anonymous, Kansas City, 1/160
Helzberg (B.C.) Fdn. Trust, Kansas City, 1/162
Heritage Fdn. of Florissant, Florissant, 1/162

Herrick Fdn., Kansas City, 1/162
Hewitt (Kate W.) Trust, Kansas City, 1/163
Higdon (Aimee V. & John C.) Charitable Trust & Fdn., Kansas City, 1/164
Hill (Vassie James) Trusts, Kansas City, 1/164
Hirsch (Florence) Educational Endowment Fund, St. Joseph, 1/165
Hirsch (Oscar C.) Fdn., Cape Girardeau, 1/166
Hocker (Mary Virginia & O. Glen) Fdn., Mexico, 1/167
Hollander Charitable Trust, St. Louis, 1/167
Holmes (Mary Brooks) Charitable Fund, St. Louis, 1/169
Holmes-McDonald Fdn., Kansas City, 1/171
Home Mission, St. Joseph, 1/171
Honigberg (Samuel) Fdn., St. Louis, 1/171
Hospital Saturday & Sunday Association, St. Louis, 1/172
Huber (John B.) Trust, St. Louis, 1/173
Humane Society of St. Joseph & Buchanan County, St. Joseph, 1/173
Hyer (Lewis Wilkins) Trust, St. Louis, 1/174
Hyer (Lewis W.) Trust, St. Louis, 1/175
Iglauer (Henry S.) Memorial Fund, St. Louis, 1/176
Ingersoll (A.C.), Jr. Memorial Trust, St. Louis, 1/177
Ingram (Joe) Trust, Kansas City, 1/178
Interco Incorporated Charitable Trust, St. Louis, 1/178
Irving (Anna Elno) Trust f/b/o Mercy Hospital, Kansas City, 1/181
Jackes Fdn., St. Louis, 1/181
Jaeger Charitable Fdn., St. Louis, 1/183
J.J.C.T.M. Fdn., Kansas City, 1/183
Joconat Fdn., Kansas City, 1/184
Johnson (Gunnard & Charlotte) Fdn., Kansas City, 1/184
Johnson (James Lee) Charitable Trust, St. Louis, 1/185
Jones (C.W.) Fdn., Independence, 1/187
Jones (Addison E.) Trust, St. Louis, 1/188
Jones (Herbert Vincent), Jr. Fdn., Kansas City, 1/188
Jones (R. Harry) Trust, Kansas City, 1/189
Jordan (Ettie Amelia) Trust, St. Louis, 1/190
Jordan (Mary Ranken & Ettie A.) Charitable Fdn., St. Louis, 1/191
Jordan (Mary A.L. Ranken) Trust, St. Louis, 1/193
Juvenile Improvement Club Trust, Kansas City, 1/195
Kalish (Claire E. & Lionel), Jr. Fdn., Clayton, 1/196
Kansas City General Hospital & Medical Center Fdn., Kansas City, 1/196
Kansas City Life Employees Welfare Fund, Kansas City, 1/197
Kansas City Star Public Activities Assoc., Kansas City, 1/197
Kaplan (Abe & Catherine) Fdn., Kansas City, 1/198
Katz (Isaac & Minnie) Fdn., Kansas City, 1/199
Kemper (R.C.) Charitable Trust & Fdn., Kansas City, 1/199
Kemper (R.C. & Cynthia Warrick), Jr. Charitable Trust & Fdn., Kansas City, 1/200
Kemper (David Woods) Memorial Fdn., Kansas City, 1/201
Kerckhoff Fdn., St. Louis, 1/202
Kerens (R.C.) Mortuary Chapel Fund, St. Louis, 1/202
Kiener (Harry J.) Trust, St. Louis, 1/203
Kirkwood (Laura Nelson) Residuary Trust, Kansas City, 1/203
Kirkwood Rotary Fund, Kirkwood, 1/203
Kieselhorst (June) Trust, St. Louis, 1/203
Kittredge (Ida) Trust, St. Louis, 1/204
Knapp Monarch Fdn., St. Louis, 1/205
Koplar (Sam & Janet) Fdn., St. Louis, 1/206
Kotany (Ludwig) Fund, St. Louis, 1/207
Kraehe (Oliver R.) Trust, St. Louis, 1/207
Krasne (Hyman & Esther) Fdn., Kansas City, 1/207

Krupnick Fund, St. Louis, 1/208
Kutten (Joseph & Carolyn) Fdn., Clayton, 1/209
Kurz Charitable Trust & Fdn., Kansas City, 1/210
Labarque Charitable Trust, St. Louis, 1/211
Laclede Steel Company, St. Louis, 1/211
Ladies Union Benevolent Association, St. Joseph, 1/212
Land (Arthur L.) Charitable Trust, Kansas City, 1/213
Land (Frank S.) Fdn., Kansas City, 1/213
Landwehr (Frank) Trust, St. Louis, 1/214
Lang Fdn., St. Louis, 1/215
Larner (Irvin & Sara) Charitable Trust, Creve Coeur, 1/217
Lasec Trust Fund, St. Louis, 1/217
Laski (Viola Aloe) Charitable Trust, St. Louis, 1/218
Latshaw (John) Fdn., Kansas City, 1/220
Lazaroff (Morris & Ann) Fdn., St. Louis, 1/220
Leader Fdn., St. Louis, 1/221
Leatherbury (Evelyn J.) Charitable Trust, St. Louis, 1/223
Levin (Richard M.) Fdn., Kansas City, 1/223
Levitt (William & Ida) Fdn., Clayton, 1/224
Josal Fund, St. Louis, 1/224
Lewis (David S.), Jr. Family Charitable Trust, St. Louis, 1/225
Liberty Loan Fdn., St. Louis, 1/226
Lichtenstein (David B.) Fdn., St. Louis, 1/227
Lincoln Engineering Company Charitable Trust, St. Louis, 1/228
Linhart (Charlotte Marie) Memorial Fund, St. Louis, 1/229
Lockwood (Ira H. & Jessie King) Trust, Kansas City, 1/229
Logan (John Sublett) Fdn., St. Joseph, 1/230
Logan (Helen R.) Memorial Fund, Kansas City, 1/230
Logan (James E.) Mercy Hospital Trust, Kansas City, 1/231
Logan (Mildred T.) Memorial Fund, Kansas City, 1/232
Long (R.A.) Fdn., Kansas City, 1/233
Longmire Fund, St. Louis, 1/233
Loomis Fdn., Kansas City, 2/001
Loose (Carrie J.) Trust, Kansas City, 2/001
Loose (Ella C.) Trusts, Kansas City, 2/004
Loose (Jacob L.) Million Dollar Charity Fund Trust, Kansas City, 2/007
Loose (Jacob L.) Million Dollar Charity Fund Association, Kansas City, 2/008
Lopata (Stanley & Lucy) Fdn., St. Louis, 2/010
Lorber (Edward A.) Jewish Religious Education Fdn., Kansas City, 2/011
Lucas (Lottie King) Trust, Kansas City, 2/012
Lyons (Charles) Memorial Fdn., Lexington, 2/014
Lyons (Sidney) Charitable Fdn., St. Louis, 2/014
Mag Fdn., Kansas City, 2/015
Mallinckrodt Fund, St. Louis, 2/016
Mallinckrodt (Edward), Jr. Trust, St. Louis, 2/017
Manne (Max & Thelma) Fdn., St. Louis, 2/017
Martin (Jacob & Nettie) Charitable Fdn., St. Louis, 2/018
McBride Fdn., Clayton, 2/018
Love (William McBride) Charitable Fdn., St. Louis, 2/019
McGee Fdn., Kansas City, 2/020
Frederic (Lettie B. Mc Ilvain) Fund, Kansas City, 2/021
McMillan - Avery Fdn., Clayton, 2/022
McMillan (Lillian C.) Trusts, St. Louis, 2/023
Manassa Timber Company Charitable Trust, St. Louis, 2/027
Manchester Bank Charitable Trust, St. Louis, 2/028
Marian Fdn., Clayton, 2/028
Martin (Donelia Evaline) Trust, Kansas City, 2/029

Massman Fdn., Kansas City, 2/030

May (David) Employees Trust Fund, St. Louis, 2/031

McCleary Fdn., Excelsior Springs, 2/031

McComb Manufacturing Fdn., St. Louis, 2/032

McDonnell Fdn., St. Louis, 2/032

McDonnell Scholarship Fdn., St. Louis, 2/033

Meadowood Charitable Trust, St. Louis, 2/034

Medical Fdn. Fund Trust, Kansas City, 2/035

Melcher (Harold S.) Fdn., Kansas City, 2/035

Metropolitan Church Federation of St. Louis, St. Louis, 2/035

Melcher (Luther) Fdn., Kansas City, 2/036

Memorial Home, St. Louis, 2/036

Mercantile Trust Company Charitable Trust, St. Louis, 2/037

Messing (Roswell), Jr. Charitable Fdn., Maryland Heights, 2/038

Milgram Fdn., Kansas City, 2/041

Nichols (Miller) Fdn., Kansas City, 2/042

Miller (Jack & Helyn) Fdn., Kansas City, 2/042

Missouri Council on Family Law, University City, 2/043

Missouri Pharmacy Fdn., Jefferson City, 2/043

Missouri Society of Professional Engineers Educational Fdn., Jefferson City, 2/043

Hickey - Mitchell Company Charitable Trust, St. Louis, 2/043

Monsanto Fund, St. Louis, 2/044

Morton (Leonard) Trust, St. Louis, 2/047

Putnam (Karl F.) Trust, St. Louis, 2/048

Moseley (Frank W.) Fdn., Kansas City, 2/048

Moseley (Ray F.) Charities Fund, Kansas City, 2/049

Mount Hope Church Trust Fund, St. Louis, 2/050

Mount Hope Mauseleum Endowment Fund, St. Louis, 2/051

Mullins (Fristoe) Charitable Trust, St. Louis, 2/052

Neenan (James P. & Helen D.) Charitable Trust, Kansas City, 2/052

Nelson (Oscar D. & Florence L.) Fund, Kansas City, 2/053

Newcomers (D.W.) Sons Fdn., Kansas City, 2/055

Nichols Company Charitable Trust, Kansas City, 2/055

Norquist - Robinson Fdn., Kansas City, 2/056

Novoson Charitable Fdn., St. Louis, 2/057

Noyes (Charles W.) Trust, St. Joseph, 2/058

Noyes (Sarepta Ward) Testamentary Trust, St. Joseph, 2/058

Olin (Evelyn B.) Charitable Trust, St. Louis, 2/059

Olin (Evelyn Brown) Charitable Trust, St. Louis, 2/060

Olin (John M.) Charitable Trust, St. Louis, 2/061

Olin (Spencer T. & Ann W.) Fdn., St. Louis, 2/062

Ostermoor (Ida & Alexis) Fund, St. Louis, 2/063

Davis (G.H. & Elizabeth O.) Endowment Fund f/b/o Park College, Kansas City, 2/063

Parker (Anita B.) Trust, St. Louis, 2/064

Parker (Charles W.) Trust, St. Louis, 2/064

Parmelee Fdn., Kansas City, 2/064

Patterson (Frances) Trust, Kansas City, 2/065

Pauline - Morton Fdn., Kansas City, 2/066

Pearson (Donna S. & Sam C.) Fdn. Formerly D.S.S.S. Fdn., St. Louis, 2/067

Peet (H.O.) Fdn., Kansas City, 2/068

Persons (W.R.) Fdn., Clayton, 2/068

Peters (Earl) Award Trust Fund, Benton, 2/069

Peters (F.H.) Trust, St. Louis, 2/070

Pet Milk Fdn., St. Louis, 2/070

Pettus (James T.) Charitable Trust, Clayton, 2/070

Pettus (James T.), Jr. Fdn., Clayton, 2/071

Piazzek (Deforrest F.) Trust, Kansas City, 2/071

Pierson (Elmer F.) Fdn., Kansas City, 2/073

Pierson (John T.) Fund, Kansas City, 2/074

Pollak Charitable Fdn., St. Louis, 2/074

Pott (Herman T.) Fdn., St. Louis, 2/076

Powell Fdn., Kansas City, 2/077

Powell Family Fdn., Kansas City, 2/077

Powell (Ruth & Robert R.), Jr. Fdn., Kansas City, 2/078

Preston (Frederick M.) Trust, Neosho, 2/078

Pryor (Belle Findley) Trust, St. Louis, 2/078

Public Library of St. Louis, Steedman Architectural Library Fund, St. Louis, 2/079

Putnam (Ann Elizabeth) Trust, St. Louis, 2/079

Queeny (John & Olga) Educational Fdn., St. Louis, 2/080

Ramacciotti (Frank L.) Charitable Trust, St. Louis, 2/081

Rarick (James E.) Fdn., St. Louis, 2/081

Raycon Fdn., St. Louis, 2/081

Rayhill (Charles T.) Fdn., St. Louis, 2/083

Ready (Margaret R.) Trust, St. Louis, 2/083

Robinson (Lizzie W.) Trust, St. Louis, 2/083

Rechner (Carl B.) Fdn., Kansas City, 2/083

Reed (Nell Quinlan) Fdn., Kansas City, 2/085

Reeder Fdn., Kansas City, 2/085

Repelmar Fdn., St. Louis, 2/085

Reproductive Biology Research Fdn., St. Louis, 2/086

Reynolds (J.B.) Fdn., Kansas City, 2/087

Richardson (L.F.) Fdn., Nevada, 2/087

Roberts (Sam E. & Mary F.) Fdn., Kansas City, 2/088

Roblee (Florence A.) Trust, St. Louis, 2/089

Ross Charitable Trust, St. Louis, 2/089

Roth (Alice Eiseman) Memorial Scholarship Fund, St. Louis, 2/090

Roth (Frederick S.) Trust, St. Louis, 2/091

Rothbarth Charity Fdn., St. Louis, 2/092

Sachar Fdn., St. Louis, 2/093

Rothschild Fund, Kansas City, 2/093

R.Q.S. Fdn., Kansas City, 2/094

Rust (John B.) Charity Trust, Kansas City, 2/095

Sachs Fund, St. Louis, 2/096

St. Louis Community Trust, St. Louis, 2/098

St. Louis Delta Gamma Alumnae Fund, St. Louis, 2/099

St. Louis Girl Scouts Trust, St. Louis, 2/100

St. Louis Journalism Fdn. Charitable Trust, St. Louis, 2/100

St. Louis Mercantile Library Association, St. Louis, 2/101

St. Louis Otological Fdn., St. Louis, 2/102

St. Louis Post-Dispatch Fdn., St. Louis, 2/102

St. Louis Regional Planning & Construction Fdn., St. Louis, 2/103

St. Louis Union Trust Company Charitable Trust, St. Louis, 2/105

St. Paul Evangelical Church Trusts, St. Louis, 2/110

Schiffman (John & Althea) Fdn., St. Louis, 2/111

Schneeberger (Leroy C.) Charitable Trust, St. Louis, 2/112

School of the Ozarks Trust, St. Louis, 2/112

Schutte (Victor E. & Caroline E.) Fdn., Kansas City, 2/112

Scott (Oreon E.) Fdn., St. Louis, 2/113

Sealright-Oswego Falls Fdn., Kansas City, 2/114

Seay Fdn., St. Louis, 2/115

Seitz (Pansy A.) Trust f/b/o Grace Holy Trinity Church, Kansas City, 2/116

Seitz (Pansy A.) Trust f/b/o Mercy Hospital, Kansas City, 2/117

Seven-Up Company Charitable Trust, Clayton, 2/118

Shank (William C. & Mariee S.) Charitable Trust, Kansas City, 2/118

Shenker (Morris A. & Lillian) Fdn., St. Louis, 2/119

Sherman (David) Fdn., North Kansas City, 2/120

Shirkey (Helen & Howard) Fdn., Richmond, 2/121

Shoemaker (Ella S.) Trust, St. Louis, 2/121

Shoenberg Fdn., St. Louis, 2/122

Shutz Fdn., Kansas City, 2/123

Siemers (Agnes) Trust, St. Louis, 2/125

Simon (John E.) Fdn. Formerly Simon Fdn., St. Louis, 2/125

Sligo Charitable Trust, St. Louis, 2/126

Slough Fdn., Kansas City, 2/128

Smith (Jerry) Charitable Trust, Kansas City, 2/128

Smith (Ralph L.) Fdn., Kansas City, 2/129

Snyder (William D.) Fdn., Kansas City, 2/129

Sosland Fdn., Kansas City, 2/130

Souers (Sidney W. & Sylvia N.) Charitable Trust, St. Louis, 2/131

Southern States Steel Corporation Charitable Trust, St. Louis, 2/133

Speas (John W. & Effie E.) Memorial Trust, Kansas City, 2/133

Speas (Victor E.) Fdn., Kansas City, 2/134

Spector Fdn., St. Louis, 2/135

Spencer (George A.) Memorial Trust, Centralia, 2/136

Spiegel (Edwin J.) Fdn., Frontenac, 2/136

Spielberg (Frank & Bessie) Fdn., St. Louis, 2/136

Spillane (Thomas J.) Memorial Fund, St. Louis, 2/137

Springmeier Fdn., St. Louis, 2/137

Starr Fdn., Kansas City, 2/138

Starr (Raymond H.) Family Fdn., Kansas City, 2/139

Stein (Elliott H. & Mary Ann) Fdn., St. Louis, 2/139

Steinberg Charitable Trust, St. Louis, 2/140

Steinberg Charitable Fund, St. Louis, 2/141

Stevenson (Virginia E.) Scholarship Trust, St. Louis, 2/142

Storckman (Clem F.) Trust, St. Louis, 2/143

May Stores Fdn., St. Louis, 2/143

Stuart Four Square Fund, St. Louis, 2/145

Sunderland (Lester T.) Fdn., Kansas City, 2/146

Sunline Fdn., St. Louis, 2/147

Sunnen Fdn., Maplewood, 2/147

Sutherland (Herman & Helen) Fdn., Kansas City, 2/150

Sutton (Walter S.) Trust, Kansas City, 2/151

Sverdrup & Parcel Charitable Trust, St. Louis, 2/151

Swift (John S.) Company Charitable Trust, St. Louis, 2/153

Swinney (E.F.) Trust f/b/o Employees, Kansas City, 2/154

Swinney (E.F.) Trust f/b/o Nettleton Home, Kansas City, 2/155

Swinney (Edward F.) Student Loan, Kansas City, 2/156

Swinney (Edward F.) Fdn., Kansas City, 2/160

Sycamore Tree Trust, Clayton, 2/161

Tatman Fdn., St. Louis, 2/162

Tegeler Fdn., St. Louis, 2/162

Templin (Walter Wayne) Trust, St. Louis, 2/164

Tension Envelope Fdn., Kansas City, 2/165

Ten-Ten Fdn., Kansas City, 2/166

Thornhill (Edward A.) Fdn., Kansas City, 2/167

Timmons (Bess Spiva) Fdn., Joplin, 2/169

Tower Grove Bank & Trust Company Employees Benefit Trust, St. Louis, 2/170

Townsend (R.E.) Educational Fund, St. Joseph, 2/171

Benjamin (David) Trust, Kansas City, 2/172

McBeth (Catherine) Trust, Clinton, 2/172

Trustees of the Home for Little Wanderers, St. Joseph, 2/173

Tucker (Patricia Aloe) Charitable Trust, St. Louis, 2/173

Turner (Courtney S.) Fdn., Kansas City, 2/174

23 West Tenth Street Fdn., Kansas City, 2/174

Union Electric Company Charitable Trust, St. Louis, 2/175

Universal Printing Fdn., St. Louis, 2/177

Valley Dolomite Corporation Charitable Trust, St. Louis, 2/177

Schapiro Fdns., St. Louis, 3/111
Scharff Fdn., Clayton, 3/111
Schattner (Chas) Fund Trust, Kansas City, 3/112
Scheibe (Irven M. and Irven B.) Fdn., St. Louis, 3/112
Schonfeld (Dr. Alexander and Helena) Fdn., St. Louis, 3/113
Schwartz (Edward K.) Fdn., St. Louis, 3/114
Shampaine Fdn., St. Louis, 3/114
Siteman Charitable Fdn., Clayton, 3/115
Small (Harry L.) Fdn., Kansas City, 3/116
Smith (Cyril H. & Kathryn S.) Charitable Trust, St. Louis, 3/116
Smith (J. Herndon and Lida Wallace) Fund, St. Louis, 3/116
Spencer (Kenneth A. and Helen F.) Fdn., St. Louis, 3/118
Stark Bros. Nurseries and Orchards Company Charitable Tr., Louisiana, 3/120
Charitable Trust of Stark Bros. Nurseries and Orchards Co., St. Louis, 3/120
Stern-Slegman-Prins Fdn., Kansas City, 3/121
St. Louis Altenheim, St. Louis, 3/122
St. Louis Bible Society, St. Louis, 3/125
St. Louis Girl Scouts Fund, St. Louis, 3/125
St. Louis Regional Open Space Fdn., St. Louis, 3/125
St. Louis Regional Recreation and Conservation Fdn., St. Louis, 3/126
Stupp (Norman J.) Fdn., Ladue, 3/128
Swinney (Edward F.) K.C. University Gymn. Fdn., Kansas City, 3/128
Swinney (Edward F.) Student Loan, Kansas City, 3/129
Switzer (Fred M.) Sr., Fund, St. Louis, 3/136
Tegeler Fdn., St. Louis, 3/137
Thesaurus Fdn. of Ches. Todd, St. Louis, 3/137
Tilles (Rosalie) Non-Sectarian Charity Fund Trust, St. Louis, 3/139
Tober (Abraham & Anna) Charitable Trust, St. Louis, 3/140
Tower Grove Bank and Trust Co., St. Louis, 3/142
Traffic Club of St. Louis, St. Louis, 3/142
Dorsey B. Heer Trust, St. Louis, 3/143
Trustees for the Gillis Opera House under the Will of Mary A. Troost, deceased, Kansas City, 3/143
Trustees of the Home for Little Wanderers, St. Joseph, 3/143
Tyler-Gunther Fdn., Kansas City, 3/144
United Fdn., St. Louis, 3/144
Van Verwolde (Alma Vanderborch) Tr. U/I, St. Louis, 3/144
Vatterott Fdn., St. Ann, 3/145
Walker (W.C.) for American Bible Society, Kansas City, 3/145
Wolferman Family Fdn., Kansas City, 3/146
Walsh (Edward J.), Jr. Trust, St. Louis, 3/147
Westwood Charitable Fdn., St. Louis, 3/147
Wilson (Victor) Trust, Kansas City, 3/148
Wolff (John M.) Fdn., St. Louis, 3/148
Woolford Fdn., Kansas City, 3/150
World Color Press Charitable Fdn., Maryland Heights, 3/151
Theta XI Fdn., St. Louis, 3/152
Judson Young Memorial Fdn., Salem, 3/153
Young Mens Christian Assn. Tr., Kansas City, 3/153
Young Womens Christian Assn. Tr., Kansas City, 3/153
Youth Palisades Fdn., Goodman, 3/154

MONTANA

First Filming

Allan Fdn., Great Falls, 1/002
Fort Benton Community Improvement Association, Fort Benton, 1/002

Brown (Edith L.) Scholarship Trust, Miles City, 1/003
Boy Scouts of America North Central Montana Council Trust, Great Falls, 1/003
Covenant Lodge 6 I.O.O.F., Missoilla, 1/004
Dean (Maria M.) Fdn., Helena, 1/004
Dufresne Fdn., Great Falls, 1/005
Elm (Henry) Trust, Sidney, 1/005
Falls Creek Environmental Education Fdn., Condon, 1/006
Flathead 4-H Fdn., Kalispell, 1/006
Fortin Fdn. of Montana, Billings, 1/006
Fox Fdn., Billings, 1/008
Gallagher (W.J.) Fdn. Trust, Helena, 1/009
Griffis Scholarship Fdn., Kalispell, 1/009
Hawkins Scholarship Fdn., Great Falls, 1/010
Hanford (Norris) Family Fdn., Fort Benton, 1/010
Heisey Fdn., Great Falls, 1/010
Jones Fdn., Wibaux, 1/011
Leuthhold Fdn., Billings, 1/012
MacIntyre Fdn., Billings, 1/012
Morledge Fdn., Billings, 1/012
Niels (Arthur J.) Family Fdn., Libby, 1/013
Peters (Julius C.) Jr., Fdn., Great Falls, 1/013
Quarterback Club, Great Falls, 1/014
Ryan (Robert J.) Fdn., Great Falls, 1/015
Sears (William E.) Fdn., Superior, 1/015
Svarre Fdn., Sidney, 1/015
Towe Fdn., Circle, 1/016
Treacy Co., Helena, 1/016
English (Michael M.) Deceased Trust, Under Will of, Great Falls, 1/017

Second Filming

Buttrey (Jane) Memorial Trust Number 11, Great Falls, 2/002
Christie (Kenneth) Educational Fund, Helena, 2/002
Clark (Paul) Home, Butte, 2/002
Cowley Endowment, Great Falls, 2/003
Gallatin County Youth Fdn., Bozeman, 2/003
Globe Fdn., St. Louis, Mo., 2/004
Hanford (Norris) Family Fdn., Fort Benton, 2/004
Harris (George M.) & Faye Taber Harris Charitable Fdn., Helena, 2/006
Haynes Fdn., Bozeman, 2/005
Johnson (Ray and Nell) Scholarship Fund of Harlowton High School, Helena, 2/006
Kahrs (Augusta) Memorial Fdn., Helena, 2/006
Maronick (Edward P.) Charitable Fdn., Helena, 2/006
Maronick (Stephen J.) Charitable Fdn., Helena, 2/007
McKee (John W.) Education Trust, Glasgow, 2/007
McLaughlin Fdn., Great Falls, 2/010
Montana Chamber of Commerce Fdn., Helena, 2/011
Montana Masonic Fdn., Helena, 2/011
Pioneer Memorial Scholarship Fund, Helena, 2/011
Ruffcorn (William M.) Charitable Fdn., Helena, 2/012
Ryan (Robert J.) Fdn., Valier, 2/012
Schoknecht Family Fdn., Kalispell, 2/012
Yellowstone Art Center Fdn., Billings, 2/014
Youth Palisades Fdn., Goodman, Mo., 2/015

NEBRASKA

First Filming

Abbott Fdn., Alliance, 1/001
Abel Fdn., Lincoln, 1/001
Abrahams Charitable Trust, Omaha, 1/002
Albin (Don E. & Dona June) Charitable Trust, Broken Bow, 1/003
Aller (Dudley & Agnes) Fdn., Omaha, 1/003

Anderson (Carl A. & Eda A.) Fdn., Omaha, 1/003
Anderson (Irene) Trust, Lincoln, 1/004
Babcock Memorial Trust Fund, Ord, 1/006
Beck (Tad) Fund, Lincoln, 1/006
Beebe (Walter) Employees Trust, Omaha, 1/007
Benevolent Fdn., Lincoln, 1/008
Bernstein (Robert & Frances) Fdn., Omaha, 1/008
Bleicher (Jerome E. & Freda) Fdn., Omaha, 1/009
Brownell - Talbot Library Fund, Omaha, 1/009
Burket Fdn., Omaha, 1/009
Cary (Daniel & Cornelia) Research Fdn., Omaha, 1/010
Chandler Charitable Fdn., Bellevue, 1/010
Chapman (Gertrude & Isadore) Fdn., Omaha, 1/011
Cherniack Fdn., Omaha, 1/011
Cherniack (Harold & Harriet) Fdn., Omaha, 1/012
C & H Fdn., Omaha, 1/012
Christian Fdn., Norfolk, 1/013
Coleman Fdn., Diller, 1/013
Coryell (L.L.) & Son Park Fdn., Lincoln, 1/014
Dawson (Doris) Fdn., Schuyler, 1/015
Dillon Fdn., Omaha, 1/015
Dodge (N. Phillips & Virginia L.) Fdn., Omaha, 1/015
Douglas (James A.) Memorial Fdn., Omaha, 1/015
Dunklau (Rupert) Fdn., Fremont, 1/016
Eckert Fdn., Omaha, 1/017
Ferer (Aaron) & Sons Fdn., Omaha, 1/017
Ferris (Walter Cutler) Fund, Lincoln, 1/017
Foster (Charles E.) Crippled Children Memorial Fund, Omaha, 1/018
Foxley Fdn., Omaha, 1/018
Fremont Y.M.C.A. Fdn., Fremont, 1/019
Gallagher Fdn., Omaha, 1/019
Garfield County Fdn., Burwell, 1/020
German Old People's Home, Omaha, 1/020
Gifford Fdn., Omaha, 1/021
Glorious Gospel Hour Society, Columbus, 1/021
Gross (Daniel J.) Testamentary Trust for Creighton University, Omaha, 1/022
Hastings Court #152 Royal Order of Jesters, Hastings, 1/022
Haun (Francis R.) Fund for Language Disability Students, Wayne, 1/023
Hengstler Scholarship Loan Fund, Creighton, 1/023
Hinky Dinky Fdn., Omaha, 1/023
Hitchcock (Gilbert M. & Martha H.) Fdn., Omaha, 1/024
Jirdon (John R.) Fdn., Morrill, 1/027
Kaplan (Cecilia M. & David J.) Fdn., Omaha, 1/028
Kaslow Charitable Trust, Omaha, 1/029
Katz (Louis) Fdn., Omaha, 1/030
Brown - Kelley Fdn., Morrill, 1/031
Kiewit Fdn., Omaha, 1/031
Kiewit (Peter) Sons Company Fdn., Omaha, 1/032
Kirkpatrick, Pettis, Smith, & Polian Charitable Fdn., Omaha, 1/032
Kistler Charitable Fdn., Omaha, 1/033
Kiwanis Club Fdn., Lincoln, 1/033
Kugel (Josephine) Fdn., Omaha, 1/033
Landen Fdn., Omaha, 1/034
Leavitt (Edna & Ira) Fdn. Trust, Alliance, 1/034
Levitt Fdn., York, 1/035
Lied Fdn., Omaha, 1/035
Livingston (Milton S. & Corinne N.) Fdn., Omaha, 1/036
Lockwood Fdn., Gering, 1/037
Lubin (Irene W. & Donald S.) Fdn., Omaha, 1/038
Lueder Construction Company Fdn., Omaha, 1/038
Malmsten (C.J.) Charitable Trust, Lincoln, 1/038

Malmsten (Salina E.) Charitable Trust, Lincoln, 1/040
Mellam (Leo L. & Laural D.) Fdn., Omaha, 1/041
Milder (Hymie & Ella) Fdn., Omaha, 1/041
Millard (W.B.) Memorial Fund, Omaha, 1/042
Moore (Robert E. & Elmie E.) Trust, Lincoln, 1/042
M.T.S. Fund, Lincoln, 1/043
Nebraska Cross Counties Girl Scout Council, Grand Island, 1/043
Nebraskaland Fdn., North Platte, 1/044
Nelsen Fdn., Omaha, 1/044
Nicholas (Sidney R.) Memorial Scholarship Fund, Maxwell, 1/045
Old West Trail Fdn., Lincoln, 1/045
Omaha Livestock Fdn. Charitable Trust, Omaha, 1/046
Omaha National Bank Charitable Fdn. Trust, Omaha, 1/046
Omsteel Fdn., Omaha, 1/047
Peoples City Mission, Lincoln, 1/047
Quirk Family Fdn., Hastings, 1/047
Ressegieu Fdn., Alliance, 1/048
Rice (Don) Fdn., Omaha, 1/049
Riekes (John M.) Fdn., Omaha, 1/049
Rogers (R.H.) Family Fund, Lincoln, 1/050
Rosenfeld (Harry & Blanche) Fdn., Omaha, 1/051
Scott (Walter), Jr. Charitable Fdn., Omaha, 1/052
Seacrest Fdn. #2, Lincoln, 1/053
Silver (Ben D. & Madeline C.) Fdn., Omaha, 1/053
Steinhart Fdn., Nebraska City, 1/054
Smith (Julia Regina) Fdn., Omaha, 1/055
Stewart (Don W.) Family Fund, Lincoln, 1/056
Storz (Adolph G.) Fdn., Omaha, 1/056
Storz (Arthur C.) Fdn., Omaha, 1/057
Storz (Robert Herman) Fdn., Omaha, 1/057
Stuart Fdn., Lincoln, 1/058
Swanson (Carl & Caroline) Fdn., Omaha, 1/059
Swanson (Gilbert C.) Fdn., Omaha, 1/060
Thieszen Fdn., Henderson, 1/061
Morse (Herman O.) Endowment Trust, Lincoln, 1/061
Urban League Housing Fdn., Omaha, 1/062
Volpe Charitable Fdn., Bellevue, 1/062
Walker Fdn., Fremont, 1/063
Wander Fdn. for Medical Research, Lincoln, 1/064
Welsh (James LeRoy & Helen V.) Fdn., Omaha, 1/065
Wenger Fdn., Lincoln, 1/066
Woods Charitable Fund, Lincoln, 1/066
World - Herald Fdn., Omaha, 1/068
Y - K Fdn., Omaha, 1/070

Second Filming

Anderson (Roger L.) Charitable Fdn., Lincoln, 2/001
Andrews Cemetery, Lincoln, 2/001
Bay State Fdn., Mitchell, 2/001
Beasom Fdn., Omaha, 2/003
Bernstein (David & Muriel) Fdn., Omaha, 2/003
Bingel (Arthur & Dora) Fdn., Omaha, 2/003
Boys Clubs of Omaha Endowment Fund, Omaha, 2/004
Bucholz (Naomi T.) Charitable Trust, Omaha, 2/004
Buckstaff (Aaron H.) Charitable, Lincoln, 2/005
Buffett Fdn., Omaha, 2/005
Brandeis (E. John) Fdn., Omaha, 2/006
Brown (Mary H.) #2, Lincoln, 2/007
Cropsey (Frank), Lincoln, 2/007
Daugherty (Robert B.) Fdn., Omaha, 2/008
DeWitt Development Fdn., DeWitt, 2/008
Dill (George W. & Mae K.) Fdn., Omaha, 2/008
Dobbins (Harry T.), Lincoln, 2/009

Dodge (N.P. & Laura W.) Fdn., Omaha, 2/009
Dowd (Leo J.) Fdn., Columbus, 2/010
Dowd (Leo) Student Aid Funds, Columbus, 2/011
Dworak Charitable Fdn., Lincoln, 2/011
Eppley (Eugene C.) Fdn., Omaha, 2/012
Erck Charitable Fdn., Lincoln, 2/013
Fairmont Fdn., Omaha, 2/013
Feinberg (Robert M.) Fdn., Omaha, 2/014
Ferer (Aaron) & Sons Fdn., Omaha, 2/015
Fink (Bernard & Margaret) Fdn., Omaha, 2/015
Finley (R.A.) Charitable Trust, Omaha, 2/016
Fremont Y.M.C.A. Fdn., Fremont, 2/016
Gallimore (Clarence & Kathleen) Charitable Fdn., Omaha, 2/016
Gilroy (James F.) Trust, Geneva, 2/017
Hall (F.M.) Charitable Trust, Lincoln, 2/017
Holland (M.B.) - Holland Families, Lincoln, 2/017
Holland (M.B.) - St. Joseph's, Lincoln, 2/018
Hunt (Loren T.) - Baptist, Lincoln, 2/018
Hunt (Loren) - Friend Institutions, Lincoln, 2/018
Hyte (William) Board of Regents, Lincoln, 2/019
Imig Trust, Omaha, 2/019
Katzman (Daniel & Ruth) Fdn., Omaha, 2/020
Katzman (Meyer) Fdn., Omaha, 2/021
Kinder - Porter Fdn., Lincoln, 2/022
Lincoln City Library Fdn., Lincoln, 2/023
Lindquest (Katherine T.) Trust - Edward Whittingham Thomas Memorial Fund, Omaha, 2/023
Lukens (Richard & Hazel) Charitable Fdn., Omaha, 2/024
Maenner Fdn., Omaha, 2/024
May (Louis E.) Trust, Fremont, 2/025
McGrew Charitable Fdn., Lincoln, 2/025
McKee (Mary) Scholarship Trust, Lincoln, 2/026
Medical Research Fdn., Lincoln, 2/026
Miller Fdn., Omaha, 2/027
Miller (Katherine C.) Trust, Lincoln, 2/027
Minard Community Fdn., Omaha, 2/027
Nebraska Medical Education Fund, Omaha, 2/028
Newman (Esther K.) Memorial Fdn., Omaha, 2/028
Heimer (Octavia) Perpetual Trust, Lincoln, 2/030
Omsteel Fdn., Omaha, 2/030
Opitz (Paul) - Hannah Endebrock Educational Fdn., Omaha, 2/030
Osco Cemetery, Lincoln, 2/031
Paine (B.L.) Evangelist Residue, Lincoln, 2/031
Paine (Bartlett L.) for Others, Lincoln, 2/031
Paine (B.L.) Running Expense Residue, Lincoln, 2/032
Paine (B.L.) - St. Paul's Church, Lincoln, 2/032
Paxson Fdn., Omaha, 2/033
Pomerine Student Loan Fund, Lincoln, 2/034
Priesner (Anna M.) Southminster Methodist, Lincoln, 2/034
Salvation Charitable Trust, Omaha, 2/034
Silver Charitable Trust, Ralston, 2/035
Speier (Millard & Harriet) Fdn., Omaha, 2/036
St. Joseph's Catholic Church (M.B. Holland), Lincoln, 2/036
Maher (Blake) - St. Patrick's Cemetery, Lincoln, 2/038
Sunnyside, Inc., Hastings, 2/038
Swanson (Gretchen) Family Fdn., Omaha, 2/039
Tifereth Israel Fdn., Lincoln, 2/039
Trinity Lutheran Cemetery & Property Association of Indianola, Dartley, 2/040
Wilson Charitable Income Trust, Fremont, 2/040
Young (Jean G. & H.C.) Fdn., Omaha, 2/041

NEVADA

First Filming

Beebe (Lucius M.) Memorial Fdn., Reno, 1/001
Borestone Mountain Poetry Award Fdn., Reno, 1/001
Brinker (Dorethea) Scholarship Fund, Las Vegas, 1/002
C-B Fdn., Reno, 1/003
Cord Fdn., Reno, 1/004
Crummer (Roy E.) Fdn., Reno, 1/004
Dunham-Mason Fdn., Reno, 1/005
Episcopal Relief Fund, Elko, 1/006
Faith Fdn., Las Vegas, 1/007
Forest Economics Fdn., Las Vegas, 1/007
Jones (Clifford A. and Oklabelle) Charitable Fdn. Trust, Las Vegas, 1/008
Korg Fdn., Las Vegas, 1/008
Kutzen (Donna) Youth Fdn., Las Vegas, 1/009
Forrester (Mary McClave) Fdn., Reno, 1/009
Mission Ridge Fdn. of Nevada, Reno, 1/010
Moore (Robert T. and Margaret C.) Memorial Trust, Reno, 1/010
Nevada Humane Society, Reno, 1/011
Rasmussen (Barbara) Memorial Scholarship Fdn., Las Vegas, 1/012
Saturno Trust, Reno, 1/012
Straub (Glenn R.) Fdn., Las Vegas, 1/013
Von Tobel (Ed and Mary) Fdn., Las Vegas, 1/013
Woitishek (Louis A.) Education Fund, Las Vegas, 1/015

Second Filming

Breliant Fdn., Las Vegas, 2/001
Coson (James R.) Fdn., Las Vegas, 2/003
Fawcett (Walter C.) Trust, Reno, 2/004
Fleischmann (Max C.) Fdn., Reno, 2/004
Gross (Harvey A.) Charitable Fdn., Stateline, 2/007
Heart of Variety Trust Fund, Las Vegas, 2/008
Laub Fdn., Las Vegas, 2/008
Lin-Abe Fdn., Las Vegas, 2/009
Nevada Southern University Land Fdn., Las Vegas, 2/090
Saturno-Sunny Acreas Trust, Reno, 2/010

NEW HAMPSHIRE

First Filming

Anctil (J. Wilfred) Fdn., Nashua, 1/001
Bank of New Hampshire Fdn., Concord, 1/001
Barker Fdn., Nashua, 1/002
Chase (Mildred Bassett) Memorial Fund, Concord, 1/003
Bean Fdn., Jaffrey, 1/004
Gile (Helen Blake) Trust, Concord, 1/005
Brown Fund, Keene, 1/006
Brown Memorial Field, Keene, 1/007
Buffington (Nell T.) Charitable Trust, Concord, 1/007
Burbank Associates, Nashua, 1/008
Burroughs Fdn., Manchester, 1/008
Carter (Elizabeth B.) Fdn., Nashua, 1/010
Chase-Miller Charitable Fdn., Manchester, 1/011
Cogswell Benevolent Trust, Manchester, 1/011
Cohen (Zvi & Deborah) Charitable Trust, Bedford, 1/012
Concord National Bank Fdn., Concord, 1/013
Daniels Fdn., Peterborough, 1/013
Dartmouth National Bank Charitable Fdn., Hanover, 1/014
Doehla (Harry) Educational Fdn., Nashua, 1/014
Edgcomb Steel Fdn., Nashua, 1/014

First National Bank Charitable Fdn., Derry, 1/015
Foundation for the Preservation of Historic Keene, Keene, 1/015
Good Neighbor Stations' Fdn., Manchester, 1/015
Halfway Home, Salem, 1/016
Hermsdorf Fdn., Manchester, 1/017
Hogan (Coleman F. & Margaret M.) Fdn., Exeter, 1/017
Hubbard Farms Charitable Fdn., Walpole, 1/018
Greggs (Hugh) Fdn., Nashua, 1/018
Hurlin Fdn., Antrim, 1/019
Iafolla (John) Charitable Fdn., Portsmouth, 1/019
Indian Head Bank Fdn., Nashua, 1/019
International Narrow Fabric Fund, Keene, 1/020
Jackman (Charles H.) Trust, Nashua, 1/020
Jaffrey-Gilmore Fdn., Jaffrey, 1/021
Kaltenborn Fdn., Hill, 1/021
Kennett Fdn., Conway, 1/022
Lonnberg (Alfred E.) Fdn., Francestown, 1/022
Marchand (Janice I.) Trust, Rochester, 1/023
Lane (Charles H.) Christmas Fund, Portsmouth, 1/024
Lane (Charles H.) Trust, Portsmouth, 1/024
Fernald (Lulu A.) Trust, Rochester, 1/025
Martin Charity Fund, Wolfeboro, 1/025
McIninch Fdn., Manchester, 1/026
Mork (Arnold P.) Charitable Fdn., Littleton, 1/026
Morrison (Cecil & Harriet M.) Trust, Rochester, 1/027
Mosher (Anna H.) Charitable Trust, Concord, 1/027
Nashua Corporation Fund, Nashua, 1/028
Pearson (John H.) Trust, Concord, 1/029
Polish American Citizen Club of Claremont, Claremont, 1/030
Potter (Marion Spaulding) Charitable Trust, Concord, 1/031
Powersbridge Fdn., Nashua, 1/032
Randolph Fdn., Randolph, 1/033
Reed Fdn., North Conway, 1/034
Reilly (John J.) Charitable Trust, Manchester, 1/034
R E L Corporation, Manchester, 1/034
Rockingham Bank Fdn., Exeter, 1/035
Rockingham Park Fdn., Manchester, 1/035
Rolfe & Rumford Home of Concord, Concord, 1/035
Rust (W.F.) Fdn., Manchester, 1/036
Salem Historical Society, Salem, 1/037
Shepard (John Sanford) Fdn., Franklin, 1/037
Spaulding (Harriet M.) Charitable Trust, Concord, 1/038
Shieling Trust, Manchester, 1/039
Spaulding (Huntley N.) Charitable Trust, Concord, 1/040
Stevens (David and Anna) Memorial Fund, Salem, 1/041
Sullivan (David Alexander) Testamentary Trust, Portsmouth, 1/041
Treat Fdn., Hampton, 1/042
Balcom (Sarah M.) Trust, Concord, 1/042
Gile (Helen Blake) Trust, Concord, 1/042
Camp Carpenter Trust, Manchester, 1/043
Union Leader Fund, Manchester, 1/043
Wheelwright Trust, Exeter, 1/044
Verney (Gilbert) Fdn., Bennington, 1/044
Wadleigh Fdn., Manchester, 1/044
Verney (Gilbert) Fdn., Bennington, 1/045
Wheeler (Glenn L.) Trust, Laconia, 1/045
Woodman (Annie E.) Institute, Dover, 1/046
Woodman (Annie E.) Testamentary Trust, Dover, 1/048
Bretton Woods Charitable Trust, Bretton Woods, 1/049
Young (Sarah E.) Trust, Rochester, 1/049
Zopfi Fdn., Manchester, 1/050

Second Filming

Allen - Rogers Fdn., Laconia, 2/001
Barnhart (William G. & Elizabeth J.) Fdn., Plymouth, 2/002
Baybutt Fund, Keene, 2/003
Bean (Norwin S. & Elizabeth N.) Fdn., Manchester, 2/004
Berry (Charles H.) Fund, New Durham, 2/005
Berry (William G.) Trust, Manchester, 2/005
Brookshire Fdn., Manchester, 2/006
Chase (Mildred Bassett) Memorial Fund, Concord, 2/006
Chase (Samuel Myron) Forests & Bird & Animal Sanctuaries, Concord, 2/006
Chertok (Rose) Charitable Trust Formerly District of Columbia, Laconia, 2/007
Clark (George Gallup) Testamentary Trust, Plymouth, 2/008
Cohn (Irwin & Mary) Fdn., Nashua, 2/008
Cummings (Charles H.) Trust, Concord, 2/009
Cunningham Charitable Trust, Hanover, 2/010
Dale (Charles M.) Trust, Nashua, 2/010
Deerfield Education Fund, Deerfield, 2/011
Doehla (Harry) Fdn., Nashua, 2/011
Emmet (Beulah) Fdn., Wilton, 2/013
Exeter Historical Society, Exeter, 2/014
Family Service of Concord, New Hampshire, Concord, 2/014
Folsom (Elvirus F.) Trust, Concord, 2/015
Foundation for Biblical Research & Preservation of Primitive Christianity, Charlestown, 2/015
Gale (Napoleon B.) Trust, Laconia, 2/016
Blanchard (George Gardner & Fanny Whiting) Scholarship Fund, Nashua, 2/017
Gile (Helen Blake) Trust, Concord, 2/017
Gilman Home for the Aged, Laconia, 2/017
Gordon (J. S.) Family Fdn., Manchester, 2/018
Granger (Alfred T.) Student Art Trust Fund, Hanover, 2/018
Green (Frank E.) Trust, Manchester, 2/019
Greenspan Fdn., Manchester, 2/019
Griffin (Abbie M.) Educational Fund, Nashua, 2/020
Griffin (Abbie M.) Hospital Fund, Nashua, 2/021
Hillside Cemetery Association of South Weare, South Weare, 2/021
Invalids' Home, Keene, 2/022
Jenness (Charles G.) Boys Club House Trust Fund, Rochester, 2/023
Jenness (Charles G.) Donation Fund, Rochester, 2/024
Macallen Fdn., Newmarket, 2/025
Manchester Bank Charitable Fund Formerly Manchester Savings Bank Charitable Fund, Manchester, 2/025
Manchester Historic Association, Manchester, 2/026
Martin (Mary R.) Testamentary Trust, Wolfeboro, 2/027
McMillan (Bessie B. Torr) Scholarship Fund, Rochester, 2/027
M.P.B. Fund, Keene, 2/028
Nakos (Arthur J.) Scholarship Fund, Nashua, 2/029
New Hampshire Historical Society, Concord, 2/029
Page Belting Company Fdn., Concord, 2/030
Rice (Hamilton) Charitable Trust, Manchester, 2/031
Robichaud (Wilfred H.) Testamentary Trust, Nashua, 2/031
Robichaud (Wilfred H.) Testamentary Trust, Nashua, 2/032
Rochester High School Class of 1905 Fiftieth Reunion Fund, Rochester, 2/033
Rochester Historical Society, Rochester, 2/033
Sargent (Abbie) Memorial Scholarship, Concord, 2/034
Speare (Sceva) Fdn., Nashua, 2/034
Shepard (Alan B.) Scholarship Fund, Manchester, 2/034
Smith (Ray Winfield) Fdn., Dublin, 2/035
Springfield Fund, Rochester, 2/035

Students Scholarship Fund, Hanover, 2/036
Taylor Home, Laconia, 2/036
Tober (Benjamin A.) Scholarship Fund, Portsmouth, 2/038
Town (Col. F. L.) Trust Fund, Lancaster, 2/038
Harrington (William) Trust, Manchester, 2/039
Tsedakah Trust, Laconia, 2/039
Turcotte Fdn., Manchester, 2/039
Woodward Home, Keene, 2/040
Young (Josh) Memorial Fund, Newport, 2/041

NEW JERSEY

First Filming

Abrams Fdn., Trenton, 1/001
Adler (Max) Fdn., Ocean City, 1/001
Agar (Calvin A.) Fdn., Newark, 1/002
Alliance Fdn., Chatham, 1/002
American Hungarian Citizens Club, Clark, 1/003
Amerio Charitable Fdn., Hackensack, 1/003
Ankentom Fdn., Newark, 1/004
Arenberg (Claire & Albert) Fund, Metuchen, 1/004
Aresty Fdn., Trenton, 1/006
Aronson (Louis V., II) Fdn., Far Hills, 1/006
Arzyl Fund, Wyckoff, 1/007
Asbury Park Press Fdn., Asbury Park, 1/009
Atlantic Fdn., Trenton, 1/010
Atlas Fdn., Rutherford, 1/011
Avon Fund, Newark, 1/011
Badenhausen (Otto & Hildegarde) Fdn., Newark, 1/012
Badenhausen (Carl & Dorothy) Fdn., Newark, 1/012
Baker (Augustus Lynn) Memorial Fund, Dover, 1/013
Ballantine (P.) & Sons Fdn., Newark, 1/013
Banc Fund, South Orange, 1/014
Bartels (Theodore R. & Grayce W.) Fdn., Ho-Ho-Kus, 1/014
Bassett Fdn., Bernardsville, 1/015
Becton, Dickinson Fdn., Rutherford, 1/016
Belleville Fdn., Belleville, 1/016
Bellock (J.) Family Fdn., Newark, 1/017
Bergen Evening Record Fund, Hackensack, 1/018
Berlin (B. S.) Fdn., Princeton, 1/019
Thomas & Betts Charitable Trust, Elizabeth, 1/020
Bethell (Marjorie) Scholarship Fund, Montclair, 1/020
Bick (George N.) Fdn., South Orange, 1/021
Bickett (Dr. William J.) Memorial Scholarship Fund, Trenton, 1/021
Birnberg Fdn., Clifton, 1/022
Bladis Fdn., Springfield, 1/022
Blancke (Harold) Fdn., Blairstown, 1/023
Blauvelt-Demarest Fdn., Westwood, 1/024
Block (Adele & Leonard) Fdn., Jersey City, 1/024
Block (Melvin A.) Family Fdn., Jersey City, 1/025
Blotner (Carl & Rita) Fdn., South Orange, 1/026
Blotner (Maxwell & Anne) Family Fdn., East Orange, 1/027
Bluestein (Iris W. & Sanfurd G.) Fdn., Montclair, 1/027
Bolger Fdn., Ridgewood, 1/027
Bonomo Fdn., Jersey City, 1/028
Booth (J. & M.) Fund, Essex Fells, 1/029
Borden (Mary Owen) Memorial Fdn., Newark, 1/029
Borks (Ruth & Bernard) Charitable Trust, Livingston, 1/032
Elrich Fdn., Short Hills, 1/032
Brady Fdn., Gladstone, 1/033
Brandt Fdn., Millburn, 1/034

Bridgeton Rotary Club Student Award and Loan Fund, Bridgeton, 1/035

Bristol-Myers Fund, Hillside, 1/035

Britton Family Charitable Fdn., Montclair, 1/038

Broad National Bank Fdn., Newark, 1/038

Broderson-Melander Fdn., Montclair, 1/039

Brook Fdn., West Orange, 1/039

Brown (Edith & Maurice) Fdn., Fair Lawn, 1/040

Brucker (Manuel & Carolyn) Family Fdn., Belleville, 1/041

Brundage (Charles E. & Edna T.) Charitable, Scientific, and Wild Life Conservation Foundation, Newark, 1/041

Bulidema Trust, Princeton, 1/042

Bunn (Howard S.) Fdn., Short Hills, 1/043

Burr Fdn., Elizabeth, 1/044

Butts (Gertrude) Memorial Home Association, Newark, 1/045

Byas (Hugh Fulton) Memorial Fdn., Jersey City, 1/045

Caplan (Alexander & Sylvia) Fdn., Chatham, 1/046

Cape Branch Fdn., Trenton, 1/047

Cash (Mary B.) Trust, Montclair, 1/047

Casser (Benjamin & Rose) Philanthropic Fdn., Cresskill, 1/048

Casser (Julius & Evelyn) Philanthropic Fdn., Teaneck, 1/048

Century Fund, Vineland, 1/049

Chubb Fdn., Short Hills, 1/049

Churg (Wolfe & Gita) Fdn., Teaneck, 1/051

Clofine Fdn., Atlantic City, 1/052

Cohen (Ruth & Nathaniel) Fdn., Elizabeth, 1/053

Cohn (Julius H. & Bessie R.) Fdn., Newark, 1/053

Colgate (Russell) Fund, Jersey City, 1/054

Congdon Art Education Fdn., Medford Lakes, 1/055

Cooper (Eugene S.) Family Fdn., Newark, 1/055

Cooper (R. C.) Fdn., Washington, 1/056

Corbin-Carter Fdn., Westfield, 1/056

Cozad (Samuel) Trust, Montclair, 1/056

Cramer (Gerald B. & Barbara) Fdn., Franklin Lakes, 1/057

Cumberland County Historical Society, Greenwich, 1/057

Cumberland County Medical Society Health and Educational Fund, Vineland, 1/058

Damico (Anthony M.) Memorial Fund, West Orange, 1/059

Danzis (Max) Medical Education Fdn., Newark, 1/059

Davimos Fdn., West Orange, 1/059

Davis (Morton & Mildred) Family Fdn., South Orange, 1/060

Davis (Sarah T. L.) Trust, Montclair, 1/061

Davlin Fdn., Princeton, 1/061

Day (Ernest N.) Fdn., Dunellen, 1/062

Decatur Fdn., Newark, 1/063

Densen (Max) Fdn., Clifton, 1/063

Dern Family Fdn., Livingston, 1/064

Diamond Fdn., Elizabeth, 1/064

Diener (Leonard & Beatrice) Fdn., Elizabeth, 1/065

Diener (Juda & Miriam) Fdn., Elizabeth, 1/065

Doll Charitable Fdn., Mendham, 1/066

Dresdner Fdn., Upper Montclair, 1/066

Dreyfuss (Alice & Leonard) Fdn., Newark, 1/067

Duffy (Alfred & Elizabeth) Fdn., Montclair, 1/068

Durex Fdn., Hillside, 1/068

East Branch Fdn., Trenton, 1/068

Eighteen Seventy Fdn., Passaic, 1/069

Eiseman Family Fdn., Englewood, 1/070

Eisner Fdn., Red Bank, 1/070

Electrons Inc., Fdn., Newark, 1/071

Eljabar Fdn., East Orange, 1/071

Wallace-Eljabar Fund, East Orange, 1/072

Ellerslie Fund, Princeton, 1/075

Ellis (Abraham) Fdn., Belleville, 1/076

Engle Oostdyk Fdn., East Paterson, 1/077

Engstrom Fdn., Trenton, 1/077

Entin (Herman) Charity Fdn. of the Kiwanis Club of Belleville, Belleville, 1/079

Epstein (Rose & Maurice) Fdn., Morristown, 1/079

Fanwood Fdn., Plainfield, 1/080

Fatzler (Fred) Fdn., Maplewood, 1/080

Feins Fdn., Maplewood, 1/081

Feldman (Sol & Minna) Family Fdn., Belleville, 1/082

Feldman (I.J.), Ridgefield, 1/082

Essex Fells Welfare Fdn., New Vernon, 1/083

Felson (Alfred & Lillian) Fdn., Hoboken, 1/084

Fidelity Union Fdn., Newark, 1/084

Field Studies Trust Fund, Monclair, 1/085

First Baptist Church Trust, Montclair, 1/086

Fishberg (Joseph) Fdn., Trenton, 1/086

F L P Fund, Summit, 1/087

Flunison Fund, Princeton, 1/087

Forbes Fdn., Far Hills, 1/088

Foster (Ethel Pratt) Fdn., Scotch Plains, 1/089

Foundation for Microbiology, New Brunswick, 1/089

Foundation Chapter of Theta Chi Fraternity, Trenton, 1/090

Foundation for World Servers, Englewood, 1/091

Fox Fdn., Newfield, 1/091

Frazer (Margaret) Scholarship Fund, Vineland, 1/093

Freas Fdn., Montvale, 1/093

Freeman (Grace) Art Trust, Montclair, 1/093

Frelinghuysen Fdn., Far Hills, 1/094

Friedland Fdn., South Orange, 1/095

Futeran (Morris & Manya) Fdn., Cranford, 1/096

G B G S Charitable Fdn., West Orange, 1/096

Geller (Herman & Yetta) Fdn., Verona, 1/097

Gerard Fdn., Newark, 1/097

Gerney (Joseph) Fdn., Newark, 1/097

Gilbert (Charles B.) Fdn., Trenton, 1/098

Gilbert (Linus R.) Fdn., Trenton, 1/098

Ginsburg (Abe & Sylvia) Fdn., Union City, 1/099

Ginsburg (Jacob) Fdn., West New York, 1/099

Ginsburg (Martin & Natalie) Fdn., West New York, 1/100

Gitlin (Benjamin) Fdn., Newark, 1/100

Glassford (Bess) Fdn., Ridgewood, 1/101

Glazier (Alfred S.) Family Charitable Fdn., Fort Lee, 1/101

Gloucester County College Fdn. Fund, Sewell, 1/101

Goldberg (Abraham) Fdn., Perth Amboy, 1/101

Goldberg (Sidney & Edna) Fdn., Hackensack, 1/102

Goldfarb (Louis & Rose) Fdn., South Orange, 1/103

Goldfarb (Morris & Lydia) Fdn., Perth Amboy, 1/103

Goldfuss (Doctors Max & Rose Bass) Fdn., East Orange, 1/104

Goldstein (Harold & Jean) Fdn., Palisade, 1/104

Goodall Rubber Company Charitable and Welfare Fdn., Trenton, 1/104

Goodbody (Marcus) Fdn., Madison, 1/105

Goodman (Charles S.) Fdn., Paterson, 1/106

Goodman (Leon) Scholarship Trust, Highland Park, 1/106

Goodman (Sol & Vera) Family Fdn., Short Hills, 1/106

Goodstein Fund, Millburn, 1/107

Gordon (Ben & Dolly) Fdn., Harrison, 1/107

Granet Fdn., Union, 1/107

Greene (David & Selma) Fdn., West Orange, 1/109

Grace Fund, Short Hills, 1/109

Greenburg (Harry) Fdn., North Bergen, 1/110

Griffith (F. Willard & Theodora A.) Fdn., Union, 1/111

Gross Fdn., West Orange, 1/111

Gross (Henry & Augusta) Fdn., Trenton, 1/112

Gross (Meyer P.) Fdn., East Orange, 1/112

Gruber Fdn., Paterson, 1/112

Gumpert-Janover Fdn., Jersey City, 1/113

Gutkin (Beatrice M.) Fdn., Newark, 1/113

Hackman (William M.) Fdn., Newark, 1/114

Hahn Fdn., Montclair, 1/114

Hano (Louis C.) Fdn., Trenton, 1/115

Harbor Branch Fdn., Trenton, 1/115

Harder (Howard Charles & Julia Johns) Fdn., Alpine, 1/116

Hardy Trust, Cedar Grove, 1/117

Harris (Grace) Memorial, Maplewood, 1/118

Hartley Fdn., Morristown, 1/119

Hauser Fund, Short Hills, 1/119

Henderson (William T. & Marie J.) Fdn., South Orange, 1/120

Herald News - Drukker Fdn., Passaic, 1/120

Hesseltine (Clair Emmett) Fdn., South Amboy, 1/121

Heyman Fdn., Kenilworth, 1/122

Hoffmann - La Roche Fdn., Nutley, 1/122

Heyman (Horace W.) Memorial Scholarship Fund, Kenilworth, 1/123

Hilgert (Hans W.) Fdn., Clifton, 1/124

Hodnett Fdn., Peapack, 1/124

Hoffman (Florence L. & Philip E.) Fdn., Newark, 1/125

Holtz (Isadore & Frieda) Fdn., West Orange, 1/125

Homasote Fdn., Trenton, 1/126

Homebound Pilots, Paterson, 1/127

Honeybrook Fdn., Princeton, 1/127

Hosteller Fdn., Short Hills, 1/128

Hubbard (John C. & Susan K.) Fdn., Madison, 1/128

Huber Fdn., Rumson, 1/129

Hunt Charitable Trust, Chatham, 1/131

Hyde (Lilia Babbitt) Fdn., Elizabeth, 1/131

I. B. E. W. 1158 Welfare Plan Fund, Bloomfield, 1/134

International Fdn., Metuchen, 1/134

Iselin Fdn., Oceanport, 1/135

Ix Fdn., Union City, 1/136

Ix (Charles William) Charitable Trust, Englewood, 1/137

Jackson (Frank & Helen) Fdn., Westfield, 1/138

Jacob (Michael & Barbara) Fdn., Rumson, 1/139

Jacobson Fdn., Englewood, 1/140

Janet Fdn., East Orange, 1/141

Jay Fdn., Orange, 1/141

Jelinek (Ulric) Fdn., Newark, 1/142

Jessup Fdn., Convent Station, 1/143

Jiljon Fund, Verona, 1/143

J N S Fdn., Margate, 1/144

Jobar Fdn., Orange, 1/145

Johanson (John E.) Fdn., Boonton, 1/146

Johnson (Charles, Jr. & Dorothy) Fdn., Clifton, 1/146

Johnson (Gertrude H. & Ralph L.) Fdn., Ridgewood, 1/147

Johnson (Joan & Edward) Charitable Trust, Englewood, 1/148

Johnson (John Stewart) Charitable Trust, Trenton, 1/148

Johnson (Robert Wood) Fdn., New Brunswick, 1/149

Johnston (W. S.) Fdn., Bay Head, 1/150

Jones Fdn., Bordentown, 1/151

Kanter Family Fdn., Jersey City, 1/152

Kaplan (Meyer & Morris) Fdn., Trenton, 1/152

Kaplan (R. & B.) Fdn., Englewood, 1/153

Katz (Rubin) Fdn., Atlantic City, 1/153

Kaufman (Felix) Fdn., West New York, 1/153

Keating Fdn., Lyndhurst, 1/154

Keating Family Fdn., Lyndhurst, 1/156

Keats Fdn. for Research and Education, West Orange, 1/158

Kennedy (John R.) Fdn., Montvale, 1/161

Kerney (James) Fdn., Trenton, 1/162

Kessler Fdn., Newark, 1/164

Kidde (Walter) and Company Fdn., Clifton, 1/164

Kindle Fdn. for Education, Westwood, 1/165

Kirkman Fdn., Atlantic City, 1/166

Kirshbaum (Carolyn & Irving) Fdn., Deal, 1/166

Klauber Fdn., West Orange, 1/167

Klebanoff Fdn., Newark, 1/167

Kleitman Fdn., Morristown, 1/168

Klinkenstein Fdn., Newark, 1/168

Klipstein (Ernest Christian) Fdn., New Vernon, 1/168

Kluge (Willard G.) Fdn., Pompton Lakes, 1/169

Kohl (Louis) Fdn., Newark, 1/171

Kolarsey (Emil W.) Camp Fund, Paterson, 1/171

Kolodny (Joseph) Fdn., Tenafly, 1/172

Kosh Fdn., East Orange, 1/172

Koven Fdn., Dover, 1/173

Kramer (Harold) Fdn., Trenton, 1/174

Kramer (Selma & Raymond) Fdn., Clifton, 1/175

Kramer - Englander Fdn., Trenton, 1/176

Kroll Fdn., Highland Park, 1/176

Krusen (H. Stanley & Elizabeth H.) Fdn., Summit, 1/177

Kuehm (Frederick W. & Frieda L.) Fdn., Wayne, 1/177

Kyle (Barbara Auer) and John Parsons Auer Trust, Montclair, 1/178

Labov Fdn., Ridgefield, 1/179

La Fera Charitable Fdn., Newark, 1/179

Langworthy Fdn., Camden, 1/180

Large Fdn., Flemington, 1/184

Leach (Richard C.) Fdn., Plainfield, 1/185

Leavens Fdn., Kearney, 1/186

Leavitt (N. R.) Fdn., Elizabeth, 1/187

Leek (Donald J. C.) Fdn., Egg Harbor, 1/187

Leek (John E.) Fdn., Egg Harbor, 1/188

Leiwant Fdn., East Orange, 1/188

Lenk (Thomas T.) Fdn., Teaneck, 1/189

Lesnik (Seymour & Stanley) Fdn., Newark, 1/189

Glazer-Levin Fdn., Trenton, 1/190

Levin (Paul) Fdn., Short Hills, 1/191

Levin (Louis) Fdn., Union, 1/191

Levmore Fdn., Dover, 1/192

Levy (Charles) Fdn., Trenton, 1/192

Levy (Emanuel & Ethel) Fdn., West Englewood, 1/193

Levy (Iris & Milton L.) Fdn., Elizabeth, 1/193

Levy (Leon L.) Fdn., Trenton, 1/194

L'Hommedieu (Frances B. & Paige D.) Trust, Princeton, 1/195

Lichtman Fdn., Newark, 1/195

Lichtman (Harry & Gussie) Fellowship Fdn., South Orange, 1/197

Lillian (Edwin) Fdn., Jersey City, 1/197

Lincoln (Robert J.) Fdn., Mountainside, 1/198

Lindberg Fdn., Convent Station, 1/198

Lippman (Alfred J.) Fdn., Shrewsbury, 1/199

Lipton (Thomas J.) Fdn., Englewood Cliffs, 1/199

Liss Fdn., Summit, 1/201

Lockwood Fdn., Plainfield, 1/202

Loosli Fdn., Plainfield, 1/203

Losam Fund, Princeton, 1/203

Lovell (Gordon P.) Fdn., Montclair, 1/203

Luchars (Alexander) Trust, Montclair, 1/204

Lucky Hollow Animal Welfare Society, Paramus, 1/205

L V H Fdn., Maplewood, 1/205

MacDonald (Nestor J. & Helen J.) Fdn., Elizabeth, 1/206

Mack Fdn., Moonachie, 1/206

Mack (Martin & Judy) Fdn., East Orange, 1/208

Malesardi Fdn. Charitable Trust, Englewood, 1/208

Mann (Bernard & Rosalind) Fdn., Edgewater, 1/208

Mannheimer Primatological Fdn., Toms River, 1/209

Marantz Fdn., Hillside, 1/209

Marfran Fdn., West Orange, 1/210

Margetts Fdn., Morristown, 1/210

Marian Fdn., Red Bank, 1/211

Marron (Louis E. & Eugenie M.) Fdn., Newark, 1/211

Martin (H. Bradley) Charitable Fdn., Newark, 1/212

Martin (Kenneth & Florence) Fdn., Westfield, 1/212

Matthew's Memorial Fund, Bishop, Princeton, 1/213

May (Ernest M.) Fdn., Newark, 1/213

Mayne (Earl H.) Trust, Newark, 1/214

Mayne Educational Fund, Sparta, 1/215

M.C. Scholarship Fdn., Far Hills, 1/215

McCutchen Fdn., Plainfield, 1/215

Ketcham & McDougall Fdn., Roseland, 1/216

McGraw (Curtis W.) Fdn., Princeton, 1/217

McLane (Dorothea VanDyke) Association, Princeton, 1/217

McMurray - Bennett Fdn., Newark, 1/218

Mecray Family Charitable Fdn., Haddonfield, 1/219

Mekeel (Bud) Scholarship Fund, Montclair, 1/219

Mercer Memorial House, Atlantic City, 1/220

Merck Company Fdn., Rahway, 1/222

Merck Family Fund, Newark, 1/223

Messing (Morris M. & Helen F.) Fdn., Nutley, 1/224

Minnig (Carl J.) Fdn., Rumson, 1/225

Mitchell Family Fdn., Fort Lee, 1/226

Mitchell (James Ewing) Fdn., Newark, 1/226

Monroe (Jay R.) Memorial Fdn., Millburn, 1/227

Montclair Lions Club Student Aid Fund Trust, Montclair, 1/228

Morello Fdn., Vineland, 1/228

Morrison (James C. & Mary S.) Fund, Short Hills, 1/229

Mortgage Bankers Association of New Jersey Educational Fdn., Newark, 1/230

Morris County Children's Home, Morristown, 1/230

Moss Family Charitable Fdn., Montclair, 1/231

Motolinsky (Melvyn H.) Research Fdn., New Brunswick, 1/232

Munn Fdn., Passaic, 1/232

Naisby Fdn., Cinnaminson, 1/232

Nash (Philip W.) Fdn., Edison, 2/001

New Jersey Bank & Trust Company Fdn., Paterson, 2/001

North Branch Fdn., Trenton, 2/002

Norton (James F.) Memorial Fund, Jersey City, 2/002

Norwood Fdn., Hackensack, 2/003

Nunlist (Winifred M.) Corporation, Newark, 2/003

Ohl (George A.) Cancer Fund Trust, Newark, 2/004

Ohl (George A.) Infantile Paralysis Fund, Newark, 2/004

Okonite Fdn., Ramsey, 2/005

Orange Orphan Society, South Orange, 2/006

Ortner Fdn., Newark, 2/007

Oschwald Fdn., Rumson, 2/007

Parr Fdn., Englewood, 2/008

Parsons (J. Lester) Fdn., Short Hills, 2/008

Pathy (O. L.) Educational & Charitable Fdn., Newark, 2/009

Peaslee Fdn., Clarksboro, 2/010

Peet (Gerald D.) Fdn., Montclair, 2/010

Pettinos (Charles E. & Joy C.) Fdn., Elizabeth, 2/010

P.H.A. Scholarship Fund, Mendham, 2/013

Phillips Fdn., Montclair, 2/013

Phipps (Howard) Family Charitable Fdn., Newark, 2/014

Physicians Endowment Fund Committee, Newark, 2/015

Picone (Joseph) Fdn., Leonia, 2/015

Platoff (Marvel S.) Fdn., Union City, 2/015

Platten Fdn., Princeton, 2/016

Plumber Local #24 Welfare Fund, Newark, 2/017

Pocumtuck Company, Princeton, 2/017

Pollack (Rita H. & Monroe W.) Fdn., Wayne, 2/017

Pollak Fund, Newark, 2/018

Pollak Fdn., Kearny, 2/019

Pope (Generoso), Jr. Fdn., Englewood Cliffs, 2/019

Presbyterian Charitable Fdn., Glen Ridge, 2/020

Prospect Fdn., Summit, 2/021

Prupis (Robert & Edythe) Fdn., West Orange, 2/021

Quaker Hill Fdn., Edison, 2/022

Raritan Fdn., New Brunswick, 2/023

Red Bank Fdn., Lincroft, 2/023

Red Devil Fdn., Union, 2/024

Reich (Jerome & Phyllis) Family Fdn., Short Hills, 2/025

Reighley (Ellen Elizabeth) Fdn., Montclair, 2/025

Reimann (Kurt P.) Fdn., Rutherford, 2/026

Rice (David & Rebecca) Fdn. for Vocational Guidance & Aid, Irvington, 2/026

Rettig Fdn., Maplewood, 2/026

Richman Fdn., Hackensack, 2/027

Ring Fdn., Trenton, 2/027

Ring Fdn. of Trenton, New Jersey, Trenton, 2/028

Ritter (Dr. Morton D.) Fdn., Atlantic City, 2/029

Robbins Fdn., Union, 2/029

Robison Fdn., Fairview, 2/030

Rogers (W. Leslie) Library Fdn., Pennsauken, 2/031

Rogosin Fdn., Allenhurst, 2/031

Rohrer (William G., Jr.) Charitable Trust, Camden, 2/032

Rohrer (William G., Jr.) Educational Fdn., Camden, 2/033

Rosen (Howard T.) Fdn., Newark, 2/033

Rosen (Saul & Helen) Fdn., Paterson, 2/04

Rosenberg (Harold N. & Frances L.) Fdn., Englewood, 2/034

Ross (Irene H. & Harper G.) Fdn., New Brunswick, 2/035

Roth (Aaron H. & Molly) Fdn., Newark, 2/036

Roxiticus Fund, Morristown, 2/037

Rubens (Louis) - Filigree Fdn., Lyndhurst, 2/038

Rubinstein (Frank & Tina) Fdn., Livingston, 2/039

Rubenstein (Howard J.) Charitable Trust, Jersey City, 2/039

Rubin (Leonard & Syril) Fdn., Edgewater, 2/039

Rudolph Fdn., Newark, 2/040

Rukin (David & Eleanore) Philanthropic Fdn., Saddle River, 2/041

Ryan (Richard Nelson) Fdn., Sea Girt, 2/042

Safran Brothers Fdn., Perth Amboy, 2/043

Sagamore Fdn., Newark, 2/043

Sagan Fdn., Newark, 2/043

Saltzman Fdn., Deal, 2/045

Sanders Fdn., Plainfield, 2/045

Savary & Glaeser Fdn., Greenbrook, 2/046

Schachter Fdn., Millburn, 2/046

Schatzkin Ceramic Fdn., Interlaken, 2/047

Schering Fdn., Bloomfield, 2/047

Schiavone-Bonomo Fdn., Jersey City, 2/048

Schlenger (Joan & Robert) Fdn., Millburn, 2/048

Schonbrunn Fdn., Palisades Park, 2/049

Schumann (Florence & John) Fdn., Montclair, 2/049

Schuster (Max & Blanche) Fdn., Edgewater, 2/051

Schwartz (Albert A. & Suzanne) Fdn., Edison, 2/051

Schwarz Family Fdn., Newark, 2/052

Segal (Milton H. & Helen) Fdn., Avenel, 2/052

Seiden Fdn., Moonachie, 2/052

Sellars (R. B.) Fdn., Peapack-Gladstone, 2/053

Sellew Trust for Italian Presbyterian Church of Montclair, Montclair, 2/053

Sellew Trust for Italian Presbyterian Church of Upper Montclair, Montclair, 2/054

Sellew Trust for Women's Aid & Missionary Society-Chapel Ground, Montclair, 2/055

Sellew Trust for Women's Aid & Missionary Society-Home Mission Work, Montclair, 2/055

Shiman Fdn., Newark, 2/056

Shreve (William A. & Mary A.) Fdn., Newark, 2/056

Shuster (Ralph & Clara) Fdn., Old Bridge, 2/057

Signal Corps Educational Fdn., Fort Monmouth, 2/058

Silby (Martin V. & Frieda) Fdn., Perth Amboy, 2/058

Silvers (Earl Reed) Fdn., Ridgewood, 2/059

Simkin (Charles) Fdn., Perth Amboy, 2/059

Singer (Michael) Fdn., Newark, 2/060

Sisselman (H. Jerome) Torah Fdn., East Rutherford, 2/061

Skalka Fdn., Short Hills, 2/062

Sleesman (Peter) Trust for Education of Children, Bridgeton, 2/062

Slobodien Fdn., Cranford, 2/062

Snyder (Theresa O.) Fdn., Jersey City, 2/063

South Branch Fdn., Morristown, 2/064

Spivack (William A.) Fdn., Elizabeth, 2/064

Standish Fdn., Elizabeth, 2/064

Stuart (Acheson) Fdn., Newark, 2/065

Stevens (Helen Ward) S.I.T. Student Trust, Montclair, 2/065

Stone Fund, Newark, 2/066

Stringer Fdn., Ridgewood, 2/066

Stroock (May & Stephen) Fdn., Deal, 2/067

Structural Steel & Ornamental Iron Assoc. Scholarship Fund, Newark, 2/067

Stuckler (Fred & Emma) Charitable Fdn., Wayne, 2/068

Sugarman (Morris & Pauline) Fdn., Passaic, 2/068

Sunnyvale Fdn., East Orange, 2/068

Swanson (Robert S.) Fdn., Totowa, 2/069

Tatem (J. Fithian) Scholarship Fund, Haddonfield, 2/069

Tau Chapter Fdn., Franklin, 2/070

Teeters Fund, Tenafly, 2/070

Tenenbaum (Morris) Charitable Trust, Dumont, 2/071

Terhune (Albert Payson) Fdn., Passaic, 2/071

Theta Fdn., Jersey City, 2/072

Thirteen Twenty-five Fdn., Plainfield, 2/072

Thomas (Louis J.) Charitable Fdn., Newark, 2/073

Thurnauer (Martin & Leni) Fdn., Teaneck, 2/073

Tiger Fund, West Orange, 2/074

Tindell Fdn., Short Hills, 2/075

Tobelmann Fdn., Westfield, 2/075

Todd (W. Parsons) Fdn., Morristown, 2/076

Tomasulo (Joseph) Fdn., Elizabeth, 2/077

Torah Perpetuation Fdn., Elizabeth, 2/077

Troast (Paul L. & Eleanor M.) Fdn., Clifton, 2/077

Atkins (Charlotte B.) Trust, Newark, 2/078

Bottier (Louise J.) Trust, Newark, 2/078

Brokaw (Elvira G.) Trust, Montclair, 2/079

Brown (Robert A.) Trust, Newark, 2/079

Cutler (Altha H.) Trust f/b/o J. W. Roberts Memorial Fund, Montclair, 2/079

Clark (Margaretta) Trust, Newark, 2/080

Colgate (R.M.) Trust f/b/o Wash Playground, Newark, 2/081

Cutler (A.H.) Trust f/b/o Morris Plains Library Association, Montclair, 2/081

Cutler (A.H.) Trust f/b/o W.W. Cutler Memorial Fund, Montclair, 2/082

Dart (Mary G.) Trust, Newark, 2/082

Endowment Fund Christ Episcopal Church, Newark, 2/083

Farrow (Willard) Trust, Montclair, 2/083

Jeffery (Clara L. D.) Charitable Residuary Trust, Summit, 2/084

Harrison (Kate D.) Trust, Montclair, 2/084

Lanning (L. M.) Trust f/b/o United Methodist Church Trust, Newark, 2/085

Lanning (L. M.) Trust f/b/o Summerfield Methodist Church, Newark, 2/085

Lillie (Emily M.) Trust, Newark, 2/085

Ott (Florence P.) - Nicholas Power Fund, Newark, 2/086

Sayre (Hannah M.) Trust, Summit, 2/086

Ritter (Etta Louise) Trust, Newark, 2/087

Ritter (William H.) Trust, Newark, 2/088

Sherin (Bess Wood) Trust, Newark, 2/090

Sherman (Harriet S.) Trust, Montclair, 2/090

Stern (Herman) Trust, Summit, 2/091

Styer (Wilford) Memorial Scholarship Fund, Newark, 2/091

Vanderhoven (Clara) Trust, Newark, 2/091

Vaughan (Lucy M.) Fund, Newark, 2/091

Wells (Charles H.) Trust, Newark, 2/092

Whitney (Alfred R.) Trust f/b/o Home for Destitute & Worthy Women & Children, Montclair, 2/092

Turrell Fund, East Orange, 2/093

Unger Fdn., Wayne, 2/098

Union Fdn., Elizabeth, 2/099

Union County Historical Society, Elizabeth, 2/099

Upton (Lucy & Eleanor S.) Charitable Fdn., Newark, 2/100

Vahlsing Fdn., Newark, 2/101

Valley Brook Fdn., Elizabeth, 2/101

Venneri (Arthur) Fdn., Cranford, 2/102

Victoria Fdn., Montclair, 2/102

Vinik Fdn., Newark, 2/103

W.A.K. Fdn., Rockleigh, 2/104

Wachstein Fdn., South Orange, 2/105

Wallerstein (Jane & Bernard) Fdn., South Orange, 2/106

Wallerstein (Julian W.) Fdn., Newark, 2/107

Walter (A.) Fdn., Paterson, 2/107

Warner-Lambert Charitable Fdn., Morris Plains, 2/108

Warrick (Frances S.) Fdn., Englewood, 2/109

Warshauer Fdn., Tenafly, 2/110

Wasserson (Edward & Sara) Family Fdn., Short Hills, 2/110

Watson (John Jay & Eliza) Fdn., Elizabeth, 2/111

Wegard Fdn., Willingboro, 2/114

Weiner (Martin) Fdn., Paterson, 2/114

Weisberger (Joseph & Helen) Home for the Elderly, Vauxhall, 2/115

Wellington (Cary L.) Fdn., Englewood, 2/117

Wetterberg (Harold) Fdn., Newark, 2/117

White Family Trust, Englewood, 2/118

White (Thomas H.) Fdn., Margate City, 2/118

Whitehead (E. R.), Jr. Fdn., West Allenhurst, 2/118

Whitfield (Howard) Fdn., Red Bank, 2/119

Hayes-Wigton Fdn., Plainfield, 2/120

Wilf Family Fdn., Hillside, 2/121

Willowwood Fdn., Gladstone, 2/121

Wolf (Alice K.) Memorial Scholarship, Camden, 2/122

Wolff (Irving) Fdn., Trenton, 2/122

Wood (Mary F. & Charles O.) Fdn., Ho-Ho-Kus, 2/123

Worthington Fdn., Harrison, 2/124

Wright, Saddle River, 2/124

Yablick (Gershon Nison & Shaineh) Charities, Jersey City, 2/124

Yankner (Louis) Fdn., Paterson, 2/125

Yegen (Christian C.) Fdn., Teaneck, 2/125

Yeskel (William) Fdn., Newark, 2/126

Yoeckel Fdn., Stockholm, 2/127

Young (Edward M.) Trust f/b/o Edward & Alice Young Scholarship Fund, Montclair, 2/127

Young (H. R.) Fdn., Fair Haven, 2/128

1920 Fdn. Princeton University, Jersey City, 2/129

Second Filming

Abrams (Meyer L. & Rhoda S.) Fdn., Cherry Hill, 3/001

Adams Fdn., Margate, 3/002

Adams (Adam A.) Fdn., Newark, 3/002

Africano (Dr. Scipio H.) Scholarship Fund, Union City, 3/003

Anton (Adele B.) Fdn., Whippany, 3/004

Aidekman Fdn., Elizabeth, 3/004

Alford Fdn., Fort Lee, 3/005

Alpha Tau Chapter, Sigma Theta Tau, Newark, 3/005

Altschuler (Irving M.) Memorial Fund, Bayonne, 3/006

Altshuler Fdn., Englewood, 3/006

American Institute of Food Distribution, Fair Lawn, 3/006

Animal Care Fund, Toms River, 3/007

Animal Shelter, New Brunswick, 3/008

Apple Fdn., Newark, 3/008

Lockerly Arboretum Fdn., Elizabeth, 3/009

Armitage (Arthur E.) Fund, Medford, 3/009

Armstrong (Arthur A.) Memorial Fd. Trust, Newark, 3/010

Barse (Dane & Josephine) Fdn., Vineland, 3/010

Bart (Clara) Fdn., Newark, 3/010

Bartenders Union Local 488 Insurance & Welfare Fund, Jersey City, 3/011

Barth Fdn., Newark, 3/011

Basic Foods Fdn., Englewood, 3/012

Bauer (George W.) Family Fdn., Roselle, 3/013

Beck (Joseph W. & Elsie E.) Fdn., Newark, 3/013

Becker (Moe) Fdn., Newark, 3/014

Beer Fdn., Tenafly, 3/014

Berger (Sol & Margaret) Fdn., Clifton, 3/014

Berkowitz (Edith C. & Bernard S.) Fdn., Newark, 3/015

Besser (Hyman & Fannie B.) Fdn., East Orange, 3/016

Besserman (Dorothy & Jules R.) Fdn., Upper Montclair, 3/016

Blonder - Tongue Fdn., Old Bridge, 3/017

Bluestein (Iris W. & Sanford G.) Fdn., Montclair, 3/017

Bowen Engineering Charitable Fund, North Branch, 3/018

Brawer Philanthropic Fdn., Haledon, 3/018

Beck (Felix M. & Doris L.) Fdn., Livingston, 3/019

Brenner (Jerome & Muriel) Fdn., Fort Lee, 3/020

Bristol (John W.) Fund, Far Hills, 3/020

Broad National Bank Fdn., Newark, 3/021

Broadway Tire Company Fund, North Hackensack, 3/021

Brody (Frances) Fdn., Woodbridge, 3/022

Brody (Leo) Fdn., Newark, 3/023

Brody (Sophie & Arthur) Fdn., South Orange, 3/023

Brookwood Fdn., Orange, 3/023

Brotman Family Fdn., Newark, 3/023

Brown Fdn., Vineland, 3/024

Brucker (Henry & Elizabeth) Corporation, Newark, 3/024

Buck (Junior C.) Fdn., Montclair, 3/026

Burlington County Historical Society, Burlington, 3/026

Button Fdn., East Rutherford, 3/027

Conference Charitable Trust of Morristown Pediatric, Mendham, 3/027

Campbell Soup Fund, Camden, 3/028

Carson Fdn., Sparta, 3/029

Carteret China Company Fdn., Carteret, 3/030

Cass (Elizabeth R. Lee) Trust, Newark, 3/031

Cedar Hill Golf & Country Club, Livingston, 3/031

Center for Analysis of Public Issues, Princeton, 3/031

Faulks (Theodosia P.) Trust, Elizabeth, 3/032

Chapin (Frances) Fdn., Maplewood, 3/032

Christ Church of East Orange Trust, Newark, 3/033

Cinnaminson Home, Cinnaminson, 3/033

Class of 1913, Princeton University Fdn., Westfield, 3/034

Cogliati Charitable Trust, Newark, 3/035

Cohn (J. H.) & Company Fdn., Newark, 3/035

Cohen (Abram B.) Fdn., Fair Lawn, 3/036

Coles (J. A.) Trust, Newark, 3/036
Conklin (Franklin), Jr. Trusts, Newark, 3/037
Cooper (Florence & Harry A.) Fdn., Hillside, 3/037
Cooper (Max & Dora) Family Fdn., Newark, 3/038
Creamer (Frank T.) Trust, Newark, 3/038
Cumberland County Medical Society Health & Educational Fund, Vineland, 3/038
Davis (Joseph & Sadie) Fdn., South Orange, 3/039
D'Olier Fdn., Morristown, 3/039
Dotson (Marjorie) Fund, Englewood, 3/040
DuBoff (Stanley & Rochelle) Charitable Trust, Rockaway, 3/041
Dutcher (Edward H.) Fellowship Fdn., Newark, 3/041
East Millstone Reformed Church Endowment Fund, Newark, 3/041
Eastern Sociological Society, Teaneck, 3/042
Economics Education Institute, East Orange, 3/042
Edell (Morton) Fdn., Newark, 3/044
Edgar (Alyce R.) Rutgers Fdn., Newark, 3/045
Edgar (Harold T.) Trust, Newark, 3/045
Egenalf (Tena) Trust, Newark, 3/045
Eigen (Hugh Allen) Memorial Scholarship Fdn., Passaic, 3/045
Eldridge (Sarah K.) Trust, Newark, 3/046
Elizabethtown Historical Fdn., Elizabeth, 3/046
Ellden Health & Aid Fund for the Benefit of Saddle River, Saddle River, 3/046
Engelhard (Charles) Fdn., Newark, 3/047
Essex County Committee, American Legion Trust, Newark, 3/049
Essex County Community Trust, Newark, 3/049
Fischer (Bernard & Anne) Fdn., Fort Lee, 3/050
Fischer (Morris & Nellie) Fdn., Union City, 3/050
Flagg Fdn., Fort Lee, 3/051
Frazer (Margaret) Scholarship Fund, Vineland, 3/052
Franco (Isaac H.) & Sons Fdn., Deal, 3/052
Friends of Venezia Fdn., North Bergen, 3/053
Picone (Joseph) Fdn., North Bergen, 3/053
Four Oaks Fdn., Somerville, 3/053
Garbe Fdn., Westfield, 3/055
Gehrie Fdn., Montclair, 3/056
Gleason (H. P.) Trust, Newark, 3/056
Golber (Arnold) Fdn., Newark, 3/056
Goldsmith (Bertram M.) Fdn., Annandale, 3/058
Goodman (Abraham, Mollie & Anna) Fdn., Kearny, 3/058
Goodman (Jacob & Libby) Fdn., Kearny, 3/060
Grad Fdn., Newark, 3/061
Greenberg (Mark D.) Fdn., Newark, 3/061
Greenberg (Reuben) Memorial Scholarship Fund, Hopatcong, 3/062
Greer (Annie S.) Fdn., Newark, 3/062
Groff (Frank & Louise) Fdn., Red Bank, 3/064
Gronim Fdn., West Orange, 3/065
Guennol Charitable Fdn., Newark, 3/065
Guest (Raymond R.) Charitable Fdn., Newark, 3/065
Hackensack Rotary - Newman Fund, Hackensack, 3/066
Haire (John R. & Doris J.) Fdn., Hillside, 3/066
Hansen (Edward C.) Fdn., Ridgefield Park, 3/067
Harmony Fdn., Newtown, 3/068
Harris (Sidney E.) Fdn., South Orange, 3/068
Hartley Fund, Newark, 3/068
Herr (Louis J. & Ruth G.) Fdn., Newark, 3/069
Hillside Industrial Fdn., Hillside, 3/070
Hill - Snowdon Fdn., Plainfield, 3/071
Horg (Sidney S.) Trust, Newark, 3/072
Holden (Audrey P.) Charitable Fdn., Newark, 3/072
Jockey Hollow Fdn., Jersey City, 3/073

Holman (S. C.) Fdn., Pennsauken, 3/073
Holzer (Richard H.) Memorial Fdn., Demarest, 3/074
Home for Aged Women, Jersey City, 3/074
Hudson Fdn., Montclair, 3/076
Igoe (Peter J. & Virginia E.) Fdn., Newark, 3/076
Industrial Products Suppliers Fdn., Englewood, 3/076
Iozia (Garry D. & Louise) Fdn., East Paterson, 3/077
Isele (Joseph) Fdn., Ho-Ho-Kus, 3/077
Weill (Teresa Jackson & Milton) Fdn., West New York, 3/078
Jacquelin Fdn., Princeton, 3/079
Jaycee Fdn., Livingston, 3/080
Johnson (Herbert R.) Trust U/A A.S.D. Johnson Fund, Englewood, 3/080
Kane Lodge Fdn., Hoboken, 3/081
Kanouse (Mary F.) Trust, Newark, 3/081
Kasser Family Fdn., Montclair, 3/081
Kearns (Thomas F.) Fdn., Alpine, 3/082
Kel Fdn., Saddle River, 3/082
Kelsey (Frederick W.) Trust, Newark, 3/082
Kirshbaum (Carolyn & Irving) Fdn., Deal, 3/082
Klausmann Corporation, Newark, 3/083
Kramer, Hirsch & Carchidi Fdn., Trenton, 3/084
Krieger (Charles K. & Esther) Fdn., Jersey City, 3/084
Kucklinsky (Fred & Esther) Fdn., Madison, 3/085
Kugler Fdn., Tenafly, 3/085
Ladd (Kate Macy) Fund, Newark, 3/086
Ladies Home of Plainfield, Plainfield, 3/087
Laurentian Fdn., Kearny, 3/088
Lautenberg Fdn., Montclair, 3/088
Lehr (Gussie & Harry) Fdn., North Bergen, 3/089
Leslie Fdn., Parsippany, 3/090
Lesnik Fdn., Newark, 3/091
Lester Fdn., Union, 3/092
Levin (Frances & George) Fdn., Irvington, 3/092
Lichtenfels (Robert) Trust, Newark, 3/093
Schultz (William Lightfoot) Fdn., Clifton, 3/093
Litwin (David & Minna) Fdn., Newark, 3/094
Livingston Fdn., Montvale, 3/094
L & S Fdn., Livingston, 3/095
Lorello (Robert) Fdn., Maplewood, 3/095
Madan (F.) Fdn., Cranford, 3/096
Malakoff (Herbert David) Memorial Fdn., Union City, 3/096
Marcus (Robert G. & Natalie S.) Charitable Trust, Trenton, 3/097
Margulies (William) Fund, South Orange, 3/097
Margulis Family Fdn., Maplewood, 3/098
Marian (Joseph & Ophelia) Trust, Asbury Park, 3/098
Mayne Educational Fund, Sparta, 3/098
McCarter (Jane L.) Trust, Newark, 3/099
McGraw (Curtis W.) Fdn., Princeton, 3/099
Medical Economics Fdn., Oradell, 3/099
Meisselbach (A. F.) Trust, Newark, 3/101
Menger (Carl & Eleanor) Fdn., Newark, 3/101
Mettler (John W.) Trust, Newark, 3/102
Metuchen Golf & Country Club, Edison, 3/102
Meyer (Aaron & Rachel) Memorial Fdn., Newark, 3/102
Benedict - Miller Fdn., Newark, 3/103
Millman Fdn., South Orange, 3/103
Morris Scholarship Fdn. for Boys' Club of Newark, Newark, 3/103
Moss (George H., Jr. & Mary Alice) Fdn., Rumson, 3/104
Mueller (C. F.) Company Scholarship Fdn., Jersey City, 3/104
Muscarelle (Joseph L.) Fdn., Maywood, 3/105
National Youth Science Fdn., South Orange, 3/106
Nesler (C. F.) Newark Community Trust, Newark, 3/106

New Jersey Branch of the Shut-In Society, Irvington, 3/107
New Jersey Golf Clubs Association, Totowa, 3/107
New Jersey Press Association, New Brunswick, 3/108
New Jersey Psychoanalytic Fdn., Englewood, 3/108
New Jersey Social & Academic Federation, Newark, 3/109
Newspaper Fund, Princeton, 3/109
Newton Area Scholarship - Leadership Fund, Newton, 3/111
Nichols (Douglas R.) Fdn., Califon, 3/112
Niebling (Charles) Trust, Newark, 3/113
Noyes Fdn., Smithville, 3/113
Ohl (George A.) Trust, Newark, 3/113
Okin (Robert) Fdn., West Orange, 3/115
Old Tennant Church Trust, Newark, 3/116
Olivia Fdn., Red Bank, 3/116
Order of Colonial Lords of Manors in America, Englewood, 3/116
Packard Fdn., Hackensack, 3/117
Pascoe (Herbert J.) Educational Fdn., Newark, 3/118
Passaic County Children's Aid & Society for Prevention of Cruelty to Children, Paterson, 3/119
Penick (Albert) Fund, Cedar Grove, 3/119
Perkins (F. Mason) Trust, Hackensack, 3/120
Perlmutter Family Fdn., Woodbridge, 3/121
Phipps (Howard) Fdn., Newark, 3/121
Premillenial Fdn., Lakewood, 3/122
Mannheimer Primatological Fdn., Toms River, 3/122
Princeton Regional Scholarship Fdn., Princeton, 3/123
Radeen (Abraham & Clara) Fdn., Millburn, 3/123
Randolph Fdn., Saddle River, 3/123
Reade (Walter) Fdn., Oakhurst, 3/124
Reilly (Thomas F.) Trust, Newark, 3/125
Reinfeld (Samuel & Pauline) Charitable Trust, South Orange, 3/125
Reinfeld (Saul & Evelyn) Charitable Trust, South Orange, 3/126
Reisen Fdn., Union, 3/126
Reisman Fdn., Pennsauken, 3/127
Foundation for Research in Philosophy of Science, Trenton, 3/128
Ricketts (Leslie C.) Fdn., Newark, 3/128
Rineberg Family Fdn., Deal, 3/129
Rippel (Fannie E.) Fdn., Newark, 3/130
Robins (Bernard) Fdn., Westfield, 3/133
Rockingham Fdn., Newark, 3/133
Vander Roest (H.) Trust, Newark, 3/133
Rose (Lenox S.) Trust, Newark, 3/133
Rosenberg (Arthur) Fdn., Englewood Cliffs, 3/133
Rosendahl (Edward & Sophia C.) Fdn., Tenafly, 3/134
Rotary Club of Trenton, Trenton, 3/135
Runkle (William) Trust, Newark, 3/135
Saibel Fdn., Clifton, 3/135
Salamensky (Carl) Fund, Wayne, 3/136
Salierno (Vincent & Rose) Fdn., Newark, 3/136
Sandler & Worth Charitable Fund, Springfield, 3/137
Satsky Fdn., Newark, 3/138
Sawtelle (Virginia Harkness) Fdn., Montclair, 3/138
Schamach (Milton) Fdn., Paterson, 3/140
Schenck (Lillian P.) Fund, Englewood, 3/140
Scher (Norman & Nancy) Fdn., South Orange, 3/141
Schultz Fdn., Clifton, 3/141
Seton Fdn., Newark, 3/142
Shulton Fdn., Clifton, 3/143
Sigma Theta Tau, Inc. - Alpha Tau Chapter, Newark, 3/144
Silberman (Curt C. & Else) Fdn., East Orange, 3/144
Slater (Albert H.) Fdn., East Paterson, 3/145
S.M.S. Fdn., New Vernon, 3/145

Snelbaker (Ashbrook D.) Home, Woodstown, 3/146
Snider (E. L.) Charitable Trust, Trenton, 3/146
Snow (John Ben) Fdn., Westfield, 3/146
Spitalny Fdn., Asbury Park, 3/148
Stavisky (Samuel F.) Family Fund, Newark, 3/148
Steele (Franklin A.) Fdn., Princeton, 3/148
Steinhardt (Lincoln & Bernice) Family Fdn., South Orange, 3/149
Stern Fdn., South Orange, 3/149
Stern (Dr. Gershon A. & Lois) Fund, Vineland, 3/150
Strauss (Howard G.) Fdn., Union, 3/151
Strawbridge (Duncan H.) Trust, Hackensack, 3/152
Stutchin (Bessie) Memorial Fdn. for Narcotic Research & Treatment, Paterson, 3/152
Summit Home for Children, Chesebrough Fdn., Summit, 3/152
Szerup Fdn., Union, 3/152
Tamburelli (Ercole & Irma) Fdn., Englewood, 3/153
Tarbell (Martha) Trust, Newark, 3/154
Taub (Henry & Marilyn) Fdn., Tenafly, 3/154
Taub (Joseph & Arlene) Fdn., Union, 3/155
Templeton Fdn., Englewood, 3/156
Thermoid Charitable Trust, Trenton, 3/156
Thomases (Florence & Fred) Fdn., Englewood, 3/156
Titsworth (C. G.) Trust, Newark, 3/157
To-le-da Fdn., Paterson, 3/157
Triangle Fdn., New Brunswick, 3/158
Twenty-Two Fdn., Princeton University, Newark, 3/159
Union County Trust Fdn., Elizabeth, 3/159
Visceglia Fdn., Newark, 3/160
Visiting Nurse Association of Summit, New Providence & Berkeley Heights, Summit, 3/161
Waldman (Joseph) Fdn., Parsippany, 3/161
Walters (William J.) Scholarship Fund, Newark, 3/161
Ward (Moses) Trust, Newark, 3/161
Warner Fdn., Short Hills, 3/162
Water & Wastewater Equipment Manufacturers Association, Newark, 3/162
Weidberg (Joseph M. & Evelyn R.) Fdn., West Atlantic City, 3/163
Weil (Jeanette W.) Fdn., Wayne, 3/164
Weiner - Wishengrad Fdn., Newark, 3/164
Weisberger (Joseph & Yetta) Fund for the Aged Poor & Needy, Newark, 3/165
Weiss (Doris & Milton) Fdn., Clifton, 3/166
Wheaton Historical Association, Millville, 3/166
Whittington (Anna E.) Memorial for Negro College Fund, Newark, 3/167
Williams (Henry) Trust, Montclair, 3/167
Willits Fdn., New Providence, 3/168
Willner (Albert & Blanche) Fdn., South Orange, 3/168
Wilson (Mary Blair) Fdn., Mantoloking, 3/169
Wilson (Robert) Trust, Newark, 3/169
Wood-Rdige Memorial Fdn., Wood-Rdige, 3/169
Wilson (Woodrow) Fdn., Princeton, 3/170
Wrightson - Besch Fdn., Newark, 3/170
Young Israel of Newark Trust, Newark, 3/171

NEW MEXICO

First Filming

American Tank and Steel Fdn., Farmington, 1/001
Bureau of Charities, Inc., Albuquerque, 1/002
Christian Fellowship, Inc., Albuquerque, 1/002
Communications and Electronics Fdn., Raton, 1/003
Dowling Family Foundation, Inc., Carlsbad, 1/003

Kruger (W. C.) Fdn., The, Santa Fe, 1/004
McCutchen (Paul) Fdn., Roswell, 1/004
Miller (Dr. H. A.) Fdn., Clovis, 1/004
Moody (Robert) Fdn., Inc., Santa Fe, 1/005
Petty (Norman), Clovis, 1/005
Roswell Lodge #969, B. P. O. Elks, Roswell, 1/005
Sabre-Pinon Educational Fdn., Santa Fe, 1/006
Sacred Heart Fdn., Inc., Clovis, 1/007
Spain (W. C.) Fdn., Santa Fe, 1/007

Second Filming

Campbell Family Foundation, Albuquerque, 2/001
Faris (Chester E.) Educational Foundation of the Jicarilla Apache Tribe of New Mexico, Albuquerque, 2/001
Fdn. of the 1st Cavalry Division Association, Albuquerque, 2/002
Korber (J.) Fdn., Albuquerque, 2/003
Liberman (Isaac) Fdn., Albuquerque, 2/003
Lippett (Jerome) Memorial Trust, Albuquerque, 2/004
Lovelace Fdn. for Medical Education and Research, Albuquerque, 2/005
Maddox (J. F.) Fdn., Hobbs, 2/007
Meadors (Max) Fdn., Clovis, 2/008
Miller (Otto A. and Nellie C.) Charitable Fdn., Albuquerque, 2/008
Muir (John) Institute, Albuquerque, 2/009
New Mexico Foundation, Las Cruces, 2/009
Rad Water Users Cooperative, Tucumcari, 2/010
Reeve Fdn., North Branch, N.J., 2/010
Roswell Lodge #969 B.P.O. Elks, Roswell, 2/011
Sandia Fdn., Albuquerque, 2/011
Seward (Robert) Fdn., Carlsbad, 2/012
Viles Fdn., Las Vegas, 2/012
Wurlitzer (Helene) Fdn. of New Mexico, Taos, 2/013

NEW YORK

First Filming

Aaron (Bernard J. & Sylvia) Fdn., Brooklyn, 1/001
Aaron & Ida Fdn., NYC, 1/002
Abbene (Rita) Memorial Fdn., Rockville Centre, 1/002
Abbott (George) Education Fdn., NYC, 1/003
Abelard Fdn., NYC, 1/003
Abelow Fdn., NYC, 1/005
Abelove (Martin) Fdn., NYC, 1/006
Abex Fdn., NYC, 1/007
Abner (Howard J.) Fdn., NYC, 1/008
Abramovitz (William) Fdn., NYC, 1/009
Abrams (Benjamin and Elizabeth) Fdn., NYC, 1/010
Abrams (Max & Helen) Fdn., NYC, 1/011
Abrons (Richard & Mimi) Fdn., NYC, 1/013
A - C Trust, Albany, 1/014
Achelis Fdn., NYC, 1/015
Ackerman (Jerome & Barbara) Fdn., Bronx, 1/017
Acorn Fdn., NYC, 1/017
Adam, Meldrum & Anderson Charity Fd., Buffalo, 1/018
Adams (James S.) Fdn., NYC, 1/018
Adams (Emma J.) Memorial Fdn., NYC, 1/020
Addison (Viola G.) Fdn., NYC, 1/021
Adelphi Fdn., NYC, 1/021
Addison (Viola G.) Fdn., NYC, 1/021
Adelson (Jane L. and Charles R.) Fdn., NYC, 1/021
Adenbaum (Leo, Claire & Robert), Glen Cove, 1/023
Ades Fdn., NYC, 1/023
Adler Fdn. (Louis & Bessier), NYC, 1/024

Adolphus (Gustavus) Lutheran Church, NYC, 1/025
A & E Fdn., Scarsdale, 1/026
AEM Fdn., NYC, 1/026
Aeroflex Fdn., NYC, 1/027
Agate (S & A) Fdn., NYC, 1/028
Agricultural Development Council, NYC, 1/029
Aibel (Irving J.) Fdn., NYC, 1/032
Akbar Fund, NYC, 1/033
Akston (Ziuta & Joseph James) Fdn., NYC, 1/034
Alamatuck Fund, NYC, 1/035
Albert (Eli D.) Fdn., NYC, 1/036
Albion Fdn., NYC, 1/036
Aldan (Richard Steven) Fdn., Brooklyn, 1/037
Aldrich (Larry) Fdn., NYC, 1/037
Alexander (Oakey L. & Ethel W.) Fdn. Trust, NYC, 1/037
Alexander (Shepard L.) Fdn., NYC, 1/038
Allade, NYC, 1/039
Allaverdy Fdn., NYC, 1/040
Allen Fdn., NYC, 1/040
Allen Fdn., Mineola, 1/042
Allen (Sheila) Fdn., NYC, 1/042
Allen (Vivian B.) Fdn., NYC, 1/043
Allerhand (Ida & Irving), Brooklyn, 1/045
Alleynian Fdn., NYC, 1/046
Allied Chemical Fdn., NYC, 1/046
Allied Stores Fdn., NYC, 1/051
Allyn Fdn., Skoneateles, 1/052
Alper Fdn., NYC, 1/053
Alpern Family Fdn., Bronx, 1/054
Alpern Fdn., NYC, 1/054
Alpert Fdn., NYC, 1/055
Alpha Chi Rho Educational Fdn., NYC, 1/055
Alpha Epsilon Pi Fdn., NYC, 1/056
Alpha Fund, Corning, 1/056
Alsberg Fdn., NYC, 1/057
Alson (Elaine & Ernest) Fdn., Orangeburg, 1/057
Alter (Francis & Margaret) Fdn., NYC, 1/058
Altman Fdn., NYC, 1/059
Altman (Jack & Sylvia) Fdn., NYC, 1/061
Altman-Stiller Fdn., NYC, 1/062
Altshul (Stephen L.) Fdn., NYC, 1/062
Amato Opera Circle, NYC, 1/063
Amax Aid Fund, NYC, 1/063
American Agriculturist Fdn., Ithaca, 1/064
American Airlines Fdn., NYC, 1/065
American Artists Ad Astra Fdn., NYC, 1/068
American Chinese Medical Society Educational Fund, Old Westbury, 1/068
American Conservation Association, NYC, 1/069
American Electric Power System Educational Trust Fund, NYC, 1/071
American European Fdn., NYC, 1/072
American Express Fdn., NYC, 1/072
American Export Industries Fdn., NYC, 1/074
American Fdn. for Art Research, NYC, 1/075
American Fdn. for Ecumenical Studies & Relations, NYC, 1/076
American Fdn. for Mental Hygiene, NYC, 1/076
American Friends of Israel, NYC, 1/077
American International Association for Economic & Social Development, NYC, 1/078
American Israeli Fdn., NYC, 1/079
American Life Fdn. & Study Institute, Watkins Glen, 1/079
American Moroccan Educational Fdn., White Plains, 1/082
American National Standards Institute, NYC, 1/082
American Philanthropic Fdn., NYC, 1/083
American Railway Car Institute, NYC, 1/084
American Scholarship Fdn. for Israel, Roslyn, 1/084
America's Future, New Rochelle, 1/085
Ametek Fdn., NYC, 1/088
AMF Fdn., NYC, 1/089
AMK Fdn. (n/k/a United Brands Fdn.), NYC, 1/091
Amos Fdn., Syracuse, 1/092
Andason Fdn., NYC, 1/093

Anderson Fdn., Elmira, 1/094
Anderson (Herbert R.) Fdn., Yorktown Heights, 1/095
Andretta Fdn., Kingston, 1/095
Andrus (Julia Dyckman) Memorial, Yonkers, 1/096
Angelus Fdn., NYC, 1/103
Anita Fdn., NYC, 1/104
Ansorge (Monte S.) Fdn., Hollis, 1/105
Anthropos Academy, NYC, 1/105
Appleton (Grace G.) Student Loan Fund, Albany, 1/106
Appley (Lawrence A.) Fdn., Hamilton, 1/106
Applied Resources, NYC, 1/107
Aquinas Fund, NYC, 1/109
April (Gloria) Fdn., NYC, 1/111
Arabel Fdn., NYC, 1/111
Aramino (John N.) Memorial Fund, Rochester, 1/113
Arapahoe Fdn., Port Washington, 1/113
ARCA Fdn., NYC, 1/113
Arcadia Fdn., Rochester, 1/114
Archbishopric of NY, NYC, 1/116
Arditti (Albert A.) Fdn., NYC, 1/117
Ariowitsch Family Fdn., NYC, 1/117
Arkell Hall Fdn., Canajoharie, 1/118
Arkville Erpf Fund, NYC, 1/118
Arlen (Harold) Fdn., NYC, 1/120
Armenian Educational Council, Troy, 1/121
Armour (George & Frances) Fdn., NYC, 1/121
Armour (Nathan Z.) Fdn., NYC, 1/123
Aron (J.) Charitable Trust, NYC, 1/123
Aronow (David) Fdn., NYC, 1/126
Arts Concepts Fdn., NYC, 1/127
Arts Trust Fund, NYC, 1/127
Artwill Burde Fdn., NYC, 1/128
Arwood Fdn., NYC, 1/128
A & S Fdn., NYC, 1/129
Asarco Fdn., NYC, 1/131
Ascher Fdn., NYC, 1/133
Ascoli (Marion R.) Fund, NYC, 1/134
Ascoli (Max) Fund, NYC, 1/136
Ash (Sol & Lillian) Fdn., NYC, 1/138
Askin (Fannie & Arnold) Fdn., NYC, 1/139
Associated Metals & Minerals Fdn., NYC, 1/140
Associates Fdn., NYC, 1/141
Association of Russian Cadets Graduated Outside Russia, NYC, 1/141
Astor (Vincent) Fdn., NYC, 1/142
Atkins (R.R.) Fdn., NYC, 1/144
Atlantic Richfield Fdn. (NY), NYC, 1/145
Atlas (Edythe & Sol G.) Fund, Mineola, 1/150
Atomic Research, Central Islip, 1/150
Atran Fdn., NYC, 1/151
Attwood (Arthur P.) Scholarship Fund, Albany, 1/152
Auchincloss (Lily) Fdn., NYC, 1/153
Auer (Louis) Fdn., NYC, 1/154
Aufiero (J. M.) Fdn. for Charitable Purposes, NYC, 1/155
Augsbury Fdn., Ogdensburg, 1/156
Augustine Family Charitable Trust, NYC, 1/157
Aurelio Fdn., NYC, 1/157
Aurora Fund, NYC, 1/158
Auslander (George) Fdn., Valley Stream, 1/159
Averick Fdn., NYC, 1/160
Avery (Maxwell) Fdn., Syracuse, 1/160
Avon Family Fdn., NYC, 1/161
Avon Products Fdn., NYC, 1/162
AVR Fdn., NYC, 1/164
Axelrod (Charles) Fdn., NYC, 1/165
Ayer Fdn., NYC, 1/166
B Fund, NYC, 1/166
Bach Aria Group Association, NYC, 1/167
Bache Corporation Fdn., NYC, 1/168
Bache (H. L.) Fdn., NYC, 1/170
Bache (Jules) Fdn., NYC, 1/171
Bachmann Fdn., NYC, 1/172
Bachmann (Julian & Emmy) Fdn., NYC, 1/173
Backman (Jules) Fdn., Scarsdale, 1/174
Backster Research Fdn., NYC, 1/174
Bado Fdn., NYC, 1/174

Baer Fdn., NYC, 1/175
Baerwald (Herman & Shirley) Fdn., NYC, 1/177
Bagby Music Lovers Fdn., NYC, 1/177
Baier (Marie) Fdn., NYC, 1/178
Bailey (Frank & Marie Louise) Fdn., NYC, 1/179
Baird Family Fund, Syosset, 1/180
Baird Fdn., Buffalo, 1/180
Baird (William C. & Mary Edwards N.) Trust, Rochester, 1/182
Baker (George F.) Trust, NYC, 1/182
Baldwin (Robert H.) Fdn., NYC, 1/185
Baldwin (Bill) Fund, Troy, 1/186
Ballin (Charles & Pauline G.) Fdn., NYC, 1/186
Ballon (Harriet & Charles) Fdn., NYC, 1/187
Balmoral Fdn., NYC, 1/188
Banbury Fund, NYC, 1/189
Banker (Dean) Fdn., NYC, 1/190
Bankers Trust Co. Fdn. Trust, NYC, 1/190
Baptist Church of Sidney Center Trust, Walton, 1/191
Barash (Mitchell) Fdn., Roslyn, 1/192
Barchoff (Mollie) Fdn., Bronx, 1/193
Barclay Fdn., NYC, 1/193
Bardon-Cole Fdn., NYC, 1/194
Baris (Paul H. & Sharon D.) Trust, NYC, 1/194
Barish (Sol) Fdn. in Memory of His Parents, NYC, 1/195
Barjac Fund, Loudonville, 1/195
Barker (James M. & Margaret R.) Fdn., NYC, 1/196
Barkey Fdn., NYC, 1/196
Barnard (Christian) Research Fdn., NYC, 1/197
Barnett (Sarah) Fdn., Yonkers, 1/197
Barney (N. J.) Fdn., NYC, 1/198
Barotz (Barbara) Memorial Fdn., NYC, 1/199
Barr (Martin & Rhoda) Fdn., Hastings on Hudson, 1/199
Barrett (Edmund E. & Lois S.) Fdn., NYC, 1/199
Barron (Gloria M.) Fdn., Muttontown, 1/200
Barson (William & Charlotte) Fdn., Scarsdale, 1/200
Bart (Philip) Fdn., NYC, 1/201
Barth (Theodore H.) Fdn., NYC, 1/202
Barvoets (E.A.) Fund, Albany, 1/204
Bassage (Winfield S.) Trust, Rochester, 1/205
Bassine Fdn., NYC, 1/206
Batcheller (Highland G.) Jr. Memorial Fdn., Albany, 1/207
Bateh (Eissa A.) & Brothers Fdn., NYC, 1/207
Bauer (Harry & Lore) Fdn., North Woodmere, 1/208
Baumgold Bros. Fdn., NYC, 1/209
Bausch & Lomb Fdn., Rochester, 1/210
Bayard Cutting Arboretum Endowment Fund, NYC, 1/211
Bayley (Dorothy & George) Fdn., Hempstead, 1/212
Bayne (Howard) Fund, NYC, 1/213
Beane Fdn., NYC, 1/214
Beaumont (Louis D.) Fdn., NYC, 1/214
Beck Fdn., NYC, 1/216
Beck (Belle) to Combat Malignant Diseases, NYC, 2/001
Becker (Adam & J.S.) Fdn., NYC, 2/002
Becker (Ellen L. & Otto L.) Charitable Trust, Bronx, 2/003
Becker (Isadore and Adele) Fdn., NYC, 2/003
Becker (Morris & Gerald) Fdn., NYC, 2/004
Beecher Fdn., Buffalo, 2/005
Beer-Friedland Fdn., NYC, 2/006
Beha (James A.) Fdn., NYC, 2/006
Behrens (Herbert R.) Fdn., NYC, 2/007
Beir Fdn., NYC, 2/007
Belfer Fdn., NYC, 2/008
Belgian Society of Benevolence, NYC, 2/009
Bell Fdn., NYC, 2/010
Beller (Louis K.) Fdn., Brooklyn, 2/010
Bellin (Harry, Sophie & Mollie) Fdn., NYC, 2/010
Belmont Fdn., Brooklyn, 2/010

Belock (Lilyan & Harry D.) Fdn., Kings Point, 2/012
Bendheim (Doris & Frank) Charitable Trust, NYC, 2/013
Bendheim (Charles & Els) Fdn., NYC, 2/013
Bendheim (Siegfried & Nannette) Fdn., NYC, 2/014
Bendit (Leo H.) Charitable Fdn., NYC, 2/014
Benedek Fdn., NYC, 2/015
Benedek (A. Richard) Fdn., NYC, 2/016
Benenson (Robert & Nettie) Fdn., NYC, 2/016
Angola Benevolent Fund, Gloversville, 2/017
Benjamin Family Fdn., NYC, 2/017
Benjamin (Audrey & Bruce) Fund, NYC, 2/018
Bennett (James Gordon) Memorial Corp., NYC, 2/019
Bensley (Charles J.) Fdn., NYC, 2/021
Benton (William) Fdn., NYC, 2/021
Berch (Barnett & Anne) Fdn., NYC, 2/024
Bercow (Herman & Rhoda) Fdn., NYC, 2/024
Berger (Fdn. of Ethel P.), NYC, 2/024
Bergler (Edmund & Marianne) Psychiatric Fdn., NYC, 2/025
Bergman (Rabbi Yesucher Dov) Fdn., NYC, 2/025
Bergstein (Sol & Judith) Fdn., Brooklyn, 2/026
Berk (David & Minnie) Fdn., Brooklyn, 2/027
Berkman Fund, Hempstead, 2/028
Berlin (Irving) Charitable Fund, NYC, 2/028
Berman Fdn., NYC, 2/029
Berman (Elias & Sheva) Fdn., NYC, 2/030'
Berman (Harry & Mabel) Fdn., Rye, 2/031
Berman (Moses & Bernice) Fdn., Lawrence, 2/031
Bernard (Esther R.) Fdn., NYC, 2/031
Bernard (Herbert & Eileen) Fdn., NYC, 2/032
Bernard (Jack & Nancy) Fdn., NYC, 2/032
Bernbach (Bill) Fdn., NYC, 2/032
Bernhardt (Max E.) Charitable Trust, NYC, 2/034
Bernheim Fdn., NYC, 2/034
Bernstein (Alex A. & Sarah) Fdn., NYC, 2/035
Bernstein (Bernard) Family Fdn., NYC, 2/035
Bernstein (Edythe Blanksteen) Fdn., NYC, 2/036
Bernstein (Samuel & Julia) Fdn., Brooklyn, 2/037
Bernstein (Arnold & Jeanne) Fund, NYC, 2/038
Bernstein (Theodore & Aline) Fund, NYC, 2/040
Berol Fdn., NYC, 2/040
Berse (Harry & Sylvia) Fdn., NYC, 2/040
Bershad Fdn., White Plains, 2/041
Besskind (Dorothy M.) Fdn., NYC, 2/042
Beta Sigma Rho Fdn., NYC, 2/043
Bethesda-By-The-Sea et al Trust, NYC, 2/043
Bettin Fdn., Webster, 2/044
Beyer & Cahn Fdn., Manhasset, 2/045
Bezalel Fdn., NYC, 2/045
Bialkin Family Fdn., NYC, 2/047
Bibliographical Society of America, NYC, 2/048
Biddle (Clement & Grace) Fdn., NYC, 2/049
Biddle (Margaret T.) Fdn., NYC, 2/050
Biddle (Mary Duke) Fdn., NYC, 2/051
Biederman Fdn., NYC, 2/053
Bienenfeld (Benjamin, Lillian & Mae) Fdn., Belle Harbor, 2/053
Bienenfeld (Gertrude & Morris) Charitable Trust, NYC, 2/054
Bier Fdn., NYC, 2/054
Bierman (Jacquin D.) Fdn., NYC, 2/055
Bigar (Raymond & Nicole) Fdn., NYC, 2/055
Bigelow Charitable Trust Fund, NYC, 2/056
Billington (Amy) & Henderson (George L.) Scholarship Fund, White Plains, 2/057
Bilo Fund, NYC, 2/057
Birnbaum Fdn., NYC, 2/058
Bisco (Leonard) Fdn., NYC, 2/059
Bismarck (Mona) Fdn., NYC, 2/060
Bissing (Bessie L.) Trust, NYC, 2/062
Bitensky (Halina & Samson) Fdn., NYC, 2/063
B & L Fdn., NYC, 2/064

Black Oak Fdn., NYC, 2/065
Black (Katharine A. & Clinton R.) Jr. Fdn., NYC, 2/066
Blackmer (Henry M.) Fdn., NYC, 2/067
Blackstone Corporation Trust--Lenna (Oscar A.) Fdn., Buffalo, 2/069
Blaine (Robert & Doris) Fdn., Forest Hills, 2/069
Blaine (Walter F.) Fdn., NYC, 2/069
Blair Fdn., NYC, 2/070
Blair (John) Fdn., NYC, 2/071
Blank (Morris & Sadie) Fdn., Great Neck, 2/072
Blankley (Thomas & Susanne) Fund, NYC, 2/073
Blanksteen (William) Fdn., NYC, 2/073
Blechner (Max) Charitable Fund, NYC, 2/074
Blickman Fdn., NYC, 2/074
Blinken Fdn., NYC, 2/075
Bliss (Cornelius N.) Memorial Fund, NYC, 2/076
Blitzer (Terese N.) Fdn., NYC, 2/078
Blumenkrantz Fdn., NYC, 2/079
Blumenthal Family Fdn., NYC, 2/079
Blitzer (Edward H. R.) Fund, NYC, 2/079
Blitzer (Jeremiah) Fund, NYC, 2/080
Blitzer (William F.) Fund, NYC, 2/080
Bloch (Herman) Fdn., NYC, 2/081
Block (Marvin A. & Lillian K.) Fdn., Buffalo, 2/082
Block (Paul & Dina W.) Fdn., NYC, 2/082
Block (Herman W.) Fund, NYC, 2/084
Blodgett (Margaret Kendrick) Fdn., NYC, 2/085
Bloom (Aaron & Rose) Fdn., NYC, 2/086
Bloom (Charles) Fdn., NYC, 2/087
Bloom (Norman & Herbert) Fdn., NYC, 2/087
Bloom (Sol) Family Fdn., NYC, 2/088
c/o Bloom--Zinn (Eleanor & Oscar) Fdn., NYC, 2/089
Bloomberg Fdn., NYC, 2/089
Bloomer (James J.) Trust, Elmira, 2/090
Bloomingdale (Lyman G.) Fdn., NYC, 2/090
Blue Hill Fdn., NYC, 2/091
Blueberry Cove Scholarship Fund, NYC, 2/092
Bluestein (Jacob) Fdn., NYC, 2/092
Bluhdorn (Charles & Yvette) Charitable Trust, NYC, 2/093
Blum (Adolfo) Fdn., NYC, 2/093
Blum (Henry L.) Fdn., NYC, 2/093
Blum (Lawrence S.) Fdn., NYC, 2/094
Blum (Morris) Fdn., NYC, 2/096
Blume (Alvin L. & Dorothea S.) Fdn., Hartsdale, 2/096
Blume (Jack Teigh) Fdn., NYC, 2/097
Blumenthal (Morris J.) Fdn., NYC, 2/098
Blumstein (William) Family Fdn., NYC, 2/098
Blythmour Fdn., NYC, 2/099
Bobrow (Janet Goldberg) & Marion Goldberg, Goldberg Memorial Fund, NYC, 2/101
Bobst (Elmer & Mandouha) Fdn., NYC, 2/101
Bloomingdale (Betty & Alfred) Fdn., NYC, 2/102
Bloomingdale Store Fdn., NYC, 2/102
Blue Bird Fdn., NYC, 2/103
Bocklet (Charles J. & Mary B.) Fdn., Rockville Center, 2/103
Bodenheim Fdn., NYC, 2/104
Bodman Fdn., NYC, 2/105
Bloomingdale (Lyman G.) Fdn., NYC, 2/106
Bloomingdale (Samuel J.) Fdn., NYC, 2/106
Bloomingdale (Betty & Alfred) Fdn., NYC, 2/107
Bloomingdale Store Fdn., NYC, 2/108
Blue Bird Fdn., NYC, 2/109
Bodman Fdn., NYC, 2/109
Boehm (Lillian) Fdn., NYC, 2/111
Bogen Fdn., NYC, 2/112
Bohemia Fdn., NYC, 2/114
Bohm (Alexander & Renee) Fdn., Brooklyn, 2/115
Bohrer Fdn., NYC, 2/115
Bokharian Jewish Aid Society, NYC, 2/115
Bollingen Fdn., NYC, 2/116
Bonsal (Alonzo F. & Jennie W.) Fdn., NYC, 2/116

Booth Ferris Fdn., NYC, 2/118
Boquet Fdn., NYC, 2/121
Borak (Shirley) Fdn., NYC, 2/121
Bordon (Abraham & Ethel) Fdn., NYC, 2/122
Borgenicht (Max & Helen) Fdn., NYC, 2/122
Bossong Trust Fund, NYC, 2/123
Bostwick (Albert C.) Fdn., Westbury, 2/124
Boulware (Lemuel R.) Charitable & Educational Trust, NYC, 2/126
Bourne (S. H.) Fdn., NYC, 2/128
Bowers Fdn., Binghamton, 2/128
Bowne (Robert) Fdn., NYC, 2/128
Bowron (John Walker) Scholarship Fund, Albany, 2/129
Ward (Robert Boyd) Fund, White Plains, 2/130
Boyle (Sheila & William J.) Fdn., Garden City, 2/131
Boynton Fdn., NYC, 2/132
Brabson (Rodney and Mary) Fdn., NYC, 2/133
Brace-Mueller-Huntley Fdn., Syracuse, 2/133
Brady (Charles F.) Memorial Fund, Syracuse, 2/134
Brakman Aid Fund, NYC, 2/135
Braloff (Herman M.) Fdn., NYC, 2/135
Branch-Wilbur Fund, Rochester, 2/136
Brand (Martha & Regina) Fdn., NYC, 2/136
Brandt (Elsie L. & Peter H.), NYC, 2/137
Brandt (Gusti) Fdn., NYC, 2/138
Brant Lake Camp Scholarship Fdn., NYC, 2/139
Brauer Fdn., Kings Point, 2/139
Braun (Philip N.) Fdn., Syracuse, 2/139
Bravmann (L.) Fdn., NYC, 2/139
Braver Fdn., NYC, 2/140
Brecher (Eva Tuttman) Fdn., Long Island City, 2/141
Breck (Henry C.) Fund, NYC, 2/142
Brecker (Dorothy & Louis J.) Fdn., NYC, 2/142
Bregman (Oscar H.) Fdn., White Plains, 2/143
Brehmer (Franklin George) Fdn., Red Hook, 2/143
Brez Fdn., NYC, 2/144
Brenner Fdn., NYC, 2/150
Bressler Family Fdn., NYC, 2/150
Breswick Fdn., NYC, 2/151
Briggs (Lillian) Fdn., Binghamton, 2/151
Briggs (Theodore C. & Ruth C.) Fund, Rochester, 2/152
Brimberg Fdn., NYC, 2/153
Brinker (Arthur C. & Rose R.) Fdn., Brooklyn, 2/153
Broad Street Fdn., NYC, 2/154
Broderick (Patrick J.) Memorial Fdn., NYC, 2/155
Brodhead Fdn., NYC, 2/156
Brodkin (Herbert H. & Patricia M.) Fdn., NYC, 2/157
Bronfman (Samuel) Fdn., NYC, 2/158
Brookgreen Gardens, NYC, 2/159
Brookgreen Gardens Trust, NYC, 2/160
Brooklyn Home for Aged, Brooklyn, 2/161
Brooklyn Institute for Arts & Sciences, NYC, 2/163
Brooklyn Urological Research Fund, Brooklyn, 2/165
Brooks (Harrison M.) Trusts, Buffalo, 2/165
Brooks (Max) Fdn., NYC, 2/165
Brothers Ashkenazi Fdn., NYC, 2/166
Browdy Fdn., NYC, 2/167
Brown (Jack R.) Fdn., NYC, 2/167
Brown (Peter A.) Cultural Fdn., NYC, 2/167
Brown (Alice & Harry) Fdn., NYC, 2/168
Brown (A. S. & L. M.) Fdn., New Rochelle, 2/169
Brown (Laura & Arthur) Fdn., NYC, 2/169
Brown (Lillian & A. Milton) Fdn., NYC, 2/170
Bruckner Society of America, NYC, 2/171
Brugler (Mercer & Bernice) Charitable Trust, Rochester, 2/172
Brunner (Bertram F. & Susie) Fdn., NYC, 2/173
Bruner Fdn., NYC, 2/175

Brunner (Robert) Fdn., NYC, 2/177
Brush (Thomas S.) Fdn., NYC, 2/178
Brush-Day Fdn., NYC, 2/179
Brushwood Fund, NYC, 2/179
Buchwalter (Louis & Gertrude) Fdn., NYC, 2/180
Buckner Fdn., NYC, 2/181
Bucky (Jacob & Eugenie) Memorial Fdn., NYC, 2/182
Buffalo Equity Fdn., Buffalo, 2/185
Buffalo Tennis & Squash Club, Buffalo, 2/185
Buitoni (Giovanni & Letizia) Fdn., NYC, 2/186
Bull's Head Fdn., NYC, 2/187
Bulova Fund, NYC, 2/188
Bulova (Arde) Memorial Fund, NYC, 2/188
Bunbury Company, NYC, 2/189
Bunderoff (Harry & Jean) Fund, NYC, 2/191
Burchfield (Charles E.) Fdn., Buffalo, 2/191
Burden (Florence V.) Fdn., NYC, 2/192
Burden (Frances & Townsend) Fdn., NYC, 2/194
Burger (Alexander & Sarah) Fdn., NYC, 2/195
Burnett (Belle C.) Fdn., Salem, 2/196
Burnett (William O.) Fdn., NYC, 2/196
Butensky (Burten) Fdn., NYC, 2/197
Butler Fdn., NYC, 2/198
Butler (Abbey J.) Fdn., NYC, 2/199
Butler J. E. & Z. B.) Fdn., NYC, 2/200
Butler (Marshall D.) Fdn., Melville, 2/201
Butler (William V.) Fdn., NYC, 2/203
Butterman-Goldsmith Fdn., Brooklyn, 2/203
Buxbaum (Belle & Charles) Fdn., Jackson Heights, 2/204
Byck Fdn., NYC, 2/205
Bydale Fdn., NYC, 2/205
Bynum Family Fdn., Fayetteville, 2/206
Caesar Fdn., NYC, 2/206
C.A.L. Fdn., NYC, 2/207
Caleb Fdn., NYC, 2/208
Calkins (Daniel H.) Memorial Fund, Rochester, 2/209
Calm Fdn., NYC, 2/210
Cahn (Harry) Fdn., NYC, 2/210
Camargo Fdn., NYC, 2/210
Cameron Baird Fdn., Buffalo, 2/211
Camp (Erwin) Fdn., NYC, 2/212
Campe (Ed Lee & Jean) Fdn., NYC, 2/212
Campe (Sam & Louise) Fdn., NYC, 2/214
Canada Dry Fdn., NYC, 2/216
Cancer Research Fdn. Forence Kaufman, Brooklyn, 2/216
Canno (Leonard & Irma) Fdn., NYC, 2/217
Cantor (H. B.) Fdn., NYC, 2/217
Caplan (I.J.) Fdn., NYC, 2/218
Cappellino (Charles M.) Fdn., Brooklyn, 2/219
Caputo (Lorenzo) Memorial Fdn., Lindenhurst, 2/219
Caro (Herman & Kate) Fdn., NYC, 2/220
Carduner (Leonard & Harriet) Fdn., Great Neck, 2/221
Carey (Richard J.) Fdn., NYC, 2/221
Carey (W. Gibson) Jr. Fdn., NYC, 2/222
Caritas Fund, NYC, 2/222
Carity (Chester) Fdn., NYC, 2/224
Carl Company Fdn., Schenectady, 2/225
Carnegie (Dorothy) Fdn., NYC, 2/225
Carolyndale, NYC, 2/226
Carp (Louis & Florence) Memorial Fdn., NYC, 3/001
Carr (Frank J.) Medical Fdn., Buffalo, 3/001
Carson (J. H. & E. R.) Fdn., NYC, 3/001
Carson (Samuel) Fdn., White Plains, 3/003
Carter Fund, NYC, 3/003
Carthage Fund, Scarsdale, 3/004
Case (Hadley & Julie M.) Fdn., NYC, 3/004
Case-Hoyt Fdn., Rochester, 3/004
Casella (P. J. & Palmina) Fdn., Binghamton, 3/005
Casey (Annie E.) Fdn., NYC, 3/006
Casey (Sophia & William J.) Fdn., NYC, 3/006
Casket Makers Insurance Trust Fund, NYC, 3/007
Cassel (Hugh) Fdn., NYC, 3/008
Castaldo (Pasquale A.) Fdn., Bronx, 3/008

Cuyler (David B.) Memorial Scholarship Fund, Rochester, 3/171
Cynthiana Fdn., NYC, 3/172
Dabro Fdn., Brooklyn, 3/172
Da Costa Fdn., NYC, 3/172
Dadourian (Jack & Alice) Fdn., Richmond Hill, 3/172
Daitch (Herbert & Hilda) Fdn., NYC, 3/173
Dale Fdn., NYC, 3/174
Dalsemer (Leonard & Emily) Fdn., NYC, 3/174
Daly (Joseph R.) Fdn., NYC, 3/175
Dammann Fund, NYC, 3/176
Damroth Fdn., NYC, 3/177
Dane (Eli) Fdn., NYC, 3/178
Dane (Maxwell & Belle) Fdn., NYC, 3/178
Danenberg Fdn., Long Island City, 3/179
Danforth (Josiah H.) Memorial Fund, Gloversville, 3/180
Daniel (Gerard & Ruth) Fdn., New Rochelle, 3/181
Dansker Fdn., NYC, 3/182
Danziger Family Fdn., Inc., Lawrence, 3/183
Danziger (Gloria & Sidney) Fdn., NYC, 3/183
Darcy Fdn., NYC, 3/184
Darlington Fdn., NYC, 3/185
Darlington (Sibyl H.) Fdn., NYC, 3/185
Davenport Memorial Hsop. Children's Fund Trust #28053, Rochester, 3/186
Davenport West Memorial Fdn., NYC, 3/187
David (Ben) Fdn., NYC, 3/188
Davidowitz Fdn., NYC, 3/188
Davidson (Aaron & Ida) Fdn., Brooklyn, 3/189
Davidson (Abraham E.) Memorial Fdn., Brooklyn, 3/189
Davidson (Ellis) Fdn., Mineola, 3/190
Davidson (Marvin H.) Fdn., NYC, 3/190
Davidson-Hooker (S. W. Davidson for) Fund, NYC, 3/191
Davidson (Philip) Fdn., Brooklyn, 3/192
Davis (Aaron W.), NYC, 3/193
Davis (Donald L.) Fdn., Buffalo, 3/194
Davis (Jacob) Fdn., NYC, 3/195
Davis (Leonard & Sophie) Fdn., NYC, 3/195
Davis (Simon & Annie) Fdn., NYC, 3/196
Davisdale Fdn., Central Valley, 3/197
Davison-Foreman (W. F. Davison for) Fdn., NYC, 3/197
Daw Fund, NYC, 3/199
Day is Done Fdn., NYC, 3/199
Dean Fdn., White Plains, 3/200
Dean (Gordon) Memorial Fellowship Fund Trust, NYC, 3/201
Dean (Howard B.) Fdn., NYC, 3/201
Dean (Joel), Hastings-on-Hudson, 3/202
Deborah Fdn., NYC, 3/202
De Forest (Charles M.) Fdn., NYC, 3/204
De Jonge (Solomon & Blanche) Fdn., NYC, 3/205
De Jur (Harry) Fdn., NYC, 3/206
De Jur (Ralph & Frances), NYC, 3/206
Deke Fdn., NYC, 3/207
Delacorte (Valerie & George) Fdn., NYC, 3/207
Delacorte (Margarita V.) "M.V.D. Fund", NYC, 3/209
Delahaye Fund, NYC, 3/210
Delaran Family Fund, NYC, 3/211
Dell Publishing Co. Fdn., NYC, 3/212
Delta Phi Educational Fund, NYC, 3/213
Dember Fdn., NYC, 3/213
Denberg (Louis) Fdn., NYC, 3/215
Dent Fdn., NYC, 3/215
Derfner (Samuel & Ray) Fdn., NYC, 3/216
Detecto Scales Fund, Brooklyn, 3/217
Detweiler Fund, NYC, 3/217
Deutsch Fdn., NYC, 3/218
Deutsch (Ernst & Paula) Fdn., NYC, 3/218
Deutsch (Louis) Fdn., NYC, 3/219
Deutschmann Fdn., NYC, 3/220
Devine (C. J.) Charitable Trust, NYC, 3/220
Devine (Christopher J.) Fdn., NYC, 3/221
Devine (Tura E.) Fdn., NYC, 3/222
Dewar (James A. & Jessie Smith) Fdn., Oneonta, 3/222

Dewey (John) Fdn., NYC, 3/223
Dewey (Thomas E., Jr. & Ann) Fdn., NYC, 3/223
Dewey (Thomas E.) Fund, NYC, 3/224
D H J Fdn., NYC, 3/225
Dial (Morse G.) Fdn., NYC, 3/226
Diamond (Aaron) Fdn., NYC, 4/002
Diamond (Diana & Theodore) Fdn., NYC, 4/002
Diamond Family Fdn., NYC, 4/002
Diamond (Philip & Gussie) Fdn., NYC, 4/003
Diamond Jubilee Fund of King Solomon Lodge, NYC, 4/005
Diarbekirian Fdn., NYC, 4/005
Dickenson (Harriet Ford) Fdn., NYC, 4/006
Dickey (Charles D.) & Catherine C. Dickey Charitable Trust, NYC, 4/007
Dietz (Arthur O.) & Sarah G. Dietz Fdn., NYC, 4/008
Di Giacomo (William A.) Fdn., NYC, 4/008
Digney (Harry P.) Fdn., Syracuse, 4/008
Dillon Fund, NYC, 4/008
Dillon (Robert E.) Fdn., Buffalo, 4/010
Dillon (Bertha)--Susan Douglass Fdn., NYC, 4/011
Di Loreto Fdn., Jamaica, 4/011
Dixon Educational Trust, NYC, 4/012
Dixon (Peter T.) Fdn., NYC, 4/012
Dixon (Hugo) Trust, NYC, 4/013
D.M. Fdn., NYC, 4/014
Doane (William H.) Trust, NYC, 4/014
Dobrow Fdn., NYC, 4/015
Dobson Fdn., NYC, 4/016
Dodge Charitable Trust, NYC, 4/017
Dodge (William H.) Trust of 12/28/44 for Y.W.C.A. of Niagara Falls, Buffalo, 4/018
Doering Family Fdn., NYC, 4/019
Doft (Beryl H.) Fdn., Lawrence, 4/019
Doherty (Henry L. & Grace) Charitable Fdn., NYC, 4/020
Doherty (Henry L.) Educational Fdn., NYC, 4/022
Dolan Fdn., Syracuse, 4/024
Dolan (E. John) Fdn., Bronx, 4/025
Dolgin Fdn., Brooklyn, 4/025
Dolkart-Bernstein Charitable Trust, NYC, 4/026
Doll Fdn., NYC, 4/026
Dollinger (Lewis L., Jr. & Katherine) Charitable Trust, Rochester, 4/026
Donmarel Fdn., Jamestown, 4/028
Donnell Fdn., NYC, 4/029
Donovan (J. Timothy) Fdn., NYC, 4/029
Dorne (Albert) Memorial Fdn., NYC, 4/030
Dorr Fdn., NYC, 4/030
Dorsky (Samuel) Fdn., NYC, 4/031
Doubleday (Russell & Janet) Fund, NYC, 4/032
Doughnut Fdn., NYC, 4/032
Douglas (Hunter) Fdn., NYC, 4/033
Douglas (Leonard & Elaine) Fdn., NYC, 4/033
Dowley (Roy) Fdn., Syracuse, 4/033
Downtown Brooklyn Development Committee, Brooklyn, 4/035
Downe Fdn., NYC, 4/036
Doyle Fdn., NYC, 4/037
Drachman Fdn., NYC, 4/038
Draddy (Vincent De Paul) Fdn., NYC, 4/038
Dramatists Guild Fund, NYC, 4/039
Drafer (Mary Childs) Fund, NYC, 4/040
Dreier Fdn., NYC, 4/041
Dreitzer (Albert J.) Fdn., NYC, 4/042
Dreyfus (Camille & Henry) Fdn., NYC, 4/042
Dreyfus (Max & Victoria) Fdn., Bronxville, 4/044
Dreyfus Medical Fdn., NYC, 4/045
Dryer (Leora M.) Trust f/b Notre Dame de Paris Fund, Rochester, 4/046
DSB Fdn., NYC, 4/047
Duberstein (Mitchell & Lillian) Fdn., NYC, 4/047
Dubin (Abe & Henny) Fdn., NYC, 4/048
Dubin (Elinor) Memorial Fdn., New Rochelle, 4/049
Dublin Fund, NYC, 4/050

DuBois (Peter & Maria) Fdn., NYC, 4/051
Ducks Unlimited Fdn., NYC, 4/051
Duffy (George) Fdn., NYC, 4/052
Dukas Memorial Fund, NYC, 4/055
Duke (Doris) Fdn., NYC, 4/055
Dula (Caleb C. & Julia W.) Educational & Charitable Fdn., NYC, 4/057
Barry (Charles Dummer & Ida Morton) Fdn., NYC, 4/061
Dun & Bradstreet Fdn., NYC, 4/061
Dunkak Aid Fund, NYC, 4/063
Hines (Duncan) Fdn., Ithaca, 4/064
Dunlap (Charles J.) Endowment Fund, NYC, 4/065
Dunlap (Charles J.) Memorial Fund, NYC, 4/065
Milbank (Dunlevy) Fdn., NYC, 4/066
DuNouy (Pierre LeComte) American Fdn., NYC, 4/066
DuNouy (Pierre LeComte) French Fdn., NYC, 4/067
Dunphy Fdn., NYC, 4/068
Dunwody (William Elliott) Jr. Fdn., NYC, 4/069
Duplan Corporation Fdn. Trust, NYC, 4/069
Du Pont (A. Rhett) Trust, NYC, 4/070
du Pont (Francis I.) & Co. Charitable Trust, NYC, 4/071
Durand (Samuel E.) Charitable Trust, Rochester, 4/072
Durham (Rosalie & Stanley) Fdn., Rye, 4/073
Durst Fdn., NYC, 4/073
Dushey Family Fdn., Brooklyn, 4/075
Dworkin Fdn., NYC, 4/076
Dyett (Herbert T.) Fdn., Rome, 4/076
Dym (Allan) Fdn., NYC, 4/077
Dynaton Fdn., NYC, 4/078
Dyson Fdn., NYC, 4/078
Dyson Fund, NYC, 4/079
Dzus (William) Fund, West Islip, 4/081
Eagle Fdn., Brooklyn, 4/081
East Island Planning Corporation, NYC, 4/081
East Main Fdn., NYC, 4/082
East River Fdn., NYC, 4/082
Eastman Kodak Charitable Trust, Rochester, 4/083
Eastman (Lucius & Eva) Fund, NYC, 4/084
Eberstadt (Vera & Walter) Fdn., NYC, 4/085
Eckhouse (Joseph L.) Fdn., NYC, 4/086
E. D. Fdn., NYC, 4/086
Edanros Research Fdn., White Plains, 4/087
Eddy (Russell J.) Fdn., NYC, 4/089
Edelman (Ethel & Irvin) Fdn., NYC, 4/089
Edelstein (George) Fdn., Bronx, 4/089
Edersheim Fdn., NYC, 4/090
Edipa Fdn., NYC, 4/091
Edmonds (Dean S.) Fdn., NYC, 4/092
Educational Facilities Laboratories, NYC, 4/092
Educational Fdn. of Theta Delta Chi, NYC, 4/098
Educational Opportunity Fund, NYC, 4/099
Edwards Educational Fund, NYC, 4/099
Edwards Fdn., Harrison, 4/100
Edwards Fdn., NYC, 4/100
Edwards Fdn., Syracuse, 4/101
Hammer (G. A.) E. E. L. Fdn., Patchoque, 4/102
Ehrenkranz (Joel & Anne) Fdn., NYC, 4/102
Ehrlich (Doris & Nathan) Fdn., Bronx, 4/103
Ehrman (Fred & Susan) Fdn., NYC, 4/103
Ehrman (Sender) Fdn., NYC, 4/104
Ehrmann (Herman & Amelia S.) Fdn., NYC, 4/104
Eichler Fdn., Monsey, 4/105
Einbender (Alvin H.) Fdn., Scarsdale, 4/106
Electrical & Electronic Research Fdn., Westbury, 4/106
Eisemann (Henry G. & Florence E.) Fdn., Hicksville, 4/107
Eisenberg (Alex & Irene) Fdn., NYC, 4/108
Eisenberg (Joseph H.) Fdn., Sands Point, 4/108
Eisenberg (Moe) Memorial Fdn., Brooklyn, 4/109
Eisenhart (Edward C.) Fund, Rochester, 4/109

Frankel (Ferdinand & Lucille) Fdn., NYC, 5/037

Frankel (William & Selma) Fdn., NYC, 5/039

Franklin Fdn., Syracuse, 5/039

Freed Fdn., Brooklyn, 5/040

Freedman (Andrew) Home, NYC, 5/041

Freedman (Harry A. & Etta) Fdn., NYC, 5/043

Freedman (Louis & Bert) Fdn., NYC, 5/043

Freeman Fdn., Bronx, 5/044

Freeman (Merrill D. & Elizabeth T.) Fdn., NYC, 5/045

French (D. E.) Fdn., Auburn, 5/046

Frese (Arnold D.) Fdn., NYC, 5/047

Freund (Joseph L. & Ray L.) Fdn., NYC, 5/048

Freund (Patricia W. & John H.) Fdn., NYC, 5/049

Fribourg Fdn., NYC, 5/049

Frick Art Reference Library, NYC, 5/050

Fried Fdn., NYC, 5/051

Fried (Moses) Fdn., NYC, 5/051

Friedberg (C. K. & G.) Fdn., NYC, 5/052

Friedlander (Marcus S. & Madeline S.) Charitable Trust, NYC, 5/052

Friedlaender (Eugen) Fdn., NYC, 5/053

Friedman (Arthur) Fdn., NYC, 5/054

Friedman (Eugene W. & Geraldine) Fdn., NYC, 5/054

Friedman (Howard & Lee) Fdn., NYC, 5/055

Friedman (Joseph & Gertrude) Fdn., Jamaica, 5/056

Friedman (L. & M.) Fdn. Trust, NYC, 5/056

Friedman (Leopold & Ruth) Fdn., NYC, 5/057

Friedman (Norman P.) Fdn., Babylon, 5/058

Friedman (Paul & Wanda) Fdn., NYC, 5/058

Friedman (Ruth E. & Ralph) Fdn., NYC, 5/059

Friedman (William R. & Erica) Fdn., NYC, 5/060

Frieman (Reuben & Ethel) Fdn., NYC, 5/060

Friends of the Philippines Fdn., NYC, 5/061

Friendship Builders, Utica, 5/061

Frindel Fdn., NYC, 5/061

Froelich (Louis B. & Harry S.) Fdn., NYC, 5/062

Frohlich (Ludwig W.) Charitable Trust, NYC, 5/063

Fromer (Leon & Gina) Fdn., NYC, 5/063

Fruchthandler (Alex & Ruth) Fdn., Brooklyn, 5/064

Frost - Corwin Fdn., Bronxville, 5/065

FRU Fdn., NYC, 5/066

Frueauff (Charles A.) Fdn., NYC, 5/067

Frumkes (Alana & Lewis) Fdn., NYC, 5/070

Fuchsberg Family Fdn., NYC, 5/070

Fuhrman Charitable Fdn., NYC, 5/071

Fuld Fdn., NYC, 5/072

Fuller (Wayne) Fdn., NYC, 5/072

Fullerton Fdn., NYC, 5/073

Stempfle (Evelyn E.) Fund, Gloversville, 5/073

Fulton (Hugh) & Jessie C. Fulton Fdn., NYC, 5/073

Fund for Area Planning and Development, NYC, 5/074

Fund for Astrophysical Research, NYC, 5/075

Fund for Contemporary Music, NYC, 5/076

Fund for New Priorities in America, NYC, 5/076

Fund for Peaceful Atomic Development, NYC, 5/076

Furbay (Doctor John H.) International Scholarship Fund, West Hempstead, 5/077

Furman Family Charitable Trust, NYC, 5/077

Furman (Saul) & Anne L. Furman Fdn., NYC, 5/078

Gadebusch Fdn., NYC, 5/079

Gaffney (Miller S. & Adelaide S.) Fdn., Binghamton, 5/079

Gage Fund, Pound Ridge, 5/080

Gaisman Fdn., Hartsdale, 5/080

Galasso Fdn., Cobleskill, 5/081

Gallagher (Alice P.) Fdn., Mineola, 5/082

Gallery (Arnot Art) Association, Elmira, 5/083

Galpeer Fdn., NYC, 5/083

Galuten Fdn., NYC, 5/083

Galewitz Family Fdn. Trust, NYC, 5/084

Gambrell (Sarah Belk) Fdn., Charlotte, N.C., 5/085

Ganek (Howard & Judith) Fdn., NYC, 5/085

Gannett (Frank E.) Newspaper Fdn., Rochester, 5/086

Gannett (Frank) Newspaperboy Scholarships, Rochester, 5/091

Gantz (Philip & Emanuel) Fdn., Hartsdale, 5/092

Garay (Mary & Arnold) Memorial Fdn., Hewlett, 5/093

Garbarino (Helen & Charles) Fdn., NYC, 5/093

Gardner (Robert L.) Fdn., NYC, 5/094

Garfinkle (Henry & Anne) Fdn., NYC, 5/095

Garlock Charitable Trust, Rochester, 5/096

Garner Fdn., NYC, 5/097

Garrett (Ann & Richard) Fdn., Rochester, 5/097

Garrett (Margaret Dodge) & Johnson Garrett Fdn., NYC, 5/098

Garrison (Lena Howard) Educational Trust, Binghamton, 5/098

Garrison (Lena Howard) Religious Trust, Binghamton, 5/099

Gartman Fdn., Mt. Kisco, 5/100

Gary Fdn., NYC, 5/101

Gaston (George A.) Charitable Trust, NYC, 5/102

Gateposts Fdn., NYC, 5/103

Gaylord Fund, NYC, 5/104

G. D. S. Fdn., NYC, 5/106

Gebhard-Gourgaud (Eva) Fdn., NYC, 5/107

GED Fdn., Rye, 5/107

Geer (M. L. & F. G.) Fdn., NYC, 5/108

Geffen (Florence & Maxwell) Fdn., NYC, 5/108

Gefen (Rosalind & Bernard) Fdn., Albany, 5/109

Geisman (Jess & Stella) Fdn., NYC, 5/110

Gelb (Lawrence M.) Fdn., NYC, 5/111

Genealogical Study, Rochester, 5/112

Geller (Monroe) Charity Fdn., NYC, 5/112

Gellert Family Charitable Trust, NYC, 5/113

General Cable Fund, NYC, 5/114

General Electric Employees Share Fund of Schenectady, N.Y., Schenectady, 5/115

General Electric Fdn., Schenectady, 5/119

General Foods Fund, White Plains, 5/123

General Host Corp. Employee's Trust Estate, NYC, 5/127

General Telephone & Electronics Fdn., NYC, 5/128

Genorese Family Fdn., Long Island City, 5/134

Georgian Charitable Trust, NYC, 5/135

Georgia Warm Springs Fdn., NYC, 5/136

Gepeto Charitable Trust, NYC, 5/136

Gerli (Charles L. & Elizabeth P.) Fdn., NYC, 5/136

Gerli (P. & P.) Fdn., NYC, 5/137

Gerstenzang (Leo & Ziuta) Fdn., NYC, 5/138

Gettner (Clare & Herman) Fdn., NYC, 5/139

Getzler Fdn., NYC, 5/140

Gevirman (Jerome) Fdn., NYC, 5/140

Geyer (B.B.) Fdn., NYC, 5/141

G G D Fdn., NYC, 5/142

G G M Fdn., NYC, 5/143

Giannelli (S.) & S. Ayers Trust for New York Cardio-Respiratory Center, NYC, 5/143

Gibber (Louis & Molly) Fdn., Kiamesha Lake, 5/144

Gibbs Brothers Fdn., NYC, 5/145

Giebel Fdn., NYC, 5/147

Gies (William J.) Fdn. for Advancement of Dentistry, NYC, 5/147

Gifford (Rosamond) Charitable Fdn., Syracuse, 5/148

Gilbert Fdn., NYC, 5/151

Gilbert & Snyder Fdn., NYC, 5/151

Gillen (Conrad H. & Anna Belle) Trust Fund, Gloversville, 5/152

Gillam (Beatrice Arkell) Memorial Scholarship Fund, NYC, 5/153

Gillfield Fdn., NYC, 5/154

Gimbel (Bernard F. & Alva B.) Fdn., NYC, 5/155

Gimbel Brothers Fdn., NYC, 5/156

Gimbel (Bruce A.) Fdn., NYC, 5/156

Gimbel (Sophie & Adam) Fdn., NYC, 5/157

Gimbel (Elinor Steiner) Fund, NYC, 5/158

Gimbel-Saks Fdn., NYC, 5/158

Gimbel-Saks Trust Fund, NYC, 5/159

Ginkel Fdn., Rochester, 5/159

Ginsberg (Harry) Family Fdn., NYC, 5/160

Ginsberg (Louis) Scholarship Fund, NYC, 5/161

Ginsberg (Moses) Family Fdn., NYC, 5/161

Ginsberg (Teresa & Jack) Fdn., NYC, 5/162

Ginsburg (Arnold Lewis) Fdn., NYC, 5/164

Gish (Lillian) Fdn., NYC, 5/164

Gitenstein (Kermit) Fdn., Atlantic Beach, 5/165

Gitlow (Samuel & Esther) Fdn., NYC, 5/165

Gittleson Fdn., New Hyde Park, 5/165

Gittleson (Frank) Fdn., Hicksville, 5/166

Gittlin (Richard D.) Fdn., NYC, 5/167

Gladstein (Mathew & Edythe) Fdn., NYC, 5/167

G. L. & C. Fdn., NYC, 5/168

Gleason (James E. & Eleanor) Trust, Rochester, 5/168

Gleason Works Fdn., Rochester, 5/170

Gleason Fund Life Benefit Plan, Rochester, 5/170

Glekel (Jacob S.) Fdn., Belle Harbor, 5/173

Root Glen Fdn., Clinton, 5/173

Glenwood Fdn., NYC, 5/174

Glickenhaus Fdn., Scarsdale, 5/174

Glickstein Fdn., NYC, 5/175

Glorney (Corlette) Fdn., NYC, 5/175

Gluck (Joseph) Fdn., NYC, 5/176

Gluck (Max H.) Fdn., NYC, 5/177

Gluckman Fdn., NYC, 5/177

God Bless America Fund, NYC, 5/178

Gadfly Fdn., NYC, 5/178

Goelet (Anne Marie) Fdn., NYC, 5/178

Goelet (Francis) Fdn., NYC, 5/180

Goelet (John) Fdn., NYC, 5/181

Goelet (Robert G.) Fdn., NYC, 5/183

Gold (David H.) Fdn., Hewlett, 5/185

Gold (Harry) Research Fund, NYC, 5/186

Gold (Max & Rosa) Fdn., NYC, 5/186

Goldbaum (Arnold & Marjorie) Fdn., Roslyn, 5/187

Goldberg (Henry L.) Fdn., NYC, 5/187

Goldberger (Edward & Marjorie) Fdn., NYC, 5/188

Golden (John) Fund, NYC, 5/189

Goldberg (Samuel) & Sons Fdn., NYC, 5/191

Goldberger Fdn., New Rochelle, 5/192

Golden (Sibyl & William T.) Fdn., NYC, 5/191

Goldenberg (Lewis & Helen) Fdn., NYC, 5/193

Goldfarb (Bertha & Jack) Fdn., NYC, 5/194

Goldfein (Philip & Pauline) Fdn., NYC, 5/195

Goldfine (William) Fdn., NYC, 5/195

Goldin (Joan & Jerrold) Fdn., NYC, 5/196

Golding (Jerrold R. & Shirley) Fdn., NYC, 5/196

Golding (Lawrence) Fdn., NYC, 5/197

Golding (Samuel H. & Sue) Fdn., NYC, 5/197

Goldman (Louis & Dorothy) Fdn., NYC, 5/198

Goldman (Morton R. & Dorothy I.) Fdn., NYC, 5/198

Goldman (William P.) & Brothers Fdn., NYC, 5/199

Goldrich (Nathan J. & Helen) Fdn., NYC, 5/200

Goldring Fdn., NYC, 5/200

Goldschmidt Fdn., NYC, 5/201

Goldsmith (Clarence E.) Fund, NYC, 5/202

Goldsmith Fdn., NYC, 5/202

Goldsmith (Bernard M.) Fdn., Pelham Manor, 5/203

Goldsmith (C. Gerald & Barbara) Fdn., NYC, 5/204

Goldsmith (Horace W.) Fdn., NYC, 5/205

Harris, Upham Fdn., NYC, 6/122
Harris Trust, Glen Head, 6/122
Harrow School Fdn., NYC, 6/123
Hart (Alfred & Ida) Fdn., Rochester, 6/123
Harteveldt Fdn., NYC, 6/123
Hartford (John A.) Fdn., NYC, 6/124
Hartman (Alexander & Sima) Family Fdn.,
    Bronx, 6/125
Hartman (Jesse) Fdn., NYC, 6/126
Hartman (William H.) Trust, Rochester, 6/127
Harweb Fdn., NYC, 6/127
Haskel (William & Rose) Memorial Fdn., NYC,
    6/128
Hatfield (William B.) Fdn., Melville, 6/128
Hauppauge Community Scholarship & Loan
    Fund, Hauppauge, 6/129
Haupt Fdn., NYC, 6/130
Hausman (M.) & Sons Fdn., NYC, 6/131
Haussamen (Carol W.) Fdn., NYC, 6/131
Haven of Peace, Owego, 6/132
Havens Relief Fund Society, NYC, 6/132
Hawes (F. & G.) Fdn., NYC, 6/137
Hayes (Arthur & Florence) Fdn., NYC, 6/138
Hayes (William J. & Harriet A.) Trust Fund,
    Troy, 6/138
Hays (Florence & James) Fdn., NYC, 6/139
Hazan (Alfred) Fdn., NYC, 6/140
Hazan (Fred) Fdn., NYC, 6/140
Hazen (Joseph H.) Fdn., NYC, 6/141
Hearst Fdn., NYC, 6/142
Hecht-Parents Magazine Fdn. for Child
    Welfare, NYC, 6/143
Heckscher Fdn. for Children, NYC, 6/144
Heermance Memorial Library, Coxsackie, 6/147
Heidenberg (J. & S.) Fdn., NYC, 6/147
Held Family Corporation, Jericho, 6/147
Hefferman (Joseph & Marion) Fund, NYC,
    6/148
Heights Charitable Fdn., NYC, 6/148
Heimerdinger (Jane R.) Fdn., NYC, 6/149
Heimerdinger (John F. & Suzanne S.) Fdn.,
    NYC, 6/150
Heinemann (Lore & Rudolf) Fdn., NYC,
    6/151
Heineman Fdn. for Research, Educational,
    Charitable & Scientific Purposes, NYC,
    6/151
Heinze Fdn., NYC, 6/152
Trites (Florence Smith) Trust f/b/o Searing
    Memorial Methodist Church, NYC, 6/153
Helene Fdn., NYC, 6/154
Heller Brothers Fdn., NYC, 6/154
Heller (Max & Rose) & Anna Heller Fdn.,
    NYC, 6/155
Heller (William) Fdn., NYC, 6/155
Hellman (Paul) Fdn., NYC, 6/156
Hellman (Richard) Fdn., Scarsdale, 6/157
Helm Fdn., NYC, 6/158
H E M Charitable Trust, Port Washington,
    6/158
Belding Heminway Fdn., NYC, 6/159
Hemmerdinger Fdn., NYC, 6/161
Berish Henckes Fdn., Jamaica, 6/161
Henderson (William D. & Marion C.) Fdn.,
    Rochester, 6/161
Henderson (William J.) Memorial Fund, NYC,
    6/162
Hendrickson Bros. Fdn., Valley Stream, 6/162
Hendrickson (Arthur J.) Fdn., Valley Stream,
    6/164
Henfield Fdn., NYC, 6/165
Henlen Charitable Trust, Scarsdale, 6/166
Hennessy Fdn., NYC, 6/167
Henry Fdn., Great Neck, 6/168
Henshel Fdn., NYC, 6/168
Henshel (Colonel Harry D.) Fdn., NYC, 6/168
Hentz (H.) Company Fdn., NYC, 6/169
Herbert (Katharine) Fund, NYC, 6/169
Hermitage Fdn. Trust, NYC, 6/169
Heroy (W. W. & R. L.) Fdn., Huntington,
    6/170
Herrman (Herbert Erlanger) Fdn., Larchmont,
    6/171
Herrmann (Vincent H.) Fdn., NYC, 6/171
Hersheopf (Rose) Cancer Fdn., NYC, 6/171
Herskowitz (Marvin J.) Fdn., NYC, 6/172

Hertz (Helmut & Ruth) Charitable Trust,
    Rochester, 6/172
Hertzberg (Benjamin & Lilian) Fdn., NYC,
    6/173
Herzfeld Fdn., NYC, 6/174
Herzig (Leonard & Margot) Fdn., NYC, 6/174
Herzog (Edwin H. & Helen Louise) Fdn., NYC,
    6/175
Hess (Audrey S. & Thomas B.) Fdn., NYC,
    6/176
Hess (Haskel) Fdn., Manhasset, 6/178
Hessberg (Mrs. Samuel) Memorial Scholarship
    Fund, Albany, 6/178
Hettinger Fdn., NYC, 6/178
Hewitt (Bernard & Florence) Fdn., Jamaica,
    6/180
Hewlett Fdn., Valley Stream, 6/181
Heyman Family Fund, NYC, 6/181
Heyman (George H. & Edythe F.) Family Fdn.,
    NYC, 6/182
Heymann (Eric--Emily) Fdn., Forest Hills,
    6/182
Heymsfeld (Eleanor & Ralph) Fdn., Woodmere,
    6/183
Hidary (Jacob) Fdn., NYC, 6/183
Higgins (Walter J.) Research & Charitable
    Fund, Hempstead, 6/184
High Winds Fund, NYC, 6/184
Hilary Fund, NYC, 6/185
Hilf Fdn., Brooklyn, 6/186
Hill (Eleanor K.) Animal Rescue, Binghamton,
    6/186
Hill (John & Helen) Fdn., NYC, 6/186
Hill (John W.) Fdn., NYC, 6/187
Hill (June) Fund, NYC, 6/188
Hillaire Fdn., NYC, 6/188
Hillman (Alex) Family Fdn., NYC, 6/188
Hillman (Carol & Joel) Fdn., NYC, 6/190
Hillson Fund, NYC, 6/190
Himoff (Jack & Dorothy) Fdn., Long Island
    City, 6/190
Hinerfeld Trust, Larchmont, 6/191
Hinman (Hazen B.) Sr. Fdn., Rome, 6/192
Hill (The Savage) Fdn., NYC, 6/193
Hirschfeld (Isador & Pauline) Fdn., NYC,
    6/193
Hirschhorn (Jean & Fred) Jr. Fdn., NYC,
    6/194
Hirshhorn (Joseph H.) Fdn., NYC, 6/195
Hinrichs (Hans & Minnie) Fdn., NYC, 6/199
Hirsch (Harold E.) Fdn., NYC, 6/200
Hirsch (Howard C.) Fdn., NYC, 6/201
Hirsch (Mary & Alexander) Fdn., NYC, 6/202
Hirsch (Regina) Fdn., Brooklyn, 6/202
Hirsh (Steven S.) Charitable Trust, NYC,
    6/203
Hirschfeld (Herman) Fdn., NYC, 6/204
Hirst (Edward H. & Edna J.) Fund, NYC,
    6/205
Historical Research Fdn., NYC, 6/206
H L M Fdn., Great Neck, 6/206
Hoard (Mary Tucker) & Sarah Tucker Wilson
    Memorial Fund, Lockport, 6/207
Hochschild Fund, NYC, 6/207
Hochstein Fdn., NYC, 6/209
Hodes Family Fdn., NYC, 6/210
Hodes (Robert M. & Doris B.) Fdn., Elmsford,
    6/211
Hoffman Fdn., NYC, 6/212
Hoffman (Byrd) Fdn., NYC, 6/213
Hoffman (Josef & Violet) Fdn., NYC, 6/214
Hoffman (Leon) Fdn., Scarsdale, 6/214
Hofheimer (Nathan) Fdn., NYC, 6/215
Hogate Fdn., Mt. Kisco, 6/216
Holiatric Fdn., Albany, 6/217
Holland Lodge Fdn., NYC, 6/217
Hollins Fdn., NYC, 6/217
Holman Libby Fdn., NYC, 6/218
Holmiel Fdn., NYC, 6/218
Holstein Fdn., Baldwinsville, 6/219
Holtzmann (Jacob L. & Lillian) Fdn., NYC,
    6/220
Holzer (Marcell M.) Fund for Education, NYC,
    6/220
Honig Family Fdn., Lawrence, 6/220
Hood (John & Anne) Trust, NYC, 6/221

Hooker (Roger Wolcott) Fdn., NYC, 6/221
Home for Aged People, Croton, 6/222
Honig Family Fdn., NYC, 6/222
Honig (Jack L.) Fdn., NYC, 6/223
Honig (Paul) Fdn., NYC, 6/224
Hoover (Herbert) Fdn., NYC, 6/225
Hope Fdn., NYC, 6/226
Hopeman Memorial Fund, Rochester, 6/227
Hopewell Fdn., NYC, 6/227
Horizon Two Thousand, NYC, 6/228
Hornblow Fdn., NYC, 6/228
Horowitz (Stanley & Ruth) Fdn., Great Neck,
    6/228
Horney (Edward & Edna Mae) Fdn., Old
    Westbury, 6/229
Hornung (Gerald & Virginia) Family Fdn.,
    NYC, 7/000
Horowitch (Maurice & Sheldon) Fdn.,
    Binghamton, 7/000
Horowitz (Louis J. & Mary E.) Fdn., NYC,
    7/001
Hospitalization Trust Fund of the Electrical
    Manufacturing Industry, Flushing, 7/001
Horer (John C.) Fdn., NYC, 7/001
Houdaille Fdn., Buffalo, 7/003
Harris (John Houghton) Fdn., NYC, 7/004
Howard Fdn., New Rochelle, 7/004
Howard (Bernard) Fdn., NYC, 7/005
Howard Memorial Fund, NYC, 7/005
Howard (Loretta H.) Charitable & Educational
    Fund, NYC, 7/007
Howatt (Glenn N.) Fdn., NYC, 7/008
Howe (David A.) Public Library, Wellsville,
    7/008
H R M Fdn., NYC, 7/008
H S G Fdn., NYC, 7/009
Hubbard (Thomas J. & Anne A.) Charitable
    Trust, NYC, 7/011
Hubbard (G. Morrison) Jr. Fdn., NYC, 7/011
Hubshman (Henry & Sylvia) Fdn., NYC,
    7/012
Hughes (Ethel Charlotte) Testamentary Trust,
    Hamilton, 7/013
Hughes (Doctor Joseph E.) Scholarship Fund,
    White Plains, 7/013
Hugoton Fdn., NYC, 7/014
Huguenot Historical Association Fdn., New
    Rochelle, 7/014
Hulbert (Nila B.) Fdn., Oneota, 7/015
Hull (Elizabeth)--Kate Warriner Award, NYC,
    7/015
Hull (Roger & Rosalie) Fdn., NYC, 7/016
Humanist Trust, Flushing, 7/016
Hunt (Richard M.) Fdn., NYC, 7/017
Hunter (Graham) Fdn., NYC, 7/018
Huntington (Archer M.) No. 6, NYC, 7/018
Huntington (Archer M.) Charitable Trust A,
    NYC, 7/019
Huntington (Archer M.) Charitable Trust B,
    NYC, 7/020
Hull (Helen Huntington) Fund, NYC, 7/021
Huntington's Chorea Fdn., NYC, 7/021
Humanities Fund, NYC, 7/022
Humanities Old Age Fdn., NYC, 7/023
Hunter Fdn., NYC, 7/024
Huntington Hartford Family Fund, NYC,
    7/025
Huntington Hartford Fdn., NYC, 7/025
Huntington Hospital, NYC, 7/026
Hurley Recreation Association, Hurley, 7/026
Hutcheson (Marjory Weld) Memorial Fund,
    NYC, 7/026
Hutchins (Frank A.) Trust Fund, Rochester,
    7/027
Hutchins (F. Irving) Charitable Trust,
    Rochester, 7/028
Hutchins (Mark J.) Fdn., NYC, 7/029
Hutner (Bernie) Fdn., NYC, 7/030
Hutton (Edward F.) Fdn., NYC, 7/031
Hyams Fdn., NYC, 7/031
Hyams (Estelle T.) Fdn., NYC, 7/031
I B E W Local #836, Potsdam, 7/032
I F F Fdn., NYC, 7/032
I & L Association Fdn., NYC, 7/033
I. M. M. Charities, NYC, 7/035
Iglehart Health Fund, NYC, 7/036

Indian Head Fdn., NYC, 7/037
Ingersoll Rand Fund, NYC, 7/038
Inglenook Fdn., NYC, 7/039
Inisfad Fdn., NYC, 7/040
Inmont Fdn., NYC, 7/042
Institute of Fiscal & Political Education, NYC, 7/042
Institute of Oceanography & Marine Biology, Oyster Bay, 7/043
Institute of Society, Ethics & Life Sciences, Hastings-on-Hudson, 7/044
Interchange Fdn., NYC, 7/044
International Chamber Music Fdn., NYC, 7/045
International Film Fdn., NYC, 7/045
International Fund for Monuments, NYC, 7/045
International Rowing Course Fdn., NYC, 7/046
International Society for the History of Ideas, NYC, 7/047
Interreligious Fdn. for Community Organization, NYC, 7/047
Interstate Fdn., NYC, 7/048
Irish Emigrant Society of New York, NYC, 7/049
Iroki Fdn., NYC, 7/049
Irving One Wall Street Fdn., NYC, 7/050
Irwin (Harry & Florence) Fdn., Brooklyn, 7/051
Isaacs (I. Robert & Sophie) Fdn., NYC, 7/052
Isaacson (Reuben & Lillian) Charitable Fdn., NYC, 7/052
Isaacson (Joseph & Evelyn) Fund, NYC, 7/053
Isaacson (Nathan & Lena) Fdn., NYC, 7/054
Isak (Mishpahat) & Frieda Fish, NYC, 7/055
Iselin (Alan V.) Family Fdn., Albany, 7/055
Islands Research Fdn., NYC, 7/056
Israel (Abraham Ben) Memorial Fund, Long Beach, 7/056
I T T Fdn., NYC, 7/057
I T T Rayonier Fdn., NYC, 7/057
Ittleson Beneficial Fund, NYC, 7/058
Ittleson Family Fdn., NYC, 7/059
Ivanhoe Benevolences, Brooklyn, 7/061
Ivy Fund, NYC, 7/061
Ix (Helen & William E.) Charitable Trust, NYC, 7/062
Jackbryer Fdn., Merrick, 7/063
Jackson Hole, NYC, 7/064
Jackson (Peter A. H. & Esther) Memorial, NYC, 7/066
Jacobs (Bernard & Betty) Fdn., NYC, 7/068
Jacobs (Charles B. & Irene B.) Fdn., NYC, 7/068
Jacobs (Harry & Rose) Fdn., NYC, 7/069
Jacobson Family Trust, NYC, 7/069
Jacobson (Franz & Rose) Fdn., NYC, 7/070
Jacobus (Daniel C.) Cemetery Trust, NYC, 7/070
Jaffe (Teri & Leo) Fdn., NYC, 7/071
Jakobson (John R.) Fdn., NYC, 7/072
Jocobus Fdn., NYC, 7/072
Jackson (Adrian H.) Charitable Trust, NYC, 7/073
Jaffe (Natalie & Jeff) Fdn., Hewlett Bay Park, 7/074
Jaffe (Sam) Fdn., Brooklyn, 7/074
Jaffin (George & Janet) Fdn., NYC, 7/074
Jaglom (Simon & Marie) Fdn., NYC, 7/075
Jamison (Margaret A.) Memorial, New Paltz, 7/075
Janin (Harry) Fdn., NYC, 7/076
Jandon Fdn., NYC, 7/077
Janel Fdn., NYC, 7/077
Janeway Fdn., NYC, 7/078
Japilan Fdn., NYC, 7/078
Jaspan (Joseph) Fdn., Woodmere, 7/079
J. C. Fdn., NYC, 7/079
Jeffee Fdn., NYC, 7/080
Jeffrey Fdn., NYC, 7/082
Jenrette (Richard Hampton) Fdn., NYC, 7/083
Jensam Fdn., NYC, 7/083
Jeroboam Fdn., NYC, 7/083
Jewish Children's Home of Rochester, N.Y., Rochester, 7/084

Jewish Philanthropic Fund of 1933, NYC, 7/085
J. & H. E. Fund, Fulton, 7/086
J. I. Fdn., NYC, 7/086
J. K. Fdn., NYC, 7/087
J. K. M. Fdn., NYC, 7/087
Jobarr Fdn., NYC, 7/088
Jockey Club Fdn., NYC, 7/088
Joffe (A. B.) Fdn., NYC, 7/089
Johns--Manville Fund, NYC, 7/090
Johnson (Mark & Hilda) Fdn., NYC, 7/091
Johnson (R. B.) Fdn., NYC, 7/091
Johnson (Margaret & Milton G.) Fdn., Hartsdale, 7/092
Johnson (Robert H.) Fdn., NYC, 7/092
Johnson (Walter L.) & Isabelle M. Johnson Fdn., NYC, 7/093
Johnstown Historical Society, Johnstown, 7/094
Johnson (Walter L.) & Isabelle M. Johnson Fdn., NYC, 7/094
Johnston (James Graham) & Marcelle Launay Johnstion Fdn., NYC, 7/095
Johnston (Andrew M.) Award Fund, Albany, 7/096
Joint Fund for Higher Education, NYC, 7/096
Joley Fdn., Pittsford, 7/097
Jonas (Donald & Barbara) Fdn., NYC, 7/097
Jonas (Harriet H.) Fdn., NYC, 7/097
Jonas (James A.) Fdn., NYC, 7/098
Jondith Fund, NYC, 7/098
Jonas (Louis August) Fdn., Walden, 7/099
Jones (Daisy Marquis) Fdn., Rochester, 7/100
Jones (Elizabeth L.) Charitable Trust, Rochester, 7/101
Jones (W. Alton) Fdn., NYC, 7/101
Joseph Family Fdn., NYC, 7/103
Joseph (Dr. Rudolph) Fdn., Freeport, 7/103
Joselow Fdn., NYC, 7/104
Joyner (James Craig) Fdn., NYC, 7/105
J S O Fdn., Scarsdale, 7/105
Juberon Fdn., NYC, 7/106
Judelson (David N.) Family Charitable Trust, NYC, 7/106
Jurzykowski (Alfred) Fdn., NYC, 7/106
Justice Fdn., NYC, 7/108
K. A. in V. C. Fdn., Ithaca, 7/108
Kade (Max) Fdn., NYC, 7/108
Kaelber Fdn., Rochester, 7/112
Kafka (Melvin & Sylvia) Fdn., NYC, 7/113
Kahn (Harry & Margery) Fdn., NYC, 7/113
Kahn (Pauline & Henry L.) Fdn., NYC, 7/115
Kahn (Polly & Gilbert) Fdn., NYC, 7/115
Kahn (Sidney B.) Family Fdn., Woodmere, 7/116
Kaish Fdn., Long Island City, 7/116
Wood Kalb Fdn., Long Island City, 7/116
Kalish Fdn., NYC, 7/117
Kallir (Otto & Fanny) Fdn., NYC, 7/118
Kallish (Louis) Fdn., NYC, 7/118
Kalman Klein & David Teicholz Fdn., NYC, 7/119
Kalman Sunshine Fund, NYC, 7/119
Kalnick Fdn., NYC, 7/119
Kaltman Family Fdn., Long Island City, 7/120
Kamber (Abraham) Fdn., NYC, 7/120
Kamman (Frank F.) Cemetery Trust, Buffalo, 7/121
Kandell Fdn., NYC, 7/122
Kane Paper Corporation Scholarship Fund, Baldwin, 7/122
Kann Fdn., NYC, 7/123
Kanter-Kallman Fdn., NYC, 7/123
Kanter (Joseph) Memorial Fund, NYC, 7/124
Kantor (Lucille & Martin) Fdn., Great Neck, 7/125
Kaplan (Joseph A.) Fdn., Yonkers, 7/125
Kaplan (J. M.) Fund, NYC, 7/126
Kaplan (M. C.) Fund, White Plains, 7/129
Kaplan (M. P.) Family Fdn., NYC, 7/130
Karasik Brothers Fdn., Chicago, Illinois, 7/130
Karagheusian (Howard) Commemorative Corp., NYC, 7/130
Karasik (Marjorie & Charles) Fdn., NYC, 7/134
Karger (Eleanor G. & John S.) Fdn., NYC, 7/134

Karlson (George C.) Fdn., Hicksville, 7/135
Karp Fdn., NYC, 7/135
Karpas Charitable Trust, NYC, 7/136
Karpas (Irving D. & Janet S.) Fdn., NYC, 7/137
Katcoff Family Fdn., Patchoque, 7/138
Kates Fdn., NYC, 7/138
Kates (Barbara Anne) Fdn., NYC, 7/138
Kates (Louis & Mildred) Fdn., NYC, 7/139
Katz (Louis & Ida) Fdn., NYC, 7/139
Katzenbach (L. E.) Fund, NYC, 7/141
Katzenstein (Eric & Ruth) Fdn., NYC, 7/141
Katzenstein (Theo) Memorial Fund, NYC, 7/142
Katzin Fdn., NYC, 7/143
Kaufmann (Evelyn & Fred) Fdn., NYC, 7/144
Kaufman (Henry & Elaine) Fdn., NYC, 7/144
Kaufman (Irving & Gladys) Fdn., NYC, 7/145
Kaufmann (Nanette & Richard K.) Fdn., NYC, 7/147
Kavir Institute, NYC, 7/147
Kavookjian (Haik & Alice) Fdn., NYC, 7/147
Kavy Fdn., Brooklyn, 7/148
Kayden Fdn., Great Neck, 7/149
Kaye (Louis C.) Fdn., NYC, 7/149
Kearney-National Fdn., NYC, 7/150
Keats (Ezra Jack) Fdn., NYC, 7/151
Keck (William M.) Jr. Fdn., NYC, 7/151
Keeler (Gaynor) Trust, Albany, 7/152
Keenan (Delbert & Selma) Family Fdn., NYC, 7/153
Keeley (Calvin N.) Trust, 7/153
Keller Contribution Account, NYC, 7/153
Kellman (Rabbi Isaac) Fdn., NYC, 7/154
Kellogg Free Library, Cincinnatus, 7/155
Kelly (Daniel & Helen) Fdn., NYC, 7/156
Kemper (Richard M.) Fdn., Scarsdale, 7/157
Kempner (Paul & Nancy) Fdn., NYC, 7/158
Kend (David & Elaine) Fdn., Kings Point, 7/159
Kanmar Fdn., NYC, 7/159
Kennard (Charles W.) Fdn., NYC, 7/159
Kennedy (F. T.) Fdn., NYC, 7/160
Kennedy (Joseph E.) Fdn., NYC, 7/160
Kennedy (Joseph P.) Jr. Fdn., NYC, 7/161
Kenney (F. Donald) Fdn., NYC, 7/161
Kennedy (Laurence & Helen) Fdn., Mt. Kisco, 7/161
Kenton Fdn., NYC, 7/163
Kenwood Benevolent Society, Kenwood, 7/164
Kenyon College, NYC, 7/164
Kerbs (Jeanne E.) Fdn., NYC, 7/165
Keresey (Edward J.) Fdn., NYC, 7/166
Kerman (Rustam K.) Fdn., Albany, 7/166
Kern (George W.) Fdn., NYC, 7/167
Kern (George W.) & Lolita D. Kern Fdn., NYC, 7/168
Kern (Paul Emery) Fdn., NYC, 7/168
Kerry Fdn., NYC, 7/169
Kessel (Lawrence & Marie) Fdn., NYC, 7/170
Kevorkian Fdn., NYC, 7/170
Kibel Fdn., Bronx, 7/172
Kidde (Walter) Constructors Fdn., NYC, 7/172
Kiff (Charles Everett) Scholarship Fund, Delhi, 7/173
Kimbel (William & L. Maud) Fdn., 7/175
Kimelman (Oscar) Fdn., NYC, 7/175
Kimmelman Fdn., NYC, 7/176
Kings Daughters Home for Children, Cortland, 7/177
Kings Point Richmond Fdn., NYC, 7/178
Kingsley (The Stevens) Fdn., NYC, 7/179
Kingston Fdn., NYC, 7/180
Kinney (G. R.) Fdn., NYC, 7/181
Kirch (Hyman) Fdn., Brooklyn, 7/181
Kirschenbaum (Charles & Esther) Fdn., New Rochelle, 7/182
Kissam (Leo T.) Fdn., NYC, 7/183
Kissinger Family Fdn., Huntington Bay, 7/183
Kittay Fdn., NYC, 7/184
Kirschenbaum (Irving) Fdn., NYC, 7/185
Kirshen Fdn., NYC, 7/186
Kit-ed Fund, NYC, 7/186
Kiwanis (Elma) Youth Fdn., Elma, 7/187
Klau (David & Sadie) Fdn., NYC, 7/188

Klee Fund, NYC, 7/189
Kleiger Fdn., NYC, 7/190
Klein (Louis) Jr. Fdn., NYC, 7/191
Klein (Moses) Fdn., NYC, 7/192
Klein (Roger) Fdn., NYC, 7/192
Klein (Walter C.) Family Fdn., NYC, 7/193
Kleinbard (Martin & Joan) Fdn., NYC, 7/193
Kleinman (Isidor & Rosi) Fdn., NYC, 7/194
Kleinoder (Jack) Fdn., Albertson, 7/195
Klimpl (Emanuel & Evelyn) Fdn., NYC, 7/196
Klineman (Emery & Julia) Fdn., NYC, 7/196
Klineman (Erwin & Anne) Fdn., NYC, 7/197
Klingenstein (Paul & Selma) Fdn., Scarsdale, 7/198
Klorfein (Julius & Rose) Fdn., NYC, 7/199
Klugman-Blockton Fdn., NYC, 7/199
Kneiger (S & M) Fdn., Cedarhurst, 7/200
Knickerbacker (John) Trust--Troy Cemetery Association, Troy, 7/201
Knickerbacker (John) Trust (Trophy Fund), Troy, 7/203
Knickerbacker (John) Trust--Waterford Rural Cemetery, Troy, 7/204
Knight Aid Fund, Scarsdale, 7/205
Knight (Harry E.) Scholarship Fund, Albany, 7/206
Kobrick (Jack & Rose) Fdn., NYC, 7/207
Knight (Ruth H.) Fdn., NYC, 7/207
Knitown Fdn., NYC, 7/208
Knox (Seymour H.) Fdn., Buffalo, 7/209
Kodak Employees Association, Rochester, 7/211
Koenigsberg Family Fdn., NYC, 7/211
Koegel Fdn., Granite Springs, 7/212
Koempel (Bertha) Fdn., NYC, 7/213
Koff (S. J.) Fdn., NYC, 7/214
Koffman (Burton I.) Fdn., Binghamton, 7/215
Kogel (George) Fdn., Kings Point, 7/215
Kogos (Frederick) Fdn., Great Neck, 7/216
Kohns (Robert Lee) Fdn., NYC, 7/216
Kohnstamm (Paul L.) Family Charitable Trust, NYC, 7/217
Kolber (Sam) Fdn., Hewlett Bay Park, 7/217
Komanoff (Hannah & Isidore) Fdn., Long Beach, 7/218
Kopf Fdn., NYC, 7/219
Koplik Fdn., NYC, 7/219
Koppel (G. & R.) Fdn., NYC, 7/220
Kippel (Rudolph & Greta) Fdn., NYC, 7/221
Korean International Educational Fdn., NYC, 7/221
Koret (Richard) Fdn., NYC, 7/221
Korn (Irving & Lee) Fdn., Great Neck, 7/222
Kornfeld (Joseph S.) Memorial Alcove, NYC, 7/223
Korzenik (Harold) Fund, Brooklyn, 7/223
Koshland Fund, NYC, 7/224
Kourland (Alexander) Memorial Fdn., Harrison, 7/225
Kramer Fdn., NYC, 7/225
Kramer (Julia Adler) Fdn., NYC, 7/227
Kramer (Philip & Sarah) Charitable Trust, NYC, 7/227
Kramer (Murray) Fdn., Woodmere, 8/001
Kramer-Levinson Memorial Scholarship Fund, Bronx, 8/001
Krasne (Abraham) Fdn., Bronx, 8/001
Krasnow Fdn., NYC, 8/002
Krasnow (David) Scholarship Fund, Malverne, 8/003
Krasnow (Elaine Beth) Fdn., Scarsdale, 8/003
Smith-Krass Fdn., NYC, 8/005
Kraus Fdn., NYC, 8/005
Kraus (Louis J.) Fdn., NYC, 8/005
Kreier (Robert A.) Fdn., NYC, 8/006
Kreissman Trust, White Plains, 8/006
Kreizel (Ann & Arthur) Fdn., Sands Point, 8/007
Kresevich Fdn., Bronx, 8/007
Kress (Herman) Fdn., NYC, 8/008
Krim Fdn., NYC, 8/008
Krevit Fdn., NYC, 8/010
Kronish (Fred) Fdn., Brooklyn, 8/010
Kronovet (Samuel & Kate) Fdn., NYC, 8/011
Krueger (Harvey & Constance) Fdn., NYC, 8/012

Krug (Stewart L.) Fdn., NYC, 8/013
Krumbein Fdn., NYC, 8/013
Krumholz (Nathan A. & Gertrude) Fdn., NYC, 8/014
Krygier Family Fdn., NYC, 8/014
Kuchai (Hyman & Janet) Fdn., Harrison, 8/015
Kudler (Helen & Daniel) Fdn., Jericho, 8/016
Kudner Fdn., NYC, 8/016
Kugel (David & Beatrice S.) Fdn., NYC, 8/016
Kugel (Erwin) Fdn., NYC, 8/017
Kuller (Irving) Fdn., NYC, 8/018
Kunsberg (Stanley H. & Marcella) Fdn., Scarsdale, 8/018
Kupfer (Milton P.) Fdn., NYC, 8/019
Kurtz-Deknatel Fdn., Woodmere, 8/020
Kurtz Family Welfare Fund, NYC, 8/021
Kurz (Benjamin) Fdn., Long Island City, 8/021
Kurzon (Joseph & Esther) Fdn., NYC, 8/022
Lachman (Charles R.) Fdn., NYC, 8/023
Ladies Charity Guild of Manhattan, NYC, 8/023
LaFarge (John) Fdn., NYC, 8/024
Lagemann Fdn., NYC, 8/024
Lagin (Stanley Jay) Fdn., Westbury, 8/025
Lagowitz (Isidor) Fdn., Bronx, 8/025
Laidlaw (Elliot C. R.) Fdn., NYC, 8/026
Lakeview Fund, NYC, 8/026
Lamb Fdn., Ossining, 8/027
Lamb (Grace F.) Trust A, NYC, 8/028
Lamb (Grace F.) Trust B, NYC, 8/029
Lambert (Abbott L.) Fdn., NYC, 8/030
Lamm-Miller-Fox College Fund, NYC, 8/031
Lamport (Samuel C. & Miriam D.) Fdn., NYC, 8/031
Landau Fdn., NYC, 8/032
Landau (Emil & Erna) Fdn., Oceanside, 8/033
Lander (Margaret F. & Raymond A.), Jr. Charitable Trust, Rochester, 8/033
Landis (Ira L.) Fdn., Brooklyn, 8/034
Lane Family Fdn., NYC, 8/034
Lane (Harlod M.), Jr. & Renee Lane Fdn., NYC, 8/035
Lane Fdn., NYC, 8/035
Langbert (H. Thomas & Evelyn) Fdn., NYC, 8/036
Lange (Linda B.) Scholarship Fund, Albany, 8/036
Langner (Ruth & Herbert), NYC, 8/037
Langson (Lillian & Ira N.) Fdn., NYC, 8/038
Lan-Nor-Grene Fdn., NYC, 8/038
Lanvin-Charles of the Ritz Fdn., NYC, 8/039
Lanyi Fdn., NYC, 8/040
Larsen Fund, NYC, 8/041
Lasdon Fdn., NYC, 8/042
Lasker (B. J.) Fdn., NYC, 8/043
Lasry Fdn., NYC, 8/043
Lasser Fdn., NYC, 8/043
Latham Fdn. for Promotion of Humane Education, NYC, 8/044
Laube (Herbert L. & Lois M.) Fdn., Camillus, 8/045
Lauder (Estee & Joseph) Fdn., NYC, 8/046
Laufer (Rebeka) Memorial Fdn., NYC, 8/046
Laurel Fund, NYC, 8/046
Lautz (S.) For C. L. Mausoleum, Buffalo, 8/048
Lavenburg Corner House, Inc., NYC, 8/048
L. A. W. Fund, NYC, 8/050
Lawrence-Myden Fdn., NYC, 8/051
Lawrence (Edward & Lee) Fdn., Pt. Washington, 8/051
Lawrence (Gertrude) Memorial Fdn., NYC, 8/052
Lawrence (Dr. Joseph J.) Trust, NYC, 8/052
Lauria Fdn., NYC, 8/053
Lazar Fdn., NYC, 8/054
Lazarus (Rosalind) & Norman Aunet for American Federation of the Arts, NYC, 8/055
Lazarus (Rosalind) & Norman Aunet for American-Israel Cultural Fdn., NYC, 8/055
Lazarus (Rosalind) & Norman Aunet for Columbia University, NYC, 8/056

Lazarus (Rosalind) & Norman Aunet for Repertory Theater of Lincoln Center, NYC, 8/057
Lazarus (Rosalind) & Norman Aunet for Union of American Hebrew Congregation, NYC, 8/057
Lazarus (Rosalind) & Norman Aunet for University of Poughkeepsie, NYC, 8/058
Lazar (Mary & Leonard) Family Fdn., NYC, 8/058
Lazrus (Benjamin) Fdn., NYC, 8/059
LBT Fdn., NYC, 8/060
LCP Fdn., NYC, 8/060
Lea (Helen Sperry) Company, Brooklyn, 8/060
Faigel Leah Fdn., NYC, 8/061
Lean (Roy A.) Estate Scholarship Trust, Rochester, 8/061
Leaton (Edward K.) Charitable Trust, NYC, 8/062
Leavy (Nathan & Doris) Fdn., NYC, 8/062
Ledcote Charity Fdn., Port Jefferson, 8/063
Lederer Fdn., White Plains, 8/063
Lee Memorial Hospital, NYC, 8/064
Leiter Family Cemetery Trust, Rochester, 8/065
Leff Fdn., NYC, 8/066
Leff (N. M.) Fdn., NYC, 8/067
Lefrak (Harry & Sarah) Fdn., Rego Park, 8/067
Lefrak (Samuel J. & Ethel) Fdn., Rego Park, 8/068
Lehman (Adele & Arthur) Fdn., NYC, 8/069
Lehman (Edith & Herbert) Fdn., NYC, 8/070
Georgian-Lehman Philanthropic Fund, NYC, 8/071
Lehman (Golda & Isaac) Fdn., NYC, 8/071
Lehman (Orin) Fdn., NYC, 8/071
Lehne (Peter & Jessie) Memorial Fdn., NYC, 8/072
Lehr (Benjamin) Fdn., NYC, 8/072
Leib (Mendel) Fund for Education, NYC, 8/074
Leibowitz (Samuel H.) Fdn., NYC, 8/074
Leichtman Fdn., NYC, 8/075
Leidesdorf Fdn., NYC, 8/075
Leighton (Frank J.), NYC, 8/076
Leighton (Leida E.) Trust, Rochester, 8/077
Leinen (Raymond F.) Trust, Rochester, 8/077
Lemberg Fdn., NYC, 8/078
Leonard (Charles R. and Jessie H.) Fdn., NYC, 8/079
Lepercq Fdn., NYC, 8/079
Lerner (Alfred and Roslyn) Fdn., NYC, 8/080
Lerner (Herbert B.) Fdn., NYC, 8/081
Lerner (Robert Z. & Helen) Fdn., NYC, 8/081
Lerner-Gray Fdn., NYC, 8/081
Lese (Marion and Joseph J.) Fdn., NYC, 8/082
Lesko (John and Mary) Fdn., Westbury, 8/083
Lessmann Fdn., NYC, 8/083
Leenow (Jack) Family Fdn., Rockville Centre, 8/084
Levenson Fdn., NYC, 8/085
Leventhal Bros. Fdn., NYC, 8/086
Leventritt (Edgar M.) Fdn., NYC, 8/086
Levick Fdn., Buffalo, 8/087
Levin Fdn., NYC, 8/088
Levin (Elisabeth & John) Fund, NYC, 8/089
Levin (Harold & Juliet) Fdn., NYC, 8/090
Levin (Nathan & Pam) Fund, NYC, 8/090
Levine (Bernard and Anna) Fdn., Malverne, 8/091
Levine (Harry) Memorial Fdn., NYC, 8/092
Levy (Florence C. and Leo J.) Fdn., NYC, 8/093
Levine (Irving J.) Fdn., NYC, 8/094
Levine (Jacob and Abner) Fdn., Lawrence, 8/094
Levine (Carolyn & Leo) Fdn., Roslyn, 8/095
Levine (Joseph E.) Fdn., NYC, 8/095
Levitt (Arthur), Jr. Charitable Trust, NYC, 8/096
Levitt (David M. and Norma U.) Fdn., NYC, 8/096
Levitt Fund, NYC, 8/097
Levkoff (Evelyn and David) Fdn., Jackson Heights, 8/098

Levy (Adele R.) Fund, NYC, 8/099
Levy (Benjamin J. and Anna) Family Fdn., NYC, 8/101
Levy (I. Montefiore) and Otten Fdn., NYC, 8/102
Lewson Fdn., NYC, 8/102
Levy (Shaya Shabot) Fdn., NYC, 8/103
Lewenstein Fdn., NYC, 8/104
Lewin (Juliette S. & George J.) Fdn., NYC, 8/104
Lewine (Cara & Hiram S.) Fdn., 8/104
Lewis Fdn., Delmar, 8/105
Lewis Fdn. (120 Broadway), NYC, 8/105
Lewis Fdn. (One Wall Street), NYC, 8/105
Lewis Fdn. (880 Fifth Avenue), NYC, 8/106
Lewis (George E. and Edith S.) Fdn., Buffalo, 8/107
Lewis (Sarah J.) Fdn., East Hampton, 8/107
Lewison (Peter & Harold) Fdn., NYC, 8/107
Lewyt Fdn., NYC, 8/108
Li Fdn., NYC, 8/109
Libby Fdn., NYC, 8/110
Liberian Fdn., NYC, 8/111
Liberian Institute of the American Fdn. for Tropical Medicine, NYC, 8/112
Librett (Charles and Clara) Fdn., New Rochelle, 8/112
Licht-Schleifer Fdn., NYC, 8/112
Lichtenstein (Anne Boyd) Fdn., NYC, 8/112
Liebman Fdn., NYC, 8/114
Liebman (Herman) Fdn., NYC, 8/114
Liebowitz (J. S.) Fdn., NYC, 8/115
Liese (Harry & Sylvia) Fdn., NYC, 8/116
Life Extension Fdn., NYC, 8/116
Life Saving Benevolent Assn. of N.Y., NYC, 8/117
Lilco Charitable Trust, Mineola, 8/117
Lilienthal (Muriel & Felix) Fdn., NYC, 8/119
Lilly (Evan F.) Memorial Trust, NYC, 8/120
Limburg Fdn., NYC, 8/121
Linbuan Fdn., NYC, 8/122
Lincoln Rochester Charitable Fund, Rochester, 8/123
Lindemann Fdn., NYC, 8/124
Lindenbaum (Armand & Jean) Fdn., NYC, 8/125
O'Connor (A. Lindsay and Olive B.) Fdn., Binghamton, 8/125
Lindsley (John) Fund A, NYC, 8/126
Lindsley (John) Fund B, NYC, 8/128
Lindsley (Thayer) Trust, NYC, 8/130
Linton Fdn., NYC, 8/131
Lions Blind & Charity Fund, Kenmore, 8/132
Lipschitz (Jacques & Yulla) Fdn., Hastings-on-Hudson, 8/133
Lipkins Fdn., NYC, 8/133
Lipman Fdn., Wyandanch, 8/134
Lipper Fdn., NYC, 8/134
Lipton Fdn., NYC, 8/136
Liss (Harold I. & Faye B.) Fdn., Long Island City, 8/137
Lissner (Herman) Fdn., NYC, 8/138
List-Glenn Charitable Trust, Rochester, 8/138
Littauer (Lucius N.) Fdn., NYC, 8/139
Little Mother's Aid Association, NYC, 8/142
Living Arts Fdn., NYC, 8/143
Livingston (Mollie Parnis) Fdn., NYC, 8/143
Livingston (Richard M. & Mimi S.) Fdn., Scarsdale, 8/144
L & L Fdn., NYC, 8/144
Lobel Fdn., NYC, 8/145
Lobsenz (Harry Leon) Fdn., NYC, 8/145
Local 802 Musicians Emergency Relief Fund, NYC, 8/146
Loeb (Frances & John L.) Fdn., NYC, 8/147
Loeb (Henry & Louise) Fund, NYC, 8/148
Loeb (John L.), Jr. Fdn., NYC, 8/149
Loeb (Lucille & Carl) Fdn., NYC, 8/150
Loew (Arthur M.) Fdn., NYC, 8/151
Loewy (Raymond) Associates Fdn., NYC, 8/152
Logos Fdn. of New York, NYC, 8/152
Lohengrin Fdn., NYC, 8/153
Lombardi (Tarky) Fdn., Syracuse, 8/153
London (Ellin & Robert) Fdn., Scarsdale, 8/154

London (Theodore & Iris) Fdn., NYC, 8/155
Longhill Charities, NYC, 8/155
Longine-Willnauer Fdn., NYC, 8/156
Longlein Fdn., NYC, 8/156
Longview Fdn., NYC, 8/158
Lonner (Max & Lea) Fdn., NYC, 8/158
Lonoff (Shumer S.) Fdn., NYC, 8/159
Looker Fund, NYC, 8/159
Lookout Fund, NYC, 8/160
Loomis Fdn., NYC, 8/161
Lorberbaum Fdn., NYC, 8/162
Lorch Fdn., NYC, 8/163
Lord (Mary) Fdn., NYC, 8/163
Lorenz Fdn., NYC, 8/164
Lorillard Corporation Fdn., NYC, 8/164
Walska (Ganna) Lotusland Fdn., NYC, 8/165
Louis (Jack & Gloria) Fdn., NYC, 8/165
Louis (S. M.) Fund, NYC, 8/167
Lovejoy (Frederic F. & Georgiana) Charitable Fdn., Rochester, 8/167
Low (Evlynne & Max) Fdn., NYC, 8/168
Low (Madeleine M.) Fund, NYC, 8/169
Lowe (Joe & Emily) Fdn., NYC, 8/170
Lowenstein (Ernest) Fdn., Cedarhurst, 8/172
Lowenstein (Leon) Fdn., NYC, 8/172
Lowenthal (Edith & Milton) Fdn., NYC, 8/174
Lowy (Michael) Fdn., NYC, 8/175
Lubin (Joseph I. & Evelyn J.) Fdn., NYC, 8/176
Luce (Henry) Fdn., NYC, 8/177
Lucerna Fund, Port Washington, 8/179
Ludwig (Virginia & D. K.) Fdn., NYC, 8/180
Lukashok (Milton & Muriel) Fdn., NYC, 8/181
Lukin Fdn., NYC, 8/181
Luria (Herbert B.) Fdn., NYC, 8/182
Lusskin (Lillian S.) Orthopaedic Fdn., NYC, 8/183
Lutheran Emigrants House Association of N.Y., NYC, 8/183
Lybrand Fdn., NYC, 8/183
Lynch (Edmund C.) Fund, NYC, 8/185
Lyons Fdn., Claverack, 8/186
Lyric Fdn. (For Traditional Poetry), NYC, 8/187
MacDonald (James A.) Fdn., NYC, 8/188
MacDonald (Marquis George) Fdn., NYC, 8/189
Mack (Ted) Fdn. for Young Americans, NYC, 8/192
Maclean (Charles & Lee) Fund, NYC, 8/192
Madison Square Boys Club Trust, NYC, 8/192
Mad River Fdn., NYC, 8/194
Maes-Heller Fdn., NYC, 8/195
Maggin Fdn., NYC, 8/195
Maferr Fdn., NYC, 8/195
Maguire (Russell) Fdn., NYC, 8/196
Mahoney Fdn., NYC, 8/197
Mahshala Fdn., Brooklyn, 8/197
Mailman Fdn., NYC, 8/198
Major Fdn., NYC, 8/199
Malamut (Stephen G.) Fdn., NYC, 8/200
Malcom (Wilbus G.) Fdn., Grand View-on-Hudson, 8/201
Malcam Trust, NYC, 8/202
Maleh-Shalom Fdn., NYC, 8/202
Malkin (Peter & Isiabel) Fdn., NYC, 8/203
Mallas (Louis J.) Fdn., NYC, 8/204
Mallory (P. R.) Family Fdn., NYC, 8/205
Mallory (Rebecca Sealy) Fdn., NYC, 8/206
Malsin (Lane Bryant) Fdn., NYC, 8/207
Mancher Family Fdn., NYC, 8/207
Mancini Charitable Fdn., Rochester, 8/208
Mandel (Ber) Family Fdn., Brooklyn, 8/209
Mandelbaum (Samuel) Fdn., NYC, 8/209
Meltzer (Manford & Theda) Fdn., NYC, 8/210
Mangan (Nancy S. & James F.) Charitable Trust, Rochester, 8/211
Mangel Stores Fund, NYC, 8/211
Manischewitz (Meyer & Min) Fdn., NYC, 8/214
Mann (Honey and Norman) Fdn., NYC, 8/214
Mann (John T.) Fdn., NYC, 8/215

Manoff (Lucy and Richard K.) Fdn., NYC, 8/217
Manufacturers Hanover Fdn. (formerly Manufacturers Hanover Trust Company Fdn.), NYC, 8/217
Cavanagh (John G.) Trust, 8/222
Riegel (Lelia E.) Trust for Religious Education, Charitable and Scientific Purposes, NYC, 8/225
Manufacturers and Traders Trust Company Fdn., Buffalo, 8/226
Maple Lawn Cemetery Association Trust, Buffalo, 8/227
Mar Dan Fdn., NYC, 8/227
Mar (Lil) Charitable Trust, NYC, 8/228
Marbill Fdn., NYC, 9/001
Marble Fund, NYC, 9/001
March Fdn., NYC, 9/002
March (Ruth H.) Fdn., NYC, 9/003
Marcus (Judy & Wayne) Fdn., NYC, 9/004
Marcuse Fund, NYC, 9/004
Margolin (Boris) Fdn., NYC, 9/005
Margolis Fdn., NYC, 9/006
Marine Tobacco Fdn., Long Island City, 9/011
Marjart Fdn. Ltd., NYC, 9/012
Marjon Fdn., NYC, 9/013
Mark Family Fdn., NYC, 9/014
Markel Family Fdn., Buffalo, 9/014
Markel (Pauline Yuells) Charitable Trust, NYC, 9/015
Markert (Genevieve J. & Leonard P.) Fdn., Syracuse, 9/016
Kahn (Max H.) & Harry Markowitz Fdn., NYC, 9/017
Marks Fdn. f/k/a Annette & Richard Lee Marks Fdn., NYC, 9/017
Marks (Aaron) Fdn., Woodmere, 9/018
Marks (Doris & David) Jr. Fdn., NYC, 9/019
Marks (George L.) Fdn., NYC, 9/019
Markus (Frits) Fdn., NYC, 9/020
Markus (Rita) Fdn., NYC, 9/021
Marrow Fund, NYC, 9/022
Marrus (David & Judith) Fdn., NYC, 9/022
Markus (Jacob & Mary) Fdn., Far Rockaway, 9/023
White Scholarship Fund, Cooperstown, 9/023
Marsicano Fdn., NYC, 9/024
Martin Fdn., NYC, 9/024
Martin (Glenn L.) Fdn., NYC, 9/025
Martin (Jack) Fund, Lawrence, 9/027
Martin (Sylvia) Fdn., NYC, 9/028
Martin-Marietta Corporation, NYC, 9/029
Markel Family Fdn., Buffalo, 9/033
Martinson (Joseph) Memorial Fund, NYC, 9/033
Marx Fdn., NYC, 9/033
Marx (Virginia & Leonard) Fdn., Scarsdale, 9/035
Maslow Fdn., NYC, 9/035
Maslow (Arthur & Barbara) Fdn., Great Neck, 9/036
Maslow (Charles) Fdn., NYC, 9/036
Maslow (Lester) Fdn., Great Neck, 9/037
Maslow (Norman & Selma) Fdn., Hewlett Harbor, 9/037
Maslowski (John M.) Scholarship Fund, Albany, 9/038
Mason (Birny) Jr. Fdn., NYC, 9/039
Masujoka Fdn., NYC, 9/040
Matanah Fdn., NYC, 9/040
Matchette (Franklin J.) Fdn., Mineola, 9/041
Mather (Richard) Fund, Syracuse, 9/041
Matthews (Hale) Fdn., NYC, 9/042
Matthews (John N.) Family Fdn., NYC, 9/043
Matouk (John & Maude) Charitable Fdn., NYC, 9/044
Matz Fdn., Brooklyn, 9/044
Matz (Israel) Fdn., NYC, 9/046
Maurer Fdn., NYC, 9/047
Mautner (Irwin & Flora) Fdn., Hartsdale, 9/047
Maxwell Endowment Fund, Buffalo, 9/048
May (Benjamin M.) & Great S. May Fdn., NYC, 9/048
May (Joseph M.) Memorial Association, NYC, 9/049

May (Mitchell) Fdn., NYC, 9/050
May-Serman Fdn., NYC, 9/051
Maya Corporation, NYC, 9/052
Mayer (A. & C.) Fdn., NYC, 9/054
Mayer (Alfred & Lee) Fdn., Forest Hills, 9/054
Mayer (Leonard) Fdn., NYC, 9/055
Mayer (General William) Fdn., NYC, 9/055
Mayers (Lawrence S.) Fund, NYC, 9/056
Maynard (Theodore E.) Fdn., NYC, 9/057
Mayne Fdn., Roslyn Heights, 9/057
Mayo (Bocko) & Anna Mayo Fdn., Roslyn Heights, 9/057
Mazer (Jacob & Ruth) Fdn., NYC, 9/058
Mazer (Joseph & Ciel) Fdn., NYC, 9/059
M C A Fdn., NYC, 9/060
McAfee Fdn., NYC, 9/061
McCaddin--McQuirk Fdn., NYC, 9/061
McCain Trust Fund, NYC, 9/063
McCandless Fdn., NYC, 9/063
McCann Fdn., Poughkeepsie, 9/064
McCartny Charities, Troy, 9/064
McCartny (Michael W.) Fdn., NYC, 9/065
McCormack (Emmet J.) Fdn., NYC, 9/065
McCormick (Anne O'Hare) Memorial Fund, NYC, 9/066
McCurdy (Gilbert & Virginia) Charitable Trust, Rochester, 9/066
McDonell (Alexander Angus) Fdn., NYC, 9/067
McDonnell & Company Fdn., NYC, 9/068
McDonnell (Charles E.) Fdn., NYC, 9/068
McDonnell (Peggy & Murray) Fdn., NYC, 9/069
McFarland (A. R. & E. M.) Fdn., NYC, 9/070
McGonagle (Dextra Baldwin) Fdn., NYC, 9/071
McGraw (Donald C.) Fdn., NYC, 9/072
McHugh Fdn., NYC, 9/072
McIntosh (Josephine C.) Fdn., NYC, 9/073
McKee (Frank W. & Mary) Trust Fund, Rochester, 9/074
Cattell (James McKeen) Fund, NYC, 9/074
McKnight (William G.) Fund, NYC, 9/075
McLoughlin (Martha) Fdn., Brooklyn, 9/076
McLouth Charitable Trust, Rochester, 9/076
McMillin (John M.) Fdn., NYC, 9/077
McNees Fdn., Rye, 9/078
Meade (Joseph P.) Memorial Science Fund, Rochester, 9/078
Meadowbrook Fdn., NYC, 9/079
Meadowhill Fund, NYC, 9/080
Meals-on-Wheels of Syracuse, N.Y., Syracuse, 9/081
Mecox Fdn., NYC, 9/081
Medical Research Trust, NYC, 9/082
Medical Society of the County of N.Y. Physician's Loan & Relief Fund, NYC, 9/083
Medina (Harold R.) Fund, NYC, 9/083
Medwick Fdn., Larchmont, 9/084
Meers (Henry W.) Fund, NYC, 9/084
Meier (Madeleine & Edwin) Fdn., Mt. Vernon, 9/085
Melamid Fdn., NYC, 9/085
Melanol Fdn., NYC, 9/086
Melcher (Herbert H.) Fdn., NYC, 9/086
Mele Fdn., Richmond Hill, 9/086
Melflor Fund, Bronxville, 9/087
Mellon (Andrew W.) Fdn., NYC, 9/088
Melnick (J. A.) Fdn., NYC, 9/094
Melnick (J. B.) Fdn., NYC, 9/094
Melville (Frank) Memorial Fdn., Stony Brook, 9/095
M. E. M. Fdn., NYC, 9/096
Memorial Fdn. for Jewish Culture, NYC, 9/096
Memorial Fund, Inc., NYC, 9/096
Menke (Joan R.) Fdn., Scarsdale, 9/097
Mercantile Library Association of the City of N.Y., NYC, 9/097
Mercer (Henry D.) Fdn., NYC, 9/098
Messinger (Philip) Fdn., NYC, 9/099
Meyer (Edward & Sandra) Fdn., NYC, 9/099
Merck (John) Fund, NYC, 9/099
Mercy (Sue & Eugene), Jr. Fdn., NYC, 9/100

Mercury Aircraft Fdn., Hammondsport, 9/101
Meresman Fdn., NYC, 9/101
Merin (Herbert & Rita) Fdn., Great Neck, 9/101
Merkel (Henry) Fdn., Old Westbury, 9/102
Merkeri Fdn., NYC, 9/103
Mernan Fdn., Buffalo, 9/103
Meron Fund, Spring Valley, 9/103
Merrill, Lynch, Pierce, Fenner & Smith Fdn., NYC, 9/104
Mertz Fdn., NYC, 9/105
Mertz (Martha) Fdn., NYC, 9/106
Mertz Art Fund, Port Washington, 9/107
Messer Fdn., Buffalo, 9/107
Messinger (Abe & Gertrude) Fdn., Lawrence, 9/108
Metals Fdn., NYC, 9/109
Metcalf (Stanley W.) Fdn., Auburn, 9/109
Michael Fdn., Bronx, 9/110
Michael (Jakob & Edna) Fdn., NYC, 9/111
Paul (Josephine Bay) & C. Michael Paul Fdn., NYC, 9/112
Meyer (Andre & Bella) Fdn., NYC, 9/113
Meyer (Helen & Abraham) Fdn., NYC, 9/114
Meyer (Julian & Alexa) Fdn., NYC, 9/115
Meyer (M. & E.) Fund, NYC, 9/116
Meyer (Maurice & Carolyn) Fdn., NYC, 9/117
Meyer (Richmond F. & Margaret S.) Fdn., Salt Point, 9/117
Meyer (Ruth) Fund, NYC, 9/118
Michael Fdn., Bronx, 9/118
Michael (Jakob & Edna) Fdn., NYC, 9/119
Michel (Barbara & Clifford) Fdn., NYC, 9/120
Comunita Gioranile San Michele, NYC, 9/121
Middlebrook (John O. & Gladys T.) Trust, NYC, 9/123
Middlebury College--John H. Fulton Memorial Fund, NYC, 9/123
Middlebury College--Fulton Lecture Fund, NYC, 9/124
Middlebury College--Jean T. Fulton Memorial Fund, NYC, 9/125
Middletown Fund, NYC, 9/126
Midgard Fdn., NYC, 9/126
Midnight Mission, NYC, 9/127
Midwood Memorial Scholarship Fund, Brooklyn, 9/130
Milano Fdn., NYC, 9/130
Milbank Memorial Fund, NYC, 9/130
Milk (Harry & Martin) Fdn., NYC, 9/135
Millbrook Free Library, Millbrook, 9/136
Millbrook Free Library, NYC, 9/136
Miller (Charles T.) Fdn., NYC, 9/137
Miller (David) Fdn., NYC, 9/137
Miller (Grace B.) & J. Bernard Miller Fdn., NYC, 9/138
Miller (Kathryn & Gilbert) Fund, NYC, 9/138
Miller (Louis & Sylvia) Family Fdn., Bronxville, 9/139
Miller (Michael B.) Fdn., Port Chester, 9/140
Miller (Mitch) Fdn., NYC, 9/140
Miller (Murray) Fdn., NYC, 9/141
Miller (Stanley R.) Fdn., NYC, 9/141
Milliken (Deering) Fdn., NYC, 9/142
Mills Fdn., NYC, 9/143
Mills (J. Clawson) Charitable Trust, NYC, 9/144
Miner (Alice T.) Masonic Memorial Trust Fund, Albany, 9/144
Minkoff (Lena) Memorial Fdn., Great Neck, 9/145
Minskoff (Sam) Fdn., NYC, 9/146
Minton Fdn., NYC, 9/147
Minton Fund, NYC, 9/148
Minton Trust, NYC, 9/149
Mintzer (Joseph G. & Hortense L.) Trust, Troy, 9/150
Mishcon Fdn., NYC, 9/150
Mishkin Fdn., NYC, 9/151
Mission Trust Fund, NYC, 9/152
Mitchell (Samuel & Rose) Fdn., NYC, 9/152
Mitrani Family Fdn., NYC, 9/153
Mitileman (J. & G.) Fdn., Old Brookville, 9/154
M. & J. Fdn., NYC, 9/155
M. L. B. Fdn., Latham, 9/156

Mobil Fdn., NYC, 9/156
Model (Leo) Fdn., NYC, 9/158
Midel (Jane & Leo) Fdn., NYC, 9/158
Modlin (Elihu & Dorothy) Fdn., North Woodmere, 9/159
Mohansic Fdn., Yonkers, 9/159
Mohasco Memorial Fund, Amsterdam, 9/160
Molinari (Anthony C.) Fdn., Oneonta, 9/162
Monadnock Fund, NYC, 9/162
Montargent Fdn., NYC, 9/163
Moog (William C.) Fdn., East Aurora, 9/164
Moore (Albert V.) Fdn., NYC, 9/165
Moore (Edward S.) Fdn., NYC, 9/165
Moore (James A.) Fdn. for Otologic Research, NYC, 9/166
Morelos Fdn., Ithaca, 9/167
Morey (Dana W.) Fdn., NYC, 9/167
Morfit (T. Garrison & Eleanor L.) Fdn., NYC, 9/168
Morgan Guaranty Trust Company of New York Fdn., NYC, 9/170
Morgan Guaranty Trust Company of New York Charitable Trust, NYC, 9/171
Morgenstern (Morris & Celia) Fdn., NYC, 9/174
Morgenstern (Morris) Fdn., NYC, 9/174
Morris (Alice V. & Dave H.) Memorial, NYC, 9/175
Morris (Norman M.) Fdn., NYC, 9/176
Morris (Harold & Edythe) Fdn., Scarsdale, 9/177
Post-Morrow Fdn., Brookhaven, 9/178
Morse (Carl A.) Fdn., NYC, 9/178
Morse (Earl & Irene) Fdn., NYC, 9/178
Mortimer (Charles G. & Elizabeth A.) Fdn., NYC, 9/179
Mosbacher Fdn., NYC, 9/180
Moser (Marvin & Joy) Fdn., Scarsdale, 9/181
Moses (Henry & Lucy) Fund, NYC, 9/182
Mosler (Edwin H.) Jr. Fdn., NYC, 9/183
Moskowitz Fdn., Kew Gardens, 9/184
Mosler (John & Sheila) Fdn., NYC, 9/185
Mostyn Fdn., NYC, 9/186
Mott (Stewart R.) Charitable Trust, NYC, 9/187
Moul (Clifford W.) Scholarship Fund, Albany, 9/188
Mount Moriah Benevolent Fund, Jamestown, 9/188
Mowry (James M.) Trust #27004, Rochester, 9/188
Mowry (James M.) Trust #27005, Rochester, 9/189
M S I Fund, NYC, 9/190
Muehlstein (Herman) Fdn., NYC, 9/191
Mueller (Carl M. & Suzanne C.) Charitable Trust, NYC, 9/192
Muench-Kreuzer Fdn., Syracuse, 9/193
Mulvey (James A.) Fdn., White Plains, 9/193
Munson Fdn., NYC, 9/194
Munzer Family Fdn., Lindenhurst, 9/195
Murel Fdn., NYC, 9/196
Murray Fdn., Jericho, 9/197
Murray Hill Memorial, NYC, 9/198
Murray (Lynne) Sr. Educational Fdn., Houston, Texas, 9/198
Murray-MacDonald Fdn., NYC, 9/199
Murrow (Edward R.) Fdn., NYC, 9/200
Musa Alami Fdn. of Jericho, NYC, 9/201
Musher (Hadassah & Sidney) Fdn., NYC, 9/201
Muskiwinni Fdn., NYC, 9/202
Myden (Lawrence) Fdn., NYC, 9/204
Myers (H. Herbert) Memorial Fdn., Brooklyn, 9/204
Myrin Institute, NYC, 9/204
Myser Fdn. Fund, Maspeth, 9/204
Nabi Fdn., Great Neck, 9/205
Nabra Fdn., Oyster Bay, 9/206
Nadler (Aaron) Fund, NYC, 9/206
Nager (Edward F.) Fdn., Brooklyn, 9/207
NaHas Fdn., NYC, 9/208
Namm Fdn., NYC, 9/208
Narrangansett Charitable Land Trust, NYC, 9/210
Nass (Max & Eva) Fdn., NYC, 9/210

Nathanson (Irwin B. & Sally L.) Fdn.,
   Harrison, 9/210
National Academy of Education, Syracuse,
   9/211
National Association of Electrical Distributors
   Education Fdn., NYC, 9/212
National Biscuit Company Fdn. Trust, NYC,
   9/213
National City Fdn., NYC, 9/215
Aiken (Herbert W.) Fdn., Van Olinda
   Scholarship Fund, Albany, 9/216
Albany League of Arts, Albany, 9/217
National Distillers & Chemical Fdn., NYC,
   9/218
National Dye Works Fdn., Brooklyn, 9/219
National Early Childhood Research Council,
   NYC, 9/220
National Fdn. for Arts & Sciences, NYC,
   9/220
National Performing Arts Fdn., NYC, 9/220
National Fdn. for Ileitus & Colitis, NYC,
   9/221
National Genetics Fdn., NYC, 9/221
National Lead Fdn., NYC, 9/222
Near Eastern Art Research Center, NYC,
   9/224
Necarsulmer (Henry & Betty) Fdn., NYC,
   9/225
Necarsulmer (Mary & Edward), Jr. Fdn., NYC,
   9/226
Neisner Brothers Fdn., Rochester, 9/227
Neloner Fund, NYC, 9/227
Nellany (Charles V.) Fdn., Buffalo, 9/228
Nelson (Leonard) Fdn., NYC, 9/228
Nerken Fdn., NYC, 9/229
Nermie Fdn., NYC, 9/229
Netherland-America Fdn., NYC, 10/000
Netter (Alice & Fred) Fdn., NYC, 10/000
Netzorg (Sidney M. & Leah H.) Fdn., NYC,
   10/001
Neu (Hugo & Doris) Fdn., NYC, 10/002
Neuberger (Roy R. & Marie S.) Fdn., NYC,
   10/003
Neugass (Ludwig) Fdn., NYC, 10/005
Neuman (I & B) Fdn., NYC, 10/006
Neurological Disease Fdn., Jamaica, 10/006
Neustadter (Arnold & Dorothy) Fdn., NYC,
   10/007
Nevins (J. F. H.) Estate--H. C. Nevins Home
   Trust, NYC, 10/008
Haas (A.) et al Trust for D. Haas Memorial,
   NYC, 10/010
New Castle Fdn., NYC, 10/010
New Court Securities Fdn., NYC, 10/010
New Hermes Fdn., NYC, 10/011
New Hope Fdn., NYC, 10/012
New-Land Fdn., NYC, 10/013
New Rochelle Hospital No. 1, NYC, 10/015
New Rochelle Hospital No. 2, NYC, 10/015
New World Fund, NYC, 10/016
New York City Jaycees Fdn., NYC, 10/016
New York Conservation Council & American
   Game Association Fdn., Palmyra, 10/017
New York Fdn., NYC, 10/018
New York Fund for Children, NYC, 10/022
New York Genealogical & Biographical Society
   et al Trust, NYC, 10/023
New York Post Fdn., NYC, 10/024
N.Y. State Association of Transportation
   Engineers, Schenectady, 10/026
N.Y. State Hospitality Educational Fund,
   Buffalo, 10/027
New York Times Fdn., NYC, 10/028
New York University, NYC, 10/029
New Zion Fdn., NYC, 10/030
Newark Neighbors, Newark, 10/030
Newburger (May & Morris) Fdn., NYC,
   10/031
Newburger (Robert & Ann) Fdn., NYC,
   10/032
Newcombe Fdn., NYC, 10/033
Newell (Albert P.) Fdn., Ogdensburg, 10/034
Newhall (Donald V.) Fdn., NYC, 10/034
Newman (Clara) Memorial Fund, Brooklyn,
   10/035
Newman (William R.) Fdn., Jamaica, 10/035

Newmark (Allan J.) Fdn., NYC, 10/035
Newmont Fdn., NYC, 10/036
Newsday Athletic Association, Garden City,
   10/037
NFL Alumni Fdn. Fund, NYC, 10/037
Nias (Henry) Fdn., NYC, 10/038
Nichols Fdn., NYC, 10/038
Nichols (Thomas S.) Fdn., NYC, 10/040
Nickerson (Albert L.) Charitable Trust, NYC,
   10/041
Niedelman (Samuel & Hilda) Fdn., NYC,
   10/041
Niemeyer (Gustav) Memorial Educational
   Fund, NYC, 10/042
24 Emergency Fund, NYC, 10/042
Nieweg Fdn., NYC, 10/042
United States--Nigerian Fdn. for Ojike Medical
   Center, NYC, 10/042
Nirenberg (Bertram & Sally) Fdn., Loudonville,
   10/043
Nizer Fdn., NYC, 10/043
Noall (Roger) Fdn., NYC, 10/044
Norcross (Augusta) Fdn., NYC, 10/044
Norcross Wildlife Fdn., NYC, 10/044
Norr Fund, NYC, 10/046
Norry Family Fdn., Rochester, 10/047
North Star Fdn., White Plains, 10/047
Northome Fund, Scarsdale, 10/048
Norumbega Fund, NYC, 10/049
Norwood Fdn., NYC, 10/050
Notine (Donald D.) Trust, Oyster Bay Cove,
   10/050
Noyes (A. B. & J.) Fdn., NYC, 10/050
Noyes (Jessie Smith) Fdn., NYC, 10/051
Nurses House, NYC, 10/053
"The N. Y. B. F. S. Fdn.", NYC, 10/054
Oaklands Fund, Mt. Kisco, 10/055
Oaklawn Fund, NYC, 10/056
Oakley (Walter W.) Trust, Rochester, 10/057
Oaktree Fdn., NYC, 10/058
Oberlin (Abe) Fdn., NYC, 10/058
O'Brien (Henry L.) Fdn., West Hampton
   Beach, 10/059
O'Connell (Walter F.) Fdn., NYC, 10/059
Oestreicher (Carl & Lucile) Fdn., NYC, 10/060
Offin (Charles Z.) Art Fund, NYC, 10/060
Ogden (Ralph E.) Fdn., Mountainville, 10/061
O'Haire (Frances A. & Mary G.) Prize Fund,
   Troy, 10/062
O'Hara Fdn., NYC, 10/063
O H L Fund, Sands Point, 10/063
Ohrbach's Department Store Fund, NYC,
   10/064
Oishei (John R.) Appreciation Charitable Trust,
   Buffalo, 10/065
Oken (Benjamin M.) Memorial Fund,
   Rochester, 10/065
Old Republic Charitable Fdn., NYC, 10/066
Old Westbury College Fdn., Oyster Bay,
   10/067
Olin Fdn., NYC, 10/067
Olive Bridge Fund, NYC, 10/070
Olsa Fdn., Brooklyn, 10/071
Olsan Medical Research Fund, Rochester,
   10/071
Olsen Memorial Fund, Utica, 10/072
Olun (Jacob & Rose) Fdn., Binghamton,
   10/073
O'Neil (Cyril F. & Marie E.) Fdn., NYC,
   10/073
O'Neill (J. J.) Fdn., NYC, 10/074
Open Space Institute, NYC, 10/075
Oppenheimer (Minnie K.) Fdn., NYC, 10/075
Oppenheimer (M. & N.) Fdn., NYC, 10/077
Orchestra of America, NYC, 10/077
Orda (Max & Bertha) Fdn., NYC, 10/078
Order of Minor Conventuals (u/a with George
   Korb), Rensselaer, 10/078
Orenstein (Albert) Fdn., NYC, 10/079
Orentreich Fdn. for the Advancement of
   Science, NYC, 10/080
Origo (Iris M.) Charitable Trust, NYC, 10/081
Orisha Fund, NYC, 10/082
O'Shei (Emmett) Trust, Buffalo, 10/083
Osher Fdn., NYC, 10/084
Osofsky (Meyer & Aileen) Fdn., NYC, 10/084

Osterer (David G.) Fdn., NYC, 10/085
Ostrau (Bertram M.) Fdn., Harrison, 10/085
Ostreich (Leonard L. & Ellen S.) Fdn., Roslyn,
   10/086
Ostwald (Adolph) Fdn., Staten Island, 10/087
Otis Fdn., NYC, 10/087
Ottens Family Fdn., NYC, 10/088
Ottinger Fdn., NYC, 10/089
Our Lady of Lourdes Fund, Poughkeepsie,
   10/090
Overbrook Fdn., NYC, 10/091
Overlook Fund, NYC, 10/093
Overseas Chinese Music & Arts Center, NYC,
   10/094
Owens Fdn., Syracuse, 10/095
Ox Hollow Fdn., NYC, 10/096
Pack (Howard M.) Fdn., NYC, 10/097
Paffendorf Fdn., Roslyn Heights, 10/098
Page (F. Lemoyne) Memorial Fdn., NYC,
   10/098
Page (Robert G.) Charitable Trust, NYC,
   10/098
Palanbee Fund, NYC, 10/099
Palestine (Lester & Anna) Fdn., NYC, 10/100
Paley (Barbara) Fund, NYC, 10/100
Paley (William S.) Fdn., NYC, 10/101
Pall Fdn., NYC, 10/102
Palmer (Arthur C. & Lucia S.) Fdn., Waverly,
   10/103
Palmer (Lowell M.) Fdn., NYC, 10/103
Pan Am Charitable Fdn., NYC, 10/104
Panny Fdn., NYC, 10/105
Paragon Fdn., Brooklyn, 10/106
Paragon Fund, NYC, 10/106
Paragraph Twelfth Trust u/w Margaret T.
   Biddle, NYC, 10/108
Parisier (Maurice I.) Fdn., NYC, 10/108
Park Fdn., NYC, 10/109
Park Fdn., Ithaca, 10/109
Park (David C.) Fdn. Trust, Syracuse, 10/110
Parker (Albert & Jeannette) Fdn., NYC,
   10/110
Parker (Jack) Fdn., Forest Hills, 10/111
Parkinson (Joy Hirshon) Fdn., NYC, 10/111
Parks Fdn., Staten Island, 10/112
Parshelsky (Moses L.) Fdn., Brooklyn, 10/113
Parthenon Fdn., NYC, 10/115
Paskus (Katherine & Benjamin C.) Fdn., NYC,
   10/116
Paskus (Martin) Fdn., NYC, 10/116
Pastorale Fund, NYC, 10/117
Patterson (Alicia) Fdn., NYC, 10/118
Patterson (James J.) Charitable Fdn., NYC,
   10/120
Patterson (Joseph M.) Charitable Fdn., NYC,
   10/121
Patterson (Susan) Trust--Westfield Cemetery
   Association, Buffalo, 10/122
Pauker (Michael & Frieda) Family Fdn., NYC,
   10/122
Paul (Josephine Bay) & C. Michael Paul Fdn.,
   NYC, 10/123
Pauker (Michael & Frieda) Family Fdn., NYC,
   10/124
Pavlo (Sophia) Fdn., NYC, 10/124
Pavone (Father) Memorial Fdn., Port
   Washington, 10/125
Pax America Fdn., NYC, 10/125
Payne (Oliver H. & Lola G.) Trust, NYC,
   10/125
Kidder Peabody Fdn., NYC, 10/126
Peapaction Fdn., NYC, 10/127
Pearlman Family Fdn., NYC, 10/128
Pearlman (Henry) Fdn., NYC, 10/129
Pearson (Frederick F. A.) Fdn., NYC, 10/129
Pechman Fdn., NYC, 10/129
Peck (Barney & Helen) Fdn., NYC, 10/130
Peckman Fdn., White Plains, 10/131
Peco Fdn., Elmont, 10/132
Peierls Fdn., NYC, 10/132
Peltz (Maurice) Family Fdn., Bronx, 10/133
Pemberton Fdn., NYC, 10/134
Penney (Charles Rand) Fdn., Olcott, 10/134
Penney (James C.) Fdn., NYC, 10/135

Pension Fund of the Columbia Univ. Presbyterian Hospital School of Nursing Alumnae Assoc., NYC, 10/136
Pentagon Fdn., Flushing, 10/137
Peo Fdn., Buffalo, 10/138
Pepper (Stella & Arthur) Fdn., Scarsdale, 10/138
Pepsi Co. Fdn., Purchase, 10/139
Performing Arts Fdn., NYC, 10/141
Performing Dance Fdn., Merrick, 10/142
Perkin Fund, NYC, 10/142
Perkins (George W.) Memorial Fdn., NYC, 10/143
Perkins (Clarence W.) Trust, Rochester, 10/144
Perlbinder (J.) Fdn., NYC, 10/144
Perman (Edith & Paul) Fdn., Rockville Centre, 10/145
Perrin (M. D.) Fdn., NYC, 10/145
Perry (Hart) Fdn., NYC, 10/147
Perry (W. Haggin) Fdn., NYC, 10/147
Pershing (Muriel R. & Francis W.) Fdn., NYC, 10/148
Peters (Betty M. & Leone J.) Fdn., NYC, 10/149
Peterson (Karl) Fdn., Jamestown, 10/151
Petrie (Miriam & Milton) Fdn., NYC, 10/152
Petschek (Hans & Eva) Trust, NYC, 10/153
Pettit (John H.) Fdn., Ridgewood, 10/154
Pforzheimer (Carl & Lily) Fdn., NYC, 10/155
Pfeiffer (Gustavus & Louise) Research Fdn., NYC, 10/157
Pfizer Fdn., NYC, 10/159
Pforzheimer (Lily O.) Memorial Fund, NYC, 10/160
Phelps Dodge Fdn., NYC, 10/161
Philippe Fdn., NYC, 10/162
Philipson (Max & Ruth C.) Fdn., Utica, 10/164
Phillips (Charlotte Palmer) Fdn., NYC, 10/164
Phillips (Nathan & Sylvia) Fdn., NYC, 10/166
Pibly Fund, Bronx, 10/166
Picker (Blanche & Jerome W.) Fdn., NYC, 10/167
Picker (James) Fdn., White Plains, 10/167
Pierce (John B.) Fdn., NYC, 10/169
Pierce (Mal) Fdn., Huntington, 10/171
Pincus (Hannah Moisha) Fdn., Brooklyn, 10/172
Pincus (Lionel I.) Fdn., NYC, 10/172
Pinecrest Fund, 10/173
Pinto Fdn., NYC, 10/173
Pitkow (Jerome D.) Memorial Fdn., NYC, 10/174
PKL Fdn., NYC, 10/174
Planned Expenditures Fdn., NYC, 10/176
Plant (Henry B.) Memorial Fund, NYC, 10/176
Pleasantville Fdn., NYC, 10/177
Plehn (Henry M.) Fdn., East Rockaway, 10/178
Plesser Fdn., Brooklyn, 10/179
Plymouth Fdn., NYC, 10/179
Plymouth Fund, NYC, 10/180
Poet's Fdn., NYC, 10/181
Polachek (John) Fdn. for Medical Research, NYC, 10/181
Pollack (David & Ray) Fdn., NYC, 10/183
Pollitzer Fdn., NYC, 10/183
Pollock Fdn., NYC, 10/184
Polsky Fdn., NYC, 10/185
Pomerance (Leon & Harriet) Fdn., Great Neck, 10/185
Poole Fdn., Island Park, 10/186
Poor Clare Monastery #1, NYC, 10/186
Pope Fdn., NYC, 10/187
Pope Fund, 10/188
Poses (Jack I. & Lillian L.) Fdn., NYC, 10/189
Posner Fdn., NYC, 10/190
Post (Kenneth) Fdn., Etna, 10/190
Post (Marjorie Merriweather) Fdn., NYC, 10/191
Potts Memorial Fdn., Hudson, 10/192
Powell Fdn., NYC, 10/193
Pratt (Guertha) Home Endowment Fund, Rochester, 10/194

Pratt-Northam Fdn., Syracuse, 10/194
Prentice (Mr. & Mrs. Robert Kelly) Fund, NYC, 10/195
Press (Jacob) Fdn., NYC, 10/195
Tenny Press Fdn., NYC, 10/196
Pressner (Max & Anna) Fdn., NYC, 10/196
Price-Warren (Elizabeth H.) Mortuary Chapel, Troy, 10/197
Price (Louis & Harold) Fdn., NYC, 10/198
Price (Theodore H. & Nancy) Fdn., NYC, 10/199
Price Waterhouse Fdn., NYC, 10/200
Princeton Class of 1937 Fdn., NYC, 10/202
Princeton 1918 Fdn., NYC, 10/202
Prizer (John C.) Jr. Charitable Trust, NYC, 10/203
Procter (Patricia M.) Fdn., NYC, 10/204
Proff Fdn., NYC, 10/205
Proff (Morris & Anna) Sons Fund, NYC, 10/206
Prospect Hill Fdn., NYC, 10/208
Prutzman Fdn., Manhasset, 10/209
Finch Pruyn Fdn., Glen Falls, 10/209
Psi Upsilon Scholarship Trust, Rochester, 10/210
Puckett (B. Earl) Fund for Retail Educ., NYC, 10/211
Puro Fdn., NYC, 10/211
Pyramid Fdn., NYC, 10/212
Quarry Lake Trust, NYC, 10/212
Quartararo (Jack M. and Anthony M.) Fdn., Poughkeepsie, 10/213
Quarte Fdn., NYC, 10/213
Rabin Fdn. Corp., NYC, 10/215
Rabinor (George B.) Fdn., Woodmere, 10/215
Rabinowitz (Abraham & Sara) Fdn., NYC, 10/215
Radin (Abraham J.) Fdn., NYC, 10/216
Radow Fdn., NYC, 10/216
Rafco Associates, NYC, 10/217
Raff (Isadore & Clair) Fdn., NYC, 10/218
Rafsky (Henry A.) Research Fund, NYC, 10/220
Raible Fdn., NYC, 10/220
Raisler (Harold K.) Fdn., NYC, 10/221
Raisler (H.N.) Fund, NYC, 10/221
Raisler (Robert K.) Fdn., NYC, 10/222
Raizen (Charles S.) Fdn., New Rochelle, 10/223
Ramsay (C.B.) Fdn., Forest Hills, 10/224
Rand Fdn., Brooklyn, 10/224
Rappaport (Rose & Morris) Fdn., Bronx, 10/225
Raskin Fdn., NYC, 10/226
Rath (John E.) Fdn., Franklin Square, 10/227
Rattner (Bessie) Fdn., NYC, 10/227
Rauch Fdn., Old Westbury, 10/228
Ray (William F.) Fdn., NYC, 10/228
Raymond Fdn., Greene, 10/228
Raymond (Sidney & Martha) Fdn., NYC, 11/002
Raynie Fdn., NYC, 11/002
R & D Fund, NYC, 11/003
Read (Charles L.) Fdn., NYC, 11/004
Reader's Digest Fdn., Pleasantville, 11/005
Realm Fdn., NYC, 11/007
Redwood Fdn., NYC, 11/007
Reflection Fdn., Hartsdale, 11/008
Reich (June & Jay) Fdn., NYC, 11/008
Reichenstein (Victor & Elyse) Fdn., Great Neck, 11/008
Reicher (Anne & Harry J.) Fdn., NYC, 11/009
Reid Fdn., Purchase, 11/009
Reid (Mary Scott) & L. Bagley Reid Trust, NYC, 11/010
Reilly (John A.) & Marjorie J. Reilly Fdn., NYC, 11/011
Reinach (Anthony M.) Fdn., NYC, 11/011
Reinhardt Fdn., NYC, 11/011
Reinhardt (Jack & Jeane) Fdn., NYC, 11/012
Reiss (Jacob L.) Fdn., NYC, 11/012
Reiss (Julian) Fdn., Lake Placid, 11/013
Relin (Morris) Fdn., NYC, 11/014
Remark, Great Neck, 11/014
Rembrandt Corporation, NYC, 11/015

Remington (Carolyn L.) Charitable Trust, Rochester, 11/016
Remington (Mr. & Mrs. John W.) Trust, Rochester, 11/017
Remmel (Harmon L.) Fund, NYC, 11/018
Renfield (Joseph H.) Charitable Trust, NYC, 11/019
Renker-Moss Fdn., Kingston, 11/020
Renshaw (Dora) Fdn., McKownsville, 11/020
Research for Individual Advancement Fdn., Mineola, 11/020
Research Institute for the Study of Man, NYC, 11/021
Resnick (Louis B.) Fdn., NYC, 11/022
Reves (Weny & Emery) Fdn., NYC, 11/022
Revits (Harry) Fdn., Flushing, 11/022
Revlon Fdn., NYC, 11/023
Revoir (Frank G. & Frances) Fdn., Syracuse, 11/024
Revson (Martin) Fdn., NYC, 11/024
Rexford Fund, NYC, 11/025
Reynolds (Christopher) Fdn., NYC, 11/026
Rhoades (John M.) Fdn., NYC, 11/028
Rhodes Fdn., NYC, 11/028
Rice (Jacob & Sophie) Family Fdn., NYC, 11/028
Rice (Stanley R.) Fdn., NYC, 11/028
Rich (Robert E.) Company, Buffalo, 11/030
Richard Fdn., NYC, 11/030
Richard (Henry & Ida) Fdn., NYC, 11/032
Richards (Irving and Rosalind) Fdn., NYC, 11/032
Richards (Miriam and Harold) Fdn., NYC, 11/033
Richendal Fdn., NYC, 11/034
Richmond (Henry A.) Trust-Teacher's Relief Fund, Buffalo, 11/035
Ridings (Peter A.) Memorial Fdn., Cazenovia, 11/035
Riegel (John L. & Margaret M.) Fdn., NYC, 11/036
Riegel Paper Corporation Fdn., NYC, 11/036
Riegelman Fdn., NYC, 11/037
Ries (Bernadette and Hans) Fdn., Port Washington, 11/038
Riese (S & M) Fdn., NYC, 11/039
Riley (H.W.E.) Fdn., Ardsley-on-Hudson, 11/039
Riley (Nancy L.) Fdn., NYC, 11/040
Rimberg (Anita Adolf) Fdn., Bronx, 11/040
Rinehart (Mary Roberts) Fdn., NYC, 11/041
Rittenberg (Newman L.) Fund, NYC, 11/041
Ritter (May Ellen & Gerald) Fdn., NYC, 11/042
Rittmaster Fdn., NYC, 11/043
Riverside Fdn., NYC, 11/045
Rizzuti Medical & Eye Research Fdn., Brooklyn, 11/045
RKO General Fdn., NYC, 11/046
RME Fdn., NYC, 11/046
RMG Fdn., NYC, 11/046
Roaman (Alan & Joyce) Fdn., Great Neck, 11/048
Roaman (Irving & Luzela) Fdn., NYC, 11/048
Roaman (Richard & Barbara) Fdn., NYC, 11/048
Robanna Charitable Trust, NYC, 11/049
Robbins Charitable Fdn., NYC, 11/050
Robbins (Herman) Memorial Fdn., NYC, 11/050
Roberts (Louis & Edith) Fdn., NYC, 11/051
Roberts (Richard & Doris) Charitable Trust, NYC, 11/051
Robey Fdn. Trust u/d C.L. Robey, NYC, 11/051
Robin Fdn., Brooklyn, 11/053
Robins Family Fdn., Point Lookout, 11/053
Robinson (Lewis G.) Charitable Trust, Troy, 11/054
Robinson (Lewis G.) Para 6th A, Troy, 11/055
Robison (James E.), NYC, 11/056
Roby (Sidney B.) Charitable Trust, Rochester, 11/056
Rochester Jobs Incorporated, Rochester, 11/057
Rochester Opportunities Fdn., Rochester, 11/059

Scharf (Blanche & Aaron M.) Fdn., NYC, 11/221

Scheider (Julius) & Marie Scheider Fdn., NYC, 11/222

Scheinbart Fdn., NYC, 11/223

Scheinberg Fdn., NYC, 11/223

Schell (Alice A.) Memorial Fund, NYC, 11/233

Schenck (Nicholas and Pansy) Fdn., NYC, 11/224

Schenectady Local 105 Educational and Apprenticeship Fund, Schenectady, 11/225

Schenley Fund, NYC, 11/225

Schegler (Sylvan) Trust Fdn., NYC, 11/226

Scher Family Fdn., NYC, 11/226

Schetzen (Harry & Mae) Fdn., NYC, 11/227

Scheuer Associates Fdn., NYC, 11/227

Scheuer (S. H. & Helen R.) Family Fdn., NYC, 11/228

Schickel (Caroline) Trust u/w, Buffalo, 12/001

Schiff Fdn., NYC, 12/001

Schiff (Lawrence & Sidney L.) Fdn., NYC, 12/003

Schildkraut Fdn., NYC, 12/004

Schimmel Fdn., NYC, 12/004

Schimmel (Michael) Fdn., NYC, 12/005

Schimper (Frederick & Amelia) Fdn., NYC, 12/006

Schlang Fdn., NYC, 12/007

Schlein Fdn., Merrick, 12/008

Schlosser (Jack & Dorothy) Fdn., Great Neck, 12/009

Schmidt (Arthur W. and Nellie W.) Charitable Fdn., Spring Valley, 12/009

Schmidt (Thomas Payne) Fdn., NYC, 12/010

Schneider Fdn., NYC, 12/011

Schneider (Harry and Sylvia) Fdn., Far Rockaway, 12/012

Schneider (Walter J.), NYC, 12/013

Lippman Schnurmacher Fund, NYC, 12/014

Schoellkopf (J.F.) IV, Berkshire Scholarship Fund, NYC, 12/015

Schoellkopf (Judith Abbott) Fdn., Buffalo, 12/016

Schoellkopf (J.F.) Trust for Western, 12/016 N.Y. Section American Chemical Society, Buffalo, 12/016

Achoen Fdn., Bronx, 12/016

Schoengold Fdn., Woodmere, 12/017

Schoff Family Fund, NYC, 12/018

Scholarship Fdn., NYC, 12/019

Scholarship Fund of the Men's Club of The Town of Pelham, Pelham, 12/020

Schorr (Esther) Fdn., NYC, 12/020

Schott (Lewis & Marcia) Fdn., NYC, 12/021

Schrader (Abe & Rose) Fdn., NYC, 12/021

Schrader (Edward A.) Fdn., NYC, 12/022

Schrag (Carl I.) Scholarship Fdn., Brooklyn, 12/022

Schulman Fdn., NYC, 12/023

Schreiber (Aaron M.) Family Fdn., NYC, 12/024

Schreiber (Adolph H.) Family Fdn., NYC, 12/025

Schreiber (Louis J.) Family Fdn., NYC, 12/026

Schreiber (Max) Family Fdn., NYC, 12/027

Schreier (Sandra & Fred) Charitable Trust, Scarsdale, 12/027

Schulman (Jacob) Fdn., Gloversville, 12/028

Schulman (Samuel & Bertha) Fdn., NYC, 12/028

Schultz (Michael & Lora) Fdn., NYC, 12/029

Schutz (Sigmund) Fdn., NYC, 12/030

Schuman (Allan R.) Fdn., NYC, 12/032

Schupf Family Fund, NYC, 12/033

Schur Fdn., Bronx, 12/033

Schur (Lawrence H.) Fdn., Bronx, 12/035

Schustek (Samuel & Hannah) Fdn., Jamaica, 12/035

Schwab (Martin & Betty) Fdn., NYC, 12/035

Schwartz (Arnold) Charitable Fdn., NYC, 12/036

Schwartz (Arnold) Charitable Trust, NYC, 12/036

Schwartz (Milton I. & Harriet) Fdn., Great Neck, 12/037

Schwarzhaupt (Emil) Fdn., NYC, 12/038

Schweitzer (Herbert) Fdn., NYC, 12/038

Schuster Charitable Trust, NYC, 12/039

Schwab (Jack) Fdn., NYC, 12/040

Schwab (Willy & Bertha) Fdn., NYC, 12/040

Schwab (Albert S.) Fdn., Rochester, 12/041

Schwab (J. E.) Fdn., NYC, 12/042

Schwadron (Arthur & Marjorie) Fdn., Scarsdale, 12/043

Schwalbe Brothers Fdn., NYC, 12/043

Schwartz (Alvin & Dorothy) Fdn., Great Neck, 12/044

Schwartz (A. J.) Fdn., Greenvale, 12/044

Schwartz (Barbara H.) Charitable Trust, NYC, 12/045

Schwartz (Harry A.) Family Fdn., NYC, 12/045

Schwartz (Joseph H. & Rose) & Milton & Barbara Schwartz Fdn., NYC, 12/046

Schwartz (Leo & Bea) Fund, NYC, 12/047

Schwartz (Morna R.) Fdn., NYC, 12/048

Schwartz (Nathan S.) Typographical Union No. 6 Award, NYC, 12/049

Schwartzstein Fdn., NYC, 12/049

Schwartzschild (Molly & Alfred) Fdn., NYC, 12/049

Schwebel (Irene & Mac) Fdn., NYC, 12/050

Schweitzer (Peter J.) Fdn., NYC, 12/050

Schweitzer (William P.) Fdn., NYC, 12/051

Scientific Research Fdn., NYC, 12/052

Scotese Family Fdn., NYC, 12/053

Scott (David B.) Fdn., Norwich, 12/053

Scott (Earle M.) Family Fdn., Lancaster, 12/054

Scott (S. Spencer) Fund, Scarsdale, 12/055

Scott (Walter) Fdn., NYC, 12/056

Scott (William & Edith) Fdn., NYC, 12/057

Scottish Women's Society Trust, Rochester, 12/058

Scull (Mr. & Mrs. Robert C.) Fdn., Corona, 12/059

Sealantic Fund, NYC, 12/059

Seamprufe Fdn., NYC, 12/062

Seedman (George J.) Fdn., NYC, 12/062

Seely (Hart I.) Memorial Student Loan Fund of Waverly, New York, Waverly, 12/062

Segal Medical Research Fund, Rochester, 12/063

Segal (Rosa & Harry) Fdn., NYC, 12/063

Seiden & deCueras Fdn., NYC, 12/063

Seidman Fdn., NYC, 12/064

Seiffert Fdn., Bronx, 12/065

Seiler (Jack & Muriel P.) Fdn., NYC, 12/065

Sejlee Fdn., Scarsdale, 12/066

Selden (Florence & Carl) Fdn., NYC, 12/067

Seley Fdn., Atlantic Beach, 12/067

Seley (Louis E. & Theresa S.) Fdn., Atlantic Beach, 12/068

Selgreen Fdn., NYC, 12/068

Selkowitz (Sam & Julia) Fdn., Binghamton, 12/069

Service to Adolescents through Release of Tension, NYC, 12/069

Setze (Josephine) Trust, NYC, 12/069

Service Lodge Fdn. Fund, NYC, 12/071

Seven Lamps Fdn., NYC, 12/071

Seventh Regiment Fund, NYC, 12/072

Shafer Research Fdn., NYC, 12/072

Shafiroff (Martin D.) Fdn., NYC, 12/073

Shaker (Ann Maytag) Fdn., NYC, 12/073

Shalen (Robert E. & Howard H.) Fdn., NYC, 12/073

Shankman (Richard Allan) Memorial Fund, NYC, 12/074

Shapiro Fdn., NYC, 12/074

Shapiro Fund, NYC, 12/075

Shapiro (A. & I.) Fdn., Brooklyn, 12/076

Shapiro (I. & L.) Fdn., NYC, 12/u78

Shapiro (Robert H. & Muriel A.) Charitable Trust, Scarsdale, 12/079

Sharfman (Isidore) Fdn., NYC, 12/080

Sharing (B. L.) Association, Brooklyn, 12/080

Sharpe Family Fdn., NYC, 12/081

Shatford (J. D.) Memorial Trust, NYC, 12/082

Shattuck (George & Sheila) Charitable Trust, Syracuse, 12/083

Shearson, Hammill Fdn., NYC, 12/083

Sheckman (Mina Bronfman) Fdn., NYC, 12/084

Shedlin (Allan) Fdn., NYC, 12/085

Sheib (Simon & Stella) Fdn., NYC, 12/086

Sheils Fdn., New Rochelle, 12/087

Sheinberg (Eric P.) Fdn., NYC, 12/087

Sheldon Fdn., NYC, 12/087

Sheldon (Max) Fdn., NYC, 12/088

Shell Companies Fdn., NYC, 12/088

Sheltering Arms Children's Service--Gould Fund, NYC, 12/093

Shenstone Branch Fdn., NYC, 12/094

Shepherd Fdn., NYC, 12/095

Sheriff Fund, Chappaqua, 12/095'

Sherman Fdn., Flushing, 12/096

Sherman (Florence) Fdn., NYC, 12/097

Sherman (Max) Fdn., NYC, 12/098

Sherman (Walter) Fdn., Brooklyn, 12/099

Sherr Fdn., NYC, 12/099

Sherr (Abraham I. & Jean) Fdn., NYC, 12/100

Sherrill Fdn., NYC, 12/101

Sherwood (Arvilla) Trust, Rochester, 12/102

Shethar Fdn., NYC, 12/103

S & H Fdn., NYC, 12/103

Shields (Elizabeth Bayne) Fund, NYC, 12/108

Shields (Richard) Charitable Trust, NYC, 12/109

Shields (Richard) Fund, NYC, 12/111

Shikes Fdn., NYC, 12/112

Shipper Fdn., Brooklyn, 12/113

Shults (Otto A.) Fdn., Rochester, 12/113

Shuman (Stanley S.) Fdn., NYC, 12/114

Shumway (Frank & Shirley) Fdn., Rochester, 12/115

Siebert (Muriel F.) Fdn., NYC, 12/115

Siegadi Fdn., Hempstead, 12/116

Siegel (Benjamin & Rachel) Charitable Trust, Rochester, 12/117

Siegel (Herbert J. & Ann L.) Fdn., NYC, 12/118

Siegel (Jacob & Amelia) Fdn., NYC, 12/118

Siegman (Simon) Fund, NYC, 12/119

Sigall (Leon & Hertha) Fdn., NYC, 12/119

Sigma Chi Fdn./Rochester Gamma Pi, Rochester, 12/120

Silber Fdn., Woodmere, 12/120

Silberberg Fdn., NYC, 12/121

Silberkleit (Louis H.) Fdn., NYC, 12/122

Silberman (J. Sidney) Fdn., NYC, 12/122

Silbermann (Max) Fdn., NYC, 12/123

Silberstein Fdn., NYC, 12/124

Sills (Philip & Helen) Fdn., NYC, 12/125

Silman (David) Fdn., NYC, 12/125

Silver (Robert J. & Sandra K.) Fdn., NYC, 12/126

Silver (Israel & Clara) Fdn., NYC, 12/127

Silver (Roslyn & Julius) Fdn., NYC, 12/127

Silvera (David) Fdn., NYC, 12/128

Silverberg (Blanche) Memorial Fdn., NYC, 12/129

Silverman Fdn., NYC, 12/129

Silverman (Jack) Fdn., Jamaica, 12/130

Silverman (Jeffrey S.) Fdn., NYC, 12/131

Silverman (Morris & Arthur O.) Fund, NYC, 12/131

Silverman (Richard Lynn) Fdn., Locust Valley, 12/132

Silvershein Charitable Trust, NYC, 12/132

Silverstein (Joseph & Beatrice) Fdn., NYC, 12/133

Silverstein (Lt. Joseph) Memorial Fund, NYC, 12/134

Silverstone (Estelle & Sidney M.) Fdn., Harrison, 12/134

Simmonds Fdn., NYC, 12/135

Simon Fdn., Albany, 12/135

Simon Fdn., NYC, 12/136

Simon (Hermann E.) Charitable Trust, NYC, 12/137

Simon (Irving L.) Fdn., Albany, 12/138

Simon (Robert & Anne) Fdn., NYC, 12/138

Simon (Stanley & Marcelle K.) Charitable Trust, NYC, 12/138
Simon (William E.) Fdn., NYC, 12/139
Simson (Walter H.) Fdn., NYC, 12/141
Singer (Carl & Marion) Charitable Fdn., NYC, 12/142
Singer Company Fdn., NYC, 12/143
Singer (Dorothy & Sidney) Fdn., NYC, 12/145
Singer (B. Barrett) Fdn., Amsterdam, 12/146
Singer (Everett) Fdn., Amsterdam, 12/147
Singer (Harry & Anna) Fdn., Bronx, 12/147
Singer (Herbert T.) Fdn., Amsterdam, 12/147
Sinnet (Herman) Fdn., NYC, 12/148
Singer (Maurice) & Company, Port Chester, 12/148
Sirow (Melvin & Doris) Fdn., Great Neck, 12/149
Sisters of Third Order of St. Francis, Rochester, 12/150
Skaneateles Central School Endowment Fdn., Skaneateles, 12/151
Skerryvore Fdn., NYC, 12/152
Sklar (Max H.) Fdn., Long Island City, 12/153
Skutch (Judith & Robert) Fdn., NYC, 12/154
Slaner Fdn., NYC, 12/154
Slater (Murray) Fdn., NYC, 12/155
Sleepy Hollow Restorations, Irvington, 12/155
Slifka (Alan B.) Fdn., NYC, 12/158
Slifka (Irving) Fdn., NYC, 12/158
Sloan (Alfred P.) Fdn., NYC, 12/158
Slocum-Dickson Fdn., Utica, 12/164
Sloman Fdn., New Rochelle, 12/165
Slotkin Fdn., NYC, 12/165
Smachlo Fdn., NYC, 12/166
Small (David H.) Fdn., NYC, 12/166
Small (Irving & Myrna) Fdn., NYC, 12/167
Small (Rita F.) Memorial Fdn., NYC, 12/168
Smigel Charitable Fdn., Cortland, 12/168
Smith, Barney Fdn., NYC, 12/169
Smith (George Graham) & Elizabeth Galloway Smith Fdn., Buffalo, 12/170
Earl (Harrison) & Frances Smith Scholarship Fund, Elmira, 12/171
Smith (Josephine Rudy) Memorial Fdn., Syracuse, 12/171
Smith (George D.) Fund, NYC, 12/171
Smith (Matthew E. & Gladys C.) Trust, NYC, 12/172
Smithers (Christopher O.) Fdn., NYC, 12/173
Smoler (Irwin C.) Fdn., NYC, 12/176
Smutny (Rudolf & Florence M.) Family Fdn., Garden City, 12/177
Sneider-Magid Fdn., NYC, 12/178
Snell (Albert C.) Research Fund, Scarsdale, 12/178
Society of Art Theatre of Ballet Fdn., NYC, 12/179
Socolow Fdn., NYC, 12/180
Socolow (Lena) Palestine Scholarship Fund, NYC, 12/180
Sohn (Harry & Dora F.) Fdn., Far Rockaway, 12/181
Sokoloff Fdn., NYC, 12/181
Sokolsky (George E.) Silurian Contingency Fund, NYC, 12/182
Solinger (David M. & Hope G.) Fdn., NYC, 12/182
Sollar Fdn., NYC, 12/183
Solomon (Caspar L.) Fdn., Rochester, 12/184
Solomon (Jacob & Yetta) Fdn., NYC, 12/184
Solomon (Philip & Edward) Fdn., Great Neck, 12/185
Solomon (Sally & Alta) Fdn., NYC, 12/186
Solomon (Sidney L.) Fdn., NYC, 12/187
Solomon (Morris J.) Sunshine Fund, Brooklyn, 12/188
Solow (Samuel) Fdn., NYC, 12/189
Solzberg Fdn., Brooklyn, 12/189
Sonderling (Catherine & Egmont) Fdn., NYC, 12/190
Sontag Fdn., NYC, 12/191
Soriano (Andres) Cancer Research Fund, NYC, 12/191
Soros (George) Charitable Trust, NYC, 12/192
South Bay Fund, NYC, 12/193
Spaeth Fdn., NYC, 12/193

Spear (Arthur & Stella) Fund, Briarcliff Manor, 12/194
Spectemur Agendo, Inc., NYC, 12/195
Spector (Julian & Frances) Fdn., Forest Hills, 12/196
Spector (Solomon) Fdn., Syracuse, 12/197
Spector Fdn., NYC, 12/197
Spektor Family Fdn., NYC, 12/198
Spencer (Girard L.) Family Fdn., NYC, 12/198
Spengler Educational Fdn., Brooklyn, 12/199
Sperling (Paul & Julia) Fdn., NYC, 12/199
Sperry (Paul J.) Charitable Fund, NYC, 12/201
Sperry Rand Corporation Fdn., NYC, 12/201
Spiegel (Ike D.) Fdn., NYC, 12/202
Spielberg Fdn., Jamaica, 12/203
Spielman (Lillian S. & William B.) Fdn., NYC, 12/204
Spilky Fdn., NYC, 12/205
Spilky (A. H. & E. G.) Fdn., Brooklyn, 12/205
Spill Fdn. Trust, NYC, 12/205
Spingold (Nate B. & Frances) Fdn., NYC, 12/206
Spirer Fdn., NYC, 12/206
Spitalnik Fdn., New Rochelle, 12/207
Sprayregen Fdn., NYC, 12/207
Springate Corporation (f/k/a Leonard Bernstein Fdn.), NYC, 12/208
Spofford (Carolyn S.) Fdn., NYC, 12/208
Sprague (Julian & Helene) Fdn., NYC, 12/209
Sprague (Seth) Fdn., NYC, 12/210
Srybnik Fdn., Brooklyn, 12/215
Staley (Thomas F.) Fdn., NYC, 12/216
Stamer (Frank B. & Emilie E.) Fdn., Brooklyn, 12/218
Standard Packaging Fdn., NYC, 12/218
Stanger (Wesley A.) Jr. Fund, NYC, 12/219
Stanley (Alfred T.) Fdn., NYC, 12/219
Stanley (Morgan) Fdn., NYC, 12/220
Stanley-Timolat Fdn., NYC, 12/221
Stanlinco Ltd. Fdn., Brooklyn, 12/222
Stanmar Fund, NYC, 12/222
Stern (Michaels) Fdn., Rochester, 12/223
Star Supermarkets Fdn., Rochester, 12/223
Stark (Virgil & Judith) Fdn., NYC, 12/225
Starr Fdn., NYC, 12/225
Statler Fdn., Buffalo, 12/227
Statler (Ellsworth M.) for Ellsworth Morgan Statler, Buffalo, 13/001
Statler (Ellsworth M.) Trust for Marian Frances Statler-Milton Howland Statler Portion, Buffalo, 13/001
Statler (Ellsworth M.) Trust for Marion-Idesta Statler Portion, Buffalo, 13/002
Statter (Amy Plant) Fdn., NYC, 13/002
Staub (Marshal G.) Fdn., NYC, 13/003
Stavisky Family Fdn., NYC, 13/003
Stearns (Janet Upjohn) Charitable Trust, NYC, 13/003
Stears (Janet Upjohn) Fdn., NYC, 13/004
Stebbins Fund, Syosset, 13/005
Stedman Fdn., Portchester, 13/007
Steeplechase Fund, Elmont, 13/008
Steffan (Walter J.) Fdn., Hamburg, 13/009
Stein (Benjamin M.) Fdn., Great Neck, 13/010
Stein (Joseph F.) Fdn., NYC, 13/011
Steinberg (Julius) Fdn., Great Neck, 13/012
Steinberg (Meyer) Fdn., NYC, 13/013
Steinberg (Saul) Fdn., NYC, 13/013
Steinberger-Mayer Fdn., NYC, 13/014
Steindecker (John D. & Rebecca) Fdn., NYC, 13/015
Steinert (Albert & Marie) Fdn., NYC, 13/015
Steinman (David B.) Fdn., NYC, 13/016
Stern (Charles M.) Award Trust, Albany, 13/017
Stern (Herbert M.) Charitable Trust, Rochester, 13/018
Stern Edwin & Eve) Fdn., NYC, 13/018
Stern (Erna & Isaac) Fdn., Brooklyn, 13/019
Stern (Frederick & Lotte) Fdn., NYC, 13/020
Stern (Isidore) Fdn., NYC, 13/021
Stern (Leo & Marjorie) Fdn., NYC, 13/022
Stern Max) Charitable Trust, NYC, 13/023

Stern (Robert L. & Ellen D.) Fdn., NYC, 13/024
Stern (Siegfried) Fdn., NYC, 13/025
Stern (Walter P. & Elizabeth M.) Fdn., NYC, 13/025
Sternlight (Hugo C.) Fdn., NYC, 13/026
Stetten (Edwin) Fdn., NYC, 13/027
Stettenheim (Flora & Isidor M.) Fdn., NYC, 13/028
Stevenson (Burton E.) Endowment for Children, NYC, 13/028
Stevenson (John) Fdn., NYC, 13/029
Stevenson Fdn. Trust, Rochester, 13/030
Stevens (Caroline H.) Trust, Rochester, 13/031
Stewart (Charles & Maud) Fdn., NYC, 13/032
Stifel Fdn., NYC, 13/033
Stillman (Leland) Fdn., NYC, 13/034
S T M Fdn., NYC, 13/034
Stolbach (Rose & Dora) Fdn., NYC, 13/036
Stone Fence Fund, NYC, 13/036
Stone Fdn., NYC, 13/037
Stone Fdn., NYC, 13/037
Stone (Gerald & Helen) Fdn., NYC, 13/038
Stone (Hannah & Leonard) Fdn., NYC, 13/038
Stone (Louis) Fdn., NYC, 13/039
Stonehill (Norma L. & Harold S.) Fdn., NYC, 13/039
Stony Brook Community Fund, Stony Brook, 13/040
Stoolfire Trust Estate, Granville, 13/041
Storm King Art Center, Mountainville, 13/042
Stovroff Fdn., Buffalo, 13/043
Stowell Fdn., NYC, 13/043
Strasenburgh Fdn., Rochester, 13/044
Straus (Glayds G.) Family Fund, NYC, 13/045
Straus (Irma N.) Fdn., NYC, 13/046
Straus (Margaret & Jack I.) Fdn., NYC, 13/047
Straus (Oscar & Marion) Fdn., NYC, 13/047
Straus Trust Fund, NYC, 13/048
Strauss (David & Lois) Fdn., NYC, 13/049
Strauss (Max & Ida) Fdn., NYC, 13/050
Streeter (Leora Y.) Scholarship Award Trust, Rochester, 13/050
Streisand (Emanuel) Fdn., NYC, 13/051
Strelsin Fdn., NYC, 13/052
Strichman Fdn., NYC, 13/053
Stroock (Alan & Katherine) Fund, NYC, 13/053
Strum (Irving & Esther) Fdn., NYC, 13/054
Stuart (Harry) Fdn., NYC, 13/054
Studley Fdn., NYC, 13/055
Studner (Myron M.) Fdn., NYC, 13/056
Stulman Fdn., Brooklyn, 13/057
Stuttman (Sol & Beatrice) Fdn., NYC, 13/057
Suarez (Evelyn Marshall) Fdn., NYC, 13/058
Suchman (Joseph) Memorial Fdn., NYC, 13/059
Sudman (Solomon I. & Fannie) Fdn., NYC, 13/059
Sugden (Herbert J. & Margaret S.) Fdn., Saranac Lake, 13/061
Sukenik Fdn., NYC, 13/061
Sullivan (Algernon Sydney) Fdn., NYC, 13/061
Sullivan (Glayds L.) Charitable Trust, Rochester, 13/064
Sullivan (William Matheus) Musical Fdn., NYC, 13/065
Sulzbach Fdn., NYC, 13/066
Sulzberger Fdn., NYC, 13/067
Sulzberger (Louise B. & David H.) Fdn., NYC, 13/068
Sulzberger (Marion B.) Fdn., NYC, 13/068
Summerfield (Solon E.) Fdn., NYC, 13/069
Sumner Fdn. for the Arts, NYC, 13/071
Sun-Bulletin Fund, Binghamton, 13/071
Sun Chemical Fdn., NYC, 13/071
Sunshine Biscuits Fdn., NYC, 13/072
Supenat Fdn., New Rochelle, 13/073
Superba Cravats Charitable Trust, Rochester, 13/073
Surut (Richard) Fdn., NYC, 13/074
Suslak Family Charitable Fdn., NYC, 13/075

Sussman (Murray & Miriam) Fdn., NYC, 13/076

Sutton (Abraham ben Jacob) Fdn., Long Beach, 13/076

Sutton Fund for Educational Research, NYC, 13/077

Sudakoff (Harry) Fdn., Forest Hills, 13/078

Swanson Fdn., NYC, 13/079

Schwartz (Samuel & Bertha) Fdn., Auburn, 13/079

Swartzman (Harry & Edna) Fdn., NYC, 13/081

Sweig (Morton & Charlotte) Fdn., NYC, 13/081

Swenson (Olof C.) Charitable Trust, NYC, 13/081

Swiger Fdn., NYC, 13/082

Swiss Society of Sciences in U.S.A., NYC, 13/082

Switzer Fdn., NYC, 13/083

Swope Gift Corporation, NYC, 13/084

Grant (Elizabeth Swords) Research Fdn., NYC, 13/085

Sybron Community Fund, Rochester, 13/085

Sykes (Wadsworth C.) Charitable Trust, Rochester, 13/085

Sykes (W. C.) Trust Fund, Rochester, 13/086

Sylvester (Allie L.) Fund, NYC, 13/086

Syracuse Home Association, Syracuse, 13/087

Syracuse Jewish Children's Fdn., Syracuse, 13/088

Syracuse Supply Company Fdn., Syracuse, 13/089

Syroco-Holstein Fdn., Baldwinsville, 13/090

Szerlip (Judith & Jack) Fdn., NYC, 13/090

Tachna (Ensign Lionel J.) Memorial Fund, NYC, 13/091

Tager-Joffe Fdn., Buffalo, 13/092

Tailors' National Home, NYC, 13/093

Tai-Ping Fdn., NYC, 13/094

Taishoff (Jerome) Fdn., NYC, 13/095

Tait (Mr. & Mrs. Robert C.) Charitable Fund, Rochester, 13/096

Talcott (James) Fund, NYC, 13/097

Talisman Fdn., NYC, 13/104

Talmage Charitable Trust, NYC, 13/105

Tambil Fdn. Trust, NYC, 13/106

Lockhart (J. M.) Trust, NYC, 13/107

Tamis (Abraham & Lillian) Fdn., NYC, 13/107

Tananbaum (Stanley & Doris) Fdn., NYC, 13/108

Tanenbaum (Barnett & Rae) Fdn., NYC, 13/109

Tannenbaum (Nathan) Fdn., NYC, 13/109

Tanner Fdn., Scarsdale, 13/110

Target Rock Fdn., NYC, 13/110

Tarnoff (Arline V. & Norman H.) Fdn., Yonkers, 13/111

Task Fdn., NYC, 13/112

Tausend (Stanley) Fdn., NYC, 13/112

Tavlin (Michael N.) Charitable Trust, Great Neck, 13/113

Taylor Scholarship Fdn., NYC, 13/113

Taylor (Hilda D.) Fund, Rochester, 13/114

Taylor (Moses) Fdn., NYC, 13/115

Tebil Fdn., NYC, 13/116

Teitelbaum (David & Sylvia) Fund, NYC, 13/121

Tekakwitha Fdn., Waterford, 13/121

Telfeyan Evangelical Fund, Plandome, 13/123

Tenmain Fdn., NYC, 13/123

Tennant (John S.) Charitable & Educational Fund, NYC, 13/124

Tennant Fdn., NYC, 13/125

Tennyson (Jean) Fdn., NYC, 13/125

Terrace Park Dairy Fdn., Sioux Falls, So. Dak., 13/126

Terwilliger (Donald L.) Fdn., NYC, 13/127

Thannhauser Fdn., NYC, 13/127

Theatre Communications Group, NYC, 13/128

Third Dakota Fund, NYC, 13/128

Thompson (H.E.) Fdn., NYC, 13/129

Thompson (John F.) Fdn., NYC, 13/130

Thompson (J. Walter) Company Fund, NYC, 13/131

Thompson (Otis A.) Fdn., Norwich, 13/133

Thomson (James E.) Fdn., NYC, 13/134

Thompson (Wm. B.) Trust, Yonkers, 13/135

Thorne Fdn., NYC, 13/135

Thors (J. Emerson & Marthe M.) Fdn., NYC, 13/136

Three Seas Fdn., NYC, 13/137

Tiffany (Louis Comfort) Fdn., NYC, 13/138

Tillinghast Fund, NYC, 13/138

Tingle (Leonard) Fdn., NYC, 13/140

Tinker Fdn., NYC, 13/140

Tinker (Annie Rensselaer) Memorial Fund, NYC, 13/143

Tioga Fdn., NYC, 13/144

Tishman (Alexander & Amy) Fdn., NYC, 13/145

Tishman (Edward & Jeanette) Fund, NYC, 13/146

Tishman (Norman--Rita) Fund, NYC, 13/147

Tishman (Peter & Ellen) Fund, NYC, 13/148

Tishman (Paul) Trust, NYC, 13/148

Titelbaum (Joseph L.) Fdn., NYC, 13/149

T. O. C. C. Fdn., East Meadow, 13/149

Tod (Sarah) Fund, NYC, 13/149

Todd (George L. & Elizabeth C.) Trust, Rochester, 13/150

Hamlin (T. O.) Trust for Soldiers & Sailors Memorial Hospital, Rochester, 13/151

Todd (Walter L. & George L.) Trust, Rochester, 13/151

Tode (Arthur M. & Kate E.) & Arthur M. & Olga T. Eisig Fdn., NYC, 13/152

Toffel Fdn., NYC, 13/152

Tolchin (Arthur & Mary Frances) Fdn., Harrison, 13/152

Tolkin (Irving N.) Fdn., Woodhaven, 13/153

Tomleen Fdn., NYC, 13/154

Tomshinsky (Fannie & Victor Fdn., NYC, 13/155

Tona Fdn., NYC, 13/156

Topol Fdn., Mamaroneck, 13/156

Townsen (Mr. & Mrs. Douglas C.) Trust Fund, Rochester, 13/156

Townson (Mr. & Mrs. Kenneth C.) Fund, Rochester, 13/157

Tracy Fdn., Harrison, 13/159

Tracy Fdn., Coeymans Hollow, 13/160

Traeger (Jacqueline & Charles H.) Fdn., NYC, 13/160

Traina (Teal) Fdn., NYC, 13/161

Trainor (Bertha) Memorial Bed for Children Fdn., Albany, 13/162

Trajean Fdn., NYC, 13/163

Travis (Judson & Helen) Charitable Fund, NYC, 13/164

Treisman (Jerome E.) Charitable Fund, NYC, 13/164

Treitel (Nathan & Eva) Fdn., NYC, 13/165

Trent (Edwin & Terese) Fdn., NYC, 13/165

Trenton-New Brunswick Theatres Welfare Fund, NYC, 13/166

Tremain (Hon. Charles) Memorial Trust, NYC, 13/166

Treuenfels (Rudy) Educational Fdn., NYC, 13/167

Triantafillu (Harry D.) Fdn., White Plains, 13/168

Trippe Fund, NYC, 13/168

Triumph Fund, NYC, 13/169

Tropham Fdn., Bronx, 13/169

T R R Fdn., NYC, 13/170

Trump (Fred C.) Fdn., Jamaica, 13/171

Anderson (Marcus) Trust u/w, for Lakeview Cemetery, Jamestown, 13/172

Andrews (Anna May) Trust u/w, f/b/o The Buffalo Fdn., Buffalo, 13/172

Ball (Albert) Trust u/a, f/b/o First Baptist Church, Buffalo, 13/173

Bassett (Nehemiah B.) Trust u/w, Schenectady, 13/173

Beinecke (Doris K.) Fdn., Trust u/a, NYC, 13/173

Brown (Irene M.) Trust u/w, f/b/o John & Irene Scholarship Fund, Buffalo, 13/174

Burkett (Jessie S.) Trust u/w, Delhi, 13/175

Chamberlain (Sarah A.) Trust u/w, f/b/o American Association of University Women, Buffalo, 13/175

Trustees of the Children's Endowment Fund of The Fifth Masonic District of Manhattan, NYC, 13/176

Cobb (Helen Anderson) Trust u/w, Buffalo, 13/176

Crane (Charles R.) Trust u/w, f/b/o Institute of Current World Affairs, NYC, 13/176

Trust for Employees of United Paramount Theatres, NYC, 13/176

Trust for Employees of Paramount Pictures Theatre Corporation, NYC, 13/177

Ewell (Carrie F.) Trust u/w, Buffalo, 13/178

Grant (Harriet W.) Trust u/w, Buffalo, 13/178

Grant (Elmer L.) Trust u/w for First Society, Buffalo, 13/178

Harriman (Mary W.) Trust, Trustees under, NYC, 13/179

Hopkins (Edward D.) Trust u/w, Buffalo, 13/181

Hubes (Henry) Trust u/w for First Presbyterian Church Society, Buffalo, 13/181

Klinck (Fred F.) Trust u/w, f/b/o Fred F. Klinck Memorial Fund, Buffalo, 13/182

Lang (James H.) Trust u/w Cemetery Trust, Buffalo, 13/183

Maclay (Alfred B.) Gardens, Trustees of, Tallahassee, Fla., 13/183

Mahoney (James N.) Trust u/w, f/b/o Crippled Childrens' Camps, Buffalo, 13/183

Marshall (Lida T.) Trust u/w for, Buffalo, 13/184

Marshall (Lida T.) Trust u/w for Board of First Presbyterian Church, Buffalo, 13/184

Marshall (Lida T.) Trust u/w for First Presbyterian Society, Buffalo, 13/185

McCann (James J.) Trust u/w, Poughkeepsie, 13/185

Moore (Eleanore A.) Trust u/w, Buffalo, 13/186

Oppenheim (Max) Trust u/w, Buffalo, 13/187

Siegert (Wilhelmina C.) Trust under Item 12 of Will, Forest Hills, 13/188

Sussman (Otto) Trust u/w Article V, NYC, 13/188

Shea (John T. & Mina) Memorial Fund, Trust u/w, Utica, 13/190

Talcott (Maria L.) Trust u/w for First Presbyterian Church of Silver Creek, Buffalo, 13/191

Townsend (Charlotte K.) Trust u/w for First Baptist Church of Leroy, Buffalo, 13/192

Townsend (Charlotte K.) Trust u/w for Leroy Red Cross, Buffalo, 13/192

Vogelstein (#####) Trust u/w for Heinemann & Rosa Vogelstein Fdn., NYC, 13/193

Walker (Anne) Trust u/w for Scholarship Fund for Dunbar High School Boys, Buffalo, 13/193

Weir (Harry N.) Trust u/w for Village of Hoosick Falls, Albany, 13/193

Laid Fdn. (Trust u/d Joan Whiteside for the), NYC, 13/194

Whitney (Helen H.) Trust u/d dated May 10, 1943 for Charitable Purposes, NYC, 13/194

Whitney (John Hay) Trust u/d dated December 29, 1959 for Charitable Purposes, NYC, 13/197

Whitney (John Hay) Trust u/d dated December 29, 1958 for Charitable Purposes, NYC, 13/198

Women's Medical Association of N.Y.C. (Trust u/a, m/b) and The Mary Putnam Jacobi Fellowship Committee of the Women's Medical Association of N.Y.C., NYC, 13/199

Wright (Nathanial, Trust u/w), Buffalo, 13/200

Tsolainos (K. P. & Phoebe) Fdn., NYC, 13/201

Tuch (Michael) Fdn., NYC, 13/202

Tucker (Marcia Brady) Fdn., Mt. Kisco, 13/203

Tulcin (Robert & Doris) Fdn., Scarsdale, 13/205

Tully (Edward A. & Pauline H.) Fdn., Flushing, 13/205

Tully (William J.) Fdn., Pelham, 13/206

Tumpeer (Victor & Pearl) Fdn., NYC, 13/207

Tunick (Stanley B.) Fdn., Rockville Centre, 13/209

Turner (Lewis & Marjorie) Fdn., NYC, 13/210

Tuscan Fdn., Brooklyn, 13/211

Tuvin Fdn., NYC, 13/211

Wender (Phyllis B. & Ira T.) Fdn., NYC, 13/211

Twin Industries Employee's Good Neighbor Fund, Buffalo, 13/212

Twinbrook Fdn., NYC, 13/212

Tyson (Robert & Lucy) Fdn., NYC, 13/213

Ullman (W. A.) Fdn., Scarsdale, 13/213

Ullmann (Sigfried & Irma) Fdn., NYC, 13/214

Ullmann Fdn., NYC, 13/215

Ulrick (Charles & Josephine Bay) Fdn., NYC, 13/216

U M C Industries Fdn., NYC, 13/217

Underhill (Mr. & Mrs. Dudley Field) Charitable Trust, NYC, 13/218

Underwood (Trust u/d J.T.)-J.T. Underwood Fdn., NYC, 13/218

Ungar (S. J.) Fdn., NYC, 13/219

Unger (Clara Buttenweiser) Memorial Fdn., NYC, 13/220

Unicorn Fdn. for Advancement of Education, NYC, 13/221

Union Bay Charitable Trust, NYC, 13/221

Union Camp Charitable Trust, NYC, 13/223

Union Carbide Education Fund, NYC, 13/224

Union Pacific Railroad Fdn., NYC, 13/224

United Armenian Charities, NYC, 13/226

United Jewish Appeal, NYC, 13/226

United States Trust Company of New York Scholarship Fund, NYC, 13/228

Unity Fdn., NYC, 13/229

Unterberg (Bella & Israel) Fdn., NYC, 13/229

Upson (Maxwell M.) Fdn. Trust, NYC, 14/001

Urend (Genet) Jr. Trust, Buffalo, 14/002

Usdan (Suzanne & Nathaniel H.) Fdn., NYC, 14/002

U S G A Junior Gulf Fdn., NYC, 14/003

Ushkow Fdn., Garden City, 14/003

United States Trust Company of New York Fdn., NYC, 14/004

Uptopia Fund, NYC, 14/005

Utter (David H.) Memorial Scholarship Fund, Rochester, 14/006

Valenstein (Lawrence) Fund, NYC, 14/007

Valley Fdn., NYC, 14/007

Valley Fdn., NYC, 14/008

van Ameringen Fdn., NYC, 14/009

van Ameringen (H.) Fdn., NYC, 14/011

Hansford (Van Buren N.) Charitable Trust, Rochester, 14/012

Van Hornesville Community Corporation, Van Hornesville, 14/012

Van Itallie Fdn., NYC, 14/013

Marsh (Cornelia Van Rensselaer) Memorial Fund, Mt. Kisco, 14/014

Van Slyke (Joan D.) Testamentary Trust for State College for Teachers, Albany, 14/014

Van Vechten (Lester) Trust u/w for St. John's Lutheran Church, Troy, 14/015

Vandium Corporation Charitable Trust, NYC, 14/016

Vanderbilt (R. T.) Trust, NYC, 14/017

Vanguard Fdn., NYC, 14/018

Venetos Fdn., New Rochelle, 14/018

Verby (Stanley M. & Marjorie S.) Fdn., Jamaica, 14/019

Vernon Fdn., NYC, 14/019

Vernon (Miles Hodsdon) Fdn., NYC, 14/020

Vert (May M.) Memorial Fund, Albany, 14/021

Vert (Sarah S.) Student Fund, Albany, 14/021

Vila (George R.) Fdn., NYC, 14/022

Vinmont Fdn., NYC, 14/022

Virgil (Richard & Susan) Fdn., Flushing, 14/023

Vly Pond Fdn., NYC, 14/024

Vogel (Harold & Hilda) Fdn., NYC, 14/024

Vogel (Irving H.) Fdn., NYC, 14/025

Vogel (Edwin C. & Florence G.) Fund, NYC, 14/025

Vollmer Fdn., NYC, 14/027

Von Schrenk Fund, Jamaica, 14/028

Voorhees (Enders M.) Fdn., NYC, 14/029

Vorchheimer (Julius) Fdn., NYC, 14/030

Wachtel (Noah & Sadie) Fdn., Bronx, 14/031

Wagman (Stanley & Harriett) Family Fdn., NYC, 14/031

Wagner (Harry M. & Sylvia) Fdn., NYC, 14/032

Wagner (Senator Robert F.) & Susan Wagner Memorial Fdn., NYC, 14/032

Waldbaum (I.) Family Fdn., NYC, 14/033

Walden Fund, NYC, 14/034

Waldheim (Aaron) Fdn., NYC, 14/035

Waldman Fdn., NYC, 14/036

Waldron (Frederick C.) Fdn., NYC, 14/037

Waldron Fund, NYC, 14/037

Waldron Memorial Fund, NYC, 14/038

Walker Fund, NYC, 14/039

Walker (Caroline Shields) Fund, NYC, 14/039

Walker (Donald S.) Fund, NYC, 14/041

Walker (George Herbert) Fdn., NYC, 14/042

Walker (Lillian & Marty) Fdn., NYC, 14/044

Walker (Maurice) Fdn., Bayside, 14/045

Wallace-Murray Education & Welfare Fund, NYC, 14/045

Wallace-Murray Fdn., NYC, 14/046

Wallace (DeWitt) Fund, NYC, 14/048

Wallace (John & Amelie) Fdn., NYC, 14/049

Walston (V. C.) Memorial Scholarship Fdn., NYC, 14/049

Walter Fdn., NYC, 14/049

Walter (William L.) & Elinor F. Walter Fdn., Mamaroneck, 14/050

Walters Family Fdn., NYC, 14/051

Walworth (Alice C.) Memorial Free Bed Trust Fund, Albany, 14/052

Wanger (Etta L. & Henry F.) Fdn., NYC, 14/053

Warburg (Edward & Mary) Fund, NYC, 14/053

Warburg (Mr. & Mrs. Paul Felix) Fund, NYC, 14/055

Ward (Jess) Fdn., NYC, 14/056

Ward (C. P.) Charitable Fdn., Rochester, 14/056

Ward (Joseph A.) Jr. Scholarship Fund, NYC, 14/056

Waring Fdn., NYC, 14/057

Warner (Albert & Bessie) Fund, NYC, 14/057

Warner (Florence Weithorn) Fdn., NYC, 14/058

Warner (Reuben) Fdn., Bronx, 14/058

Warnshuis (Margaret Chambers) Fdn., Bronxville, 14/059

Warshaw (Nathan & Zipporah) Fdn., NYC, 14/059

Warren (Glenn B. & Gertrude P.) Fdn., Schenectady, 14/060

Wartels (Elias) Fdn., Scarsdale, 14/062

Washington Square Fdn., NYC, 14/062

Wass (Harold S.) Fdn., NYC, 14/063

Wasserman (Dale) Fdn., NYC, 14/063

Wasserman (Dr. Rene D.) Fdn., Flushing, 14/064

Wasserman (John & Miriam) Fdn., NYC, 14/064

Wasserman (Lucius P.) Fdn., NYC, 14/065

Wassner (Abraham) & Sons Fdn., NYC, 14/065

Waterman (George H.) Fdn., NYC, 14/066

Watson (Emitom) Fdn., Port Washington, 14/067

Watson (Thomas J.) III Fund, NYC, 14/067

Wattles (Gordon W.) Fund, NYC, 14/068

Webb (Electra Havemeyer) Fund, NYC, 14/069

Weber (Charles R. & Winifred R.) Fdn., NYC, 14/071

Webster Fdn., Long Island City, 14/071

Webster (Emma Reed) Trust u/a for the Webster Aid Association of Albion, New York, 14/072

Webster Kiwanis Charitable Fdn., Rochester, 14/073

Wechsler (Sammy & Betty) Fdn., NYC, 14/073

Wechsler (Arnold J. & Miriam) Fdn., NYC, 14/074

Weekes (Arthur D.) Jr. Charitable Trust, NYC, 14/075

Weezie Fdn., NYC, 14/076

Wegman (John F.) Fdn., Rochester, 14/077

Wehle (Elizabeth R. & Louis A.) Charitable Trust, Rochester, 14/079

Wehle (John L. & Marjorie Strong) Charitable Trusts, Rochester, 14/080

Wehle (Robert G.) Charitable Trust, Rochester, 14/081

Wehle (Richard) Fdn., Buffalo, 14/082

Wehmann (Gilbert H.) Fund, NYC, 14/082

Weicker (Theodore & Elizabeth) Fdn., NYC, 14/083

Weight Watchers Fdn., Great Neck, 14/084

Weil (Henrietta & Frank) Fdn., NYC, 14/084

Weil (Hermann) Memorial Fdn., NYC, 14/085

Weiler (F.) Charity Fund, NYC, 14/085

Weiler (Elizabeth L.) Fdn., NYC, 14/087

Weill (Sanford I.) Charitable Fdn., NYC, 14/087

Weinberg (John L.) Fdn., NYC, 14/088

Weinberg (Marshall M.) Fdn., NYC, 14/089

Weinberger (Oscar & Della) Fdn., NYC, 14/089

Weinburg (Louis) Fdn., Troy, 14/089

Weiner & Bauer Fdn., NYC, 14/091

Weiner (Joan & Horton D.) Fdn., NYC, 14/091

Weinman (Isak & Rose) Fdn., NYC, 14/092

Weinman Family Fdn., Norwich, 14/093

Weinstein (Alex J.) Fdn., Croton-on-Hudson, 14/094

Weinstein (J.) Fdn., Brooklyn, 14/094

Weinstock (Murray & Evelyne) Fdn., NYC, 14/095

Weir (Ernest & Mary Hayward) Fdn., NYC, 14/096

Weir (Harry N.) Trust for Town of Hoosick Community Center, Albany, 14/098

Weisberg (Mark & Edna) Charitable Fdn., NYC, 14/098

Weisberg Fdn., NYC, 14/099

Weisbuch Aid Fund, Great Neck, 14/100

Weisl (Alicereyed) Fdn., NYC, 14/101

Weisman (Lawrence I.) Fund, Brooklyn, 14/103

Weiss (Daniel & Gloria) Fdn., NYC, 14/103

Weiss (Morton N.) Fdn., Roslyn Heights, 14/104

Weiss (Stephen H.) Fdn., NYC, 14/105

Weissmann Fdn., NYC, 14/105

Weissman (Samuel & Sophie) Fdn., Hewlett Bay Park, 14/106

Welby (Glen) Fund, NYC, 14/106

Welch (Mark W.) Charitable Trust, Rochester, 14/106

Welfare Trust Fund of the Twenty-Five Year Club of L.D. Inc., NYC, 14/107

Weller Fdn., Fort Plain, 14/108

Wellington Fdn., NYC, 14/108

Wells (A. Eugene & Roberta S.) Fdn., Atlantic Beach, 14/109

WElls (Jay) Fdn., NYC, 14/109

Wellsville Rotary Education Fund, Wellsville, 14/109

Welsh (William E., Jr. & Barbara Ann) Fdn., NYC, 14/110

Weltz (S. Robert) Jr. Fdn., NC, 14/111

Wend (A. Mary) Library Fund of N.Y. State Training School for Girls, Hudson, 14/111

Wend (E.) Memorial Fund--Hudson Area Association Library, Hudson, 14/112

Wenner-Gren Fdn. for Anthropological Research, NYC, 14/112

Werblow (Nina & Robert) Fdn., NYC, 14/118

Werksman (Irving & Rejene) Fdn., NYC, 14/119

Wertheim Fund, NYC, 14/119

Wessel Fdn., White Plains, 14/120

West (Dorothy Phelps) Fund, NYC, 14/120

Westab Inc. Charitable Trust, NYC, 14/121

Western Electric Fund, NYC, 14/123

Wetzler (Benjamin) Fdn., NYC, 14/124

Wexler (Irving) Fdn., Long Island City, 14/125

Wheelan Fdn., Great Neck, 14/125

White Fdn., NYC, 14/126

White Fund, NYC, 14/127

White (Minnie Marsh) Trust, Cooperstown, 14/128

White (James L.) Fdn., Port Washington, 14/128

White (Marcelle Picard) Fdn., NYC, 14/129

White (Captain Charles) Memorial, u/d Eastern Airlines for, NYC, 14/129

Whiteacre Charitable Trust, Rochester, 14/130

Whiting (Harry H.) & Leah Grace Whiting Memorial Fdn., Buffalo, 14/131

Whitney (Eleanor Searle) Charitable Trust, NYC, 14/131

Whitney (Julia A.) Fdn., NYC, 14/132

Whitney (William C.) Fdn., NYC, 14/133

Whittaker (Wallace S.) Fdn., NYC, 14/135

Whittier Avenue Fdn., Yonkers, 14/136

Widder (Adolph) Fdn., NYC, 14/137

Widder (Samuel) Fdn., NYC, 14/137

Widenmann (Hans & Dorothy) Fund, NYC, 14/138

Widmer Charitable Trust, Rochester, 14/139

Widows' Consultation Center, NYC, 14/141

Wiener (Murray L. & Sylvia Z.) Fdn., Great Neck, 14/141

Wiener (Seymour) Family Fdn., NYC, 14/143

Wiggin (Albert H. & Jessie D.) Fdn., NYC, 14/144

Wikstrom Fdn., Albany, 14/144

Wildner Fdn., NYC, 14/145

Wilhelmina Fdn., NYC, 14/147

Williams Fdn., NYC, 14/147

Williams (A. E.) Fund, NYC, 14/147

Williams (Albert Lynn) Fdn., Bronxville, 14/148

Williams (Elizabeth Stillman) Benevolent Fund, NYC, 14/148

Williams (Emma J.) Fdn., NYC, 14/149

Williams (Monsignor Francis J.) Fdn., NYC, 14/149

Williams (Joseph P.) Fdn., Mill Neck, 14/150

Williams (Ruth Bloom) Memorial Fdn., Bronxville, 14/151

Williams (Sherman Camp) Fdn., Pearl River, 14/152

Williams-Adler Fdn., NYC, 14/152

Wilson (Elaine P. & Richard U.) Fdn., Rochester, 14/154

Wilson (H. W.) Fdn., Bronx, 14/155

Wilson (John D.) Family Fdn., Syracuse, 14/155

Wilson (Marie C. & Joseph C.) Fdn., Rochester, 14/156

Wilson (Robert G.) Fdn., NYC, 14/157

Wilson (Robert Latchworth) & Linda Collens Wilson Fdn., Boston, 14/158

Wilson (Mr. & Mrs. Robert W.) Fdn., Brooklyn, 14/158

Wilson (Edward G. & Jane J.) Trust u/a, NYC, 14/158

Windsor Fdn., NYC, 14/159

Winick-Schiffer Fdn., NYC, 14/160

Winkelman (Dwight W.) Fdn., Syracuse, 14/160

Winley Fdn., NYC, 14/161

Winslow (John) Fdn., Millbrook, 14/162

Winston (N. K.) Fdn., NYC, 14/162

Winston (Norman & Rosita) Fdn., NYC, 14/162

Winter (Philip L. & Sarah L.) Fdn., NYC, 14/163

Winthrop (John) Fdn., NYC, 14/164

Winthrop (Sarah T.) Memorial Fund, NYC, 14/164

Winton (Sydney C.) Family Fund, NYC, 14/166

Wire-O Fdn., Poughkeepsie, 14/166

Wise (W.) et al Trust f/b/o Guertha Pratt Home, Rochester, 14/167

Wise (William N.) Trust, Rochester, 14/168

Wishnick (Eli) Fdn., NYC, 14/168

Witco Chemical Corporation Fdn., NYC, 14/170

Witting Family Fdn., Syracuse, 14/172

Wivenhoe Fund, NYC, 14/172

Woelfel (E. R.) Memorial Scholarship Fund, Rochester, 14/173

Wohl Fdn., NYC, 14/174

Wohlgemuth (Esther & Morton) Fdn., Monroe, 14/174

Wolf (David) Fdn., NYC, 14/177

Wolf (Fradel & Henry) Fdn., NYC, 14/177

Wolfson (Erwin & Rose F.) Fdn., NYC, 14/177

Wolfe (Herbert O.) Fdn., Brooklyn, 14/178

Wolfe (Lester & Kathlyn) Fdn., NYC, 14/179

Wolin (Louis) Fdn., Forest Hills, 14/179

Wolk (Ernie) Charitable Trust, Rochester, 14/180

Wolk (Isadore) & Rebecca Wolk Fdn., Buffalo, 14/181

Wolk (Louis S.) Fdn., Rochester, 14/181

Wollman (Jodi Ann) Glioblastoma Fdn., NYC, 14/182

Wolosoff Fdn., Flushing, 14/182

Women's Aid for the Relief of Widows & Orphans, NYC, 14/183

Anco Wood Fdn., Glendale, 14/184

Wood (Roy A.) Fdn., Brooklyn, 14/184

Wood (Samuel J. & Evelyn L.) Fdn., NYC, 14/185

Woodfin Fdn., NYC, 14/186

Woodland Fdn., NYC, 14/186

Woodmere Educational Fund, NYC, 14/187

Woodner Fdn., NYC, 14/187

Woodstock Fdn., NYC, 14/188

Woodward (Harper) Fdn., NYC, 14/190

Woodward Fund, Rochester, 14/191

Woolley-Clifford Fdn., NYC, 14/191

Word Fdn., NYC, 14/193

Workman (Israel) Fdn., Great Neck, 14/193

World Arts Fdn., NYC, 14/194

World Institute Council, NYC, 14/195

Wouk (Abe) Fdn., NYC, 14/195

Wrightson-Ramsing Fdn., NYC, 14/196

W. S. P. & R. Charitable Trust Fund, NYC, 14/197

W U I Fdn., NYC, 14/197

Wuderman Fdn., NYC, 14/198

Wunsch Fdn., Brooklyn, 14/199

Wunsch (Samuelsie) Fdn., Glen Cove, 14/199

Wurzweiler (Gustav) Fdn., NYC, 14/199

Wyandotte Industries Fdn., NYC, 14/204

Wyler (Alfred & Marguerite) Fdn., NYC, 14/204

Wyman-Potter Fdn., Rochester, 14/205

Wynd (Alice & Clarence) Trust, Rochester, 14/206

Yager Fdn. (f/k/a Goergen Mackwirth Fdn.), Buffalo, 14/207

Yager (M. H.) Fdn., Niskayuna, 14/207

Yale 1947 Fdn., NYC, 14/208

Yank Fdn., NYC, 14/209

Yardney Fdn., NYC, 14/209

Yassen (Roger & Janet) Fdn., NYC, 14/211

Kamlet (Abram & Anna) Yeshivos Fdn., NYC, 14/211

Yokel (Walter & Julis) Fdn., Great Neck, 14/212

Yonkers Fdn., Yonkers, 14/212

Young (F. & J.) Fdn., NYC, 14/213

Young (Morgan-Jackson) Fdn., NYC, 14/214

Young & Rubicam Fdn., NYC, 14/215

Young & Rubicam Scholarship Fund, NYC, 14/216

Young (Betty) & Sol Young Fdn., NYC, 14/216

Young (Wallace) Fdn., Waverly, 14/217

Youth Fdn., NYC, 14/218

Youths' Friends Association, NYC, 14/219

Yuker Fdn., Hempstead, 14/221

Yurowitz (Andy & Helen) Fdn., Brooklyn, 14/222

Zachary Trust, Bronx, 14/222

Zahn Fdn., Great Neck, 14/222

Zausner Fdn., NYC, 14/223

Zedukah Vechesed Fdn., Brooklyn, 14/224

Zeigen (Bess & Sam) Fdn., NYC, 14/224

Zell (Annette W.) & Daniel D. Zell Fdn., Mamaroneck, 14/224

Zeughauser (Phyllis & Milton) Fdn., New Rochelle, 14/225

Ziegler (Matilda) Publishing Company for the Blind, NYC, 14/226

Zimmerman (Charles S. E.) Fdn., NYC, 14/227

Zirinksy (Gertrude) Fdn., NYC, 14/227

Zirinsky (Paul) Memorial Fdn., NYC, 14/227

Zeughauser (Phyllis & Milton) Fdn., New Rochelle, 14/228

Ziegler (E. Matilda) Fdn. for the Blind, NYC, 14/229

Zimmerman (Anna & David) Fdn., NYC, 14/229

Zimmerman (Meyer) Charitable Trust, Roslyn Heights, 14/230

Zimmerman (Marie & John) Fund, NYC, 14/230

Zimtbaum (Arthur) Fdn., Brooklyn, 14/231

Zorn (Norma & Milton J.) Fdn., NYC, 14/232

Zuckerman Smith Fdn., NYC, 14/232

Zuckerwar (Marguerite & Jacob) Fdn., Gloversville, 14/232

24 Emergency Fund, NYC, 14/234

1907 Fdn., NYC, 14/234

Second Filming

Albert & Greenbaum Fdn., Brooklyn, 15/001

American Educational Fund, NYC, 15/001

A.A.A.A. Educational Fdn., NYC, 15/002

Abelson (Ben & Ida) Fdn., Scarsdale, 15/002

A&B Fdn., NYC, 15/003

Abrams (Solomon & Mollie) Fdn., NYC, 15/003

Abrons (Louis & Anne) Fdn., NYC, 15/004

Ace Fdn., NYC, 15/006

ACG Trust of 7/1/59, Buffalo, 15/006

Ackerman (Myron H.) Fdn., NYC, 15/007

Adams (Lovell A.) Student Memorial Fund, Rochester, 15/007

Adirondack Historical Association, NYC, 15/008

Adler (Carol) Fdn., NYC, 15/010

Adler (Irma & Martin) Fdn., NYC, 15/011

Adler (Marcus & Gertrud) Charitable Trust, NYC, 15/011

Adler (Ruth & Ernest) Fdn., Port Chester, 15/012

Aeolian Fdn., NYC, 15/012

Africa Fund, NYC, 15/013

Agway Fdn., DeWitt, 15/015

Aisenberg Family Fdn., New Rochelle, 15/015

Altschul Fund, NYC, 15/016

Ailborn Foundation, NYC, 15/016

AKC Fund, NYC, 15/018

Albee (Edward) Fdn., NYC, 15/019

Alexander (Norman & Marjorie) Fdn., NYC, 15/020

A.L.T. Charitable Fund, NYC, 15/021

Alka Charity Organization, NYC, 15/022

Allen (Rita) Fdn., NYC, 15/022

Alpert (Zusman) Family, Brooklyn, 15/023

Alpha Theta Educational Fdn., NYC, 15/023

Alter (Louis W. & Catherine M.) Fdn., NYC, 15/024

Altschul Fdn., NYC, 15/025

Alumni Assoc. of the State Univ. of N.Y. Agricultural and Technical College of Farmingdale, Farmingdale, 15/026

Amerace Fdn., NYC, 15/027

American Academy of Arts & Letters, NYC, 15/027

Amelingmeir (Werner & Arline) Educational Fdn., Merrick, 15/031

American Association for the International Commission of Jurists, 15/031

American Catholic Association of Paris Trust, NYC, 15/032

American Chai Trust, NYC, 15/033

American Society of the French Legion of Honor, NYC, 15/034

American Fdn. for Management Research, NYC, 15/034

American Geriatrics Society Research Fdn., NYC, 15/035

American Health Education for African Development, NYC, 15/035

American Indian Educational Fdn., NYC, 15/036

American Legion Post 0730 Williams Greengrass, Addison, 15/037

American Medical Society on Alcoholism, NYC, 15/037

American School in London Fdn., NYC, 15/038

American Seamen's Friend Society, NYC, 15/039

Burnett (Louisa Ames) Fdn. Trust, NYC, 15/040

Ames Fdn., Freeport, 15/041

Anderson (A.E.) Fdn., Cheektowaga, 15/042

Architects Technical Assistance Center, NYC, 15/043

Arents (u/d George), Jr. for the Arents Fdn., NYC, 15/043

A.R.F. Fund, NYC, 15/044

A.R.F. Fund, NYC, 15/045

Arkin (Alvin & Ann) Fdn., NYC, 15/046

Arlan's Dept. Store Fdn., NYC, 15/046

Argentine American Fdn., NYC, 15/047

Aronowitz Fdn., NYC, 15/048

Aronson & Oresman Fdn., NYC, 15/048

Aronson (David & Bertha) Fdn., Great Neck, 15/049

Arthur Fdn., NYC, 15/049

Murray (Arthur) Fdn., NYC, 15/050

Art Institute of Chicago Trust, NYC, 15/051

Arts Fund, NYC, 15/053

Arts of the Theatre Fdn., NYC, 15/053

Asnes (Paul) Fdn., NYC, 15/053

ARW Fdn., NYC, 15/054

A&S Fdn., Brooklyn, 15/056

Ashton Fdn., NYC, 15/059

Askin (Seymour) Fdn., NYC, 15/060

Association for the Aid of Crippled Children, NYC, 15/061

Astor (William Waldorf) Fdn., NYC, 15/063

Axe-Houghton Fdn., NYC, 15/066

Babe Ruth Fdn., NYC, 15/068

Bacon (George Wood) Fund for the School for Social Research, Cornell Univ. & American Friends Service Comm., NYC, 15/068

Baer (Charles & Margaret) Fdn., Manhasset, 15/069

Bainbridge Free Library Trust, NYC, 15/071

Baird (Flora M.) Fdn., Buffalo, 15/071

Baird (Frank B.), Jr. Fdn., Buffalo, 15/073

Bajus Fdn., Syracuse, 15/074

Baldwin-Yates County Humane Society Trust, Rochester, 15/075

Ballet Institute, NYC, 15/075

Hazzard (Walter & Grace) Educational Fund, Jamestown, 15/076

Barash (Herman) Fdn., NYC, 15/077

Barber Memorial Building Trust, Rochester, 15/078

Barber (Marion Isaacs) Fdn., NYC, 15/078

Barocas (Rebecca & Victor) Fdn., NYC, 15/079

Barotz (Barbara) Memorial Fdn., NYC, 15/079

Bardon-Cole Fdn., NYC, 15/080

Barkin (Dan W.) & Dave Lerm Fdn., NYC, 15/080

Barnard-Needy Mountaineers of Middle Southern States Trust, Rochester, 15/081

Bizer Charitable Trust, Detroit, Mich., 15/081

Barnard Scholarship Fund, Rochester, 15/082

Barnard-St. James Episcopal Church, Rochester, 15/082

Barnes (Joshua) Fdn., NYC, 15/083

Baron (Salo W. & Jeannette M.) Fdn., NYC, 15/083

Barrack (Florence & Ben) Fdn., NYC, 15/084

Barmore (u/w Fred L.) Trust, Jamestown, 15/084

Barrie (George) Fdn., NYC, 15/084

Baruch (Belle W.) Fdn., NYC, 15/085

Bassine (David P.) Fdn., NYC, 15/087

Baten (Charles & Rita) Fdn., NYC, 15/091

Battin (Victor & Clara C.) Fdn., NYC, 15/092

Bauman (Lionel & Sylvia) Fdn., NYC, 15/092

B & B Fdn., NYC, 15/094

Bear Fdn., NYC, 15/095

Bear (Mary) Cemetery Trust, Harrisburg, Pa., 15/096

Beaupre Charitable Trust, NYC, 15/096

Becker Family Fdn., NYC, 15/098

Becker (Isidore & Adele) Fdn., NYC, 15/098

Beckerman (Stanley H. & Ruth) Fdn., Roslyn, 15/099

Dickinson & Becton Family Fdn., NYC, 15/100

Bedford Fund, Scarsdale, 15/100

Bedient (u/w Melvin F.) Trust, Jamestown, 15/101

Bedminster Fund, NYC, 15/101

Beldoch (Albert) Fdn., NYC, 15/102

Belgian Art Fdn. in the United States, NYC, 15/103

Bellow Fdn., NYC, 15/104

Benach (Henry & Shirlee) Fdn., Scarsdale, 15/104

Benevolent Lodge Sunshine Fdn., Flushing, 15/105

Benevolent Nursing Assistance Association, Gloversville, 15/105

Benjamin (Henry Rogers) Fund, NYC, 15/105

Bennahum Fdn., NYC, 15/106

Bentley Educational Fdn., NYC, 15/106

Bentley Fund, Pine Plains, 15/107

Bercar Fdn., NYC, 15/107

Berdon (Laura & Matthew) Fdn., NYC, 15/107

Berglas (Louis) Fdn., Brooklyn, 15/108

Berkson (Seymour & Eleanor) Fdn., NYC, 15/108

Berlin (David A. & Rebecca I.) Artists & Students Assistance Fund, NYC, 15/109

Berlinger (Rhonie & George) Fdn., NYC, 15/110

Berman Fdn., Great Neck, 15/111

Bernajean Charity, NYC, 15/111

Bernard Public Library Trust, Rochester, 15/111

Berne (Gustave M.) Fdn., Far Rockaway, 15/112

Bernstein Fund, NYC, 15/112

Bernstein (David & Ruth) Fdn., Scarsdale, 15/113

Bernstein (I. Jack & Elsie L.) Fdn., NYC, 15/114

Bernstein (Sanford C.) & Co. Fdn., NYC, 15/115

Berolzheimer (Charles P.) Fdn., NYC, 15/115

Berra Charitable Fdn., NYC, 15/116

Berry (Joan) Fdn., NYC, 15/117

Bened Besel Fdn., NYC, 15/118

Bieber (Siegfried & Josephine) Fdn., NYC, 15/118

Billet (Leo) Family Fdn., NYC, 15/120

Birkenau Jewish Cemetery Trust, NYC, 15/120

Birsh Fdn., NYC, 15/121

Bishop (Mabel W.) Fdn., Utica, 15/121

Black (E.M.) Fdn., NYC, 15/122

Black (William M.) Fdn., NYC, 15/122

Blackman Scholarship Fdn., Flushing, 15/123

Blackstone (Henry) Fdn., Syosset, 15/123

Blaine (Walter F.) Scholarship Fund, NYC, 15/124

Blank (Robert & Adele) Fdn., NYC, 15/125

Blankman Fdn., Port Washington, 15/126

Block (Burton & Renee) Fdn., NYC, 15/126

Block (H. & M.) Fdn., NYC, 15/127

Blumberg Fdn., NYC, 15/127

Blumberg (Gerald) Fdn., NYC, 15/128

Board of Foreign Missions of the Protestant Episcopal Church Trust, NYC, 15/128

Bobb (Mildred E.) Fund, NYC, 15/128

Bookshin (Harry & Margaret A.) Fdn., NYC, 15/129

Boone (Ben B. & Mary) Fdn., NYC, 15/130

Borden Fdn., NYC, 15/131

Borg (Janice Hellman) Memorial Fund, NYC, 15/132

Borris Fdn., NYC, 15/132

Boscop Fdn., NYC, 15/133

Bowles (Sylvan E.) Scholarship Fund, Great Neck, 15/134

Bowman (Christ E.) Cemetery t/w Trustee, Harrisburg, Pa., 15/135

Bowman (Christ E.) t/w Tresslers Home Trustee, Harrisburg, Pa., 15/135

Brafman (Abraham & Ruth) Fdn., Brooklyn, 15/135

Bram (William B. & Jane E.) Fdn., NYC, 15/136

Brandeis Lodge Fdn., NYC, 15/137

Brandt (Harry) Fdn., NYC, 15/137

Branta Fdn., White Plains, 15/138

Brandt (Rose & William) Fdn., NYC, 15/139

Braun (Philip & Laura) Fdn., NYC, 15/140

Braverman (Irving & Josephine) Fdn., NYC, 15/140

Bregman (Abner) Fund, NYC, 15/141

Breth (Ferdinand W.) Fdn., NYC, 15/141

Bricker Fdn., Harrison, 15/142

Brickner (Barbara & Balfour) Fdn., NYC, 15/142

Bridge to Freedom, Kings Park, 15/143

Briggs (Julia A.) Memorial Fund, Harrisburg, Pa., 15/143

Bristol Fund, NYC, 15/144

Britenstool (Dr. Harry) Scholarship Fund -- Greater N.Y. Council Boy Scouts of America Trust, NYC, 15/144

Britenstool (Dr. Harry) Scholarship Fund -- Girl Scouts Council of Greater N.Y. Trust, NYC, 15/145

Britenstool (Dr. Harry) Scholarship Fund -- College of Physicians & Surgeons, NYC, 15/146

Brizel Fdn., NYC, 15/146

Broadcast Institute of North America, NYC, 15/147

Bro-Con Charitable Trust, Albany, 15/148

Brock Fdn., Great Neck, 15/148

Brockway Fdn. for the Needy of the Village & Township of Homer, Homer, 15/149

Bronfman (Ann & Edgar) Fdn., NYC, 15/149

Bronner Fdn., NYC, 15/150

Brookdale Fdn., NYC, 15/151

Brooklyn Bar Association Fdn., Brooklyn, 15/152

Brooklyn Institute of Arts & Sciences Trust, NYC, 15/152

Brooklyn Police Medal Fund, NYC, 15/153

Brose (C. & K.) Fdn., Poughkeepsie, 15/154

Brown University Club in New York, NYC, 15/154

Brown (Arthur J.) Family Fdn., NYC, 15/154

Brown (Grandma) Fdn., Mexico, 15/155

Brownstone (Lucien & Ethel) Fdn., NYC, 15/156

Brownstone (Walter & Sylvia) Fdn., NYC, 15/157

Buckley (Henry C.) Foundation Trust, NYC, 15/158

Brumberger Fdn., Brooklyn, 15/158

Brunckhorst Fdn., Brooklyn, 15/159

Buffalo Tennis Fdn., Buffalo, 15/160

Bunge Fdn., NYC, 15/160

Burnett (Walter J.) Fdn. Trust, NYC, 15/160

Burns Fdn., Alton, 15/161

Burrows Fdn., NYC, 15/161

Busch (Charles L.) Charitable Fdn., NYC, 15/162

Butler (H. H.) Fdn., NYC, 15/163

Butler (J. Homer) Fdn., NYC, 15/163

Byrne Fdn., Syracuse, 15/164

Cabot (F. Higginson) Fdn., NYC, 15/164

Cahn (Alice & Maurice) Fdn., Bronx, 15/165

Cameo Fdn., NYC, 15/165

Camillus Fdn., Camillus, 15/166

Cannold (Sidney) Charitable Fdn., Harrison, 15/167

Cannon (Henry W.) Educational Fund Trust, NYC, 15/167

Cantor (B. G.) Fdn., NYC, 15/168

Cantor (Sol W. & Hermina) Fdn., NYC, 15/169

Carborundum Employees Benefit Fund, Niagara Falls, 15/169

Cardamylian Shipowners Fdn., NYC, 15/169

Cardiac Surgery Research Fdn., NYC, 15/170

Carnegie Fdn. for the Advancement of Teaching, NYC, 15/171

Carnegie Endowment for International Peace, NYC, 15/174

Carnegie Fund for Authors, NYC, 15/178

Caron (John B.) Fdn., NYC, 15/178

Carr (u/w Daniel L.) Trust, Jamestown, 15/179

Carpat Fdn., NYC, 15/179

Cartown (Harriet & Fred) Fdn., NYC, 15/180

Cary (Mary Flagler) Charitable Trust, NYC, 15/181

Catz (Isidor B.) Fdn., NYC, 15/183

Cavior Fdn., NYC, 15/184

Center for Understanding Media, NYC, 15/184

Central Hanover Educational Fund, NYC, 15/185

Barbieri (Cesare) Dixie Cup Employees Fdn. Trust, NYC, 15/185

C F & I-Roebling Fdn., NYC, 15/190

Chambers-White Fdn., NYC, 15/191

Chautauqua Co. Council Inc., Boy Scouts of America Trust, Jamestown, 15/193

Checkver Fdn., Douglaston, 15/193

Chesed, Inc., NYC, 15/193

Chesky (Ruth & Ezra) Fdn., NYC, 15/194

Chisholm Fund, NYC, 15/194

Christenfeld (Samuel H.) Fdn., NYC, 15/195

Citizens Union Research Fdn. Inc., of the City of New York, NYC, 15/195

Civic Trust of Lebanon-Harmon, NYC, 15/197

Abrams (Rose L.) Gemilith Chesed Assoc., Brooklyn, 15/198

Childrens Aid Association of Amsterdam New York, Amsterdam, 15/198

Childrens Fdn. of Columbia County, Hudson, 15/199

C.I.T. Fdn., NYC, 15/201

City Stores Fdn., NYC, 15/204

Clark (Edna McConnell) Fdn., NYC, 15/205

Charles (Justin) Fdn., NYC, 15/207

Clark Fdn., NYC, 15/209

Champlain and Clarke (Rachel Fiero) Scholarship Funds, Albany, 15/213

Clifford (Margaret) t/w, White Plains, 15/214

Climenko (Jesse & Pearl) Fdn., NYC, 15/214

Clipper & Landsberger Fdn., NYC, 15/214

Cobble Pond Fdn., NYC, 15/215

Cohan & Gilbert Fdn., Bronxville, 15/215

Cohen (Blanche & David) Fdn., Hicksville, 15/216

Cohen (Edward I.) Fdn., NYC, 15/216

Etelman (Harry I.) Fdn., Tenafly, N.J., 15/217

Cohen (Florence & Ben) Fdn., Hicksville, 15/217

Cohen (Louis) Fdn., NYC, 15/218

Cohen (Wilfred P.) Fdn., NYC, 15/218

Cohn & Tubetex Fdn., NYC, 15/220

Cohn (Marion E.) Fdn., NYC, 16/001

Cohn (Max B.) Family Fdn., NYC, 16/002

Cohn (Sol) Fdn., Great Neck, 16/003

Bardon-Cole Fdn., NYC, 16/005

Cole Fdn., NYC, 16/005

Cole (Irene K. & Harry S.) Charitable Fdn., NYC, 16/006

Colegrove-Presbyterian Church of Bargett, Rochester, 16/007

Coleman (Gregory S.) Fdn., East Norwich, 16/007

Coleman (Julian S.) Fdn., NYC, 16/008

Coleman (Alvin & Kathryn) Fdn., NYC, 16/008

Coler (Marcus & Bertha) Fdn., NYC, 16/010

College of St. Francis Xavier Trust, NYC, 16/011

College Community Services Inc-Brooklyn College, Brooklyn, 16/012

Collins (Joseph) Fdn., NYC, 16/012

Commission for the United World Colleges, NYC, 16/015

Commonwealth Fund, NYC, 16/015

Cooperberg (Seymour) Family Fdn., Mt. Vernon, 16/021

Connolly (James T.) Fdn., NYC, 16/022

Connor-First Methodist Church of Mt. Morris Trust, Rochester, 16/022

Consumers Technical Institute, New Rochelle, 16/022

Contempo Productions Fdn. for the Arts, NYC, 16/023

Conway (Carle C.) Scholarship Fdn., NYC, 16/023

Cooper (Milton & Ida) Fdn., NYC, 16/025

Copeland Fdn., Albany, 16/026

Cornell Delta Phi Educational Fund, NYC, 16/026

Cornell (Angeline W.) Trust U/A, F/B/O Methodist Episcopal Church of Marmaroneck, White Plains, 16/027

Cornerhouse Fund, NYC, 16/027

Corning Museum of Glass, Corning, 16/028

Cornish (Selma C.) Fund, NYC, 16/029

Corporation of Yaddo, Saratoga Springs, 16/030

Corpus Christi Church Trust, Rochester, 16/031

Cos Cob Fdn., NYC, 16/032

Cotton Bay Fdn., NYC, 16/032

Council for Middle Eastern Affairs, Elmont, 16/033

Covey (Lois Lensky) Fdn., NYC, 16/034

Cowan (Louis & Pauline) Fdn., NYC, 16/035

Cox-Big Springs Historical Society Trust, Rochester, 16/037

Coyne (Maurice) Fdn., NYC, 16/038

Craft Associates Trust, Ithaca, 16/039

Cremona Fund, NYC, 16/039

Crownlet Fdn., NYC, 16/040

Cruise-St. Bernards Seminary Trust, Rochester, 16/041

Cryonics Society of New York, Sayville, 16/041

Cullen Family Fdn., NYC, 16/041

Culinarians Home Fdn., NYC, 16/042

Culligan (U/W Catherine) Trust, Jamestown, 16/043

Cummings (James H.) Fdn., Buffalo, 16/044

Curtice-Burns Charitable Fdn., Rochester, 16/044

Curtis (Allan & Myrna) Fdn., NYC, 16/045

Cutler-Boy Scouts Residue Trust, Rochester, 16/046

Cutler-Boy Scouts Trust, Rochester, 16/047

Cutler-Childrens Nursery Trust, Rochester, 16/047

Cutler-Convalescent Hospital Trust, Rochester, 16/047

Cutler-Episcopal Diocese Trust, Rochester, 16/048

Cutler-Episcopal Diocese Residue Trust, Rochester, 16/048

Cutler Humane Society Trust, Rochester, 16/049

Cutler-St. Paul's Church Trust, Rochester, 16/049

Cyjo Fdn., NYC, 16/050

Dadourian Fdn., NYC, 16/051

Daly Fdn. for World Peace, NYC, 16/052

Danforth (Robert S.) Fdn., NYC, 16/052

Dap Fdn., NYC, 16/052

Darby Fdn., NYC, 16/053

Darling Fdn. of New York State Early American Silversmiths & Silver, Buffalo, 16/053

Darmstadter (Fritz & Emily) Fdn., NYC, 16/054

Daughters of the Cincinnati, NYC, 16/056

Daughtry (Merwin) Fdn., Brooklyn, 16/056

Daum Fdn., NYC, 16/057

Davant Fdn., NYC, 16/057

Davenport-Hatch Fdn., Rochester, 16/058

Davidson (Viola J.) (Baldwin Cemetery) Trust, Harrisburg, Pa., 16/059

Davis (Harold M.) Trust, NYC, 16/059

Davis (Kolman C. & Mildred) Fdn., New Rochelle, 16/060

Davis (Shelby Cullom) Fdn., NYC, 16/060

Davis & Warshow Scholarship Fdn., NYC, 16/061

Dawn Fdn., NYC, 16/061

Deanin Fdn., NYC, 16/062

Debany (Edgar & Marie) Trust, Brooklyn, 16/063

DeCoppet & Doremus Fund, NYC, 16/063

Deitz Fund, NYC, 16/063

Dejur (Jerome Lowell) Fellowship Trust, NYC, 16/064

Dental Society Memorial Education Fdn., Buffalo, 16/065

Dew (Donald Hicks) Fdn., Canastota, 16/065

Diefendorf Fund, Syracuse, 16/067

Detmold (William L.) Trust, NYC, 16/067

De Kerchove (Maisie) Fdn., NYC, 16/067

Delacorte (George & Margarita) Fdn., NYC, 16/068

Dental Hygienists Association NYC, Bronx, 16/070

Dental Hygienists Association of the State of New York, Brooklyn, 16/070

Deerfield Fdn., NYC, 16/070

De Puy (Charles T. & Gwyneth F.) Charitable Trust, Rochester, 16/071

de Rothschild (Edmond) Fdn., NYC, 16/071

Diamond Brothers Fdn., NYC, 16/072

Diamond Distributors Fdn., NYC, 16/073

Diamond (Diana & Theodore) Fdn., NYC, 16/074

Diamond (Louis & Juliet) Fdn., NYC, 16/075

Diefendorf Fund, NYC, 16/075

Dikaia Fdn., Syracuse, 16/075

Diker (Valerie & Charles) Fund, NYC, 16/076

Di Lee Fdn., NYC, 16/076

Dilmaghani Fdn., Scarsdale, 16/077

Di Loreto Fdn., Jamaica, 16/078

Dinsmore Fdn., NYC, 16/078

Dixie Club of New York Charitable & Educational Trust, NYC, 16/080

Dixon (Joan & Palmer) Fund, NYC, 16/080

D.J.B. Fdn., Scarsdale, 16/081

DLJ Fdn., NYC, 16/082

Dodge (Cleveland H.) Fdn., NYC, 16/083

Doelger (Peter) Fdn., NYC, 16/085

Doft (Frank J.) Fdn., NYC, 16/085

Dollard (Elizabeth K.) Second Charitable Trust, NYC, 16/087

Donaldson (Oliver S. & Jennie) Charitable Trust, NYC, 16/087

Doniger (Sundel & Margaret) Fdn., Long Island City, 16/087

Dorf Fdn., NYC, 16/088

Doud (Margaret J.) Trust, Rochester, 16/088

Dow Jones Fdn., NYC, 16/089

Dresdner Fdn., NYC, 16/090

Dretzin (Nathan A. & Lillian) Fdn., NYC, 16/091

Drexel Harriman Ripley Charitable Trust, NYC, 16/093

Dreyer (Saul) Charitable Fund Trust, NYC, 16/093

Drimmer (H. L.) Fdn., NYC, 16/094

Duck Harbor Fdn., NYC, 16/094

Dudley Fdn., NYC, 16/095

Duhl (Benjamin & Ethel) Fdn., NYC, 16/096

Dungannon Fdn., NYC, 16/097

Dunwalke (Clarence & Anne Dillon) Trust, NYC, 16/098

Dyer (Helen H.) Fdn., NYC, 16/099

Dzus (William) Fund, West Islip, 16/099

Eagan (Edward G. & Mary M.) Fdn., Syracuse, 16/100

Eagan (Leo T. & Eleanor D.) Fdn., Syracuse, 16/101

East Harlem Recreation Center, NYC, 16/102

Eastman, Dillon, Union Securities & Co. Fdn., NYC, 16/102

Dishy Easton Fdn., NYC, 16/104

Eaton (Joseph & Lillian) Fdn., NYC, 16/106
Ebsary Charitable Fdn., Rochester, 16/107
Eddy (Edgar) Cemetary Trust, Jamestown, 16/107
Edson-Wheatland Chili C.S.D. #1 Trust, Rochester, 16/108
Educational Fdn. of Theta Delta Chi, NYC, 16/108
Educational Partnerships Incorporated, NYC, 16/110
Eichelberger (Charles) Trust, Harrisburg, Pa., 16/111
Eisenstein (Shelda) Scholarship Fund, Levittown, 16/112
Elias Fdn., NYC, 16/112
Elliott (Edward) Fdn., NYC, 16/113
Elmaleh (Victor) Fdn., NYC, 16/114
Elmaleh Fdn., NYC, 16/115
Elow (Louis & Sadie) Fdn., NYC, 16/116
Enslein (Robert E.) Fdn., NYC, 16/117
Environment Mobilization Fund, NYC, 16/118
Environmental Defense Fund, NYC, 16/118
Eisner (Richard A.) Fdn., NYC, 16/118
Engel (Louis) Fdn., Scarborough, 16/120
Epstein (Henry D. & Dasha A.) Fdn., NYC, 16/120
Epstein (Mollie & Jack) Fdn., NYC, 16/121
Epstein (Paul H.) Fdn., NYC, 16/122
Erdmann Fund, NYC, 16/122
Esco Fund Committee, NYC, 16/123
Esh (Rachael & Barnett) Fdn., NYC, 16/124
Espen (Helen E.) T/W Paxton Graveyard, Harrisburg, Pa., 16/125
Esso Education Fdn., NYC, 16/125
Esterline Charitable Fdn., NYC, 16/126
Eta Chapter of Sigma Alpha Mu Fdn., NYC, 16/127
Ettinger Fdn., NYC, 16/127
Evangelical Theological Seminary, NYC, 16/128
Evans (Richard & Rebecca) Fdn., Johnstown, 16/129
Evinger (Eliza) Cemetery Fund, Harrisburg, Pa., 16/130
Evins (David & Lee) Fdn., NYC, 16/130
Eyre (Edith K.)-Answorth Scholarship Trust, NYC, 16/131
Fabrikant (Irving) Fdn., NYC, 16/132
Fairview Fdn., Hartsdale, 16/132
Faith Home Fdn., Brooklyn, 16/133
Falk (Charles & Charlotte) Fdn., NYC, 16/134
Faller (Leon & Kaethe) Fdn., NYC, 16/135
Fanton Fdn., NYC, 16/136
Farber (Jack) Family Fdn., Riverdale, 16/137
Farber (Max & Molly) Family Fdn., Brooklyn, 16/138
Farber (Sam & Anna) Family Fdn., Brooklyn, 16/138
Faris Fdn., NYC, 16/138
Farrell Fdn., NYC, 16/138
Fatato (Luigi) Fdn., Brooklyn, 16/139
Feder Family Charitable Trust, NYC, 16/140
Feder (Henry & Nell) Fdn., NYC, 16/140
Feder (Steven) Memorial Fund, Bayside, 16/141
Feinberg (Jac & Eva) Fdn., Mt. Vernon, 16/141
Feinstein (Al) Charitable Fdn., NYC, 16/142
Feinstein (Edward) Fdn., NYC, 16/143
Feld (Morris & Eva) Fdn., NYC, 16/143
Feldman Fdn., Brooklyn, 16/144
Feldman (Samuel & Esther) Fdn., Garden City Park, 16/145
Fell (John R. & Josephine L.) Fdn., NYC, 16/146
Female Charitable Society of Baldwinsville, Baldwinsville, 16/147
Fenton Fdn., New Suffolk, 16/147
Ferguson Fdn., Buffalo, 16/147
Ferrin (Barbara Hogate) Fdn., Scarsdale, 16/148
Fertig (Lawrence) Fdn., NYC, 16/149
Fetsch Family Fdn., Sands Point, 16/150
Feuerstein (Sidney & Charlotte) Charitable Fdn., NYC, 16/151
F.H.W. Fdn., NYC, 16/152

Fialkov (Herman & Elaine) Fdn., NYC, 16/152
Field (Albert J.) Fdn., Albany, 16/152
Fields (Ralph A.) Fdn., NYC, 16/153
Field (Ruth P.) Fund, NYC, 16/153
Fife (Elias & Bertha) Fdn., Long Island City, 16/153
Fife (Joseph & Martin) Fdn., NYC, 16/154
Findlay (Mary B. & D.C.) Fdn., NYC, 16/155
Fine (Norman & Sandra) Fdn., NYC, 16/156
Finkle Fdn., NYC, 16/156
Finkelstein (Jerry) Fdn., NYC, 16/156
Finn (David & Laura) Family Fdn., New Rochelle, 16/157
Firemen's Medal Fund Trust, NYC, 16/158
First National City Bank Financial Trustee U/A 12/27/60 with Dorothy P. Freeman et al f/b/o/ Perkins Gardens, NYC, 16/159
Fisher Brothers Fdn., NYC, 16/159
Fitterer (Dorothy D. & John C., Jr.) Fdn., NYC, 16/160
Five Towns Fdn., NYC, 16/161
Fine (Sidney A. & Libby) Fdn., NYC, 16/162
First Presbyterian Church Society of Seneca Falls, Rochester, 16/163
Fischer Fdn., NYC, 16/163
Fisher Family Fdn., NYC, 16/164
Fisher (Welthy) Fund, NYC, 16/164
Fishman (George N. & Endys S.) Fdn., Latting Town, 16/165
Flanagan (Thomas M. & Esther C.) Charitable Trust, Norwich, 16/165
Flateau (Felix) - Rosenbaum (Alex) Fund, NYC, 16/166
Flah Fdn., Syracuse, 16/166
Flax (Anna & Nathan) Fdn., NYC, 16/167
Fleischman (Charles II) Memorial Trust, NYC, 16/167
Fleschner (Janice & Malcolm) Fdn., NYC, 16/168
Flug (Alfred & Fortune) Fdn., NYC, 16/168
Flushing Hospital & Medical Center Trust, NYC, 16/169
Fogelman (Raymond) Fdn., NYC, 16/169
Folsom (Maud Glover) Fdn., Mineola, 16/170
Football Medical Trust, NYC, 16/171
Forcheimer (Rudolph & Hilda V.) Fdn., Scarsdale, 16/172
Forton Scholarship Fdn., NYC, 16/173
Foundation Family Isaac Youssef Levy (See Reel 18/109),
Foundation For Art, Science & Education, White Plains, 16/173
Foundation for Charity, NYC, 16/174
Foundation for Clinical Research, NYC, 16/174
Foundation for Education in the Humanities, NYC, 16/175
Foundation for a Graphic History of Jewish Literature, NYC, 16/175
Foundation for Hearing Aid Research, Woodstock, 16/176
Foundation for the Investigation of Chronic Pulmonary Disease, Mt. Kisco, 16/177
Foundation for Medical Technology, NYC, 16/177
Foundation for Modern Dance, NYC, 16/178
Foundation for the Study of American Yoga & Tibetan Buddhist Doctrines, NYC, 16/178
Foundation for the Study of Human Organization, NYC, 16/178
Foundation for Research in Preventive Psychiatry, Portchester, 16/179
Samuels (Fan Fox & Leslie R.) Fdn., NYC, 16/179
Fox (William Sr.) Fdn., NYC, 16/180
Fraad (Rita & Daniel) Fdn., NYC, 16/181
Franck (Charles) (Holophane) Fdn., NYC, 16/181
Franco (Regina & Irving) Fdn., Brooklyn, 16/183
Frank (Ruth & Walter) Fdn., NYC, 16/183
Frank (Walter N., Jr.) Fdn., NYC, 16/184
Frankel (George & Elizabeth F.) Fdn., NYC, 16/184
Franklin Fdn., Syracuse, 16/185

Franklin Fdn., NYC, 16/186
Freeman Fdn., Ithaca, 16/186
Freeman (Jack & Pauline) Fdn., Poughkeepsie, 16/187
Freefam Fdn., NYC, 16/188
Frick Collection, NYC, 16/189
Fried (Brita & Walter) Charitable Trust, NYC, 16/191
Fried (Louis & Goldie) Fdn., NYC, 16/192
Frieda Fdn., NYC, 16/192
Friedman (Arthur S. & Betty Lucas) Fdn., Chappaqua, 16/193
Friedman Fdn., NYC, 16/194
Friedman Memorial Fdn., NYC, 16/195
Friedman (Harold & Sylvia) Fdn., NYC, 16/195
Friedman (Max & Sadie) Fdn., NYC, 16/196
Friedricks (Henry) Fdn., NYC, 16/197
Friends of A.D.I.R., NYC, 16/198
Friends of the Institute of Commercial Art, NYC, 16/199
Friends of Teachers Training & Research Institutions of Israel, NYC, 16/200
Frischer (Charles) Fdn., Scarsdale, 16/201
Fried Fdn., NYC, 16/201
Friedman (Harold & Sylvia) Fdn., NYC, 16/202
Frumkes (Herbert M.) Fdn., NYC, 16/202
Fuchs (Solomon & Rebecca) Fdn., Bronx, 16/203
Full Circle Fdn., NYC, 16/204
Fuller (Bernard & Helen) Fdn., Whitestone, 16/204
Fund for Adult Education, NYC, 16/206
Fund for the City of New York, NYC, 16/206
Furman (Morris & Gertrude) Fdn., NYC, 16/207
Furst (Sol & Hilda) Fdn., NYC, 16/208
Furtherance Fund, Greenvale, 16/209
Furthermoor Fdn., NYC, 16/210
Futterman (Harry) Fund, NYC, 16/211
Gabby Fdn., NYC, 16/212
Gadfly Fdn., NYC, 16/212
Gallager (James H.L.) School Fund Trust, Rochester, 16/213
Gadsby Fund, NYC, 16/214
Gallop (M. Robert) Fdn., NYC, 16/214
Gamma Phi Beta Sorority Alpha Chapter, Syracuse, 16/215
Gamma Phi Beta Sorority, Syracuse University Society, Syracuse, 16/215
Gandhian Fdn., NYC, 16/215
Ganlee Fdn., NYC, 16/215
Gant (Donald R. & Jane T.) Fdn., NYC, 16/217
Gardner (Anna & Meyer) Scholarship Fund, Utica, 16/218
Garfinkel (Sam) Family Fdn., Great Neck, 16/218
Gary Fdn., NYC, 17/001
Gash (Frederick) Fdn., NYC, 17/001
Gavrin (Arthur J.) Fdn., Scarsdale, 17/002
Geare-First Methodist Church of Pittsford, Rochester, 17/003
Geare-Poor of Pittsford Trust, Rochester, 17/003
Gehr (George W.) Cemetery Trust, Harrisburg, Pa., 17/003
Gehring Fdn., Dolgeville, 17/003
Gelardin Fdn., NYC, 17/004
Gelfand (Maxwell L.) Research Fund, NYC, 17/005
Gellert (Leopold R.) Family Trust, NYC, 17/005
Gellert (Michael E.) Trust, NYC, 17/006
General Semantics Fdn., NYC, 17/008
Genesee County Museum, Rochester, 17/008
Gerry Fdn., NYC, 17/009
G.F.R. Fdn., NYC, 17/011
Gildesgame Fdn., Mt. Kisco, 17/012
Gilman Fdn., NYC, 17/012
Gilmour Fdn., Brooklyn, 17/014
Ginsberg Fdn., Tupper Lake, 17/015
Ginsburg (Morris) Fdn., NYC, 17/015
Giordano (Salvatore) Fdn., NYC, 17/015

Given (Irene Heinz & John LaPorte) Fdn., NYC, 17/017

Glazier Fdn., NYC, 17/018

Glazer (Adele & Benjamin) Fdn., NYC, 17/019

Gleason Fund, Rochester, 17/020

Glickman (Morris) Fdn., Poundridge, 17/023

Gluck (Doris & Arthur) Fdn., NYC, 17/024

Godden (Lucy) & Julia Grace Trust, Jamestown, 17/025

Goelet (Robert) Fdn., NYC, 17/029

Gold (Alter) Memorial Fdn., Bronx, 17/030

Goldberg (Murray) Scholarship Fdn., Brooklyn, 17/031

Golden (Sibyl & William T.) Fdn., NYC, 17/031

Goldfein (Stanley F.) Fdn., NYC, 17/032

Goldman Sachs Fund, NYC, 17/033

Goldman Fund, NYC, 17/034

Goldman (Herman) Fdn., NYC, 17/036

Goldman (Mathilda & Charles) Fdn., NYC, 17/038

Goldstein (Alfred & Ann) Fdn., NYC, 17/039

Goldstein (Samuel & Abraham) Fdn., Plainview, 17/041

Goldstone Fund, NYC, 17/042

Goldhirsch (David & Regina) Fdn., NYC, 17/043

Goldin (Barry Lawrence) Fdn., NYC, 17/044

Goldman (Nathan) Fdn., NYC, 17/044

Goldner Charity Fund, NYC, 17/045

Goldring (Joseph G.) Fdn., Brooklyn, 17/045

Goldsmith (Warren R.) Family Fdn., NYC, 17/046

Goldstein (t/w Adolf) County Trust Co., White Plains, 17/047

Gondelman Fdn., NYC, 17/047

Goodman (Andrew) Fdn., NYC, 17/049

Goodman (David & Rebecca) Fdn., Brooklyn, 17/049

Goodman (Edward A.) Fdn., NYC, 17/049

Goodman (Herman & Ruth) Fdn., NYC, 17/051

Goodstein (David) Family Fdn., NYC, 17/051

Gootter (Shirley) Fdn., Brooklyn, 17/053

Gorovoy (Sam) Fdn., NYC, 17/053

Gottleib Fdn., NYC, 17/053

Gould (Edwin) Trust for Dobbs Ferry Hospital, NYC, 17/054

Gould (Harry E.) Fdn., NYC, 17/055

Gould Memorial Reformed Church Trust, NYC, 17/056

Gourary Fund, NYC, 17/056

Grace (David R. & Nancy E.) Fdn., NYC, 17/057

Graham (t/w Deborah L.) f/b/o Hawthorn Reformed Church, White Plains, 17/058

Institute for Creative Research, NYC, 17/058

Gralnick Fdn., NYC, 17/059

Gramercy Park Fdn., NYC, 17/059

Grant (William R.) Fdn., Oyster Bay, 17/060

Great Mountain Forest Corporation, NYC, 17/061

Green Scapular Fdn., Valley Stream, 17/061

Greenaway Fdn., NYC, 17/061

Greenberg (Alan C.) Fdn., NYC, 17/062

Greenman (Elsie & Nathan) Fdn., Farmingdale, 17/063

Greenman (Phyllis & Bernard) Fdn., Roslyn, 17/064

Greenspan (Benjamin & Sara) Fund, NYC, 17/065

Grenard Fdn., NYC, 17/067

Gellert (Greta) Charitable Account, NYC, 17/067

Grolier Fdn., NYC, 17/070

Gross (Benjamin & Rose M.) Fdn., Hartsdale, 17/072

Gross (Emily Jane) Book Fund, East Rockaway, 17/073

Gross (House of) Fdn., NYC, 17/074

Gross (Julia & Seymour) Fdn., NYC, 17/075

Grossman (Isidore) Fdn., NYC, 17/075

Grossman Fdn., NYC, 17/077

Grossman (Irwin & William) Fdn., NYC, 17/077

Gruber (Maurice & Marian A.) Fdn., NYC, 17/078

Gruenberg (Leonard S.) Fdn., NYC, 17/078

Grumbacher (Stanley) Trust "C", NYC, 17/079

Grumbacher (Stanley & Kathleen) Fdn., NYC, 17/080

Grund Fdn., NYC, 17/081

Grunfeld (Herbert) Trust 1953, NYC, 17/082

Grunfeld (Herberg) Trust of 2-1-66, NYC, 17/082

Gruss (Joseph & Caroline) Charitable Fdn., NYC, 17/083

Guggenheim (Daniel & Florence) Fdn., NYC, 17/084

Guggenheim (Murray & Leonie) Fdn., NYC, 17/086

Guggenheim (Harry Frank) Fdn., NYC, 17/088

Guggenheim (Peggy) Fdn., NYC, 17/090

Gulbenkian Fdn., NYC, 17/090

Gulf & Western Fdn., NYC, 17/091

Gurwin (J.) Fdn., Great Neck, 17/094

Guterman (A.S.) Fdn., NYC, 17/094

Gutterman (Milton H.) Fdn., NYC, 17/095

Gutfreund (Joyce & John) Fdn., NYC, 17/095

Gutman (Edna & Monroe C.) Fdn., NYC, 17/097

Guttman (Stella & Charles) Fdn., NYC, 17/098

Guttman (Stella & Charles) Breast Diagnostic Trust, NYC, 17/100

Hahn (Philip Y.) Fdn., Rochester, 17/102

Haft (Morris W. & Fannie B.) Fdn., NYC, 17/103

Haft (Robert) Fdn., Great Neck, 17/104

Halldon Fdn., NYC, 17/104

Halper (Norman H.) Fdn., NYC, 17/105

Halperin (Meyer) Fdn., Brooklyn, 17/106

Halpert (Edith Gregor) Fdn., NYC, 17/106

Hammer Fdn., NYC, 17/107

Hansley Fdn., NYC, 17/107

Harkness Ballet, NYC, 17/107

Harriet Aid Society, Jackson Heights, 17/108

Harris (Jacqueline S. & Edward), Jr. Trust, Rochester, 17/109

Harris (Helen) et al. Trust, NYC, 17/110

Harrisburg Welfare Federation Trust, Harrisburg, Pa., 17/110

Harrison (Alfred & Pauline) Charitable Trust, NYC, 17/111

Harrison (Wallace K.) Architectural Fdn., NYC, 17/111

Belafonte (Harry) Fdn., NYC, 17/112

Hart (t/w L.M.) Art. 2 f/b/o St. Paul's Methodist Church (See Reel 18/127),

Hart (Mark M.) Family Fdn., Lake Success, 17/112

Hart (Milton) Fnd., Rye, 17/113

Hasenfeld (A. & Z.) Fdn., NYC, 17/113

Hastings (Merrill G. & Emita E.) Fdn., NYC, 17/113

Hartog (Ada F.) Fdn., NYC, 17/114

Harlyn Fdn., NYC, 17/115

Hatcher Fund, NYC, 17/118

Hatch (Alfrederic S.) Charitable Trust, NYC, 17/120

Hazen (Harry) Fdn., White Plains, 17/120

Spencer (H.D. & R.B.) Fdn. Trust, Poughkeepsie, 17/121

Health & Welfare Security Fund of Local 343 H.R.E. & B.U., Kingston, 17/121

Hearing Fdn. of Buffalo, Buffalo, 17/122

Hearn (Murray) Fund, Remsenburg, 17/122

Hersh (Albert & Dolores) Fdn., Jamaica, 17/122

Hearst (William Randolph) Fdn., NYC, 17/123

Heart Education & Research Fdn., Brooklyn, 17/126

Hebrew University (Jerusalem) Trust, NYC, 17/126

Heckert Cemetery Trust, Harrisburg, Pa., 17/127

Heckler (David) Fdn., Long Island City, 17/127

Heijmans (Justus) Fdn., NYC, 17/128

Heimlich Fdn., New Rochelle, 17/128

Heineman & Co. Fdn., NYC, 17/130

Heineman (U/w Louis) Trust, Jamestown, 17/131

Heiser Fdn., NYC, 17/131

Heitner (Lee) Memorial Fdn., NYC, 17/131

Heller (Elizabeth & Herbert C.) Fdn., NYC, 17/132

Hellman (Lotte & Harold) Fdn., Roslyn, 17/133

Hellmuth (Clara & Kurt) Fdn., NYC, 17/134

Herbert Fdn., NYC, 17/135

Helmsley (Harry B.) Fdn., NYC, 17/135

Hebrew University Association Trust, NYC, 17/136

Herbert (Katharine) Fund, NYC, 17/137

Herbert (Victor) Fdn., NYC, 17/137

Holmes Fdn., NYC, 17/138

Henderson (Theodora G.) Trust #4, NYC, 17/142

Herrman (Herbert Erlanger) Fdn., Larchmont, 17/145

Herman Fdn., NYC, 17/145

Herrman (William H.) Fdn., NYC, 17/146

Herzfeld (Emy & Emil) Fdn., NYC, 17/147

Herzman Fdn., NYC, 17/149

Herzog (Paul & Suschka) Fdn., NYC, 17/150

Hess Family Fdn., NYC, 17/150

Hess (Linnie A.) Trust, Harrisburg, Pa., 17/151

Hess (Simon B.) Family Fdn., Manhasset, 17/151

Heyman (Ruth & Ralph) Fdn., Scarsdale, 17/152

Hickey (Paul K.) Fdn., NYC, 17/152

Hickrill Fdn., NYC, 17/153

Higgins (John D. & Lynn) Fdn., Glen Head, 17/154

Higier (Julius & Edna) Fdn., Gloversville, 17/155

Hillson (Max & Ida) Fdn., NYC, 17/155

Hill-Stead Museum, NYC, 17/157

Hillery (Judge John D.) Memorial Scholarship Fund, Buffalo, 17/157

Hipple (Henrietta) Cemetery Trust, Harrisburg, Pa., 17/158

Hirsch Memorial Fdn., NYC, 17/159

Hirsch (R. David) Fdn., NYC, 17/159

Hirschfield (Alan & Berte) Fdn., NYC, 17/161

Hirsler (t/w Suie V.) for Clearfield Methodist Church & Cemetery, Lancaster, Pa., 17/162

Hittner Fdn., NYC, 17/162

Hoart (Francis & Gladys) Fdn., NYC, 17/163

Hodgkins Fdn., Syracuse, 17/163

Hoffman (Bernard & Dorothy) Fdn., Belle Harbor, 17/164

Hoffritz (Edwin J.) Fdn., NYC, 17/165

Hollard Fdn., Brooklyn, 17/165

Holmes (Byron C.) Cemetery Trust, Albany, 17/166

Holt (t/w Wainright) f/b/o Laurel Grove Cemetery, White Plains, 17/167

Home for the Friendless - t/w Daniel W. Dull, Harrisburg, Pa., 17/167

Home for Old Men & Aged Couples Trust, NYC, 17/168

Homeland Fdn., NYC, 17/169

Honig (Martin & Sarah R.) Fdn., Forest Hills, 17/171

Hooper Fdn., Hamburg, 17/172

Hoppin (Jane & Henry) Fdn., NYC, 17/172

Hormone Research Fdn., NYC, 17/173

Horowitz (Sidney & Grace) Fdn., Great Neck, 17/174

Horowitz-Slotkin Fdn., Brooklyn, 17/175

Hossan (Samra, William & Rose) Endowment Fund, NYC, 17/175

Hotel & Motel Educational Fdn., NYC, 17/175

Howard (Cecil) Charitable Trust, NYC, 17/176

Howe Fdn., Buffalo, 17/176

Hoyt (Clare J.) Memorial Fdn., Walden, 17/177

H.S.L. Fdn., NYC, 17/177

Hudson Valley Girl Scout Council Inc. Trust, Albany, 17/178

Hudson Valley Paper Fdn., Albany, 17/178

Hulbert (Madeline) Scholarship Trust, Rochester, 17/179

Hultquist Fdn., Jamestown, 17/179

Human Sciences Fdn., NYC, 17/180

Hungarian Cultural Fdn., Buffalo, 17/180

Huguenot Historical Association Fdn., New Rochelle, 17/181

Huyer (Edmund Niles) Preserve, Rensselaerville, 17/181

Hyde Fdn., Buffalo, 17/182

Hyde (W.T.) Charitable Trust, Pleasantville, 17/183

I.B.F.W. Local #351 Electrical Joint Apprenticeship & Training Trust Fund, Olean, 17/183

Industrial Relations Counselors, NYC, 17/183

Inmont Fdn., NYC, 17/185

Institute for Gravitational Strain Pathology, NYC, 17/186

Institute of Current World Affairs (See Reel 18/164),

Inter-Faith Better Homes Development Corporation, Albany, 17/187

International Association of Cleaning & Dye House Workers Welfare Trust Fund, Buffalo, 17/187

International Fdn. for Art Research, NYC, 17/187

International Fdn. for Ewha Womans University, NYC, 17/188

International Legal Center, NYC, 17/189

Interracial Council for Business Opportunity Fund, NYC, 17/198

Institute for Educational Development, NYC, 17/198

IOS Fdn. of Delaware, NYC, 17/200

Isaacs (David L. & Harriet) Trust, East Hills, 17/200

Isaacs (Mark B.) Fdn., NYC, 17/203

Iselin-Jefferson Fdn., NYC, 17/204

Israel (Lawrence J.) Fdn., NYC, 17/205

J.H.L. Fdn., NYC, 17/205

Jacobowitz Fdn., Buffalo, 17/206

Jacobs (Samuel & Anna) Fdn., NYC, 17/206

Jacobs (Stanley R. & Helene B.) Fdn., NYC, 17/207

Jacobson (Franz & Rose) Fdn., NYC, 17/208

Jaffin (Barney) Fdn., NYC, 17/208

Jamestown Boys Club Inc. Trust, Jamestown, 17/209

Jinishian (Vartan H.) Trust #2, NYC, 17/209

Joelson Fdn., NYC, 17/209

Kennedy (Joseph P.), Jr. Fdn., NYC, 17/210

J.M. Fdn., NYC, 17/211

Johnson City Teachers Memorial Fdn., Binghamton, 17/212

Junior Citizens of America, NYC, 17/212

Jacobs (John, Mary & Bernard) Fdn., NYC, 17/213

Jacobson (Benjamin) & Sons Fdn., NYC, 17/214

Jedra Charitable Fdn., NYC, 17/215

Jephson Educational Trust, NYC, 17/215

Grossinger (Jennie) Fdn., NYC, 17/216

Jesselson Fdn., NYC, 17/217

Jewish Charities Fund, NYC, 17/218

Jewish Fdn. for Education of Girls, NYC, 17/218

J.H.S. Fdn., NYC, 18/001

Johnson City Teachers Memorial Fdn., Johnson City, 18/002

Jones (Blanche & George) Fund, NYC, 18/002

Jones (Ernest A.) Fdn., NYC, 18/003

Klein (David A.) Memorial Fdn., NYC, 18/004

Klein (George & Adele) Fdn., Brooklyn, 18/005

Klein (Ruth & Seymour) Fdn., NYC, 18/005

Klein (Stephen & Regina) Fdn., Brooklyn, 18/006

Kleinbaum Fund, NYC, 18/007

Josten Fund, NYC, 18/009

K.A. in V.C. Fdn., Ithaca, 18/010

Kadin (William) Fdn., NYC, 18/011

Kahal Fdn., NYC, 18/012

Kahn (Herman & Ruth) Fdn., NYC, 18/012

Kahn Performing Arts Fdn., NYC, 18/013

Kahn (Joseph & Susan) Fdn., NYC, 18/014

Kahn (Malcolm B. & Sandra) Fdn., Hewlett, 18/014

Pack-Kahn Fdn., NYC, 18/015

Kahn (Samuel & Ethel) Fdn., NYC, 18/015

Kahn (S. Sidney) Fdn., NYC, 18/016

Kahn (Robert & Sandra) Fdn., Rockville Centre, 18/017

Kahn (Wilfred R.) Fdn., Mamaroneck, 18/017

Kalil (Elias) Fdn., Manhasset, 18/018

Kalikow (Harold & Juliet) Fdn., Forest Hills, 18/019

Kalman (Henry) Fdn., NYC, 18/019

Kanter (Samuel & George) Fdn., NYC, 18/020

Kaplan (Lazare & Charlotte) Fdn., NYC, 18/021

Kaplan (Richard) Fdn., NYC, 18/022

Kappel (Samuel & Minnie J.) Fdn., NYC, 18/022

Karp (Harvey & Beverly) Fdn., NYC, 18/023

Kaspar & Esh Fdn., NYC, 18/024

Katz (Matilda & Samuel) Family Fdn., NYC, 18/024

Katz (Samuel & Marion) Fdn., NYC, 18/025

Kaufman Family Fdn., NYC, 18/026

Kaufmann (Elizabeth S. & Irving G.) Fdn., NYC, 18/027

Kaufmann (Henry) Fdn., NYC, 18/028

Kaufman (Richard) Scholarship Fund, NYC, 18/029

Kaufman (William & Esther) Fdn., NYC, 18/030

Kayser-Roth Fdn., NYC, 18/030

Kemp Benevolent Fund, NYC, 18/031

Keller (Charles S.) Scholarship Fund, NYC, 18/033

Kelly (Julia) Trust, Jamestown, 18/033

Kempner Fdn., NYC, 18/033

Kennedy Educational Fdn., NYC, 18/034

Kennedy (Dav-d & Phyllis) Fdn., Brooklyn, 18/035

Kenworthy (Marion E.)-Swift (Sarah H.) Fdn., NYC, 18/036

Kerby Realty Fdn., Syracuse, 18/037

Chernovsky (Keren Bertha), NYC, 18/037

Kerrigan-Teich Fdn., Brooklyn, 18/037

Kessel (Morris & Jeanette) Fund, NYC, 18/038

Kidd (Elizabeth L. & J. Howard), Jr. Charitable Trust, Rochester, 18/038

Kiesewetter Charitable Fdn., Syracuse, 18/039

Kimball Public Library Trust, NYC, 18/039

Kingsberg Fdn., NYC, 18/039

Kinney (Emma D.) t/a Baldwin Cemetery, Harrisburg, Pa., 18/040

Kinzer (Anna M.) t/w Evangelical Lutheran Church, Lancaster, Pa., 18/040

Kirshner (Samuel) Fdn., Woodside, 18/041

Kivelson (Eva & Harvey) Fdn., NYC, 18/042

Kleid (Lewis) Fdn., NYC, 18/042

Klein (Stephen & Regina S.) Fdn., Brooklyn, 18/043

Kleyman (Leslie) Fdn., NYC, 18/044

Klorfein (Julius & Rose) Fdn., NYC, 18/044

Klugmann (Alfred) Fdn., NYC, 18/045

Knapp (David B.) Fdn., NYC, 18/046

Knowlton Brothers Fdn., Watertown, 18/047

Knox Gelatine Fdn., Johnston, 18/047

Koenigsberg (Joshua S.) Memorial Fdn., NYC, 18/048

Korn (Irene & Bernard), Oceanside, 18/049

Korn (Richard & Peggy) Fdn., NYC, 18/049

Berger (Kornel) Fdn., Maspeth, 18/051

Kosh (David & Ruth) Fdn., NYC, 18/051

Kraft, Fischman & Assael Fdn., NYC, 18/051

Kramer (C.L.C.) Fdn., NYC, 18/052

Kramer (Murray) Fdn., Woodmere, 18/052

Krause (Sydney & Marjory) Fdn., Scarsdale, 18/053

Krauss (Max) Fdn., NYC, 18/054

Kreiss (Sidney & Mildred) Fdn., Woodmere, 18/054

Krejtman Family Fdn., NYC, 18/055

Kriendler (Maxwell A.) Fdn., NYC, 18/056

Kriger Fund, New Rochelle, 18/056

Krimendahl (H. Frederick) II Fdn., NYC, 18/057

Kriser (Charles) Fdn., NYC, 18/057

Kudler (Helen & Daniel) Fdn., Jericho, 18/058

Kuhlmann (August M.) Fdn., Buffalo, 18/059

Kuichling (Emil) Fund Trust, Rochester, 18/059

Labrenz Fdn., Orchard Park, 18/059

Lado, Inc., NYC, 18/059

Laing-Emma L. Stevens Hospital Trust, Rochester, 18/060

Lamon Fdn., NYC, 18/060

Landau (George & Roberte) Fdn., NYC, 18/061

Landegger Fdn., NYC, 18/062

Landorf & Glottstein Fdn., NYC, 18/063

Landis (Aaron & Lucille) Family Fdn., NYC, 18/063

Landowne Fdn., Brooklyn, 18/064

Landsman (Charles) Fdn., NYC, 18/065

Lang (Eugene M.) Fdn., NYC, 18/066

Lang (Pearl) Dance Fdn., NYC, 18/067

Langie (Louis A.) Fdn. Trust, Rochester, 18/067

Lann Fdn., NYC, 18/068

Lansingburgh Historical Society, Troy, 18/069

Lapkin Fdn., NYC, 18/070

LaRocque Bey School of Dance Theatre, NYC, 18/072

Larkin--First Methodist Church of LeRoy Trust, Rochester, 18/073

Larkin-Prize Speaking Trust, Rochester, 18/073

Larsen (Irgens) Fdn., NYC, 18/073

Lassalle Fund, NYC, 18/074

Lasker (Albert & Mary) Fdn., NYC, 18/076

Lattimer Family Fund, NYC, 18/078

Lauro Fdn., NYC, 18/079

Lavanburg (Fred L.) Fdn., NYC, 18/079

Lawrence (John S. & Florence G.) Fdn., NYC, 18/080

Lazare (Louis) Fdn., NYC, 18/081

Lazare (Marie) Fdn., NYC, 18/082

Lazrus (Oscar M.) Fdn., NYC, 18/083

Lazarus (Rosalind) & Avnet (Norman) t/u/a f/b/o Jewish Theological Seminary of America, NYC, 18/084

League of Lutheran Women of Albany, Albany, 18/085

Aaron Eliezer Dvorah & Leah Fdn., Flushing, 18/087

Ledkote Charity Fdn., Port Jefferson, 18/087

Lee (Edward & Elaine L.) Fdn., NYC, 18/088

Leeds Fdn., Lake Ronkonkoma, 18/088

Lefkowitz (Sally & Nat) Fdn., NYC, 18/089

Lehman (Jack & Sara) Fdn., NYC, 18/090

Lehman (Philip) Fdn., NYC, 18/090

Lehman (Robert) Fdn., NYC, 18/092

Lehman (William H. & Leona B.) Trust, Mt. Kisco, 18/093

Leness (G. J.) Fdn., NYC, 18/094

Leonard Fdn., NYC, 18/094

Leonhardt Fdn., NYC, 18/095

Lesser (Max M. & Eleanor) Fdn., NYC, 18/096

Leubsdorf (Karl & Bertha) Charitable Trust, NYC, 18/096

Lever Brothers Company Fdn., NYC, 18/096

Levick (Judith & Ronald) Fdn., NYC, 18/097

Levidare Fdn., NYC, 18/097

Levien Fdn., NYC, 18/098

Levin (Isabel & Russell) Fdn., Scarsdale, 18/099

Levine (Arthur J. & Marilyn) Fdn., NYC, 18/100

Levine (Mike & Edith) Fdn., NYC, 18/101

Levinson (Louis A.) Fdn., Woodmere, 18/102

Levinson (Morris L.) Fdn., NYC, 18/103

Leviton Fdn., Brooklyn, 18/104

Leviton Fdn. Inc. - Delaware, Brooklyn, 18/104

Levitt Fdn., NYC, 18/105

Levitt (Mortimer) Fdn., NYC, 18/106

Levy (Arthur & Janet) Fdn., Forest Hills, 18/107

Levy (Betty & Norman F.) Fdn., NYC, 18/108

Levy (Irving & Estelle) Fdn., NYC, 18/108

Levy, Foundation Family Isaac Youssef, NYC, 18/109

Levy (Jacob) Fdn., NYC, 18/109

Levy (Jacques M.) & Co. Fdn., NYC, 18/110

Garlick (Lewis & Jewel) Fdn., Great Neck, 18/110

Lewis (Merwin) Fdn., NYC, 18/111

Lewis (Milton F. & Rita C.) Fdn., NYC, 18/111

Lewis (Mortimer B.) Fdn., NYC, 18/112

Lewittes Fdn., NYC, 18/113

Liberman (Bertha & Isaac) Fdn., NYC, 18/113

Licht Brothers Fdn., Forest Hills, 18/114

Lief, Werle, Alston Fdn., NYC, 18/115

Life Saving Benevolent Association of New York, NYC, 18/115

Lift Fdn., Rochester, 18/117

Lightolier Fund, NYC, 18/117

Limon (Jose) Dance Fdn., NYC, 18/119

Lindburn Fdn., NYC, 18/119

Lincoln Fund, NYC, 18/120

Linder (Albert A. & Bertram N.) Fdn., NYC, 18/121

Linder (Maurice) Fdn., NYC, 18/123

Link Fdn., Binghamton, 18/124

Lipman (Howard & Jean) Fdn., NYC, 18/125

Lipsig (Harry H.) Fdn., NYC, 18/126

Litt Fdn., NYC, 18/127

Hart (t/w L.M.) Art. 2 f/b/o St. Paul's Methodist Church, White Plains, 18/127

Lloyd (Edmund S.) Fdn., Middletown, 18/128

Stanley Lodge Relief Fund, NYC, 18/128

Loeb Rhoades Employees Welfare Fund, NYC, 18/129

Lober Charitable Fund, NYC, 18/130

Loeb (Carol Buttenweiser) Fdn., NYC, 18/131

Loew's Theatres Welfare Fund, NYC, 18/132

Loewy Family Fdn., NYC, 18/133

Loch Graveyard Deed of Trust, Harrisburg, Pa., 18/134

Loeb (Robert Lester & Ann G.) Fdn., NYC, 18/135

Local 802 Senior Musicians Fund, NYC, 18/135

Local 802 Senior Musicians Fund (See Reel 20/099),

Logan Fdn., NYC, 18/136

Lomart Educational Fdn., Brooklyn, 18/137

Lonberg-Silard Fund, Pleasantville, 18/137

Long Island Historical Society, Brooklyn, 18/138

Long Island Volunteers, Riverhead, 18/139

Loo (C.T.) Chinese Educational Fund, NYC, 18/139

Lopin (Sam & Anna) Fdn., NYC, 18/140

Lotsch (Dr. Joseph M.) Fdn., NYC, 18/141

Loudoun Memorial Hospital Trust, NYC, 18/142

Loudoun Memorial Hospital Trust U/A Walter S. Fox, NYC, 18/142

Loudoun Memorial Hospital Trust U/A Eleanor C. Fox, NYC, 18/143

Love (Joseph) Fdn., NYC, 18/145

Lovell Family Ltd., NYC, 18/146

Louwana Fund, NYC, 18/146

L-T Fdn., NYC, 18/147

Lowe Family Foundation, NYC, 18/148

Lubin (Louis & Anna P.) Fdn., Peekskill, 18/149

Luckman (Dave) Memorial Fdn., Mineola, 18/149

Lunt-Fontanne Fdn., NYC, 18/150

Lurge (Schaina & Josephine) Memorial Fdn., NYC, 18/151

Lowey Fdn., NYC, 18/151

Lynch (Cornelius T. & Elizabeth M.) Scholarship Trust, Rochester, 18/151

Lynch (Joseph B.) Fdn., NYC, 18/152

Lynn (Amy & Eugene) Fdn., NYC, 18/153

Maas Fdn., NYC, 18/153

Mabey (Anna L.) Fdn., Sidney, 18/154

Macbeth Fdn., Newburgh, 18/154

Macdonald (Alexander J.) Family Fdn., Orchard Park, 18/155

Mahood (David M.) Ttee U/A 10-28-43, NYC, 18/156

Mainzer (Max) Memorial Fdn., Flushing, 18/156

Maisel (Melvin L.) Family Fdn., Mt. Vernon, 18/157

Major Fdn., NYC, 18/157

Make New York Beautiful, Inc., NYC, 18/158

Malanowicz (Edmund E.) Memorial Scholarship Fund, Cheektowaga, 18/159

Malbin Fdn., White Plains, 18/159

Malina Fdn., NYC, 18/159

Mallon (George Barry) Memorial Corporation, NYC, 18/160

Malman (Seymour) Fdn., Great Neck, 18/160

Malmed (Charles J. & Martha) Fdn., Long Island City, 18/161

Maslow (Elsie & Lewis) Fdn., NYC, 18/162

Maslin (Raphael & Elaine) Fdn., NYC, 18/162

Manacher (Irving A. & Bella) Fdn., NYC, 18/163

Manufacturers Hanover Trust Company Ttee for Institute of Current World Affairs, NYC, 18/164

Management Institute for National Development, NYC, 18/164

Manealoff (William & Dorothy) Fdn., NYC, 18/165

Mandle (Henry H. & Florence B.) Trust, Bronx, 18/165

Mangel (Martin Elliot) Fdn., NYC, 18/166

Manheim Fdn., NYC, 18/167

Mann (Mary) Philanthropic League, NYC, 18/170

Mann (Samuel J.) Memorial Fund Trust, Rochester, 18/171

Marin (Norma & John C.) Fdn., NYC, 18/171

Markle (John & Mary R.) Fdn., NYC, 18/172

Marks (Carl) Fdn., NYC, 18/176

Marblette Fdn., Long Island City, 18/177

Martin Fdn., NYC, 18/177

Marcus (Jacob & Rachel) Memorial Fdn., Jamestown, 18/178

Marcus (James S.) Fdn., NYC, 18/179

Marinbach (Samuel & Bertha) Fdn., NYC, 18/180

Markelson (Dora) Fdn., NYC, 18/180

Marks (Joseph) Fdn., Portchester, 18/181

Marcellus Family Fund, Syracuse, 18/182

Martin Family Fdn., NYC, 18/183

Marx (L.E.) Fdn., NYC, 18/184

Marx (Louis) Fdn., NYC, 18/184

Masaryk Institute, NYC, 18/186

Maslow (Robert) Fdn., NYC, 18/186

Masonic Charity Fdn. of Connecticut, NYC, 18/187

Master Heart Fdn., NYC, 18/187

Mastronardi (Charles A.) Charitable Fdn., Brooklyn, 18/188

Mathewson (Joseph B. & Christina A.) Fdn., Ithaca, 18/189

Matheson (William J.) Fdn., NYC, 18/189

Matlick (Max & Goldye) Fdn., NYC, 18/193

Matthews (Mark) Fdn., NYC, 18/194

Mawar Fdn., NYC, 18/194

Maxwell (Eva & Oscar) Fdn., Portchester, 18/195

Mayer Family Fdn., NYC, 18/195

Mayer (Cecile L.) Medical Fdn., NYC, 18/196

Mayer (Cyrus & Sylvia) Fdn., NYC, 18/196

Mayers Fund, NYC, 18/197

Mayfield Trust, NYC, 18/198

Maymar Corporation, NYC, 18/198

McCarthy (Julia) Tuition Scholarship, Albany, 18/199

McConnell (Neil A.) Fdn., NYC, 18/200

McCrory Corporation Needy & Worthy Employees Trust, NYC, 18/202

McCrory Fdn., NYC, 18/203

McElnea (William H., Jr.) Fdn., NYC, 18/204

McKee (James W. & Jayne A.) Fdn., NYC, 18/205

McLellan (Mary A.) Trust, Jamestown, 18/205

Mead Greenwood Cemetery, T/A, F/B/O, White Plains, 18/207

Mearin Fdn., Brooklyn, 18/207

Medical Services International, NYC, 18/208

Medico Educational TV & Radio Fdn., NYC, 18/209

Medina (Harold R.) Fund F/B/O Westhampton Free Library, NYC, 18/209

Megna Fdn., Brooklyn, 18/209

Melis (F. Kenneth) Fdn., Garden City, 18/210

Melly (L. Thomas) Fdn., NYC, 18/210

Melnick (Julius) Fdn., Bronx, 18/210

Memton Fund, NYC, 18/211

Merrill (Ingram) Fdn. Trust, NYC, 18/212

Met Council Community Improvement Fund, NYC, 18/214

Metropolitan Applied Research Center, NYC, 18/215

Metropolitan Museum of Art Trust PT 18263, NYC, 18/217

Metropolitan Museum of Art Trust PT 7933, NYC, 18/218

Meyer-Raeburn (N.S.) Fdn., NYC, 18/219

Meyer (Franz & Gertrude) Fdn., NYC, 19/011

Meyer (Walter E.) Research Institute of Law, NYC, 19/002

Michaels Philanthropic Fdn., Brooklyn, 19/003

Miley (Thomas J. & Margaret) Fdn., NYC, 19/005

Miller Fdn. Charitable Trust, NYC, 19/005

Miller (Maurice & May) Fdn., NYC, 19/006

Mirabelle Fdn., NYC, 19/006

Molin (Richard) Memorial Fdn. for Cancer, Rockville Centre, 19/007

Moller (Ferdinand & Catherine) Trust u/a f/b/o Dutch Evangelical Reformed Church of Canarsie, NYC, 19/007

Monell (Ambrose) Fdn., NYC, 19/008

Montague Fdn., NYC, 19/010

Montebello Trust, NYC, 19/011

Monterey Fund, NYC, 19/012

Moore (Arlee N.) Trust, Jamestown, 19/013

Perlman (Morris & Luba) Fdn., Brooklyn, 19/015

Morris (William J.) Fdn., NYC, 19/015

Morrow Fdn., NYC, 19/016

Mountain (James S.) Memorial Fund, Thornwood, 19/017

Murphy (Daniel J.) Fdn., NYC, 19/017

Cohen (Murray) Fdn., NYC, 19/018

Tomcheho Mushor Fdn., NYC, 19/019

Myers Trust, Troy, 19/020

Meyers (Rose Steefel) Fund, Rochester, 19/021

MFN Fdn., NYC, 19/021

Michener Fdn., NYC, 19/021

Middlesex Baptist Church Trust, Rochester, 19/021

Millard-First Presbyterian Church of Dundee, Rochester, 19/022

Millard (Mark J.) Fdn., NYC, 19/022

Miller (Irving & Mildred L.) Fdn., Lawrence, 19/022

Miller (Robert P.) Fdn., NYC, 19/023

Miller (Jerome & Irma) Fdn., NYC, 19/023

Millonzi (Robert & Eleanor) Fdn., Buffalo, 19/024

Milton (Leonard) Fdn., Lake Success, 19/025

Milvan Fdn., NYC, 19/025

Miniaci (Alfred & Rose) Fdn., NYC, 19/025

Mission of the Immaculate Virgin Trust, NYC, 19/026

Mission Trust Fund, NYC, 19/026

Mitchell (Jan) Fdn., NYC, 19/027

McHarg Fdn., Binghamton, 19/028

Morgens East Fdn., NYC, 19/028

Morgenstern (Sigmund) Charity Trust, NYC, 19/029

Morse (Enid & Lester S., Jr.) Fdn., NYC, 19/029

Morris (Vera & Walter) Fdn., NYC, 19/030

Morris (William) Agency Fdn., NYC, 19/030

Morrow Fdn., NYC, 19/031

Moses (Henry L.) Trust, NYC, 19/031

Mosler Fdn., NYC, 19/033

Moss (Estelle & Benjamin S.) Fdn., NYC, 19/034

Moyer Fdn., Scarsdale, 19/035

Mulligan-Rochester General Hospital Trust, Rochester, 19/036

Mulligan (Mary S.) Charitable Trust, Rochester, 19/036
Fund for Multinational Management Education, NYC, 19/037
Munitalp Fdn., NYC, 19/037
Museum of Music, Scarsdale, 19/038
Murphy Fdn., NYC, 19/038
Musicians Foundation, NYC, 19/039
Myers (John) Fdn., NYC, 19/040
NAMSB Fdn., NYC, 19/041
NAPA Purchasing Educational Fdn., NYC, 19/042
Nasper (Doris F.) Fdn., New Hyde Park, 19/043
National Committee of the Young Men's Christian Association of China, NYC, 19/043
National Friends of Public Broadcasting, NYC, 19/044
National Institute of Arts & Letters, NYC, 19/046
National Self Government Committee, Brooklyn, 19/049
National Sports Alliance Relief Fund, NYC, 19/050
National Vitamin Fdn., NYC, 19/051
Naumburg (Cecile & George) Fdn., NYC, 19/051
Naumburg (Walter W.) Fdn., NYC, 19/052
Neinken Fdn., NYC, 19/053
Nelco Fdn., NYC, 19/053
Nelkin Fdn., NYC, 19/054
Neumark (Arthur J.) Fdn., NYC, 19/055
Newcomb (E.W.) Estate Stony Wold Corporation Article 15th Trust, NYC, 19/055
Noyes (Charles F.) Trust u/a 9/11/63, NYC, 19/056
New York Alpha Phi Kappa Psi Fdn., Ithaca, 19/058
New York Association for the Blind Trust, NYC, 19/058
New York Classical Clubs Greek & Latin Scholarship Fund, Jamaica, 19/059
New York Genealogical & Biographical Society, NYC, 19/059
New York State Scottish Rite Charities, Rochester, 19/061
New York Society for Ruptured & Crippled Trust, NYC, 19/061
New York University Jewish Culture Fdn., NYC, 19/061
Newman (Jerome A. & Estelle R.) Assistance Fund, NYC, 19/062
New York Chamber of Commerce Educational Fdn., NYC, 19/062
New York Genealogical & Biographical Society, NYC, 19/063
NFL Alumni Fdn. Fund, NYC, 19/064
Niagara Frontier Builders Association, Buffalo, 19/065
Nicholson (Gunnar & Lillian) Fdn., NYC, 19/066
Nickerson (Albert L.) Charitable Trust, NYC, 19/066
Nizer Fdn., NYC, 19/067
Noble (John H. & Ethel G.) Charitable Trust, NYC, 19/068
Noland Fdn., NYC, 19/069
Noon Fdn., NYC, 19/069
NONA Charitable Corporation, NYC, 19/070
Norman Fdn., NYC, 19/071
Normandie Fdn., NYC, 19/075
North Shore Hospital Medical Staff Scholarship Fund, Manhasset, 19/077
Northeastern New York Community Trust, Albany, 19/078
N.S.C. Fdn., NYC, 19/079
NVE Shalom Fdn., NYC, 19/080
Nye (Jane & Richard) Fdn., NYC, 19/081
Oesting (William C.) Trust, White Plains, 19/082
Oestreicher (Sylvan) Fdn., NYC, 19/083
Ohrbach (Nathan M.) Fdn., NYC, 19/083
Olian (Cyrus & Jacob) Fdn., NYC, 19/084
Ollesheimer (Sarah S.) Fund, NYC, 19/085

Olmsted-Genesee Gospel Society Trust, Rochester, 19/085
Olmsted-LeRoy High School Scholarship Fund, Rochester, 19/085
Oppenheim-Smith Fdn., NYC, 19/086
Oltarsh (Max & Ruth) Fdn., NYC, 19/087
Open Key Fund, Buffalo, 19/087
Oppco Fdn., NYC, 19/088
Oppenheim Students Fund, Niagara Falls, 19/089
Orchestra Fdn., NYC, 19/089
Organic Reactions, Flushing, 19/090
Osborn (Miriam) Memorial Home Association, Rye, 19/091
Osceola Fdn., NYC, 19/093
Ostriker (A.J.) Fdn., NYC, 19/094
Otlet (James & Helene) Fdn., NYC, 19/095
Otten (Albert) Fdn. Trust, NYC, 19/096
Overseas Fdn., NYC, 19/097
Lehman (Robert Owen) Fdn., NYC, 19/099
Ozai-Durrani Charitable Trust, NYC, 19/101
Pack (Howard M.) Fdn., NYC, 19/102
Pack (Jay J. & Sheila) Fdn., NYC, 19/103
Pakula (Benjamin) Fdn., NYC, 19/104
Pakula (Jeanette & Paul) Fdn., NYC, 19/105
Palisades Geophysical Institute, Blauvelt, 19/105
Palmer (Francis Asbury) Fund, NYC, 19/106
Pantke-Giebler Fdn., NYC, 19/107
Parapsychology Fdn., NYC, 19/107
Parapsychology Research Fund, NYC, 19/110
Borchard (Samuel) Fdn., NYC, 19/110
Parker & Co. International Fdn., NYC, 19/111
Parker (Minnie) Charitable Trust, NYC, 19/111
Parker (Pauline R.) Trust, Binghamtom, 19/113
Parnes (Louis) Fdn., NYC, 19/114
Parry (George K.) Fdn., Old Brookville, 19/114
Parsons Memorial Library Trust, NYC, 19/115
Patrick (Elizabeth) Fdn., NYC, 19/117
Patricof (Alan) Fdn., NYC, 19/117
Patterson (Harry W.) Fdn., Pike, 19/118
Paul (Josephine Bay & C. Michael) Fdn., NYC, 19/118
Pearlman (S. & K.) Fdn., NYC, 19/119
Peat, Marwick, Mitchell Fdn., NYC, 19/120
Peck Fund Trust, NYC, 19/121
Pelham Visiting Nurses Service, Pelham, 19/121
Pelz (Robert L.) Fdn., NYC, 19/121
Perlman (Joseph & Grace) Fdn., NYC, 19/122
Perlman (Morris & Luba) Fdn., Brooklyn, 19/123
Petschek (Walter & Franziska) Family Trust, NYC, 19/123
Simonoff, Peyser & Citrin Fdn., NYC, 19/124
Pflugfelder (John G. & Anne) Fdn., NYC, 19/125
Pelz (Robert L.) Fdn., NYC, 19/126
Penick (S.B.) Fdn., NYC, 19/127
Peregrine White Sanctuary, NYC, 19/128
Perley (Victor E.) Fund, NYC, 19/129
Perlman (A.) Iron Works Fdn., Bronx, 19/130
Perrin A., Fdn., NYC, 19/131
Peterson (Henry) Fdn., NYC, 19/131
Petschek Fdn., NYC, 19/132
Petschek (William) Fdn., NYC, 19/134
Alan Philanthropies, Inc., Mamaroneck, 19/135
Philatelic Fdn., NYC, 19/135
Philatelic Hobbies for the Wounded, Bronx, 19/136
Philips (Herman & Rita) Fdn., NYC, 19/141
Phillips (Ellis L.) Fdn., Ithaca, 19/142
Phillips (Harry & Marjorie) Trust, NYC, 19/143
Phipps (Howard) Charitable Fdn., NYC, 19/144
Phipps (John S.) Fdn., NYC, 19/144
Piatigorsky Family Fdn., NYC, 19/145
Picker (Celia C. & David V.) Fdn., NYC, 19/146
Pickman Fdn., Hollis, 19/146
Pied Piper Fdn. for Performing Arts, St. Albans, 19/147

Pi Lambda Phi Fraternity (Upsilon Chapter), NYC, 19/147
Pinkerton Fdn., NYC, 19/147
Plant (Henry B.) Memorial Fund, NYC, 19/149
Planting Fields Fdn., NYC, 19/151
Plattdeutsche Old Folks Home Society of Brooklyn & Vicinity, Brooklyn, 19/152
Pluta Family Fdn., Rochester, 19/153
Podell (Jules) Fdn., NYC, 19/153
Poliak (Saul & Janice) Fdn., NYC, 19/154
Pokoik (Abraham & Rebecca) Fdn., NYC, 19/155
Polikoff (Jean & Benet, Jr.) Fund, NYC, 19/156
Pollack (Milton & Lillian) Fdn., NYC, 19/156
Pomerantz Fdn., NYC, 19/157
Popper (Eric R.) Fdn., NYC, 19/158
Popper (Robert & Hermine) Fdn., NYC, 19/159
Porter (Mrs. Cheever) Fdn., NYC, 19/160
Post (Marjorie Merriweather) Fdn., NYC, 19/160
Potter (John Taft) Fdn., Plainview, 19/162
Pollak (Bernard E. & Mildred C.) Fdn., NYC, 19/163
Poughkeepsie Area Fund, Poughkeepsie, 19/163
Prager (David & Annabelle) Fund, NYC, 19/164
Pratt-Shad Fdn., NYC, 19/164
Pren-Hall Fdn., NYC, 19/165
Presbyterian Hospital in the City of New York Trust, NYC, 19/166
Preston (Madge) Scholarship Fund, Rochester, 19/166
Price (Arthur & Lucille H.) Charitable Fdn., NYC, 19/166
Prince (Frank J. & Elizabeth M.) Fdn., NYC, 19/167
Princeton Class of 1937 Fdn., NYC, 19/168
Princeton University - Barrington Spear Paine Memorial Fund, NYC, 19/168
Print Council of America, NYC, 19/169
Project Return Fdn., NYC, 19/170
Psychosynthesis Research Fdn., NYC, 19/171
Public Library of Charles City, Iowa, NYC, 19/171
Punch-Rochester Community Chest Trust, Rochester, 19/172
Queens College Fund, Flushing, 19/172
Rabinowitz Fdn., Brooklyn, 19/173
Rabinowitz (Louis M.) Fdn., NYC, 19/173
Rabow Fdn., Buffalo, 19/175
Radio Therapy Cancer Research Fund, NYC, 19/175
Ramallah Fdn., NYC, 19/176
Randen Fdn., White Plains, 19/176
Randleigh Fdn., NYC, 19/177
Raphelda Fdn., NYC, 19/178
Raphael (Sidney O. & Thelma) Fdn., NYC, 19/179
Rapid-American Fdn., NYC, 19/179
Raskin (Hirsch & Braine) Fdn., NYC, 19/179
Realty Fdn. of New York, NYC, 19/181
Reed (Philip D.) Fdn., NYC, 19/183
Reeves (Benjamin M.) Fdn., NYC, 19/184
Reeves Brothers Fdn., NYC, 19/185
Reichman Fund, NYC, 19/187
Rednor (Daniel & Helen) Fdn., NYC, 19/188
Reichman (Henry) Fdn., NYC, 19/189
Reilley (Ewing W.) Charitable Trust, NYC, 19/190
Reindel Fund, NYC, 19/191
Resnik (Regina) Scholarship Fund, NYC, 19/191
Revson (Charles H.) Fdn., NYC, 19/191
Reynolds (Paul S.) Fdn., NYC, 19/193
R.H.M. Fdn., NYC, 19/195
Richard (A. & E.) Fdn., Poughkeepsie, 19/195
Richel Fdn., NYC, 19/196
Ridenour Endowment Fund, NYC, 19/197
Ridgefield Fdn., NYC, 19/198
Riecker (William F.) Fdn., NYC, 19/199
Right Hand Fdn., NYC, 19/199
Riklis Fdn., NYC, 19/200

Rittmaster (David H. & Ethel) Fdn., NYC, 19/201

Rivas - University of Rochester Trust, Rochester, 19/202

Rivas - Woodward Memorial Trust, Rochester, 19/202

Riverside Fdn., NYC, 19/203

Rixson (Oscar C.) Fdn., Bronxville, 19/203

Robbins (Louis) Family Fund, NYC, 19/204

Robbins Fdn., NYC, 19/204

Roberts (Dudley) Fdn., NYC, 19/206

Roberts Family Fdn., NYC, 19/207

Robertson (Andrew W.) Trust, Jamestown, 19/207

Robinson (Maurice R.) Fund, NYC, 19/208

Robinson (Stuart M.) Fdn., NYC, 19/209

Rochester Historical Society, Rochester, 19/210

Rockette Alumnae Charitable Trust, Glen Cove, 19/212

Rodgers & Hammerstein Fdn., NYC, 19/212

Rogers (Emil & Stelle) Fdn., NYC, 19/212

Rogers (W. James IV) Memorial Scholarship Fund, Buffalo, 19/213

Rogowsky (Herbert) Fdn., Port Chester, 19/213

Role Fdn., NYC, 19/214

Rome Cable Fdn., Rome, 19/215

Romer (Harry) Fdn., NYC, 19/217

Roon Fdn., Olean, 19/217

Roosevelt School P.T.A. (New York State Congress of Parents & Teachers), New Rochelle, 19/218

Root Glen Fdn., Clinton, 19/218

Rose (Henry) Fdn., NYC, 20/001

Rose (Marion) Fdn., North Bellmore, 20/002

Rose (Theodore T. & Hilda) Fdn., NYC, 20/003

Rosemore Fdn., NYC, 20/004

Rosen (Reb Moishe) Fund, NYC, 20/004

Rosenbaum (Edward & Ruth) Fdn., New Rochelle, 20/005

Rosenberg (Abraham & Lillian) Fdn., NYC, 20/005

Rosenblatt (Louis & Emanuel G.) Fdn., NYC, 20/007

Rosenblatt (Samuel & Dorothy) Fdn., NYC, 20/007

Rosenberg (Sunny & Abel) Fdn., NYC, 20/008

Rosenblat Charitable Trust, Mt. Vernon, 20/009

Rosenborg (Ralph M.) Art Fdn., NYC, 20/010

Rosenfeld (Alfred & Rita) Fdn., NYC, 20/010

Rosenstiel Fdn., NYC, 20/010

Rosenstein (Neil & Miriam) Fdn., NYC, 20/013

Rosensteil (Dorothy H. & Lewis) Fdn., NYC, 20/013

Rosenthal (Juliet) Fdn., NYC, 20/015

Rosenthal (Myer & Joseph) Memorial Fdn., Hollis Park Gardens, 20/016

Rosewater Fdn., NYC, 20/016

Rosner (Benjamin F.) Fdn., Long Iland City, 20/017

Rossman (Melvin & Barbara) Fdn., NYC, 20/018

Roth (Alan) Fdn., NYC, 20/019

Roth (Marvin & Ronnie) Fdn., NYC, 20/020

Roth (William) Fdn., NYC, 20/020

Rothenberg Fdn., NYC, 20/021

Rothenberg (Harvey & Elaine) Fdn., NYC, 20/022

Rothko (Mark) Fdn., NYC, 20/023

Rothman (Harry) Fdn., NYC, 20/023

Rothschild (B. de) Fdn. for the Advancement of Science in Israel, NYC, 20/024

Rothschild (Marcus A.) Fdn., NYC, 20/025

Routh (J.P.) Fdn., NYC, 20/025

Rowe (Ellis L.) Trust for Eastern New York Orthopaedic Fdn., Troy, 20/026

Rowman (Walter & Frieda) Fdn., NYC, 20/027

Royal College of Surgeons Fdn., NYC, 20/027

RRR Fdn., NYC, 20/028

Rubenstein (Frank) Fdn., Bronx, 20/029

Rubinstein (Frank & Alice) Fdn., NYC, 20/031

Rubinstein (Helena) Fdn., NYC, 20/033

Rueckwald Fdn., Bowmansville, 20/035

Russo (Isaac & Doris) Fdn., NYC, 20/035

R.W.S. Fdn., NYC, 20/036

Ryan (Theresa A.) f/b/o Memorial Methodist Episcopal Church of White Plains, White Plains, 20/036

Sachs Fdn., Bronx, 20/037

Sackler (Mortimer D.) Fdn., NYC, 20/037

Safro (Paul & Miriam) Fdn., NYC, 20/038

Sakel (Manfred) Institute, NYC, 20/038

Saltzman Fdn., NYC, 20/040

Salute to the Seasons Fund for a More Beautiful New York, NYC, 20/041

Sanders-St. Paul Episcopal Church Trust, Rochester, 20/042

Sandler (Joseph & Gwendolyn) Fdn., NYC, 20/042

Santvoord (Peg) Fdn., NYC, 20/042

East (Sarita Kenedy) Fdn., NYC, 20/044

Saul & Eleanor Fdn., Hewlett Harbor, 20/044

Saw Mill Fund, NYC, 20/045

Saxe (Morris D.) Fdn., Albany, 20/045

Schaefer (B.F.S.) Fdn., Melville, 20/045

Schaffer Society, Schenectady, 20/046

Schafler Fdn., NYC, 20/046

Schalkenbach (Robert) Fdn., NYC, 20/047

Schapiro (Tobias & Lina - Jacques) Fdn., NYC, 20/049

Schary Fdn., NYC, 20/049

Schattner (Nuchin H. & Mina) Fdn., NYC, 20/050

Schechter Torah Fdn., NYC, 20/050

Scheffres Fdn., NYC, 20/050

Scheider (Henrietta Rinaldo) Fdn., NYC, 20/053

Schell (Alice A.) Memorial Fund, NYC, 20/054

Schenck (Jane I.) Estate, Norwich, 20/054

Schenley Fdn., NYC, 20/055

Schenley Wholesalers Fdn., NYC, 20/055

Schepp (Leopold) Fdn., NYC, 20/056

Scherman Fdn., NYC, 20/059

Schiff (Jacob R.) Charitable Trust, NYC, 20/062

Schiffman (Jozefine & Stanley) Fdn., NYC, 20/063

Schlang (Joseph) Fdn., NYC, 20/064

Schlang (Maurice H.) Fdn., NYC, 20/065

Schmeidler Fdn., New Rochelle, 20/065

Schmitt (Kilian J. & Caroline F.) Fdn., Rochester, 20/066

Schneider (Helen & Irving) Fdn., NYC, 20/067

Schocken Fdn., NYC, 20/068

Schoenberger (Alvin & Elizabeth) Fdn., White Plains, 20/069

Scholar Advancement Fdn., NYC, 20/069

Scholarship Fund of the Society of Women Engineers, Port Washington, 20/069

Schonholtz (Jack) Philanthropic Fund, Brooklyn, 20/069

Schottland Fdn., NYC, 20/070

Schreiber Fdn., NYC, 20/071

Schroeder (Aldine W.) Fdn., NYC, 20/071

Schulder (Bertie & Mannie) Fdn., Cedarhurst, 20/072

Schulder (Israel & Eva) Fdn., Brooklyn, 20/074

Schulder (Jack & Hilda) Fdn., NYC, 20/074

Schuman (Seymour) Fdn., NYC, 20/074

Schur (Lawrence H.) Fdn., Bronx, 20/075

Schwartz Fdn., NYC, 20/075

Schwartz (Bernard & Irene) Fdn., Great Neck, 20/076

Schwartz (Irving W. & Goldie) Fdn., NYC, 20/077

Schwartz (Leo & Bea) Fund, NYC, 20/078

Schwartz (Leo S.) Medical Research Fdn., NYC, 20/079

Schwartz (Robert B. & Estelle) Fdn., NYC, 20/080

Schwarz (Robert & Sylvia) Fdn., NYC, 20/081

Schwartz (Samuel & Bertha) Fdn., Auburn, 20/081

SCM Fdn., NYC, 20/083

Scott (David B.) Fdn., Norwich, 20/083

Scriven Fdn., NYC, 20/084

Seacoast Fdn., NYC, 20/087

Seamus Dance Fdn., NYC, 20/088

Second District Dental Society State of New York Benevolent Fund, Brooklyn, 20/088

Second District Dental Society State of New York Relief Fund, Brooklyn, 20/089

Segno (Tiro A.) Fdn., NYC, 20/090

Seligman (Henriette) Memorial Fund Trust, Rochester, 20/090

Selter Fdn., Great Neck, 20/091

Local 802 Senior Musicians Fund, NYC, 20/091

Seventh Regiment Fund, NYC, 20/092

71 Fund, NYC, 20/092

Shaftsbury Corporation, NYC, 20/093

Shaekther (Benyumen) Fdn., Bronx, 20/095

Shapiro (Sara & Morris A.) Fdn., NYC, 20/095

Shapiro-Viertel Fdn., White Plains, 20/096

Sharp (Evelyn) Fdn., NYC, 20/097

Shaw (Leo G. & Margaret B.) Fdn., NYC, 20/098

Shea (Harrie T.) Fdn., NYC, 20/099

Sheehan (Joseph E.) Fdn., NYC, 20/100

Seldon (Ralph C.) Fdn., Jamestown, 20/100

Shelter Rock Fdn., NYC, 20/101

Shepard (Richard & Susan) Fdn., New Rochelle, 20/103

Sherman (Calude & Jeannine) Fdn., NYC, 20/103

Shiftan (Ernest & Carola) Fdn., Scarsdale, 20/104

Shiman (Abraham) Memorial Fund, Mt. Vernon, 20/105

Shlom Bonayich, Brooklyn, 20/105

Shlomm (Gregory & Raissa) Fdn., NYC, 20/105

Shorin Fdn., Brooklyn, 20/106

Shub (George & Ruth) Fdn., Wingdale, 20/106

Shubert (Sam S.) Fdn., NYC, 20/107

Shumway (Hettie & Ritter) Community Fund, Rochester, 20/108

Sibley-Spencer Good Samaritan & District Nurse Trust, Rochester, 20/109

Sichel (Franz W.) Fdn., NYC, 20/109

Siegel (Philip & Jeanette) Fdn., NYC, 20/110

Siegel (William & Sadie) Fdn., NYC, 20/111

Sienna Fdn., NYC, 20/112

Siegel (Augustus J.) Trust, NYC, 20/113

Silberman (Marvin J. & Ruth V.) Fund, NYC, 20/113

Silberstein (Leopold D.) Fdn., NYC, 20/113

Silberstein (William & Sylvia) Fdn., Mamaroneck, 20/114

Silbert Fdn., Great Neck, 20/115

Silbert Fund, NYC, 20/115

Silbert (Theodore H. & Sylvia F.) Fdn., NYC, 20/117

Silver (Harry & Shirley) Fdn., NYC, 20/118

Silver (Louis & Martha) Fdn., NYC, 20/119

Silver Cross Philanthropic Society, NYC, 20/120

Silverstein Bros. Fdn., NYC, 20/121

Simons-Greene Fdn., NYC, 20/121

Simon (Hugo & Rose) Fdn., NYC, 20/122

Simpson Fdn., NYC, 20/123

Simpson (Nathan & Augusta) Fdn., NYC, 20/123

Singer (Frances A.) Fdn., Cazenovia, 20/124

Singer (Saul) Fdn., NYC, 20/125

Sinrich Fdn., Hartsdale, 20/125

Sinsheimer (Alexandrine & Alexander L.) Fund, NYC, 20/125

Sinsheimer (Warren J. & Florence) Fdn., NYC, 20/128

Sirota Fdn., NYC, 20/129

Skating Club of New York Educational Fund, NYC, 20/130

Skin Research Fdn., NYC, 20/131

Slade (C.F. Roe) Fdn., NYC, 20/131

Slattery (James M.) Fdn., Maspeth, 20/134

Slocum-Dickerson Fdn., Utica, 20/135

Smadbeck (Warren & Violeta) Fdn., NYC, 20/135

Small Fdn., Poughkeepsie, 20/136

Smith (A. Mabelle) Trust, Rochester, 20/136

Smith (Eugene A.T.) Testamentary Trust, Patchogue, 20/136

Smith (George Graham & Elizabeth Galloway) Fdn., Buffalo, 20/137

Smith-First Presbyterian Church Trust, Rochester, 20/137

Smith-First Presbyterian Society Trust, Rochester, 20/137

Smith (Robert T.) Fdn., Ogdensburg, 20/138

Smith (W. Russell) Fdn., Garden City, 20/139

Smolowe (Richard E.) Fdn., NYC, 20/139

Snyder (Sarah Duduit) Memorial Fund, NYC, 20/140

Snyder (Burdette E.) Fdn. Trust, NYC, 20/140

Social Education Fdn., NYC, 20/142

Society of French Professors in America, NYC, 20/142

Society of the Friendly Sons of Saint Patrick in the City of New York, NYC, 20/142

Society for the Promotion of Jewish Education, NYC, 20/144

Society of St. Mary of the Snow, Brooklyn, 20/144

Society of Woman Geographers, NYC, 20/145

Sofia American Schools, Inc., NYC, 20/146

Solomon (Max) Fdn., NYC, 20/148

Solomon (Peter J. & Linda N.) Fdn., NYC, 20/149

Solomon (Richard H.) Charitable Fdn., NYC, 20/150

Sommer (M. & H.) Fdn., Bronxville, 20/151

Sonhil Fund, NYC, 20/151

Sonnenblick Fdn., NYC, 20/153

Sorg Printing Co. Inc. Fdn., NYC, 20/154

Southern Education Fdn., NYC, 20/154

Southern New York Medical Education & Research Fdn., Brooklyn, 20/159

South Parish Congregational Church Trust, NYC, 20/160

Sovereign Senators Charity Fund, NYC, 20/160

Spatt (Moses) Fdn., Brooklyn, 20/160

Spears (Jackson E. & Evelyn G.) Fdn., NYC, 20/161

Speedwell Services for Children Trust, NYC, 20/162

Spektor Family Fdn., NYC, 20/162

Spenadel (Henry) Fund for Advancement of Education in Dentistry, NYC, 20/163

Spence Chapin Adoption Service Endowment Fund Trust, NYC, 20/164

Spencer (H.D. & R.B.) Fdn. Trust, Poughkeepsie, 20/164

Spiegel (Jerry) Fdn., Hicksville, 20/164

Spiegel (Sam) Fdn., NYC, 20/165

Spiegelberg (William & Virginia) Fdn., NYC, 20/165

Spiritual Science Fdn., Spring Valley, 20/166

Spiro Family Fdn., Kings Point, 20/166

Spittler (Henry A.) Fdn., Monroe, 20/167

Sports Fdn., NYC, 20/168

Sprecher (Emily B.) t/w Evangelical Lutheran Church, Lancaster, Pa., 20/168

S.S. Family Fdn., NYC, 20/169

St. Agnes Hospital Trust, NYC, 20/170

Stamm (A.L.) Fdn., NYC, 20/170

Standard Brands Charitable Scientific & Educational Fdn., NYC, 20/171

Stanton Fdn., NYC, 20/172

Star Textile & Research Fdn., Cohoes, 20/174

Star Welfare Fdn., NYC, 20/175

Starr (Gerald) Family Fdn., Garden City Park, 20/177

State Bank of Albany Fdn., Albany, 20/177

Statler (Ellsworth M.) Trust, Buffalo, 20/178

Stauffer Chemical Company Fdn., NYC, 20/179

Steckler (Philip H. & Lois R.) Fdn., NYC, 20/180

Stein (Alan L. & Ruth) Fdn., NYC, 20/181

Stein (Louise & Mike) Fdn., Kings Point, 20/182

Steinberg Charitable Fdn. Trust, NYC, 20/183

Steinberg (Miriam & Harold) Fdn., NYC, 20/183

Steinberg (Robert M.) Fdn., NYC, 20/184

Steinmetz (B. & M.) Fdn., Brooklyn, 20/184

Stempel Fdn., NYC, 20/185

Stern (Gustav) Fdn., NYC, 20/186

Stern (Herbert E.) Family Fdn., NYC, 20/186

Stern (Jerome L. & Jane) Fdn., NYC, 20/187

Stern (Martin) Fdn., NYC, 20/188

Stern (Robert H.) Fdn. for Cancer Research, NYC, 20/188

Sternberg Family Fdn., NYC, 20/188

Sterret (Marjorie) Battleship Fund, NYC, 20/189

Stevens (Doris) Fdn., NYC, 20/189

Stewart (John W. & Laura S.) Fdn., NYC, 20/189

St. Faith's House, Tarrytown, 20/191

Stillman (Chauncey) Benevolent Fund, NYC, 20/192

Stinchfield (Frank & Margaret) Fdn., Riverdale, 20/194

St. Lawrence Council, Inc., B.S.A., Canton, 20/195

St. Luke's Episcopal Church of Jamestown N.Y. Trust, Jamestown, 20/196

St. Mark's Episcopal Church Trust, NYC, 20/197

Stone (Edward Durell) Fdn., NYC, 20/197

Stone (Hannah & Leonard) Fdn., NYC, 20/197

Stony Wold Corporation, NYC, 20/198

Stott (Robert L.) Fdn., NYC, 20/199

Stradivarius Fund, NYC, 20/200

Stradivartous Memorial Association, NYC, 20/201

Stratton (Henry M. & Lillian) Fdn., NYC, 20/201

Straus (Philip A. & Lynn) Fdn., Larchmont, 20/202

Straus (Roger Williams) Memorial Fdn., NYC, 20/203

Strausberg (Samuel) Memorial Fdn., NYC, 20/204

Strauss (Jacob) Fdn., Jamaica, 20/204

Strauss (Joseph) Fdn., Bronx, 20/205

Strong (Margaret Woodburg) Museum of Fascination, Rochester, 20/206

Strong Fdn. of New York, NYC, 20/207

St. Seraphim Fdn., NYC, 20/207

Stuart (Mark), Jr. Fdn., NYC, 20/208

Stuart (Mark) Fdn., NYC, 20/209

Strum (Hyman & Rose) Fdn., Bronx, 20/210

Stupell Fdn., NYC, 20/210

Su Crest Fdn., NYC, 21/001

Suffolk County Happy Landing Fund, Bay Shore, 21/002

Sugden (Herbert J. & Margaret S.) Fdn., Saranac Lake, 21/002

Sullivan Fdn., NYC, 21/003

Sunshine (Leonard) Fdn., NYC, 21/003

Surdna Fdn., NYC, 21/003

Survival in Freedom (SURFREE), Penn Yan, 21/008

Susseles Family Philanthropies, NYC, 21/008

Sussman (Arthur & Estelle) Fdn., Long Island City, 21/009

Sussman (Emanuel & Ethel) Fdn., Briarcliff Manor, 21/011

Swarzman Fdn. Corp., Brooklyn, 21/011

Sweet Briar Alumnae Club of New York, NYC, 21/011

Sydney Fdn., NYC, 21/012

Sykes (Edward) Endowment Trust, NYC, 21/013

Szyfra Miriam Fdn., Brooklyn, 21/014

Taconic Fdn., NYC, 21/015

Tang (Hamburg) Fdn., Upper Brookville, 21/017

Taraknath Das Fdn., NYC, 21/018

Tarnopol (Michael & Lynne) Fdn., NYC, 21/018

Taxin (Louis H. & Gertrude R.) Fdn., Scarsdale, 21/019

Taylor (Howard D. & Sandra) Family Fdn., NYC, 21/019

Taylor (Ruth) Award Fund, NYC, 21/020

Teagle Fdn., NYC, 21/020

Teamkin (Jerome) Fdn., Great Neck, 21/023

Tempelsman Fdn., NYC, 21/023

Tenzer, Greenblatt, Fallon & Kaplan Fdn., NYC, 21/024

Thannhauser Fdn., NYC, 21/024

Thayer Family Fund, NYC, 21/025

Theater Genesis Inc., NYC, 21/027

Theta Delta Chi Educational Fdn., NYC, 21/027

Thomas (Martha P. & Joseph A.) Fdn., NYC, 21/028

Thomas (Marion B.) T/W, Harrisburg, Pa., 21/029

Thompson (Otis A.) Fdn., Norwich, 21/029

Thomson-Leeds Fdn., NYC, 21/030

399 East 72nd Street Trust, NYC, 21/031

Tishman Realty Fdn., NYC, 21/032

Titan Industrial Fdn., NYC, 21/032

Titus (William & Dorothea) Fdn., NYC, 21/033

Tobin (Stella) Fdn., Forest Hills, 21/034

Todd (Robert B.) T/A Lancaster General Hospital, Lancaster, Pa., 21/034

Tooley (Norman & Charlotte) Benevolent Fund, Rochester, 21/035

Tone (Frank J.) Incentive Fund, Niagara Falls, 21/036

Topstone Fund, NYC, 21/036

Torrence Fdn., Scarsdale, 21/037

Tosei Fdn., Ardsley, 21/038

TMCA Supplemental Unemployment Benefit Trust, NYC, 21/038

Travis (David A.) Fdn., NYC, 21/039

Trott (Donald & Frances) Fdn., NYC, 21/040

Troupiansky (Harry) Fdn., Lawrence, 21/040

Trudeau Institute, NYC, 21/041

Alston (U/D Mary Niven) 1/25/66 for Convent of Saint Helena, NYC, 21/041

Barmore (U/W Fred L.) Trust, Jamestown, 21/044

Beattie (U/W/O Agnes) Trust F/B/O St. Agnes Church, NYC, 21/044

Bedient (U/W Melvina) Trust, Jamestown, 21/045

Bingham (U/D William II) Trust for Charity, NYC, 21/045

Bingham (U/W William II) Betterment Fund, NYC, 21/048

Black (U/W H.S.), NYC, 21/050

Blackmar (U/D Lillian), NYC, 21/051

Hannan (Water S.) et al, Trust U/A 3/28/27 for Blakely Memorial Scholarship Fund, NYC, 21/052

Bolton (U/D Frances P.) for Payne Fund, NYC, 21/053

Bookstaver (U/W Mabel L.) Trust Bookstaver, Jamestown, 21/054

Burnett-Timken Memorial Fdn. & Research Fund Trust, NYC, 21/056

Bush (U/W Frank B.) Trust, Jamestown, 21/057

Brady (U/W James Cox) Trust for Instituto Pontificio Delle Maestre Pie Filippini, NYC, 21/058

Brady (U/W James Cox) Trust for Board of Trustees, Our Lady of Perpetual Help, NYC, 21/061

Brown (U/W J.J.) Trust F/B/O Brown Family Plot, Banks Cemetery, White Plains, 21/062

Carr (U/W Daniel L.) Trust, Jamestown, 21/063

Chadwick (U/D Dorothy J.) 6/11/57, NYC, 21/063

Childs (Eversley & Mary) Trust U/A 6/14/27 for Setauket Community House, NYC, 21/065

Clark (U/A Jennifer H. & Bracket David) Trust, Rochester, 21/066

Considine (U/W Leo) Trust F/B/O St. Joseph's Hospital, Elmira, 21/066

Tuchman (B.W.) Fund, NYC, 21/172
Tucker (Allen) Memorial, NYC, 21/173
Tucker Scholarship Fdn., Mt. Kisco, 21/173
Tudor Fdn., NYC, 21/174
Turetsky (Solomon & Rose) Fdn., Hollis, 21/175
Turner (John B.) Fdn., Norwich, 21/176
Tuttle (Forbes S.) Fdn., Syracuse, 21/176
Twentieth Century Fund, NYC, 21/177
Tyler (Clarence A.) Scholarship Fund, Alden, 21/182
Tyson (David) Fdn., NYC, 21/182
Tuxedo Club, Tuxedo Park, 21/182
Ungar (S.J.) Fdn., NYC, 21/183
Ungerleider (Joy & Samuel) Fdn., NYC, 21/183
United Armenian Charities, NYC, 21/184
United Merchants Fdn., NYC, 21/184
United Merchants & Manufacturers Employees Welfare Fdn., NYC, 21/185
United States Plywood Fdn., NYC, 21/186
United States Steel Fdn., NYC, 21/186
Urban Affairs Fdn., NYC, 21/188
Valenstein (Alice) Fund, NYC, 21/188
Valhalla Scholarship Assistance Fund, Valhalla, 21/189
Valley Stream Fdn., Valley Stream, 21/189
Van Alstyne (Lt. David III) Fdn., NYC, 21/190
Vanneck Fdn., NYC, 21/191
Van Orden (T/W May E.) Par. 8, White Plains, 21/192
Vascular Research Fdn., East Hills, 21/193
Veritism Fdn., Hauppauge, 21/193
Verrazzano Fdn., NYC, 21/194
Vert (May M.) Park Fund, Albany, 21/194
Vietor-Woodward Memorial Trust, Rochester, 21/195
Vetlesen (G. Unger) Fdn., NYC, 21/195
Vogel (Jerry) Fdn., NYC, 21/197
Vogelstein (Heinemann & Rosa) Fdn., NYC, 21/197
Vogelstein (Ludwig) Fdn., NYC, 21/199
von Humboldt (Alexander) Fdn., NYC, 21/200
Wachtel (Harry H.) Fdn., NYC, 21/200
Wagner (C.) Estate - Heinbach - Wagner Trust, NYC, 21/201
Waldelco Fdn., NYC, 21/202
Waldman Fdn., NYC, 21/203
Waldorf Education in the West of the World, NYC, 21/204
Walker Environmental Institute, NYC, 21/205
Wallace (Marcel) Fdn., NYC, 21/205
Walden (George H.) Memorial Fund Trust, Rochester, 21/206
Wally Fdn., NYC, 21/206
Walsh (Thomas J., Jr. & Ann L.) Charitable Trust, NYC, 21/207
Walter (Bruno) Memorial Fdn., NYC, 21/214
Wantagh 7-12 Association, Wantagh, 21/214
Wappler Fdn., NYC, 21/215
Warburg (Paul M.) Fund, NYC, 21/216
Warner Fdn. of Buffalo, Buffalo, 21/217
Warner Home for the Aged, Jamestown, 22/002
Washington Avenue Fdn., NYC, 22/004
Wasserman (David) Fdn., Amsterdam, 22/004
Wasserman (David) Scholarship Fund, Amsterdam, 22/005
Wasserman (Jack) Fund, NYC, 22/006
Waterman Fund, NYC, 22/007
Waterman (Edmund) Fdn., NYC, 22/007
Waterman (Philip M.) Fdn., NYC, 22/008
Watson (Thomas J.) Fdn., NYC, 22/011
Wawepex Society of Cold Spring Harbor, Cold Spring Harbor, 22/012
Waxman (Harry) Fdn., Brooklyn, 22/013
Weatherhead Fdn., NYC, 22/014
Webb (Earle W., Jr.) Memorial, NYC, 22/015
Webster Benevolent Fund, NYC, 22/016
Wechsler-Forrest-Slater Fdn., Bronx, 22/016
Wehle (Louis A.) Fdn., Rochester, 22/017
Weil, Duffy Fdn., NYC, 22/018
Weiler (Theodore & Renee) Fdn., NYC, 22/019
Weinberg Charitable Fdn., Brooklyn, 22/019

Weinberg (David & Rhoda) Fdn., Jamaica, 22/019
Weinberg (Harold & Anna M.) Family Fdn., NYC, 22/019
Weinberg (Sidney J.), Jr. Fdn., NYC, 22/020
Weiner Family Charitable Trust, NYC, 22/021
Weinman Family Fdn., Norwich, 22/022
Weinstein (Abba A.) Memorial Scholarship Fund, West Islip, 22/023
Weinstein (Samuel & Irving) Fdn., NYC, 22/024
Weisberger Fdn., NYC, 22/024
Weissblatt Fdn., NYC, 22/025
Weissman (Paul M.) Family Fdn., NYC, 22/025
Weitzenhoffer (Mark & Edith C.) Fdn., NYC, 22/026
Weld Fund, NYC, 22/027
Wells - LeRoy Community Chest Trust, Rochester, 22/027
Wells - LeRoy Methodist Church Trust, Rochester, 22/028
Wendt (Margaret L.) Fdn., Buffalo, 22/028
Werblin (David A. & Leah Ray) Fdn., NYC, 22/029
Werner Fdn., NYC, 22/030
Westchester Good Guys Fdn., NYC, 22/032
Western New York Fdn., Buffalo, 22/032
Davis (Westmoreland) Memorial Fund, NYC, 22/033
Weston Road Charitable Trust Fdn., NYC, 22/035
Westport Women's Club, Inc. Trust, NYC, 22/035
Whitaker (William A.) Fdn. Trust, NYC, 22/036
White (Dorothy & Robert B.) Fdn., NYC, 22/037
White & Maske Fund, NYC, 22/037
White (Rodney L.) Fdn., NYC, 22/037
Whiting Fdn., Buffalo, 22/038
Whitney (Helen Hay) Fdn., NYC, 22/038
Whitney (John Hay) Fdn., NYC, 22/041
Wide Waters Fund, New Rochelle, 22/042
Widgeon Fdn., NYC, 22/043
Wiener (David & Rae) Fdn., NYC, 22/044
Wilder (Robert O.) Fdn., NYC, 22/045
Wile Memorial Fund Trust, Rochester, 22/046
Wilfred Fund, NYC, 22/046
Wilkerson (Miriam) Trust #2, NYC, 22/047
Williams (Percy) Home, NYC, 22/047
Williams (Rose Isabel) Fdn., NYC, 22/048
Williams (Sophie Frances) Fdn., NYC, 22/048
Willsea-Hillside Children's Center Trust, Rochester, 22/049
Wilson (T/W Frances M.), White Plains, 22/049
Wilson (Clark W.) Library Trust, Syracuse, 22/050
Wilson (Mr. & Mrs. Robert W.) Fdn., Brooklyn, 22/050
Windward Fdn., NYC, 22/052
Winkhaus (John T.) Fund, NYC, 22/052
Winston (Harry) Fdn., NYC, 22/053
Wise (George & Florence) Fdn., NYC, 22/054
Wohl (Ignatz) Family Fdn., Great Neck, 22/054
Wohlstetter Fdn., NYC, 22/055
Wolberg Fdn., NYC, 22/055
Wolf Fdn., NYC, 22/057
Wolf (Max & Edith) Fdn., NYC, 22/057
Wolf (Thomas P. & Marian G.) Trust, NYC, 22/057
Desenberg - Wolff Fdn., NYC, 22/058
Wolfowski Fdn., NYC, 22/059
Wolfred Fdn., Scarsdale, 22/059
Wolfston (G. William) Fdn., NYC, 22/060
Woolner (Adolph) Fdn., Hartsdale, 22/061
Womans Round Lake Improvement Society, Albany, 22/061
Avis (Minnie Wood) Trust, Harrisburg, Pa., 22/062
Woodward (Ann Eden) Fdn., NYC, 22/062
Woodward Charitable Fdn., NYC, 22/063
Woodward - 1st Methodist Church of LeRoy, Rochester, 22/063

Woodward - LeRoy Central School #1, Rochester, 22/064
Woodward Memorial Trust #1, Rochester, 22/064
Woodward Memorial Trust #2, Rochester, 22/065
Woodward - St. Marks Church of LeRoy Trust, Rochester, 22/065
Woolman Family Fdn., Albany, 22/066
Woolsey - S. Perinton Cemetery Ass'n Trust, Rochester, 22/066
Woolsey - S. Perinton Methodist Episcopal Church Trust, Rochester, 22/066
World Health Fdn. of the United States of America, NYC, 22/067
Wyler (Paul & Friedell Fdn.), Scarsdale, 22/067
Wyler (Fran & Sig) Fdn., NYC, 22/068
Wyler (Paul & Friedel) Fdn., NYC, 22/068
Wyn Fdn., Larchmont, 22/068
Jarvie (U/W James M.) Trust U/Par. 14 F/B/O Jerusalem YMCA, NYC, 22/069
Keren Yaldenu, Inc., NYC, 22/070
Yang (Ho-Ching) Memorial Fdn., NYC, 22/071
Yonderbrook Fdn., NYC, 22/072
Young (Arthur) Fdn., NYC, 22/073
Young Men's Christian Association of Westport Trust, NYC, 22/075
Young Presidents Fdn., NYC, 22/075
Zacharia (Herman I.) & Son Fdn., NYC, 22/076
Zaifert (Harry & Rose S.) Fdn., NYC, 22/077
Zankel (Arthur & Nancy) Fdn., Scarsdale, 22/078
Zarin (Murray I. & Florence) Fdn., Great Neck, 22/079
Zatorina Benevolent Society, NYC, 22/079
Zauderer (George) Fdn., NYC, 22/079
Zeitz Fdn., Brooklyn, 22/081
Zelinka (David & Ruth) Fdn., NYC, 22/082
Zimmer Fdn., NYC, 22/083
State Board of Control of the State of Florida & Protestant Episcopal Church in the Diocese of Florida Trust, NYC, 22/084
Zuckerman (Gail I.) Fdn., NYC, 22/084
Zuflacht (Phyllis) Memorial Scholarship Fdn., NYC, 22/085

NORTH CAROLINA

First Filming

Applebaum Fdn., Greensboro, 1/001
Akers Fdn., Gastonia, 1/001
Anderson (Robert C. & Sadie G.) Fdn., Charlotte, 1/002
Andrews (A.B.) Fdn. - Trust, Raleigh, 1/004
Bank of Granite Fdn., Granite Falls, 1/005
Baptist Hill Fdn., Wilmington, 1/005
Baptist Ministers Trust, Charlotte, 1/006
Barium Springs Home, Charlotte, 1/007
Barnhardt Fdn., Charlotte, 1/007
Battle Fdn., Rocky Mount, 1/008
Beam (C.C.) Trust Fund, Charlotte, 1/008
Bear (Emanuel I. & Samuel N.) Trust, Wilmington, 1/009
Belk (John M.) Fdn. - Trust, Charlotte, 1/010
Belk (Thomas Milburn) Fdn. - Trust, Charlotte, 1/011
Belk - Tyler Fdn., Rocky Mount, 1/012
Bernard Fdn., High Point, 1/012
Best (Munroe) Fdn., Goldsboro, 1/013
Borden Manufacturing Company Fund, Goldsboro, 1/014
Borden (Frank & Sallie) Fdn. - Trust, Raleigh, 1/015
Bridges (Henry P.), Jr. Fdn., Charlotte, 1/016
Brown Fdn., Troutman, 1/016
Broyhill Educational Fund, Lenoir, 1/017
Bryan Family Fdn., Greensboro, 1/018
Burney Trust Fund, Southern Pines, 1/019

Caldwell County Medical Society Educational Fund, Lenoir, 1/020
Cannon (Arch) Memorial Endowment, Winston-Salem, 1/021
Cannon (Martin) Family Fdn., Charlotte, 1/021
Association of Capitular Masons, Charlotte, 1/022
Carolina Steel Fdn., Greensboro, 1/023
Carswell Fdn., Charlotte, 1/024
Case (Fannie Mit) Scholarship Fund, Asheville, 1/024
Cassell Fdn., High Point, 1/025
Carter Fdn., Greensboro, 1/025
Chapman Charitable Trust, Charlotte, 1/026
Chatham Fdn., Elkin, 1/027
Cheatham Fdn., Statesville, 1/028
Cherokee Fdn., Marble, 1/028
Children's Home of Winston-Salem, Charlotte, 1/029
Coharie Fdn., Winston-Salem, 1/029
Coley (S.B.) Fdn., Raleigh, 1/030
Cone (Bernard M.) Family Fdn., Greensboro, 1/030
Cosby Fdn., Charlotte, 1/032
Cowan Fdn., Charlotte, 1/032
Cozart Fdn., Raleigh, 1/033
Crist Fdn., Charlotte, 1/034
Tate - Culbertson Fund, Charlotte, 1/035
Dave (Joseph) Fdn., Asheville, 1/035
Davidson Community Trust, Davidson, 1/036
Davis (Alex R.) Fdn., Charlotte, 1/036
Davis - Faircloth Memorial Fund, Wake Forest, 1/037
Davis (H. Wayne) Fdn., High Point, 1/037
Davis (Champion McDowell) Charitable Fdn., Wilmington, 1/037
Davis (Dr. James W.) Trust, Charlotte, 1/039
Brown (DeWitt & Othel) Charitable Trust, Charlotte, 1/040
Dickson (Rush S.) Family Fdn., Charlotte, 1/041
Devotion Fdn., Winston-Salem, 1/042
Peacock (Dred) Memorial Student Loan Fund, High Point, 1/043
Drexel Fund, Drexel, 1/043
Duke Endowment, Charlotte, 1/044
Duke University, Charlotte, 1/047
Durham Fdn., Durham, 1/048
Durham Fdn. - Fletcher Heart Fund, Durham, 1/050
Earle (John D.) Fdn., Asheville, 1/050
Ek-Partin Trust, Asheville, 1/051
Ervin Fdn., Charlotte, 1/051
Faison (Elias S.) Fdn., Charlotte, 1/052
Fass Family Fdn., Asheville, 1/053
Fassett (Mary K.) Memorial Trust, Durham, 1/054
F C & R Fdn., Greensboro, 1/054
Feldman (Ruth & Leon) Fdn., Asheville, 1/055
Ferguson (Howard & Mescal) Fdn., Randleman, 1/055
Fieldcrest Fdn., Eden, 1/056
Finch (Brown F. Fdn., High Point, 1/057
Finch (Thomas Austin) Fdn., High Point, 1/059
Finley (A.E.) Fdn., Raleigh, 1/061
First - Citizens Fdn., Smithfield, 1/062
First Union Fdn., Charlotte, 1/063
Fishman Family Fdn., Greensboro, 1/065
Fleshman-Pratt Fdn., Winston-Salem, 1/065
Foam Industries Fdn., Mount Airy, 1/067
Foscue Fdn., High Point, 1/067
Foundation for Community Development, Durham, 1/069
Foundation for Religious Action, Pinehurst, 1/070
Francis (W.J.) Memorial Scholarship Fund, Asheville, 1/071
Freeze (Baxter P.) Fdn., High Point, 1/071
Fryman Fdn., Greensboro, 1/072
Finch - Gaddy Fdn., Raleigh, 1/073
Gallimore Charitable Fund, Greensboro, 1/074
Garrett (Elizabeth Wagg) Fdn., Greensboro, 1/074

Gaskin Fdn., Charlotte, 1/075
Gaylord Fdn., Charlotte, 1/075
Ginter (Karl & Anna) Fdn., Charlotte, 1/075
Girard (Dorothy & Cy) Fdn., Gastonia, 1/076
Girard (Phyllis & Herbert) Fdn., Gastonia, 1/077
Girl Scout Council of Coastal Carolina, Goldsboro, 1/077
Goodman Fdn., Salisbury, 1/077
Goodwill Industries of Guilford, Greensboro, 1/078
Graham (Frank) Fund, Charlotte, 1/078
Gravely Fdn., Rocky Mount, 1/079
Gregg (G.E.) Benevolence Fund, Greensboro, 1/080
Guardsman's Assistance Fund, North Wilkesboro, 1/080
Handi-Clean Family Fdn., Greensboro, 1/081
Hanes (John Wesley & Anne Hodgin) Fdn., Winston-Salem, 1/081
Hanes (P.H.) Fdn., Winston-Salem, 1/083
Harrison (Nathaniel Mason) Fdn., High Point, 1/084
Hauser (Arless B.) Church Fund, Winston-Salem, 1/085
Hayworth (Charles E.), Jr. Fdn., High Point, 1/085
Hayworth Fdn., High Point, 1/087
Heinig (Anne) Memorial Park Fdn., Charlotte, 1/089
Belk (Henderson) Fdn., Charlotte, 1/089
Helder (Horatio A. & Adah C.) Scholarship, Asheville, 1/090
Henkel (Vance) Fdn., Statesville, 1/091
Hembly (Alex) Fdn., Charlotte, 1/091
Hickory Chair Fdn., Hickory, 1/092
Hickson (Lillian E.) Memorial Fund, Durham, 1/093
Holderness Fdn., Greensboro, 1/094
Holding (Robert P.) Fdn., Smithfield, 1/095
Hopper Fdn., Monroe, 1/097
Huffman - Cornwell Fdn., Morganton, 1/097
Ivey's Trust Fund, Charlotte, 1/099
Jenkins - Tapp Fdn., Kingston, 1/100
J.J.B.L. Fdn., Raleigh, 1/101
Johnson Fdn., Salisbury, 1/101
Johnston Motor Lines Fdn., Charlotte, 1/102
Kadis Fdn., Goldsboro, 1/102
Keiner Fdn., Salisbury, 1/103
Kemp Fdn., Goldsboro, 1/104
Kenan (Sarah Graham) Fdn., Chapel Hill, 1/105
Kiwanis Education Fund, Burlington, 1/106
Frasch (Kolker) Family Fdn., Murphy, 1/106
Kyser Fdn., Chapel Hill, 1/107
LaFar Benevolent Fdn., Gastonia, 1/107
Landis Community Fdn., Landis, 1/107
Latta Baptist Church, Charlotte, 1/108
LaRose (S. & Elizabeth) Fdn., Greensboro, 1/109
Latta (E.D.) Trust, Charlotte, 1/109
Lawndale Fdn., Lawndale, 1/110
Lavitt (Louis) Fdn., Wilmington, 1/111
Leverton (Ann & Morris) Fdn., New York, N.Y., 1/111
Lewallen (A. Thad) Fdn., Winston-Salem, 1/112
Lineberger Fdn., Belmont, 1/112
Logan Preaching Mission of the First Methodist Church of Rutherfordton, N.C., Charlotte, 1/113
Love (Martha & Spencer) Fdn., Greensboro, 1/114
Lynch (Alice B. & James S.) Fdn., Winston-Salem, 1/115
Manetta Mills Fund, Monroe, 1/116
Marsh Fdn., Charlotte, 1/116
Marvin (Lucile Murchison) Fdn., Wilmington, 1/118
Matheson Lecture Fdn., Charlotte, 1/118
Matthews (Raymond E. & Byrd D.) Memorial Fdn., Asheville, 1/119
May Memorial Library Annex Trust, Burlington, 1/120
McAdenville Fdn., McAdenville, 1/120

McAlister (Alexander Worth) Fdn., Greensboro, 1/121
McClure (James G.K.) Educational & Development Fund, Asheville, 1/122
McHenry Fdn., Charlotte, 1/123
McNair (John F.) Memorial Fund Trust, Raleigh, 1/124
Methodist Fdn. of the Western North Carolina Conference, Mount Airy, 1/125
Methodist Home for the Aged Trust, Charlotte, 1/125
M H D Fdn., Morganton, 1/126
Moffitt (Ralph & Aleen) Fdn., Lexington, 1/127
Murray Fdn., Mocksville, 1/127
Boddie - Noell Fdn., Rocky Mount, 1/128
Mims (Allan C.) Fdn., Rocky Mount, 1/128
Mint Museum of Art Trust, Charlotte, 1/128
Mims (Allan C.) Fdn., Rocky Mount, 1/129
M & J Fdn., Goldsboro, 1/129
Morganton Park & Recreation Fdn., Drexel, 1/130
Moore (B.C.) & Sons Fdn., Charlotte, 1/130
Moore County Charitable Fdn., Aberdeen, 1/131
Morrow (Mary) Scholarship Fund, Raleigh, 1/131
Moss (William O. & Virginia) Fdn., Greensboro, 1/132
Murrill Fdn., Monroe, 1/133
Myers Family Fdn., Greensboro, 1/133
Myers Fdn., Charlotte, 1/134
Myers (Dennis) Fdn., Charlotte, 1/134
Nalle Clinic Fdn., Charlotte, 1/135
Neisler Fdn., Charlotte, 1/136
New Perth Associate Reformed Presbyterian Church Cemetery Fund, Charlotte, 1/137
News & Observer - Raleigh Times Fdn., Raleigh, 1/137
New Salem Methodist Church Trust, Charlotte, 1/138
Boddie - Noell Fdn., Rocky Mount, 1/139
North Charlotte Fdn., Charlotte, 1/139
Odell Fdn., Charlotte, 1/141
O'Herron Fdn., Charlotte, 1/141
Ozanne (Charles E.) Trust, Durham, 1/142
Pace (Karl B.) Fdn., Greenville, 1/144
North Charlotte Fdn., Charlotte, 1/144
Patla-Straus Family Fdn., Asheville, 1/144
Peden Fdn., Raleigh, 1/145
Pension Planners Fdn., Charlotte, 1/146
Peoples Bank Fdn., Rocky Mount, 1/146
Perry (Ely J.) Fdn., Kinston, 1/147
Pharr (William J. & Catherine Stowe) Fdn., McAdenville, 1/147
Physical Therapy Association Scholarship & Loan Fund, Chapel Hill, 1/148
Pierson (M. Everett) Fdn., Charlotte, 1/148
Pierson (Mary Jane) Memorial Trust, Charlotte, 1/149
Pi Kappa Phi Memorial Fdn., Charlotte, 1/149
Pilot Freight Carriers Fdn., Winston-Salem, 1/150
Pinnix Fdn., Gastonia, 1/150
Greensboro Police Dependents Fdn., Greensboro, 1/151
Presbyterian Journal Fdn., Weaverville, 1/152
Pritchard Memorial Baptist Church Trust, Charlotte, 1/153
Puett (Minnie Stowe) Trust, Charlotte, 1/153
Rankin (Elizabeth S. & E. Roy) Trust, Charlotte, 1/154
Rauch Fdn., Bessemer City, 1/155
Ransome Fdn., Cornwells Heights, Pa., 1/156
Reeves (Myrtle S.) Memorial Fund, Durham, 1/156
Reynolds (Z. Smith) Fdn., Winston-Salem, 1/157
Robinson Fdn., Greensboro, 1/159
Robinson (Eloise) Scholarship Fund, Raleigh, 1/160
Robinson (Ralph S.) Family Fdn., Gastonia, 1/161
Robinson Scholarship Fund, Raleigh, 1/162
Rogers (Florence) Charitable Trust, Fayetteville, 1/165

Rowan County Medical Scholarship Fund, Salisbury, 1/166

Rowan County United Fund, Salisbury, 1/166

Shank (Marie) Scholarship Fund, Asheville, 1/166

Schoenith Fdn., Charlotte, 1/167

Sevier Fdn., Marion, 1/168

Shaw (H.M.), Sr. Trust, Raleigh, 1/169

Shrago (Jacob P. & Ruth L.) Fdn., Goldsboro, 1/171

Smith (Hobart) Family Fdn., Charlotte, 1/171

Smith (Marvin B.), Jr. Memorial Scholarship Fund, Greensboro, 1/172

Smith (Jennie H.) Testamentary Trust, Raleigh, 1/173

Snyder (E.J.) Family Fdn., Albemarle, 1/174

Speizman Fdn., Charlotte, 1/174

Sprunt (Annie Gray) Charitable Trust, Wilmington, 1/175

Steele Creek Presbyterian Church, Charlotte, 1/175

Stein (Kalman & Fannie) Fdn., Fayetteville, 1/175

Stowe (Daniel J.) Fdn., McAdenville, 1/176

Stowe (Robert Lee), Jr. Fdn., Belmont, 1/177

Straus (Martha Washington & Harry H.) Fdn., Asheville, 1/178

Superior Fdn., Raleigh, 1/180

Swindell (Ella & Les) Fdn., Greensboro, 1/184

Sylvan Fdn., Rosman, 1/185

Tanglewood Park, Clemmons, 1/185

Tannenbaum (A.J. & Leah Louise B.) Fdn., Greensboro, 1/186

Terrence (Michael) Fdn., Fayetteville, 1/187

Thank You Fdn., Charlotte, 1/188

Thomasville Furniture Industries Fdn., High Point, 1/188

Thompson Orphanage Trust, Charlotte, 1/193

Thrower (Edwin K.) Fdn., High Point, 1/193

Thruston Fdn., Charlotte, 1/194

Ragland (Trent), Jr. Trust, Raleigh, 1/195

Ragland (Trent) Trust, Raleigh, 1/198

Baucom (Henry) Memorial Trust, Winston-Salem, 1/199

Brown (George T.) Trust, Winston-Salem, 1/199

Duke (Benjamin N.) Trust f/b/o Laurinburg Normal Industrial Institute, Durham, 1/200

Flowers (William W.) Trust f/b/o Durham Charities, Durham, 1/201

Freeze (Baxter P.) Fdn., High Point, 1/203

Hanes (Elizabeth P.) Trust f/b/o Duke University, Winston-Salem, 1/203

Harmon (Tilla) Trust f/b/o Foreign Missionary Society of the Moravian Church, Winston-Salem, 1/204

Kistler (Mary C.) Trust f/b/o Morganton-Burke Library Association, Morganton, 1/204

Kistler (Mary C.) Trust f/b/o Grace Episcopal Church, Morganton, 1/205

Pipkin Fdn., Winston-Salem, 1/205

Reynolds (W.N.) Residuary Trust, Winston-Salem, 1/206

Robin (Stefan H.) Memorial Fund, Winston-Salem, 1/208

Tufts Fdn., Pinehurst, 1/209

Tyler (Arthur L.) Fdn., Rocky Mount, 1/210

Valdese Manufacturing Company Fdn., Valdese, 1/210

Van Every (Philip L.) Fdn., Charlotte, 1/210

Verna Fdn., Charlotte, 1/211

Vreeland Fdn., Charlotte, 1/212

Turrentine Memorial Educational Fund, Winston-Salem, 1/213

Wachovia Fdn., Winston-Salem, 1/215

Waldroup (R.M. & Hattie L.) Educational Fund, Asheville, 1/216

Warshawsky (Roy I.) Family Fdn., Chicago, Illinois, 1/216

Wayne Fdn., Goldsboro, 1/217

Wellons Fdn., Dunn, 1/217

Whiston Fdn., Mt. Gilead, Ohio, 1/218

Wilson (Rufus D.), Jr. Trust, Charlotte, 1/218

Wilson (Thomas Henry & Dell Bernhardt) Fdn., Winston-Salem, 1/219

Woltz Charitable Trust, Mount Airy, 1/220

Wood (Elliott S.) Fdn., High Point, 1/220

Wray (A.M.) Heart Services Fund, Charlotte, 1/221

Wren Fdn., Siler City, 1/221

York (William M.) Benevolence Fund, Greensboro, 1/223

York Fdn., Raleigh, 1/223

Young (Buck) Fdn., Lexington, 1/223

Second Filming

Adams (Charles B.) Family Fdn., Greensboro, 2/001

Advertising Club of Charlotte, Charlotte, 2/002

Agape Trust, Charlotte, 2/002

Alba-Waldensian Fdn., Valdese, 2/003

Alebasco Fdn., Greensboro, 2/003

Altrusa Trust Fund, Greensboro, 2/004

Alwinell Fdn. of Charlotte, N.C., Charlotte, 2/005

Baker (Allen & Sallie H.) Memorial Scholarship Fund, Greenville, 2/005

Balthis (Pearl Dixon) Fdn., Charlotte, 2/006

Bankers Educational Fdn., Charlotte, 2/008

Barbour (William I.) Trust, Raleigh, 2/008

Barium Springs Presbyterian Orphanage, Wilmington, 2/011

Baxter (George W.) Fdn., Charlotte, 2/012

Beacon Fdn., Swannanoa, 2/013

Beam (D.F.) Fdn. Trust, Gastonia, 2/014

Belk Fdn., Charlotte, 2/014

Bellany (Robert R.) Memorial Fdn., Wilmington, 2/018

B & H Fdn., Greensboro, 2/019

Bingham (Callie) Fdn., Jacksonville, 2/020

Bishop of the Diocese of East Carolina of the Episcopal Church, Greenville, 2/021

Blackenship (A.V.) Fdn., Charlotte, 2/021

Block (William) Memorial Fdn., Wilmington, 2/022

Blumenthal Fdn. for Charity, Religion, Education and Better Inter-Faith Relation, Charlotte, 2/023

Borne (Orton A.) Fdn., Pleasant Garden, 2/024

Boshamer (Cary C.) Fdn., Gastonia, 2/025

Braswell-Gordon Fdn., Rocky Mount, 2/025

Breman (Sara & Joseph) Fdn., Asheville, 2/026

Brenner Fdn., Winston Salem, 2/027

Brody (Reuben) Fdn., Kinston, 2/028

Broome (T.J.W.) Memorial Fund, Monroe, 2/029

Brown-Wooten Fdn., Burlington, 2/029

Bryan (James E. & Mary Z.) Fdn., Raleigh, 2/030

Bryan (W. Carroll) Memorial Trust, Jacksonville, 2/031

Burroughs Wellcome Fund, Research Triangle, 2/031

Bird (Carolina) Club, Tryon, 2/033

Carolina Plywood Fdn., Lexington, 2/034

Carpenters Health and Welfare Fund, Charlotte, 2/034

Carter (Wilbur Lee) Charitable Trust, Greensboro, 2/035

Celanese Fdn., Charlotte, 2/035

Challenge Fund, Greensboro, 2/036

Chapin Fdn., Charlotte, 2/037

Children's Rehabilitation Fdn., Charlotte, 2/037

Chittum-Colonial Fdn., Mt. Holly, 2/038

Chowan Educational Fdn., Edenton, 2/038

Roanoke-Chowan Educational Fdn., Windsor, 2/040

Chowanook Fdn., Merry Hill, 2/041

Columbus Lions Club, Columbus, 2/041

Community Service Corporation, High Point, 2/041

Cone (Sydney M.), Jr. Family Fdn., Greensboro, 2/042

Connemara Fund, Greensboro, 2/042

Coppridge Research Laboratory, Durham, 2/043

Roxboro Cotton Mills Scholarship Fdn., Roxboro, 2/043

Cornelious (J.B.) Fdn., Davidson, 2/044

Culler Fdn., High Point, 2/044

Dalton (Harry L.) Fdn., Charlotte, 2/045

Duplin Country Club, Warsaw, 2/047

Davis (Suzanne M.) Educational Fund, Cherokee, 2/047

Davis (B.S.), III Family Fnd., Charlotte, 2/048

Davis (Cornelia Nixon) Home, Wilmington, 2/048

Dickson Fdn., Charlotte, 2/049

Durham Clinic Fdn. Corporation, Durham, 2/049

Durham Fdn., Durham, 2/050

Efird Fdn., Charlotte, 2/050

Enka Fdn., Enka, 2/051

Ficklen Fund, Greenville, 2/052

First Presbyterian Church u/w James S. Ficklen, Greenville, 2/053

Fishman Family Fdn., Greensboro, 2/054

Fox (Jared C.) Family Fdn., Greensboro, 2/054

Fund for the Advancement of Neuro Surgery, Charlotte, 2/055

Gardner (O. Max) Fdn., Shelby, 2/055

Gocking (Minnie L.) College Educational Fund for the Children of Thompson Orphanage & Training Institution of Charlotte, Charlotte, 2/056

Good Works Fdn., Greensboro, 2/056

Harold Institute, Winston-Salem, 2/057

Harriss Fdn., High Point, 2/058

Harvey (Felix) Fdn., Kinston, 2/059

Hatteras Fdn., Manteo, 2/060

Haywood County Medical Fdn., Asheville, 2/060

Herman (Charles F.) Educational Fund, Raleigh, 2/061

Herman Fdn., Conover, 2/062

Hickson (Lillian E.) Memorial Fund, Durham, 2/062

Hillsdale Fund, Greensboro, 2/064

Historic Darden Hotel Fdn., Williamston, 2/065

Holt (Ralph M.) Fdn., Burlington, 2/066

Horne (J.L.) Trust, A part of Rocky Mount Fdn., Rocky Mount, 2/067

Hunt (Malcolm H.) Educational Trust, Raleigh, 2/067

Ingold Charitable Trust, Morganton, 2/067

International Arthur Schnitzler Research Association, Durham, 2/068

Jackson (John Herrick) Memorial Fdn., Greensboro, 2/069

James (William Daniel) Memorial Fdn., Hamlet, 2/070

Raleigh Jaycee Zoological Fdn., Raleigh, 2/071

Jefferson Standard Business Education Fund, Greensboro, 2/071

Jewel Box Fdn., Greensboro, 2/072

Jones (Ralph N.) Fdn., Charlotte, 2/072

Karyae Benevolent Fdn., Gastonia, 2/074

Kennedy (Wallace A. and Velna B.) Fdn., Greensboro, 2/074

Lackey Fdn., Winston Salem, 2/075

Lamb (Kirkland S. and Rena B.) Fdn., Charlotte, 2/076

Lance Fdn., Charlotte, 2/076

Little (Effie Allen) Fdn., Wadesboro, 2/077

Lundy Fdn., Clinton, 2/077

McCrary-Acme Fdn., Asheboro, 2/078

McLendon (Len) Memorial Fund, Greensboro, 2/079

M.H.D. Fdn., Morganton, 2/080

Mills Family Fdn., Asheville, 2/080

Ministering Circle Memorial Fund, Wilmington, 2/081

Minor Fdn., Charlotte, 2/081

Morgan Trust for Charity, Religion, and Education, Laurel Hill, 2/083

Morgantown Kiwanis Fdn., Morgantown, 2/084

Morrison Charitable Trust, Asheville, 2/085

Morehead (John Motley) Fdn., Charlotte, 2/085

Mt. Olive Jr. College Memorial Library, Greenville, 2/089

National Sportscasters and Sportswriters Fdn., Salisbury, 2/090

North Carolina Delta Upsilon Fdn., Liberty, 2/090

New Hanover Humane Society, Wilmington, 2/091

Ness (Edda & Philip) Fdn., Asheville, 2/092

New Bern Golf and Country Club, New Bern, 2/092

New Life, Goldsboro, 2/092

North Carolina Dental Society Relief Fund, Raleigh, 2/094

North Carolina Leadership Institute, Inc., Greensboro, 2/094

Occidental Charitable Fdn., Raleigh, 2/095

Oconee Fdn., Swannanoa, 2/095

Patterson Memorial Fund, Durham, 2/096

Perry Fdn., Wilmington, 2/097

Perry-Griffin Fdn., Oriental, 2/098

Person County United Fund, Roxboro, 2/099

Phillips (David E.) Fdn., High Point, 2/099

Piedmont Aviation Fdn., Winston-Salem, 2/099

Piedmont Publishing Co. Fdn., Winston-Salem, 2/099

Planters Cotton Oil & Fertilizer Co. Scholarship Fund, Rocky Mount, 2/100

Printing Industries of the Carolinas Fdn., Charlotte, 2/100

Provident Charitable Fdn., Sanford, 2/100

Preyer (Mary Norris) Fund, Greensboro, 2/101

Prickett (Lynn R. and Karl E.) Fund, Greensboro, 2/102

Purpose Fdn., Raleigh, 2/103

Public Scholarship Fdn., Henderson, 2/103

Rankin (O'H.) Fdn., Charlotte, 2/103

Richardson (Grace Jones) Trust, Greensboro, 2/104

Richardson (Grace) Fund, Greensboro, 2/105

Richardson (Mary Lynn) Fund, Greensboro, 2/106

Richardson (Smith) Fdn., Greensboro, 2/107

Richmond Temperance and Literary Society Commission, Laurinburg, 2/109

Robinson (J. B.) Memorial Fdn., Jacksonville, 2/109

Ross Foundation of Charlotte, Charlotte, 2/110

Samsons Fdn., Kinston, 2/110

Sandhills College Fdn., Southern Pines, 2/112

Sheldon (Dr. W. F. & Joan Scott) Scholarship Fund, Raleigh, 2/112

Scottish Fund, Charlotte, 2/114

Shapiro (Carole) Memorial Fdn., Asheville, 2/116

Sharon Fdn., Hickory, 2/117

Sinclair (J. F.) Memorial Endowment, West End, 2/117

Smith Educational Loan Fdn., Laurinburg, 2/117

Smith (W. Jasper) Memorial Scholarship Fund, Greenville, 2/117

Smith (Edward C.) Fdn., Lexington, 2/118

S. N. C. I. Fdn., Belmont, 2/119

Sofofk Fdn., Greensboro, 2/119

Solomon (Amelia & Ben) Charity Fund, Wilmington, 2/120

Spangler (C. D.) Fdn., Charlotte, 2/120

Spindale Mills Fdn., Rutherfordton, 2/121

Stadler (Leroy) Fdn., Greensboro, 2/122

Starnes (William Edward) Educational Fund, Raleigh, 2/123

Stedman Fdn., Greensboro, 2/124

Sternberger (Emanuel) Educational Fund, Greensboro, 2/125

Sternberger (Sigmund) Fdn., Greensboro, 2/126

Stewart (Lindsay) Memorial Fund, Greensboro, 2/128

St. John's Cemetery Trustee U/W Smith (Lydia C.), Greenville, 2/129

Stowe (S. P.) Sr., Fdn., Belmont, 2/129

Superior Cable Fdn., Hickory, 2/130

Synod of North Carolina Presbyterian Fdn., Raleigh, 2/130

Taylor Fund, Greensboro, 2/131

AAtlantic Christian College ETAL U/W Ange (A. W.), Greenville, 2/131

Thrower (Edwin K.) Fdn., High Point, 2/132

Trust Under AGreement with Drake (James B.) F/B/O Lincoln Hospital, Durham, 2/134

Trust Under Agreement with Duke (Benjamin N.) F/B/O Louisburg College, Durham, 2/135

Trust Under Agreement with Efland Memorial Association F/B/O Efland Methodist Church, Durham, 2/137

Trust Under Agreement with Duke (Benjamin N.) F/B/O Greensboro College, Durham, 2/138

Trust U/A Dwelle (Mary M.), Charlotte, 2/138

Trust U/W Faulk (Maurice) for The Blind, Charlotte, 2/139

Trust U/W Faulk (Maurice) for Salvation Army, Charlotte, 2/139

Trust U/W Flowers (William W.) F/B/O Durham Charity, Durham, 2/140

Trust U/A Mecklenburg Sanatorium, Charlotte, 2/140

Virginia Trust, Greensboro, 2/141

Waverly Fdn., Laurinburg, 2/141

Williamson (William H.) Charitable Fdn., Charlotte, 2/142

Wilmington Industrial Development Inc., Wilmington, 2/143

Winston-Salem Urban Coalition, Incorporated, Winston-Salem, 2/143

Wiscasset Assoc., Albemarle, 2/147

Wise (Jessie Kenan) Fdn., Wilmington, 2/147

Woltz Charitable Trust, Mount Airy, 2/149

Woodson (Margaret C.) Fdn., Salisbury, 2/149

Wright Refuge, Durham, 2/150

Zageir (Helen & Coleman) Fdn., Asheville, 2/150

NORTH DAKOTA

First Filming

Bloedow (Myrtle) Memorial Fdn., Fargo, 1/003

Bismarck Medical Fdn., Bismarck, 1/004

Brown (Gabriel J.) Trust, Bismarck, 1/004

Dawson Fdn., Fargo, 1/005

Eckert (Fred & Clara) Fdn. for Children, Williston, 1/005

Farnham Fdn., Fargo, 1/006

Finlayson (Christine) Graduate Scholarship Fund, Fargo, 1/007

Goldberg (Max & Anne) Fdn., Fargo, 1/007

Gough (Helen) Fdn. Trust, Fargo, 1/007

Haggart (George E.) Fdn., Fargo, 1/008

Haggart (W.R.) Fdn., Fargo, 1/008

Herbst Family Fdn., Fargo, 1/009

Hoghaug (Paul) Scholarship Fund, Grand Forks, 1/009

Ireland (Guy & Bertha) Fdn., Grand Forks, 1/009

Julyn (Frank) Trust, Fargo, 1/010

Kwako (Mary Jo) Memorial Trust, Fargo, 1/011

Leach (Tom & Frances) Fdn., Bismarck, 1/011

League for Animal Welfare, Bismarck, 1/011

Mattson (Edgar P.) Trust, Fargo, 1/012

Myra Fdn., Grank Forks, 1/012

Pardau Fdn. for Advanced Education, Fargo, 1/013

Reineke (Earl C.) Fdn., Fargo, 1/013

Person (Paul B. & Helen B.) Fdn., Fargo, 1/013

Powell Charitable Trust Fund, Cando, 1/014

Rosendahl (Peder) Trust, Harvey, 1/014

Stern (Alex) Family Fdn., Fargo, 1/014

Wilk (Mortimer and Agnes) Fdn., Fargo, 1/014

Zlevor (Rosamund) Trust, Fargo, 1/015

Second Filming

Arneberg (John G.) Trust, Grank Forks, 2/006

Bismarck Drug Abuse Fdn., Bismarck, 2/007

Black (Norman) Fdn., Fargo, 2/008

Campbell (Robert D.) Fdn., Grand Forks, 2/009

Fargo-Moorhead Area Fdn., Fargo, 2/009

Geller (Sam & Toba) Fdn., Fargo, 2/013

Jorgenson (Austa) Scholarship Trust, Grand Forks, 2/013

Julyn (Frank) Trust, Fargo, 2/014

Leach (Tom & Frances) Fdn., Bismarck, 2/014

Martell (C.F.) Memorial Fdn., Fargo, 2/015

Medora Fdn., Bismarck, 2/017

Merritt (Sam & Bertha) Memorial Trust, Fargo, 2/017

North Dakota Association of the Blind Trust, Fargo, 2/018

Olson (Jessie) Trust f/b/o Argusville Congregational Church, Fargo, 2/018

Olson Trust 1 - Crippled Children Home of Jamestown, Fargo, 2/019

Olson Trust 2 - Childrens Village of Fargo, Fargo, 2/019

Olson Trust 3 - Good Samaritan Home of Arthur, Fargo, 2/020

Springer (Henry A.) Educational Fdn,, Dickinson, 2/020

Zion Lutheran Church Maintenance Trust Fund, Fargo, 2/021

OHIO

First Filming

Abel Fdn., Columbus, 1/001

Acme Cleveland Fdn., Cleveland, 1/003

Adult Mental Health Clinic Trust, Youngstown, 1/004

Agnew Fdn., Cambridge, 1/004

Airolite Fdn., Marietta, 1/005

Akron Clinic Fdn., Akron, 1/005

Allyn Fdn., Dayton, 1/006

Alpha Rho Fdn., Columbus, 1/007

American Association Against Addiction, Akron, 1/007

American Fdn., Cleveland, 1/008

American Greetings Fdn., Cleveland, 1/009

American Home Missionary Church, Cleveland, 1/010

American Psychology Archives Fdn., Akron, 1/010

American Technical Institute Student Loan Fund, Akron, 1/011

American Welding & Manufacturing Co. Fdn., Warren, 1/011

America's Future Trees Fdn., Cleveland, 1/012

Anderson (Carl E. & Delores) Fdn., Canton, 1/012

Andrews Fdn., Cleveland, 1/013

Andrews (Matthew) Memorial Fdn., Cleveland, 1/014

Anesthesia Fdn., Youngstown, 1/015

Antrim (Everett) Memorial Kiwanis Scholarship Trust, Columbus, 1/016

Anvil Fdn., Toledo, 1/017

Apple Fdn., Dayton, 1/018

Applebaum (Abel A.) Family Fdn., Toledo, 1/019

Area Betterment Council, Niles, 1/019

Armco Fdn., Middletown, 1/020

Armington (Evenor) Fund, Cleveland, 1/022

Armington (George & Clara) Fund, Cleveland, 1/023

Art Iron Fdn., Toledo, 1/024

Ashman Fdn., Brecksville, 1/025

Aslan Fdn., Cincinnati, 1/025

Associated Charities of Findlay, Ohio, Findlay, 1/026

Astatic Fdn., Conneaut, 1/026

Augustus Fund, Cleveland, 1/027

Dougherty (Thomas & Mildred) Fdn.,
Cleveland, 1/183
Dunn Fdn., Cleveland, 1/184
Douglas (Frederick Melvin) Fdn., Toledo,
1/184
Downtown Catholic Club, Cleveland, 1/185
Dreidame (Ruth H. & Robert F.) Fdn.,
Cincinnati, 1/185
Drew (Elizabeth S.) Fdn., Cincinnati, 1/186
Duberstein Fdn., Dayton, 1/187
Durrell (Richard & Lucile) Fund, Cincinnati,
1/187
Dyson Fdn., Eastlake, 1/188
Eaton (Cyrus S.) Fdn., Cleveland, 1/188
East Dayton Tool Fdn., Dayton, 1/190
Eaton Charitable Fund, Cleveland, 1/191
Education for Freedom Fdn., Columbus, 1/192
Educational & Musical Arts, Dayton, 1/194
E H Fdn., Cincinnati, 1/195
EL-AN Fdn., Columbus, 1/195
Eleven Twenty-Four Fdn., Cincinnati, 1/196
Elliott (E. Allen) Family Fdn., Cincinnati,
1/196
Ellman (Edwin M.) Trust, Columbus, 1/197
Ellman (Geraldine R.) Trust, Columbus, 1/197
Ellman Fdn., Columbus, 1/198
Eltra Fdn., Toledo, 1/198
Emeny (Caroline Bush & Frederick L.) Fdn.,
Shaker Heights, 1/199
Emery (Thomas J.) Memorial, Cincinnati,
1/200
Emsheimer (Louis E. & Marcia M.) Charitable
Trust, Shaker Heights, 1/203
Ernst & Ernst Fdn., Cleveland, 1/203
Ernsthausen (John F. & Doris E.) Charitable
Fdn., Cleveland, 1/205
Ensten (Harold V. & Esther Ruth) Fdn.,
Cleveland, 1/206
Estonian Cultural Garden Association,
Cleveland Heights, 1/206
Euclid General Hospital Fdn., Cleveland, 1/207
Evans (Elizabeth W. & Raymond F.)
Charitable Fdn., Cleveland, 1/207
Evans (Thomas J.) Fdn., Newark, 1/209
Everett Fdn., Chagrin Falls, 1/210
Everett (Homer) Fund, Cleveland, 1/210
Evergreen Fdn., Toledo, 1/212
Eyman (Jesse) Trust, Washington Court House,
1/213
Faber Fdn., Wyoming, 1/214
Fairhill Fund, Cleveland, 1/214
Falsgraf Fdn., Cleveland, 1/215
Farran (Charles) Fdn., Cleveland, 1/215
Faulkner Charity Fund, Bucyrus, 1/216
Federated Department Stores Fdn., Cincinnati,
1/216
Fergus (Robert H. & Elizabeth) Trust,
Columbus, 1/217
Figgie Family Fdn., Cleveland, 1/218
Hynes-Finnegan Fdn., Youngstown, 1/218
Finnegan (John D.) Fdn., Youngstown, 1/219
Firestone (J.B.) Charitable Trust, Elyria, 1/220
Firestone (J.B.) Civic Trust, Elyria, 1/222
Firestone Fdn., Akron, 1/223
Firman Fund, Cleveland, 1/225
First Educational & Charitable Trust of Canton,
Ohio, Canton, 1/226
First National Bank of Cincinnati Fdn.,
Cincinnati, 1/227
First National Fdn., Steubenville, 1/228
Fisher Fdn., Canton, 1/229
Fisher (William C. & Lillye T.) Memorial
Fund, Cleveland, 1/229
Fleischman (Charles) Endowment Fund,
Cincinnati, 1/230
Fleishmann Fdn., Cincinnati, 1/231
Flickinger Memorial Trust, Lima, 2/001
Flowers (Albert W. & Edith V.) Charitable
Fdn., Canton, 2/001
Flowers (H. Fort) Fdn., Findlay, 2/002
Forbes (James & Carol) Fdn., Cleveland,
2/003
Libbey-Owens- Ford Philanthropic Fdn.,
Toledo, 2/003
Fort Steuben Burial Estates Association,
Wintersville, 2/004

Foster (Clyde T. & Lyla C.) Fdn., Cleveland,
2/004
Foster (William E., Jr.) Fdn., Elyria, 2/005
Founders Trust, Cleveland, 2/006
Four-Shra-Nish Fdn., Arcanum, 2/006
Fox Fdn., Lancaster, 2/007
Foy (Madelyn B. & Norman W.) Fdn., Chagrin
Falls, 2/008
Franco-American Cultural Fdn., Cleveland,
2/009
Frankhauser (Grace G.) Trust, Bettsville, 2/010
Franklin Fdn., Cleveland, 2/010
Franklin Hills Memorial Gardens, Columbus,
2/011
Franklin (Sidney & Beatrice) Charitable Trust,
Cleveland, 2/011
Fraternal Order of Police, Columbus, 2/012
Frease (Donald W.) Fdn., Dover, 2/013
Freelander (A. L.) Fdn., Dayton, 2/013
Freelander Fdn., Wooster, 2/014
Fremont Community Fdn., Toledo, 2/014
Friedman (Sol H.) Charitable Trust, Cleveland,
2/015
Friends of the Chagrin Falls Library, Chagrin
Falls, 2/016
Friendship Fund, Tiffin, 2/016
Frisch (R.S.F. & S.) Fdn., Cincinnati, 2/017
Fritzsche Fdn., Elyria, 2/017
Frohman (Sidney) Fdn., Sandusky, 2/018
Frohring (Paul & Maxine) Fdn., Chagrin Falls,
2/018
Frohring (William O. & Gertrude Lewis) Fdn.,
Newbury, 2/019
Frost (Meshech) Testamentary Trust, Columbus,
2/021
Gabele (Robert F. & Anne) Fdn., Cleveland,
2/021
Gale Charitable Fdn., Cincinnati, 2/022
Galion Community Fdn., Columbus, 2/023
Galvin Fdn., Lima, 2/023
Gardner (Colin) Fdn., Middletown, 2/024
Gallon (J.) Fdn., Toledo, 2/024
Gardner (Edward T.) Fdn., Dayton, 2/025
Gardner (Della B.) Trust, Middletown, 2/026
Gay (Virginia) Home for Aged Women,
Columbus, 2/026
Gellin (Rosemary) Fdn., Cleveland, 2/028
General Fireproofing Fdn., Youngstown, 2/028
General Tire Fdn., Akron, 2/028
Genshaft Family Fdn., Canton, 2/029
Gerlach Fdn., Columbus, 2/029
Gerson (Benjamin S.) Family Fdn., Cleveland,
2/030
Gibbens (C.A.) Memorial Scholarship Fund,
Elyria, 2/031
Gibbs Investment Fund, Canton, 2/031
Gilbert Fdn., Columbus, 2/032
Giles (Charles H. & Fannie M.) Fdn.,
Cleveland, 2/033
Gintert (Raymond C. & Mary) Trust, Warren,
2/034
Goldberg (Jack & Esther) Fdn., University
Hgts., 2/034
Goodyear Tire & Rubber Company Fund,
Akron, 2/036
Gordon (Ada L. Talbott) Fdn., Columbus,
2/038
Gradison Fdn., Cincinnati, 2/040
Grady (Mary) Charitable Trust, Columbus,
2/041
Graefe (Carl F.) Fdn., Akron, 2/041
Gram (Harry G.) Fdn., Springfield, 2/042
Grandin Farm Fdn., Cincinnati, 2/042
Graves Fdn., Akron, 2/042
Gray (G. A.) Fdn., Cincinnati, 2/043
Green Family Fdn., Cincinnati, 2/044
Greene (Helen Wade) Charitable Trust,
Cleveland, 2/044
Green (Jack & Norma) Fdn., Shaker Heights,
2/045
Gregg Fdn., Lima, 2/045
Gregory Fdn., Toledo, 2/046
Gregory (Eleanor) Trust, Cleveland, 2/047
Greiser (Melvin R. & Ada C.) Fdn., Cincinnati,
2/047
Griesinger Fdn., Cleveland, 2/048

Gries (Lincoln H. & Lillian D.) Charitable
Trust, Akron, 2/049
Gries (Lucile & Robert H.) Charity Fund,
Cleveland, 2/049
Grimes Fdn., Urbana, 2/051
Griswold-Eshleman Charitable Fund, Cleveland,
2/051
Gross (Walter L. & Nell R.) Charitable Trust,
Cincinnati, 2/051
Gullia Fdn., Cleveland, 2/052
Hadley (John B. & Ruth R.) Fdn., Toledo,
2/052
Hall (Joseph B.) Fdn., Cincinnati, 2/053
Halvorson Charitable Fdn., Gates Mills, 2/055
Hamilton (Esther) Alias Santa Claus Club
Scholarship Fund, Youngstown, 2/056
Hamilton Foundry Fdn. Formerly Hamilton
Foundry, Inc. Fdn., Hamilton, 2/056
Hassensall (Otallie E.) Testamentary Trust,
Toledo, 2/057
Hamilton (Henrietta) Fdn., Kent, 2/058
Hamlet Fdn., Chagrin Falls, 2/059
Hamlin (Mary L.) - Madeleine Hamlin Hughes
Fund, Cleveland, 2/059
Hancock (W. Wayne & Mary Fisher) Fdn.,
Cleveland, 2/060
Hanna Mining Company Fund, Cleveland,
2/061
Hansen (Fred E.) Charitable Fund, Cleveland,
2/062
Harbarger (Arthur L.) Charitable Trust, Akron,
2/062
Hardee Fdn., Toledo, 2/063
Harkins Medical Research Fdn., Cleveland,
2/064
Harrington (Grace & John T.) Fdn.,
Youngstown, 2/064
Harteveld's, Inc., Cincinnati, 2/065
Hartzmark (Lee) Fdn., Shaker Heights, 2/066
Haskell Fund, Cleveland, 2/066
Haskell (Gertrude H.) Memorial Trust F/B
John D. Archbold Memorial Hospital,
Cleveland, 2/067
Harvard Business School Club of Cleveland
Fund, Cleveland, 2/069
Hauck (Frederick A.) Fdn., Cincinnati, 2/070
Hauserman (Frederick K.) Charitable Trust,
Cleveland, 2/071
Hausman Fdn., Toledo, 2/072
Hauss-Helms Fdn., Wapakoneta, 2/073
Hayes Historical Society, Toledo, 2/074
Hayden Fdn., Cincinnati, 2/075
Hayfields Fdn., Cincinnati, 2/076
Hayward Distributing Company Charitable
Trust, Columbus, 2/077
Hazen (Roland) Fund, Lebanon, 2/078
H. C. S. Fdn., Cleveland, 2/078
Heffner Fund, Cleveland, 2/079
Heldman (George L.) Fdn., Cincinnati, 2/080
Helfrich Family Fund, Bucyrus, 2/081
Helping Hand Fdn., Baltic, 2/081
Heltzel Fdn., Warren, 2/082
Herbruck (Wendell) Educational Trust, Canton,
2/083
Herrlinger (Roth F., Jr.) Charitable Fdn.,
Cincinnati, 2/083
Herschede (Jane T. and Mark P.) Fdn.,
Cincinnati, 2/084
Hershik (Clifford B.) Fdn., Cleveland, 2/085
Hervey Charitable Fdn., Canton, 2/086
Hetherington Fdn., Cincinnati, 2/086
Heymann Fdn., Toledo, 2/087
Hibbert Fund, Toledo, 2/089
High (Charles F.) Fdn., Bucyrus, 2/089
Highland Fdn., Greenfield, 2/090
Hildreth Fdn., Columbus, 2/091
Hill Acme Company Fdn., Cleveland, 2/092
Hipple Fdn., Dayton, 2/092
Hirschheimer Charitable Trust, Canton, 2/093
Hobart (C. C.) Fdn., Troy, 2/093
Hoke Fdn., Lorain, 2/094
Holdstein (Milo S. and Edith A.) Fund, Shaker
Heights, 2/094
Holl (Logan) Fdn., Logan, 2/095
Homan Fdn., Cincinnati, 2/095
Hook (Charles R.) Fdn., Middleton, 2/096

Hoover (David C.) Charitable Trust, Canton, 2/096
Hoover Fdn., Canton, 2/097
Hoover (Frank G.) Charitable Trust, Canton, 2/101
Hoover (Herbert W., Jr.) Fdn. Trust, Canton, 2/102
Hoover Management Employees Charitable Fund Trust, Canton, 2/103
Hoover (Richard S.) Charitable Trust, Canton, 2/104
Hoover (Thomas H.) Charitable Trust, Canton, 2/105
Hoover (W. Henry) Fund, Canton, 2/106
Horvitz (Samuel A.) Memorial Fdn., Cleveland, 2/107
Hostetler (Gordon and Phoebe) Fdn., Akron, 2/107
Howley Fdn., Cleveland, 2/108
Jones (Thomas Hoyt & Katherine Brooks) Fdn., Cleveland, 2/109
Hub of Steubenville Fdn., Steubenville, 2/109
Huffman Fdn., Dayton, 2/110
Humphrey (George M. and Pamela S.) Fund, Cleveland, 2/110
Hunter Fund, Cleveland, 2/111
Hunter (Deshler) Fund, Columbus, 2/112
Hunter (Kate Deshler) Fund, Columbus, 2/113
Huntington (Mariett L.) Residue Fund, Cleveland, 2/113
Huron Medical Fdn., Cleveland, 2/114
Huttenbauer Fdn., Cincinnati, 2/115
Hybres Fdn., Youngstown, 2/115
Hynes (John F. and Loretta A.) Fdn., Youngstown, 2/116
I. E. Industries Fdn., Minster, 2/116
Isaacson (Max and Sylvia) Fdn., Dayton, 2/117
Ingalls (Louise H. and David S.) Fdn., Cleveland, 2/117
Ingram (Edgar W.) Fdn., Columbus, 2/119
Institute for Purchasing Research, Dayton, 2/119
Interlake Yachting Association Youth Fund, Toledo, 2/120
Ireland Fdn., Cleveland, 2/120
Ireland (James D. and Cornelia W.) Fund, Cleveland, 2/121
Isaac Fdn., Bryan, 2/122
Itts Fdn., Warren, 2/122
Jackson (Norma Witt) Charitable Fdn., Cleveland, 2/123
Jacobson (Jack) Memorial Fdn., Cleveland, 2/123
Jarson (Isaac N. and Esther M.) Charitable Trust, Cincinnati, 2/124
Jefferson Educational Fdn., Columbus, 2/124
Jeffery (E. T.) Fdn., Cleveland, 2/125
Jenbek Fdn., Cincinnati, 2/125
Jennings (Martha Holden) Fdn., Cleveland, 2/126
Jenkins (Edward C.) Fdn., Columbus, 2/129
J. M. S. Fdn., Canton, 2/131
Johnson (Marvin) Fdn., Shaker Heights, 2/131
Joseph and Feiss Co. Charity Fund, Cleveland, 2/131
Joseph (Maddy Sue and Frank E., Jr.) Charitable Fdn., Cleveland, 2/132
J. P. W. Fdn., Dayton, 2/133
Juilfs Fdn., Cincinnati, 2/133
Junior Achievement for Northwestern Ohio, Toledo, 2/134
Kaighin (Helene P.) Charitable Trust, Warren, 2/134
Kann Fdn., Cleveland, 2/135
Kaplan-Halpert Fdn., Cleveland, 2/136
Karp (Joseph & Fannie) Fdn., Cincinnati, 2/136
Karb (Kate M.) Trust, Columbus, 2/137
Kaufman Fdn., Akron, 2/137
Keating (Charles H., Jr.) Fdn., Cincinnati, 2/138
Keckley Rural Life Center, Marysville, 2/138
Keith (Walter P. & Fama N.) Fdn., Akron, 2/138
Kelley (Horace) Art Fdn., Cleveland, 2/139

Kelly-Springfield Supplemental Unemployment Benefits Trust, Akron, 2/141
Kenzie Family Fdn., Peninsula, 2/141
Kessler Fdn., Youngstown, 2/142
Kiefaber (W. H.) Fdn., Dayton, 2/142
Kilcawley (William H.) Fund, Youngstown, 2/143
Kilroy Fdn., Cleveland, 2/144
King (Woods & Louise B.) Fdn., Mentor, 2/144
Kleinman Family Fdn., Cleveland, 2/145
Kloepfer (Fred & Pearl) Fdn., Bucyrus, 2/145
Knight Center Corporation, Cleveland, 2/146
Knight (Edward F.) Family Fdn., Toledo, 2/146
Knight Fdn., Akron, 2/147
Knight (William & Elsie) Fdn., Toledo, 2/149
Kobacker (Jerome) Charities Fdn., Toledo, 2/150
K-9 Kollege Fdn., Canton, 2/151
Kramer (Louise) Fdn., Dayton, 2/151
Krause Family Fdn., Cleveland, 2/152
Krauss Fdn. Charitable Trust, Springfield, 2/153
Krebs Fdn., Rocky River, 2/154
Krieger (Leonard) Charitable Fdn., Cleveland, 2/154
Kreinbring (Edward W. & Violet) Charitable Trust, Solon, 2/155
Kroehle (Ralph) Fdn., Warren, 2/155
Kuck (E. R.) Fdn. Trust, Cincinnati, 2/156
Kuhns Brothers Company Fdn., Dayton, 2/157
Kulas Fdn., Cleveland, 2/157
Kuntz Fdn., Dayton, 2/159
Landt (Josephine Berting) Fdn., Cincinnati, 2/160
Lange Fdn., Dayton, 2/160
Larsh Fdn., Dayton, 2/161
Larson (W. O.) Fdn., Grafton, 2/162
Lake Community Student Loan Fdn., Hartville, 2/162
Lamb (John Otis) Fdn., Cincinnati, 2/163
Lamson & Sessions Co. Charitable Trust, Cleveland, 2/164
Landers Fdn., Toledo, 2/166
Lathrop Fdn., Toledo, 2/166
Laub Charitable Trust, Akron, 2/167
Lauer Fdn., Cincinnati, 2/167
Lavine (Joseph E.) Fdn., Warren, 2/167
Lawrence (John T., Jr.) Fdn., Cincinnati, 2/168
Lawson Baptist Fdn., Akron, 2/168
Lazarus (Simon) Family Fdn., Columbus, 2/169
Lazarus (Adelaide & Jeffrey) Fdn., Cincinnati, 2/169
Lazarus (Charles Y. and Frances N.) Fdn., Columbus, 2/170
Lazarus (Hattie W. and Robert) Fdn., Columbus, 2/170
Lazarus (Jeffrey L., Jr.) Family Fdn., Cincinnati, 2/171
Lazarus (Fred, Jr.) Fdn., Cincinnati, 2/171
Lazarus Store Fdn., Columbus, 2/172
Le Blond Fdn., Cincinnati, 2/173
Lecture Recital Scholarship Fdn., Cleveland, 2/174
Leitch (Robert Ingram and Carrie Scott) Fdn., Cleveland, 2/174
Lenhert (Martha) Fdn., Englewood, 2/175
Lennon (Fred A.) Fdn., Solon, 2/175
Le Suer (William and Arlene) Charitable Trust, Cleveland, 2/176
Le Suer (William and Arlene) Scholarship Trust, Moreland Hills, 2/177
Leustig (Frederick F., Jr.) Memorial Scholarship Fdn., Cleveland, 2/177
Levine (A. and A.) Fdn., Toledo, 2/178
Levinson (Robert E.) Fdn., Cincinnati, 2/179
Levison (Stanley K.) Fdn., Toledo, 2/179
Levy (Seymour) Family Fdn., Cleveland, 2/180
Lewis (Chauncey G.) Trust, Columbus, 2/181
L. G. B. Fdn., Toledo, 2/181
Libwall Fdn., Cincinnati, 2/182
Lincoln Electric Fdn., Cleveland, 2/182
Lincoln (J. F.) Family Fdn., Cleveland, 2/183

Lincoln Heights Fdn., Cincinnati, 2/185
Linden Trust, Shaker Heights, 2/186
Lindner (Carl H.) Fdn., Cincinnati, 2/186
Lindner (Robert D.) Fdn., Cincinnati, 2/187
Lindseth Fdn., Shaker Heights, 2/187
Lippman (Jerome and Goldie) Fdn., Akron, 2/188
Litchfield (Paul W.) Fdn., Cleveland, 2/189
Lloyd (C. T.) Fdn., Cleveland, 2/189
Local Chapter of American Red Cross of Delaware, Ohio Trust, Columbus, 2/190
Lockhart (George and Mary) Fdn., Canton, 2/191
Lockshin (Louis) Family Fdn., Akron, 2/192
Lockwood (W. B.) Fund, Youngstown, 2/193
Lodge and Shipley Fdn., Cincinnati, 2/193
Lone Star Fdn., Akron, 2/194
Long (Augustine J.) Fdn., Cleveland, 2/195
Louise Fdn., Cleveland, 2/195
Loveman-Burdett Oxygen Fdn. & Charitable Trust, Cleveland, 2/197
Lowe-Marshall Trust, Chesterhill, 2/197
Lubrizol Fdn., Wickliffe, 2/197
Lucas County State Fdn., Toledo, 2/198
Lumb (H. C.) Charitable Trust, Shaker Heights, 2/198
Lunkenheimer Fdn., Cincinnati, 2/200
Lyons Memorial Fund, Cincinnati, 2/200
M Fdn., Toledo, 2/202
Mac Gregor (B. N.) Fdn., Warren, 2/202
MacNichol Fund, Toledo, 2/203
Madden Fdn., Toledo, 2/204
Madow Family Fdn., Cleveland, 2/204
Main Line Fdn., Cleveland, 2/205
Maltby (Martha J.) Trust, Columbus, 2/205
Melton (S. M.) Trust, Columbus, 2/206
Manchester Family Fdn., Toledo, 2/206
Mandel (Jack N. & Lilyan) Fdn., Cleveland, 2/207
Mandel (Joseph & Florence) Fdn., Cleveland, 2/209
Mandel (Morton & Barbara) Fdn., Cleveland, 2/210
Manes (Louis L.) Fdn., Akron, 2/211
Manners Fdn., Cleveland, 2/212
Maradele Fdn., Cleveland, 2/212
Marathon Oil Fdn., Findlay, 2/213
Marcus (Elton D.) Fdn., Cleveland, 2/215
Margolis (Abe) Fdn., Dayton, 2/215
Marion County Historical Association and the Stengel-True Museum, Marion, 2/216
Markey Fdn., Bryan, 2/217
Mares, Inc., Cincinnati, 2/217
Markus (Roy & Eva) Fdn., Cleveland, 2/218
Marsh (Michael) Trust, Columbus, 2/218
Marsh (Joseph H. & Jessie M.) Charitable Trust, Dover, 2/219
Marsh (Victor R. & Gladys P.) Charitable Trust, Dover, 2/219
Marshall (C. Frank & Virginia Jordan) Fdn., Akron, 2/220
Martin Brothers Electric Fdn., Cleveland, 2/221
Mashburn (J. Cromer) Family Fdn., Cincinnati, 2/221
Masonic Blood Bank, Dayton, 2/222
Mastin (Lillian & Thomas) Charitable Trust, Cleveland, 2/222
Mather (Elizabeth Ring & William Gwinn) Fund, Cleveland, 2/223
Mather (S. Livingston) Charitable Trust, Cleveland, 2/224
Maxon Construction Company Fdn., Dayton, 2/225
Maxon Family Fdn., Dayton, 2/225
Mazza (Peter) Fdn., Cleveland, 2/226
McAnly Fdn., Cleveland, 2/227
McCollough (William G.) Trust, Steubenville, 2/227
McDonald (C. B.) Charitable Trust, Cleveland, 2/228
McDowell (Robert C.) Fund, Cleveland, 2/228
McDonald (Walter A. & George) Fdn., Cincinnati, 2/229
McFawn (Lois Lisler) Trust, Cleveland, 2/229
McKelvey (G. M.) Company Charitable Fdn., Youngstown, 2/230

Schneier Fdn. of Akron, Akron, 3/159
Schneider (Henry G.) Family Fdn., Dayton, 3/159
Schneider Trust, Canton, 3/160
Schonberg (Alan & Maria) Fdn., Cleveland, 3/161
Schoonover Charitable Fdn., Lima, 3/161
Schott (Joseph J.) Fdn., Cleveland, 3/162
Schottenstein (Jerome & Geraldine) Fdn., Columbus, 3/163
Schriber (Louis & Isabel) Fdn., Dayton, 3/163
Schubert (A. W.) Fdn., Cincinnati, 3/163
Schulman (Alex) Fdn., Akron, 3/164
Schultz Fdn., Cleveland, 3/164
Schulzinger (Joseph N.) Memorial Fdn., Cincinnati, 3/165
Schumacher (F. E.) Company Fdn., Canton, 3/165
Schumacher Fdn., Columbus, 3/166
Schumacher Lumber Company Fdn., Canton, 3/166
Scott (Louise Orr) Trust, Columbus, 3/167
Scott & Fetzer Fdn., Lakewood, 3/167
Scott (O. M.) Fdn., Columbus, 3/168
Scripps-Howard Fdn., Cincinnati, 3/169
Sealy Fdn., Cleveland, 3/170
Sealy-Wuliger Fdn., Cleveland, 3/172
Sears Family Fdn., Cleveland, 3/173
Sebald (Weber W.) Fdn., Middletown, 3/174
Sebald (Weber W. & Elmina McK.) Fund, Middletown, 3/175
Second Sohio Fdn., Cleveland, 3/175
Seeman (Alvin E. & Margaret H.) Charitable Fdn., Toledo, 3/177
Seelbach (Charles F.) Educational Fdn., Cleveland, 3/178
Dayton Sertoma Club Sponsorship Fund, Dayton, 3/178
Shafer (Richard H. & Ann) Fdn., Columbus, 3/179
Shanman (Moses D. & Esther L.) Charitable Trust, Cleveland, 3/179
Sheller-Globe Fdn., Toledo, 3/180
Shelton (Mary P.) Library Fund, Cincinnati, 3/181
Shepard Fdn., Euclid, 3/181
Shillito Store Fdn., Cincinnati, 3/182
Shoolroy (Ross K.) Fdn., Wooster, 3/183
Shore (T. Spencer) Fdn., Cincinnati, 3/183
Shunk (John Q.) Association, Bucyrus, 3/184
Shouvlin Fdn., Springfield, 3/185
Showalter (Helen M.) Fdn. Trust, Akron, 3/185
Siebert (Professor Wilber H.) Fdn., Columbus, 3/185
Siff (David M.) Fdn., Akron, 3/186
Sloane (Ulric) Trust, Columbus, 3/186
Sindell Fdn., Cleveland, 3/187
Sister City Fdn., Dayton, 3/188
Skeggs Fdn., Cleveland, 3/188
Smart (Charles Allen) Scholarship Trust, Chillicothe, 3/188
Smith (Curtis Lee) Family Fdn., Cleveland, 3/189
South Waite Fdn., Cleveland, 3/190
Speyer (Howard B.) Fdn., Toledo, 3/191
Spitzer (Louis & Julia) Memorial Fund, Youngstown, 3/192
Springfield Fdn., Springfield, 3/192
Stambaugh (Avanell C.) Fund, Youngstown, 3/194
Stanley (Lawrence D.) Fdn., Columbus, 3/194
Stark (Donald A. & Jane C.) Charitable Trust, Mentor, 3/195
Steinbrenner Fdn., Lorain, 3/196
Steinharter (Stanley S. & Augusta K.) Fdn., Cincinnati, 3/196
Stellhorn Fdn., Sandusky, 3/196
Sterling (Frederick C.) Trust, Cleveland, 3/197
Stern (Max, Martha, and Alfred M.) Fund For Medicines and Appliances, Cincinnati, 3/199
Stern (Morton H.) Fdn., Columbus, 3/200
Stern (Joseph S., Jr.) Family Fund, Cincinnati, 3/200
Stewart (John H., Jr.) Fdn., Canton, 3/202

Stockholders Anonymous, Inc., Findlay, 3/202
Stone Fdn., Cincinnati, 3/203
Stone (Walter) Fdn., Wyoming, 3/203
Stouch (Clyde W.) Fdn. Fund, Steubenville, 3/204
Stores (Mr. Wiggs) Fdn., Cleveland, 3/204
Strait (James & William) Trust, Columbus, 3/205
Stranahan (Robert A., Jr.) Charitable Trust, Toledo, 3/205
Strawbridge (Robert & Martha) Fdn. Formerly New York, Highland Heights, 3/206
Strietmann Fdn., Cincinnati, 3/207
Sunnyslope Fdn., Akron, 3/209
Surface Combustion Division, Midland-Ross Corporation Supplemental Unemployment Benefit Trust Fund, Toledo, 3/209
Taft (Robert, Jr.) Fdn., Cincinnati, 3/210
Tait (Frank M.) Fdn., Dayton, 3/212
Talbott (Eva V.) Fdn., Columbus, 3/214
Tamarkin Fdn., Youngstown, 3/215
Technical Education Fdn., Columbus, 3/216
Taplin (Thomas E.) Fund, Cleveland, 3/217
Taylor Fdn., Dayton, 3/218
Taylor (Clarence M. & Clara A.) Fund, Cleveland, 3/219
Taylor Fdn., Dayton, 3/219
Taylor Metal Products Company Trust, Mansfield, 3/220
Taylor-Winfield Fdn., Warren, 3/220
Tecca Fdn., Cleveland, 3/221
Tell (Paul P.) Fdn., Akron, 3/222
Tennant (Byron L.) Memorial Fund, Columbus, 3/223
Thal (Joseph) Family Fdn., Dayton, 3/223
Thomas (Edwin J.) Fdn., Akron, 3/224
Thompson Center Vocation & Rehabilitation Trust, Columbus, 3/225
Thompson (Joseph H.) Fund, Cleveland, 3/226
Tillman (Nancy) Memorial Fund, Toledo, 3/227
Times Company Fdn., Marietta, 3/227
Timken Company Educational Fund, Canton, 3/228
Timken Fdn. of Canton, Canton, 3/229
Timken (Henry & Louise) Fdn., Canton, 3/231
Timken International Fund, Canton, 3/231
Timken Company Charitable Trust, Canton, 3/232
Timmons Fdn., Columbus, 3/232
Tinnerman Products Fdn., Berea, 4/001
Tobias (A. I. & Sadie) Fdn., Cleveland, 4/002
Tod Fdn., Youngstown, 4/003
Toledo Community Participation Fund, Toledo, 4/003
Toledo Fdn., Toledo, 4/004
Toledo Stamping Charitable Fdn., Toledo, 4/005
DeVilbiss Company Supplemental Unemployment Benefit Plan, Toledo, 4/005
Toledo Trust Fdn., Toledo, 4/006
Tool Steel Gear & Pinion Fdn., Cincinnati, 4/007
Towmotor Fdn., Cleveland, 4/008
Tracy Fdn., Columbus, 4/009
Transplantation Society of Northeastern Ohio, Cleveland, 4/009
Tremco Fdn., Cleveland, 4/009
Trout (Charles) Trust, Columbus, 4/010
True (Henry A.) Trust, Marion, 4/011
Baker (Ethel Smith) Trust, Toledo, 4/012
Miller (Laura H.) Trust, Ashtabula, 4/012
Roberts (Helen E.) Trust, Columbus, 4/012
Schonthal (Joseph) f/b/o Colored Folks Home, Columbus, 4/013
Sikaras (Charles G.) Trust f/b/o Village of Mollaus, Greece, Warren, 4/013
T R W Fdn., Cleveland, 4/017
Tucker (Samuel A. & Louise K.) Family Fdn., Cleveland, 4/019
Turkish-American Association, Columbus, 4/019
Turner (Ione) Charitable Trust, Canton, 4/019
Tyler (Marion C.) Fdn., Cleveland, 4/020
Tyler (W. S.) Fdn., Cleveland, 4/021
Ulery (O. B.) Fdn., Springfield, 4/021

Ullner (Ry) Family Fdn., Cincinnati, 4/022
Ungar Fdn., Cincinnati, 4/023
Union Corwin de Ford Memorial Scholarship Fund, Youngstown, 4/023
Union Metal Charitable Trust, Canton, 4/024
Union Steel Fdn., Cincinnati, 4/025
United States Shoe Fdn., Cincinnati, 4/025
University of Toledo Student Investment Fund, Toledo, 4/026
V & V Fdn., Gates Mills, 4/027
Van Huffel (I. J.) Fdn., Warren, 4/027
Vaughn Family Fdn., Akron, 4/028
Verkamp Fdn., Cincinnati, 4/029
Vermiilion Fdn., Toledo, 4/030
Vernay Fdn., Yellow Springs, 4/030
Veterans of Foreign Wars, Newton Falls, 4/031
Viny (Louis) Family Fdn., Cleveland, 4/031
McFawn (Lois Sisler) Trust, Cleveland, 4/031
Viny (Louis) Family Fdn., Cleveland, 4/032
Vista Fdn., Cincinnati, 4/032
Vogelgesang (Edythe Hasler) Scholarship Fund, Canton, 4/033
Wabash (Weston) Fdn., Dayton, 4/033
Wade Fund, Cleveland, 4/035
Waite-Brand Fdn., Toledo, 4/036
Walker (Roe) Charitable Trust, Cincinnati, 4/037
Walnut Hall Fdn., Cincinnati, 4/038
Warburton (Ralph T. & Esther L.) Fdn., Canton, 4/038
Ward (Harry H.) Trust, Cleveland, 4/039
Warner (Harry B.) Charitable Trust, Akron, 4/040
Warnock Charity Fund, Bucyrus, 4/041
Washburn (Grace High) Trust, Bucyrus, 4/041
Washington (George) Memorial Fdn., Cleveland, 4/042
Wasmer (John C.) Fdn., Lakewood, 4/043
Wasserstrom Fdn., Columbus, 4/043
Watson (Walter E. & Caroline H.) Fdn., Youngstown, 4/045
Watterson Fdn., Cleveland, 4/045
Wean (Raymond John) Fdn., Warren, 4/046
Weber (E. Clare & Grace) Charitable Fdn., Shaker Heights, 4/050
Weeks (James & Edna) Fund, Cleveland, 4/051
Wehrle Fdn., Newark, 4/051
Weinberger (Adolph) Fdn., Cleveland, 4/053
Weiss (Clara) Fund, Rocky River, 4/054
Wellman (S. K.) Fdn., Cleveland, 4/054
West (Burton L.) Educational Fund, Columbus, 4/055
Westlake Fdn., Cleveland, 4/056
Weston (David F. & Sara K.) Fund, Cincinnati, 4/057
White (Helen B. & Charles M.) Charitable Trust, Cleveland, 4/060
White (J. Austin) Charitable Trust, Cincinnati, 4/061
White Motor Company Charitable Trust, Cleveland, 4/062
Whitewater Fdn., Cincinnati, 4/062
Whitinsville Fdn., Cleveland, 4/063
Whiting (Augustus N.) Trust, Columbus, 4/064
Wiener Family Fdn., Toledo, 4/066
Wildfowl Conservancy Inc., Cincinnati, 4/066
Wildermuth (E. F.) Fdn., Columbus, 4/067
Wilhelm (Kay Kelly) Memorial Scholarship Fund, Cardington, 4/068
Williams (Birkett L.) Fdn., Cleveland, 4/068
Williams (Richard Francis) Fdn., Cincinnati, 4/069
Williams-Matthews Fdn., Portsmouth, 4/070
Williamson Company Fdn., Cincinnati, 4/070
Willo (Veronica) Scholarship Fund, Youngstown, 4/070
Willson (Alfred L.) Charitable Fdn., Columbus, 4/071
Wilson (H. F. & Julia M.) Charitable Fdn., Lima, 4/073
Wilson (Marguerite M.) Fdn., Cleveland, 4/074
Wine (William E.) Trust, Toledo, 4/074
Winegardner Fdn., Cincinnati, 4/075

WKBN Broadcasting Fdn., Youngstown, 4/076
Wodecroft Fdn., Cincinnati, 4/076
Wood Fdn., Columbus, 4/077
Wooster (George A.) Memorial Fund for the
  Blind of Ross County, Chillicothe, 4/078
Wright Fdn., Cleveland, 4/079
Wright (Jennison) Fund, Toledo, 4/080
Yeck (John & Willa) Fund, Dayton, 4/081
Yeiser (Charles F. & Mary) Fdn., Cincinnati,
  4/081
Yoder Charitable Fdn., Wooster, 4/084
Young (M. A.) Fdn., Youngstown, 4/085
Young Men's Mercantile Library Association,
  Cincinnati, 4/085
Youngstown Welding & Engineering Fdn.,
  Youngstown, 4/087
Zeller Trust Fdn., Toledo, 4/088
Zoological Garden Fdn./Edna Ford Knight
  Memorial, Toledo, 4/089
Zoological Garden Fdn./General Garden Fund,
  Toledo, 4/090
Zusman Fdn., Dayton, 4/091
Zverina (Anton & Rose) Fund, Cleveland,
  4/091
Zychick (Julius & Sarah) Charitable Fdn.,
  Beachwood, 4/092
6050 Fdn., Cincinnati, 4/092
6320 Fdn., Dayton, 4/093

Second Filming

Abbot Home, Zanesville, 5/001
Abrahamson Fdn., Cincinnati, 5/002
Abrams (Howard & Estelle) Fdn., Shaker
  Heights, 5/002
Acme Cleveland Fdn., Cleveland, 5/003
Adler (Thomas & Emily) Fdn., Cincinnati,
  5/004
Aerie No. 2291 F.O.E., Clyde, 5/005
Albers (William H.) Fdn., Cincinnati, 5/005
ADler (Herbert & Dorothy) Fdn., Cleveland,
  5/006
Allen (D. P.) Trusts, Cleveland, 5/007
Alloy Fund, Marion, 5/011
Altshuler (Oscar H.) Fdn., Youngstown, 5/011
American Aggregates Fdn., Greenville, 5/012
American Dental Association, Cleveland, 5/013
American Safe Driving Institute, Dayton, 5/013
American Turners Instructors' Fund, Cleveland,
  5/013
Anderson Fdn., Maumee, 5/014
Andrews (J.H.) Trust for Chruch of Our
  Saviour, Akron, Ohio, Cleveland, 5/015
Angell (George & May M.) Trust, Cleveland,
  5/016
Apollo Real Estate Charitable Trust, Cleveland,
  5/018
Armogida (James & Velia) Scholarship Fund,
  Canton, 5/018
Arnovitz Fdn., Dayton, 5/019
Aronson (Harold J.) Fdn., Cleveland, 5/019
Art Institute of Zanesville, Zanesville, 5/020
A S P A Fdn., Berea, 5/021
Austin (Samuel & Sarah J.) Trust, Cleveland,
  5/021
Austin (Wilbert J.) Professorship of
  Engineering, Cleveland, 5/021
Barrows Fund, Cincinnati, 5/022
Babcock (Caroline A.B.) Library Fund,
  Cleveland, 5/023
Babcock (Caroline A.B.) Academy Fund,
  Cleveland, 5/024
Baldwin (J.) Trust, Cleveland, 5/024
Baldwin Memorial Library Fund, Cleveland,
  5/025
Meldrum (Barclay) - Joseph Fewsmith Fdn.,
  Cleveland, 5/026
Bardes Fund, Cincinnati, 5/026
Barth (Robert J.) Fdn., Dayton, 5/027
Beacon Journal Fund, Akron, 5/028
Beinke (George C.) Scholarship Fund, Toledo,
  5/028
Bell (J.G.) Fdn., Lakewood, 5/029
Bell (Samuel W.) Home for Sightless,
  Cincinnati, 5/029

Benjamin (Eudalia H.) Trusts, Cleveland,
  5/031
Bernhard (Elizabeth) Trust, Cleveland, 5/038
Berk (S. Bernard) Charitable Fdn., Akron,
  5/038
Berry (Marie D.) Trust, Cleveland, 5/039
Bicknell (John E. & Ida G.) Memorial Fund,
  Cleveland, 5/039
Biggar (Hamilton F.) Trusts, Cleveland, 5/041
Gingham (C. W.) Trust, Cleveland, 5/046
Bingham (William) Trust, Cleveland, 5/047
Binz (Emma & Frank) Memorial Fund,
  Cleveland, 5/047
Bishop (George T.) Trust, Cleveland, 5/049
Black (D. S.) Fdn., Cleveland, 5/049
Black Swamp Historical Museum, Paulding,
  5/050
Blackall (R.H. & S.B.) Trust, Cleveland, 5/051
Blossom (D. S.) Trusts, Cleveland, 5/051
Bodman Widows Home, Cincinnati, 5/053
Bonda (Alva T. & Marie) Fdn., Cleveland,
  5/053
Boswell (William P.) Fdn., Cincinnati, 5/054
Boyce (Julia F.) Trust, Cleveland, 5/054
Boyd (Ida Wood) Trust, Cleveland, 5/054
Boys' Village, Smithville, 5/055
Bramson Fdn., Cleveland, 5/055
Braun Fdn., Toledo, 5/056
Bridge Street Fund, Cincinnati, 5/056
Brown (Euna) Trust, Marietta, 5/056
Hathaway - Brown School - Mothers &
  Daughters Trust, Cleveland, 5/057
Browning (John N.) Family Fund, Cincinnati,
  5/058
Browning (L. L.) Memorial Fund, Cincinnati,
  5/059
Buckeye International Fdn., Columbus, 5/060
Bunts (Frank E.) Trust, Cleveland, 5/061
Burke (E. S.), Jr. Trust, Cleveland, 5/061
Burkons (Jerome & Lenore) Fdn., Cleveland,
  5/062
Burnham (Walter S.) Trusts, Cleveland, 5/062
Burt Fdn., Akron, 5/064
Burton (Theodore E.) Trust, Cleveland, 5/064
Buse (Raymond L.) Memorial Fdn., Cincinnati,
  5/066
Cahoon (Ida M.) Memorial Park Trust,
  Cleveland, 5/067
Cahoon (Ida M.) Library of Dover Trust,
  Cleveland, 5/067
Caldwell (James) Scholarship Fund, Wooster,
  5/068
Camden Fdn., Cincinnati, 5/068
Canaday (Ward M. & Mariam C.) Educational
  & Charitable Fund, Toledo, 5/068
Canfield (Nellie H.) Trust, Cleveland, 5/070
Carey (Robert S. & Judith F.) Charitable Fdn.,
  Cleveland, 5/070
Carkhuff Charitable Trust, Cleveland, 5/071
Carlin Fdn., Cleveland, 5/072
Carmel of Mary Immaculate & St. Mary
  Magdalen Trust, Cleveland, 5/073
Cassano Fdn., Kettering, 5/074
Daley (William R. & F. Cassie) Trust,
  Cleveland, 5/074
Casto (Don M.) Fdn., Columbus, 5/075
Chalker (Newton) Trust, Akron, 5/076
Charitable Assistance Fdn., Columbus, 5/079
Charities Fdn., Toledo, 5/079
Charity School of Kendal, Massillon, 5/081
Chesterton Fdn., Cleveland, 5/082
Chew (J.A.) Fdn., Xenia, 5/082
Choffin (C.C.) Trust, Youngstown, 5/083
Christ Church Episcopal, Hudson, Ohio Trust,
  Cleveland, 5/084
Christ United Presbyterian Church General
  Endowment Fund, Canton, 5/084
Christian Residences Fdn., Cleveland, 5/085
Christian REsidences Fdn. Fund, Cleveland,
  5/086
Christopher Fdn., Cleveland, 5/087
Cincinnati Fdn. for the Aged, Cincinnati,
  5/089
Clements (Vida S.) Fdn., Columbus, 5/090
Cleveland Automobile Club Orphans Outing
  Fund, Cleveland, 5/090

Cleveland Fdn., Cleveland, 5/091
Cleveland - Cliffs Fdn., Cleveland, 5/099
Cleveland Crane & Engineering Division,
  McNeil Corp. Charitable Trust Fund,
  Cleveland, 5/101
Cleveland Revolving Fund, Cleveland, 5/102
Sokol Cleveland, Warrensville Heights, 5/103
Clopay Corporation Fdn., Cincinnati, 5/103
Cole (Joseph E. & Marcia) Charitable Fdn.,
  Cleveland, 5/103
Community Fdn., Toledo, 5/104
Cook (Nettie) Fund, Cleveland, 5/106
Copperweld Steel Company's Warren
  Employees Trust, Warren, 5/106
Copperweld Steel Company's Warren
  Supervisory Salaried Employees Trust,
  Warren, 5/108
Corrigan (James W.) Memorial Fund,
  Cleveland, 5/108
Corrigan (Laure Mae) Trusts, Cleveland, 5/109
Coulby (Jane E.) Trust, Cleveland, 5/115
Coven (Jack & Hortense) Fdn., Beachwood,
  5/115
Cox (Jacob D.) Trust, Cleveland, 5/115
Cox (James M.) Fdn., Dayton, 5/116
Crosley Fdn., Cincinnati, 5/117
Daniels (William R.) Scholarship Trust Fund,
  Lakewood, 5/118
Danner Fdn., Akron, 5/119
Darsky Fdn., Youngstown, 5/119
Dauby (N. L.) Charity Fund, Cleveland, 5/120
Dayco Charitable Fdn., Dayton, 5/121
Deaconess Hospital & Health Fdn., Cleveland,
  5/122
Deeds (Edward A.) Carillon Trust, Dayton,
  5/123
Delta Omicron Fdn., Cincinnati, 5/124
DeWitt (Clinton & Margaret) Endowment
  Fund, Cleveland, 5/124
DeWitt (Margaret) Estate Trust, Cleveland,
  5/125
Dienstberger (Mr. & Mrs. Arnold C.) Charity
  Trust Fund, Lima, 5/126
Dively (George S.) Fdn., Cleveland, 5/127
Doctors Hospital Fdn., Columbus, 5/128
Donahue (Mary B.) Trust, Cleveland, 5/128
Donnell Fdn., Findlay, 5/130
Duff Family Fdn., Lima, 5/131
Duff (Alfred) Memorial Fund, Port Clinton,
  5/132
Bowman (George A. & Edith Duncan) Fdn.,
  Kent, 5/133
Durkin Fdn., Cleveland, 5/133
Dworkin (Harry J. & Claire S.) Fdn.,
  Cleveland, 5/134
Eckert (Denver M.) Educational & Charitable
  Trust, Defiance, 5/134
Eckler (Edith Mae) Trust, Akron, 5/135
Economy Engineering Fdn., Cleveland, 5/135
Edmont Fdn., Coshocton, 5/136
Edwards (J. T.) Company Fdn., Columbus,
  5/137
Electric Furnace Fdn., Salem, 5/137
Ellsworth (J. W.) - Western Reserve Academy
  Funds, Cleveland, 5/138
Everett Fdn., Chagrin Falls, 5/140
Ellsworth (J. W.) - Western Reserve Academy
  Funds, Cleveland, 5/140
Emery Industries, Inc. Fdn., Cincinnati, 5/141
Epp (Otto C. & Maude Willey) Fdn.,
  Cincinnati, 5/142
Ernsthausen (Doris E.) - Item Six Fund,
  Cleveland, 5/142
Evans (Phyllis H. & William H.) Charitable
  Fdn., Cleveland, 5/143
Fahrion (S. May) Trust, Cleveland, 5/144
Fairview Memorial Park Funds, Columbus,
  5/144
Feldman Fdn., East Liverpool, 5/145
Felman (Morris P.) Fdn., Dayton, 5/145
Fenn (S. P.) Trust, Cleveland, 5/146
Fergus (Robert H. & Elizabeth) Fdn.,
  Columbus, 5/148
Ferro Fdn., Cleveland, 5/148
Fickinger (Sarah A.) Trust, Cleveland, 5/149
Fifth Third Fdn., Cincinnati, 5/149

Finn Foundries Fdn., Dayton, 5/150
Firestone Trust Fund, Cleveland, 5/151
Firestone (Harvey S.) Trust, Cleveland, 5/153
Fishel Fdn., Columbus, 5/154
Flesh (Alfred L.), Jr. Memorial Trust, Piqua, 5/155
Fling (Russell S.) Fdn., Columbus, 5/155
Fordham (Thomas B.) Fdn., Dayton, 5/155
Foss (Donald J.) Memorial Employees' Trust, Wooster, 5/157
Foundation for World Law, Cleveland, 5/158
Fox (Harry K. & Emma R.) Charitable Fdn., Cleveland, 5/158
France (Nona) Fdn., Toledo, 5/159
Pack (Frances) Trust, Cleveland, 5/160
Franklin Fdn., Cleveland, 5/161
Fraser (Fleming B.) Fdn., Norwood, 5/161
Fraternal Order of Eagles, Toronto, 5/162
Freeman Fdn., Lakewood, 5/162
Freeman (Emma D.) Trusts, Cleveland, 5/163
Friedlander Family Fund, Cincinnati, 5/164
Friedman (Sam & Esther) Fdn., Cleveland, 5/164
Frodsham (Stanley) Memorial Trust, Cincinnati, 5/165
Fullgraf Family Fdn., Cincinnati, 5/166
Gale (Albert E.) Charity Trust Fund, Lima, 5/166
Gardner Fdn., Middletown, 5/167
Gericke (Dr. Alfred J. & Rose O.) Fdn., Medina, 5/169
Gerzeny World Missions Fund, Brecksville, 5/169
Gibbs (Elmer W.) Memorial Trust, Canton, 5/170
Gibbs (Mr. & Mrs. Lewis) Memorial Trust Fund, Canton, 5/171
Giller Fdn., Akron, 5/171
Goerlich Family Fdn., Toledo, 5/173
Goldner (Leo) Fdn., Toledo, 5/174
Goldsmith (Louis) Fdn., Cincinnati, 5/174
Goldsmith (William & Minnette) Fdn., Canton, 5/175
Gollan (Marie Louise) - Winston P. Burton Trusts, Cleveland, 5/176
Gorman (J. C.) Fdn., Mansfield, 5/177
Gottshall - Rex Memorial Scholarship, Holland, 5/178
Goudvis (T. L.) Fund, Vermilion, 5/179
Gray (Ethel) Trust, Marietta, 5/179
Cleveland Neighborhood Centers Association (Greater), Cleveland, 5/180
Guggenheim (Joan Y.) Fdn., Cincinnati, 5/181
Gund (George) Fdn., Cleveland, 5/182
Gund (George) Trusts, Cleveland, 5/185
Hadden Fdn., Cleveland, 5/186
Halapleus (James G.) Testamentary Trust, Toledo, 5/187
Halle Brothers Company Fdn., Cleveland, 5/188
Hamlin (E.B. & Madeleine) Funds, Cleveland, 5/188
Hankins Fdn., Shaker Heights, 5/189
Feltes (Hannah Voell) Fdn., Cincinnati, 5/190
Hare Charity Trust Fund, Columbus, 5/191
Harris - Intertype Fdn., Cleveland, 5/191
Hartland Consolidated School Fdn., Cleveland, 5/192
Hartzmark (Lee) Fdn., Shaker Heights, 5/193
Hauserman (E. F.) Charitable Trust, Cleveland, 5/194
Hauserman (Frederic Z.) Charitable Trust, Cleveland, 5/195
Hays (Robert L. & Lois M.) Fdn., Shaker Heights, 5/195
Hayward (George E. & Katherine) Trust, Marietta, 5/196
Hebron Community Fdn., Hebron, 5/197
Heldman (Robert W.) Fdn., Cincinnati, 5/197
Herenden (Ellen C.) Trust, Cleveland, 5/198
Herrlinger Fdn., Dayton, 5/199
Hickox Fdn., Cleveland, 5/199
Hill (Hal H.) Memorial Fund, Cleveland, 5/201
Hinsch Fdn., Cincinnati, 5/202

Hoover - Price (Milligan College) Trust, Canton, 5/203
Hord (John H.) Trust, Cleveland, 5/203
Hosford (Donald M. & Helen F.) Charitable Fdn., Cleveland, 5/204
Hough Fdn., Cleveland, 5/205
Housing Now, Inc., Dayton, 5/206
Hyde (Howard & Katharine) Fund, Cleveland, 6/001
Howland Athletic Club, Warren, 6/002
Huenefeld Memorial, Cincinnati, 6/002
Hulsken (Elizabeth L.) Trust, Lima, 6/004
Hunkin Fdn., Cleveland, 6/004
Hunter Fdn. Trust, Youngstown, 6/005
Huntington (John) Art & Polytechnic Trust, Cleveland, 6/006
Huntington (John) Fund for Education, Cleveland, 6/011
Hurley (F. E.) Trust, Cleveland, 6/014
Huron Medical Fdn., Cleveland, 6/015
I. E. Industries Fdn., Minster, 6/016
Imperial Electric Fdn., Akron, 6/016
Industrial Nut Fdn., Cleveland, 6/017
Institutional Housekeepers Educational Trust, Gallipolis, 6/019
Iten (Charles J.) Trusts, Cleveland, 6/019
I T T Wakefield Fdn., Vermilion, 6/020
Irwin Auger Bit Company Fdn., Wilmington, 6/020
Jacob (Richard J.) Family Charitable Fdn. Corporation, Dayton, 6/022
Jacob (Robert B.) Family Charitable Fdn. Corporation, Dayton, 6/023
Jacobs Family Fdn., Cincinnati, 6/024
Jaffe Charitable Fdn., Cleveland, 6/024
Jasam Fdn., Columbus, 6/025
Jeffrey (Joseph A.) Endowment Fund, Columbus, 6/026
Jenkins (Samuel R. & Mary W.) Fund, Cleveland, 6/026
Jobst (Conrad) Fdn., Toledo, 6/027
Johnson (Katherine H.) Trust, Akron, 6/028
Jones Home for Children, Cleveland, 6/029
Jones (George & Cora) Memorial Fund, Cleveland, 6/029
Jones (George & Cora) Memorial Trust Fund, Cleveland, 6/031
Jones (Gertrude) Trust, Cleveland, 6/032
Jones (Orville L.) Trust, Cleveland, 6/032
Palmer (Judson) Home, Findlay, 6/034
Kachelmacher Memorial, Logan, 6/035
Kahn (William V. & Therese) Fdn., Columbus, 6/036
Kalb (Gus) Memorial Fund Charity, Lima, 6/036
Kanter (Joseph H.) Fdn., Cincinnati, 6/037
Kaplin Fdn., Toledo, 6/037
Kargher - Schaffer Fdn., Cleveland, 6/038
Karp (Joseph & Fannie) Fdn., Cincinnati, 6/039
Katz (Herman M. & Myrtle) Fdn., Columbus, 6/040
Kaye (George & Alice) Fdn., Pepper Pike, 6/041
Kelley (Hermon A.) Scholarship Trust, Cleveland, 6/042
Kelley (Hermon A.) Art Library Fund, Cleveland, 6/042
Kelso (John B.) Trusts, Cleveland, 6/043
Kendall (Frederick Augustus) Scholarship Trust, Cleveland, 6/044
Kendall (Hayward) Trust, Cleveland, 6/045
Kendall (Nathan) Trust, Cleveland, 6/046
Kendall (Virginia) Scholarship Trust, Cleveland, 6/047
Kettering Family Fdn., Dayton, 6/048
Kettering Fund, Dayton, 6/050
Kilburger (Charles) Scholarship Fund, Lancaster, 6/050
Kilfoyl (Abby) Testamentary Trust, Cleveland, 6/052
Killgallon Fdn., Bryan, 6/053
Kobacker (Arthur J. & Sara Jo) Fdn., Brilliant, 6/054
Knights of Columbus Home of Canton, Ohio, Canton, 6/055

Konigslow (Ella) Testamentary Trust, Cleveland, 6/055
Krieger (Leonard) Charitable Fdn., Cleveland, 6/056
Kroger Company Charitable Trust, Cincinnati, 6/056
Kuhns Brothers Company Fdn., Dayton, 6/057
Kunkel Fund, Cincinnati, 6/058
Kangesser (Robert E., Harry A., & M. Sylvia) Fdn., Cleveland, 6/059
Kanter (Joseph H.) Fdn., Cincinnati, 6/063
Lake County Fdn., Painesville, 6/063
Lakewood High School Alumni Loan Fund, Lakewood, 6/064
Freeman (Ruth) Memorial Fund - Lakewood Hospital Trust, Cleveland, 6/064
Lakewood Securities Fdn. Charitable Trust, Lakewood, 6/065
Lamb (Edward) Fdn., Toledo, 6/065
Saenger (Therese Lange) & Sidney Lange Fdn., Cincinnati, 6/066
Laub Fdn., Rocky River, 6/067
Lazarus (Frank I.) Fdn., Cincinnati, 6/068
Lazarus (Fred), III Fdn., Cincinnati, 6/068
Lazarus (Ralph) Fdn., Cincinnati, 6/069
Leslie Scholarship Fund, Toledo, 6/069
House (Letha E.) Fdn., Medina, 6/070
Levinson (Ben) Benevolent Fund, Cincinnati, 6/070
Leyman Fdn., Cincinnati, 6/070
Lichter Fdn., Cincinnati, 6/071
Liebowitz Fdn., Cincinnati, 6/071
Lilly (Emma) Trust, Cleveland, 6/072
Lima Community Fdn., Lima, 6/072
Lincoln (James F.) Arc Welding Fdn., Cleveland, 6/073
Linderme (Emil M.) Fdn., Cleveland, 6/074
Lions Club of Dayton, Ohio Fdn., Dayton, 6/076
Lion Knitting Mills Company Charity & Educational Fund, Cleveland, 6/076
Lippy Fdn., Warren, 6/076
Litchfield Welfare Fund, Akron, 6/077
Litwin Fdn., Cincinnati, 6/077
Lloyd Library Maintenance Fund, Cincinnati, 6/077
Lloyd Library Books & Binding Trust, Cincinnati, 6/077
Lloyd Library Building Fund, Cincinnati, 6/078
Lloyd Library Publication Fund, Cincinnati, 6/078
Loth (C.) Fdn., Cincinnati, 6/078
Lutz (Philip P. & Faye) Fdn. Trust, Akron, 6/079
Macdonald Fdn., Lima, 6/080
Mahoning County Medical Society Fdn., Youngstown, 6/080
Mansfield Tire & Rubber Company Supplemental Employment Benefits Trust, Mansfield, 6/081
Marcliff Fdn., Cincinnati, 6/081
Marks (Amelia & Julius) Charitable Fdn., Columbus, 6/081
Markey (John C.) Charitable Fund, Bryan, 6/083
Marsh (John J.) Charitable Trust Fund, Dover, 6/083
Marsh (Michael) Non Exempt Charitable Trust, Columbus, 6/084
Masonic Relief Assoc. of Cincinnati, Ohio, Cincinnati, 6/084
Mattlin Fdn., Columbus, 6/084
Mazer (Shirley & Marshall) Fdn., Dayton, 6/085
McArthur (Bruce E.) Fdn., Canfield, 6/087
McBride (Harriet E.) Trust, Cleveland, 6/087
McClain (J. Allen) Trust, Eaton, 6/087
Young (Helen McClain) Fund, Cleveland, 6/088
McGill (Rose) Fund, Columbus, 6/088
McGinness Fdn., Cleveland, 6/089
McGregor (Joanne J. & H. Laird) Fdn., Findlay, 6/090
McGunagle Family Fdn., Cleveland, 6/090
McIntosh Fdn., Cleveland, 6/091
McIntire (John) Trust, Zanesville, 6/091

Sherwin (Frances McIntosh) Trust, Cleveland, 6/093

McKee (Arthur G.) & Company Charitable Trust, Cleveland, 6/093

McKinley High School Class of 1924 Trust, Canton, 6/094

Mead Corporation Fdn., Dayton, 6/094

Mead (George), Jr. Fdn., Dayton, 6/095

Meeks (Jack N.) Fdn., Columbus, 6/096

Melton (Samuel Mendel) Fdn., Columbus, 6/096

Messer, Perin, Sundahl & Associates Fdn., Cincinnati, 6/097

Merrill Fdn., Cleveland Heights, 6/098

Metzenbaum (Bessie Benner) Fdn., Cleveland, 6/098

Meyers (Lowell M.) Family Fdn., Columbus, 6/099

Miami Valley Educational Television Fdn., Dayton, 6/100

Miami Valley Speech & Hearing Association Scholarship Fund, Middletown, 6/100

Michel (Bertha A.) Trust, Cleveland, 6/100

Midwest Fdn., Cleveland, 6/101

Milan Historical Museum Trust, Cleveland, 6/101

Miller (Polly & Leon Gordon) Fdn., Cleveland, 6/101

Mitchell (Elizabeth Myers) Trust, Cleveland, 6/102

Monnett (Frank S.) Public Educational Fund, Columbus, 6/103

Montgomery Fdn., Coshocton, 6/103

Moore (Alfred A.) Fdn., Cincinnati, 6/105

Morgan Fdn., Akron, 6/105

Morgens (Howard) Fdn., Cincinnati, 6/105

Morgenthaler (David T. & Lindsay J.) Fund, Lakewood, 6/106

Morely (Charles R.) Trust, Cleveland, 6/106

Morley Library Endowment Fund, Cleveland, 6/107

Morris (Calvary) YMCA Fund, Cleveland, 6/107

Morris (Willard & Mary) Fdn., Columbus, 6/108

Moul (Charles) Trusteeship Trust, Canton, 6/108

Murrer Fund, Cincinnati, 6/109

Musica Sacra Fdn., Cincinnati, 6/109

Myers (Harry D. & Grace) Fdn., Pepper Pike, 6/109

Nance (James J.) Fdn., Akron, 6/109

National Association of Collegiate Directors of Athletics, Rocky River, 6/111

National Kidney Fdn., Inc. of Central Ohio, Columbus, 6/111

Neiman Family Fdn. Formerly Illinois, Warren, 6/111

Newberry (Virginia Kelly) Scholarship Trust, Cleveland, 6/112

Newton (Isaac) - Church Fund, Cleveland, 6/112

Nichols Fdn., Cincinnati, 6/113

Noble (Elmore S.) Trust, Cleveland, 6/114

Noll (Philip R.) Fdn., Cleveland, 6/114

Noonan Fdn., Springfield, 6/115

North Canton Cemetery Association Trust, Canton, 6/115

Northeast Ohio Boy Scout Trust, Painesville, 6/116

Northern Ohio Children's Performing Music Fdn., Westlake, 6/116

Nussbaum Charitable Trust, Cincinnati, 6/116

Oberhelman - Ritter Foundry Company Fdn., Cincinnati, 6/118

O'Bleness (Charles) Fdn., Columbus, 6/118

Oettinger Fdn., Cincinnati, 6/120

Ohio Law Opportunity Fund, Columbus, 6/121

Ohio Lions Eye Research Fund, Jackson, 6/121

Ohio Valley Fdn., Cincinnati, 6/123

Omi Brotherhood Fdn. of America, Dayton, 6/123

O'Neil (M. G.) Fdn., Akron, 6/123

Ormet Fdn., Hannibal, 6/124

Osborn (Arthur B.) Trust, Cleveland, 6/124

Osborn (Mary K.) Trusts, Cleveland, 6/125

Over - the - Rhine Recreation Fdn., Cincinnati, 6/126

Oxford Museum Association, Oxford, 6/127

Pack (George L.) Trust, Cleveland, 6/127

Painter (Leilla M.) Trust, Cleveland, 6/128

Parker Fdn., Cleveland, 6/129

Parmalee (James) Trust, Cleveland, 6/130

Parson (Richard C.) Trust, Cleveland, 6/131

Pauline Home for the Aged, Columbus, 6/131

Peirce Construction Company Charitable Fdn., Holland, 6/132

Penfield Memorial Endowment Fund, Cleveland, 6/133

Penton (J. A.) - Kenyon College Trust, Cleveland, 6/134

Perkins (General Simon) Fund, Cleveland, 6/134

Pfening Fdn., Columbus, 6/134

Phi Kappa Psi Fraternity Endowment Fund, Cleveland, 6/135

Philada Home Fund, Cincinnati, 6/136

Philips (Jesse) Fdn., Dayton, 6/137

Opp (Phillip) Trust, Cleveland, 6/138

Phillips (Dr. A. K.) Fdn., Youngstown, 6/139

Plate (Robert J.) Commemorative Trust, Lima, 6/139

Porthouse Fdn., Kent, 6/141

Prayer Unlimited International, Cleveland, 6/142

Prentiss (Elizabeth S.) Fund, Cleveland, 6/143

Prentiss (Elizabeth Severance) Fdn., Cleveland, 6/144

Prentiss (Elizabeth Severance) Funds, Cleveland, 6/147

Prescott Fdn., Cleveland, 6/155

Price (Mary F.) Trust, Columbus, 6/156

Proctor & Gamble Fund, Cincinnati, 6/156

Psychiatric Research Fdn. of Cleveland, Cleveland, 6/158

Randall Fdn., Cincinnati, 6/159

Raab (Manda) Trust, Cleveland, 6/159

Rangela Fdn., Cincinnati, 6/160

Ranney Scholarship Fund, Cleveland, 6/161

Ratner (Harry) Fdn., Cleveland, 6/162

Rauh (Florence E. L.) Trusts, Cleveland, 6/162

Reed (Etta J.) Trust, Cleveland, 6/166

Reinberger Fdn., Cleveland, 6/167

Republic Steel Corporation Educational & Charitable Trust, Cleveland, 6/169

Richman Brothers Fdn., Cleveland, 6/171

Richman (Edith & George) Fund, Shaker Heights, 6/174

Richman (Nathan G.) Trust, Cleveland, 6/175

Rio Grande College Endowment Fund, Columbus, 6/175

Ritchie (Clara Belle) Trust Funds, Cleveland, 6/176

Rittenhouse (Curtis W.) Trust, Cleveland, 6/178

Riverside Hospital Medical Residents Fund, Columbus, 6/179

Roadway Fdn., Akron, 6/179

Robbins Fdn., Gates Mills, 6/179

Robertson (Reuben B.) Fdn., Hamilton, 6/180

Rollins (Beulah P.) Trust, Cleveland, 6/182

Romanian Orthodox Charity Union A/K/A Charity Romanian Orthodox Union, Cleveland, 6/182

Rose (Mary Upson) Funds, Cleveland, 6/183

Rosenblum Fdn., Steubenville, 6/187

Rosenwasser (Marcus) Trust, Cleveland, 6/187

Rutz (Fred C.) Fdn., Cleveland, 6/188

Sacks Family Charitable Fdn., Akron, 6/189

St. Christopher's Fund, Cleveland, 6/190

St. Frances Cabrini Heart Fdn., Cleveland, 6/191

St. Gerard Fdn., Cleveland, 6/191

St. John's Episcopal Church General Fund, Cleveland, 6/192

Sauder Museum, Archbold, 6/192

Savage (Mary T.) Trust, Cleveland, 6/193

Share Fdn., Reading, 6/194

Schmidlapp (Jacob G.) Trust, Cincinnati, 6/195

Schmidlapp (C. R.) Fund, Cincinnati, 6/196

Schmidlapp Memorial Dormitory Trust, Cincinnati, 6/198

Schneider (Elizabeth M.) Trust, Cleveland, 6/199

Schroh (Evelyn A.) Trust, Cleveland, 6/199

Sears (Ruth P.) Trust, Cleveland, 6/200

Seely (Warner) Trust f/b/o United Appeal of Greater Cleveland, Cleveland, 6/201

Seymour (Harold F. & Helen Sullivan) Memorial Fund, Cleveland, 6/201

Haas (Samual T.) Charitable Trust, Cleveland, 6/202

Scholarship Fund, Toledo, 6/204

Schott (Charles J.) Fdn., Cincinnati, 6/205

Schottenstein (Jacob & Gussie) Fdn., Columbus, 6/206

S C O A Fdn., Columbus, 6/206

Seiberling Rubber Co. Supplemental Unemployment Benefits Plan Trust, Akron, 7/001

Sheadle (J. H.) Trust, Cleveland, 7/001

Shelby County Cancer & Health Fdn., Sidney, 7/003

Sherman Church Cemetery Trust, Canton, 7/003

Sherwin (H. A.) Fund, Cleveland, 7/003

Shinnick (William M.) Trust, Zanesville, 7/004

Shull (Robert C. & Alma Lee) Fdn., Westlake, 7/005

Shulman (Bernard & Theresa) Fdn., Cleveland, 7/005

Siller (Ernest Jacob) - Geminde Haus Fund, Cleveland, 7/006

Skeel (Annie P.) Trust, Cleveland, 7/007

Skilken (Joseph & Helen) Fdn., Columbus, 7/007

Skirball Fdn., Cleveland, 7/009

Slach (Peter J.) Trust, Cleveland, 7/010

Slepm (C. Bascom) Trust, Cincinnati, 7/011

Smith (Alida Attwell) Trust, Wooster, 7/013

Smith (Robert Munro) Fdn., Akron, 7/014

Smucker (Willard E.) Fdn., Orrville, 7/014

Smythe (Alan W.) Trust - Mausoleum Fund, Cleveland, 7/015

Society Fdn., Cleveland, 7/016

Solrob Fdn., Cleveland, 7/017

Spaeth (Phil D.) Fdn., Cincinnati, 7/017

Spero Fdn., Cleveland, 7/018

Spero (B. E. & Gertrude) Fdn., Cleveland Heights, 7/018

Spero - Mendelsohn Charitable Fdn., Youngstown, 7/019

Spieker Charitable Fdn., Toledo, 7/020

Sprankle (John G.) Memorial Fund Trust, Canton, 7/020

Springdale Women's Club, Cincinnati, 7/020

Spring Hill Fdn. Trust, Akron, 7/021

Stanita Fdn., Lima, 7/021

Squire (Andrew) Trust, Cleveland, 7/023

Stambaugh (John & Rhea W.) Fdn., Mansfield, 7/024

Stark (John) Family Fdn., Cincinnati, 7/024

Standard Products Fdn., Cleveland, 7/026

Semple (Louise Taft) Fdn., Cincinnati, 7/027

Taft (Hubert), Jr. Memorial Scholarship Fdn., Cincinnati, 7/028

Swasey (Eben) Memorial Endowment Fund, Cleveland, 7/029

Taft (Elizabeth Sutphin) Charitable Trust, Cincinnati, 7/029

Swasey (Ambrose) Trusts, Cleveland, 7/030

Swanbeck (Ethel G.) Education Fund, Sandusky, 7/033

Stark, Carroll, Tuscarawas County Academy of General Practice, Canton, 7/033

Starling (Kenyon) Fdn., Dayton, 7/033

Starn Fdn., Northfield, 7/034

Stearns & Foster Fdn., Cincinnati, 7/035

Steel Foundry Research Fdn., Rocky River, 7/035

Steiner Fdn., Cincinnati, 7/036

Stern (Joseph & Ruth E.) Fdn., Steubenville, 7/037

Stern (Robert D.) Fund, Cincinnati, 7/037

Steudel (Frieda M. & Arthur W.) Fdn., Parma, 7/039

Steubenville Electrical Welfare Fund, Steubenville, 7/040
Stone (Ella A.) Trusts, Cleveland, 7/040
Stone (Harry H.) Fdn., Cleveland, 7/042
Stock (Fred F.) Trust, Marietta, 7/042
Stouffer Foods Corporation Fund, Cleveland, 7/043
Stranahan Fdn., Toledo, 7/044
Strangward (Mary) Trust, Cleveland, 7/046
Stuck (Violet E.) Trust, Akron, 7/046
Schloss (Ann L. & Stuart A.) Fdn., Cincinnati, 7/047
Sula Aca Fund, Cincinnati, 7/047
Summit County Medical Society Educational & Charitable Trust Fund, Akron, 7/047
Summit County Society for Crippled Children & Adults, Akron, 7/048
Taplin Fund, Cleveland, 7/048
Taunt - Tuttle Scholarship Fund, Toledo, 7/049
Thomas (Joseph C.) Trusts, Cleveland, 7/050
Thomas (Layte H.) Trust, Cleveland, 7/051
Thomas (William H.) Fdn. of Delta Theta Phi, Cleveland, 7/052
Thornberry (S. Starr) Trust, Toledo, 7/052
Timken Roller Bearing Co. Charitable Trust, Canton, 7/052
Toledo Automobile Dealers Association, Toledo, 7/053
Toledo Soldiers Memorial Association, Toledo, 7/053
Toledo Repertoire Theatre Fdn., Toledo, 7/054
Tomcinoh Fdn., Hamilton, 7/054
Treuhaft (Elizabeth M. & William C.) Fdn., Cleveland, 7/055
Turner (Burton Benns) Trust, Cleveland, 7/055
Tyler (Washington S. & Marion C.) Memorial Fund, Cleveland, 7/056
Alberty (E. G.) Trust, Columbus, 7/057
Babcock (Fannie M.) Trust, Akron, 7/058
Barber (Alfred M.) Trust, Akron, 7/059
Baughman (Frank C.) Trust, Akron, 7/059
Frick (Laura B.) Trust, Wooster, 7/060
Gibbs (Eleanor B.) Trust, Akron, 7/060
Hansen (Hermine Z.) Trust, Akron, 7/061
Marx (Robert S.) Trust, Cincinnati, 7/062
Moffitt (Lucian Q.) Trust, Akron, 7/063
Myers (Herman E.) Trusts, Akron, 7/064
Myers (Mary H.) Trust, Wooster, 7/066
Noble (Ormond C.) Endowment, Akron, 7/067
Overholt (Maria O.) Trust, Wooster, 7/067
Palmer (Edith H.) Trust, Akron, 7/068
Ranney (Mary S.) Trust, Cleveland, 7/068
Taft (Rosalyn) Gift Trust, Cincinnati, 7/069
Reed (Frank C.) Trust, Akron, 7/070
Rittenhouse (Curtis W.) Memorial Trust, Wooster, 7/070
Ruckel (Delia B.) Trust, Akron, 7/071
Schell (C. E.) Fdn. for Education, Cincinnati, 7/072
Schneider (Philip H.) Welfare Fdn. Trust, Akron, 7/072
Swetland (Mary Ann) Trust, Cleveland, 7/073
Warner (Augustus) Trust, Akron, 7/073
Tuneberg (Robert F. & Mary) Fdn., Westlake, 7/074
Tyne Fdn., Cincinnati, 7/075
Ukrainian Museum-Archive, Cleveland, 7/075
Unitcast Fdn., Cleveland, 7/076
University School Father & Son Trust, Cleveland, 7/076
Valentine (Lucretia J.) Trust, Cleveland, 7/077
Van Wert County Fdn., Van Wert, 7/078
Vedensky Family Fdn., Cleveland, 7/080
Stouffer (Vernon) Fdn., Cleveland, 7/080
Visintine - McCabe - Igoe Trust, Columbus, 7/081
Wade (Ellen Garretson) Memorial Fund, Cleveland, 7/081
Wagnalls Memorial, Lithopolis, 7/083
Baldwin (J.) - Baldwin Wallace College, H.T. Baldwin Fund, Cleveland, 7/085
Ward (William E.) Trust, Cleveland, 7/085
Warner (Cornelia B.) Library & Equipment Fund, Cleveland, 7/086
Warner (Marvin L.) Fdn., Cincinnati, 7/087

Warner (Worcester R. & Cornelia B.) Library & Endowment Fund, Cleveland, 7/087
Warner (Worcester R.) Trust, Cleveland, 7/088
Warner & Swasey Fdn., Cleveland, 7/089
Warren - Trumbull County Soap Box Derby, Warren, 7/090
Weatherhead (Albert J.) Trust, Cleveland, 7/091
Webb (Scott A.) Trust, Columbus, 7/092
Weber (Gustav C. E.) Memorial Fund, Cleveland, 7/092
Webster (Eleanor) Fdn., Canton, 7/093
Western Reserve Association Trusts, Cleveland, 7/093
Western Reserve Herb Society, Hudson, 7/095
Whitehaven Park Association, Cleveland, 7/096
Wiggs (Mr.) Store Fdn., Cleveland, 7/096
Wilford (John) Trust, Cleveland, 7/097
Williams College Cincinnati Scholarship Fund, Cincinnati, 7/097
Williams County Charitable Trust, Bryan, 7/098
Williams (Louise M.) Trust, Cleveland, 7/098
Williams (T. Henry) Trust, Akron, 7/099
Willoughby Memorial Company, Cleveland, 7/100
Willson (Alfred L.) Children's Center, Columbus, 7/100
Wings Over Africa Formerly in Indiana, Troy, 7/101
Winters Employee Charitable Fund, Canton, 7/101
Wise (Samuel D. & May W.) Fdn., Cleveland, 7/102
Wolcott (Joseph L.) Scholarship Fund, Toledo, 7/103
Wolf (Florence B. & James B.) Fdn., Cleveland, 7/103
Woltz (Darl L.) Charitable Fdn., Columbus, 7/104
Women of Moose #101, Cincinnati, 7/104
Women's Christian Association, Troy, 7/104
Women's Philanthropic Union, Cleveland, 7/105
Woodward Engineering Society Alumni Association Scholarship Fdn., Toledo, 7/105
Woolpert (Lyall) Fdn., Dayton, 7/105
Worrallo (Francelia M.) Trust, Cleveland, 7/106
West Park Congregational Church Endowment Fund, Cleveland, 7/107
Western Reserve Historical Society - Palmer Fund, Cleveland, 7/107
Yoder (Harvey O.) Fdn., Cleveland, 7/108
Youngstown Fdn., Youngstown, 7/108
Zenith Fdn., Toledo, 7/113
Zimmerman (J. Milton & Doris F.) Fdn., Dayton, 7/113
Zychick (Julius & Sarah) Charitable Fdn., Beachwood, 7/114
6320 Fdn. Formerly Smith (Frederick C.) Fdn., Dayton, 7/114

OKLAHOMA

First Filming

Aaronson (Alfred and Millicent) Fund, Tulsa, 1/001
Adams (K. S.) Foundation, Bartlesville, 1/002
Alexander Memorial Fund, Tulsa, 1/002
Allison Foundation, Tulsa, 1/003
American Medical Fdn., Oklahoma City, 1/003
Anderson Fdn., Oklahoma City, 1/004
Bailey (H. E.) Fdn., Oklahoma City, 1/004
Bartlett (Edward E. & Helen Turner) Fdn., Sapulpa, 1/004
Bartlett (Hu & Eva Maud) Fdn., Sapulpa, 1/005
Bass (John Harvey) Nursing Scholarship Fund, Norman, 1/006

Beatty (Cordelia Lunceford) Trust, Blackwell, 1/006
Benson Foundation, Pawhuska, 1/007
Birnses (Grace & Franklin) Fdn., Tulsa, 1/007
Blackwood (C. I.) Memorial Fund, Edmond, 1/008
Blair Fdn., Tulsa, 1/008
Bolen Fdn., Oklahoma City, 1/009
Boudreau Fdn., Tulsa, 1/009
Bovaird (The Mervin) Fdn., Tulsa, 1/010
Boys & Girls 4 H Club Murray Co. Oklahoma Trust, Oklahoma City, 1/011
Brennan (G. L.) Fdn., Inc., Tulsa, 1/011
Briles Educational Foundation Fund, Ada, 1/012
Broken Arrow Fdn., Broken Arrow, 1/013
Buck (The J. Frank) Fdn., Shawnee, 1/013
Campbell (Max & Tookah) Fdn., Inc., Tulsa, 1/013
Cherokee Fdn., Bartlesville, 1/014
Collins (George Fulton, Jr.) Fdn., Sapulpa, 1/016
Collins (The George & Jennie) Fdn., Sapulpa, 1/017
Cook (Hahn) Fdn., Oklahoma City, 1/018
Daniel (The William T.) Fdn., Oklahoma City, 1/018
DeMolay Youth Scholarship Fund, Bartlesville, 1/018
Detrick (O. K.) Fdn., Tulsa, 1/019
Dickinson Fdn. of Ardmore, Ardmore, 1/020
Dillingham Fdn., Enid, 1/020
Drumwright Memorial Hospital Fdn., Drumwright, 1/021
Dusek (Raymond J.) Fdn., Oklahoma City, 1/022
Egan Fdn., Muskogee, 1/022
Elliot Charitable Fdn., Oklahoma City, 1/023
Endacott Fdn., Bartlesville, 1/024
Everett (Mark Allen) Fdn., Oklahoma City, 1/025
Faglin (George & Maxine) Charitable Fdn., Oklahoma City, 1/025
Feldman (Nancy G.) and Raymond G. Feldman Fdn., Tulsa, 1/026
Felt (The Howard E.) Fdn., Tulsa, 1/026
Fife Fdn., Oklahoma City, 1/026
First National Fdn., Oklahoma City, 1/027
Flint (Charles W. & Pauline) Fdn., Tulsa, 1/027
Food for India Fund, Oklahoma City, 1/028
Frontier Fdn., Oklahoma City, 1/029
Gallery Fdn., Bartlesville, 1/029
Gimp Fdn., Tulsa, 1/029
Goldstein (August & Barbara) Fdn., Tulsa, 1/030
Goldstein (Harry A.) Fdn., Tulsa, 1/031
Griffin Fdn., Muskogee, 1/031
Gussman (Herbert & Roseline) Fdn., Tulsa, 1/032
Hackney Fdn., Enid, 1/032
Harris Fdn., Oklahoma City, 1/033
Harrison (Thos. J.) and Beal Harrison Trust, Pryor, 1/033
Haven House Fdn., Tulsa, 1/034
Hudson (The John T.) Fdn., Pawhuska, 1/035
Hunzicker Charitable Fdn., Oklahoma City, 1/036
Hyde Fdn., Oklahoma City, 1/036
Johnston (The P.X.) Fdn., Oklahoma City, 1/037
Kane (Robert) Hi-Y Memorial Trust, Bartlesville, 1/037
Kane (Robert) High School Scholarship Memorial Trust, Bartlesville, 1/037
Kirkpatruck Fdn., Oklahoma City, 1/037
Kirkpatrick (Hesper) Testamentary Trust, Tulsa, 1/039
Kravis (Raymond F. & Bessie R.) Fdn., Tulsa, 1/040
LaFortune (The J.A.) Fdn., Tulsa, 1/041
LaFortune Park Development Fund Trust Corrine Chil, Tulsa, 1/041
Learned (The Mary & Stanley) Fdn., Bartlesville, 1/042
Lewis Foundation, Tulsa, 1/042

Livingston (Julius & Gertrude) Fdn., Tulsa, 1/043

L & L Fdn., Enid, 1/043

Macklanburg (Robert A. Jr.) Fdn., Oklahoma, 1/044

McBride (Earl D.) Fdn., Oklahoma City, 1/045

McAlester Clinic Fdn., McAlester, 1/045

McCasland Fdn., Duncan, 1/045

McCollum-Scott Fdn., Oklahoma City, 1/046

Merrick Fdn., Ardmore, 1/046

Merritt Fdn., Enid, 1/048

Miller (Charles & Fannie) Trust, Tulsa, 1/048

Milligan (James H.) Fdn., Oklahoma City, 1/048

Munds (Louise B.) Trust, Oklahoma City, 1/049

M & J T Fdn., Norman, 1/049

Morris Fdn., Oklahoma City, 1/049

Nadel (I.) & Sophia Nadel Fdn., Tulsa, 1/050

National Society of Colonial Dames of America in the State of Oklahoma, Tulsa, 1/050

Neustadt Charitable Fdn., Ardmore, 1/051

Noble (The Vivian Bilby) Fdn., Ardmore, 1/051

Oklahoma County Medical Society Community Fdn., Oklahoma City, 1/052

Oklahoma Cowbelles, Oklahoma City, 1/052

Oklahoma Gas & Electric Co, Fdn., Oklahoma City, 1/052

Otasco Fdn., Tulsa, 1/054

Oxley Fdn., Tulsa, 1/054

Pan American Petroleum Fdn. (name changed to Amoco Production Foundation, effective February 1, 1971), Tulsa, 1/055

Pawnee & Noble Counties Community Action Fdn., Inc., Pawnee, 1/056

Pennington (The Steve) Fdn., Oklahoma City, 1/057

Peters (Harold) Scholarship Fund, Oklahoma City, 1/057

Phillips (The Frank) Fdn., Bartlesville, 1/057

Phillips (Frank) YMCA Trust, Bartlesville, 1/059

Pioneer Fdn., Oklahoma City, 1/059

Porter Watchorn Fdn., Inc., Shawnee, 1/061

Price Fdn., Inc., Bartlesville, 1/061

Puterbaugh Fdn., McAlester, 1/062

Quapaw (Benjamin), Miami, 1/063

Rapp (Robert Glenn) Fdn., Oklahoma City, 1/064

Edwards (R. J.) Rural Medicine Trust, Oklahoma City, 1/065

Sanditen (Ely) Fdn., Tulsa, 1/066

Sanditen (The Ira E.) Fdn., Tulsa, 1/066

Schwab Fdn., Enid, 1/067

Schweitzer Fdn., Oklahoma City, 1/068

Schroggs (Arthur E.) Scholarship Fdn., Stillwater, 1/068

Scroggs (Arthur E.) YMCA & Less Privileged Child, Stillwater, 1/068

Skelly Oil Co. Fdn., Tulsa, 1/069

Snyder (C. Don) Fdn., Oklahoma City, 1/069

Soday Research Fdn., Tulsa, 1/070

Springfield (The Mabel W.) Trust, Sayre, 1/070

Stambaugh Fdn., Tulsa, 1/071

Taubman (Herman P. & Sophia) Fdn., Tulsa, 1/071

T G & Y Fdn., Oklahoma City, 1/072

Tietze (Irving B.) Memorial Scholarship Trust of Bartles, Bartlesville, 1/073

Titus (C. W.) Fdn., Tulsa, 1/074

Tri-County Tech Endowment Fund, Bartlesville, 1/074

Tuepker Fdn., Tulsa, 1/075

Tulsa Boys Home Endowment Fund, Tulsa, 1/075

Tulsa Royalties Co., Tulsa, 1/076

United Fund of Shawnee, Shawnee, 1/077

University Scholarship Fdn., Oklahoma City, 1/077

Vinson Fdn., Tulsa, 1/077

Warr Fdn., Oklahoma City, 1/078

Warren (The William K.) Fdn., Tulsa, 1/079

Wave Fdn., Oklahoma City, 1/081

Wegener (The Herman & Mary) Fdn., Oklahoma City, 1/082

Wetzel (Louise) Fdn., Ponca City, 1/082

Wheeler Fdn., Tulsa, 1/082

Young (R. A.) Fdn., Oklahoma City, 1/083

Young (Stanton L.) Fdn., Oklahoma City, 1/084

Young Women's Christian Association Trust, Bartlesville, 1/085

Youngblood (Laurence S.) Fdn., Oklahoma City, 1/085

Second Filming

American Legion Post 0308, Tulsa, 2/001

Bass (John Harvey) Nursing Scholarship Fund, Norman, 2/001

Benham (David Blair) Fdn., Oklahoma City, 2/003

Bolger (E. C.) Trust B, Tulsa, 2/004

Broadhurst Fdn., Tulsa, 2/005

Bryan Fdn., Tulsa, 2/006

Charities Inc., Oklahoma City, 2/007

Chozen (Linda & Harvey) Fdn., Tulsa, 2/007

Classen Awards Fdn., Oklahoma City, 2/008

Cocking (Walter D.) Loan Fund, Stillwater, 2/008

Coleman Fdn., Wister, 2/008

Community Hospital Fdn., Elk City, 2/009

Cuesta Fdn., Tulsa, 2/009

Dale (E. E.) Library Fdn., Guymon, 2/009

Daniel (William T.) Fdn., Oklahoma City, 2/010

Daube Fdn., Ardmore, 2/010

Detrick (O.K.) Fdn., Tulsa, 2/012

Dulaney Fdn., Oklahoma City, 2/012

Fields (Laura) Trust, Lawton, 2/013

Gaylord Philanthropies, Oklahoma City, 2/013

Geary Cemetery Trust, Geary, 2/015

Goddard Youth Fdn., Ardmore, 2/015

Goddard (The C.B.) Art Center Trust, Ardmore, 2/016

Hall Fdn., Norman, 2/018

Harmon (Pearl M. & Julia J.) Fdn.-Trust, Nowata, 2/020

Helt (Vernon L.) Fdn., Edmond, 2/024

Holy Family Fdn., Tulsa, 2/024

James (Guy H.) Fdn., Oklahoma City, 2/025

Johnson (Jimmy) Fdn., Oklahoma City, 2/026

Johnston (Williard) Fdn. Inc., Oklahoma City, 2/026

Kaiser (Herman & Kate) Fdn., Tulsa, 2/027

Kantot Fdn., Tulsa, 2/027

Kernke (Joe C. & Blanche J.) Fdn., Oklahoma City, 2/028

Kerr-McGee Fdn., Oklahoma City, 2/028

Leflore (Louie) Scholarship Fund, Muskogee, 2/029

Loy Foundation, Pawhuska, 2/029

Macklanburg-Duncan Fdn., Oklahoma City, 2/029

Macklanburg-Hulsey Fdn., Oklahoma City, 2/030

Maxwell Fdn., Oklahoma City, 2/031

McGee Fdn., Oklahoma City, 2/031

McMahon Fdn., Lawton, 2/032

Miller (The Meyer C.) Fdn., Tulsa, 2/034

Miller Meyers Rothbaum Fdn., Tulsa, 2/035

Moorer (W.D. & G.B.) Fund, Tulsa, 2/035

Myers (The Gertrude Jo) and Louis P. Meyers Foundation, Tulsa, 2/036

Naifeh Fdn., Oklahoma City, 2/037

Nichlos Fdn., Chickasha, 2/037

Norris Fdn., Ada, 2/037

Oklahoma Allergy Clinic Fdn., Oklahoma City, 2/038

Oklahoma City Charted Life Underwriter Education, Oklahoma City, 2/039

Oklahoma Methodist Home - 862, Oklahoma City, 2/039

Oklahoma Methodist Home for the Aged, Inc. - 861, Oklahoma City, 2/040

Oklahoma Psychiatric Fdn., Spencer, 2/040

Osborne (Beverly and Rubye) Fdn., Oklahoma City, 2/041

Oven Fund, Enid, 2/042

Page (Charles) High School Scholarship Fdn., Tulsa, 2/042

Parman (Robert A.) Fdn. Rose Elizabeth Parman, Oklahoma City, 2/043

Pariott (F. B.) Educational Fund, Tulsa, 2/046

Pariott (F. B.) Trust, Tulsa, 2/046

Peters (Harold) Scholarship Fund, Oklahoma City, 2/047

Philson Fdn., Bartlesville, 2/047

Phi Beta Phi Scholarship Fdn., Oklahoma City, 2/047

Robberson (The R. W.) Fdn., Oklahoma City, 2/048

Robinowitz Fdn., Tulsa, 2/049

Robinowitz (Sol) Fdn., Tulsa, 2/050

Sand Springs Home, Sand Springs, 2/050

Scholarship Fund of Tulsa County Medical Society, Tulsa, 2/056

School of the Ozarks-860, Oklahoma City, 2/057

Share (Charles Morton) Trust No. 461, Oklahoma City, 2/057

Shepard Fdn., Oklahoma City, 2/058

Singer (Morris & Libby) Fdn., Oklahoma City, 2/059

Skelly (Gertrude) Trust - 1, Tulsa, 2/060

Snedaker (Bertha E.) Charitable Trust, Spavinaw, 2/061

Stuart Fdn., Tulsa, 2/061

Tissue Culture Association, Ardmore, 2/061

Tulsa Boys Home Educational Fund Trust, Tulsa, 2/063

Tyler (D. M.) Fdn., Dewey, 2/063

Weitzenhoffer (Aaron M.) Fdn., Oklahoma City, 2/064

Willard (Frances E.) Home, Oklahoma City, 2/065

Williams (Ira) Fdn., Oklahoma City, 2/065

Woods- Star Fdn., Oklahoma City, 2/066

Young Encore Fdn., Oklahoma City, 2/067

Ungerman (Arnold H. & Bess Zeldich) Charitable Trust, Tulsa, 2/067

Zink (John) Fdn., Tulsa, 2/068

OREGON

First Filming

Adams Fdn., Portland, 1/001

Alaska-Yukon Society of Oregon, Portland, 1/001

Page (Albina) Fund, Salem, 1/002

Aldrich (Donna W.) Trust No. 291, Salem, 1/002

Allied Christian Fdns., Portland, 1/003

Annual Community Scholarship Fund, Portland, 1/003

Archdiocese of Portland in Oregon, Portland, 1/004

Aronson (Fred G.) Dec'd fbo American Cancer Society, Portland, 1/005

Autzen Fdn., Portland, 1/005

Beane (Walter H. and Beatrice M.) Trust, Portland, 1/006

Beam Family Fdn., Portland, 1/007

Binford (Peter) Fdn., Portland, 1/007

Boone Fund, Portland, 1/008

Bounds (Roger J.) Fdn., Hermiston, 1/009

Brady (Robert) Trust, Portland, 1/010

Broadmead Farms Fdn., Portland, 1/011

Brown (E. C.) Trust #4 1200, Portland, 1/012

Bueerman-John B. Champion Memorial Lecture Fund, Rev. Frederick, Portland, 1/013

Bueerman (Winifred H.) Religious Fdn. Trust Fund, Portland, 1/013

Cammack (Archie C. and Gertrude C.) Medical Research Fund, Portland, 1/014

Campbell (W. C.) Charitable Trust, Portland, 1/014

Caufield (Robert & Jane) Fund for Elderly People of Clackamas County, Portland, 1/015

McClintock (L. A.) Memorial Fdn., Salem, 2/025
McCready (W. J.) Sons Fdn., Forest Grove, 2/025
McDaniel (Delilah H.) Trust, Portland, 2/026
Metals Research Fdn., Portland, 2/026
Meyer Fdn., Portland, 2/027
Michel Fdn., Portland, 2/028
Mikkelson Fdn., Albany, 2/029
Moore (Ralph Vernon), Deceased, Portland, 2/031
Nydia Temple No. 4 Daughters of the Nile, Portland, 2/032
Oregon Shakespearean Festival Endowment Fund, Ashland, 2/032
Pike (Albert) Memorial Fund, Portland, 2/032
Plummer (O. M.) Scholarship Fund, Portland, 2/032
Polly Fdn., Salem, 2/033
Portland Foursquare Education Loan Fund, Portland, 2/033
Richardson (Charles P.) Deceased, Portland, 2/034
Roberts (Annie) Fdn., Portland, 2/034
Roberts (Henry) Fdn., Portland, 2/034
Rogers (Clyde O.), Deceased, Portland, 2/035
Salzer (Joe) Kappa Sigma Memorial Fund, The, Eugene, 2/036
Schnitzer Fdn., Portland, 2/037
Schultz (Ida), Deceased--Trust of, Portland, 2/037
Southworth (Mabel) Scholarship Fund, Portland, 2/038
Stevens (Mertie and Harley) Memorial Fund, Portland, 2/038
Tennant (John J.) Fdn., Portland, 2/040
Thompson (C. H.) Fund for Girls U. S. National Bank of, Portland, 2/041
Tualatin Hills Park Fdn., Beaverton, 2/042
Vierani (Louis A.), Deceased--Vierani Family Fund, Portland, 2/042
Wade (R. M.) Fdn., Portland, 2/043
Wadsworth (Walter W.) Trust, Portland, 2/043
Walton (William S.) Charitable Trust, Portland, 2/043
Wardin Fdn., Portland, 2/044
Wilcox (A. D.) Trust, Salem, 2/045
Willamette Trust, Salem, 2/045
Wise (Dr. S. H.) Fellowship Fund in Internal Medicine, Portland, 2/046
Women of Rotary Fdn., Portland, 2/046
Woodward (W. A.) Fdn., Cottage Grove, 2/047

PENNSYLVANIA

First Filming

Abes (Michael Gary) Memorial Scholarship Loan Fund, Pittsburgh, 1/001
A & B Fdn., Allentown, 1/001
Abraham (Fredericks) Fdn., Philadelphia, 1/002
Abrams (Curry & Rudolf) Charitable Trust, Boyertown, 1/003
Abrams (Samuel L.) Fdn., Harrisburg, 1/004
Adams (Mabel A.) Charitable Trust, Kutztown, 1/005
Adams Fdn., Bethlehem, 1/005
Adco Fdn., Philadelphia, 1/006
Adler (Jack & Jean) Fdn., Philadelphia, 1/007
Aequanimitas Fdn., Reading, 1/008
Alcoa Fdn., Pittsburgh, 1/008
Alexander (H.B.) Fdn., Harrisburg, 1/013
Allegheny Fdn., Pittsburgh, 1/013
Alnwick Fdn., Bryn Athyn, 1/017
Althouse Fdn., Reading, 1/017
Altoona Fdn., Altoona, 1/017
Alwine (Harry K.) Residuary Trust, Hershey, 1/019
American Anti Vivisection Society Trust, Philadelphia, 1/020

American Bank & Trust Company of Pennsylvania Fdn., Reading, 1/021
American Humane Association Trust, Philadelphia, 1/022
American Legion Home Association Trevorton Post -92, Trevorton, 1/023
American Research Fdn., Gladwynne, 1/023
Founders Memorial Fund of American Sterilizer Company, Erie, 1/023
American War Mothers, Upper Darby, 1/025
Amity, Inc., Philadelphia, 1/025
Anathan (Bessie F.) Fdn., Pittsburgh, 1/026
Anderson (Mary) Trust, Philadelphia, 1/026
Apple (Benjamin & Lillie E.) Fdn., Sunbury, 1/028
Apple (John A.) Fdn., Sunbury, 1/029
Applegarth Fdn., Plymouth Meeting, 1/030
Arbee Fdn., Manheim, 1/030
Ardbridge Fdn., Philadelphia, 1/031
Arentzen Charitable Fund, Pittsburgh, 1/032
Armistead (W.M.) Fdn., Philadelphia, 1/033
Armon Fdn., Cornwells Heights, 1/034
Arnold Fdn., Red Lion, 1/036
Aronson (Jacob H.) Annual Award, Pittsburgh, 1/036
Aronson Grave Maintenance Fund, Pittsburgh, 1/036
Atlantic Richfield Employees' Emergency Fund, Philadelphia, 1/038
Atlantic Richfield Fdn., Philadelphia, 1/041
Auner (Michael Bill) Memorial Fdn., Pittsburgh, 1/041
Aylesboro, Pittsburgh, 1/042
Babcock Charitable Trust, Pittsburgh, 1/043
Bache (William) Memorial Fund, Wellsboro, 1/044
Bailey (Helen L.) Fdn., Pittsburgh, 1/044
Ball (Joseph A.) Fdn., Philadelphia, 1/045
Baird (Edith L.W.) T/D, Philadelphia, 1/046
Barakat (Lavyah A.) Home for Orphan Girls, Inc., Philadelphia, 1/047
Barber (Mgt. M.) TD Jones (H.M.) End Fdn., Philadelphia, 1/047
Barber (Mgt. M.) TD Parsels (Addie) Memorial Fdn., Philadelphia, 1/047
Barbieri (Andrea Mills) Fdn., Philadelphia, 1/048
Bard College Class of 1950, Pittsburgh, 1/048
Barg (Alvin & Elaine) Fdn., Philadelphia, 1/049
Barg (Bernard & Helen) Fdn., Philadelphia, 1/050
Barg (Herbert & Marilyn) Fdn., Philadelphia, 1/050
Barkay Fdn., Reading, 1/051
Barnwell (Mary) Fdn., Philadelphia, 1/051
Barra Fdn., Philadelphia, 1/051
Bartschi Fdn., Malvern, 1/053
Bass (Samuel) Fdn., Reading, 1/055
Bast Family Fdn., Philadelphia, 1/056
Batchelar (Eugene C.) Memorial Fund, Pittsburgh, 1/057
Baxter (Harold) Fdn., Wynnewood, 1/058
B.C. Fdn., Philadelphia, 1/058
Beau Family Fund, Elkins Park, 1/059
Bear Run Fdn., Pittsburgh, 1/060
Bechtel (Richard C.) Fdn., Philadelphia, 1/060
Bechtel (R.M.) Trust, Reading, 1/061
Beck (Frances) Memorial Fund, Sayre, 1/061
Beck (John A.) Memorial Church Fund, Pittsburgh, 1/062
Beck (John A.) Memorial Scholarship Fund, Pittsburgh, 1/062
Becker (Cindy) Stambaugh Fund, York, 1/063
Bell (Herbert C.), Philadelphia, 1/063
Bell (Frank & Mary) Charitable Trust, Pittsburgh, 1/064
Bellows (Adelaide Cole) Scholarship Fund, West Chester, 1/064
Benedum (Claude Worthington) Fdn., Pittsburgh, 1/065
Benevolent Investments, Inc., Pittsburgh, 1/069
Benner (Carl O.) Memorial Fund, Coatesville, 1/069
Beresin (Jacob) Fdn., Pittsburgh, 1/069

Beresin (Jay G. & Minnie) Fdn., Philadelphia, 1/070
Bergson (Betty)-Kook Memorial Fdn., Philadelphia, 1/071
Bergstrom Fdn., Pittsburgh, 1/071
Berks Products Fdn., Reading, 1/072
Berman (Bernard & Audrey) Fdn., Allentown, 1/072
Berman (Philip & Muriel) Fdn., Allentown, 1/073
Biddle (James G.) Company Fdn., Plymouth Meeting, 1/073
Billirene Fund, Philadelphia, 1/074
Binder Scholarship Fund, Philadelphia, 1/074
Binswanger (Frank G.) Fdn., Philadelphia, 1/076
Birdsboro Fdn., Birdsboro, 1/078
Bishop (Vernon & Doris) Fdn., Lebanon, 1/078
Bisiker Charitable Trust, Butler, 1/079
Bitner (H.M.) Charitable Trust, Pittsburgh, 1/079
Black (Arthur O.) Fdn., Butler, 1/080
Black (Max & Bella) Fdn., Philadelphia, 1/081
Blaisdell (Philo & Sarah) Fdn., Bradford, 1/081
Blank (Ruth & Samuel A.) Fdn., Philadelphia, 1/083
Blasbank (Alfred) Fdn., Philadelphia, 1/084
Blessing (John A.) Fdn., Harrisburg, 1/084
Bloom (Frederick S.) Charitable Trust, Pittsburgh, 1/085
Blough (Roger & Helen) Fdn., Hawley, 1/086
Bluestone-Netzer Fdn., Pittsburgh, 1/088
Boehm Inter-Cultural Education Fdn., Morrisville, 1/088
Bolich (Mary Margaret) Fdn., Allentown, 1/088
Bollman (George W.) Memorial Fund, Allentown, 1/089
Bonner (Monsignor John J.) Fdn., Philadelphia, 1/090
Booth Fdn., Philadelphia, 1/090
Bornstein Fdn., Philadelphia, 1/090
Borowsky Fdn., Philadelphia, 1/091
Boyer Fdn., Boyertown, 1/091
Boyer (John) First Troop Philadelphia City Cavalry Memorial Fund, Philadelphia, 1/092
Boy Scout Trust Fund, Towanda, 1/093
Boy Scouts of America Trust / under Agreement of Allegheny Council, Pittsburgh, 1/093
BPO Elks No. 970 Scholarship Fund, Levittown, 1/096
Brahm (W. Walter) for Westminster College, Pittsburgh, 1/096
Brait (Charles & Fan) Fdn., Bala Lynwyd, 1/096
Brand Fdn., McKeesport, 1/097
Brasley (Ben Paul) Fdn., Pittsburgh, 1/097
Breinig (Alfred O.) Fdn., Jenkintown, 1/098
Brenner Fdn., Harrisburg, 1/099
Brenner (Jeanette M. & Joseph F.) Fdn., Harrisburg, 1/100
Breyer Fdn., Philadelphia, 1/100
Bridges of Understanding Fdn., Penns Park, 1/101
Brindle Education Fdn., Waynesboro, 1/101
Brockway Glass Company Fdn., Brockway, 1/101
Brooks Fdn., Pittsburgh, 1/102
Brody (Israel I.) & Birdye Brodie Fdn., Indiana, 1/104
Broomall A.E. Decd Del Co Hist T/W, Philadelphia, 1/104
Brotherhood's Relief & Compensation Fund, Harrisburg, 1/104
Brown (John A.), Philadelphia, 1/105
Bruder (Michael A.) Fdn., Philadelphia, 1/106
Brundred (W.J.) Charitable Fund, Oil City, 1/107
Buck (Caroline Alexander) Fdn., Philadelphia, 1/109
Buckingham Mountain Fdn., Philadelphia, 1/109

Bucks County Historical Society, Doylestown, 1/110

Bulletin Contributionship, Philadelphia, 1/111

Burrel TWP Scholarship Fund-Brooks, Pittsburgh, 1/113

Burstin Albert Charities, Pittsburgh, 1/115

Butcher (W. W. Keen and Madeleine A.K.) Family Fdn., Philadelphia, 1/116

Butz (William & Alice) Memorial Fund, Allentown, 1/116

Caddie Welfare Fdn. of W.P.G.A., Pittsburgh, 1/118

Caesar (Mollie M. & Abraham D.) Fdn., Philadelphia, 1/118

Cairncrest Fdn., Bryn Athyn, 1/119

Calhoun (Ernest N. & Cynthia S.) Fdn., Pittsburgh, 1/120

Camp Fdn., Reading, 1/124

Campbell (John Russell) Memorial Fund, Oil City, 1/124

Caplan (Julius H.) Charity Fdn., Lebanon, 1/125

Capuzzi (Domenico) Perpetual Fdn. Trust, Philadelphia, 1/126

Carbeau (C.W.) Family Fdn., Zelienople, 1/127

Carnegie Hero Fund Commission, Pittsburgh, 1/127

Carlton (Kershow M.) Dec'd Church Soc. Trust, Philadelphia, 1/130

Carter (Charles Wentz) Memorial Fdn., Philadelphia, 1/031

Carthage Fdn., Pittsburgh, 1/133

Case Western Reserve University Plaisance, Pittsburgh, 1/134

Cassatt Fdn. T/U/D 11/21/69, Philadelphia, 1/135

Cassett (Louis N.) Fdn., Philadelphia, 1/135

Caster Family Fdn., Reading, 1/136

Catherwood Fdn., Bryn Mawr, 1/137

Catherwood (E.R.) Trust, Philadelphia, 1/139

CCNB Fdn., New Cumberland, 1/140

Centaur Fdn., Philadelphia, 1/141

Central Valley Fdn., Philadelphia, 1/141

CEPA Fdn., Philadelphia, 1/141

Certain-Teed Products/Corp. Fdn., Valley Forge, 1/142

Chalfant Fdn., Pittsburgh, 1/143

Charleroi Sportsmen Association, Charleroi, 1/143

Childs (Otis H.) Trust, Pittsburgh, 1/144

Central Pennsylvania Chapter of Chartered Life Underwriters, Williamsport, 1/145

Chilmark Fdn., Philadelphia, 1/145

Christian Schmidt Fdn., Philadelphia, 1/146

Citizen's National Bank of Blossburg, Pa., T.D., Philadelphia, 1/147

Clark (A.B.) Fdn., Hastings, 1/148

Clark (Charles H.) Fdn., Harrisburg, 1/149

Clark (James P.) Fdn., Philadelphia, 1/149

Claster Fdn., Williamsport, 1/150

Clasier (Joel) Fdn., Philadelphia, 1/151

Clearfield Area United Fund, Clearfield Borough, 1/153

Clonmel Fdn., Philadelphia, 1/153

Cochran (Fanny T.) Bryn Mawr College Trust, Philadelphia, 1/153

Cockran (Fanny T.) Pennsylvania Prison Society, Philadelphia, 1/154

Cockran (Robert Spencer) Trust, Philadelphia, 1/155

Cochrane (Andrew R.) & Dorothy L. Cochrane Fdn., Pittsburgh, 1/155

Cohen (Abram) Fdn., Erie, 1/156

Cohen (Abram) Fdn., Philadelphia, 1/156

Cohen (Harold H.) Fdn. Charitable Trust, Erie, 1/157

Cohen (Nathan) Fdn., Philadelphia, 1/157

Cohen (William J.) Upland M.E. Charitable Trust, Philadelphia, 1/158

Cohn (Lillian) Fdn., Cynwyd, 1/159

Colteryahn (Louise) Charities, Pittsburgh, 1/159

Columbia-Summerhill Fdn., Pittsburgh, 1/160

Concordia Fdn., Philadelphia, 1/160

Connelly Fdn., Philadelphia, 1/161

Contributors Charitable Fdn., Philadelphia, 1/162

Cook (Joseph & Lillian) Fdn., Monroeville, 1/163

Cooper (Nathaniel F.) & Roslyn Cooper Fdn., Philadelphia, 1/164

Cooper (Sidney A.) Fdn., Philadelphia, 1/164

Coplex Fdn., Philadelphia, 1/165

Corson Fdn., Plymouth Meeting, 1/165

Coslett Fdn., Swarthmore, 1/166

Cote Fdn., Greensburg, 1/168

Cox (George S.) Dec'd, T/W, Philadelphia, 1/169

Coxe (Sophia G.) Charitable Trust, Philadelphia, 1/170

Craig (Earle M. & Margaret Peters) Trust, Pittsburgh, 1/171

Crawford (E.R.) Estate Trust Fund, Duquesne, 1/172

Crawford (H.J.) for Elizabeth Crawford Memorial School, Oil City, 1/173

Crels Fdn., New Holland, 1/173

Cresson (Emlen) Trust, Philadelphia, 1/174

Crowther (Elizabeth) Dec'd T/W, Philadelphia, 1/175

Crozer Fdn., Philadelphia, 1/176

Crozer (Robert H.) Dec'd, Upland Poor T/W, Philadelphia, 1/176

Curley (Walter) Fdn., Pittsburgh, 1/177

Curran (Wm.) Dec'd Lafayette College Fund Trust, Philadelphia, 1/179

Curran (William) T/W, Philadelphia, 1/180

Currens (Robert M.) & Grace A. Currens Trust, Shippensburgh, 1/181

Curtis (Ford E.) & Harriet R. Curtis Fdn., Pittsburgh, 1/181

Dackerman (Savena & Harry C.) Fund, Philadelphia, 1/182

Dailey (Charles A.) Fdn., Erie, 1/183

Psaly Dairy Charitable Trust, Pittsburgh, 1/183

Dana Fdn., Buck Hill Falls, 1/184

Daniel (Zaccheus) Fdn., Pittsburgh, 1/185

Dauphin Deposit Trust Fdn., Harrisburg, 1/187

David (Arthur Vining) Fdn., Pittsburgh, 1/188

Daylor (Edward A.) Fdn., Coatesville, 1/191

D & C N Trust, Haverford, 1/192

Deal (Seraph J.) Dec'd Arch St. Pres. Charitable Trust, Philadelphia, 1/193

Degen (Renie) fbo Jewish Organized Charities Trust u/w, York, 1/194

Degn (Alice S.) Dec'd Hope Lodge Fdn., Philadelphia, 1/194

Delaware Terminal Fdn., Philadelphia, 1/196

Delfinger (Max & Eva) Fdn., Philadelphia, 1/196

Delta Delta Fdn., Drumore, 1/197

Demarest (Eben) Trust, Pittsburgh, 1/197

Dentist's Supply Co., Fdn., York, 1/198

Denton (Frank R.) Fdn., Pittsburgh, 1/198

De Porres (Martin) Fdn., Philadelphia, 1/199

Dickinson School of Law-Kline Account, Reading, 1/201

Dickson (Allan H. & Kate P.) Memorial Trust, Wilkes-Barre, 1/201

Dietrich Fdn., Incorporated, Philadelphia, 1/202

Dietrich (Daniel W.) Fdn., Philadelphia, 1/203

Dinardo (Daniel) Fdn., Pittsburgh, 1/204

Divinity School of P.E. Ch. in Philadelphia Trust, Philadelphia, 1/205

Dodge (Herbert C.), M.D. Charitable Trust, Bala Cynwyd, 1/206

Dolbear (Frank T.) Memorial Fund, Scranton, 1/206

Dolfinger-McMahon Fdn. T/D, Philadelphia, 1/207

Donahue (John F.) Fdn., Pittsburgh, 1/208

Douty (Alfred & Mary) Fdn., Lafayette Hill, 1/208

Downs Fdn., Willow Grove, 1/209

Dravo Corporation & Subsidiaries Charitable Trust, Pittsburgh, 1/210

Dunwoody Home, Philadelphia, 1/210

Eastwick (Joseph & Suzanne) Fdn., Philadelphia, 1/213

Eavenson (Ada J.) Charitable Trust, Pittsburgh, 1/213

Eberhard Fdn., Philadelphia, 1/214

Eberly Fdn., Uniontown, 1/214

Eden Fdn., Philadelphia, 1/215

Edgcomb Steel Company Fdn., Philadelphia, 1/215

Edgewater Steel Charitable Trust, Pittsburgh, 1/216

Educational Medical & Good Will Fund, New Bethlehem, 1/218

Edwin Fdn., Harrisburg, 1/219

Ehrlich (Jack) Fdn., Philadelphia, 1/219

Eichleay Fdn., Pittsburgh, 1/220

Elks Home Association of Shamokin, Shamokin, 1/221

Ellis (Abraham M. & Rose) Fdn., Philadelphia, 1/221

Ellis (Herman M. & Elinor G.) Fdn., Philadelphia, 1/222

Ellis (Rudolph) Gratuity Fund of the Foundation, Philadelphia, 1/222

Engelberg (Max) Family Fdn., Pittsburgh, 1/223

Kirby (Fred M. & Jessie A.) Episcopal House, Inc., Wilkes-Barre, 1/224

Erie Memorial, Erie, 1/224

Eshelman Welfare Fund, Lancaster, 1/225

Esperanti League for North America, Meadville, 1/225

Euler (Ralph S. & Bertha G.) Fdn., Pittsburgh, 1/225

Evans (Thomas Raymond) Fdn., Pittsburgh, 1/225

Everest Fdn., Marion Station, 1/227

E2K Fund, Philadelphia, 1/227

Faber (Eberhard L.) Fdn., Wilkes-Barre, 1/228

Fairbanks-Horix Charitable Trust, Pittsburgh, 1/228

Falk (Leon) Family Trust, Pittsburgh, 1/229

Fazio (A.J.) Memorial Fdn., Pittsburgh, 1/230

Fehr Fund, Bryn Mawr, 1/231

Feinstein (Myer & Rosaline) Fdn., Philadelphia, 1/232

Feith Family Fdn., Elkins Park, 1/232

Feldman (A. Harry) Fdn., Philadelphia, 1/234

Feldman (Miriam R. & Israel C.) Fdn., Philadelphia, 1/234

Feldman Fund, Philadelphia, 1/235

Feller Family, Harrisburg, 1/235

Ferree (Clifford B.) Memorial Fdn., Pittsburgh, 1/235

Ferst Fdn., Philadelphia, 1/236

Finkelstein (George & Mina) Charitable Trust, Allentown, 2/001

First National Bank Fdn., Wilkes-Barre, 2/001

First Pennsylvania Charitable Trust, Philadelphia, 2/001

Fischer Fdn., Philadelphia, 2/003

Fisher Charitable Trust, Pittsburgh, 2/003

Fisher (Wilbur E.) Trust, Pittsburgh, 2/005

Fishman (Morris & Rachel) Fdn., Philadelphia, 2/007

Fishon (Irving J.) Memorial Fdn., Philadelphia, 2/007

Fitch (William Henry) Memorial Fund, Pittsburgh, 2/008

Fitzpatrick (Ann) T/W, Philadelphia, 2/011

FJA Fdn., Philadelphia, 2/011

Flaherty Fdn., New Castle, 2/011

Fleekop (Isadore & Minnie) Fdn., Philadelphia, 2/012

Fleekop & Leff Charitable Fdn., Philadelphia, 2/012

Fleisher (Robert H. & Janet S.) Fdn., Philadelphia, 2/013

Fluhrer (William) fbo Children's Home, York, 2/014

Fluhrer (William) fbo Gospel Herald Society, York, 2/014

Fluhrer (William) fbo Grace & Hope Mission, York, 2/014

Fluhrer (William) fbo Salvation Army, York, 2/014

Fluhrer (Blanche S.) fbo S.P.C.A., York, 2/015

Hurwitz (Solomon & Martha) Charitable Fund, Harrisburg, 2/150

Ind Home Blind Women & Home Incur Trust, Philadelphia, 2/151

Indiana Kiwanis Club Fdn., Indiana, 2/152

International Textbook Company Employers Charities Fund, Scranton, 2/152

Irvin (Mary Ann) Scholarship Fdn., Indiana, 2/152

Irwin (Grace I.) Fund, Pittsburgh, 2/153

Italian Beneficial Society - S.A. Ma Victor, Donora, 2/153

Jackson (John E. & Sue M.) Charitable Trust, Pittsburgh, 2/154

Jackson (Ruth H.) Charitable Trust, Pittsburgh, 2/154

Jackson (William R. & Lucille) Charitable Trust, Pittsburgh, 2/155

Jacobs (Theresa & Stanley) Fdn., Philadelphia, 2/156

Jamison (Dorothy & David) Fdn., Philadelphia, 2/157

J.D.B. Fund, North Wales, 2/157

Jenks (John W.) Memorial Fdn., Punxsutawney, 2/158

Jennings (Mary Hillman) Fdn., Pittsburgh, 2/159

Jerome Fdn., Pittsburgh, 2/159

Jerrehian Fdn., Wynnewood, 2/160

J.M.F. Trust, Philadelphia, 2/161

John & Sara Fund, Meadowbrook, 2/162

Johnson (A.L.) Dec'd Bristol Free Library Grundy Fdn., Philadelphia, 2/163

Johnson (A.L.) Dec'd St. James Church Trust, Philadelphia, 2/164

Johnson (Grace Phillips) Fdn., Pittsburgh, 2/164

Johnson (Margaret J.) Dec'd, Philadelphia, 2/165

Johnson (Paul J.) Fdn., Philadelphia, 2/165

Johnson (Isabel Beck) Loan Fund, Pittsburgh, 2/166

Johnson (R.G.) Charitable Fdn., Pittsburgh, 2/166

Jones (Donald P.) Fdn., Media, 2/166

Jones (Edmund A.) Scholarship Fund, Swarthmore, 2/168

Jones (Wilbur K.) Fdn., Harrisburg, 2/169

Joseph (Bertha M. Noss) f/b/o Childrens Home, York, 2/169

Joseph (Bertha M. Noss) f/b/o Visiting Nurse Association Trust u/w, York, 2/170

Joseph (Bertha M. Noss) f/b/o York Benevolent Association Trust u/w, York, 2/170

Joseph (Bertha M. Noss) f/b/o York Hospital Trust u/w, York, 2/171

Kable (Edgar P.) Fdn., York, 2/171

Kadis (Abraham & Sarah) Fdn., Philadelphia, 2/171

Kahaner (Charles A.) Fdn., Philadelphia, 2/172

Kahl (J. Oscar) & Mary E.S. Kahl Fund, Philadelphia, 2/172

Kahn (David & Annie) Fdn., Orwigsburg, 2/172

Kaiserman (Kevy K. & Hortense M.) Fdn., Wynnewood, 2/174

Kamin (S. Irwin) Fdn., Inc., Pittsburgh, 2/175

Kamis (David) Fdn., Merion, 2/175

Kaplan (Morris & Anna) Fdn., Allentown, 2/176

Kardon (Samuel) Fdn., Philadelphia, 2/177

Karlshof Fund, Philadelphia, 2/177

Katz Fdn., Pittsburgh, 2/178

Katz (Lawrence & Selma) Fdn., Philadelphia, 2/180

Katzen (Paul & Belle H.) Charitable Trust, Pittsburgh, 2/181

Katzenberg Fdn., Jenkintown, 2/182

Kauffman (Virgil) Fdn., Yardley, 2/182

Kaufman (David E. & Morgan S.) Fdn., Philadelphia, 2/183

Kaufmann (Arthur C.) Fdn., Philadelphia, 2/184

Kaufmann (Edgar J.) Charitable Fdn., Pittsburgh, 2/184

Kaufmann (Oliver M.) Family Charitable Trust, Pittsburgh, 2/187

Kaul (Andrew) Fdn., Inc., St. Marys, 2/188

Kavanagh (T. James) Fdn., Philadelphia, 2/189

Kelley (Kate M.) Fdn., Pittsburgh, 2/189

Kelley (John B.) Fdn., Philadelphia, 2/190

Kelly Memorial Hospital Staff Room-McKeesport Hospital, Pittsburgh, 2/191

Kennedy (Dr. Russell G. & Blanche M.) Fdn., Butler, 2/192

Kenridge Fdn., Bethlehem, 2/192

Kewanee Oil Fdn., Bryn Mawr, 2/193

Keyworth (William A.) Fdn., York, 2/194

Keyworth (William A.) f/b/o St. Paul's Lutheran Church, York, 2/194

Kimberton Farms School Trust, Philadelphia, 2/194

King Fifth Wheel Fdn., Mountaintop, 2/195

King (Harry M.) f/b/o Children's Home, York, 2/195

King (Harry M.) f/b/o Visiting Nurse Association, York, 2/196

King (Harry M.) f/b/o York Benevolent Association, York, 2/196

Kipphen Field Fund, Doylestown, 2/197

Kirkwood Fdn., Bryn Mawr, 2/197

Kirschner (Michael S. & Fannie) Fdn., Philadelphia, 2/198

Kiwanis Fdn. of Eastern Pa., Inc., Easton, 2/198

Klatzkin Fdn., Johnstown, 2/199

Klevan (Philip) Fdn., Altoona, 2/201

Kline (C. Mahlon) Memorial Fdn., Philadelphia, 2/202

Kline (Hess & Helyn) Fdn., Philadelphia, 2/202

Kline (J. Alexander & Reba C.) Fdn., Philadelphia, 2/203

Kline (Josiah W. & Bessie H.) Fdn., Inc., Harrisburg, 2/204

Ketchum, MacLeod & Grove Fdn., Pittsburgh, 2/204

Knobloch (Ellis T.) Trustee under Declaration of Charitable Trust, Erie, 2/205

Knollbrook, Philadelphia, 2/206

Knudsen (Earl) Charitable Fdn., Pittsburgh, 2/207

Kohn Fdn., Philadelphia, 2/207

Koppers Fdn., Pittsburgh, 2/208

Korman (Hyman) Family Fdn., Jenkintown, 2/211

Kossman (Curtis I. & Paul) Charitable Fdn., Pittsburgh, 2/212

Kraftsow Fdn., Philadelphia, 2/213

Krasnov (Samuel) Fdn., Bethlehem, 2/214

Krumholz Fdn., West Reading, 2/214

Krumrine (G.D.) & Mary J. Krumrine Fdn., State College, 2/215

Kunkel (Dr. George B.) Memorial Fund, Harrisburg, 2/215

Kunkel (John Craine) Fdn., Harrisburg, 2/216

Kurz Fdn., Philadelphia, 2/217

Kynett (Edna G.) Memorial Fdn., Philadelphia, 2/218

Lamade (Howard J. & George R.) Fdn., Williamsport, 2/219

Lamme (Benjamin Garver) Scholarship Fund, Pittsburgh, 2/219

Landau (Leonard & Ethel) Fdn., Philadelphia, 2/220

Landfall Fdn., Pittsburgh, 2/221

Lansford Legion Home Association, Lansford, 2/224

Lashner (Terri Barbara) Memorial Charitable Trust, Philadelphia, 2/224

Latrobe Steel Charitable Trust, Latrobe, 2/224

Laub (Richard M.) Fdn., Jenkintown, 2/225

Laughlin (Alexander M. & Judith) Fdn., Pittsburgh, 2/226

Laurel Fdn., Pittsburgh, 2/227

Lavin (Katherine Masland) Fdn., Philadelphia, 2/230

Leavitt (Boris & Sophie) Fdn., Hanover, 2/230

Lebovitz Fdn., Pittsburgh, 2/231

Leech (Most Rev. George C.) & King St. Ferdinand III-College Scholarship Fdn. u/d/t, Harrisburg, 2/231

Leeland Fdn., Conshohocken, 2/232

Lefco Fdn., Wyncote, 2/232

Lefton (Al Paul) Company Fdn., Philadelphia, 2/233

Lehigh Portland Cement Company Charitable Trust, Allentown, 2/233

Leidner (Nelson J.) Fdn., Huntingdon Valley, 2/234

Leisser (Martin B.) Art Fund, Pittsburgh, 2/234

LeMaistre (Philip M.) Fdn., Pittsburgh, 3/001

Leopold (Irving & Eunice) Fdn., Philadelphia, 3/001

Lesher (Margaret & Irvin) Fdn., Oil City, 3/001

Levin (Benjamin B. & Natalie O.) Charitable Trust, Philadelphia, 3/002

Levine (Joseph & Bessie) Fund, Philadelphia, 3/003

Levitties (Samuel W.) Fdn., Philadelphia, 3/004

Levy (Jacob & Mary) Fdn., Scranton, 3/004

Levy (Leon) Fdn., Philadelphia, 3/005

Levy (Leon M.) Fdn., Scranton, 3/006

Lewin (Walter G.) & Mary B. Lewin Charitable Fdn., Hummelstown, 3/006

Lewis (Jennie S.) Fund, Reading, 3/006

Lieber (Sara) Fdn., Pittsburgh, 3/007

Limbach Fdn., Pittsburgh, 3/007

Linch (Mary E.) f/b/o Greenmount Cemetery Association, York, 3/008

Linch (Mary E.) f/b/o Prospect Hill Cemetery, York, 3/008

Liscom (Dean & Louise) Fdn., Lansdowne, 3/008

Lizars Fdn., Philadelphia, 3/009

Lockhart Iron & Steel Co. Charitable Trust, Pittsburgh, 3/009

Loeb (William S. & Nancy A.) Fdn., Philadelphia, 3/010

Loewenstein (Louis & Helen K.) Fund, Philadelphia, 3/011

Loftus (Mary & Peter) Fdn., Pittsburgh, 3/011

London (Max) Fdn., Johnstown, 3/012

Long (Sara) Charity Fund, Philadelphia, 3/013

Lord (Thomas) Charitable Trust, Erie, 3/014

Lotman (Samuel & Gertrude) Fdn., Scranton, 3/015

Louchheim (Henry S.) Fund, Philadelphia, 3/015

Love (George E. & Margaret McC) Fdn., Pittsburgh, 3/016

Lovett Fdn., Philadelphia, 3/017

Lowengard (Leon) Scholarship Fdn., Harrisburg, 3/118

Lowry Home for Smaller Animals Trust, Philadelphia, 3/021

Loyalhanna Fdn., Pittsburgh, 3/021

Luggage Workers Union of Philadelphia and Vicinty #61-Health Benefit Fund, Pittsburgh, 3/024

Lukens Steel Fdn., Coatesville, 3/024

Luria (A.L. & Jennie L.) Fdn., Philadelphia, 3/025

Luria (William J. & Josephine M.) Fund, Bala Cynwyd, 3/026

Lutheran Children's Home, Pittsburgh, 3/027

Lycoming House, Philadelphia, 3/028

MacBeth (George D. & Beatrice H.) Fdn., Pittsburgh, 3/029

Mack (Harvey F.) & Florence S. Mack Educational & Charitable Trust, Easton, 3/030

Mackey (Thomas R.) Memorial Scholarship Fund, Pittsburgh, 3/033

Mack (J.S.) Fdn., Homer City, 3/033

Madway Fdn., Philadelphia, 3/035

Madway (Hillard & Janet) Fdn., Merion, 3/035

Magnetics Inc., Student Loan Fund, Pittsburgh, 3/036

Maneely Fund, Philadelphia, 3/037

Stern (I. Jerome) Family Fdn., Philadelphia, 4/083

Sternfeld (Albert H.) Fdn., Philadelphia, 4/084

Stevens (Lewis M.) Conference Trust, Philadelphia, 4/085

Stewart (Glen) for Johns Hopkins Hospital, Pittsburgh, 4/086

Stewart (William G.) Fdn., Pittsburgh, 4/086

Stornoway Fdn., Ligonier, 4/087

Stough (Edna D.) f/b/o Greenmount Cemetery, York, 4/088

Strauss Fdn., Philadelphia, 4/088

Strawbridge (Margaret Dorrance) Fdn., Philadelphia, 4/089

Stroud (Susan C.) Dec'd Women's SPCA Trust, Philadelphia, 4/090

Strouse (Evelyn P. & Benjamin A.) Fdn., Philadelphia, 4/091

Strumia Fdn., Bryn Mawr, 4/093

Struthers Wells Fdn., Warren, 4/093

Strumia Fdn., Bryn Mawr, 4/093

Subin Fdn., Philadelphia, 4/094

Suhr (Charles L.) Charitable Trust, Oil City, 4/095

Sunoco Fund, Philadelphia, 4/095

Sunstein (D.) Fdn., Philadelphia, 4/096

Sunstein (Leon C.) Fdn., Philadelphia, 4/097

Sunstein (Leon), Jr. Fund, Philadelphia, 4/099

Superior-Pacific Fund, Wynnewood, 4/100

Susquehanna-Pfaltzgraff Fdn., York, 4/101

Sutherland (J.B.) Memorial Fund, Pittsburgh, 4/103

Swartz (Mary E.) Dec'd T/w, Philadelphia, 4/103

Swendenborg Fund, Pittsburgh, 4/104

Swartzlander (Rebecca H.) Testamentary Trust, Doylestown, 4/105

Swensrud (S.A.) Charitable Trust, Ligonier, 4/106

Swope (Charles S.) Memorial Scholar-Fund, West Chester, 4/106

Syntron Fdn., Homer City, 4/107

Tasty Baking Fdn., Philadelphia, 4/108

Taylor (T.R.) & Company Fdn., York, 4/109

Techalloy Fdn., Rahns, 4/110

Techalloy Scholarship Fdn., Rahns, 4/110

Tecosky (Evelyn R. & J. Lawrence) Fund, Philadelphia, 4/111

Temple Baptist Church Mt. Oliver, Pittsburgh, 4/111

Temple (Joseph E.) TD, Philadelphia, 4/111

Teti (Joseph A.), Jr., Fdn., Philadelphia, 4/112

Textron Charitable Trust, Pittsburgh, 4/112

Thayer Corporation, Philadelphia, 4/115

Thomas (L.G.L. & Florance S.) Fdn., Philadelphia, 4/116

Thomas (Morgan H. & Aimee) Fdn., Philadelphia, 4/117

Thomson (J. Edgar), Estate of, Philadelphia, 4/117

Thomson (Frank) Scholarship Fund, Philadelphia, 4/119

Tinicum Medical Research Fdn., Ottsville, 4/120

Titelman Welfare Fund, Altoona, 4/121

Tobin (Sylvan M. & Frances E.) Fdn., Philadelphia, 4/121

Tolz Family Fdn., Bala Cynwyd, 4/122

Tonkin-Egbert Memorial Fund, Oil City, 4/122

Toren (James W. & May) Fdn., Haverford, 4/123

Tose Fdn., Bridgeport, 4/123

Tri-County Conservancy of the Brandywine Inc., Chaddsford, 4/124

Trion Charitable Fdn., Mckees Rocks, 4/125

Alwine (Harry K.) Trust of Elizabethtown High School Scholarship Fund, Hershey, 4/125

Arner (Julia C.) Trust u/w Item 3, Philadelphia, 4/127

Arner (Julia C.) Residuary Trust, Philadelphia, 4/128

Battenberg (D.) Fund, Trust u/w H. William, Scranton, 4/128

Behrend (E.R) Trust Fund, Erie, 4/129

Berenato (Anthony F. & Dena Marie) Charitable Trust, Bala Cynwyd, 4/131

Cathcart (Eliza) Home for Incurables Trust, Philadelphia, 4/131

Clarke-Aff-League Memorial Fund, Philadelphia, 4/132

Crawford (H.J.) Trust u/ind 10/15/40 Crawford Hall Grove City College, Grove City, 4/133

Crawford (H.J.) Trust u/ind 8/8/39 for Oil City Hospital, Oil City, 4/134

Croasdale (Helen) Dec'd T/W, Philadelphia, 4/134

Deshong (Alfred O.) Trust u/w, Chester, 4/135

Entrekin Fdn. Trust, Philadelphia, 4/135

Tower United Presbyterian Church u/w of Jennie H. Glend, Oil City, 4/136

Hallowell (Lillian C.) Dec'd T/W, Philadelphia, 4/136

Guckert (Matilda) T/W, Philadelphia, 4/138

Henretta Memorial Public School Library Building Fund, Oil City, 4/138

Higbee (Clinton A.) T/W, Philadelphia, 4/140

Jackson (A.L.) Dec'd Charity Trust T/W, Philadelphia, 4/141

Justus (Edith C.) Trust, Oil City, 4/141

Kelsey-Hayes Company Fdn., Philadelphia, 4/142

Kerling (Teddie L.) Scholarship Fund Trust u/w, Scranton, 4/145

Kirkwith (Mike) Trust of Hershey Post #386 of the American Legion, Hershey, 4/145

Rhoads (Leidy) Fdn. Trust, Philadelphia, 4/147

Levy (Leon M.) Trust u/w, Scranton, 4/149

Lizzie (Kelley) T/W, Philadelphia, 4/149

Lindsey (J. Walter) T/W, Philadelphia, 4/150

Lownes (George B.) Dec'd T/W, Philadelphia, 4/151

Marc & Friends Charitable Trust, Pittsburgh, 4/151

McCarter (Samuel B.) Charitable Trust, Pittsburgh, 4/152

McCarthy (John A.) Res. T/W, Philadelphia, 4/152

McCombes (Eugene J.) Dec'd Trust u/w, Philadelphia, 4/153

Mong (William) Memorial Fund Trust u/w, Oil City, 4/154

Nineteen Fifty Seven Charity Trust, Philadelphia, 4/155

Parmly Trust Fund, Philadelphia, 4/156

Peberdy (Charles), Jr. Trust u/d, Philadelphia, 4/158

Penn (Margaret A. & Dorothy M.), Oil City, 4/159

Scranton Protective Surface Association, Scranton, 4/160

Reeves (Sophia) Fdn. Trust, Philadelphia, 4/160

Schorman (Gustav) Memorial Trust, Oil City, 4/162

Shortridge (Eliz J.) Dec'd Charity Fund T/W, Philadelphia, 4/162

Smith (Emma Strouss) Fund u/w William T. Smith, Oil City, 4/163

Steffee (John) Memorial Trust Fund u/w Eleanor Steffee, Oil City, 4/164

Stern (Samuel) u/w and Court Order September 1909 Term, Oil City, 4/165

Good (William), Jr. Memorial Fund u/w of Lauretta Good Strayer, Oil City, 4/166

Taylor (Elizabeth) Charitable Trust, Jenkintown, 4/166

Young (Horace L.) Trust u/w Deceased, Philadelphia, 4/166

Taylor Fdn. Trust, Philadelphia, 4/167

Taylor Memorial Arboretum, Philadelphia, 4/169

Truth Fdn., Beaver, 4/171

Tucker (Elizabeth) T/W, Philadelphia, 4/172

Wanamaker (J.) Dec'd Beth College Pres. Church Trust, Philadelphia, 4/172

Wanamaker (J.) Dec'd Bethany Brotherhood Trust, Philadelphia, 4/173

Wanamaker (M.B.) Dec'd Grace Pres. Church Trust, Philadelphia, 4/174

Twersky (Sigmund & Lea) Fdn., Philadelphia, 4/175

Tyler (John J.) Arboretum, Philadelphia, 4/175

Tyson Fdn., Philadelphia, 4/178

United Refining Company Charitable Fdn., Warren, 4/178

United Service Fdn., Inc., New Holland, 4/179

Unruh (Emaline) T/W, Philadelphia, 4/179

Valentine-Kline Fdn., Philadelphia, 4/180

Van Bomel (Catherine Breyer) Fdn., Philadelphia, 4/181

Vanderbilt (Oliver) Fdn., Philadelphia, 4/182

Vang Memorial Fdn., Pittsburgh, 4/184

Vanity Fair Mills Fdn.-Choctaw, Reading, 4/185

Vanity Fair Mills Fdn.-Escambia, REading, 4/185

Vanity Fair Mills Fdn.-Marengo, Reading, 4/186

Veterans Hospital Committee-Shaw 6788-0, Pittsburgh, 4/186

Vicary Fdn, Incorporated, Erie, 4/187

Vickers (Rachel B.) Dec'd T/W, Philadelphia, 4/188

Virginia Concrete Foundation, Inc., Allentown, 4/189

Visiting Nurse Association of York, Pennsylvania, York, 4/190

Waber-Odell Fdn., Wynnewood, 4/190

Waber (Morris) Fund, Philadelphia, 4/191

Wald Fdn., Inc., Huntingdon, 4/192

Walden Trust, Pittsburgh, 4/192

Waldorf Educational Fdn., Philadelphia, 4/193

Waldorf School Trust, Philadelphia, 4/194

Walmar Fdn., Scranton, 4/195

Walnut Street Corporation, Philadelphia, 4/196

Walton (Rachel Mellon) Fdn., Pittsburgh, 4/196

Warden (Barbara) Fdn., Philadelphia, 4/197

Warwick Fdn., Doylestown, 4/198

Wasserman (Richard & Helene) Fdn., Philadelphia, 4/198

Waters (Robert S.) Charitable Trust, Pittsburgh, 4/199

Water (George & Elizabeth) Trust, Pittsburgh, 4/200

Wawasset Benefical Society Special Fund, Coatesville, 4/201

Way (Anna L.) Dec'd T/W, Philadelphia, 4/201

Weaver (Margaret Criag) Fdn., Pittsburgh, 4/202

Webb (Charles J.) Fdn., Jenkintown, 4/203

Wechsler (Irving A. & Thelma W.) Charitable Fdn., Pittsburgh, 4/204

Weinberg (Benjamin B.) and Gertrude Weinberg Fdn., Homestead, 4/204

Weir (Edgar V.) Family Fdn., Butler, 4/204

Weir Lake Development Company, Kunkletown, 4/205

Weisbrod (Robert & Mary) Fdn., Pittsburgh, 4/205

Weisser (Edward A.) Memorial Opthalmic Fdn., Pittsburgh, 4/206

Wells (Struthers) Fdn., Warren, 4/207

Welsh (Lulu A.), York, 4/207

Werner (Charles) Life Institute Trust, Reading, 4/207

Wesel Fdn., Scranton, 4/207

West Coast Fund, Wynnewood, 4/208

Western Pennsylvania Council on Drug Abuse, Sewickley, 4/208

Westinghouse Airbrake Fdn., Pittsburgh, 4/210

Westinghouse (H.H.) Bequest Fund, Pittsburgh, 4/211

Westinghouse Electric Fund, Pittsburgh, 4/212

Wheeler (Morris) Fdn., Philadelphia, 4/212

Whitaker Fund, Bala Cyn, 4/213

Whiteford (William) Fdn., Pittsburgh, 4/215

Whitelay (George H.) f/b/o American Fund for Dental Education, York, 4/215

Whiteley (Ida O.) First Presbyterian Church, York, 4/216

Whiteley (Purdon S.) f/b/o Country Club of York, Pa., York, 4/216

Whiteley (Purdon S.) f/b/o Prospect Hill Cemetery, York, 4/217

Whiteley (Purdon S.) f/b/o Y.M.C.A., York, 4/217

Whitner (C.K.) Fdn., Reading, 4/217

Widener Memorial Fdn. in Aid of Handicapped Children, Philadelphia, 4/217

Wiener-Glazer Fdn., Philadelphia, 4/219

Willary Fdn., Scranton, 4/219

Williams (John C.) Charitable Trust, Pittsburgh, 4/219

Williams (C.K.) Fdn., Easton, 4/220

Willis (Hilda M.) Fdn., Pittsburgh, 4/222

Wills (David Gordon) Memorial Fdn., Allentown, 4/223

Wilson (Thomas A.) Charitable Trust, McKeesport, 4/223

Wilson (William R.) Charitable Trust, Philadelphia, 4/223

Wilson (Irving W.) Fdn., Pittsburgh, 4/223

Wilson (Kate H.) Trust, Philadelphia, 4/224

Winkelman (Nathaniel W. & Lillie G.) Fdn., Philadelphia, 4/225

Winter (Jacob C.) Fdn., Red Lion, 4/226

Winters (Samuel & Emma) Fdn., Pittsburgh, 4/226

Wittmar (Buzzy) Scholarship Fund, Philadelphia, 4/227

Woelpper (George G.) T/W, Philadelphia, 4/228

Wolcott Fdn., Philadelphia, 4/229

Wolffe (Joseph B. & Evelyn) Fdn., Norristown, 4/229

Women in the Urban Crisis, Pittsburgh, 4/230

Womens Aid of the Penn Central Transportation Company, Philadelphia, 4/231

Wood (Alan) Steel Company, Conshocken, 4/232

Wright (Daisy C.) T/W-St. Francis Church, Philadelphia, 4/233

Wunderly Fdn., Pittsburgh, 4/234

Wurtz (Henrietta Tower) Memorial, Philadelphia, 4/235

Wyomissing Fdn., Wyomissing, 4/237

Yarnall (Lydia) Dec'd Rush Hospital T/W, Philadelphia, 4/238

Yarnall (Lydia) Dec'd Del Co. SPCA T/W, Philadelphia, 4/239

Yarway Fdn., Blue Bell, 4/240

Yavapai Fdn., Pittsburgh, 4/241

Yellow Cab Fdn., Philadelphia, 4/242

Yentis Fdn., Philadelphia, 4/242

York County Medical Society Educational Trust, York, 4/242

Wyomissing Fdn., Wyomissing, 5/001

Yarnell (Lydia) Dec'd Rush Hospital T/W, Philadelphia, 5/003

Yarnell (Lydia) Dec'd Del Co. SPCA, Philadelphia, 5/004

Yarway Fdn., Blue Bell, 5/004

Yavapai Fdn., Pittsburgh, 5/005

Yellow Cab Fdn., Philadelphia, 5/006

Yentis Fdn., Philadelphia, 5/007

York County Medical Society Educational Trust, York, 5/007

York Society to Protect Children & Aged Persons, York, 5/007

Young (Pearl) Fdn., Philadelphia, 5/008

Young Great Society Building Fdn., Philadelphia, 5/008

Zacks (E.A.) Charitable Fdn., Erie, 5/009

Zalfsne-Wilke Fdn., Philadelphia, 5/010

Zeidman (Leonard) Fdn., Norristown, 5/010

Ziegler (Issaac) Charitable Trust, Scranton, 5/011

Zimmermann (Barbara S.) Charitable Trust, Philadelphia, 5/012

Zurn Fdn., Erie, 5/013

1718 Fdn., Philadelphia, 5/014

Second Filming

Abington Memorial Hospital Tr. #68500, Philadelphia, 6/002

ACME Markets Inc. Fdn., Philadelphia, 6/003

Ahl (Lydia G.) Cemetery Tr., Harrisburg, 6/004

Alex (Pres. C. H.) Pa. Poor Relief Fdn. Tr., Philadelphia, 6/004

Allegheny High School World War Mem'l Fdn., Pittsburgh, 6/005

Allen (Elizabeth) Cemetery Fund, Harrisburg, 6/006

Allman (Sydney K.) Jr., Fdn., Philadelphia, 6/006

Alpern (Simon) Family Fdn., Pittsburgh, 6/007

American Assn. For The History of Medicine, Philadelphia, 6/007

American Fdn. Incorp., Philadelphia, 6/008

American Guild of Organists, Philadelphia, 6/011

American Leaders Fdn., Scranton, 6/012

American Sterilizer Co. Fdn., Erie, 6/012

American Sunday School Union, Philadelphia, 6/013

American S. S. Union/John C. Green Fund Trust, Philadelphia, 6/014

Ames (Harriet) Charitable Trust, Radnor, 6/015

Amsterdam Fdn., Philadelphia, 6/016

Annenberg Fund, Radnor, 6/017

Annenberg (M. L.) Fdn., Radnor, 6/018

Apple (Benjamin and Lillie E.) Fdn., Sunbury, 6/020

Apple (John A.) Fdn., Sunbury, 6/023

Archbold Expeditions, Philadelphia, 6/024

Archer Fdn., Harleysville, 6/024

Armon Fdn., Cornwells Heights, 6/025

Arner (Julia C.) Trust U/4th Item of Will of Surviving Trustee, Philadelphia, 6/025

Arnold Fdn., Wilkes Barre, 6/026

A & S Fdn., Philadelphia, 6/026

Trustee for Ashland Cemetery Assn. - Issac T. Osmond, Harrisburg, 6/027

Ashland Cemetery Assn. T/A of Annie Oberdier and Lizzie Hackenberg, Harrisburg, 6/027

Trustee For Ashland Cemetery Assn. - Sarah Motts, Harrisburg, 6/027

Trustee For Ashland Cemetery Assn. - S.K. Ege, Harrisburg, 6/028

Trustee For Ashland Cemetery Assn. Darland Lot, Harrisburg, 6/028

Ashland Cemetery Assn. T/W of Herbert K. Line, Harrisburg, 6/028

Trustee for Ashland Cemetery Assn. - Estate of J. Gudshall, Harrisburg, 6/028

Ashland Cemetery Assn. T/W of Alexander Lindsay, Harrisburg, 6/028

Trustee for Ashland Cemetery Assn. - Anne M. Richards, Harrisburg, 6/028

Trustee for Ashland Cemetery Assn. - Estate of S. W. Searight, Harrisburg, 6/029

Trustee for Ashland Cemetery Cemetery Assn. - Zuleima A. Grove, Harrisburg, 6/029

Asplundh Fdn., Jenkintown, 6/029

American Assoc. for Education of the Visually Handicapped, Philadelphia, 6/030

Tashjian Jeanette Bach T. W., Philadelphia, 6/030

Bacon (Dr. Harry E.) Proctologic Residents Research Fdn., Philadelphia, 6/032

Baer (Howard D.) Charity Tr., York, 6/032

Bailey Memorial Fund, Harrisburg, 6/033

Bailis (Anna) Fdn., Philadelphia, 6/033

Baird (Edith L. W.) No. 2, Philadelphia, 6/033

Baird Memorial Trust First Pa. Bank & Tr. Co. Trustee, Philadelphia, 6/034

Baird (Walter T.) Trust, Philadelphia, 6/035

Trustee for Alice Baker Estate, Harrisburg, 6/036

Baker (Margaret) Memorial Fund, Philadelphia, 6/036

Balch (Edwin Swift) Trust, Philadelphia, 6/037

Balch (Emily Swift), Philadelphia, 6/038

Estate T. W. Balch Portrait Fund, Philadelphia, 6/040

Balch (Thomas) Library Building and Upkeep, Philadelphia, 6/040

Baldwin Cemetery Assn. Couffer, Harrisburg, 6/041

Bangert (John J.) Trust, Pittsburgh, 6/041

Barg (Herbert & Marilyn) Fdn., Philadelphia, 6/041

Barg (William and Yetta) Fdn., Merion, 6/042

Barnes (Butcher) Fdn., Media, 6/043

Bear (Ida A.) T/W, Harrisburg, 6/043

Beaver (Thomas) Free Library, Danville, 6/044

Bedford (Elizabeth Richards) T/W, Harrisburg, 6/044

Beidel (George S.) Trust, Harrisburg, 6/044

Benedum (Claude Worthington) Fdn., Pittsburgh, 6/044

Beneficia Fdn., Byrn Athyn, 6/050

Berenato (Anthony F & Dena Marie) Charitable Trust, Bala Cynwyd, 6/052

Berger (David and Harriet) Fdn., Philadelphia, 6/052

Berkowitz (Edward and Florence) Family Fdn., Chareloi, 6/052

Berks County Tuberculosis Soc., Reading, 6/053

Berman Charitable Fdn., Pottstown, 6/054

Berman (Philip and Muriel) Fdn., Allentown, 6/054

Berman (Sol and Naomi) Charitable Fdn., Pottstown, 6/055

Bennett (Joseph M.), Philadelphia, 6/057

Bernstein (Robert M. and Marshall A.) Fdn., Philadelphia, 6/058

Beth-Con Fdn., Bath, 6/058

Betser (Carrie Miller) TW Home For The Friendless, Harrisburg, 6/059

Betts Fdn., Warren, 6/059

Biddle (Mary L. C. & Chapman) Fund For Reduced Ladies, Philadelphia, 6/061

Bishop (Jacob) Cemetery Trust, Harrisburg, 6/062

Trust U/A S. Fordham Bixler, Bethlehem, 6/062

Bixler and Woodward Cemetery Trust, Harrisburg, 6/063

Bliley Electric Fdn., Erie, 6/063

Blair County Historical Society, Altoona, 6/064

Block (Alice) Fdn., Philadelphia, 6/064

Bloom Fdn., Pittsburgh, 6/064

Bloom (Frederick S.) Charitable Trust, Pittsburgh, 6/065

Blum (Jerrold S.) Fdn., Pittsburgh, 6/066

Bockius (Morris R.) T/W J. M. Clarke Fdn., Philadelphia, 6/067

Bok (Mary Louise Curtis) Fdn., Philadelphia, 6/068

Bonner (Monsignor John J.) Fdn., Philadelphia, 6/069

Boy Scouts of America Yohogania Area Council, Pittsburgh, 6/069

Boyd (John T.) T/W Old Seceder Burial Ground, Harrisburg, 6/070

Brachfeld (Jonas and Rosalind) Fdn., Bala Cynwyd, 6/070

Brahin Family Fund, Levittown, 6/071

Breckenridge (Amanda L.) Cemetery Fund, Harrisburg, 6/071

Brenner (Jacob A.) T/W St. Marks Evangelical Lutheran Church of Lancaster, Lancaster, 6/072

Breinig (Alfred O.) Fdn., Jenkintown, 6/072

Brier (Jack and Irene E.) Fdn., Philadelphia, 6/072

Brier (Samuel & Elizabeth) Fdn., Philadelphia, 6/074

Brill (David D.) Fdn., Philadelphia, 6/074

Brooks Fdn. Charity Religion, Pittsburgh, 6/075

Brooks Fdn. Education Fund, Pittsburgh, 6/076

Brooks Fdn. Miscellaneous Charities, Pittsburgh, 6/076

Brown (Alexander) TD, Philadelphia, 6/077

Brubaker (Roland H.) T/W Lancaster General Hospital, Lancaster, 6/078

Brubaker (Roland H.) T/W St. Joseph Hospital, Lancaster, 6/079

Bryan (John E.) T/A VFW National Home Et Al, Harrisburg, 6/079

Buchanan (Pitt) Charitable Trust, Jenkintown, 6/080

Buchmiller (D. F.) Park, Lancaster, 6/080

T/D Bucks Co. Lodge, 6/081

Budd Company Fdn., Philadelphia, 6/081

Buhl Fdn., Pittsburgh, 6/082

Bunten (William H.) Memorial Fdn., Philadelphia, 6/084

Burnell (John H.) #2, Philadelphia, 6/084

Wauwatosa Knights of Columbus Council #3702, Wauwatosa, 6/084

Butt (James C. and Dorothy G.) Fdn., Paoli, 6/085

Cadeau Fdn., Philadelphia, 6/085

Callin (M. Alice) Cemetery Fund, Harrisburg, 6/086

Cameron (Mary) TR U/W (Paragraph), Harrisburg, 6/086

Cantor (Betty and Gil) Fdn., Philadelphia, 6/086

Carnaham W.C.M.S.McK. C. Trust, Pittsburgh, 6/087

Carborundum Charitable Fdn., Pittsburgh, 6/087

Card Catlin Scholarship Trust, Erie, 6/089

Carlson (Fred M. and Helen M.), Erie, 6/089

Carlisle Hospital T/W of Laura D. Weaver #1, Harrisburg, 6/089

Carlisle Hospital T/W of Robert B. Weaver #2, Harrisburg, 6/090

Carlisle Hospital T/W #3, Harriisburg, 6/091

Carlisle Hospital T/W of Agnes Woods #4, Harrisburg, 6/091

Carlson (Gunard Berry) Memorial Fdn., Inc., Thorndale, 6/092

Carnell (Althea J.) for Medical Students, Philadelphia, 6/094

Carolann Trust, Hazleton, 6/094

Carpenter (Joseph G.) Fdn., Philadelphia, 6/095

Centenary United Brethern, Harrisburg, 6/097

Central Montgomery County Fdn., Philadelphia, 6/097

Cerebral Stereotoxis Institute, Philadelphia, 6/097

Change Fdn., Philadelphia, 6/097

Chapman (John W. and Alice M.) Fdn., Washington, 6/098

Charlestein (Julius and Ray) Fdn., Philadelphia, 6/098

Chase (Gertrude Homer) #11 Charities, Philadelphia, 6/099

Chestnut Fdn., Glenshaw, 6/099

Chit Chat Fdn., Wernersville, 6/100

Christ Church Danville, Pa. No. #2 Trust, Philadelphia, 6/101

Christ Church Danville, Pa. No. #1 Trust, Philadelphia, 6/103

Church of Good Samaritan, Philadelphia, 6/103

Church of God North Middleton Township Trust U/W of Minnie W. Weitzel, Harrisburg, 6/104

Church of Covenant in City of Detroit Trust, Philadelphia, 6/104

Churchville Cemetery Assn. Tr., Harrisburg, 6/105

Churchville Cemetery Assn. (Ralph) Trust, Harrisburg, 6/106

City of Philadelphia, Philadelphia, 6/106

Claneil Fdn., Philadelphia, 6/107

Morris, J. For Clark Med. Ed. Fdn., Pittsburgh, 6/108

Clary (Patrick T.), Pittsburgh, 6/109

Clay (R. Edey) Decd. TW, Philadelphia, 6/110

Clements (H. Loren) Scholarship Fund, Scranton, 6/110

Coble (Aaron C.) T/W Heckton Cemetery Fund, Harrisburg, 6/111

Cochran (J.) Decd. Chester Poor T/W, Philadelphia, 6/111

Coen (Charles S. and Mary) Family Fdn., Washington, 6/112

Cohen (Cecil and Czerna) Fdn., Pittsburgh, 6/113

Cohen (David) Fdn., Philadelphia, 6/113

Cohen (Harris) Cemetery Fund, Harrisburg, 6/114

Cohen (Mary T.), Philadelphia, 6/114

Cohen (Wm. J.) T/D, Philadelphia, 6/114

Cohen (William J.) Decd. T/W, Philadelphia, 6/115

Coleman Fdn., Philadelphia, 6/116

College Aid Program For A Greater Philadelphia, Philadelphia, 6/117

Collins (Michael) Cemetery Fund, Harrisburg, 6/117

Colonial Flying Corps. Museum, Inc., Philadelphia, 6/117

Colwell (Lila J.) T/W Cemetery, Harrisburg, 6/118

Commins (Burton E.) T/W Humane Society of Harrisburg, Harrisburg, 6/119

Commings (Burton E.) T/W Forster St YMCA, Harrisburg, 6/119

Commings (Burton E.) T/W Dauphin County Assn. For the Blind, Harrisburg, 6/119

Fisher (Elizabeth) T/W Church of God, Harrisburg, 6/120

Fetrow Cemetery Fund U/W of Edna E. Kilmore, Harrisburg, 6/120

Foundation For Community Health, Philadelphia, 6/120

Congregational Homes Berg Fund, Pittsburgh, 6/120

Conston Fdn., Philadelphia, 6/121

Cook (Francis J.) T/W Home for the Friendless, Harrisburg, 6/123

Cooper (Harry and Anna) Fdn., Elkins Park, 6/123

S. S. of S. D. Cooper Memorial M.E. Church Trust, Philadelphia, 6/124

Coover (Eli H.) Cemetery Fund, Harrisburg, 6/125

Copperweld Steel Compnay's Glassport Employees' Trust, Glassport, 6/125

Cornman (W. S.) T/W, Harrisburg, 6/126

Coyle (J. Andrew) T/W, Harrisburg, 6/126

Coyle (J. Andrew) TW First Presbyterian Church, Harrisburg, 6/126

Craighead (Margaret E.) T/W, Harrisburg, 6/127

Crane (John A.) Decd, Philadelphia, 6/127

Crary Home, Warren, 6/128

Cross (Samuel and Anna) Fdn., Philadelphia, 6/128

Crozer (Robert H.) T/W, Philadelphia, 6/129

Crozer (S. A.) Decd. Upland Baptist T/W, Philadelphia, 6/130

Crozer (Sallie L.) Decd. Upland Poort T/W, Philadelphia, 6/131

Croft (Anna N.), Harrisburg, 6/131

Crouse (George Jackson) Tr. U/W, Harrisburg, 6/132

Vesuvius Crucible Co. Charitable Foundation, Pittsburgh, 6/132

Cumbler (George W. and Elizabeth H.) T/A Hill Cemetery, Harrisburg, 6/133

Cumbler (Melvin Bent) T/W Evangelical Lutheran Church, Harrisburg, 6/133

Cumbler (Melvin Bent) T/W St. Peters Church, Harrisburg, 6/133

Cutalar Fdn., Philadelphia, 6/134

Curtis (Ford E.) and Harriet R. Curtis Fdn., Pittsburgh, 6/134

Cyclops Fdn., Pittsburgh, 6/134

Dale (Kate C.) T/A for Second Presbyterian Church, Harrisburg, 6/135

Myer Davidow Fdn., Scranton, 6/135

Day (Charles W.) Cemetery Fund, Harrisburg, 6/135

Dean Fdn., Philadelphia, 6/136

Deichler (Emma J.) Cemetery Fund, Harrisburg, 6/136

Delaware County Medical Society Public Health Fund, Lansdowne, 6/136

Delaware Old Mennonite Congregation T/A, Harrisburg, 6/136

Delong (Benjamin F.) T/W, Philadelphia, 6/137

Denenberg (Gertrude) Charitable Trust, Philadelphia, 6/137

Derry Township School District Trust, Hershey, 6/138

Devens Charities, Pittsburgh, 6/138

Dibeler (Minnie) T/W Falmouth Cemetery Assoc., Harrisburg, 6/140

Dicenso (Alfred A.) and Robert L. Ellison Fdn., Inc., Williamsport, 6/140

Dickstein (Harry) Family Fdn., Scranton, 6/141

Dillon Charitable Fdn., Pittsburgh, 6/141

Dissinger (Eva M.) T/W Christ Lutheran Church, Harrisburg, 6/142

Dissinger (Milton V.) Cemetery Fund, Harrisburg, 6/142

Dodge (Herbert C.) M. D. Charitable Trust, Bala Cynwyd, 6/142

Dodson (E. R.) T/W Smicksburg Methodist Church, Harrisburg, 6/142

Dodson (E. R.) TW Smicksburg Lutheran Cemetery, Harrisburg, 6/143

Dogole (Irving M.) Fdn., Philadelphia, 6/144

Dole (Ida W.), Philadelphia, 6/144

Donnelly (Mary J.) Fdn., Pittsburgh, 6/145

Dougherty (Frank) TW Mary Dougherty Educational Purse, Lancaster, 6/145

Doyle (E.) Dec'd Memorial Trust Fund, Philadelphia, 6/146

Doyle (E.) Dec'd T/W Pastor Lady Mt. Carmel, Philadelphia, 6/147

Doyle (Elizabeth) Dec'd T/W Masses Fund, Philadelphia, 6/148

Dozer (Harry T. & Shirley W.) Fdn., Philadelphia, 6/148

Dozzi (Eugene) Charitable Fdn., Pittsburgh, 6/149

Drake (Annie) Dec'd T/W, Philadelphia, 6/151

Dubrow Fdn., Philadelphia, 6/151

Duncannon Presbyterian Church T/A Clara R. Zimmerman Mem., Harrisburg, 6/152

Eafco Fdn., Philadelphia, 6/153

Easton Home for Aged Women, Easton, 6/154

Eaton-Dikeman Educational Fdn., Mount Holly Springs, 6/155

Eckrich (Conrad) T/W, Harrisburg, 6/155

Eckert (Margaret) T/W, Harrisburg, 6/155

Eckstein (Wm.) Dec'd Nurses Relief Fd. Tr., Philadelphia, 6/156

Eckstein (Wm.) Dec'd Soldiers Fd. Tr., Philadelphia, 6/156

Eden Fdn., Philadelphia, 6/157

Eshleman (Anna M.) TA Tressler Orphans Home, Harrisburg, 6/157

Eichelberger (E. A.) T/W St. Johns Evangelical Lutheran, Harrisburg, 6/158

Eighteenth Zone Veterans #1, Pittsburgh, 6/158

Eisenbrey (M. E.) T/W St. Mark P.E. Church, Philadelphia, 6/158

Ellenbogen (Joseph) & Eva Ellenbogen Fdn., Pittsburgh, 6/159

Elliot (William) Educational Fdn., Philadelphia, 6/159

Elliotsburg Lutheran Church Cemetery Fund, Harrisburg, 6/160

Ellis (Morris) Fdn., Bala Cynwyd, 6/160

Engelberg (Max) Family Fdn., Pittsburgh, 6/161

English (Mary E.) Fund Trust, Philadelphia, 6/162

English Presbyterian Church T/W of Sara E. McCauley, Harrisburg, 6/163

Epstein (Wallace Jay) Fdn., Philadelphia, 6/163

Erie Clinic Fdn., Erie, 6/163

Erie Dry Goods Compnay Contribution Fund, Erie, 6/163

Erie Foundry Co. Fdn., Erie, 6/164

Erie Technological Products Inc., Fdn., Erie, 6/164

Ervite-Vicary Fdn., Erie, 6/165

E. S. B. Fdn., Philadelphia, 6/165

Eschol Lutheran Church Cemetery Fund, Harrisburg, 6/166

Eshleman (Anna M.) T/A St. Pauls Lutheran Church of Newport, Harrisburg, 6/166

Evans (D. A. & J. A.) Memorial Fdn., Ellwood City, 6/167

Failor (Minerva F.) T/W Ashland Cemetery
Assn., Harrisburg, 6/168
Fatima Vocations Fund, Canonsburgh, 6/168
Faylor Fdn., Selinsgrove, 6/168
Feldman (Richard Mace) Memorial Fdn.,
Pittsburgh, 6/168
Fenstermaker (Suzanne Mae) Nephritis Fdn.,
Fogelsville, 6/169
Fischer Memorial Burial Park, Philadelphia,
6/170
First Pres. Ch. New Castle Cmty Fund Tr.,
Philadelphia, 6/170
First Reformed Evangelical Ch. (Annie M.
Smith Fdn.), Harrisburg, 6/170
First Troop Phila. Cavalry Endowment Fund,
Philadelphia, 6/171
Fishburn (Salome A.) T/W, Harrisburn, 6/171
Fisher-Mumford Fdn., Pittsburgh, 6/171
Foerderer (Percival E. and Ethel Brown) Fdn.,
Philadelphia, 6/172
Food Fair Stores Fdn., Philadelphia, 6/174
Fortin (Susan B.) Dec'd 2 T/W, Philadelphia,
6/176
Fortin (Susan B.) Dec'd 3 TW, Philadelphia,
6/177
Foster (Benjamin) Fund, Philadelphia, 6/177
Foster (Solomon) Trust, Pittsburgh, 6/178
Fdn. in Refractories Education, Pittsburgh,
6/180
Fownes (Jessie Gaither) TD, Philadelphia,
6/180
Fox (Mary Ann) Estate, Lock Haven, 6/181
Franconia Fdn., Harleysville, 6/182
Frank (Chas J.) A. E. Frank Fdn., Philadelphia,
6/182
Frederick (Howard G.) Tr. U/W (Residuary),
Harrisburg, 6/182
Fox (James Frederic) Fdn., Meadowbrook,
6/183
Friends Freedman's Assoc. of Philadelphia,
Philadelphia, 6/184
Freeman (William C. and Alice M.) T/A St.
Lukes Episcopal Church, Lebanon,
Harrisburg, 6/184
Frick Art Reference Library Trust, Mellon
Square Pi, 6/185
Frick (Henry C.) Educational Commission,
Pittsburgh, 6/185
Frick (H.) for Frick Art Ref. Library Trustee,
Mellon Square Pi, 6/188
Trustee U/Dt of Helen C. Frick Dated 11/18/
31 for Iron Rail Vacation Homes,
Pittsburgh, 6/189
Friedman (Leon and Beatrice) Fund, Easton,
6/190
Friends Freedman's Assoc. of Philadelphia,
Philadelphia, 6/190
English (Mary E.) Fund, Philadelphia, 6/191
Fund for Research Therapeutics, Wayne, 6/191
Gallun (Richard A.) Fund, Milwaukee, 6/192
Gamma Fdn., Philadelphia, 6/192
Garfield Fdn., Fort Washington, 6/192
Garber (Alexander) Fdn., Lancaster, 6/192
Garrett (George A.) Decd T/W, Philadelphia,
6/193
Garrett (G.A.) for St. Pauls Church T/W,
Philadelphia, 6/194
Garrett Williamson Lodge, Philadelphia, 6/194
Garrison Fdn., Philadelphia, 6/196
Geddes (Carrie) Dec'd T/W, Philadelphia,
6/197
German Baptist Society, Philadelphia, 6/197
Gibbons Home, Swarthmore, 6/198
Gilbert (Bertha G.) T/W Quincy UB
Orphanage & Home, Harrisburg, 6/199
Gilbert (Bertha G.) T/W Shiremanstown UB
Church, Harrisburg, 6/199
Gilbert (George) Cemetery Fund, Harrisburg,
6/200
Gimbel (Ellis A.) Charitable Trust,
Philadelphia, 6/200
Glantawe Hospital Mgment. Committee,
Pittsburgh, 6/201
Glatco Student Loan Fund P. H. Glatfelter
Truste, Spring Grove, 6/201
Glen (Lester) Fdn., Birchunville, 6/201

Glendorn Fdn., Bradford, 6/202
Glosser (David A.) Fdn., Johnstown, 6/203
Goetter (Bertha A.) Fdn., Sharon, 6/204
Gold (Aaron & Claire) Fdn., Philadelphia,
6/204
Goldman (George B.) Fdn., Philadelphia,
6/205
Golsmith Fdn., Philadelphia, 6/205
Good (H. Martin) TW Millersville Mennonite
Childrens' Home, Lancaster, 6/206
Gorgas (Kate F.) T/A Harrisburg Community
Chest, Harrisburg, 6/207
YWCA T/A of Gorgas ((Kate F.), Harrisburg,
6/207
Moody Bible Institute of Chicago S. R. Grabill
T/W, Lancaster, 6/208
Graduate Radiology Research Fund,
Philadelphia, 6/208
Graham (Arthur) T/W, Harrisburg, 6/208
Greater Hazleton Improvement Fund, Hazleton,
6/209
Green Clover Fdn., Siking Spring, 6/209
Greiner (Daisy P.) TW Evangelical Lutheran
Ch., Lancaster, 6/209
Griffith (Morgan) Mem. Fund, Pittsburgh,
6/210
Groff (Lillian Z.) Memorial Fund TA Quincy
Orphanage and Home of U.B.C., Lancaster,
6/211
Groff (John S. & Lillian Z.) Men Fd. T/A
Grand Lodge, Lancaster, 6/211
Gross (Ida B.) Cemetery Fund, Harrisburg,
6/212
Grove City Fdn., Grove City, 6/212
Grumbine (Harvey C.) Fdn., Lebanon, 6/212
Grundy Fdn., Philadelphia, 6/213
Gund (Eleanora M.) Charity Trust, Pittsburgh,
6/215
Habbyshaw (William E.) Memorial Fund T/A,
Harrisburg, 6/216
Hagan (W. Clark), Pittsburgh, 6/216
Hahnemann Hospital Trust, Philadelphia,
6/217
Hallowell Fdn., Rydal, 6/218
Hallowell (Wm.) Dec'd Gwynedd. Mtg. Frnds.
Tr., Philadelphia, 6/218
Hamaker (George E.) Cemetery Fund,
Harrisburg, 6/219
Hamaker (Lina H.) Cemetery Fund, Harrisburg,
6/219
Hambay (James T.) Fdn. Co. Trustee U/W,
Harrisburg, 6/219
Hammermill Fdn., Erie, 6/219
Haney (J. L.) Class of 1895 Central High
School, Philadelphia, 6/220
Haney (J. L.) - E. Z. Davis Memorial Fund,
Philadelphia, 6/221
Hansen Fdn., MaCungie, 6/222
Harling (F. H.) T/W Swartz Harling Cemetery
Trust, Harrisburg, 7/001
Hoffer (Sue S.) Cemetery Trust, Harrisburg,
7/001
Harner Fdn., Boyertown, 7/001
Harnish (Martin M.) T/W Lancaster County
Fdn., Lancaster, 7/002
Harris (John H.) Fdn., Pittsburgh, 7/003
Harris (Milton E. and Ruth K.) Charitable
Fdn., Pittsburgh, 7/004
Harris Park Fund T/W of Simon Cameron,
Harrisburg, 7/004
Harrisburg Academy of Medicine Trust,
Harrisburg, 7/005
Harrisburg Fdn. T/W of E. J. Stack Pole,
Harrisburg, 7/005
Harrisburg Hospital T/W of A. A. Pancake,
Harrisburg, 7/006
Haskell (Joseph M.) Fdn., Pittsburgh, 7/006
Haupt (Enid A.) Charitable Tr., Radnor, 7/006
Rixstine (Mary Amanda Hawke), West Chester,
7/008
Hazen (Lita) Charitable Tr., Radnor, 7/008
Hebrew Cemetery Assn. Endowment Fund
U/A, Harrisburg, 7/009
Heiman (Cynthia Ann) Fdn., Allentown, 7/009
Held (Elizabeth) Tuesday Misical Fund,
Pittsburgh, 7/010

Hendel (Robert and Marie) Fdn., Pittsburgh,
7/011
Hering (Walter E.) Charitable Fd.,
Philadelphia, 7/011
Hershey (Henry L.) Cemetery Fund, Harrisburg,
7/012
Hess (Max) Fdn., Allentown, 7/012
Heyl (Jacob E.) #6, Philadelphia, 7/013
Hibshman (J. Harry) Scholarship Fund,
Ephrata, 7/014
Hillman Fdn., Inc., Pittsburgh, 7/014
Himes (George W.) Cemetery Fund,
Harrisburg, 7/015
Hirsh (Jack) Fdn., Philadelphia, 7/015
Historic Fallsington Inc., Fallsington, 7/016
Hochheimer (George M. & Anna W.)
Educational Trust, Uniontown, 7/016
Hocker (Catherine M.) Cemetery Fund,
Harrisburg, 7/017
Hocker (Catherine M.) T/W Zion Lutheran
Church, Harrisburg, 7/017
Hoffman (Bob) Fdn., York, 7/017
Hogg (George) Medical Fdn., Pittsburgh,
7/017
Hofmann (Catherine V. & Martin) Fdn.,
Wyomissing, 7/018
Trust U/W Rosanna L. Holl for Gen. Council
of Assemblies of God, Kutztown, 7/019
Holy Sacrament Episcopal Mission Trust,
Philadelphia, 7/019
Holy Trinity Church Trust, Philadelphia, 7/019
Home for the Friendless T/W of D.M. Dull
(Jane J. Dull), Harrisburg, 7/020
719 Charitable Trust, Pittsburgh, 7/021
Harrisburg Welfare Federation Trust,
Harrisburg, 7/021
Hooper (Elizabeth S.) Fdn., Philadelphia,
7/022
Hooper Fdn., Philadelphia, 7/022
Hoopes (Lida Y.) Scholarship Fund T/W,
Philadelphia, 7/023
Glen Stewart for John Hopkins Hospital,
Pittsburgh, 7/024
Horn (Joseph V.) Scholarship Fund 40,028,
Philadelphia, 7/024
Houghton-Carpenter Fdn., Philadelphia, 7/024
House of Rest for the Aged, Philadelphia,
7/025
Houstin Fdn., Philadelphia, 7/026
Houston (S. F.) Dec'd T/W Cdrl. Ch. Christ,
Philadelphia, 7/027
Houston (Sam F.) Dec'd Tr. Houston Com.
Center, Philadelphia, 7/028
Houston (S. F.) Dec'd T/W Epis. Dio. of Pa.,
Philadelphia, 7/029
Houston (S. F.) Dec'd H.H.H.II #3 T/W,
Philadelphia, 7/030
Houston (S. F.) Dec'd T/W St. Martin Fld.,
Philadelphia, 7/030
Huber (Ira & Doris) T/A Marticville Cemetery
Assn., Lancaster, 7/031
Huebner (S. S.) Fdn. for Insurance Education,
Philadelphia, 7/032
Hughes (Annie M.) T/W Catholic Diocese of
Harrisburg, Lancaster, 7/033
Hughes Fdn., East Stroudsburg, 7/033
Hunsicker (Robert F.) Fdn., Allentown, 7/034
Hunt (Roy A.) Fdn., Pittsburgh, 7/035
Huston Fdn., Coatesville, 7/036
T/W Hutchinson (Jane), Philadelphia, 7/036
Hyman Family Fdn., Pittsburgh, 7/037
Ideal Fdn., Sykesville, 7/037
Imbt (Herbert R.) Charitable Trust,
Philadelphia, 7/038
INA Fdn., Philadelphia, 7/038
Independence Fdn., Philadelphia, 7/040
Industrial Home for Crippled Children,
Pittsburgh, 7/042
Irvine (Kate) Cemetery Fund, Harrisburg,
7/043
Integrity Fdn., Philadelphia, 7/043
Irwin (Agnes and Sophy) Memorial Fdn.,
Philadelphia, 7/043
Jackson (Percy H.) Td., Philadelphia, 7/045
Jacobson (David R.) Estate Cemetery Fund,
Harrisburg, 7/045

Jaegle (C.) Jr. for Catholic Diocese, Pittsburgh, 7/046

Jaffe (Evelyn) Charitable Trust, Radnor, 7/046

James (Frank) Residuary Tr., Philadelphia, 7/047

Janssen (Henry) Fdn., Inc., Reading, 7/048

Javitch (David & Jennie) Fdn., Carlisle, 7/050

Trust U/W J. L. Jeanes, Philadelphia, 7/050

Jen Fdn., Philadelphia, 7/051

Johnson (Alice A.) Scholarship Home Economic Assoc. of Phila., Philadelphia, 7/051

Johnston (A. R.) T/W for Presbyterian Church of New Bloomfield, Harrisburg, 7/052

Haines (Henrietta) Jahnson, Philadelphia, 7/052

Johnstone Trust, State Dollege, 7/052

M. C. Jones Fdn., Gettysburg, 7/053

Arthur Judson Fdn., Philadelphia, 7/053

Karnavas (A.) Fdn., Pittsburgh, 7/053

Kassab (J. G. and Helen) Fdn., Canonsburgh, 7/054

Katz Fdn., Meadow Brook, 7/054

Katz (J. Jerome) & Clara G. Katz Scholarship Fund, Philadelphia, 7/055

Kaub (Linda S.) Dec'd A. L. Kaub Charitable Trust, Philadelphia, 7/056

Kaub (Linda S.) Dec'd Daniel Stine Fd. Tr., Philadelphia, 7/057

Kauffman (Jessie E.) T/W Lodge 43 Free and Accepted Masons, Lancaster, 7/058

Keasbey (Henry G. & Anna G.) Memorial Fdn., Philadelphia, 7/058

Keehmle (M. Theresa) T/W, Philadelphia, 7/060

Keen (Emma L.) Dec'd Phila Miss. & Ch. Soc. Tr., Philadelphia, 7/060

Keim (Bertha G.Y.) T/W for Womens Foreign Missionary Society of Grace Methodist Episcopal Church, Harrisburg, 7/061

Keim (Bertha G.Y.) T/W for Womens Home Missionary Society of Grace Methodist Episcopal Church, Harrisburg, 7/061

Keim (Bertha G.Y.) T/W for Conestoga Methodist Church Lancaster County, Harrisburg, 7/061

Keister (William A. and Arvilla) Memorial Fdn., Harrisburg, 7/062

Kelly (Catherine M.) T/W # 59 St. Marys Parochial School, Lancaster, 7/062

Kelly (Catherine M.) T/W # 67 St. Marys Parochial School, Lancaster, 7/062

Kempel (A.B.) Memorial Fund, Oil City, 7/063

Kendall Fdn., Bradford, 7/064

Kennametal Fdn., Latrobe, 7/064

Kennedy (Friend) Educ. Fund, Pittsburgh, 7/065

Keystone Fdn., Philadelphia, 7/067

Kift-Thomas (Robert L.) R. Mullen Jr., Allentown, 7/067

Kilmore (Edna E.) T/W St. Johns Cemetery, Harrisburg, 7/068

Kinzer (Anna M.) TW Ladies Doscas Society of Lancaster, Lancaster, 7/068

United Penn Bank, Trustee for Angeline Elizabeth Kirby Memorial Health Center, Wilkes-Barre, 7/069

Angeline Elizabeth Kirby Memorial Health Center, Wilkes-Barre, 7/070

Kirkbride Fund, Philadelphia, 7/071

Kirsopp Fdn., Philadelphia, 7/072

Klein Fdn. Julius Klein Robert Klein and Jos, Wyncote, 7/073

Klein Fdn., Philadelphia, 7/074

Klein (Louis) Fdn., Philadelphia, 7/074

Klein (Raymond and Miriam) Fdn., Wyncote, 7/075

Kobrovsky (Bernard and Florence) Charitable Fdn., Allentown, 7/075

Kohn (Joseph and Mollie) Fdn., Philadelphia, 7/075

Koppelman (Theodore) Fdn., Scranton, 7/076

Korman (Hyman) Family Fdn., Jenkintown, 7/076

Kraftsow Fdn., Philadelphia, 7/078

Kralle (Wilhelmine) Endowment Fund, Philadelphia, 7/079

Kramer (Frederick C.) Cemetery Fund, Harrisburg, 7/079

Krauskoph Fdn., Philadelphia, 7/080

Kroungold Fdn., Wynnewood, 7/080

Kulicke (Lieut. F.W.) III, Fund Koli, Ft. Washington, 7/081

Kunkel (Elizabeth Crain) Tr. for HBG Hospital, Harrisburg, 7/081

Kunkel (Elizabeth Crain) T/W for Historical Society of Dauphin County, Harrisburg, 7/081

Kunkel (Elizabeth Crain) T/W Eng. Pres. Cong. Sunday Schl., Harrisburg, 7/081

Kunkel (Elizabeth Crain) T/W Market Sq. Presby. Ch., Harrisburg, 7/082

Kunkel (John C.) Fdn., Harrisburg, 7/082

Kunkel (John Crain) Fdn., Harrisburg, 7/082

Lake (William B.) Fdn., Philadelphia, 7/082

Laley (George A.) T/W, Harrisburg, 7/083

Lambrecht (Annette Bailey) T/W For Middle Paxton Township Library Fund, Harrisburg, 7/084

Landisburg (Trustee for) Church of God, Harrisburg, 7/084

Laros (R. K.) Fdn., Philadelphia, 7/084

Larson (Oscar) & Annie H. Larson Fdn., Pittsburgh, 7/085

Larue (John H.) Dec'd, Philadelphia, 7/085

Lavetan Fund, York, 7/086

Lavino (T/D E.G.) #44658, Philadelphia, 7/087

Tecosky (Evelyn R. and J. Lawrence) Fund, Philadelphia, 7/088

Lazear (Martha Edwards) Fdn., Pittsburgh, 7/088

Lea (A. H.) Dec'd T/W First Unitarian Ch., Philadelphia, 7/089

Lebanon Steel Foundry Fdn., Lebanon, 7/090

Lee (Bridget) Religious and Charitable Trust, Pittsburgh, 7/091

40,071 Leeds and Northrup Fdn., Philadelphia, 7/091

Leffman (Henry) TD, Philadelphia, 7/092

Lehigh Valley Cardio Vascular Research Assn., Allentown, 7/093

Lehigh Valley Helping Hand Fdn., Allentown, 7/093

Lehman-Epstine Trust, Pittsburgh, 7/095

Lepperd (W. Abner) T/W Waggoners Evangelical Ch., Harrisburg, 7/095

Levee (Pearl) Charitable Tr., Radnor, 7/096

Levin (Harry and Reba) Fdn., Philadelphia, 7/098

Levine (Arnold I. and Adelyne Roth) Fdn., Pittsburgh, 7/099

Levine (Morris M.) Fdn., Philadelphia, 7/100

Levinson (James & Rachel) Fdn., Pittsburgh, 7/100

Levinson (Ralph) Family Fund, Reading, 7/100

Levy (Jacob and Mary) Fdn., Scranton, 7/101

Liberty Sport Togs Fdn., Philadelphia, 7/101

Lieberman (Elizabeth L. and Albert H.) Fdn., Philadelphia, 7/101

Liebman (Joseph) Fdn., Philadelphia, 7/102

Life Insurance Medical Research Fund, Philadelphia, 7/102

Lindback (T/W Mary F.) Residuary Trust, Philadelphia, 7/103

Linebaugh (Emily T.) T/W Womens Foreign Missionary Society, Harrisburg, 7/104

Linebaugh (Emily T.) T/W, Harrisburg, 7/104

Lingle (Irwin D.) Tr. U/W, Harrisburg, 7/105

Lipsky (Rubin) Fund, Philadelphia, 7/105

Litras (T/W John) #66040, Philadelphia, 7/105

Little Quakers, Inc., Philadelphia, 7/105

Lockard (William F.) Tr. Fund, Columbia, 7/106

Loomis (Eliza) Cemetery Fund, Harrisburg, 7/107

Long (Ida A.) Trust, Harrisburg, 7/107

Long (Mary S.) TA Bloomfield Presbyterian Church, Harrisburg, 7/107

Lowengard (Leon) Cemetery Fund, Harrisburg, 7/107

Lower Frankford Stone Church T/W Mildred Shugart, Harrisburg, 7/107

Lustgarten (Benjamin and Hilda) Fdn., Bala Cynwyd, 7/108

Lutheran Reformed Church of Dellville Tr., Harrisburg, 7/108

Machinery Associates Fdn. T/D, Narberth, 7/108

Magee (Harry L.) T/A B. Magee Fdn., Harrisburg, 7/108

Mandell (Samuel P.) Fdn., Philadelphia, 7/109

Marcus (Mildred) Fdn., Philadelphia, 7/110

Marcus (Myer) Fdn., Philadelphia, 7/110

Maris (Anne Gerhard) Fund, Philadelphia, 7/110

Markovitz (Regina N.) Charity Fund, Philadelphia, 7/111

Markoe (Matilda C.) Memorial Fund, Philadelphia, 7/111

Marple (Emily M.) T/W Grace Methodist Church, Harrisburg, 7/112

Marple (Emily M.) T/W Children's Industrial Home, Harrisburg, 7/112

Marsim Fund, Philadelphia, 7/112

Masonic Building Corp. of Easton, Easton, 7/113

Massey Charitable Tr., Pittsburgh, 7/113

Master Brewers Assn. of America Philadelphia District, Philadelphia, 7/113

Mathews (Felix A.) T/W Cemetery, Harrisburg, 7/113

Matzkin (Forman) Fdn., Philadelphia, 7/114

Maynard Fdn., Pittsburgh, 7/114

Mayr (Chrissie B.) Educational Trust Fund Trust, Montoursville, 7/115

McAlister (Emma) T/W Bloomfield Cemetery, Harrisburg, 7/116

McAnall (Anna M.) Dec'd T W, Philadelphia, 7/116

McBride (Thurlow and Harriet) Fdn., Philadelphia, 7/116

McClure (C. G.) Dec'd McClure School, Philadelphia, 7/117

McCormick (Anne) Trustee U/W, Harrisburg, 7/117

McCormick (Anne) Tr. U/W Family & Children Serv. of Harrisburg, Harrisburg, 7/117

McCormick (Anne) Tr. U/W Trustees of the Dr. John M. T. Finney Fund, Harrisburg, 7/118

McCormick (Anne) Tr. U/W Harrisburg Hosp., Harrisburg, 7/118

HcCormick (Anne) Tr. U/W Trustees of Penna State Coll., Harrisburg, 7/118

McCormick (Anne) Trust U/W Tr. of Presbyterian Ch. of Harrisburg, Harrisburg, 7/118

McCormick (Anne), Trustee U/W (Residuary Trust), Harrisburg, 7/118

McCormick (Anne) Tr. U/W Silver Springs Church of Cumberland County, Pa., Harrisburg, 7/118

McCormick (J. S.) Company Charitable Trust, Pittsburgh, 7/119

McCormick (Vance) Tr. U/W Local Charities, Harrisburg, 7/119

McCormick (Vance C.), Tr. U/W Presbyterian Church Hbg., Harrisburg, 7/120

McCormick (Vance C.) Tr. U/W Residuary Trust, Harrisburg, 7/120

McDaniel (Ruth A.) T/A Paxtang Cemetery Assn., Harrisburg, 7/120

McDonald (Caroline G.) T/A, Harrisburg, 7/121

McDowell and McClellan Cemetery T/A, Harrisburg, 7/121

McEldowney (Jane Smith) T/D, Philadelphia, 7/121

McIlhenny (James and Sena) T/A Bloomfield Cemetery, Harrisburg, 7/122

McKee (Jessie W.) T/W Bloomfield Presbyterian Ch., Harrisburg, 7/122

McKee Memorial Westmore Land Hospital, Pittsburgh, 7/122

Rittenhouse (E. K.) Music and Altar Fdn., Philadelphia, 7/212

Rittenhouse (E. K.) Symphony Society FKD, Philadelphia, 7/212

Ritter (A. May) T/A Trindle Springs Lutheran Church, Harrisburg, 7/213

Ritter (R. A.) Fdn., Rydal, 7/213

Ritzman (Allen Z.) Trustee U/W, Harrisburg, 7/214

Roberts (Rebecca A.) T/A Gailey Burial Ground, Harrisburg, 7/214

Trust U/W Warren Roberts, Bethlehem, 7/214

Roberts (W. L.) T/A Gailey Cemetery Assn., Harrisburg, 7/214

Robbins (Jerome W. and Patricia D.) Fdn., Lancaster, 7/215

Robinson Fdn., Philadelphia, 7/215

Robinson (Alex and Leona) Fdn., Monroeville, 7/216

Robinson (Sarah M. W.) Cemetery Fund T/W, Harrisburg, 7/216

Robinson (Harold and Shirley) Fdn., Pittsburgh, 7/217

Rodgers (Harry N.) #2, Philadelphia, 7/217

Rodstein (Albert M. and Miriam) Fdn., Wyncote, 7/217

Rose (Leon and Louise) Family Fund, Philadelphia, 7/218

Rosen (Maurice M.) Fdn., Philadelphia, 7/218

Rosen (Rose and Harry) Fdn., Pittsburgh, 7/219

Rosen (Tallu) Fdn., Philadelphia, 7/220

Rosenau (Jeremy A.) Fdn., Philadelphia, 7/221

Rosenbloom (Solomon) for Orthodox Synagogues, Pittsburgh, 8/002

Rosenfeld (Mary & Emanuel) Fdn. Td., Philadelphia, 8/002

Rosenthal (E. N.) Family Fdn., Pittsburgh, 8/003

Rosenlund Family Fdn., Philadelphia, 8/004

Rosenwald (Lessing and Edith) Fdn., Philadelphia, 8/005

Rosewater Fund, Elkins Park, 8/007

Rotary International Book Fdn. (World Wide Book Fdn. of the Rotary Club of Souderton-Telford), Souderton, 8/007

Rotary Fdn. of Philadelphia, Philadelphia, 8/007

Royston Fdn., Philadelphia, 8/008

Ruck (George) Trust, Philadelphia, 8/009

Russ (William) T/W Ice Fund, Harrisburg, 8/009

Rutherford (Elizabeth Martha) T/W Cemetery, Harrisburg, 8/010

Rutherford (Howard A.) T/W Cemetery Fund, Harrisburg, 8/010

Rutherford (Isabella P. and Margaret B.) T/A Paxton Presbyterian Church, Harrisburg, 8/010

Rutherford (Josh E. & Margaret M.) T/A Paxton Presbyterian Church, Harrisburg, 8/010

Rutherford (Matthew R.) T/A Paxton Presbyterian Church, Harrisburg, 8/010

St. Christophers Hospital for Children Trust, Philadelphia, 8/012

St. Gabriels Episcopal Church Tr., Philadelphia, 8/012

St. James Church Perkiomen Tr., Philadelphia, 8/013

St. Johns Episcopal Church T/A, Harrisburg, 8/014

St. Marys Catholic Fdn., St. Marys, 8/014

St. Pauls Lutheran Ch. of Millersville Pa., Harrisburg, 8/015

St. Thomas Church Whitemarsh Trust, Philadelphia, 8/016

T/W Robert Saintclair, Philadelphia, 8/016

Saltsburg Community Memorial Assn., Saltsburg, 8/017

Samuels (A.) Fdn., Allentown, 8/018

Sanders (Alice J.) T/A Paxtang Cemetery Assn., Harrisburg, 8/019

Sandridge Fdn., Bryn Mawr, 8/019

Sandy Hill Reformed Church TW LC Bixler, Harrisburg, 8/019

Sol Satinsky Fdn., Philadelphia, 8/019

Saunders (Dorothy Love & Lawrence), Philadelphia, 8/020

Tait (S. D.) Dec'd Ind Widows Etc. Soc. T/W, Philadelphia, 8/021

Schiffman (Dr. Frederic C.) T/A Harrisburg Hospital, Harrisburg, 8/021

Schimmel (Rose and Joseph H.), Philadelphia, 8/022

Schadt (George H.) TW Middletown Cemetery, Harrisburg, 8/022

Schadt (Emma G.) TW Middletown Cemetery, Harrisburg, 8/023

Scherger Fdn. Ralph Scherger Et Al Trustees, Pittsburgh, 8/023

Schlegelmilch (Charles W.) Tr. for Kinderhook Evangelical Cong. Church, Lancaster, 8/024

Schmidt (Oscar C.) T/W, Philadelphia, 8/024

Scholl (T. J.) T/W Cemetery, Harrisburg, 8/025

Scholl (Tolbert J.) TA Central Pa. Conference of the Methodist, Harrisburg, 8/026

Scholl (T. J.) TW Wesly United Methodist Ch., Harrisburg, 8/026

Schwoyer (John A.), Trust U/W for "4 Churches", Kutztown, 8/026

Segal (Bernard G.) Fdn., Philadelphia, 8/026

Seybert (Adam and Maria Sarah) Institution for Poor Boys and Girls, Philadelphia, 8/027

Schweiker (Malcolm A.) Jr., Memorial Fdn., Philadelphia, 8/028

Segall (Herman & Sophia) Fdn. Trust Under Will, Philadelphia, 8/029

Seibert (S. W.) TW Cemetery, Harrisburg, 8/030

Siebert (William H.) T/A Harrisburg Academy of Medicine, Harrisburg, 8/030

Seidle (David W.) T/W Seidle Memorial Hospital, Harrisburg, 8/030

Seidle (David W.) T/W Cemetery, Harrisburg, 8/031

Scholl (T. J.) TW Seidle Memorial Hospital, Harrisburg, 8/032

Seifert (John A.) T/W Cemetery, Harrisburg, 8/032

Shallway Fdn., Connellsville, 8/032

Shaffer-Liss Fdn., Philadelphia, 8/033

Shapiro (Zalman and Evelyn) Charitable Trust, Reading, 8/034

Shaull (Clyde L. & Mary C.) Education Trust, Mechanicsburg, 8/034

Sharpe (Elizabeth G.) T/W Cemetery, Harrisburg, 8/035

Sheibley (Mary E.) Reformed Church, Harrisburg, 8/035

Sheller (Samuel B.) T/W Ashbury Methodist Ch., Harrisburg, 8/035

Shelly (Roberts) Fdn., Drexel Hill, 8/035

Shetter (Florence) T/A First United Church of Christ, Harrisburg, 8/035

Shires (Harry B.) T/A Baldwin Cemetery, Harrisburg, 8/035

Shoemaker (Manai) Cemetery Trust, Harrisburg, 8/036

Shoemaker (Ray S.) Scholarship Fdn., Harrisburg, 8/036

Shoops Cemetery Assn. Trust, Harrisburg, 8/036

Shoops Cemetery Assn. Special Care Fund T/A, Harrisburg, 8/037

Shuler (Annie P.) T/W Crumlich Lot Springville Cemetery, Harrisburg, 8/038

Shy (G. Milton) Memorial Fund, Philadelphia, 8/038

Silberman (Alexander) Fdn., Philadelphia, 8/039

Silberstein (Nathan) Fund, Philadelphia, 8/040

Silco Fdn., Huntingdon Valley, 8/040

Simon (Esther) Charitable Tr., Radnor, 8/041

Sipe (Elmer) T/W Salem Stone Church Cemetery, Harrisburg, 8/042

Slagen (Raymond S.) T/W Lancaster Heart Haven, Lancaster, 8/042

Smith (Alfred) Trust, Philadelphia, 8/043

Smith (C. K.) T/W Woodmere Art Gallery, Philadelphia, 8/044

Smith (Charles K.) Trust, Philadelphia, 8/045

Smith (Emma) T/W Cemetery, Harrisburg, 8/046

Smith (Henry D.) Trust, Harrisburg, 8/046

Smith (Samuel) Fdn., Allentown, 8/046

Smith (U. Grant) Trust, Philadelphia, 8/047

Smith (W. W.) Fdn., Bryn Mawr, 8/047

Smulowitz (Ted) Family Fdn., Kingston, 8/048

Snyder (David & Margaret A.) T/A Methodist Church of Millerstown, Harrisburg, 8/048

Snyders UB Church of Wheatfield Trust, Harrisburg, 8/049

S. & R. Fdn., Washington Cross, 8/049

Sofield (Alice D.) TW Jersey Shore Cemetery, Harrisburg, 8/050

Sofield (Alice D.) TW Paxtang Cemetery, Harrisburg, 8/050

Solanco Day Care Service, Quarryville, 8/051

Solomon (Daniel D.) Fdn., Philadelphia, 8/051

Spackman (Isabel M.) Trust, Philadelphia, 8/053

Spangler (William G.) T/W Carlisle Cemetery, Harrisburg, 8/053

Spellissy Fdn., Philadelphia, 8/053

Spielman (Selma and Samuel) Fdn., Cheltenham, 8/054

Sportwood (S. B.) T/W Presbyterian Ch. of New Ca., Philadelphia, 8/054

Sprenkle (Edna M.) T/W Cemetery, Harrisburg, 8/055

S. S. Arch St. Me. Church Phila. Tr., Philadelphia, 8/055

Staats Fdn., Malvern, 8/056

Stackpole (Edward J.) T/W Market Square Pres. Church, Harrisburg, 8/057

Stallman (J. Kenneth) Fdn., York, 8/057

Standen Fdn., Philadelphia, 8/058

Stannard (Barbara) Residuary Estate, Pittsburgh, 8/058

Steelton Cemetery Assn. Heugy Trust, Harrisburg, 8/059

Steelton School Board Calder Trust, Harrisburg, 8/059

Steelmet Fdn., Pittsburgh, 8/060

Steelton Welfare Assn. (A. M. Siebert) Trust, Harrisburg, 8/060

Steelton YMCA Endowment, Harrisburg, 8/061

Stein (Gertrude) Fdn., Pittsburgh, 8/061

Stephens (Isaiah E.) TW Cemetery, Harrisburg, 8/061

Stern (Harry L.) Trust, Philadelphia, 8/061

Johnson (Stewart M.) Mausoleum Fund, Harrisburg, 8/062

Stewart (J. H.) Pres. Ch. Falling Sp. Trust, Philadelphia, 8/063

Duncan (B. Stiles & Grace N.) Assoc. T/A Duncannon Cemetery, Harrisburg, 8/064

Stokes (Francis J. & Lelia W.) Fdn., Philadelphia, 8/065

Stokes (Lydia B.) Fdn., Philadelphia, 8/065

Stoner (Eva Florence) Trust, Harrisburg, 8/066

Stott (Elizabeth P.) Testamentary Trust, Philadelphia, 8/066

Stout (Edward W.) T/W Baldwin Cemetery, Harrisburg, 8/067

Strauss (Ruth Bryan) Memorial Fdn., State College, 8/067

Strick (Frank) Fdn., Meadowbrook, 8/067

Stroud Fdn., Philadelphia, 8/069

Stroud (S. C.) Dec'd Amer. Anti Vivi Soc. Tr., Philadelphia, 8/069

Sturges Fdn., Pittsburgh, 8/070

Succop (William G. and Gladys Marie D.) Tr., Pittsburgh, 8/072

Summers (Dallas) T/W Carlisle Cemetery, Harrisburg, 8/072

Sutleff (Ellis) T/W Benton Cemetery, Harrisburg, 8/072

Sutliff (Ellis) T/W Coles Creek Cemetery, Harrisburg, 8/073

Sutton (James) Home for Aged and Infirm Men Tr., Wilkes-Barre, 8/074

Swarner (Catherine P.) TW Cemetery Trust, Harrisburg, 8/075

Swedenborg Scientific Assn., Bryn Athyn, 8/075

Swigart Fdn., Huntingdon, 8/075

Switzer (Mary L.) T/W Baldwin Cemetery, Harrisburg, 8/076

Sylk Brothers Fdn., Philadelphia, 8/076

Taubel (A.) Dec'd Cal. Ort. Pres. Ch. WW N. J. T. W., Philadelphia, 8/076

Taubel (A.) Dec'd Christ West Hope Ch. TW, Philadelphia, 8/077

Tausig (Edwin F.) T/A Mt. Moriah Cemetery Assn., Harrisburg, 8/078

Tausig (Herman) T/A Mt. Moriah Cemetery Assn., Harrisburg, 8/078

Taubel (A.) Dec'd Phila. Ger. Protest Home, Philadelphia, 8/078

Taubel (A.) Dec'd Palatinate Reform Ch., Philadelphia, 8/078

Tausig (Pearl G.) T/W Cemetery, Harrisburg, 8/080

Taylor (Elizabeth T.) Trust Fund, Jenkintown, 8/080

Teck Fund, Philadelphia, 8/080

Temple University Law Fdn., Philadelphia, 8/081

Thorpe Brothers Charitable Tr., Pittsburgh, 8/081

Thress (Minnie K.) Trust, Philadelphia, 8/082

Thomas (Marion B.) T/W Cemetery, Harrisburg, 8/083

Thompson (Edward Shippen) T/W Cemetery, Harrisburg, 8/083

Thorofare Markets Charitable Fdn., Murrysville, 8/083

Thumma (W. H.) T/W Opposum Hill Cemetery, Harrisburg, 8/084

Timmins (Edward Jackman) Memorial Fund, Pittsburgh, 8/084

Timmons (John S. and Jane McC.) Fdn., Philadelphia, 8/085

Todd (Robert B.) T/W Lancaster General Hospital, Lancaster, 8/086

Townsend (Annie P.) Dec'd A. P. Townsend Fd., Philadelphia, 8/087

Treen (Henrietta S.) Fund Trust, Philadelphia, 8/088

Trees (Edith L.) Charitable Tr., Pittsburgh, 8/089

Tri-County Conservancy of the Brandywine, Chadds Ford, 8/089

Trexler (Harry C.) Estate, Allentown, 8/090

Trexler (Harry C.) Trust Fund-Masonic Lodges Library and Romper Day, Allentown, 8/096

Tressler (Frank E.) T/W Student Prize Fund, Harrisburg, 8/097

Todd (C. R. and B. G.) T/A First Reformed Church, Harrisburg, 8/097

Boyd (John Y.), Tr., Harrisburg, 8/097

Bretz (Robert P.), Trustee, Harrisburg, 8/098

Brown (George L.), Tr. U/W Harrisburg and Polyclinic Hospital, Harrisburg, 8/098

Einstein (Richard F.), Sur. Tr. U/W (Tr. #2 Charitable), Harrisburg, 8/098

Conners (Laura Line) Trust, Harrisburg, 8/098

Brown (George L.), Tr. U/W (Dickinson College), Harrisburg, 8/098

Erdman (Florence Waring) Dec'd Trust, Philadelphia, 8/098

Gambold (Thomas R. and Nellie J.), Trust f/b/o First Presbyterian Church, Wilkes-Barre, 8/100

Ferguson (Rose Entler), Tr. U/W (Harrisburg Hospital), Harrisburg, 8/100

Gorgas (Kate F.) T/A Home for the Friendless, Harrisburg, 8/101

Trust U/W/O Amy E. Reno, Clearfield, 8/101

O. Raymond Grimley Trust U/W (Item 6) for St. Paul's Church of Christ, Kutztown, 8/101

Trust Under Item Fifth B-I of Will of Bernard L. Salesky, Philadelphia, 8/101

Trust U/W of Anne West Strawbridge, Philadelphia, 8/101

T/D Julia M. Turner-Arch St. Presbyterian, Philadelphia, 8/102

Tyson Fdn., Ambler, 8/103

Voss (Elsa Horne) Animal Welfare Fund, Pittsburgh, 8/104

Ulrich (Barbara) T/A Cemetery Fund, Harrisburg, 8/104

Underwood (Anna H.) TW Carlisle Cemetery, Harrisburg, 8/105

Union Benevolent Assn., Philadelphia, 8/105

Union Cemetery of Fayette County, Philadelphia, 8/107

Union Deposit Lutheran Reformed Church Trust, Harrisburg, 8/108

Union M. E. Church TD, Philadelphia, 8/108

Union School and Childrens Home Trust, Philadelphia, 8/108

United Assn. of Journeymen and Apprentices of The Plumbing and Pipefitting Industry-Local #655, Gilbert, 8/109

United Brethren Church of Duncunnon Trust, Harrisburg, 8/110

United Daughters of Confederacy TD, Philadelphia, 8/110

United Presbyterian Home for Aged, Pittsburgh, 8/110

Urguhart (Marion W.) Mem. Fdn., Philadelphia, 8/111

Venango County Assn. for The Blind, Oil City, 8/111

Vincent (Anna M.) Trust, Philadelphiia, 8/112

Wagman (Nancy) Fdn., Philadelphia, 8/115

Walker Fdn., Erie, 8/116

Walton (Margaret H.) Fund, Philadelphia, 8/116

Wanamaker (Mary B.) Trust, Philadelphia, 8/117

Wanamaker (Rodman) TD #112040-1, Philadelphia, 8/118

Wanamaker (Rodman) T/D #112050-1, Philadelphia, 8/119

Ware (Sampson G.) Trust, Philadelphia, 8/119

Warne (Emma L.) Trust, Philadelphia, 8/120

Warne Fdn., Skytop, 8/121

Warner (Lydia Fisher) Trust, Philadelphia, 8/122

Watson (Elizabeth P.) Trust, Philadelphia, 8/123

Watson Memorial Home, Warren, 8/124

Wayne Athletic Fdn., Inc., Honesdale, 8/125

Weaver (Laura) Fund TW, Harrisburg, 8/125

Weinberger Fund Fdn., Old Forge, 8/126

Weinstein (Matthew B.) and Fred L. Rosenbloom Trust, Merion, 8/126

Weir (Sibyl M.) T/A YMCA of Harrisburg, Harrisburg, 8/126

Weir (Sibyl M.) T/A Home for The Friendless, Harrisburg, 8/126

Welch (Mary H. & Edwin T.) Memorial Trust Fund, Oil City, 8/127

Welfare Fund of United Carpenters and Joiners of America, Philadelphia, 8/127

Wentz (William B.) T/A Blain Cemetery Assn., Harrisburg, 8/127

Wentz (William B.) T/A Zion Lutheran Church of Blain, Harrisburg, 8/127

Wesley United Methodist Church Trust, Harrisburg, 8/128

West (Helen A.) T/W First Lutheran Choi Carlisle, Harrisburg, 8/128

West (Helen A.) T/W Nat'l Lutheran Home for Aged, Harrisburg, 8/129

West (Helen A.) T/W First Lutheran Church of Carlisle, Harrisburg, 8/131

West (Helen A.) T/W Melk & West Cemetery Plots, Harrisburg, 8/132

West (Helen A.) T/W First Lutheran Church Sunday School, Harrisburg, 8/132

West (Helen A.) T/W First Evangelical Lutheran Ch., Harrisburg, 8/132

Westbury Lutherary & Historical Soc. Tr., Philadelphia, 8/133

Westinghouse Educational Fdn., Pittsburgh, 8/133

Westtown Boarding School No. 2 Tr., Philadelphia, 8/135

Wexler (Sylvia G. & Morris M.) Fdn., Philadelphia, 8/136

Whalen (A. Floyd) T/A English Presbyterian Ch., Harrisburg, 8/137

Whalley Charitable Tr., Windber, 8/138

Wheeling-Pittsburgh Steel Fdn., Inc., Pittsburgh, 8/139

Williams (James and Mary) T/W Monaghan Presby. Ch., Harrisburg, 8/140

Whelan (Sarah Yeates) T/D, Philadelphia, 8/140

Whitman (Nathanial W.) T/W Kindle Spring Cemetery Assn., Harrisburg, 8/141

Whitman (Nathanial W.) TW Trindle Spring Evangelical, Harrisburg, 8/141

Widener Memorial Fdn., Philadelphia, 8/142

Widener Memorial Fdn. In Aid of Handicapped Children, Philadelphia, 8/143

Smith (William Wikoff) TD #174820-1, Philadelphia, 8/143

Williamson (Clara G.) Trust, Philadelphia, 8/144

Williamson (Frederick B.), Jr. Trust, New Hope, 8/144

Willisbrook Trust, Malvern, 8/146

Willits Trust #43578, Philadelphia, 8/147

Wilson (Joseph D.) Trust, Philadelphia, 8/148

Winter (Charles R.) Fdn., Lancaster, 8/149

Witman (Emma) T/W Cemetery Fund, Harrisburg, 8/150

Witmer (Ann C.) Home, Lancaster, 8/150

Woldow Family Fdn., Philadelphia, 8/150

Wolf (Benjamin and Fredora K.) Memorial Fdn., Philadelphia, 8/151

Wolf (Howard A. & Martha R.) Fund, Philadelphia, 8/153

Wolf (Lillie K. C.) Trust, Harrisburg, 8/154

Wolf (Michael Annie and Beckie) T/A Cemetery, Harrisburg, 8/154

Womans Missionary Fund T/W Emma L. Bickel, Harrisburg, 8/154

Womens Penna S. P. C. A. Tr., Philadelphia, 8/155

Wood Fdn. of Chambersburg, Chambersburg, 8/155

Woodbridge (Louise Deshong) Trust, Philadelphia, 8/156

Woods (Agnes S.) T/W Ashland Cemetery, Harrisburg, 8/157

Woods-Marchand Fdn., Greensburg, 8/157

Woods (William M. and Margarite J.) T/A Newville Cemetery, Harrisburg, 8/157

Worley (Kate) Trust, Philadelphia, 8/158

Worth (John S. & Francis R.) Trust, Bethlehem, 8/158

Wright (A. J. and Fanny) T/A Baldwin Cemetery, Harrisburg, 8/159

Wright (Annie) Seminary, Philadelphia, 8/159

Wunderlich (Albert) Dec'd, Philadelphia, 8/160

Wunderlich (Albert) Church Tr., Philadelphia, 8/160

Wurster (Charles S. B.) Trust Fund, Oil City, 8/161

Wurster (Irene Payne) Trust Fund, Oil City, 8/161

Yarnell (Lydia) Dec'd #24471.0-0 Colored Home Trust, Philadelphia, 8/162

Yinger (Ida F.) T/W Cemetery Fund, Harrisburg, 8/162

Yost (Charles H.) T/W Cemetery, Harrisburg, 8/162

Young (Elizabeth A.) Cemetery, Harrisburg, 8/163

Young (Elizabeth A.) T/W St. Peters Lutheran Church, 8/163

Young (Mary) T/W First Baptist Church, Harrisburg, 8/163

Yount (Carl C.) Charitable Tr., Pittsburgh, 8/165

Y. M. C. A. T/W Sarah McCauley, Harrisburg, 8/164

Y. W. C. A. Camp for Girls T/A of Kate F. Gorgas, Harrisburg, 8/164

Yount (Charles C.) Char. Trust, Pittsburgh, 8/164

Youth Tennis Foundation of Erie, Erie, 8/165

Zeigler (Effie M.) T/A St. Pauls Evan. Lutheran Ch., Harrisburg, 8/167

RHODE ISLAND

First Filming

Abrams (Anna S.) Memorial Fdn., Providence, 1/002
Abrams (Saul) Fdn., Providence, 1/003
Ancient Arabic Order Nobles of the Mystic Shrine, Cranston, 1/004
Armbrust Fdn., Providence, 1/005
Ashaway Charitable Trust, Westerly, 1/006
Baxt (Victor J. & Gertrude) Fund, Providence, 1/007
Beckett (Thomas) Fdn., Providence, 1/008
Church (Benjamin) Home for Aged Men, Providence, 1/008
Bernstein (Alice & Bo) Charitable Fdn., Providence, 1/008
Berry Family Fund, Providence, 1/009
Blacher Fdn., Providence, 1/010
Blackall Fdn., Woonsocket, 1/011
Bonte Fdn., Woonsocket, 1/012
Brown & Sharpe Fdn., North Kingstown, 1/012
Brown (Sarah S.) Fund, Providence, 1/013
Bristolite Fdn., Bristol, 1/013
Burgess (Laura A.) Fund, Providence, 1/015
Carol Fdn., Providence, 1/015
Carpenter Fdn., Providence, 1/016
Carr (Arthur H.) Trust, Bristol, 1/017
Chace Fund, Providence, 1/018
Chernick Fdn., Providence, 1/019
Chornyei (Ernest J.) Charitable Fdn., Watch Hill, 1/020
Citizens Charitable Fdn., Providence, 1/021
Clapp (Charles & Elinor) Charitable Trust, Barrington, 1/022
Cohen (B.) & Sons Fdn., Woonsocket, 1/022
Collyer Fdn., Lincoln, 1/022
Company of Military Historians, Providence, 1/023
Corkin (Robert Lloyd) Charitable Fdn., Providence, 1/026
Counting House Corporation, Providence, 1/026
Danforth (Helen M.) Charitable Fdn., Providence, 1/027
Darman Fdn., Woonsocket, 1/027
DeAngelis (John A. & Elsa J.) Charitable Trust, Lincoln, 1/027
Dexter (Louisa) Fund, Providence, 1/028
Egavian (Edward V. & Larry V.) Fdn., Providence, 1/028
Eppley Fdn. for Research, Newport, 1/029
Ewing Fdn., Providence, 1/030
Federal Products Fdn., Providence, 1/031
Finkelstein (Jacob) & Sons Fdn., Woonsocket, 1/032
Fox Family Fdn., Providence, 1/032
Galkin (Ira & Anna) Charitable Trust, Providence, 1/033
Goldstein Fdn., Woonsocket, 1/034
Grant (Max L.) Fdn., Providence, 1/034
Greenhalgh Charitable Fdn., Pawtucket, 1/034
Gregson Fdn., Providence, 1/035
Fain (Irving Jay & E. Macie) Fund, Providence, 1/036
Fain (Norman & Rosalie) Fund, Providence, 1/037
Finkelstein (Joseph M.) Fdn., Providence, 1/037
Gross (Anna C. and G. Mason) Fdn., Providence, 1/038
Haffenreffer Family Fund, Providence, 1/039
Hail (Mary Kimball) Testamentary Trust, Providence, 1/040
Heritage Fdn. of Rhode Island, Providence, 1/041
Hassenfeld Fdn., Pawtucket, 1/041

Hazard (Frank B.) General Charity Fund, Providence, 1/042
Heritage Fdn. of Rhode Island, Providence, 1/043
Hodgson Fdn., Pawtucket, 1/043
Holcombe (R. W.) Charitable Trust, Providence, 1/044
Hope Fdn., Providence, 1/044
Howard (George A. & Eliza Gardner) Fdn., Providence, 1/045
India Point Fdn., Providence, 1/045
Industrial Charitable Trust, Providence, 1/046
Kimball (Fanny A.) Trust, Providence, 1/047
Krause Fdn., Providence, 1/048
Lawton (Abbie Frances) Memorial Home, Central Falls, 1/048
Lawton (Isaac B.) Trust f/b/o Abbie Frances Lawton Memorial Home, Providence, 1/048
Lederer (B. B.) Sons Fdn., Providence, 1/049
Levin (Leonard) Fdn., Providence, 1/050
Levinger Fdn., Providence, 1/051
Leviten Family Fdn., Pawtucket, 1/052
Levy (June Rockwell) Fdn., Harrisville, 1/052
Lord (Inez Clarke) Scholarship Fund, Providence, 1/053
Low (I. S.) Fdn., Providence, 1/053
MacColl Benevolent Fund, Providence, 1/054
Macktez Fdn., Woonsocket, 1/055
Marsello (Alfred) Family Fdn., Providence, 1/056
McMahon Fdn., Pawtucket, 1/056
McWhirter Fdn., Providence, 1/057
Meehan Fdn., Providence, 1/057
Lawton (Isaac B.) Trust f/b/o Memorial Baptist Church, Pawtucket, Providence, 1/058
Moore Fdn., Westerly, 1/059
Moore (Harriet Chappell) Fdn., Westerly, 1/060
Newport National Bank Fdn., Newport, 1/061
Nicholson File Fdn., East Providence, 1/061
Old Meeting House Fdn., Providence, 1/062
Old Stone Bank Educational Fdn., Providence, 1/062
Old Stone Charitable Fdn., Providence, 1/062
Paley (Lawrence A. & Jewel) Fdn., Providence, 1/063
Papitto (Ralph R.) Fdn., Cranston, 1/063
Peerless Fdn., Providence, 1/063
Pell (Claiborne & Nuala) Fund, Newport, 1/064
Picchione-Dome (Nicholas) Fdn., Providence, 1/065
Providence Journal Charitable Fdn., Providence, 1/066
Ramsay Fdn., Pawtucket, 1/066
Paine (Almond M.) Residuary Trust, Providence, 1/067
Ress Family Fdn., Providence, 1/068
Rhode Island Hospital Department of Ophthalmology Fdn., Providence, 1/069
Rosen (Samuel) Family Fdn., Providence, 1/069
Roswin Fund, Providence, 1/070
Royal Arts Fdn., Newport, 1/070
Royal Robes Fdn., Woonsocket, 1/071
Samdperil (Isadore & Sophie) Family Fdn., Pawtucket, 1/072
Sapinsley Family Fdn., Providence, 1/072
Shepard Fdn., Providence, 1/073
Taradash Charitable Fdn., Little Compton, 1/074
Clarke (John) Trust, Providence, 1/074
Sherburne (Grant) Fund, Providence, 1/075
Steinert (Albert M.) Trust, Providence, 1/076
Sholes (Leonard J.) Fdn., Cranston, 1/076
Smithfield Sportsman's Club, Greenville, 1/077
Soforenko (Edwin S.) Fdn., Providence, 1/077
Sylmer Fdn., Pawtucket, 1/077
Taco Fdn., Cranston, 1/078
Taft-Peirce Fdn., Woonsocket, 1/079
Tanner (Fred) Fdn., Providence, 1/079
Tanner (C. Milton) Charitable Fdn., Warwick, 1/080
Troop 82 Providence Charitable Trust, Providence, 1/080

Trustees of Long Wharf and Public Schools, Newport, 1/080
Tupper Fdn., Providence, 1/080
Vernon Court Fdn., Providence, 1/081
Vigneron Memorial Fund, Providence, 1/081
Wilson Fdn., Saunderstown, 1/083
Wolf (Ruth & W. Irving, Jr.) Fdn., Pawtucket, 1/083
Bingham (Worth) Memorial Fund, Providence, 1/085

Second Filming

Abrahamian (George) Fdn., Providence, 2/001
Alperin Fdn., Providence, 2/001
American Universal Insurance Co. Fdn., Providence, 2/002
Armbrust Fdn., Providence, 2/003
Ayers (Lucy C.) Home for Nurses, Providence, 2/004
Bernstein (Alice & Bo) Charitable Fdn., Providence, 2/005
Bonte Fdn., Woonsocket, 2/006
Brite Fdn., Providence, 2/007
Broadbent Charitable Fdn., Rumford, 2/008
Brownell & Field Fdn., Providence, 2/008
Bruin Charitable Fdn., Providence, 2/009
Cohen (J.L. & R.) Fdn., Cranston, 2/010
Congdon & Carpenter Fdn., Providence, 2/011
Dexter (Mary) Fund, Providence, 2/011
Federal Products Fdn., Providence, 2/012
Green (Arthur Leslie) Scholarship Trust, Newport, 2/013
Grinell (Russell) Fund, Providence, 2/014
Heritage Fdn. of Rhode Island, Providence, 2/015
Kane (Howard) Fdn., Providence, 2/015
Langrock (David T.) Fdn., Providence, 2/015
Leach (Harry) Family Fdn., Providence, 2/016
Leesona Charitable Fdn., Warwick, 2/016
Louttit Fdn., Providence, 2/017
Molly Fund, Block Island, 2/019
Narrangansett Preservation & Improvement Association, Narragansett, 2/019
Newport Restoration Fdn., Newport, 2/020
Oster (Aaron J.) Family Fdn., Providence, 2/021
Pilavin (Albert & Selma F.) Fund, Providence, 2/022
Providence Building, Sanitary & Educational Association, Providence, 2/022
Providence Fund, Providence, 2/023
Riesman Fdn. of Rhode Island, Providence, 2/024
St. Dunstan's College of Sacred Music, Providence, 2/026
Salmanson Fdn., Pawtucket, 2/027
Smith Family of Providence Fdn., Providence, 2/028
Spear (Alfred & Esther) Fdn., Providence, 2/028
Townsend Aid for the Aged, Providence, 2/029
Trifari, Krussman & Fishel Fdn., East Providence, 2/030

SOUTH CAROLINA

First Filming

Abney (John Pope) Memorial Fund, Greenwood, 1/001
Alexander (Saul) Fdn., Charleston, 1/002
Arcadia Fdn., Arcadia, 1/005
Arkwright Fdn., Spartanburg, 1/005
Arnold (Ben) Memorial Fdn., Columbia, 1/007
Asnip (George) Fdn., Hilton Head Island, 1/008
Athelp Fdn., Clover, 1/008
Ballenger Fdn., Greenville, 1/009
Bears Bluff Laboratories, Inc., Charleston, 1/010
Beverage-Air Fdn., Spartanburg, 1/010

Blackman Fdn., Spartanburg, 1/010
Branyon Charitable Fund, Greenville, 1/011
Brown (Edgar A.) Fdn., Columbia, 1/011
Burgess (James F. & Nelle E.) Fdn., Greenville, 1/012
Burgiss (W.W.) Charities, Greenville, 1/013
Buxton (Julian T. & Lucy W.) Fdn., Sumter, 1/014
Charleston Scientific & Cultural Educational Fund, Charleston, 1/015
Church Street Historic Fdn., Charleston, 1/016
Clifton Fdn., Spartanburg, 1/017
Columbia Hospital of Richland County Research & Educational Fdn., Columbia, 1/019
Cone Fdn. of South Carolina, Greenville, 1/019
Cothran (Jane) High School Fund, Greenville, 1/021
Daniel Fdn., Greenville, 1/021
Davenport (Dan D.) Fund, Greer, 1/023
Defore (Ernest O.) Fdn., Clemson, 1/024
Dowling Fdn., Beaufort, 1/024
Doyle (Edgar Clay & Mary Cherry) Memorial Fund, Seneca, 1/025
Edgefield Advertiser Fdn., Edgefield, 1/026
Gambrill Fdn., Greenville, 1/026
Gunter (Dorothy Hipp) Fdn., Greenville, 1/027
Hamrick Companies Fdn., Gaffney, 1/027
Harris (Robert & Myrtle) Charitable Trust, Lancaster, 1/028
Her Majesty Company Fdn., Mauldin, 1/028
Hipp (Herman N.) First Fdn., Greenville, 1/029
Hipp (B. Calhoun) First Fdn., Greenville, 1/030
Hipp (Francis M.) Fdn. Formerly Hipp Fdn., Greenville, 1/031
Huffines (Robert L.), Jr. Fdn., Walterboro, 1/031
Hughes Fdn., Greenville, 1/033
Humphrey (William G.) Fdn., Spartanburg, 1/033
Joanna Fdn., Joanna, 1/034
Jolley Fdn., Greenville, 1/035
Keys Fdn., Greenville, 1/036
Koebig (Hans K. & Helen F.) Trust, Charleston, 1/037
Littlejohn (Broadus & Evelyn) Fdn., Spartanburg, 1/037
Mangini (Antoinette) Fdn., Gaffney, 1/038
Marion (William Boyce) Christian Service Trust Fund, Columbia, 1/038
Mathews Fdn., Greenwood, 1/039
Maxwell (Robert J.), Jr. Fdn., Greenville, 1/040
McEachern Fdn., Florence, 1/041
Meehan (Joseph A.) Fdn., Union, 1/041
Hamrick Mills Fdn., Gaffney, 1/042
Moore (Alfred) Fdn., Wellford, 1/042
Napoleon Hill Fdn., Charleston, 1/043
New (Alfred G.) Fdn., Spartanburg, 1/044
Moore Scholarship Fund, Charleston, 1/044
Norman (Jacque B.) Fdn., Greenville, 1/045
Norris Fdn., Greenville, 1/045
Orders Fdn., Greenville, 1/047
Ouzts (Jesse & Elizabeth) Fdn., Greenwood, 1/048
Pacolet Fdn., Spartanburg, 1/048
Park (Mary Barratt) Fdn., Greenwood, 1/048
Pate Fund, Greenville, 1/048
Peace Fund, Greenville, 1/049
Pearce (Bobby) Memorial, Greenville, 1/051
Pellett Fdn., Greenville, 1/052
Phelps Fdn., Aiken, 1/052
Pitts (Ira S.) Fdn., Clemson, 1/053
Pitts Fund, Camden, 1/054
Poynor (Wilmer S. & Mamie S.) Memorial Trust, Florence, 1/054
Quinn (Kirby) Fdn., Greenville, 1/055
Real Estate Education Fdn. of South Carolina, Columbia, 1/055
Reedy River Charitable Trust Formerly Furman Charitable Trust, Greenville, 1/056
Repokis (Henry) Fdn., Clemson, 1/057

Risher (Harold B.) Fdn., Spartanburg, 1/057
Roe Fdn., Greenville, 1/058
South Carolina Federation of Women's Clubs Progress Fdn., Columbia, 1/059
SCN Charitable & Educational Fdn., Columbia, 1/060
Self Fdn., Greenwood, 1/061
Shealy Fdn., Florence, 1/064
Sibley Fdn., Union, 1/064
Simmons (J. Clyde) Fdn., Spartanburg, 1/065
Simpson Fdn., Greenville, 1/066
Belk-Simpson Fdn., Greenville, 1/067
Sirrine (William G.) High School Fund, Greenville, 1/070
Sisson (Clyde) Fdn., Columbia, 1/070
Small (Thomas G.) Fdn., Greenville, 1/071
Smith (Aug W.) Company & McGee-Smith Company Fdn., Spartanburg, 1/072
Solomons (Maude C.) Trust, Sumter, 1/072
Sottile Fdn., Charleston, 1/072
South Carolina Press Association Journalism Fdn., Columbia, 1/073
Springs (Elliott White) Fdn., Lancaster, 1/073
Springs (Frances Ley) Fdn., Lancaster, 1/075
Stringer Fdn., Anderson, 1/076
T-Fund, Greenwood, 1/076
Thomas Educational Fdn., Beaufort, 1/077
Thomason Fdn., Greenville, 1/077
Thurmond (Strom) Fdn., Aiken, 1/078
Dumas (Mendel) Trust, Charleston, 1/079
Wiggins (Pauline & Lee) Fdn., Hartsville, 1/080
Winthrop College Alumnae Association, Greenville, 1/080
Yaschik (Henry) Charitable Fdn., Charleston, 1/081
Yeargin Fdn., Greenville, 1/081

Second Filming

Aiken Fdn., Florence, 2/002
Aldrich Fund, Greenwood, 2/002
Anderson (C.W.) Fdn., Clinton, 2/003
Greenville County Art Association, Greenville, 2/003
Bailey Fdn., Clinton, 2/004
Beverage Air Fdn., Spartanburg, 2/006
Byrnes (James F.) Fdn., Columbia, 2/006
Citizens and Southern National Bank of South Carolina Fdn., Charleston, 2/007
Clifton Fdn., Spartanburg, 2/007
Dreher (William Thurmond) Memorial Scholarship Fund, Columbia, 2/008
Edgefield Advertiser Fdn., Edgefield, 2/008
Evins (Elizabeth & Tom) Fdn., Spartanburg, 2/009
Fair (Annie A. & Charles H.) Fund, Greenville, 2/009
Fraser Fdn., Hilton Head Island, 2/009
Fulp Fdn., Greenwood, 2/011
First National Bank of South Carolina Agricultural Fdn., Anderson, 2/011
Goudelock (Bill) Scholarship Fund, Columbia, 2/012
Gregg-Graniteville Fdn., Graniteville, 2/012
Gregg Fdn., Graniteville, 2/013
Hilton Head Island Charitable Fdn., Hilton Head County, 2/014
Horne (Dick) Fdn., Orangeburg, 2/014
Joanna Fdn., Joanna, 2/015
Liberty Corporation Fdn., Greenville, 2/017
McCall Fund, Easley, 2/018
Riversel Charities, Rock Hill, 2/018
Sargent Fdn., Greenville, 2/018
Scurry (D.L.) Fdn., Greenville, 2/019
Services Council of Aiken County, Aiken, 2/019
Sirrine (J. E.) Textile Fdn., Greenville, 2/020
Sottile Fdn., Charleston, 2/021
South Carolina Federation of Womens Clubs Progress Fdn., Columbia, 2/021
Southeastern Photoplatemakers Association, Clinton, 2/022

SOUTH DAKOTA

First Filming

Brockelsby Fdn., Rapid City, 1/004
Dow (Baron and Emilie) Home Inc., Sioux Falls, 1/005
Burgess (Carl T. and Catheryn L.) Fdn., Rapid City, 1/005
Economics Scholarship Fund, Rapid City, 1/006
Fredrickson (George & Gertrude) Fdn., Sioux Falls, 1/006
Griffin (John & Sara) Fdn., Sioux Falls, 1/006
Gunderson Fdn., Vermillion, 1/007
Hatterscheidt Fdn., Aberdeen, 1/007
Hayward Memorial Testamentary Trust, Sioux Falls, 1/008
Kennedy (Bruce-John) Fdn., Sioux Falls, 1/009
Kramer (Louie & Frank) Educational Fund, Sioux Falls, 1/009
Memorial Scholarship Fund for A Squad Cheer Leaders of 1967-1968, Rapid City, 1/009
Solen (John E.) Scholarship Testamentary Trust, Sioux Falls, 1/010
Wood (A.R.) Educational Trust, Sioux Falls, 1/010

Second Filming

Fire House, Sioux Falls, 2/003
Foster-Bell Charitable Fdn., Sioux Falls, 2/003
Howard Memorial Fund, Aberdeen, 2/004
Lambda Chi Alpha Fraternity, Vermillion, 2/005
Scandinavian Mutual Fire Insurance, 2/005
Shobolm (C.E.) Charitable Trust, Rapid City, 2/005

TENNESSEE

First Filming

Aladdin Industries Fdn., Nashville, 1/001
Allan Fdn., Memphis, 1/001
Alexander (John T.) American Legion Post 17, Callatin, 1/001
American Paper and Twine Co. Charitable Tr., Hashville, 1/002
American Snuff Co. Charitable Tr., Memphis, 1/002
Baird (William O.) Fdn., Memphis, 1/003
Baptist World Missions Tr., Memphis, 1/004
Belz (Philip & Sarah) Fdn., Memphis, 1/004
Benwood Fdn., Chattanooga, 1/006
Bernal Fdn., Nashville, 1/008
Binswanger (Milton S.), Jr. Fdn., Memphis, 1/009
Black (Tom and Katherine) Fdn., Knoxville, 1/010
Block (Richard) Fund, Memphis, 1/011
Bondurant Fdn., Memphis, 1/011
Botto (Elsie) Trust, Memphis, 1/012
Bowers Surgical Society, Memphis, 1/013
Boy Scouts Trust, Knoxville, 1/013
Boyle (J. Bayard) Fdn., Memphis, 1/013
Bradford Fdn., Nashville, 1/014
Brayton Fdn., Dyersburg, 1/015
Brinkley Fdn., Memphis, 1/016
Brown (Dora MacLellan) Charitable Trust, Memphis, 1/017
Bullard (George Newton) Fdn. (formerly Hayes (Ella A.) Fund), Nashville, 1/018
Caldwell Fdn., Chattanooga, 1/020
Camp Columbus, Chattanooga, 1/021
Campbell Fdn., Memphis, 1/022
Carrier (Robert M. & Lenore W.) Fdn., Memphis, 1/023
Cavalier Fdn., Chattanooga, 1/025
Chattanooga Times Fdn., Chattanooga, 1/025
Cheek-Eason Fdn., Nashville, 1/025

Chenoweth (Elizabeth) Fdn., Paris, 1/026
Choctow Charitable Fdn., Memphis, 1/027
Christian Education Fdn., Chattanooga, 1/027
Christian Home, Lawrenceburg, 1/028
Civic Research Committee, Memphis, 1/028
Civitan Child Welfare Auxiliary, Chattanooga, 1/028
City's Greater Memphis Fund, Memphis, 1/029
Clark Fdn., Chattanooga, 1/031
Cockrill (M. S.) School Medal Fund, Nashville, 1/032
Commerce Union Fdn., Nashville, 1/032
Condra (Robert M.) Fdn., Nashville, 1/032
Crook (Mamie Wills) Charitable Trust, Nashville, 1/033
Cumberland Charitable Trust, Nashville, 1/034
Cumberland Clinic Fdn., Crossville, 1/035
Currey (Brownlee) Fdn., Nashville, 1/035
Daniel (Jack) Fdn., Nashville, 1/036
Day Fdn., Memphis, 1/036
DeHaven (Anna H.) Trust, Memphis, 1/037
Dixie Yarns Fdn., Chattanooga, 1/038
D. J. Fdn., Nashville, 1/039
Dlugach (Harry) Memorial & Educational Fdn., Memphis, 1/040
Dobbs Fdn., Memphis, 1/041
Dobson (Allen) Fdn., Nashville, 1/041
Dyer-(Arthur J.)-Nashville Bridge Company Fdn., Nashville, 1/042
Estes (Paul C.) Fdn., Murfreesboro, 1/043
Evans Fdn., Chattanooga, 1/043
Faholo Fdn., Chattanooga, 1/044
Forbes (Felder F.) Memorial Fdn., Chattanooga, 1/046
Fidelity Fdn., Chattanooga, 1/047
Finley (W. Max) Fdn., Chattanooga, 1/048
First Fdn., Nashville, 1/048
First Nat'l Bank of Memphis Charitable Trust, Memphis, 1/049
Fisher Trust, Knoxville, 1/050
Fleming Fdn., Nashville, 1/051
Fogelman Family Fdn., Memphis, 1/051
Fort (Dr. Rufus E.) & Louise Clark Fort Charitable Trust, Nashville, 1/051
Foshee (J. Clinton) Fdn., Nashville, 1/052
Franklin Builders Scholarship, Nashville, 1/053
Gamble (Guy) Estate, Memphis, 1/053
Glenn (John S.) Fdn., Nashville, 1/054
Goldsmith Fdn., Memphis, 1/054
Golightly Fdn., Memphis, 1/055
Griffith Fdn., Nashville, 1/056
Guardian Fdn., Memphis, 1/056
Hale Charitable Trust, Nashville, 1/057
Halverstadt (Herbert & Gertrude) Fdn., Nashville, 1/058
Hand Fdn., Chattanooga, 1/059
Harbert (P. M.) Scholarship Trust Fund, Savannah, 1/061
Harris Fdn., Johnson City, 1/061
Hart (Patricia & Rodes) Fdn., Nashville, 1/062
Prater (Otto & Mattie M.) Fdn., Nashville, 1/064
Haspel Fdn., Memphis, 1/064
Hassenfeld (Rita and Harold) Fdn., Shelbyville, 1/065
Haws Fdn., Nashville, 1/066
Hearthstone Fdn., Knoxville, 1/067
Herff (Herbert) Fdn., Memphis, 1/067
Hillsboro Enterprises Fdn., Nashville, 1/068
Hooker Family Fdn., Nashville, 1/069
Hooker (John J.) Fdn., Nashville, 1/069
Hotaling Fdn., Dyersburg, 1/070
Hubbard (G. W.) Trust for Meharry Medical College, Nashville, 1/071
Hughes (Maurice L.) Trust, Nashville, 1/072
Hussey Fdn., Memphis, 1/072
Hyde (Joseph R.), Jr. Fdn., Memphis, 1/073
Isbell (W. J. and Nell) Fdn., Memphis, 1/073
Jack and Jill of America Fdn., Chattanooga, 1/074
Jamison Fdn., Nashville, 1/074
Jarman Fdn., Nashville, 1/074
Johnson (Loren W.) Trust, Memphis, 1/075
Johnson (Victor), Jr. Fdn., Nashville, 1/076
Johnson (Wallace E.) - E. B. McCool Fdn., Memphis, 1/077

Kian (John G.) Memorial Fdn., Chattanooga, 1/078
Kaplan (Dr. Edward S.) Family Fdn., Memphis, 1/078
Katz (Benjamin S.) Family Fdn., Nashville, 1/078
Katz (Edward & Dorothy) Fdn., Sparta, 1/081
Keeble Fdn., Nashville, 1/083
Kempkau (C. W.) Trust for Jr. League Home of Nashville, Nashville, 1/083
Kempkau (C. W.) Trust for Monroe Harding Scholarship Fund, Nashville, 1/084
Kempkau (C. W.) Trust for Middle Tenn Council B. S. A., Nashville, 1/085
King Fdn., Kingsport, 1/085
King (Mrs. J. M.) Trust for Junior League Home, Nashville, 1/086
Kopald Family Fdn., Memphis, 1/086
Layne and Bowler, Inc. Charitable Trust, Memphis, 1/087
Lewis (Joseph) & Louise Lewis-Charitable Trust, Memphis, 1/087
Lewis (Sarah) Trust, Nashville, 1/088
Little Bahala Baptist Church Cemetery, Memphis, 1/089
Lowenstein (Wm. P. & Marie R.) Fdn., Memphis, 1/090
Lovell (Charles & Frances) Fdn., Nashville, 1/090
Lyon (Kate L.) Trust for Meharry Medical College, Nashville, 1/091
MacLeilan (Cora L.) Charitable Trust for the MacLellan Fdn., Chattanooga, 1/091
MacLellan Fdn., Chattanooga, 1/092
MacLellan (R. J.) Trust for the MacLellan Fdn., Chattanooga, 1/094
Maddox Fdn., Nashville, 1/095
Malco Charity Trust, Memphis, 1/096
Markus (Marton & Gale) Fdn., Nashville, 1/096
Martin (Judge John D.) Fdn., Memphis, 1/097
Massengill-Defriece Fdn., Bristol, 1/097
Massey (Jack C.) Fdn., Nashville, 1/098
McClure (W. K.) Fdn. for The Study of World Affairs, Knoxville, 1/099
McKee (Thomas Preston) Fdn., Johnson City, 1/099
Meade Haven Charitable Trust, Nashville, 1/099
Meeman (Edward J.) Fdn., Memphis, 1/100
Melrose Fdn., Knoxville, 1/101
Memorial Welfare Fdn., Chattanooga, 1/101
Memphis Sunshine Home for Aged Men, Memphis, 1/104
Mercer (Louise) Fdn., Memphis, 1/104
Mid-South Cardiovascular Surgical Research Fdn., Memphis, 1/105
Miller (J. B.) and Louise Perkins Miller Trust, Nashville, 1/106
Mills Fdn., Chattanooga, 1/106
Moore (R. L.) Fdn., Chattanooga, 1/107
Morrison (Margaret) Fdn., Chattanooga, 1/108
Morin Fdn., Lookout Mountain, 1/109
Morton Fdn., Knoxville, 1/109
Motlow (Conner) Fdn., Nashville, 1/110
Motlow (D. E.) Fdn., Nashville, 1/111
Notlow (Robert) Fdn., Nashville, 1/111
Nashville Academy Medical Fdn., Nashville, 1/112
Nashville Childrens Fdn., Nashville, 1/112
Navarre Fdn., Chattanooga, 1/112
Neely (Theodora) Trust, Memphis, 1/112
Nid Charitable Trust, Chattanooga, 1/112
Oak Hall Trust, Memphis, 1/113
Old Gray Cemetery Historic & Memorial Assn., Knoxville, 1/114
Old Womans Home, Nashville, 1/114
Owen (Ralph & Lulu) Fdn., Nashville, 1/115
Osborne (Weldon F.) Fdn., Chattanooga, 1/116
Pallas (William C.), M. D. Fdn., Chattanooga, 1/116
Perel Fdn., Memphis, 1/116
Pioneer Fdn., Chattanooga, 1/117
Plough (Sam) Fdn., Memphis, 1/117
Potter (Edward) Fdn., Nashville, 1/117

Potter (Justin & Valere) Fdn., Nashville, 1/118
Ridgeview Fdn., Nashville, 1/119
Ridr Fdn., Nashville, 1/119
River Oil Co. and James L. Fri, Jr. Family Charitable Fdn., Memphis, 1/120
Rodes (Battle) Fdn. Allan Battle Rodes, Trustee, Nashville, 1/121
Rogers Memorial Fund-Cordova Cemetery, Memphis, 1/121
Rose Fdn., Nashville, 1/122
Rosen (Lester A.) Trust, Memphis, 1/122
Rozier Charitable Trust, Memphis, 1/123
Russ (Manuel) Fdn., Chattanooga, 1/124
Sanford Fdn., Knoxville, 1/125
Santa Claus, Memphis, 1/125
Sauer (Sarah) Fdn., Memphis, 1/126
Schadt Fdn., Memphis, 1/126
Seidman (P. K.) Trust, Memphis, 1/127
Shepherd (Eliz. Burford) Scholarship Committee, Nashville, 1/128
Shulman (Barbara J. & Herbert L.) Fdn., Elizabethton, 1/129
Skinner (Raymond) Scholarship Fund, Memphis, 1/130
Day-Smith Fdn., Memphis, 1/131
Southern Benefit Fdn., Nashville, 1/131
Speech Fdn. of America, Memphis, 1/132
Speed (J. Spencer) Scholarship Fund Fdn., Memphis, 1/133
Stevenson (Alec Brock & Elise M.) Fdn., Nashville, 1/134
Stevenson (Eldon), Jr. Fdn., Nashville, 1/135
Thomas (Mamie)/Elmwood Cemetery, Memphis, 1/135
Tilford (H. C.) Fdn., Shelbyville, 1/136
Smith (M. J.) Family Fdn., Nashville, 1/136
Kempkau (C.W.) Trust for Vanderbilt Univ., Nashville, 1/137
Kennedy (Mrs. John C.) Trust U/W for Mt. Olivet Cemetery, Nashville, 1/137
Nestor (Mrs. M. A.) Trust U/W for Mt. Calvary Cemetery, Nashville, 1/137
Parmer (W.O.) Educational Fund, Nashville, 1/138
Pike (H.M.) Trust, Nashville, 1/138
Porter (F.G.) Trust for Downtown Presbyterian Ch., Nashville, 1/139
Preston (Thomas Ross) Charitable Trust, Chattanooga, 1/139
Shook Heirs Trust for Shook Medal Fund, Nashville, 1/140
Stallworth (Hugh W. & Anita) Fdn., Nashville, 1/140
Sullivan (Robert E.) Charitable Trust, Nashville, 1/141
Thomas (John W.) Memorial Fund, Nashville, 1/141
Tigrett (I. B.) Memorial Trust Fund, Jackson, 1/142
Wells (Pearl) Charitable Trust, Nashville, 1/142
Williamson County Memorial Gardens Inc., Nashville, 1/142
Womack (William C.) Trust for 1st Presbyterian Ch., Nashville, 1/143
Turnley Fdn., Nashville, 1/143
Union Planters Nat'l Bank of Memphis Charitable Tr., Memphis, 1/144
Unobsky (Bert) Fund, Memphis, 1/144
Van Vleet Fdn., Memphis, 1/145
Walkem Fdn., Memphis, 1/145
Walker (Mamie) Trust, Memphis, 1/146
Waller (M. & W.) Fund, Nashville, 1/147
Washington Fdn., Nashville, 1/147
Watkins (Hattie G.) Education Fund, Memphis, 1/148
Watson Fdn., Knoxville, 1/149
Webster Fdn., Nashville, 1/149
Webster Fdn., Nashville, 1/150
Weems (G. H.) Educational Fund, Knoxville, 1/151
Weil (Alvin B.) Fund, Memphis, 1/151
Werthan Fdn., Nashville, 1/152
Werthan (Joe & Howard) Fdn., Nashville, 1/152
Westend Fdn., Chattanooga, 1/154

White (Irene Ward) Fdn., Nashville, 1/155
Whitehead Charitable Trust, Memphis, 1/156
Wiener (Donald B.) Fund, Memphis, 1/156
Willis (Horace H.) Scholarship, Memphis, 1/157
Wilson Charitable Trust, Nashville, 1/157
Wurzburg (Abe) Fdn., Memphis, 1/158
Wurzburg (Reginald) Fund, Memphis, 1/159
Wurzburg (Reginald) Fdn., Memphis, 1/159

Second Filming

Anderson (Alice Petway) Fdn., Nashville, 2/002
American Paper and Twin Co. Char. Trust, Nashville, 2/003
American Society for Surgery of the Hand Memorial Fund, Memphis, 2/003
American Vision Research Fdn., Memphis, 2/003
Ashcraft Fdn., Memphis, 2/003
Baird (William O.) Fdn., Memphis, 2/004
Beauchamp (Mrs. D.V.) Trust for Vanderbilt University, Nashville, 2/004
Bell (W.M.) Fdn., Memphis, 2/006
Bowen (Victor) Fdn., Madison, 2/007
Bradford Fdn., Nashville, 2/007
Bristol Rotary Student Loan, Bristol, 2/009
Brown Fdn., Chattanooga, 2/009
Bullard (George Newton) Fdn. (formerly Ella P. Hayes Fund), Nashville, 2/010
Caldwell Fdn., Chattanooga, 2/011
Caldwell (Hardwick) Fdn., Chattanooga, 2/012
Brown (Grover C.) Fdn., Cleveland, 2/012
Brown (L.P.) Fdn., Memphis, 2/013
Cardiac Research Fdn., Nashville, 2/014
Cartinhour Fdn., Chattanooga, 2/015
Chai Fdn., Chattanooga, 2/016
Chapman Fdn., Memphis, 2/017
Chattanooga Area Fdn. for Research Training, Treatment and Teaching in the Mental Health Disciplines, Chattanooga, 2/017
Cherokee Fdn., Signal Mountain, 2/018
C.I.O.S. Inc., Memphis, 2/019
Cleveland Lodge No. 134, F. & A.M., Cleveland, 2/020
Cooley (J.S.) Tr. for Benefit of Protestant Orphanage, Nashville, 2/020
Cooley (J.S.) for Protestant Orphanage Fdn., Nashville, 2/021
Cooper (Sam) Fdn., Memphis, 2/021
Crystal Fdn., Chattanooga, 2/022
Dale Fdn., Nashville, 2/024
Delta Fdn., Memphis, 2/024
DiPrima (Francis R.) Mem. Fund, Memphis, 2/025
Dobson (Allen) for Youth, Nashville, 2/025
Dobson (Matt H.) Fdn., Nashville, 2/026
Dozier (Mattie E.) Trust for Old Womans Home, Nashville, 2/026
Eastern Christian Fdn., Nashville, 2/027
Ewing (Elizabeth O.) Trust Protestant Orphanage Fdn., Nasvhille, 2/027
Farmers Mutual Exchange of Cleveland Inc., Cleveland, 2/028
Farris (Mary L.) Trust B for Ridgeview Fdn., Nashville, 2/028
Feinstone (W. Harry) Fdn., Memphis, 2/029
Fensterwald Fdn., Nashville, 2/029
Flippin (John R.) Charitable Trust, Memphis, 2/031
Freeburg Brothers Trust, Memphis, 2/033
Gattas (Fred P.) Co. Inc. Fdn., Memphis, 2/034
Gerson Fdn., Morristown, 2/035
Gooch (C. M.) Fdn., Memphis, 2/036
Goodwin (W. A.) for University of the South, Nashville, 2/036
Halle (A. Arthur) Mem. Fdn., Memphis, 2/037
Hamico Inc., Chattanooga, 2/038
Hamilton (Arthur) Educational Tr. Fund, Dyersburg, 2/039
Hamilton Nat'l Bk. Tr. U/A Emma B. Hurlbut Orion Hurlbut (Orion L. & Emma B.) Memorial Fund, Chattanooga, 2/040

Hardeman (Nannie B.) Christian Fdn., Chattanooga, 2/041
Harrell (Clyde W.) Educational Fund, Kingsport, 2/041
Hart (Patricia & Rodes) Fdn., Nashville, 2/041
Hartzog (Thomas S.) & Joye B. Hartzog Fdn., Memphis, 2/043
Health & Welfare Trust, Nashville, 2/044
Hohenberg Charity Trust, Memphis, 2/045
Hooker (John J.) Fdn., Nashville, 2/045
Houston (P. D.), Jr. and Elsie L. Houston Fdn., Nashville, 2/046
Houston (Anna Safley) Memorial, Chattanooga, 2/047
Howard-Buckingham Friendship Fdn., Memphis, 2/048
Hutcheson (Hazel Montague) Fdn., Chattanooga, 2/048
Hyde (J. R.) Fdn., Memphis, 2/049
Hyde (Joseph R.), Jr. Fdn., Memphis, 2/050
Incorporation Fdn., Johnson City, 2/051
Jemison Fdn., Memphis, 2/052
Johnson Scholarship Fdn., Inc., Lewisburg, 2/052
Kendall Welfare Fdn., Chattanooga, 2/053
King (Mrs. J. M.) f/b/o Peabody College for Teachers, Nashville, 2/054
King (Mrs. J. M.) Trust for Old Womans Home, Nashville, 2/055
King (Mrs. J. M.) for George Peabody College for Teachers, Nasvhille, 2/055
King (Mrs. J. M.) Trust f/b/o Woman's Home, Nashville, 2/056
Kirshner (A.) Trust for Fifth Avenue Synagogue, Nashville, 2/056
Lance Fdn., Franklin, 2/056
Lee (Arthur K. and Sylvia S.) Scholarship Fdn., Nashville, 2/057
Ligon Fdn., Memphis, 2/058
Magic Chef Fdn., Cleveland, 2/059
Magness (Elizabeth J.) Home for Aged and Indigent Tr., Nashville, 2/059
Magness (W. H.) Trust for Nashville Agricultural and Normal Institute, Nashville, 2/060
Magness (W. H. & Edgar) Community House and Library Trust, Nashville, 2/060
Margolin Bros., Memphis, 2/061
Master's Fdn., Chattanooga, 2/061
McGuire (Maurine F.) Fdn., Nashville, 2/062
Memphis Zoological Society, Memphis, 2/063
Motlow (D.C.) Fdn., Nashville, 2/063
Motlow (Robert) Fdn., Nashville, 2/063
N. A. W. I. C. Founders' Scholarship Fdn. #6523-62, Chattanooga, 2/064
North American Royalties Inc. Welfare Fund, Chattanooga, 2/066
Oak Manor, Chattanooga, 2/067
Opportunity Fdn. Trust, Memphis, 2/067
Osborne (Weldon F.) Fdn., Chattanooga, 2/068
Panded Fund, Nashville, 2/069
Phillips (Albert & Elizabeth) Fdn., Nashville, 2/070
Precision Rubber Products Fdn., Lebanon, 2/070
Quin (Mrs. M. G.) for Old Womens Home, Nashville, 2/070
Quin (Mrs. M. G.) Trust F/B/O Old Womans Home, Nashville, 2/071
Salvation Army Magness Trust Fund Commerce Union, Nashville, 2/071
Salova King Fdn., Chattanooga, 2/072
Samaritan Fdn., Nashville, 2/073
Scholze (Virginia & George), Jr. Fdn., Chattanooga, 2/074
Shook Heirs Medal Fund, Shook Sch., Nashville, 2/074
Stephens Fdn., Nashville, 2/075
Stockell (George W.) Trust for Old Womans Home, Nashville, 2/076
Student Loan Fund of Rotary Educational Fdn. of Memphis, Memphis, 2/077
Tennessee Fdn., Nashville, 2/077
Thomas (John W.) Memorial Fund, Nashville, 2/078

Thomas (Mamie) Farm Account Trust, Memphis, 2/080
Thruston (G. P.) for Nashville Museum of Art, Nashville, 2/080
Thruston (G. P.) for Tennessee Historical Society, Nashville, 2/081
Thruston (G. P.) F/B/O Nashville Museum of Art, Nashville, 2/081
Toms Fdn., Knoxville, 2/082
Tonya Memorial Fdn., Chattanooga, 2/084
Tri-ni Toastmistress Club, Chattanooga, 2/090
Trippeer Fdn., Memphis, 2/090
T. N. V. I. Fdn., Chattanooga, 2/091
Volunteer Toastmistress Club, Chattanooga, 2/091
Wells (Pearl) Charitable Trust, Nashville, 2/091
Westend Fdn., Chattanooga, 2/092
Wexner Fdn., Memphis, 2/093
White (Irene Ward) Fdn., Nashville, 2/093
Willey Fdn. 122 Union Ave., Memphis, 2/095
Wilson (Anne & David) Fdn., Nashville, 2/095
Womack (W.C.) for First Presbyterian Church of McMinnville, Tennessee, Nashville, 2/095
Wunderlich (Alvin) Fdn., Memphis, 2/096
Yankey (Andrew G.) Scholarship Fund, Inc., Nashville, 2/096
Burt (Nellie A.) Hospital, Enosburg, Vt., 2/096
Chelsea High School Scholarship Fund, Bradford, Vt., 2/096
Christian Evangelical Trust, So. Newbury, Vt., 2/096
Clark (Harry E.) Scholarship Trust U/a, Brattleboro, Vt., 2/097

TEXAS

First Filming

Aaronson Brothers Fdn., El Paso, 1/002
Abercrombie (J.S.) Fdn., Houston, 1/003
Aberrant Behavior Center, Dallas, 1/003
Abundance Fdn., Houston, 1/004
Adam (Paul J. & Adrienne) Fdn., Dallas, 1/005
Alamo Heights Memorial Library Fund, San Antonio, 1/005
Alpha Xi Delta Foundation of Texas, Houston, 1/005
Alexander (Eloise) Foundation, San Antonio, 1/006
Alexander (Kathleen Jones) Fdn., San Antonio, 1/007
American Founders Educational Fdn., Austin, 1/007
Anchorage Fdn., Houston, 1/007
Anderson (Carl C., Sr. & Mary Jo) Charitable Fdn., Houston, 1/008
Anderson (M.D.) Fdn., Houston, 1/009
Angelina Fdn., Lufkin, 1/011
Angelina Fund, Lufkin, 1/012
Rockwell (Lillian) Endowment Fund of the Arabia Temple Crippled Children's Clinic, Houston, 1/013
Barnhart (Joseph & Wilhelmina Arnold) Fdn., Houston, 1/014
A R X Fdn., Austin, 1/014
Askin (Simon) Fdn., Houston, 1/014
Atkerson Fdn., Dallas, 1/014
Augzasis Fdn., Houston, 1/015
Baker Fdn., Austin, 1/016
Baldwin (Peter W. & Martha V.) Fdn., Dallas, 1/016
Baptist World Missions Trust, Memphis, Tenn., 1/017
Barber Fdn., Abilene, 1/017
Barrett Fdn., Houston, 1/017
Bass Fdn., Dallas, 1/018
Bass Fdn., Fort Worth, 1/019
Battelstein Charities Corp., Houston, 1/019
Battelstein Fdn., Houston, 1/020
Battelstein (Jerry) Fdn., Houston, 1/021

Baylor School of Law Fdn., Waco, 1/021
Bayshore Fdn., Corpus Christi, 1/021
Beal Fdn., Midland, 1/022
Beard (W.N.) Trust, Fort Worth, 1/022
Beasley (Theodore & Beulah) Fdn., Dallas, 1/023
Bee Fund, Dallas, 1/023
Belden (Mary Mosher) Memorial Fund, Dallas, 1/024
Bell Trust, Dallas, 1/025
Belle Ann Fdn., Lubbock, 1/026
Bennett (Anthony R.) Educ. Trust, Tyler, 1/029
Benlowitz Fdn., Houston, 1/029
Berne (Ira) Fdn., Houston, 1/029
Bertha Fdn., Graham, 1/030
Bertner Fdn., Houston, 1/030
Berwin (Celia) Memorial Fdn., Brownsville, 1/031
Bettes Fdn., Houston, 1/032
B.F. Fdn., Dallas, 1/032
Biehl Fdn., Houston, 1/032
Bintliff (Alice & David) Fdn. Formerly - Bintliff (David C.) Fdn., Houston, 1/033
Biological Humanics Fdn., Dallas, 1/034
Blackketter (Donald E.) Educ. & Charitable Fdn., Shamrock, 1/034
Blaffer Fdn., Houston, 1/035
Blaffer (Sarah Campbell) Fdn., Houston, 1/036
Bledsoe (Marc) Fdn., Dallas, 1/037
Blucher (Marie M.V.) Fdn., Corpus Christi, 1/037
Bond (Roland S. & Sadie A.) Fund, Dallas, 1/037
Boswell Fdn., Fort Worth, 1/038
Boswell (V.W.) Fdn., Fort Worth, 1/038
Boy Scout Fdn. of Sam Houston Area Council, Houston, 1/039
Boyd Fdn., El Paso, 1/039
Boyd (W. L. & Mrs.) Schooling Fund, McKinney, 1/040
Brachman (Elias) Memorial Fdn., Fort Worth, 1/040
Brackenridge (George W.) Fdn., San Antonio, 1/041
Braden (Albert H. & Kathleen O'Connor) Fdn., Houston, 1/043
Bray Milk Fund, El Paso, 1/043
Brazonia County Medical Educational Fdn., Houston, 1/044
Bridwell (J.S.) Fdn., Wichita Falls, 1/045
Briscoe (Elizabeth & Wylie) Fdn., Lubbock, 1/046
Brodsky Fdn., Houston, 1/046
Brooks (A.L., Jr.) Charitable Fdn., Bellville, 1/046
Brookview Fdn., Dallas, 1/047
Brown (Bernie) Fdn., Houston, 1/047
Brown (Robert J. & Clara) Fdn., Abilene, 1/048
Brown (M.K.) Fdn., Pampa, 1/048
Bruins (Addie) Educational Trust, Orange, 1/049
Bryant (Joe H. & Mary Lee) Fdn., Lubbock, 1/050
Buckner (R.C. & Sallie Frances) Fdn., Jacksonville, 1/051
Bunnell (Pat) Fdn., San Angelo, 1/051
Burch-Settoon Loan Fund Trust, Dallas, 1/052
Bush (J. E.) Fdn., Dallas, 1/052
Butler (George & Anne) Fdn., Houston, 1/053
Butler (J. R. & Mary Trout) Fdn., Houston, 1/053
Butrijamp Fdn., Dallas, 1/054
Caldwell Fdn., Chattanooga, Tenn., 1/055
Campbell Fdn., Dallas, 1/055
Cameron (W. W.) Fdn., Waco, 1/056
Capital National Fdn., Houston, 1/056
Carpenter Fdn., Houston, 1/056
Carruth Charitable Trust, Houston, 1/056
Carter (Amon G.) Fdn., Fort Worth, 1/057
Carysmith Fdn., Houston, 1/061
Castleberry (Paris & Helen) Fdn., Fort Worth, 1/061
Cates (Paul & Alta) Religious Fdn., Lubbock, 1/062

Catto Fdn., San Antonio, 1/063
Chambers Fdn., Houston, 1/064
Chandler Memorial Home, San Antonio, 1/064
Chappell Fund, Lubbock, 1/066
Chester (John B. & Charlotte) Fdn., Dallas, 1/066
Childers (Betty Bivins) Fdn., Amarillo, 1/067
Chilton Fdn. Trust, Dallas, 1/067
Christian Child Help Fdn., Houston, 1/068
Christian Fdn., Houston, 1/068
Christian Fdn., Dallas, 1/068
Civic Fdn. of San Marcos, San Marcos, 1/069
Clampitt Fdn., Dallas, 1/069
Clark (Anson L.) Charitable Trust, Dallas, 1/070
Clark (Curtis) Fdn., Corpus Christi, 1/071
Clark Fdn. Trust, Dallas, 1/071
Clayton Fund, Houston, 1/073
Clift (Hubert E.) Fdn., Houston, 1/074
Clive (C. L. & Henriette F.) Fdn., Austin, 1/075
Coates (George H., Mr. & Mrs.) Fdn., San Antonio, 1/075
Cockrell Fdn., Houston, 1/075
Cohen-Blum Fdn., Houston, 1/076
Collie Fdn., The - Amended Return 1969, Houston, 1/076
Collie Fdn., The - Amended Return 1970, Houston, 1/076
Collins (Ben & Jane) Home for Women, Texarkana, 1/077
Collins (Paul & Mary) Trust No. 2, Austin, 1/078
Collins (Calvert K.) Fdn., Dallas, 1/079
Collins (James M.) Fdn., Dallas, 1/079
Collins (Ruth Woodall) Fdn., Dallas, 1/081
Collins (Carr P.) Fdn., Dallas, 1/081
Colpitts (B. Vernon & Gwendolyn) Trust, Houston, 1/082
Cone Fdn., Houston, 1/082
Conner (William C.) Fdn., Fort Worth, 1/082
Constantin Fdn., Dallas, 1/083
Conway (J. W., Mrs.) Cemetery Trust, Fort Worth, 1/084
Cook Fdn., Houston, 1/084
Cooper Industries Fdn., Houston, 1/085
Costa (Aubrey M.) Fdn., Dallas, 1/086
Costello Fdn., Dallas, 1/086
Cox (Ed) Fdn., Dallas, 1/087
Creel Fdn., Houston, 1/088
Creston Fdn., Dallas, 1/089
Crippled Children's Fdn. of America, Dallas, 1/089
Crow (Trammell) Fund, Dallas, 1/090
Cullen Fdn., Houston, 1/090
Cullen (Roy Henry) Fdn., Houston, 1/091
Culleoka Water Supply Corp., McKinney, 1/091
Curtis Fdn., Longview, 1/092
Czech Education Fdn. of Texas, College Station, 1/092
Dail (Leigh D.) - TCU Trust, Fort Worth, 1/092
Dail (Mary) - W. I. Cook Children's Hospital Trust, Fort Worth, 1/092
Dail (Mary) TCU Trust, Fort Worth, 1/093
Daily Benevolent Corp., Houston, 1/093
Dallas Cotton Exchange Trust for Employees & Former Employees, Dallas, 1/094
Dallas Cotton Exchange Trust, Dallas, 1/094
Dallas Universal Trust Fund, Dallas, 1/095
Dart Fdn., Austin, 1/095
Davidson Fdn., Dallas, 1/096
Davidson (Josephine) Memorial Trust, Dallas, 1/097
Davidson (M. N.) Fdn., Houston, 1/098
Davis (H. C.) Fund, San Antonio, 1/099
Dealey (G. B.) Fdn., Dallas, 1/100
Deford Fdn. Trust, Austin, 1/102
Denison Methodist Fdn., Brownfield, 1/102
Denton Rotary Club Ray Chapman Scholarship Fund, Denton, 1/102
Detering (Lenora) Fdn., Houston, 1/104
Deutser Fdn., Houston, 1/104
Dickson (Raymond) Fdn., Hallettsville, 1/104

Dietert (Harry W. & Alma D.) Educational Fdn., San Antonio, 1/105
Dingle (Lucille H. & Gil) Fdn., Brazoria, 1/106
D L R Trust, Houston, 1/106
Donnell Fdn., Wichita Falls, 1/107
Donsky (Ervin & Frances) Fdn., Dallas, 1/108
Donsky (Nathan & Sylvia) Fdn., San Angelo, 1/108
Doss (M.S.) Fdn., Fort Worth, 1/109
Dove Creek Fund, Houston, 1/109
Dowd (Una Chapman) Fdn. Tr., Corpus Christi, 1/110
Dugger (Anne E.) Scholarship Fund, San Antonio, 1/110
Dupre (Naason K. & Florrie S.) Permanent Education Scholarship Fund, Lubbock, 1/110
Dye (F.W. & Bessie A.) Fdn., Dallas, 1/111
Earthman Memorial Fund, Houston, 1/114
East Texas Fdn., Silsbee, 1/115
Eastland Industrial Fdn., Eastland, 1/115
Educational Advancement Fdn., Houston, 1/116
Educational Fdn. of the Southwest, Dallas, 1/116
Edwards Fdn., Dallas, 1/116
Edwards (M.C.) Trust, El Paso, 1/117
Employees of Continental-Emsco Trust, Dallas, 1/117
E S R C Fdn., Dumas, 1/117
Estate of C.C. Gibbs, San Antonio, 1/118
Esteve (Ramon M.) Fdn., Dallas, 1/119
Estill (Mary King) Fdn., Corpus Christi, 1/120
Fain Fdn., Wichita Falls, 1/120
Fair Fdn., Dallas, 1/121
Fair (R.W.) Fdn., Tyler, 1/121
Faith Fdn., Houston, 1/123
Fasken, Midland, 1/124
Favrot Fund, Houston, 1/124
Feinberg Fdn., El Paso, 1/125
Feldman Fdn., Dallas, 1/126
Fenwick (Marin B.), San Antonio, 1/127
Ferrell (Charles Robert), Houston, 1/128
Fields (Leo) Family Fdn., Dallas, 1/128
Fiji Fdn. of Texas, Dallas, 1/128
Fikes (Leland) Fdn., Dallas, 1/128
Finger Fdn., Houston, 1/130
Finklestein (M.B. & Fannie) Fdn., Houston, 1/131
Ewing (Finley & Gail) Fund, Dallas, 1/131
Finney (Susan) Memorial Fund, Dallas, 1/132
First Bank & Trust Co. Char. Tr., Booker, 1/132
First National Fdn. of Waco, Waco, 1/133
Flake (Maria Boswell) Home for Old Women Trust, Houston, 1/133
Fleming (Mary Irene) Educ. Fund, Corsicanna, 1/134
Fleming Fdn., Fort Worth, 1/134
Flewellen Charitable Fdn., Longview, 1/135
Fomby (Ed) Memorial Fund, San Antonio, 1/136
Fomby (Harriet) Memorial Fund, San Antonio, 1/136
Forbes (D.W. & Josephine S.) Fund, Dallas, 1/136
Forrest (Ora C.) Fdn., Slaton, 1/138
Fort Worth Benevolent Home, Fort Worth, 1/138
Fort Worth Benev. Home Educ. Fund, Fort Worth, 1/138
Fort Worth Classroom Teachers Assoc., Fort Worth, 1/139
Fort Worth Country Day, Inc. Benefit Tr., Fort Worth, 1/139
Foster Fdn., San Antonio, 1/140
Foundation for the Arts, Dallas, 1/141
Foundation of Faith, Tyler, 1/141
Frankel (Maurice) Fdn., Houston, 1/142
Frankel (Pearl & Frank) Fdn., Houston, 1/143
Frankel (Robert K., Jr.) Fdn., Houston, 1/143
Free People Fdn., Dallas, 1/144
Fuller Fdn., Inc., Fort Worth, 1/144
Furr Fdn., Lubbock, 1/145
Gailo Trust, Houston, 1/146

Levy (Milton P., Jr.) Foundation, Irving, 2/050

Lewer Foundation, Raymondville, 2/050

Lewis (Lillian Kaiser) Foundation, Houston, 2/051

Lewis (Richard Spencer) Memorial Foundation, San Antonio, 2/051

Lichtenstein Charitable & Educational Trust, Corpus Christi, 2/051

Lind (Dr. Carl J.) Memorial Foundation, Houston, 2/052

Lindsey (S. A.) Foundation, Tyler, 2/052

Lindsey-Wolf Foundation, Tyler, 2/052

Link Charitable Trust, Houston, 2/052

Lipnick Foundation, Houston, 2/053

Lipscomb (Virginia Collins) Scholarship Fund, Dallas, 2/053

Lipshy Foundation, Dallas, 2/053

Little (Rufus L.) Fdn., Houston, 2/054

Livermore (Mary L.) Trust, Lubbock, 2/054

Livermore Religious Trust, Lubbock, 2/055

Lone Star Steel Foundation, Dallas, 2/055

Long (Joe & Edith Trotter) Foundation, Dallas, 2/056

Longview Foundation, Longview, 2/056

Looney Foundation, Edinburg, 2/057

Lott Foundation, Lubbock, 2/057

I Love Foundation, Lubbock, 2/058

Lubbock Electrical Workers Building Association, Lubbock, 2/058

Luling Foundation, Luling, 2/058

Luse (W. P. & Bulah) Foundation, Dallas, 2/060

Luttrell Trust, Arlington, 2/060

Lynch Foundation, Dallas, 2/061

Lynch (S. H.) Foundation, Dallas, 2/062

Lynn Foundation, Dallas, 2/062

Lyons Foundation, Houston, 2/062

Mac Gregor (George L.) Foundation, Dallas, 2/063

Mac Lay Foundation, Dallas, 2/064

Maher Foundation, Dallas, 2/064

Malcolm (David) Foundation, Houston, 2/065

Mano Trust, San Antonio, 2/065

Manske (Otto & Edna Witte) Trust, Brownsville, 2/066

Manx Foundation, Austin, 2/066

Marcus (Mr. & Mrs. Edward) Foundation, Dallas, 2/066

Marcus (Mr. & Mrs. Stanley) Foundation, Dallas, 2/067

Mares Foundation, Dickinson, 2/067

Marshall Foundation, Houston, 2/068

Martel (Marian and Speros) Foundation, Houston, 2/069

Martin (Retha R.) Foundation, Lubbock, 2/069

Martin (Fred A.) Foundation, Fort Worth, 2/070

Martin (W. L.) Foundation, Dallas, 2/071

Mathes (Burke) Family Fdn., Athens, 2/071

Matthews Special Fund, Pland, 2/071

Maurin Foundation for Parapsychology, Houston, 2/071

Maynard Foundation, Amarillo, 2/072

McAshan Educational & Charitable Trust, Houston, 2/072

McBurney Foundation, Dallas, 2/073

McCormick (Eddie Hill) Trust, Houston, 2/073

McCreless (Sollie Emmitt & Lilla Marr) Foundation, San Antonio, 2/075

McCullough (M. & A.) Foundation, Wichita Falls, 2/075

McCullough Foundation, Houston, 2/076

McDermott Foundation, Dallas, 2/077

McDermott (R. Thomas & Ethel L.) Foundation, Houston, 2/078

McGaha Foundation, Wichita Falls, 2/078

McGlothlin Foundation, Abilene, 2/078

McGown Charitable Trust, San Antonio, 2/079

McKee (Robert E. & Evelyn) Fdn., El Paso, 2/079

McKenna (George) Trust, Fort Worth, 2/080

McKenzie Fdn., Tyler, 2/080

Bowman-McLean Fdn., San Antonio, 2/081

McLean (Marrs) Scholarship Trust, Junction, 2/082

McManus Mission Fund, Houston, 2/082

McMillan (Mary Moore) Fdn., Overton, 2/083

McNutt (V. H.) Memorial Fdn., San Antonio, 2/084

McQueen (Adeline & George) Fdn. of 1960, Fort Worth, 2/084

Meadows Fdn., Dallas, 2/085

Medical Arts Publishing Fdn., Houston, 2/086

Melton Fdn., San Antonio, 2/088

Menil Fdn., Houston, 2/088

Meredith Fdn., Mineola, 2/090

Merrick (Louise Lindsey) Fdn., Tyler, 2/091

Midland Country Club, Midland, 2/091

Midland Chapter Associates of Lubbock Christian College, Midland, 2/092

Midland County Medical Society, Midland, 2/092

Miller (I. L. & Bertha Gordon) Fdn., Houston, 2/092

Miller (Martin G. & Glendora) Fdn., Houston, 2/093

Mind Science Fdn., San Antonio, 2/094

Minzer Family Fund, Dallas, 2/094

Mitchell Bros. Charitable Trust, Dallas, 2/095

Mohr (F. B.) Fdn., Dallas, 2/095

Montgomery Fdn., Edinburg, 2/096

Moore Fdn., El Paso, 2/097

Moore (Charles & Katherine) Fdn., Dallas, 2/097

Morrison Fdn., Austin, 2/098

Morrison (Ollege & Minnie) Fdn., Houston, 2/099

Morton (Granville C.) Charitable Fdn., Dallas, 2/099

Mosesman (Morris) Family Fdn., Dallas, 2/100

Mosher Fdn., Houston, 2/100

Mosher (Harriett) Memorial Fund, Houston, 2/102

Moss Foundation Trust, Lubbock, 2/104

Mullen Fdn., Alice, 2/104

Munson (W. B.) Fdn., Denison, 2/104

Murchison Fund, Dallas, 2/105

Mosesman (Ben) Family Fdn., Dallas, 2/105

Mutual Benefit Foundation, Houston, 2/105

Mutual Benevolent Association, Houston, 2/107

Nadig (Dr. Perry & Rowena) Fdn., San Antonio, 2/108

Nasher Fdn., Dallas, 2/108

Navarro Community Fdn., Corsicana, 2/108

Neal (James Robert) Memorial Trust, Houston, 2/109

Neal (Margaret Ophelia) Trust, Houston, 2/109

Neuhoff Fdn., Dallas, 2/110

Newby Memorial Students Loan Fund, Fort Worth, 2/111

Newell (W. P. & Dell Andrews) Charitable Trust, Fort Worth, 2/112

Nicholson (Harold E.), Jr. Fdn., Shamrock, 2/113

Nicholson (Harold E.), Jr. Memorial Hospital, Shamrock, 2/113

Nine Eleven Fdn., Houston, 2/114

Nine Star Fdn., Dallas, 2/115

North (Janis & Phil) Fdn., Fort Worth, 2/116

Oakland Cemetery Lot Owners Association Permanent Endowment, Dallas, 2/116

O'Brien Fdn., Refugio, 2/117

O'Donnell Fdn., Dallas, 2/117

O'Loughlin Fdn., Amarillo, 2/118

Open Hand Fund, Inc., San Antonio, 2/118

Oppenheimer (Jesse H. & Susan R.) Fdn., San Antonio, 2/119

Opportunity Plan Fdn., Inc., Canyon, 2/120

Oshman Fdn., Houston, 2/121

Paducah (M. S. Wells) Scholarship Trust, Fort Worth, 2/121

Page (Jack C. & Imogene S.) Charitable Trust, Dallas, 2/121

Page (G. H.) Fdn., Waco, 2/122

Parker (J. E. & Bessie Ola) Fdn., Odessa, 2/127

Parry Foundation, Houston, 2/127

Patterson (Helen) Trust, Junction, 2/128

Payne (Robert & Virginia) Fdn., Dallas, 2/128

Pearle (Elsie & Stanley C.) Charitable Fdn., Dallas, 2/129

Peavy (Stanley H.) Benevolent Fdn., Graham, 2/130

Pembroke Fund, Houston, 2/130

Pennzoil United Fdn., Houston, 2/131

Perkins (Joe & Lois) Fdn., Wichita Falls, 2/131

Permian Basin Petroleum Museum, Library and Hall of Fame, Midland, 2/132

Permian Charitable Fdn. of Midland, Texas, Midland, 2/133

Perot Fdn., Dallas, 2/134

Perrenot-Burges Fdn., El Paso, 2/134

Peterson (Mary Katherine) Fdn., Houston, 2/135

Phelps-McEwen Fund, Dallas, 2/136

Phillips (John Roberts & Rebecca Jane Hall) Fdn., Houston, 2/136

Pilot Fdn., Dallas, 2/136

Piper (Minnie Stevens) Fdn., San Antonio, 2/137

Polemanakos Fdn., Houston, 2/139

Pollock Fdn., Dallas, 2/140

Popular Fdn., El Paso, 2/140

Poth (Robertson) Fdn., Austin, 2/141

Prado Fdn., Corpus Christi, 2/141

Prairie Fdn., Midland, 2/142

Press Club of Dallas Fdn. Fund, Dallas, 2/142

Pressler (Nancy & Paul) Fdn., Houston, 2/144

Price (R. B.) Family Fdn., El Paso, 2/144

Prometheus Corporation, Houston, 2/144

Radiant Fdn., Dallas, 2/145

Rambaud (Lulu Bryan) Charitable Trust Agency, Houston, 2/145

Rayzor (J. Newton) Fdn., Houston, 2/146

Redfern (John J. & Rosalind) Fdn. No. 2, Midland, 2/147

Resler Fdn., El Paso, 2/148

Reynolds (Alice & Dick) Fdn., Austin, 2/148

RGK Fdn., Austin, 2/149

Richardson (Sid W.) Fdn., Fort Worth, 2/149

Richardson (Sid) Memorial Fund, Fort Worth, 2/152

Rickel (Cyrus K. & Ann C.) Fdn., Fort Worth, 2/154

Ricketts (R. D. & H. A.) Fdn., Houston, 2/155

Rienzi Fdn., Houston, 2/155

Ripley (Danield & Edith) Fdn., Houston, 2/157

Roberts (Dora) Fdn., Fort Worth, 2/158

Robertson (Lora A.) Trust, Dallas, 2/159

Rockwell Brothers Endowment, Houston, 2/160

Rockwell Fund, Houston, 2/161

Roderick Fdn., El Paso, 2/162

Rooke Fdn., Woodsboro, 2/163

Rooth Fdn., Dallas, 2/164

Rosen Fdn., Houston, 2/165

Rothschild (Miriam & Joseph) Fund, Dallas, 2/165

Rounds (George) Trust, West Columbia, 2/165

Rowland (James A. & Mayme H.) Fdn., Dallas, 2/166

Caudill, Rowlett, & Scott Fdn., Houston, 2/167

Rudman Fdn., Tyler, 2/168

Rudy Fdn., Houston, 2/169

Runnells Fund, Bay City, 2/169

Runyon (Grace & John W.) Fdn., Dallas, 2/171

Rupe Fdn., Dallas, 2/172

Rushing (W. B. & Mozelle) Fdn., Lubbock, 2/173

Russell Fdn., Houston, 2/173

Russell (Lester Asa) Fdn., Dallas, 2/173

Rutherford Fdn., Houston, 2/174

St. Joachim Fdn., Pampa, 2/175

San Antonio Loan & Trust Fund, San Antonio, 2/175

San Antonio Tennis Educational Fdn., San Antonio, 2/177

Sandefer (J. Marguerite) Scholarship Trust, Wichita Falls, 2/177

Sands Fdn., Dallas, 2/177

Sangreal Fdn., Dallas, 2/178

Scaler Fdn., Houston, 2/178

Second Filming

Alexander (Kathleen Jones) Fdn., San Antonio, 4/008

Alexander (Robert D. and Catherine R.) Family Fdn., Fort Worth, 4/008

Alford (John R.) and Susan Landon Alford Fdn., Henderson, 4/009

American Founders Educational Fdn., Austin, 4/010

Anchorage Fdn., Houston, 4/011

Anderson (Mary Munnerlyn) Fdn. Fund, Houston, 4/011

Andrews (Celeste B.) Endowment Fund, Houston, 4/013

Angelina Fdn., Lufkin, 4/014

Antonian Educational Fdn., San Antonio, 4/014

Anthony (Martha Jane and James Edward) Fdn., Fort Worth, 4/014

Army Lodge-Thagard Fdn., San Antonio, 4/014

Assistance League of Houston, Houston, 4/015

Austin (Tilley and Frank) Charitable Trust, Dallas, 4/016

Austin Woman's Club, Austin, 4/016

Auxiliaries to the Devotion of the Holy Infant of Good Health, Laredo, 4/017

Baer (Sylvan T.) Fdn. Trust, Dallas, 4/017

Bailey (Nell V.) Charitable Trust, Fort Worth, 4/018

Baldwin (Peter W. and Martha V.) Fdn., Dallas, 4/019

Ballas (Helen) - Smith (Jennie) Fund, Dallas, 4/019

Barger (Dennis) Fdn., Dallas, 4/019

Barnett (Ben G.) Fdn., Dallas, 4/020

Barnett (Madlyn B. and Louis H.) Fdn., Fort Worth, 4/024

Barrick Fdn. Trust Dept. First National Bank, Amarillo, 4/024

Beaumont Area Pipe Fitters Joint Educational Trust Fund, Beaumont, 4/025

Beissner Fdn., Houston, 4/026

Belden (Mary Mosher) Memorial Fund, Dallas, 4/026

Bell County Medical Society Scholarship Fund, Temple, 4/027

Bell Trust, Dallas, 4/027

Belle Ann Fdn., Lubbock, 4/028

Bennett (Anthony R.) Educational Trust, Tyler, 4/028

Beren (Carl M. and Mattie) Fdn., Dallas, 4/029

Beretta Fdn., San Antonio, 4/029

Berlowitz Fdn., Houston, 4/030

Berne (Ira) Fdn., Houston, 4/030

B. G. S. Fdn., Dallas, 4/031

Bivins (Mary E.) Trust, Amarillo, 4/031

Bivins (Mary E.) Fdn., Amarillo, 4/032

B. J. and R. Fdn., Austin, 4/036

Blaffer (Robert Lee) Trust, Houston, 4/036

Blum Trust, Dallas, 4/037

Bolton Fdn., Waco, 4/038

Bond (Roland S. and Sadie A.) Fund, Dallas, 4/038

Bonner Price Student Loan Fund Trust, Plainview, 4/039

Boys Club Fdn., Houston, 4/040

Boys Harbor Fdn., La Porte, 4/040

Brackins (Charles T. and Katie B.) Scholarship Fdn., Dallas, 4/041

Bright Star Fdn., Dallas, 4/041

Brinegar (Franklin I.) Fdn., Dallas, 4/043

Brochstein (Harry & Ellery) Fdn., Houston, 4/043

Brooks (Pierce) Gospel Fdn., Dallas, 4/044

Brookshire-Kleberg (B. C. and Addie) County Charitable Fdn., Corpus Christi, 4/044

Brown Memorial Trust, Fort Worth, 4/045

Brown (T. J.) and C. A. Lupton Fdn., Fort Worth, 4/046

Bruner Fdn., San Antonio, 4/047

Buck (Raymond E.) Fdn., Fort Worth, 4/047

Burch-Settoon First Methodist Church of Plainview, Dallas, 4/048

Burford Fdn., Tyler, 4/048

Boykin (Burwell and Bella) Memorial Fund, Beaumont, 4/049

Butcher Fund, Houston, 4/049

Butt (H. E.) Fdn., Corpus Christi, 4/050

Byars Fdn., Tyler, 4/052

Cain Fdn., Houston, 4/052

Caldwell (D. K.) Fdn., Tyler, 4/053

Cameron (Harry S. and Isabel C.) Fdn., Houston, 4/055

Cannan (Helen & Darrold) Fdn., Wichita Falls, 4/056

Carr (Dougherty) Arts Fdn., Corpus Christi, 4/056

Carter (Samuel Fain) Fellowship Trust No. 37-12-5, Houston, 4/057

Carter (Amon G.) Star Telegram Employees Fund, Fort Worth, 4/058

Caruth Fdn., Dallas, 4/059

Carver Fdn., Houston, 4/060

Castleberry (Paris and Helen) Fdn., Fort Worth, 4/061

Chapel (Margarite Bright) Parker Endowment Trust, San Antonio, 4/061

Charity Ball Association of Baton Rouge, Houston, 4/062

Charlton (Margaret J. and George V.) Fdn., Dallas, 4/062

Chase Field Child Care Center, Beeville, 4/063

Childrens Clinic of Sherman-Trust, Sherman, 4/063

Chilton Fdn., Dallas, 4/064

Christian Heritage Fdn., Waco, 4/064

Christian Fdn., Dallas, 4/065

Cigarroa (Dr. Joaquin Gonzalez) Sr., Memorial Fdn., Laredo, 4/065

Clark (James H. and Lillian) Fdn., Dallas, 4/066

Clark (Lester) Fdn., Breckenridge, 4/067

Clay (Ann E.) Fund Trust, Galveston, 4/067

Clear Fork Charitable Fdn., Fort Worth, 4/068

Coale Fdn., Houston, 4/069

Cohen (Jacob A. and Charlene) Fdn., Houston, 4/069

Collins-Griffin-Beardsley Educational Trust, Austin, 4/070

Combe (Carrie Moore) Fdn., San Antonio, 4/070

Comfort Public Schools Trust, San Antonio, 4/071

Commerce Lodge #439 A. F. & A. M., Commerce, 4/072

Commonwealth Fdn., El Paso, 4/072

Constantin Trust, Dallas, 4/073

Loring Cook Fdn., McCallen, 4/074

Coonly (William J. and Genevieve H.) Fdn., El Paso, 4/074

Copano Research Fdn., Victoria, 4/074

Cope (Millard) Scholarship Trust, Dallas, 4/075

Corpus Christi Heart Assoc., Corpus Christi, 4/076

Corrigan Fdn., Dallas, 4/076

Cossabroom (J. V. and Cora B.) Fdn., Houston, 4/077

Council of Citizens Who Care, Houston, 4/078

Cowden (Ida Fay) Fdn., Midland, 4/079

Cronin-Bauer Fdn., Houston, 4/080

Crooker Charitable Fdn., Houston, 4/081

Crosbyton Industrial Fdn., Crosbyton, 4/081

Crump (Joe and Jessie) Fund, Fort Worth, 4/081

Crump (J. L.)-Taylor and Brown Trust, Fort Worth, 4/082

Dakin (David Norris) Memorial Educational Loan Fund, Houston, 4/082

Dallas Bankers Wives Charitable Trust, Dallas, 4/082

Dallas Theological Seminary Fdn., Dallas, 4/083

Danciger (Dan) Fund, Dallas, 4/084

Danner (Elmer H.) Scholarship Trust, Dallas, 4/084

Davidson Family Charitable Fdn., Fort Worth, 4/085

Davidson (M. N.) Fdn., Houston, 4/086

Del Barto-Tramonte Fdn., Houston, 4/088

Derrico Neurosurgical Trust, Dallas, 4/088

Dickinson Fdn., Wichita Falls, 4/089

Dickson (Sallie) Memorial Fund Trust, Dallas, 4/090

Dietrich (Edward B.) Fdn. for Medical Research & Education, Houston, 4/090

Dodge Jones Fdn., Abilene, 4/091

Donors Anonymous Fdn., Dallas, 4/092

Dorset Fdn., Sherman, 4/094

Dougherty Fdn., Beeville, 4/095

Dove Creek Fund, Houston, 4/096

Dresser Fdn. Republic Natl. Bank of Dallas, Dallas, 4/096

Drummet Intercontinental Center, Houston, 4/097

Duncan Fdn., Waco, 4/097

Duncan (A. J. & Jessie) Fdn., Fort Worth, 4/098

Duncan (Anne & C. W.) Jr., Fdn., Houston, 4/098

Duncan (Jeaneane & John H.) Fdn., Houston, 4/100

Dyche Fdn., Houston, 4/100

Early Fdn., Dallas, 4/101

Easter Seal Society for Crippled Children and Adults of Tarrant County, Fort Worth, 4/101

Educational & Charitable Fdn., Houston, 4/102

Educational Opportunities, Dallas, 4/102

Ehlers (V. M.) Memorial Fund, Temple, 4/103

Elburt Fund, Dallas, 4/104

Elkins (Mr. & Mrs. J. A.) Jr., Houston, 4/104

Ellis (Lionel J.) Memorial Library, Houston, 4/105

El Paso Elk Endowment Fund for Crippled and Handicapped, El Paso, 4/106

Eshleman Fdn., Corpus Christi, 4/106

Evangelia Settlement, Waco, 4/107

Fabian Fund, Dallas, 4/107

Farish Scholarship Fund, Houston, 4/108

Farish (William Stamps) Fund, Houston, 4/109

Finney (Susan) Memorial Trust Fund, Houston, 4/110

First Capitol Historical Fdn., Inc., West Columbia, 4/110

First Dallas Charitable Corporation, Dallas, 4/110

Fish (Bess N.) Charitable Fdn., Houston, 4/111

Fish (Ray C.) Fdn., Houston, 4/112

Fleming (Mary Irene) Educational Fund, Corsicana, 4/115

F. & M. Charities "A" Inc., Abilene, 4/115

Foley Brothers Store Fdn., Houston, 4/116

Fondren Fdn., Houston, 4/119

Ford (Ralph V.) Charitable Trust, Houston, 4/119

Foree Fdn., Dallas, 4/120

Forrest Fdn., Lubbock, 4/120

Fort Bend County Unit of The Texas State Teachers Association Student Loan Fund, Rosenberg, 4/121

Foster Fdn., El Paso, 4/121

Freedman (Margaret Bloom) Fdn., Dallas, 4/122

Fridia Educational Fund, Waco, 4/122

Fritz Trust Harvey L. Davis Trustee, Dallas, 4/122

Frio Charitable Fdn., Houston, 4/123

Fort Worth Childrens Hospital Trust, Fort Worth, 4/124

Fulbright, Crooker, Freeman, Bates & Jaworski Charitable Fdn., Houston, 4/125

Garrett (Gavin R.) Fdn., Lampasas, 4/126

Garson (Greer) Fund, Dallas, 4/126

Gate Foundation, Houston, 4/126

Gee (Raymond C. and Margaret S. Fdn., Fort Worth, 4/128

Gembler (V. L.) Trust Good Shepard Evangelical Lutheran Church, San Antonio, 4/128

Gembler (V. L.) Trust-St. Johns Evangelical Lutheran Church, San Antonio, 4/129

Gembler (V. L.) Trust-Grace Lutheran Hospital, San Antonio, 4/130

Gembler (V. L.) Trust Texas Lutheran College, San Antonio, 4/130

Genecov (A. S.) Fdn., Tyler, 4/131

George (Albert F.) Fdn., Houston, 4/131

Germany Fdn., Dallas, 4/132

Glazer (Stevie) Nurses Fund, Dallas, 4/133

Goddard (Charles B.) Fdn., Dallas, 4/133

Goeth Fdn., Austin, 4/134

Goldsobel (Sam) Fdn., Dallas, 4/135

Goldston Endowment Inc., Houston, 4/135

Goldston (Wm. J.) Fdn., Houston, 4/136

Goodrich (Esther Florence Whinery) Charitable Fdn. For the Advancement of Art, Houston, 4/137

Gordon (Charles & Susan) Educational Memorial Trust, San Antonio, 4/138

Gordon (Meyer and Ida) Fdn., Houston, 4/138

Grace (W. E. - Bill) Fdn., Fort Worth, 4/139

Graves Fdn., Austin, 4/141

Greentree Fund, Houston, 4/141

Griswold Fdn., Lake Jackson, 4/141

Gross Fdn., Houston, 4/142

Gulf Oil Fdn., Houston, 4/143

Haby Charitable Trust, San Angelo, 4/146

Haggar Fdn., Dallas, 4/146

Hall (David Graham) Trust, Honey Grove, 4/149

Halsell (Ewing) Fdn., San Antonio, 4/150

Hamman (George & Mary Josephine) Fdn., Houston, 4/151

Handy-Andy Fdn. of Texas, San Antonio, 4/153

Hanley (Sue Terrell) Memorial Fund, Fort Worth, 4/154

Hansbro (Mervin G.), Houston, 4/154

Hansen (Elizabeth Rhea) Trust, Austin, 4/154

Hardie (Elizabeth K.) Fdn., San Antonio, 4/155

Harding Fdn., Raymondville, 4/155

Harris (Ann K.) Fdn., El Paso, 4/156

Harris (S. T. & Margaret) Fdn., Dallas, 4/156

Hartman-Edgar (Albert W.) L. Frazell Fdn. for Medical Research, San Antonio, 4/157

Harvest Queen Fdn., Plainview, 4/158

Hastings (William H. and Margaret P.) Trust, Corsicana, 4/159

Hatheway (Mary) and Robert James Abell Fdn., Midland, 4/159

Hawley (John B.) Memorial Scholarship Fund, Fort Worth, 4/159

Heard (John S. & Rachel) Fdn. of Collin County, McKinney, 4/160

Heights Fdn., Houston, 4/160

Hein (Sue) Memorial Trust Fund, Fredericksburg, 4/161

Heitmann (F. A. and Blanche) Fdn., Houston, 4/162

Henderson (Robert W.) Fdn., Houston, 4/162

Henna (Louis M.) Fdn., Round Rock, 4/162

Hervey Fdn., El Paso, 4/163

Herzfeld Charitable Trust, Houston, 4/163

Heusinger (Julia) McCall Musical Fdn., San Antonio, 4/163

Herzstein (Albert and Ethel) Charitable Fdn., Houston, 4/164

Hexter (Louis J.) Fdn., Dallas, 4/164

Hill Fdn., Dallas, 4/165

Hill Memorial Park Fdn., Weimar, 4/165

Hillcrest Fdn., Dallas, 4/166

Hobby-Crafters Fdn., Dallas, 4/167

Hoblitzelle Fdn., Dallas, 4/168

Hodges (Donald W.) Fdn., Dallas, 4/173

Hohlt (R. B. and Katherine M.), Houston, 4/173

Holubec (Kenneth) Memorial Educational Fund, San Angelo, 4/173

Holubec (Kenneth) Memorial Trust, San Angelo, 4/174

Homcare Fdn., Houston, 4/174

Hood (Josephine and Forrest) Scholarship Fund, Mission, 4/174

Houston Baby Oilers, Houston, 4/175

Houston Endowment, Houston, 4/175

Howard Fdn., Texarkana, 4/179

Houston Library of Arts, Houston, 4/179

Hudson Fdn., Brownsville, 4/180

Hudson Fdn., Houston, 4/181

Hughes (Vincent A. and Margaret E.) Fdn., Dallas, 4/182

Hurlock (Charles H.) Sr., Educational Fdn., Houston, 4/182

Hutchins (Jack) Fdn., Wharton, 4/183

Hygeia Fdn., Harlingen, 4/184

Institute For Aid and Rehabilitation, Houston, 4/185

Foundation for Institutes of Research and Advanced Studies, Galveston, 4/186

Institutional Psychiatric Research Fdn., Dallas, 4/186

International Southwest Fdn., San Antonio, 4/187

Ivey (Tom F.) Memorial Scholarship Fund, Sinton, 4/187

Issleib (Hertha) Fdn., San Antonio, 4/187

Jackson County Fdn., Ganado, 4/187

Jackson (Ruth) Research Fdn., Dallas, 4/189

Jaworski (Leon) Fdn., Houston, 4/189

Johnson (F. Kirk) Fdn., Fort Worth, 4/190

Johnston (Ralph A.) Fdn., Houston, 4/191

Jones-O'Donnell Fdn., Dallas, 4/192

K. A. Educational Corp., Austin, 4/192

Karcher (Lydia K.) Fdn., Dallas, 4/193

Karsten (Floyd L.) Junior Fdn., Houston, 4/194

Kay (Mary) Fdn., Dallas, 4/195

Keith (Ben E.) Fdn. Trust, Fort Worth, 4/196

Kempner (Harris & Eliza) Fund, Galveston, 4/197

Kimbell Art Fdn., Fort Worth, 4/199

King (Thomas A.) and Ethel King Educational Fdn., Vernon, 4/201

Kiwanis Trust Fund, Witchita Falls, 4/201

Kleberg (Caesar) Fdn. for Wildlife Conservation, Kingsville, 4/202

Kleberg (Robert J.) Jr., and Helen C. Kleberg Fdn., Kingsville, 4/203

Knapp Fdn., Weslaco, 4/204

Koehler (Otto) Fdn., San Antonio, 4/204

Koehler (Otto A.) and Marcia Koehler Fdn., San Antonio, 4/204

Koening (Emiland Meta) Fdn., Houston, 4/205

Kohfeldt Fdn., Denison, 4/205

Kopper-Smith Fdn., Houston, 4/205

Kratzenstein (Simon) Fund, Corpus Christi, 4/206

Krost (Max) Charitable Trust, Houston, 4/206

Krupp (M. B.) Fdn., El Paso, 4/207

Lakeside Fund, Dallas, 4/207

Lakeville Corp., Dallas, 4/207

Laity Lodge, San Antonio, 4/208

Lamar (Percy & Zina) Fdn., Lubbock, 4/209

Lanier (Robert C.) Fdn., Houston, 4/210

Larkin Fdn. (TFY-2946), Dallas, 4/211

Laurent Fdn., Houston, 4/212

Law Fdn., Houston, 4/212

Leadership Fdn., Houston, 4/214

Legion Oil Co., Dallas, 4/215

Lemens (Vernon) Charitable Fdn., Austin, 4/215

Letourneau Fdn., Longview, 4/216

Levin (J. K. & Libbie) Scholarship Trust, Houston, 5/002

Levine (Sol and Doris) Fund, Dallas, 5/002

Levy (Addie) Trust Continental, Fort Worth, 5/003

Lifshutz Fund, San Antonio, 5/003

Ling (James J.) Fdn., Dallas, 5/005

Littaver (Helen Irwin) Educational Trust, Fort Worth, 5/005

Locke Charitable Fdn., Miami, 5/005

Long (L. A.) Trust, Wichita Falls, 5/006

Love (Margaret and Ben) Educational Fdn., Houston, 5/007

Lubbock Women's Club, Lubbock, 5/007

Lutheran Students Assistance Fund, Inc., Houston, 5/008

Lynch (S. H.) Fdn., Dallas, 5/009

Lynn Fdn., Dallas, 5/010

MacIntosh Murchison Memorial Trust, El Paso, 5/010

Moffett (Minnie L.) Scholarship Trust, Dallas, 5/011

Main Street Charities, Dallas, 5/012

Mansur (Harl & Evelyn) Fdn., Wichita Falls, 5/013

Maperaus Trust, Houston, 5/013

Marcus (Lawrence) Fdn., Dallas, 5/014

Marsh Fdn., Amarillo, 5/015

Martin (A. D.), Dallas, 5/016

Martin (Katherine Boland) Charitable Trust, Fort Worth, 5/017

Masonic Home Scholarship Fund, Fort Worth, 5/017

Massie Memorial Fdn., San Angelo, 5/018

Mathes (Burke) Family Fdn., Athens, 5/018

Mathis (Lester W. and Lucille) Fdn., Fort Worth, 5/018

Mayborn (Frank W.) Fdn., Temple, 5/019

Mayer (Frederick and Mildred) Fdn., Dallas, 5/020

McAdams Fdn., Austin, 5/021

McAshan Educational & Charitable Trust, Houston, 5/025

McCall (Julia Heusinger) Musical Fdn., San Antonio, 5/025

McCartt (Helen and Gene) Fdn., Amarillo, 5/026

McClurkan (W. B. & Azalee), Sr. Memorial Trust, Denton, 5/026

McCollum (Leonard and Margaret) Fdn., Houston, 5/027

McCoy Charitable Trust, Dallas, 5/028

McDermott (Eugene & Margaret) Fund, Dallas, 5/030

McDermott (R. Thomas and Ethel L.) Fdn., Houston, 5/030

McMullin Fdn., Dallas, 5/032

McMillan (Bruce), Jr. Fdn., Overton, 5/033

Means (Robert Craig) Fdn., Valentine, 5/035

Menil Fdn., Houston, 5/035

Meyer (Paul J.) Fdn., Waco, 5/037

Michaux Corp., Houston, 5/037

Midland Charities, Midland, 5/038

Midland National Endowment Fund of The First Presbyterian Church, Midland, 5/039

Mirza Trust of San Antonio, San Antonio, 5/039

Mission Road Fdn. School for Exceptional Children, San Antonio, 5/040

Modesett Fdn., Corpus Christi, 5/040

Molloy Fdn., Houston, 5/041

Montgomery (Ray) Fdn., Dallas, 5/041

Moody Fdn., Galveston, 5/042

Northen (Mary Moody), Dallas, 5/047

Moody (Shearn) Fdn., Galveston, 5/048

Moor (Lee) Childrens Home, El Paso, 5/049

Moore (William R. and Carolyn P.) Charitable Trust, Dallas, 5/050

Moran Fdn., Houston, 5/051

Morbow Fdn., Houston, 5/051

Morrison (Ollege and Minnie) Fdn., Houston, 5/052

Morrow (Kyle and Josephine) Fund, Houston, 5/052

Moshana Fdn., Austin, 5/053

Mossler (Candace) Corporation, Houston, 5/053

Murrary (Sid) Charitable Trust No. 1, Corpus Christi, 5/054

Munson (W. B.) Fdn. Trust, Denison, 5/054

National Home Fashions League, Dallas, 5/055

Marcus (Neiman) Fdn., Dallas, 5/055

Ney (Elizabet) Texas Fine Arts Association McClendon Fdn., Austin, 5/056

New Braunfels Textile Mills Hospital Trust, New Braunfels, 5/056

Newton (Carl) Fdn., San Antonio, 5/056

Nichols [Robert L. (Bob)], Jr. Scholarship Fdn., Terrell, 5/058

Novy (Jim) Fdn., Austin, 5/058

O'Connor (Kathryn) Fdn., Victoria, 5/059

O'Connor (Junie) Fdn., Victoria, 5/060

Officers Wives Club at Fort Hood, Fort Hood, 5/061

Oldham (Ida Mae) Trust, Lubbock, 5/061

Oliver (Cluthe & William Oliver) Fdn., Dallas, 5/062

Olsan (Frances) Fdn., Dallas, 5/063

Zelrich Co. Profit Sharing Retirement Plan,
Dallas, 5/187
Ziegler (Samuel E.) Educational Fund, Dallas,
5/187
Zuber (Abe and Stella) Fdn., Houston, 5/188
Zuber (Philip and Florence) Fdn., Houston,
5/189

UTAH

First Filming

Bamberger (Eleanor) Special Achievement
Award Trust, Salt Lake City, 1/002
Bamberger (Ruth E. and John E.) Memorial
Foundation, Salt Lake City, 1/002
Bamberger Special Achievement Award Trust
No. 2, Salt Lake City, 1/003
Bardsley (William J.) Charitable Trust, Salt
Lake City, 1/004
Battson (Edwin and Leah) Fdn., Salt Lake
City, 1/004
Beesley (John O. and Effie E.) Charitable
Foundation, Salt Lake City, 1/005
Big Horn Stake Charitable Trust, Salt Lake
City, 1/006
Benevolent Trust Fund of B.P.O.E., Salt Lake
City, 1/006
Broadbent Fdn., Cedar City, 1/007
Buehner (Paul) Fdn., Murray, 1/007
Burton (Edward L.) Fdn., Salt Lake City,
1/008
Carleson (Harry E. and Vera F.) Benefit Trust,
Salt Lake City, 1/009
Carleson Benefit Trust, Salt Lake City, 1/009
Clayton (C. Comstock) Fdn., Salt Lake City,
1/010
Clyde Fdn., Springville, 1/011
Cody Ward Murals Charitable Trust, Salt Lake
City, 1/011
Cook (Melvin A.) Charitable Fdn., Salt Lake
City, 1/012
Daft (Sarah) Home, Salt Lake City, 1/012
Dee (Annie Taylor) Fdn., Ogden, 1/013
Dumke (Dr. Ezekiel R. and Edna Wattis) Fdn.,
Salt Lake City, 1/014
Dupler Fdn., Salt Lake City, 1/015
Eccles (George S. and Dolores Dore') Fdn., Salt
Lake City, 1/015
Eggertsen (S. B.) Fdn., Salt Lake City, 1/016
Episcopal Church in Utah Trust, Salt Lake City,
1/018
First Security Fdn., Salt Lake City, 1/019
Flint (Leland B. and Dora T.) Fdn., Salt Lake
City, 1/019
Garco Fdn., Salt Lake City, 1/020
Girt (Lester H.) Charitable Trust, Salt Lake
City, 1/020
Handley (G. Kenneth and Ethel L.) Fdn., Salt
Lake City, 1/021
Hansen (Glen L.) Memorial Trust, Ogden,
1/021
Harris (Mattie Wattis) Fdn., Ogden, 1/021
Harris (William H.) Fdn., Ogden, 1/023
Hogle Fdn., Salt Lake City, 1/023
Hubbard (Dr. John C. an' Bliss L.) Fdn., Salt
Lake City, 1/024
Hughes (Preston G.) Fdn., Spanish Fork,
1/025
Hunter (Dulany) Fdn., Vernal, 1/025
Intermountain-Saltmount Employees Trust, Salt
Lake City, 1/026
Kelson Fdn., Salt Lake City, 1/026
Kibbie (William Patrick) Memorial Fund, Salt
Lake City, 1/027
King (Walter G. and Walter E. Ware
Memorial Fdn., Salt Lake City, 1/028
Knight (Jesse) Charitable Trust, Salt Lake City,
1/028
Lane (Rose) Charitable Trust, Salt Lake City,
1/029

Liljenquist (Raymond V.) Fdn., Salt Lake City,
1/029
Masonic Fdn. of Utah, Salt Lake City, 1/029
Meagher Family Charitable Trust, Salt Lake
City, 1/030
Moreton Family Fdn., Salt Lake City, 1/031
Movitz (Samuel A. and Richard D.) Fdn., Salt
Lake City, 1/032
National Institute for Research and
Developement, Salt Lake City, 1/032
Peterson (Virgil V.) Fdn., Salt Lake City,
1/033
Radium Company, Salt Lake City, 1/033
Richards (Franklin D. and Helen K.) Memorial
Trust Fund, Salt Lake City, 1/034
Roe (Bernice and Ben) Fdn., Salt Lake City,
1/034
Rosenblatt Memorial Fdn., Salt Lake City,
1/035
Rozelle (Mack Thomas) Charitable Trust, Salt
Lake City, 1/036
St. Marks Hospital Charitable Trust, Salt Lake
City, 1/036
Shaw (Mary Elizabeth Dee) Charitable Trust,
Ogden, 1/037
Stewart (Elizabeth Dee Shaw) Charitable Trust,
Ogden, 1/037
Shaw (Mary Elizabeth Dee) Charitable Trust,
Ogden, 1/037
Stokes (Allen W. and Alice H.) Charitable
Trust, Logan, 1/039
Tanner (Obert C. and Grace A.) Fdn., Salt
Lake City, 1/039
Teton Youth Improvement Fdn., Provo, 1/040
Trust for Employees of Publix-Rickards-Nace
Inc., Salt Lake City, 1/040
Utah State Medical Association Fdn., Salt Lake
City, 1/041
Van Evera (Dewitt) Fdn., Salt Lake City,
1/042
Wattis (Everetta L.) Fdn., Ogden, 1/042
Walker Bank and Trust Charitable Fdn., Salt
Lake City, 1/043
Wallace (John M. and Glenn Walker) Fdn.,
Salt Lake City, 1/044
White-Smith Fdn., Salt Lake City, 1/045
Winder (George and Lorna) Charitable Trust,
Salt Lake City, 1/046
Young (Thomas) Fdn., Salt Lake City, 1/046

Second Filming

Beam (Josephine) Educational Fund, Salt Lake
City, 2/004
Beuhner (Paul) Fdn., Murray, 2/005
Cartwright (Victor I.) Family Fdn., Provo,
2/006
Castle Fdn., Salt Lake City, 2/007
Clark (Allie W.), Salt Lake City, 2/007
Cunningham (Dora E.) Memorial Fund, Salt
Lake City, 2/008
England (G. Eugene) Fdn., Salt Lake City,
2/008
Hansen (Glen L.) Memorial Trust, Ogden,
2/009
Hansen (George T.), Salt Lake City, 2/010
Kibbie (William Patrick) Memorial Fund, Salt
Lake City, 2/010
Lindholm (Claire E. and George) Fund, Salt
Lake City, 2/010
Michael (Herbert I. & Elsa B.) Fdn., Salt Lake
City, 2/011
Spratling (Ronald N.) Fdn., Salt Lake City,
2/011
Steiner American Foundation, Salt Lake City,
2/012
Stevens (O. C.) Memorial Fdn., Provo, 2/013
Widtsoe (John A.) Educational Fdn., Salt Lake
City, 2/014

VERMONT

First Filming

Barrows (Augustus & Kathleen) Memorial &
Trust Fund, Burlington, 1/002
Bloomer (Asa) Fdn., Rutland, 1/003
Bostwick (Dunbar W.) Fdn., Shelburne, 1/004
Bryandt Chucking Grinder Company, Charitable
Fdn. of the, Springfield, 1/004
Bryant (William L.) Fdn., Springfield, 1/005
Cone Automatic Machine Company Charitable
Fdn., Windsor, 1/005
Converse Home, Burlington, 1/006
Fellows Gear Shaper Fdn., Springfield, 1/007
Five-Twenty-Five Fdn., Londonderry, 1/008
Lyon (Edward A.) Trust, Brattleboro, 1/009
Morton (Alice E.) Memorial Scholarship Fund,
St. Albans, 1/009
National Survey Employee Benefit Fund,
Chester, 1/010
Roth (Louis K. & Rae E.) Fdn., Burlington,
1/010
Stranahan Memorial Fund, St. Albans, 1/010
Sun of Justice Trust, Benson, 1/011
Vermont Transit Fdn., Burlington, 1/012
V B T C O Charities, Brattleboro, 1/012
Vermont Bank & Trust Company Trust f/b/o
Rutland Hospital, Rutland, 1/013
Vermont Structural Steel Fdn., Burlington,
1/013
Vermont Wild Land Fdn., Charlotte, 1/014
White (Eleanor) Trust, Rutland, 1/014
Wilson (John R.) Trust, Bennington, 1/015
Windham Fdn., Grafton, 1/015

Second Filming

Burt (Nellie A.) Hospital Fund, Enosburg Falls,
2/001
Chelsea High School Scholarship Fund,
Bradford, 2/001
Christian Evangelical Trust, South Newbury,
2/001
Clark (Harry E.) Scholarship Trust, Brattleboro,
2/001
Davison (Dr. R. Winthrop) Scholarship Trust,
Brattleboro, 2/002
Five Twenty Five Fdn., Londonderry, 2/002
Fletcher Memorial Library, Ludlow, 2/003
Flower (David A.) Memorial Scholarship Fund,
West Rupert, 2/003
Free Press Fdn., Burlington, 2/003
Lamson - Howell Fdn., Randolph, 2/004
May (Louise Breason) Fdn., Springfield, 2/004
Mores (William A.) Fund, Brattleboro, 2/005
St. Johnsbury Fdn., St. Johnsbury, 2/005
Scott (Olin) Fund, Bennington, 2/006
Shelburne Industries Fdn., Shelburne, 2/006
Springfield Hospital Auxiliary, Springfield,
2/007
Stol (Florence Louchheim) Fdn., Brattleboro,
2/007

VIRGINIA

First Filming

Agecroft Association, Richmond, 1/001
American Paper Company Fdn., Richmond,
1/002
Anderson (Isabel S. & Edward C.) Trust,
Richmond, 1/003
Archbold Fdn., Upperville, 1/003
Arlington County Medical Society Fdn.,
Arlington, 1/004
Armstrong Fdn., Winchester, 1/005
Arnold (Minnie M.) Charitable Fdn.,
Alexandria, 1/006
Arthur (Barney) Fdn., Altavista, 1/007
Bank of Virginia Fdn., Richmond, 1/007

Bayside Charity Fund, Norfolk, 1/008
Bendall (Harry) Fdn., Alexandria, 1/008
Berlin (Norman & Harriet) Fdn., Norfolk, 1/009
Binswanger Glass Fdn., Richmond, 1/009
Blackwell (Mary Ball) Fdn., Richmond, 1/010
Carter (Beirne Blair & Elisabeth Reed) Trust, Roanoke, 1/011
Bliley (Joseph W.) Memorial Fund, Richmond, 1/012
Stickley Institute, Board of Trustees of, Strasburg, 1/013
Carter (Bessie Bocock & Robert) Trust, Richmond, 1/014
Bocock (Frederic Scott & Roberta Bryan) Trust, Richmond, 1/015
Bocock (Elizabeth Scott & John H.) Trust, Richmond, 1/015
Bowman Fdn., Sunset Hills, 1/016
Boyd (Miss Lizzie E.) Foreign Missionary Trust, Richmond, 1/017
Boyd (Miss Lizzie E.)-Student Educational Fund, Richmond, 1/018
Brawley (Francis P. & Norma B.) Trust, Charlottesville, 1/018
Brothers (George R. & Evelyn W.) Trust, Richmond, 1/019
Brown (Donald S.) Fdn., Richmond, 1/021
Brown (Rives S.) Charitable Fdn., Martinsville, 1/022
Bryan (John Stewart) Memorial Fdn., Richmond, 1/023
Bryan (Jonathan) III Trust, Richmond, 1/023
Brown (Donald S.) Fdn., Richmond, 1/024
Bryan (Thomas P. & Alice W.) Trust, Richmond, 1/025
Hayes (Belle Bryan & John G., Jr.) Trust, Richmond, 1/026
Bryant Fdn., Alexandria, 1/026
Burwell-van Lennep Fdn., Winchester, 1/027
Byrd (Anne Douglas Beverley) Educational and Charitable Trust, Winchester, 1/027
Cabell (Robert G., III & Maude Morgan) Fdn., Richmond, 1/028
Calasia Fund, Arlington, 1/029
Camp Fdn., Franklin, 1/030
Camp (Carrie S.) Fdn., Franklin, 1/032
Camp (J. L.) Fdn., Franklin, 1/033
Camp (John & Mary) Fdn., Richmond, 1/033
Campbell (Ruth Camp & Henry) Fdn., Richmond, 1/034
Castle (Virginia) Fdn., Charlottesville, 1/035
Charles (Marjorie Smith) Fdn., Norfolk, 1/036
Christian Missions' Aid, Arlington, 1/036
Cohen (LeRoy R., Jr. & Rosalie M.) Fund, Richmond, 1/037
Cohen (Sarah) Scholarship Fund, Norfolk, 1/037
Coons (James Robertson & Ollie Terrill) Memorial Fund, Richmond, 1/037
Covington (James E.) Trust, Richmond, 1/038
Craigie (Walter Williams) Trust, Richmond, 1/038
Crittenton Mission, National Florence, Alexandria, 1/039
Dan River Mills Fdn., Danville, 1/040
Danmoore Fdn., Richmond, 1/042
Darling (James S.) Memorial Fund, Hampton, 1/043
Denney Fdn., Lynchburg, 1/044
Dennis Fdn., Richmond, 1/044
Di Giulian (A. P.) Fdn., Fairfax, 1/045
Doyle Fdn., Martinsville, 1/045
Dudley (Estes) Fdn., Richmond, 1/046
Echols (John C.) Memorial Fund, Lynchburg, 1/046
Edson Family Fdn., Waynesboro, 1/047
Elkin (Mildred L.) Fdn., Richmond, 1/048
Elmwood Fund, Richmond, 1/048
English Fdn., Altavista, 1/049
Enterprise - Black Diamond Fdn., Bristol, 1/049
Erwin (William J.) Charitable Trust, Danville, 1/050
Estes Fdn., Richmond, 1/051

Fatherree (Mildred M.) Fdn., Richmond, 1/051
F E B S Fdn., Richmond, 1/052
Fenton Fdn., Richmond, 1/053
Ferebee (J. Smith) Fdn., Richmond, 1/054
Fifer (Carson Lee) Fdn., Alexandria, 1/054
First & Merchants Fdn., Richmond, 1/055
Flournoy Fdn., Portsmouth, 1/058
Forest Community Fdn., Harrisonburg, 1/059
U. S. S. Forrestal Memorial Educational Fdn., Norfolk, 1/059
Foundation Boys Club, Portsmouth, 1/060
Fraley (William Elbert) Memorial Trust, Richmond, 1/060
Frank Charitable Fdn., Newport News, 1/060
Fried (Herbert) Fdn., Richmond, 1/061
Gibson (George D.) Fdn., Richmond, 1/062
Gill Memorial Hospital Fdn., Ronaoke, 1/062
Godfrey (Arthur) Fdn., Paeonian Springs, 1/064
Goldrich (Lawrence J.) Fdn., Norfolk, 1/064
Gollsby Educational Fund, Marion, 1/065
Gosnell (Fred A., Sr.) Fdn., Arlington, 1/066
Gray (Garland) Fdn., Richmond, 1/066
Green (R. J.) Scholarship Fund, Richmond, 1/067
Hampton Fdn., Richmond, 1/067
Hardy - Harris Fdn., Richmond, 1/068
Harris (Holbert L.) Fdn., Alexandria, 1/071
Harris (Holbert L.) Testamentary Trust, Alexandria, 1/072
Hastings Trust, Newport News, 1/073
Hedley - Thomas Fdn., Richmond, 1/074
Herndon Fdn., Richmond, 1/075
Hinks (Kennett W.) Trust, Ivy, 1/075
Historic Fredericksburg, Inc., Fredericksburg, 1/076
Hitz (Frederick P. & Mary Buford) Trust, Richmond, 1/077
Hobbie (Warren W.) Fdn., Roanoke, 1/077
Hooker Fdn., Martinsville, 1/078
Houser Fdn., Fredericksburg, 1/079
Hunter Fdn., Norfolk, 1/079
International Communication of Orthodox Nations, Vienna, 1/080
Ironworkers Apprentice Fund of the Richmond, Virginia Area, Richmond, 1/080
Ivakota Association, Alexandria, 1/081
Ix (Alice D. & Frank J.) Charitable Trust, Charlottesville, 1/082
Jackson (Herbert Worth) Scholarship Fund, Richmond, 1/083
Jeffress (Thomas F.) Memorial, Richmond, 1/083
Johns (Frank S.) Fdn., Richmond, 1/084
Johnson (Earl, Jr. & Margery Scott) Endowment Trust, Richmond, 1/085
Kaplan (Harry & Jessie S.) Student Memorial Fund, Annandale, 1/085
Kilham Trust, Charlottesville, 1/086
Kincaid (Rose) Fund, Hot Springs, 1/086
King (Donald P.) Fdn., Richmond, 1/087
King William Associates, King William, 1/087
Klingstein Fdn., Harrisonburg, 1/087
Landmark Charitable Fdn., Norfolk, 1/088
Lane Fdn., Altavista, 1/089
Lane (Edward H.) Fdn., Altavista, 1/091
Porter (William Lane & Elisabeth Scott) Charitable Trust, Richmond, 1/091
Williams (Langbourne) Fund, Rapidan, 1/092
Laverge (Henriette A. & Jan) Charitable Trust, Richmond, 1/093
Pratt (John Lee & Lillian Thomas) Fdn., Fredericksburg, 1/093
Leggett Fdn., Danville, 1/094
Lester (J. R.) Educational Fund, Martinsville, 1/095
Looney Fdn., Rural Retreat, 1/095
Lowry Fdn., Richmond, 1/096
Luria (Anna & Louis) Fdn., Falls Church, 1/097
Mann (Herbert Agnew) Memorial Fund for Sick Children of the Poor, Richmond, 1/098
Marlowe Fdn., Falls Church, 1/098
Markel Fdn., Richmond, 1/099

Mars Fdn. Formerly District of Columbia, McLean, 1/100
McCarthy (Judge Walter T.) Fund, Arlington, 1/103
McElroy Family Trust, Richmond, 1/103
Meador (James A.) Fdn., Salem, 1/103
Meyers-Krumbein Fdn., Richmond, 1/104
Miller & Rhoads Fdn., Richmond, 1/105
Monticello Association Endowment Fund, Richmond, 1/106
Morgan (A. D. & Annye Lewis) Memorial Scholarship Fund, Norfolk, 1/106
Morris (Lewis Z.) Memorial Fund, Richmond, 1/107
Moss Memorial Baptist & Fairview Presbyterian Trust, Alexandria, 1/107
Scott (Mary Nixon and Buford) Trust, Richmond, 1/108
Noland Company Fdn., Newport News, 1/109
Noland Memorial Fdn., Newport News, 1/109
Nordan (Fred C. & Virginia H.) Memorial Music Fund, Richmond, 1/110
Old Dominion University Research Fdn. Formerly Old Dominion College Research Fdn., Norfolk, 1/110
Olmstead (George) Fdn., Arlington, 1/111
Olsson (Elis) - Chesapeake Fdn., West Point, 1/112
Olsson (Elis) Memorial Fdn., Richmond, 1/114
Oxford Charitable Trust, Richmond, 1/114
Pan-Rhodian Society Apollon of America, Arlington, 1/116
Pendleton Construction Corporation Fdn., Wytheville, 1/116
Perry Fdn., Charlottesville, 1/116
Pioneer Fdn., Arlington, 1/118
Plymale Fdn., Lynchburg, 1/119
Pritchett (Mary Roberts) Scholarship Fund, Lynchburg, 1/119
Pusey (Paul H.) Fdn., Richmond, 1/119
Reinsch (Emerson G. & Dolores G.) Fdn., Arlington, 1/120
Research Analysis Corporation, McLean, 1/120
Richmond Corporation Fdn., Richmond, 1/122
Richmond Fdn. a/c Parke C. Bagby Memorial Relief Fund, Richmond, 1/123
Richmond Fdn. a/c General Account, Richmond, 1/124
Richmond Fdn. a/c A. D. Williams and Sue W. Massie Fund, Richmond, 1/124
Richmond Fdn. a/c Ella Rowley Pizzini Charity Fund, Richmond, 1/125
Richmond Fdn. a/c Sheltering Arms Hospital Fund, Richmond, 1/125
Richmond Hotels Fund, Richmond, 1/126
Robertshaw Controls Company Charitable & Educational Fund, Richmond, 1/126
Robertson (Mary Taylor & Walter S.) Trust, Richmond, 1/128
Robins Fdn., Richmond, 1/129
Rogers (Ralph L. & Rose F.) Fdn., Richmond, 1/129
Rosenbaum Fdn., Richmond, 1/130
Rosenbaum (Harry L.) Fdn., Roanoke, 1/130
Rosenthal Fund, Richmond, 1/131
Rosenthal (Leo) Fdn., Richmond, 1/132
Safer (John) Charitable Fdn., Arlington, 1/133
St. Catherine's School Fdn., Richmond, 1/133
Sands (Sally) Fdn., Petersburg, 1/165
Schmidt Fdn., Richmond, 1/166
Schwarzschild Fdn., Richmond, 1/167
Schwarzschild (Kathryn & W. Harry) Fund, Richmond, 1/168
Scott (Susan Bailey & Sidney Buford) Endowment Trust, Richmond, 1/169
Scott (Alice W. & James H.) Trust, Richmond, 1/170
Seward (Simon) Fdn., Petersburg, 1/171
Shepherd (Kathleen Ann Kelley) Trust, Charlottesville, 1/171
Shingleton (N. B.) Scholarship Fund, Winchester, 1/171
Shuster (Grace Greinert) Fdn., Reston, 1/172
Slack Fdn., Roanoke, 1/172
Snell Fdn., Arlington, 1/173

Snyder-Dupre Scholarship Fund, Wofford College Alumni Association, Arlington, 1/173

Starke Fdn., Richmond, 1/174

Steinman (Max) Fdn., Portsmouth, 1/175

Stone (Roy C., Evelyn H. & James C.) Charitable Fdn., Martinsville, 1/175

St. Paul's Church Home, Richmond, 1/177

Strause (M. L. & B. H.) Fdn., Richmond, 1/178

Stern Fdn., Richmond, 1/178

Sproul Charitable Trust, Staunton, 1/179

Sulgrave Fdn., Richmond, 1/179

Swain-Grousbeck Sight Trust, Danville, 1/180

Sydnor (Lucy and Eugene) Fdn., Richmond, 1/181

Talley (D. D.) III Fdn., Richmond, 1/181

Taubman (Arthur & Grace W.) Fdn., Roanoke, 1/182

Taylor Fdn., Norfolk, 1/183

Taylor Fdn., Richmond, 1/184

Thalhimer (Morton G. & Ruth W.) Fdn., Richmond, 1/184

Titmus Fdn., Petersburg, 1/186

Tros-Dale Fdn., Charlottesville, 1/186

Truland Fdn., Arlington, 1/187

Van Clief (Eleanor Cameron) Fdn., Charlottesville, 1/188

Virginia Association of Insurance Agents, Richmond, 1/188

Virginia Iron Fdn., Roanoke, 1/189

Virginia Realtor's Fdn., Richmond, 1/190

Virginia Scrap Iron & Metal Company Charitable Fdn., Roanoke, 1/190

Virginia Trust for Historic Preservation, Richmond, 1/191

Warwick (Pierre C. & Sarah M.) Charitable Trust, Richmond, 1/191

Washington Suburban Institute, Fairfax, 1/192

Wayside Fdn. for the Arts, Middletown, 1/192

West (Caleb D.), Jr. Trust, Newport News, 1/193

Whitfield Fdn., Richmond, 1/193

Whitner (Anna Church) Fellowship Fund, Richmond, 1/194

Weedon (Ellen Bayard) Fdn., Charlottesville, 1/194

Wesleymen Fdn., Norfolk, 1/195

Wilkinson (J. Harvie, Jr.) Charitable Fdn., Richmond, 1/195

Wilson-Neel Fdn., Fairfax, 1/196

Wilton (E. Carlton) Fdn., Richmond, 1/196

Willhob Fdn., Richmond, 1/196

Winkler (Mark & Catherine) Fdn., Falls Church, 1/197

Wise Fdn., Charlottesville, 1/197

Witt (Isabel Luke) Fund, Richmond, 1/198

Youth Development Fdn., Arlington, 1/199

Second Filming

Askin (Albert) Fdn., Richmond, 2/001

Ancient & Accepted Scottish Rite of Free-Masonry Southern Jurisdiction, U.S.A., Portsmouth, 2/002

Barton (Robert T., Jr. & Eleanor P.) Educational & Charitable Fund, Richmond, 2/002

Baskerville (Hamilton) Trust, Richmond, 2/003

Bassett (Lucy Brown) Fdn., Bassett, 2/003

Bassett (Patricia E. & John D.), III Fdn., Bassett, 2/003

B C J Fdn., Alexandria, 2/003

Beazley Fdn., Portsmouth, 2/004

Beaulah Baptist Church Cemetery Trust, Richmond, 2/005

Bradley (Frances Sage) Fdn., Alexandria, 2/006

Brandon Church Cemetery Trust, Richmond, 2/007

Broadwater Fund, Accomac, 2/008

Brody Family Fdn., Norfolk, 2/008

Browder (Basil D.) Health Fdn., Danville, 2/008

Brown Fdn., Richmond, 2/009

Bruington Baptist Church Trust, Richmond, 2/009

Bundoran Fdn., North Garden, 2/009

Cave Spring Recreation Fdn., Roanoke, 2/011

Christian Children's Hong Kong Fund, Richmond, 2/011

Cohen (LeRoy R., Jr. & Rosalie M.) Fund, Richmond, 2/011

Coiner (H. E.) Trust, Staunton, 2/012

Colonial Historical Fdn., Alexandria, 2/012

Crippled Children's Hospital Trust, Richmond, 2/013

Crompton - Shenandoah Company Employees Welfare Fund, Waynesboro, 2/014

Currie (John) Trust, Richmond, 2/015

Daingerfield (John H.) Cemetery Fund, Richmond, 2/015

Dalis Fdn., Norfolk, 2/016

Reed (Martha Davenport & Frederic Scott) Fdn., Manakin - Sabot, 2/017

Dawbarn (H. D.) Fdn., Charlottesville, 2/018

Delta Sigma Delta Educational Fdn. Formerly Michigan, Richmond, 2/018

Dere Fdn., Richmond, 2/019

deWolf (Bradford C. & Susanne R.) Fund, McLean, 2/020

Dice (Charles S.) Trust, Staunton, 2/021

Donovan (Herbert A. "Mike") Scholarship Fund, Charlottesville, 2/021

Downman (John Y.) Trust, Richmond, 2/022

Dudley (R. M.) Trust, Staunton, 2/023

Easley (Andrew Horsley & Anna Owen) Charitable Trust, Lynchburg, 2/023

Ann Elizabeth Fdn., Richmond, 2/024

Elmore Fdn., Richmond, 2/024

Emmaneul Protestant Episcopal Church Trust, Richmond, 2/025

English (W. C.) Fdn., Altavista, 2/026

Ephesus Baptist Church Trust, Richmond, 2/026

Evans (Hester E. R.) Trust, Staunton, 2/026

Faith Home, Richmond, 2/027

Medical College of Virginia - Feamster Fdn., Richmond, 2/027

Fifer (Kate L.) Trust, Staunton, 2/028

Fisher (Bruce Crane) Charitable Trust (see also 089), Richmond, 2/028

State Planters Charitable Trust, Richmond, 2/029

Flight Safety Fdn., Arlington, 2/029

Frazier Scholarship Fund, Charlottesville, 2/031

Friedman (Dan & Teal) Fdn., Richmond, 2/032

Gooch (Claiborne W.), Jr. Charitable Trust, Lynchburg, 2/033

Parsons (James H.) Greenbrier Memorial Fund, Charlottesville, 2/033

Grim (Clifford D. & Virginia S.) Educational Fund, Winchester, 2/033

Gunst Fdn., Richmond, 2/034

Halcyon Fdn., Charlottesville, 2/034

Hands for Christ, Roanoke, 2/035

Hermitage Fdn., Norfolk, 2/036

Higginbotham (A. T.) Trust, Staunton, 2/036

Hirschler Fdn., Richmond, 2/037

Historic Richmond Fdn., Richmond, 2/038

Hofheimer (H. C.), II Family Fdn., Norfolk, 2/039

Hope House Fdn., Norfolk, 2/040

Houser (Dr. A. A.) Trust, Richmond, 2/041

Houser Fdn., Fredericksburg, 2/041

Howard (Jane Colston) Trust, Staunton, 2/042

Human Resources Research Organization, Alexandria, 2/043

Hupman (John L.) Trust, Staunton, 2/044

Hurt Public Schools Trust, Richmond, 2/044

Inorganic Syntheses, Williamsburg, 2/045

Institute for Research in the Social Sciences & Humanities, McLean, 2/046

Irvington Baptist Church Trust, Richmond, 2/047

Irvington Methodist Church Trust, Richmond, 2/047

Iseman (Hulda & I.) Trust, Staunton, 2/048

Jones (George M.) Library Association, Lynchburg, 2/048

Kiwanis Fdn. of Arlington, Arlington, 2/050

Kline Fdn., Norton, 2/050

Kyle Memorial Student Loan Fund, Orange, 2/051

Lane Fdn., Norfolk, 2/051

Lane (Minnie & Bernard) Fdn., Altavista, 2/052

Larrymore Fdn., Norfolk, 2/053

Lenasa Fdn., Richmond, 2/055

Lewis Fdn., Richmond, 2/055

Lincoln Fdn., Norfolk, 2/055

Loudon Memorial Hospital Trust, Arlington, 2/057

Lynch Fdn., Springfield, 2/057

Macamor Fdn., McLean, 2/058

Randolph Macon College Trust, Richmond, 2/059

Marks Fdn., Richmond, 2/060

Marshall (George C.) Research Fdn., Lexington, 2/060

King (Martin Luther), Jr. Memorial Fund, Harrisonburg, 2/061

Masonic Home of Virginia Trust, Richmond, 2/061

Mathews (Frank L.) Trust, Staunton, 2/061

May Fdn., McLean, 2/061

May (L. Cutler), Jr. Memorial Fund, Richmond, 2/062

McCrea Fdn., Richmond, 2/062

McGuire (Edward) Memorial Assn., Richmond, 2/062

McMahon (Father John J.) Charitable Trust Fund, Falls Church, 2/063

Mandelson (Alfred G. & Ida) Family Fdn., Alexandria, 2/064

Miller (J. Mason) Trust, Staunton, 2/064

Miller (J. Clifford & Lizora Schoolfield) Fdn., Richmond, 2/064

Morgan (Marietta McNeill & Samuel Tate), Jr. Trust, Richmond, 2/065

Myerley (Louis D.) Trust, Staunton, 2/067

Myraid Fdn., Richmond, 2/067

National Association of Foundations, Alexandria, 2/067

Nordan (Fred C. & Virginia H.) Memorial Music Fund of Comfort Presbyterian Church, Fayetteville, N. C., Richmond, 2/068

Lowry (Harold L. & Brooke Neilson) Memorial Fund [Norfolk Fdn.], Norfolk, 2/068

Norfolk Society of Arts, Norfolk, 2/068

Nunnally Fdn., Richmond, 2/069

Oakwood Hebrew Cemetery Association, Richmond, 2/069

Ohrstrom Fdn., The Plains, 2/069

Roberts (William A.) Trust, Lynchburg, 2/071

Palmer (Harry A.) Trust, Staunton, 2/071

People's National Educational Fdn., Charlottesville, 2/072

Perel (Ruth & Milton) Fdn., Richmond, 2/072

Perkins Fdn., Roanoke, 2/072

Petersburg Home for Ladies, Petersburg, 2/073

Piney Woods Country Life School, Richmond, 2/073

Pitts (Benjamin T.) Fdn., Fredericksburg, 2/073

Poor Lands of Lower Parish, Chuckatuck, 2/074

Poster Fdn., Dayton, 2/075

Randolph (Virginia) Fdn., Richmond, 2/076

McGuire (Alice Reed & Hunter Holmes), Jr. Endowment Trust, Richmond, 2/077

Reynolds (Richard S.) Fdn., Richmond, 2/078

Richmond Food Store Educational Trust, Richmond, 2/079

Russell County Cooperative, Lebanon, 2/080

Sadler (William A.) Cemetery Fund, Richmond, 2/080

St. James Episcopal Church Trust, Arlington, 2/080

St. Luke's Episcopal Church Trust, Richmond, 2/080

St. Olive's School for Mountain Girls, Charlottesville, 2/081

St. Peter's Episcopal Church Trust, Richmond, 2/081

Sampson (Mayme W.) Trust, Staunton, 2/082
Saunders - Miller Fdn., Richmond, 2/082
Schwarzchild Brothers, Inc. Fdn., Richmond, 2/083
Reed (Mary Ross Scott & William T.), Jr. Trust, Manakin - Sabot, 2/084
Seay (George J. & Effie L.) Trust, Richmond, 2/085
Seventh Street Christian Church Trust, Richmond, 2/085
Sharp (Alice) Trust, Staunton, 2/086
Sheet Metal Workers International Association Local Union 87 Health & Welfare Fund, Norfolk, 2/086
Sherwood Forest Shores Association, Alexandria, 2/086
Shuster (Grace Greinert) Fdn., Reston, 2/086
Smith (Ola B.) Memorial Educational Trust, Charlottesville, 2/086
Snyder - DuPre Scholarship Fund, Arlington, 2/087
Stettinius - Gray Trust, Richmond, 2/088
State Planters Charitable Trust (See also 029), Richmond, 2/088
Fisher (Bruce Crane) Charitable Trust, Richmond, 2/089
Swartz Fdn., Roanoke, 2/089
Sutton (W. A.) Trust, Staunton, 2/089
Townsend (Helen Scott) & William T. Reed, III Fdn., Manakin - Sabot, 2/089
Adams (Jack) Trust, Richmond, 2/091
Arents (G.) Trust, Richmond, 2/092
Bogert (H. T.) Trust, Richmond, 2/092
Branch (Effie) Trust for Sheltering Arms Hospital, Richmond, 2/093
Cole (Quincy) Trust, Richmond, 2/093
Cox (Hallie H.) Trust for Blue Ridge Sanatorium, Richmond, 2/093
J. F. Trust for Crippled Children's Hospital, Richmond, 2/094
Downman (John Yates) Trusts, Richmond, 2/094
Zinke (Charles) Trust for Richmond Area Community Chest, Richmond, 2/095
Hudgens (Julian A.) Trust, Richmond, 2/095
Hunton (Eppa), Jr. Trust, Richmond, 2/095
Hunton (Virginia P.) Trust, Richmond, 2/095
J.F.B. Trust for Children's Milk Fund, Richmond, 2/095
Massie (Sue W.) Charitable Trust, Richmond, 2/096
Sadler (William A.) Cemetery Fund, Richmond, 2/096
Van Clief (Ray Alan) Burial Plot Trust, Richmond, 2/096
W C W Trust for Virginia Museum of Fine Arts, Richmond, 2/097
Williams (Mrs. Wilkins C.) Trust, Richmond, 2/097
Williams (A. D.) Trusts, Richmond, 2/097
Zimmer (Alverda) Trust, Petersburg, 2/100
Zincke (Margaret L.) Trust, Richmond, 2/100
Grace & Holy Trinity Episcopal Church Trust, Richmond, 2/101
Treakle (J. Edwin) Fdn., Gloucester, 2/101
Mountain Mission School Trust, Richmond, 2/101
N S P Trust for Loudon Memorial Hospital, Arlington, 2/102
Trigg (Landon W.) Charitable Trust, Richmond, 2/102
Truland Fdn., Arlington, 2/102
Upper Shirley Fdn., Charles City, 2/103
Van Clief (Margaret Good) Burial Plot Trust, Richmond, 2/104
Virginia Forests Educational Fund, Richmond, 2/104
Virginia Home for Incurables Trust, Richmond, 2/105
Washington Forest Fdn., Arlington, 2/105
Webb Family Fdn., Annandale, 2/106
Williamson (Mary) Educational Loan Fund, New Market, 2/106
Winans (Juliet M.) Trust, Staunton, 2/107
Woodbury Forest School-Lord Fund Trust, Richmond, 2/107

Womack Fdn., Danville, 2/108
Woodbury Forest School-Walker Fund Trust, Richmond, 2/108
Yancey (J. P.) Fdn., Newport News, 2/109

WASHINGTON

First Filming

American Home Fdn., Seattle, 1/001
Anderson (Agnes H.) - R. M. Riley Fund, Seattle, 1/001
Anderson (Agnes H.) - Loan & Scholarship Fund, Seattle, 1/002
Anderson (Agnes H.) - Research Fellowship Fund, Seattle, 1/002
Anderson (Duncan A. & Sophia L.) Fdn., Seattle, 1/003
Anderson (Sophie L.) Educational Trust, Seattle, 1/004
Arboretum Fdn., Seattle, 1/005
Arhil Fdn., Kent, 1/005
Bar 41 Ranch Fdn., Wilbur, 1/005
Bashore (David) Relief Board, Walla Walla, 1/006
Bassan Fdn., Seattle, 1/006
Bathiany (Steven) Memorial Scholarship Fund, Federal Way, 1/007
Beezley (P. C. & Esther W.) Fdn., Seattle, 1/007
Benson (Arvid C. - Arthur J.) Memorial Fdn., Seattle, 1/008
Benson (Edna G.) Fund, Seattle, 1/008
Bergstrom (Alex) Trust, Seattle, 1/009
Bigler (Melina) Trust, Seattle, 1/010
Blanchette (Frederic J.) Fdn., Seattle, 1/011
Block Fdn., Seattle, 1/011
Boeing Company Charitable Trust, Seattle, 1/012
Boeing Employees Disaster Relief Fund and Trust, Seattle, 1/014
Boyce (Harry B.) Trust, Seattle, 1/014
Bresee (Darius) Trust, Seattle, 1/015
Breunsbach Fdn., Vancouver, 1/015
Broadway High School Alumni Fdn., Seattle, 1/016
Brockman (Leo J.) Trust, Seattle, 1/016
Brown Assitance Fund Trust, Seattle, 1/017
Buhrman (F. W.) Educational & Scholarship Trust, Mount Vernon, 1/018
Burke (Caroline) Testamentary Trust, Seattle, 1/018
Burkowsky (Henrietta) Trust, Seattle, 1/019
Button (Dr. Reuben A.) Scholarship Fund, Puyallup, 1/020
Campbell (Susan E.) Trust, Seattle, 1/020
Cardiac Muscle Society, Seattle, 1/021
Carman (Nellie M.) Trust, Seattle, 1/021
Carrington (Glenn) Fdn., Seattle, 1/022
Casey Family Program, Seattle, 1/023
Cawsey Trust, Everett, 1/024
Challman Fdn. Trust, Seattle, 1/024
Clapp (Wilhelmina) Trust, Seattle, 1/025
Collins (I. Sidwell) Memorial Library Fund, Spokane, 1/026
Comstock Fdn., Spokane, 1/027
Conner (Leona) Library Fund, Seattle, 1/029
Consolidated Charities, Seattle, 1/030
Cook (Ben & Louella) Fdn., Seattle, 1/031
Cooney (Neil) Memorial School Fund, Seattle, 1/031
Cooper (Isaac) Trust, Seattle, 1/032
Culbertson (Essa) Remedial School Fdn., Seattle, 1/033
Davis (Norman & Amelia) Fdn. Trust, Seattle, 1/033
Delany (Alice & Henry) Trust, Seattle, 1/034
Douglas (Donald) Scholarship Fund, Yakima, 1/034
Duecy Trust, Everett, 1/035
Duffy - Williams Corporation, Seattle, 1/036

Dunlap (Anna C.) Scholarship Trust, Seattle, 1/036
Edson (Eugene J.) Trust, Seattle, 1/038
Egtvedt Charitable Trust, Seattle, 1/039
Ehrlich - Donnan Fdn., Seattle, 1/041
Elden (Arthur C.)-Rochester Medical School Fund, Seattle, 1/042
Elrod Fdn., Tacoma, 1/042
Culbertson (Essa) Fdn., Seattle, 1/043
Erickson (Carl J.) Educational Fund, Yakima, 1/043
Euclid Fdn., Seattle, 1/044
Evergreen Fund, Bainbridge Island, 1/045
Exchange Club of Spokane Fdn., Spokane, 1/045
Farwell Fdn., Sunnyside, 1/046
Fassett - Graham Trust, Seattle, 1/046
Faulding (Chalres) Trust, Spokane, 1/046
Fir Charitable Fund, Tacoma, 1/047
Fisher (O. D.) Charitable Fdn., Seattle, 1/048
Foss Fdn., Tacoma, 1/048
Foundation 28, Seattle, 1/048
Friedlander Fdn., Seattle, 1/049
Friedlander (Margery & Paul) Fdn., Seattle, 1/049
Friends of University School, Seattle, 1/050
Fuchs (Gottfried & Mary) Fdn., Tacoma, 1/050
Galbraith (William Shaw)-Medical Student Fund, Seattle, 1/051
Galland Fdn. for Establishing Fellowships & Scholarships, Spokane, 1/052
Glaser Fdn., Edmonds, 1/053
Glenhome Trust, Seattle, 1/053
G M L Fdn., Port Angeles, 1/054
Golub (Stanley D.) Fdn., Seattle, 1/055
Goodfellow Fund, Seattle, 1/055
Greater Lakes Mental Health Fdn., Tacoma, 1/056
Green (Joshua) Fdn., Seattle, 1/056
Greenacres Memorial Park, Seattle, 1/057
Greer (Ida M.) Scholarship, Tacoma, 1/058
Gwin (William F. & Lugarda H.) Memorial Fund, Seattle, 1/059
Hagen (Larry) Memorial Scholarship Fund, Seattle, 1/059
Hall (Mildred C.) Estate, Seattle, 1/060
Hamilton (T. S.) Fund, Seattle, 1/060
Hansen (Carl M.) Fdn., Spokane, 1/061
Harrington - Schiff Fdn., Seattle, 1/061
Harrington - Schiff Charitable Trust, Seattle, 1/062
Harrison (Angie W.) Trust, Seattle, 1/062
Harvard Club of Seattle Scholarship Fund, Seattle, 1/063
Hemmerling (Chris) Estate - Odessa Memorial Hospital Trust, Seattle, 1/063
Hemmerling (Chris) Estate - United Congregational Church Fund, Seattle, 1/064
Hitchcock (C. G.) Charitable Trust, Yakima, 1/065
Holmes (Norman) Memorial Scholarship, Cosmopolis, 1/065
Holy Trinity Church, Seattle, 1/065
Howell Fdn., Seattle, 1/065
Hutchinson (Eileen M.) Trust, Seattle, 1/066
Johnston Fdn., Spokane, 1/066
Johnson (Charles) Memorial Fund, Seattle, 1/068
Johnson (Louis) Trust, Seattle, 1/068
Johnston (Catherine) Testamentary Trust, Seattle, 1/068
Jones (Franke Tobey) Home, Tacoma, 1/069
Jones (Lavina) Trust, Yakima, 1/070
Keller (Martha May & Fred) Trust, Seattle, 1/071
Keller Memorial Park & Museum Fund, Seattle, 1/071
Kern (Louisa) Fund, Seattle, 1/072
Kotkins (Henry L. & Marion F.) Charitable Trust, Seattle, 1/072
Laird Fdn., Seattle, 1/072
Lanham Fdn., Seattle, 1/073
Larson (A. E.) Trust for People of Yakima City, Yakima, 1/074

Larson (A. E.) Trust for Rotary Club of Yakima Crippled Children Fund, Yakima, 1/075

Larson (A. E.) Trust for Salvation Army, Yakima, 1/075

Lewis (Jerome L.) Scholarship Fund, Seattle, 1/076

Lindberg Fdn. Trust, Tacoma, 1/076

Lockwood (Byron W. & Alice L.) Fdn., Seattle, 1/077

Longshoremen's Benevolent Association, Longview, 1/078

Longview Fdn., Longview, 1/079

Loudon (James Agnew & Minnie Larsen) Trust, Yakima, 1/079

Luce (Charles)-Nancy Oden Fund, Seattle, 1/080

MacDonald-Will Fdn., Tacoma, 1/080

Mayer (Markus & Mildred) Scholarship Fund, Seattle, 1/081

Marsh (Louis & Katherine) Scholarship Fund, Seattle, 1/082

Martin Fdn., Seattle, 1/083

McEachern (A. B. & Flavia B.) Charitable Trust, Seattle, 1/083

McGill Fdn., Seattle, 1/085

McMahon (Edward & Theresa S.) Trust, Seattle, 1/085

McIntosh (Jessie O'Bryan) Trust, Seattle, 1/086

Meadowdale Fdn., Tacoma, 1/087

Medina Fdn., Seattle, 1/088

Meikle (William & Edith) Trust, Seattle, 1/089

Meikle (Edith) Trust, Seattle, 1/089

Mell (Moy) Fdn., Edmonds, 1/090

Meyer (Estelle R.) Charity Fund, Seattle, 1/091

Meyer (Estelle) Park Fund, Seattle, 1/091

Miller (Alexander) Trust for Yakima Rotary Club, Yakima, 1/092

Miller (Lila) Scholarship Trust, Yakima, 1/092

Miller (Lila J.) Trust, Yakima, 1/093

Millicent Fdn., Vancouver, 1/094

Minerva Building Corporation, Tacoma, 1/096

Mittelstaedt (Lester W.) Fdn., Seattle, 1/096

Morria (William B. & Mattie L.) Fdn., Walla Walla, 1/097

Mowrer (William E.) Scholarship Fund, Seattle, 1/097

Murray Fdn., Tacoma, 1/098

Mutual Charitable Trust, Tacoma, 1/099

Myers (Margaret) Trust, Seattle, 1/100

Myhre (Loretta & Leonard A.) Fdn., Seattle, 1/100

Naramore Fdn., Seattle, 1/101

Nicoulin (Claude X.) Trust, Seattle, 1/101

Norcliffe Fund, Seattle, 1/101

O'Donnell (H. J.) Philantropic Trust, Seattle, 1/102

Osterman (A. J.) Scholarship Fund, Seattle, 1/103

Ostrander Fdn., Seattle, 1/103

Pacific Car & Foundry Company Fdn., Bellevue, 1/104

Palmer Charitable Fdn., Seattle, 1/105

Perkins (Harry A.) Trust, Seattle, 1/106

Permanent Endowment Fund of Seattle Symphony Orchestra, Seattle, 1/106

Perry (Marian Morgan) Library Fund, Yakima, 1/107

Pierce (David & Dorothy) Trust, Spokane, 1/107

Pleuthner (Augustus J.) Religious Fdn., Bellingham, 1/108

Polack Fdn., Seattle, 1/108

Poncin Scholarship Fund, Seattle, 1/109

Powers (Robert K.) Charitable Fdn., Spokane, 1/109

Rainwater (K.) Trust for First Christian Church, Yakima, 1/110

Raymond (Leslie V. & Stella J.) Fdn., Raymond, 1/111

Reed (Simpson) Fdn., Seattle, 1/111

Reed (Mark E.) Scholarship Fdn., Seattle, 1/112

Reno (George Henry) Scholarship Trust Fund, Seattle, 1/113

Renshaw Fdn., Seattle, 1/113

Rider Masonic Home, Rosalia, 1/114

Ridgway Graphic Arts Fdn., Redmond, 1/114

Robertson (David Allan) Memorial Scholarship Fund, Seattle, 1/115

Rubinstein (Sam & Gladys) Charitable Trust, Seattle, 1/116

Saberhagen Trust Fund, Seattle, 1/116

Seblen (Nina) Scholarship Fund, Seattle, 1/117

Shamberger (Martha) Trust, Seattle, 1/117

Shank (Gertrude McEachern) Charitable Trust, Seattle, 1/118

Shemanski (Tillie & Alfred) Fdn., Seattle, 1/119

Shuchart (George) Trust, Everett, 1/119

Shyman (Alfred & Etta) Charitable Trust, Seattle, 1/120

Siders (Frances E.) Trust, Seattle, 1/120

Sidney Fund, Seattle, 1/121

Sievers Fdn. Trust, Everett, 1/122

Simpson Timber Company Fdn., Seattle, 1/122

Simpson (Mervin) Trust, Seattle, 1/123

Skinner Fdn. Trust, Seattle, 1/124

Snyder (Frost & Margaret) Fdn., Tacoma, 1/126

Souther Fdn., Ridgefield, 1/128

Spokane Children's Home, Spokane, 1/129

Staufenbeil (Gladys) Trust, Seattle, 1/129

Stern (Edward) Family Fdn., Seattle, 1/129

Stuart (Charles E.) Scholarship Fund, Seattle, 1/130

Stuart (Mary Horner) Fdn., Seattle, 1/130

Stubblefield (Joseph L.) Trust, Walla Walla, 1/131

Sullivan Fdn., Seattle, 1/132

Sundquist (Ralph & Elaine) Charitable & Educational Trust, Yakima, 1/132

Talbot (Marie) Trust, Seattle, 1/133

Teachers Fdn., Seattle, 1/133

Tenzler Fdn., Tacoma, 1/134

Tenzler (Flora B.) Memorial Trust for the Benefit of the Frank Tobey Jones Home, Tacoma, 1/138

Tjelde (Odin & Gunhild) Fdn., Morton, 1/138

Torque Chapter - Women's Health League, Seattle, 1/139

Torrence (George R. & Jeanette H.) Charitable Trust, Seattle, 1/139

Trident Fdn., Everett, 1/140

Trimble (George W.) Trust, Seattle, 1/140

Trinity Parish Church Memorial Endowment Fund, Seattle, 1/141

Edson (Eugene J.) Trust, Seattle, 1/142

United Pacific Fdn., Tacoma, 1/142

Utter (Fred B.) Fdn., Spokane, 1/143

Vanguard Fund, Seattle, 1/144

Wageman (Don H. & Blanche) Trust, Seattle, 1/145

Wall (Katherine E. & Caron) Trust f/b/o St. James Catholic Parish, Seattle, 1/145

Washington Association for Retarded Children, Seattle, 1/146

Weisfield's Fund, Seattle, 1/147

Weisfield (Richard and Blanche) Fdn., Seattle, 1/147

Welborn (John F.) Shriners Hospital Fund, Seattle, 1/147

Wells (A. Z.) Fdn., Seattle, 1/148

Weyerhaeuser Company Fdn., Tacoma, 1/148

Wiborg Fdn., Tacoma, 1/149

Wickersham (May L.) Trust, Seattle, 1/150

Williams (Luke), Jr. Family Fdn., Spokane, 1/151

Wilson (John & Mary) Fdn., Seattle, 1/151

Woodbridge Fdn., Tacoma, 1/152

Wright (Howard) Trust, Seattle, 1/152

Wyman Youth Trust, Seattle, 1/153

Zahn (Daniel W.) Memorial Fd., Seattle, 1/153

Second Filming

Anacortes Community Theater, Anacortes, 2/001

Anderson Fdn., Seattle, 2/001

Anderson (Nellie) Trust, Seattle, 2/002

Anderson (Sophie L.) Trust, Seattle, 2/003

Angel (John P.) Fdn., Seattle, 2/003

Anti-Tuberculosis League, Seattle, 2/004

Asia Charitable Trust, Seattle, 2/004

Bengel (Pauline) King County Humane Soceity Fdn., Seattle, 2/005

Bengel (Pauline)-Seattle Goodwill Industries Fdn., Seattle, 2/005

Bengel (Pauline)-Seattle Symphony Fund, Seattle, 2/006

Boeing Employees Disaster Relief Fund Tr., Seattle, 2/007

Bloedel Fdn., Bainbridge Island, 2/007

Booker (Leon C.) Trust, Yakima, 2/008

Bradshaw (William B.) Trust, Seattle, 2/008

Brechemin Family Fdn., Seattle, 2/009

Royal Broughan Fdn., Seattle, 2/010

Bullitt Fdn., Seattle, 2/012

Cady (George A.) Educational Trust, Chehalis, 2/013

Carkeek (Florence Lewis) Trust, Seattle, 2/014

Castle (William L. "Leo") Fdn., Seattle, 2/015

Prior (Clementine) Scholarship Fund, Yakima, 2/015

Clise (Charles F.) Fund, Seattle, 2/016

Collins (I. Sidwell) Memorial Library Fund, Spokane, 2/016

Colman Charity Fund, Seattle, 2/017

Come & Help Club, Yakima, 2/019

Congregation Temple DeHirsch & Jewish Family & Child Service, Seattle, 2/019

Cooperative Community of Seattle, Seattle, 2/021

Council for the Advancement of Human Welfare, Seattle, 2/021

Cowles (Harriet Cheney) Fdn., Spokane, 2/021

Cowles (William H.) Fdn., Spokane, 2/022

Drain (Patrick) Testamentary Trust, Spokane, 2/025

Dupar Charitable Fdn., Seattle, 2/026

Duryee Charitable Trust, Everett, 2/027

Edmonds Lodge No. 165 F. & A. M. Charitable Fund, Edmonds, 2/028

Edwards (Dr. A. F.) Trust, Seattle, 2/028

Elks Building Association of Walla Walla, Walla Walla, 2/028

Evergreen Fund, Seattle, 2/029

Family Fdn., Seattle, 2/029

Ferris (Joel E.) Fdn., Spokane, 2/030

Firland Volunteer Fdn., Seattle, 2/030

Fisher (O. D.) Charitable Fdn., Seattle, 2/030

Fisher (Virginia W.) Fdn., Seattle, 2/031

Foresight Fdn., Gig Harbor, 2/031

Forest Clinic Fdn., Spokane, 2/032

Fuller (Margaret E.) Trust Fund, Seattle, 2/033

Fuller (Richard E.) Trust Fund, Seattle, 2/034

Gardner (Rebecca Schoenfeld & Jospeh) Fdn., Seattle, 2/035

Geneva Fdn. Formerly Albers Fdn., Seattle, 2/036

Gonzaga University Perpetual Trust, Seattle, 2/036

Haas (Saul) Fdn., Seattle, 2/037

Hamilton (Marie H.) Scholarship Fund, Seattle, 2/037

Harvard Club of Seattle Scholarship Fund, Seattle, 2/038

Hauberg Fdn., Seattle, 2/039

Hawkes (Mr. & Mrs. S. O.) Trust, Yakima, 2/039

Heffernan (Eleanor) Educational Fund, Yakima, 2/039

Hickman (Leona) Trust, Seattle, 2/040

Highline Youth Fdn., Seattle, 2/041

Hinman (Walter & Hazel) Fdn., Seattle, 2/041

Heath Church & Mission Trust, Tacoma, 2/042

Heath Kiwanis Trust, Tacoma, 2/043

Hitchock (C. G.) Charitable Trust, Yakima, 2/043

Hunt (Reed & Sarah) Fund Formerly California, Gig Harbor, 2/044

Irvine (Lizzie Brownell & John H.) Testamentary Trust, Seattle, 2/045

Johnston (T. Leman & Ruth C.) Education Trust, Seattle, 2/046

Johnson (Sarah Harris) Seattle Day Nursey
   Fund, Seattle, 2/046
Johnson (Sarah Harris) Wash. State Heart Ass.
   Fd., Seattle, 2/047
Kennedy (John F.) Memorial High School,
   Seattle, 2/049
Killian (Baxter) Memorial Scholarship Fund,
   Seattle, 2/050
Kingsley (Mary E.) Trust, Spokane, 2/050
Leavenworth (Emma E.) Trust, Seattle, 2/051
Leuthold Fdn., Spokane, 2/052
Levine Family Fdn., Bellevue, 2/053
Manson Community Library, Mason, 2/054
McEachern (A. B. & Flavia B.) Charitable
   Trust, Seattle, 2/054
Merriwether Fdn., Kirkland, 2/056
Merrill (R. D.) Fdn., Seattle, 2/056
Mittelstaedt (Lester W.) Fdn., Seattle, 2/057
Moss (Albert & Rosemond A.) Fdn., Seattle,
   2/058
Munson (John P.) Scholarship Fund, Yakima,
   2/058
Naramore Fdn., Seattle, 2/059
Nelson (R. E.) Family Fdn., Spokane, 2/059
North Tacoma Business & Professional
   Women's Club, Gig Harbor, 2/059
Olsen (Emma Smith) Trust, Seattle, 2/059
Olympia - Tumwater Fdn., Tumwater, 2/060
Pauze (L. George) Scholarship, Hoquiam,
   2/061
People-to-People, Seattle Chapter, Seattle,
   2/062
Price (Andrew) Charitable Trust, Seattle, 2/062
Pullman Fdn., Spokane, 2/062
Royston (Rachel) Permanent Scholarship Fdn.
   of Alpha Sigma State of Delta Kappa
   Gamma Society International, Seattle,
   2/063
Radiologic Research Fdn., Vancouver, 2/064
Rice (Ren H.) Fdn., Spokane, 2/065
Schafer (Carl & Mabel) Scholarship Fund,
   Seattle, 2/067
Schafer (Peter & Marie) Memorial Scholarship
   Fund, Seattle, 2/068
Scharff (Gaston) Memorial Trust, Spokane,
   2/069
Schluenz (William & Etta M. C.) Trust, Seattle,
   2/071
Jones (Florence) Memorial Scholarship Trust of
   Spokane Central Lions Club, Spokane,
   2/071
Miller (Alexander) Trust for the Board of
   County Commissioners of Yakima City for
   Tuberculosis Control, Yakima, 2/072
Miller (Alexander) Trust for YMCA, Yakima,
   2/072
Schoknecht Charitable Trust, Spokane, 2/074
Sigma Tau Fdn. of University of Washington,
   Seattle, 2/074
Spokane Fdn., Spokane, 2/075
Staley (Jessie P. & E. Fletcher) Scholarship
   Fdn., Yakima, 2/077
Suskin (Howard H.) Fdn., Seattle, 2/078
Stimson (C. D.) Highlands School Fund,
   Seattle, 2/079
Turnbull (Benjamin F.) Trust, Seattle, 2/079
Sealander (Torvig) Trust, Seattle, 2/079
Wagner Fund, Tacoma, 2/081
Walla Walla Union - Bulletin Fdn., Walla
   Walla, 2/082
Washington (George) Fdn., Yakima, 2/082
Weber (Philip P. & Lucy) Children's Home
   Fund, Spokane, 2/083
Weber (Philip P. & Lucy) Scholarship Fund,
   Spokane, 2/084
V W R United Fdn., Seattle, 2/084
Watson (H.) Scholarship Fund, Seattle, 2/085
Watson (H.) Loan Fund, Seattle, 2/085
Welch Fdn., Spokane, 2/086
Wilson (Gertrude) Charitable Trust, Seattle,
   2/087
Wright (Virginia) Fund, Seattle, 2/087
Wood (Clark M.) Fdn., Seattle, 2/088
Yakima County Tuberculosis Association,
   Yakima, 2/088
Yakima Fdn. Trust, Yakima, 2/088

Yakima Valley Memorial Fund for Nursing
   Education, Yakima, 2/089
Young Men's Christian Association of Yakima
   Trust Fund, Yakima, 2/089
Sundquist (Ralph) Scholarship Fund, Yakima,
   2/090
Brown (Roy C. & Ruth C.) Scholarship Fund,
   Yakima, 2/090
Anthon (S. I.) Scholarship Fund, Yakima,
   2/091
Robertson (W. W.) Memorial Scholarship
   Fund, Yakima, 2/091

WEST VIRGINIA

First Filming

Acme Fishing Tool Co. Supplemental
   Unemployment Benefit Plan, Parkersburg,
   1/001
Benevolent Fund of Kanawha County Bar
   Association, Charleston, 1/002
Berman (Fanny C.) Family Fdn., Charleston,
   1/002
Blaydes Fdn., Bluefield, 1/003
Bloch Fund, Wheeling, 1/003
Bloch Tobacco Fdn., Wheeling, 1/003
Woodbridge-Brown Fund, Charleston, 1/004
Carbon Fuel Fdn., Charleston, 1/005
Carr (Dr. & Mrs. Hugh) Scholarship Fund,
   Wheeling, 1/006
Children's Farm Trust, Wheeling, 1/007
Children's Home of Wheeling, Wheeling,
   1/007
Daywood Fdn., Charleston, 1/009
Dillon (Frances Polk) Trust, Charleston, 1/010
Fenton Fdn., Williamstown, 1/010
Foster Fdn., Huntington, 1/011
Funkhouser (R. J.) Fdn., Hedgesville, 1/011
Garrison (Forest L.) Trust, Charleston, 1/012
Gebhart (Florence V.) Testamentary Trust for
   the Children's Home Society, Charleston,
   1/012
Gebhart (Annie E.) Union Mission et al Trust,
   Charleston, 1/013
Guill (A. J.) Estate Trust, Charleston, 1/014
General Electronics Fund, Wheeling, 1/015
Harless (Jamey) Fdn., Gilbert, 1/016
Harron (Ray V.) Fdn., Bridgeport, 1/016
Herscher Fdn., Charleston, 1/017
Jacobson (Bernard H. & Blanche E.) Fdn.,
   Charleston, 1/018
Scott (A. M.) Trust, Charleston, 1/018
Kanawha Valley Fdn., Charleston, 1/019
Keystone Fund, Parkersburg, 1/020
Kirkland (Mr. & Mrs. John Long) Scholarship
   Fund, Wheeling, 1/021
Koontz (Patrick D.) Trust, Charleston, 1/022
Laughlin (George A.) Trust, Wheeling, 1/022
Laughlin (George A.) Scholastic Prizes,
   Wheeling, 1/023
Lavenia Home for Old Ladies Trust, Charleston,
   1/024
Matthews (Armstrong Robertson) Memorial
   Fund, Bluefield, 1/024
McCamic (Charles) Fdn., Wheeling, 1/025
McDonough (Bernard) Fdn., Parkersburg,
   1/026
McJunkin Family Fdn., Charleston, 1/027
Memorial Education Trust Fund, Charleston,
   1/028
Minor (Berkeley & Susan Fontaine) Fdn.,
   Charleston, 1/028
Mu Mu Fdn., Charleston, 1/030
Nugent (Adaline C.) Trust, Parkersburg, 1/031
Paull (Lee C.) Fdn., Wheeling, 1/031
Permanent Endowment Fund of Sunrise Fdn.,
   Charleston, 1/032
Robin Hood Burial Fund, Twilight, 1/032
Robin Hood Relief Fund, Twilight, 1/033
Nelson (Edwin Robson) Fdn., Huntington,
   1/033

Ruby Enterprises Fdn., Morgantown, 1/033
Scott (Kate C.) Fdn., Charleston, 1/033
Stone (W. E.) Fdn., Wheeling, 1/034
Scott (A. M.) Trust, Charleston, 1/035
Shaw (John C.) Trust, Wheeling, 1/036
Steenbergen (Peter H.) Scholarship Fund,
   Charleston, 1/036
Teass (Mae Mason) Testamentary Trust,
   Charleston, 1/037
Thomas (A. S.) Memorial Fund, Charleston,
   1/037
Upper Ohio Valley Self-Help Fdn., Parkersburg,
   1/038
Voice of the Hills Fdn., Fairmont, 1/038
Wehrle (Elizabeth H. & H. B.) Fdn.,
   Charleston, 1/039
Weiss (William E.) Fdn., Wheeling, 1/040
Westmoreland Coal Company - Penn Virginia
   Corporation Scholarship Fund, Madison,
   1/041
West Virginia University Service Club Loan
   Fund, Morgantown, 1/042
Wilbet Fund, Wheeling, 1/042

Second Filming

Ceredo-Kenova Fdn., Ceredo, 2/001
Chambers (James B.) Memorial, Wheeling,
   2/001
Charleston Fdn. for Research, Charleston,
   2/002
Delta Tau Delta Fdn., Fairmont, 2/003
Fostoria Glass Company Fdn., Moundsville,
   2/003
Kanawha Valley Fdn. (Greater), Charleston,
   2/003
Humphrey's (A. J.) Trust, Charleston, 2/007
Lamb (F. B.) Trust, Charleston, 2/007
Moore (Dr. Phoebia G.) Memorial Library
   Trust Fund Association, Mannington, 2/007
Fish (J. T. & C. B.) Fdn., Logan, 2/008
Moore Fdn., Charleston, 2/008
Mu Mu Fdn., Charleston, 2/010
Carter (Norval) Memorial Trust Fund,
   Huntington, 2/010
Beren (Max) Prize Fdn., Parkersburg, 2/010
Parsons (Bernice Pickens) Fdn. Trust,
   Charleston, 2/010
Partnership Fdn., Capon Springs, 2/011
Sneddon (Lizbeth Calder) Trust, Charleston,
   2/011
Randolph County Archers, Elkins, 2/011
Snyder (Alicia Watchorn) Fdn., Mount Hope,
   2/011
Starvaggi Charities, Weirton, 2/012
West Virginia State Dental Relief Fund,
   Charleston, 2/012
Wilbet Fund, Wheeling, 2/012
Withrow (Frank H.) Trust, Charleston, 2/013

WISCONSIN

First Filming

Abbot Machine Company Charitable Fdn.,
   Milwaukee, 1/001
Alano Fdn., Milwaukee, 1/001
Albrecht (Gilmon F.) Fdn., Madison, 1/001
Alexander Charitable Fdn., Port Edwards,
   1/002
Alexander (Walter) Fdn., Wausau, 1/002
Allis-Chalmers Emergency Fund, Inc., West
   Allis, 1/003
Allis (Louis) Co. Fdn., Milwaukee, 1/005
Ampco Fdn., Milwaukee, 1/005
Andrews (George E.) Trust, Beloit, 1/007
Apple Family Fdn., Milwaukee, 1/008
Appleton Coated Fdn., Appleton, 1/008
ARPS Fdn., New Holstein, 1/008
Ashland Fdn., Ashland, 1/009
Ashley (Charles David) Fdn., Milwaukee,
   1/009

Atkins Fdn., Milwaukee, 1/010
Bacon (Frank Rogers) Fdn., Milwaukee, 1/010
Badger State Advancement Assn. of the Blind, Milwaukee, 1/012
Baird Fdn., Milwaukee, 1/013
Baird (Kenneth) Fdn., Whitefish Bay, 1/014
Bamberger Fdn., Milwaukee, 1/014
Marshall & Ilsley Bank Fdn., Milwaukee, 1/015
Banta Company Fdn., Menasha, 1/016
Bardon Fdn., Milwaukee, 1/017
Barker (Helen and Leland H.) Fdn., Inc., Milwaukee, 1/018
Barry (James W. T.) Fdn., Milwaukee, 1/018
Baudhuin (George J.) Fdn., Sturgeon Bay, 1/019
B.C. Fdn., Milwaukee, 1/019
Beach (Olive & Emmitt H.) Charitable Trust, Sheboygan, 1/020
Beals (Vina S.) Charitable Trust, Neenah, 1/021
Becker (George J.) Fdn., Inc., Fond du Lac, 1/022
Beloit Fdn., Beloit, 1/022
Bergstrom Fdn., Neenah, 1/023
B/G Fdn., Milwaukee, 1/023
Bickel Family Fdn., Milwaukee, 1/024
Birnschein (Alvin & Marion) Fdn., Milwaukee, 1/025
Bitker (Arthur J.) Memorial Fdn. Charitable Trust, Milwaukee, 1/025
Block (Robert S.) Family Fdn. Fund, Milwaukee, 1/026
Block (Robert S.) Family Fdn., Milwaukee, 1/026
Bockl Fdn., Milwaukee, 1/026
Boesel (Charles M.) Fdn., Milwaukee, 1/027
Borg (George W. & Effie) Scholarship Fund, Delavan, 1/027
Boston Store Welfare Fdn., Milwaukee, 1/028
Bosworth Family Fdn., Milwaukee, 1/028
Bowman (Jonathan) Home for Women, Milwaukee, 1/029
Boyd (Lois & Charles) Fdn., Appleton, 1/029
Braun (Victor F.) Fdn., Milwaukee, 1/030
Braun Fdn., Milwaukee, 1/031
Briggs & Stratton Corp. Fdn., Wauwatosa, 1/031
Broeren (Jean C. and Mary Ellen) Fdn., Thorp, 1/032
Brill Family Charitable Fdn., Milwaukee, 1/032
Brook Hill Fund, Gensesee Depot, 1/033
Brown (R. & E.) Fdn., Milwaukee, 1/033
Brumder (Thekla U.) Fdn., Milwaukee, 1/034
Bucyrus-Erie Fdn., South Milwaukee, 1/034
Buettner (Erhard H.) Fdn., Milwaukee, 1/036
Buettner (Erhard) Fdn., Milwaukee, 1/036
Berger (H. E.) Fdn., Manitowoc, 1/037
Burmester Fdn., Janesville, 1/037
Butter (Earl) Fdn., Menomonee Falls, 1/038
Cahco Fdn., Madison, 1/038
Camp (H. H.) Fdn., Milwaukee, 1/039
Carleton Willet Mason Trust, Milwaukee, 1/040
Cedar Ridge Fdn., Milwaukee, 1/040
Cedarburg Friends of The Library, Cedarburg, 1/041
Cenco Fdn., Janesville, 1/041
Center for International Life, Milwaukee, 1/042
Cern Fdn., Madison, 1/042
Chapin Fdn. of Wisconsin, Milwaukee, 1/044
Chapman Fdn., Milwaukee, 1/045
Chapman (Donald S.) Fdn., Milwaukee, 1/046
Childrens Fdn. of Milwaukee, Milwaukee, 1/046
Scholarship Fund of Milwaukee Alumnae Chaper of Chi Omega, Thiensville, 1/047
Chipstone Fdn., Milwaukee, 1/048
Chou (Rev. T. S.) Educational & Charitable Trust, Madison, 1/048
Clarner Fdn., Wauwatosa, 1/048
Cohen (Arthur A.) Family Fdn., Milwaukee, 1/048
Cohen (Melvin S.) Fdn., Eau Claire, 1/049
Commercial State Fdn., Madison, 1/049

Commerical State Bank Fdn., Madison, 1/050
Community Trust, West Bend, 1/050
Consolidateds Civic Fdn., Wisconsin Rapids, 1/051
Conway (Mr. & Mrs. Francis J.) Fdn., Thorp, 1/053
Cornell Products Fdn., Milwaukee, 1/053
Cox (R. M.) Fdn., Racine, 1/054
Craig Family Fdn., Milwaukee, 1/055
Creative Church Fdn., Madison, 1/055
Cremer Fdn., Madison, 1/055
Cron (Roland & Florence) Fdn., Milwaukee, 1/056
Croxson (Arthur & Ann S.) Charitable Trust, Neenah, 1/056
Cudahy (Patrick and Anna M.) Fund, Milwaukee, 1/057
Cudahy (Patrick) Institute, Milwaukee, 1/060
Cullister Fdn., Janesville, 1/060
Cuna Mutual & Cumis Charitable Fdn., Madison, 1/061
Cutler-Hammer Fdn., Milwaukee, 1/061
Dade Fdn., La Crosse, 1/062
Dahl (Howard) Fdn., La Crosse, 1/062
Dairyland Fdn., Madison, 1/063
Danad Corp., Milwaukee, 1/063
Daniels Fdn., Rhinelander, 1/064
Davids Fdn., Milwaukee, 1/065
Davidson (Gordon M.) Charitable Trust, Wauwatosa, 1/065
Davidson (Robert J.) Charitable Trust, Elm Grove, 1/067
Davidson (Walter C.) Charitable Trust, Brown Deer, 1/067
Delong (James E.) Charitable Fdn., Waukesha, 1/068
Demmer (Edward U.) Fdn., Marine Plaza, 1/069
De Rance, Milwaukee, 1/069
De Witt (Charles and Marion) Fdn., Racine, 1/072
Dexter-Kranick Fdn., Milwaukee, 1/073
D & G Fdn., Milwaukee, 1/074
Diercks (Margaret) Memorial Trust, Antigo, 1/075
Discoverers Fund, Milwaukee, 1/075
Doerr (Edwin) Fdn., Milwaukee, 1/075
Doerr (Emmett J.) Fdn., Milwaukee, 1/075
Doerr (Lee A.) Fdn., Milwaukee, 1/076
Douglas County Disaster and Welfare Fund, Superior, 1/076
Downing Fdn., Milwaukee, 1/076
Duhamel (Mae L.) Trust, Lancaster, 1/077
Dumore Fdn., Racine, 1/078
Earle Fdn., Racine, 1/078
Ebin (Louis) Charities, La Crosse, 1/079
Edel Charitable Fdn., Milwaukee, 1/079
Eder (Ralph and Louise) Fdn., Milwaukee, 1/080
Eilcar Fdn., Milwaukee, 1/081
Eisner (William) Fdn., Hales Cornors, 1/082
Elizabeth Trust, Milwaukee, 1/083
Elliot (Herbert H. & Fern) Family Fdn., Milwaukee, 1/084
Elmwood Fdn., Kohler, 1/084
Elser (Mathilde U. and Albert) Fdn., Milwaukee, 1/085
Elwell Fdn., Milwaukee, 1/086
Emch Family Fdn., Milwaukee, 1/086
Enger-Kress Fund, West Bend, 1/087
Epstein (H. L.) Family Fdn., Milwaukee, 1/087
Esch Fdn., Sheboygan, 1/088
Evangelical Fdn., Appleton, 1/089
Everest (D. C.) Fdn., Wausau, 1/089
Fahrenkrug (Anna G.) Memorial Fund, Green Bay, 1/090
Faith Fdn., Evansville, 1/091
Falk (Harold F. and Suzanne D.) Fdn., Milwaukee, 1/091
Falk (Herman W.) Memorial Fdn., Milwaukee, 1/092
Fellner (Phillip J.) Fdn., Racine, 1/093
Ferris (Walter) Fdn., Milwaukee, 1/093
Findley (K. E.) Fdn., Milwaukee, 1/094
Findorff Fdn., Madison, 1/095

First Civic Fdn., Milwaukee, 1/095
First Wisconsin Fdn., Milwaukee, 1/096
First Wisconsin National Bank Madison Fdn., Madison, 1/097
Fitch Research Fund, Milwaukee, 1/098
Fitch (John Grant) Fdn., Milwaukee, 1/098
Fitzgerald (Elizabeth Bacon)-Kenshire Fdn., Milwaukee, 1/099
Fond du Lac YMCA Fdn., Fond du Lac, 1/099
Ford (Guy Stanton) Educational Fdn., Madison, 1/100
Forman (Harry & Rose) Fdn., Milwaukee, 1/100
Formrite Fdn., Manitowoc, 1/100
Forward Fdn., Wausau, 1/100
Fox-Henze Fdn., Port Washington, 1/101
Foxwood Fdn., Milwaukee, 1/101
Frackelton Fdn., Milwaukee, 1/102
Franzen (William R.) Charitable Trust, Milwaukee, 1/102
Franzen (William R.) Supplemental Charitable Trust, Milwaukee, 1/103
Free Family Fdn., Milwaukee, 1/103
Freeman (L. L. and Cornelia G.), Racine, 1/104
French (Bill) Memorial Scholarship Fund, Sheboygan, 1/105
Fulton Fdn., West Allis, 1/105
Fusfeld (Mil & Jay) Fdn., Wausau, 1/106
Gabel (Frank M.) Fdn., Sheboygan, 1/106
Gabrielse-Hermann Charitable Fdn., Sheboygan, 1/107
Gallum Fdn., Milwaukee, 1/107
Gallun (Richard A.) Fund, Milwaukee, 1/108
Garber Family Fdn., Milwaukee, 1/108
Gardner Fdn., Milwaukee, 1/109
Gaston (Omar L.) Memorial Trust, Madison, 1/110
Gehl Fdn., West Bend, 1/111
General Charities, Milwaukee, 1/111
Giddings & Lewis Fdn., Fond du Lac, 1/112
Gisholt (John A. Johnson) Fdn., Madison, 1/113
Gitzen (Joseph A.) Fdn., Milwaukee, 1/116
Glen Fdn., Milwaukee, 1/116
Globe-Union Fdn., Milwaukee, 1/116
Godfrey Fdn., Waukesha, 1/118
Good Hope Fdn., Milwaukee, 1/119
Graber Fdn., Madison, 1/119
Grant Street Fdn., Wasau, 1/120
Greater Waukesha United Fund, Waukesha, 1/121
Grede Fdn., Milwaukee, 1/121
Gruett Scholarship Trust, Merrill, 1/122
Grunau Fdn., Milwaukee, 1/123
Gruszynski Fdn., Thorp, 1/123
Habush (Robert L.) Family Fdn., Milwaukee, 1/124
Hagge (H. J.) Fdn., Wausau, 1/124
Hahn Fdn., Racine, 1/125
Hall (Alma G.) Fdn., Milwaukee, 1/126
Halmbacher Fdn., Milwaukee, 1/126
Hamilton (Agusta) Fdn., Manitowoc, 1/127
Hamilton Memorial Fdn., Two Rivers, 1/127
Hansen-Von Hagke Fdn., Milwaukee, 1/128
Harnischfeger Fdn., Milwaukee, 1/129
Hayssem Family Fdn., Sheboygan, 1/129
Hecht (David M. & Joyce F.) Fdn., Milwaukee, 1/130
Heider Fdn., Wauwatosa, 1/131
Heileman Old Style Brewery Fdn., La Crosse, 1/131
Heller Fdn., Oshkosh, 1/132
Henoch (Willard F.) Fdn., Milwaukee, 1/132
Henry (Walter) Fdn., Milwaukee, 1/133
Herbst Fdn., Milwaukee, 1/133
Herlin Family Fdn., Ripon, 1/134
Herman (Helen K.) Scholarship Trust, Sheboygan, 1/134
Hershoff Family Fdn., Milwaukee, 1/134
Hayden (Vander) Fdn., Elm Grove, 1/135
High Cliff Forest Park Assoc., Kaukauna, 1/136
Hill (Robert) Fdn., Milwaukee, 1/136
H & M Charities, Milwaukee, 1/137

Hoan (Daniel W.) Fdn., Milwaukee, 1/137
Hoard (W. D.) Fdn., Fort Atkinson, 1/138
Hobbs Fdn., Eau Claire, 1/138
Hoffman Fdn., Milwaukee, 1/139
Hoffman (Harri & Herta) Fdn., Milwaukee, 1/140
Holbrook (J. and J.) Family Fdn., Milwaukee, 1/140
Homan (Gus) Memorial Fund, Sheboygan, 1/140
Hood Fdn., Green Bay, 1/141
Hood (Wayne) Fdn., La Crosse, 1/141
Horn Fdn., Sheboygan, 1/142
Horwitz (Frank) Trust, Sheboygan, 1/142
Hummitzsch (Jerry) Memorial Scholarship Fund, Sheboygan, 1/143
Humphrey Fdn., Milwaukee, 1/143
Hunkel (Philipp L.) Memorial Research Fund, Wauwatosa, 1/144
Hutter (George F.) Charitable Trust, Fond du Lac, 1/145
Hyland-Hall & H & H Electric Fdn., Madison, 1/145
Hyslop Fdn., Kenosha, 1/146
Irving (Jim and Ada) Fdn., Stoughton, 1/146
Jaclyn Memorial Fdn., Milwaukee, 1/147
Janesville Fdn., Janesville, 1/148
Jensen Fdn., Madison, 1/149
Eauterbach (Wilma Heath) Fdn., Delaven, 1/149
Jerome (Wallace H.) Fdn., Barron, 1/149
Johnson (Herman E.) Charitable Fdn., Racine, 1/150
Kidney Fdn. of Wisconsin, Madison, 1/150
Johnson (Roy W.) Fdn., Milwaukee, 1/150
Johnson (Water A. & Lydia) Scholarship Trust, Monroe, 1/151
Johnson Service Fdn., Milwaukee, 1/151
Jones of Fort Atkinson Fdn., Fort Atkinson, 1/154
Jones (Alan P.) Trust for St. Peter's Episcopal Church, Fort Atkinson, 1/154
J.P.K. Fdn., Milwaukee, 1/155
Jungbluth Fdn., Wauwatosa, 1/156
Katherine and William Corp., Milwaukee, 1/156
Katz Fdn., La Crossee, 1/157
Katz (Gary) Fdn., Milwaukee, 1/157
Kelley Fdn., Milwaukee, 1/158
Kerscher (Francis) Fdn., Manitowoc, 1/158
Kimball (Miles) Fdn., Oshkosh, 1/158
Kimberly-Clark Fdn., Neenah, 1/159
Klug & Smith Co. Charitable Trust, Racine, 1/162
Knights Fdn., Milwaukee, 1/162
Knudsen Fdn., Milwaukee, 1/163
Knuth (Erv and Lou) Fdn., Menomonee Falls, 1/164
Koehring Fdn., Milwaukee, 1/164
Kohler Fdn., Kohler, 1/165
Kohl (Edwin Phillips) Memorial Fund, Milwaukee, 1/167
Kootz (Arthur C.) Fdn., Milwaukee, 1/167
Kopmeier Family Fdn., Milwaukee, 1/168
Krause (Chas A.) Fdn., Milwaukee, 1/169
Krause (Charles A.) Scholarship Fund, Milwaukee, 1/171
Kraut Fdn., Fond du Lac, 1/172
Kravit Family Fdn., Milwaukee, 1/172
Kress (George) Fdn., Green Bay, 1/173
Kritzik (David) Family Fdn., Milwaukee, 1/175
Kritzik (Reuben) Family Fdn., Oak Creek, 1/176
Kritzik (Stanley) Family Fdn., Milwaukee, 1/176
Kritzik (Robert) Fdn., Milwaukee, 1/177
Kubousek (James J.) Fdn., Brookfield, 1/177
Kultgen (John and Mary) Fdn., Brookfield, 1/178
Kurth (Herbert), Katherine Kurth, and Elisabeth Kurth Wrean Tinetka Kurth Messinger Trustees of Religious Trust, Milwaukee, 1/178
Kurzawa Family Fdn., Wauwatosa, 1/179
Lafayette Masonic Fdn., Milwaukee, 1/180

Lakeland Fdn., Sheboygan, 1/181
Lakeside Fdn., Milwaukee, 1/182
Lange Memorial Fdn., Baraboo, 1/182
Langenfeld (Paul W.) Fdn., New Holstein, 1/183
Langenfeld Fdn., New Holstein, 1/184
Lardner (Lucile & Lynford) Fdn., Milwaukee, 1/185
Laskin (Arhtur J. & Nancy L.) Fdn., Milwaukee, 1/186
Laub (Rudolf A.)/Agency Fdn., Milwaukee, 1/186
Lauterbach (Wilma Heath) Fdn., DeLaven, 1/187
Law (William L.) Fdn., Cudahy, 1/187
Lawset Inc., Milwaukee, 1/188
Leach (Elmer) Fdn., Oshkosh, 1/189
Leichts Fdn., Green Bay, 1/189
Leverenz Fdn., Sheboygan, 1/190
Liebenson (David and Mildred) Fdn., Oshkosh, 2/001
Lindsay Fdn., Milwaukee, 2/001
Litsheim-Sorensen Fdn., Eau Claire, 2/002
LMLSP Fdn., Milwaukee, 2/002
Loewi & Co. Fdn., Milwaukee, 2/003
Loock (Margaret & Fred) Fdn., Milwaukee, 2/003
Lorentz (Adelaide Prahl) Memorial Scholarship Trust, Milwaukee, 2/004
Love (Elaine) 1956 Educational Fund, Milwaukee, 2/005
Lubar Family Fdn., Milwaukee, 2/005
Luedke-Smith Fdn., Shorewood, 2/005
Lutz (Werner) Fdn., Milwaukee, 2/006
Lyle (Paul H.) Fdn., Racine, 2/006
Madison Gas & Electric Fdn., Madison, 2/007
Madison-Kipp Fdn., Madison, 2/008
Madson (George L.) Family Charitable Trust, Neenah, 2/008
Maeefund, Milwaukee, 2/009
Maher (Roy W.) Fdn., Milwaukee, 2/010
Manegold (Robert L. & Sally S.) Fdn., Milwaukee, 2/011
Maitowoc Savings Bank Fdn., Manitowoc, 2/012
Manpower Fdn., Milwaukee, 2/013
Marathon Electric Fdn., Wausau, 2/014
Mark Fdn., Wausau, 2/014
Markham (Marianne & George) Fdn., Milwaukee, 2/015
Marquette Electronics Fdn., Milwaukee, 2/016
Marin (Juan R.) Memorial Fdn., Milwaukee, 2/016
Mason (Edna Louise) Scholarship Fund, Waukesha, 2/017
Lowe Fdn., Milwaukee, 2/017
Mason (B. A.) Trust, Chippewa Falls, 2/018
Mason (Edna Louise) Scholarship Fund, Waukesha, 2/019
Master Fdn. Trust, Wauwatosa, 2/019
Master Lock Fdn., Milwaukee, 2/019
M. B. & T. Fdn., Madison, 2/021
McBeath (Faye) Fdn., Milwaukee, 2/021
McBeath (Faye) Fund for Aid of the Blind, Milwaukee, 2/023
McCanna Fdn., Burlington, 2/024
McCaffey (Jere D.) Family Fdn., Milwaukee, 2/024
McGiveran Family Fdn., Milwaukee, 2/024
McKelvey (Jeannette) Fdn., Milwaukee, 2/025
Medford Student Loan and Scholarship Fdn., Medford, 2/026
Menasha Corporation Fdn., Menasha, 2/026
Menn (Gregory) Fdn., Appleton, 2/027
Mequon Methodist Scholarship Fund, Thiensville, 2/027
Messmer Fdn., Milwaukee, 2/027
Meyer (George L. N.) Family Fdn., Milwaukee, 2/028
Miba Inc., Milwaukee, 2/029
Midland Fdn., Milwaukee, 2/030
Mielke Family Fdn., Appleton, 2/031
Miller (Robert J.) Fdn., Milwaukee, 2/031
Miller Fdn., Marshfield, 2/032
Miller Fdn., St. Nazianz, 2/033

Miller (Dr. Harold L.) and Margaret Miller Fdn., Milwaukee, 2/033
Miller High Life Fdn., Milwaukee, 2/034
Milwaukee Gear Fdn., Milwaukee, 2/035
Milwaukee Music Scholarship Fdn., Milwaukee, 2/036
Milwaukee Operetta Guild, Milwaukee, 2/036
Ministrare Inc., Milwaukee, 2/037
Moebius (C. & J.) Fdn., Milwaukee, 2/037
Morley-Murphy Fdn., Green Bay, 2/038
Morse (Colonel Robert H.) Fdn., Beliot, 2/038
Mosinee Paper Mills Foundation Inc., Mosinee, 2/038
Milberger (Lorraine) Fdn., Milwaukee, 2/039
Munkwitz Fdn., Trust, Milwaukee, 2/039
Murco Fdn., Wausau, 2/040
Murphy (Eugene W. & Marjorie P.) Fdn., La Crosse, 2/041
Musebeck (G. E.) Fdn., Oconomowoca, 2/041
Naleid Charitable Fdn., Racine, 2/041
Nash Fdn., Manitowoc, 2/042
National League Baseball Club of Milwaukee Fdn., Milwaukee, 2/043
Neenah Foundry Fdn., Neenah, 2/044
Neese Fdn., Beliot, 2/045
Nekoosa-Edwards Fdn., Port Edwards, 2/046
Nickoll (Benjamin E.) Family Fdn., Milwaukee, 2/047
N. N. Fdn., Milwaukee, 2/047
Nordberg Fdn., Milwaukee, 2/048
North Shore Bank Fdn., Shorewood, 2/049
Northern Laboratories Fdn., Manitowoc, 2/049
Northland Missions, Pound, 2/050
Northwoods Fdn., Milwaukee, 2/054
Nymeyer Library Memorial Trust, Milwaukee, 2/055
Old Boys Scholarship Fdn., Milwaukee, 2/055
Oshkosh Motor Trust Fdn., Oshkosh, 2/056
Oster (John) Family Fdn., Milwaukee, 2/056
Our Lady of the Lake Fdn. 1870 Marine Pl., Milwaukee, 2/057
Pabst Breweries Fdn., Milwaukee, 2/058
Pabst (Fred) Fdn., Oconomowoc, 2/059
Pabst (William F.) Fdn., Milwaukee, 2/061
Palmer (Henry L.) Fdn., Milwaukee, 2/062
Parker Fdn., Janesville, 2/062
Peck Family Fdn., Milwaukee, 2/062
Pelton Fdn., Milwaukee, 2/064
Perfex Fdn., Milwaukee, 2/064
Peters (Arthur N.) Fdn., Milwaukee, 2/065
Peters (R. D. and Linda) Fdn., Brillion, 2/065
Phillips (Henry and Gladys) Fdn., Wausau, 2/066
Pickard (S. N.) Charitable Trust, Neenah, 2/066
Pieper (Robert W.) and Josephine Pieper Fdn., Milwaukee, 2/067
Port Ulao Fdn., Milwaukee, 2/068
Post (Major Arthur L.) Memorial Fdn., Milwaukee, 2/069
Pieper Power Fdn., Milwaukee, 2/069
Pollybill Fdn., Milwaukee, 2/070
Portage Hosiery Company Fdn., Portage, 2/071
Posner (Gene) Family Fdn., Milwaukee, 2/071
Powiazer (Goldie) Fdn., Milwaukee, 2/072
Prange (H. C.) Company Fund, Sheboygan, 2/072
Prince (Mollie and Edward) Fdn., Milwaukee, 2/074
Primakow (Harry) Family Fdn., Milwaukee, 2/074
Pritzlaff (Elinor Gallum) Fdn., Hartland, 2/074
Puelicher Fdn., Milwaukee, 2/075
Purity Fdn., Mayville, 2/075
Raylen Fdn., Wauwatosa, 2/076
Raymond (Dr. R. G.) & Sarah Raymond Fdn., Oshkosh, 2/077
Reigle (J. O.) Fdn., Kewaskum, 2/077
Reiss Fdn., Sheboygan, 2/078
Rennebohn (Oscar) Fdn., Madison, 2/078
Resnick Fdn., Milwaukee, 2/080
Richardson Paint Company Scholarship Fund, Baraboo, 2/080
Richter Fdn. Richter (Oscar A.) Et Al Trustees, Manitowoc, 2/081
Riverlea Fdn., Menasha, 2/081

Riverside Paper Fdn., Appleton, 2/081
Robinson (Clara Stiles) Trust, Beliot, 2/082
Rose (Clifford M.) Scholarship Fdn., Kewaskum, 2/082
Rosenberg (A. P. and Ida) Fdn., Milwaukee, 2/083
Rosenberg (Henry & Blanche) Fdn., Milwaukee, 2/083
Rosenberg (Joseph & Edith) Fdn., Milwaukee, 2/084
Ross (Will) Memorial Fdn., Milwaukee, 2/084
Rothe (Joseph W. & Martha M.) Fdn., Green Bay, 2/085
Roussy Fdn., Milwaukee, 2/085
Rueping (Fred) Fdn., Fond du Lac, 2/085
Ruhar Inc., Milwaukee, 2/085
Sacul Fdn., Milwaukee, 2/086
Saltzstein (Joan and Irving) Fdn., Milwaukee, 2/086
Schafer (Forest H.) Fdn., Clintonville, 2/087
Scheinfeld (James D. & Audrey F.) Fdn., Milwaukee, 2/088
Schield Family Fdn., Milwaukee, 2/088
Schimenz (Mathias G.) Memorial Law Scholarship Fund, Milwaukee, 2/089
Schlitz Fdn., Milwaukee, 2/089
Schneider (D. J.) Family Fdn., Oconomowoc, 2/091
Schoenleber Fdn., Milwaukee, 2/091
Schroeder (John E. & Gertrude) Fdn., Milwaukee, 2/092
Schwartz (Simon) Fund, Two Rivers, 2/092
Seaman Fdn., Bayside, 2/093
Seaman (Irving) Family Fdn., Milwaukee, 2/094
Seaman (Douglas) Fdn., Milwaukee, 2/095
Segel Family Fdn., Milwaukee, 2/095
Seidel Fdn., Milwaukee, 2/095
Seng Stock Fdn., Green Bay, 2/096
Sentry Fdn., Stevens Point, 2/096
Settlement Cook Book Company, Milwaukee, 2/097
Shapiro (Michael and Rae) and Family Fdn., Milwaukee, 2/097
Shattuck (James & Martha) Charitable Trust, Neenah, 2/098
Sheboygan Clinic Fdn., Sheboygan, 2/100
Sheboygan County Medical Society Utilization Committee Charitable Trust, Sheboygan, 2/101
Sherry (Avery & Betty) Fdn., Milwaukee, 2/101
Shiloh Fdn., Oconomonoc, 2/102
Shimonek (Mary) Trust, Green Bay, 2/102
Shoup Fdn., Racine, 2/102
Siebert Lutheran Fdn., Brookfield, 2/103
Sigma Phi Fraternity of the United States, Oshkosh, 2/104
Silver Family Fdn., Racine, 2/104
Slichter (Allen M.) Fdn., Milwaukee, 2/105
Smith (Clarence B.) Fdn., La Crosse, 2/106
Smith (Theda Clark) Family Fdn., Menasha, 2/106
Smith (David B.) Family Fdn., Wausau, 2/107
Smith (L. B.) Family Fdn., Milwaukee, 2/107
Smith (T. L.) Fdn., Milwaukee, 2/108
Smith (Wieland) Fdn., Milwaukee, 2/109
Snyder (Donald A.) Special Fund, Neenah, 2/109
Spindler (Walter E.) Fdn., Milwaukee, 2/110
Stahmer (Albert H.) Fdn., Wausau, 2/112
Stamp (H. O.) Fdn., Fox Point, 2/112
Stangel (Arthur G.) Fdn., Manitowoc, 2/113
Stearns Fdn., Milwaukee, 2/114
Steffen-Antigo Memorial Fund, Antigo, 2/114
Stainman Lumber Co. Fdn., Milwaukee, 2/115
Stern (Harold M.) Family Fdn., Milwaukee, 2/115
Stiefel Fdn., Green Bay, 2/116
Stiemke (Walter and Olive) Fdn., Milwaukee, 2/116
Stillman (Edward and Ruth) Family Fdn., Milwaukee, 2/117
Stolper Weinsink Fdn., Menomonee Falls, 2/118

Stone (Stanley and Polly) Fdn., Milwaukee, 2/118
Stratton (Margaret Elizabeth) Memorial Fdn., Milwaukee, 2/120
Stryker (Clinton E.) Fdn., Milwaukee, 2/121
Stull (Charles E.) Fdn., Milwaukee, 2/122
Suckle (Henry & Esther) Fdn., Madison, 2/122
Suder-Pick Fdn., Milwaukee, 2/123
Superior Die Set Fdn., Oak Creek, 2/124
Swoboda Fdn., Milwaukee, 2/125
Taylor Family Fdn., Kenosha, 2/126
Thauer (Muriel) Scholarship Fund, Watertown, 2/126
Thornhill Fdn., Sheboygan, 2/127
Tolibia Fdn., Fond du Lac, 2/127
Town Club Junior Tennis Fdn., Milwaukee, 2/128
Trane Family Fdn., La Crosse, 2/128
Trane Company Fdn., La Crosse, 2/129
Triss Charitable Trust, Neenah, 2/129
Trostel (Albert & Kendrick) Fdn., Milwaukee, 2/130
Trostel Charities Limited, Milwaukee, 2/131
Turner (James E.) Family Trust, Waukesha, 2/132
Uhrig (Edward A.) Fdn., Milwaukee, 2/132
Union Toy & Prescription Fdn., Milwaukee, 2/133
Uihlein (William B.) Family Fdn., Milwaukee, 2/134
Uihlein (Robert A.) Fdn., Milwaukee, 2/135
Uihlein (Joseph E.) Fdn., Milwaukee, 2/136
Usinger Fdn., Milwaukee, 2/136
Van Kooy (Cornelia) Memorial Trust Fund, Milwaukee, 2/137
Vennstra (Garrett) Fdn., Racine, 2/138
Verhulst (Jacob P.) Fdn., Sheboygan, 2/138
Vogel Fdn., Milwaukee, 2/139
Voigt Charitable Fdn., Racine, 2/139
Vollrath (Walter J.) Family Fdn., Sheboygan, 2/140
Von Schleinitz (Rene) Fdn., Milwaukee, 2/141
Wahlberg Fdn., Milwaukee, 2/142
Waisman (Morris S.) Charitable Fdn., Racine, 2/142
Wanderer Forum Fdn., Marshfield, 2/143
Inbusch (Charles E. and Dorothy Watkins) Fdn., Milwaukee, 2/144
Waukesha Motor Company Fdn., Waukesha, 2/144
Wauwatosa Knights of Columbus Fdn., Milwaukee, 2/145
Wisconsin Moose Breeders & Exhibitors Corporation, Milwaukee, 2/145
Wausau Fdn. Wisconsin Valley Trust Co., Wausau, 2/145
W. D. Fdn., Milwaukee, 2/146
Weber Fdn., Kiel, 2/146
Weber (Clarence J.) Fdn., Sheboygan, 2/146
Wehr Corp. Fdn., Milwaukee, 2/147
Wehr (Todd) Fdn., Milwaukee, 2/148
Weil (Richard & Lucille) Family Fdn., Milwaukee, 2/148
Weill (Stefanie H.) Charitable Trust, Sheboygan, 2/149
Weisel Fdn., Milwaukee, 2/149
Weisenthal (Charles L. & Shirley A.) Fdn., Milwaukee, 2/150
Wendt (Dr. Floyd A.) Scholarship Trust, Milwaukee, 2/151
Wermuth (John M.) Family Fdn., Elm Grove, 2/151
West Allis State Bank Fdn., West Allis, 2/152
St. John (Ruth) & John Dunham West Fdn., Manitowoc, 2/152
Western Publishing Company Fdn., Racine, 2/153
Weyenberg (Frank L.) Charitable Fdn., Milwuakee, 2/154
Wheeler Fdn., Mequon, 2/154
W. & H. Fdn., Milwaukee, 2/154
Whitewater Kiwanis Fdn., Whitewater, 2/155
Wiechers (Jerome C. and Margaret) Charitable Fdn., Racine, 2/155
Wiechers (Glenn S.) Fdn., Racine, 2/156
Wieczorek (E. E.) Fdn., Racine, 2/157

Wiler Fdn., Milwaukee, 2/157
Wilken-Harding Educational Fdn., Milwaukee, 2/158
Wisconsin Bridge & Iron Fdn., Milwaukee, 2/159
Wisconsin Hospital Association Research & Education Fdn., Madison, 2/159
Wisconsin Public Service Fdn., Green Bay, 2/160
Wisconsin State Dental Society Relief Fund, Milwaukee, 2/161
Wisconsin Tissue Mills Fdn., Menasha, 2/161
Wolff Kubly & Hirsig Fdn., Madison, 2/161
Wood (Lester G.) Fdn., Green Bay, 2/162
Woyahn (Henry) Memorial Fdn., Waukesha, 2/162
Wright (Alma Smith) Fdn., Milwaukee, 2/163
Wright (Charles W.) Fdn. of Badger Meter, Milwaukee, 2/164
Wuethrich Fdn., Greenwood, 2/165
Younger Family Fdn., Milwaukee, 2/166
Ziegler Fdn., West Bend, 2/167
Ziemann Fdn., Milwaukee, 2/168
Zien (Robert) Family Fdn., Milwaukee, 2/170
Zimmermann (F. J.) Fdn., Wausau, 2/170
Zion Cemetery Assoc. Trust, Appleton, 2/170
Zwicker Fdn., Appleton, 2/171
1800 Fdn., Milwaukee, 2/172

Second Filming

Albridght (Charles Edgar) and Uihlein Albright Fdn., Milwaukee, 3/001
Allen-Bradley Fdn., Milwaukee, 3/002
Alvord (Grace C.), Milwaukee, 3/002
American Appraisal Trust, Milwaukee, 3/003
Appleton Memorial Hospital Endowment Trust Fund, Appleton, 3/003
Appleton Rotary Fdn., Appleton, 3/003
Ariens Fdn., Brillion, 3/004
Arps (Helmuth F.), Milwaukee, 3/004
Aytchmonde Woodson Fdn., Wausau, 3/005
Bamberger Fdn., Milwaukee, 3/007
Barkow (August G.) Family Fdn., Milwaukee, 3/007
Bassett (Norman) Fdn., Madison, 3/007
Baye Fdn., Milwaukee, 3/008
Bemis Fdn., Shelboygan Falls, 3/008
Bennett (Margaret), Milwaukee, 3/009
Benstead Fdn., Racine, 3/009
Bjorksten Research Fdn., Madison, 3/010
Blatland Fdn., Delafield, 3/010
Blatz (Emil), Milwaukee, 3/011
Bowen (M. P.) for Greenwood Cemetery, Milwaukee, 3/011
Bowman (J.) for Spring Grove Cemetery, Milwaukee, 3/012
Bowman (Jennie) for Jonathan Bowman Memorial Park, Milwaukee, 3/012
Bowman (Jennie) for U. of W. Memorial Fund, Milwaukee, 3/013
Bowman (Jennie) for 1st Pres. Meth. Ep. Churches, Milwaukee, 3/013
Brandenburg Fdn., Madison, 3/014
Brann (Ethel M.) Fdn., Green Bay, 3/015
Brewer (A. Keith) Fdn., Richland Center, 3/015
Brillion Fdn., Brillion, 3/015
Brooks (Jane) Fdn., Milwaukee, 3/016
Brown (Ellen M.) Trust, Milwaukee, 3/016
Burger Fdn., Manitowoc, 3/017
Buscheck (Alfred J.) Memorial Trust, Milwaukee, 3/017
Cavanaugh (Catherine F.) Memorial Fdn., Milwaukee, 3/019
Christ Church Eau Claire, Milwaukee, 3/019
Christensen (Col. L. C.) Chairtable & Religious Fdn., Racine, 3/019
Christensen (Arthur J. & Cecelia L.) Fdn., Racine, 3/020
Coddington Memorial Fdn., Milwaukee, 3/020
Cohn (Sam) Memorial Scholarship Fund, Walworth, 3/021
Community Associates Fdn., Milwaukee, 3/021
Connell (James A.) Endowment Fund, Milwaukee, 3/022

Connor (William D.) Educational Fund, Marshfield, 3/022

Connor Fdn., Wausau, 3/022

Cranston (Joseph P.) Trust, Milwaukee, 3/023

Cudahy (Helen M.), Milwaukee, 3/023

Cudahy (Patrick) Fdn., Milwaukee, 3/024

Curry (J. & M.) Endowment Fund, Milwaukee, 3/024

Davidson (Robert J.) Char. Trust, Elm Grove, 3/025

Dekoven Fdn. for Church Work, Racine, 3/025

Derfus (Joseph) Fdn., Milwaukee, 3/026

Doepke (Fred C.) Fdn., Milwaukee, 3/026

Draeger (Herman A.) Trust, Green Bay, 3/027

Dough Boy Fdn., New Richmond, 3/027

Engstrom (Irma S.) Scholarship Trust, Milwaukee, 3/028

Evinrude (Ole) Fdn., Milwaukee, 3/028

Evjue Fdn., Madison, 3/029

Fairchild Fdn., Milwaukee, 3/030

Fazen Charitable Fdn., Racine, 3/031

Feitler Family Fund, Milwaukee, 3/031

Fink (Robert J.) Fdn., Eau Claire, 3/032

Fliel (Clara), Milwaukee, 3/032

Lindbaum (Maude F.), Milwaukee, 3/034

Fliel (Clara), Milwaukee, 3/035

Foley (Leon F.) Fdn., Milwaukee, 3/035

Fox River Fdn., Appleton, 3/034

Fahrenkrug Memorial Fund, Green Bay, 3/035

Freeman (Michael & Susan) Family Fdn., Milwaukee, 3/035

Friday Fdn., New Richmond, 3/036

Friends of the Museum Endowment Fund, Milwaukee, 3/036

Fristche (G. R.) Memorial Scholarship Fund, Milwaukee, 3/036

Fromstein Fdn., Milwaukee, 3/037

Gardner Charitable Trust, Madison, 3/038

Garton Fdn., Sheboygan, 3/038

Garver Memorial Trust, Madison, 3/039

Gelatt Fdn., La Crosse, 3/041

German Language & School Society Wisconsin, Milwaukee, 3/042

Glen (Stanley & Ethel) Family Fdn., Cedarburg, 3/043

Glinberg (Harry & Rose) Family Fdn., Milwaukee, 3/043

Goldberg (I. E.) Memorial Trust, Milwaukee, 3/044

Greene Manufacturing Company Fdn., Racine, 3/044

Gregory (Ella K.) for Childrens Hospital, Milwaukee, 3/045

Gregory (E.) for Family Service of Milwaukee, Wisconsin, Milwaukee, 3/046

Grudem (Arden E.) Family Fdn., Eau Claire, 3/046

G.S. Fund, Milwaukee, 3/047

Guell Fdn., Thorp, 3/048

Gund (Henry), Sr., Milwaukee, 3/048

Habush (Robert L.) Fam. Fdn., Milwaukee, 3/048

Handicapped Students of Wisconsin, Madison, 3/049

Harmon (E. T.), Milwaukee, 3/049

Harmon (Hester Ann) Trust, Milwaukee, 3/050

Hatch Enterprises, Milwaukee, 3/051

Heath Fdn., Milwaukee, 3/052

Helz (Bessie Shaad), Estate of, Milwaukee, 3/053

Heyden (Vander) Fdn., Elm Grove, 3/054

Hoeppner (E. G.) Charities, Eau Claire, 3/054

Hoffer Fdn., Wausau, 3/054

Hooper Fdn., Manitowoc, 3/055

Horsman (J. E.) for Grace Episcopal Church, Milwaukee, 3/055

Horsman (J. E.) for Nora Cemetery, Milwaukee, 3/055

International Dental Research Fdn., Milwaukee, 3/056

Irving (Jim & Ada) Fdn., Stroughton, 3/057

Jacobus Fdn., Milwaukee, 3/058

Johnson Fdn. Trust, Racine, 3/058

Johnsons Wax Fund, Racine, 3/059

Junior House Fdn., Milwaukee, 3/060

Kahn (Herbert and Elise) Fdn., Milwaukee, 3/061

Kearney Negro Welfare Fdn., Milwaukee, 3/061

Kenosha Lions Fdn. of Kenosha, Wisconsin, Kenosha, 3/062

Kimball (Emma K.), Milwaukee, 3/062

Kings Daughters Fdn., Neenah, 3/063

Klug & Smith Co. Charitable Tr., Racine, 3/064

Kolinski (Maximillian C.), Milwaukee, 3/064

Kiaut Fdn., Fond du Lac, 3/065

Kradwell Trust for Nashotah Episcopal Seminary, Milwaukee, 3/065

Ladish (Herman W.) Family Fdn., Milwaukee, 3/066

Ladish (Herman W.) Fdn., Milwaukee, 3/067

Ladish Malting Co. Fdn., Milwaukee, 3/069

Larsen Company Fdn., Green Bay, 3/069

Wilma Heath Lauterbach Fdn., Delavan, 3/071

Lawrence (E. R. Reid) College Librarian Scholarship, Milwaukee, 3/071

Lawrence (E. R. Reid) College Art Scholarship, Milwaukee, 3/072

Levy (Irving E.) Charities, Madison, 3/072

Lewis (W. Mitchell) Memorial Fund, Milwaukee, 3/073

Lilly (George C. H.) in Memory of Emma Sabina Heney Maria Lilly, Milwaukee, 3/073

Leyhe Fdn., Oshkosh, 3/074

Lieberman (Jay M. & Joan K.) Family Charitable Fdn., Milwaukee, 3/074

Lindbaum (Maude F.), Milwaukee, 3/074

L.P.L. Fdn., Oconomowoc, 3/075

Luchsinger (May L.) Trust for Veterans Home at King Wisconsin, Monro, 3/076

Maher (Roy W.) Fdn., Milwaukee, 3/076

Rector, Wardens & Vestrymen of St. Lukes Protestant Episcopal Church of Racine, Wisc., Milwaukee, 3/076

Marathon Box Fdn., Wausau, 3/076

Marsden Park Trust, Fennimore, 3/078

Mautz Paint Fdn., Madison, 3/078

Rankin (May Nichel) Fellowship Fund, Milwaukee, 3/079

McGaffey (Jere D.) Family Fdn., Milwaukee, 3/080

McIver-Prittie Fdn., Ashland, 3/080

Meachem (DRS) Fdn. Fund, Milwaukee, 3/080

Meachem (Eliza S.), Milwaukee, 3/081

Meachem (John G.), Jr. Endowment Fund, Milwaukee, 3/081

Meachem (John G.), Jr. Trust, Milwaukee, 3/082

Meachem (John G.), III Trust, Milwaukee, 3/083

Meachem (John G.), III Decd, Rector Wardens Vestrymen of St. Lukes Protestant Episcopal Church, Milwaukee, 3/084

Medalist Industries Fdn., Milwaukee, 3/085

Mengel Fdn., Wisconsin Rapids, 3/085

Meyer (George J.) Fdn., Cudahy, 3/086

Meyer (George T.) Fdn., Milwaukee, 3/086

Meyers Charitable Fdn. Trust, Milwaukee, 3/086

Milwaukee Fdn., Milwaukee, 3/087

Milwaukee Scientific Educational Fdn., Milwaukee, 3/093

Moen (O. T.) Fdn., Greendale, 3/093

Schandein (Claire) for Milwaukee Childrens Hospital Assoc., Milwaukee, 3/094

Murphy (Morley) Fdn., Green Bay, 3/095

Motor Castings Fdn., West Allis, 3/095

Mueller (August G.) Trust, Milwaukee, 3/095

Muetzel Educational Fdn., Tomah, 3/096

Muth (K. W.) Fdn., Sheboygan, 3/097

Neenah Rotary Fdn., Neenah, 3/097

Nine Juda Angels Memorial Scholarship Fund Charitable Trust, Monroe, 3/098

N.M.C. Projects, Madison, 3/099

North (Etta) Trust, Milwaukee, 3/100

Our Lady of Lourdes Charitable Trust, Neenah, 3/100

Overton (Adah C.) Scholarship Fund, Janesville, 3/101

Pauly Fdn., Manitowoc, 3/101

Pavalon (Wesley D.) Fdn., Milwaukee, 3/101

Pehrson (Robert Neil) Literary Memorial Association, Manitowoc, 3/103

Pfister & Vogel Tanning Co. Fdn., Milwaukee, 3/103

Phillips (L. E.) Charities, Eau Claire, 3/104

Phi Delta Epsilon Fdn. of Milwaukee, Milwaukee, 3/106

Pierce (A. J. W.) Endowment Fund, Milwaukee, 3/106

Plankinton (Elizabeth A.) Trust for Calvary Presbyterian Church of Milwaukee, Milwaukee, 3/106

Plotkin Fdn., Milwaukee, 3/107

Pokras (Adolph & Edith) Fdn., Mequon, 3/107

Port Washington Kiwanis Fdn., Port Washington, 3/108

Presto Fdn., Eau Claire, 3/108

Price Fdn., Milwaukee, 3/111

Project Christopher, Appleton, 3/111

Pugh (W. H.), Racine, 3/111

Quirk (Earl and Eugenia) Fdn., Watertown, 3/112

Reid (E. R.) for Childrens Service Society of Wisconsin, Milwaukee, 3/113

Reid (E. R.)-Thomas B. Reid Journalistic Scholarship, Milwaukee, 3/113

Ritz (Maurice and Esther Leah) Fdn., Milwaukee, 3/113

River Tennis Club Junior Tennis Fdn., River Hills, 3/114

Robbins (Sena R.), Milwaukee, 3/114

Roddis (Hamilton) Fdn., Wisconsin Rapids, 3/115

Roehl Fdn., Oconomowoc, 3/116

Rohde Fdn., Sheboygan, 3/117

Rondeau (Francis) Fdn., Mosinee, 3/117

Rosenberg (George & Dorothy E.) Fdn., Milwaukee, 3/118

Rosenberg (Pierce & Mildred) Fdn., Milwaukee, 3/118

Ross (Will) Fdn., Milwaukee, 3/119

Rounys Fun Fund Committee, Madison, 3/119

Rubenstein Fdn., Milwaukee, 3/119

Rutledge (Edward) Charity, Chippewa Falls, 3/119

Rutledge (Hannah M.) Home for The Aged, Chippewa Falls, 3/121

Sadoff (Ben) Fdn., Fond du Lac, 3/123

Oster (P. J.) for St. Boniface Cemetery, Milwaukee, 3/123

St. Francis Hospital Fdn. of Milwaukee, Milwaukee, 3/124

St. Lukes Guild of Racine, Milwaukee, 3/124

St. Pauls Episcopal Church of Ashippuny, Milwaukee, 3/124

St. Pius X Charitable Fdn., Appleton, 3/125

Sattler Research & Charitable Fdn., Kenosha, 3/125

Schelble (James A. & Lorna G.) Family Fdn., Milwaukee, 3/126

Schenk (William C.) Trust, Milwaukee, 3/126

Schimenz (Mathias G.) Law Memorial Scholarship Fund, Milwaukee, 3/126

Schroeder (Walter) Fdn., Milwaukee, 3/126

Schuette Family Fdn., Green Bay, 3/127

Schuster (John K.) Trust, Milwaukee, 3/129

Schuster (Ed) & Co. Fdn., Milwaukee, 3/129

Schwartz Fdn., Manitowoc, 3/130

Shaler (C. A.) Scholarship Fund, Milwaukee, 3/131

Shattuck (Frank C.) Charitable Trust, Neenah, 3/131

Sheldon (Angie) Memorial Scholarship Fund, Stevens Point, 3/132

Stanek Fdn., Milwaukee, 3/132

Stangel (J. J.) & Co. Fund, Manitowoc, 3/133

Steffen-Antigo Memorial Fund, Antigo, 3/133

Steven Fdn., Eau Claire, 3/134

Stevenson (Robert & Cleo) Fdn., Elm Grove, 3/134

Stickney (Frances C.), Milwaukee, 3/135

Storey (Dan) Fdn., Wausau, 3/138

Sivyer (Ida M.) for Boys Trade Technical High
  School, Milwaukee, 3/139
Stratton Fdn., Milwaukee, 3/140
Sturm (A.) and Sons Fdn., Manawa, 3/141
Sturtevant (J. C.) Fdn., Wausau, 3/141
Taylor (Emerline), Milwaukee, 3/142
Taylor (James A.) Family Fdn., Milwaukee,
  3/143
Thorp Finance Fdn., Thorp, 3/145
Tilarids Fund, Milwaukee, 3/146
Tobin Fdn., Fond du Lac, 3/147
Turnbull (Andrew B.) Fdn., Green Bay, 3/147
Triangle Fraternity Marquette Chapter,
  Milwaukee, 3/148
Trustees of the Trust Fund for the Girls of
  Stevens Point, Stevens Point, 3/148
Truth, Inc., Milwaukee, 3/148
United Temple Association, La Crosse, 3/149
Wymelenberg (Arnold Van Den) Fdn., Green
  Bay, 3/150
Wadewitz (W. R.) Charitable Fdn., Racine,
  3/150
Walters (Bernard and Mildred) Fdn.,
  Milwaukee, 3/151
Waukesha Rotary Club Charitable Fund,
  Waukesha, 3/152
Wauwatosa Knight of Columbus Fdn.,
  Milwaukee, 3/152
Wausau Paper Mills Fdn., Brokaw, 3/152
Webcrafters-Frautschi Fdn., Madison, 3/153
Weisbrod (Henry G.) Scholarship Fdn., Racine,
  3/154
Whitewater Kiwanis Fdn., Whitewater, 3/154
Whyte Fdn., Milwaukee, 3/154
Wichmann Fdn., Appleton, 3/155
Wiese (Ludwig and Pearl) Educational Fdn.,
  Racine, 3/155
Wildwood Fdn., Milwaukee, 3/156
Windway Fdn., Sheboygan, 3/157
Winter (Jack and Muriel) Fdn., Milwaukee,
  3/158
Wisconsin Centrifugal Fdn., Waukesha, 3/158
Wisconsin-Cornell Scholarship Fund,
  Milwaukee, 3/159
Wisconsin Dental Association Fdn., Milwaukee,
  3/159
Wisconsin Eastern Star Fdn., Beaver Dam,
  3/159
Wisconsin Natural Resources Fdn., Madison,
  3/160
Wisconsin State Council Knights of Columbus
  Fdn., Prairie du Sac, 3/167
Wustum (Jennie E.), Milwaukee, 3/161
Young (Irvin L.) Fdn., Neenah, 3/163
Youth Fdn., Milwaukee, 3/164
Zahns Fdn., Milwaukee, 3/165
Zilber (Joseph J.) Family Fdn., Milwaukee,
  3/165

WYOMING

First Filming

Bryan (Dodd and Dorothy L.) Fdn., Sheridan,
  1/002
Johnson (Libby) Memorial Scholarship,
  Rawlins, 1/003
Neilson Fdn., Cody, 1/003
Odell (Ray) Fdn., Casper, 1/004
Perkins (B. F. and Rose H.) Fdn., Sheridan,
  1/004
Scott Fdn., Sheridan, 1/006
Thorne-Rider Fdn., Sheridan, 1/006
Whedon (Earl and Bessie) Cancer Detection
  Fdn., Sheridan, 1/007

Second Filming

Goodstein Fdn., Casper, 2/002
Greater Fdn., Laramie, 2/003
Morton Fdn., Douglas, 2/003
Nicoli (A. J.) Charitable Fdn., Moran, 2/004
Sheridan Community Building Corp., Sheridan,
  2/005
Stock (Paul) Fdn., Cody, 2/006
Tonkin (Tom & Helen) Fdn., Casper, 2/006
Whitney Benefits, Sheridan, 2/008
Wyoming State Dental Assoc., Casper, 2/009

OFFICE OF INTER-
NATIONAL OPERATIONS

First Filming

Bachrach (Jerome C. & Monique L.) Charitable
  Trust, Israel, 1/001
Batchworth Trust, England, 1/003
Beder Trust, England, 1/006
Daugherty (Julie C.) Charitable Foundation, St.
  Croix, 1/010
de Freitas (Helen & Godffrey) Charitable Trust,
  England, 1/017
Ditchley Foundation, England, 1/021
Jackson Foundation, St. Thomas, 1/023
Lorenz (Paul & Harriet) Foundation, England,
  1/031
McConnell (J. W.) Foundation, Canada, 1/034
Steiner (Rudolf) Cultural Foundation, France,
  1/040
WA - CHE - YO - CHA - PA Foundation,
  Canada, 1/042
Weston (W. Garfield) Charitable Foundation,
  Canada, 1/047
World Law Foundation, Canada, 1/051
Zeller Family Foundation, Canada, 1/054

29th May 61 Charity Trust, England, 1/063

Second Filming

Atherton (Kate M.) Trust Estate for Salvation
  Army Boys & Girls Home, Honolulu,
  Hawaii, 2/000
Les Amis De La Banlieue, France, 2/002
Beit Trust, England, 2/003
Board of Scholarship for the Mackenzie King
  Travelling Scholarship Fund, Canada, 2/003
Canadian Princeton Alumn Fund, Canada,
  2/004
Cooke (Charles M. & Anna C.) Trust,
  Honolulu, Hawaii, 2/005
Cowett Family Charitable Trust, Switzerland,
  2/006
Wright (H. Dudley) Research Fdn.,
  Switzerland, 2/007
Dulverton Trust, England, 2/007
Federation of World Health Fdns., Switzerland,
  2/008
Ferre (Luis A.) Fdn., Puerto Rico, 2/010
Fundacao Calouste Gulbenkian Parque De
  Santa Gertr, Portugal, 2/011
Harvey Fdn., Puerto Rico, 2/021
Helping Hand Fdn., Vietnam, 2/021
Ironbridge (George) Museum Trust Limited,
  England, 2/021
Fdn. Beni Israel, Switzerland, 2/022
Jewish Colonization Assoc., England, 2/025
Kaiulani Home for Girls Trust, Honolulu,
  Hawaii, 2/027
Keller (Arthur R.) Trust Estate, Honolulu,
  Hawaii, 2/027
Kennedy (Laura V.) Trust, Hilo, Hawaii,
  2/028
Lester Fdn., Belgium, 2/030
Neilson (Francis) Trust, England, 2/030
McConnell (John) & Margaret Ann Wilson
  McConnell Fdn., Canada, 2/030
Ontario Paper Company Fdn., Canada, 2/031
Queen's University, Canada, 2/032
Royal Pinner School Fdn., England, 2/032
Association Saint Christophe, France, 2/033
Stichting Singer Memorial Fdn., Netherlands,
  2/033
Steiner (Rudolf) Cultural Fdn., France, 2/034
Stiftung (Herbert Grunfeld), Liechtenstein,
  2/034
Trustees of the Will of Dr. John Radcliffe,
  England, 2/035
Tulloch (Alexander R.) Trust, Honolulu,
  Hawaii, 2/035
Wa Che Yo Cha Pa Fdn., Canada, 2/035
Webster (R. Howard) Fdn., Canada, 2/035
Widtsoe (John A.) Education Fdn., Korea,
  2/036
Zaidan Hojin Biseibutsu Kagaku Kenkyukai,
  Japan, 2/037